CONTENTS

Acknowledgements

The creation of this book was a large undertaking, and many people contributed to our efforts. First, Nancy Green, Jane Clarenbach, and the NAGC Publications Committee, chaired at different times by Joseph Renzulli and Nicholas Colangelo, provided helpful guidance and oversight throughout the process. From negotiating the contract to reviewing materials, the help of these individuals was a critical factor in the successful completion of this volume. In particular, Jane Clarenbach provided encouragement and helpful insights as the book and individual chapters evolved.

The book obviously would have not been possible without the contributions of the many authors. Their task was not easy, with a restrictive format, tight page limit, multiple revisions, and long periods of waiting as the book progressed through multiple rounds of review. Many authors also wrote on very challenging topics, including some on which there is little research available. Yet, every author produced a high-quality chapter that effectively summarizes what we know and what we need to know.

We are especially grateful for the contributions of authors who stepped in at the eleventh hour to to complete several chapters. Given the selflessness of these authors, we would like to thank them by name: Joyce Alexander, Brenda Linn, Sharlene Newman, Angela Schnick, and Bruce Shore.

In order to produce the highest quality work, we relied on the expertise of several reviewers. We appreciate their candid and insightful reviews and suggestions, all of which helped strengthen the book. A complete list of the reviewers is included below.

The production process on a book of this size is quite difficult, and we benefited from the guidance and talents of Joel McIntosh, Jennifer Robins, and their colleagues at Prufrock Press. Jennifer's careful copyediting helped to polish the chapters and allowed us to put our best foot forward.

Last, but certainly not least, Leigh Kupersmith served as the managing editor for this project. Leigh kept the process organized and on track, and the highly complicated process of tracking drafts, reviews, and revisions for the 50 chapters simply would have taken far longer without Leigh's considerable talents. We thank her for her contributions.

REVIEWERS

Cheryll M. Adams
Edward R. Amend
Ronald A. Beghetto
Catherine M. Brighton
Richard M. Cash
Elizabeth S. Caylor
Molly A. Chamberlin
Kim Chandler
Trudy L. Clemons
Larry J. Coleman
Rita R. Culross
David Yun Dai
Felicia A. Dixon
Sally M. Dobyns
Lori J. Flint
Françoys Gagné
Marcia Gentry
Tarek C. Grantham
Miraca U. M. Gross
E. Jean Gubbins
Joanne Haroutounian
Holly Hertberg-Davis
Nancy B. Hertzog

Eunsook Hong
Scott L. Hunsaker
Joan K. Jacobs
Susan K. Johnsen
Robert Kunzman
Jann Lappien
Jacob T. Levy
Matthew C. Makel
Rebecca S. Martinez
Dona J. Matthews
Michael S. Matthews
Matthew T. McBee
Jay A. McIntire
Erin Morris Miller
Tonya R. Moon
Maureen Neihart
Stuart N. Omdal
Barry A. Oreck
Jean Sunde Peterson
Rebecca L. Pierce
Marion Porath
Kelly Rapp
Sylvia Rimm
Anne N. Rinn
Robert A. Schultz
Kenneth Seeley
Elizabeth Shaunessy
Bruce M. Shore
Bharath Sriraman
Vicki B. Stocking
Julie D. Swanson
Mary Tallent-Runnels
Carol L. Tieso
Grace R. Waitman
Karen L. Westberg
Frank C. Worrell

INTRODUCTION

Jonathan A. Plucker
and Carolyn M. Callahan, Editors

The field of gifted education is plagued with assertions based on "research" without a clear and unbiased sourcebook that can be referenced by scholars and practitioners alike. Despite a century of research on giftedness, the enthusiasm and rhetoric surrounding various programming options, curricular models, instructional approaches, and other practices in schools and through other services offered to gifted students often exceeds the level of available empirical support—or even contradicts the available evidence. This volume is designed to serve as a concise reference book for those trying to identify what the research does, in fact, say about a particular topic. The intention is to present, in digest form, a summary of relevant research and a guide on how the research applies to the field. The chapters do not represent full and detailed reviews of the literature or meta-analyses of a particular set of studies. Rather they are synopses that reflect an evaluation of the empirical data on the topic, a brief overview of the important implications for practice, and an outline of studies or data that are still needed to fully inform our practice. Each of the chapters reflects a rigorous, empirically grounded approach to inform the reader's understanding of the research in gifted education.

THE ORGANIZATION OF THE TEXT

The book is organized alphabetically by chapter topic for convenience of searching for information on a particular topic, and the topics were derived from identifying seven general areas commonly addressed in understanding the development of gifted students and in making decisions about appropriate educational and psychological services. These areas include:
- conceptual and foundational issues,
- curricular issues,
- cognitive issues,
- affective issues,
- programmatic issues,
- teacher and parent issues, and
- special populations of gifted students.

Within these general areas, specific topics (determined in consultation with representatives of the Research and Evaluation Division of the National Association for Gifted Children) are reflective of a broad range of interest areas that may be useful in informing administrators, teachers, parents, psychologists, or counselors.

The compendium of final topics does not address particular instructional strategies such as curriculum compacting, problem-based learning, and the like. Rather, we asked authors of all relevant chapters (specifically those dealing with curricular issues) to address research on the use of instructional strategies within specific content areas such as mathematics, science, and social studies. Our thought in doing so was to mirror both contemporary educational psychology scholarship, which focuses on learning within specific contexts as opposed to generalizable learning strategies, and to reflect the way in which education practitioners and parents are most likely to use the book. For example, we surmised that they would more likely look for research on teaching gifted students in social studies rather than seek research on problem-based learning across all content areas. In making the final selection of topics to include in the volume, we considered three broad categories of topics: those that are historically of interest to the field, those that are currently popular, and those that we anticipate becoming more important—or that we believe *should* be more important. Although there are certainly many overlapping concepts, issues, and research studies across topics, we have made every attempt to minimize overlap of content across the entries.

There is no question that there are a few topics that are not included here that some would wish we had included (and that we wish we could have included). In some cases, there simply was an insufficient body of literature to warrant a chapter; in others the topic may be of interest to researchers or some other group, but did not seem to be worthy of inclusion in a volume that had to be limited in size and scope.

AUTHORS

The authors of the individual chapters represent a range of experience levels, from senior scholars, to promising, early career researchers (i.e., more than a dozen of the participating authors are junior faculty or graduate students). Although most authors are active within the field of gifted education, we also invited scholars working primarily outside of the field when we determined that their input would provide a valuable perspective. Regardless of their experience or their relationship to gifted education, each of the authors has prepared a defensible and clear guide to and evaluation of the existing evidence to support the educational practice or theory examined.

CHAPTER ORIENTATION
AND ORGANIZATION

In the interest of creating consistency across the chapters, the authors were given the charge of preparing their research summaries by:

1. defining the terms as used in the research on the topic under review,
2. identifying the major questions that are addressed in the research on this topic,
3. specifying conclusions that can be drawn with some confidence from the research on this topic based on empirical support,
4. frankly evaluating the limitations of the research on the topic,
5. providing a discussion of the practical implications of the research on this topic, and
6. enumerating the major resources and references that are credible sources on the research on this topic.

Some of the authors adhered strictly to these guidelines in preparing their chapters; others found that the literature and research on the topic did not lend itself to clear interpretation within that framework. Therefore, each chapter addresses all aspects of the charge, but not all chapters conform to the exact same format.

USE OF THE MATERIAL

Like an encyclopedia, the chapters are presented alphabetically for easy access. The Table of Contents lists the titles of all of the chapters and a key word index provides the reader a reference to key areas covered within each chapter.

We recognize that the compendium may not be exhaustive, but we hope this book will serve as a quick reference for practitioners looking for ideas that are easy to grasp and guidance in key areas of gifted education. We also hope that the many areas that were identified as still too ill-defined are developed and investigated in the near future, and we hope that the many unanswered questions identified by our authors will serve as guides for future research in the field.

Chapter 1

ACADEMIC COMPETITIONS

Stuart N. Omdal and M. R. E. Richards

rom spelling bees to sophisticated research in the sciences, academic competitions have existed for centuries. Highlighting the academic and intellectual proficiencies of students was viewed as a way to inspire others to greater achievement and to encourage students to pursue further education and career choices in their particular area of expertise. During the mid-20th century, professional organizations, businesses with interests in scientific research, and universities started new competitions, many being in the realm of talent searches. These competitions and scholarship opportunities were regarded as a method of helping students fund college or create more potential employees to meet the growing demands of science and technology. Today the search for talent continues and many new individual or small-group competitions are used as a form of enrichment for gifted and talented learners. These challenging activities are commonly extracurricular activities and/or designed as summer programs. Somers and Callan

(1999) estimated that annually nearly 3 million students in the United States alone participate in science or math competitions.

TERMS AS USED IN THE RESEARCH

The basic terminology describing academic competitions in the literature varies. For the purposes of clarity in this chapter, the terms commonly used are defined below.

Academic Competitions

This category refers to a variety of events whereby individuals or small groups of students display projects previously completed (i.e., *fairs*, defined below) or events where students compete in activities for honors or awards (i.e., *contests*, defined below). Participants may send original writing or photographs of art for judging, submit projects online, or compete in a variety of content or performance areas in the same place and time with individuals or teams. In this chapter, the term does not refer to academic competitiveness by individual students in a class or school, nor does it refer to programs requiring an entrance examination prior to participation (e.g., the Center for Talented Youth's Talent Search). Published research on the longitudinal effects of such specialized academic acceleration, such as Stanley and Benbow's (1983) article, "SMPY's First Decade: Ten Years of Posing Problems and Solving Them," and the follow-up report by Swiatek and Benbow (1991), "A 10-year Longitudinal Follow-Up of Participants in a Fast-Paced Mathematics Course," cannot be generalized to address the effects or benefits of academic competitions as defined in this chapter.

Another line of research excluded from this chapter consists of research conducted on participants of academic competitions not related to the competitions. For example, a study by Lamont, Kaufman, and Moody (2000) analyzed essays and conducted interviews with Presidential Scholars composed of college students who had scored in the top 1% on the Scholastic Aptitude Test (SAT) and entered an essay contest. Students were prompted to write a conversation between themselves and a famous person. The researchers analyzed the essays for implicit or explicit indications of the students' perceptions on what the "ideal self" is for a learner in the American education system. Because the connection with an academic competition was only an eligibility requirement to be a participant in a study unrelated to academic competitions, this and other similar research was not considered.

Fairs

This category refers to events in which individual or small groups of students participate first at the local level and often can advance through state, national, and sometimes international levels. Products are displayed in a common place or are submitted online (e.g., ThinkQuest) and are judged independently of each other using specific criteria. A fair may or may not be a competition, although many are. Examples include science fairs, Intel (formerly Westinghouse) Science Talent Search, International Science and Engineering Fair, and National History Day.

Contests

This category includes events in which individuals or small groups of students participate in activities and compete for honors or awards. The competition may be of a problem-solving nature (e.g., Odyssey of the Mind, DestiNation Imagination, Future Problem Solving, Math Olympiad); information retrieval (e.g., National Science Bowl, Panasonic Academic Challenge); performance (e.g., Music Teachers National Association competitions); or interdisciplinary (e.g., Academic Decathlon). These competitions are usually held in a geographically central location, and others may be conducted online (e.g., Math Olympics). Another approach is for entries such as creative writing, poetry, or visual arts (e.g., Scholastic Art and Writing Awards) to be submitted electronically or via standard mail for judging by experts.

Between 250 and 300 fairs and contests are available for students across all academic areas in multiple formats. Recognition for winners varies from a certificate, to scholarships worth many thousands of dollars. Universities often recruit high school students who attain the highest awards. There are several resources listing these competitions located at the end of this chapter. Educators in gifted education have regarded these competitions as an extracurricular means of developing and nurturing the talents of children (Karnes & Riley, 1996) and view these as a method to allow for in-depth study and real-world application of knowledge and the application of research skills.

MAJOR QUESTIONS ADDRESSED IN THE RESEARCH

1. What are the immediate benefits or effects for students who participate in academic competitions?
2. What are the long-term benefits or effects for students who participate in academic competitions?

3. In what ways do personal characteristics of participants in academic competitions vary?
4. How do students regard academic competitions?

EMPIRICALLY BASED CONCLUSIONS

Much of the research conducted in the area of academic competitions is based on anecdotal evidence. Although this adds to our understanding of the importance of competitions, these informal evaluations do not provide evidence of attribution of effects or generalizability of the findings. For example, a report by Riley and Karnes (1999) highlights the benefits of competitions for students with disabilities, but these results cannot be generalized to gifted children. An in-depth search of the research provided few articles on the effects, short or long term, of academic competitions and contests on gifted participants. In general, these reports were based on anecdotal evidence of the participants as reported by the authors. A search shows that the majority of articles available explore the types of competitions and the expectations of those competitions. The following sections address what research has been found.

Immediate Benefits or Effects

Creativity and Problem Solving. Fishkin (1989) examined the influence of the Odyssey of the Mind (OM) competitions. The major finding was that the creativity of the participants did significantly increase as measured by Similes, a test to measure literary creativity; the Torrance Tests of Creative Thinking, Figural and Verbal; the Sears Self-Concept Inventory; and the Intellectual Achievement Responsibility Questionnaire. She also found that creative self-concept and internal locus of control were higher at the end of the year than at the beginning and that consideration of difference in amount of effort as rated by the teacher/facilitator exerted in the activities of OM accounted for differences in measured creativity and in affect (self-concept). The lack of a control group may allow for the conclusion that gains were the result of growth effect. The results did not show a significant increase on subject knowledge based on the test instrument utilized. Shook's (1997) examination of OM found that the experimental group scored significantly higher than the control group as measured by the Torrance Tests of Creative Thinking, with no commensurate increase in problem-solving skills.

Long-Term Benefits or Effects

Several follow-up studies have been conducted with winners in two science competitions. Campbell, Feng, and Verna (1999) collected data from winners of the American Math, Physics, and Chemistry Olympiad programs (n = 229). In addition to collecting information about universities attended, degrees earned, and accomplishments in their careers, questions were asked about the impact of the Olympiad programs. Seventy-six percent of the Olympians and 70% of their parents stated that they would not have accomplished as much without the programs, and 76% of the Olympians and 76% of their parents judged the program as a help to them in accepting their talents. Four percent of the Olympians and none of the parents believed that the program impeded the development of their talent. Most of the Olympians and their parents responded that they thought the program raised their awareness of educational possibilities, increased their confidence, validated their exceptional ability, and helped them set higher goals for their futures.

Personal Characteristics of Participants in Academic Competitions

Baird and Shaw's (1996) examination of the Science Olympiad found that the use of an assessment of prior knowledge and skills of potential team members by the team coach was of little use in predicting the potential team member's actual performance in a competition setting. Baird and Shaw's (1996) study was designed to determine if a student's success in selected events of the Science Olympiad correlated with his or her scores on two different skill and reasoning instruments, the Test of Integrated Process Skills (TIPS) and the Group Assessment of Logical Thinking (GALT). The study was conducted separately for each instrument and coordinated with the student's success on the preselected events of the Science Olympiad. The findings indicated that there was no correlation between the skills the coaching manual stated would be required of the students and the student scores on tests assessing their actual skill level with the required skills.

In her master's thesis, Weeks (2003) conducted a qualitative study with five students currently involved with Odyssey of the Mind, five college students who had previously participated in the program, and two OM coaches. In this study, she proposed an examination of the impact of OM on the cognitive and psychosocial development of adolescents. Through interview analysis, she grouped participant statements by theme and deduced that an OM "program design providing a balance of challenge and support appears to accelerate students' psychosocial and cognitive development" (p. 4). Based on the data, Weeks speculated that the OM directives, including the use of small teams, mentors, open-ended problems, and the exclusive execution of all work to be done by students, contributed to the student's cognitive and psychosocial development.

Students' Perceptions of Academic Competitions

Frasier, Winstead, and Lee (1997) surveyed 205 students and 32 teacher-coaches eliciting perceptions of the degree to which the Future Problem Solving Program (FPSP) was actually meeting their stated goals of helping students enhance their creative thinking abilities, awareness of and interest in the future, communication, problem solving, teamwork, and research skills. Both students and teacher-coaches deemed the program successful in meeting its goals. Responses of teacher-coaches were significantly more positive than those of students. Younger students (grades 4–6) were significantly more positive than middle grade students and more positive than high school students.

Abernathy and Vineyard's (2001) study examined the junior and senior high school participants' perceptions of their experience in science academic competitions. The study found that the overall experience was not positive for the students. When the participants of science fair and Science Olympiad where asked if they would choose to be in the same activity 26.24% of the science fair participants and 35.71% of the Science Olympiad participants indicated they would continue in those activities. For some students, engagement in the competition can be enjoyable. However, it was the belief of all of the adults, parents, and teachers that science fairs and project contests are beneficial to students, and thus support the popularity of these fairs and projects. Some supportive findings from the Abernathy and Vineyard (2001) study found that when asked on a survey to rank their preferences of 12 different academic competitions, about one third of the students (n = 943) ranked science fair or Science Olympiad as their first choice. A survey on reasons for participating in science fair and Science Olympiad incorporated students ranking perceived rewards (benefits). The first two rankings for both the science fair and Science Olympiad were (1) "fun" and (2) "learning new things." For science fair, the number three ranking was "competing against other students" and for Science Olympiad it was "working with my friends."

Tallent-Runnels and Yarborough (1992) compared the responses of a group of students in a gifted education program that had participated in the Future Problem Solving Program with comparable students who had not participated. The authors reported significant differences in students' perceptions of their control over the future and their concerns about the future. The students participating in FPSP indicated a greater interest in global issues and viewed their control over the future more positively.

LIMITATIONS OF THE RESEARCH

The published literature on the educational effects and influences of academic competitions has relied on anecdotal testimonials, survey research, and a few case studies. The lack of a body of solid research, either quantitative or qualitative, makes it nearly impossible to draw conclusions from the studies on this topic. It appears that the studies available lacked rigor in the research design (e.g., lack of control groups, vague items on surveys, and other confounding factors). One of the reasons one might want to cite research on academic competitions is to recommend their use in school systems. It is a difficult task to do that when few recent studies are available.

Little research has been conducted on the relationship of participation in an academic competition and scholastic achievement or other growth outcomes as a result of participation. Before drawing conclusions about the outcomes of participation in competitions, experimental and/or comparative data on these outcomes are needed. A second line of research that examines the ways in which competitions affect psychosocial outcomes for gifted students would provide further understanding of the ways competitions impact these students. Although a very small number of studies suggest that academic competitions can have significant impact on participants' academic self-concept and future college and career plans, expansion and replication of this line of research would also help make more accurate assessments of the degree to which the stated goals of many of the competitions are achieved.

PRACTICAL IMPLICATIONS OF THE RESEARCH

One study suggests that participants in academic competitions emphasizing creative thinking and/or problem solving do show an increase in creative thinking (Fishkin, 1989). Students participating in the Future Problem Solving Program had more positive perceptions about the future and viewed their control over the future more positively. About one third of the students surveyed who participated in science fair and Science Olympiad reported enjoying the experience and working with others. Some enjoyed the competition and would do it again. Publications with an anecdotal basis are generally very positive in their reports of the efficacy of academic competitions based on comments from students, parents, and coaches/facilitators.

Although the literature documents a wide variety of academic competitions available for students representing all subject matter areas with choices to work individually or with a team, further experimental research is needed to validate these popular activities.

RESOURCES

There are a number of books and Internet links that provide listings of competitions and the topic of the contests. Below is a small sampling.

Internet Sources

Hoagies' Gifted Education Page: Contests and Awards
http://www.hoagiesgifted.org/contests.htm

Destination ImagiNation
http://www.destinationimagination.org

National History Day
http://www.nationalhistoryday.org

National Geographic Bee
http://www.nationalgeographic.com/society/ngo/geobee

Odyssey of the Mind
http://www.odysseyofthemind.com

Books

Karnes, F. A., & Riley, T. L. (2005). *Competitions for talented kids: Win scholarships, big prize money, and recognition.* Waco, TX: Prufrock Press.

REFERENCES

Abernathy, T. V., & Vineyard, R. N. (2001). Academic competitions in science: What are the rewards for students? *The Clearing House, 74,* 269–276.

Baird, W. E., & Shaw, E. L., Jr. (1996). Predicting success in selected events of the Science Olympiad. *School Science & Mathematics, 96,* 85–93.

Campbell, J. R., Feng, A., & Verna, M. (1999, August). *United States Olympiad studies: Math, physics, chemistry.* Paper presented at the 13th Biennial World Conference of the World Council for Gifted and Talented Children.

Fishkin, A. (1989). Efforts of Odyssey of the Mind creative problem-solving teams: Effects on creativity, creative self-concept, locus-of-control and general self-concept in gifted children. *Dissertation Abstracts International, 51*(01), 135. (UMI No. AAT9004004)

Frasier, M. M., Winstead, S., & Lee, J. (1997). Is the Future Problem Solving program accomplishing its goals? *Journal of Secondary Gifted Education, 8,* 157–163.

Karnes, F. A., & Riley, T. L. (1996). Competitions: Developing and nurturing talents. *Gifted Child Today, 19*(2), 14–15, 49.

Lamont, M., Kaufman, J., & Moody, M. (2000). The best of the brightest: Definitions of the ideal self among prize-winning students. *Sociological Forum, 15,* 187–224.

Riley, T. L., & Karnes, F. A. (1999). Competitions and exceptional children: A great combination. *Teaching Exceptional Children, 31*(5), 80–84.

Shook, D. N. (1997) *The effect of participation in the Odyssey of the Mind program on student creative thinking and problem solving skills*. Unpublished doctoral dissertation, Georgia State University.

Somers, L., & Callan, S. (1999). *An examination of science and mathematics competitions*. Retrieved January 20, 2006, from http://www.wmich.edu/evalctr/competitions.pdf

Stanley, J. C., & Benbow, C. P. (1983). SMPY's first decade: Ten years of posing problems and solving them. *Journal of Special Education, 17*, 11–25.

Swiatek, M. A., & Benbow, C. P. (1991). A 10-year longitudinal follow-up of participants in a fast-paced mathematics course. *Journal for Research in Mathematics Education, 22*, 138–150.

Tallent-Runnels, M. K., & Yarborough, D. W. (1992). Effects of the Future Problem Solving Program on children's concerns about the future. *Gifted Child Quarterly 36*, 190–194.

Weeks, D. M. (2003). *The impact of Odyssey of the Mind on the cognitive and psychosocial development of adolescents*. Unpublished master's thesis, Central Connecticut State University.

Chapter 2

ADHD

M. Layne Kalbfleisch and
Meredith Banasiak

his summary will explore the coexistence of intellec-
tual giftedness and Attention Deficit/Hyperactivity
Disorder (ADHD), two disparate, complex conditions that present additional complexities when they
are present in the same person. Because these complexities manifest themselves uniquely and on an
individual basis, and because of the limited research on the
combined gifted/ADHD condition, it is necessary to understand each construct singly in order to frame a discussion of
the combined condition. Research pertaining to the underlying physiology, diagnostic methods, and intervention strategies that are relevant to the combined condition will be the
focus of this discussion.

It is important to understand that ADHD is different
than and separate from a learning disability. Although in many
cases, a diagnosis of ADHD does occur together with specific
learning disabilities (Barkley, 1998; Biederman, Newcorn, &
Sprich, 1991; Shaywitz et al., 1995), these diagnoses do not
denote intellectual boundaries (Daley, 2006; Furman, 2005;

Garber, Garber, & Freedman Spizman, 1995). An individual can have both ADHD and exceptional intelligence. The combined condition, however, presents characteristics and challenges, as well as instances where this type of person may perform better on certain tasks distinct from those individuals having ADHD only or giftedness only.

WHAT IS ADHD?

There is much discrepancy across the literature about the characterization of ADHD, ranging from whether or not it is a disability, or even a valid diagnosis (Kohn, 1989; Reid, Maag, & Vasa, 1993). Moreover, it has been implied that the diagnosis of ADHD is a social invention (Breggin, 1998; Diller, 1998), or that ADHD is a misinterpretation of giftedness or creative behavior (Baum, Olenchak, & Owen, 1998; Lind, 1993; Rimm, 1999). To refute these perspectives, in 2002, the American Psychiatric Association released the International Consensus Statement on ADHD that stated, in part, that,

> As a matter of science, the notion that ADHD does not exist is simply wrong. All of the major medical associations and government health agencies recognize ADHD as a genuine disorder because the scientific evidence indicating it is so overwhelming. (Consortium of International Scientists, 2002, p. 89)

ADHD is the most common neuropsychiatric disorder of childhood (American Psychiatric Association, 2000) and is characterized by the following three core symptoms: inattention, and/or hyperactivity, and/or impulsivity (American Psychiatric Association, 2000) across the life cycle. Because ADHD symptoms may manifest themselves in different combinations of the above symptoms, and to different degrees, the APA has recognized three specific categories of ADHD in the 2000 *Diagnostic and Statistical Manual for Mental Disorders* (DSM-IV-TR): Predominantly Hyperactive/Impulsive Type, Predominantly Inattentive Type (commonly known as Attention Deficit Disorder, or ADD), and Combined Type.

Although the exact cause of ADHD is not known, behavioral symptoms are attributed to both biological and environmental factors. For instance, there is evidence to support the theory that a neurotransmitter dysfunction is the underlying cause of ADHD. Neurotransmitters are chemicals produced, released, and utilized by neurons in the brain that support different types of motor, emotional, and cognitive functions. Psychostimulant drugs that regulate the amount of certain neurotransmitters have been shown to reduce the symptoms of ADHD (Spencer et al., 1996).

The two neurotransmitters linked to ADHD are dopamine and norepinephrine. Dopamine, needed for movement control, can contribute to excess physical activity and possibly hyperactivity when it is present at abnormally high levels in the brain (Castellanos et al., 1994; Castellanos et al., 1996). Some studies propose that the excess dopamine results from an overabundance of dopamine transporters (D1) in the brain. Dopamine transporters remove dopamine that has been released into the system, so that it cannot be used by the brain. Some empirical support for this comes from studies that have found much higher concentrations of dopamine transporters in adults with ADHD than in adults without ADHD (Dougherty et al., 1999). Furthermore, dopamine binding decreased in subjects after a 4-week treatment regiment of low-dose methylphenidate (commonly known as Ritalin; Krause, Dresel, Krause, Kung, & Tatsch, 2000). Research indicates that the motor and cognitive symptoms of ADHD, while linked to the same neurotransmitters, are regulated by different brain processes (Solanto, 2002) and respond to drug therapy differently (Meador-Woodruff, Damask, & Watson, 1994; Spencer et al., 1996). This would account for the predominance of the two distinct ADHD subtypes: hyperactive/impulsive and inattentive (Lahey et al., 1994). Current research efforts are attempting to resolve the issue of whether ADHD results from a single neuropsychological deficit, or whether it results from a combination of deficits defined by these subtypes (Pennington, 2005).

The most widely accepted hypothesis correlates ADHD with a core defect that results in difficulties with executive function (Castellanos, Glaser, & Gerhardt, 2006). The executive function model accounts for the brain's ability to excite or inhibit responses, initiate and sustain activity, set priorities, and organize goal-oriented behaviors (Barkley, 1998; Denckla, 1996). It is proposed that there is a deficiency of both the neurotransmitters dopamine and norepinephrine. While dopamine assists with the organization of motor movement, norepinephrine is needed to sustain attention (Ernst, Zametkin, Matochik, Jons, & Cohen, 1998). Problems with the regulation of these two neurotransmitters contribute to some of the executive function difficulties seen in ADHD. When considering the relationship of brain structure to function, executive function is usually ascribed to the frontal cortex. There is evidence to suggest that the frontal cortex of the brain is altered in children with ADHD (Mostofsky, Cooper, Kates, Denckla, & Kaufmann, 2002; Murias, Swanson, & Srinivasan, 2007). However, there is strong evidence to show that the cerebellum, located at the base of the brain, is also a part of this support system. The cerebellum supports functions related to fine motor control, balance, and movement coordination. But, it also improves the efficiency of executive function by communicating with the frontal lobes during tasks that require attention (Anderson, Polcari, Lowen, Renshaw, & Teicher, 2002; Berquin et al., 1998; Castellanos et al., 2001; Mostofsky, Reiss, Lockhart, & Denckla, 1998). Research that continues to define the physiology of executive function in the normal brain will contribute much to the understanding of how this theoretical process is operating differently in the ADHD population.

Because ADHD is prevalent across families, generations (Biederman, Faraone, Mick, & Lelon, 1995), and among twins (Goodman & Stevenson, 1989), dopamine dysfunction is attributed to genetic factors. Specifically, one variation (allele) of the DRD4 gene that produces a dopamine receptor in areas associated with attention and self-regulation was found in populations with ADHD (Faraone, Doyle, Mick, & Biederman, 2001; Grady et al., 2005). Other groups are examining the gene abnormality of the DAT 1 gene, which codes for a dopamine transporter (Cook et al., 1995; Gill, Daly, Heron, Hawi, & Fitzgerald, 1997). There is growing evidence supporting the involvement of multiple genes associated with ADHD (Faraone et al., 2005; Swanson, Kinsoburne, et al., 2007). Thus, it is not prudent to conclude that certain genes will predetermine a diagnosis or result in an eventual diagnosis of ADHD.

DIAGNOSING ADHD

An objective evaluation tool for a diagnosis of ADHD seems unrealistic until the physiology of ADHD and its complexities become more succinctly defined. In current practice, ADHD only can be evaluated on the basis of behavior. For those who seek additional information, cognitive testing with a Wechsler Intelligence Scale for Children (WISC-IV) or other assessments such as the Test of Variables of Attention (TOVA), Gordon Diagnostic, or Conners' Continuous Performance Test (CPT), which tap into working memory and executive function and are sources of a more objective evaluation of attention and concentration. The terms *executive function* (Norman & Shallice, 1980/2000), *working memory* (Baddeley, 1986), and *attention* (Posner & Snyder, 1975) have varying definitions in the research literature, but they essentially address the core intellectual functions that come into question with ADHD (such as the ability to manage and prioritize information, the ability to attend to relevant information, and the ability to commit intellectual resources to tasks that are subjectively relevant and interesting to the individual) and are the basis of cognitive strengths seen in some gifted individuals with ADHD. The most widely adopted diagnostic measure is the DSM-IV-TR (American Psychiatric Association, 2000), which provides a list of behavioral criteria that identify ADHD. In order to be characterized as one of the three ADHD subtypes, the DSM-IV-TR states that, "Six or more of the listed symptoms of inattention, and six or more of the listed symptoms of hyperactivity-impulsivity must have been present for at least 6 months to a point that is disruptive and inappropriate for developmental level" (American Psychiatric Association, 2000). Additionally, the following conditions must be met:

- some symptoms that cause impairment were present before age seven;
- some impairment from the symptoms is present in two or more settings;
- there must be clear evidence of significant impairment in social, school, or work functioning;
- the symptoms do not happen only during the course of a pervasive developmental disorder or a psychotic disorder; and

- the symptoms are not better accounted for by another mental disorder (American Psychiatric Association, 2000).

It is imperative that a qualified clinician make the ADHD diagnosis because so many of the symptoms overlap with other conditions and learning disabilities. It is important to distinguish ADHD symptoms in terms of tasks that require effort (Borcherding et al., 1988) and not automatic tasks such as watching television or playing video games (Douglas & Parry, 1994). Although there are legitimate concerns that ADHD is overdiagnosed (Wolraich et al., 1990), a missed diagnosis is equally serious and especially relevant in the case of gifted ADHD children, where a child's cognitive strengths can obscure the symptoms. Some examples of situations that lend themselves to overdiagnosis include seeking diagnosis too early in childhood (prior to age 7), failing to assess how intellectually engaging an environment is before judging the hyperactivity of a child who may just be bored and restless, or failing to detect that hyperactivity may be the result of another problem (e.g., steroid inhalers, sleep disorders, allergies, or emotional trauma). In cases of gifted children with ADHD, regardless of their talents, it is just as critical for them to be correctly diagnosed as it is for nongifted children with ADHD, in order to develop their strengths and compensate for their difficulties.

The DSM-IV-TR acknowledges that "individuals with ADHD may show intellectual development in the above-average or gifted range" (American Psychiatric Association, 2000, p. 88) but does not provide any behavioral descriptions or epidemiological statistics for this combined condition. Thus, a comprehensive knowledge of ADHD, as well as an understanding of giftedness, is integral and necessary in determining an appropriate diagnosis.

GIFTEDNESS AND ADHD

Giftedness and ADHD, as separate constructs, can share many similar traits including rapid speech, impulsive actions, overindulgence, extra sensitivity to environmental stimuli, intense curiosity, melodrama, tendency to mix truth with fiction, use of image and metaphor, behavior extremes, somatic complaints, and difficulty adjusting to new environments (Kaufmann, Kalbfleisch & Castellanos, 2000). Given these similarities, it is important to understand the subtleties that distinguish the gifted child with overexcitabilities from the gifted child with ADHD. Developmentally, gifted children without ADHD are more likely to be socially, cognitively, and/or emotionally advanced at the mental age of children 2–4 years older (Neihart, Reis, Robinson, & Moon, 2002), whereas ADHD children experience a developmental lag 2–3 years behind their peers (Barkley, 1998; Kinsbourne, 1973). Furthermore, it is extremely important to note that giftedness can potentially moderate and/or enhance the function of a person with ADHD, and when it does, it can be positive. The presence of a benefit, however, is also typically present with some of the classic difficulties a person with ADHD experiences.

In comparing gifted children with ADHD to gifted peers without ADHD, children with the combined condition tend to exhibit inconsistency in academic performance (Webb & Latimer, 1993), and difficulty with handwriting, and prefer group or participatory activities to working alone (Zentall, Moon, & Hall, 2001). In comparing the combined gifted/ADHD condition with peers having ADHD only, the combined group typically experiences high-level interest and functioning in at least one subject area as opposed to a general dislike for school (Zentall, 1997) and sustained inattention.

One of the hallmarks of giftedness is the speed at which someone acquires new information. Conversely, one of the most pronounced consequences of ADHD is an inability to produce (Sergeant, Oosterlaan, & Van der Meere, 1999). Thus, there is a gap between rapid knowledge acquisition and what a gifted individual with ADHD may be able to demonstrate. To bridge this paradoxical gap, experimenting with various ways to make their "process" their "product" (e.g., allowing verbal presentations to replace or supplement written recall) will help them demonstrate their knowledge at a high proficiency level (Kaufmann et al., 2000).

POTENTIAL BENEFITS OF THE COMBINED CONDITION

Although ADHD symptoms can mask talent, it is also true that giftedness can mask ADHD. There is evidence that intelligence promotes skills that help to overcome some of the challenges of ADHD, such as allowing children with ADHD to channel excess activity constructively, to maintain focus and attention within areas of interest, and to avoid the urge to interrupt (Barkley, 1998; Phelan, 1996). Moreover, the combined condition poses its own set of gifts unique to this group.

Another observation is that highly creative qualities are linked to ADHD (Cramond, 1994, 1995; Kalbfleisch, in press; Lovecky, 1994; White & Shah, 2006). Specifically, individuals with ADHD tend to be comfortable with chaos or ambiguity and are not bounded by convention when it comes to creative expression (Hallowell & Ratey, 1995). These qualities manifest themselves in novel ways of combining dissimilar or unrelated things. Creative individuals are said to be able to achieve a state of "flow" or complete immersion in a task (Csikszentmihalyi, 1996); similarly, a state of "hyperfocus" has been attributed to individuals with ADHD (Hallowell & Ratey, 1994). One study found that boys with giftedness and ADHD experienced significantly more difficulty than boys with ADHD when shifting their attention between reading and divergent thinking (Kalbfleisch, 2000), suggesting that the gifted child with ADHD may be disposed to this state of hyperfocus. Interestingly, when the boys with both giftedness and ADHD were measured on their ability to shift between two very different divergent thinking tasks, they appeared more adept. Their shift measures looked similar to their gifted peers without ADHD and the typically performing children in the study. This lends support for the idea that gifted children with ADHD possess cognitive strengths that make them more adept in creative and divergent problem-solving tasks and situations. Although this state of hyperfocus can be a cognitive or intellectual benefit, it can make these children socially vulnerable because they lack the ability to "go with the flow" when in social situations with siblings, classmates, and friends (Moon, Zentall, Grskovic, Hall, & Stormont, 2001).

TREATMENT/INTERVENTION

Historically, a basic measure of giftedness is determined by a score on a standardized IQ test. Unfortunately, the behavioral symptoms associated with ADHD undermine certain aspects of performance in the testing environment that often results in IQ scores unrepresentative of an individual's actual ability. For this reason, giftedness is not always identified in this population (Gardner & Walters, 1993) and sometimes there is confusion about a diagnosis of ADHD and/or giftedness (Hartnett, Nelson, & Rinn, 2004). Given these limitations, how is it possible to assess and identify gifted individuals with ADHD? Specific research is needed to begin to capitalize on existing methods of assessment and to further identify testing trends present in children with giftedness and those with both giftedness and ADHD (Chae, Kim, & Noh, 2003). This type of normed information will provide a way to compare the gifted child to peers and to performance profiles associated with ADHD. One such study examined the relationship between ADHD, IQ, and divergent thinking, and found that boys with giftedness and ADHD used more diverse and nonverbal information in problem solving and showed aptitude in creativity, scoring higher on the Torrance Tests of Creative Thinking–Figural Forms (Torrance, 1990) than a group of gifted boys without ADHD (Shaw & Brown, 1991). Thus, a broader range of skills could be assessed if cognitive domains related to creativity could be assessed alongside traditional measures of intelligence. This would open the door to support nontraditional methods of assessment to allow this special population to display its unique skill sets and to compare and contrast with academic achievement measures (Volpe et al., 2006), which are likely to be incongruent with abilities in those with giftedness and ADHD. Until alternative tools are established, the use of multiple diagnostic methods, including standard achievement tests, teacher reports, and peer and parent nomination, in addition to intelligence tests will produce a more comprehensive portfolio in assessing an individual's intelligence (Webb & Latimer, 1993).

Intervention should address social, emotional, and cognitive aspects of both conditions (Neihart, 2003) and be individualized according to the degree of impairment and specific experience of each child. In the educational setting, there is a need for challenge in the area of giftedness balanced with a need for structure, stimulation, and individualization (Flick, 1998; Lerner, Lowenthal, & Lerner, 1995). Limited amounts of information on treatment-intervention models currently exist for the gifted/ADHD subgroup (Leroux & Levitt-Perlman, 2000). A program that accommodates different learning/processing styles and means of output (Gardner, 1991; Kaplan & Gould, 1995; Renzulli, 1994; Sternberg, Ferrari, Clinkenbeard, & Grigorenko, 1996) will be most able to challenge the gifts and support the limitations. How to best proceed on a pedagogical level has not been the subject of research to date. There are no data to inform which specific methods or strategies will provide successful intervention, accommodation, or enrichment in this twice-exceptional population. However, based upon observed strengths and weaknesses of these types of students, Kaufmann and colleagues (2000) suggest an approach that adapts existing gifted instructional models to accommodate for ADHD. For example:

- When practicing or presenting Synectics (Synectics being an approach to creative thinking through analogy or metaphor), perform the stages in small increments to maintain attention and focus (Gordon, 1960, 1974; Gordon & Poze, 1972).
- During Creative Problem Solving (CPS) and Future Problem Solving (FPS), refer to rules and vocabulary written on posters as visual supplements instead of using verbal instruction exclusively (Eberle & Stanish, 1985; Isaksen & Treffinger, 1985; Torrance & Sisk, 1997).
- In addition to specific contexts mentioned above, important interventions such as providing visual supplements to reinforce verbal instruction and guidance to perform tasks in small increments to maintain focus can support performance in circumstances across academic tasks and environments.
- Announce each stage and transition of the CPS/FPS or Synectics process before moving to the next.
- Within each enrichment cluster and in the regular classroom, assign buddies to assist each other in reviewing the work just undertaken and the work expected for the next day (Renzulli, 1994; Renzulli & Reis, 1997).
- Create and identify daily compacting procedures in addition to, or instead of, longer term goals in order to provide a schedule and practice organizational skills (Reis, Burns, & Renzulli, 1993; Renzulli, 1994).
- Employ alternative technologies such as computers or video rather than rely exclusively on in-person relationships and mentorships (Clasen & Clasen, 1997; Noller & Frey, 1994).
- Create a quiet area for student-teacher conferences rather than hold meetings at the teacher's desk or other high-traffic areas in order to reduce visual or noise distraction (Betts, 1991; Kaplan & Gould, 1995; Schlichter, 1997).

- Promote social skills by encouraging students to present their work to a variety of audiences (Reis et al., 1993; Renzulli, 1994).
- Present biographies of eminent persons and fictitious gifted characters that focus on learning and problem solving rather than solitary successes and find, when possible, models of people who have triumphed over disabilities to learn about coping skills (Frasier & McCannon, 1999; Schlichter, 1997).
- Have the students prepare a perfect day fantasy, allowing them to identify those factors that interrupt their focus and interfere with the achievement of their goals to help them identify distractions they encounter in the environment (Eberle, 1996; Torrance & Safter, 1999).
- Allow students to select challenging, high-interest rewards such as reading or puzzles as stimulating reinforcers (Renzulli, 1994).
- To bridge the paradoxical gap between the difficulties caused by ADHD and the strengths in divergent productive thinking, experimenting with various ways to make "process" their "product" (Kaufmann et al., 2000).

Mechanisms that address both strengths and weaknesses of the discrete and combined conditions will improve classroom efficiency and provide long-range benefits and skills to this special population. Because these conditions affect social and emotional development in addition to cognitive development, a team involving parents, physicians, counselors, teachers, and specialists in both ADHD and gifted education will be able to combine resources to meet the unique and changing requirements of these types of children.

Although this discussion is largely concerned with reviewing nonmedical interventions, it is acknowledged that data supporting positive outcomes for those with ADHD who have been appropriately prescribed psychostimulant drugs is coming on line (Castellanos et al., 2002; Solanto, 2002). But, this must be considered in the context of preliminary findings from longitudinal studies of the effects of stimulant medication that indicate decreases in physical growth associated with long-term use of these medications (Swanson, Elliot, et al., 2007). There is a paucity of data on this outcome in gifted individuals with ADHD. Because these medications are a commonly recommended intervention strategy in the treatment of ADHD, it is important to find the appropriate dose of the right medication for the individual, which can take some time and discomfort. Such medications act to reduce the core symptoms of inattention, impulsivity, and hyperactivity and offer much benefit in terms of motor, social, emotional, and executive functioning. The intake of medication should be accompanied by cognitive, behavioral and/or social therapies, and academic tutoring, if needed, to maximize the opportunity for permanent learning and acquiring compensatory skills (Barkley, 1998).

CONCLUSION

The coexistence of giftedness and ADHD presents its own unique challenges and benefits. Much basic research is still required to understand the complex physiology of ADHD and how it interacts with giftedness.

What We Know

- The underlying cause of ADHD is based on the regulation of the neurotransmitters dopamine and norepinephrine. Psychostimulant medications work to adjust this neurotransmitter imbalance and, in cases of appropriate medicine and dose, provide positive gains for the individual.
- ADHD and giftedness can and do coexist.
- Children with ADHD and giftedness are subject to both potential intellectual benefits and social vulnerabilities promoted by the state of flow or hyperfocus that this combination appears to lend.
- Ideally, diagnosing the combined condition requires a team of qualified experts from the fields of school psychology (preferably those who have expertise in gifted education), pediatrics, psychiatry, and curriculum and instruction. Under current circumstances, the parent needs to be the advocate who will initiate these interactions and coordinate the information on behalf of his or her child.

What We Should Study

- What are the underlying causes of ADHD? How does the ADHD brain differ from a normal brain structurally and functionally? (Biology)
- Why do individuals with ADHD and giftedness display strengths in creative or divergent thinking tasks? (Biology)
- How can we qualitatively diagnose this combined condition? Do current intelligence tests accurately reflect the aptitude of those with ADHD? The development of testing profiles for a comparison of the three groups (i.e., ADHD, gifted/ADHD, and gifted) are needed to better characterize them. (Diagnostic Tools)
- How can we best support this combined condition in educational curricula? (Intervention)
- There is a paucity of basic data on the prevalence of ADHD in the gifted population. Demographic studies are needed to more clearly outline this population and sharpen our strategic ability to advocate on their behalf. (Epidemiology)

RESOURCES

Children and Adults with Attention Deficit Hyperactivity Disorder (CHADD)
http://www.chadd.org

Council for Exceptional Children
http://www.cec.sped.org

Education Resources Information Center
http://www.eric.ed.gov

REFERENCES

American Psychiatric Association. (2000). *Diagnostic and statistical manual of mental disorders* (4th ed.) Washington, DC: Author.

Anderson, C. M., Polcari, A. M., Lowen, S. B., Renshaw, P. F., & Teicher, M. H. (2002). Effects of methylphenidate on functional magnetic resonance relaxometry of the cerebellar vermis in children with ADHD. *American Journal of Psychiatry, 159*, 1322–1328.

Baddeley, A. D. (1986). *Working memory.* Oxford, England: Clarendon Press.

Barkley, R. A. (1998). *Attention Deficit and Hyperactivity Disorder: A handbook for diagnosis and treatment* (2nd ed.). New York: Guilford Press.

Baum, S. M., Olenchak, F. R., & Owen, S. V. (1998). Gifted students with attention deficits: Fact or fiction? Or, can we see the forest for the trees? *Gifted Child Quarterly, 42*, 96–104.

Berquin, P. C., Giedd, J. N., Jacobsen, L. K., Hamburger, S. D., Krain, A. L., Rapoport, J. L., et al. (1998). The cerebellum in Attention-Deficit/Hyperactivity Disorder: A morphometric study. *Neurology, 50*, 1087–1093.

Betts, G. (1991). The autonomous learner model for the gifted and talented. In N. Colangelo & G. Davis (Eds.), *Handbook of gifted education* (pp. 142–153). Boston: Allyn & Bacon.

Biederman, J., Faraone, S., Mick, E., & Lelon, E. (1995). Psychiatric comorbidity among referred juveniles with major depression: Fact or artifact? *Journal of the American Academy of Child and Adolescent Psychiatry, 34*, 579–590.

Biederman, J., Newcorn, J., & Sprich, S. (1991). Comorbidity of Attention Deficit Hyperactivity Disorder with conduct, depressive, anxiety, and other disorders. *American Journal of Psychiatry, 148*, 564–577.

Borcherding, B., Thompson, K., Kruesi, M. J. P., Bartko, J., Rapoport, J. L., & Weingartner, H. (1988). Automatic and effortful processing in Attention Deficit Hyperactivity Disorder. *Journal of Abnormal Child Psychology, 16*, 333–345.

Breggin, P. R. (1998). *Talking back to Ritalin: What doctors aren't telling you about stimulants for your children.* Monroe, ME: Common Courage Press.

Castellanos, F. X., Elia, J., Kruesi, M. J. P., Gulotta, C. S., Meffors, I. N., Potter, W. Z., et al. (1994). Cerebrospinal fluid monamine metabolites in boys with Attention Deficit Hyperactivity Disorder. *Psychiatry Research, 52*, 305–316.

Castellanos, F. X., Elia, J., Kruesi, M. J. P., Marsh, W. L., Gulotta, C. S., Potter, W. Z., et al. (1996). Cerebrospinal homovanillic acid predicts behavioral response to stimulants in 45 boys with Attention Deficit Hyperactivity Disorder. *Neuropsychopharmacology, 14*, 125–137.

Castellanos, F. X., Giedd, J. N., Berquin, P. C., Walter, J. M., Sharp, W., Tran, T., et al. (2001). Quantitative brain magnetic resonance imaging in girls with Attention-Deficit/Hyperactivity Disorder. *Archives of General Psychiatry, 58*, 289–295.

Castellanos, F. X., Lee, P. P., Sharp, W., Jeffries, N. O., Greenstein, D. K., Clasen L. S., et al. (2002). Developmental trajectories of brain volume abnormalities in children and adolescents with Attention-Deficit/Hyperactivity Disorder. *Journal of the American Medical Association, 288*, 1740–1748.

Castellanos, F. X., Glaser, P. E., & Gerhardt, G. A. (2006). Towards a neuroscience of Attention-Deficit Hyperactivity Disorder: Fractionating the phenotype. *Journal of Neuroscience Methods, 151*, 1–4.

Chae, P. K., Kim, J., & Noh, K. (2003). Diagnosis of ADHD among gifted children in relation to KEDI-WISC and T.O.V.A. performance. *Gifted Child Quarterly, 47*, 192–201.

Clasen, D., & Clasen, R. (1997). Mentoring: A time-honored option for education of the gifted and talented. In N. Colangelo & G. Davis (Eds.), *Handbook of gifted education* (2nd ed., pp. 218–229). Needham Heights, MA: Allyn & Bacon.

Consortium of International Scientists. (2002). International consensus statement on ADHD. *Clinical Child and Family Psychology Review, 5*, 2, 89–111.

Cook, E. H., Stein, M. A., Krasowski, M. D., Cox, N. J., Olkon, D. M., Kieffer, J. E., et al. (1995). Association of Attention Deficit Disorder and the dopamine transporter gene. *American Journal of Human Genetics, 56*, 993–998.

Cramond, B. (1994). Attention-Deficit Hyperactivity Disorder and creativity—What is the connection? *Journal of Creative Behavior, 28*, 193–210.

Cramond, B. (1995). *The coincidence of Attention Deficit Hyperactivity Disorder and creativity* (Research-Based Decision Making Series No. 9508). Storrs: National Research Center on the Gifted and Talented, University of Connecticut.

Csikszentmihalyi, M. (1996). *Creativity: Flow and the psychology of discovery and invention.* New York: HarperCollins.

Daley, D. (2006). ADHD: A review of essential facts. *Child: Care, Health & Development, 32*, 193–204.

Denckla, M. B. (1996). A theory and model of executive function: A neuropsychological perspective. In G. R. Lyon & N. A. Krasnegor (Eds.), *Attention, memory, and executive function* (pp. 263–278). Baltimore: Paul H. Brookes.

Diller, L. H. (1998). *Running on Ritalin: A physician reflects on children, society and performance in a pill.* New York: Bantam Books.

Dougherty, D. D., Bonab, A. A., Spencer, T. J., Rauch, S. L., Madras, B. K., & Fischman, A. J. (1999). Dopamine transporter density is elevated in patients with Attention Deficit Hyperactivity Disorder. *The Lancet, 354*, 2132–2133.

Douglas, V. I., & Parry, P. A. (1994). Effects of reward and nonreward on frustration and attention in Attention Deficit Disorder. *Journal of Abnormal Child Psychology, 22*, 281–302.

Eberle, R. (1996). *SCAMPER: Games for imagination development.* Waco, TX: Prufrock Press.

Eberle, R., & Stanish, B. (1985). *CPS for kids.* Carthage, IL: Good Apple.

Ernst, M., Zametkin, A. J., Matochik, J. A., Jons, P. H., & Cohen, R. M. (1998). DOPA decarboxylase activity in Attention Deficit Hyperactivity Disorder adults: A [fluorine-18] fluorodopa positron emission tomographic study. *Journal of Neuroscience, 18,* 5901–5907.

Faraone, S. V., Doyle, A. E., Mick, E., & Biederman, J. (2001). Meta-analysis of the association between the 7-repeat allele of the dopamine d(4) receptor gene and Attention Deficit Hyperactivity Disorder. *American Journal of Psychiatry, 158,* 1052–1057.

Faraone, S. V., Perlis, R. H., Doyle, A. E., Smoller, J. W., Goralnick, J. J., Holmgren, M. A., et al. (2005). Molecular genetics of Attention-Deficit/Hyperactivity Disorder. *Biological Psychiatry, 57,* 1313–1323.

Flick, G. L. (1998). *ADD/ADHD behavior-change resource kit.* New York: Simon & Schuster.

Frasier, M., & McCannon, C. (1999). Using bibliotherapy with gifted children. *Gifted Child Quarterly, 25,* 81–85.

Furman, L. (2005). What is ADHD? *Journal of Child Neurology, 20,* 994–1102.

Garber, S. W., Garber, M. D., & Freedman Spizman, R. (1995). *If your child is hyperactive, inattentive, impulsive, distractible: Helping the ADD hyperactive child.* New York: Villard Books.

Gardner, H. (1991). *The unschooled mind: How children think and how schools should teach.* New York: Basic Books.

Gardner, H., & Walters, J. (1993). A rounded version. In H. Gardner (Ed.), *Multiple intelligences: Theory into practice* (pp. 13–34). New York: Basic Books.

Gill, M., Daly, G., Heron, S., Hawi, Z., & Fitzgerald, M. (1997). Confirmation of association between Attention Deficit Hyperactivity Disorder and a dopamine transorter polymorphism. *Molecular Psychiatry, 2,* 311– 313.

Goodman, R., & Stevenson, J. (1989). A twin study of hyperactivity. II. The aetiological role of genes, family relationships and perinatal adversity. *Journal of Child Psychology and Psychiatry, 30,* 691–709.

Gordon, W. J. (1960). *Synectics.* New York: Harper & Row.

Gordon, W. J. (1974). *Making it strange.* New York: Harper & Row.

Gordon, W. J., & Poze, T. (1972). *Teaching is listening.* Cambridge, MA: SES Associates.

Grady, D. L., Haraxhi, A., Smith, M., Flodman, P., Spence, M. A., Swanson, J. M., et al. (2005). Sequence variants of the DRD4 gene in autism: Further evidence that rare DRD4 7R haplotypes are ADHD specific. *American Journal of Medical Genetics, Part B (Neuropsychiatric Genetics), 136B:* 33–35.

Hallowell, E., & Ratey, J. (1994). *Answers to distraction.* New York: Simon & Schuster.

Hallowell, E., & Ratey, J. (1995). *Driven to distraction.* New York: Simon & Schuster.

Hartnett, D. N., Nelson, J. M., & Rinn, A. N. (2004). Gifted or ADHD? The possibilities of misdiagnosis. *Roeper Review, 26,* 73–77.

Isaksen, S. G., & Treffinger, D. J. (1985). *Creative problem solving: The basic course.* Buffalo, NY: Bearly.

Kalbfleisch, M. L. (2000). *Electroencephalographic differences between males with and without ADHD with average and high aptitude during task transitions.* Unpublished doctoral dissertation, University of Virginia.

Kalbfleisch, M. L. (in press). The neural plasticity of giftedness. In L. Shavinina (Ed.), *Handbook on giftedness.* New York: Springer Science.

Kaplan, S., & Gould, B. (1995). *Frames: Differentiating the core curriculum.* Calabasas, CA: Educator to Educator.

Kaufmann, F. A., Kalbfleisch, M. L., & Castellanos, F. X. (2000). *Attention Deficit Disorders and gifted students: What do we really know?* (Research Monograph No. 00146). Storrs: National Research Center on the Gifted and Talented, University of Connecticut.

Kinsbourne, M. (1973). Minimal brain dysfunction as a neurodevelopmental lag. *Annals of the New York Academy of Sciences, 205,* 268–273.

Kohn, A. (1989, October). Suffer the restless children. *Atlantic Monthly,* 90–100.

Krause, K. H., Dresel, S. H., Krause, J., Kung, H. F., & Tatsch, K. (2000). Increased striatal dopamine transporter in adult patients with Attention Deficit Hyperactivity Disorder: Effects of methylphenidate as measured by single photon emission computed tomography. *Neuroscience Letters, 285,* 107–110.

Lahey, B. B., Applegate, B., McBurnett, K., Biederman, J., Greenhill, L., Hynd, G. W., et al. (1994). DSM-IV field trials for Attention Deficit Hyperactivity Disorder in children and adolescents. *American Journal of Psychiatry, 151,* 1673–1685.

Lerner, J. W., Lowenthal, B., & Lerner, S. R. (1995). *Attention Deficit Disorders: Assessment and teaching.* Pacific Grove, CA: Brooks/Cole.

Leroux, J. A., & Levitt-Perlman, M. (2000). The gifted child with ADD: An identification and intervention challenge. *Roeper Review, 22,* 171–176.

Lind, S. (1993). Something to consider before referring for ADD/ADHD. *Counseling & Guidance, 4,* 1–3.

Lovecky, D. (1994). The hidden gifted learner: Creativity and Attention Deficit Disorder. *Understanding Our Gifted, 6*(6), 3, 18–19.

Meador-Woodruff, J. H., Damask, S. P., & Watson, S. J. (1994). Differential expression of auto-receptors in the ascending dopamine systems of the human brain. *Proceedings of the National Academy of Sciences, 91,* 8297–8301.

Moon, S. M., Zentall, S. S., Grskovic, J. A., Hall, A., & Stormont, M. (2001). Emotional and social characteristics of boys with AD/HD and/or giftedness: A comparative case study. *Journal for the Education of the Gifted, 24,* 207–247.

Mostofsky, S. H., Reiss, A. L., Lockhart, P., & Denckla, M. B. (1998). Evaluation of cerebellar size in attention-deficit hyperactivity disorder. *Journal of Child Neurology, 13,* 434–9.

Mostofsky, S. H., Cooper, K. L., Kates, W. R., Denckla, M. B., & Kaufmann, W. E. (2002). Smaller prefrontal and premotor volumes in boys with Attention-Deficit-Hyperactivity Disorder. *Biological Psychiatry, 52,* 785–794.

Murias, M., Swanson, J. M., & Srinivasan, R. (2007). Functional connectivity of frontal cortex in healthy and ADHD children reflected in EEG coherence. *Cerebral Cortex, 17,* 1788–1799.

Neihart, M., Reis, S., Robinson, N., & Moon, S. (Eds.). (2002). *The social and emotional development of gifted children: What do we know?* Waco, TX: Prufrock Press.

Neihart, M. (2003). *Gifted children with Attention Deficit Hyperactivity Disorder (ADHD).* Arlington, VA: ERIC Clearinghouse on Disabilities and Gifted Education. (ERIC Document Reproduction Service No. ED482344)

Noller, R., & Frey, R. (1994). *Mentoring: Annotated bibliography.* Sarasota, FL: Center for Creative Learning.

Norman, D. A., & Shallice, T. (2000). Attention to action: Willed and automatic control of behaviour. In M. Gazzaniga (Ed.), *Cognitive neuroscience: A reader* (pp. 376–390). Malden, MA: Blackwell. (Original work published 1980)

Pennington, B. (2005). Toward a new neuropsychological model of Attention-Deficit/ Hyperactivity Disorder: Subtypes and multiple deficits. *Biological Psychiatry, 57,* 1221–1223.

Phelan, T. (1996). *All about Attention Deficit Disorder.* Minneapolis, MN: Child Management Press.

Posner, M. I., & Snyder, C. R. R. (1975). Attention and cognitive control. In R. Solso (Ed.), *Information processing and cognition: The Loyola Symposium* (pp. 55–85). Hillsdale, NJ: Lawrence Erlbaum.

Reid, R., Maag, J., & Vasa, S. F. (1993). Attention Deficit Hyperactivity Disorder as a disability category: A critique. *Exceptional Children, 60,* 198–214.

Reis, S. M., Burns, D., & Renzulli, J. S. (1993). *Curriculum compacting: The complete guide for modifying the regular curriculum for high ability students.* Mansfield Center, CT: Creative Learning Press.

Renzulli, J. S. (1994). *Schools for talent development: A practical plan for total school improvement.* Mansfield Center, CT: Creative Learning Press.

Renzulli, J. S., & Reis, S. M. (1997). The schoolwide enrichment model: New directions for developing high end learning. In N. Colangelo & G. Davis (Eds.), *Handbook of gifted education* (2nd ed., pp. 136–153). Needham Heights, MA: Allyn & Bacon.

Rimm, S. (1999, March). Attention Deficit Disorder: A difficult diagnosis. *Parenting for High Potential,* 12–13, 28.

Schlichter, C. (1997). Talents unlimited model in programs for gifted students. In N. Colangelo & G. A. Davis (Eds.), *Handbook of gifted education* (2nd ed., pp. 318–328). Needham Heights, MA: Allyn & Bacon.

Sergeant, J., Oosterlaan, J., & Van der Meere, J. (1999). Information processing and energetic factors in Attention Deficit Hyperactivity Disorder. In H. C. Quay & A. E. Hogan (Eds.), *Handbook of disruptive behavior disorders* (pp. 75–104). New York: Plenum Press.

Shaw, G. A., & Brown, G. (1991). Laterality, implicit memory and attention disorder. *Educational Studies, 17,* 15–23.

Shaywitz, B. A., Fletcher, J. M., Holahan, J. M., Schneider, A. E., Marchione, K. E., Stuebing, K. K., et al. (1995). Interrelationships between reading disability and attention deficit hyperactivity disorder. *Child Neuropsychology, 1,* 170–186.

Solanto, M. V. (2002). Dopamine dysfunction in ADHD: Integrating clinical and basic neuroscience research. *Behavioral Brain Research, 130,* 65–71.

Spencer, T., Biederman, J., Wilens, T. E., Harding, M., O'Donnell, D., & Griffin, S. (1996). Pharmacotherapy of Attention Deficit Hyperactivity Disorder across the life cycle. *Journal of the American Academy of Child and Adolescent Psychiatry, 35,* 409–432.

Sternberg, R., Ferrari, M., Clinkenbeard, P., & Grigorenko, E. (1996). Identification, instruction and assessment of gifted children: A construct validation model. *Gifted Child Quarterly, 40,* 129–137.

Swanson, J. M., Elliott, G. R., Greenhill, L. L., Wigal, T., Arnold, E., Vitiello, B., et al. (2007). Effects of stimulant medication on growth rates across 3 years in the MTA follow up. *Journal of American Academy of Child and Adolescent Psychiatry, 46,* 1015–1027.

Swanson, J. M., Kinsoburne, M., Nigg, J., Lanphear, B., Stefanatos, G. A., Volkow, N., et al. (2007). Etiologic subtypes of ADHD: Brain imaging, molecular genetic, and environmental factors and the dopamine hypothesis. *Neuropsychological Reviews, 17,* 39–59.

Torrance, E. P. (1990). *Torrance Tests of Creative Thinking, directions manual, figural forms A and B*. Bensenville, IL: Scholastic Testing Service.

Torrance, E. P., & Safter, T. (1999). *Making the creative leap beyond . . .* Buffalo, NY: Creative Education Foundation Press.

Torrance, E. P., & Sisk, D. S. (1997). *Gifted and talented children in the regular classroom*. Buffalo, NY: Bearly.

Volpe, R. J., DuPaul, J. G., DiPerna, J. C., Jitendra, A. K., Lutz, J. G., Tresco, K. E., et al. (2006). ADHD and scholastic achievement. *School Psychology Review, 35*, 47–61.

Webb, J. T. & Latimer, D. (1993). ADHD and children who are gifted. *Exceptional Children, 60*, 183–185.

White, H. A., & Shah, P. (2006). Creativity in adults with ADHD. *Personality and Individual Differences, 40*, 1121–1131.

Wolraich, M. L., Lindgren, S., Stromquist, A., Milich, R., Davis, C., & Watson, D. (1990). Stimulant medication use by primary care physicians in the treatment of Attention Deficit Hyperactivity Disorder. *Pediatrics, 86*, 95–101.

Zentall, S. (1997, March). *Learning characteristics of boys with Attention Deficit Hyperactivity Disorder and/or giftedness*. Paper presented at the annual meeting of the American Educational Research Association, Chicago. (ERIC Document Reproduction No. ED407791)

Zentall, S. S., Moon, S. M., & Hall, A. M. (2001). Learning and motivational characteristics of boys with AD/HD and/or giftedness. *Exceptional Children, 67*, 499–519.

Chapter 3

ADVANCED PLACEMENT AND INTERNATIONAL BACCALAUREATE PROGRAMS

*Holly Hertberg-Davis and
Carolyn M. Callahan*

THE ADVANCED PLACEMENT PROGRAM

nitial development of the Advanced Placement (AP) program was predicated on a perceived need to provide students with an opportunity to earn college credit while still in high school. The major impetus for the creation of the AP courses and exams came from a group of educators convened to respond to concerns that an innovative program developed by the Ford Foundation providing scholarships to high school sophomores to attend prestigious colleges was taking the most promising students away from their secondary schools. Noting that there was "a failure of the school and college to see their jobs as a continuous process" (General Education in School and College, 1952, as cited in Rothschild, 1995, p. 26), the group recommended that able students take freshman college courses in their home high schools during their senior years. In 1954, the Educational

Testing Service was given a contract to: (a) develop exams to assess outcomes in experimental schools using college-level syllabi, and (b) compare results of the high school students' scores on the exams to those of freshmen in the 12 colleges involved in the endeavor. The resulting favorable comparison provided an impetus to expand efforts to develop individual courses allowing motivated students to earn college credit while still in high school.

Currently, the AP program consists of 35 courses and exams offered by the College Board to provide students with exposure to college-level work and the potential to earn college credit while still in high school. Students may elect to take any number of AP courses and exams across the 35 subject areas that are offered, depending upon the availability and timing of the AP courses offered in their schools. Schools are not required to offer any specific number or sequence of AP courses.

In order to receive college credit for an AP course, students must take a standardized end-of-course exam. These exams are developed by the College Entrance Examination Board (CEEB) and scored by independent, trained examiners. Scores range from 1 to 5 on each exam. College credits are assigned according to the policy of the college or university to which the student applies for credit. A score of 3 or greater is described by the College Board as acceptable to most colleges for granting credit for Advanced Placement (Morgan & Ramist, 1998), although the acceptable score varies widely by college and department. The AP Program Web site advises students that a grade of 3 on an AP exam is equivalent to a C in an introductory college course and that a 5 is equivalent to an A (College Board, 2005b).

AP courses are developed in consultation with college faculty and high school teachers who are experienced in Advanced Placement teaching. The College Board also provides workshops for teachers on strategies for teaching AP courses and preparing students for the AP exams. Additionally, for each of the 35 AP courses, course syllabi—including topical outlines and recommended texts and readings, specifications of what is emphasized on the end-of-course examinations, recommended laboratory time and exercises, and sample exam questions—are provided for teachers.

In 2005, 1.2 million students from 15,000 schools took 2.1 million AP exams.

THE INTERNATIONAL BACCALAUREATE PROGRAM

Early descriptions of the International Baccalaureate (IB) program asserted that the program was "a rigorous pre-university course of study, leading to examinations, that meets the needs of highly motivated and academically gifted secondary school students" (International Baccalaureate North America, 1986, p. 1). The initial aim of the program, as its name implies, was to provide "an international university entrance examination that could be taken in any country and recognized in any country" (p. 1). However, the most recent literature of the diploma program no longer includes *gifted* as a descriptor of its target population, but rather describes its focus as "highly motivated students who hope to attend university" (International Baccalaureate Organization, 2004).

Funded by major grants from the Ford Foundation and the Twentieth Century Fund, the program was initiated by educators in international schools who were faced with multiple entrance exams required by the nations where their students were considering postsecondary education. These educators were also concerned about the "increasing emphasis on education as the delivery of information, the fragmentation of knowledge, and the de-emphasis on aesthetic and creative education" (International Baccalaureate North America, 1986, p. 2).

The IB program aims to provide a rigorous course of study focusing on active learning, citizenship, internationalism, and respect for other cultures. Unlike the Advanced Placement program, which allows students to choose from individual courses, the IB program is designed to be a comprehensive program of studies (for further distinctions between the AP and IB programs, see Table 1). Students in the program are expected to complete a course of study following specific requirements including study in both the humanities and sciences. Students seeking the IB diploma must select one subject from each of six categories (Language, Second Language, Individuals and Societies, Experimental Sciences, Mathematics and Computer Science, and Arts and Electives). Courses are designated as either Higher Level (HL) or Subsidiary Level (SL). To earn the IB diploma, students must successfully complete at least three (but not more than four) subjects at the Higher Level and three courses at the Subsidiary Level. All IB diploma candidates must also take the Theory of Knowledge course. Taken over the course of the 2 years of the program, this course is designed to provoke students to examine the nature of knowledge and knowing. Students take end-of-course exams in each of the IB subjects. These exams are evaluated by independent IB examiners.

In addition to the required coursework, IB diploma candidates must also complete an extended essay of 4,000–5,000 words on an independent study topic and successfully complete an approved creative, aesthetic, or social service activity.

In order to offer the IB program, a school must be approved through a formal application and review process. The application requires the school to offer all of the courses in the IB program leading to the diploma. Participation in the IB program also requires an application fee and an annual participation fee, obligatory participation in teacher training, and the provision of an IB coordinator in the school.

In 2005, more than 50,000 students from 1,597 schools in 122 countries worldwide were enrolled in the IB Diploma Program.

TABLE 1

Distinctions Between the AP and IB Programs

	The Advanced Placement Program	The International Baccalaureate Program
Coursework	The AP program consists of courses independent of one another. Students may take as many or as few as they like.	In order to earn an IB diploma, students must take a program of required courses.
Adoption of the program	No application or review process is necessary for adopting the AP program, but audits are now being conducted to ensure that courses bearing the AP label align with AP quality standards.	A formal application and review process is necessary for a school to adopt the IB program.
Cost to schools	No cost is associated with the AP program. Students pay an exam fee.	School must pay an application and annual participation fee to have IB program.
Teacher training	Teacher training is offered, but not required in order to offer AP courses.	Teacher training is mandatory in order to offer IB courses.
Personnel	No AP coordinator is required to oversee AP courses.	An IB coordinator is required in a school to oversee IB program.

MAJOR QUESTIONS ADDRESSED IN THE RESEARCH

Although AP and IB courses have become the primary service models for gifted high school students, little research has been conducted on their appropriateness for these learners. Of the research that has been conducted, the primary questions have focused on satisfaction with the courses/programs and success of students in college. Of the research that has been conducted, the primary methodologies used have been surveys of student and teacher satisfaction with the programs, as well as comparisons of college success among those students who have earned credit for college courses through the AP or IB exams and those who have not. Recent studies have examined the appropriateness of AP and IB courses for minority students.

CONCLUSIONS FROM THE RESEARCH

Student Satisfaction

Research on student perceptions of AP and IB courses reveals that students feel satisfied with the challenge offered in these courses, particularly as they are compared to nonaccelerated high school options. The Oregon Early Options Study (Oregon University System, Oregon State Department of Education, and Office of Community College Services, 1999), which included an examination of student satisfaction with AP courses and IB programs, cited "relief of high school boredom" (p. 3) as among the benefits of AP, IB, and other early college credit options. In another study of students' perceptions of AP and IB courses, students reported feeling better prepared for college as a result of taking these courses (Hellerman, 1994). Casserly (1986) reported overall high student satisfaction with AP courses; however, there were large standard deviations on each rating (close to 1 on a 5-point scale) and considerable numbers of students assigned ratings below the middle of the scale. A recent study investigating the "fit" of AP and IB courses for gifted students (Hertberg-Davis, Callahan, & Kyburg, 2006) found that, overwhelmingly, students taking AP and IB courses believed that these courses were the most challenging courses offered in high school and preferred these courses over any others they had taken. However, while the AP students interviewed in the study expressed overall satisfaction with the courses, they indicated that there was too much emphasis on the end-of-course AP exams. Hertberg-Davis et al. (2006) also found that students who expressed dissatisfaction with their AP and IB courses pointed to the lack of fit between their learning styles and the way in which material was presented in the courses.

Teacher Opinion

In 1986, the College Board reported that 92% of a national sample of teachers rated the AP program excellent or good, and 78% agreed that the courses challenged both the teachers and students. Similarly, 92% of the teachers in a limited 1985 California sample rated AP programs as good or excellent (Casserly, 1986). Data were not analyzed by course in these studies. In a more recent survey of AP teachers that yielded more than 32,000 responses, the College Board reported that ethnic minority teachers were heavily underrepresented, and that most teachers appeared to have financial access to professional development activities prior to teaching AP, but limited time to take them. These teachers described the five most pressing issues they faced as a result of teaching AP as (1) keeping up with changing discipline content, (2) integrating new teaching methods, (3) preparing students for state assessments, (4) dealing with lack of family involvement, and (5) accessing good professional development (Milewski & Gillie, 2002). Hertberg-Davis et al. (2006) found that AP and IB teachers perceived many advantages to the courses they taught and believed that their courses provided college-level challenge to advanced high school learners. The AP teachers in this study also noted disadvantages to the courses, including concerns that the need to prepare students for the end-of-course exams limited their ability to address students' interests, forced them to rush through material, and limited the range of instructional strategies that they could use to a primarily lecture-oriented format. Based on a self-report study of teachers who were experienced AP science teachers, Herr (1992) concluded that AP teachers introduce a wider range of topics than teachers in honors classes do and cover them in greater detail. But, because of the need to cover topics to be tested, they adopt a "strong lecture format and minimize time-consuming, student-centered activities such as laboratory experiments, student projects, and student presentations" (p. 530). Furthermore, one third of AP science teachers judged the pace of AP to be too fast and indicated a preference to switch to honors if given a choice. They also indicated that they failed to spend time on topics that pique the interests of students because of content coverage demands.

Impact on College Performance

Research studies provide tentative evidence that students who take AP and IB courses perform as well or better in college than students who do not take these courses. Some research indicates that, regardless of student success within AP courses, merely taking AP courses may have an impact on students' educational paths. The National Center for Educational Accountability, a collaborative effort of the Education Commission of the States, the University of Texas at Austin, and Just for the Kids, reports that based on data from Texas schools, even students who scored less than 3 on an AP examination in high school were twice as likely to graduate from college within 5 years as students who did not take AP courses (Mathews, 2004). Clifford Adelman's study, "Answers in the Toolbox" (1999), found that the strength of a student's high school curriculum was a stronger predictor of college success and college graduation than were socioeconomic status, test scores, or high school grade point average.

Research studies on college success report "good" correlations between scores on AP exams and grades in subsequent college courses and also document that AP students continue to pursue knowledge in the subject areas in which they took exams at a higher rate than other students (Morgan & Crone, 1993). Students who received credit for introductory courses based on success on AP exams have been compared in subsequent courses to those who took the college introductory courses. Those students who earned AP credit received significantly higher grades than those students who took the college courses (Breland & Oltman, 2001; Morgan & Ramist, 1998). However, subsequent examination of these studies by a panel of the National Research Council (NRC; 2002) resulted in the conclusion that

> The methodology used in conducting the studies makes it difficult to determine how often and under what circumstances there is a positive advantage for AP students.... [The methodological flaws also] make it difficult to determine whether any apparent advantage held by AP students is a function of the college they attend, the classes they enter, their own academic backgrounds and abilities, or the quality of the AP courses they took in high school. (p. 193)

As with AP courses, research on the impact of the IB program on students' performance in college is very limited. Like the AP research, research on IB programs is characterized by lack of control for aptitude and motivational variables. Poelzer and Feldhusen (1996) compared students enrolled in IB higher level [HL] courses in physics, biology, and chemistry; students enrolled in subsidiary level [SL] courses in the same subjects; and students enrolled in regular school courses. Even though sample sizes were small, an ANOVA repeated measure pre-post comparison showed students in the HL (studying the subject 2 years before sitting for the examination) and SL courses (studying the subject for 1 year before sitting for the examination) outperforming students in the traditional courses on Advanced Placement tests. However, the mean score of IB physics students (27%) fell well below the mean for AP students (43%).

A study of IB students at the University of Virginia documented that the grade point averages of IB students during their college years exceeded those of AP students by .2 points and exceeded students who were in neither IB nor AP programs by .3 points (Grexa, 1988). The author concluded that "IB students perform at least as well as their counter-parts from the same or other schools that do not offer IB" (p. 5).

A report prepared by the Center for Undergraduate Education in Science, Mathematics, and Engineering (1999) cautions that even high scores on the AP examinations cannot be equated with deep understanding. Part of the concern about the preparedness of students for college courses stems from the conclusion that the College Board courses are based on "*typical* [emphasis in the original] college introductory courses, rather than the best college courses or educational practices based on learning and pedagogy" (p. 24). The National Academy panel studying Advanced Placement mathematics and science courses likewise challenged the "assumption that AP courses uniformly reflect the content coverage and conceptual understanding that is developed in good college courses" (National Research Council, 2002, p. 192). The International Baccalaureate program does not claim that its courses are based on college introductory courses, yet many colleges and universities grant credit for courses based on scores on the IB exams. No independent research documents the equivalence of AP and IB courses, and the literature does not present evidence that the IB exam score predicts or does not predict success in upper level college courses, nor that the preparation in IB courses provides (or does not provide) the depth of understanding equivalent to that of introductory college courses (National Research Council, 2002).

In reviewing the mathematics and science curriculum offered in AP and IB programs, the National Academy of Sciences (NAS) panel (National Research Council, 2002) concluded that there were shortcomings in these curricula, particularly with respect to developing deep understandings of concepts and key ideas from the disciplines: "Excessive breadth of coverage (especially in 1-year science programs) and insufficient emphasis on key concepts in final assessments contribute to the problem in all science fields. . . [I]n mathematics, further improvement is needed" (p. 8). There is no clear delineation of the specific prior knowledge needed for success in the sciences. Further, they conclude, many of the programs and courses are not effective in helping students develop metacognitive skills.

The Advanced Placement Program and Equity Concerns

It is well-documented that African Americans and Hispanics are underrepresented in AP courses (e.g., Gándara, 2004; Miller, 2004; National Study Group for the Affirmative Development of Academic Ability, 2004). A recent study at the University of Texas at Austin's Charles A. Dana Center investigated Calculus courses with high enrollment of minority students in high-poverty schools to understand the specific factors associated with this high enrollment (Picucci & Sobel, 2002). The study found that these courses were situated in districts with a culture of high expectations for student achievement; a commitment to training teachers and advanced-level content; and a partnership with an outside agency that provided resources, training, and support for teachers and students. The teachers in these schools had high expectations for their students and used varied instructional techniques to make the high-level content accessible to students. In turn, students in these schools took the initiative to enroll in AP courses and persisted in the face of difficulty. The study did not examine student success within the courses or on the AP exams.

Increasing the number of minority students participating in advanced-level courses—particularly AP courses—has been a major focus of the College Board and of the federal and state governments in recent years (e.g., Borman, Stringfield, & Rachuba, 2000; Kinlaw, 2006; White House Press Release, 2004). As a result of these strenuous efforts, the number of Black and Latino students participating in AP courses has increased significantly. The number of Black students taking AP exams nearly doubled between 2000 and 2005 to approximately 62,000, and the number of Latino students taking AP exams more than doubled to approximately 135,000 during that same time period (Epstein, 2006).

This increased access to AP courses and the challenging curriculum within them for Black and Latino students represents an important movement toward achieving equity at the highest levels of school achievement. However, while minority participation in AP courses has increased dramatically, the large increase in participation has not been matched by dramatic increases in performance on AP exams. In fact, the percentage of Black students receiving a 3 or higher on AP exams has dropped. In 2004, 32% of the AP exams taken by Black students received a score of 3 or higher (College Board, 2005), compared to 39% in 1997 (College Board, 1997). In contrast, 96% of White students scored 3 or higher on AP exams in 2004, down from 99% in 1997 (College Board, 1997, 2005). The College Board suggests that scores ranging from 3 to 5 indicate students are "qualified" to "extremely well qualified" in terms of their abilities to tackle the challenges of college coursework (College Board, 2005). These findings cause concern in light of a recent study at the National Center for Educational Accountability (Dougherty, Mellor, & Jian, 2006) that found that higher college graduation rates among low-SES and minority students are related to AP course enrollment only for those students who took and passed AP exams. These findings echo those of Geiser and Santelices (2004), who found that the number of AP courses a student took in high school did not predict higher GPAs in college or college completion, but that success on AP exams did.

These findings, when coupled with the disparities in AP exam performance between White students and Black and Latino students, highlight the importance not only of expanding the number of students taking AP courses, but of providing support structures within and beyond these courses to ensure that students are equipped with the appropriate tools to learn the material within the courses (Beitler, 2004; Dougherty et al., 2006). Because gifted programs and honors courses offered in elementary and middle schools—the "feeder" programs for AP and other high-level high school courses—are also notably lacking in ethnic, racial, and socioeconomic diversity (Borland, 2004; U.S. Department of Education, Office of Civil Rights, 2000), many Black and Latino students come to AP courses with the aptitude, but not the background skills such as writing, study, and time-management skills, necessary for successful performance (Hertberg-Davis et al., 2006). Emerging research indicates that providing support structures such as focused study and writing skills training, peer study and support groups, and pre-AP courses is crucial to expanding the numbers of students succeeding in AP and other advanced courses (Beitler, 2004; Burton, Whitman, Yepes-Baraya, Cline, & Kim, 2002; Hertberg-Davis et al., 2006; Kyburg, Hertberg-Davis, & Callahan, 2007). Studies also indicate that efforts to increase minority student participation and success in AP courses are most effective when situated within a broader context of high expectations for minority students (Kyburg et al., 2007; Picucci & Sobel, 2002).

Further complicating the question of whether increasing access to AP courses does indeed result in positive, long-term educational outcomes for Black and Latino students is the fact that there is a great deal of variation in the quality of AP courses offered (Aluri, Winecoff, & Lyday, 1991; California

State University Institute for Educational Reform, 1999; Hertberg-Davis et al., 2006; Mathews, 1998; National Research Council, 2002). Concerns over the lack of consistency in course quality have caused the College Board to commit to reviewing AP courses to ensure alignment with intended AP course content and quality (Honowar, 2005). Several studies have indicated that the quality of an AP course depends largely on the individual teacher teaching the course (Burton et al., 2002; National Research Council, 2002). Unfortunately, research indicates that the quality of AP courses offered in schools tends to correlate with the SES level of the students served by the school, resulting in the existence of lower quality AP courses in schools serving primarily low-SES populations (Dougherty et al., 2006). Whether the quality of the AP courses a student takes impacts later college performance has yet to be examined.

LIMITATIONS OF THE RESEARCH

Major questions remain concerning AP and IB courses. First, the question of whether AP and IB courses do indeed prepare students as well as introductory-level college courses has not been investigated thoroughly. The question of whether the *quality* of the AP or IB courses a student takes affects later college performance has not been investigated. Additionally, no studies that control for prior differences in achievement and motivation have been conducted to test the impact of taking AP and IB courses on student performance in college. Finally, more research is needed on the question of whether the curriculum and instruction in AP and IB courses is appropriate for a broad range of advanced learners, or if the courses or their delivery have presented barriers to the successful participation of groups underrepresented in these courses.

PRACTICAL IMPLICATIONS

The body of research on AP and IB courses carries with it several implications for practice.

Infuse Greater Challenge Into the K–12 Curriculum for Advanced Learners

The research indicates that students taking AP and IB courses enjoy these courses because of the high level of challenge offered, challenge that they have craved but not found in other courses during their educational careers. This indicates that advanced students often have to wait until the latter years of high school to encounter the type of academic challenge that they need. This finding suggests that appropriately serving advanced learners requires an infusion of greater challenge into the sequence of courses they will encounter throughout their years in school.

⌐ Provide Other Options for Advanced Learners Beyond AP and IB in High Schools

Research indicates that currently, AP and IB courses serve as the primary methods of serving advanced students in high school. High schools need to provide additional options (such as independent studies, externships, internships, and in-depth seminars on topics of student interest) for advanced learners whose learning needs do not fit with the fast-paced, lecture-oriented style of Advanced Placement and International Baccalaureate courses.

Provide Academic Scaffolding to Minority Students Taking AP and IB Courses

Although research indicates that the number of minority students participating in advanced high school courses is increasing, there is by no means parity in enrollment, and minority students continue to underperform on the end-of-course exams. Schools committed to increasing equity in advanced courses must be thoughtful about providing these students with the supports that they need to succeed in these courses: pre-AP and IB experiences focused on developing study, writing, and time-management skills; training of AP and IB teachers on differentiating instruction to meet the needs of the broad range of learners now taking these courses; and cohort groups of other minority students taking advanced coursework to provide peer support.

RESOURCES

The following are two recommended resources, in addition to those in the reference list, for those interested in learning more about AP and IB programs.

Callahan, C. M. (2003). *Advanced Placement and International Baccalaureate programs for talented students in American high schools: A focus on science and math* (Research Monograph No. 03276). Storrs: National Research Center on the Gifted and Talented, University of Connecticut.

National Research Council, Gollub, J. P., Bertenthal, M. W., Labov, J. B., & Curtis, P. C. (Eds.). (2002). *Learning and understanding: Improving advanced study of mathematics and science in U.S. high schools*. Washington, DC: National Academy Press.

CONCLUSION

Research indicates that AP and IB courses present the highest level of challenge of the courses offered in secondary public schools, and that most AP and IB students, as well as their teachers, are satisfied with the content and classroom environment within these courses.

We still need to investigate whether AP and IB courses prepare students for postintroductory college courses, as well as the introductory college courses that they often replace, and whether the content and teaching methodologies in AP and IB courses present barriers to the successful participation of underrepresented groups.

REFERENCES

Adelman, C. (1999). *Answers in the toolbox: Academic intensity, attendance patterns, and bachelor's degree attainment.* Washington, DC: U.S. Department of Education.

Aluri, R. S., Winecoff, H. L., & Lyday, W. J. (1991). The Advanced Placement experience in small rural high schools in South Carolina. *Journal of Rural and Small Schools, 4*(3), 14–19.

Beitler, A. (2004, December). Making this team. *Principal Leadership,* 24–28.

Borland, J. H. (2004). *Issues and practices in the identification and education of gifted students from under-represented groups* (Research Monograph No. 04186). Storrs: National Research Center on the Gifted and Talented, University of Connecticut.

Borman, G. D., Stringfield, S., & Rachuba, L. (2000). *Achieving minority high achievement: National trends and promising programs and practices.* New York: College Board.

Breland, H. M., & Oltman, P. K. (2001). *An analysis of Advanced Placement (AP) examinations in economics and comparative government and politics* (College Board Research Report 2001-4; ETS RR-01-17). New York: College Board.

Burton, N. W., Whitman, N. B., Yepes-Baraya, M., Cline, F., & Kim, R. M.-i. (2002). *Minority student success—The role of teachers in Advanced Placement courses.* Retrieved March 20, 2007, from http://apcentral.collegeboard.com

California State University Institute for Educational Reform. (1999). *The Advanced Placement program: California's 1997–98 experience.* Sacramento, CA: Author.

Casserly, P. L. (1986). *Advanced Placement revisited* (College Board Research Report 86-6). New York: College Board.

Center for Undergraduate Education in Science, Mathematics, and Engineering Education. (1999). *Transforming undergraduate education in science, mathematics, engineering and technology.* Retrieved March 20, 2007, from http://books.nap.edu/openbook/0309062942/html/24.html

College Board. (1997). *National summary reports 1997.* New York: Author.

College Board. (2005). *Exam scoring: What an AP grade means.* Retrieved August 2, 2005, from http://apcentral.collegeboard.com/article/0,3045,152-167-0-1994,00.html

Dougherty, C., Mellor, L., & Jian, S. (2006). *The relationship between Advanced Placement and college graduation.* Retrieved July 10, 2007, from http://www.

just4kids.org/en/files/Publication-The_Relationship_between_Advanced_Placement_and_College_Graduation-02-09-06.pdf

Epstein, D. (2006, February 8). *Tons of test takers*. Retrieved July 10, 2007, from http://www.insidehighered.com/news/2006/02/08/ap

Gándara, P. C. (2004). *Latino achievement: Identifying models that foster success* (Research Monograph No. 04194). Storrs: National Research Center on the Gifted and Talented, University of Connecticut.

Geiser, S., & Santelices, V. (2004). *The role of Advanced Placement and honors courses in college admissions*. Berkeley, CA: Center for Studies in Higher Education.

Grexa, T. (1988). A case for the International Baccalaureate. *Journal of College Admissions, 121*, 2–6.

Hellerman, S. B. (1994). *Getting the best precollege education*. Baltimore: Johns Hopkins University.

Herr, N. E. (1992). A comparative analysis of the perceived influence of Advanced Placement and honors programs on science instruction. *Journal of Research in Science Teaching, 29*, 551–552.

Hertberg-Davis, H., Callahan, C. M., & Kyburg, R. M. (2006). *Advanced Placement and International Baccalaureate programs: A "fit" for gifted learners?* (Research Monograph No. 06222). Storrs: National Research Center of the Gifted and Talented, University of Connecticut.

Honowar, V. (2005). U.S. leaders fret over students' math and science weaknesses. *Education Week, 25*(3), 1.

International Baccalaureate North America. (1986). *International Baccalaureate*. New York: Author. (ERIC Document Reproduction Service No. ED285450)

International Baccalaureate Organization. (2004). *The diploma programme*. Retrieved March 20, 2007, from http://www.ibo.org/ibo/index.cfm?page=/ibo/programmes&language=EN

Kinlaw, A. B. (2006). *Achieving equity*. Retrieved March 20, 2007, from http://apcentral.collegeboard.com/apc/public/program/initiatives/2200.html

Kyburg, R. M., Hertberg-Davis, H., & Callahan, C. M. (2007). Advanced Placement and International Baccalaureate programs: Equity and excellence for students from diverse backgrounds in urban environments? *Journal of Advanced Academics, 18*, 172–215.

Mathews, J. (1998, March 22). The challenge index. *The Washington Post*, p. W14.

Mathews, J. (2004, November 23). *A chart exposes high school malpractice*. Retrieved July 31, 2007, from http://www.washingtonpost.com/wp-dyn/articles/A6900-2004Nov23.html

Milewski, G. B., & Gillie, J. M. (2002). *What are the characteristics of AP teachers? An examination of survey research* (No. 2002-10). New York: The College Board.

Miller, L. S. (2004). *Promoting sustained growth in the representation of African Americans, Latinos, and Native Americans among top students in the United States at all levels of the education system* (Research Monograph No. 04190). Storrs: National Research Center on the Gifted and Talented, University of Connecticut.

Morgan, R., & Crone, C. (1993). *Advanced Placement examinees at the University of California: An examination of the freshman year course and grades of examinees in biology, calculus, and chemistry* (Statistical Report 93-210). Princeton, NJ: Educational Testing Service.

Morgan, R., & Ramist, L. (1998, February). *Advanced Placement students in college: An investigation of course grades at 21 colleges*. Retrieved July 27, 2005, from http://apcentral.collegeboard.com/apc/public/repository/ap01.pdf.in_7926.pdf

National Research Council, Gollub, J. P., Bertenthal, M. W., Labov, J. B., & Curtis, P. C. (Eds.). (2002). *Learning and understanding: Improving advanced study of mathematics and science in U.S. high schools*. Washington, DC: National Academy Press.

National Study Group for the Affirmative Development of Academic Ability. (2004). *All students reaching the top: Strategies for closing the academic achievement gap*. Naperville, IL: Learning Point Associates.

Oregon University System, Oregon State Department of Education, and Office of Community College Services. (1999). *Oregon early options study*. Eugene, OR: Author. (ERIC Document Reproduction Service No. ED430470)

Picucci, A., & Sobel, A. (2002). *Executive summary: Collaboration, innovation, and tenacity: Exemplary high-enrollment AP Calculus programs for traditionally underserved students*. Austin, TX: Charles A. Dana Center.

Poelzer, G. H., & Feldhusen, J. F. (1996). An empirical study of the achievement of International Baccalaureate students in biology, chemistry, and physics in Alberta. *Journal of Secondary Gifted Education, 8*, 28–40.

Rothschild, E. (1995). Aspiration, performance, reward: The Advanced Placement program at 40. *College Board Review,176–177*, 24–32.

U.S. Department of Education, Office of Civil Rights. (2000). *2000 annual report to Congress*. Accessed March 20, 2007, from http://www.ed.gov/about/offices/list/ocr/AnnRpt2000/edlite-contents.html

White House Press Release. (2004, January). *Fact sheet: Jobs for the 21st century*. Retrieved July 10, 2007, from http://www.whitehouse.gov/news/releases/2004/01/20040121.html

Chapter 4

ALTERNATIVE ASSESSMENT

Tonya R. Moon

ontemporary thinking in the field of cognition suggests that classroom assessment should be based on current conceptions of knowledge about a particular content area (Bass, Magone, & Glaser, 2002). Concurrently, there also is a movement within the broader fields of measurement and assessment in developing assessments that assess students on four basic cognitive activities (e.g., Bass et al., 2002). These four activities include students demonstrating: (1) an understanding of a problem grounded in a particular topic of study; (2) the application of organized, goal-oriented strategies to solve the problem; (3) a variety of monitoring techniques for progress; and (4) explanations that demonstrate understanding of principles supportive of the area of study. One assessment technique that allows students to demonstrate these four cognitive activities is alternative assessment.

Although the term *alternative assessment* is used in special education settings to denote alternatives or assessment substitutes to traditional assessment for students with disabilities, its use in general and gifted education does not connote the same meaning. In general education, roots of the term can be traced back to the mid-1980s when alternatives to standardized educational assessment were being discussed due to the extreme focus on multiple-choice testing in the American educational system. One also can trace a shift in terminology, going from alternative assessment, to performance-based assessment, to authentic assessment by advances in the understanding of how people learn. The National Research Council (Bransford, Brown, & Cocking, 1999) suggests that learning depends upon a number of factors, some of which include: (1) understanding is more likely to occur when transfer is involved rather than simply memorizing information from a text or lecture, and (2) for in-depth learning to occur, it must also be active and contextual. Today, the three terms often are used synonymously and are meant to convey assessments in which students create a response to a given situation rather than simply selecting from a list of answer options. This chapter presents an overview of the most commonly used terms in the field of alternative assessment (see Appendix A), as well as what the current research base indicates relative to classroom applications of alternative assessments.

CONCLUSIONS FROM THE RESEARCH

A tremendous amount of research has focused on the use of alternative assessments at an accountability level and, in particular, the technical aspects of using them (e.g., Boscardin, Aguirre-Muñoz, Chinen, Leon, & Shin, 2004; Moon & Hughes, 2002). This research suggests that using alternative assessments for accountability purposes comes at great costs. The costs are not only in terms of monetary investments (Hardy, 1996), but also in terms of reduced generalizability and validity of the scores obtained from them (e.g., Cronbach, Linn, Brennan, & Haertel, 1997). The benefit of alternative assessments, however, is the requirement of transfer of school learning to real-life, or simulated real-life, problems.

Although it is limited, the research focusing on the various aspects of classroom alternative assessment is both promising and worrisome. When investigating the factors that impede the use of such assessments in the classroom, several studies have concluded that the lack of time; teacher beliefs about students and the content area; and teacher interest, understanding, and skill (Flexer, Cumbo, Borko, Mayfield, & Marion, 1995) are factors that present major obstacles.

Lack of Time for Implementation

One consistent theme that arises in the research on alternative assessment is the issue of teachers feeling that they cannot accomplish all of the required curriculum while incorporating alternative assessments into their routine instructional practices. Factors that interfere with the implementation include a lack of thorough understanding of the content area, not being able to devise a system to acquire and keep track of information about individual students, and lacking facility with managing a classroom where multiple events are occurring simultaneously. Although these factors can be overcome through appropriate and high-quality professional development, it does take time, support, and collaboration. Studies investigating these issues suggest that at least one year of professional development with release time be provided so that teachers can participate with the intensity, including appropriate scaffolding based on readiness, needed to make more than superficial changes to their practices and beliefs (Borko, Mayfield, Marion, Flexer, & Cumbo, 1997). The time spent in professional development is not just telling teachers about "how to" conduct alternative assessments but also allowing them the experiences of implementing alternative assessments in an actual teaching and learning context, which is emphasized and supported in the field of cognition.

Teachers' Beliefs About Students and Learning

Teachers' beliefs about students serve as either facilitators or impediments to using alternative assessments in the classroom (Flexer et al., 1995). If teachers believe that students have the ability to do, think, reason, communicate, and generalize, they are more likely to incorporate alternative assessments in their instructional repertoire. On the other hand, if teachers believe students are only developmentally ready to receive information but not transmit and transfer evidence of learning, they are less likely to incorporate alternative assessments into their instructional plans.

In addition to teachers' beliefs about students, their beliefs about what is important to teach also affect their willingness to incorporate alternative assessment into their classroom practices (Flexer et al., 1995). For example, if a teacher believes that knowing facts is what is important rather than developing a conceptual understanding, then the teacher is less likely to implement alternative assessment in the classroom. On the other hand, teachers who believe that focusing on big ideas and conceptual understanding is important have an easier time considering and implementing alternative assessment in the classroom.

Effects on Content and Pedagogy

When investigating the use of alternative assessments over an extended period of time, results are convincing that teachers can adopt many positive changes to both to the depth of content and appropriate use of pedagogy (Flexer et al., 1995). Positive shifts in instructional practices include increasing the use of manipulatives, hands-on small-group activities, and activities that require students to use problem-solving skills and to provide explanations. This shift is away from the predominant model of textbook-driven content and paper-and-pencil worksheet activities. Over time, teachers begin to see inadequacies of the textbook, not only in terms of content coverage but also in terms of topics.

Effects of Students

Research focusing on students' reactions to alternative assessments suggest that they find them more meaningful, interesting, and motivating than traditional assessments (e.g., multiple-choice tests; Moon, Brighton, Callahan, & Robinson, 2005), and students who engage in alternative assessments are more likely to be motivated to learn in school overall (Flexer et al., 1995). If students have increased interest and see the relevance of the assessments to their world, students are more likely to invest in the assessment by explaining their understandings of the content learned more completely and accurately. Other research suggests that economically advantaged students are more comfortable with the demands of alternative assessments (in terms of their attitudes toward problems with more than one solution and in their abilities to use appropriate disciplinary thinking to solve problems; Shepard et al.,1995).

In investigations looking at the cognitive complexity of alternative assessments and the aspects of reasoning involved with them, results suggest that there is a difference between students who have deep and enduring knowledge of a content area as opposed to those students who do not. Students with deeper and more enduring knowledge provide concept-based explanations and use correct terminology similar to the explanations and terminology of experts.

MAJOR QUESTIONS ADDRESSED IN THE RESEARCH

Research questions relating to alternative assessments can be divided into two broad areas. The first focuses on issues associated with using alternative assessments at an accountability level (e.g., state, district). Research questions within this area address one of three themes: (1) development of alternative assessments and alignment to content standards; (2) technical issues associated with alternative assessments (i.e., generalizability, rater training, equating, validity); and (3) effects of using alternative assessments (e.g., costs, administrative convenience, and practicality). Research questions in each of these themes include:

Theme 1: Development of Alternative Assessments
- What does a given alternative assessment measure?
- How applicable is the novice to expert continuum in evaluating students' responses to alternative assessments?

Theme 2: Technical Issues Associated With Alternative Assessments
- How do different statistical procedures for assessing interrater reliability and scorer reliability compare?
- What is the exchangeability of different types of alternative assessments (e.g., hands-on versus computer-simulated)?
- What features of tasks determine their difficulty?
- What factors affect the validity of alternative assessments?
- What factors affect the generalizability of alternative assessments?
- To what degree do raters affect student scores? How consistent are raters in evaluating students' scores?
- Do different methods of training raters result in differences in students' scores?

Theme 3: Effects of Alternative Assessments
- What administrative factors must be considered in the implementation of large-scale alternative assessments? For example, what budgetary costs must be accounted for in order to implement large-scale alternative assessments?
- What are the instructional effects associated with implementing large-scale alternative assessments for all students and for particular groups of students?

The second area of research on alternative assessment focuses on issues associated with factors that facilitate and impede the implementation of alternative assessments at the classroom level for instructional purposes and teachers' and students' reactions to such assessments. It is important to note that there exists a dearth of research on classroom assessment in general, regardless of the type of assessment. Example questions include:
- What cognitive activity do students engage in when completing an alternative assessment in a particular content area?
- What aspects of reasoning are needed to complete an alternative assessment in a particular content area?
- What factors facilitate and impede teachers designing and implementing alternative assessments for instructional purposes?
- What teachers' beliefs about students mediate their investment in using alternative assessments in their classrooms?
- What are teachers' and students' reactions to the implementation of classroom alternative assessments?
- What effects do alternative assessments have on student learning?

LIMITATIONS OF THE RESEARCH

The ability to make informed decisions about the use of an alternative assessment is limited by the scarcity of evidence from research studies on the effects of their use in classroom settings and their technical qualities. However, the research that has been conducted indicates that alternative assessments may be used to obtain reliable and valid information about student learning and achievement of academic learning standards.

Not only are there a very limited number of studies on the classroom use of alternative assessment, issues in interpreting the evidence also include the lack of sufficient sample sizes, which affects the generalizability of research findings, and lack of replication across grade levels and content areas.

PRACTICAL IMPLICATIONS OF THE RESEARCH

Practical implications of the research on alternative assessment primarily rest in areas related to their development, as well as the benefits and drawbacks of using them. In the ideal world, authentic assessment closely resembles authentic contexts where students are provided opportunities to demonstrate sophisticated interdisciplinary understandings. However, practitioners with limited content knowledge, an incomplete understanding of how the content is applicable to the real world, or limited understanding of the developmental levels of students have tremendous difficulty designing or implementing authentic, relevant, or meaningful alternative assessments. What these practitioners typically develop or implement are assessments that measure only surface-level knowledge and understandings and not assessments that measure deep understanding of a particular content area.

Another practical implication of the use of classroom alternative assessment comes from the overemphasis on standardized multiple-choice tests and in particular the drill-and-kill rote curriculum most children are exposed to. The decontextualized curriculum has put all students, in particular, students of poverty, at a disadvantage in terms of developing their cognitive and reasoning abilities, which in turn affect not only their performance but also their willingness to engage in the processes needed to be successful on such assessments.

WHAT WE KNOW ABOUT ALTERNATIVE ASSESSMENT

- Teachers' beliefs about students facilitate or impede their use of alternative assessments in the classroom.
- Positive shifts (e.g., use of manipulatives) in teachers' instructional practices can occur as a result of using alternative assessments.
- Students' reactions to alternative assessments suggest that alternative assessments are more meaningful, interesting, and motivating to them.

- Students with a deeper understanding of an area are able to provide explanations similar to experts when responding to an alternative assessment.
- Although limited, studies suggest that the information obtained from classroom alternative assessments can be used to make informed instructional decisions about students.

AREAS NEEDING RESEARCH

One area in this body of literature that needs additional research is clear documentation of the depth of knowledge a teacher must possess in order to effectively develop and implement alternative assessments. For example, within a heterogeneous classroom, students have varying readiness levels, interests, and learning profiles. What depth of content knowledge and understanding of student development must teachers have in order to develop differentiated alternative assessments? What are the management skills that a teacher needs to have in order to implement differentiated alternative assessments in mixed-ability classrooms? What are the curricular and instructional changes that need to occur in order for teachers to consistently implement alternative assessments in their classrooms?

RESOURCES

In addition to the valuable resources that are included in the reference list, the following Web sites and articles are suggested resources.

Web Sites

The National Research Center on the Gifted and Talented
http://curry.edschool.virginia.edu
The NRC/GT conducted a national, large-scale study on the development and implementation of classroom alternative assessments and has reports available, as well as approximately 40 alternative assessments spanning the four core content areas.

North Central Regional Educational Laboratory
http://www.ncrel.org
The North Central Regional Educational Laboratory is a federally funded center with many alternative assessment resources available in the areas of mathematics and science.

Articles

Moon, T. R. (2002). Using performance assessment in the social studies classroom. *Gifted Child Today, 25*, 53–59.

Moon, T. R., & Callahan, C. M. (2001). Classroom performance assessment: What should it look like in a standards-based classroom? *NASSP Bulletin, 85*, 48–58.

Moon, T. R., & Callahan, C. M. (2000). Performance assessment and its role in instruction of able learners, *Tempo, 20*(4), 6–7, 19–21.

REFERENCES

Bass, K. M., Magone, M. E., & Glaser, R. (2002). *Informing the design of performance assessment: A content process analysis of two NAEP science tasks* (CSE Technical Report 564). Los Angeles: National Center for Research on Evaluation, Standards, and Student Testing (CRESST).

Borko, H., Mayfield, V., Marion, S., Flexer, R., & Cumbo, K. (1997). *Teachers' developing ideas and practices about mathematics performance assessment: Successes, stumbling blocks, and implications* (CSE Technical Report 423). Los Angeles: National Center for Research on Evaluation, Standards, and Student Testing.

Boscardin, C. K., Aguirre-Muñoz, Z., Chinen, M., Leon, S., & Shin, H. S. (2004). *Consequences and validity of performance assessments for English learners: Assessing opportunity to learn (OTL) in grade 6 language arts* (CSE Technical Report 635). Los Angeles: National Center for Research on Evaluation, Standards, and Student Testing (CRESST).

Bransford, J. D., Brown, A. L., & Cocking, R. R. (Eds.). (1999). *How people learn: Brain, mind, experience, and school.* Washington, DC: National Academy Press.

Cronbach, L. J., Linn, R. L., Brennan, R. L., & Haertel, E. D. (1997). Generalizability analyses for performance assessments of student achievement or school effectiveness. *Educational & Psychological Measurement, 57*, 373–399.

Flexer, R. J., Cumbo, K., Borko, H., Mayfield, V., & Marion, S. F. (1995). *How "messing about" with performance assessment in mathematics affects what happens in classrooms* (CSE Technical Report 396). Los Angeles: National Center for Research on Evaluation, Standards, and Student Testing.

Hardy, R. (1996). Performance assessment: Examining the costs. In M. B. Kane & R. Mitchell (Eds.), *Implementing performance assessments: Promises, problems, and challenges* (pp. 107–118). Mahwah, NJ: Lawrence Erlbaum.

Moon, T. R., Brighton, C. M., Callahan, C. M., & Robinson, A. E. (2005). Development of authentic assessments for the middle school classroom. *Journal of Secondary Gifted Education, 16*, 119–133.

Moon, T. R., & Hughes, K. R. (2002). Training and scoring issues involved in large-scale writing assessments. *Educational Measurement: Issues and Practice, 21*(2), 15–19.

Shepard, L., Flexer, R., Hiebert, E., Marion, S., Mayfield, V., & Weston, T. (1995). *Effects of introducing classroom performance assessments on student learning* (CSE Technical Report 394). Los Angeles: National Center for Research on Evaluation, Standards, and Student Testing (CRESST).

APPENDIX A
GLOSSARY OF USEFUL TERMS WITH ALTERNATIVE ASSESSMENT

Alternative assessment (authentic assessment; performance assessment): Assessments that require students to generate a response to an open-ended question rather than selecting from a set of provided responses. Alternative assessments include investigations, exhibitions, oral presentations, written presentations, and portfolios. Ideally, alternative assessments require students to be actively engaged with meaningful, authentic, and relevant questions that require application of prior knowledge and relevant domain skills, and acquisition of new knowledge.

Analytic scoring: A method of scoring a student's response to an alternative assessment across multiple domains (or dimensions) of performance. For example, analytic scoring of a mathematics alternative assessment might include scores for the following domains: conceptual understanding, strategies and reasoning, computation and execution, and communication.

Anchors (exemplars): Anchor papers are concrete examples of student performance that provide explicit exemplars of each score level. The purpose of the papers is to illustrate the intent of each point of the score scale. Raters use anchor papers to evaluate student work by comparing the student's performance to the anchor papers.

Assessment (prompt; task; test): The process of gathering quantitative or qualitative data about an individual or a group of individuals for the purpose of guiding the instructional process and/or providing feedback to stakeholders. The process of gathering the data may be formal (e.g., state testing) or informal (e.g., teacher observation) and the uses of the data gathered may be formative or summative.

Authentic assessment: See alternative assessment.

Benchmark: A description of a specific, expected level of student performance in a content area at particular grades, ages, or developmental levels. Benchmarks are used to measure student progress.

Bias: Bias is the presence of some characteristic in an assessment (or item) that unfairly influences students' scores. The result of the bias is differences in performance for individuals of the same ability but from different ethnic/cultural, gender, age groups, or other unique groups.

Content standards: The curricular knowledge, skills, and understandings that define goals for student learning or mastery.

Content-related validity: Evidence that indicates that an assessment instrument reflects the content domain that it is intended to represent as defined by the assessment description.

Cut score (performance standards): A specified score on a scale that indicates the minimum performance level needed to demonstrate proficiency or mastery.

Constructed response: A student's answer to an alternative assessment requiring student-created response rather than a choice from a set of provided options.

Construct-related validity: Evidence that supports a posited hypothetical construct and the degree to which an assessment instrument measures the intended construct.

Criteria: Characteristics that are used to evaluate the quality of a student's performance.

Criterion-referenced assessment: An assessment where a student's performance is compared to clearly defined objectives, skill levels, or areas of knowledge, rather than to a norm group. Criterion-referenced assessments indicate how well a student has mastered a specified assessment domain.

Criterion-related validity: The degree of relationship between two assessments intended to measure the same construct.

Dimension: Categories that reflect desired knowledge, skills, and understandings measured in an alternative assessment. For example, in an alternative assessment focusing on effects of the Nazi regime during War World II, dimensions that student work might be assessed on could include historical accuracy, historical relevancy, authenticity of recommendations, bibliography, and writing style.

Essay test: A test requiring students to respond to questions in writing rather than choosing the correct answer from a set of options. The form of the essay test can be restricted response, which typically requires students to list, define, describe, or give reasons, or the form of the essay may be extended response, which often requires students to compose, summarize, formulate, compare/contrast, or interpret. Extended response essays provide less structure and allow more creativity than restricted response essays.

Exemplar: See anchor.

Formative assessment: Assessments (e.g., tests, observations) used for the purposes of providing ongoing information about what a student knows, understands, and is able to do relative to a given learning objective. The intent of the information obtained from a formative assessment is to provide instructional feedback for the purpose of modifying instruction and improving student learning.

Generalizability theory: A psychometric theory that allows investigation of the sources of variation in alternative assessment scores. For example, assessing the extent to which differences among raters affect students' scores has implications for rater training.

Holistic scoring: The method of scoring alternative assessments that calls for an overall judgment about the quality of a student's response using synthesized multiple criteria.

Interrater reliability: The consistency with which two or more judges rate the work of the same students.

Measurement: The process of quantifying student learning without making judgments.

Performance assessment: See alternative assessment.

Performance standards: See cut score.

Performance task: See alternative assessment.

Portfolio: A systematic and organized collection of student work that demonstrates direct evidence of a student's achievement and progress over a period of time. Portfolios may be gathered in the form of videos, CD-ROMS, or a physical collection of materials. The collection of work can be exemplary ("my best work") or a collection of work demonstrating progress.

Product: A tangible result of a student responding to an alternative assessment.

Prompt: The part of an alternative assessment that describes what it is that the student should do to demonstrate his or her knowledge, skills, understandings, and/or dispositions.

Rater training: The process of preparing raters to evaluate students' performances on alternative assessments.

Rubrics: Scoring guidelines based on explicit definitions used to evaluate the quality of students' responses.

Scoring criteria: In an alternative assessment situation, a rubric.

Standards: Agreed-upon statements in a content domain that specify what a student should know, understand, and be able to do.

Standardization: A consistent set of procedures for designing, administering, and scoring an assessment. The purpose of standardization is to assure that all students are assessed under the same conditions so that their scores have similar meaning and are not influenced by differing conditions.

Summative assessment: Assessments administered at the conclusion of a unit of instruction (or activity) to determine the effectiveness of instruction and a students' achievement of specified knowledge, skills, and understandings.

Validity: The degree to which evidence supports the accuracy of inferences (decisions) about students based on their performances.

Writing sample: A student-generated composition to determine a student's writing abilities.

Chapter 5

Cognitive Characteristics of the Gifted

Pau-San Hoh

ognition is often regarded as being synonymous with thinking. But, what is thinking? We can go on and on listing all of the things that count as "thinking" without ever reaching a coherent answer. To get a better handle on the concept, consider the opening statement in a book on cognition: "If you root yourself to the ground, you can afford to be stupid" (Churchland, 1986, p. 13). Because we *do* move around in the world, we need cognition to survive. We have to be able to navigate on uneven terrain, to remember how to find our way home, to problem solve when we encounter obstacles, to imagine various scenarios before deciding on a course of action, to infer from subtle signs that danger is lurking around the corner, and so on. All of these are part of cognition. It entails having the know-how to deal with an ever-changing environment. The term *environment* is used in the broadest sense here. It includes new demands from higher levels of education—important aspects of the life of a gifted child in society. The environmental aspect is emphasized because the discussion of cognition in this chapter is confined only to those traits that are deemed important or useful to our type of culture. Cognitive characteristics, therefore, may be viewed as propensities to employ one's mental resources in certain ways when performing culturally pertinent tasks.

We all use cognition to function in the world. The investigation of how human beings process and apply information through the senses (called *information processing*) is regarded by researchers as the study of *intelligent behavior*. We all exhibit intelligence by being able to function in an environment that is ever-changing, either because we move from situation to situation or because we have to deal with new demands. Even the simple tasks we do every day cannot be simulated easily in artificial intelligence and hence reflect intelligent behavior. The study of intelligent behavior is complicated by the fact that different fields investigating different areas of human performance do not share a common language. The term *visual cognition* is used in vision research, but *verbal* or *linguistic intelligence* (not *cognition*) is employed in language study. Nevertheless, as shown below, excellence in one domain usually involves cognitive characteristics that also appear in other kinds of superior performance (e.g., language, mathematics, music, fine art). Although research in gifted education currently cannot account for these similarities, eventually it will have to explain why the same cognitive characteristics appear across diverse domains of talent. Efforts to integrate models describing processing of different types of information are already underway in research on the general population.

WHO ARE THE GIFTED?

The problem of deciding what criteria to use to identify giftedness remains an intractable one in the field. Giftedness has traditionally been taken to mean *intellectual giftedness*, and the gifted have often been identified through IQ, achievement, or other formal tests of school-based skills. Obviously, this poses a fundamental problem for any investigation of cognitive characteristics. The traits found will correlate directly with intellectual ability if this is how the gifted have been identified in the first place.

To avoid an IQ bias, the discussion in this chapter relies heavily on studies whose gifted subjects were selected by other means. The verbally gifted were identified through their creative products (Piirto, 1992) and spontaneous speech (Hoh, 2005). The work of Krutetskii (1976) and his associates (Dubrovina, 1992; Shapiro, 1992) represents an important source of information on mathematical giftedness. Even though their findings are drawn primarily from test-like settings, these researchers' observations of the students' thinking processes are detailed and comprehensive, thus allowing for comparisons with information from other sources. Other studies on mathematical ability use performance in class and in competitions and not formal testing alone to identify the gifted (Shavinina & Kholodnaja, 1996). In studies where IQ was used as an identification criterion, other distinctive traits such as humor, focused concentration, and motivation were also considered (Sankar-DeLeeuw, 2004). There is one research area, however, that employs experimental subjects identified mainly through IQ or general achievement, and that is the investigation of metacognitive awareness (Alexander, Carr, & Schwanenflugel, 1995). To counter this IQ bias in research on metacognitive awareness, findings from other types of studies are supplemented here. A relatively new area of investigation is spatial-temporal intelligence. Cooper's (2000) interviews with inventors identified through their nationally recognized products form the basis of discussion of spatial-temporal ability. Winner's (1996) case studies offer much in-depth information on gifted children's behaviors and propensities in their natural environment.

The following discussion takes into consideration not only intellectual abilities but also artistic talents in cases where both share similar cognitive characteristics. Studies on artistic talent use subjects who had distinguished themselves through class performance, auditions, or products (Baum, Owen, & Oreck, 1996; Freeman, 2000; Oreck, Owen, & Baum, 2003; Porath, 1997).

COGNITIVE CHARACTERISTICS

Many of the cognitive characteristics commonly associated with giftedness do have empirical support but a few still lack confirming evidence despite being cited widely. Each substantiated characteristic can be found in at least several if not all domains of performance. The characteristics listed in this chapter are obviously not mutually exclusive; interrelationships amongst them, if present, are spelled out in the relevant sections below. Each characteristic is defined first, and illustrations are given where necessary to make the concepts clear. In many cases, the terms are mainly descriptive and are not associated with any particular theory or model unless otherwise noted.

The definition of cognition given above encompasses the abilities of all humans and not just the gifted. Recent research on human cognition is included where relevant to highlight some of the questions that should be raised and pursued for a deeper understanding of the gifted population.

Precocity

For giftedness to manifest itself, precocious physical development is a prerequisite for many of the domains. Reports of early speech provide the clearest calibration of precocious development. Verbal precocity depends heavily on physiological readiness. It takes fine control over a complex set of muscles to produce comprehensible speech. In Terman's (1925) classic study of more than a thousand high-IQ individuals, parents reported retrospectively that the subjects started speaking about 3 ½ months ahead of schedule. In analyzing drawings by 50 artistically talented children aged 20 months to 8 years, Harrison

(1999) noted that advanced fine motor development enables good eye-hand coordination, which in turn makes exemplary work possible.

Precocity can be more easily confirmed in some areas than in others. In fields where extensive knowledge exists for the developmental stages of typical children, definitive comparisons can be made. This would be true for verbal precocity, with child language study (called *first language acquisition*) being an established field, partly so for mathematical ability, and less so for the other areas.

Now, let us review the research literature for evidence that the gifted are exceptionally strong in the following areas.

Perceptual Sensitivity

Sternberg and Lubart (1992) stated that the gifted are good at detecting critically relevant, or salient cues. That is, the observant precocious child actively perceives—through whichever sense(s) she is strong in—what others often fail to notice. Supposedly, the gifted are more perceptually sensitive.

Sternberg and Lubart's (1992) claim has been borne out by evidence from many quarters. In verbal tests conducted on 42 typically developing and 49 gifted third and fourth graders, McBride-Chang, Manis, and Wagner (1996) found that those with strong cognitive skills are also more aware of the sound features of English (phonological awareness). Because phonological awareness has been shown to be a strong indicator of reading ability in many studies (see review by Adams, 1990), McBride-Chang et al.'s finding helps explain why gifted children tend to be early readers.

Consider for a moment what it means to be able to distinguish the approximately 24 consonants and 14 vowels (monophthongs and diphthongs) in English: The young child has to be able to pick out salient language cues from the conversations around her. Bear in mind that these rapid, continuous conversation streams are not explicitly segmented into words and syllables, let alone single consonants or vowels. Therefore, a salient cue also implies a subtle one because the critical difference between, say, "p" and "b" is only in a single dimension, voicing.

The ability to discriminate subtle rhythmic patterns, melodic shapes, and tonal colors is crucial for musical talent (Haroutounian, 1995). Although children younger than 5 typically have difficulty matching the pitches of commonly heard tunes, Revesz (1925/1970) reported that musically gifted children can sing with accuracy by their second year. When 12 musically talented children aged 8 to 11 were tested for pitch perception and aesthetic discrimination of music styles, Freeman (2000) found their performance to be superior to that of the control group. Baum et al. (1996) similarly confirmed that their musically capable subjects in third grade were better at perceiving subtle differences in tone and pitch when tested.

Heightened visual awareness accounts for the attention to detail in the drawings of talented young artists. In an evaluative study of the drawings of

217 children ages 4 to 10, including 12 gifted individuals distributed across these ages, Porath (1997) described the higher degree of elaboration in the figures produced by the talented, indicating awareness of details missed by others. Freeman's (2000) tests on artistically talented children between the ages of 8 and 11 demonstrated their keener perception in identifying a painter's style. Realistic drawings can show up early at age 2 or 3 among the talented (Harrison, 1999; Winner, 1996), when others are still using schematic forms (e.g., a circle for the head, lines for limbs) at 5 or 6 (Thomas & Silk, 1990).

Persistent Concentration

Active seeing—the noticing of details invisible to others—requires patience and concentration, as observed by Root-Bernstein and Root-Bernstein (2004, p. 138), who studied many eminent artists and scientists. The term *persistent concentration* as used here implies the ability to attend to a task intensively and for an unusually long time without being distracted by "noise" in the environment and without showing signs of mental fatigue. Related terms used in the literature include *tenacity, perseverance,* and *persistence.* These often are regarded as personality traits separate from cognition in giftedness research. Another related concept, *task commitment* (Renzulli, 1977), is seen as a motivational factor, also considered distinct from cognition.

The technical term used in research is *attention,* and research on human attention has a relatively long history. Of current interest is the relationship between attention and learning (Jiménez, 2003), which has implications on the study of giftedness. With only isolated experiments on gifted subjects, findings on attention pertain primarily to the general population. The focus in most investigations has been on very basic processes: the ability to pick out particular information from a mass of data (focused or selective attention) and the ability to attend to two or more tasks simultaneously (divided attention) (see Lund, 2001). The older experiments concentrated on hearing; more recent ones focus on vision. Using analogies from computational models, researchers in visual cognition now regard attention as being an intricate composite of many processes and subcomponents. That is, many forms of attention are involved in human functioning. This new view poses new questions for giftedness research: Which types of attention are essential to superior performance, and in which domains are they crucial? These are the kinds of questions that should be explored in giftedness research, but much still needs to be discovered about typical behavior before superior performance can be defined at this level of description.

Be that as it may, the sketchy evidence presently available on gifted individuals' ability to attend to a task is suggestive. Tests done on 239 school children ages 9 to 13 show a significant positive correlation between giftedness and the ability to direct one's visual attention to extract an embedded figure from a picture (Baillargeon, Pascual-Leone, & Roncadin, 1998).

Tenacity to practice at length has been reported in all domains, including mathematics (Sriraman, 2004), music and dance (Baum et al., 1996), fine art (Harrison, 1999), writing (Piirto, 1992), and reading (Winner, 1996). Research on mathematical talent by Krutetskii (1976) and his colleagues (Dubrovina, 1992; Shapiro, 1992) gives us further insight on this trait. For more than a decade, these Soviet researchers conducted in-depth studies on the psychology of mathematical learning among school children in grades 2–10. Based on the students' performance on mathematical problem solving, their verbal discourse during problem solving, and their responses when interviewed, the researchers consider extended concentration without fatigue as one of the distinguishing traits of the mathematically gifted. Their mathematically able subjects showed signs of mental rejuvenation by doing comparatively better in other disciplines they usually did not fare well in *after* doing challenging mathematical problems (Krutetskii, 1976, pp. 310–312).

Obsessive Fascination

Curiosity is often listed as a characteristic of giftedness in identification instruments. The term does not fully convey the giftedness trait in question. Gifted persons often display an extreme fascination with their domain of talent that borders on the obsessive. They often actively translate experience into terms that fit into their area of interest to a degree that the average person would not. Winner (1996, p. 39) aptly referred to the "mathematizing of everyday experience" for those with quantitative ability, whereby the routine task of living becomes a source for yet more computational problems to mull over. Seeing the world in quantitative terms has also been mentioned by Krutetskii (1976), whose high-ability subjects created their own mathematical problems from everyday situations.

Piirto's (1992) portfolio of works by writing prodigies in elementary and middle school highlighted this group's fascination with language, as shown in their language play, trying out new words over and over, and exploring linguistic meanings from multiple angles. More than mere fascination, perhaps the gifted individual understands the world best through her chosen medium. Seeing the prodigious works created by a child artist, Golomb commented, "to draw is to know and understand" (1990, p. 13).

Superior Memory

Research in cognitive psychology in the last two decades has yielded many fascinating observations about the various forms of memory we all rely on to guide intelligent behavior. We depend, for example, on associations to recall past experiences (associative memory) and on representations stored mentally in abstract form to guide immediate behavior (working memory; see Goldman-

Rakic, 1990). As with attention, memory is now viewed as a composite of many subprocesses. The questions raised by research on human memory are similar to the ones on attention posed earlier: Which ones are critical for superior performance, and for which domains?

Present research on giftedness only can offer the general observation that gifted children have exceptional memories in their areas of talent, as Winner (1996) concluded from her case studies and review of Terman's research. This has been supported by several studies. The linguistically talented are comparatively better at retrieving verbal information (Dark & Benbow, 1991). The mathematically talented, on the other hand, excel at using stored quantitative, spatial, and visual information (Hermelin & O'Connor, 1986). Mathematically able students retain general information about types of problems, solution methods, reasoning schemes, and logical patterns. That is, mathematically talented students' memory is distinguished from that of the nongifted, not in the amount of information stored but in the *type* of information retained. Retaining information in generalized and abbreviated form "does not load the brain with surplus information and thus permits it to be retained longer and used more easily" (Krutetskii, 1976, p. 300). This is different from mechanically remembering a lot of numerical facts, which is not a distinguishing characteristic of capable mathematicians.

Talented dancers by third grade exhibit superior kinesthetic (body) memory by being able to remember and replicate movement sequences precisely (Baum et al., 1996). Their same-age peers with an "ear for music" can hold tonal sequences better than others (Baum et al., 1996; Freeman, 2000), which explains why they are able to play back a tune after hearing it only once or twice (Winner, 1996).

The gifted individual's superior memory may be restricted to the domain of excellence only. For example, child chess experts' superior memory is confined to chess positions and does not extend to numbers (Chase & Ericsson, 1982; Chi, 1978).

Cooper's (2000) interview of seven adult inventors offered an insider's view of superior nonquantitative, nonverbal memory. The inventors could store, transform, and apply images in various forms and ways. Some of these thinkers stored past experience as images. The images were not only visual; some were based on kinesthetic and sensory experience. Previous hands-on experience provided the inventors with the "body knowledge" to form new ideas (Cooper, 2000, p. 180), and all of them had vast storehouses of such information.

Dynamic Imaging

The term *spatial-temporal intelligence* more accurately describes the inventors' abilities than the commonly used phrase *spatial intelligence* (Gardner, 1983). Cooper's inventor subjects mentally manipulated the spatial features of stored images by transforming size, shape, and the like. That is, spatial-temporal thinkers employ mental imagery in a dynamic way, reorienting their perspectives to "view" the object from many angles—all the while moving fluidly back and forth in time. They may move mentally into the past to retrieve stored information or into the future to find a solution from an imagined scenario. Throughout, the images are not held in fixed form but are manipulated and transformed flexibly.

Other studies also hint at imaging abilities that go beyond the typical. If artistically talented children can imagine the whole picture, it may explain some of the behaviors observed. Whereas preschoolers typically draw additively with short, hesitant strokes, precocious artists as young as 3 can draw the whole object with one fluid contour line (Winner, 1996, p. 77). Talented young artists also are adept at drawing objects from any starting point without slowing down, as Picasso could (Richardson, 1991). Harrison (1999, pp. 190–193), who studied 50 talented artists ages 20 months to 8 years, reported that this group tended to decentralize, conceptualize, and depict objects from multiple imagined perspectives. Talented young musicians who are able to improvise heard scores spontaneously (Winner, 1996) presumably possess a similar ability to manipulate whole structures mentally, as do gifted dancers (Baum et al., 1996). Young gifted writers play with reverse structure (Piirto, 1992) and the precocious 4-year-old can alter word order to achieve thematic continuity, whereas typical children still find these linguistic forms difficult at 12 (Hoh, 2005).

Mental imagery, even for those who are visually gifted, should not be regarded as pictures on a screen. Rather, the imagery involves abstract forms in which essential properties have been coded for later use (see below). Researchers in visual cognition consider imaging fundamental to normal, and not just gifted, perception (Kosslyn, 1994). Currently, researchers are examining the relationships amongst vision, attention, and memory in normal functioning (Henderson & Hollingworth, 2003). Their findings may help address the question as to what is distinctive about imaging in gifted performance.

Abstraction and Generalization

Not only are the gifted sensitive to the cues in their areas of talent, evidence suggests that they perceive external stimuli (objects or events) as being *organized* information. Observation and imaging create a mass of data that have to be organized and streamlined for successful problem solving (Wertheimer, 1945/1982). Good problem solvers simplify by focusing only on a few essential features. Perceiving the essence of a thing or process in this way is called *abstraction*. Abstracting from concrete details enables good thinkers to grasp the internal structure of a problem, a prerequisite to solving it successfully. The problem situation is understood effectively as a whole rather than viewed haphazardly in a piecemeal manner. Next, to deal with new problems successfully, good thinkers recognize fundamental similarities between these and the ones already encountered. This is called *generalization*.

Current research on human vision offers insight on our ability to abstract away from the concrete and the particular and apply the idealized information to new situations. Based on experimental results, as well as neurological and anatomical investigations, vision researchers posit that we all—not just the gifted—abstract away from concrete properties of the objects and scenes we see (Peterson & Rhodes, 2003). Coding visual properties such as object shape and position, and even color, in abstract form for more efficacious storage and retrieval is part of intelligent behavior. Perhaps the gifted happen to be particularly efficient in this essential task.

Research on mathematical talent provides compelling evidence for both abstraction and generalization in the thinking of gifted children. In fact, Krutetskii (1976) considered abstraction and generalization as important defining criteria for mathematical talent. Krutetskii's high-ability subjects in sixth and seventh grades reported a déjà vu feeling when given new problems to solve—if they had encountered problems of the same type before containing different quantities. Krutetskii (1976, p. 248) said it succinctly: "in solving the first concrete problem of a given type, they—if one can so express it—were thereby solving all problems of that type." Retaining information in idealized, rather than concrete, form enables capable students to detect similarities flexibly even when the problems presented later are not exact replicas but variations of the original (Solso, 1998).

Shavinina and Kholodnaja (1996) drew similar conclusions from examining the responses of 43 high schoolers gifted in physics and mathematics and 34 controls, who were all given open-ended problems testing their verbal and spatial skills. The researchers noticed that the gifted subjects asked more generalized questions, their knowledge was organized around general categories rather than specific items, and their thinking was directed to general principles and laws. In contrast, the thinking of the average students was more concrete in nature. Sriraman's recent (2004) study of four mathematically gifted students in ninth grade underscored this group's tendency to think comprehensively of all possible cases.

Other studies involving formal testing of younger children's abstract reasoning also have differentiated between the intellectually gifted and the average. For example, Ablard and Tissot's (1998) study of 150 academically talented students in grades 2–6 concluded that their reasoning ability is comparable to that of average students four grade levels higher. Gifted adults also think holistically: Cooper (2000, p. 183) said that her spatial-temporal subjects "grasped the *whole*" to create their inventions. Thinking holistically in this way instead of getting lost in a lot of complicated details partly accounts for the appearance of speedy processing discussed below.

The two processes, abstraction and generalization, are sometimes combined under the label *pattern recognition,* a term that aptly describes the ability to grasp the whole structure. Winner's (1996, p. 88) 7-year-old musically talented subject was able to make his improvisations fit into the background because he could hear the musical structure easily. Winner's other musically talented subject was able to read and write by 3 and learn other notational systems such as programming and foreign languages by 8—all of which require pattern recognition.

The suppression of irrelevant information—enabling more efficient use of mental resources—is being investigated in the field of cognitive development, with intelligence being reported as a factor in preliminary results (Hettinger & Carr, 2003). A similar theme runs through other areas of research such as language acquisition. Language acquisition involves not only the addition of neural material but heavy pruning of the growing brain's architecture. Conservation of mental resources is an important consideration because, at the biological level, the brain is a voracious consumer, gobbling up one fifth of the body's oxygen and similar amounts of its calories (Pinker, 1994).

Efficient Coordination

To describe how we perceive and think, cognitive scientists use models that comprise many interconnected subcomponents or modules arranged in a multitiered fashion, each performing a specific function. In many of these models, the subcomponents operate simultaneously, with higher level modules continuously modifying their outputs in response to feedback from low-level modules that are running concurrently. This is called *parallel processing*, and parallel computation to simulate human behavior is a robust area of study (see, e.g., Arbib & Robinson, 1990). The brain itself is regarded as a massively parallel structure, with many subareas being activated simultaneously when performing a task.

Parallel processing provides a major advantage because it allows us to interpret and respond quickly to external stimuli and changing environments, bring multiple bodies of knowledge together to create new ideas, coordinate several subtasks at the same time, and so forth. As such, parallel processing would be one area worth exploring in the search for giftedness traits. At present, giftedness research unfortunately lacks information at the level of specificity that is applied to studies on the typical population.

What we do have from the literature are general observations of gifted individuals' ability to coordinate multiple tasks. The term *coordination* is used in a nontechnical sense here, simply to capture what has been observed in overt behavior: the juggling of several things at the same time or performance that can only come from handling two or more mental tasks simultaneously.

Efficient coordination can be inferred from reports of precocious children who read fluently and expressively. Reading requires coordination of multiple processes, including relating letters to sounds, retrieving stored words, and integrating meaning and experience. Experimental evidence shows that even beginning readers have to process simultaneously two different pathways, one for spelling and sound, the other for spelling and meaning (Laing & Hulme, 1999). Typically developing children read hesitantly with a lot of errors and repairs, thereby revealing the challenge of trying to juggle several processes at the same time. Precocious readers, on the other hand, not only coordinate these processes flawlessly but add extra flourishes such as reading with emotion and emphasis while still in kindergarten (Sankar-DeLeeuw, 2004).

To create literary devices such as metaphors and allusions, writers have to integrate two or more previously separate bodies of knowledge. In Piirto's (1992) portfolio, a 6-year-old writing prodigy compared raindrops to liquid caterpillars and a 9-year-old likened a rabbit's fur to suede. Even greater coordinative dexterity is displayed when a 3-year-old creates metaphors spontaneously (Hoh, 2005), considering that typical children still have difficulty understanding them at 5.

The ability to coordinate two or more tasks is in fact taken as an accurate criterion for identifying talent in the performing arts (Baum et al., 1996). As described earlier, Cooper's (2000) inventor subjects created 3-D images mentally while moving fluidly back and forth in time to search for solutions. To construct and maintain mental laboratories in this way, spatial-temporal thinkers have to multitask.

Curtailed Learning and Reasoning

Some of the cognitive advantages mentioned above—abstraction, generalization, superior memory, and efficient coordination—should affect speed of learning and reasoning. The impression of speedy processing among the gifted may also be due to the abbreviated steps taken in reaching a solution. Krutetskii (1976) called this *curtailed reasoning*, whereby his gifted subjects seemed to "intuit" solutions without working through mathematical problems step by step. Similar behavior has also been observed in Winner's (1996) mathematically precocious case studies, who, even at age 2, could solve arithmetic problems by "intuitive leaps" instead of formal algorithms, but could not explain the steps taken.

Precocious artists seem to grasp the three-quarters view without being taught the formal principles involved, and they may apply this perspective comfortably in half of their figure drawings by age 6—even when this view appears only 15% of the time in the works of typical adolescents who had learned it explicitly in class (Milbrath, 1995).

Reasoning that seems "intuitive" has proven particularly useful to spatial-temporal thinkers because it short-cuts endless digressions from getting lost in a maze of stored and imagined information (Cooper, 2000, p. 185). This capacity for curtailed reasoning has led Cooper's (2000, p. 183) inventor subjects to produce what appeared to others as "instant solutions."

Because the brain is very limited in its capacity to process information compared to a computer, curtailed reasoning may be critical in distinguishing amongst those with high and low abilities. Krutetskii (1976) suggested that superior performance may be due to curtailed reasoning freeing the gifted person to pursue more sophisticated abstract thinking. As such, curtailed learning and reasoning warrants more attention in giftedness research, especially for domains in which it is barely mentioned.

Although learning with minimal instruction is one of the most widely cited characteristics of gifted children (Gross, 1993), the common basis for this claim also happens to be the most problematic upon close scrutiny. Many researchers use fluent reading before school age as evidence for this trait (Gottfried, Gottfried, Bathurst, & Guerin, 1994; Price, 1976; Roedell, Jackson, & Robinson, 1980; VanTassel-Baska, 1983). It is not clear in reading precocity that curtailed learning is actually involved. It seems just as likely that at least some intellectually able preschoolers have been exposed to comparatively more reading opportunities once they signal to caretakers their readiness for this activity. Some reports do hint at children learning from reading with their parents (e.g., Hodge & Kemp, 2000). And, most claims of precocious reading are based on caretakers' retrospective reports instead of researchers' longitudinal observations of children in their natural settings.

How much of the information in the environment (i.e., input) is meaningful to precocious children as opposed to that received by their nongifted peers? Such comparisons have yet to be made, especially in home settings where the child hears intellectual discussions, observes an expert at work, or participates in adult problem solving. The issue is not just the amount of exposure but exposure to input *meaningful* to the child. Remember, too, that the other traits of the gifted—perceptual sensitivity, persistent concentration, obsessive fascination, and perseverance—make it more likely that the precocious child has been "in training" in her domain of talent for longer and with more intensity than the general population.

Flexible Thinking

Intelligent functioning in our everyday world, which is central to the definition of cognition in this chapter, calls for flexible thinking and appropriate application of past knowledge. Often, the typical real-world situation has yet to be defined as a "problem" needing a solution. There are certainly no ready-made rules to be applied in most cases. Ritchhart (2001, p. 144) expressed it well when he says that to be effective, we need "an attitude of awareness or a sensitivity to occasions." This is referred to as *flexible thinking*—knowing when to call upon one's inner resources and deciding which resources to apply for optimal result.

Researchers have been investigating the relationship between flexible thinking and intelligence for some time, but interpreting the experimental evidence is tricky owing to differences in definitions of flexibility. Flexibility has been treated as association of a given concept with concepts in other knowledge areas, perception of a problem from multiple angles, appropriate strategy selection from a wide repertoire, tendency to switch to another strategy when the one in use seems ineffective, or as ability to reach a solution through a reverse operation (see Jaušovec's 1994 review).

Be that as it may, flexibility in its diverse forms can be inferred from analyses of gifted students' performance in mathematics and science. Krutetskii (1976) described how his mathematically gifted subjects easily switched from one mental operation to another, used diverse approaches to solve problems, stayed free from conventional methods, and confidently reconstructed established thought patterns and systems of operation. Krutetskii's finding is echoed in the investigations of Shavinina and Kholodnaja (1996) and Sriraman (2004) in the same domain. Adult mathematicians also seem to think flexibly, working problems both ways by constructing examples to verify truth and counterexamples to uncover falsity (Sriraman, 2003). Similarly, 17- and 18-year-olds identified as gifted (through test scores or exceptional performance) in Jaušovec's (1994) experiments were less likely to get stuck applying familiar but ineffective methods compared to average and low-performing students. In addition, Jaušovec finds that the gifted students applied different types of strategies (e.g., using subgoals, working backward, using memory recall, generating an analogy) to different classes of problems whereas the average subjects' responses showed no discernible pattern, indicating little planning.

Those who have a strong sense of humor are particularly good at detecting when to apply certain types of stored knowledge (McGhee, 1979). Gifted children's widely cited love for humor shows up in language, as well as other domains. The drawings of talented young artists often display this quality, as in the sketch of a "Scottish" octopus in plaid by one of Harrison's (1999) subjects at 4 1/2 years. Winner (1996) stated that these children do not copy slavishly but add their own whimsical touches, possibly to create the visual stimulation their minds crave. In music and dance too, the ability to improvise well distinguishes talented performers from the less able (Baum et al., 1996).

Flexibility and efficiency in dealing with novel situations has been cited as one of the hallmarks of giftedness (English, 1992; Sternberg & Davidson, 1986). As shown above, flexibility in application of knowledge and skills does appear in performance across many domains. Moreover, infant research also suggests that preference for novelty may be correlated with intelligence (Rose & Feldman, 1995). However, there are two important points worth noting here. First, flexibility also underlies *normal* human processing. Researchers studying visual processing propose models that are flexible, allowing for back-and-forth checking between higher and lower levels of operation. Without this built-in flexibility feature, they cannot explain how we all adapt to ever-changing input from an ever-modifying environment to "see" (Sabah, 2002). Second, most cases reviewed in the gifted literature involve bringing what is *known* to bear on the situation. The degree of "novelty" has not been defined clearly in the field. As shown below, experiments investigating how the gifted deal with novelty have produced inconclusive results.

Metacognitive Awareness

Metacognition is awareness of one's own thinking and its regulation. It comprises, among other processes, keeping track of one's understanding of the problem, focusing attention on appropriate aspects of the problem at different stages, organizing mental resources and external tools for optimal use, reviewing one's own progress, and choosing more promising approaches when current ones fail (Frederiksen & Collins, 1996). Because metacognition determines planning and influences outcome, some theorists hypothesize that it is essential for superior performance (Sternberg, 1985, 1988) and that it separates the gifted from the nonidentified (Shore & Kanevsky, 1993). Yet, experiments comparing metacognition in gifted and nongifted groups have yielded mixed results.

Experimental research on the relationship between metacognition and giftedness has been limited to investigating several narrow aspects only. Studies have examined what children consider as factors affecting memory, attention, and reading comprehension (declarative metacognitive knowledge), and how well they can transfer strategies from one problem situation to another on their own or with instruction (strategy regulation). Some investigations also have been done on how well children can "read" their own mental states (cognitive monitoring). In a comprehensive review of such experiments, Alexander et al. (1995) found that the presence or absence of intelligence differences depends on the aspect of metacognition studied and the age of the subjects. In the studies reviewed, gifted children did not appear more advanced than their same-age peers in their understanding of the factors affecting mental processes. The one exception is in questions pertaining to memory, where the gifted group could be distinguished from the nongifted. The two groups fared about the same in their ability to read their own mental states. Gifted and nongifted subjects in elementary school also could not be distinguished by their ability to transfer strategies learned in one situation to another (strategy regulation). There are some hints, though, of giftedness emerging as a differentiating factor for strategy regulation in the early teens (Alexander et al., 1995, p. 18). Alexander et al. (1995, p. 25) concluded in their review:

> Young gifted children do not appear to be more spontaneously strategic nor do they seem to use more complex strategies than nongifted children. Young gifted children do not show a vastly superior ability to benefit from minimal strategy training nor are they better able to benefit from more explicit training.

In a later experiment using kindergartners and first graders, Schwanenflugel, Stevens, Moore, and Carr (1997) tried to address some of the lingering questions from the earlier metacognitive research. Again, the empirical evidence does not confirm a giftedness advantage (although Schwanenflugel et al.'s concluding statements appear to indicate otherwise). Closer examination of the methodology and results of this study shows why investigations of this type are prone to many difficulties. To begin, the child subjects were asked to talk about their own mental activities. The verbally advanced (i.e., gifted) were better at explaining, say, how contextual information helped memory. However, no significant differences between the gifted/nongifted groups were uncovered on whether they forgot things. On the one hand, it is questionable whether typical young children can assess their mental states accurately. On the other hand, gifted children, being perfectionistic, may be more critical in judging their own mental abilities (see below). This would explain why the gifted subjects' responses were not reliably consistent even when the questions were closely related (Schwanenflugel et al., 1997, p. 33).

In short, conclusive evidence is elusive in experimental studies on metacognition due to many confounding factors. Familiarity with the topic or task, especially given the broad knowledge base of the gifted, can positively affect strategy use (Alexander et al., 1995). Personality traits such as tenacity may help the gifted see a task to completion while their less able peers may abandon the struggle halfway without demonstrating their ability to the fullest extent (Kanevsky, 1992).

There is, nevertheless, one area in which the gifted do seem to excel. Ewers and Wood (1993) concluded from their study of fifth graders that the gifted were more accurate in judging their ability to solve challenging problems whereas the others overestimated their abilities. Other studies have also noted this self-assessment accuracy of the gifted (Coleman & Shore, 1991; Shore & Dover, 1987), suggesting more advanced metacognitive development.

A stronger relationship between metacognition and giftedness is shown in studies on students who are gifted and learning disabled. In these studies, learning disabled gifted children and adolescents outperformed their average, nondisabled peers on metacognitive tasks (Hannah & Shore, 1995; Montague, 1991).

Gifted individuals' metacognitive awareness of their ability or performance is more apparent in exploratory-type studies. Krutetskii's (1976) mathematically talented subjects used plans to search for the best solution. They did this deliberately, intentionally suspending the final solution while analyzing the problem from various perspectives. In this way, the students could cull auxiliary information from each trial before selecting the best method. This can be inferred from statements such as "I am not solving the problem yet; I want to get to know it better" (Krutetskii, 1976, p. 292). Winner (1996, p. 89) similarly related her musical prodigy's running commentary of his own performance and how he did slides, octave changes, and harmonics. The success of the inventors Cooper (2000, p. 184) interviewed came partly from their metacognitive perspective: their ability to stand outside of themselves and "watch" themselves manipulate mental imagery.

Speedy Processing

Given the time constraint in IQ testing, it is easy to presume that those who score well (and by extension the gifted) process information speedily. Careful examination of the experimental evidence yields a more complex picture. Shavinina and Kholodnaja (1996) found that their intellectually capable subjects actually delayed solving problems to evaluate alternatives carefully unlike other students. Their performance, according to these researchers, was aided by their capacity to differentiate essential from unimportant features (abstraction). Thus, the *appearance* of speedy processing may be the result of abstraction as well as other processes defined above.

Some tasks are better suited to speedy resolution than others. For example, Sternberg (1988) concluded that better reasoners in analogy tests were quicker in making comparisons but slower in meaning identification. Shore and Lazar (1996) concluded from their study of students in seventh and eighth grades that the high-IQ group's overall speed advantage resulted from spending relatively less time on the execution phase of problem solving compared to the exploration stage. Allocating more time for planning also allows them to weigh more strategic options flexibly in order to pick the most appropriate one. In criticizing IQ tests, Sternberg (1988, p. 26) said, "intelligence is not defined by speed alone but, more important, by knowing when to be quick and when to take time to deliberate. Strictly timed tests often force an individual to behave impulsively—unintelligently, in a sense." Not surprisingly, Swanson (1992) reported that the gifted and high average students tested took more than 45 seconds longer than low average 9- and 10-year-olds to solve problems. Elementary-age studies by Shore (2000) and his colleagues revealed that accuracy is a stronger predictor of IQ scores compared to speed.

Processing speed, nevertheless, is required in some tasks. This would apply to tasks where processing is automatic at lower levels (i.e., fast and done without requiring conscious attention) so as to free up mental resources for processing at higher levels of thinking. Reading is one such task. Quick recognition of spelling patterns frees the reader from analyzing words letter by letter, leading to fluent reading (Levy, Bourassa, & Horn, 1999). This is why experiments on word identification (rapid automatized naming) show a positive relationship between speed and reading fluency (Bowers, 1993). Studies on infant cognition demonstrate that those who look at a stimulus for a shorter time actually get more, not less, information out of it than those who look for a long time (Mitchell & Horowitz, 1988). Conversely, slow readers tend not to transfer previously encountered information to new words, indicating that less learning takes place with this group compared to their speedier counterparts (Levy et al., 1999). In fact, reading too slowly actually hinders comprehension because the reader may forget earlier parts of the text. Possibly, some tasks such as reading require a certain degree of speediness to enable integration of input and stored information.

Empirical evidence linking processing speed with intelligence is also found in the field of cognitive development. Studies in this field indicate that speed only correlates with intelligence (as measured by IQ) when subjects have to coordinate several (simple) tasks simultaneously (see Hettinger & Carr's 2003 summary). In essence, for any field, processing speed should be measured for different stages of problem solving and for different types of tasks. Additionally, processing speed should be considered in relation to the other cognitive characteristics that affect task completion time, such as abstraction and generalization, coordination, and curtailed reasoning.

Philosophical Thinking

Young children typically focus on the here and now in their speech (Brown, 1973), which is why we tend not to notice what they do not know or cannot do. Young gifted children, on the other hand, think more broadly about abstract topics. They think philosophically, concerning themselves with larger questions and ideas that go beyond the needs of daily living. These questions often involve things that have no observable or ready-made answers, such as the nature or future of humankind and the cosmos—questions in which the child herself is not at the center of the inquiry. Reports of philosophical thinking among gifted children have mainly been anecdotal, which is why the documented evidence is mentioned here.

Sankar-DeLeeuw (2004) reported that all of the kindergartners studied have thought philosophically about the universe, religion, and mythology from an early age. Hoh (2005) gave a sample of the philosophical questions recorded at age 4, such as, "What's life about?" Interest in the beyond is naturally most apparent in the expressive domains. Thus, it shows up in fine art, where Harrison (1999, pp. 192–193) noted "a fascination to represent that which is not readily observable, to go beyond the obvious . . . and extrapolate from the known to the unknown." Piirto (1992) considered philosophical thinking a common characteristic of the writing of talented students.

OUTCOMES

Vast Knowledge Base and Vocabulary

Having a vast knowledge base often has been listed as one of the cognitive traits of gifted children. It is more accurate to view it as the confluence of the characteristics identified above. Traits such as perceptual sensitivity, obsessive fascination, superior memory, abstraction, and generalization lead to quick acquisition of the symbolic system of written language. Extensive reading is likely a major source of knowledge for high-ability children. Most of Terman's

(1925) early readers started at age 4, giving them a head start in knowledge acquisition, especially if they read omnivorously. This explains the high scores of the intellectually capable in vocabulary tests (Gardner, 1990).

Superior performance may be dependent on speed of knowledge acquisition, organization of stored knowledge, and efficiency of knowledge retrieval, but little attention has been paid to this area in giftedness research. Therefore it is not clear at present how gifted children use their vast knowledge base to excel in complex problem solving.

Advanced Strategic Knowledge and Ability

The same cognitive characteristics mentioned above also may be responsible for the giftedness advantage evident in numerous studies on problem-solving strategies amongst varied age groups (Hettinger & Carr, 2003). Curtailed learning and reasoning, superior memory, ability to abstract and generalize, speedy processing, and flexible thinking contribute to a wider repertoire of strategies and their appropriate application during problem solving. Expert-like behavior can show up as early as elementary age, with high-ability children using the adults' strategies of working with a plan and employing metacognition (Shore, 2000).

RELEVANT PERSONALITY TRAITS

Self-Challenging Nature, Tenacity, and Perfectionism

The cognitive characteristics of the gifted work hand in hand with their personality traits to contribute to superior performance. Of particular relevance is gifted students' need to challenge themselves continually and unflaggingly. Various researchers have observed this behavior in experimental problem solving (Kanevsky, 1992) and natural settings (Winner, 1996). Evidence abounds in different domains. Talented young artists create their own visuo-spatial challenges (Freeman, 2000); mathematically gifted students are driven in their quest for the most elegant mathematical solutions (Krutetskii, 1976). Gifted subjects' verbalizations during problem solving (think-aloud protocols) confirm that they do not simply aim for one final solution but toward increasing the given problem's complexity by considering various solutions, especially when the problem is ill-defined (Jaušovec, 1994, p. 72).

The need for a stimulating environment may explain the observed relationship between giftedness and humor. Humor offers an intellectual form of pleasure derived from the cognitive challenge of creating it (McGhee, 1979). Gifted children's cognitive characteristics enable them to sustain this internally motivated drive to challenge themselves. Abstraction and generalization, curtailed learning and reasoning, efficient coordination, and superior memory probably work in combination to create the impression that the gifted have a preference for complexity (Hettinger & Carr, 2003). Bear in mind, though, that "complexity" is relative to the observer's point of view. What may seem complex to most may not appear so to one who can see the overall pattern amongst the myriad details, recognize the familiar hidden in a new situation, draw together various mental resources with ease, and so forth. Indeed, given the exceptional abilities described above, it would be surprising if gifted individuals do *not* prefer complexity.

THEORETICAL ISSUES

General Intelligence or Multiple Intelligences?

On the surface, the preceding discussion may seem paradoxical: an individual's talent tends to be concentrated within a particular domain but cognitive characteristics cut across areas of performance. At issue is whether a common factor underlies giftedness (general intelligence) or whether there are different and separate types of intelligence (multiple intelligences). If there is a general intelligence factor, then high ability should show up in more than one area for each gifted individual. If multiple intelligences are involved, then superior performance could be restricted to certain domains. This issue is far from settled in the field.

The abilities of the academically gifted do tend to be less balanced than those of other groups (Benbow & Minor, 1990; Mueller, Dash, Matheson, & Short, 1984; Silver & Clampit, 1990), whether we compare verbal to numerical (Terman, 1925) or verbal to spatial abilities (Lewis, 1985). Talents may be so focused that they do not extend into areas that may seem related to us. For example, Goldsmith and Feldman (1989) described a Chinese child artist whose painting skills were close to an adult's but whose calligraphy was still juvenile.

Nevertheless, academically gifted students may still perform above their nongifted peers overall even when the abilities of the former are uneven. For instance, mathematically precocious children usually perform far above older, typical students in verbal tests even when it is not their strongest area (Benbow & Minor, 1990). Krutetskii (1976) similarly observed that verbal abilities are well-developed in *all* mathematically gifted pupils.

The correlation between mathematical and spatial abilities has been noted by many researchers (Benbow & Minor, 1990; Benbow, Stanley, Kirk, & Zonderman, 1983; Fennema & Sherman, 1977; Hermelin & O'Connor, 1986). However, Krutetskii (1976) stressed that mathematical precocity is not homogeneous; some mathematically able individuals have spatial strengths and others do not. Fennema and Tartre (1985) also cautioned that spatial skills are applicable to certain types of mathematical problems but not to others.

The above findings on verbal, quantitative, and spatial relationships may be reconciled by Robinson, Abbott, Berninger, Busse, and Mukhopadhyay's (1997) analysis of the test scores of 276 first and second graders. The researchers concluded that, although a relationship exists between quantitative and verbal abilities among gifted children, correlations between their quantitative and spatial abilities are significantly stronger.

Kindergartners identified as advanced in mathematical and spatial reasoning and language were reported by parents as being developed in memory and fine motor skills, as well (Pletan, Robinson, Berninger, & Abbott, 1995). The interconnections become even more prominent among adult experts. Through more than a decade of research of hundreds of creative individuals, Root-Bernstein and Root-Bernstein (1999, 2004) proposed that experts across disciplines use similar thinking tools such as observing, pattern recognizing, pattern forming, imaging, dimensional thinking, modeling, body thinking, transforming, synthesizing, abstracting, analogizing, and empathizing—many of which are listed in this chapter as common cognitive characteristics of the gifted. Sternberg, Grigorenko, and Singer (2004) also observed these traits across the artistic and scientific domains in their work on creativity, as did Eiduson (1962) when testing and interviewing groups of artists and scientists.

Restrictions Leading to Domain Specificity

Evidently, the different domains of talent share common cognitive abilities and processes (Runco, 1994). So, how can this be reconciled with the fact that the accomplishments of high-achieving individuals tend to be restricted to specialized disciplines? The answer lies partly in the fact that research tends to focus on the end products unique to each discipline (Csikszentmihalyi, 1996; Gardner, 1999), not on the processes common to their creation. Root-Bernstein and Root-Bernstein (2004, p. 145) noted that many famous innovators in the arts and the sciences are superior in several areas: "Creative artifacts and expressive products are transformations of thought and therefore unreliable guides to the processes by which those thoughts are generated."

Intuitive, nonverbal thinking has to be translated into a mode that can be communicated to others and therefore determines the area one chooses in which to work (Sternberg et al., 2004, p. 202). Other restrictions are imposed by environmental factors and the type and length of training needed to perform in a field.

Investigations of human functioning outside of giftedness research raise even more questions that cannot be addressed by the current state of knowledge. On the one hand, new computational models use similar basic processes to describe how we process a variety of information types, for example, language, visual scenes, and music (McKevitt, 2002). Yet, on the other hand, any in-depth study (e.g., on processing peripheral vision or sentence structure) involves a network of subcomponents that are semi-autonomous in nature. These subcomponents handling highly specific parts of a task are posited to be semi-autonomous (hence modular) because this would then allow for the quick decision making that has to take place at all stages of an operation; otherwise, we would not be exhibiting the kind of speedy and smooth performance that we humans typically do display. In short, human cognition seems to be driven by these semi-autonomous agents interacting with each other cooperatively and often competitively in a massively parallel system (Klimesch, 1994). Modularity *and* connectivity both characterize cognitive processing at this stage of knowledge.

METHODOLOGICAL LIMITATIONS

Recall that the definition of cognition at the beginning of this chapter embodies the idea of effective functioning in a fluid environment. Empirical evidence of the mental operations of gifted individuals as they function in the real world would have been welcome. It would have revealed how they perform in situations that are open-ended, less structured, and ambiguous. But, such evidence is scarce in this field.

Experimental studies tend to test very limited aspects of the abilities under investigation. For example, McBride-Chang et al.'s (1996) test of speech perception covered only three factors out of a multitude of dimensions comprising natural language processing. Studies that do include nontesting data rely heavily on retrospective parental reports, such as Terman's (1925) seminal research. More recent work that supplements caretakers' recollections with present-time observations uses very few subjects; for example, Sankar-DeLeeuw's (2004) qualitative case study used only five subjects.

Most domains have barely been explored. There are more investigations of mathematical ability than any other, but even here, early giftedness in this area has been neglected (Robinson et al., 1997). Furthermore, research is drawn to the exceptional at the expense of those who are moderately gifted even though the latter group is considerably larger (Livne & Milgram, 2000).

Qualitative case studies combined with quantitative analyses are needed for deeper insight on the inner workings of numerous talented minds, perhaps along the lines of Krutetskii's (1976) decade-long research. However, it is highly laborious and labor-intensive to transcribe and analyze the verbal discourse (or behavior) of subjects, when even 10 minutes of recording can easily consume hours of study. Much work, therefore, lies ahead for this relatively young field.

SUMMARY

- The same cognitive characteristics appear in superior performance across domains, from the intellectual to the artistic.
- Empirical evidence from many domains indicate that the gifted are particularly strong in perception, concentration, memory, imaging, abstraction and generalization, learning and reasoning, and task coordination as these terms are defined here.
- The gifted also tend to be obsessively fascinated with their domains of talent and to think philosophically.
- The evidence is less clear-cut for the oft-cited characteristics of speedy processing, learning with minimal instruction (especially for reading precocity), ability to deal with novelty (flexible thinking), and metacognitive awareness—suggesting the need for further study of subcomponents of these traits in certain age groups.
- Other traits commonly mentioned—having a vast knowledge base, displaying advanced strategic ability, and preferring complexity—are outcomes of the interplay of the cognitive characteristics identified in this chapter.
- Research on human cognition in nontraditional areas such as visual and spatial processing can help formulate more precise questions to direct future inquiry on the cognitive characteristics of the gifted.

REFERENCES

Ablard, K. E., & Tissot, S. L. (1998). Young students' readiness for advanced math: Precocious abstract reasoning. *Journal for the Education of the Gifted, 21*, 206–223.

Adams, M. (1990). *Beginning to read: Thinking and learning about print.* Cambridge, MA: MIT Press.

Alexander, J. M., Carr, M., & Schwanenflugel, P. J. (1995). Development of metacognition in gifted children: Directions for future research. *Developmental Review, 15*(1), 1–37.

Arbib, M. A., & Robinson, J. A. (Eds.). (1990). *Natural and artificial parallel computation.* Cambridge, MA: MIT Press.

Baillargeon, R., Pascual-Leone, J., & Roncadin, C. (1998). Mental-attentional capacity: Does cognitive style make a difference? *Journal of Experimental Child Psychology, 70*, 143–166.

Baum, S. M., Owen, S. V., & Oreck, B. A. (1996). Talent beyond words: Identification of potential talent in dance and music in elementary students. *Gifted Child Quarterly, 40*, 93–101.

Benbow, C. P., & Minor, L. L. (1990). Cognitive profiles of verbally and mathematically precocious students: Implications for identification of the gifted. *Gifted Child Quarterly, 34*, 21–26.

Benbow, C. P., Stanley, J. C., Kirk, M. K., & Zonderman, A. B. (1983). Structure of intelligence of intellectually precocious children and in their parents. *Intelligence, 7,* 129–152.

Bowers, P. G. (1993). Text reading and rereading: Determinants of fluency beyond word recognition. *Journal of Reading Behavior, 25,* 133–153.

Brown, R. (1973). *A first language: The early stages.* Cambridge, MA: Harvard University Press.

Chase, W. G., & Ericsson, K. A. (1982). Skill and working memory. In G. H. Bower (Ed.), *The psychology of learning and motivation* (Vol. 16, pp. 1–58). New York: Academic Press.

Chi, M. (1978). Knowledge structures and memory development. In R. S. Siegler (Ed.), *Children's thinking: What develops?* (pp. 73–96). Hillsdale, NJ: Lawrence Erlbaum.

Churchland, P. S. (1986). *Neurophilosophy: Toward a unified science of the mind-brain.* Cambridge, MA: MIT Press.

Coleman, E. B., & Shore, B. (1991). Problem solving processes of high and average performers in physics. *Journal for the Education of the Gifted, 14,* 366–379.

Cooper, E. E. (2000). Spatial-temporal intelligence: Original thinking processes of gifted inventors. *Journal for the Education of the Gifted, 24,* 170–193.

Csikszentmihalyi, M. (1996). *Creativity.* New York: Harper.

Dark, V. J., & Benbow, C. P. (1991). Differential enhancement of working memory with mathematical versus verbal precocity. *Journal of Educational Psychology, 83,* 48–60.

Dubrovina, I. V. (1992). The nature of abilities in the primary school child. In V. A. Krutetskii (Ed.) & J. Teller (Trans.), *Soviet studies in mathematics education* (Vol. 8, pp. 65–96). Chicago: University of Chicago School Mathematics Project.

Eiduson, B. (1962). *Scientists: Their psychological world.* New York: Basic Books.

English, L. (1992). Children's use of domain-specific knowledge and domain-general strategies in novel problem solving. *British Journal of Educational Psychology, 6,* 203–216.

Ewers, C. A., & Wood, N. L. (1993). Sex and ability differences in children's math self-efficacy and prediction accuracy. *Learning and Individual Differences, 5,* 259–267.

Fennema, E., & Sherman, J. (1977). Sex-related differences in mathematics achievement, spatial visualization, and sociocultural factors. *Journal of Educational Research, 14,* 51–71.

Fennema, E., & Tartre, L. A. (1985). The use of spatial visualization in mathematics by girls and boys. *Journal for Research in Mathematics Education, 16,* 184–206.

Freeman, J. (2000). Children's talent in fine art and music—England. *Roeper Review, 22,* 98–101.

Frederiksen, J. R., & Collins, A. (1996). Designing an assessment system for the workplace of the future. In L. B. Resnick, J. Wirt, & D. Jenkins (Eds.), *Linking school and work: Roles for standards and assessment* (pp. 193–221). San Francisco: Jossey-Bass.

Gardner, H. (1983). *Frames of mind: The theory of multiple intelligences.* New York: Basic Books.

Gardner, H. (1999). *Intelligence reframed.* New York: Basic Books.

Gardner, M. F. (1990). *Expressive one-word picture vocabulary test* (Rev. ed.). Novato, CA: Academic Therapy.

Goldman-Rakic, P. (1990). Parallel systems in the cerebral cortex: The topography of cognition. In M. A. Arbib & J. A. Robinson (Eds.), *Natural and artificial parallel processing* (pp. 155–176). Cambridge, MA: MIT Press.

Goldsmith, L. T., & Feldman, D. H. (1989). Wang Yani: Gifts well given. In W. C. Ho (Ed.), *Yani: The brush of innocence* (pp. 51–62). New York: Hudson Hills Press.

Golomb, C. (1990, August). *Eytan: The development of a precociously gifted child artist*. Paper presented at the Annual Convention of the American Psychological Association, Boston.

Gottfried, A. W., Gottfried, A. E., Bathurst, K., & Guerin, D. W. (1994). *Gifted IQ: Early developmental aspects: The Fullerton Longitudinal Study*. New York: Plenum Press.

Gross, M. U. M. (1993). *Exceptionally gifted children*. London: Routledge.

Hannah, C. L., & Shore, B. M. (1995). Metacognition and high intellectual ability: Insights from the study of learning disabled gifted students. *Gifted Child Quarterly, 39*(2), 95–109.

Haroutounian, J. (1995). Talent identification and development in the arts: An artistic/educational dialogue. *Roeper Review, 18,* 112–117.

Harrison, C. (1999). Visual representation of the young gifted child. *Roeper Review, 21,* 189–194.

Henderson, J. M., & Hollingworth, A. (2003). Eye movements, visual memory, and scene representation. In M. A. Peterson & G. Rhodes (Eds.), *Perception of faces, objects, and scenes* (pp. 356–383). Oxford, England: Oxford University Press.

Hermelin, B., & O'Connor, N. (1986). Spatial representations in mathematically and in artistically gifted children. *British Journal of Educational Psychology, 56,* 150–157.

Hettinger, H., & Carr, M. (2003). Cognitive development in gifted children: Toward a more precise understanding of emerging differences in intelligence. *Educational Psychology Review, 15,* 215–246.

Hodge, K. A., & Kemp, C. R. (2000). Exploring the nature of giftedness in preschool children. *Journal for the Education of the Gifted, 24,* 46–71.

Hoh, P.-S. (2005). The linguistic advantage of the intellectually gifted child: An empirical study of spontaneous speech. *Roeper Review, 27,* 178–185.

Jaušovec, N. (1994). *Flexible thinking: An explanation for individual differences in ability*. Cresskill, NJ: Hampton Press.

Jiménez, L. (2003). *Attention to implicit learning*. Philadelphia: John Benjamins.

Kanevsky, L. (1992). The learning game. In P. S. Klein & A. J. Tannenbaum (Eds.), *To be young and gifted* (pp. 204–243). Norwood, NJ: Ablex.

Klimesch, W. (1994). *The structure of long-term memory: A connectivity model of semantic processing*. Hillsdale, NJ: Lawrence Erlbaum.

Kosslyn, S. M. (1994). *Image and brain*. Cambridge, MA: MIT Press.

Krutetskii, V. A. (1976). *The psychology of mathematical abilities in school children* (J. Teller, Trans. and J. Kilpatrick & I. Wirszup, Eds.). Chicago: University of Chicago Press.

Laing, E., & Hulme, C. (1999). Phonological and semantic processes influence beginning readers' ability to learn to read words. *Journal of Experimental Child Psychology, 73,* 183–207.

Levy, B. A., Bourassa, D. C., & Horn, C. (1999). Fast and slow namers: Benefits of segmentation and whole word training. *Journal of Experimental Child Psychology, 73,* 115–138.

Lewis, M. (1985). Gifted or dysfunctional: The child savant. *Pediatric Annals, 14*, 733–742.

Livne, N. L., & Milgram, R. M. (2000). Assessing four levels of creative mathematical ability in Israeli adolescents utilizing out-of-school activities: A circular three-stage technique. *Roeper Review, 22*, 111–116.

Lund, N. (2001). *Attention and pattern recognition.* New York: Routledge.

McBride-Chang, C., Manis, F. R., & Wagner, R. K. (1996). Correlates of phonological awareness: Implications for gifted education. *Roeper Review, 19*, 27–30.

McGhee, P. E. (1979). *Humor: Its origin and development.* San Francisco: W. H. Freeman.

McKevitt, P. (Ed.). (2002). *Language, vision, and music. Selected papers from the 8th International Workshop on the Cognitive Science of Natural Language Processing, Galway, 1999.* Philadelphia: John Benjamins.

Milbrath, C. (1995). Germinal motifs in the work of a gifted child artist. In C. Golomb (Ed.), *The development of artistically gifted children. Selected case studies* (pp. 101–134). Hillsdale, NJ: Lawrence Erlbaum.

Mitchell, D. W., & Horowitz, F. D. (1988, April). Processing of high- and low-saliency stimulus features by 3- and 4-month-old infants. Paper presented at the International Conference on Infant Studies, Washington, DC.

Montague, M. (1991). Gifted and learning-disabled gifted students' knowledge and use of mathematical problem-solving strategies. *Journal for the Education of the Gifted, 14*, 393–411.

Mueller, H. H., Dash, U. N., Matheson, D. N., & Short, R. H. (1984). WISC-R subtest patterning of below average, average and above average IQ children: A meta-analysis. *Alberta Journal of Educational Research, 30*, 68–85.

Oreck, B. A., Owen, S. V., & Baum, S. M. (2003). Validity, reliability, and equity issues in an observational talent assessment process in the performing arts. *Journal for the Education of the Gifted, 27*, 62–94.

Peterson, M. A., & Rhodes, G. (Eds.). (2003). *Perception of faces, objects, and scenes.* Oxford, England: Oxford University Press.

Pinker, S. (1994). *The language instinct.* New York: HarperCollins.

Piirto, J. (1992). *Understanding those who create.* Dayton: Ohio Psychology Press.

Pletan, M. D., Robinson, N. M., Berninger, V. W., & Abbott, R. D. (1995). Parents' observations of kindergartners who are advanced in mathematical reasoning. *Journal for the Education of the Gifted, 19*, 30–44.

Porath, M. (1997). A developmental model of artistic giftedness in middle childhood. *Journal for the Education of the Gifted, 20*, 201–223.

Price, E. H. (1976). How thirty-seven gifted children learned to read. *The Reading Teacher, 30*(1), 44–46.

Renzulli, J. (1977). *The enrichment triad model.* Mansfield Center, CT: Creative Learning Press.

Revesz, G. (1970). *The psychology of a musical prodigy.* Freeport, NY: Books for Libraries Press. (Original work published 1925)

Richardson, J. (1991). *A life of Picasso.* New York: Random House.

Ritchhart, R. (2001). From IQ to IC: A dispositional view of intelligence. *Roeper Review, 23*, 143–150.

Robinson, N. M., Abbott, R. D., Berninger, V. W., Busse, J., & Mukhopadhyay, S. (1997). Developmental changes in mathematically precocious young children: Longitudinal and gender effects. *Gifted Child Quarterly, 41*, 145–158.

Roedell, W. C., Jackson, N. E., & Robinson, H. B. (1980). *Gifted young children.* New York: Teachers College Press.

Root-Bernstein, R. S., & Root-Bernstein, M. M. (1999). *Sparks of genius: The thirteen thinking tools of the world's most creative people.* Boston: Houghton Mifflin.

Root-Bernstein, R., & Root-Bernstein, M. (2004). Artistic scientists and scientific artists: The link between polymathy and creativity. In R. J. Sternberg, E. L. Grigorenko, & J. L. Singer (Eds.), *Creativity: From potential to realization* (pp. 127–151). Washington, DC: American Psychological Association.

Rose, S. A., & Feldman, J. F. (1995). Prediction of IQ and specific cognitive abilities at 11 years from infancy measures. *Developmental Psychology, 31,* 685–696.

Runco, M. A. (Ed.). (1994). *Problem finding, problem solving, and creativity.* Norwood, NJ: Ablex.

Sabah, G. (2002). The respective roles of conscious and subconscious processes for interpreting language and music. In P. McKevitt (Ed.), *Language, vision, and music. Selected papers from the 8th International Workshop on the Cognitive Science of Natural Language Processing, Galway, 1999* (pp. 241–254). Philadelphia: John Benjamins.

Sankar-DeLeeuw, N. (2004). Case studies of gifted kindergarten children: Profiles of promise. *Roeper Review, 26,* 192–207.

Schwanenflugel, P. J., Stevens, T., Moore, P., & Carr, M. (1997). Metacognitive knowledge of gifted children and nonidentified children in early elementary school. *Gifted Child Quarterly, 41,* 25–35.

Shapiro, S. I. (1992). A psychological analysis of the structure of mathematical abilities in grades 9 and 10. In V. A. Krutetskii (Ed.) & J. Teller (Trans.), *Soviet studies in mathematics education* (Vol. 8, pp. 97–142). Chicago: University of Chicago School Mathematics Project.

Shavinina, L. V., & Kholodnaja, M. A. (1996). The cognitive experience as a psychological basis of intellectual giftedness. *Journal for the Education of the Gifted, 20,* 3–35.

Shore, B. M. (2000). Metacognition and flexibility: Qualitative differences in how gifted children think. In R. C. Friedman & B. M. Shore (Eds.), *Talents unfolding: Cognition and development* (pp. 167–187). Washington, DC: American Psychological Association.

Shore, B. M., & Dover, A. C. (1987). Metacognition, intelligence, and giftedness. *Gifted Child Quarterly, 31,* 37–39.

Shore, B. M., & Kanevsky, L. S. (1993). Thinking processes: Being and becoming gifted. In K. A. Heller, F. J. Mönks, & A. H. Passow (Eds.), *International handbook of research and development of giftedness and talent* (pp. 133–147). New York: Pergamon Press.

Shore, B. M., & Lazar, L. (1996). IQ-related differences in time allocation during problem solving. *Psychological Reports, 78,* 848–850.

Silver, S. J., & Clampit, M. K. (1990). WISC-R profiles of high ability children: Interpretation of verbal-performance discrepancies. *Gifted Child Quarterly, 34*(2), 76–79.

Solso, R. L. (1998). *Cognitive psychology.* Boston: Allyn & Bacon.

Sriraman, B. (2003). The characteristics of mathematical creativity. *The Mathematics Educator, 14,* 19–34.

Sriraman, B. (2004). Gifted ninth graders' notions of proof: Investigating parallels in approaches of mathematically gifted students and professional mathematicians. *Journal for the Education of the Gifted, 27*, 267–292.

Sternberg, R. J. (1985). *Beyond I.Q.: A triarchic theory of human intelligence.* New York: Cambridge University Press.

Sternberg, R. J. (1988). *The triarchic mind: A new theory of human intelligence.* New York: Viking.

Sternberg, R. J., & Davidson, J. E. (1986). *Conceptions of giftedness.* New York: Cambridge University Press.

Sternberg, R. J., Grigorenko, E. L., & Singer, J. L. (Eds.). (2004). *Creativity: From potential to realization.* Washington, DC: American Psychological Association.

Sternberg, R. J., & Lubart, T. I. (1992). Creative giftedness in children. In P. S. Klein & A. J. Tannenbaum (Eds.), *To be young and gifted* (pp. 33–51). Norwood, NJ: Ablex.

Swanson, H. L. (1992). The relationship between metacognition and problem solving in gifted children. *Roeper Review, 15*(1), 43–48.

Terman, L. M. (1925). *Mental and physical traits of a thousand gifted children. Genetic studies of genius: Vol. 1.* Stanford, CA: Stanford University Press.

Thomas, G. V., & Silk, A. M. J. (1990). *An introduction to the psychology of children's drawings.* New York: Harvester Wheatsheaf.

VanTassel-Baska, J. (1983). Profiles of precocity: The Midwest Talent Search finalists. *Gifted Child Quarterly, 27*(3), 139–145.

Wertheimer, M. (1982). *Productive thinking.* Chicago: University of Chicago Press. (Original work published 1945)

Winner, E. (1996). *Gifted children: Myths and realities.* New York: Basic Books.

Chapter 6

COGNITIVE DEVELOPMENT

Felicia A. Dixon

he study of cognitive development focuses on changes in mental skills that occur through increasing maturity and experience (Sternberg & Williams, 2002). In general, it involves the regular, age-related changes in children's cognition over time. Without doubt, the most well-known theories of cognitive or intellectual development are those of Piaget and Vygotsky. In addition, the Neo-Piagetian viewpoint concerning cognitive development must be examined relative to how it contributes to clarification of the construct. Piaget viewed the child as "a young intellectual, constructing ever more powerful theories of the world as a result of applying a set of logical tools of increasing generality and power" (Case, 1992, p. 4). In his work, Piaget attempted to specify the nature of these tools, the process by which they are acquired, and the knowledge of the world that they encompass. Piaget posited certain very basic and discrete cognitive operations that were acknowledged to be present from birth. However, with experience these operations were seen as gradually becoming differentiated and

coordinated into systems of increasing complexity and coherence. Cognitive development, then, was divided into four stages, each anchored at specific points in the child's development. He termed these four stages as sensorimotor stage (0–2 years); preoperational stage (2–7 years); concrete operational stage (7–10 years); and formal operational stage (11–adulthood). These stages represented qualitative changes in cognitive development with each successive stage (Sternberg & Williams, 2002). Piaget suggested that children transitioned from one stage to another through active reflection on the products of their current mental activity and on the inherent contradictions that this reflection revealed. Piaget's theory is domain general; that is, it predicts that children who show cognitive development in one area generally should show comparable cognitive development in other areas. Although Piaget's theory of cognitive development is widely embraced as the single most influential theory of cognitive development offered, it does not specifically address the needs of gifted students as developmentally different from the regular population of learners. However, Cohen and Kim (1998), in synthesizing much research stated,

> [many researchers] found that gifted children do not generally enter a higher stage of development (either on traditional Piagetian tasks or in specific areas such as moral development, humor, social development or analogical reasoning) much earlier than their typically-developing peers, though the quality or breadth of ability within stage is evident. (p. 201)

The Neo-Piagetian view of cognitive development is based on reactions and responses to Piaget's theory. Neo-Piagetians build on Piaget's theory, although they disown the parts of the theory that have not held up to close scrutiny. Suggesting that there may be other stages that extend beyond formal operations, Neo-Piagetians, including Riegel (1973), Pascual-Leone (1990) and Sternberg (1988), suggest a stage called *dialectical thinking*, which is built on the premise that as people mature through adolescence and into early adulthood, they recognize that most real-life problems do not have a unique solution that is fully correct. Rather, the idea is that thinking about problems evolves as students propose a thesis as a solution to the problem. Perhaps with further examination of the problem, either by these students themselves or by others, an antithesis to the thesis is proposed that directly contradicts it. Eventually, someone may propose a synthesis that somehow integrates what had appeared to be two opposing and irreconcilable points of view. The Neo-Piagetian view seems to consider higher stages of thinking as people develop, and it implies a connection to processes thought to connect with giftedness (Dixon, 2005).

Whereas Piaget viewed development as occurring largely from the inside, outward, Lev Vygotsky's view was that cognitive development occurred from the outside, inward. Vygotsky posited that a person's intrapersonal or internal processes were based on interactions with others (Sternberg & Williams, 2002). Children observe interactions between people in their world, interact with people themselves, and then make use of all of the interactions to further their own development. Thus, Vygotsky's theory is a sociocultural theory. Although Piaget focused on the individual's maturation as key to understanding cognitive development, Vygotsky recognized that developmental accomplishments depended as much on the influence of the social and environmental contexts as they did on maturation. Much of Vygotsky's theory applies to understanding gifted students, but the theory itself is not specifically focused on the gifted population and how it is different in terms of advanced cognitive development.

Cognitive development does not always increase gradually over time, but in some domains it might reach adult levels early, remaining stable thereafter (Bjorklund, 2005). Cognition refers to the processes or faculties by which knowledge is acquired and manipulated; these are mental processes and therefore cannot be directly observed. Relative to gifted children, it is important to understand average developmental patterns so that advanced and accelerated development can be noticed (Clark, 1997). However, as Mönks and Mason (1993) advised, existing and ongoing research demonstrates that only longitudinal studies can provide evidence about the relative contribution of nature and nurture to the development of gifted individuals. Always comparing the gifted to the average does not explain the differences specific to gifted individuals; that comes with studying them and their own developmental changes. According to Kanevsky (1992), gifted children are "playful masters of the learning game" (p. 205), and this chapter reviews the research on how cognitive development enables these children to play this game with style and ease.

According to Winner (2000),

> Research on retardation is more advanced and more integrated into the field of psychology than is research on giftedness. Research on retardation is more likely to find its way into mainstream developmental journals than is research on giftedness, which is often to be found in specialized and hence less widely read journals. (p. 159)

The research on cognitive development and giftedness reveals some interesting issues. Hettinger and Carr (2003) stated that the fields of gifted education and cognitive development have had little communication; traditionally these fields have stood far apart, sharing few ideas and little discourse among researchers. "Both fields have separately examined common factors believed to contribute to cognitive development and giftedness but have not integrated their findings" (Hettinger & Carr, 2003, p. 216). Further, Hettinger and Carr stated that although the research community has some knowledge of the developmental path cognition takes in gifted children, the body of research has significant gaps, including the types of studies conducted. Most of the research on the development of giftedness is based on studies comparing same-age groups of gifted and average students rather than carefully researching the same gifted students in longitudinal studies.

In order to keep the topic of cognitive development in perspective, it is useful to review the following seven general "truths" identified by Bjorklund (2005) before proceeding to examine the research available on this topic as it relates to gifted children:

1. Cognitive development proceeds through the dynamic and reciprocal transaction of a child's biological constitution (including genetics) and his or her physical and social environment (including culture).
2. Cognitive development is a constructive process, with children playing an active role in the constructions of their own minds.
3. Cognition is multifaceted, and different cognitive skills show different patterns of developmental function and stability of individual differences.
4. Cognitive development involves changes in both domain-general and domain-specific mechanisms.
5. Cognitive development involves changes in the way information is represented, although children of every age possess a range of ways in which to represent experiences.
6. Background knowledge, or knowledge base, has a significant influence on how children think.
7. Children's problem solving becomes increasingly strategic with age; children have a broad selection of strategies to choose from, and they become more effective with age in their selection and monitoring of problem-solving strategies (pp. 499–505).

This chapter is organized according to the following divisions: definition of relevant terms; major questions addressed on the topic of cognitive development in gifted children; conclusions from the research based on empirical support; limitations of the research; practical implications; and credible resources on the research of cognitive development.

DEFINITION OF RELEVANT TERMS

Cognition refers to the processes or faculties by which knowledge is acquired and manipulated; these are mental processes and therefore cannot be directly observed (Bjorklund, 2005). Although one cannot directly observe the processes, the developmental aspect can be observed. Cognitive development focuses on changes in mental skills that occur through increasing maturity and experience (Sternberg & Williams, 2002). In understanding this development in gifted students, research studies frequently use several important terms that are defined below.

  *   *Information processing* is a term that provides an understanding of cognitive development through specification of how knowledge, mental representations, mental processes, and strategies develop with age.

Individual differences are understood in terms of differences in the effectiveness of these elements (Sternberg, 2002).

- *Problem solving* refers to the process of moving from a situation in need of resolution to a solution, overcoming any obstacles along the way (Reed, 2000).
- *Metacomponents of problem solving* (Sternberg, 1981) are higher order control processes used for executive planning and decision making in problem solving, both in academic situations and in everyday life. The first process includes choosing problems need to be solved. Decisions depend on the recognition of the nature of the problem that needs to be solved. The second process is selection of the components to solve the problem. In this process, the student must select what information is necessary for solving the problem. Strategy selection comes next and is the step in which the student must select what steps are necessary to solve the problem and place them in the proper sequence to know how to apply the relevant principles for solution of the problem. Priority selection is the step in the process in which the student must set priorities to take in solving a problem (Rogers, 1986). Next, selection of representations of information refers to the process of learning ways within a given discipline to represent information and then building on the representations in effective problem solving (i.e., emulate the experts). The sixth process involves making decisions about what resources to allocate to the problem-solving task. This step refers to making the decisions that are the most productive and being cognizant of what requires the most energy and time allocation for efficient solutions. Finally, evaluation of the solution systematically is the step that is necessary to assess the effectiveness of a solution.
- *Insight problems* are problems that require a major intuitive leap for their solutions (Sternberg, 1999). These are problems that require the problem solver to think in novel ways not obvious from the way the problem is presented.
- *Metacognition* is the student's knowledge and awareness of his or her own cognitive processes and the ability to monitor and evaluate his or her own thinking (Shore & Dover, 1987).
- *Speed of processing* is the actual time it takes for students to process information.
- *Knowledge base* refers to the breadth and depth of knowledge that learners possess (Hettinger & Carr, 2003).
- *Similar stage hypothesis* refers to the fact that all learners traverse the same stages (Piagetian) of cognitive development in the same order, but the gifted progress at a significantly accelerated rate within each stage (Rogers, 1986).
- *Task variability hypothesis* posits that gifted learners excel in the performance of certain tasks within each of Piaget's stages of development (Rogers, 1986).

A knowledge of these terms helps the reader understand the ways that students develop cognitively and helps to establish the language that refers to these important processes.

MAJOR QUESTIONS ASKED

The major questions raised by researchers interested in cognitive development of gifted children and adolescents include the following:

1. Do the gifted differ in the ages or stages of cognitive development (Rogers, 1986; Webb, 1974)?
2. Do the gifted differ in the cognitive strategies they select and use in problem-solving tasks, and do these strategies indicate advanced cognitive development (Hettinger & Carr, 2003; Kanevsky, 1992; Rogers, 1986; Shore, 1986; Shore, Koller, & Dover, 1994; Shore, Rejskind, & Kanevsky, 2003)?
3. Is studying the relationship of IQ to problem solving important to understanding cognitive development (Shore & Lazar, 1996)?
4. What is the relationship between metacognition and problem-solving tasks (Dover & Shore, 1991; Kanevsky, 1990; Swanson, 1992; Tarshis & Shore, 1991)?
5. What is the relationship between cognitive development and context in gifted students (Barab & Plucker, 2002)?
6. How do gifted students think that is indicative of advanced cognitive development (Dixon, 2005; Dixon et al., 2004)?

The research investigations based on these questions take a variety of different formats, but they all seek to find out if gifted students are truly different in their cognitive development from average children and adolescents.

WHAT CONCLUSIONS CAN BE DRAWN FROM THE RESEARCH?

Gifted education teachers and researchers can draw several reasonable conclusions from the research on cognitive development.

1. Speed of processing does correlate with both IQ and achievement (Kranzler, Whang, & Jensen, 1994; Roberts, Beh, & Stankov, 1988; Spiegel & Bryant, 1978).
2. In terms of time spent on certain aspects of problem-solving tasks, Davidson and Sternberg (1984) found that a gifted group of 9- to 11-year-old students took longer to solve insight problems than did an average group. Shore and Lazar (1996) found that while a gifted

group of 12- and 13-year-old students took significantly less time in the execution phase of problem solving, they spent more time on the problem exploration and planning stages of the tasks. Both of these important studies indicate that attention to detail and accuracy impact time spent in solving the problems.

3. Empirical studies on the use of metacognitive strategies in the gifted population have yielded mixed results. Metacognitive differences favoring the gifted were found in preschool-age children, elementary school children, and adolescents (see Shore, 2000, for a review). Hettinger and Carr (2003) stated that perhaps the varied results in empirical studies based on metacognitive strategies and gifted students point to the fact that most studies of gifted children use IQ or achievement scores as the sole measure of giftedness, making it unclear whether metacognition is related to intelligence or IQ test performance.

4. In terms of strategy use in general in problem-solving tasks, studies by Davidson and Sternberg (1984), Scruggs and Mastropieri (1985), and Montague (1991) all indicated that gifted students used a wider variety of strategies in solving problems than did their nongifted comparison groups.

5. Relative to Piaget's theory, researchers continue to explore the ways this theory applies to gifted students' advanced cognitive processes (Cohen & Kim, 1998; Webb, 1974).

6. Expert thinking in any domain requires an appreciation of dialectical thinking, described as one stage beyond formal operations (Dixon, 2005; Riegel, 1973; Sternberg & Williams, 2002).

LIMITATIONS OF THE RESEARCH

Although research from both gifted and cognitive development supports the inclusion of speed of processing as a variable in cognitive development and more expert performance, processing speed is difficult to isolate and its effects are confounded by other factors (Hettinger & Carr, 2003). Although theories of giftedness include processing speed as a catalytic factor (e.g., Sternberg's triarchic theory), knowledge base is also very important. The knowledge base issue is not really fully explored in the literature on cognitive development and is a definite gap. For instance, it is still not understood why some children and adolescents acquire knowledge more readily.

Hettinger and Carr (2003) noted that gifted children differ from their average age-mates in the amount and the quality of their knowledge. However, researchers working with gifted populations have not examined the development of knowledge base in gifted populations using the methods developed by researchers examining expertise. In fact, as mentioned at the beginning of this chapter, the bulk of research on the development of giftedness is based on studies comparing same-age groups of gifted to average children (Shore et al.,

2003). It may be more productive and less of a limitation in the conclusions of the research to follow the development of gifted individuals in longitudinal studies to more fully understand what they do differently as they develop. In fact, longitudinal studies are a necessity in clarifying what qualitatively happens over time to the cognitive development of gifted individuals.

Because cognitive development rests on change over time, it seems that Mönks and Mason (1993) are absolutely correct when they state the importance of longitudinal research as the way to uncover these changes. Only with a focus on the progression of abilities with time will we be able to directly observe what the gifted do differently from their nongifted counterparts.

PRACTICAL IMPLICATIONS OF RESEARCH ON COGNITIVE DEVELOPMENT AND GIFTED STUDENTS

We want to know what makes these students different from other students. We want to know how giftedness can be explained relative to the major theories of cognitive development (Piaget, Vygotsky, and the Neo-Piagetian view). We want to know if the IQ definitions make more sense than other definitions and help us truly isolate a group of students who need different services in the schools. And, we want to know how to understand the cognitive processes of gifted children as they are developing so that we can advocate for services in schools and understandings in the context in which these students find themselves. All of these issues point to the practical importance of why this field of gifted education needs to have a better grasp of the developmental processes of gifted children.

Further, the Columbus Group (1991) described giftedness as asynchronous development in which advanced cognitive abilities and heightened intensity combine to create inner experiences and awareness that are qualitatively different from the norm. Asynchrony increases with higher intellectual capacity. It further explained that the uniqueness of the gifted renders them particularly vulnerable and requires modifications in parenting, teaching, and counseling in order for them to develop optimally. If asynchrony has a part in understanding gifted students at all, it must be to help us understand what we need to know to serve the child better.

We must look to the field of cognitive development for patterns in research that might better help us to conduct our research more effectively. Mönks and Mason (1993) stated that human development is generally regarded as a process of interaction between individual characteristics and environmental opportunities. What results from the interaction of specific individual traits and experiences in a given social and environmental context directly impacts how the child develops. These are at the core of what we do in the field of gifted education to understand, educate, nurture, and advocate for special programming for an essential subset of the population. Much more longitudinal research should be conducted to help us understand this very important developmental process.

MAJOR RESOURCES AND REFERENCES ON COGNITIVE DEVELOPMENT AND GIFTED STUDENTS

The literature on this topic focused on several resources. It is essential to look to the general topic of cognitive development in order to understand the general issues. Bjorklund (2005) is an excellent reference on cognition and cognitive development. In addition, Sternberg's many works serve to highlight the aspects of cognition and help us to focus on the development of the gifted individual. Hettinger and Carr (2003) provided an excellent lens from which to view both strands of research: cognitive development in gifted literature and cognitive development in the developmental literature. The review of studies provided in this article was a wonderful point of departure for this chapter. The vast amount of literature on cognitive processes, problem solving, and metacognition conducted by Shore and his colleagues and Kanevsky (e.g., Kanevsky, 1990; Shore & Dover, 1987; Shore et al., 2003) were very helpful in examining the research base for cognitive development.

In conclusion, this field has much to do in order to advance the knowledge base in cognitive development. We must do more longitudinal research—maybe not as extensive as Terman's studies, but certainly along those lines—so that we can follow the progression of those who exhibit giftedness early on in their lives. We need to gather more empirical data to support what we intuitively expound about the cognitive differences in gifted children. We must look to the developmental theories that apply to all children and continually test them for relevance to and explanation of the cognitive development of gifted students so that we can subsequently tailor their education for maximum cognitive growth. Most of all, we must continually seek to know if the developmental path of the gifted child is quantitatively different (i.e., the same path with faster progress from the age peer) or qualitatively different (i.e., a totally different path from that of the age peer). It seems that each of these positions makes sense, but each has different and important educational ramifications for the student.

REFERENCES

Barab, S. A., & Plucker, J. A. (2002). Smart people or smart contexts? Cognition, ability, and talent development in an age of situated approaches to knowing and learning. *Educational Psychologist, 37,* 165–182.

Bjorklund, D. F. (2005). *Children's thinking.* Belmont, CA: Wadsworth/Thomson.

Case, R. (1992). General and specific views of the mind, its structure, and its development. In R. Case (Ed.), *The mind's staircase: Exploring the conceptual underpinnings of children's thought and knowledge* (pp. 3–15). New Jersey: Lawrence Erlbaum.

Clark, B. (1997). *Growing up gifted* (5th ed.). Columbus, OH: Charles E. Merrill.

Cohen, L. M., & Kim, Y. M. (1998). Piaget's equilibration theory and the young gifted child: A balancing act. *Roeper Review, 21,* 201–206.

Columbus Group. (1991, July). Unpublished transcript of the meeting of the Columbus Group, Columbus, Ohio.

Davidson, J. E., & Sternberg, R. J. (1984). The role of insight in intellectual giftedness. *Gifted Child Quarterly, 28,* 257–273.

Dixon, F. A. (2005). Critical thinking: A foundation for challenging content. In F. Dixon & S. Moon (Eds.), *The handbook of secondary gifted education* (pp. 323–341). Waco, TX: Prufrock Press.

Dixon, F. A., Prater, K. A., Vine, H. M., Wark, M. J., Williams, T., & Hanchon, T. (2004). Teaching to their thinking: A strategy to meet the critical thinking needs of gifted students. *Journal for the Education of the Gifted, 28,* 56–76.

Dover, A. C., & Shore, B. M. (1991). Giftedness and flexibility on a mathematical set-breaking task. *Gifted Child Quarterly, 35,* 99–105.

Hettinger, H., & Carr, M. (2003). Cognitive development in gifted children: Toward a more precise understanding of emerging differences in intelligence. *Educational Psychology Review, 15,* 215–245.

Kanevsky, L. S. (1990). Pursuing qualitative differences in the flexible use of problem-solving strategy by young children. *Journal for the Education of the Gifted, 13,* 115–140.

Kanevsky, L. S. (1992). The learning game. In P. S. Klein & A. J. Tannenbaum (Eds.), *To be young and gifted* (pp. 204–241). Norwood, NJ: Ablex.

Kranzler, J. H., Whang, P. A., & Jensen, A. R. (1994). Task complexity and the speed of efficiency of elemental information processing: Another look at the nature of intellectual giftedness. *Contemporary Educational Psychology, 19,* 447–459.

Mönks, F. J., & Mason, E. J. (1993). Developmental theories and giftedness. In K. Heller, F. J. Mönks, & A. Passow (Eds.), *International handbook of research and development of giftedness and talent* (pp. 89–101). Oxford, England: Pergamon.

Montague, M. (1991). Gifted and learning-disabled gifted students' knowledge and use of mathematical problem-solving. *Journal for the Education of the Gifted, 14,* 393–411.

Pascual-Leone, J. (1990). An essay on wisdom: Toward organismic processes that make it possible. In R. J. Sternberg (Ed.), *Wisdom: Its nature, origin, and development* (pp. 52–83). New York: Cambridge University Press.

Reed, S. K. (2000). Problem solving. In A. E. Kazdin (Ed.), *Encyclopedia of psychology* (pp. 75–77). New York: Oxford University Press.

Riegel, K. (1973). Dialectical operations: The final period of cognitive development. *Human Development, 16,* 346–370.

Roberts, R. D., Beh, H. C., & Stankov, L. (1988). Hick's law, competing task-performance and intelligence. *Intelligence, 12,* 111–130.

Rogers, K. B. (1986). Do the gifted think and learn differently? A review of recent research and its implications for instruction. *Journal of the Education of the Gifted, 10,* 17–39.

Scruggs, T. E., & Mastropieri, M. A. (1985). Spontaneous and verbal elaboration in gifted and nongifted youths. *Journal for the Education of the Gifted, 9,* 1–10.

Shore, B. M. (1986). Cognition and giftedness: New research directions. *Gifted Child Quarterly, 30,* 24–32.

Shore, B. M. (2000). Metacognition and flexibility: Qualitative differences in how gifted children think. In R. C. Friedman & B. M. Shore (Eds.), *Talents unfolding: Cognition and development* (pp. 167–187). Washington, DC: American Psychological Association.

Shore, B. M., & Dover, A. C. (1987). Metacognition, cognition, and giftedness. *Gifted Child Quarterly, 31,* 37–39.

Shore, B. M., Koller, M., & Dover, A. C. (1994). More from the water jars: A reanalysis of problem solving performance among gifted and nongifted children. *Gifted Child Quarterly, 38,* 179–183.

Shore, B. M., & Lazar, L. (1996). IQ related differences in time allocation during problem solving. *Psychological Reports, 78,* 848–850.

Shore, B. M., Rejskind, F. G., & Kanevsky, L. S. (2003). Cognitive research on giftedness: A window on creativity. In D. Ambrose, L. Cohen, & A. J. Tannenbaum (Eds.), *Creative intelligence: Toward theoretic integration* (pp. 181–210). New York: Hampton Press.

Spiegel, M. R., & Bryant, N. D. (1978). Is speed of processing information related to intelligence and achievement? *Journal of Educational Psychology, 70,* 904–910.

Sternberg, R. J. (1981). A componential theory of intelligence. *Gifted Child Quarterly, 25,* 86–93.

Sternberg, R. J. (1988). A three facet model of creativity. In R. J. Sternberg (Ed.), *The nature of creativity* (pp. 125–147). New York: Cambridge University Press.

Sternberg, R. J. (1999). Intelligence as developing expertise. *Contemporary Educational Psychology, 24,* 359–375.

Sternberg, R. J. (2002). Individual differences in cognitive development. In U. Goswami (Ed.), *Blackwell handbook of childhood cognitive development* (pp. 600–619). New York: Oxford University Press.

Sternberg, R. J., & Williams, W. M. (2002). *Educational psychology.* Boston: Allyn & Bacon.

Swanson, H. L. (1992). The relationship between metacognition and problem solving in gifted children. *Roeper Review, 15,* 43–48.

Tarshis, E., & Shore, B. M. (1991). Differences in perspective taking between high and above average IQ preschool children. *European Journal of High Ability, 2,* 201–211.

Webb, R. A. (1974). Concrete and formal operations in very bright 6–11 year olds. *Human Development, 17,* 292–300.

Winner, E. (2000). The origins and ends of giftedness. *American Psychologist, 55,* 159–169.

Chapter 7

COLLEGE PROGRAMMING

Anne N. Rinn

ollege programs for gifted students can be separated into two categories: honors programs and early entrance programs (Rinn & Plucker, 2004). Both types of programs largely provide gifted students with academic and social opportunities that may be unavailable in a regular setting.

DEFINITIONS

Gifted College Students

Defining or identifying giftedness in college students is as complex as defining giftedness in children or adolescents. Although younger gifted students often are identified by achievement test scores, intelligence quotient (IQ) scores, and/ or teacher recommendations, among other criteria (Davis & Rimm, 2004), the criteria available for identifying gifted college students is likely limited to high school performance, scores on the SAT and/or ACT tests, and college grade point average. Using students' SAT/ACT scores as indicators of intellectual giftedness is recognized by the National Collegiate Honors Council as a standard way to identify gifted college students, largely for lack of a better option (Digby, 2002).

Selectivity

The term *selectivity* is often used to describe the average academic ability of a college or university's entering freshman class (Astin & Henson, 1971). Typically, the notion of selectivity refers to the selectivity of an entire institution of higher education, and research on selectivity usually pertains to the institutional environment as a whole. However, programs or colleges within an institution of higher education also can be selective. And, while an overall campus environment may exhibit certain characteristics, a particular subenvironment may exert an influence in another direction (Strange & Banning, 2001). For example, programs for gifted college students can be described as selective programs, or at least more selective than their host university, because of the higher academic ability of the members of the program as compared to those members of the host university at large.

Honors Programs

An honors program can be defined as a planned set of arrangements, including curriculum differentiation and close faculty-student relationships, to meet the needs of a college or university's most able students (Austin, 1986). Most institutions of higher education have honors programs, but others provide actual colleges that grant their own diplomas, and so are referred to as honors colleges (Digby, 2003). Most researchers use the terms *honors program* and *honors college* interchangeably, as the programmatic/administrative benefits of participating in such programs are generally the same (e.g., special housing, honors advising, early registration). The "philosophic underpinning" of honors programs "is the belief that academically talented students have scholarly and developmental needs and interests that are best served by course work, living arrangements, and activities that differ from the usual college offerings" (Gerrity, Lawrence, & Sedlacek, 1993, p. 43). Requirements for admission to an honors program are generally based on some combination of the following: minimum SAT/ACT scores, a minimum high school grade point average or class rank, one or more essays, and letters of recommendation (Digby, 2002; Sullivan & Randolph, 1994).

Early Entrance Programs

An early entrance program can be defined as a program that allows gifted adolescents the opportunity to enter college early while omitting all or part of their high school years. Some early entrance programs, for example, allow for the completion of the junior and senior years of high school, as well as the freshman and sophomore years of college, in only 2 years (Stephens, 1998). Like honors programs, early entrance programs are generally housed within a college or university. Some programs are, however, separate from an institution of higher education (Olszewski-Kubilius, 1995). Programs vary with regard to age of admission and in amount of academic, social, and emotional support provided to the students. As with honors programs, special arrangements may include a designated residence hall, student lounges, and special advisors, among other arrangements (Boothe, Sethna, Stanley, & Colgate, 1999). Requirements for admission to an early entrance program are similar to the requirements for admission to an honors program (Boothe et al., 1999). In addition, interviews often are conducted to assess readiness for college, maturity, independence, and other characteristics considered necessary for success (Olszewski-Kubilius, 1995).

Major Research Questions and Findings

Research on college programming for gifted students includes the study of characteristics of students who participate in specific programs and the effects of specific programs on various academic, social, and emotional outcomes. However, very little research has focused on the gifted student in college (Rinn & Plucker, 2004), and thus insufficient data exists from which we can draw conclusions regarding the characteristics of gifted students who participate in special programs at the college level. Research on the effects of honors programs and early entrance programs on gifted students largely focuses on academic outcomes and social/emotional outcomes, but many of these findings are inconclusive, as well. Thus, the following review of the literature provides research on both characteristics of gifted college students and effects of special programs.

Honors Programs and Academic Constructs

Academic Achievement. Pflaum, Pascarella, and Duby (1985), in a study of freshmen honors students, found honors program participation is associated with high academic achievement during the first year of college. Shushok (2003) found gifted honors students have higher academic achievement than gifted nonhonors students. Rinn (2007) found the same results, even after controlling for precollege ability levels. In addition, honors students who participate in a gifted program as a child or adolescent usually have even higher grade point averages in college than those honors students who did not participate in a gifted program (Longo, 1996).

These current research findings are in contrast to prior findings, which indicate students who participate in a selective program will likely receive lower grades than they would in a less selective program as a result of some combination of a more challenging and rigorous curriculum and/or increased competition with high-ability peers (Davis, 1966; Werts & Watley, 1969). Alexander and Eckland (1977), for example, found college selectivity had a negative effect on undergraduate grade performance. The research findings regarding the academic achievement of honors college students are thus inconclusive, although the three- or four-decade gap in these findings should lead researchers to focus on more recent findings.

Aspirations. Participation in an honors program is linked with greater retention in higher education, as well as increased aspirations for a graduate or professional degree (Malaney & Isaac, 1988; Shushok, 2003). Indeed, research indicates that gifted college students are most likely to participate in an honors program in order to prepare for graduate school (Gerrity et al., 1993). In a recent study, Rinn (2005) found that the majority of honors students aspired to earn a doctorate degree. Living in an honors residence hall likely enhances these effects (Rinn, 2004). In addition, upon graduation, honors students indicate higher satisfaction with their jobs than nonhonors students (Sturgess & Fleming, 1994), and are more likely to complete graduate or professional school than nonhonors students (Jahnke, 1976).

Using 1,772 students enrolled at 140 different colleges and universities, Thistlethwaite and Wheeler (1966) studied the effects of the college environment on students' aspirations to seek graduate-level degrees. In controlling for sex, degree aspirations at the beginning of college, and National Merit Qualifying Test scores, among other variables, the authors found the selectivity of an institution or program has a direct positive effect on aspirations, "since an undergraduate will perform best and aim highest at a school where most of his fellow students have high aspirations and are superior academically" (Drew & Astin, 1972, p. 1152). Thus, students participating in a selective program would perhaps develop the desire to attend graduate school, or be reinforced for already desiring to attend graduate school, if most of the other students in the selective program were also interested in doing so. Again, however, this research might be outdated and researchers might want to focus on more recent findings.

Honors Programs and Social/Emotional Constructs

Very little research has examined honors programs in relation to social and/or emotional constructs. Prior research has indicated that honors students have considerable confidence in their academic abilities (Mathiasen, 1985). More recently, Rinn (2007) found honors students had significantly higher academic self-concepts than nonhonors students of equal ability, even after controlling for SAT score.

Early Entrance Programs and Academic Constructs

Academic Achievement. In general, early entrants are successful with regard to academic achievement (Brody & Stanley, 1991; Gross & van Vliet, 2005; Janos, Robinson, & Lunneborg, 1989). In a study of 24 early entrants, for example, 18 students earned a freshman year grade point average greater than 3.5 (on a 4.0 scale; Brody, Lupkowski, & Stanley, 1988). In addition, relative to regular college students, early entrants are more likely to earn general and/or departmental honors (Stanley, 1985).

Aspirations. Compared to average-ability college students, early entrants are more likely to aspire to attend graduate or professional school (Noble, Robinson, & Gunderson, 1993), as well as actually attend graduate or professional school (Gross & van Vliet, 2005).

Early Entrance Programs and Social/Emotional Constructs

"Historically, acceleration has been a controversial topic, largely as a result of concern about social and emotional development" (Brody et al., 1988, p. 348). However, detrimental effects of early entrance programs have not been documented. A cross-sectional study of students in the University of Washington's Early Entrance Program reveals first- and second-year early entrants may be more likely to interact with one another than with traditional-aged college students, but by their third year, early entrants interact much more frequently with traditional-aged college students (Janos et al., 1988). These findings support prior research indicating the social development of early entrants is not very different from that of their nonaccelerated peers, in that both groups must learn to navigate social relations by "taking risks and experiencing setbacks," and "problems in social adaptation . . . tend to be relatively minor and overcome within a few years" (Janos et al., 1988, p. 211). Early entrants may even experience a slight decrease in self-esteem during their first year in an early entrance program, but this decrease is similar to that found in most college freshmen (Lupkowski, Whitmore, & Ramsay, 1992). However, in the vast research of early entrants from the Study of Mathematically Precocious Youth (SMPY), researchers report early entrants generally experience high self-esteem and generally do not experience social or emotional difficulties (Richardson & Benbow, 1990). Major reviews of the literature pertaining to early entrants report the same findings: Early entrants generally experience positive social and emotional development (Colangelo, Assouline, & Gross, 2004; Gross & van Vliet, 2005; Noble et al., 1993; Olszewski-Kubilius, 1995, 2002).

LIMITATIONS OF THE RESEARCH

A lack of comparison between programs, ignoring selective mortality, and a lack of control for precollege characteristics are major limitations of the research on honors and early entrance programs.

Lack of Comparison Between Programs

Most literature on honors programs is descriptive or evaluative in nature, and usually only includes students in a single program (Rinn & Plucker, 2004). Similarly, most studies of early entrance programs examine achievement during a particular course or describe the overall attainment of a cohort of early entrants within a particular program (Brody et al., 1988). Although these studies are certainly useful, they do not provide a comprehensive analysis of varying types of programs. A comprehensive overview, such as a meta-analysis or a multiprogram comparison study, would allow researchers and educators to develop a clearer understanding of the experiences of gifted students participating in these programs. This deeper understanding would certainly aid in program development.

Ignoring Selective Mortality

Students with negative experiences (poor grades, poor social experiences) may leave an honors program or an early entrance program early; students remaining in a program may be those who have high grade point averages, high self-concepts, or high motivation. Reynolds (1988) argues an increase in academic self-concept seen from the first to the last year in college, for example, is due to both general maturation and selective mortality, which occurs when students with poor grades and poor adjustment drop out of college. House (1993) found students' academic self-concepts to be a strong predictor of subsequent school withdrawal, indicating those with low academic self-concepts may indeed drop out of school. Yet, many research studies of honors programs do not include data from students who have dropped out. The attrition rates within honors programs are largely unknown, except at an anecdotal level. Research findings may be due to selective mortality rather than to the effects of the program. Including data on attrition rates would serve to clarify the potential effects of selective mortality.

Lack of Control for Precollege Characteristics

Research regarding the effectiveness of college-level programs often fails to control for precollege characteristics of students. Astin (1970) emphasizes the importance of preenrollment student characteristics in studying college impact, arguing preenrollment characteristics will influence which experiences students choose while in college, as well as scores on outcome measures.

Practical Implications

Research regarding honors programs and early entrance programs and the academic and social/emotional development of gifted students has many practical implications. First and foremost, understanding the effectiveness, or the lack thereof, of college programs can help assist educators, school counselors, and parents, among others, in deciding whether or not to encourage gifted students to participate in such programs. Although little research has experimentally documented the effectiveness of these college programs, we do know that students enrolled in honors programs and early entrance programs are likely to experience positive academic, social, and emotional characteristics. Thus, gifted students perhaps ought to be encouraged to join such programs, if possible.

Understanding the effects of honors programs and early entrance programs on factors such as academic achievement, aspirations, and self-concept also may help administrators in issues related to student retention. Although attrition from a selective program is largely unexpected (Hermanowicz, 2004), it nonetheless occurs. Honors students, for example, make important contributions to their institutions, at least anecdotally, by offering "positive peer effects for their classmates" and by influencing "the school's appeal to faculty members" (Long, 2002, p. 4). Institutions should, naturally, focus on attracting and retaining gifted college students. An understanding of the factors affecting the retention of gifted students may aid in this task.

What We Know

What Research Tells Us
- Gifted college students likely have higher grade point averages than average-ability college students (Brody et al., 1988; Pflaum et al., 1985; Rinn, 2005; Shushok, 2003; Stanley, 1985).
- Gifted college students likely have higher aspirations than average-ability college students (Malaney & Isaac, 1988; Noble et al., 1993; Rinn, 2007; Shushok, 2003; Thistlethwaite & Wheeler, 1966).

- Gifted college students likely experience positive social and emotional development (Gross & van Vliet, 2005; Mathiasen, 1985; Olszewski-Kubilius, 1995; Rinn, 2007).

What Needs to be Studied in the Future
- Studies that experimentally validate the effectiveness of honors programs and early entrance programs are greatly needed.
- Current research needs to be conducted using traditionally aged, gifted college students, as very little research exists in this area.
- Across-program comparisons need to be made among both honors programs and early entrance programs.
- Longitudinal and/or cross-sectional research needs to be conducted in order for researchers and educators to gain a deeper understanding of the academic, social, and emotional development of gifted college students enrolled in honors programs and/or early entrance programs.

REFERENCES

Alexander, K. L., & Eckland, B. L. (1977). High school context and college selectivity: Institutional constraints in educational stratification. *Social Forces, 56*, 166–188.

Astin, A. W. (1970). The methodology of research on college impact. *Sociology of Education, 43*, 223–254, 437–450.

Astin, A. W., & Henson, J. W. (1971). New measures of college selectivity. *Research in Higher Education, 6*, 1–9.

Austin, C. G. (1986). Orientation to honors education. In P. G. Friedman & R. C. Jenkins-Friedman (Eds.), *Fostering academic excellence through honors programs* (pp. 5–16). San Francisco, CA: Jossey-Bass.

Boothe, S., Sethna, B. N., Stanley, J. C., & Colgate, S. O. (1999). Special opportunities for exceptionally able high school students: A description of eight residential early-college-entrance programs. *Journal of Secondary Gifted Education, 10*, 195–202.

Brody, L. E., Lupkowski, A. E., & Stanley, J. C. (1988). Early entrance to college: A study of academic and social adjustment during the freshman year. *College and University, 63*, 347–359.

Brody, L. E., & Stanley, J. C. (1991). Young college students: Assessing factors that contribute to success. In W. T. Southern & E. D. Jones (Eds.), *The academic acceleration of gifted children* (pp. 102–132). New York: Teachers College Press.

Colangelo, N., Assouline, S. G., & Gross, M. U. M. (2004). *A nation deceived: How schools hold back America's brightest students* (Vol. 1). Iowa City, IA: The Connie Belin & Jacqueline N. Blank International Center for Gifted Education and Talent Development.

Davis, J. A. (1966). The campus as a frog pond: An application of the theory of relative deprivation to career decisions of college men. *American Journal of Sociology, 72*(1), 17–31.

Davis, G. A., & Rimm, S. B. (2004). *Education of the gifted and talented* (5th ed.). Boston: Pearson.

Digby, J. (2002). *Honors programs and colleges: The official guide of the National Collegiate Honors Council* (3nd ed.). Princeton, NJ: Peterson's.

Digby, J. (2003, September). Gifted education: The road to honors programs at the college level. *Parenting for High Potential,* 10–14.

Drew, D. E., & Astin, A. W. (1972). Undergraduate aspirations: A test of several theories. *American Journal of Sociology, 77,* 1151–1164.

Gerrity, D. A., Lawrence, J. F., & Sedlacek, W. E. (1993). Honors and nonhonors freshman: Demographics, attitudes, interests, and behaviors. *NACADA Journal, 13*(1), 43–52.

Gross, M. U. M., & van Vliet, H. E. (2005). Radical acceleration and early entry to college: A review of the research. *Gifted Child Quarterly, 49,* 154–171.

Hermanowicz, J. C. (2004). The college departure process among the academically elite. *Education and Urban Society, 37*(1), 74–94.

House, J. D. (1993). The relationship between academic self-concept and school withdrawal. *Journal of Social Psychology, 133,* 125–127.

Jahnke, C. L. (1976). A comparative study of honors program and non-honors program graduates. *Forum for Honors, 7*(1), 28–44.

Janos, P. M., Robinson, N. M., Carter, C., Chapel, A., Cufley, R., Curland, M., et al. (1988). A cross-sectional developmental study of the social relations of students who enter college early. *Gifted Child Quarterly, 32,* 210–215.

Janos, P. M., Robinson, N. M., & Lunneborg, C. E. (1989). Markedly early entrance to college: A multi-year comparative study of academic performance and psychological adjustment. *Journal of Higher Education, 60,* 495–518.

Long, B. T. (2002). *Attracting the best: The use of honors programs to compete for students.* Chicago: Spencer Foundation. (ERIC Document Reproduction Service No. ED465355)

Longo, F. C. (1996). Gifted education: Its effect on college functioning (Doctoral dissertation, University of Southern Mississippi, 1996). *Dissertation Abstracts International, 56*(11-A), 4327.

Lupkowski, A. E., Whitmore, M., & Ramsay, A. (1992). The impact of early entrance to college on self-esteem: A preliminary study. *Gifted Child Quarterly, 36,* 87–90.

Malaney, G. D., & Isaac, P. D. (1988). The immediate post-baccalaureate educational plans of outstanding undergraduates. *College and University, 63,* 148–161.

Mathiasen, R. E. (1985). Characteristics of the college honors student. *Journal of College Student Personnel, 26,* 171–173.

Noble, K. D., Robinson, N. M., & Gunderson, S. A. (1993). All rivers lead to the sea: A follow-up study of gifted young adults. *Roeper Review, 15*(3), 124–130.

Olszewski-Kubilius, P. (1995). A summary of research regarding early entrance to college. *Roeper Review, 18,* 121–126.

Olszewski-Kubilius, P. (2002). A summary of research regarding early entrance to college. *Roeper Review, 24,* 152–157.

Pflaum, S. W., Pascarella, E. T., & Duby, P. (1985). The effects of honors college participation on academic performance during the freshman year. *Journal of College Student Personnel, 26,* 414–419.

Reynolds, W. M. (1988). Measurement of academic self-concept in college students. *Journal of Personality Assessment, 52,* 223–240.

Richardson, T. M., & Benbow, C. P. (1990). Long-term effects of acceleration on the social-emotional adjustment of mathematically precocious youths. *Journal of Educational Psychology, 82,* 464–470.

Rinn, A. N. (2004). Academic and social effects of living in honors residence halls. *Journal of the National Collegiate Honors Council, 5*(2), 67–79.

Rinn, A. N. (2005). Trends among honors college students: An analysis by year in school. *Journal of Secondary Gifted Education, 16,* 157–167.

Rinn, A. N. (2007). Effects of programmatic selectivity on the academic achievement, academic self-concepts, and aspirations of gifted college students. *Gifted Child Quarterly, 51,* 232–245.

Rinn, A. N., & Plucker, J. A. (2004). We recruit them, but then what? The educational and psychological experiences of academically talented undergraduates. *Gifted Child Quarterly, 48,* 54–67.

Shushok, F. X., Jr. (2003). Educating the best and the brightest: Collegiate honors programs and the intellectual, social and psychological development of students. *Dissertation Abstracts International, 63*(11-A), 3880. (UMI No. 3070562)

Stanley, J. C. (1985). Young entrants to college: How did they fare? *College and University, 60,* 219–228.

Stephens, K. R. (1998). Residential math and science high schools: A closer look. *Journal of Secondary Gifted Education, 10,* 85–92.

Strange, C. C., & Banning, J. H. (2001). *Educating by design: Creating campus learning environments that work.* San Francisco: Jossey-Bass.

Sturgess, J., & Fleming, J. (1994). A survey about completing an honours degree and future occupational therapy career paths. *Australian Occupational Therapy Journal, 41,* 65–72.

Sullivan, R. R., & Randolph, K. R. (1994). *Ivy League programs at state school prices.* New York: Prentice Hall.

Thistlethwaite, D. L., & Wheeler, N. (1966). Effects of teacher and peer subcultures upon student aspirations. *Journal of Educational Psychology, 57,* 35–47.

Werts, C. E., & Watley, D. J. (1969). A student's dilemma: Big fish-little pond or little fish-big pond. *Journal of Counseling Psychology, 16,* 14–19.

Chapter 8

CONCEPTIONS OF GIFTEDNESS

Erin Morris Miller

onceptions of giftedness are central to gifted education. The conception or theory of giftedness that is adopted by a school system should drive all other aspects of gifted programming including identification, curricula, and instruction. Thus, it is essential that there be a clear understanding of conceptions of giftedness. A discussion of all of the different conceptions of giftedness is beyond the scope of this chapter; therefore, only those conceptions for which there is evidence of use in the U.S. school system and/or those conceptions with evidence of empirical validation are described here. In addition to presenting a general overview of the influence of an individual's personal conception of giftedness, this chapter will address the terms used in the literature, particularly as these are associated with the major theorists in the field; the major questions that are addressed in research and the available empirical support for different conceptions; the limitations and the practical implications of the research; and the major references and resources for obtaining further information.

TERMS USED IN THE RESEARCH

- *Theory*: A hypothesis or set of hypotheses used to promote discussion, guide research, and/or provide a basis for explaining behavior.
- *Formal/explicit theory of giftedness*: An explicit theory of giftedness results from a combination of the theorist's personal conceptions and research in the field of giftedness and/or intelligence. An explicit theory is explained or spelled out in the literature of the field.
- *Informal/implicit theory of giftedness*: An implicit theory of giftedness is a personal conception of giftedness that resides in a person's mind. These models are formed through the sum of a person's experiences with gifted education and gifted individuals.
- *Inclusive/broadened theory of giftedness*: A theory that moves beyond a one-dimensional conception of giftedness (i.e., high IQ) to include multiple elements such as different aspects of intelligence, different ways of expressing intelligence, personality traits, and/or social factors.
- *Research-based theory of giftedness*: A theory is said to be research-based when different elements of the theory were suggested and supported by prior research—often from several fields of study such as psychology, sociology, education, and history.
- *Research-validated theory of giftedness*: When research has been conducted after development of the theory specifically to test different aspects of the theory or hypotheses upon which the theory rests, and that research supports the hypotheses suggested by the theory, it is said to be research-validated.
- *General intelligence (g)*: Denotes the idea of a general or common intellectual ability that arose from the observation that there are positive correlations among different measures of achievement and ability.

MAJOR THEORISTS

- *Terman*: Defined giftedness as scoring two standard deviations above the norm on the Stanford-Binet intelligence test.
- *Sternberg*: Defined giftedness in relation to his triarchic theory of intelligence that posits three distinct forms of intelligence: analytic, creative, and practical. He has extended this information processing approach in his discussion of how the mental processes of gifted children resemble the cognitive processes of persons who, through study and work, have become experts in their fields.
- *Gardner*: Defines giftedness as a sign of precocious potential in one or more of independent multiple intelligences including linguistic, log-

ical-mathematical, spatial, musical, bodily-kinesthetic, interpersonal, intrapersonal, and naturalistic intelligence.

- *Renzulli*: Defines giftedness as manifesting itself in two different kinds of persons: the schoolhouse-gifted person, who excels at test-taking and learning school lessons, and the creative-productive gifted person, whose giftedness manifests itself through the development of original products that have an impact on society. Creative-productive giftedness is thought to arise from three interdependent constructs: well-above-average ability, task commitment (energy expended on a particular problem or specific performance area), and creativity (fluency, flexibility, and originality of thought; openness to experience; curiosity; and sensitivity to aesthetics). These factors make up Renzulli's three-ring conception of giftedness.

- *Gagné*: Proposes a distinction between the concept of giftedness and the concept of talent in his Differentiated Model of Giftedness and Talent (DMGT). Giftedness denotes untrained and spontaneously expressed superior natural abilities in at least one ability domain. The natural abilities of giftedness can develop over time through an interaction with intrapersonal and environmental catalysts and chance, leading to systematically developed skills or talent in a field of human endeavor. For both giftedness and talent, performance places the individual in the top 10% of age peers.

- *Feldman*: Proposes that giftedness manifests itself in the process of development and reorganization of a specific domain (i.e., language arts, mathematics, physics) through creative processes. These domains themselves are evolving and transforming at the same time as the individual is changing.

MAJOR QUESTIONS ADDRESSED IN THE RESEARCH

Explicit theories of giftedness lead to different sets of research questions than do implicit theories. Research on explicit theories is directed mainly toward questions to provide empirical validation of the theory. These questions include:

- Are the ability/cognitive/personality structures of gifted students organized in the way the theorist proposes?
- Can the theory predict later performance?
- Can the theory clearly and consistently differentiate between gifted students and students who are not gifted according to the theory?

Research on implicit theories of giftedness deals mainly with description and comparisons in order to look for patterns within and among groups (i.e., teachers vs. nonteachers) and addresses such questions as:

- What is the nature of different groups' implicit theories of giftedness?
- Are there similarities in implicit theories among/between groups?
- Do individuals' implicit theories predict their later decisions and actions?

EMPIRICAL SUPPORT FOR RESEARCH ON CONCEPTIONS OF GIFTEDNESS

Explicit Theories

Although all major theories of giftedness arose out of the base of research, not all theories of giftedness have been investigated through subsequent research specifically testing the theory. Therefore, this section will focus on Renzulli's (1978) three-ring conception of giftedness, and the applications of Gardner's (1983) theory of multiple intelligences and Sternberg's (1986) triarchic theory of intelligence.

Are the ability/cognitive/personality structures of gifted students organized in the way that the theorist proposes? This is a fundamental question regarding the different theories. The ability/cognitive/personality structures are the latent constructs that instruments are designed to measure. The measurement of latent constructs calls for the use of exploratory and confirmatory factor analysis (Loehlin, 1998). Factor analysis has been used by researchers seeking to validate assessments based on multiple intelligences (Callahan, Tomlinson, Moon, Tomchin, & Plucker 1995) and on the triarchic theory of intelligence (Sternberg, Ferrari, Clinkenbeard, & Grigorenko, 1996). Factor analysis is beneficial because it is a sound way to answer questions regarding the structure of theories. One possible limitation comes in the naming of the factors that are extracted as a result of the procedure. Identification of the factors is based on the researchers' knowledge and understanding of the area in question. It is also at the researchers' discretion as to what factor analysis techniques to employ.

As part of a study designed to validate Sternberg's triarchic theory of giftedness as operationalized through the Sternberg Triarchic Abilities Test (STAT), Sternberg et al. (1996) conducted a principal-components analysis followed by varimax rotation on the multiple choice items of the STAT. Results indicated independent factors for each of the intelligences (analytic, creative, and practical) without a general ability factor. The data suggest that these constructs seem to be independent of each other and represent unique processes. Independent verification of these factors has not been conducted.

An example of the issue of choice of technique and interpretation can be seen in the series of articles about factor analyses of assessments designed to measure the dimensions of giftedness proposed by Gardner (Gridley, 2002; Plucker, Callahan, & Tomchin, 1996; Pyryt, 2000). The data set in the original study consisted of results from scores on performance-based assessments and teacher rating scales designed to measure linguistic, logical-mathematical, spatial, and interpersonal intelligence as defined in Gardner's theory of multiple intelligences (Plucker et al., 1996). Plucker et al. used principal factors extraction with orthogonal (Varimax) rotation and extracted four factors, which they interpreted as Linguistic, Logical-Mathematical, Spatial-General, and Spatial-Tangrams. The choice of orthogonal rotation indicates that these researchers saw the factors as being theoretically uncorrelated. However, they also conducted a confirmatory factor analysis. These results suggested that the best fitting model is one that contains a higher order factor such as general intelligence (g).

Pyryt (2000) reanalyzed the correlation matrix reported in the earlier (Plucker et al., 1996) article using maximum likelihood extraction with oblique rotation. The resulting structure matrix was interpreted as indicating four factors. Pyryt interpreted these factors as a general ability factor, a spatial factor, a low-ability factor, and a second general ability factor. A subsequent higher order factor analysis resulted in a single general factor accounting for 55% of the variance. Pyryt used this data to support the existence of g, or general intelligence. The correlation matrix was analyzed yet again by Gridley (2002) using confirmatory factor analysis. The model that best fit the data was one that consisted of logical-mathematical, linguistic/interpersonal, and spatial factors with an overlying g factor. The implication is that the assessment technique measures more than general intelligence, but that general intelligence is a latent construct that is connected to the other factors. These results seem to be similar to the confirmatory factor analysis conducted by Plucker et al. It should be noted that factor analysis is based on finding what is common among data (Loehlin, 1998). Finding general factors, particularly if one conducts a higher order factor analysis, is an expected result.

In sum, the same data can yield different results depending on the choices made about how to conduct and interpret the factor analysis. Further, the interpretation of the results depends on the goals and purposes of the researcher. It also is possible to interpret the results as indicating that the assessments did not document the constructs of multiple intelligences well.

Can the theory predict later performance? This question is important when evaluating theories of giftedness because this is what school districts are looking for in a gifted theory as applied to identification. Schools want to know which kinds of tests will accurately predict achievement and success in gifted programs. The most direct way to answer questions related to prediction is through regression analysis. Yet, few researchers have used regression to see how well the operationalization of their theory predicts success. One exception is Sternberg's study (Sternberg et al., 1996) of the construct validity of an identification model based on his theory of triarchic intelligences. Scores on the Sternberg Triarchic Abilities Test accounted for 40–44% of the variance in achievement in a college-level psychology course, which is considered a large effect in social science research (Cohen, 1988).

Can the theory clearly and consistently differentiate between gifted students and students who are not gifted according to the theory? This question is likely to be most important to those who are charged with defending the choices made as to who will participate in a gifted program in a school system and who will not. Defending this choice is difficult for programs with very stringent requirements, but it also is essential that programs based on more broadened conceptions of giftedness also are able to defend the inclusion of a wider range of students. Researchers studying applications of Renzulli's (1978) three-ring conception of giftedness have attempted to do just that by comparing the products created by students from the top 5% ability level and those scoring above average (10–25% range) but below a 5% cutoff. The focus on student products is based on the fact that the three-ring theory of giftedness describes one type of giftedness as creative productivity (Renzulli, 1978). Reis and Renzulli (1982) found that ratings of the products of students scoring in the top 5% on standardized tests of intelligence were not significantly different from ratings of the products of students who scored above average (15–20%) but not in the top 5%.

Another method for analyzing differences between groups of students is discriminant function analysis. This statistical method was used by Delisle and Renzulli (1982) to explore which characteristics discriminated between students ranked in the top 25% of a class who completed projects in the gifted classroom and those who did not complete their projects. They found that academic self-concept, not academic ability, was the factor that distinguished between these two groups. These studies support the notion that above-average and not just exceptional students should be given the opportunity to participate in the kinds of enrichment activities described in the model of services suggested by Renzulli.

Implicit Theories of Giftedness

Examination of implicit theories of giftedness is a relatively new area of study. Very little research has been conducted thus far. However, as indicated earlier, there are essential questions that arise when evaluating implicit theories of giftedness including:
- Do implicit theories of giftedness exist?
- Are there similarities in implicit theories among/between groups? and
- Do implicit theories of giftedness predict later decisions and actions?

It is these questions that will organize the discussion of this area of inquiry.

Do implicit theories of giftedness exist? (i.e., Do people or particular groups of people hold implicit theories of giftedness that are specific to their understanding and experiences with gifted students?) This is the first and fundamental question that must be addressed in terms of the study of implicit theories. Teachers are one group whose perceptions of giftedness have been studied. Because this topic is relatively new and hypotheses about teachers' implicit theories are at a developmental stage, the research questions remain general in nature. Further, data about teachers' perceptions of giftedness have generally been gathered through in-depth, open-ended interviews (i.e., Campbell & Verna, 1998; Hunsaker, 1994; Peterson & Margolin, 1997; Rohrer, 1995; Singer, Houtz, & Rosenfield, 1992). Studies of teachers' beliefs about giftedness indicate that, in general, teachers seemed to be either unaware of the traits associated with broader and more inclusive definitions of giftedness, and/or were unable to recognize how these traits are manifested, or did not focus on these kinds of traits as indicators of giftedness (Campbell & Verna, 1998; Copenhaver & McIntyre, 1992; Frasier, Hunsaker, Lee, Findley, et al., 1995; Guskin, Peng, & Simon, 1992; Hunsaker, 1994; Hunsaker, Finley, & Frank, 1997; Peterson & Margolin, 1997; Rohrer, 1995).

Are there similarities in implicit theories of giftedness among/between different groups? The similarities and differences between and among different groups such as teachers versus nonteachers or people from different cultural groups is important because it allows for a greater understanding of which characteristics are valued by different groups of people. There appear to be differences among different cultures in their descriptions of giftedness (Frazier, Hunsaker, Lee, Mitchell, et al., 1995; Peterson, 1999; Scott, Perou, Urbano, Hogan, & Gold, 1992; Zhang & Hui, 2003.)

Do implicit theories of giftedness predict later decisions and actions? The question of whether implicit theories of giftedness predict later decisions and actions has not been thoroughly addressed in research on giftedness. Analysis of teachers' responses to different case studies and profiles indicates that teachers respond differently to different kinds of students (Guskin et al., 1992; Siegle & Powell, 2004). However, whether the differences found in studies of teachers' perceptions can be predicted from teachers' implicit theories of giftedness has not been researched.

There is research on the use of implicit theories of intelligence that is relevant to the study of giftedness because of the link between giftedness and intelligence. Lim, Plucker, and Im (2002) conducted a series of experiments to study implicit theories of intelligence among a sample of adults. In the course of their study, they explored participants' beliefs about academic intelligence, everyday intelligence, and intelligence in general. The results suggested that the implicit theories of the participants differed for each of the kinds of intelligence but were also similar in several ways. For all three implicit theories, social competence and problem-solving ability accounted for the majority of the explained variance. Results of a subsequent experiment on the extent to which the participants used these components of their theories when evaluating others' intelligence indicated that the coping with novelty, problem-solving ability, and self-management ability factors are the dominant factors predicting participants' evaluation of the intelligence of individuals presented in hypothetical profiles. Participants seemed to use their implicit theories when evaluating others.

LIMITATIONS OF THE RESEARCH

In the simplest of terms, conceptions of giftedness are ideas. This is both the strength and weakness of this aspect of the field. On one hand, the carefully considered ideas of learned researchers and theorists are the fuel that propels a field further. On the other hand, what can be conceptualized in the mind cannot always be translated into researchable hypotheses. The complexity of conceptions of giftedness provides elegance and intellectual appeal, but often our ability to conceive an idea outstrips our ability to measure it. Thus, the major limitation of research on conceptions of giftedness is the difficulty in operationalizing the different elements of the theories, whether they are explicit theories or implicit theories and beliefs. And, in the event that one is able to operationalize the elements of a conception of giftedness into assessments, there is still the difficulty in demonstrating that the new instrument is reliable and valid. This is particularly difficult when one is trying to find innovative ways to both define and measure giftedness. These limitations present fundamental challenges when it comes to research. Therefore, this is a topic with a great deal of opportunity for further study.

The lack of research that seeks to test empirically different theories of giftedness is surprising considering the primacy of definition in determining appropriate services for gifted students. It is impossible to serve what you cannot define. Each of the questions proposed as essential to studying explicit theories seem to be straightforward and answerable. Renzulli (1990) has written, "the proof of the pudding is in the eating" (p. 319), meaning that validation of the three-ring conception of giftedness can be gleaned from the success of the models that are based on this theory. And, yet, to reproduce the pudding, one must understand the ingredients and how they come together. To do this, more empirical research is needed on different conceptions of giftedness.

PRACTICAL IMPLICATIONS
OF THE RESEARCH

Research on conceptions of giftedness has tremendous implications for practitioners in the field, particularly school administrators working to develop their programs for gifted students. The conception of giftedness used by a school system is the foundation for all subsequent decisions made about issues such as identification, curricula, and programming. The conception of giftedness adopted by a school system provides the compass that guides the program. Research on different conceptions of giftedness provides administrators with information to help them make decisions about which model best fits their school population, philosophy, and goals. At the current time, the limited research base and information to guide identification procedures may contribute to limited adoption of more inclusive models of giftedness at the state and local level as compared to more traditional definitions based almost entirely on a high IQ score (Hunsaker, Abeel, & Callahan, 1991; Stephens & Karnes, 2000.)

RESOURCES

Although the base of research directly supporting the various conceptions of giftedness is small, there are several individual studies and books that are credible sources of research on conceptions of giftedness (in addition to the reference list to this chapter) including the following listed below.

Feldman, D. H. (1994). *Beyond universals in cognitive development* (2nd ed). Norwood, NJ: ABLEX.

Friedman, R. C., & Shore, B. M. (1998). *Talent in context: Historical and social perspectives on giftedness.* Washington, DC: American Psychological Association.

Friedman, R. C., & Shore, B. M. (2000). *Talents unfolding: Cognition and development.* Washington, DC: American Psychological Association.

Gagné, F. (2004). Transforming gifts into talents: The DMGT as a developmental theory. *High Ability Studies, 15,* 119–147.

Heller, K. A., Mönks, F. J., Sternberg, R. J., & Subotnik, R. F. (2000). *International handbook of giftedness and talent* (2nd ed.). Kindlington, Oxford, England: Elsevier Science Ltd.

Hollingworth, L. S. (1942). *Children above 180 IQ Stanford-Binet.* Yonkers-on-Hudson, NY: World Book Company.

Sternberg, R. J., & Davidson, J. E. (Eds.). (1986). *Conceptions of giftedness.* Cambridge, England: Cambridge University.

Sternberg, R. J., & Davidson, J. E. (Eds.). (2005). *Conceptions of giftedness* (2nd ed.) Cambridge, England: Cambridge University.

Sternberg, R. J., & Williams, W. M. (1998). *Intelligence, instruction, and assessment: Theory into practice.* Mahwah, NJ: Lawrence Erlbaum.

Terman, L. M. (1925). *Mental and physical traits of a thousand gifted children.* Stanford, CA: Stanford University Press.

REFERENCES

Callahan, C. M., Tomlinson, C. A., Moon, T. R., Tomchin, E. M., & Plucker, J. A. (1995). *Project START: Using multiple intelligences model in identifying and promoting talent in high-risk students* (Research Monograph No. 95136). Charlottesville, VA: National Research Center on the Gifted and Talented.

Campbell, J. R., & Verna, M. A. (1998, April). *Messages from the field: American teachers of the gifted talk back to the research community.* Paper presented at the annual meeting of the American Educational Research Association, San Diego, CA.

Cohen, J. (1988). *Statistical power analysis for the behavioral sciences* (2nd ed.). Hillsdale, NJ: Lawrence Erlbaum.

Copenhaver, R. W., & McIntyre, D. J. (1992). Teachers' perceptions of gifted students. *Roeper Review, 14,* 151–153.

Delisle, J. R., & Renzulli, J. S. (1982). The revolving door identification and programming model: Correlates of creative production. *Gifted Child Quarterly, 26,* 89–95.

Frasier, M. M., Hunsaker, S. L., Lee, J., Findley, V. S., Frank, E., Garcia, J. H., et al. (1995). *Educators' perceptions of barriers to the identification of gifted children from economically disadvantaged and limited English proficient backgrounds.* (Research Monograph No. 95216). Storrs: National Research Center on the Gifted and Talented, University of Connecticut.

Frasier, M. M., Hunsaker, S. L., Lee, J., Mitchell, S., Cramond, B., Krisel, S., et al. (1995). *Core attributes of giftedness: A foundation for recognizing the gifted potential of minority and economically disadvantaged students* (Research Monograph No. 95210). Storrs: National Research Center on the Gifted and Talented, University of Connecticut.

Gardner, H. (1983). *Frames of mind: The theory of multiple intelligences.* New York: Basic Books.

Gridley, B. E. (2002). In search of an elegant solution: Reanalysis of Plucker, Callahan, and Tomchin with respects to Pyryt and Plucker. *Gifted Child Quarterly, 46,* 224–234.

Guskin, S. L., Peng, C-Y. J., & Simon, M. (1992). Do teachers react to "multiple intelligences"? Effects of teachers' stereotypes on judgments and expectancies for students with diverse patterns of giftedness/talent. *Gifted Child Quarterly, 36,* 32–37.

Hunsaker, S. L. (1994). Creativity as a characteristic of giftedness: Teachers see it, then they don't. *Roeper Review, 17,* 11–15.

Hunsaker, S. L., Abeel, L. A., & Callahan, C. M. (1991, June). *Instruments used in the identification of gifted and talented children.* Paper presented at the meeting of the Jacob K. Javits Gifted and Talented Education Program Grant Recipients, Washington, DC.

Hunsaker, S. L., Finley, V. S., & Frank, E. L. (1997). An analysis of teacher nomination and student performance in gifted programs. *Gifted Child Quarterly, 41,* 19–24.

Lim, W., Plucker, J. A., & Im, K. (2002). We are more alike than we think we are: Implicit theories of intelligence with a Korean sample. *Intelligence, 30,* 185–208.

Loehlin, J. C. (1998). *Latent variable models: Factor, path and structural analysis.* Mahwah, NJ: Lawrence Erlbaum.

Peterson, J. S. (1999). Gifted—Through whose cultural lens? An application of the postpositivistic mode of inquiry. *Journal for the Education of the Gifted, 22,* 354–383.

Peterson, J. S., & Margolin, L. (1997). Naming gifted children: An example of unintended "reproduction." *Journal for the Education of the Gifted, 21*, 82–100.

Plucker, J. A., Callahan, C. C., & Tomchin, E. M. (1996). Wherefore art thou, multiple intelligences? Alternative assessments for identifying talent in ethnically diverse and low income students. *Gifted Child Quarterly, 40*, 81–92.

Pyryt, M. C. (2000). Finding "g": Easy viewing through higher order factor analysis. *Gifted Child Quarterly, 44*, 190–192.

Reis, S. M., & Renzulli, J. S. (1982). A case for a broadened conception of giftedness. *Phi Delta Kappan, 63*, 619–20.

Renzulli, J. S. (1978). What makes giftedness: Reexamining a definition. *Phi Delta Kappan, 60*, 180–184, 261.

Renzulli, J. S. (1990). "Torturing the data until they confess": An analysis of the analysis of the three-ring conception of giftedness. *Journal for the Education of the Gifted, 13*, 309–331.

Rohrer, J. C. (1995). Primary teacher conceptions of giftedness: Image, evidence, and nonevidence. *Journal for the Education of the Gifted, 18*, 269–283.

Scott, M. S., Perou, R., Urbano, R. Hogan, A., & Gold, S. (1992). The identification of giftedness: A comparison of White, Hispanic, and Black families. *Gifted Child Quarterly, 36*, 131–139.

Siegle, D., & Powell, T. (2004). Exploring teacher biases when nominating students for gifted programs. *Gifted Child Quarterly, 48*, 21–29.

Singer, E. M., Houtz, J. C., & Rosenfield, S. (1992). Teacher-identified characteristics of successful gifted students: A Delphi study. *Educational Research Quarterly, 15*, 5–14.

Stephens, K. R., & Karnes, F. A. (2000). State definitions for the gifted and talented revisited. *Exceptional Children, 66*, 219–238.

Sternberg, R. J. (1986). A triarchic theory of intellectual giftedness. In R. J. Sternberg & J. Davidson (Eds.), *Conceptions of giftedness* (pp. 223–243). Cambridge, England: Cambridge University.

Sternberg, R. J., Ferrari, M., Clinkenbeard, P., & Grigorenko, E. L. (1996). Identification, instruction, and assessment of gifted children: A construct validation of a triarchic model. *Gifted Child Quarterly, 40*, 129–137.

Zhang, L., & Hui, S. K. (2003). From pentagonal to triangle: A cross-cultural investigation of an implicit theory to giftedness. *Roeper Review, 25*, 78–82.

Chapter 9

COUNSELING

Jean Sunde Peterson

A decade ago, Moon and Hall (1998), in their overview of existing literature (e.g., Colangelo, 1997; Genshaft, Birely, & Hollinger, 1995; Kerr, 1991; Milgram, 1991; Moon, Kelly, & Feldhusen, 1997; Shore, Cornell, Robinson, & Ward, 1991), noted that "gifted children, especially the most highly talented, often need specialized counseling services to deal with psychological problems related to their giftedness and actualize their potential" (p. 59). Regardless of that scholarly support for services, Moon (2003) noted the heavy emphasis in the field of gifted education on achievement outcomes, to the neglect of "other important outcomes such as happiness, well-being, and life satisfaction" (p. 16). In that regard, Moon argued for "helping students develop self-awareness and skills in decision making and self-regulation" (p. 16). Such support can indeed occur in schools through school counselors (Peterson, 2006a, 2006b), gifted education personnel, and classroom teachers (Peterson, 2003); in university-based counseling centers specializing in concerns related to giftedness (Colangelo & Assouline, 2000); indirectly through parent groups (Webb & DeVries, 1993); and through professional counselors in private practice or community agencies (Mahoney, 2007; Mendaglio, 2007; Saunders, 2007).

This review will summarize research related to counseling gifted individuals—major questions addressed, empirical support for conclusions drawn, limitations of the research, practical implications, and credible resources in this area. The discussion will consider both prevention-oriented counseling and intervention-oriented counseling. It will also present research and other scholarly writing related to issues that gifted individuals potentially bring to counseling. Proactive strategies might help to avoid specific or general concerns, and reactive strategies can be tailored to fit particular presenting issues.

DEFINING THE TERMS USED IN THE RESEARCH

Several terms used above, as well as some that will appear later in the chapter, should be defined. *Affective* refers to social and emotional, rather than physical and cognitive, dimensions of child and adolescent development. *Developmental guidance* involves school-based psychoeducational activities that promote healthy development and are developmentally appropriate for the students who are served. In counseling, *proactive* strategies are implemented so that problems do not develop or become worse. *Prevention* refers to programs and strategies that foster healthy social and emotional development, proactively providing opportunities to develop skills and self-understanding related to effective living. *Reactive* approaches address existing problems. *Intervention* refers to reactive strategies intended to ameliorate difficult situations. A *systems perspective* is one in which situations are viewed within various contexts (e.g., family, school) as phenomena involving complex reciprocal and recursive interactions among various players. In *outcome studies*, researchers focus on the effectiveness of counseling approaches and interventions. *Differentiated counseling approaches* are approaches tailored to populations served (e.g., altering traditional counseling approaches to respond to characteristics common among gifted youth and their families). *Presenting issues* are concerns that clients bring to counseling. *Maladjustment* refers to problems with social and emotional adjustment, which in turn contribute to problems in living. *Psychopathology* denotes the presence of a diagnosable psychological disorder. *Resilience* reflects the ability to thrive in spite of adversity. *Clinical populations* include individuals who seek help from counselors, therapists, psychologists, and psychiatrists. *Generalizing*, in research and in this chapter, refers to applying conclusions and drawing inferences, based on a sample of individuals, to a broader population.

MAJOR QUESTIONS ADDRESSED IN THE RESEARCH

Major questions addressed by researchers in the area of counseling strategies are as follows:

- What are potential counseling needs and presenting issues of gifted children and adolescents?
- What kinds of counseling approaches are effective with various gifted populations and with various presenting issues?
- What models of counseling have been developed that incorporate understanding of child and adolescent development, giftedness, and systems?

CONCLUSIONS FROM THE RESEARCH

Counseling Needs and Presenting Issues of Gifted Children and Adolescents

In Mendaglio and Peterson's (2007) edited volume, eight clinicians working largely with gifted individuals were asked to list common presenting issues. Half mentioned anxiety and depression, underachievement, and relationships. A wide array of other issues mentioned included social, emotional, and behavioral disturbances; problems related to attention deficit; conduct problems; adjustment disorders in response to life events; chemical dependency; perfectionism; thought disorders; developmental issues for both achievers and underachievers; Asperger's syndrome; sexual and other abuse; and managing extreme sensitivities.

One study (Moon et al., 1997), involving a needs-assessment survey of 335 parents, school personnel, and related counseling professionals, found that all three respondent groups believed that gifted and talented youth have concerns that need differentiated counseling services. However, in the research literature in general, no consensus exists regarding whether gifted youth have greater or fewer counseling needs than those who are not identified as gifted. Both anecdotal and empirical literatures suggest that "gifts" can be both positive and negative (cf. Reynolds & Piirto, 2005); yet, until recently, the "burden" side of giftedness received little research attention, compared to the "asset" side (Yoo & Moon, 2006). Studies that have indeed explored vulnerabilities associated with high capability have yielded inconsistent results.

Giftedness as Asset. Several empirical studies have supported the perception that giftedness is an advantage socially and emotionally. Terman's (1925) conclusions about gifted individuals' better psychological health than less able peers have been supported empirically (Nail & Evans, 1997). Neihart (2002), summarizing research, noted that gifted individuals' cognitive capacities can help them cope with stressors (e.g., Baker, 1995; Scholwinski & Reynolds, 1985). Intelligence often has been found to be a factor of resilience (e.g., Higgins, 1994; Werner, 1984). When gifted students are compared with less able age peers, differences generally favor gifted students. They appear to be more independent, intrinsically motivated, flexible, self-accepting, and psychologically well adjusted, although there is also some limited evidence to suggest that young adolescent gifted students are somewhat lower on measures of general well-being than their same-age peers (VanTassel-Baska & Olszewski-Kubilius, 1989). Giftedness also has been associated with higher self-confidence (Ablard, 1997), fewer behavior problems (Ludwig & Cullinan, 1984), cooperative play patterns in preschoolers (Lupkowski, 1989), and greater self-awareness (Jacobs, 1971). Scholwinski and Reynolds's large study found that gifted children had comparatively lower levels of anxiety. Kennedy's (1962) study of 100 participants in a selective summer math institute found that gifted adolescents scored within normal limits on the Minnesota Multiphasic Personality Inventory (MMPI) unless factors other than intelligence were salient. Nevertheless, it is important for parents, teachers, and counselors to recognize that gifted youth may need and seek counseling services because of problems related to behavior, anxiety, low self-confidence, and lack of coping skills, for instance.

Similar to Others. Other studies have found that gifted individuals are similar to less capable age peers—for example, in psychological well-being (Neihart, 1999), self-concept (Hoge & McSheffrey, 1991; Tong & Yewchuk, 1996), distress and maladjustment (LoCicero & Ashby, 2000), and coping with stressors, although they use problem-solving strategies more often (Preuss & Dubow, 2003). Neihart (1999) examined empirical studies of depression among children identified as gifted (e.g., Baker, 1995; Berndt, Kaiser, & Van Aalst, 1982) and concluded that gifted individuals exhibited similar or lower levels of depression and similar levels of suicidal ideation. Gust-Brey and Cross (1999) also found no empirical evidence that rates of depression or suicide were higher among gifted youth than in epidemiological studies. In a national study of gifted victims and perpetrators of bullying (Peterson & Ray, 2006a, 2006b), findings regarding prevalence were similar to those in other studies. However, the concerns discussed here and in the next section are all potential presenting issues when gifted students are involved in counseling, regardless of venue.

Burdens and Needs. In contrast to studies that have found positive results are those that have illuminated dark aspects of giftedness. When researchers have compared gifted and less able samples on various common presenting issues, findings have indicated higher prevalence among gifted respondents in the areas of anxiety (Tong & Yewchuk, 1996) and perfectionism (Orange, 1997; Roberts & Lovett, 1994; Schuler, 1997).

Other concerns, illuminated in noncomparative studies, include depression and suicidal ideation in profoundly gifted youth (Jackson & Peterson, 2003); suicide (Cross, Gust-Brey, & Ball, 2002); distress related to sexual orientation (Peterson, 2001a; Peterson & Rischar, 2000); high expectations, teasing, and confusion about abilities (Ford, 1996); heightened sensitivity (Hébert, 2000a); social isolation for exceptionally gifted children (Gross, 1993); loneliness (Kaiser & Berndt, 1985); females' denial of giftedness as a social coping strategy (Swiatek, 2001); control and choice as related to boredom (Kanevsky & Keighley, 2003); learned helplessness (Ziegler, Finsterwald, & Grassinger, 2005); fear of failure (Speirs Neumeister & Finch, 2006) and self-perceptions of inadequacy (Rice, Leever, Christopher, & Porter, 2006) related to perfectionism; psychological vulnerability related to creativity (Csikszentmihalyi, 1996); school dropout (Renzulli & Park, 2002); homesickness related to early entrance to college, but balanced by better relationships with parents and new relationships with college students (Muratori, Colangelo, & Assouline, 2003); and the short-term negative social impact of relocation (Plucker & Yecke, 1999). A case study of a prolific child writer (Edmunds & Edmunds, 2005) illuminated the "double-edged sword" of sensitivity, and in an exploratory study (Alsop, 2003), anxiety, tension, "easily frustrated," "easily upset," "overly sensitive," and "self-critical" clustered under "intensity." The latter study concluded that gifted individuals need resilience to deal with asynchronous development, which contributes to a comparatively different child-by-environment interaction, with the asynchrony increasing as intellectual capacity increases. Scholars have also found a sense of differentness from peers (Ford, 1993) and negative outcomes because of lack of support for personality characteristics (Baker, 1995; Neihart, 1999). A longitudinal study (Peterson, 2007c) of life events and challenges found that social concerns and stress related to accelerated classes, overcommitment, and expectations were significant challenges. Life events ranged from deaths in the extended family and serious illness in the family or self to drug treatment and parental incarceration. Themes regarding what participants thought teachers and parents should know included stress, sensitivity, family stress, and social struggles. Significant to all of these potential concerns is the finding that these students are not likely to tell adults of their distress (Peterson & Ray, 2006a, 2006b; Peterson & Rischar, 2000).

Yoo and Moon's (2006) study of counseling concerns parents of gifted children noted on an intake protocol at a university-based counseling center found that school concerns related to boredom, educational planning (e.g., grade acceleration), and talent-development programming were cited most frequently. Gifted adolescents were perceived to have high needs for career planning. Across all ages, most parents had pursued counseling for their children because they wanted assessment and recommendations to help them advocate for school services.

Multicultural issues also are related to the counseling process, not only in terms of being a factor in the therapeutic relationship (Atkinson & Hackett, 2004), but also regarding counselor awareness of the potential impact of cultural values on classroom behavior and teacher-student relationships, fit in the typically dominant-culture-driven school environment (Peterson, 1999), and even counselor assumptions about giftedness and achievement (Peterson, 2006b). In one ethnographic study (Peterson & Margolin, 1997), themes in the language of dominant-culture teachers, as they explained nominations of children in their classrooms for a hypothetical gifted program, reflected dominant-culture values. Their ad hoc criteria were evident in the five major themes that emerged (behavior, verbal ability and assertiveness, family and socioeconomic status, perceived work ethic, and social skills). Any of these might preclude attention to children from cultures that do not value verbal assertiveness and "standing out," as well as students with low English proficiency, behavior problems, low socioeconomic status, or poor social skills. A parallel, follow-up study of individuals in nonmainstream cultures (Peterson, 1999) found values that differed from those reflected in the teachers' language, such as service to others, expressive arts, handiwork, and nonbookish wisdom. List and Renzulli (1991) found that family values related to creativity also can be at odds with values supported by the school. The findings regarding differing cultural values provoke questions related to potential counseling issues, including lack of affirmation of capability from self and others. It should be noted here, however, that high-achieving females with low socioeconomic status in one study (Reis & Diaz, 1999) supported each other, were involved in activities, and were independent, resilient, and career-focused.

Factors with impact on achievement also have been explored. Findings in Peterson and Rischar's (2000) study of gifted young adults who were gay, lesbian, bisexual, or transgendered raised awareness that distress can be masked—even by hyperachievement. Although 71% experienced significant depression, only 29% of parents and no teachers were told about it. Counselors played important roles for 78%, with 79% of those viewing counseling as helpful.

Low academic achievement is a more common cause for concern. Colangelo (2003) noted that underachievement was the issue brought to counseling most frequently by gifted youth at a university-based clinic. Yet, varying definitions and identification methods and often contradicting conclusions about what characterizes underachievers continue to create confusion about this complex and highly idiosyncratic population. For example, studies associating low self-concept with underachievement (e.g., Kanoy, Johnson, & Kanoy, 1980; Van Boxtel & Mönks, 1992) differ from those who have found that underachievers do not have lower self-concepts than achievers (e.g., Holland, 1998). McCoach and Siegle (2003) found differences between achievers and underachievers in attitudes toward school and teachers, motivation and self-regulation, and goal valuation, but not in academic self-concept. Speirs Neumeister and Hébert (2003) also found a healthy self-concept in a gifted underachiever in a university.

A study of the school files of gifted achievers and underachievers (Peterson & Colangelo, 1996) found both episodic and chronic underachievement, with 20% of underachievers becoming achievers or resuming academic achievement before graduation. A follow-up study (Peterson, 2000) found that 82% of underachievers had attended college for 4 years, and 41% had achieved at a level higher than they did during high school. These two studies support the notion that (complex) developmental factors might be among factors involved in reversal. Affective issues that were reported in the latter study included autonomy-, career-, and identity-related developmental concerns, peer-relational concerns, and concerns related to critical life events. Nice (2006), in a study of average-ability female adolescent underachievers, with implications for gifted underachievers, concluded that asynchrony played a role. Bravado regarding independence and serious romantic relationships kept significant adults at arm's length, just at a time when they needed guidance and support. Energy was focused on filling relational needs, with relationships tending to be more toxic and less egalitarian than those of their achieving counterparts.

A few studies of underachievers represent movement away from correlational studies of common characteristics and toward "linkages and flow of causality among these different characteristics and students' achievement" (Reis & McCoach, 2000, p. 205). One retrospective study of underachievement (Emerick, 1992) found that out-of-school interests, personal changes, and being able to pursue topics of interest were among factors associated with reversing underachievement, all of these potentially the focus of counseling. With attention to developmental task accomplishments, Peterson's 4-year follow-up study (2000) and two qualitative 4-year longitudinal studies (2001a, 2002) explored underachievement developmentally. In the latter, resolving family conflict, a counseling issue, was always one of the accomplishments when developmental successes converged, and convergence was associated with motivation for academic achievement. Peterson's (2001b) retrospective study of underachievers who became professionally successful as adults revealed that having achieving mentors and models was important, that "feistiness" in response to difficult family circumstances was an asset for females, and that an achievement-oriented peer milieu also was associated with later success. Hébert's studies of gifted students in rural poverty (Hébert & Beardsley, 2001) and in urban settings (Hébert, 2000a, 2001) called attention to counseling issues, counselors' views of underachievers, the need to increase their awareness of diverse cultures, the need to advocate for underachievers and intervene early, and factors of resilience. Peterson's (2007b) 15-year longitudinal study of a gifted survivor of multiple trauma found impact on social and emotional development, with the subject's intelligence, ability to engage support from others, and counselors being factors of resilience. These developmental studies call attention to issues and supportive factors that schools and other counselors can be alert to when working with bright underachievers.

Gifted students' advanced career maturity requires differentiated career counseling (Kelly & Colangelo, 1990), with one counseling concern being early decisions that potentially limit further exploration (Kerr, 1991). In regard to career development, counselors should be aware of the controversial concept of multipotentiality (Achter, Benbow, & Lubinski, 1997), as well as the potential impact of asynchronous development (Kelly & Colangelo, 1990), lack of decision-making skills (Achter et al., 1997), and even safety concerns related to sexual orientation in future careers (Peterson & Rischar, 2000).

Studies of gifted populations with particular concerns, such as gifted Asian American students (Plucker, 1996), African American (Ford, 1992; Grantham & Ford, 1998; Hébert, 1995, 2000a, 2001; Hébert & Beardsley, 2001) and Hispanic (Cordeiro & Carspecken, 1993; Diaz, 1998) students, gifted children of alcoholics (Peterson, 1997), and gifted students with learning disabilities (Reis & Colbert, 2004), underscore the potential salience of resilience in research and counseling of troubled gifted youth. Related to the concept of "fit" in the school context, Seeley (1984) found gifted delinquents with high creative and fluid intelligence, combined with relatively lower verbal and crystallized intelligence and school performance.

It also should be noted here that gifted individuals with dual diagnoses may be misassessed. They may find the interaction of the two diagnoses confusing (Olenchak & Reis, 2002), and high intellectual ability can mask symptoms, potentially leading to missed services, including those for learning disabilities. Focusing on dual-exceptionality, Rizza and Morrison (2003) found that emotional and behavioral disabilities may preclude attention to talent development in gifted students when unidimensional criteria are used for identifying disabilities and talent.

Regarding Attention Deficit/Hyperactivity Disorder (ADHD), Zentall, Moon, Hall, & Grskovic (2001) concluded that intelligence did not protect gifted children from problematic behaviors related to academic work, and emotional maturity lagged behind intellectual and imaginational talents, although talent domains offered hope for long-term improvement. On the other hand, behavioral issues that counselors see may in fact reflect hypersensitivity to the environment, hyper-intense reactions, and developmental asynchrony, rather than disability or pathology. The stress of inappropriate school environments and difficulty relating to peers may contribute to depression and anxiety, although professionals may not recognize underlying issues related to giftedness (Webb et al., 2005). In general, misinterpretation of behaviors can lead to emotional distress (Moon, 2002).

Approaches Effective With Various Populations and Presenting Issues

Reis and Moon (2002) noted the lack of "empirical research on patterns and interventions that promote the healthy development of gifted students into gifted adults who lead satisfying personal and professional lives. . . . what works best, under what circumstances, for what types of gifted students and their families" (p. 262). Studies attempting to ascertain what kinds of issues are of concern to them are also rare. Reis and McCoach (2000) concluded, in their review of three decades of research on underachievement, a common presenting issue—that counseling probably should be part of interventions attempting to reverse it. Yet, counseling treatments have received scant research attention.

A number of psychoeducational approaches, however, are part of the literature. To help classroom teachers promote social and emotional development, VanTassel-Baska (2006) offered a prototypical lesson with a metacognitive orientation, focusing on emotional intelligence. The emphasis was on being able to perceive, appraise, and express emotion; use emotions to facilitate thinking; apply emotional knowledge; and regulate emotion. Greene (2002), in summarizing career literature related to giftedness, emphasized the importance of addressing nonacademic components, such as personality, values, desired lifestyle, and trends, in addition to the importance of recognizing that gifted youth should be prepared to accommodate chance factors. Kerr's (1991) work has supported the importance of a good fit among personality, interests, values, and career context.

In regard to facilitating personal development, Moon and Thomas (2003) described the function of a "talent coach." Persson's (2005) qualitative Swedish case study suggested that "received mentorship" may be the only way to counsel a gifted individual in an uncomfortable egalitarian school setting. Similarly, Hébert (1995), Hébert and Olenchak (2000), and Ford (1996) found support for involving male mentors for gifted males across cultural groups, and Hébert (2000a) concluded that providing meaningful community service opportunities as an outlet for sensitive young men can be beneficial. School and other counselors can also offer support and guidance for social and emotional development. Hébert (1991, 2000b) found empirical support for the effectiveness of bibliotherapy with gifted clients.

Peterson's (2001a, 2002) longitudinal study of underachievers focused on the developmental tasks of finding career direction, establishing a mature relationship, achieving autonomy, and resolving conflict with family, all areas with potential to be part of proactive counseling approaches. In addition, calling attention to factors of resilience, such as being able to attract the attention of adults, having a confidant, having a stable primary caretaker during one's first 2 years, having a proactive impulse, and being able to envision a better future (Higgins, 1994), may affirm strengths in gifted children and adolescents and contribute to feelings of hope.

Outcome research for various counseling modalities has been conducted largely outside of the field of gifted education. In family therapy, for example, only a few therapists with expertise in giftedness have written about their approaches (e.g., Wendorf & Frey, 1985) or presented case studies (Moon, Nelson, & Piercy, 1993; Thomas, 1995; Thomas, Ray, & Moon, 2007). In contrast, as noted by Moon and Thomas (2003), one special issue of the *Journal of Marital and Family Therapy* in 1995 focused on the effectiveness of marital and family therapy. In that issue, a meta-analysis (Shadish, Ragsdale, & Glaser, 1995) of 163 randomized outcomes studies indicated positive outcomes, with the effect size of family therapy at .47 across 44 studies. However, insufficient evidence precluded determination of the effectiveness of family therapy for school-achievement problems. Common factors seem to be more important in creating change than specific orientations (Blow & Sprenkle, 2001; Sprenkle, Blow, & Dickey, 1999), and, although nonempirical articles have described approaches effective with specific presenting problems, empirical support for particular models is lacking in the literature. In general, according to Moon and Thomas, although no randomized, controlled studies have examined family-therapy efficacy with gifted individuals and their families, significant empirical evidence of efficacy with the general population suggests that family work can be effective with the gifted population, as well. Clinicians working with families should include school, peer, and giftedness issues in their case conceptualizations and treatment plans.

Models Developed

Clinicians and scholars have advocated for differentiated counseling services for gifted children and adolescents and their families (e.g., Colangelo, 2003; Moon et al., 1997; Peterson, 2003, 2006a; Silverman, 1993). Some have offered models for addressing social and emotional concerns of gifted students.

Several proactive school-based, differentiated, affective-curriculum approaches to developmental guidance have been developed. Two dimensions of the Autonomous Learner Model (Betts, 1985; Betts & Kercher, 1999) attend to affective concerns of gifted adolescents. In Buescher's (2004) two-tier model for counseling gifted adolescents, key developmental issues form a proactive curriculum for adolescents and their parents, teachers, and counselors. The model purposefully increases knowledge about self-development, social realities, and the interaction of conflict and intimacy. Peterson (2003) presented a multifaceted affective curriculum for gifted adolescents, including weekly discussion groups focusing on developmental tasks (see Peterson, 2008), guest lectures by community professionals on developmental concerns, and regularly encouraging self-reflection after engaging in program and academic activities. Rimm's (1995, 2003) Trifocal method for addressing underachievement, with collaboration between teachers and parents, has some empirical support.

Regarding models applicable to clinical practice, each of the eight contributors to the Mendaglio and Peterson (2007) volume presented conceptions of giftedness and personality, a model of counseling, and a case study. Some of their specific techniques are described as follows. Mahoney's (2007) model detailed a framework of several systems that have impact on, and four constructs that are related to, gifted-identity formation. Mendaglio's (2007) affective-cognitive model included confrontation to increase self-awareness; didactic information about giftedness and Dabrowskian concepts; cognitive restructuring; fostering an empirical attitude in clients; and emotion awareness and expression. Kerr's (2007) model included powerful techniques to generate motivation for rapid change, mind/body techniques, and healing ceremonies. Boland and Gross (2007) used Socratic questioning, thought-challenging, point-counter-point, exaggeration, and eliciting automatic thoughts and schemas. Saunders (2007) helped underachievers to establish routines, worked to unify parental support, and used Transactional Analysis to help families improve communication. Thomas et al.'s (2007) model employed role-plays, consultation with teachers, a structural-strategic approach, scaling, and reframing, as well as an imaginative-postmodern approach, helping families to restructure their stories. Ziegler and Stoeger (2007), focusing on development of exceptional talent, used individual and group sessions with significant adults. Peterson (2007a) used a brief, solution-focused approach with individuals, focusing on strengths and resilience, purposefully externalizing the problem, and using semi-structured small-group work with gifted students in schools. In Silverman's (1993) developmental model for counseling the gifted, career and talent development, preparing for marriage, and learning skills for conflict resolution were potential areas of focus. She encouraged individual psychotherapy when gifted students act out sexually, have problems with anger, show symptoms of abuse, underachieve, or seem depressed.

However, although these models offer interesting and practical guidance for school and community counselors, almost none have been studied empirically. In general, researchers have not attended to even what kinds of counseling services parents, educators, and counselors deem beneficial. In fact, there is little in the research literature to guide the process of counseling.

LIMITATIONS OF THE RESEARCH

Like much of the research in the field about characteristics of gifted students, the scant research about counseling needs and approaches may not be based on populations that are inclusive enough of individuals with high ability to warrant broad generalization. Students at typical residential schools for highly able students and at summer residential or commuter programs are essentially convenience samples, not likely to be demographically representative of high-capability children and adolescents across cultural and socioeconomic groups, across various levels of academic performance, and across differing family circumstances, including disruptions related to unemployment, changes in family structure, health, death of someone close to the students, or relocation, for instance. In addition, school programs for gifted and talented students may be limited to those who have high scores on standardized achievement tests and/ or high grades in classroom work (Moore, Ford, & Milner, 2005), leaving out highly capable students who, for any number of reasons, are not able or willing to focus on standardized group tests or achieve well academically.

Therefore, not only have counseling needs and approaches not been studied enough, but, especially in terms of ascertaining characteristics of gifted children and potential presenting issues in counseling, not enough of the gifted population has been studied to generalize findings. Obviously it is difficult to access gifted students beyond selective programs, and, given the seeming rarity of counseling centers geared to issues of gifted youth and their families, it also is not easy to access clinical populations. Furthermore, findings in studies of accessible students in special programs and in clinical populations may be skewed in the direction of either mental health or psychopathology, depending on which population is studied.

PRACTICAL IMPLICATIONS OF THE RESEARCH

The practical implications of the research in the area of counseling strategies are largely related to the *lack* of pertinent empirical support for various approaches and models. Future researchers can assume a veritable open field to explore, although a scarcity of mental-health practitioners who specialize in concerns of gifted youth and of these clinicians who write for publication will likely remain a significant constraint. Gifted education teachers who develop and employ affective curricula may be more accessible by researchers for studying presenting issues and effectiveness of approaches, although those teachers also may not be plentiful. School counselors currently are being trained in developmental guidance and can cofacilitate or facilitate activities with gifted education personnel. Practitioners, including gifted education teachers, who accept the reality that there is much that has not been ascertained by researchers, can be part of a continuing process of discovery about social and emotional development of gifted youth. They might seek out and collaborate with university researchers on research projects and share their concerns and successes at conferences and in publications.

Certainly, the intersection of giftedness and various counseling issues represents a research direction with great potential—for example, in connection with eating disorders, self-mutilation, substance abuse, sexual abuse, obsessive-compulsive disorder, oppositional-defiant disorder, parent-child conflict, developmental stuckness, physical disability, and response to life events (e.g., loss and grief, divorce, serious illness, accident, relocation). These areas have not received research attention within the field of gifted education, and therefore little is known about whether there are qualitative differences in how gifted individuals experience these phenomena. Timing, in terms of age, of the appearance of various psychiatric disorders among gifted individuals also warrants attention. Researchers also might explore the effect of giftedness on both the family system and the therapeutic system, as well as how counselors differentiate their services for gifted youth in general and also across cultures and socioeconomic levels. Embracing the complexity of the broad, highly idiosyncratic population of interest, researchers should endeavor to employ samples that include those with exceptional ability who are typically not likely to be identified for programs for gifted students. In addition, longitudinal studies need to be conducted in order to allow practitioners (and children and parents, as well) to see how issues develop over time, the effect of various interventions over time, and whether various presenting issues appear to be related to developmental shifts, relatively transient. Attitudes of counselors toward giftedness is another promising area for exploration—for example, whether they can embrace it, affirm it, be comfortable with it, not need to compete with it, and be aware of potential risk factors (Peterson, 2006a).

It is important for counselors in schools, summer programs, and various other venues to be aware of the counseling models that have been described in the literature related to giftedness, albeit usually without empirical support. Each of these models highlights one or more important dimensions of the social and emotional development of gifted students and can provide helpful perspectives to those working with gifted youth. According to Thompson and Rudolph (1996), highly able children, although able to compensate for or disguise many concerns, and although often wanting to solve their problems independently, can be responsive clients.

Gifted children and adolescents are continuously developing, just as their less-able age peers are, with an assumed need for support, but likely with a qualitatively different subjective developmental experience and therefore with a need for differential services (Peterson, 2006a). The developmental template, an important aspect of some of the models mentioned earlier, is certainly an important framework for all responses to affective concerns. Increased scholarly attention to these concerns of gifted youth, particularly with a focus on delivery of services in schools and other venues, can help parents, teachers, and clinicians be alert to general developmental concerns, as well as mental-health issues.

MAJOR, CREDIBLE RESOURCES AND REFERENCES ON THE RESEARCH

Major, credible resources are included in the extensive references used in this chapter. However, noted here are those that are comprehensive and include references to empirical studies: the edited Neihart, Reis, Robinson, and Moon (2002) review of scholarship related to social and emotional development of gifted children; Colangelo and Davis's (2003) *Handbook of Gifted Education*, with several chapters related to counseling the gifted; Kerr's (1991) *A Handbook for Counseling the Gifted and Talented*; Whitmore's (1980) *Giftedness, Conflict and Underachievement*; and Mendaglio and Peterson's (2007) *Models of Counseling Gifted Children, Adolescents, and Young Adults*, which presents international scholar-practitioners' models.

REFERENCES

Ablard, K. E. (1997). Self-perceptions and needs as a function of type of academic ability and gender. *Roeper Review, 20,* 110–115.

Achter, J. A., Benbow, C., & Lubinski, D. (1997). Rethinking multipotentiality among the intellectually gifted: A critical review and recommendations. *Gifted Child Quarterly, 41,* 5–15.

Alsop, G. (2003). Asynchrony: Intuitively valid and theoretically reliable. *Roeper Review, 25,* 118–127.

Atkinson, D. R., & Hackett, G. (2004). *Counseling diverse populations* (3rd ed.). Boston: McGraw-Hill.

Baker, J. A. (1995). Depression and suicidal ideation among academically gifted adolescents. *Gifted Child Quarterly, 39,* 218–223.

Berndt, D. J., Kaiser, C. F., & Van Aalst, F. (1982). Depression and self-actualization in gifted adolescents. *Journal of Clinical Psychology, 38,* 142–150.

Betts, G. T. (1985). *Autonomous learner model for the gifted and talented.* Greeley, CO: Autonomous Learning Publications and Specialists.

Betts, G., & Kercher, J. (1999). *Autonomous learner model: Optimizing ability.* Greeley, CO: Autonomous Learning Publications and Specialists.

Blow, A. J., & Sprenkle, D. H. (2001). Common factors across theories of marriage and family therapy: A modified Delphi study. *Journal of Marital and Family Therapy, 27,* 385–402.

Boland, C. M., & Gross, M. U. M. (2007). Counseling highly gifted children and adolescents. In S. Mendaglio & J. S. Peterson (Eds.), *Models of counseling gifted children, adolescents, and young adults* (pp. 153–198). Waco, TX: Prufrock Press.

Buescher, T. M. (2004). Counseling gifted adolescents: A curriculum model for students, parents, and professionals. In S. M. Moon (Ed.), *Social/emotional issues, underachievement, and counseling of gifted and talented students* (pp. 221–228). Thousand Oaks, CA: Corwin Press.

Colangelo, N. (1997). Counseling gifted students: Issues and practices. In N. Colangelo & G. A. Davis (Eds.), *Handbook of gifted education* (2nd ed., pp. 353–365). Boston: Allyn & Bacon.

Colangelo, N., & Assouline, S. G. (2000). Counseling gifted students. In K. A. Heller, F. J. Mönks, & R. J. Sternberg (Eds.), *International handbook of giftedness and talent* (pp. 595–607). Amsterdam: Elsevier.

Colangelo, N., & Davis, G. A. (2003). *Handbook of gifted education* (3rd ed.). Boston: Allyn & Bacon.

Cordeiro, P. A., & Carspecken, P. F. (1993). How a minority of the minority succeed: A case study of twenty Hispanic achievers. *Qualitative Studies in Education, 6,* 277–290.

Cross, T. L., Gust-Brey, K., & Ball, P. B. (2002). A psychological autopsy of the suicide of an academically gifted student: Researchers' and parents' perspectives. *Gifted Child Quarterly, 46,* 247–264.

Csikszentmihalyi, M. (1996). *Creativity: Flow and the psychology of discovery and invention.* New York: HarperCollins.

Diaz, E. I. (1998). Perceived factors influencing the academic underachievement of talented students of Puerto Rican descent. *Gifted Child Quarterly, 42,* 105–122.

Edmunds, A. L., & Edmunds, G. A. (2005). Sensitivity: A double-edged sword for the pre-adolescent and adolescent gifted child. *Roeper Review, 27,* 69–77.

Emerick, L. J. (1992). Academic underachievement among the gifted: Students' perceptions of factors that reverse the pattern. *Gifted Child Quarterly, 36*, 140–146.

Ford, D. Y. (1992). Determinants of underachievement among gifted, above-average, and average Black students. *Roeper Review, 14*, 130–136.

Ford, D. Y. (1993). An investigation of the paradox of underachievement among gifted Black students. *Roeper Review, 16*, 78–84.

Ford, D. Y. (1996). *Reversing underachievement among gifted Black students.* New York: Teachers College Press.

Genshaft, J. L., Birely, M., & Hollinger, C. L. (Eds.). (1995). *Serving gifted and talented students: A resource for school personnel.* Austin, TX: ProEd.

Grantham, T. C., & Ford, D. Y. (1998). A case study of the social needs of Danisha: An underachieving gifted African-American female. *Roeper Review, 21*, 96–101.

Greene, M. J. (2002). Career counseling for gifted and talented students. In M. Neihart, S. M. Reis, N. M. Robinson, & S. M. Moon (Eds.), *The social and emotional development of gifted children: What do we know?* (pp. 93–102). Waco, TX: Prufrock Press.

Gross, M. U. M. (1993). *Exceptionally gifted children.* London: Routledge.

Gust-Brey, K., & Cross, T. L. (1999). An examination of the literature base on the suicidal behaviors of gifted children. *Roeper Review, 22*, 28–35.

Hébert, T. P. (1991). Meeting the affective needs of bright boys through bibliotherapy. *Roeper Review, 13*, 207–212.

Hébert, T. P. (1995). Coach Brogan: South Central High School's answer to academic achievement. *Journal of Secondary Gifted Education, 7*, 310–323.

Hébert, T. P. (2000a). Defining belief in self: Intelligent young men in an urban high school. *Gifted Child Quarterly, 44*, 91–114.

Hébert, T. P. (2000b). Helping high ability students overcome math anxiety through bibliotherapy. *Journal of Secondary Gifted Education, 8*, 164–178.

Hébert, T. P. (2001). "If I had a notebook, I know things would change": Bright underachieving young men in urban classrooms. *Gifted Child Quarterly, 45*, 174–194.

Hébert, T. P., & Beardsley, T. M. (2001). Jermaine: A critical case study of a Black child living in rural poverty. *Gifted Child Quarterly, 45*, 85–103.

Hébert, T. P., & Olenchak, F. R. (2000). Mentors for gifted underachieving males: Developing potential and realizing promise. *Gifted Child Quarterly, 44*, 196–207.

Higgins, G. O. (1994). *Resilient adults: Overcoming a cruel past.* San Francisco: Jossey-Bass.

Hoge, R. D., & McSheffrey, R. (1991, December-January). An investigation of self-concept in gifted children. *Exceptional Children*, 238–245.

Holland, V. (1998). Underachieving boys: Problems and solutions. *Support for Learning, 13*, 174–178.

Jackson, S. M., & Peterson, J. S. (2003). Depressive disorder in highly gifted adolescents. *Journal of Secondary Gifted Education, 14*, 175–186.

Jacobs, J. C. (1971). Rorschach studies reveal possible misinterpretation of personality traits of gifted students. *Journal of Personality Assessment, 47*, 303–304.

Kaiser, C. F., & Berndt, D. J. (1985). Predictors of loneliness in the gifted adolescent. *Gifted Child Quarterly, 29*, 74–77.

Kanevsky, L., & Keighley, T. (2003). To produce or not to produce? Understanding boredom and the honor in underachievement. *Roeper Review, 26*, 20–28.

Kanoy, R. C., Johnson, B. W., & Kanoy, K. W. (1980). Locus of control and self-concept in achieving and underachieving bright elementary students. *Psychology in the Schools, 17*, 395–399.

Kelly, K., & Colangelo, N. (1990). Effects of academic ability and gender on career development. *Journal for the Education of the Gifted, 13*, 168–175.

Kennedy, W. A. (1962). MMPI profiles of gifted adolescents. *Journal of Clinical Psychology, 18*, 148–149.

Kerr, B. A. (1991). *A handbook for counseling the gifted and talented.* Alexandria, VA: American Counseling Association.

Kerr, B. (2007). Science, spirit, and talent development. In S. Mendaglio & J. S. Peterson (Eds.), *Models of counseling gifted children, adolescents, and young adults* (pp. 231–252). Waco, TX: Prufrock Press.

List, K., & Renzulli, J. S. (1991). Creative women's developmental patterns through age thirty-five. *Gifted Education International, 7*, 114–122.

LoCicero, K. A., & Ashby, J. S. (2000). Multidimensional perfectionism in middle school age gifted students: A comparison to peers from the general cohort. *Roeper Review, 22*, 182–185.

Ludwig, G., & Cullinan, D. (1984). Behavior problems of gifted and nongifted elementary school girls and boys. *Gifted Child Quarterly, 28*, 37–39.

Lupkowski, A. E. (1989). Social behaviors of gifted and typical preschool children in laboratory school programs. *Roeper Review, 11*, 124–127.

Mahoney, A. S. (2007). Gifted identity formation: A therapeutic model for counseling gifted children and adolescents. In S. Mendaglio & J. S. Peterson (Eds.), *Models of counseling gifted children, adolescents, and young adults* (pp. 199–230). Waco, TX: Prufrock Press.

McCoach, D. B., & Siegle, D. (2003). Factors that differentiate underachieving gifted students from high-achieving gifted students. *Gifted Child Quarterly, 47*, 144–154.

Mendaglio, S. (2007). Affective-cognitive therapy for counseling gifted individuals. In S. Mendaglio & J. S. Peterson (Eds.), *Models of counseling gifted children, adolescents, and young adults* (pp. 35–68). Waco, TX: Prufrock Press.

Mendaglio, S., & Peterson, J. S. (Eds.). (2007). *Models of counseling gifted children, adolescents, and young adults.* Waco, TX: Prufrock Press.

Milgram, R. M. (1991). *Counseling gifted and talented children: A guide for teachers, counselors, and parents.* Norwood, NJ: Ablex.

Moon, S. M. (2002). Gifted children with attention-deficit/hyperactivity disorder. In M. Neihart, S. M. Reis, N. M. Robinson, & S. M. Moon (Eds.), *The social and emotional development of gifted children: What do we know?* (pp. 193–201). Waco, TX: Prufrock Press.

Moon, S. M. (2003). Personal talent. *High Ability Studies, 14*, 1–21.

Moon, S. M., & Hall, A. S. (1998). Family therapy with intellectually and creatively gifted children. *Journal of Marital and Family Therapy, 24*, 59–80.

Moon, S. M., Kelly, K. R., & Feldhusen, J. F. (1997). Specialized counseling services for gifted youth and their families: A needs assessment. *Gifted Child Quarterly, 41*, 16–25.

Moon, S. M., Nelson, T. S., & Piercy, F. P. (1993). Family therapy with a highly gifted adolescent. *Journal of Family Psychotherapy, 4*, 1–16.

Moon, S. M., & Thomas, V. (2003). Family therapy with gifted and talented adolescents. *Journal of Secondary Gifted Education, 14*, 107–113.

Moore, J. L., Ford, D. Y., & Milner, H. R. (2005). Recruitment is not enough: Retaining African American students in gifted education. *Gifted Child Quarterly, 49*, 51–67.

Muratori, M., Colangelo, N., & Assouline, S. (2003). Early-entrance students: Impressions of their first semester of college. *Gifted Child Quarterly, 47*, 219–237.

Nail, J. M., & Evans, J. G. (1997). The emotional adjustment of gifted adolescents: A view of global functioning. *Roeper Review, 20*, 18–22.

Neihart, M. (1999). The impact of giftedness on psychological well-being: What does the empirical literature say? *Roeper Review, 22*, 10–17.

Neihart, M. (2002). Gifted children and depression. In M. Neihart, S. M. Reis, N. M. Robinson, & S. M. Moon (Eds.), *The social and emotional development of gifted children: What do we know?* (pp. 93–102). Waco, TX: Prufrock Press.

Neihart, M., Reis, S. M., Robinson, N. M., & Moon, S. M. (Eds.). (2002). *The social and emotional development of gifted children: What do we know?* Waco, TX: Prufrock Press.

Nice, J. B. (2006). *Academically underachieving and achieving adolescent girls: Quantitative and qualitative differences in self-efficacy, planning, and developmental asynchrony.* Unpublished dissertation, York University, Toronto, Canada.

Olenchak, F. R., & Reis, S. M. (2002). Gifted students with learning disabilities. In M. Neihart, S. M. Reis, N. M. Robinson, & S. M. Moon (Eds.), *The social and emotional development of gifted children: What do we know?* (pp. 177–191). Waco, TX: Prufrock Press.

Orange, C. (1997). Gifted students and perfectionism. *Roeper Review, 20*, 39–41.

Persson, R. S. (2005). Voices in the wilderness: Counselling gifted students in a Swedish egalitarian setting. *International Journal for the Advancement of Counseling, 27*, 263–276.

Peterson, J. S. (1997). Bright, troubled, and resilient, and not in a gifted program. *Journal of Secondary Gifted Education, 8*, 121–136.

Peterson, J. S. (1999). Gifted—through whose cultural lens? An application of the post-positivistic mode of inquiry. *Journal for the Education of the Gifted, 22*, 354–383.

Peterson, J. S. (2000). A follow-up study of one group of achievers and underachievers four years after high school graduation. *Roeper Review, 22*, 217–224.

Peterson, J. S. (2001a). Gifted and at risk: Four longitudinal case studies. *Roeper Review, 24*, 31–39.

Peterson, J. S. (2001b). Successful adults who were once adolescent underachievers. *Gifted Child Quarterly, 45*, 236–249.

Peterson, J. S. (2002). A longitudinal study of post-high-school development in gifted individuals at risk for poor educational outcomes. *Journal of Secondary Gifted Education, 14*, 6–18.

Peterson, J. S. (2003). An argument for proactive attention to affective concerns of gifted adolescents. *Journal of Secondary Gifted Education, 14*, 62–71.

Peterson, J. S. (2006a). Addressing counseling needs of gifted students. *Professional School Counseling, 10*, 1, 43–51.

Peterson, J. S. (2006b). Superintendents, principals, and counselors: Facilitating secondary gifted education. In F. A. Dixon & S. M. Moon (Eds.), *The handbook of secondary gifted education* (pp. 649–671). Waco, TX: Prufrock Press.

Peterson, J. S. (2007a). A developmental perspective. In S. Mendaglio & J. S. Peterson (Eds.), *Models of counseling gifted children, adolescents, and young adults* (pp. 97–126). Waco, TX: Prufrock Press.

Peterson, J. S. (2007b). *Gifted and traumatized: A developmental perspective.* Manuscript in preparation.

Peterson, J. S. (2007c). *Life events and other stressors for gifted youth during the school years.* Manuscript submitted for publication.

Peterson, J. S. (2008*). The essential guide to talking with gifted teens: Ready-to-use discussions about identity, stress, relationships, and more.* Minneapolis, MN: Free Spirit.

Peterson, J. S., & Colangelo, N. (1996). Gifted achievers and underachievers: A comparison of patterns found in school files. *Journal of Counseling and Development, 74*, 399–407.

Peterson, J. S., & Margolin, L. (1997). Naming gifted children: An example of unintended 'reproduction.' *Journal for the Education of the Gifted, 21*, 82–100.

Peterson, J. S., & Ray, K. E. (2006a). Bullying among the gifted: The subjective experience. *Gifted Child Quarterly, 50*, 252–269.

Peterson, J. S., & Ray, K. E. (2006b). Bullying and the gifted: Victims, perpetrators, prevalence, and effects. *Gifted Child Quarterly, 50*, 148–168.

Peterson, J. S., & Rischar, H. (2000). Gifted and gay: A study of the adolescent experience. *Gifted Child Quarterly, 44*, 149–164.

Plucker, J. A. (1996). Gifted Asian American students: Identification, curricular and counseling concerns. *Journal for the Education of the Gifted, 19*, 315–343.

Plucker, J. A., & Yecke, C. P. (1999). The effect of relocation on gifted students. *Gifted Child Quarterly, 43*, 95–106.

Preuss, L. J., & Dubow, E. F. (2003). A comparison between intellectually gifted and typical children in their coping responses to a school and a peer stressor. *Roeper Review, 26*, 105–111.

Reis, S. M., & Colbert, R. (2004). Counseling needs of academically talented students with learning disabilities. *Professional School Counseling, 8*, 156.

Reis, S. M., & Diaz, E. (1999). Economically disadvantaged urban female students who achieve in schools. *Urban Review, 31*, 31–54.

Reis, S. M., & McCoach, D. B. (2000). The underachievement of gifted students: What do we know and where do we go? *Gifted Child Quarterly, 44*, 152–170.

Reis, S. M., & Moon, S. M. (2002). Models and strategies for counseling, guidance, and social and emotional support of gifted and talented students. In M. Neihart, S. M. Reis, N. M. Robinson, & S. M. Moon (Eds.), *The social and emotional development of gifted children: What do we know?* (pp. 251–266). Waco, TX: Prufrock Press.

Renzulli, J. S., & Park. S. (2002). *Giftedness and high school dropouts: Personal, family, and school-related factors* (Research Monograph No. 2168). Storrs: National Research Center on the Gifted and Talented, University of Connecticut.

Reynolds, R. C., & Piirto, J. (2005). Depth psychology and giftedness: Bringing soul to the field of talent development and giftedness. *Roeper Review, 27*, 164–171.

Rice, K. G., Leever, B. A., Christopher, J., & Porter, J. D. (2006). Perfectionism, stress, and social (dis)connection: A short-term study of hopelessness, depression, and academic adjustment among honors students. *Journal of Counseling Psychology, 53*, 524–534.

Rimm, S. B. (1995). *Why bright kids get poor grades and what you can do about it.* New York: Crown.

Rimm, S. B. (2003). Underachievement: A national epidemic. In N. Colangelo & G. A. Davis (Eds.), *Handbook of gifted education* (3rd ed., pp. 424–443). Boston: Allyn & Bacon.

Rizza, M. G., & Morrison, W. F. (2003). Uncovering stereotypes and identifying characteristics of gifted students and students with emotional/behavioral disabilities. *Roeper Review, 26*, 73–77.

Roberts, S. M., & Lovett, S. B. (1994). Examining the "F" in gifted: Academically gifted adolescents' physiological and affective responses to scholastic failure. *Journal for the Education of the Gifted, 17*, 241–259.

Saunders, C. L. (2007). Counseling underachieving students and their parents. In S. Mendaglio & J. S. Peterson (Eds.), *Models of counseling gifted children, adolescents, and young adults* (pp. 127–152). Waco, TX: Prufrock Press.

Scholwinski, E., & Reynolds, C. R. (1985). Dimensions of anxiety among high IQ children. *Gifted Child Quarterly, 29*, 125–130.

Schuler, P. (1997). *Characteristics and perceptions of perfectionism in gifted adolescents in a rural school environment.* Unpublished doctoral dissertation, University of Connecticut, Storrs.

Seeley, K. R. (1984). An investigation of the relationships among intellectual and creative abilities, extracurricular activities, and giftedness in a delinquent population. *Gifted Child Quarterly, 28*, 73–79.

Shadish, W. R., Ragsdale, K., & Glaser, R. R. (1995). The efficacy and effectiveness of marital and family therapy: A perspective from meta-analysis. *Journal of Marital and Family Therapy, 21*, 345–360.

Shore, B. M., Cornell, D. G., Robinson, A., & Ward, V. S. (1991). *Recommended practices in gifted education.* New York: Teachers College Press.

Silverman, L. S. (1993). A developmental model for counseling the gifted. In L. K. Silverman (Ed.), *Counseling the gifted and talented* (pp. 51–78). Denver: Love.

Speirs Neumeister, K. L., & Finch, H. (2006). Perfectionism in high-ability students: Relational precursors and influences on achievement motivation. *Gifted Child Quarterly, 50*, 238–250.

Speirs Neumeister, K. L., & Hébert, T. P. (2003). Underachievement versus selective achievement: Delving deeper and discovering the difference. *Journal for the Education of the Gifted, 26*, 221–238.

Sprenkle, D. H., Blow, A. J., & Dickey, M. H. (1999). Common factors and other nontechnique variables in marriage and family therapy. In M. A. Hubble, B. L. Duncan, & S. D. Miller (Eds.), *The heart and soul of change: What works in therapy* (pp. 329–360). Washington, DC: American Psychological Association.

Swiatek, M. A. (2001). Social coping among gifted high school students and its relationship to self-concept. *Journal of Youth and Adolescence, 30*, 19–39.

Terman, L. M. (1925). *Genetic studies of genius: Vol. I. Mental and physical traits of a thousand gifted children.* Stanford, CA: Stanford University Press.

Thomas, V. (1995). David and the family bane: Therapy with a gifted child and his family. *Journal of Family Psychology, 10*, 15–24.

Thomas, V., Ray, K. E., & Moon, S. M. (2007). A systems approach to counseling gifted individuals and their families. In S. Mendaglio & J. S. Peterson (Eds.), *Models of counseling gifted children, adolescents, and young adults* (pp. 69–96). Waco, TX: Prufrock Press.

Thompson, C. L., & Rudolph, L. B. (1996). *Counseling children* (4th ed.). Pacific Grove, CA: Brooks/Cole.

Tong, J., & Yewchuk, C. (1996). Self-concept and sex-role orientation in gifted high school students. *Gifted Child Quarterly, 40*, 15–23.

Van Boxtel, J. W., & Mönks, F. J. (1992). General, social, and academic self-concepts of gifted adolescents. *Journal of Youth and Adolescence, 21,* 169–186.

VanTassel-Baska, J. (2006). Secondary affective curriculum and instruction for gifted learners. In F. A. Dixon & S. M. Moon (Eds.), *The handbook of secondary gifted education* (pp. 481–503). Waco, TX: Prufrock Press.

VanTassel-Baska, J., & Olszewski-Kubilius, P. (Eds.). (1989). *Patterns of influence on gifted learners.* New York: Teachers College Press.

Webb, J. T., & DeVries, A. R. (1993). *Training manual for facilitators of SENG model guided discussion groups.* Scottsdale, AZ: SENG.

Webb, J. R., Amend, E. R., Webb, N. E., Goerss, J., Beljan, P., & Olenchak, F. R. (2005). *Misdiagnosis and dual diagnosis of gifted children and adults: ADHD, Bipolar, OCD, Asperger's, Depression, and other disorders.* Scottsdale, AZ: Great Potential Press.

Wendorf, D. J., & Frey, J. (1985). Family therapy with the intellectually gifted. *American Journal of Family Therapy, 13,* 31–38.

Werner, E. E. (1984). Resilient children. *Young Children, 40,* 68–72.

Whitmore, J. R. (1980). *Giftedness, conflict and underachievement.* Boston: Allyn & Bacon.

Yoo, J. E., & Moon, S. M. (2006). Counseling needs of gifted students: An analysis of intake forms at a university-based counseling center. *Gifted Child Quarterly, 50,* 52–61.

Ziegler, A., Finsterwald, M., & Grassinger, R. (2005). Learned helplessness among average and mildly gifted girls and boys attending initial high school physics instruction in Germany. *Gifted Child Quarterly, 49,* 7–18.

Ziegler, A., & Stoeger, H. (2007). The role of counseling in the development of gifted students' actiotopes: Theoretical background and exemplary application of the 11-SCC. In S. Mendaglio & J. S. Peterson (Eds.), *Models of counseling gifted children, adolescents, and young adults* (pp. 253–286). Waco, TX: Prufrock Press.

Zentall, S. S., Moon, S. M., Hall, A. M., & Grskovic, J. A. (2001). Learning and motivational characteristics of boys with AD/HD and/or giftedness. *Exceptional Children, 67,* 499–519.

Chapter 10

CREATIVITY ENHANCEMENT

Ronald A. Beghetto

reativity is a topic that has generated much interest, and for good reason. Creativity has been heralded as the highest form of human expression (Bandura, 1997), cited as the ultimate economic resource (Florida, 2004), and viewed as essential for addressing increasingly complex individual and societal issues (Plucker, Beghetto, & Dow, 2004; Runco, 2004a). As a result, researchers and educators have invested greatly in studying and developing programs aimed at enhancing student creativity. Although much work remains, there is compelling evidence that student creativity can be enhanced. In addition, researchers have identified several factors associated with successful enhancement efforts.

The aim of this chapter is to provide an overview of what is known about creativity enhancement. The chapter is organized into seven sections. First, key terms are listed and defined and then major questions addressed by research on creativity enhancement are discussed. Next, conclusions that can be drawn from creativity enhancement research are summarized.

Then, limitations and practical implications of creativity enhancement research are discussed. The chapter closes with a summary of what is known about creativity enhancement and a list of creativity research sources.

KEY TERMS USED IN CREATIVITY ENHANCEMENT RESEARCH

- *Creativity*: The ability to generate ideas, products, or solutions that are considered novel and useful for a given problem, situation, or context.
- *Creativity (Big C)*: Unambiguous creative contributions (e.g., music of Mozart, the inventions of Edison, the theories of Einstein, the social justice work of Martin Luther King, Jr. and Mother Teresa).
- *Creativity (Little c)*: Interpersonal, everyday creative contributions (e.g., a unique science fair project, a prize-winning poem at a local poetry contest).
- *Creativity (mini c)*: Intrapersonal, unique, and meaningful interpretations, conceptions, and insights (e.g., unique, personal understanding of a poem).
- *Creativity enhancement*: Formal educational efforts aimed at developing creative potential and producing creative outcomes.
- *Creative problem solving*: The ability to generate useful solutions to ill-defined or unique problems.
- *Convergent thinking*: The ability to evaluate and select the most appropriate or useful ideas, solutions, or products for a given problem, context, or situation.
- *Divergent thinking*: The ability to generate a wide array of novel ideas or solutions. Divergent thinking typically is subdivided into four components:
    - *originality* (the ability to generate novel or unique ideas and solutions),
    - *fluency* (the ability to generate many ideas and solutions),
    - *flexibility* (the ability to generate conceptually or categorically different ideas and solutions), and
    - *elaboration* (the capacity to provide detailed ideas or solutions).

MAJOR QUESTIONS ADDRESSED IN THE RESEARCH

Whether and how creativity can be enhanced is the driving question of creativity enhancement research. However, creativity scholars recognize that this question cannot be adequately addressed without first clearly developing an understanding of what is meant by creativity. Thus, scholars have focused on addressing three major questions aimed at clarifying the meaning of creativity:

- The definitional question: What is creativity?
- The magnitude question: What level of impact is necessary for a contribution to be considered creative?
- The domain question: Can someone be creative in more than one area?

Each of these questions will be addressed in the following sections.

What Is Creativity?

For more than 50 years, creativity researchers have worked on clarifying the meaning of creativity. A clear understanding of the nature of creativity is necessary for understanding, guiding, and evaluating creativity enhancement efforts. Although originality often is thought of as being synonymous with creativity, without the added criterion of appropriate or useful, it would be nearly impossible to "distinguish eccentric or schizophrenic thought from creative thought" (Feist, 1998, p. 290). Creativity researchers therefore distinguish creativity from that which is only original or out of the ordinary by adding the additional criterion of useful, appropriate, or relevant for a given context (Amabile, 1996; Plucker et al., 2004; Runco, 2004a).

Plucker and his colleagues (2004) provided the following synthesized definition, which represents attributes frequently represented in definitions of creativity found in the published literature: "Creativity is the interaction among aptitude, process, and environment by which an individual or group produces a perceptible product that is both novel and useful as defined within a social context" (p. 90). Clearly, this definition is not the final word on how creativity has or should be defined.[1] Still, the definition represents a general consensus of the key attributes of creativity and provides a basis for understanding the ultimate goal of creativity enhancement efforts, that is, increasing the capacity of students to produce novel and useful ideas, products, and solutions in a given context (e.g., a creative eighth-grade science fair project).

---

1 For instance, there is some debate as to whether creativity must take the form of perceptible product. Although a perceptible product (e.g., idea, behavior, poem, song, or painting) is extremely helpful and somewhat necessary for rendering a judgment on whether creativity has occurred, too much emphasis on product may undermine creative potential—particularly in children. Runco (2004a, 2004b) cautions that productivity is not synonymous with creativity. If creativity is defined to include productivity, then the focus is on those with high levels of productivity (e.g., Mozart) and the creative potential of those who are not necessarily productive (e.g., children) goes unrecognized (Runco, 2004b). Similarly Cramond (1994) has argued that although achievement (or productivity) may be a good way to decide who should be considered creative, it should not be used as an exclusionary criterion.

What Level of Impact Is Necessary for a Contribution to be Considered Creative?

The level of impact necessary for a contribution to be considered creative is an essential issue when considering whether and how creativity can be enhanced. Creativity scholars have distinguished three different levels of creative impact: Big-C, little-c and mini-c. *Big-C creativity* refers to the highest level of creative impact. Big-C research (e.g., Gardner, 1993; Simonton, 1984) focuses on individuals who have attained eminence in their respective field through a combination of staggering levels of productivity and lasting impact (e.g., Einstein, Mozart, Coltrane, Dickinson). Big-C research is important in that it provides insights into creative expression at the highest levels. However, Big-C work can, unintentionally, reinforce misconceptions about creativity. For instance, if creativity comes to be seen as only that which is of the Big-C level, then there is little room for recognizing the creative potential and production of noneminent individuals.

Fortunately, creativity scholars also recognize that everyday creativity also is important to consider (see Kaufman & Baer, 2006; Runco & Richards, 1998; Sternberg, Grigorenko, & Singer, 2004, for reviews). Indeed, just because someone's creative contribution is not revolutionary doesn't mean it is not creative. In this way, the novel and useful efforts of normal, everyday people are still, by definition, creative. This level of creativity is referred to as *little-c creativity* (e.g., a fourth-grade student's prize-winning drawing).

In addition to recognizing the existence of little-c creativity, creativity researchers recently have described a more personal level of creativity (Cohen, 1989; Runco, 2004b). Beghetto & Kaufman (2007) have referred to this level of creativity as *mini-c creativity*. Beghetto and Kaufman defined mini-c creativity as novel and personally meaningful interpretations of experiences, actions, and events. Mini-c creativity speaks to the creative aspects of learning and personal understanding (Beghetto & Kaufman, 2007; Beghetto & Plucker, 2006). Moreover, mini-c creativity highlights the developmental nature of creativity (Cohen, 1989; Sawyer et al., 2003) and suggests that all forms of later creative expression (both little-c and Big-C) start as novel and useful mini-c interpretations. In sum, a clear understanding of the various levels of creative impact (particularly mini-c and little-c) is necessary when evaluating the effectiveness of creativity enhancement efforts.

Can Someone Be Creative in More Than One Area?

If a student is creative in art, can he or she also be taught to be creative in science? The question of whether someone can be creative in many areas or just one has garnered much attention and debate amongst creativity scholars (see Baer, 1998; Kaufman & Baer, 2005; Plucker, 1998; Sternberg et al., 2004) and has important implications for creativity enhancement efforts. For instance, if a student's creativity is specific to a particular subject area, then enhancement programs might attain more success if they identify and target students' particular creative potentials rather than focus on more general cognitive skills (e.g., enhancing flexible thinking, elaboration, evaluation of ideas). On the other hand, if creativity is domain general, then it might be more efficient and effective to focus on general skills rather than expend the time and resources necessary for identifying and tailoring programs to students' particular creative potentialities.

This question of whether students can be creative in more than one area is thorny because it is connected to the level of creative impact being considered. For instance, if the focus is on Big-C creativity, then it seems unlikely that a student will achieve Big-C creative eminence across multiple domains. Although it is possible (e.g., Leonardo da Vinci, Thomas Edison), such examples are extremely rare. This is because, as Simonton (1984) has demonstrated, Big-C creative eminence generally requires a great deal of time invested in mastering a particular domain. Most people simply do not have the time and resources to develop the expertise and commitment necessarily to generate breakthroughs across multiple domains (e.g., art, science, dance, music).

There also is evidence that little-c creativity is limited to a single subject area or domain. For example, Baer (1991, 1993, 1994) has found that creative performance ratings, across different domains (e.g., poetry, story writing, creation of math puzzles, drawing) are weakly, if at all, related. Although this line of research provides support for domain specificity of little-c creativity (i.e., students seem to be creative in one domain rather than across domains), important domain general issues of creativity remain (e.g., the importance of environmental and personal supports for taking intellectual risks, the requisite intellectual skills and ability to generate novel ideas and select the most appropriate ideas). Also, given that students' academic interests and self-competence beliefs are still developing, caution is warranted when focusing too narrowly on a given academic context. This is because focusing too narrowly on one specific topic may result in lost opportunities for students to have experiences with creative thinking across different subject areas.

Creativity scholars have developed models of creativity that offer a more balanced perspective on how to think about the aspects of creativity specific to a domain and those aspects that contribute to creativity across domains (e.g., the componential model of creativity, Amabile 1983a, 1983b, 1996; the amusement park theoretical model, Kaufman & Baer, 2004; the hybrid model, Plucker & Beghetto, 2004). These more balanced perspectives stress the importance of enhancement efforts focusing on cultivating student skills, interest, and task commitment within domains while also recognizing the value of diverse experiences, flexible thinking, and cross-fertilization of ideas across various domains. Renzulli's (1994) Schoolwide Enrichment Model is an example of a school-based program that represents a hybrid position of domain generality and specificity.

CONCLUSIONS FROM THE CREATIVITY ENHANCEMENT RESEARCH

Research conducted over the past 50 years indicates that creativity can be enhanced through well-designed training programs and techniques (see Nickerson, 1999; Scott, Leritz, & Mumford, 2004, for recent reviews). However, this conclusion is not as clear as it may initially seem given the varying levels of creative impact, issues of domain specificity, and how creativity is defined. Consequently, the effects of training programs, processes, and techniques also vary with respect to the creative outcomes under consideration. In most cases, research on the effectiveness of creativity training has focused on divergent thinking outcomes (i.e., the ability to generate novel ideas) and outcomes associated with little-c creative problem solving, performance, and attitudes.

Table 1 summarizes[2] common elements of creativity enhancement programs found to be positively related to various creativity outcomes. Key findings with respect to each outcome also are highlighted in the sections that follow.

Divergent Thinking

Divergent thinking (DT) is a common focus and outcome of creativity training. DT represents a composite of subskills, including originality (the ability to generate novel ideas), fluency (the ability to generate many ideas and solutions), flexibility (the ability to generate conceptually or categorically different ideas and solutions), and elaboration (the capacity to provide detailed ideas or solutions).

As summarized in Table 1, research evidence suggests that gains in divergent thinking are linked with training programs that (a) take a cognitive focus; (b) use techniques to develop specific cognitive processes (e.g., idea generation, conceptual combination); and (c) teach specific thinking techniques and strategies (e.g., use of analogies, divergent and convergent thinking techniques).

In addition, the most effective approaches include programs of longer duration, those that apply a systematic model of training, and use a variety of instructional strategies (e.g., lectures, audio/visual media, individualized coaching). Importantly, divergent thinking can be undermined if training focuses too much on providing instructional feedback (Scott et al., 2004).

---

2   This summary is based on a recent, comprehensive meta-analysis of 70 prior studies of creativity conducted by Scott et al. (2004). Table 1 summarizes correlational findings from their quantitative meta-analysis. Importantly, only variables with a positive relationship with the effect size estimates of at least one outcome variable ($r > .10$) are represented in Table 1. Cells without checkmarks may include no relationship, negative relationships, or positive relationships ($r < .10$). Please refer to the full published report (Scott et al., 2004) for a more nuanced and comprehensive presentation of their study and findings. Inferences drawn from Table 1 should be done so with caution (and only after consulting the full research report of Scott et al., 2004).

T A B L E   1

Training Program Elements Related to Creativity Outcomes

Training Program Elements	Creativity Outcomes				
	Divergent Thinking	Creative Problem Solving	Creative Performance	Creative Attitude/ Behavior	Overall
Theoretical Approach					
Cognitive	√	√	—	√	√
Personality	—	—	√	—	—
Motivational	—	—	√	—	—
Confluence	—	—	√	—	—
Core Processes					
Problem identification	√	√	√	√	√
Information gathering	—	√	√	—	—
Information organization	—	√	√	√	√
Conceptual combination	√	√	—	√	√
Idea generation	√	√	√	√	√
Idea evaluation	—	√	—	√	—
Implementation planning	√	√	√	√	√
Solution monitoring	—	√	√	√	√
Techniques					
Divergent thinking	√	—	—	√	—
Convergent thinking	√	√	—	√	√
Critical thinking	—	√	—	√	√
Metacognition	—	√	—	—	√
Ideation	—	—	—	√	—
Constraint identification	√	√	√	√	√
Strength/weakness identification	√	—	—	√	—
Analogies	√	√	√	√	—
Brainstorming	—	√	—	√	—

Note. Material drawn from Scott et al. (2004). Overall = overall, cross-outcome index. √ = positive relationship.

Creative Problem Solving

Creative problem solving refers to the ability to generate original and useful solutions to novel or ill-defined problems. As summarized in Table 1, positive problem solving outcomes are associated with creativity training that uses structured models (e.g., Creative Problem Solving program, Isaksen & Treffinger, 2004); teaches specific cognitive processes (e.g., problem identification, idea evaluation, solution monitoring); and uses a blend of idea generation (e.g., brainstorming, analogies) and idea evaluation (e.g., convergent thinking, critical thinking) techniques. Also, the most effective training programs seem to afford opportunities to practice specific skills, receive instructional feedback, work with others, and actually focus on producing solutions to realistic problems. Training programs that use mass learning activities (rather than distributed) or focus on presenting information in a more holistic fashion seem to have a negative effect on creative problem solving outcomes (Scott et al., 2004). Similarly, Isaksen and Treffinger (2004) reported that the Creative Problem Solving program (CPS) is most effective when used thoughtfully and deliberatively, yet flexibly enough to respond to unique problem solving and contextual needs of individuals and groups.

Creative Performance

Creative performance represents the production of creative products. Positive creative performance outcomes are linked with enhancement programs that use a variety of theoretical frameworks (e.g., personality, motivational). Elements of successful training programs have been associated with: (a) a focus on specific processes (e.g., idea generation, solution monitoring); (b) the use of specific techniques and strategies (e.g., constraint identification, analogies); (c) the provision of instructional feedback in a rigorous, realistic practice-based experience; and (d) the use of a variety of instructional strategies (e.g., lecture, cases, social modeling) and exercises (e.g., classroom, field based, and performance/production). Notably, programs that focus on convergent thinking, idea evaluation, cooperative learning, or use less structured techniques (e.g., imaginative exercises) have been found to have a negative association with creative performance outcomes (Scott et al., 2004).

Creative Attitudes and Behaviors

Creative attitudes and behaviors represent outcomes such as individual reactions to creative ideas and the initiation of creative effort (Scott et al., 2004). Positive attitudinal and behavioral outcomes have been associated with training programs that take a cognitive focus and emphasize a variety of specific core processes (e.g., ideation generation, implementation planning). In addition, favorable outcomes have been associated with creativity training programs that: (a) apply specific techniques and skills training (e.g., brainstorming, analogies); (b) provide a rigorous experience; (c) use various instructional strategies (e.g., lecture, group work, cases); and (d) provide opportunities to engage in a wide variety of instructional exercises (e.g., classroom, field, performance, group). Favorable outcomes seem to be undermined by more holistic approaches to presenting information, too much instructional feedback, and less constrained techniques (e.g., imagery, expressive activities; Scott et al., 2004).

LIMITATIONS OF CREATIVITY ENHANCEMENT RESEARCH

Although the research available on the effectiveness of creativity training is persuasive, there are a few important conceptual and practical limitations to this research (Nickerson, 1999). Conceptually, there is still disagreement surrounding several core issues regarding the nature of creativity (e.g., domain general vs. domain specific), the criteria used to determine whether creativity has been enhanced (e.g., issues of impact, measurement issues), and potentially problematic beliefs about creativity that can lead to the abandonment or marginalization of even the most promising creativity enhancement efforts (see Beghetto & Plucker, 2006; Scott, 1999; Westby & Dawson, 1995).

A persistent limitation pertains to how creativity has been and continues to be assessed. As with all assessments, when it comes to assessing creativity, what you assess is essentially what you get. For instance, domain general features of creativity may not be recognized when creativity is assessed through a domain specific lens (and vise versa). In fact, Plucker (1998, 1999, 2004) has demonstrated that when researchers use more general psychometric measures (e.g., creativity checklists), creativity appears domain general. However, when researchers use more subjective and domain specific assessments (e.g., performance assessments), creativity appears domain specific. This "method effect" (Plucker, 2004) is an important consideration when interpreting findings surrounding the impact of creativity training.

In addition, Hunsaker and Callahan (1995) have highlighted key concerns regarding school assessments of student creativity. In particular, these scholars note that it is easy to use a creativity measurement instrument without taking the time to fully appreciate the complexity of the nature of creativity itself and the soundness of the methods being used to assess student creativity. Consequently, this may result in placing too much reliance on a single instrument or method for assessing creativity. This issue is important for educators and parents to recognize given the wide variety of creativity instruments and methods available to school personnel, including (but certainly not limited to): divergent thinking tests (e.g., Torrance Tests of Creative Thinking, Torrance, 1966); self-report checklists (e.g., Group Inventory for Finding Creative Talent, Rimm, 1980); teacher ratings of students (e.g., Scales for Rating the Behavioral Characteristics of Superior Students, Renzulli, Smith, White, Callahan, & Hartman, 1976); and instruments designed to evaluate the creativity of products (e.g., Creative Product Semantic Scale, O'Quin & Besemer, 1989).

No matter how well designed an assessment instrument, the information from such assessments can be misused both in making decisions about student creativity and in understanding the nature of creativity itself. Because of this, creativity researchers such as Cramond (1994) have asserted that the assessment of creativity should be multidimensional and use "any and all methods available to ascertain where children's strengths lie" (p. 70). This view is in alignment with Hunsaker and Callahan's (1995) admonition that educators should avoid relying on "one-quick-test approaches to assessing the creativity of students" (p. 110).

Another limitation of creativity enhancement research is, as Scott et al. (2004) note, the failure to include important and complex contextual factors (e.g., life histories, environmental opportunities, and more nuanced aspects of the instructional environment). The lack of studies is somewhat understandable given that such factors are difficult to measure and can be resource intensive. However, such factors, specifically the motivational messages sent by the environment, play an important role in determining the ultimate success of any creativity effort (Beghetto, 2005). Consider, for example, a classroom creative problem solving session in which students are encouraged to postpone initial judgment of ideas, but in actuality there is an underlying motivational climate that impedes intellectual risk-taking. It wouldn't be surprising if even the most highly creative students would be hesitant to share their ideas when they face persistent eye-rolling, giggling from peers, and dismissal of their unique ideas from teachers. Researchers will need to include such important contextual factors in their studies to better understand how such factors influence creativity training, the outcomes of that training, and the sustainability of that training.

Finally, there is a need for additional studies that synthesize and summarize research and theory on creativity and creativity enhancement, such as the meta-analysis conducted by Scott et al. (2004) and the descriptive review provided by Nickerson (1999). In addition, longitudinal and mixed-method studies that blend quantitative and more fine-grained qualitative approaches will be necessary for developing a deeper understanding of the individual experiences and broader and long-term outcomes of creativity enhancement. In this way, important questions about the outcomes of creativity enhancement can be addressed (e.g., Do students who receive consistent, high-quality creativity training go on to make important creative contributions in their future careers?).

PRACTICAL IMPLICATIONS OF CREATIVITY ENHANCEMENT RESEARCH

The practical implications that follow from creativity enhancement research should be considered in light of an important caveat: "Best practices" and implications drawn from research must be considered in light of what is "best" for whom, in what context, under what conditions, and at what cost. With this caveat in mind, there are several general implications that can be drawn from research on creativity enhancement.

- *Successful creativity enhancement efforts are guided by clear goals.* Given that creativity enhancement efforts can lead to a variety of creativity related outcomes, it is important that the goals of any enhancement effort are clearly specified and understood by all participants. This includes ensuring that there is a clear understanding of the meaning of creativity itself. This is particularly important in school settings because teachers' beliefs about creativity influence the expectations they hold for students, as well as the way in which they design educational experiences. Educators and parents committed to promoting creativity are advised to ensure that creativity enhancement efforts are guided by clear goals and sound conceptions of creativity.

- *Successful creativity enhancement efforts are based on sound methods.* Although there are no sure-fire recipes for success when it comes to creativity enhancement, the research on successful programs points to procedures that will increase the likelihood of success. Scott et al. (2004) summarize the following considerations for the delivery of cognitively based creativity training programs: (1) training programs should be based on sound conceptions of the cognitive activities underlying creativity, (2) training should be rigorous and lengthy, focusing on specific cognitive skills and strategies and how those skills and strategies lead to specific creative outcomes, (3) strategies and principles should be illustrated using realistic cases and instructional strategies (e.g., cooperative learning), and (4) trainings should include a variety of exercises in which strategies can be applied in appropriate domains and complex, realistic contexts. In addition to considering what strategies and techniques have been positively linked with creative outcomes, educators and parents are advised to not lose sight of the complex (and sometimes contradictory) nature of creativity enhancement. For instance, it is important to recognize that a particular enhancement strategy (e.g., frequent instructional feedback) can be positively linked with some creative outcomes (e.g., creative performance) and, at the same time, potentially undermine other creative outcomes (e.g., divergent thinking).

- *Successful creativity enhancement efforts ensure that the broader educational environment supports creativity.* No matter how successful a creativity enhancement program, gains made in training programs will be lost if a student's broader educational environments are not supportive of creativity. Indeed, school and classroom environments play an important role in whether students' creativity will be supported (Beghetto, 2005, 2006a, 2007). For instance, Beghetto (2006b) found that middle and secondary students' reports of teachers providing positive feedback on their creativity was the strongest unique predictor of students' beliefs in their own creativity. As such, educators have a responsibility to actively consider how the motivational messages sent by school and classroom policies, practices, and procedures support or undermine student creativity.

SUMMARY OF WHAT WE KNOW ABOUT CREATIVITY ENHANCEMENT

- Creativity training programs are effective in influencing a variety of creativity-related outcomes (e.g., divergent thinking, creative problem solving, creative performance, creative attitudes and behaviors).
- Different aspects of training programs influence creativity outcomes in differential (and sometimes opposite) ways (e.g., frequent instructional feedback can promote creative problem solving and performance, yet undermine divergent thinking).
- Creativity training programs are most effective when they use sound methods, models, and techniques and provide opportunities to apply those techniques and strategies in realistic contexts.
- Creativity enhancement efforts will be undermined to the extent that they are not based on clear conceptions of creativity and are not situated in a broader educational environment that is supportive of student creativity.
- Several important questions about creativity enhancement remain unanswered (e.g., questions of domain specificity, how to best assess creativity, and the long-term outcomes of creativity training). Therefore, parents and educators must continually stay abreast with advances in research and consider implications for the specific context and population of students.

RESOURCES AND REFERENCES FOR RESEARCH ON CREATIVITY ENHANCEMENT

Edited Volumes

Borland, J. H. (Ed.). (2003). *Rethinking gifted education.* New York: Teachers College Press.

Fishkin, A. S., Cramond, B., & Olszewski-Kubilius, P. (Eds.). (1999). *Investigating creativity in youth.* Cresskill, NJ: Hampton Press

Houtz, J. C. (Ed.). (2003). *The educational psychology of creativity.* Cresskill, NJ: Hampton Press.

Kaufman, J. C., & Bear, J. (Eds.). (2006). *Creativity and reason in cognitive development.* New York: Cambridge University Press.

Runco, M. A. (2007). *Creativity theories and themes: Research, development and practice.* Burlington, MA: Elsevier Academic Press.

Runco, M. A., & Pritzker, S. R. (Eds.). (1999). *Encyclopedia of creativity*. San Diego, CA: Academic Press.

Sternberg, R. J. (Ed.). (1999). *Handbook of creativity*. New York: Cambridge University Press.

Sternberg, R. J., Grigorenko, E. L., & Singer, J. L. (Eds.). (2004). *Creativity: From potential to realization*. Washington, DC: American Psychological Association.

Creativity-Related Journals

Creativity Research Journal (Lawrence Erlbaum)

Gifted Child Quarterly (National Association for Gifted Children)

High Ability Studies (Routledge)

Journal of Creative Behavior (Creative Education Foundation)

Korean Journal of Thinking & Problem Solving (Korean Association for Thinking Development)

Psychology of Aesthetics, Creativity, and the Arts (American Psychological Association)

Roeper Review (Roeper School)

REFERENCES

Amabile, T. M. (1983a). *The social psychology of creativity*. New York: Springer.

Amabile, T. M. (1983b). Social psychology of creativity: A componential conceptualization. *Journal of Personality and Social Psychology, 45*, 357–377.

Amabile, T. M. (1996). *Creativity in context: Update to the social psychology of creativity*. Boulder, CO: Westview.

Baer, J. (1991). Generality of creativity across performance domains. *Creativity Research Journal, 4*, 23–39.

Baer, J. (1993). *Divergent thinking and creativity: A task-specific approach*. Hillsdale, NJ: Erlbaum.

Baer, J. (1994). Divergent thinking is not a general trait: A multi-domain training experiment. *Creativity Research Journal, 7*, 35–46.

Baer, J. (1998). The case for domain specificity of creativity. *Creativity Research Journal, 11*, 173–177.

Bandura, A. (1997). *Self-efficacy: The exercise of control*. New York: Freeman.

Beghetto, R. A. (2005). Does assessment kill student creativity? *The Educational Forum, 69*, 254–263.

Beghetto, R. A. (2006a). Creative justice? The relationship between prospective teachers' prior schooling experiences and perceived importance of promoting student creativity. *Journal of Creative Behavior, 40*, 149–162.

Beghetto, R. A. (2006b). Creative self-efficacy: Correlates in middle and secondary students. *Creativity Research Journal, 18*, 447–457.

Beghetto, R. A. (2007). Does creativity have a place in classroom discussions? Prospective teachers' response preferences. *Thinking Skills and Creativity, 2*, 1–9.

Beghetto, R. A., & Kaufman, J. C. (2007). Toward a broader conception of creativity: A case for mini-c creativity. *Psychology of Aesthetics, Creativity, and the Arts, 1*, 73–79.

Beghetto, R. A., & Plucker, J. A. (2006). The relationship among schooling, learning, and creativity: "All roads lead to creativity" or "You can't get there from here"? In J. C. Kaufman & J. Baer (Eds.), *Creativity and reason in cognitive development* (pp. 316–332). Cambridge, England: Cambridge University Press.

Cohen, L. M. (1989). A continuum of adaptive creative behaviors. *Creativity Research Journal, 2*, 169–183.

Cramond, B. (1994). We can trust creativity tests. *Educational Leadership, 52*(2), 70–71.

Feist, G. J. (1998). A meta-analysis of personality in scientific and artistic creativity. *Personality and Social Psychology Review, 2*, 290–309.

Florida, R. (2004). *The rise of the creative class: And how it's transforming work, leisure, community and everyday life.* New York: Basic Books.

Gardner, H. (1993). *Creative minds.* New York: Basic Books.

Hunsaker, S. L., & Callahan, C. M. (1995). Creativity and giftedness: Published instrument uses and abuses. *Gifted Child Quarterly, 39*, 110–114.

Isaksen, S. G., & Treffinger, D. J. (2004). Celebrating 50 years of reflective practice: Versions of creative problem solving. *Journal of Creative Behavior, 38*, 75–101.

Kaufman, J. C., & Baer, J. (2004). The Amusement Park Theoretical (APT) model of creativity. *Korean Journal of Thinking and Problem Solving, 14*(2), 15–25.

Kaufman, J. C., & Baer, J. (Eds.). (2005). *Creativity across domains: Faces of the muse.* Mahwah, NJ: Lawrence Erlbaum.

Kaufman, J. C., & Baer, J. (Eds.). (2006). *Creativity and reason in cognitive development.* Cambridge, England: Cambridge University Press.

Nickerson, R. S. (1999). Enhancing creativity. In R. J. Sternberg (Ed.), *Handbook of human creativity* (pp. 392–430). New York: Cambridge University Press.

O'Quin, K., & Besemer, S. P. (1989). The development, reliability, and validity of the revised creative product semantic scale. *Creativity Research Journal, 2*, 267–278.

Plucker, J. A. (1998). Beware of simple conclusions: The case for content generality of creativity. *Creativity Research Journal, 11*, 179–182.

Plucker, J. A. (1999). Reanalyses of student responses to creativity checklists: Evidence of content generality. *Journal of Creative Behavior, 33*, 126–137.

Plucker, J. A. (2004). Generalization of creativity across domains: Examination of the method effect hypothesis. *Journal of Creative Behavior, 38*, 1–12.

Plucker, J. A., & Beghetto, R. A. (2004). Why creativity is domain general, why it looks domain specific, and why the distinction doesn't matter. In R. J. Sternberg, E. L. Grigorenko, & J. L. Singer (Eds.), *Creativity: From potential to realization* (pp. 153–168). Washington, DC: American Psychological Association.

Plucker, J. A., Beghetto, R. A., & Dow, G. T. (2004). Why isn't creativity more important to educational psychologists? Potentials, pitfalls, and future directions in creativity research. *Educational Psychologist, 39*, 83–96.

Renzulli, J. S. (1994). *Schools for talent development: A practical plan for total school improvement.* Mansfield Center, CT: Creative Learning Press.

Renzulli, J. S., Smith, L. H., White, A. J., Callahan, C. M., & Hartman, R. K. (1976). *Scales for rating the behavioral characteristics of superior students.* Mansfield Center, CT: Creative Learning Press.

Rimm, S. B. (1980). *Group inventory for finding creative talent (GIFT)*. Waterton, WI: Educational Assessment Service.

Runco, M. A. (2004a). Creativity. *Annual Review of Psychology, 55*, 657–687.

Runco, M. A. (2004b). Everyone has creative potential. In R. J. Sternberg, E. L. Grigorenko, & J. L. Singer (Eds.), *Creativity: From potential to realization* (pp. 21–30). Washington, DC: American Psychological Association.

Runco, M. A., & Richards, R. (Eds.). (1998). *Eminent creativity, everyday creativity, and health*. Norwood, NJ: Ablex.

Sawyer, R. K., John-Steiner, V., Moran, S., Sternberg, R., Feldman, D. H., Csikszentmihalyi, M., et al. (2003). *Creativity and development*. New York: Oxford University Press.

Scott, C. L. (1999). Teachers' biases toward creative children. *Creativity Research Journal, 12*, 321–328.

Scott, G., Leritz, L. E., & Mumford, M. D. (2004). The effectiveness of creativity training: A quantitative review. *Creativity Research Journal, 16*, 361–388.

Simonton, D. K. (1984). *Genius, creativity, and leadership: Historiometric inquiries*. Cambridge, MA: Harvard University Press.

Sternberg, R. J., Grigorenko, E. L., & Singer, J. L. (Eds.). (2004). *Creativity: From potential to realization*. Washington, DC: American Psychological Association.

Torrance, E. P. (1966). *Torrance tests of creative thinking: Norms technical manual*. Princeton, NJ: Personnel.

Westby, E. L., & Dawson, V. L. (1995). Creativity: Asset or burden in the classroom. *Creativity Research Journal, 8*, 1–10.

Chapter 11

CRITICAL THINKING

Brenda Linn and Bruce M. Shore

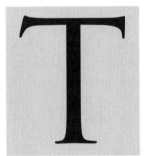he term *critical thinking*, as used in education, is frequently defined in a strikingly circular way, as "thinking critically," "reflecting critically," or "thinking reflectively." It also is frequently used to suggest an actively skeptical stance, and occasionally conflated with critical theory or critical pedagogy (Freire, 1973). But, whereas critical theory and critical pedagogy emphasize the analysis of ideas in terms of their relation to social power structures, critical thinking is concerned with the evaluation of ideas in terms of their logical and empirical foundations. The word *critical* comes from the Greek verb *krinein,* meaning to judge or evaluate. The addition of *thinking* adds a second element: the use of reason as the means of evaluation. In cognitive science and cognitive psychology, critical thinking tends to be used almost interchangeably with rational thinking or, simply, with rationality, especially those applications of rationality that have to do with evaluation.

Stanovich (2004) characterized critical (or rational, or analytical, or "System 2") thinking as rule-based, conscious, relatively slow, serial, resource-intensive, controlled, decontextualized, and acquired by cultural transmission and formal learning. He contrasted it with "System 1," which is really a set of systems that operate in an associative, parallel, automatic, often modular way. System 1, or The Autonomous Set of Systems (TASS), is relatively undemanding of cognitive capacity, relatively fast, and is acquired from biology, exposure, and personal experience. Although at times TASS arrives at the same conclusions as System 2 thinking, the processes supported by TASS tend to be based on domain-specific, automatic, and relatively low-level heuristics and on contextualized knowledge.

The distinction between System 1 and System 2, or something very close to it, has been drawn by many cognitive psychologists and cognitive scientists. Perhaps the best known of these is Fodor's (1983) distinction between modular processes and central processes, but a similar distinction is drawn by many other researchers, who identify an automatic, heuristic-based, tacit, gist, fuzzy trace, or holistic processing system on the one hand, and a systematic, rational, explicit, or analytical processing system on the other (Brainerd & Reyna, 2001; Chaiken, Liberman, & Ragly, 1989; Epstein, 1994; Evans, 1984, 1989; Evans & Over, 1996; Evans & Wason, 1976; Frankl, 1946/1973; Gibbard, 1990; Johnson-Laird, 1983; Klein, 1998; Levinson, 1995; Norman & Shallice, 1986; Posner & Snyder, 1975; Reber, 1993; Slomans, 1996; Sternberg, 2000). Although these dichotomies do not coincide on all points, they all point to the existence of two separate systems—almost two separate minds—within the human brain. One of these minds, or sets of systems, is what popular culture thinks of as intuitive, holistic, spontaneous, even reflexive; it is the locus of intelligence, as usually understood, and yet it is capable of reacting in deeply unintelligent ways (Sternberg, 2002). The second system is conscious, analytical, intentional, reflective, and relatively slow, but it supports rationality, and makes us capable of overriding the built-in biases of the older, more automatic System 1 (Stanovich, 1999).

In the context of this body of research and discussion, critical thinking may be understood as that application of System 2 primarily concerned with (a) evaluating evidence and argument, (b) evaluating and choosing a course of action, (c) evaluating goals, and (d) evaluating its own powers of evaluation (meta-rationality).

The evaluation of evidence entails what has been termed *epistemic rationality*—the ability to assess truth and validity, whereas the evaluation of courses of action also entails *practical or instrumental rationality*—the ability to predict the probable outcome of a course of action and evaluate it in terms of desired or desirable goals. The critical evaluation of goals entails a "broad" view of rationality (Nathanson, 1994), whereas a "thin" view of rationality simply accepts goals as givens and reasons from there.

CRITICAL THINKING IN EDUCATION

In the educational literature, some definitions of critical thinking avoid the trap of circularity and are compatible with the newly emerging understanding of rationality. Ennis (1987), for example, defined critical thinking as "reasonable, reflective thinking that is focused on what to believe or do" (p. 12). Ennis's taxonomy of critical thinking skills was in large measure an elaboration of the higher levels of Bloom's taxonomy (Bloom, Engelhart, Furst, Hill, & Krathwohl, 1956), though taken in a more practical, decision-oriented context. Davis and Rimm (1998), writing specifically in the context of gifted education, also focused on (a) evaluating an argument or (b) evaluating a course of action. However, theories of critical thinking that predate the two-system models of rationality do not address the way in which classic critical thinking strategies can be co-opted by TASS processes such as belief bias (Stanovich, 1999), if-only bias (Epstein, Lipson, Lostein, & Huh, 1992), or confirmation bias (Nickerson, 1998). Nor do they confront directly the challenges that have been posed by research in cognitive development (Brown, Collins, & Duguid, 1989; Lave & Wenger, 1991; Rogoff & Lave, 1984) and in evolutionary psychology (Pinker, 1997). Some of these challenges are considered in the next section of this discussion.

QUESTIONS CENTRAL TO RESEARCH IN THE FIELD OF CRITICAL THINKING

Recent research in critical thinking, especially the research that works from the two-system model, has not yet been applied to any great extent in the specific context of gifted education. However, basic critical thinking research has direct implications for the teaching of gifted students. It has been driven by two general questions that bear directly on the relationship between intelligence or giftedness and critical thinking. The first of these is, why do intelligent people believe and do such foolish things (Sternberg, 2002) and the second is, what can be done about it (Stanovich, 2004)? From the apparent paradox of foolish behavior in intelligent people, critical thinking researchers have derived a number of specific research questions that we have attempted to summarize. Stanovich (1999, 2004, 2007, in press) has presented a particularly comprehensive overview, based not only on his extensive research program but also upon converging evidence from a very wide variety of other sources. We shall therefore refer to this research frequently in the discussion that follows.

Is critical thinking really preferable to domain-specific heuristic-based thinking? One possible explanation of the fact that people, even highly intelligent people, often do not evaluate their beliefs or actions in rational, systematic ways might be that rational System 2 analysis is not really preferable to heuristic-based System 1 processing. This argument has some empirical foundations. Researchers in cognitive development (Brown et al., 1989; Lave & Wenger, 1991: Rogoff & Lave, 1984) have taken the evidence of human irrationality found in the heuristics and biases literature (Johnson-Laird, 1982, 1983; Kahneman & Tversky, 1973; Wason, 1960) and reinterpreted it as evidence of efficient strategizing. More recently, evolutionary psychologists including Pinker (1997) and Tooby and Cosmides (1992) have shown that heuristic-based reasoning has certain adaptive advantages. This conclusion is consistent with findings from the expertise research, which showed that experts tend to use domain-specific heuristics, whereas novices prefer domain-general strategies (Newell & Simon, 1972; Simon & Simon, 1978). All extrapolations from experts to beginners are, of course, problematic. More problematic, however, is the finding that students of higher cognitive ability tend to use analytic processes when heuristic-based processing would lead to biases and errors. Higher ability subjects are less likely to allow domain-specific world knowledge to interfere with argument evaluation, verbal reasoning, evidence selection, or statistical reasoning in any of the standard heuristics and biases paradigms (Stanovich, 2004).

The two-system models of thinking described at the beginning of this chapter were advanced as a way of reconciling the competing claims of heuristic-based and analytical thinking. According to two-system models, both kinds of thinking have their place and value. Each is optimal in certain situations. This insight permits a partial answer to the question with which we began. Intelligent people think or behave foolishly when they fail to override System 1 in situations requiring System 2 processing. They also may be seen as behaving foolishly when they override System 1 where its intuitive, parallel, very rapid processing is exactly what the situation requires (Stanovich, 1999, 2004).

To what extent is critical thinking ability related to IQ? In developing critical thinking skills, gifted students have something of a head start. On laboratory tasks of critical thinking, such as argument evaluation and statistical reasoning, students of higher cognitive ability tend to perform better than those of average ability. The crucial word here, however, is *tend*. The correlation between intelligence and normative performance on reasoning tasks is about .5 (Cacioppo, Petty, Feinstein, & Jarvis, 1996; Kardash & Scholes, 1996; Klaczynski, Gordon, & Fauth, 1997; Perkins, 1995; Schommer, 1990; Stanovich, in press). The correlation between SAT scores and critical thinking also is imperfect, accounting for just more than 25% of the variance on composite measures of reasoning performance (Stanovich, 1999). In other words, high IQ facilitates but by no means guarantees rationality (Stanovich, 2002) or wisdom (Sternberg, 2004). Particularly in the evaluation of goals, intellectual capacity alone may simply enable bright people to get "what they don't want, much faster" (Baron, 1985, p. 5; also see Stanovich, 2004). Newspapers are full of instances of Ivy League graduates making astonishingly poor decisions regarding the governance of their country (Sternberg, 2002). Students of high intelligence are perhaps more likely to master the principles of critical thinking with ease, but we cannot assume that they will discover and also apply them spontaneously.

What other factors affect the rationality of people's judgment and therefore their ability to think critically? Because cognitive capacity is not very malleable and does not guarantee rationality, researchers have looked for other factors that facilitate or hinder students' ability to think. These factors include a number of "thinking dispositions" (Ennis, 1987; Stanovich, 1999), "inferential propensities" (Kitcher, 1993), or "habits of mind" (Keating, 1990). Thinking dispositions that facilitate critical thinking include willingness to postpone closure, to consider alternative opinions, and to consider contradictory evidence, as well as active open-minded thinking, and the need for cognition. Dispositions that interfere with critical thinking include absolutism, dogmatism, categorical thinking, superstitious thinking, counterfactual thinking, and belief identification. These dispositions account for individual differences in reasoning beyond those explained by measures of intelligence, and they do so across a wide variety of domains (Kardash & Sholes, 1996; Klaczynski, 2001; Stanovich, 1999). Whereas cognitive capacity affects our ability to work with abstractions, thinking dispositions seem to affect our ability, or willingness, to abstract—that is, to decontextualize or disentangle the salient points of a problem from interfering context, prior opinion, irrelevant world knowledge, vivid but unrepresentative examples, and the like. Students of higher cognitive ability are more likely than others to decontextualize successfully, but their success is mediated by their thinking dispositions, which seem to be at least in part a matter of volition rather than of ability *per se*. High-ability students, for instance, were more able than lower ability students to break the response set on a series of water-jar mixture problems when the previously successful strategy was no longer optimal; on some problems before the set-breaking task, either the old or new strategy would work. The more-able students were slower on those problems and their talk-aloud protocols revealed that they had been monitoring the task demands and their response alternatives and were aware of the choice (Dover & Shore, 1991; Shore, Koller, & Dover, 1994). But, not all students chose to apply their insight that a new strategy would now be more efficient. Whether or not they used the new strategy when it was optional depended on other questions, likely including their own thinking dispositions and assumptions about the experimenters' expectations.

To what extent can critical thinking be taught and learned? Although IQ and thinking dispositions together are quite strongly related to critical thinking ability, they do not, even in combination, guarantee that students will be good critical thinkers. Critical thinking and rationality, as System 2 processes, depend heavily upon formal learning. Both critical thinking skills and dispositions can and must be taught, yet on the whole they are not being taught in most school curricula, including those intended for highly able students. In mathematics and science programs, especially those designed for the gifted, students learn to solve abstract problems. They do not, however, learn to discern and abstract the core elements from contextualized problems. This may account for the fact that correlations between university students' mathematics and statistics background and their composite scores on a range of reasoning tasks, including statistical reasoning tasks, have been found to be very low indeed (from $r = .125$ to $.162$; Stanovich, 2002).

Although the literature on the teaching of rational thinking is still rather sparse, some researchers have begun to work out the practical implications of current research (e.g., Adams, 1989; Anderson, Reder, & Simon, 1996; Baron & Brown, 1991; Beyth-Marom, Fischoff, Quadrel, & Furby, 1991; Lipman, 1991; Mann, Harmoni, & Power, 1991; Nickerson, 1998; Nisbett, 1993; Paul, Binker, Martin, & Adamson, 1989; Perkins, 1995; Perkins & Grotzer, 1997; Stanovich, 2004; Swartz & Perkins, 1989; Williams et al., 1996). Other insights into critical thinking instruction are to be found in the thinking-disposition studies mentioned earlier. These include the need to precisely identify the thinking strategies and dispositions implicated in a given type of problem.

Should the teaching of critical thinking skills be domain specific, domain general, or both? Anderson et al. (1996) identified a number of claims against domain-general teaching that purport to be derived from cognitive psychology. These included (a) the claim that action always is grounded in the concrete situation in which it occurs, (b) the claim that knowledge does not transfer between tasks, and (c) the claim that training by abstraction is of little use. They then offered ample empirical evidence for the opposite view, namely, that (a) action can be based on abstract principles; (b) knowledge does transfer, or can be made to transfer, between domains, provided that those domains share common cognitive components; and (c) training by abstraction, supported by practice in a number of contexts and across a number of domains, is frequently the most efficient and lasting form of instruction. Anderson and colleagues' answer to the question of whether domain-general thinking skills can be taught and whether they are worth the trouble was, in both cases, an unequivocal yes. Their evidence supports Davis and Rimm's (1998) contention that, in gifted education, critical thinking should be taught both as a subject of study in its own right and also as an integral part of other subjects across the curriculum.

GENERAL CONCLUSIONS FROM RESEARCH ON CRITICAL THINKING

In summary, critical thinking researchers have built a very strong case for the existence of two separate thinking systems, one that operates more or less automatically, and one that requires both education and intention. Although both kinds of thinking have their place, it is the second, more intentional system that enables us to evaluate knowledge, argument, evidence, actions, or goals in an optimal way. Reasoning biases can be independent of IQ. Thus, although highly intelligent students have a computational advantage, they still need to master the principles that underlie critical thinking and to develop thinking dispositions that foster rather than impair rationality. This mastery and development is mostly likely to take place when thinking skills and thinking dispositions are taught in both domain-general and domain-specific contexts.

Limitations

Although the basic research in critical thinking and rationality provides an excellent framework for teaching critical thinking skills and dispositions, the efficacy of different approaches to instruction at different age and ability levels has not been studied in detail. The possible interactive relationship between critical thinking and heuristic processing also is worthy of further examination. It is clear from decades of research in reading acquisition that what begins as System 2 processing—rule-based, conscious, serial, intentional, and effortful—can with time and practice become automatized and assimilated into the rapid, parallel, and effortless System 1. Whether, and how, such assimilation might take place in other domains and content areas is yet to be established.

Practical Implications

With some caveats, research vindicates the teaching of critical thinking skills, including those traditionally entailed in the study of rhetoric, the study of logic, the study of inductive reasoning, and the scientific method. The principal caveat is that some aspects of the teaching of critical thinking need to be revisited and fine-tuned in order to accommodate recent findings in the field. The kind of fine-tuning that is needed can best be illustrated by examining the kind of curriculum that was proposed in the 1980s. We shall use Ennis' (1987) curriculum as an example, not because of its weaknesses, but rather because it is carefully constructed and rather strong. Ennis began by identifying what he called critical thinking dispositions, including asking a question, asking for clarification, and acquiring relevant background knowledge. These things might indeed be regarded as dispositions, if by that term we mean habits of effective thinkers. They do not, however, correspond to what Stanovich and his colleagues mean by thinking dispositions, namely, individual differences in cognitive flexibility, need for cognition, susceptibility to various kinds of bias, and the ability to decontextualize. Rather, they seem to correspond to elements in the general process of inquiry or of logical argument. Such advice as, "Try to be well informed," "Use and mention credible sources," and "Take the whole situation into account," are elaborated in Ennis' list of "abilities" or competencies, in which he presented criteria for evaluating information, evaluating sources, and ensuring one has considered all sides of a problem. The difficulty is that people typically believe they are, in fact, following these criteria, even as they are committing serious errors in rational thought. This is not, of course, a reason to omit teaching the criteria; such an inference would itself constitute an error in critical thinking of a type all too common in education—the tendency to scrap a practice altogether either because it was not effective with all students, or because its effectiveness was diminished by glitches in its application (Anderson et al., 1996; Stanovich, 2003). The traditional criteria are still important, but they must be reinforced with practice in recognizing task characteristics and thinking dispositions that lead us to deviate from those criteria without knowing it.

The traditional approach to the teaching of critical thinking skills and of thinking skills generally (Davis & Rimm, 1998; Ennis, 1987; Novak, 1988) needs to be reinforced on at least two fronts. First, students can be taught to recognize the kinds of tasks, and the sorts of traps, that trip people up in both theoretical and in practical situations. Second, students can be taught to recognize the thinking dispositions that affect our ability to evaluate evidence in an analytical and objective way. Gifted students are less concerned about whether the material they are learning is couched in terms of practical relevance, and they prefer a higher level of cognitive complexity. They are likely, therefore, to enjoy learning about tricky tasks, deceptive arguments, and misleading kinds of evidence more than students who are less able to think abstractly and metacognitively (hannah & Shore, 1995). Less enjoyable for gifted students may be the process of critically analyzing their own thinking dispositions. Many may find "need for cognition" is one of their strengths, this disposition having been reflected in the process by which they were designated gifted in the first place. Many, however, may find just the opposite: The ability to arrive at the expected answer, rather than to wrestle with problems and formulate objective and defensible solutions, may have dominated the process by which their giftedness was identified. This discovery may be initially unpalatable, as may be the discovery of dispositions within themselves that interfere with critical thinking and rationality. Students are likely to become more willing to grapple with these dispositions as they learn more about meta-rationality, and in particular, about the human capacity to override automatic System 1 biases when they conflict with the promptings of our deepest and most reflective selves (Stanovich, 2004).

REFERENCES

Adams, M. J. (1989). Thinking skills curricula: Their promise and progress. *Educational Psychologist, 24,* 25–77.

Anderson, R., Reder, L., & Simon, H. A. (1996). Situated learning in education. *Educational Researcher, 25*(4), 5–11.

Baron, J. (1985). *Rationality and intelligence.* New York: Cambridge University Press.

Baron, J., & Brown, R. V. (Eds.). (1991). *Teaching decision making to adolescents.* Hillsdale, NJ: Lawrence Erlbaum.

Beyth-Marom, R., Fischoff, B., Quadrel, M., & Furby, L. (1991). Teaching decision-making to adolescents: A critical review. In J. Baron & R. V. Brown (Eds.), *Teaching decision making to adolescents* (pp. 19–59). Hillsdale, NJ: Lawrence Erlbaum.

Bloom, B. S., Engelhart, M. D., Furst, E. J., Hill, W. H., & Krathwohl, D. R. (1956). *Taxonomy of educational objectives. The classification of educational goals. Handbook I: Cognitive domain.* New York: McKay.

Brown, J. S., Collins, A., & Duguid, P. (1989). Situated cognition and the culture of learning. *Educational Researcher, 18*(1), 34–41.

Brainerd, C. J., & Reyna, V. F. (2001). Fuzzy trace theory: Dual processes in memory reasoning and cognitive neuroscience. In H. W. Reese & R. Kail (Eds.), *Advances in child development and behavior* (Vol. 28, pp. 41–100). San Diego, CA: Academic Press.

Cacioppo, J. T., Petty, R. E., Feinstein, J., & Jarvis, W. (1996). Dispositional differences in cognitive motivation: Life and times of individuals varying in need for cognition. *Psychological Bulletin, 119,* 197–253.

Chaiken, S., Liberman, A., & Ragly, A. H. (1989). Heuristic and systematic information within and beyond the persuasion context. In J. S. Uleman & J. A. Baugh (Eds.), *Unintended thought* (pp. 212–252). New York: Guilford Press.

Davis, G. A., & Rimm, S. B. (1998). *Education of the gifted and talented* (4th ed.). Needham Heights, MA: Allyn & Bacon.

Dover, A. C., & Shore, B. M. (1991). Giftedness and flexibility on a mathematical set-breaking task. *Gifted Child Quarterly, 35,* 99–105.

Ennis, R. H. (1987). A taxonomy of critical thinking disposition and abilities. In J. Baron & R. J. Sternberg (Eds.), *Teaching thinking skills: Theory and practice* (pp. 9–26). New York: Freeman.

Epstein, S. (1994). Integration of the psychodynamic and the cognitive unconscious. *American Psychologist, 49,* 709–724.

Epstein, S., Lipson, A., Lostein, C., & Huh, E. (1992). Irrational reactions to negative outcomes: Evidence for two conceptual systems. *Journal of Personality and Social Psychology, 62,* 328–339.

Evans, J. St. B. T. (1984). Heuristic and analytic processes in reasoning. *British Journal of Psychology, 75,* 451–468.

Evans, J. St. B. T. (1989). *Bias in human reasoning: Causes and consequences.* London: Lawrence Erlbaum.

Evans, J. St. B. T., & Over, D. E. (1996). *Rationality in reasoning.* Hove, England: Psychology Press.

Evans, J. St. B. T., & Wason, P. C. (1976). Rationalization in a reasoning task. *British Journal of Psychology, 67,* 479–486.

Fodor, J. (1983). *Modularity of mind.* Cambridge, MA: MIT Press.

Frankl, V. E. (1973). *The doctor and the soul: From psychotherapy to logotherapy.* New York: Vintage. (Original work published 1946 as *Ärztliche Seelsorge*; R. Winston & C. Winston, Trans.)

Freire, P. (1973). *Pedagogy of the oppressed.* New York: Seabury.

Gibbard, A. (1990). *Wise choices, apt feelings: A theory of normative judgment.* Cambridge, MA: Harvard University Press.

hannah, c. l., & Shore, B. M. (1995). Metacognition and high intellectual ability: Insights from the study of learning-disabled gifted students. *Gifted Child Quarterly, 39,* 95–109.

Johnson-Laird, P. N. (1982). Thinking as a skill. *Quarterly Journal of Experimental Psychology, 34A,* 1–29.

Johnson-Laird, P. N. (1983). *Mental models.* Cambridge, MA: Harvard University Press.

Kahneman, D., & Tversky, A. (1973). On the psychology of prediction. *Psychological Review, 80,* 237–251.

Kardash, C. M., & Scholes, R. J. (1996). Effects of pre-existing beliefs, epistemological beliefs, and need for cognition on interpretation of controversial issues. *Journal of Educational Psychology, 88,* 260–271.

Keating, D. P. (1990). Charting pathways to the development of expertise. *Educational Psychologist, 25,* 243–267.

Kitcher, P. (1993). *The advancement of science.* New York: Oxford University Press.

Klaczynski, P. A. (2001). Analytic and heuristic processing influences on adolescent reasoning and decision making. *Child Development, 72,* 844–861.

Klaczynski, P. A., Gordon, D. H., & Fauth, J. (1997). Goal-oriented critical reasoning and individual differences in critical reasoning biases. *Journal of Educational Psychology, 89,* 470–485.

Klein, G. (1998). *Sources of power: How people make decisions.* Cambridge, MA: MIT Press.

Lave, J., & Wenger, E. (1991). *Situated learning: Legitimate peripheral participation.* New York: Cambridge University Press.

Levinson, S. C. (1995). Interactional biases in human thinking. In E. N. Goody (Ed.), *Social intelligence and interaction: Expressions and implications of the social bias in human intelligence* (pp. 221–260). Cambridge, England: Cambridge University Press.

Lipman, M. (1991). *Thinking in education.* New York: Cambridge University Press.

Mann, L., Harmoni, R., & Power, C. (1991). The GOFER course in decision making. In J. Baron & R. V. Brown (Eds.), *Teaching decision making to adolescents* (pp. 61–78). Hillsdale, NJ: Lawrence Erlbaum.

Nathanson, S. (1994). *The idea of rationality.* Chicago: Open Court.

Newell, A., & Simon, H. A. (1972). *Human problem solving.* Englewood Cliffs, NJ: Prentice Hall.

Nickerson, R. S. (1998). Confirmation bias: A ubiquitous phenomenon in many guises. *Review of General Psychology, 2,* 175–220.

Nisbett, R. E. (1993). *Rules for reasoning.* Hillsdale, NJ: Lawrence Erlbaum.

Norman, D. A., & Shallice, T. (1986). Attention to action: Willed and automatic control of behavior. In R. J. Davidson, G. E. Schwartz, & D. Shapiro (Eds.), *Consciousness and self regulation* (pp. 1–18). New York: Plenum.

Novak, J. D. (1988). The role of content and process in the education of science teachers. In P. F. Brandwein & A. H. Passow (Eds.), *Gifted young in science* (pp. 307–319). Washington, DC: National Science Teachers Association.

Paul, R., Binker, A., Martin, D., & Adamson, K. (1989). *Critical thinking handbook: High school.* Rohnert Park, CA: Center for Critical Thinking and Moral Critique.

Perkins, D. N. (1995). *Outsmarting IQ: The emerging science of learnable intelligence.* New York: Free Press.

Perkins, D. N., & Grotzer, T. A. (1997). Teaching intelligence. *American Psychologist,* 52, 1125–1133.

Pinker, S. (1997). *How the mind works.* New York: Norton.

Posner, M. I., & Snyder, C. R. R. (1975). Attention and cognitive control. In R. L. Solso (Ed.), *Information processing and cognition: The Loyola Symposium* (pp. 55–85). New York: Wiley.

Reber, A. S. (1993). *Implicit learning and tacit knowledge.* New York: Oxford University Press.

Rogoff, B., & Lave, J. (Eds.). (1984). *Everyday cognition.* Cambridge, MA: Harvard University Press.

Schommer, M. (1990). Effects of beliefs about the nature of knowledge on comprehension. *Journal of Educational Psychology, 82,* 498–505.

Shore, B. M., Koller, M., & Dover, A. (1994). More from the water jars: Revisiting a cognitive task on which some gifted children's performance is exceeded. *Gifted Child Quarterly, 38,* 179–183.

Simon, D. P., & Simon, H. A. (1978). Individual differences in solving physics problems. In R. S. Siegler (Ed.), *Children's thinking: What develops?* (pp. 325–348). Hillsdale, NJ: Lawrence Erlbaum.

Slomans, S. A. (1996). The empirical case for two systems of reasoning. *Psychological Bulletin, 119,* 3–22.

Stanovich, K. E. (1999). *Who is rational? Studies of individual differences in reasoning.* Mahwah, NJ: Lawrence Erlbaum.

Stanovich, K. E. (2002). Rationality, intelligence, and levels of analysis in cognitive science: Is dysrationalia possible? In R. J. Sternberg (Ed.), *Why smart people can be so stupid* (pp. 124–158). New Haven, CT: Yale University Press.

Stanovich, K. E. (2003). Understanding the styles of science in the study of reading. *Scientific Studies of Reading, 7,* 105–126.

Stanovich, K. E. (2004). *Rationality and evolution: The robot's rebellion in the age of Darwin.* Chicago: University of Chicago Press.

Stanovich, K. E. (2007). *How to think straight about psychology* (8th ed.). Boston: Allyn & Bacon.

Stanovich, K. E. (in press). *What the IQ tests miss: The cognitive science of rational and irrational thinking.* New Haven, CT: Yale University Press.

Sternberg, R. J. (2000). Wisdom as a form of giftedness. *Gifted Child Quarterly, 44,* 252–260.

Sternberg, R. J. (Ed.). (2002). *Why smart people can be so stupid.* New Haven, CT: Yale University Press.

Sternberg, R. J. (2004). Why smart people can be so foolish. *European Psychologist, 9,* 145–150.

Swartz, R. J., & Perkins, D. N. (1989). *Teaching thinking: Issues and approaches.* Pacific Grove, CA: Midwest Publications.

Tooby, J., & Cosmides, L. (1992). The psychological foundations of culture. In J. H. Barkow, L. Cosmides, & J. Tooby (Eds.), *The adapted mind: Evolutionary psychology and the generation of culture* (pp. 19–136). New York: Oxford University Press.

Wason, P. C. (1960). On the failure to eliminate hypotheses in a conceptual task. *Quarterly Journal of Experimental Psychology, 12,* 129–140.

Williams, W., Blythe, T., White, N., Li, J., Sternberg, R. J., & Gardner, H. (1996). *Practical intelligence in school.* New York: HarperCollins.

Chapter 12

DIFFERENTIATED INSTRUCTION

Carol Ann Tomlinson

DEFINING THE TERM AS USED IN RESEARCH

he term *differentiation* and related forms of the word have been used in varied ways in the field of gifted education, including denoting modifications of curriculum and instruction appropriate to the needs of gifted learners (e.g., Kaplan, 1994, Ward, 1980). More recently, the term has taken on a broader meaning and refers to modifications in curriculum and instruction necessary to support students with academically diverse learning needs (Tomlinson, 1999, 2001, 2003). According to this more recent use of the term, differentiation includes adaptations in content, process, product, affect, and learning environment in response to student readiness (proximity to learning goals), interests, and learning profile (preferences for taking in, processing, and presenting ideas) to ensure appropriate challenge and support for the full range of learners in a classroom

(Tomlinson, 1999, 2003). Defensible differentiation in that context is rooted in ongoing assessment data that informs teacher planning and is applied to curriculum that helps students make meaning of essential understandings in a discipline, use essential knowledge and skill, consistently reason at high levels, and apply what they learn in authentic ways (Tomlinson & McTighe, 2006).

Relevance to Gifted Education

The topic of differentiation is germane to gifted education for at least three reasons. Many students identified as gifted spend significant portions of their school time in heterogeneous classrooms and only will be served appropriately if curriculum and instruction are differentiated for them in these settings. Second, students identified as gifted are themselves a heterogeneous population and represent learners with differing levels of ability in different subjects, different interests, and different motivational patterns (Rogers, 2002). Some students identified as gifted also carry a second label such as learning disabled, physically handicapped, behaviorally disordered, or underachieving. In addition, there are many students in schools who are not identified as gifted but who have high potential or high ability nonetheless. Among such students are African American, Hispanic, Native American, and second language learners who are persistently underrepresented in programs for gifted learners (National Research Council, 2002). Unless differentiation is an effective part of regular classrooms, as well as special programs for students identified as gifted, many such students may continue to be underrecognized and underserved.

Also in relation to gifted education, research suggests that high-ability elementary learners (as well as others) may achieve higher academic outcomes when students with similar academic needs are clustered in relatively heterogeneous settings than when clustering is not used (Gentry, 1999). Further, research indicates that differentiation in mixed-ability settings is necessary for such settings to serve high-end learners appropriately (Kulik & Kulik, 1991).

MAJOR QUESTIONS ADDRESSED IN THE RESEARCH ON THIS TOPIC

There are currently three major questions addressed in the research on the topic of differentiation of instruction for academically diverse learners: (1) what is the efficacy of differentiation practice in response to student readiness, interest, or learning profile; (2) what is the efficacy of use of a differentiation model that employs response to student readiness, interest, and learning profile in mixed-ability settings; and (3) what is the degree of use of differentiation in school settings?

CONCLUSIONS FROM THE RESEARCH

Efficacy of Differentiating for Student Readiness, Interest, and Learning Profile

Research studies from a number of educational practices suggest positive gains from teachers differentiating instruction based on learner readiness needs. In an examination of research on multiage classes, in which differentiation is a given (Miller, 1990), achievement test results favored multiage classrooms over single-grade classrooms in 75% of measures used. Gayfer (1991) examined 64 studies of nongraded classrooms, in which students moved at their own pace, and found higher achievement gains in 58% of nongraded vs. graded traditional classrooms, comparable achievement gains in 33% of comparisons of graded and nongraded settings, and achievement gains favoring graded classes in only 9% of instances. In addition, students in the differentiated (nongraded) classrooms fared better than peers in graded classrooms fared in study habits, social interaction, cooperation, attitude toward school, and general mental health. Benefits to students in multiage and nongraded classrooms appear to increase the longer students remain in those settings (Anderson & Pavan, 1993). A qualitative study of adolescents (Csikszentmihalyi, Rathunde, & Whalen, 1993) also demonstrated negative impacts of tasks poorly matched to student readiness, whether the tasks were too complex or too simple for student needs.

Interest-based differentiation is linked to student motivation, productivity, and achievement (Amabile, 1983; Torrance, 1995), and appears to result in positive impacts on learning in both the long and short term (Hébert, 1993; Renninger, 1990, 1998; Tobias, 1990). When students have the opportunity to address questions that they are highly intrinsically motivated to pursue, the groundwork is laid for creative achievement (Collins & Amabile, 1999). This initial motivation can be maintained when teachers and parents engage students in discussing the pleasure of their work and maintain environments in which learners feel free to exchange ideas and interests (Hennessey & Zbikowski, 1993). When students select reading material of interest to them, they demonstrate greater engagement in reading and thus improved reading performance (Carbonaro & Gamoran, 2002). When students do not have strong personal interests, it is likely to be beneficial to achievement to promote contextual interest, for example, through novelty or connection with past experience (Hidi, 1990; Hidi & Anderson, 1992; Hidi & Berndorff, 1998; Wade & Adams, 1990).

Csikszentmihalyi et al. (1993) conclude from their observational studies that students who are able to pursue interests in their classes are more likely to see connections between their current work and future goals and to engage in the kind of "flow" experiences, or absorption in one's work, that are strong predictors of success in the school curriculum and successful pursuit of talent development opportunities.

Learning profile refers to student preferences for learning and subsumes theory and research on impacts of learning style, intelligence preference, gender, and culture on learning. The four categories will likely overlap in an individual. For example, cultural differences may impact gender preferences and/or learning style preferences. In a meta-analysis of research on learning styles Sullivan (1993) reports that addressing a student's learning style through flexible teaching or counseling results in achievement and attitude gains in students from a variety of cultural backgrounds.

Related to intelligence preference, or thinking styles, research suggests there are achievement benefits to addressing intelligence or thinking preference during learning, even though a final assessment is not in a learner's preferred mode (Grigorenko & Sternberg, 1997; Saxe, 1990; Sternberg, Torff, & Grigorenko, 1998). Studies examining impact of addressing students' learning styles and intelligence preferences have found positive effects for many groups of learners including Native American, Hispanic, African American, Asian American, and White students (Dunn & Griggs, 1995; Garcia, 1995; Ladson-Billings, 1994; Sternberg & Grigorenko, 1997). Despite considerable writing suggesting that gender impacts learning, there is not a substantive body of research examining achievement or attitude outcomes resulting from adjustment of learning conditions based on gender.

Efficacy of Instruction Combining Attention to Readiness, Interest, and Learning Profile

Several recent studies suggest positive impacts on student achievement when teachers consistently address learner readiness, interest, and learning profiles in their classrooms. Two recent dissertations point to achievement gains on state tests in reading and math for students across economic lines in effectively differentiated classrooms (Brimijoin, 2001) and on pretest-posttest math results (Tieso, 2002, 2005). The Tieso study looks specifically at gains of students identified as gifted, as well as nonidentified students. A multi-year, multisite study conducted by the National Research Center on the Gifted and Talented (Callahan, Tomlinson, Moon, Brighton, & Hertberg, 2003) also found small but statistically significant gains for students in differentiated classrooms versus those who received an assessment-based treatment and students in control groups, even though teachers in this study were generally novices at differentiation.

An experimental study on impacts of differentiation on achievement of first-grade children in Colombia utilized the model of differentiating content, process, and product in response to student readiness, interest, and learning profiles over a 4-month period. Researchers found that students in the differentiation group had fewer oral reading errors, higher comprehension scores, fewer students scoring below grade level, and more students scoring above grade level than control students (Marulanda, Giraldo, & Lopez, 2006).

More recent multiyear studies in an elementary school and a high school suggest positive and sustained achievement gains for students in all segments of the achievement spectrum and in a range of subject areas as a result of differentiated instruction. In the high school, the student dropout rate has also fallen sharply and student participation in Advanced Placement (AP) courses has risen by almost half, with AP exam scores holding steady or rising despite the increased enrollment. In both sites, a schoolwide emphasis on differentiation has continued for at least 5 years and differentiation is a part of the culture of teaching in both schools (Tomlinson, Brimijoin, & Narvaez, in press).

Degree of Implementation of Differentiation in Classrooms

In one study, 90% of high school teachers responded that addressing students' academic differences is important or very important to student success (Hootstein, 1998); however, in a slightly earlier nationwide survey of middle school teachers, 50% of respondents said they did not differentiate instruction because they saw no need to do so (Moon, Tomlinson, & Callahan, 1995). In any case, Schumm and Vaughn (1995) have documented that general education teachers may not differentiate because they feel doing so will call attention to student differences, they believe it is not their job to do so, they are unaware of learners' needs, or they believe that special treatment is inappropriate. Others have found that in the case of advanced learners, teachers feel students do not need adaptations or they do not know how to modify curriculum for students working significantly beyond grade-level competencies (Callahan et al., 2003; Tomlinson, 1995). Even when teachers express support for inclusive classrooms, they are likely to plan for whole-class approaches to teaching (Morocco, Riley, Gordon, & Howard, 1996).

When teachers do attempt differentiation, they may do so in ways that are limited and ineffective (Schumm et al., 1995; Stradling & Saunders, 1993). Differentiation is more likely to be reactive or improvisational rather than proactive or preplanned (Hootstein, 1998; McIntosh, Vaughn, Schumm, Haager, & Lee, 1994; Schumm & Vaughn, 1992, 1995; Tomlinson, 1995). Teachers seem particularly hesitant to change material, plan lessons for individuals, and change evaluation procedures (Callahan et al., 2003; Johnsen, Haensly, Ryser, & Ford, 2002; McIntosh et al., 1994; Schumm & Vaughn, 1995; Vaughn & Schumm, 1994). Lack of teacher clarity about meaningful curricular frameworks that should serve as a basis for differentiation also impedes efforts at differentiation (Callahan et al., 2003; Schumm & Vaughn, 1995; Tomlinson, Callahan, & Lelli, 1997; Vaughn & Schumm, 1994), and high-stakes testing also likely aggravates the problem of differentiating (Callahan et al., 2003; Vaughn & Schumm, 1994).

Lack of effective differentiation seems the norm whether students need modifications for learning problems (Bennett, Desforges, Cockburn, & Wilkinson, 1984; Deno, 1994; Fuchs & Fuchs, 1998; Schumm & Vaughn, 1995; Simpson & Ure, 1994); giftedness (Archambault et al., 1993; Bennett et al., 1984; Reis et al., 1993; Westberg, Archambault, Dobyns, & Salvin, 1993); cultural variance (Burstein & Cabello, 1989; Delpit, 1995; Lasley & Matczynski, 1997); race (Perry, Steele, & Hilliard, 2003); or multiple simultaneous learning needs (Fletcher, Bos, & Johnson, 1999; Minner, 1990; Reis, Neu, & McGuire, 1997).

LIMITATIONS OF THE RESEARCH

Although there is a substantial body of research indicating achievement gains, as well as other benefits for students when learner readiness, interest, or learning profile is taken into account in teacher plans and instruction, research on implementation of a full model of differentiation in mixed-ability classrooms is still emergent, but positive. The research that does exist on impacts of differentiation tends to examine early efforts of teachers who implement differentiation (Callahan et al., 2003; Tomlinson, 1995; Tomlinson et al., 1997). Although it is important to understand the developmental process through which teachers learn to respond to student variance in classrooms, such early stage research often fails to explain middle and later stage teacher development related to differentiation. Because differentiation calls on many teachers to significantly change their practice, understanding the full process of change is critical for planning for both preservice and in-service teacher development, as well as for sustaining increased student achievement results.

Additional research also is necessary to further illuminate characteristics of leadership that serve as catalysts for pervasive and sustained teacher change toward responsive teaching across schools (Callahan et al., 2003; Tomlinson et al., in press). Such leadership is doubtless a requirement for change that will be necessary to effectively serve an increasingly diverse student population.

In addition, it would be useful for the field of gifted education to study cognitive and affective impacts of effective differentiation on high-potential and high-ability learners both in more heterogeneous and more homogeneous settings. To date, the field has accumulated research indicating benefits of acceleration and enrichment as formats for teaching high-ability learners in homogeneous settings. There is very little research studying impacts of appropriate application of those two approaches within more academically diverse settings and very little research examining impacts on high-potential and high-ability learners of other forms of differentiation in either regular classroom or specialized settings.

Further research in these areas should be an important addition to the body of research on impacts of various approaches to serving learners identified as gifted. At the very least, it would add a new dimension to older research, which tends to compare outcomes for high-ability students in "homogeneous" settings where their academic needs are addressed and "heterogeneous" settings where their needs are not addressed.

Because a number of the studies indicating teacher hesitancy to differentiate instruction were conducted 10 or more years ago and recent focus on differentiation in schools began in or after 1995, it would be useful to revisit teacher thinking about and implementation of principles and practices of differentiation. Given that instructional change is complex, it could be particularly useful to study settings in which teachers have received sustained support for implementation of differentiation to determine what, if any, changes in teacher attitude and practice have resulted.

PRACTICAL IMPLICATIONS OF RESEARCH ON DIFFERENTIATION

An earlier body of research suggests positive impacts of addressing student readiness, interest, and learning profiles through curriculum and instruction. That body of studies, however, does not examine specific impacts on students identified as gifted. A more recent, although small, set of studies points to positive impacts of differentiation on achievement of a broad range of learners, including students at the high end of achievement and aptitude.

Research from several facets of educational practice suggest that many classroom teachers lack the skill or will to modify instruction for students with varied learning needs. Nonetheless, there are examples of schools in which whole faculties have moved toward more academically responsive teaching to the benefit of a very broad range of students. These two bodies of research mirror the literature regarding change in schools, which indicates that modifying teacher beliefs and practices is complex, but possible, when teachers receive sustained and supportive leadership for making critical changes (e.g., Evans, 1996; Fullan, 2001a, 2001b; Sarason, 1995; Schlechty, 1997).

RECOMMENDED READING

The following article provides a review of literature on theory, research, and practice related to differentiation.

Tomlinson, C., Brighton, C., Hertberg, H., Callahan, C., Moon, T., Brimijoin, K. et al. (2003). Differentiating instruction in response to student readiness, interest, and learning profile in academically diverse classrooms: A review of literature. *Journal for the Education of the Gifted, 27,* 119–145.

REFERENCES

Amabile, T. (1983). *The social psychology of creativity*. New York: Springer-Verlag.

Anderson, R., & Pavan, B. (1993). *Nongradedness: Helping it to happen*. Lancaster, PA: Technomic.

Archambault, F., Westberg, K., Brown, S., Hallmark, B., Emmons, C., & Zhang, W. (1993). *Regular classroom practices with gifted students: Results of a national survey of classroom teachers* (Research Monograph No. 93102). Storrs: National Research Center on the Gifted and Talented, University of Connecticut.

Bennett, N., Desforges, C., Cockburn, A., & Wilkinson, B. (1984). *The quality of pupils' learning experiences*. London: Lawrence Erlbaum.

Brimijoin, K. (2001). *Expertise in differentiation: A preservice and inservice teacher make their way*. Unpublished doctoral dissertation, University of Virginia, Charlottesville.

Burstein, N., & Cabello, B. (1989). Preparing teachers to work with culturally diverse students: A teacher education model. *Journal of Teacher Education, 40*(5), 9–16.

Callahan, C., Tomlinson, C., Moon, T., Brighton, C., & Hertberg, H. (2003). *Feasibility of high end learning in the middle grades*. Charlottesville: National Research Center on the Gifted and Talented, University of Virginia.

Carbonaro, W., & Gamoran, A. (2002). The production of achievement inequality in high school English. *American Educational Research Journal, 39*, 801–807.

Collins, M., & Amabile, T. (1999). Motivation and creativity. In R. J. Sternberg (Ed.), *Handbook of creativity* (pp. 297–312). New York: Cambridge University Press.

Csikszentmihalyi, M., Rathunde, K., & Whalen, S. (1993). *Talented teenagers: The roots of success and failure*. New York: Cambridge University Press.

Delpit, L. (1995). *Other people's children: Cultural conflict in the classroom*. New York: The New Press.

Deno, S. (1994, February). *Effects of support conditions on teachers' instructional adaptation and student learning*. Paper presented at the second annual Pacific Coast Research Conference, LaJolla, CA.

Dunn, R., & Griggs, S. (1995). *Multiculturalism and learning style: Teaching and counseling adolescents*. Westport, CT: Praeger.

Evans, R. (1996). *The human side of school change: Reform, resistance, and the real-life problems of innovation*. San Francisco: Jossey-Bass.

Fletcher, T., Bos, C., & Johnson, L. (1999). Accommodating English language learners with language and learning disabilities in bilingual education classrooms. *Learning Disabilities Research & Practice, 14*, 80–91.

Fuchs, L., & Fuchs, D. (1998). General educators' instructional adaptation for students with learning disabilities. *Learning Disability Quarterly, 21*, 23–33.

Fullan, M. (2001a). *The new meaning of educational change* (3rd ed.). New York: Teachers College Press.

Fullan, M. (2001b). *Leading in a culture of change*. San Francisco: Jossey-Bass.

Garcia, G. (1995). Equity challenges in authentically assessing students from diverse backgrounds. *Educational Forum, 59*(1), 64–73.

Gayfer, M. (1991). *The multi-grade classroom: Myth and reality, A Canadian study*. Toronto, Canada: Canadian Education Association.

Gentry, M. (1999). *Promoting student achievement and exemplary classroom practices through cluster grouping: A research-based alternative to heterogeneous elementary classrooms* (Research Monograph No. 999138). Storrs: National Research Center on the Gifted and Talented, University of Connecticut.

Grigorenko, E., & Sternberg, R. (1997). Styles of thinking, abilities, and academic performance. *Exceptional Children, 63,* 295–312.

Hennessey, B., & Zbikowski, S. (1993). Immunizing children against the negative effects of reward: A further examination of intrinsic motivation training techniques. *Creativity Research Journal, 6,* 297–308.

Hébert, T. (1993). Reflections at graduations: The long-term impact of elementary school experiences in creative productivity. *Roeper Review, 16,* 22–28.

Hidi, S. (1990). Interest and its contribution as a mental resource for learning. *Review of Educational Research, 60,* 549–571.

Hidi, S., & Anderson, (1992). Situational interest and its impact on reading and expository writing. In K. A. Renninger, S. Hidi, & A. Krapp (Eds.), *The role of interest in learning and development* (pp. 215–238). Hillsdale, NJ: Lawrence Erlbaum.

Hidi, S., & Berndorff, D. (1998). Situational interest and learning. In L. Hoffmann, A. Krapp, K. Renninger, & J. Baumert (Eds.), *Interest and learning: Proceedings of the Seeon conference on interest and gender* (pp. 74–90). Kiel, Germany: IPN.

Hootstein, E. (1998). *Differentiation of instructional methodologies in subject-based curricula at the secondary level.* Richmond, VA: Metropolitan Educational Research Consortium (MERC). (ERIC Document Reproduction Service No. ED427130)

Johnsen, S., Haensly, P., Ryser, G., & Ford, R. (2002). Changing general education classroom practices to adapt for gifted students. *Gifted Child Quarterly, 46,* 45–63.

Kaplan, S. (1994). *Differentiating core curriculum and instruction to provide advanced learning opportunities.* Sacramento, CA: California Association for the Gifted.

Kulik, C.-L. C., & Kulik, J. A. (1991). Ability grouping and gifted students. In N. Colangelo & G. Davis (Eds.), *Handbook of gifted education* (pp. 179–196). Boston: Allyn & Bacon.

Ladson-Billings, G. (1994). *The dreamkeepers: Successful teachers of African American children.* San Francisco: Jossey-Bass.

Lasley, T., & Matczynski, T. (1997). *Strategies for teaching in a diverse society: Instructional models.* Belmont, CA: Wadsworth.

Marulanda, M., Giraldo, P., & Lopez, L. (2006, April). *Differentiated instruction for bilingual learners.* Presentation at Annual Conference of the Association for Supervision and Curriculum Development, San Francisco.

McIntosh, R., Vaughn, S., Schumm, J., Haager, D., & Lee, O. (1994). Observations of students with learning disabilities in general education classrooms. *Exceptional Children, 60,* 249–261.

Miller, B. (1990). A review of the quantitative research on multigrade instruction. *Research in Rural Education, 7,* 3–12.

Minner, S. (1990). Teacher evaluations of case descriptions of LD gifted children. *Gifted Child Quarterly, 34,* 37–39.

Moon, T., Tomlinson, C., & Callahan, C. (1995). *Academic diversity in the middle school: Results of a national survey of middle school administrators and teachers* (Research Monograph No. 95124). Charlottesville: National Research Center on the Gifted and Talented, University of Virginia.

Morocco, C., Riley, M., Gordon, S., & Howard, C. (1996). The elusive individual in teachers' planning. In G. Brannigan (Ed.), *The enlightened educator* (pp. 154–176). New York: McGraw-Hill.

National Research Council. (2002). *Minority students in special and gifted education.* Washington, DC: National Academy Press.

Perry, T., Steele, C., & Hilliard, A. (2003). *Young, gifted, and Black: Promoting high achievement among African-American students.* Boston: Beacon.

Reis, S., Neu, T., & McGuire, J. (1997). Case studies of high-ability students with learning disabilities who have achieved. *Exceptional Children, 63,* 463–479.

Reis, S., Westberg, K., Kulikowich, J., Caillard, F., Hébert, T., Plucker, J., et al. (1993). *Why not let high ability students start school in January: The curriculum compacting study* (Research Monograph No. 93106). Storrs: National Research Center on the Gifted and Talented, University of Connecticut.

Renninger, K. (1990). Children's play interests, representations, and activity. In R. Fivush & J. Hudson (Eds.), *Knowing and remembering in young children* (Emory Cognition Series, Vol. 3, pp. 127–165). New York: Cambridge University Press.

Renninger, K. (1998). The roles of individual interest(s) and gender in learning. An overview of research on preschool and elementary school-aged children/students. In L. Hoffmann, A. Krapp, K. Renninger, & J. Baumert (Eds.), *Interest and learning: Proceedings of the Seeon conference on interest and gender* (pp. 165–175). Kiel, Germany: IPN.

Rogers, K. (2002). *Re-forming gifted education: Matching the program to the child.* Scottsdale, AZ: Great Potential Press.

Sarason, S. (1995). *School change: The personal development point of view.* New York: Teachers College Press.

Saxe, G. (1990). *Culture and cognitive development: Studies in mathematical understanding.* Hillsdale, NJ: Lawrence Erlbaum.

Schlechty, P. (1997). *Inventing better schools: An action plan for educational reform.* San Francisco: Jossey-Bass.

Schumm, J., & Vaughn, S. (1992). Planning for mainstreamed special education students: Perceptions of general classroom teachers. *Exceptionality, 3,* 81–98.

Schumm, J., & Vaughn, S. (1995). Getting ready for inclusion: Is the stage set? *Learning Disabilities Research & Practice, 10,* 169–179.

Schumm, J., Vaughn, S., Haager, D., McDowell, J., Rothlein, L., & Saumell, L. (1995). General education teacher planning: What can students with learning disabilities expect? *Exceptional Children, 61,* 335–352.

Simpson, M., & Ure, J. (1994). *Studies of differentiation practices in primary and secondary schools* (Interchange Report #30). Edinburgh, Scotland: Scottish Council for Research in Education. (ERIC Document Reproduction Service No. ED380196)

Sternberg, R., & Grigorenko, E. (1997). Are cognitive styles still in style? *American Psychologist, 52,* 700–712.

Sternberg, R., Torff, B., & Grigorenko, E. (1998). Teaching triarchically improves student achievement. *Journal of Educational Psychology, 90,* 374–384.

Stradling, B., & Saunders, L. (1993). Differentiation in practice: Responding to the needs of all pupils. *Educational Research, 35,* 127–137.

Sullivan, M. (1993). *A meta-analysis of experimental research studies based on the Dunn and Dunn learning styles model and its relationship to academic achievement and performance.* Unpublished doctoral dissertation, St. John's University, Jamaica, NY.

Tieso, C. (2002). *The effects of grouping and curricular practices on intermediate students' math achievement.* (Research Monograph No. 02154). Storrs: National Research Center on the Gifted and Talented, University of Connecticut.

Tieso, C. (2005). Effects of grouping practices and curricular adjustments on achievement. *Journal for the Education of the Gifted, 29*, 60–89.

Tobias, S. (1990). *They're not dumb, they're different: Stalking the second tier.* Tucson, AZ: Research Corporation.

Tomlinson, C. (1995). Deciding to differentiate instruction in middle school: One school's journey. *Gifted Child Quarterly, 39*, 77–87.

Tomlinson, C. (1999). *The differentiated classroom: Responding to the needs of all learners.* Alexandria, VA: Association for Supervision and Curriculum Development.

Tomlinson, C. (2001). *How to differentiate instruction in mixed-ability classrooms* (2nd ed.). Alexandria, VA: Association for Supervision and Curriculum Development.

Tomlinson, C. (2003). *Fulfilling the promise of the differentiated classroom: Strategies and tools for responsive teaching.* Alexandria, VA: Association for Supervision and Curriculum Development.

Tomlinson, C., Brimijoin, K., & Narvaez, L. (in press). *Making change for schoolwide differentiation.* Alexandria, VA: Association for Supervision and Curriculum Development.

Tomlinson, C., Callahan, C., & Lelli, K. (1997). Challenging expectations: Case studies of high-potential, culturally diverse young children. *Gifted Child Quarterly, 41*(2), 5–17.

Tomlinson, C., & McTighe, J. (2006). *Integrating differentiated instruction and understanding by design.* Alexandria, VA: Association for Supervision and Curriculum Development.

Torrance, E. (1995). Insights about creativity: Questioned, rejected, ridiculed, ignored. *Educational Psychology Review, 7*, 313–322.

Vaughn, S., & Schumm, J. (1994). Middle school teachers' planning for students with learning disabilities. *Remedial and Special Education, 15*, 151–162.

Wade, S., & Adams, B. (1990). Effects of importance and interest on recall of biographical text. *JRB: A Journal of Literacy, 22*, 331–353.

Ward, V. (1980). *Differential education for the gifted.* Ventura, CA: National/State Leadership Training Institute for the Gifted and Talented.

Westberg, K., Archambault, F., Dobyns, S., & Salvin, T. (1993). *An observational study of instructional and curricular practices used with gifted and talented students in regular classrooms* (Research Monograph No. 93104). Storrs: National Research Center on the Gifted and Talented, University of Connecticut.

Chapter 13

EARLY CHILDHOOD

Nancy M. Robinson

ithin the field of giftedness, there is no less charted territory than the early years, with the exception of the elderly. In large part, young gifted children escape attention because, like other children in the United States, they are typically in scattered, parent-paid preschool/daycare sites (Robinson, Robinson, Wolins, Bronfenbrenner, & Richmond, 1973) with teachers who are not trained to recognize or respond to children's developmental advancement. In government-sponsored programs like Project Head Start, major emphasis is focused on children at risk for school failure. Once gifted children enter the public school system, however, they eventually encounter teachers who are more likely to recognize that they have already mastered much of the curriculum. Furthermore, at this point, states assume some responsibility for educating all students appropriately, whether or not there is a legal mandate in place to serve gifted children.

There are other reasons these children are ill attended to. Many professionals doubt that advanced abilities can be reliably identified when children are so young and/or see early manifestations of ability as likely to be very unstable. Later in this chapter, we will examine evidence casting doubt on these beliefs. Because of this situation, we are missing out on a precious opportunity to identify and nurture promising young children—especially those living in difficult circumstances. It is important, then, to take stock of what we do and do not know about giftedness in the early years, roughly birth to age 7.

WHAT CONSTITUTES GIFTEDNESS IN EARLY CHILDHOOD?

In general, young children who show *significantly advanced abilities and skills* in any domain can be considered gifted (Koshy & Robinson, 2006), implying that their development in that domain has been more rapid than that of their age peers (Robinson, 2005). Because even very precocious young children have seldom encountered formal training in their area(s) of talent, their advancement constitutes the *promise* of developing excellence. In this chapter, we focus on cognitive and academic giftedness because, with few exceptions— mainly case studies—that is the major kind of giftedness about which there exists coherent research-based knowledge.

THE MAIN ISSUES ADDRESSED SO FAR: WHAT CAN WE CONCLUDE WITH SOME CONFIDENCE?

Only a few topics can be said to have been targeted by a sufficient number of well-designed and executed studies to claim that our information is solid. These few topics include (1) the early childhoods of the later eminent, (2) parenting practices associated with giftedness, (3) early identification, (4) stability of general and specific abilities, (5) which cognitive abilities are accelerated during this period, and (6) early entrance to kindergarten. In addition, there are encouraging but limited indications that early intervention can be effective in enhancing cognitive abilities, although the literature on producing giftedness by such efforts is virtually nil.

Early Childhood Family Experiences of Eminent Adults

Some of the earliest and most extensive research on gifted young children consists of retrospective accounts of the early years of eminent adults (e.g., Albert, 1980; Bloom, 1985; Cox, 1926; Goertzel, Goertzel, Goertzel, &

Hansen, 2004; McCurdy, 1960; Simonton, 1998). The authors of these compendia of case studies range from those who express laudatory views of family support to those who draw very negative views of the families. Clearly, however, the eminent persons studied had exhibited precocity during their early years, some of them to astonishing degrees, and many had received strong encouragement from their families. Many from well-to-do families had not attended common schools prior to their entering universities, often at an early age. It appears likely that some degree of family stress leads to a certain self-reliance, independence, initiative, and creativity that, combined with native ability, may be necessary for exceptional long-term success and recognition (Olszewski, Kulieke, & Buescher, 1987; Olszewski-Kubilius, 2002).

Early Childhoods of Young, Gifted Children

There is surprisingly little coherent research on the early childhoods of children who are identified before adulthood as being gifted. A number of case studies describe one to a few young children who are highly precocious—some with distinctive, uneven profiles and others more generally advanced (e.g., Feldman, 1986; Ho, 1989; Hoh, 2005; Ruf, 2005; Sankar-DeLeeuw, 2004; Stainthorp & Hughes, 2004; Winner, 1996; Witty & Coomer, 1985). One exception is the longitudinal study reported by Gross (1993, 2004), who identified a group of Australian children who were highly gifted, some under the age of 8. These children had been early walkers, early talkers, and early readers. Gross concluded that those who had been radically accelerated in school had been not only academically but socially much more successful than those kept in age-determined settings.

There is no reason to believe that the favorable child-rearing practices identified for older gifted children—families that are better educated, endowed with more resources, and more child-centered and supportive than other families—should be different during the early years, and indeed, what information we have points in that direction. Young gifted children tend to come from relatively advantaged homes (Gottfried, Gottfried, Bathurst, & Guerin, 1994) and their parents spend considerable time with them in crucial activities such as reading, playing, making up rhymes and songs, and going to interesting places (Karnes, Shwedel, & Steinberg, 1984).

Three longitudinal studies of the most competent children to emerge from otherwise relatively nonselected populations also point to the importance of personal and tangible resources in the home. Robinson, Lanzi, Weinberg, Ramey, and Ramey (2002) looked at the most academically competent 3% in a primarily low-income population of more than 5,000 third graders who had attended Project Head Start, finding that the homes of this subgroup were characterized by parents with more education and somewhat higher incomes (but still, on average, barely above the poverty line), fewer children, more child-centered child-rearing attitudes, and more involvement with the children's school. The effects were even stronger in children who had tested high in first, second, and third grade.

Similarly, Oxford, Spieker, and Robinson (2006) looked at the most competent 12% of fourth and fifth graders from a population of more than 1,000 students who had been followed since infancy, with an emphasis on their daycare experiences. Of the predictors gathered at 54 months of age, those most clearly differentiating the high-achieving children were family income, maternal education, maternal progressive beliefs, and maternal sensitivity to the child. Early measures of child language and of executive control also related significantly to later attainment.

Aspects of the early environments of 20 children identified as gifted at age 8, in a cohort of 107 largely middle-class California families, provide the richest store of information about family differences between the 20 children and the remaining 87 (Gottfried et al., 1994). Social class, parental education, and parental occupational status differentiated the groups, but so did a variety of parental practices. At age 3, for example, there were significant differences in the two groups of families in the toys, games, and materials provided; language stimulation; pride, affection, and warmth; and (pre) academic stimulation. By age 8, differences had emerged in parental responsivity, active stimulation, family participation, and paternal involvement. Early childhood experiences were reflected in these children's academic motivation even in adolescence (Gottfried, Gottfried, Cook, & Morris, 2005). Parenting gifted children is clearly labor-intensive and creates long-term impact.

Accuracy of Early Identification

Investigators who have asked parents to "volunteer" their gifted children have found that the parents do a good job of identifying children whose development is advanced (Louis & Lewis, 1992), at least in domains where skills are observable and emerging. A number of parent checklists of gifted behaviors have been devised (e.g., Benito & Moro, 1999; Klein, 1992; Silverman, Chitwood, & Waters, 1986) and those that have been validated have stood up well (Louis & Lewis, 1992; Pletan, Robinson, Berninger, & Abbott, 1995). One should note that most parents using such checklists have been relatively well educated and probably more knowledgeable about giftedness than an unselected parent group would be.

Although various teacher rating scales of gifted children have been available for some time, a recently published scale (Pfeiffer & Jarosewich, 2003) is the first to be rigorously examined. Two forms are available, one of them for preschool and kindergarten children. The diagnostic validity of the form for age 6 and above has been validated by its authors by comparing teacher ratings with WISC-IV scores of the standardization sample (Pfeiffer & Jarosewich, 2007).

In the Robinson Center at the University of Washington, we have conducted three short-term longitudinal studies of very young children whose parents nominated them in response to broadcast invitations for (1) children ages 2–5 with general intellectual precocity or precocity in a specific domain (Robinson & Robinson, 1992), (2) 18-month-old toddlers with precocious language (Robinson, Dale, & Landesman, 1990), and (3) preschoolers and kindergartners with precocious mathematical reasoning (Robinson, Abbott, Berninger, & Busse, 1996). In each case, the parents' descriptions corresponded well with standardized assessments of the children's development. For example, more than half the children in the first study had initial IQs of 132 or above and others exhibited specific precocities not directly reflected in the IQs. In the second study, mothers' descriptions of their toddler's language correlated highly with observed language when the children were seen 2 months later. In the third study, more than half of the children attained math reasoning scores above the 98th percentile on one of two measures, and there were substantial correlations between parent checklists and children's test scores (Pletan et al., 1995). Note that not only do these findings validate the parent nomination method as a way of finding such children, but—reversing the logic—also demonstrate that standardized measures accurately reflect the children's home behavior as seen by the people who live with them day in and day out.

Given the accuracy of parental identification, should rating scales be substituted for more objective measures of ability, such as the Wechsler Preschool and Primary Scale of Intelligence? As mentioned, the rating scales have been used (and validated) primarily by parents with above-average education, and even in studies with quite positive findings, have not proved foolproof. Just as with older children, multiple sources of information are better than one, and this is particularly true for children of parents who are inexperienced with young children or with completing ratings, reluctant to do so, or marginally literate in English. Indeed, the use of psychometric instruments in identifying gifted children has much to recommend it (Robinson, 2005).

Stability and Differentiation of Precocious Abilities During Early Childhood

The fact that very early developmental assessments of nongifted children have tended not to be very stable has perhaps deterred investigators from looking for children with specific cognitive abilities at early ages. Evidence from the three parent-identification studies previously cited has, however, substantiated a strong trend not only for children identified for advanced general intelligence or specific abilities to remain ahead academically, but also to increase their lead over other children. For children ages 2–5 who were nominated for high general intelligence, correlations of .59 to .75 were obtained when they were retested 1 to 4 years later and the mean of the whole group rose a few points over the same period (Robinson & Robinson, 1992). Similarly, for

276 mathematically precocious children followed for 2 years, from preschool or kindergarten through grade 1 or 2, gains relative to peers were significant on most subtests of a battery tapping math, verbal, and visual-spatial reasoning and memory, a Matthew effect (the rich get richer; Robinson, Abbott, Berninger, Busse, & Mukhopadhyay, 1997). Furthermore, both the language-precocious and the math-precocious children maintained the differentiation of the abilities for which they were identified—that is, the language-precocious children remained farther ahead in language than their other abilities (Dale, Crain-Thoreson, & Robinson, 1995), and math-precocious children did the same in mathematical abilities (Robinson et al., 1997). A recently published longitudinal account of linguistic precocity in a gifted child (Hoh, 2005) further substantiates the stability of early language development.

Reading before school entry is another differentiated ability about which there is evidence of stability. Highly gifted children typically do begin to read during the preschool years (Gross, 1993), but certainly not all do so. The verbally precocious children followed in the study previously described were, with one exception, not readers by age 4 ½, but typically caught on quickly once they started. Nancy Jackson (1992) conducted a number of studies with children who were reading very well before first grade. Some were very bright and others, moderately so. The latter tended to be adept "code crackers" who "will not always be the best candidates for permanent inclusion in a program designed for children with exceptionally high verbal intelligence" (Jackson, 1992, p. 199). Even so, both Jackson and other investigators (Jackson, 1992) have found that early readers tend over time to remain good readers, their early word recognition later converting to superior reading comprehension. A recent case study (Stainthorp & Hughes, 2004) illustrates the point.

Interestingly, when very young children are identified only by scores on developmental measures, without corroboration by real-life observers, their status has not tended to remain as strong. Willerman and Fiedler (1974) identified a group of 4-year-olds with IQs of 140+ who had been tested as part of a larger population with the Bayley scales at 8 months, finding virtually no difference between their Bayley scores and those of the other children; the results were confirmed for the same children at age 7, although by then their mean IQ had dropped to slightly above 120 (Willerman & Fiedler, 1977).

Which Cognitive Skills Are Accelerated in Young Children of High Intelligence?

The perennial question in the field of giftedness—Is high ability qualitatively different from average ability, or is it simply like that of older children (Jackson & Butterfield, 1986)?—is highly researchable in early childhood, when the growth curve is steep. A critical research paradigm, comparing gifted young children not only with their average chronological-age (CA) peers (not a very interesting comparison) but also with their mental-age (MA) peers (more to the point), has, unfortunately, been employed in only a few studies. Kanevsky (1992) compared gifted 5-year-olds with average 7-year-olds (mental-age peers) and gifted 7-year-olds on a cognitive problem, the Tower of Hanoi, finding that the gifted 5-year-olds solved the problem on a level comparable to the average 7-year-olds, but their behavior (e.g., refusing help), was more like the gifted 7-year-olds. Other investigators who have looked at metacognitive skills agree (Moss, 1990, 1992; Moss & Strayer, 1990). McClelland (1982) found that preschool children with high Stanford-Binet IQs solved more verbal problems and fewer performance problems than did a MA-matched older group. Lempers, Block, Scott, and Draper (1987), comparing very bright preschoolers with both a CA-matched group and a MA-matched group, found that the younger children resembled MA-mates on a spatial projective task and perspective-taking tasks in cognitive and affective domains. Planche (1985) and Zha (1984) found bright preschoolers exceeding the problem-solving skills of older children in France and China, respectively.

A flurry of small-scale studies in the 1970s and 1980s (see Spitz, 1985; Tannenbaum, 1992) addressed Piagetian questions, particularly the age at which bright preschoolers traverse to the stage of concrete operations. On tasks meant for 6- and 7-year-olds, even bright 4-year-olds tend not to succeed (Brown, 1973; Moore, Nelson-Piercy, Abel, & Frye, 1984), although bright 5-year-olds do (DeVries, 1974; Little, 1972) and once they catch on to an idea, they need minimal practice (Porath, 1992)—they own the idea and generalize it with little further help. A recent small-scale study (Loewen, 2006) has redirected attention to the degree to which such reasoning is malleable, showing that intervention can speed up mastery of an effective mental counting line in bright 4-year-olds.

The most reliable cognitive skills to be identified on checklists in younger children are excellence in memory, both short-term and long-term, followed by long attention span, extensive vocabulary, older playmates, and personal maturity (Klein, 1992; Louis & Lewis, 1992; Robinson et al., 1990; Silverman et al., 1986). Young gifted children show fears like those of older children (Klene, 1988). Executive control (sustained attention, inhibition of incorrect responses) at 54 months was also found by Oxford et al. (2006) to be a strong predictor of high academic attainment at grades 4 and 5.

Asynchrony of Development

Like other gifted children, young gifted children show distinct asynchronies in development. Often, for example, their cognitive advancement significantly exceeds advancement in motor skills and emotional regulation. This is a phenomenon noted from the very beginning of research about giftedness (Hollingworth, 1931; Terman, 1931). The younger the child, the greater the impact of such discrepancies (Silverman, 2002).

Most of our knowledge about such asynchronies derives from clinical observation (Silverman, 2002), but empirical demonstration is not altogether lacking. The language-precocious toddlers previously described were not, for example, advanced in gross motor skills according to the Bayley Scales of Development (Robinson et al., 1990; although note that Gross [2004] describes early walking as typical of her highly gifted group). Within an array of cognitive abilities, the study of mathematically precocious children previously cited (Robinson et al., 1997) found that the children were on average more advanced in math than in either spatial or verbal abilities, but even in the latter two fields, mean scores of the group were in the neighborhood of one standard deviation above the normative sample.

Effectiveness of Early Educational Programs

There are only a few reports of early childhood programs specifically designed for gifted children, and even fewer that have used reliable scientific designs to evaluate their effectiveness. Most have targeted children whose development was demonstrably advanced (Diezmann & English, 2001 [concepts of large numbers]; Diezmann & Watters, 2000 [science]; Hertzog, Klein, & Katz, 1999 [shadows]; Morelock & Morrison, 1999; Wright & Coulianos, 1991). One study that used a comparison group (Roedell, Jackson, & Robinson, 1980) demonstrated that, just like the findings for older children (Robinson, Shore, & Enersen, 2007), simply bringing bright children together in an interesting and nurturing environment is insufficient to affect intellectual development, at least as measured by IQ.

On the other hand, the longitudinal study of mathematically precocious young children previously described (Robinson et al., 1997) was singular for its random assignment of substantial numbers of children to intervention and nonintervention groups. It did, indeed, demonstrate the effectiveness of such intervention (28 sessions over a 2-year period) in boosting math attainment.

Identification and Nurturance of Gifted Preschoolers From Ethnic Minorities

Not because of their extensiveness but because of their high priority, it is worth noting that a few studies have tried to identify very young, promising children of underserved ethnic minorities. In addition to the waste of talent if such children are not identified, the underrepresentation of minority children in classes for gifted students continues to be a huge stumbling block. Our best bet is to find such promising children as early as possible in order to promote the development of their abilities (Robinson, 2003). One such study (B. Louis, personal communication), used novel tasks such as classification/reclassification of blocks and story-telling to identify promising preschool children for an intervention program in Newark from which a few children were able to proceed to classes for gifted children. More recently, Scott and Delgado (2005) report having screened 395 preschool children, 75% of whom were Black or Hispanic, with nine cognitive tasks and then locating 262 of them during first grade. Tasks that required the children to generate rather than just select responses successfully predicted the top 3% achievers in first grade, most of whom eventually moved into classes for the gifted. There is no evidence that traditional psychological measures wouldn't be at least as effective as these in identifying gifted young minority children.

The family environment clearly plays a major role in determining young children's cognitive and academic skills. For example, during Head Start, a study of the influence of book reading by caregivers and children, as well as caregiver IQ and education, showed a major impact on children's language ability (Payne, Whitehurst, & Angell, 1994), and a subsequent longitudinal study of post-Head Start children's language and literacy skills also reflected strong connections between home environment and literacy (Storch & Whitehurst, 2001).

There is evidence that the influence of the environment on cognitive abilities is stronger in low-income families than in the rest of the population (Turkheimer, Haley, Waldron, D'Onofrio, & Gottesman, 2003), and the genetic component minimized. Appropriately, major efforts have been addressed to provide early intervention in order to optimize the progress of children from homes of poverty. It is important to remember that gifted children have been neither the focus nor the frequent outcome of this work with high-risk families. Furthermore, it is clear that such work is not easy. A report of the National Academy of Sciences (Commission on Behavioral and Social Sciences and Education, 2002) has concluded that, to be effective, intervention must start very early, must be intensive and continuous, must include direct services to children, as well as to their parents, and must target self-regulation, social skills, language, and reasoning. Indeed, in a consortium of nine early studies designed to enhance the development of low-income children, those with lasting intellectual effects had all begun before age 2 (Lazar & Darlington, 1982). Although there continues to be optimism about the extent to which abilities are malleable, the emphasis needs to shift away from race/ethnicity and toward the more powerful impact of socioeconomic status (Robinson, 2003). There is a long way to go before society appears ready to invest what it takes to make the difference needed.

Early Entrance to Kindergarten

The most extensive literature on early school options relates to early entrance to school (Robinson, 2004) and, like the rest of the literature on acceleration (Colangelo, Assouline, & Gross, 2004), results in quite a positive picture. Early entrance is the least disruptive form of acceleration, is inexpensive, and at least in the beginning can provide appropriate challenges for many academically advanced children. This alternative does require decision making early in the child's life, however, and may be difficult to reverse.

A caution is in order: Numerous investigators have looked at the status of *unselected* younger versus older children within a grade level, almost inevitably concluding that "immaturity" characterizes the younger ones (e.g., Gagné & Gagnier, 2004; Maddux, 1983). This comes as no surprise. Yet, several reviews of social-emotional outcomes for *carefully selected* early entrants (e.g., Obrzut, Nelson, & Obrzut, 1984; Proctor, Black, & Feldhusen, 1986; Rankin & Vialle, 1996; Robinson, 2004; Rogers, 2002) agree that academically, the children usually thrive after early entrance, and that social-emotional indicators tend to be slightly but not dramatically positive (i.e., the early entrants do as well as others). There appear to be some greater behavioral risks for boys (Gagné & Gagnier, 2004). The few long-term studies have tended to show early entrants in positions of leadership later on in school (Hobson, 1963; Worcester, 1956). Some safeguards to the process include: generally limiting the practice to children within a few months of the cut-off date, being more cautious with boys than girls, assuring that the youngster's development in most domains be at least equal to the mean of the class he or she is entering, and that the receiving teacher welcomes the child. A trial placement also is recommended.

SUGGESTIONS FOR FURTHER RESEARCH ON YOUNG GIFTED CHILDREN

Clearly, much less is known about young gifted children than we need to know. Here are just two from among all of the unasked or controversial questions that deserve high priority:

- *Maturity issues.* Are gifted children *qualitatively* different in their reasoning and learning from nongifted chronological age peers, or do they resemble their mental age peers? The issue is eminently open to research in the early years, when changes are so rapid and dramatic.
- *Developmental tasks.* How much are early developmental milestones affected by high intelligence? For example, does advanced ability affect the rate of acquisition of understanding how other people think (theory of mind)? Stranger anxiety in infants? Self-help skills? Self-regulation and delay of gratification? Fears?

CONCLUSIONS

What little solid knowledge we have about young gifted children gives us good reason to pursue work with these children. We can identify them; they are not a flash in the pan; they differ from other children in meaningful ways;

their homes and their parents' behavior differ from those of children who are less advanced; they can be responsive to effective early education strategies; and early entrance to school is a viable option for them. Furthermore, young gifted children provide a window on development, including questions such as the interplay of chronological age, mental age, and degree of exceptionality. In addition, if we are to nurture the talents of both the gifted and the promising, the earlier and the more intensively we intervene, the more successful we—and they—are likely to be.

RECOMMENDED READING

Jackson, N. E. (2003). Young gifted children. In N. Colangelo & G. A. Davis (Eds.), *Handbook of gifted education* (3rd ed., pp. 470–482). Boston: Allyn & Bacon.

Klein, P. S., & Tannenbaum, A. (Eds.). (1992). *To be young and gifted.* Norwood, NJ: Ablex.

Robinson, N. M. (2000). Giftedness in very young children: How seriously should it be taken? In R. Friedman & B. M. Shore (Eds.), *Talents within: Developmental and cognitive aspects* (pp. 7–26). Washington, DC: American Psychological Association.

REFERENCES

Albert, R. S. (1980). Family positions and the attainment of eminence: A study of special family positions and special family experiences. *Gifted Child Quarterly, 24,* 87–95.

Benito, Y., & Moro, J. (1999). An empirically-based proposal for screening in the early identification of intellectually gifted students. *Gifted and Talented International, 14,* 80–91.

Bloom, B. S. (Ed.). (1985). *Developing talent in young people.* New York: Ballantine.

Brown, A. L. (1973). Conservation of number and continuous quantity in normal, bright, and retarded children. *Child Development, 44,* 376–379.

Colangelo, N., Assouline, S. G., & Gross, M. U. M. (2004). *A nation deceived: How schools hold back America's brightest students* (Vol. 1). Iowa City, IA: The Connie Belin & Jacqueline N. Blank International Center for Gifted Education and Talent Development.

Commission on Behavioral and Social Sciences and Education (CBASSE). (2002). *Minority students in special and gifted education.* Washington, DC: National Academies Press.

Cox, C. M. (1926). *Genetic studies of genius: Vol. 2. The early mental traits of three hundred geniuses.* Stanford, CA: Stanford University Press.

Dale, P. S., Crain-Thoreson, C., & Robinson, N. M. (1995). Linguistic precocity and the development of reading: The role of extra-linguistic factors. *Applied Psycholinguistics, 16,* 173–187.

DeVries, R. (1974). Relationships among Piagetian, IQ, and achievement assessments. *Child Development, 43,* 746–756.

Diezmann, C. M., & English, L. D. (2001). Developing young children's multidigit number sense. *Roeper Review, 24,* 11–13.

Diezmann, C. M., & Watters, J. J. (2000). An enrichment philosophy and strategy for empowering young gifted children to become autonomous learners in science. *Gifted and Talented International, 15,* 6–18.

Feldman, D. (1986). *Nature's gambit.* New York: Basic Books.

Gagné, F., & Gagnier, N. (2004). The socio-affective and academic impact of early entrance to school. *Roeper Review, 26,* 128–138.

Goertzel, V., Goertzel, M. G., Goertzel, T. G., & Hansen, A. (2004). *Cradles of eminence: Childhoods of more than 700 famous men and women* (2nd ed.). Scottsdale, AZ: Great Potential Press.

Gottfried, A. W., Gottfried, A. E., Bathurst, K., & Guerin D. W. (1994). *Gifted IQ: Early developmental aspects.* New York: Plenum.

Gottfried, A. W., Gottfried, A. E., Cook, C. R., & Morris, P. R. (2005). Educational characteristics of adolescents with gifted academic intrinsic motivation: A longitudinal investigation from school entry through early adulthood. *Gifted Child Quarterly, 49,* 172–186.

Gross, M. U. M. (1993). *Exceptionally gifted children.* London: Routledge-Falmer.

Gross, M. U. M. (2004). *Exceptionally gifted children* (2nd ed.). London: Routledge-Falmer.

Hertzog, N. B., Klein, M. M., & Katz, L. G. (1999). Hypothesizing and theorizing: Challenge in an early childhood curriculum. *Gifted and Talented International, 14,* 38–49.

Ho, W.-C. (Ed.). (1989). *Yani: The brush of innocence.* New York: Hudson Hills Press.

Hobson, J. R. (1963). High school performance of underage pupils initially admitted to kindergarten on the basis of physical and psychological examinations. *Educational and Psychological Measurement, 23,* 159–170.

Hoh, P.-S. (2005). The linguistic advantage of the intellectually gifted child: An empirical study of spontaneous speech. *Roeper Review, 27,* 178–185.

Hollingworth, L. S. (1931). The child of very superior intelligence as a special problem in social adjustment. *Mental Hygiene, 15(1),* 1–16.

Jackson, N. E. (1992). Precocious reading of English: Origins, structure, and predictive significance. In P. S. Klein & A. J. Tannenbaum (Eds.), *To be young and gifted* (pp. 171–203). Norwood, NJ: Ablex.

Jackson, N. E., & Butterfield, E. C. (1986). A conception of giftedness designed to promote research. In R. J. Sternberg & J. E. Davidson (Eds.), *Conceptions of giftedness* (pp. 151–181). New York: Cambridge University Press.

Kanevsky, L. (1992). The learning game. In P. S. Klein & A. Tannenbaum (Eds.), *To be young and gifted* (pp. 204–241). Norwood, NJ: Ablex.

Karnes, M. B., Shwedel, A. M., & Steinberg, D. (1984). Styles of parenting among parents of young gifted children. *Roeper Review, 6,* 232–235.

Klein, P. S. (1992). Mediating the cognitive, social, and aesthetic development of precocious young children. In P. S. Klein & A. Tannenbaum (Eds.), *To be young and gifted* (pp. 245–277). Norwood, NJ: Ablex.

Klene, R. (1988, August). *The occurrence of fears in gifted children.* Paper presented at the annual meeting of the American Psychological Association, Atlanta, GA.

Koshy, V., & Robinson, N. M. (2006). Too long neglected: Gifted young children. *European Early Childhood Education Research Journal, 14*, 113–126.

Lazar, I., & Darlington, R (1982). Lasting effects of early education: A report from the consortium for longitudinal studies. *Monographs of the Society for Research in Child Development, 47*(2–3).

Lempers, J., Block, L., Scott, M., & Draper, D. (1987). The relationship between psychometric brightness and cognitive-developmental precocity in gifted preschoolers. *Merrill Palmer Quarterly, 33*, 489–503.

Little, A. (1972). A longitudinal study of cognitive development in young children. *Child Development, 43*, 1024–1034.

Loewen, S. N. (2006). *Between the steps on "The mind's staircase": Individual pathways to the development of young children's mathematical understanding.* Unpublished doctoral dissertation, University of British Columbia, Vancouver.

Louis, B., & Lewis, M. (1992). Parental beliefs about giftedness in young children and their relation to actual ability level. *Gifted Child Quarterly, 36*, 27–31.

Maddux, C. D. (1983). Early school entry for the gifted: New evidence and concerns. *Roeper Review, 5*(4), 15–17.

McClelland, S. E. (1982). *A verbal/performance analysis of the Stanford-Binet Intelligence Scale and the development of high-IQ preschoolers.* Unpublished doctoral dissertation, University of Washington, Seattle, WA.

McCurdy, H. (1960). The childhood patterns of genius. *Horizon, 2*(5), 33–38.

Moore, C., Nelson-Piercy, C., Abel, M., & Frye, D. (1984). Precocious conservation in context: The solution of quantity tasks by nonquantitative strategies. *Journal of Experimental Child Psychology, 38*, 1–6.

Morelock, M. J., & Morrison, K. (1999). Differentiating "developmentally appropriate": The multidimensional curriculum model for young gifted children. *Roeper Review, 21*,195–200.

Moss, E. (1990). Social interaction and metacognitive development in gifted preschoolers. *Gifted Child Quarterly, 34*, 16–20.

Moss, E. (1992). Early interactions and metacognitive development of gifted preschoolers. In P. S. Klein & A. Tannenbaum (Eds.), *To be young and gifted* (pp. 278–318). Norwood, NJ: Ablex.

Moss, E., & Strayer, F. F. (1990). Interactive problem-solving of gifted and non-gifted preschoolers with their mothers. *International Journal of Behavioral Development, 13*, 177–197.

Olszewski, P., Kulieke, M., & Buescher, T. (1987). The influence of the family environment on the development of talent: A literature review. *Journal for the Education of the Gifted, 11*, 6–28.

Olszewski-Kubilius, P. (2002). Parenting practices that promote talent development, creativity, and optimal adjustment. In M. Neihart, S. M. Reis, N. M. Robinson, & S. M. Moon (Eds.), *The social and emotional development of gifted children: What do we know?* (pp. 205–212). Waco, TX: Prufrock Press.

Obrzut, A., Nelson, R. B., & Obrzut, J. E. (1984). Early school entrance for intellectually superior children: An analysis. *Psychology in the Schools, 21*, 71–77.

Oxford, M., Spieker, S., & Robinson, N. M. (2006). *Preschool antecedents of high ability and academic achievement: Findings from the NICHD Study of Early Child Care and Youth Development.* Unpublished manuscript.

Payne, A. C., Whitehurst, G. J., & Angell, A. L. (1994). The role of home literacy environment in the development of language ability in preschool children from low-income families. *Early Childhood Research Quarterly, 9,* 427–440.

Pfeiffer, S. I., & Jarosewich, T. (2003). *Gifted Rating Scales.* San Antonio, TX: Harcourt Assessment.

Pfeiffer, S. I., & Jarosewich, T. (2007). The Gifted Rating Scales—School Form: An analysis of the standardization sample based on age, gender, race, and diagnostic efficiency. *Gifted Child Quarterly, 51,* 39–50.

Planche, P. (1985). Modalités fonctionelles et conduits de resolution de problemes chez des enfants precoces de cinq, sex et sept ans d'age chronologique [Functional modalities and problem solving in precocious children five, six, and seven years old]. *Archives de Psychologie, 53,* 411–415.

Pletan, M. D., Robinson, N. M., Berninger, V. W., & Abbott, R. D. (1995). Parents' observations of kindergartners who are advanced in mathematical reasoning. *Journal for the Education of the Gifted, 19,* 30–44.

Porath, M. (1992). Stage and structure in the development of children with various types of "giftedness." In R. Case (Ed.), *The mind's staircase: Exploring the conceptual underpinnings of children's thought and knowledge* (pp. 303–317). Hillsdale, NJ: Erlbaum.

Proctor, T. B., Black, K. N., & Feldhusen, J. F. (1986). Early admission of selected children to elementary school: A review of the research literature. *Journal of Educational Research, 80,* 70–76.

Rankin, F., & Vialle, W. (1996). Early entry: A policy in search of practice. *Australian Journal of Early Childhood, 21,* 6–11.

Robinson, A., Shore, B. M., & Enersen, D. L. (2007). *Best practices in gifted education: An evidence-based guide.* Waco, TX: Prufrock Press.

Robinson, H. B., Robinson, N. M., Wolins, M., Bronfenbrenner, U., & Richmond, J. B. (1973). *Early child care in the United States.* London: Gordon and Breach.

Robinson, N. M. (2003). Two wrongs do not make a right: Sacrificing the needs of academically talented students does not solve society's unsolved problems. *Journal for the Education of the Gifted, 26,* 251–273.

Robinson, N. M. (2004). Effects of academic acceleration on the social-emotional status of gifted students. In N. Colangelo, S. G. Assouline, & M. U. M. Gross (Eds.), *A nation deceived: How schools hold back America's brightest students* (Vol. 2, pp. 59–67). Iowa City, IA: The Connie Belin & Jacqueline N. Blank International Center for Gifted Education and Talent Development.

Robinson, N. M. (2005). In defense of a psychometric approach to the definition of academic giftedness: A conservative view from a die-hard liberal. In R. J. Sternberg & J. E. Davidson (Eds.), *Conceptions of giftedness* (2nd ed., pp. 280–294). New York: Cambridge University Press.

Robinson, N. M., Abbott, R. D., Berninger, V. W., & Busse, J. (1996). The structure of abilities in math-precocious young children: Gender similarities and differences. *Journal of Educational Psychology, 88,* 341–352.

Robinson, N. M., Abbott, R. D., Berninger, V. W., Busse, J., & Mukhopadhyay, S. (1997). Developmental changes in mathematically precocious young children: Matthew and gender effects. *Gifted Child Quarterly, 41,* 145–159.

Robinson, N. M., Dale, P. S., & Landesman, S. J. (1990). Validity of Stanford-Binet IV with young children exhibiting precocious language. *Intelligence, 14,* 173–186.

Robinson, N. M., Lanzi, R. G., Weinberg, R. A., Ramey, S. L., & Ramey, C. T. (2002). Factors associated with high academic competence in former Head Start children at third grade. *Gifted Child Quarterly, 46*, 281–294.

Robinson, N. M., & Robinson, H. B. (1992). The use of standardized tests with young gifted children. In P. S. Klein & A. J. Tannenbaum (Eds.), *To be young and gifted* (pp. 141–170). Norwood, NJ: Ablex.

Roedell, W. C., Jackson, N. E., & Robinson, H. B. (1980). *Gifted young children.* New York: Teachers College Press.

Rogers, K. B. (2002). Effects of acceleration on gifted learners. In M. Neihart, S. M. Reis, N. M. Robinson, & S. M. Moon (Eds.), *The social and emotional development of gifted children: What do we know?* (pp. 3–12). Waco, TX: Prufrock Press.

Ruf, D. L. (2005). *Losing our minds: Gifted children left behind.* Scottsdale, AZ: Great Potential Press

Sankar-DeLeeuw, N. (2004). Case studies of gifted kindergarten children: Profiles of promise. *Roeper Review, 26*, 192–207.

Scott, M. S., & Delgado, C. F. (2005). Identifying cognitively gifted minority students in preschool. *Gifted Child Quarterly, 49*, 199–210.

Silverman, L. K. (2002). Asynchronous development. In M. Neihart, S. M. Reis, N. M. Robinson, & S. M. Moon (Eds.), *The social and emotional development of gifted children: What do we know?* (pp. 31–37). Waco, TX: Prufrock Press.

Silverman, L. K., Chitwood, D. G., & Waters, J. L. (1986). Young gifted children: Can parents identify giftedness? *Topics in Early Childhood Special Education, 6*(1), 23–38.

Simonton, D. K. (1998). Gifted child—genius adult: Three life-span developmental perspectives. In R. Friedman & K. B. Rogers (Eds.), *Talent in context: Historical and social perspectives on giftedness* (pp. 151–175). Washington, DC: American Psychological Association.

Spitz, H. H. (1985). Extreme décalage: The task by intelligence interaction. In E. D. Neimark, R. De Lisi, & J. L. Newman (Eds.), *Moderators of competence* (pp. 117–145). Hillsdale, NJ: Erlbaum.

Stainthorp, R., & Hughes, D. (2004). An illustrative case study of precocious reading ability. *Gifted Child Quarterly, 48*, 107–120.

Storch, S. A., & Whitehurst, G. J. (2001). The role of family and home in the literacy development of children from low-income backgrounds. In P. R. Britto & J. Brooks-Gunn (Eds.), *The role of family literacy environments in promoting young children's emerging literacy skills* (pp. 53–71). San Francisco: Jossey-Bass.

Tannenbaum, A. (1992). Early signs of giftedness: Research and commentary. *Journal for the Education of the Gifted, 15*, 104–133.

Terman, L. M. (1931). The gifted child. In C. Murchison (Ed.), *A handbook of child psychology* (pp. 568–584). New York: Wiley.

Turkheimer, E., Haley, A., Waldron, M., D'Onofrio, B., & Gottesman, I. I. (2003). Socioeconomic status modifies heritability of IQ in young children. *Psychological Science, 14*, 623–628.

Willerman, L., & Fiedler, M. F. (1974). Infant performance and intellectual precocity. *Child Development, 45*, 483–486.

Willerman, L., & Fiedler, M. F. (1977). Intellectually precocious preschool children: Early development and later intellectual accomplishments. *Journal of Genetic Psychology, 131*, 13–20.

Winner, E. (1996). *Gifted children: Myths and realities.* New York: Basic Books.

Witty, P., & Coomer, A. (1985). A case study of twin gifted boys. *Exceptional Children, 22,* 104–108.

Worcester, D. A. (1956). *The education of children of above-average mentality.* Lincoln, NE: University of Nebraska Press.

Wright, L., & Coulianos, C. (1991). A model program for precocious children: Hollingworth Preschool. *Gifted Child Today, 14*(5), 24–29.

Zha, Z. (1984). A comparative study of the analogical reasoning of 3- to 6-year-old super-normal and normal children. *Acta Psychologica Sinica, 16,* 373–382.

Chapter 14

ETHNICALLY DIVERSE STUDENTS

Marcia Gentry, Saiying Hu, and Adrian T. Thomas

n this chapter, we discuss the empirical research base concerning ethnicity and K–12 gifted education in U.S. schools, with a purpose of providing an objective assessment of the available knowledge in this area. Thus, we focus on the ethnic groups for which a research base exists, namely, Black, Latino/a, and Asian American students, and to a lesser extent, Native American students, because the bulk of the literature concerning ethnicity in gifted education focuses on the problems of underrepresentation and identification of underrepresented groups directly affecting Black, Latino/a, and Native American students. In the following sections, we define terms associated with this area of research, describe our method, identify general categories of research associated with this topic, provide practical implications concerning the research to date, discuss the limitations of the existing research, and suggest directions for future research in this area. In doing so, we reference recent, peer-reviewed sources in this area.

TERMS USED IN THE STUDY OF ETHNIC DIVERSITY IN GIFTED EDUCATION

Giftedness

Giftedness is a socially constructed concept that delineates descriptive traits and characteristics (Renzulli, 2005; Sternberg, 2005), which, because of its social construction, constantly evolves (Borland, 1997, 2005). Furthermore, because of its social construction, giftedness is something conferred on children in educational settings, by educators, using measures and methods that work well with White children of educated parents (Borland, 1997, 2005). This social conferral has led to inequitable representation among ethnic groups because it fails to recognize the cultural context of giftedness (Freeman, 2005; Plucker & Barab, 2005). As early as 1988, the Javits Act acknowledged the contextual nature of giftedness and established an empirical basis for serving students traditionally underrepresented in gifted and talented programs. Furthermore, the disproportionate representation of poor and culturally diverse students in gifted education encouraged a federal definition of giftedness that encompasses the recognition of potential. This definition acknowledges the significance of potential and emphasizes the existence of giftedness in all cultural groups and across all socioeconomic levels (United States Department of Education, 1993).

Ethnicity

Although ethnicity is a broadly defined construct, we use ethnicity to refer to students' cultural heritage. Specifically, this chapter addresses issues in gifted education affecting students from Asian American, Black, Latino/a, and Native American ethnic groups. These groups exist as a de facto result of how the United States collects demographic data on ethnic groups, and they fail to distinguish among the many variable subgroups that comprise each of the larger group designations. Therefore, we cannot define what is meant by Native American, Black, Latino/a, or Asian cultural heritage because of the diversity of cultures in each group. Terms used in the literature to identify cultural heritage or ethnicity vary. In this chapter we consistently use the terms: White, Black, Asian, Latino/a, and Native American to refer to members of various ethnic groups. We use the term *ethnically diverse gifted students* to refer to the whole topic.

METHOD

Providing a concise summary of extant knowledge concerning ethnically diverse gifted students requires a deliberate and thorough method. First, we conducted an initial search of the PsychINFO, ERIC, and ECER thesauruses and an informal search of textbooks and general literature to identify the key terms associated with ethnicity and giftedness. We paired with *gifted* the following index keywords to search three relevant academic data bases (PsychINFO, ERIC, and ECER) for the years from 1990 to present: *minority, Black, African American, Asian American, Hispanic, Latino/a,* and *Native American.* We then cross-referenced our findings. In screening the findings, we included articles in this summary that (1) addressed K–12 gifted education in United States schools; (2) presented empirical data; (3) focused on issues concerning ethnicity and gifted without the confounding issues of poverty or bilingual status (which are addressed elsewhere in this encyclopedia); and (4) appeared in peer-reviewed, academic journals, and thus, likely represented a high degree of professional quality (Friedman-Nimz, O'Brien, & Frey, 2005). We reviewed the articles that met these criteria and classified them by major content. Current empirical studies are identified in five general categories addressing five major issues or representing certain types of study regarding ethnically diverse gifted students: underrepresentation, identification, characteristics and experiences, achievement, and studies of programs or interventions.

ETHNICALLY DIVERSE GIFTED STUDENTS: WHAT WE KNOW

Underrepresentation

Study, concern, and debate regarding underrepresentation exists in the recent gifted education literature. Underrepresentation of ethnically diverse gifted students in gifted programs is severe, longstanding, exists in all levels of the educational system, and is documented by every traditional means of academic achievement (i.e., grade point average, standardized test scores, class rank; Miller, 2004). As of 1993, the U.S. Department of Education reported that Black, Latino/a, and Native American students were underrepresented by 50–70% in gifted education programs (Ford, 1998). As reported by the U.S. Department of Education (2000), Blacks, Latinos, and Native Americans represent 8.23%, 9.54%, and .91%, respectively, of elementary and secondary students in gifted and talented (GT) programs, whereas these student groups represent 16.99%, 16.13%, and 1.16%, respectively, of the nations' student population. Conversely, Asian or Pacific Islander students represent 7.08% of students in gifted programs and 4.14% of the nation's student population.

Gifted education research literature has provided evidence that ethnically diverse gifted students generally remain underrepresented in gifted education programs. As both Ford (1998) and Miller (2004) found, underrepresentation and underidentification of ethnically diverse students from Black, Native

American, and Latino/a backgrounds in gifted programs remains a serious problem across the United States. Conversely, students from Asian backgrounds are often identified as gifted at rates greater than their peers (Kitano & DiJiosia, 2002). Recently, McBee (2006) analyzed referral sources used for gifted identification screening by race and socioeconomic status, using a dataset containing demographic information, gifted nomination status, and gifted identification status for all elementary school students in the state of Georgia. He concluded that inequitable nominations, rather than assessment, were the primary source of the underrepresentation of ethnically diverse and low-income students in gifted programs. Specifically, McBee found that Asian and White students were much more likely to be nominated than Black or Latino/a students, and that students receiving free or reduced-price lunches were less likely to be nominated than students paying for their own lunches.

Another potential explanation for nomination inequities is the use of Black English. Black English, for some a symbol of ethnic identity (Ogbu, 1995, 2003), is used in formal and informal settings (Fordham, 1999; Ogbu, 2003). Fordham (1999) noted its use by a Black female, who scored 96% on the verbal PSAT, during her research interview. Similarly, Ogbu (2003) noted its use among Black students and their parents from an affluent suburb during a community social gathering. As reported by Fordham, Black English frustrates school officials. When its use frustrates those charged with recommending students to gifted programs, qualified students may be overlooked.

Evidence exists that the traditional tools used in identifying students for placement in gifted programs lack effectiveness when used with students from diverse ethnic backgrounds resulting in underrepresentation (e.g., Borland & Wright, 1994; Feiring, Louis, Ukeje, Lewis, & Leong, 1997; Lidz & Macrine, 2001; Naglieri & Ford, 2003; Plucker, Callahan, & Tomchin, 1996; Reyes, 1996; Sarouphim, 2001, 2002, 2004; Scott, 1996; Scott & Delgado, 2005). These tools typically include standardized measures of achievement and ability, as well as criterion-referenced achievement tests. Broadening definitions and conceptions of giftedness and the associated procedures used for identification have offered promise in addressing the problem of underrepresentation (e.g., Naglieri & Ford, 2003; Sarouphim, 2002). Evidence exists that professional development used with educators can enhance understanding and potentially increase the nomination of children from diverse ethnic backgrounds. In a general education study conducted by McAllister and Irvine (2002), teachers reported increased use of culturally relevant pedagogy and greater tolerance and respect for students' cultural differences after completing 40 hours of a multicultural professional development program geared to fostering culturally responsive practices.

Researchers have widely acknowledged the underrepresentation of ethnically diverse gifted students in gifted programs and recognized the ongoing struggle concerning the issues of underidentification and underrepresentation that remains in the field of gifted education. Evidence exists that the traditional tools and methods used in identifying students for gifted programs lack effectiveness when used with ethnically diverse students and thus contribute to underrepresentation. Broadening definitions and conceptions of giftedness and the associated identification procedures, as well as professional development, have been recommended as actions necessary to solve the problem of underrepresentation. The issue of underrepresentation is inextricably linked to identification methods and procedures; therefore, more research regarding identification might help mitigate underrepresentation.

Identification

Much discussion and research concerning ethnically diverse gifted students has focused on identification (Plucker, 1996). Analysis of current literature revealed that a large proportion of research on ethnically diverse gifted students focused on identification procedures, approaches, measures, and models, as well as the examination of the validity and effectiveness of these methods in identifying ethnically diverse gifted students. Extensive and varied empirical support exists for alternative means of identifying ethnically diverse gifted students. These means are primarily based on the theory of multiple intelligences (Gardner, 1983) or on methods using nonverbal means of identification. They include performance tasks in Project STAR (VanTassel-Baska, Johnson, & Avery, 2002); dynamic assessment (Borland & Wright, 1994; Lidz & Macrine, 2001); the DISCOVER Project (Sarouphim, 2001, 2002, 2004); Brigance K & 1 Screen (Feiring et al., 1997); multidimensional approach (Reyes, 1996); cognitive battery and verbal response to identify primary-aged students (Scott, 1996; Scott & Delgado, 2005); portfolio assessment (Coleman, 1994); the System of Multicultural Pluralistic Assessment (SOMPA; Matthew, 1992); the Naglieri Nonverbal Ability Test (NNAT; Naglieri & Ford, 2003); peer nomination (Cunningham, Callahan, Plucker, Roberson, & Rapkin, 1998); the Multiple Intelligence Assessment Technique (Plucker et al., 1996); and whole class tryout procedures (Jatko, 1995). Each of these methods relies on something other than traditional measures used to identify gifted children. Promising results from these studies underscore the importance of using alternative pathways to identify ethnically diverse students.

Parents, teachers, and tests all affect identification. Scott (1992) reported that more White than Latino/a or Black parents requested an evaluation of their child for gifted program placement. However, few intergroup differences existed among the children from these different ethnic backgrounds concerning initial or current attributions of giftedness. Then, Plata and Masten (1998) explored the issue of teacher nominations of White and Latino/a students to the gifted program in an ethnically diverse district. They found that White students received higher nomination ratings from their teachers than did Latino/a students. Scott, Deuel, Jean-Francois, and Urbano (1996) investigated whether ethnically diverse children with potential for high academic achievement could be identified by assessing cognitive abilities. They concluded that using a child's performance on a cognitive battery could be effective for identifying gifted minority children who previously have not been identified as having superior cognitive abilities. With parents who are unlikely to request an evaluation, and teachers who rate them lower, ethnically diverse children can be identified through cognitive assessment, despite research concerning test bias that has concluded that traditional testing also can result in the underidentification of ethnically diverse children. These conflicting findings underscore the need for multiple methods to identify gifted children.

Some research has identified the influences of acculturation factors and cultural understanding on the identification of ethnically diverse gifted students. For example, Hartley (1991) studied the differing perceptions of giftedness among parents and teachers of Navajo and White children, as well as the effects of acculturation on the responses. She concluded that qualitative differences existed between the teacher and the parent groups and that level of acculturation was a significant differentiating factor among responses. Further, behaviors such as leadership and competitiveness, considered gifted by Whites, would not be considered gifted by Navajos. In fact, there is no Navajo word for gifted; instead, they acknowledge the concept of outstanding in conjunction with a specific ability. Similarly, Masten and Plata (2000) examined the differences between teacher ratings of White and Latino/a students and concluded that acculturation seemed to influence teacher ratings, with teachers rating White students higher than Latino/a students in areas of learning, motivation, creativity, and leadership characteristics. Peterson (1999) suggested conceptualizing giftedness by examining themes that emerged in the language of Latino/a, Black, Native American, immigrant Asian, and low-income White individuals as they nominated children for a hypothetical gifted program. She compared the nomination language with the language of classroom teachers and concluded cultural understanding was a key to inclusive identification practices.

Although some existing procedures and approaches hold promise for identifying ethnically diverse gifted students, much work remains to fully address the issue. Patton, Prillaman, and VanTassel-Baska (1990) underscored this need when they assessed the nature and extent of programs for disadvantaged gifted students in the 50 states and the U.S. territories. They concluded that states had not addressed their concerns for equity and pluralism into the definitional and funding structures of the gifted programs, despite consistently positive philosophical orientations toward ethnically diverse and low socioeconomic gifted students. Frasier (1995) studied the perceptions that educators hold about the problems of identification of ethnically diverse gifted children from economically disadvantaged and limited English proficient backgrounds. She found that the major barriers to identification included test bias and teachers' inability to recognize indicators of potential in underrepresented groups.

Gifted education literature contains a large number of studies on identification procedures, approaches, measures, and models. Some identification procedures have been found to be generally effective in identifying and assessing ethnically diverse gifted students. For example, teacher nomination when cultural understanding is present, peer nomination, alternative measures, multidimensional assessments, cognitive assessment, and performance tasks all hold promise in addressing issues of underrepresentation. However, research also suggests that major barriers to identification include test bias and teachers' inability to recognize indicators of potential in ethnically diverse gifted students. Generally speaking, gifted education identification practices have not yet incorporated methods and procedures for equitably identifying ethnically diverse students. School personnel continue to rely on outdated procedures that create barriers to identification for ethnically diverse students. More attention and action needs to be devoted to the issue of nomination and identification of ethnically diverse students for gifted programs, with an emphasis on alternate, multiple, and culturally sensitive pathways to identification.

Characteristics and Experiences

Some researchers have examined the characteristics and experiences of ethnically diverse gifted students that distinguish them from their White peers. For example, Langram (1997) assessed how gifted, ethnically diverse, low-income, eighth-grade students self-reported on various psychosocial dimensions while attending a 3-year high school preparatory program. Four dominant psychosocial themes emerged from this study. First, gifted female students demonstrated an external locus of control while their male counterparts described an internal locus of control. Second, both boys and girls emphasized the importance of peer relationships. The third theme, leadership, revealed gender differences similar to those found in locus of control with female students being more concerned with external measures of success. Finally, male students reported a stronger sense of community than did the female students who seemed to resist being expected to embrace the community of the school. Renzulli and Park (2000) studied gifted high school dropouts and reported that dropping out of school was related to students' educational aspiration, pregnancy or child-rearing, gender, and parent's educational attainment. Many of the gifted dropouts came from low-income families and from ethnic minority groups, and few participated in extracurricular activities.

Several studies provided insights concerning the experiences of ethnically diverse gifted students (Harmon, 2002; Hébert, 1998, Hébert & Beardsley, 2001; Kloosterman, 1999). For example, Hébert (1998) reported that gifted Black male students experienced inadequate counseling, negative peer pressure, and family problems. Later, Hébert and Beardsley (2001) identified issues specific to rural Black gifted students, including the need for emotional support, mentors, and role models. In a recent study, Kao and Hébert (2006) revealed that Asian gifted adolescents experienced intergenerational cultural conflict within the families, and the conflict involved two concerns: parental expectations for academic performance and differing views regarding accul- turation. Specifically, the conflict centered on academic issues included differ- ing views of academic rigor, the value of standardized tests, time spent on the home computer, comparisons with classmates, and parents' misperceptions of gifted education. The conflict focused on acculturation issues including value differences, parental expectations regarding obedience and respect, different views of adolescent autonomy, and the importance of learning the ethnic lan- guage. These findings help explain the cultural dilemmas faced by gifted Asian American adolescents.

Research has shown that Black students can be negatively affected by a stereotype threat concerning perceptions that they are less smart than their White peers. Stereotype threat is "the threat of being judged by a negative stereotype" about one's group (Steele & Aronson, 1995, p. 798). Steele and Aronson (1995) explored the relationship between this phenomenon and stu- dents' (Black and White) performance by assigning participants to either a diagnostic (ability-assessed) or one of two nondiagnostic (no mention of abil- ity) conditions. The conditions were designed to prime negative stereotypes about Blacks' intellectual ability; thus, the researchers hypothesized poorer performance for Black students in the ability assessed group. As postulated, Black students in the ability-assessed group performed worse than both Black students in the nondiagnostic groups and White students in the ability- assessed group. Asian students, on the other hand, may be subjected to a model minority stereotype or a stereotype that they do well in math and science. This can be problematic in meeting the educational and counseling needs of this diverse population (Plucker, 1996).

Differences exist among various ethnic groups of gifted students. Ewing and Yong (1992) compared learning style preferences among ethnically diverse groups of gifted students and found many significant differences among gifted Black, Mexican American, and American-born Chinese students concerning their preferences for noise, light, visual modality, studying in afternoon, and persistence. This study revealed that Mexican American students were most characterized by responsibility, motivation, and preference for kinesthetic modality, and gifted American-born Chinese students were persistent, respon- sive, and preferred to study in the afternoon and in bright light. However, for gifted Black students, the three least preferred variables were auditory modal- ity, structure, and noise. This study supported previous findings that identified gifted students tend to be highly motivated, responsible, and persistent (Ricca, 1983; Ross & Wright, 1987; Yong & McIntyre, 1992).

Ethnically diverse gifted students have characteristics that differ from White students identified by traditional means for gifted and talented pro- grams. Some behaviors valued in the culture, such as cooperation, caregiving, and modesty, are not traditionally viewed as attributes of gifted, high-achieving students, and thus, students from Latino/a or Native American backgrounds might not be nominated by their teachers or parents. Black students may be affected by stereotype threat concerning their ability. Asian American students, in particular, can be affected by intergenerational conflicts and stereotyping about their ability in math and science and their status as a model minority. Being culturally diverse and from a low-income family increases risk of dropping out of school and of underachievement.

Achievement

Achievement of ethnically diverse gifted students remains an important area of inquiry. Ford's work has illuminated achievement issues affecting Black gifted students. In 1992, Ford examined the respective influences of psychological, social, and cultural determinants of underachievement as perceived by gifted Black students in an urban district. She concluded that underachievement, as perceived by Black gifted students, was influenced most by psychological factors (e.g., anxiety, loneliness, fear) rather than social and cultural factors. In investigating families of gifted Black students, Ford (1993) examined environmental variables and gender differences in underachievement among early adolescent gifted Black students. She found that family demographic variables, such as parents' levels of education, occupation, employment status, and caregiver status, contributed little to Black students' achievement orientation. Accordingly, she called for more emphasis on family values, beliefs, and attitudes in future studies. In 1995, Ford investigated academically diverse middle and high school Black students' perceptions of factors that affected their achievement. She concluded that the strongest predictors for discriminating among gifted, potentially gifted, average achievers, and underachievers were students' attitudes toward reading, math, and science; students' perceptions of parental achievement orientation; and students' own achievement ideology.

Much research attention has been paid to the underachievement (and subsequent underidentification) of Black students. In 1986, after studying Black students in one Washington, DC, high school, Fordham and Ogbu concluded that these students didn't live up to their academic potential for fear of being accused of "acting White." This conclusion was based in a cultural-ecological perspective in which Black children are socialized to function within their culture and in which they learn an oppositional frame of reference. One aspect of this opposition involves rejecting "White Americans' way of life" (Fordham & Ogbu, 1986, p. 181). Although early versions of the theory addressed Black Americans' socialization, later versions attempted to explain academic achievement. Accordingly, peer relations have a profound effect on Black students' academic pursuits; thus, among members of the oppositional culture, high academic achievement constitutes acting White. Some Black students learn to cope with Black peers' taunts—others fall victim to them. Those who choose academic success must overcome the burden of acting White.

Although Fordham and Ogbu's (1986) study and conclusions have been popular and have been used to explain the underachievement (and resulting underidentification) of Black students, more recent work has rejected the persuasiveness of their work. Tyson, Darity, and Castellino (2005) studied eight schools and found that in seven of these schools Black students strove to achieve in school. Like Fordham and Ogbu, Tyson et al. (2005) found that Black students were taunted for being smart; however, they also found that White students received similar taunting. Tyson et al. (2005) found that poor White students opted out of gifted programs because they did not want to be perceived as privileged, and they argued that many of the problems faced by gifted students are not unique to Black students. Finally, Fryer and Torelli (2006) conducted an empirical analysis of "acting White" and concluded that this phenomenon has a significant effect on Black student achievement, especially in schools with high interracial contact among high-achieving students, but little effect in predominantly Black or private schools. In looking at data from their eighth school, Tyson et al. (2005) conceded that school culture can create an environment of underachievement, which they observed in this setting.

Some researchers investigated the relationship between student motivation and achievement. For example, Grant, Battle, Murphy, and Heggoy (1999) explored influences on achievement motivation among nine rural Black female high school honor graduates. They found that these students reported and exhibited adaptive mastery-oriented achievement motivation patterns. Being Black was a significant factor manifested through the goal of disproving incompetence in the school setting, and peer support helped to sustain their individual efforts, in part based on the value of academic achievement. Schweigardt, Worrell, and Hale (2001) explored gender preferences, course selection, and enjoyment among academically talented students enrolled in a summer enrichment program. With the exception of Asian students, other student groups—Blacks, Latino/as, mixed ethnicity, and Whites—were more likely to enroll in traditionally male or female courses. However, these groups reported more internal reasons for course selection and greater course enjoyment.

Some researchers have identified positive and negative predictors of achievement. Datnow and Cooper (1997) studied peer networks of Black students in predominantly White elite independent schools and found that the formal and informal peer networks positively affected students by supporting their academic success, creating opportunities to reaffirm their racial identities, and facilitating their adjustment to unwelcoming settings. They also recognized the complex dynamics and ideologies of Black peer groups. Tomlinson, Callahan, and Lelli (1997) reported that mentorship, family outreach, and classroom modifications were significant factors that promoted success, both in the regular classroom and in transition to special services for gifted learners. In addition, Grantham (2004) explored the motivation of a Black male and his choice to participate in a gifted program. He concluded that social influences of teachers, peers, and the school setting, coupled with the student's belief that participating in the gifted program was worthwhile, contributed to the student's success in the program. Recently, Worrell (2007) indicated that ethnic minority groups had significantly higher ethnic identity (EI) scores than their

White counterparts but did not differ on other group orientation (OGO) attitudes. Worrell also reported that EI predicted self-esteem for the Latino/a students, and OGO predicted self-esteem for the Black students, but neither variable predicted self-esteem for Asian American and White academically talented students. According to Worrell, EI and OGO were negative and positive predictors of school achievement, respectively, but only for Black students, and neither variable predicted achievement in a summer program for academically talented youth.

While some researchers have concentrated on issues of underachievement, others have investigated ethnically diverse and high-achieving gifted students. For example, Gándara (2005) compared the characteristics of Latino/a high achievers with those of White high achievers at different points along the K–12 continuum, and described the lives and academic choices of four high-achieving Latino/a students. Gándara concluded that high-achieving Latino/a students were much more likely than high-achieving White students to have parents with very low educational levels, and thus they were not often able to obtain specific support and advice from their less-educated parents for successfully navigating through school. Only one of the four students attended college—others had family obligations and pressures to earn money. Gándara concluded that college access programs and the peer support these programs provide are essential for developing talent among high-achieving Latino/a students.

Achievement of ethnically diverse gifted students is related to both underrepresentation and identification. Research has shown that achievement or underachievement occurs in the context of the cultural setting in the school, peers, family, and community. Numerous variables concerning the achievement or underachievement of gifted Black students have been studied. Specifically, informal peer networks, mentorships, family outreach, classroom modifications, and familial, social, and cultural factors can influence achievement in positive ways, whereas variables such as test anxiety, peer pressure, negative perceptions toward school and the learning environment, and negative psychological and cultural factors can exert negative influences on achievement. The issue of acting White is both complex and not a definitive explanation for underachievement of Black students in gifted programs, although peer pressure and school climate can affect the culture of achievement. Although much research has been conducted on issues of underachievement of ethnically diverse gifted students, recent attention also has focused on high achievers from ethnically diverse backgrounds. More research concerning variables that positively influence achievement is warranted.

Studies of Programs and Interventions

Empirical program descriptions and intervention studies have played an important role in gifted education research by providing strategies and approaches to recognize and develop giftedness among children from diverse ethnic backgrounds (e.g., Datnow & Cooper, 1997; Grant et al., 1999; Harmon, 2002; Hébert, 1998; Hébert & Beardsley, 2001; Jones, 1997; Kloosterman, 1999; Olszewski-Kubilius & Laubscher, 1996; Tomlinson et al., 1997); studying the effects of a specific implemented program (Olszewski-Kubilius & Laubscher, 1996); discussing, reporting, or presenting the practices or processes of a program (Barnett, Gustin, & Dusel, 1996; Goertz, Phemister, & Bernal, 1996; Wright & Borland, 1992); identifying the effectiveness of certain interventions (Haensly & Lehmann, 1998; Jones, 1997); or investigating specific issues in certain programs (Cooley, 1991). For example, Jones (1997) examined a 6-year precollegiate program designed to prepare academically talented, economically disadvantaged, culturally diverse gifted students for a college education. In this program, students received a "supervised college preparatory program and annual visits to a university campus for an intensive summer institute" (Jones, 1997, p. 665). Jones found evidence to support an informal approach to science education as a strategy for reaching underserved students. He suggested similar initiatives might help attract members of historically underrepresented groups to nontraditional subject areas and to develop their interests and expertise in these areas.

Some studies, though limited, reported successful interventions in educating ethnically diverse gifted students. For example, Cartledge, Sentelle, Loe, Lambert, and Reed (2001) conducted an 18-month intervention study of Black inner-city elementary students in a gifted classroom. With goals of reducing noncompliant and disruptive behaviors and increasing academic productivity, the intervention involved positively phrased classroom behavioral expectations, social skills training, structured/systematic instruction, and preplanned positive and negative consequences for noncompliance. The results showed that the inventions resulted in reduced negative behaviors and highlighted the need for professional development to help educators address positive behavior management and thus encourage student achievement.

Similarly, Olszewski-Kubilius, Lee, Ngoi, and Ngoi (2004) reported a successful intervention effort called EXCITE, a collaborative program of a university-based gifted center and local school districts. By providing parent education and support, peer support, academic enrichment, and individualized talent development, this project was geared to prepare gifted minority elementary and middle school students for advanced high school courses in math and science. Olszewski-Kubilius et al. (2004) reported that the majority of the students in EXCITE who were retained in the program earned high grades in math and science, resulting in a 300% increase of culturally diverse children qualifying for an advanced math class in grade 6 after 2 years of involvement in the program. More recently, Swanson (2006) reported results from Project Breakthrough, which focused on curricular intervention and teacher development. Specifically, this 3-year project conducted teacher training in the use of language arts and science curriculum developed by the Center for Gifted Education at the College of William and Mary. After the training, teachers implemented the units using models of teaching designated in the project. Results from this intervention study included a threefold increase in students identified as gifted, improved student achievement, and changes in teacher perceptions of students' abilities and of their teaching practices. Swanson concluded that because teachers serve as gatekeepers for gifted programs, teacher development was a key to finding ethnically diverse gifted learners.

Program and intervention studies provide important information and knowledge by reporting successful program and intervention practices, studying effects of programs, and identifying the effectiveness of certain interventions. Research has identified some successful interventions, which include teacher development, implementation of challenging curricula, parent education and support, peer support, academic enrichment, and individualized talent development services. In summary, studies of program and intervention hold promise for better serving ethnically diverse gifted children.

LIMITATIONS AND FUTURE DIRECTIONS: WHAT WE NEED TO KNOW

Ethnic diversity in gifted education programs represents a field relatively new to educational research. Much work remains as researchers seek to understand gifted children from diverse ethnic backgrounds and the interaction of gifted education with the varying ethnic cultures. By far, the bulk of the research has provided valuable knowledge and insights for ethnically diverse gifted students with regard to defining the problem, developing alternative means of identification, describing their characteristics and experiences, or defining their achievement issues. However, it is noteworthy that research regarding ethnic groups is limited by demographic categories of ethnicity collected by the government, school districts, and researchers. It is a fact that the majority of the time, the ethnic groups by which students are identified or grouped for study include only large sweeping groups such as those reported in this chapter: Black, Asian, Native American, Latino/a. Such general groups fail to distinguish among the many differing subgroups that comprise each larger category, and thus mask potentially meaningful differences or findings within particular categories. For example, there is a need to investigate why Asian students are overrepresented and more frequently identified for placement in gifted programs, while at the same time distinguishing among different Asian cultures. Just as Japanese American students are overrepresented in gifted programs, the more recent Hmong refugee immigrants are underrepresented in the same programs. Grouping these entirely different cultures together as Asian masks important differences among various groups, and fails to facilitate study of the nuances of the cultures that can lead to understanding of student achievement, belonging, and success. There also is a need to continue the work of Hrabowski, Maton, & Greif (1998), and Hrabowski, Maton, Green, & Greif (2002), which explores social, psychological, and familial factors related to the academic success of high-achieving Black students.

Another limitation to the extant research involves confounding the variables of ethnicity or race with other variables such as poverty or English language status. When researchers confound these variables, they unintentionally contribute to a prevailing stereotype that achievement disparities exist as a function of socioeconomic status, when in fact, for Black students from high socioeconomic backgrounds and with high ability, the achievement gap is wider (Miller, 2004). They also prevent a more complete understanding of the nuances associated with diverse ethnic groups and giftedness.

With the majority of the literature and research focusing on underrepresentation, identification, characteristics and experiences, and achievement issues, the gifted education field lacks a good body of high-quality intervention research. Although identification remains an important issue, so too is the recruitment, retention, and development of ethnically diverse students into programs, schools, classes, and universities that will help them realize their potential. More research is needed on high-quality curriculum and enriching experiences that foster the development of talent among ethnically diverse children and youth. Larger scale studies, combined with what has been learned from the qualitative case study inquiries, could serve to inform practice concerning effective interventions that might work across states, groups, and schools. Research is needed that addresses identification working in tandem with effective programming. Based on the extant literature, effective programming should consider the child and his or her context and culture, involve the family and community, create a safe and challenging learning environment responsive to the child's strengths and differences, and put into place structures that create belonging, success, and achievement for the child. Such programs not only need to be developed and implemented, but their efficacy needs to be studied. The current research base concerning ethnic diversity in gifted education represents a solid foundation upon which to build much needed further study.

REFERENCES

Barnett, L. B., Gustin, W. C., & Dusel, J. C. (1996). Community challenge: Enhancing the academic achievement of children and youth. *Roeper Review, 19*, 111–114.

Borland, J. H. (1997). The construct of giftedness. *Peabody Journal of Education, 72*, 6–20.

Borland, J. H. (2005). Gifted education without gifted children: The case for no conception of giftedness. In R. J. Sternberg & J. E. Davidson (Eds.), *Conceptions of giftedness* (pp. 1–19). New York: Cambridge University Press.

Borland, J. H., & Wright, L. (1994). Identifying young, potentially gifted, economically disadvantaged students. *Gifted Child Quarterly, 38*, 164–171.

Cartledge, G., Sentelle, J., Loe, S., Lambert, M. C., & Reed, E. S. (2001). To be young, gifted, and Black?: A case study of positive interventions within an inner-city classroom of African-American students. *Journal of Negro Education, 70*, 243–254.

Coleman, L. J. (1994). Portfolio assessment: A key to identifying hidden talents and empowering teachers for young children. *Gifted Child Quarterly, 38*, 65–69.

Cooley, M. R. (1991). Peer acceptance and self-concept of Black students in a summer gifted program. *Journal for the Education of the Gifted, 14*, 166–177.

Cunningham, C. M., Callahan, C. M., Plucker, J. A., Roberson, S. C., & Rapkin, A. (1998). Identifying Hispanic students of outstanding talent: Psychometric integrity of a peer nomination form. *Exceptional Children, 64*, 197–209.

Datnow, A., & Cooper, R. (1997). Peer networks of African American students in independent schools: Affirming academic success and racial identity. *The Journal of Negro Education, 66*, 56–72.

Ewing, N. J., & Yong, F. L. (1992). A comparative study of the learning style preferences among gifted African-American, Mexican-American, and American-born Chinese middle grade students. *Roeper Review, 14*, 120–123.

Feiring, C., Louis, B., Ukeje, I., Lewis, M., & Leong, P. (1997). Early identification of gifted minority kindergarten students in Newark, NJ. *Gifted Child Quarterly, 41*, 76–82.

Ford, D. Y. (1992). Determinants of underachievement as perceived by gifted, above-average, and average Black students. *Roeper Review, 14*, 130–136.

Ford, D. Y. (1993). Black students' achievement orientation as a function of perceived family achievement orientation and demographic variables. *Journal of Negro Education, 62*, 47–66.

Ford, D. Y. (1995). *A study of achievement and underachievement among gifted, potentially gifted, and average African-American students.* Storrs: National Research Center on the Gifted and Talented, University of Connecticut. (ERIC Document Reproduction Service No. ED429394)

Ford, D. Y. (1998). The under-representation of minority students in gifted education: Problems and promises in recruitment and retention. *Journal of Special Education, 32*, 4–14.

Fordham, S. (1999). Dissin' "the standard": Ebonics as guerrilla warfare at Capital High. *Anthropology & Education Quarterly, 30*, 272–293.

Fordham, S., & Ogbu, J. U. (1986). Black students' school success: Coping with the "burden of 'acting White.'" *The Urban Review, 18*, 176–206.

Frasier, M. M. (1995). *Educators' perceptions of barriers to the identification of gifted children from economically disadvantaged and limited English proficient background.* Storrs: National Research Center on the Gifted and Talented, University of Connecticut. (ERIC Document Reproduction Service No. ED402707)

Freeman, J. (2005). Permission to be gifted: How conceptions of giftedness can change lives. In R. J. Sternberg & J. E. Davidson (Eds.), *Conceptions of giftedness* (pp. 80–97). New York: Cambridge University Press.

Friedman-Nimz, R., O'Brien, B., & Frey, B. B. (2005). Examining our foundations: Implications for gifted education research. *Roeper Review, 28*, 45–52.

Fryer, R. G., & Torelli, P. (2006). An empirical analysis of "acting White" (Working Paper No. 11334). New York: National Bureau of Economic Research.

Gándara, P. (2005). *Fragile futures: Risk and vulnerability among Latino high achievers.* Princeton, NJ: Educational Testing Service.

Gardner, H. (1983). *Frames of mind.* New York: Basic Books.

Goertz, M. J., Phemister, L., & Bernal, E. (1996). The new challenge: An ethnically integrated enrichment program for gifted students. *Roeper Review, 18*, 298–300.

Grant, D. F., Battle, D. A., Murphy, S. C., & Heggoy, S. J. (1999). Black female secondary honor graduates: Influences on achievement motivation. *Journal of Secondary Gifted Education, 10*, 103–119.

Grantham, T. C. (2004). Rocky Jones: Case study of a high-achieving Black male's motivation to participate in gifted classes. *Roeper Review, 26*, 208–215.

Haensly, P. A., & Lehmann, P. (1998). Nurturing giftedness while minority adolescents juggle change spheres. *Journal of Secondary Gifted Education, 9*, 163–178.

Harmon, D. (2002). They won't teach me: The voices of gifted African American inner-city students. *Roeper Review, 24*, 68–75.

Hartley, E. A. (1991). Through Navajo eyes: Examining differences in giftedness. *Journal of American Indian Education, 31*, 53–64.

Hébert, T. P. (1998). Gifted Black males in an urban high school: Factors that influence achievement and underachievement. *Journal for the Education of the Gifted, 21*, 385–414.

Hébert, T. P., & Beardsley, T. M. (2001). Jermaine: A critical case study of a gifted Black child living in rural theory. *Gifted Child Quarterly, 45*, 85–103.

Hrabowski, F. A., Maton, K. I., & Greif, G. L. (1998). *Beating the odds: Raising academically successful African American males.* New York: Oxford University Press.

Hrabowski, F. A., Maton, K. I., Green, M. L., & Greif, G. L. (2002). *Overcoming the odds: Raising academically successful African American females.* New York: Oxford University Press.

Jatko, B. P. (1995). Using a whole class tryout procedure for identifying economically disadvantaged students in three socioeconomically diverse schools. *Journal for the Education of the Gifted, 19*, 83–105.

Jones, L. S. (1997). Opening doors with informal science: Exposure and access for our underserved students. *Science Education, 81*, 663–677.

Kao, C., & Hébert, T. P. (2006). Gifted Asian American adolescent males: Portraits of cultural dilemmas. *Journal for the Education of the Gifted, 30*, 88–117.

Kitano, M. K., & DiJiosia, M. (2002). Are Asian and Pacific Americans overrepresented in programs for the gifted? *Roeper Review, 24*, 76–80.

Kloosterman, V. I. (1999). *Social-cultural contexts for talent development: A qualitative study on high ability, Hispanic, bilingual students.* Storrs: National Research Center on the Gifted and Talented, University of Connecticut. (ERIC Document Reproduction Service No. ED443214)

Langram, C. M. (1997). Adolescent voices—who's listening? *Journal of Secondary Gifted Education, 8*, 189–199.

Lidz, C., & Macrine, S. L. (2001). An alternative approach to the identification of gifted culturally and linguistically diverse learners: The contribution of dynamic assessment. *School Psychology International, 22*, 74–96.

Masten, W. G., & Plata, M. (2000). Acculturation and teacher ratings of Hispanic and Anglo-American students. *Roeper Review, 23*, 45–46.

Matthew, J. L. (1992). Use of SOMPA in identification of gifted African-American children. *Journal for the Education of the Gifted, 15*, 344–356.

McAllister, G., & Irvine, J. J. (2002). The role of empathy in teaching culturally diverse students: A qualitative study of teachers' beliefs. *Journal of Teacher Education, 53*, 433–443.

McBee, M. T. (2006). A descriptive analysis of referral sources for gifted identification screening by race and socioeconomic status. *Journal of Secondary Gifted Education, 17*, 103–111.

Miller, L. S. (2004). *Promoting sustained growth in the representation of African Americans, Latinos, and Native Americans among top students in the United States at all levels of the education system* (Research Monograph No. 04190). Storrs: National Research Center on the Gifted and Talented, University of Connecticut.

Naglieri, J. A., & Ford, D. Y. (2003). Addressing underrepresentation of gifted minority children using the Naglieri Nonverbal Ability Test (NNAT). *Gifted Child Quarterly, 47,* 155–160.

Ogbu, J. U. (1995). Cultural problems in minority education: Their interpretations and consequences—part two: Case studies. *Urban Review, 27,* 271–297.

Ogbu, J. U. (2003). *Black American students in an affluent suburb: A study of academic disengagement.* Mahwah, NJ: Lawrence Erlbaum.

Olszewski-Kubilius, P., & Laubscher, L. (1996). The impact of a college counseling program on economically disadvantaged gifted students and their subsequent adjustment. *Roeper Review, 18,* 202–208.

Olszewski-Kubilius, P., Lee, S. Y., Ngoi, M., & Ngoi, D. (2004). Addressing the achievement gap between minority and nonminority children by increasing access to gifted programs. *Journal for the Education of the Gifted, 28,* 127–158.

Patton, J. M., Prillaman, D., & VanTassel-Baska, J. (1990). The nature and extent of programs for the disadvantaged gifted in the United States and territories. *Gifted Child Quarterly, 34,* 94–96.

Peterson, J. S. (1999). Gifted—through whose cultural lens? An application of the post-positivistic mode of inquiry. *Journal for the Education of the Gifted, 22,* 354–383.

Plata, M., & Masten, W. G. (1998). Teacher ratings of Hispanic and Anglo students on a behavior rating scale. *Roeper Review, 21,* 139–144.

Plucker, J. A. (1996). Gifted Asian-American students: Identification, curricular, and counseling concern. *Journal for the Education of the Gifted, 19,* 315–343.

Plucker, J. A., & Barab, S. A. (2005). The importance of contexts in theories of giftedness: Learning to embrace the messy joys of subjectivity. In R. J. Sternberg & J. E. Davidson (Eds.), *Conceptions of giftedness* (pp. 201–216). New York: Cambridge University Press.

Plucker, J. A., Callahan, C. M., & Tomchin, E. M. (1996). Wherefore art thou, multiple intelligences? Alternative assessments for identifying talent in ethnically diverse and low-income students. *Gifted Child Quarterly, 40,* 81–92.

Renzulli, J. S. (2005). The three ring conception of giftedness: A developmental model for promoting creative productivity. In R. J. Sternberg & J. E. Davidson (Eds.), *Conceptions of giftedness* (pp. 246–279). New York: Cambridge University Press.

Renzulli, J. S., & Park, S. (2000). Gifted dropouts: The who and the why. *Gifted Child Quarterly, 44,* 261–271.

Reyes, E. I. (1996). Developing multidimensional screening procedures for identifying giftedness among Mexican American border population. *Roeper Review, 18,* 208–211.

Ricca, J. (1983). Curricular implications of learning style differences between gifted and non-gifted students (Doctoral dissertation, State University of New York, Buffalo, 1983). *Dissertation Abstracts International, 44,* 1324 A.

Ross, E. P., & Wright, J. (1987). Matching teaching strategies to the learning styles of gifted students. *Reading Horizons,* 48–56.

Sarouphim, K. M. (2001). DISCOVER: Concurrent validity, gender differences, and identification of minority students. *Gifted Child Quarterly, 45,* 130–138.

Sarouphim, K. M. (2002). DISCOVER in high school: Identifying gifted Hispanic and Native American students. *Journal of Secondary Gifted Education, 14*, 30–38.

Sarouphim, K. M. (2004). DISCOVER in middle school: Identifying gifted minority students. *Journal of Secondary Gifted Education, 15*, 61–69.

Schweigardt, W. J., Worrell, F. C., & Hale, R. J. (2001). Gender differences in the motivation for and selection of courses in a summer program for academically talented students. *Gifted Child Quarterly, 45*, 283–291.

Scott, M. S. (1992). The identification of giftedness: A comparison of White, Hispanic and Black families. *Gifted Child Quarterly, 36*, 131–139.

Scott, M. S. (1996). Identifying cognitively gifted ethnic minority children. *Gifted Child Quarterly, 40*, 147–153.

Scott, M. S., & Delgado, C. F. (2005). Identifying cognitively gifted minority students in preschool. *Gifted Child Quarterly, 49*, 199–270.

Scott, M. S., Deuel, L. S., Jean-Francois, B., & Urbano, R. C. (1996). Identifying cognitively gifted ethnic minority children. *Gifted Child Quarterly, 40*, 147–153.

Steele, C. M., & Aronson, J. (1995). Stereotype threat and the intellectual test performance of African Americans. *Journal of Personality and Social Psychology, 69*, 797–811.

Sternberg, R. J. (2005). The WICS model of giftedness. In R. J. Sternberg & J. E. Davidson (Eds.), *Conceptions of giftedness* (pp. 327–342). New York: Cambridge University Press.

Swanson, J. D. (2006). Breaking through assumptions about low-income, minority gifted students. *Gifted Child Quarterly, 50*, 11–25.

Title 5, Part D. [Jacob K. Javits Gifted and Talented Students Education Act of 1988], Elementary and Secondary Education Act of 1988 (2002), 20 U.S.C. Sec. 7253 et seq.

Tomlinson, C. A., Callahan, C. M., & Lelli, K. M. (1997). Challenging expectations: Case studies of high-potential, culturally diverse young children. *Gifted Child Quarterly, 41*, 5–17.

Tyson, K., Darity, W., & Castellino, D. R. (2005). It's not "a Black thing": Understanding the burden of acting White and other dilemmas of high achievement. *American Sociological Review, 70*, 582–605.

United States Department of Education, Office of Educational Research and Improvement. (1993). *National excellence: A case for developing America's talent.* Washington, DC: United States Government Printing Office.

United States Department of Education. (2000). *OCR elementary and secondary school survey: 2000.* Retrieved February 1, 2006, from http://vistademo.beyond2020.com/ocr2000r

VanTassel-Baska, J., Johnson, D., & Avery, L. D. (2002). Using performance tasks in the identification of economically disadvantaged and minority gifted learners: Findings from Project STAR. *Gifted Child Quarterly, 46*, 110–123.

Worrell, F. C. (2007). Ethnic identity, academic achievement, and global self-concept in four groups of academically talented adolescents. *Gifted Child Quarterly, 51*, 23–38.

Wright, L., & Borland, J. H. (1992). A special friend: Adolescent mentors for young, economically disadvantaged, potentially gifted students. *Roeper Review, 14*, 124–129.

Yong, F. L., & McIntyre, J. D. (1992). A comparative study of the learning style preferences of students with learning disabilities and students who are gifted. *Journal of Learning Disabilities, 25*, 124–132.

Chapter 15

EXPERTISE

Matthew C. Makel

hen one thinks of expertise, names like Einstein, Beethoven, Kasparov, and Shakespeare come to mind. All succeeded in vastly differently fields, but share the trait of having become experts in their given field. Quite simply, as experts, all performed so exceptionally well that they have become nearly synonymous with expertise and top performance in their respective fields. However, giftedness and expertise differ in their scope; giftedness often is associated with children and general ability, whereas expertise is likened to accomplished individuals in specific domains. The two may sometimes be associated with each other, but they are distinct phenomena.

Perhaps the name most famously associated with early research on expertise is Sir Francis Galton, with his book *Hereditary Genius* (1869/1925). In his book, Galton proposed that "the concrete triple event, of ability combined with zeal and with capacity for hard labour, is inherited" (p. 34). Just more than half a century later, the famous behaviorist John B. Watson (1924) asserted, tongue-in-cheek,

> Give me a dozen healthy infants, well-formed, and my own specified world to bring them up in and I'll guarantee to take any one at random and train him to become any type of specialist I might select—doctor, lawyer, artist, merchant chief, and yes, even beggar-man thief, regardless of his talents, penchants, tendencies, abilities, vocations, and race of his ancestors. (p. 128)

Watson did not actually subscribe to such an extreme position; rather, he articulated this to illustrate the extremity of an entirely genetic viewpoint. In the more than 80 years since Watson's statement, researchers have sought to better discern how genetics and one's environment combine to lead to expertise. This chapter briefly outlines the history of research on expertise and provides examples of research merging the views of giftedness and expertise.

WHAT IS EXPERTISE?

Broadly, expertise involves mastery of a given domain at a given time; experts are the best performers in their respective fields. Obviously, expert performance (and the abilities needed to achieve expert performance) varies depending on the discipline. Simonton (2000) illustrated such disparities when he wrote, "A gymnast who repeats the same flawless performance in competition after competition will be considered remarkable, whereas a writer who writes the same novel over and over would be considered less than a hack" (p. 286). Further, criteria for expert performance at one time do not invariably continue to define expert performance in the future. Indeed, the number of records broken in every Olympics illustrates the steady improvement of expert performance. Also, the brilliance of the physics developed by Newton is not reserved for tenured professors; it is taught in introductory physics classes.

Who Is an Expert?

How experts are defined in research is frequently based on the domain being studied. In some areas, such as chess, preestablished ranking systems are used to determine expertise status (Elo, 1986). A person is an expert chess player if she has achieved a certain rank through playing in chess tournaments. Similarly, pianists are considered experts by researchers if they are professionals or are affiliated with music academies (e.g., Krampe & Ericsson, 1996). Often, as in the case of Gardner's (1993) analysis of Sigmund Freud, Albert Einstein, Pablo Picasso, Igor Stravinsky, T. S. Eliot, Martha Graham, and Mahatma Gandhi, researchers select only the most eminent individuals in a given field as their sample of experts. Other times (e.g., Ceci & Liker, 1986), researchers have deemed experts to be the top-performing group in their sample. In some cases, people are dubbed memory experts if they can perform tasks such as memorizing a list of words or digits very quickly (e.g., Wilding & Valentine, 1994). Such disparity in how expertise is defined does not necessarily imply disagreement in defining expertise; rather, it often signifies differing goals in individual research investigations. As illustrated by the diverging philosophies of Galton and Watson, the primary area of disagreement is not *who* qualifies as an expert, but *how* a person becomes an expert. Despite more than 100 years of research, questions surrounding the origin and development of expertise remain unanswered.

Deliberate Practice

One explanation proposes that the sole requisite for achieving expertise is extensive deliberate practice (Ericsson, Krampe, & Tesch-Romer, 1993). Deliberate practice is highly structured and effortful rehearsal aimed at improving performance. Deliberate practice is associated with lengthy and sustained periods of work, and requires intense motivation and commitment. However, this *expertise via acquisition* explanation should not be taken to mean "those who work more perform better." Indeed, after extensive interviews with expert musicians, Ericsson et al. (1993) concluded that optimal training might involve "only" 4 hours of deliberate practice a day combined with adequate sleep. Practicing in excess of this may lead to the development of bad performance related habits and even burnout.

A recent retrospective analysis asked chess players to report their current and previous chess playing habits to determine what facets (e.g., practice alone, coaching, tournament play) best predicted subsequent performance. Results revealed that the best chess players (i.e., grandmasters) report spending about 5,000 hours in their first decade of play practicing by themselves whereas more intermediate players averaged about 1,000 hours during that same span (Charness, Tuffiash, Krampe, Reingold, & Vasyukova, 2005). Sloboda and his colleagues (Sloboda, Davidson, Howe, & Moore, 1996) had similar findings for expert musicians; the amount of intensive practice predicts subsequent performance. (For additional recent applications, also see a special issue of *Applied Cognitive Psychology* edited by Davies, Read, & Powell, 2005.) According to the chess study, more tournament play did not drive success; rather, efficient use of individualized learning did. Tournament play did not automatically equate with an efficient use of time because much of tournament play was spent against opponents of a different (significantly higher or lower) playing level.

Innate Abilities

However, many researchers are not satisfied with a deliberate practice explanation for expertise. Many believe innate or natural abilities play a significant role in the development of expertise. Innate abilities are not a result of practice, but are inborn, and often are offered as explanations for young savants and prodigies. Some researchers (e.g., Winner, 2000) propose that youth can possess (in various degrees) innate talents and unique brain structures that facilitate performance. Similarly, many have concluded that innate abilities may dictate how quickly (and how much) performance is improved (e.g., Sternberg, 2000). This is not to say that a person is born with an innate ability to perform complex tasks such as basketball, chess, or physics at an expert level without any experience or practice. Rather, some individuals may be born with abilities, such as faster reaction times or the ability to process an abundance of information, that facilitate their experiences, and thus, increase their potential for expertise. The argument that innate talent plays a role in expertise is "one of plausibility rather than data" (Sternberg, Grigorenko, & Ferrari, 2002, p. 73). How innate abilities might play a role in expertise is discussed below.

Interaction: Multiplier Effects

Numerous researchers (e.g., Dickens & Flynn, 2001; Papierno, Ceci, Makel, & Williams, 2005; Simonton, 1999b) have proposed that environmental conditions (such as deliberate practice) and a person's genes (and associated innate abilities) can interact to create multiplier effects. Such explanations propose that even the smallest initial differences (either genetic or environmental) eventually can snowball into dramatic differences in performance—that the relatively minimal effects of several influences can multiply to create significant effects on performance. The example often given is of a boy born with a genetic predisposition for basketball-related behaviors (e.g., height, agility, hand-eye coordination). If this natural ability is noticed, perhaps one of his parents will play more basketball with him, and he will be more likely to play basketball during recess. This increased practice will lead to further improvement, and increase the likelihood that he will successfully try out for the basketball team. Once on the basketball team, the boy will be exposed to coaches with expert knowledge of the game that will further assist in his basketball performance.

This hypothetical example illustrates how even slight differences in initial conditions have the potential to lead to large differences in later performance. Dickens and Flynn (2001) also state that the initial differences need not be genetic. Say that the boy from the example above actually has no particular natural advantage to playing basketball, but his father (or mother) attended a university where basketball was particularly popular and thus incited interest in the sport in all its students. This interest could then lead the parent to be more likely to spend time playing basketball with his (or her) child. Thus, this environmental difference (increased parent interest in basketball) could be the catalyst for the same course of events as the aforementioned genetic difference.

Because of their inherent complexity, multiplier models are difficult (and costly) to test empirically. One example is Dickens and Flynn's (2006) analysis of longitudinal trends in IQ scores. They found that the IQ gap between Black and White Americans has shrunk by 5.5 IQ points over the last 30 years. They conclude that this shrinkage can largely be attributed to environmental gains for Black Americans such as increases in occupational status and education funding. However, they also note that the increase in the number of Black children in single-parent households and the relative decrease in income of those homes may attenuate some gain. Dickens and Flynn (2006) conclude that further environmental advances should lead to additional shrinking of the IQ gap. Although it does not directly discuss the acquisition of expertise, this example demonstrates the powerful impact environmental changes can have on performance.

Developing Expertise

Yet another model of expertise melds the typically disparate fields of giftedness and expertise by considering giftedness to be a form of developing expertise (Sternberg, 2000, 2001). In this model, gifted individuals are simply further along in their development than are their nongifted peers. In Sternberg's developing expertise model, individuals progress from novice to expert through the interaction of five primary elements: metacognitive skills, learning skills, thinking skills, knowledge, and motivation. *Metacognitive skills* refer to a person's understanding of what they know. A person's *learning skills* are a person's ability to learn or acquire new knowledge. Learning skills can be broken into explicit (effortful) and implicit (incidental) learning. Under Sternberg's model, there are three distinct *thinking skills*: analytical, creative, and practical; each refers to a set of abilities on how to think. Sternberg breaks *knowledge* into two components: declarative knowledge (i.e., facts or "knowing that") and procedural knowledge (i.e., process or "knowing how"). These elements, according to Sternberg, are driven by *motivation* through a series of purposeful and meaningful experiences on a task in a given context to lead to expertise.

In a demonstration study to illustrate how abilities are manifest through practice in the form of developing expertise, Sternberg et al. (2002) had participants practice designing a functional city via a computer game, but varied how much each person could practice. They found that expert design performance (i.e., receiving high ratings on predetermined measures of design quality) was simultaneously a function of both general ability (in this case, performance on a cognitive measure) and amount of practice. Thus, development of expertise was not a matter of ability *or* practice, but their interaction. Similar to the multiplier effect position, Sternberg et al. concluded that people already performing at higher levels are more likely to be engaged in performing that task and thus also show greater motivation to further develop their performance.

Motivation

The importance of motivation in expertise is not unique to Sternberg's theory; motivation is a common theme among explanations of expertise. The deliberate practice model of expertise proposed by Ericsson and colleagues (1993) requires individuals to maintain a strict regimen of practice over long periods of time to become an expert. Additionally, models involving multiplier effects require individuals to stick with the given area because otherwise the initial favorable condition will not have the opportunity to flourish. Further, Gottfried and Gottfried (2004) have proposed that motivation itself is a construct in which some individuals are gifted. The group of individuals gifted in motivation is distinct from (but often overlapping with) gifted individuals in general, but is uniquely related to achievement.

The Fullerton Longitudinal Study (Gottfried, Gottfried, Bathurst, & Guerin, 1994) followed 130 infants and their families, administering a multitude of developmental, cognitive, and behavioral measures. To test the idea of gifted motivation, students who consistently scored the highest on the Children's Academic Intrinsic Motivation Inventory while they were teens were compared to a cohort comparison group (Gottfried, Gottfried, Cook, & Morris, 2005). Members of the gifted motivation group were significantly more likely to perform better than their peers on a wide range of variables (e.g., higher grades, SAT scores, teacher ratings of classroom functioning, and self-concept scores), and 50% of students in the gifted motivation group earned a bachelor's degree by age 24 compared to only 32% of the comparison group. Moreover, students in the gifted motivation group were not necessarily the students in the intellectual gifted group. In their sample, only 21% of the students in the gifted motivation group were also in the gifted intellectual group and 87% of the variance in overall academic intrinsic motivation was not accounted for by intelligence. Although expertise is not specifically addressed in the gifted motivation literature, their findings support a position that motivation plays a role in subsequent performance.

WHAT CAN WE CONCLUDE BASED ON RESEARCH?

Numerous reports across a variety of domains have reported that expert status is typically achieved only after about 10 years of sustained deliberate practice (Ericsson et al., 1993; Gardner, 1993; Simon & Chase, 1973). Given the time commitment necessary to achieve expert status, many have concluded that individuals who may show initial promise may not achieve expertise because of burnout or developing interest in other areas (e.g., Schneider, 2000).

Further supporting the narrow breadth of expertise is the research illustrating expertise to be domain- and situation-specific. For example, Ceci and Liker (1986) studied horse-race gamblers and discovered that, although experts in that area were cognitively sophisticated, expertise and general cognitive performance were not correlated. Also, chess masters, one of the most commonly studied groups in expertise research, can accurately recall the positions of briefly presented chess games qualitatively better than novices can—if the pieces are arranged in a plausible way, according to the rules of the game. However, if the pieces are randomly arranged, chess masters perform comparably to novices (Chase & Simon, 1973; Gobet & Simon, 1996). Examples such as these show that expertise does not imply high performance in areas outside the scope of what has been practiced.

There have also been numerous studies on comparing how high- and low-performing people rate their own performance. In general, people tend to overestimate their ability to perform tasks, ranging from basic math problems, to knowledge of geography, to the ability to recognize humor (see Dunning, 2005, for a review). Dunning and others have provided numerous reasons for such overconfidence; they have suggested limited metacognitive ability in areas where knowledge is limited and errors of omission (one doesn't miss what one doesn't know exists). However, a lesser known finding is that individuals who actually perform well above average tend to underestimate the relative rank of their performance. This is not to say that high performers underestimate their own ability (they don't); they simply underestimate their relative ability, believing themselves to be less above average than they actually are.

LIMITATIONS OF RESEARCH ON EXPERTISE

Researchers agree (for the most part) on who is or isn't an expert in a given domain, but disagreement emerges when explanations for the necessary and sufficient conditions to achieve expertise are discussed. Some researchers (e.g., Ericsson et al., 1993; Simonton, 2000) cite similar examples as support for drastically different explanations of how expertise is achieved. Such disagreement severely diminishes the ability to set a clear agenda on how to address future research questions and how the development of expertise best can be facilitated.

In the past, the methods researchers used to address giftedness and expertise have varied greatly. The standard model in gifted research has been the prospective model. Prospective studies (e.g., Terman, 1925) follow high-performing youth longitudinally to see if early high performance predicts later performance. Results of such studies have been fairly consistent. For the most part, Terman's gifted participants grew up to be successful relative to the average population. However, it is often noted that two future Nobel laureates (William Shockley and Luis Alvarez) were not selected to participate in Terman's study because they did not score high enough on the IQ test used to select the sample (Winner, 1996). In expertise research, on the other hand, the methods used typically have been retrospective or biographic in nature (e.g., Gardner, 1993; see review by Simonton, 1999a). Relying on such methods is sometimes necessary (not to mention more expedient and more economic than following thousands of children throughout their lives waiting to see who become experts), but these investigations often are considered less reliable and less informative than longitudinal and prospective research studies.

Also, many of the explanations of expertise are theories only. The authors of these models support their claims with examples and data, but all are debated in the field and call for further research. Expertise theories are difficult to support, not just because of the need for prospective, longitudinal research, but also because theories involving multiplier effects require the measurement of myriad relevant traits to be measured. Surely, height has very little (possibly nothing) to do with chess performance, but traits such as mental processing speed, mathematical calculation ability, the ability to simultaneously consider multiple alternatives, and the ability to judge preferable moves all likely play a part in a person's chess performance. However, how those abilities can combine with each other (not to mention the many other possible relevant abilities) to form a person's ability to play chess is difficult to calculate, particularly because researchers only can approximate each of these abilities in a single person.

PRACTICAL IMPLICATIONS OF RESEARCH ON EXPERTISE

Research on expertise (and youth who show promise) informs researchers and policy makers on how to best foster and facilitate the development of performance. However, both should be cautioned against mistakenly conflating expertise and giftedness. For example, in school, giftedness often equates with mastering what one is told to accomplish. On the other hand, in adulthood, expertise is often associated with generating new solutions to new problems. This fundamental difference could explain why many gifted youth do not become expert adults. They are simply measured using different criteria. With a developing expertise model or a multiplier effect explanation of expertise, many people can become an expert in something given the right situations. However, each person's rate of development and his or her maximum potential will vary. Performance differences at any given time do not necessarily show differences in absolute potential or future performance. Certainly, this has practical implications in the expectations and evaluation of a person's performance.

CONCLUSIONS

- The primary area of disagreement is not *who* qualifies as an expert, but *how* a person becomes an expert.

- Expert status is typically achieved only after about 10 years of deliberate practice.
- There exist numerous well-supported theories of expertise, but all call for further research to facilitate the development of expertise.
- Expertise does not imply high performance in areas outside the scope of what has been practiced.

MAJOR RESOURCES AND REFERENCES ON EXPERTISE

Ericsson, K. A., Krampe, R. T., & Tesch-Romer, C. (1993). The role of deliberate practice in the acquisition of expert performance. *Psychological Review, 100*, 363–406.

Gardner, H. (1993). *Creating minds: An anatomy of creativity seen through the lives of Freud, Einstein, Picasso, Stravinsky, Eliot, Graham, and Gandhi.* New York: Basic Books.

Simonton, D. K. (1999). Talent and its development: An emergenic and epigenetic model. *Psychological Review, 106*, 435–457.

Sternberg, R. J. (2001). Giftedness as developing expertise: A theory of the interface between high abilities and achievement. *High Ability Studies, 12*, 159–179.

REFERENCES

Ceci, S. J., & Liker, J. K. (1986). A day at the races: A study of IQ, expertise, and cognitive complexity. *Journal of Experimental Psychology: General, 115*, 255–266.

Charness, N., Tuffiash, M., Krampe, R., Reingold, E., & Vasyukova, E. (2005). The role of deliberate practice in chess. *Applied Cognitive Psychology, 19*, 151–165.

Chase, W. G., & Simon, H. A. (1973). The mind's eye in chess. In W. G. Chase (Ed.), *Visual information processing* (pp. 215–281). New York: Academic Press.

Davies, G., Read, D., & Powell, M. (Eds.). (2005). Recent advances in expertise research [Special issue]. *Applied Cognitive Psychology, 19*(2).

Dickens, W. T., & Flynn, J. R. (2001). Heritability estimates versus large environmental effects: The IQ paradox resolved. *Psychological Review, 108*, 346–369.

Dickens, W. T., & Flynn, J. R. (2006). Black Americans reduce the racial IQ gap. *Psychological Science, 17*, 913–920.

Dunning, D. A. (2005). *Self-insight: Roadblocks and detours on the path to knowing thyself.* New York: Psychology Press.

Elo, A. E. (1986). *The rating of chessplayers, past and present* (2nd ed.). New York: Arco.

Ericsson, K. A., Krampe, R. T., & Tesch-Romer, C. (1993). The role of deliberate practice in the acquisition of expert performance. *Psychological Review, 100*, 363–406.

Galton, F. (1925). *Hereditary genius: An inquiry into its laws and consequences.* London: Macmillan and Co. (Original work published 1869)

Gardner, H. (1993). *Creating minds: An anatomy of creativity seen through the lives of Freud, Einstein, Picasso, Stravinsky, Eliot, Graham, and Gandhi.* New York: Basic Books.

Gobet, F., & Simon, H. A. (1996). Recall of rapidly presented random chess positions is a function of skill. *Psychonomic Bulletin Review, 3,* 159–163.

Gottfried, A. E., & Gottfried, A. W. (2004) Toward the development of a conceptualization of gifted motivation. *Gifted Child Quarterly. 48,* 121–132.

Gottfried, A. W., Gottfried, A. E., Bathurst, K., & Guerin, D. W. (1994). *Gifted IQ: Early developmental aspects. The Fullerton longitudinal study.* New York: Plenum Press.

Gottfried, A. W., Gottfried, A. E., Cook, C. R., & Morris, P. E. (2005). Educational characteristics of adolescents with gifted academic intrinsic motivation: A longitudinal investigation from school entry through early adulthood. *Gifted Child Quarterly, 49,* 172–186.

Krampe, R. T., & Ericsson, K. A. (1996). Maintaining excellence: Deliberate practice and elite performance in young and older pianists. *Journal of Experimental Psychology: General, 125,* 331–359.

Papierno, P. B., Ceci, S. J., Makel, M. C., & Williams, W. M. (2005). The nature and nurture of talent: A bioecological perspective on the ontogeny of exceptional abilities. *Journal for the Education of the Gifted, 28,* 312–332.

Schneider, W. (2000). Giftedness, expertise, and (exceptional) performance: A developmental perspective. In K. A. Heller, F. J. Mönks, R. J. Sternberg, & R. F. Subotnik (Eds.), *International handbook of giftedness and talent* (pp. 165–177). Amsterdam: Elsevier.

Simon, H. A., & Chase, W. G. (1973). Skill in chess. *American Scientist, 61,* 394–403.

Simonton, D. K. (1999a). Significant samples: The psychological study of eminent individuals. *Psychological Methods, 4,* 425–451.

Simonton, D. K. (1999b). Talent and its development: An emergenic and epigenetic model. *Psychological Review, 106,* 435–457.

Simonton, D. K. (2000). Creative development as acquired expertise: Theoretical issues and an empirical test. *Developmental Review, 20,* 283–318.

Sloboda, J. A., Davidson, J. W., Howe, M. J. A., & Moore, D. G. (1996). The role of practice in the development of performing musicians. *British Journal of Psychology, 87,* 287–309.

Sternberg, R. J. (2000). Giftedness as developing expertise. In K. A. Heller, F. J. Mönks, R. J. Sternberg, & R. F. Subotnik (Eds.), *International handbook of giftedness and talent* (pp. 55–66). Amsterdam: Elsevier.

Sternberg, R. J. (2001). Giftedness as developing expertise: A theory of the interface between high abilities and achievement. *High Ability Studies, 12,* 159–179.

Sternberg, R. J., Grigorenko, E. L., & Ferrari, M. (2002). Fostering intellectual excellence through developing expertise. In M. Ferrari (Ed.), *The pursuit of excellence through education* (pp. 57–83). Mahwah, NJ: Lawrence Erlbaum.

Terman, L. M. (1925). *Genetic studies of genius: Volume 1. The mental and physical traits of a thousand gifted children.* Stanford, CA: Stanford University Press.

Watson, J. B. (1924). *Behaviorism.* Chicago: University of Chicago Press.

Wilding, J., & Valentine, E. (1994). Memory champions. *British Journal of Psychology, 85,* 231–244.

Winner, E. (1996). *Gifted children: Myths and realities.* New York: Basic Books.

Winner, E. (2000). The origins and ends of giftedness. *American Psychologist, 55,* 159–169.

Chapter 16

GIFTED GIRLS

Margie K. Kitano

DEFINING THE TERMS AS USED IN THE RESEARCH

otivational variables such as self-efficacy and stereotype threat have been studied in the general population and investigated among high-achieving girls and women. *Self-efficacy* refers to self-appraisal of ability to succeed at a task and may be domain-specific (Dai, 2002). *Stereotype threat* (Steele, 1997) describes a fear of inadvertently confirming a negative stereotype, for example, when a woman feels anxiety about a mathematics test because her performance might confirm the stereotype that women are inferior in math. Most studies investigating gender differences among the gifted define giftedness in terms of high achievement. Other literature proposing conceptual models on women and giftedness offers more inclusive and transformative definitions based on women's goals and choices.

MAJOR QUESTIONS ADDRESSED IN THE RESEARCH

Some 15 years ago, *How Schools Shortchange Girls* (AAUW, 1992) and *Failing at Fairness: How America's Schools Cheat Girls* (Sadker & Sadker, 1994) raised national awareness of gender bias in America's schools and the potential impact on girls' self-esteem and achievement. These reports summarized research suggesting that girls receive less attention, praise, and helpful feedback than boys in the classroom; are subject to sexual harassment; and are less likely to pursue careers in mathematics and science. Today, gender bias remains an issue in general education, with increasing recognition of the deleterious effects on both girls and boys (Sadker & Zittleman, 2005).

Over the same period, the topic of gifted girls has received some, though not extensive, attention in the literature, and much of the literature is analytic rather than empirical and embedded in the context of gender differences among the general population. The major research questions addressed include:

1. Are there continuing gender gaps in school achievement and educational and career attainment among the gifted?
2. What factors contribute to persistent gender gaps, especially in pursuit of careers in mathematics and science?
3. What are the characteristics of gifted girls?
4. Do gifted girls from racially diverse and low-income backgrounds have different needs compared to gifted girls from White and middle-class backgrounds?
5. What are the most appropriate conceptual models for investigating and understanding the characteristics and needs of gifted girls and women?

WHAT THE RESEARCH SAYS

Current Status of Girls and Women

Recent data on gender differences in the United States in school achievement, educational attainment, earnings, and employment indicate that females have achieved parity to ascendancy in some areas and are narrowing the gap in others. Yet, some gaps persist. Nationally, programs for gifted students serve proportionately more girls than boys. However, proportionately more boys achieve at the highest levels on standardized tests of mathematics. Women continue to be underrepresented among leaders in a range of disciplines.

Test Scores. Gender differences in standardized test scores vary by subject area, age at testing, and the measure used. At ages 13 and 17, girls outscored boys on the 2004 National Assessment of Educational Progress (NAEP) reading test. Boys in both age groups scored higher than girls on the NAEP math and science assessments (C. E. Freeman, 2004). Although more females than males took the AP examination in English in 2002, their average score was lower. In the same year, more males took AP exams in science and calculus and achieved higher scores than females in these areas and in social studies, calculus, and computer science (C. E. Freeman, 2004). Average ACT scores for women (21.0) and men (21.2) were similar in 2006. However, average scores for men on the SAT verbal (513) and math (538) exceeded those for women (505 and 504) in 2006 (*The Chronicle of Higher Education*, 2006).

Educational Progress and Attainment. In 2003, females had a higher rate of high school completion than males, were less likely to repeat a grade or drop out of school, reported higher aspirations in high school, and were more likely to enroll in college immediately following graduation (C. E. Freeman, 2004). In 1959–1960, females received only 35% of all bachelor's (and first-professional), 32% of all master's, and 10% of all doctoral degrees. By 2001–2002, some 57% of bachelor's, 59% of master's, and 46% of doctoral degrees were awarded to females (Fox, Connolly, & Snyder, 2005). Although their numbers are increasing, women are far less likely than men to major in computer science, engineering, and physical science (C. E. Freeman, 2004). In education, social sciences, history, psychology, biology/life sciences, and business management, women have achieved relative gender parity or disproportionately greater representation. Still, in 2003–2004, women received only a fraction of doctoral degrees awarded in engineering and engineering technologies (18%), mathematics and statistics (28%), and physical science and science technologies (28%; National Center for Education Statistics, 2005).

Employment and Earnings. A narrowing but persistent gender gap in median earnings for full-time workers ages 25–34 exists at all levels of educational attainment. In 2002, males earned 18% more than females, compared to 56% more in 1971. Race differences occur in employment. In 2004, the unemployment rate for White females ages 20–24 was lower (8%) than the rate for Hispanic females (11%), which was lower than the unemployment rate for Black females (19%; Fox et al., 2005).

Gifted Girls. Within this larger context, how have gifted females fared? Projections from the 2002 U.S. Office of Civil Rights Elementary and Secondary School Survey (see Table 1) suggest that proportionately more girls than boys are served by gifted programs across racial/ethnic groups. The percentages of girls and boys enrolled in AP mathematics and science courses suggest equitable enrollment rates for girls. Still, a disproportionately low number of American Indian, Latino, and African American girls and boys are enrolled in programs for the gifted and math/science AP courses.

Despite gender parity in enrollment in gifted programs, including Advanced Placement math and science courses, data from a long-term study

TABLE 1

Office of Civil Rights Elementary and Secondary School Survey: 2002 National Projections for Enrollment by Race/Ethnicity and Sex

Race/Ethnicity	General Enrollment		In Gifted and Talented Programs		Mathematics Advanced Placement		Science Advanced Placement	
	Female	Male	Female	Male	Female	Male	Female	Male
American Indian or Alaska Native	0.59	0.62	0.49	0.44	0.23	0.24	0.30	0.27
Asian or Pacific Islander	2.14	2.38	3.39	3.71	7.39	7.52	7.68	7.50
Hispanic	8.67	9.13	5.36	5.05	4.14	3.92	4.53	3.82
Black, not Hispanic	8.46	8.70	4.78	3.65	3.32	2.29	4.04	2.42
White, Not Hispanic	28.81	30.61	36.71	35.88	33.43	37.51	34.95	34.50
All Races	48.67	51.33	51.27	48.73	48.52	51.48	51.49	48.51

Note. From U.S. Office of Civil Rights (2002) *Elementary and Secondary School Survey: 2002.* The values represent percentages.

of mathematically precocious youth (Benbow, Lubinski, Shea, & Eftekhari-Sanjani, 2000; Benbow & Stanley, 1983; Lubinski, Webb, Morelock, & Benbow, 2001) identified gender gaps at the highest levels of mathematics performance. Among those scoring 700 or more on the SAT Math before age 13, a male to female ratio of 13:1 was reported in 1983, and a ratio of 4:1 in 2005 (Williams & Ceci, 2006). These data suggest a continuing though declining difference in ratios of men to women at the high end of ability. The gap may begin as early as third grade. Olszewski-Kubilius and Turner (2002) found small but significant gender differences for elementary age-gifted students on an off-level achievement test, with a 2:1 ratio of males to females achieving very high scores in math.

Longitudinal studies of gifted individuals born in the 1910s (Tomlinson-Keasey & Little, 1990), 1940s (Subotnik, Karp, & Morgan, 1989), and 1960s (Arnold, 1993) document dramatic increases in gifted women's educational and career opportunities and accomplishments over time. Yet, even in literature, where girls excel during the school years, men are more productive in adulthood, writing more books than women (Reis, 2002a). Relatively few women hold the highest leadership positions in government and the private sector. According to the Center for American Women and Politics (n.d.), in 2005, only 80 women were serving in the U.S. Congress: 14 in the Senate and

66 in the House. One fourth of the 80 were women of color. The percentage of women serving in state legislatures was 22.6; less than one fifth of this percentage were women of color. During the same year, only 19 women held CEO positions in FORTUNE 1000 corporations (*Fortune*, 2005).

In sum, females have made remarkable progress relative to males across several indicators of K–12 school achievement and higher education degrees awarded. Across racial and ethnic groups, girls are at least equitably represented in programs for the gifted in terms of enrollment proportions. However, gifted African American and Latina girls continue to be significantly underserved in programs for the gifted. Girls tend to score lower than males on standardized assessments in mathematics and the physical sciences, and they are less likely to pursue advanced degrees in these areas. Of significance for gifted education is a persistent gender gap favoring males at the highest levels on tests of mathematics. Despite their relatively greater success on several indicators of school achievement, fewer females are found at the highest levels of leadership across several domains. Considerable progress has been achieved in equity for women. Yet, the data indicate that exceptional school achievement does not necessarily guarantee commensurate occupational attainment or salary equity.

Factors Affecting Achievement Differences in Mathematics and Science

The early and persistent differences in male to female ratios at the highest levels of achievement in mathematics have given rise to hypotheses of biological and genetic cognitive sex differences (Spelke, 2005). A recent compilation of essays (Ceci & Williams, 2006) by leading researchers positing a range of perspectives on this topic suggests that there are no clear-cut answers. Biological differences between sexes that may affect mathematics performance include male superiority in spatial ability (especially mental rotation) and mechanical reasoning (Newcombe, 2006) and in brain structure and function (Gur & Gur, 2006; Haier, 2006). Haier reported that for men, but not women, the harder the temporal lobes were working, the better they scored on a test of math reasoning. The sample included men and women scoring more than 700 on the SAT-Math. Gur and Gur found sex differences in hemispheric symmetries and hypothesized that male brains are optimized for connectivity within hemispheres and female brains for communication between hemispheres.

Presenting an environmental perspective on sex differences in mathematics and science, Spelke (2005) argued that SAT-Math test items systematically favor the types of problems on which boys perform better. Moreover, the smaller number of boys taking the test results in greater selectivity, and equal performance of males and females (in both average and talented pools) in high school and college mathematics classes attests to equal math ability. Dweck (2006) concluded from her investigations that gender differences in math at the highest levels could be explained by gender differences in coping with setbacks and confusion. Dweck also found that when the environment encourages females to view their math abilities as competencies that can be developed, they perform as well as males. Attitudinal contributions include gender differences in value placed on various occupations (Eccles, 2006) and differences in interests and willingness to work long hours (Lubinski & Benbow, 2006). Hyde (2006) summarized external, sociocultural forces that contribute to underrepresentation of women in physical sciences, including stereotype threat (Steele, 2003); sex discrimination; and family, neighborhood, peer, and school influences.

Williams and Ceci (2006) concluded that the research findings are complex and nuanced, leaving open the possibility that both cultural and biological contributions lead to fewer women in mathematics and the physical sciences. Findings depend on the age of cohorts studied, cultural context, measures used, ranges examined within score distributions, definitions of high performance (e.g., test scores or persistence in major or profession, magnitude of differences), and malleability of differences.

The reported lack of gender differences in mathematics and science test scores in several countries outside the United States argue against genetic differences in mathematics and science ability. In 2003, data from the Organization for Economic Cooperation and Development (OECD) indicated that males scored higher than females in 21 countries on math assessment and in 11 for science assessment. However, no gender differences occurred in 7 countries for math and in 16 for the science assessment. Average reading achievement scores in all participating countries were higher for females than males (Fox et al., 2005).

J. Freeman (2004) described gifted girls in British schools as recently achieving at higher levels than gifted boys in both the liberal arts *and* hard sciences (physics, math, chemistry) on curriculum-based standardized achievement tests and nationwide public exams. According to Freeman, these data refute the idea of genetically determined sex differences in ability. Rather, nations differ in cultural attitudes toward women as manifested in policies and practices. The author attributes the gender shift of superiority in math and science scores to gender equity policies in schools, whole staff support of these policies, teaching practices that counter gender stereotypes, single-sex teaching groups, and appropriate role models. Still, disproportionately fewer girls choose to specialize in physics and engineering.

Characteristics of Gifted Girls

Much of the research specifically addressing gifted girls has sought to examine their characteristics relative to those of gifted boys to explain disparities in achievement outcomes (e.g., careers in mathematics and sciences). Some studies also include comparisons with students from the general population. A number of authors (Callahan, 1986, 1991; Dai, 2002; Kerr, 1994; Kerr & Nicpon, 2003; Reis, 1995, 1998, 2002a; Reis & Callahan, 1989) have summarized at different points in time sex differences in motivational variables such as self-efficacy, self-perceptions, attitudes, and aspirations. As noted above, stereotype threat may also affect test performance of high-achieving girls and women.

Self-Efficacy. Although the research literature reveals some inconsistencies in outcomes (Dai, 2002), in general it suggests that gifted girls in this country tend to report higher self-efficacy in mathematics than their average-achieving counterparts and similar levels to that of gifted boys. Pajares (1996) examined self-efficacy of middle school gifted and average-achieving girls and boys. Results revealed no significant differences between gifted girls and boys on self-efficacy, although the gifted girls outperformed their male peers in mathematical problem solving. The gifted students reported higher mathematics self-efficacy than did students in the general population. In a study of 10th and 11th graders taking mathematics courses, Hong and Aqui (2004) found that both males and females who are academically gifted or creatively talented in math reported having greater self-efficacy compared to their average peers and using cognitive strategies more often. Academically gifted girls also reported working harder than academically gifted boys.

Self-Perceptions. In the Pajares (1996) study, both gifted boys and girls in middle school displayed more accurate self-perceptions, although the latter evidenced bias toward underconfidence. Olszewski-Kubilius and Turner (2002) also found accurate perceptions of academic abilities among elementary-age gifted girls and boys. Follow-up of adolescents gifted in mathematics (Benbow et al., 2000) indicated no gender differences in self-esteem, and both males and females reported high levels of success and satisfaction.

Attitudes. Studies of attitudes among gifted girls and boys suggest that gifted boys may hold gender stereotypes concerning future wives' roles. In a study of attitudes at middle school, Reis, Callahan, and Goldsmith (1994) reported that gifted girls and boys held similar levels of confidence in their ability to do almost anything. However, they found pronounced sex differences in expectations about future career and family. Gifted boys tended to express the belief that their spouses should spend more time taking care of children and the home. The authors noted that encountering such stereotypes may negatively affect gifted girls.

Cultural factors may contribute to both gender stereotyped opinions and course selection. Campbell and Connolly (1984) compared Asian American and White high school students enrolled in advanced science and mathematics classes. Asian males held few negative stereotypes of gifted girls in their classes, whereas White males reported many negative perceptions. More recently, Schweigardt, Worrell, and Hale (2001) also found more stereotypical enrollment rates among non-Asian students in traditionally male and female courses in a summer program for gifted youth. Enrollment among Asian American students was more gender-balanced than among non-Asian students, and both male and female Asian American participants enrolled in traditionally male courses (math, natural and computer sciences) in greater numbers than in traditionally female courses (writing, literature, languages, social sciences).

Attitudes toward science may influence gifted girls' course-taking choices. Farenga and Joyce (1998) examined attitudes toward science of high-achieving 9- to 13-year-old students attending predominantly White, middle-class suburban schools. Results indicated that science-related attitudes were important predictors of the number of science courses selected by girls but not by boys.

Aspirations and Interests. Recent investigations have addressed perceptions of career options and occupational interests of gifted girls. In a study of gifted students, ages 11 to 14, Mendez and Crawford (2002) found that gifted girls demonstrate greater gender role flexibility in career aspirations and perceive a wider range of options open to them compared to gifted boys. Gifted girls were similar to their male counterparts in masculine traits (e.g., independence, assertiveness) *and* scored higher than boys on feminine traits (e.g., kindness, caring, understanding), although boys viewed competition more favorably. Findings did not support earlier characterizations of gifted girls as vulnerable to fear of success, and they were no more concerned than gifted boys that achievement would negatively affect their social standing. Subjects were primarily White, middle to upper socioeconomic status (SES) students.

Follow-up of adolescents gifted in mathematics (Benbow et al., 2000) participating in the Study of Mathematically Precocious Youth (SMPY) suggested that males exhibit greater focus on career success, and females value more balance in their priorities (career, family, friends). A comparison of mathematically talented students in SMPY and math/science graduate students with world-class talent (Lubinski, Benbow, Shea, Eftekhari-Sanjani, & Halvorson, 2001) indicated that for both sexes, choices are partly a function of ability/preference profiles. An individual's pattern of ability, interests, and values influences the decision to pursue a career in mathematics or physical sciences. Moreover, the researchers reported that the path to scientific distinction, as represented by the graduate students, is similar for males and females and requires exceptional mathematics reasoning ability, scientific interests, and persistence in seeking opportunities to study and develop skills in science.

Stereotype Threat. Research on stereotype threat suggests that fear of confirming a negative gender stereotype may influence female students' performance on mathematics tests, possibly beginning as young as age 5. Steele's (2003) work demonstrated that the presence or absence of stereotype threat significantly affects the mathematics test performance of female university students who are strong in math. Simply describing the test as one showing gender differences (stereotype threat condition) reduced women's performance. When the test was described as one on which women always did as well as men, female students performed as well as their male peers and significantly better than women in the stereotype threat condition. Ambady, Shih, Kim, and

Pittinsky (2001) examined stereotype threat among primarily U.S.-born Asian American (Chinese, Japanese, Korean) girls ages 5–13. Results indicated that the youngest (5–7) and oldest (11–13) girls exhibited the lowest mathematics test performance when gender identity was activated and highest when Asian identity was activated. Girls in the middle age range performed better than peers in a control condition when gender identity was activated.

In general, the research indicates that gifted girls report high levels of self-efficacy and aspirations, as well as accurate self-perceptions. Gifted girls' attitudes toward and interest in mathematics and science may affect course selection. However, girls talented in mathematics and science who opt for majors and careers in these areas, similar to their male counterparts, exhibit superior quantitative abilities and focused pursuit of learning in the discipline. There appear to be cultural differences in holding of gender stereotypes, with gifted White students more prone to stereotypical attitudes than gifted Asian students. There is some evidence that gender stereotype threat can reduce the mathematics test performance of girls and women, although not consistently over developmental periods. Gifted girls report more androgyny than gifted boys in terms of personality.

Gender, Socioeconomic Status, and Race

National reports on educational achievement and occupational attainment typically disaggregate data by race and gender separately, rendering difficult the assessment of outcomes for girls and women of color over time. Moreover, few quantitative studies in the field of gifted education have included sufficient numbers of females of color or low income to disaggregate findings by race or economic status. Yet, available studies focused on diverse girls and women, often qualitative in nature, suggest that race, ethnicity, and class add significant dimensions to understanding gifted women's educational and occupational attainment. These analyses identify specific factors requiring further investigation as possible contributors to diverse gifted women's achievement or underachievement. Ford's study (1994–1995) of fifth- and sixth-grade gifted and average-achieving African American girls indicated that most found school more exciting and interesting when they learned about Blacks. One third of the girls reported that good grades led to accusations of "acting White," and a similar proportion indicated that Blacks must work harder in school than Whites to succeed.

Arnold, Noble, and Subotnik's (1996) volume on gifted women across cultures, nations, and economic groups expanded the field's knowledge about factors affecting gifted women's achievement. They proposed a conception of giftedness (Noble, Subotnik, & Arnold, 1999) as remarkable attainment that varies with one's initial distance from the mainstream. This conception acknowledges women's differing goals and definitions of achievement, personal characteristics, talent domains, access to opportunity, and resources based on limitations imposed by geography, religious beliefs, political system, racism, sexism, and homophobia. Women initially far from the mainstream do achieve success and even eminence in their fields, despite tremendous obstacles.

Cultural factors, particularly culturally derived strengths and coping strategies, may provide additional insight into gifted women's achievement. Kitano (1997, 1998a, 1998b) and Kitano and Perkins (1996, 2000) suggested that cultural-ecological perspectives applied to lives of gifted women of color can contribute to understanding the influence of the cultural context and strengths on achievement in interaction with personal and environmental factors. Their retrospective studies of the lives of highly achieving Asian American, African American, Latino American, White, and international women identified culturally consonant coping strategies enabling these women to overcome a range of family (e.g., low expectations, death of a parent), personal (lack of self-confidence, illness), economic, and social (e.g., racial or gender discrimination) challenges to achieve high levels of occupational success. These studies suggested that earlier models of women's occupational achievement (see Kitano & Perkins, 1992), based primarily on White women, were not necessarily applicable to women of color from diverse economic backgrounds. Additional studies are needed to examine the current status of gifted females from culturally, linguistically, and economically diverse backgrounds.

Conceptual Models for Understanding Gifted Females

In examining women's achievement-related decisions, Eccles (1987) called for a reconceptualization of women's educational and vocational choices in ways that value women's goals. Eccles argued that attributing sex differences in occupational attainment to lack of self-confidence or low self-efficacy fails to recognize women's different but equally valid goals and continues to promote the view of women as "deficient males" (p. 166).

The Noble et al. (1999) definition of giftedness described above constitutes one example of reframing applied to gifted females. Reis' theory on women's creative productivity (2002b) provides another. She observes that creative productivity is more "diffused" for women than men because of the priority women give to relationships. Hence, their creative efforts are applied over several domains, often simultaneously: work, family, home tasks, hobbies, service to others, friendships, spirituality. The creative process may emerge differently in women than in men, with women's creativity diverted to and manifested in multiple areas in their lives.

LIMITATIONS OF THE RESEARCH

There is agreement in the literature that the social/cultural context affects opportunities available to women and that school and adult achievement of gifted females must be considered within this changing context.

Transformations around the globe with respect to the status of women renders difficult efforts to generalize on the basis of studies accumulated over time, place, and even within a single decade. There are few strong, empirical studies on gifted girls and women. Available studies conducted both within and outside the United States rarely include substantive numbers of gifted females from diverse racial backgrounds or economic groups allowing disaggregation of data. Investigations designed to examine unique characteristics of gifted females yield more information when including comparison groups of gifted males and average females, with controls for differences between groups in economic status. Investigators also need to define absolute, as well as relative, standards. This concern is critical with regard to characterizing outcomes for gifted girls of color, who may fare well compared to gifted boys of color, but who remain significantly underserved in absolute terms given their proportion in the general population. Additional empirical studies on gifted females from culturally, linguistically, and economically diverse backgrounds are needed to determine their current status.

PRACTICAL IMPLICATIONS OF THE RESEARCH

Practical implications of the literature should be considered with caution, as there are few empirical studies demonstrating the efficacy of specific strategies for supporting gifted girls. Much of the research on gifted girls and women is descriptive or correlational rather than causal. Moreover, practical implications assume certain values regarding goals for gifted girls. Here, the assumption is that all should have access to opportunities that encourage fulfillment of potential based on the individual's carefully considered goals that may change over a lifetime.

- Gifted girls' mathematics achievement scores benefit from learning to view mathematical abilities as competencies that can be developed rather than as gifts (Dweck, 2006).
- Gifted girls would benefit from early and continuous career counseling regarding the range of vocations and the skills, knowledge, dispositions, choices, and sacrifices required to achieve world-class status in a field (Lubinski, Benbow, et al., 2001).
- Girls with ability/interest profiles consistent with high-achievement potential in mathematics and sciences require early and continued special opportunities (e.g., research) and challenging coursework in these domains within and outside of school (Lubinski, Benbow, et al., 2001).
- Contact with role models (both face-to-face and in the curriculum) and work with mentors can encourage gifted girls' achievement (Ambady et al., 2001; Lubinski, Benbow, et al., 2001).

- Girls and boys may benefit from gender-supportive curriculum and instruction, such as connecting content to authentic problems for girls and single-sex clusters led by role models (Sax, 2005).
- School, family, and community programs encouraging high aspirations during and beyond the school years; development of culturally consonant, effective coping strategies; and guidance for higher education, including sources of financial aid, may encourage persistence among gifted girls, especially those from low-income and culturally diverse backgrounds (Kitano, 1994–1995).
- Changes in employing institutions to accommodate talented women's multiple roles and time commitments may encourage their entry and continuation in professional careers (Reis, 2002b).

WHAT THE RESEARCH TELLS US

- In the United States, women are increasingly achieving parity with men in school achievement and educational attainment, although they are not equally represented across career domains and in mathematics, physical science, and engineering.
- Factors underlying sex differences in standardized test scores at the highest levels and the underrepresentation of women in the physical sciences and engineering are complex. They include biological, environmental, social, and attitudinal differences.
- Girls are well-represented in programs for the gifted. Gender differences occur in numbers taking AP exams and in resulting scores in specific subject areas.
- Differences in self-esteem, self-efficacy, and learned helplessness do not appear to account for differences between gifted girls and boys in mathematics and science achievement. Gifted girls in general demonstrate high levels of self-efficacy, accurate self-perceptions, and greater gender role flexibility in perceived opportunities. However, activating negative gender stereotypes may lower mathematics test scores among girls and women.
- Gifted African American and Latina girls continue to be underrepresented in programs for the gifted.

AREAS FOR FUTURE STUDY

- What factors contribute to differences in test scores in mathematics and physical sciences, disaggregating by gender, gifted and average abilities, economic status, and ethnicity?
- Is the U.S. gender gap in mathematics and science achievement related to American cultural attitudes toward women?

- Can changes in gender equity attitudes, policies, and teaching practices improve girls' tests scores in mathematics and physical sciences in the U.S.?
- Does matching of instructional strategies with boys and girls' biologically based learning preferences improve their achievement?
- Do race, class, and gender interact to influence educational and occupational attainment among high-achieving students?

SUGGESTED RESOURCES

Readers interested in reviews of research on factors affecting gifted females' achievement over time are encouraged to consult Callahan (1991), Kerr and Nicpon (2003), and Reis (1998, 2002a, 2002b). For a detailed review on motivational factors, see Dai (2002). Arnold et al. (1996), Ford (1994–1995), and Kitano (1994–1995) discuss issues specific to gifted girls and women diverse in race, culture, economic status, and religion. Ceci and Williams (2006) compiled essays by researchers reflecting diverse perspectives on gender differences in science and mathematics. Sax (2005) offers a readable summary of research on biologically based gender differences and their implications for parents and teachers.

REFERENCES

American Association of University Women. (1992). *How schools shortchange girls.* Washington, DC: Author.

Ambady, N., Shih, M., Kim, A., & Pittinsky, T. L. (2001). Stereotype susceptibility in children: Effects of identity activation on quantitative performance. *Psychological Science, 12,* 385–390.

Arnold, K. D. (1993). Undergraduate aspirations and career outcomes of academically talented women: A discriminant analysis. *Roeper Review, 15,* 169–175.

Arnold, K. D., Noble, K. D., & Subotnik, R. F. (Eds.). (1996). *Remarkable women: Perspectives on female talent development.* Cresskill, NJ: Hampton Press.

Benbow, C. P., Lubinski, D., Shea, D. L., & Eftekhari-Sanjani, H. (2000). Sex differences in mathematical reasoning ability at age 13: Their status 20 years later. *Psychological Science, 11,* 474–480.

Benbow, C. P., & Stanley, J. C. (1983). Sex differences in mathematical reasoning ability: More facts. *Science, 222,* 1029–1030.

Callahan, C. M. (1986). The special needs of gifted girls. *Journal of Children in Contemporary Society, 18,* 105–117.

Callahan, C. M. (1991). An update on gifted females. *Journal for the Education of the Gifted, 14,* 284–311.

Campbell, J. R., & Connolly, C. (1984, April). *Impact of ethnicity on math and science among the gifted.* Paper presented at the Annual Meeting of the American Educational Research Association, New Orleans, LA.

Ceci, S. J., & Williams, W. M. (2006). *Why aren't more women in science? Top researchers debate the evidence*. Washington, DC: American Psychological Association.

Center for American Women and Politics. (n.d.). *Women in elected office 2005 fact sheet summaries*. Retrieved August 19, 2005, from http://www.cawp.rutgers.edu/Facts/Officeholders/cawpfs.html

The Chronicle of Higher Education. (2006). The nation. Students. *The Chronicle of Higher Education, LIII*(1), 12.

Dai, D. Y. (2002). Are gifted girls motivationally disadvantaged? Review, reflection, and redirection. *Journal for the Education of the Gifted, 25*, 315–358.

Dweck, C. S. (2006). Is math a gift? Beliefs that put females at risk. In S. J. Ceci & W. M. Williams (Eds.), *Why aren't more women in science? Top researchers debate the evidence* (pp. 47–55). Washington, DC: American Psychological Association.

Eccles, J. S. (1987). Gender roles and women's achievement-related decisions. *Psychology of Women Quarterly, 11*, 135–172.

Eccles, J. S. (2006). Where are all the women? Gender differences in participation in physical sciences and engineering. In S. J. Ceci & W. M. Williams (Eds.), *Why aren't more women in science? Top researchers debate the evidence* (pp. 199–210). Washington, DC: American Psychological Association.

Farenga, S. J., & Joyce, B. A. (1998). Science-related attitudes and science course selection: A study of high-ability boys and girls. *Roeper Review, 20*, 247–251.

Ford, D. Y. (1994–1995). Underachievement among gifted and non-gifted Black females: A study of perceptions. *Journal of Secondary Gifted Education, 6*, 165–75.

Fortune. (2005). *The 2005 Fortune 500 women CEOs*. Retrieved August 19, 2005, from http://www.fortune.com/fortune/fortune500/articles/0,15114,1046096,00.html

Fox, M. A., Connolly, B. A., & Snyder, T. D. (2005). *Youth indicators 2005: Trends in the well-being of American youth* (NCES 2005-050). Washington, DC: U.S. Government Printing Office.

Freeman, C. E. (2004). *Trends in educational equity of girls & women: 2004* (NCES 2005-016). Washington, DC: U.S. Government Printing Office.

Freeman, J. (2004). Cultural influences on gifted gender achievement. *High Ability Studies, 15*(1), 7–23.

Gur, R. C., & Gur, R. E. (2006). Neural substrates for sex differences in cognition. In S. J. Ceci & W. M. Williams (Eds.), *Why aren't more women in science? Top researchers debate the evidence* (pp. 189–198). Washington, DC: American Psychological Association.

Haier, R. J. (2006). Brains, bias, and biology: Follow the data. In S. J. Ceci & W. M. Williams (Eds.), *Why aren't more women in science? Top researchers debate the evidence* (pp. 113–119). Washington, DC: American Psychological Association.

Hong, E., & Aqui, Y. (2004). Cognitive characteristics of the gifted in math. *Gifted Child Quarterly, 48*, 191–201.

Hyde, J. S. (2006). Women in science: Gender similarities in abilities and sociocultural forces. In S. J. Ceci & W. M. Williams (Eds.), *Why aren't more women in science? Top researchers debate the evidence* (pp. 131–145). Washington, DC: American Psychological Association.

Kerr, B. A. (1994). *Smart girls two: A new psychology of girls, women and giftedness*. Dayton, OH: Psychology Press.

Kerr, B. A., & Nicpon, M. F. (2003). Gender and giftedness. In N. Colangelo & G. A. Davis (Eds.), *Handbook of gifted education* (3rd ed., pp. 493–505.). Boston: Allyn & Bacon.

Kitano, M. K. (1994–1995). Lessons from gifted women of color. *Journal of Secondary Gifted Education, 6*,176–187.

Kitano, M. K. (1997). Gifted Asian American women. *Journal for the Education of the Gifted, 21*, 3–37.

Kitano, M. K. (1998a). Gifted African American women. *Journal for the Education of the Gifted, 21*, 254–287.

Kitano, M. K. (1998b). Gifted Latina women. *Journal for the Education of the Gifted, 21*, 131–159.

Kitano, M. K., & Perkins, C. O. (1992). Factors affecting the achievement of culturally diverse gifted women. *Communicator, 22*(4), 6–10.

Kitano, M. K., & Perkins, C. O. (1996). International gifted women: Developing a critical human resource. *Roeper Review, 19*(1), 34–40.

Kitano, M. K., & Perkins, C. O. (2000). Gifted European American women. *Journal for the Education of the Gifted, 23*, 287–313.

Lubinski, D. S., & Benbow, C. P. (2006). Sex differences in personal attributes for the development of scientific expertise. In S. J. Ceci & W. M. Williams (Eds.), *Why aren't more women in science? Top researchers debate the evidence* (pp. 79–100). Washington, DC: American Psychological Association.

Lubinski, D., Benbow, C. P., Shea, D. L., Eftekhari-Sanjani, H., & Halvorson, M. B. J. (2001). Men and women at promise for scientific excellence: Similarity not dissimilarity. *Psychological Science, 12*, 309–317.

Lubinski, D., Webb, R. M., Morelock, M. J., & Benbow, C. P. (2001). Top 1 in 10,000: A 10-year follow-up of the profoundly gifted. *Journal of Applied Psychology, 86*, 718–729.

Mendez, L. M. R., & Crawford, K. M. (2002). Gender-role stereotyping and career aspirations: A comparison of gifted early adolescent boys and girls. *Journal of Secondary Gifted Education, 13*, 96–107.

National Center for Education Statistics. (2005). *Digest of Education Statistics 2005. Table 252. Bachelor's, master's, and doctor's degrees conferred by degree-granting institutions, by sex of student and field of study: 2003–04.* Retrieved March 2, 2006, from http://nces.ed.gov/programs/digest/d05/tables/dt05_252.asp?referer=list

Newcombe, N. S. (2006). Taking science seriously: Straight thinking about spatial sex differences. In S. J. Ceci & W. M. Williams (Eds.), *Why aren't more women in science? Top researchers debate the evidence* (pp. 69–77). Washington, DC: American Psychological Association.

Noble, K. D., Subotnik, R. F., & Arnold, K. D. (1999). To thine own self be true: A new model of female talent development. *Gifted Child Quarterly, 43*, 140–149.

Olszewski-Kubilius, P., & Turner, D. (2002). Gender differences among elementary school-aged gifted students in achievement, perceptions of ability, and subject preference. *Journal for the Education of the Gifted, 25*, 233–268.

Pajares, F. (1996). Self-efficacy beliefs and mathematical problem-solving of gifted students. *Contemporary Educational Psychology, 21*, 325–344.

Reis, S. M. (1995). Talent ignored, talent diverted: The cultural context underlying giftedness in females. *Gifted Child Quarterly, 39*, 162–170.

Reis, S. M. (1998). *Work left undone: Choices and compromises of talented women.* Mansfield, CT: Creative Learning Press.

Reis, S. M. (2002a). Gifted females in elementary and secondary school. In M. Neihart, S. M. Reis, N. M. Robinson, & S. M. Moon (Eds.), *The social and emotional development of gifted children* (pp. 125–135). Waco, TX: Prufrock Press.

Reis, S. M. (2002b). Toward a theory of creativity in diverse creative women. *Creativity Research Journal, 14,* 305–316.

Reis, S. M., & Callahan, C. M. (1989). Gifted females: They've come a long way—Or have they? *Journal for the Education of the Gifted, 12,* 99–117.

Reis, S. M., Callahan, C. M., & Goldsmith, D. (1994). Attitudes of adolescent gifted girls and boys toward education, achievement, and the future. *Gifted Education International, 9*(3), 144–151.

Sadker, M., & Sadker, D. (1994). *Failing at fairness. How America's schools cheat girls.* New York: Charles Scribner's Sons.

Sadker, D., & Zittleman, K. (2005). Closing the gender gap—Again! *Principal, 84*(4), 18–22.

Sax, L. (2005). *Why gender matters.* New York: Doubleday.

Schweigardt, W. J., Worrell, F. C., & Hale, R. J. (2001). Gender differences in the motivation for and selection of courses in a summer program for academically talented students. *Gifted Child Quarterly, 45,* 283–293.

Spelke, E. S. (2005). Sex differences in intrinsic aptitude for mathematics and science? A critical review. *American Psychologist, 60,* 950–958.

Steele, C. (1997). A threat in the air: How stereotypes shape intellectual identity and performance. *American Psychologist, 52,* 613–629.

Steele, C. (2003). Stereotype threat and African-American student achievement. In T. Perry, C. Steele, & A. Hilliard III (Eds.), *Young, gifted, and Black: Promoting high achievement among African-American students* (pp. 109–130). Boston: Beacon Press.

Subotnik, R. F., Karp, D. E., & Morgan, E. R. (1989). High IQ children at midlife: An investigation into the generalizability of Terman's genetic studies of genius. *Roeper Review, 11,* 139–144.

Tomlinson-Keasey, C., & Little, T. D. (1990). Predicting educational attainment, occupational achievement, intellectual skills, and personal adjustment among gifted men and women. *Journal of Educational Psychology, 82,* 442–455.

U. S. Office of Civil Rights. (2002). *Elementary and secondary school survey: 2002. Table 1 State and national projections for enrollment and selected items by race/ethnicity and sex.* [Data file]. Retrieved August 2, 2007, from http://www.ed.gov/about/offices/list/ocr

Williams, W. M., & Ceci, S. J. (2006). Introduction: Striving for perspective in the debate on women in science. In S. J. Ceci & W. M. Williams (Eds.), *Why aren't more women in science? Top researchers debate the evidence* (pp. 3–23). Washington, DC: American Psychological Association.

Chapter 17

Highly Gifted Children and Adolescents

Miraca U. M. Gross

ighly intellectually gifted children or adolescents are those who score three or more standard deviations above the mean on a test of cognitive ability. In recent years, the term has come to refer to young people with an IQ of 145 or greater regardless of whether the standard deviation of the test is 15 or 16. Within this population are two subsets: exceptionally gifted (IQ 160–179) and profoundly gifted (IQ 180+) students.

The use of these terminologies should not be seen as simply a matter of labeling. Teachers of intellectually disabled or hearing impaired students classify these young people's disabilities as *mild*, *moderate*, *severe*, and *profound* and, importantly, it is recognized that the level of the condition should dictate the degree and type of intervention educators make in response. The further students deviate from the norms for their age, the greater is the differentiation in curriculum and learning environment they require in order to learn optimally. Highly gifted students require a curriculum that differs significantly in pace, level, and complexity from that developed for age peers.

Even among the gifted, we can see enormous differences in their capacity to learn. Goldstein, Stocking, and Godfrey (1999) point out that the range of scores of children in the top 1% on IQ—from 135 to more than 200—is as broad as the range of scores from the second percentile (IQ 64) to the 98th (IQ 132). Indeed, in terms of intellectual capacity alone, the profoundly gifted child of IQ 190 differs from moderately gifted classmates of IQ 130 to the same degree that the latter differ from intellectually disabled children of IQ 70.

How do highly gifted children differ from more moderately gifted children in terms of their cognitive development and how early do these differences become evident? How do they differ in their socioaffective development and how do these differences affect socialization? What forms of educational provision are best suited to their learning and social needs? What do we know about the effects of different interventions on the children's passage through adolescence and into adulthood? This chapter will respond to these questions.

THE EARLY DEVELOPMENT OF SPEECH AND READING

Numerous researchers have noted the early development of speech and reading in the highly gifted (Barbe, 1964; Gross, 1993; Hollingworth, 1926; Terman, 1925). Critics have sometimes attributed these findings to flawed parental memory. However, since 1979 the Fullerton Longitudinal Study (Gottfried, Gottfried, Bathurst, & Guerin, 1994) has systematically recorded differences in the level of cognitive skills between children who later (at 8 years of age) were IQ tested and defined as gifted (1Q 130+) or nongifted. Significant differences appeared on psychometric testing as early as 1.5 years of age and have been sustained throughout the young people's childhood, adolescence, and young adulthood. The earliest difference was found at age one, on entrance to the study, in receptive language. Assessments of comprehension, gross and fine motor skill, memory, and personal-social development have consistently found the gifted group superior.

The Fullerton sample does not contain any subjects of IQ higher than 145; however, its strong empirical validation of parental reports of unusually early development among moderately gifted children provide support for retrospective parental assessment of the early development of cognitively mediated behaviors in the highly gifted. The children of IQ 180+ reported by Hollingworth (1926) uttered their first meaningful word between the ages of 6 and 10 months and most were speaking in sentences by their first birthday. The average age at which 50 children of IQ 160+ spoke their first word was 8.6 months (Gross, 1998).

The precocious development of reading seems to be strongly characteristic of highly gifted children. Almost 43% of Terman's subgroup of IQ 170+ was reading before age 5 compared to 18.4% of the sample as a whole (Terman

& Oden, 1947). VanTassel-Baska (1983), studying 13 and 14 year olds who had scored at the 90th percentile for college-bound seniors on the Scholastic Aptitude Test–Math (SAT–M) or Scholastic Aptitude Test–Verbal (SAT–V), found that 80% of the group had started to read before age 5 and 55% by age 4. Hollingworth's subjects of IQ 180+ were prodigious readers. In every case for which statistics on reading were reported, the child was reading short books by age 4 and in almost all cases this ability developed without formal instruction (Hollingworth, 1926). Gross similarly reported the "spontaneous" onset of reading in all her subjects of IQ 180+: "reading which is untaught and unrehearsed and which seems to appear full-blown in the child without the stages of its development, whatever they be, being perceptible to onlookers or, in some cases, to the child herself" (Gross, 1993, pp. 132–133.) Gross also noted, however, that in several cases where the school failed to respond to the child's early reading, the child interpreted this as a discouragement and responded by significantly decreasing his or her reading in the school setting and, in some cases, stopping it altogether (Gross, 1993).

Implications for Educators and Parents

The unusually early development of speech and reading is strongly predictive of high intellectual ability. Preschool teachers, and teachers in the early years of school, should not only *respond* to a young child's facility in reading but should *record* details of this for the child's subsequent teachers who can then continue to facilitate the child's reading progress—while looking out for indications of additional talents.

Teachers in the early years of school should actively look for signs of early reading. Some parents may be reluctant to tell the school that their young child is already reading, fearing that the school will attribute this to parental coaching (Gross, 1993); however, it is important that parents talk frankly to the school, at the time of enrollment, about the young child's reading advancement. Teachers can respond by placing the young child on an Individualized Educational Program (IEP), allowing her subject acceleration to work with an older class for reading lessons or, where the school has more than one class at each grade level, cluster grouping the advanced readers together with a teacher who will work to develop their reading talents.

SOCIOAFFECTIVE DEVELOPMENT IN HIGHLY GIFTED CHILDREN AND ADOLESCENTS

Highly gifted children differ both from their age peers of average ability and from more moderately gifted age peers on a range of affective variables.

Although studies of intellectually gifted students have identified a tendency toward introversion, this tendency is even more marked in the highly gifted with 75% presenting as introverted (Silverman, 1993).

Significant differences also have been noted in motivational orientation. Gross (1997), comparing academically gifted seventh graders with age peers not identified as gifted, found the gifted students to be significantly more intrinsically motivated, focusing on the task and strategies to master it rather than on the extrinsically motivated desire for high grades or academic recognition. This study also identified significant differences within the gifted group. Highly and exceptionally gifted students in a full-time ability grouped setting who also were telescoping the 6 years of secondary schooling into 5 years were very significantly more task oriented than even the moderately gifted group. In Canada, Kanevsky (1994), comparing differences between problem-solving strategies used by young children of average ability (mean IQ 104) and those used by highly gifted age peers (mean IQ 153), reported similar findings. Highly gifted children were more likely to display intrinsic motivation in enhancing their enjoyment of the problem-solving exercises by monitoring and maintaining the level of challenge available to them, whereas children of average ability appeared more extrinsically motivated by the researcher's interest in their progress. The Fullerton Study likewise found that intellectually gifted children displayed stronger academic intrinsic motivation at age 7 and 8 than nongifted age peers, and showed a stronger orientation to test themselves against challenging and rigorous tasks (Gottfried et al., 1994). Case studies provide further evidence of gifted children's passionate desire to learn more, and improve, in their talent field. The father of one of Morelock's subjects of IQ 180+ described his son's hunger for intellectual stimulus as "a rage to learn" (Morelock, 1995).

Linked to this strong intrinsic motivation is an equally strong preference for independent work. Terman's "study within a study," which traced the development of those members of the gifted group who scored at or above IQ 170 (Burks, Jensen, & Terman, 1930), found that 60% of the boys and 73% of the girls were reported by teachers and parents as preferring to work or study alone rather than with other students. Terman believed that this preference for working independently reflected a natural cognitive orientation.

This preference for independent study, combined with the findings of Schunk (1987) that children model on, and learn best from, students of similar ability to themselves, may explain why highly gifted students often are reluctant to act as tutors or assistants to children whose abilities are substantially inferior to their own. Interestingly, the reluctance to assist classmates often disappears when gifted students are placed in ability groups or accelerated settings with intellectual peers (Gross, 1993, 1998; Hollingworth, 1926).

Studies of the friendship preferences of gifted students have found that they gravitate toward either age peers who also are ability peers, or children who are older (Burks et al., 1930; Gross, 2002; Hollingworth, 1942; Janos, 1985). An empirical study of conceptions of friendship held by children of average ability, moderately gifted, and exceptionally gifted children (Gross, 2002) identified a developmental hierarchy of friendship conceptions through which primary, elementary, and middle school children pass, and found that gifted children passed through the stages much earlier and faster than their age peers. Some exceptionally gifted 7 and 8 year olds had already developed conceptions and expectations of friendship that would not develop in average-ability age peers until the later years of elementary school. This can seriously hamper the development of friendships with age peers.

Hollingworth was the first psychologist to undertake a systematic study of children's peer relationships. She defined the IQ range 125–155 as "socially optimal intelligence" (Hollingworth, 1926), finding that children scoring within this range were, in general, well-balanced, self-confident, and outgoing individuals who were accepted by age peers. She claimed, however, that above the level of IQ 160 the difference between exceptionally gifted children and their age-mates is so great that it leads to special problems of development that are correlated with social isolation (Hollingworth, 1931). She emphasized, however, that these difficulties did not arise from deficiencies within the gifted children themselves but through the unlikelihood of their easily finding others who share their abilities and interests.

Subsequent studies have confirmed Hollingworth's findings. Studies by DeHaan and Havighurst (1961), Gallagher (1958), and Janos (1983), comparing the friendship patterns of moderately and exceptionally gifted children, noted that the exceptionally gifted group tended to have significantly greater problems of social acceptance. Gallagher (1958) suggested that moderately gifted children achieve good social adjustment because they have sufficient intelligence to overcome minor social difficulties, but are not "different" enough to induce the severe problems of salience encountered by the exceptionally gifted.

The field in which the child's talent is sited can strongly influence social acceptability. Young people of IQ 160 in Gross's (2004) study who also were talented in sports or athletics were much more readily accepted by classmates than ability peers without sporting talent. Dauber and Benbow (1990), studying mathematically and verbally talented adolescents, found that students with extreme verbal talent rated themselves as having very low social standing with their age peers. The researchers attributed this both to society's higher valuing of mathematical talent than verbal talent, and to the fact that while extreme mathematical ability may be less obvious on social occasions, students who are extremely talented verbally may be conspicuous due to their sophisticated vocabulary.

Implications for Educators and Parents

Highly gifted students with a tendency to introversion may not socialize as readily or frequently with classmates as their teachers would wish; indeed, some teachers may view them, incorrectly, as "stand-offish" or antisocial. This is compounded by the fact that gifted students often gravitate toward older children and tend to prefer small, closely linked friendship groups rather than looser groups. Parents and teachers should avoid telling highly gifted students not to put all their friendship "eggs" in the one basket; it may be difficult enough to find one or two other people with whom one can share hearts and minds without being pressured to look for several.

The preference for independent work that has been noted by several researchers suggests that some highly gifted students may be temperamentally unsuited to working in mixed-ability cooperative learning groups.

EFFECTIVE INTERVENTIONS

Ability Grouping

Hollingworth (1942) was a strong advocate of ability grouping for the highly gifted, pointing out that students above IQ 170 wasted almost all of their time in the mixed-ability classroom. To ensure that gifted students in full-time ability-grouped settings did not develop an unrealistically inflated or deflated idea of their abilities, she suggested that gifted students might be grouped full time in the elementary school years with work in regular grades later in high school (Hollingworth, 1926). However, she herself was doubtful that ability grouping would lead to arrogance or conceit. "The objection that special opportunity classes for the able will make gifted students conceited is probably groundless. It seems far more likely that work with competitors of one's own caliber tends to starve conceit, rather than to feed it" (Hollingworth, 1926, p. 301).

Certainly, research is clear about the value, for academically gifted students, of well-designed ability-grouped programs. Meta-analyses of "value added" studies of the performance of gifted pupils in ability-grouped classes where the curriculum is accelerated, as well as enriched, have shown that these pupils gain in grade-level competencies at almost twice the rate of equally gifted pupils retained in the regular classroom (Kulik, 1992). The ability-grouped pupils gain, on average, 10 months additional progress over the course of a year and there is evidence to suggest that the gain may be even greater for highly gifted students. In a 3-year experimental study comparing the academic progress of two classes of gifted elementary students that she established at New York Public School 165, one class of mean IQ 146, the other of mean IQ 165, Hollingworth found that the achievement of the abler class was consistently superior (Hollingworth & Cobb, 1928).

Less formal methods of ability grouping include those facilitated by state and local associations for gifted and talented children and adolescents, which allow gifted young people to meet others with whom they have a certain commonality of abilities and interests. A number of university centers in the

United States and internationally offer summer courses for gifted students, and the Davidson Institute for Talent Development organizes regular get-togethers for highly gifted children and their parents (see the Davidson Web site http://www.GeniusDenied.com for a wealth of practical ideas). Although such occasional enrichment and socialization opportunities cannot *replace* appropriate in-school educational and social provisions, the access they can provide to developmentally appropriate curriculum and compatible age peers can lessen both the boredom of highly gifted students and their fears that they may be somehow socially unacceptable.

Acceleration

In the first half of the 20th century, acceleration was an accepted intervention with gifted students. Of Terman's 1,528 gifted students, 23% skipped a grade and 10% skipped two. In high school, these students consistently scored in the top 10% of their classes. Accelerands were more likely to enter graduate study and complete it successfully than gifted students retained with age peers. A survey of the Terman sample taken in their late 60s found that accelerands reported significantly greater life satisfaction in their work, in recreational activities, and in social activities and friendships (Cronbach, 1996). Terman and his colleagues (Terman & Oden, 1959) concluded that students of IQ 140 should be accelerated sufficiently to permit college entrance by age 17 at the latest, while the majority would be better off to enter by age 16. Hollingworth (1926) concurred; while expressing a wariness of extremely radical acceleration such as a 12-year-old entering college, she argued that children of IQ 140 could enter college by the time they were 15 or 16.

The Study of Mathematically Precocious Youth (SMPY), now in its fourth decade, is following 5,000 mathematically or verbally gifted adults who scored, as adolescents, in the top 1% of their age peers on the SAT–M or SAT–V. Talent search participants tend to retain and use their high abilities. An investigation of one cohort of talent search participants when they were in their early 30s found that 25% held doctoral degrees, as compared to 1% of the United States population (Benbow, Lubinski, Shea, & Eftekhari-Sanjani, 2000). Indeed, 50% of the highest achievers in the SMPY talent searches, young people who scored on the SAT–M or SAT–V at levels achieved by fewer than 1 in 1,000, have doctorates (Lubinski, Webb, Morelock, and Benbow, 2001). Numerous studies of the effects of acceleration, including radical acceleration (graduation from high school 3 or more years earlier than is customary), on talent search participants have found enormously beneficial academic and social outcomes.

Gross (2004) reports similar findings from her longitudinal study of 60 Australian young people of IQ 160+ that commenced in 1983. Surprisingly, given the wariness with which Australian teachers regard acceleration, 17 of the 60 young people were radically accelerated. None has regrets. Indeed, several say they probably would have preferred to accelerate still further, or have started earlier. The majority entered college between ages 11 and 15. Several won scholarships to attend prestigious universities in Australia or overseas. All have graduated with extremely high grades and, in most cases, university prizes for exemplary achievement. Almost all have gone on to obtain a doctoral degree.

In every case, the radical accelerands have been able to form warm, lasting, and deep friendships. They attribute this to the fact that their schools placed them, quite early, with older students to whom they tended to gravitate in any case. The majority are married or in permanent or serious love relationships.

By contrast, equally gifted young people who were retained in the inclusion classroom with age peers, or permitted a "token" grade advancement of a single year, have, in general, experienced significant and ongoing difficulties with peer relationships.

Hollingworth (1942) emphasized that when exceptionally gifted children who have been rejected by age peers are removed from the inappropriate grade placement, and are permitted to work and socialize with intellectual peers, the feelings of loneliness and social isolation disappear and the child is accepted as a valued classmate and friend.

It is interesting to note the positive outcomes of acceleration regardless of the frequency of its use at any given time. Acceleration was a commonly used intervention when Terman's subjects were in elementary and secondary school; however, it was much less commonly used in the first decade of the SMPY studies, and in Australia in the early 1980s, when Gross's longitudinal study commenced, it was characterized by its scarcity. Nonetheless, Terman's finding that accelerated students are more likely to earn advanced degrees also was noted by the SMPY researchers (Benbow et al., 2000), by Kulik in his meta-analyses of acceleration (Kulik, 2004), and by Gross, in her 20-year follow-up of the IQ 160+ group (Gross, 2004). The academic success of acceleration is striking. Kulik (2004), referring to the academic superiority of accelerated students over nonaccelerands of equal ability, has noted, "In a review of approximately 100 different meta-analyses of research findings in education, Chen-Lin Kulik and I were not able to find any educational treatment that consistently yielded a higher effect size than this one" (p. 20).

POINTS TO CONSIDER IN EDUCATIONAL PLANNING

- The range of abilities among the highly gifted is enormous. These students require highly individualized educational planning.
- Speech and reading develop much earlier than usual in the highly gifted. Many, perhaps the majority, of highly gifted students enter school already reading. Teachers should recognize this as predictive of high academic ability and look for other, more formal, indications.

Highly gifted children can be identified by standardized testing in their early years of school, including above-level assessment on tests normed on older students.

- The difficulties in socialization sometimes experienced by highly gifted children arise both because of the difficulties they experience in finding other children who share their abilities and interests and because they prefer the companionship of older children. When highly gifted children are grouped by ability or accelerated, difficulties in socialization are usually significantly moderated and may disappear completely.

- Young people with extreme verbal talent are more at risk for social rejection than those with extreme mathematical talent. Teachers should be sensitively aware of this and watch for students who seem to moderate their vocabulary after a few weeks in school or a few weeks in a new class.

- Acceleration is associated with long-term life satisfaction. The "smorgasbord" of acceleration procedures presented in *A Nation Deceived* (Colangelo, Assouline, & Gross, 2004) can allow for the development of highly individualized programs of acceleration.

- Radical acceleration is highly affective both academically and socially for highly gifted students.

LIMITATIONS OF RESEARCH ON HIGHLY GIFTED STUDENTS

Highly gifted children appear at ratios of fewer than 1:1,000. It would be too costly both financially and in terms of time to do a large-scale screening in the hope of finding such students. Thus, most research on the highly gifted is conducted on accessible populations; for example, students in special programs, students who have been significantly accelerated, or whose behavior or classroom performance have already indicated that they might be highly gifted. Highly gifted children with learning disabilities or other disabling conditions may not be identified—or their disability may camouflage their *degree* of giftedness. Additionally, as Richert (2003) comments, even among the research community, serving the highly gifted has been viewed as "uncompromisingly elitist" (p. 147) and highly gifted students are presumed to be White and middle class. Highly gifted children from minority populations or economically disadvantaged families may not be recognized by educators who hold such views.

The Stanford-Binet L-M allowed researchers to measure the abilities of even the most extremely gifted students. The ceilings of modern IQ tests are too low to permit this. Off-level assessment using standardized tests of aptitude and achievement, as employed by the SMPY team, seems to be a practical and highly effective substitute but this technique is currently underutilized.

REFERENCES

Barbe, W. B. (1964). *One in a thousand: A comparative study of highly and moderately gifted elementary school children*. Columbus, OH: F. J. Heer.

Benbow, C. P., Lubinski, S., Shea, D. L., & Eftekhari-Sanjani, H. (2000). Sex differences in mathematical reasoning ability: Their status 20 years later. *Psychological Science, 11*, 474–480.

Burks, B. S., Jensen, D. W., & Terman, L. M. (1930). *The promise of youth: Genetic studies of genius, Vol. 3*. Stanford, CA: Stanford University Press.

Colangelo, N., Assouline, S. G., & Gross, M. U. M. (2004). *A nation deceived: How schools hold back America's brightest students* (Vols. 1 & 2). Iowa City, IA: The Connie Belin & Jacqueline N. Blank International Center for Gifted Education and Talent Development.

Cronbach, L. J. (1996). Acceleration among the Terman males: Correlates in mid-life and after. In C. P. Benbow & D. Lubinski (Eds.), *Intellectual talent: Psychometric and social issues* (pp. 179–191). Baltimore: Johns Hopkins University Press.

Dauber, S. L., & Benbow, C. P. (1990). Aspects of personality and peer relations of extremely talented adolescents. *Gifted Child Quarterly, 34*, 10–14.

DeHaan, R. F., & Havighurst, R. J. (1961). *Educating gifted children*. Chicago: University of Chicago Press.

Gallagher, J. J. (1958). Peer acceptance of highly gifted children in the elementary school. *Elementary School Journal, 58*, 465–470.

Goldstein, D., Stocking, V. B., & Godfrey, J. J. (1999). What we've learned from talent search research. In N. Colangelo & S. G. Assouline (Eds.), *Talent Development III: Proceedings from the 1995 Henry B. and Jocelyn Wallace National Research Symposium on Talent Development*. Scottsdale, AZ: Gifted Psychology Press.

Gottfried, W., Gottfried, A. E., Bathurst, K., & Guerin, D. W. (1994). *Gifted IQ: Early developmental aspects: The Fullerton longitudinal study*. New York: Plenum Press.

Gross, M. U. M. (1993). *Exceptionally gifted children*. London: Routledge.

Gross, M. U. M. (1997). How ability grouping turns big fish into little fish—or does it? Of optical illusions and optimal environments. *Australasian Journal of Gifted Education, 6*(2), 18–30.

Gross, M. U. M. (1998). The "me" behind the mask: Intellectually gifted children and the search for identity. *Roeper Review, 20*, 167–174.

Gross, M. U. M. (2002). Gifted children and the gift of friendship. *Understanding Our Gifted, 14*(3), 27–29.

Gross, M. U. M. (2004). *Exceptionally gifted children* (2nd ed.). London: RoutledgeFalmer.

Hollingworth, L. S. (1926) *Gifted children: Their nature and nurture*. New York: Macmillan.

Hollingworth, L. S. (1931). The child of very superior intelligence as a special problem in social adjustment. *Mental Hygiene, 15*(1), 3–16.

Hollingworth, L. S. (1942) *Children above IQ 180: Their origin and development*. New York: World Books.

Hollingworth, L. S., & Cobb, M. V. (1928). Children clustering at 165 IQ and children clustering at 146 IQ compared for three years in achievement. In G. M. Whipple (Ed.), *Nature and nurture: Their influence upon achievement. The 27th Yearbook of the National Society for the Study of Education* (pp. 3–33), Bloomington, IL: Public School Publishing.

Janos, P. M. (1983). *The psychological vulnerabilities of children of very superior intellectual ability*. Unpublished doctoral dissertation, The Ohio State University, Columbus.

Janos, P. M. (1985). Friendship patterns in highly intelligent children. *Roeper Review, 8*, 46–49.

Kanevsky, L. K. (1994). A comparative study of children's learning in the zone of proximal development. *European Journal of High Ability, 5*, 163–175.

Kulik, J. A. (1992). *An analysis of the research on ability grouping: Historical and contemporary perspectives*. Storrs: The National Research Center on the Education of the Gifted and Talented, University of Connecticut.

Kulik, J. A. (2004). Meta-analytic studies of acceleration. In N. Colangelo, S. G. Assouline, & M. U. M. Gross (Eds.), *A nation deceived: How schools hold back America's brightest students* (Vol. 2, pp. 13–22). Iowa City, IA: The Connie Belin & Jacqueline N. Blank International Center for Gifted Education and Talent Development.

Lubinski, D., Webb, R. M., Morelock, M. J., & Benbow, C. P. (2001). Top 1:10,000: A 10-year follow up of the profoundly gifted. *Journal of Applied Psychology, 86*, 718–729.

Morelock, M. J. (1995). *The profoundly gifted child in family context*. Unpublished doctoral dissertation, Tufts University.

Richert, E. S. (2003). Excellence with justice in identification and programming. In N. Colangelo & G. A. Davis (Eds.), *Handbook of gifted education* (3rd ed., pp. 146–158). Boston: Allyn & Bacon.

Schunk, D. H. (1987). Peer models and children's behavioral change. *Equity and Excellence, 23*, 22–30.

Silverman, L. K. (1993). *Counseling the gifted and talented*. Denver, CO: Love.

Terman, L. M. (1925). *Mental and physical traits of a thousand gifted children: Genetic studies of genius*, Vol. 1. Stanford, CA: Stanford University Press.

Terman, L. M., & Oden, M. H. (1947). *The gifted child grows up: Genetic studies of genius, Vol. 4*. Stanford, CA: Stanford University Press.

Terman, L. M., & Oden, M. H. (1959). *The gifted group at mid-life: Genetic studies of genius, Vol. 5*. Stanford, CA: Stanford University Press.

VanTassel-Baska, J. (1983). Profiles of precocity: The 1982 Midwest Talent Search finalists. *Gifted Child Quarterly, 27*(3), 139–144.

Chapter 18

HOMESCHOOLING

Robert Kunzman

nce considered a fringe activity by cultural separatists—and not even acknowledged as legal by all 50 states until 1983—homeschooling has enjoyed dramatic growth in recent years. The National Center for Education Statistics (NCES) estimates that 1.1 million students were being homeschooled in the United States in the spring of 2003 (NCES, 2004). This represents a 29% increase from the NCES survey just 4 years earlier. Some researchers assert that more than 2 million students are being homeschooled in the United States today (Ray, 2003)—as many as 1 in 25 school-age American children. Although the total number of homeschooled students is a matter of dispute, what seems clear is the rapid relative increase of homeschooling. Even using the more conservative NCES figures, the

number of homeschooled students has increased at a rate of 10 times that of public school students during the most recent survey period.[1]

Beyond this single government survey, a look at the homeschooling landscape across the United States yields little comprehensive data on demographics, practices, and outcomes. The uncertainty (and disagreement) in this regard can be traced in part to the widely varying practices of data collection among states; less than half even have readily available data on homeschooling ("Homeschool Numbers," 2005), and many don't even know how many homeschoolers there are within their borders.[2] Furthermore, homeschoolers generally have been reluctant to provide any more information than is required by law, and homeschool advocacy groups regularly resist legislation that would increase governmental oversight. Because of this, the most frequently cited research studies have used nonrepresentative samples without controlling for variables such as household income; in addition, many of them have been sponsored by homeschool advocacy groups.

Therefore, it should not be surprising that even less empirical data are available on the subset of homeschooling gifted children. In fact, it appears that not a single, comprehensive study of gifted homeschoolers has been published—or would even be possible to conduct, given the basic uncertainty regarding homeschooling numbers and demographics overall.[3]

Nevertheless, a patchwork of partial empirical glimpses, conceptual arguments, and anecdotal reports can be assembled about homeschooling in general, and this may offer some insight into the subset of gifted homeschooling. Two questions in particular about homeschooling outcomes seem relevant to gifted education in this context. First, are homeschooled children adequately socialized? Second, what do we know about the academic achievement of homeschooled students? Both concerns resonate with themes in gifted education more generally, as parents and educators struggle with providing an educational environment that both appropriately challenges extraordinary learners and offers them opportunities to develop meaningful relationships with their peers and others.

---

1   Ray reasonably contends that many homeschool parents are reluctant to identify themselves because of their resistance to any form of government regulation (see also K. M. Welner, *Exploring the Democratic Tensions Within Parents' Decision to Homeschool*). Although some researchers have questioned Ray's objectivity—he homeschooled his own children and has been funded by the Home School Legal Defense Association—other analysts (e.g., Belfield, 2004) have criticized the NCES sampling methodology and small sample size (11,994 surveyed, revealing 239 homeschoolers) and similarly suggest that actual numbers are likely higher.

2   The inconsistency of homeschool data collection is mirrored by the variety of regulatory oversight each state exercises as well. About half of the states impose no evaluatory regulations whatsoever, although some require parents to notify authorities of their intent to homeschool. For the other half, evaluation procedures range from standardized testing (most common) to a more extensive slate of requirements including curriculum evaluation and educational attainment levels for parents.

3   The NCES survey from 2003 did ask parents about their most important reason for homeschooling. The top three responses were "concern about environment of other schools" (31%), "to provide religious or moral instruction" (30%), and "dissatisfaction with academic instruction at other schools" (16%). Although it is reasonable to assume that parents of a highly gifted child might cite school environment or academic instruction as primary concerns, these NCES data of course provide no clear sense of the proportion of homeschoolers who qualify as formally gifted.

SOCIALIZATION OF HOMESCHOOLERS

Homeschool parents are no strangers to the assumption by observers that their child won't be adequately socialized if they don't attend an institutional school. This concern continues to be raised periodically by critics, but what seems clear is that the "home" in homeschooling is rapidly becoming a misnomer. Homeschool community groups abound, mixing educational activities (such as student presentations on research topics, theatre productions, and study groups) and more informal, social-recreational activities. Local colleges and universities frequently welcome advanced homeschool students into their classrooms. Museums, libraries, and other educational organizations are increasingly oriented toward providing programming for homeschool families. Extracurricular opportunities for homeschoolers continue to grow as well. Formal homeschool athletic leagues offer competition from the local level up through national championships in basketball, soccer, volleyball, and softball.

As noted previously, however, comprehensive empirical evidence is lacking. Homeschool supporters routinely cite one particular study (Ray, 2003), commissioned by a prominent homeschool advocacy group, as evidence that homeschool graduates are engaged citizens, involved in their communities, and leading fulfilling lives. But, this study examined a small, homogeneous group of homeschoolers without controlling for parent income, education, or other variables, so neither definitive statements about homeschoolers nor reliable comparisons with the general U.S. population can be made.

The more basic question of what constitutes healthy socialization is also at issue here. Does the relative lack of constant peer interaction pose significant hurdles for socialization? Homeschool advocates point out that homeschoolers likely have greater opportunity to interact with a full range of ages—rather than almost exclusively with their peers—in a greater variety of learning settings throughout the community. This dynamic is often present with highly gifted students more generally as well; one recourse for children whose abilities extend far beyond "grade level" has been to place them with older, more academically advanced students. Parents of gifted homeschoolers, for instance, frequently report enrolling their children in university courses.

Medlin (2000) sought to bring greater precision to the question of what constitutes healthy socialization in the first place by reviewing dozens of studies focused on broader homeschooler socialization. He concluded that the evidence, while still preliminary, suggests that homeschooled children in general are engaged in their community, acquire necessary rules of behavior, and demonstrate social maturity and leadership skills. The analysis emphasized, however, that more and better research is needed before definitive conclusions about homeschooler socialization can be drawn.

ACADEMIC ACHIEVEMENT OF HOMESCHOOLERS

The question of how homeschool students compare academically with their public school peers remains a matter of dispute. Homeschool advocates can point to high-achieving individuals who win national spelling and geography bees, debate competitions, art contests, and so on. Even stalwart critics of homeschooling acknowledge that the "high end" of academic homeschooling performance compares favorably with other forms of schooling; certainly the nation's elite colleges and universities have come to think so, with admissions departments welcoming homeschooler applications, and some assigning a liaison specifically for homeschool applicants (Jones & Gloeckner, 2004; Marean, Ott, & Rush, 2005).

In terms of empirical research, the most frequently cited study by homeschool advocates confirms that at least a segment of homeschool students score two to four grade levels and 20 percentile points higher on a nationally recognized achievement test (Rudner, 1999). But, the study's author himself acknowledges that participants were an unrepresentative sample of homeschoolers and the study was not a controlled experiment; therefore, it prevents us from making reliable extrapolations to the general homeschooling population or comparing homeschoolers' performance with the broader student population (Welner & Welner, 1999). Similar limitations occur in a separate study of SAT scores (Belfield, 2004). So, while these data do not definitively conclude that homeschooling is invariably an effective educational choice for gifted students, they do suggest that the homeschool environment can provide a setting for academic acceleration and high achievement.

GIFTED EDUCATION IN HOMESCHOOLING

Not only is there scant empirical data regarding gifted homeschooling, but the formal topic of gifted education receives relatively little attention within the homeschooling community. Some commentators speculate that this may be because comparative distinctions such as "gifted" seem less relevant to parent-educators in a learning environment often distinguished by customization and self-pacing. But, as one homeschool consultant specializing in gifted and talented education notes, the typical homeschool commitment to individualized education is only one ingredient in providing an effective learning environment for a gifted child. There also needs to be intentional assessment of a child's particular and sometimes extraordinary learning needs and abilities, to identify areas of particular strength (and relative weakness) in order to customize the curricular experience most effectively (Gordon, n.d.).

Gifted education advocates often point out that although public schools recognize their obligation to provide appropriately modified programs for students with disabilities, this frequently does not hold true for highly gifted students who also need substantially different educational opportunities. Parents sometimes describe homeschooling as the "ultimate IEP," but in this case an individualized education plan is created and implemented for *every* child. The available flexibility of homeschooling allows for forms of pedagogy and curricula that resonate with gifted education: intense, in-depth focus on a particular subject or project; accelerated pacing; individual mentoring; "real-world" internships; and accessing programs and coursework within the broader community (Kearney, 1992).

In addition, advocates for homeschooling of gifted children contend that homeschooling provides vital flexibility in responding to the frequently asynchronous nature of giftedness, where students are uneven in their abilities. Categorizing homeschool children as being in a certain "grade," while sometimes necessary for paperwork requirements, holds little importance as they engage in the learning process itself. In an institutional school setting, however, it is frequently a more complicated and less flexible arrangement if a child is an average science student, a math prodigy, and struggles with reading. The homeschool flexibility in this regard need not be limited to solitary study, either. As mentioned earlier, homeschoolers frequently enjoy a network of support groups and learning co-ops. Advocates point to the makeup of these homeschool groups—which are frequently multi-age—as providing more flexibility for varying interests and abilities, with little or no attention paid to "age/grade level" classifications (Morse, 2001).

One possible concern regarding the homeschooling of gifted children is whether parents will be capable of providing instruction in specialized or advanced subject matter. (Homeschooling critics raise this issue more generally as well, with some insisting that only a licensed teacher should be entrusted with academic instruction.)[4] As suggested earlier, one way that homeschool parents address the gap between their knowledge and the many academic avenues their gifted children may wish to explore is by arranging for outside expert instruction; enrolling homeschool students in college or university courses is a common option here. But, it is also worth pointing out that such instruction is increasingly available "inside" the home as well, through the rapid growth of virtual schools and distance education. Gifted homeschool students can now access higher education regardless of their geographical location.[5]

4   Although debate continues on what constitutes effective teacher preparation, a significant body of research suggests that the quality of teacher preparation can make a difference in the academic achievement of students (see, for example, Darling-Hammond, 2006; National Commission on Teaching and America's Future, 1996; and Nye, Konstantopoulos, & Hedges, 2004).

5   This proliferation of learning options also points to the increasingly blurred boundaries of what constitutes homeschooling. Broadly speaking, homeschooling is characterized by parents (and sometimes their children) coordinating and overseeing their educational experience; this certainly can include participation in homeschooling co-ops and other learning experiences wherein instruction is provided by those other than parents (e.g., local library or museum workshops, community college classes, distance-learning courses, etc.). Although the Home School Legal Defense Association requires parents to provide direct instruction at

The proliferation of online homeschooling options, while offering greater choice, convenience, and accessibility, also raises at least two additional concerns. First, a homeschool experience dominated by "virtual classrooms" and electronic communication provides a decidedly different form of socialization than either a school building or a homeschool community group offers, one that is arguably lacking in important facets of interpersonal skills. Second, questions of quality control continue to arise, particularly in the sector of for-profit secondary education. Although "quality review" of any curriculum is one of the homeschool parents' responsibilities, quality may be more difficult for them to judge when the subject matter is beyond their expertise and the learning process does not include parent participation or facilitation.

WHAT WE KNOW . . .
AND QUESTIONS THAT REMAIN

The broader, albeit largely anecdotal, picture of homeschooling across the United States offers at least some insight into the benefits and challenges of homeschooling gifted children. At the core of the homeschooling philosophy is the conviction that parents should have primary (if not sole) responsibility for shaping the education of their children. Although this doesn't necessarily mean that parents must always directly provide instruction, the influence of an involved homeschool parent will nonetheless be enormous. In the case of a child with "special needs," this can be both an advantage or disadvantage. On one hand, parents frequently will have deep insight into the educational strengths, weaknesses, and needs of their child. On the other hand, their lack of specific expertise in gifted education may result in them overlooking useful pedagogical strategies and curricular resources.

Beyond these educated speculations, however, the current research base on homeschooling gifted children is severely limited: We have no comprehensive data on any learning outcomes for gifted homeschoolers, primarily because we have such indeterminacy on how many people homeschool in general, much less their curricula and pedagogy.

With this in mind, the research questions that remain about homeschooling gifted children are fundamental and broad. They include:

- What percentage of homeschooled children are gifted?
- What role did parents' concerns about schools meeting the advanced learning needs of their child play in their decision to homeschool?
- How do their learning outcomes (academic achievement, socialization, etc.) compare both with the wider homeschool population, as well as the gifted population more broadly?

least 51% of the time to qualify for membership, no universally accepted definition of homeschooling exists. Attendance at university classes, contrary to one reviewer's contention, is frequently seen as part of an overall homeschooling experience. It is an education orchestrated/directed by parents, even though parts of it may involve direct instruction from other adults.

- Do the benefits of individualized learning touted by homeschool advocates contribute to a better learning experience for gifted children?
- Does a lack of expertise in gifted education on the part of homeschool parents hinder the learning and growth of their children?
- If parents decide to stop homeschooling, how does their gifted child adjust to returning to a conventional classroom environment?

Clearly, the dearth of empirical research on gifted homeschooling is merely a symptom of the broader lack of comprehensive data on homeschooling in general. The current state of regulation and data collection—and the determined resistance by many homeschoolers and their organizations against outside evaluation—makes the prospects of gaining a fuller picture of gifted homeschooling quite remote. As a result, gifted education in the homeschooling context likely will remain a learning environment known primarily through anecdotal reports, and one that relies heavily on the motivation, capacity, and judgment of parents to meet the extraordinary learning needs of their children.

REFERENCES

Belfield, C. R. (2004). *Home-schooling in the US* (Occasional Paper No. 88). New York: National Center for the Study of Privatization in Education.

Darling-Hammond, L. (2006). Securing the right to learn: Policy and practice for powerful teaching and learning, *Educational Researcher, 35*(7), 13–24.

Gordon, A. S. (n.d.). *Why is assessment important if we plan on homeschooling?* Retrieved June 20, 2007, from http://giftedhomeschoolers.org/articles/testinghomeschoolers. html

Homeschool numbers growing, tracking difficult. (2005, April 6). *Penn State News* [online]. Retrieved June 20, 2007, from http://www.psu.edu/ur/2005/homeschool. html

Jones, P., & Gloeckner, G. (2004). A study of admission officers' perceptions and attitudes toward homeschool students. *Journal of College Admission, 184,* 12–21.

Kearney, K. (1992). *Homeschooling highly gifted children.* Retrieved June 20, 2007, from http://www.hollingworth.org/HomSchHG.html

Marean, J. A., Ott, M. F., & Rush, M. J. (2005). Homeschooled students and the Ivy League. In B. S. Cooper (Ed.), *Home schooling in full view: A reader* (pp. 179–197). Greenwich, CT: Information Age Publishing.

Medlin, R. G. (2000). Home schooling and the question of socialization. *Peabody Journal of Education, 75,* 107–123.

Morse, K. (2001). *When schools fail: Is homeschooling right for you and your highly gifted child?* Retrieved June 20, 2007, from http://www.hoagiesgifted.org/schools_fail. htm

National Center for Education Statistics. (2004). *1.1 million homeschooled students in the United States in 2003* (NCES Publication No. 2004115). Washington, DC: National Center for Education Statistics.

National Commission on Teaching and America's Future. (1996). *What matters most: Teaching for America's future.* New York: Author.

Nye, B., Konstantopoulos, S., & Hedges, L. V. (2004). How large are teacher effects? *Educational Evaluation and Policy Analysis, 26*, 237–257.

Ray, B. D. (2003). *Home educated and now adults: Their community and civic involvement, views about homeschooling, and other traits.* Salem, OR: National Home Education Research Institute.

Rudner, L. M. (1999). Scholastic achievement and demographic characteristics of home school students in 1998 [electronic version]. *Education Policy Analysis Archives, 7*(8). Retrieved June 20, 2007, from http://epaa.asu.edu/epaa/v7n8

Welner, K. M. (2002). *Exploring the democratic tensions within parents' decision to home-school* (Occasional Paper No. 45). New York: National Center for the Study of Privatization in Education.

Welner, K. M., & Welner, K. G. (1999). Contextualizing homeschooling data: A response to Rudner [electronic version]. *Education Policy Analysis Archives 7*(13). Retrieved June 20, 2007, from http://epaa.asu.edu/epaa/v7n13

Chapter 19

IDENTIFICATION

James H. Borland

TERMS AND ISSUES

he identification of gifted students is almost always the most controversial aspect of gifted programs in the public schools. This is inevitable because testing and other forms of assessment are involved and because the process results in some students being selected for participation in a gifted program (and thus, at least implicitly, being labeled *gifted*) and in others being left behind. Moreover, among scholars in the field of gifted education (for a small sample, see textbooks by Clark, 2002; Davis & Rimm, 2003; Gallagher & Gallagher, 1994; Howley, Howley, & Pendarvis, 1986), identification has been a perennially difficult topic, leading Tannenbaum (1983, p. 342) to refer to it as our field's "inexact science."

To what extent can research on the identification of gifted students assist practitioners in making their identification procedures more effective (and more equitable), and to what extent can it assist scholars and policy makers in their efforts?

It would seem, at first glance, that identification, which is so concerned with measurement, would be a topic ripe for empirical exploration and guidance. However, although there has been considerable research on this topic from the beginning (Terman's foundational longitudinal research conducted between 1925 and 1959 and could plausibly be considered an identification study), all identification inquiry is plagued, to one extent or another, by a serious impediment: *the problem of the criterion.*

The central issue in research on identification is whether individual assessments or identification procedures as a whole are *valid*, that is, whether they assess what they are designed to assess. To quote a classic paper by Cronbach, "validation consists of checking the test score against some other observation that serves as *criterion*" (1971, p. 443).

The identification of gifted students typically involves one of two types of validity. *Predictive validity* is concerned with whether an identification measure or process accurately predicts a future criterion, such as appropriate placement in a gifted program or what Renzulli (2005) refers to as "gifted behavior." In a more general assessment context, predictive validity is of concern with respect to measures such as the SAT, where the major question of interest is, does the score on this test, administered in the present (say, in high school), predict future behavior, such as college grade point average?

Construct validity is concerned with whether the measure or process actually assesses the construct of interest, in this case, *giftedness*. In other words, is there evidence that what is being measured is actually that which giftedness is composed of? Can we agree that there is a correspondence between the things the test assesses and the agreed-upon constituents of the construct of giftedness? But therein, of course, lies the difficulty.

As even the most cursory glance at the literature of the field of gifted education reveals, there is, to understate the situation considerably, no consensus as to what this construct, giftedness, is, how it reveals itself, or what it is composed of. Because there is no agreement as to the nature and constituents of giftedness, those conducting research into identification practices are faced with a conceptual and practical difficulty. Against what (and whose) criterion do we judge the efficacy of identification instruments and procedures?

Thus, to test whether test A or procedure B validly predicts or identifies giftedness, one needs to posit a definition of giftedness, and this is an area in which there is serious contestation. The lack of agreement on "What makes giftedness," to cite Renzulli (1978) again, makes identification research tenuous and potentially tautological.

MAJOR QUESTIONS

The potential list of questions that research on identification could address is lengthy. I will cite three that I believe are most central to our field at this time, keeping in mind that the problem of the criterion renders answering some of these questions difficult, if not impossible.

1. How well do various forms of assessment predict behaviors that are associated with gifted students or that are required of students in the gifted program in which students are placed? (This is the predictive validity problem.)

2. To what extent do various forms of assessment actually measure the constituents of giftedness? (This is the construct validity problem.)

3. To what extent can identification procedures be made more equitable with respect to issues such as race and SES? (This is a persistent problem in gifted education that is closely linked to issues of identification and that has serious implications, moral and ethical, as well as practical, for our field.)

WHAT DOES THE RESEARCH TELL US?

Although there are numerous studies that deal with the identification of gifted students, I will focus on a few that are historically significant and that have affected practice in the field of gifted education before turning to some more recent studies that exemplify current concerns.

Terman's Genetic Studies of Genius

I suggested above that Terman's *Genetic Studies of Genius* (Burks, Jensen, & Terman, 1930; Cox, 1926; Terman, 1925; Terman & Oden, 1947, 1959) could be considered an identification study. This may be a simplification, but it is true, I believe, that the notion that identification is the assessment of giftedness as a concurrent or future criterion originated with Terman. The earliest studies of giftedness in this country (e.g., Yoder, 1894) were *retrospective* in nature, focusing on adults of indisputable brilliance and accomplishment and looking back on their lives for antecedent factors that might be implicated in their genius. Terman, with the recently developed technology of mental testing at his disposal, engaged in *prospective* inquiry, identifying high-IQ children and following them longitudinally to determine whether they fulfilled what he called "the promise of youth" (Burks et al., 1930).

Terman concluded, based on the life histories of his high-IQ subjects, that tests such as the Stanford-Binet Intelligence Scale were valid identifiers of giftedness, going so far as to assert that it was only from the ranks of those children who scored in the upper ranges of IQ tests that gifted adults would emerge. An ancillary finding, but one that is related to identification and that was for a number of years quite influential, was that teachers were not particularly adept when it came to the identification of gifted students.

Terman's conclusions are problematic, as is well-known. As a group, his subjects, the "Termites," did grow up to be significantly more successful than the general population in a number of ways. However, from more than 1,000 subjects, none achieved a level of achievement remotely approaching that of Yoder's subjects or, for that matter, of those portrayed in the second volume of *Genetic Studies of Genius* (Cox, 1926). Moreover, Terman's subjects came from families that were markedly higher in socioeconomic status (SES) than the average family of the time; their fathers tended to be highly educated, to hold professional positions, and to earn high incomes. This alone would predict the level of success enjoyed by Terman's high-IQ subjects and, thus, undermine the case for the predictive validity of the Stanford-Binet as a measure of giftedness.

With respect to Terman's conclusion that teacher identification of gifted children is ineffective, we return to the problem of the criterion. In screening children to sit for the Stanford-Binet (those with Stanford-Binet IQs of 140 or higher were deemed gifted for the purposes of his study), Terman asked teachers to refer for screening the brightest, the second-brightest, and the third-brightest child in the class, as well as the youngest child (who would have been the most likely to have skipped a grade). When all was said and done, Terman found more children who met his IQ criterion in the group referred for being the youngest in the class than he did in the group teachers identified as their brightest.

Subsequent studies confirmed Terman's conclusions (see Borland, 1978), but all suffered from the same limitation: they posited high IQ as the criterion for giftedness. That teachers are less-than-perfect predictors of scores on IQ tests proves that teacher identification of gifted students is not effective only if one accepts that giftedness only consists of a high IQ, a view to which, I believe, no one in the field now subscribes. A number of studies in more recent times (e.g., Argulewicz, Elliott, & Hall, 1982; Borland, 1978; Elliott, Argulewicz, & Turco, 1986; Hunsaker, Finley, & Frank, 1997; Robinson, Shore, & Enersen, 2007; Worrell & Schaefer, 2004) have shown that teachers are much more reliable sources of identification information than Terman believed.

I referred to Terman's work above as "foundational," and that is an accurate assessment. In a real sense, the idea of identification, of using assessment data as a predictor of a future criterion or as evidence of the existence of the construct of giftedness, began with him. However, the two findings related to the issue of identification that emerged from *Genetic Studies of Genius*—that childhood IQ predicts adult giftedness and that teachers are poor identifiers of gifted students—are, at a minimum, open to doubt and debate.

Pegnato and Birch

A classic study dealing with the identification of gifted students was conducted by Pegnato and Birch (1959) in the post-Sputnik era and was published in the same year as the final volume of *Genetic Studies of Genius* (Terman & Oden, 1959). In this study, the authors defined two concepts, *effectiveness* and *efficiency*, that are criteria for identification measures. Effectiveness refers to the absence of false negatives—the greater the number of "truly gifted" students in a population a measure identifies, the more effective it is. Efficiency refers to the absence of false positives—the fewer students who are mistakenly identified as gifted by a measure, the more efficient it is. Working in a junior high school, Pegnato and Birch attempted to assess the effectiveness and efficiency of various forms of identification: teacher referral, honor roll placement, achievement tests, group IQ tests, and so forth. They computed values for effectiveness and efficiency, using individual IQ test scores as the criterion for giftedness.

Again, the problem of the criterion is salient. The values Pegnato and Birch (1959) computed for the effectiveness and efficiency of various identifiers are valid only if the criterion is valid, that is, only if giftedness can be equated with a high individual IQ test score. In essence, Pegnato and Birch designated one measure as the criterion and used it as the basis for their judgments concerning the effectiveness and efficiency of the others. Their data reveal the extent to which other measures predict individual IQ, but their values for effectiveness and efficiency are problematic.

The concepts, however, are useful. One cannot actually measure effectiveness and efficiency, as Pegnato and Birch (1959) attempted to do. The formulas for effectiveness (number of "truly gifted" students identified as gifted divided by number of "truly gifted" students in the school) and for efficiency (number of "truly gifted" students identified divided by number of students, both those who are "truly gifted" and others, identified as gifted) cannot be calculated because the number and identities of the "truly gifted" students cannot be known; if they could, identification would not be an issue. One can, nevertheless, establish a policy that emphasizes one or the other and increase effectiveness by adopting a more inclusive identification process or increase efficiency by adopting a less inclusive identification process.

Getzels and Jackson and the Identification of the Creatively Gifted

A year earlier, Getzels and Jackson (1958) published one of the most influential papers in the history of the field of gifted education. Writing in the *Phi Delta Kappan*, they described research in "a Midwestern private school" (p. 76) in which they focused on two groups of students, those who were high (in the top 20% of the sample) in IQ but not high in creativity and those who were high in creativity but not in IQ.

Their most startling conclusion was that "despite a difference of twenty-three points between the *mean* I.Q.'s of the two groups, they were *equally superior* in school achievement to the student population as a whole" (Getzels & Jackson, 1958, p. 76, italics in the original). This finding, which was widely publicized, supported the assertion that there existed a previously overlooked population of gifted students, the creatively gifted, at a time when gifted students were in great demand as a national resource in the Cold War against the Soviet Union. The implication for identification, of course, was that creativity batteries like the one used by Getzels and Jackson, which essentially measured *divergent production* (the ability to produce information in quantity and variety), should be used to identify this newly discovered and neglected group of gifted students.

Four years later, the same authors published a book (Getzels & Jackson, 1962) that included data that space limitations in the *Phi Delta Kappan* obliged them to omit. These data revealed, among other things, that the "High Creativity-Low IQ" group had a mean IQ of 127, which placed them, as a group, at the 96.7th percentile of the general population. In reality, therefore, these students were, contrary to the label Getzels and Jackson affixed to them, high-IQ students—students who had the additional benefit of having scored high on a battery of divergent-production tests. There is little wonder that they were as advanced academically as the other group and, given their IQs, little chance that they would have been overlooked had traditional identification measures been used.

The Getzels and Jackson study, flawed as it was, exerted considerable influence in gifted education. The idea that the creatively gifted constituted a separate population of gifted students gained wide acceptance,[1] and identification procedures in many schools were modified to include creativity tests based on divergent production, with the Torrance Tests of Creative Thinking (e.g., Torrance, 1966) being the most popular.

Today, many definitions of giftedness (including the two most influential, the Marland definition, 1972, and Renzulli's three-ring definition, 1978, 2005) include creativity as a component of giftedness, and Getzels and Jackson's (1958) study is probably partially responsible for that. However, measuring creativity is recognized as more difficult than it was when Getzels and Jackson published their study. As Renzulli (2005) writes,

> It is important to consider the problems researchers have encountered in establishing relationships between creativity tests and other more substantial accomplishments. . . . the research evidence for the predictive validity of such tests has been limited. . . . although divergent thinking is indeed a characteristic of highly creative persons, caution should be exercised in the use and interpretation of tests designed to measure this capacity. (p. 266)

Identification of students who are creatively gifted is, therefore, more complicated than simply administering a divergent production test. Indeed, paper-and-pencil tests of creativity have not proven to be useful owing to concerns

---

1   This idea is not contradicted by the flaws in Getzels and Jackson's (1958) research; it simply is not established empirically by the study.

about their validity. An approach that does have some empirical support was developed by Amabile (1982, 1983, 1996) and is referred to as *consensual assessment*. This involves asking experts in a field to determine, using their experience and subjective judgment, the extent to which products exemplify their producers' creativity.

That Amabile's (1982, 1983, 1996) subjective approach has fared better empirically than any objective approach to assessing creativity should not be surprising in light of the fact that her subjective approach more closely mirrors how professional creativity is assessed in the real world. For example, actors in plays, musicians in orchestras, and Nobel laureates are chosen on the basis of performances judged subjectively by experts, not on the basis of test scores.

Moreover, this underscores the fact that the term *subjective*, in a psychometric context, is not pejorative. As I stated above, validity is the essential criterion for judging an identification instrument or process. *Objectivity*, of which some educators seem to make a fetish, is neither a desirable nor an undesirable trait of such instruments and processes.

A classic definition of an objective measure, taken from Wesman's chapter in Robert Thorndike's *Educational Measurement* (1971), specifies that an objective measure is simply "one that can be scored by mechanical devices or by clerks that have no special competence in the field" (p. 81; see also Nunnally, 1964, for a classic positivist definition of *objective*).

Wiersma and Jurs (1985) elaborate further on the concept of objective tests, writing:

> The term *objective test* is really a misnomer. . . . There is actually much subjectivity in every item format. . . . The only condition that sets so-called "objective" items apart is that the scoring of the items is done objectively, with a standard scoring key, which does not call for the scorer to make subjective inferences or judgments. (p. 123; see also Payne, 1992; Sax, 1989)

In short, an objective test is one that can be scored by anyone, regardless of his or her knowledge or understanding of the test items or content, because the answers have been determined and specified in advance. The result is that, through standardization of administration and especially scoring, an objective test is the "same test" wherever it is used, provided the directions for its administration are followed faithfully.

It should be clear that meeting the standards for objectivity is not the same as meeting the standards for validity, which is more important by far. The Torrance Tests of Creative Thinking (Torrance, 1966) is an objective measure, and there are serious doubts as to its validity. Amabile's consensual assessment approach relies on subjective judgment, and there are data strongly supporting its validity. Subjective measures loom large in the "authentic assessment" movement (e.g., Darling-Hammond, Ancess, & Falk, 1995; Montgomery,

2001; Tombari & Borich, 1999) and in nontraditional approaches to identifying gifted students, as I discuss below.

The Revolving Door Approach

In the early 1980s, Renzulli, Reis, and Smith (1981) published a description of their Revolving Door Identification Model (RDIM; see also Renzulli, 1990; Renzulli & Reis, 1986). This approach to identification articulates with Renzulli's (1978, 2005) Three-Ring Conception of Giftedness, and both the conception of giftedness and the identification model designed to operationalize it were, at the time of their introduction, close to being revolutionary.

Renzulli's (1978, 2005) Three-Ring Conception posits that giftedness is an interaction among three components: task commitment, creativity, and above-average (or well-above-average) ability. It is the last of these that posed the most profound challenge to traditional thinking. Whereas Terman's IQ-based conception of giftedness focused on IQ scores attained by only one individual in 250 and his contemporary, Leta Hollingworth (1942), studied children with IQs so high they were achieved by just one person in a million, Renzulli takes the term *above-average ability* quite literally for reasons he advances in several of his publications (e.g., 1978, 2005). He explains

> when I refer to "well above average ability," I clearly have in mind persons who are capable of performance or *possess the potential for performance* that is representative of the top 15 to 20 percent of any given area of human endeavor. (2005, p. 260)

That is one of the aspects of his conception that warrants the adjective *revolutionary*, in the context of gifted education at least.

The other aspect of his conception that challenged orthodox beliefs in the field is the idea that giftedness is a transitory thing—that students are not either always gifted or always not gifted. When students with above-average ability demonstrate creativity and task commitment in response to a particular topic, idea, or challenge, they are gifted. But, when creativity and task commitment, which are not stable traits, are absent, students with above-average ability are not gifted.

The RDIM is based squarely on this way of thinking about giftedness. Students from a talent pool consisting of individuals identified as being above average in ability "revolve into" the gifted program when they have an idea for a small-group or independent project (thus demonstrating creativity). They see the project through to completion (thus demonstrating task commitment) and then "revolve out" of the program, making room for other students from the talent pool. This contrasts with the traditional approach, in which a certain, unchanging group of students is identified as gifted at one point in time and remains in the program for a full year or over a period of years.

Research on the RDIM (e.g., Reis & Renzulli, 1982; Renzulli & Reis, 1994) supports the most controversial aspect of the Three-Ring definition, above-average ability, and this lends support to the RDIM. For example, Reis and Renzulli compared two groups of students in 11 school districts. The first group consisted of students scoring in the top 5% on standardized intelligence and achievement tests. The second group consisted of students whose scores were 10 to 15 percentile points lower than the cut-off for the first group. Ratings of projects (the curricular goal of the comprehensive Renzulli model) indicated no significant differences between the two groups, nor did rating forms from different stake-holders. Other research on this model is summarized in Renzulli and Reis (1994) and on their Web site (http://www.gifted.uconn.edu).

The criterion problem is not absent from discussions of the RDIM and its related program components. The Three-Ring Conception and the identification model tied to it are valid within the context of the overall model, which posits a specific definition of giftedness and specific academic outcomes, neither of which are beyond debate. However, the internal consistency of the model of which the RDIM is a part is noteworthy, and there is evidence that, within the conceptual and practice-related constraints of the model, the identification process is valid.

WHAT CAN WE CONCLUDE FROM SEMINAL STUDIES OF IDENTIFICATION?

The foregoing review of seminal identification research in gifted education illustrates the difficulties caused by the problem of the criterion. Each of the studies is predicated on a particular definition of giftedness, and the results of each study have value only to the extent that one finds the underlying definition persuasive. For example, one can agree with Terman's findings that childhood IQ predicts adult success and that teachers cannot identify gifted students in their classrooms if one agrees that a high Stanford-Binet IQ is a valid operational definition of giftedness. Similarly, one can find Pegnato and Birch's measures of effectiveness and efficiency persuasive if, once again, individual IQ-test scores are one's criterion for giftedness. Getzels and Jackson's "discovery" of a "new" population of gifted students is eye-opening if one finds credible their characterization of a group of students whose mean IQ was nearly two standard deviations above the population mean and who scored well on a battery of tests of divergent thinking as "Low IQ–High Creativity." And, Renzulli's identification research is revelatory to the extent that one shares his belief in the validity of the three-ring conception of giftedness and that productivity in the form of small-group and independent projects is criterial for giftedness.

In short, the bulk of the research on the identification of gifted students is, probably of necessity, tautological. In logic, a tautology is a statement that is true by its own definition. For example, the statement, "If today is Wednesday and I am a male, then I am a male" is necessarily true by virtue of information posited in the sentence. One could argue that much of Terman's work is predicated on the tautology, "If giftedness consists of scoring at or above 140 on the Stanford-Binet Intelligence Scale, then scoring at or above 140 on the Stanford-Binet Intelligence Scale identifies one as gifted." In general terms, the argument supporting our research on identification seems to be, "If giftedness consists of A, B, and C, then measures of A, B, and C are valid for the identification of gifted students."

However, there is one area in which research on the identification of gifted students has moved beyond tautology to reveal issues that require our attention. This body of research concerns the chronic underrepresentation of certain segments of our society in programs for gifted students.

CURRENT RESEARCH ON IDENTIFICATION—THE PROBLEM OF EQUITY

One of the most persistent, and telling, criticisms of gifted education is directed at the chronic underrepresentation of lower SES children and children of color in gifted programs (see, for example, Borland, 2003; Borland & Wright, 1995; Ford, 1996; Ford & Harris, 1999; Frasier, 1991; Passow, 1989; Richert, 1982; Sapon-Shevin, 1994; VanTassel-Baska, Patton, & Prillaman, 1989). As Passow and Frasier (1996) wrote more than a decade ago, "the under-inclusion of economically disadvantaged and children of minority cultures in programs for the gifted has been so well documented over the years that it hardly needs further recounting here" (p. 198).

Data from the U.S. Department of Education's National Educational Longitudinal Study (1988) provide one of the clearest supports for this assertion. Focusing on eighth-grade programs for gifted students, the authors of the study report that as a student's family's socioeconomic status increases, so, too, does his or her probability of being identified as gifted. The disparities among the four SES quartiles were striking: 47.5% of eighth-grade students from the top quartile in the population with respect to SES were identified as gifted, whereas only 9.3% of students from the bottom SES quartile were identified as gifted.

In a recent monograph (Borland, 2004), I distinguished between societal factors that contribute to this problem, such as racism and the inequitable allocation of resources, over which we in the field have little immediate control, and factors endogenous to gifted education, over which we can exercise some control. Probably most critical among the endogenous factors are the various ways in which we identify students for admission to gifted programs. By modifying our practice in this area, I believe, we can make a difference with respect to the racial and socioeconomic composition of classes in gifted programs. Studies from a number of programs, many supported by the U.S. Department of Education through provisions of the Jacob Javits Gifted and Talented Students Act, support this belief (see, for example, a special issue of *Gifted Child Quarterly*, 1994, that was devoted to Javits Grant Projects). I will briefly discuss some of the alternative approaches to identification employed in these projects and advocated in the recent literature of the field of gifted education.

Multidimensional Assessment

There has been advocacy of multicriterial approaches to the identification of gifted children for some time (e.g., Baldwin, 1978). However, this has not been the norm in gifted education in the schools. Recent attention to inequities in the field has revivified efforts to include not just multiple indicators of giftedness, but indicators more sensitive to the diversity of today's student population. In addition, instead of simply adding together the scores for various indicators, computing a "giftedness index," and identifying students who exceed a cut-off score, a more clinical approach that involves examining each indicator separately and employing such concepts as best performance (Roedell, Jackson, & Robinson, 1980) has become more prominent.

Research on this approach is promising (e.g., Borland, 1994; Borland, Schnur, & Wright, 2000; Borland & Wright, 1995, 2001; Clasen, Middleton, & Connell, 1994; Feiring, Barbara, Ukeje, Lewis, & Leong, 1997; Hardaway & Marek-Schroer, 1992; O'Tuel, 1994). In our work in Project Synergy (e.g., Borland, 1994; Borland et al., 2000; Borland & Wright, 1995), we used such an approach to identify potentially gifted kindergarten students in severely underresourced schools in Central Harlem in New York City. We followed the first cohort of students quite closely and found that, of approximately 100 kindergartners in one of the lowest-ranked New York City elementary schools according to standardized reading assessments, 5 were placed in a school for academically gifted students a year and a half after identification and that their placements were successful according to every indicator (Borland et al. 2000; Borland & Wright, 1995).

Portfolio Assessment

A related approach involves using portfolios—collections of student work—as part or the totality of the identification process (see, e.g., Coleman, 1994; Feiring et al., 1997; Hardaway & Marek-Schroer, 1992; Johnsen & Ryser, 1997; Shaklee & Viechnicki, 1995; Wright & Borland, 1993). Each of the works cited reports successful outcomes, suggesting the validity, as well as the effectiveness, of this approach.

Dynamic Assessment

Dynamic assessment is based on Vygotsky's (1978) notion of the *zone of proximal development* (ZPD), the gap between what a child can do on his or her own and what that child can do with the assistance, or scaffolding, of another person, usually an adult. Dynamic assessment represents an attempt to assess the ZPD by testing, teaching, and retesting. Using dynamic assessment in the identification of gifted students, especially students from traditionally underrepresented groups, has been shown in a number of studies (e.g., Bolig & Day, 1993; Borland & Wright, 1995; Kanevsky, 1990; Kaniel & Reichenberg, 1990; Kirschenbaum, 1998; Lidz & Macrine, 2001; Sternberg & Grigorenko, 2002) to be a promising approach.

Performance- or Curriculum-Based Assessment and Observation

Yogi Berra is reported as having said, "You can observe a lot by just watching"—a statement whose essential truth cannot be gainsaid. Observation has long played a role in early childhood education (see, for example, Boehm & Weinberg, 1997; Chittenden, 1991), and its use in identifying gifted students has been advocated by a number of authors (e.g., Baum, Owen, & Oreck, 1996; Borland & Wright, 1995; VanTassel-Baska, Johnson, & Avery, 2002). Observation plays a central role in *performance-based* or *curricular-based assessment*, a process whereby students are observed responding to problem-solving tasks or curricular tasks, especially those that could be considered enrichment. The data from Project Synergy (Borland et al., 2000; Borland & Wright, 1995) support the validity of this approach, as do the data from DISCOVER (Maker, Nielson, & Rogers, 1994; Sarouphim, 1999a, 1999b, 2001, 2002) and the research by Baer (1994).

Newer and Less Traditional Psychometric Instruments

Some more recently developed standardized tests (and some that are not so new but have been used less frequently than they might be) have been studied as being possibly better able to identify a more diverse population of gifted students. One that is frequently mentioned is the Naglieri Nonverbal Ability Test (NNAT; Naglieri, 1996, 1997), which, owing to its nonverbal nature, is thought by some to be more sensitive to gifted students from minority backgrounds. In their study, Naglieri and Ford (2003) found that this test identified similar percentages of White, African American, and Latino students as gifted. Similar promising results were found by Naglieri, Booth, and Winsler (2004) and Shaunessy, Karnes, and Cobb (2004). However, critiques by Lohman (2003, 2005) challenge the research by Naglieri and Ford, leaving the question of the effectiveness of the NNAT as a valid identifier that is sensitive to the abilities of minority and English-language-learning students unresolved.[2]

Raven's Progressive Matrices (RPM; Raven & Court, 1989) is a nonverbal measure of g_f, or fluid general intelligence, the sort of general ability that those who subscribe to g-based theories of intelligence believe is innate and unaffected by acculturation, education, and other kinds of experience. Because the test is nonverbal in nature, a number of writers (e.g., Baldwin, 1987; Baska, 1986; DiJosia, 1994; MacAvoy, Orr, & Sidles, 1993; Masten, 1985; Matthews, 1988; Mills & Tissot, 1995; Pearce, 1983; Richert, 1987; Sarouphim, 2001) have advocated its use in identifying traditionally underrepresented populations of gifted students. Five of these articles (Baska, 1986; MacAvoy et al., 1993; Mills & Tissot, 1995; Pearce, 1983; Sarouphim, 2001) report empirical studies that support the use of the RPM for this purpose.

However, as Mills and Tissot (1995) point out, although the RPM does identify more children from underrepresented groups, its low correlations with traditional measures of academic aptitude and achievement could render its use problematic in programs for the academically gifted (the problem of the criterion again). Along with Matthews (1988) and Richert (1987), Mills and Tissot recommend that it be used for preliminary screening of students, not for actual placement of students in a gifted program.

The Screening Assessment for Gifted Elementary and Middle School Students, Second Edition (SAGES-2, Johnsen & Corn, 2001) is a group-administered test with subtests for Mathematics-Science, Language Arts-Social Studies, and Reasoning. According to its authors, it can be used (a) to identify gifted students in the intellectual and academic ability areas assessed, (b) to screen large groups of students relative to their possible gifted status, (c) to identify evaluated students' strengths and weaknesses in the areas assessed, and (d) to provide a psychometrically sound tool for research.

The potential utility of a test with an adequate ceiling (ceiling effects[3] being a perennial problem in the identification of gifted students) is undeniable. Moreover, in revising their test, Johnsen and Corn (2001) addressed concerns raised by reviewers of the first edition. However, reviews in the *Mental Measurements Yearbook* by Callahan (n.d.) and Knoff (n.d.) suggest that there are still kinks to be worked out.

---

2   It may be the case that nonverbal tests of aptitude will not be as much help in this respect as has been hoped. As Anastasi and Urbina (1997) write, "a growing body of evidence suggests that nonlanguage tests may be more culturally loaded than language tests. Investigations with a wide body of cultural groups in many countries found larger group differences in performance and other nonverbal tests than in verbal tests" (p. 344). If this is the case, the well-intentioned effort to reduce intergroup test-score differences through the use of nonverbal tests may exacerbate rather than ameliorate the problem.

3   Ceiling effects are encountered when a test is too easy and lacks sufficient difficult items to allow one to distinguish between more and less advanced students. For example, a ceiling effect would be encountered if one attempted to identify mathematically precocious middle school students using a test consisting of simple addition problems. All middle school students, those who are mathematically precocious and those who are not, would achieve high scores—would "hit the ceiling"—on this test, thus obscuring differences in mathematical ability that exist in this population.

As Knoff writes,

> to endorse the SAGES-2 as a psychometrically sound tool for research (much less for "practice") cannot be done at this time, especially given the breadth and depth of the research cited in the manual and the absence of any construct validity (i.e., factor analytic) data and research. In the end, the SAGES-2 is much improved but not yet ready to stand on its own.

WHAT ARE THE PRACTICAL IMPLICATIONS OF THE RESEARCH ON THIS TOPIC?

In attempting to answer the question above, it is important to keep in mind the importance of the criterion issue, that is, the question of what conception of giftedness provides the basis for the program for which students are being identified. If the definition stresses traditional forms of academic achievement and excellence, report cards and standardized achievement test results have considerable validity. However, our experience has shown that this approach leads to the underrepresentation of lower SES children and children of color in gifted programs. The question of how best to identify gifted students depends on how one defines *best* (most effectively? most efficiently? most equitably?) and, of course, *gifted students*.

Drawing conclusions about identification instruments and practices in a context-free manner tells us little and can only end up being an exercise in futility. However, pursuing this matter in the context of a conception of giftedness, a specific gifted program, or specific goal can be informative. For example, there are data supporting the validity of RDIM in programs that are based on Renzulli's three-ring conception of giftedness. There also is empirical support for Amabile's notion of consensual assessment in assessing creativity in context. In addition, there is a growing body of evidence suggesting that various nontraditional approaches to identification not only can lead to more equitable identification but also to effective identification, as well.

Identification of gifted students will never be a topic lacking in serious controversy or disputation. Given the criterion problem, the tautological nature of much of the research, and the need to approach identification issues in context, generalization from the existing body of empirical research is extremely difficult. So, what do we know that can assist practitioners in the challenging task of identifying gifted students? I offer the following suggestions somewhat tentatively:

1. Identification must be logically tied to an explicit definition of giftedness. For example, the RDIM is a logical approach to identification in a gifted program based on Renzulli's Three-Ring Conception. Simply using IQ and achievement data is not.

2. For this reason, generalizations about the validity of specific identification instruments and processes are difficult, perhaps impossible.
3. Effectiveness and efficiency cannot be measured directly, but they can be affected by a school's policy concerning identification.
4. Subjective measures should not be eschewed in the identification of gifted students. Indeed, sometimes, as in the assessment of creativity, they are the most valid measures available.
5. Traditional approaches to identification, not supplemented by more innovative, nontraditional approaches, will invariably produce a traditionally inequitable population of identified gifted students.

REFERENCES

Amabile, T. M. (1982). Social psychology of creativity: A consensual assessment technique. *Journal of Personality and Social Psychology, 43,* 997–1013.

Amabile, T. M. (1983). *The social psychology of creativity.* New York: Springer-Verlag.

Amabile, T. M. (1996). *Creativity in context.* Boulder, CO: Westview Press.

Anastasi, A., & Urbina, S. (1997). *Psychological testing.* Upper Saddle River, NJ: Prentice Hall.

Argulewicz, E. N., Elliott, S. N., & Hall, R. (1982). Comparison of behavioral ratings of Anglo-American and Mexican-American gifted children. *Psychology in the Schools, 19,* 469–472.

Baer, J. (1994). Performance assessments of creativity: Do they have long-term stability? *Roeper Review, 17,* 7–11.

Baldwin, A. Y. (1978). The Baldwin identification matrix. In A. Baldwin, G. Gear, & L. Lucito (Eds.), *Educational planning for the gifted: Overcoming cultural, geographic, and socioeconomic barriers* (pp. 33–36). Reston, VA: Council for Exceptional Children.

Baldwin, A. Y. (1987). Undiscovered diamonds: The minority gifted child. *Journal for the Education of the Gifted, 10,* 271–285.

Baska, L. (1986). Alternatives to traditional testing: The use of the Raven's Advanced Progressive Matrices for the selection of magnet junior high school students. *Roeper Review, 8,* 181–184.

Baum, S. M., Owen, S. V., & Oreck, B. A. (1996). Talent beyond words: Identification of potential talent in dance and music in elementary students. *Gifted Child Quarterly, 40,* 93–101.

Boehm, A. E., & Weinberg, R. A. (1997). *The classroom observer: Developing observation skills in early childhood settings.* New York: Teachers College Press.

Bolig, E. E., & Day, J. D. (1993). Dynamic assessment and giftedness: The promise of assessing training responsiveness. *Roeper Review, 16,* 110–113.

Borland, J. H. (1978). Teacher identification of the gifted: A new look. *Journal for the Education of the Gifted, 2,* 13–22.

Borland, J. H. (1994). Identifying and educating young economically disadvantaged urban children: The lessons of Project Synergy. In N. Colangelo, S. G. Assouline, & D. L. Ambroson (Eds.), *Talent development: Proceedings of the second biennial Wallace Conference on Talent Development* (pp. 151–172). Dayton: Ohio Psychology Press.

Borland, J. H. (2003). The death of giftedness. In J. H. Borland (Ed.), *Rethinking gifted education* (pp. 105–124). New York: Teachers College Press.

Borland, J. H. (2004). *Issues and practices in the identification and education of gifted students from under-represented groups.* Storrs: National Research Center on the Gifted and Talented, University of Connecticut.

Borland, J. H., Schnur, R., & Wright, L. (2000). Economically disadvantaged students in a school for the academically gifted: A postpositivist inquiry into individual and family adjustment. *Gifted Child Quarterly, 44,* 13–32.

Borland, J. H., & Wright, L. (1995). Identifying young potentially gifted economically disadvantaged students. *Gifted Child Quarterly, 38,* 164–171.

Borland, J. H., & Wright, L. (2001). Identifying and educating poor and under-represented gifted students. In K. A. Heller, F. J. Mönks, R. J. Sternberg, & R. F. Subotnik (Eds.), *International handbook of research and development of giftedness and talent* (pp. 587–594). London: Pergamon Press.

Burks, B. S., Jensen, D. W., & Terman, L. M. (1930). *The promise of youth: Follow-up studies of a thousand gifted children: Genetic studies of genius, Vol. 3.* Stanford, CA: Stanford University Press.

Callahan, C. M. (n.d.) Review of SAGES-2 [online]. *Mental Measurements Yearbook.* Accessed May 19, 2006, from http://web5s.silverplatter.com/webspirs/start.ws?customer=waldo&databases=YB

Chittenden, E. (1991). Authentic assessment, evaluation, and documentation of student performance. In V. Perrone (Ed.), *Expanding student assessment* (pp. 22–31). Alexandria, VA: Association for Supervision and Curriculum Development.

Clark, B. (2002). *Growing up gifted: Developing the potential of children at home and at school* (6th ed.). Englewood Cliffs, NJ: Prentice Hall.

Clasen, D. R., Middleton, J. A., & Connell, T. J. (1994). Assessing artistic and problem-solving performance in minority and nonminority students using a nontraditional multidimensional approach. *Gifted Child Quarterly, 38,* 27–31.

Coleman, L. J. (1994). Portfolio assessment: A key to identifying hidden talents and empowering teachers of young children. *Gifted Child Quarterly, 38,* 65–69.

Cox, C. M. (1926) *The early mental traits of three hundred geniuses: Genetic studies of genius, Vol. 2.* Stanford, CA: Stanford University Press

Cronbach, L. J. (1971). Test validation. In R. L. Thorndike (Ed.), *Educational measurement* (2nd ed., pp. 443–507). Washington, DC: American Council on Education.

Darling-Hammond, L., Ancess, J., & Falk, B. (1995). *Authentic assessment in action: Studies of schools and students at work.* New York: Teachers College Press.

Davis, G. A., & Rimm, S. B. (2003). *Education of the gifted and talented* (5th ed.). Newton, MA: Allyn & Bacon.

DiJosia, M. (1994). The Raven Progressive Matrices: A key to successful GATE identification. *Communicator: Journal of the California Association for the Gifted, 24*(3), 12–18.

Elliot, S. N., Argulewicz, E. N., & Turco, T. L. (1986). Predictive validity of the Scales for Rating the Behavioral Characteristics of Superior Students for gifted children from three sociocultural groups. *Journal of Experimental Education, 55,* 27–32.

Feiring, C., Barbara, L., Ukeje, I., Lewis, M., & Leong, P. (1997). Early identification of gifted minority kindergarten students in Newark. *Gifted Child Quarterly, 41,* 76–82.

Ford, D. Y. (1996). *Reversing underachievement among gifted Black students.* New York: Teachers College Press.

Ford, D. Y., & Harris J. J., III. (1999). *Multicultural gifted education.* New York: Teachers College Press.

Frasier, M. M. (1991). Disadvantaged and culturally diverse gifted students. *Journal for the Education of the Gifted, 14,* 234–245.

Gallagher, J. J., & Gallagher, S. A. (1994). *Teaching the gifted child* (4th ed.). Newton, MA: Allyn & Bacon.

Getzels, J. W., & Jackson, P. W. (1958). The meaning of "giftedness"—An examination of an expending concept. *Phi Delta Kappan, 40,* 75–77.

Getzels, J. W., & Jackson, P. W. (1962). *Creativity and intelligence.* New York: John Wiley.

Hardaway, N., & Marek-Schroer, M. F. (1992). Multidimensional assessment of the gifted minority student. *Roeper Review, 15,* 73–77.

Hollingworth, L. S. (1942). *Children above 180 IQ: Stanford-Binet.* New York: World Book Company.

Howley, A., Howley, C. B., & Pendarvis, E. D. (1986). *Teaching gifted children: Principles and strategies.* Boston: Little, Brown and Company.

Hunsaker, S. L., Finley, V. S., & Frank, E. L. (1997). An analysis of teacher nominations and student performance in gifted programs. *Gifted Child Quarterly, 41,* 19–24.

Javits grant projects. (1994). [Special issue]. *Gifted Child Quarterly, 38*(3).

Johnsen, S. K., & Corn, A. L. (2001). *Screening Assessment for Gifted Elementary and Middle School Students.* Austin, TX: Pro-Ed.

Johnsen, S. K., & Ryser, G. R. (1997). The validity of portfolios in predicting performance in a gifted program. *Journal for the Education of the Gifted, 20,* 253–267.

Kanevsky, L. (1990) Pursuing qualitative differences in the flexible use of problem-solving strategy by young children. *Journal for the Education of the Gifted, 13,* 115–140.

Kaniel, S., & Reichenberg, R. (1990). Dynamic assessment and cognitive program for disadvantaged gifted children. *Gifted Education International, 7,* 9–15.

Kirschenbaum, R. J. (1998). Dynamic assessment and its use with underserved gifted and talented populations. *Gifted Child Quarterly, 42,* 140–147.

Knoff, H. M. (n.d.) Review of SAGES-2 [online]. *Mental Measurements Yearbook.* Accessed May 19, 2006, from http://web5s.silverplatter.com/webspirs/start. ws?customer=waldo&databases=YB

Lidz, C. S., & Macrine, S. L. (2001). An alternative approach to the identification of gifted culturally and linguistically diverse learners: The contribution of dynamic assessment. *School Psychology International, 22,* 74–96.

Lohman, D. F. (2003). *A comparison of the Naglieri Nonverbal Ability Test (NNAT) and Form 6 of the Cognitive Abilities Test (CogAT): Revised 9/1/2003.* Accessed May 19, 2006, from http://faculty.education.uiowa.edu/dlohman/pdf/NNAT_vs_ CogAT6_revised2.pdf

Lohman, D. F. (2005). Review of Naglieri and Ford (2003): Does the Naglieri Nonverbal Ability Test identify equal proportions of high-scoring White, Black and Hispanic students? *Gifted Child Quarterly, 49,* 19–28.

MacAvoy, J., Orr, S., & Sidles, C. (1993). The Raven's Progressive Matrices and Navajo children: Normative characteristics and culture fair application to issues of intelligence, giftedness, and academic proficiency. *Journal of American Indian Education, 33,* 32–43.

Maker, C. J., Nielson, A. B., & Rogers, J. A. (1994). Giftedness, diversity, and problem solving: Multiple intelligences and diversity in educational settings. *Exceptional Children, 27,* 4–19.

Marland, S. P., Jr. (1972). *Education of the gifted and talented: Report to the Congress of the United States by the U.S. Commissioner of Education and background papers submitted to the U.S. Office of Education,* 2 vols. Washington, DC: U.S. Government Printing Office. (Government Documents, Y4.L 11/2: G36)

Masten, W. G. (1985). Identification of gifted minority students: Past research, future directions. *Roeper Review, 10,* 83–85.

Matthews, D. J. (1988). Raven's Matrices in the identification of giftedness. *Roeper Review, 10,* 159–162.

Mills, C. J., & Tissot, S. L. (1995). Identifying academic potential in students from under-represented populations: Is using the Raven's Progressive Matrices a good idea? *Gifted Child Quarterly, 39,* 209–217.

Montgomery, K. (2001). *Authentic assessment: A guide for elementary teachers.* New York: Longman.

Naglieri, J. A. (1996). *Naglieri Nonverbal Ability Test.* San Antonio, TX: The Psychological Corporation.

Naglieri, J. A. (1997). *Naglieri Nonverbal Ability Test: Multilevel technical manual.* San Antonio, TX: Harcourt Educational Measurement.

Naglieri, J. A., Booth, A. L., & Winsler, A. (2004). Comparison of Hispanic children with and without limited English proficiency on the Naglieri nonverbal ability test. *Psychological Assessment, 16,* 81.

Naglieri, J. A., & Ford, D. Y. (2003). Addressing underrepresentation of gifted minority children using the Naglieri Nonverbal Ability Test (NNAT). *Gifted Child Quarterly, 47,* 155–161.

Nunnally, J. Q. (1964). *Educational measurement and evaluation.* New York: McGraw-Hill.

O'Tuel, F. S. (1994). APOGEE: Equity in the identification of gifted and talented students. *Gifted Child Quarterly, 38,* 75–79.

Passow, A. H. (1989). Needed research and development in educating high ability children. *Roeper Review, 11,* 223–229.

Passow, A. H., & Frasier, M. M. (1996). Toward improving identification of talent potential among minority and disadvantaged students. *Roeper Review, 18,* 198–202.

Payne, D. A. (1992). *Measuring and evaluating educational outcomes.* New York: Merrill.

Pearce, N. (1983). A comparison of the WISC-R, Raven's Standard Progressive Matrices, and Meeker's SOI-Screening Form for Gifted. *Gifted Child Quarterly, 27,* 13–19.

Pegnato, C. W., & Birch J. W. (1959). Locating gifted children in junior high schools—A comparison of methods. *Exceptional Children, 25,* 300–304.

Raven, J., & Court, J. H. (1989). *Manual for Raven's Progressive Matrices and Vocabulary Scales, Research supplement No. 4: Additional national and American norms and summaries of normative, reliability, and validity studies.* London: H. K. Lewis.

Reis, S. M., & Renzulli, J. S. (1982). A research report on the revolving door identification model: A case for the broadened conception of giftedness. *Phi Delta Kappan, 63,* 619–620.

Renzulli, J. S. (1978). What makes giftedness? *Phi Delta Kappan, 60,* 180–184, 261.

Renzulli, J. S. (1990). A practical system for identifying gifted and talented students. *Early Childhood Development, 63,* 9–18.

Renzulli, J. S. (2005). The three-ring conception of giftedness: A developmental model for promoting creative productivity. In R. J. Sternberg & J. E. Davidson (Eds.), *Conceptions of giftedness* (2nd ed., pp. 246–279). New York: Cambridge University Press.

Renzulli, J. S., & Reis, S. M. (1986). The enrichment triad/revolving door model: A schoolwide plan for the development of creative productivity. In J. S. Renzulli (Ed.), *Systems and models for developing programs for the gifted and talented* (pp. 216–266). Mansfield Center, CT: Creative Learning Press.

Renzulli, J. S., & Reis, S. M. (1994). Research related to the schoolwide enrichment triad model. *Gifted Child Quarterly, 38,* 7–20.

Renzulli, J. S., Reis, S. M., & Smith L. H. (1981). *The revolving door identification model.* Mansfield Center, CT: Creative Learning Press.

Richert, E. S. (1982). *The national report of identification: Assessment and recommendations for comprehensive identification of gifted and talented youth.* Sewell, NJ: Educational Improvement Center South.

Richert, E. S. (1987). Rampant problems and promising practices in the identification of disadvantaged gifted students. *Gifted Child Quarterly, 31,* 149–154.

Robinson, A., Shore, B. M., & Enersen, D. L. (2007). *Best practices in gifted education: An evidence-based guide.* Waco, TX: Prufrock Press.

Roedell, W. C., Jackson, N. E., & Robinson, H. B. (1980). *Gifted young children: Perspectives on gifted and talented education.* New York: Teachers College Press.

Sapon-Shevin, M. (1994). *Playing favorites: Gifted education and the disruption of community.* Albany, NY: State University of New York Press.

Sarouphim, K. M. (1999a). Discovering multiple intelligences through a performance based assessment: Consistency with independent ratings. *Exceptional Children, 65,* 151–161.

Sarouphim, K. M. (1999b). DISCOVER: A promising alternative assessment for the identification of gifted minorities. *Gifted Child Quarterly, 43,* 244–251.

Sarouphim, K. M. (2001). DISCOVER: Concurrent validity, gender differences, and identification of minority students. *Gifted Child Quarterly, 45,* 130–138.

Sarouphim, K. M. (2002). DISCOVER in high school: Identifying gifted Hispanic and Native American students. *Journal of Secondary Gifted Education, 14,* 30–38.

Sax, G. (1989). *Principles of educational and psychological measurement and evaluation.* Belmont, CA: Wadsworth Publishing Company.

Shaklee, B. D., & Viechnicki, K. J. (1995). A qualitative approach to portfolios: The early assessment for exceptional potential model. *Journal for the Education of the Gifted, 18,* 156–170.

Shaunessy, E., Karnes, F. A., & Cobb, Y. (2004). Assessing potentially gifted students from lower socioeconomic status with nonverbal measures of intelligence. *Perceptual and Motor Skills, 98,* 11–29.

Sternberg, R. J., & Grigorenko, E. L. (2002). *Dynamic testing.* New York: Cambridge University Press.

Tannenbaum, A. J. (1983). *Gifted children: Psychological and educational perspectives.* New York: Macmillan.

Terman, L. M. (1925). *Mental and physical traits of a thousand gifted children: Genetic studies of genius, Vol. 1.* Stanford, CA: Stanford University Press.

Terman, L. M., & Oden, M. H. (1947). *The gifted child grows up: Genetic studies of genius, Vol. 4*. Stanford, CA: Stanford University Press.

Terman, L. W., & Oden, M. H. (1959). *The gifted group at mid-life: Thirty-five years' follow-up of the superior child: Genetic studies of genius, Vol. 5*. Stanford, CA: Stanford University Press.

Tombari, M. L., & Borich, G. D. (1999). *Authentic assessment in the classroom: Applications and practice*. Upper Saddle River, NJ: Merrill.

Torrance, E. P. (1966). *Torrance Tests of Creative Thinking: Technical-norms manual*. Princeton, NJ: Personnel Press.

U.S. Department of Education. (1988). *National educational longitudinal study*. Washington, DC: National Center for Educational Statistics.

VanTassel-Baska, J., Johnson, D., & Avery, L. D. (2002). Using performance tasks in the identification of economically disadvantaged and minority gifted learners: Findings from Project STAR. *Gifted Child Quarterly, 46*, 110–123.

VanTassel-Baska, J., Patton, J., & Prillaman, D. (1989). Disadvantaged gifted learners: At risk for educational attention. *Focus on Exceptional Children, 22*(3), 1–15.

Vygotsky, L. (1978). *Mind in society*. Cambridge, MA: Harvard University Press.

Wesman, A. G. (1971). Writing the test item. In R. L. Thorndike (Ed.), *Educational measurement* (pp. 81–129). Washington, DC: American Council on Education.

Wiersma, W., & Jurs, S. G. (1985). *Educational measurement and testing*. Boston: Allyn & Bacon

Worrell, F. C., & Schaefer, B. A. (2004). Reliability and validity of Learning Behaviors Scale (LBS) scores with academically talented students: A comparative perspective. *Gifted Child Quarterly, 48*, 287–308.

Wright, L., & Borland, J. H. (1993). Using early childhood developmental portfolios in the identification and education of young economically disadvantaged potentially gifted students. *Roeper Review, 15*, 205–210.

Yoder, A. H. (1894). The story of the boyhood of great men. *Pedagogical Seminary, 3*, 134–156.

AUTHOR NOTE

I would like to thank Kathleen Kelly, a recent doctoral graduate of the gifted education program at Teachers College, whose dissertation proposal, especially the review of the literature, provided a useful and scholarly resource in the writing of this chapter.

Chapter 20

IDENTIFICATION: THE AURORA BATTERY

Hilary Chart, Elena L. Grigorenko, and Robert J. Sternberg

But since I knew you trusted and believed,
I could not disappoint you and so prevailed.
—from *Encouraged*, Paul Laurence Dunbar
(1872–1906)

ost starkly underrepresented in gifted programming are minority students, students with both gifts and disabilities, and students of low socioeconomic status (SES). Similarly overlooked are those with gifts to create something new and original and to develop applications for existing knowledge. Although such contributions are honored in many theoretical definitions of giftedness, they are typically unexplored by the practical identification methods prevalent in schools. For the needs of such students to be met and their potential realized, educational systems must learn to embrace the comprehensive view of giftedness so often affirmed but so rarely applied. Educational programming can only serve these students if they are identified and can only cater to their particular strengths if these strengths are specified. Schools, then, must look further than the current "gifted" population and closer than do the current instruments in the identification process. This is precisely what our new identification battery of gifted and talented students, the Aurora Battery, is intended to make possible.

Developed from Sternberg's theory of successful intelligence (Sternberg, 1997, 1999), this group-administered assessment battery is designed to recognize abilities in analytical, creative, and practical domains using figures, words, and numbers. The augmented view of intelligence adopted by the assessment, in combination with the specificity of its tasks, is expected to capture a more diverse population of students with a more varied and better-qualified array of skills. We present here the impetus for creating this assessment: historical shifts in definitions of giftedness, the increasingly recognized ethical imperative to correct underrepresentation of certain groups, the shortcomings of current assessments, and the promise of future reward that greater investment in gifted children represents. We also discuss the assessment's theoretical grounding, development, and potential applications. The Aurora Battery may offer a new and better assessment alternative for schools interested in better recognizing all gifts and better meeting the needs of all gifted students.

HISTORICAL TRENDS: GREATER UNDERSTANDING, SHIFTING VALUES

In attempts to discover the roots of giftedness, definitions are created. In attempts to identify gifted individuals, identification procedures are established. And, in attempts to find ways to best nurture giftedness, curricula are developed. Even as such creations are intended to reflect (or at least propose) discovered truths about giftedness, they ultimately are choices dependent on context. Definitions of giftedness vary from place to place, as do the individuals identified as gifted and the ways of fostering the fulfillment of their potential. It is important to recognize that, in this way, giftedness is largely a social construct (see Borland, 2005; Freeman, 2005, Plucker & Barab, 2005; Sternberg & Grigorenko, 2002). The ways in which giftedness is defined reflect societal values as much as they do any understanding of psychology. This is not to say that any society is ever satisfied with its creations. Definitions, identification methods, or educational programming for the gifted may seem insufficient, as may the coordinated connection of all three. To understand the shortcomings of current approaches to giftedness as they are represented in the United States, many of which are the impetus for the creation of the Aurora Battery, we first briefly review the history of giftedness and the story it provides of the changing values of society.

Lewis Terman, in the 1920s, first devoted considerable effort to the study of giftedness (Hothersall, 1984). A contemporary of Spearman, who coined the term *g-factor* for the general intelligence factor (Spearman, 1927), Terman recognized giftedness simply as high general intelligence (Terman, 1925). This rather blunt and perhaps simplistic view is still the most commonly applied, if rarely exclusively supported, notion of giftedness. Actual definitions have changed considerably. The 1960s saw Drews' identification of four categories of gifted individuals (high achievers, social leaders, creative intellectuals, and rebels; Trentham & Hall, 1987) and Guilford's Structure of Intellect (SOI) model (1967) supporting multidimensionality and thereby greatly broadening the concept of giftedness (Torrance, 1970).

By the 1970s, an expanded definition was becoming widely accepted. Torrance (1970) emphasized the importance of identifying creative individuals, and the emerging trend toward the recognition of increasingly diverse abilities was reflected in the national report generated by then-U.S. Commissioner of Education Marland (1972). Marland's insistence on the consideration of *potential* for achievement as part of giftedness was a significant contribution, as were the six domains of achievement he specified (general intelligence, specific academic ability, creativity, leadership, arts, and psychomotor; Brody & Mills, 1997). Stanley's (1974, 1976) work on targeted instruction for specified academic areas of ability influenced the ways in which programming was adapted to broader definitions. Toward the end of the decade, Renzulli (1978) emphasized the importance of interactions between creativity, above-average ability, and task commitment in his three-ring model.

With the U.S. government publication of *A Nation at Risk* (National Commission on Excellence in Education, 1983), understanding and cultivating giftedness reached a new level of national priority. Gardner's (1983) theory of multiple intelligences introduced the many domains in which gifts operate and other models shifted focus to *processes*, as well as domain expertise (Ericsson, 2005). Sternberg's (1984, 1985) original triarchic theory of intelligence, and Feldhusen's (1986) four-part conception emphasized the application of abilities in real-world settings. Dimensions of giftedness couched in social contexts were suggested in Tannenbaum's (1983) psychosocial model and Mönks' (1992, 2005) multifactor model. Sternberg's (1997, 1999) expanded theory of successful intelligence emphasized analytical, creative, and practical abilities. The Differentiated Model of Giftedness and Talent (DMGT) proposed by Gagné (1995) parsed *natural* from *systematically developed abilities*. Cross and Coleman's (2005) school-based conception of giftedness (SGC) and Callahan and Miller's (2005) child-responsive model paid particular attention to giftedness in the classroom setting.

Over time, definitions of giftedness have increased both in number and complexity (see Ziegler's [2005] actiotope model). They have become both broader and more specific and have retained elements of the original *g*-factor (see Carroll's [1996] Three Stratum Theory), even as claims to eminence sometimes have been discarded. Although the above theories are predominantly grounded in research and represent significant contributions to scientific understanding, their emergence and popularity also is a testament to shifting values with regard to giftedness. Although the field has achieved no single consensus (nor is one likely or even desirable), it is clear that a greater variety of abilities now comprise giftedness and, therefore, so do a greater diversity of individuals than in the first half of the 20th century. This development is not independent of increased dedication to providing equal opportunity to gifted education for underrepresented groups, or of a greater appreciation for diverse abilities in the professional world. Such trends are evident in the federal definition as found in the Jacob K. Javits Gifted and Talented Education Act (U.S. Department of Education, 1993):

> Children and youth with outstanding talent perform or show the potential for performing at remarkably high levels of accomplishment when compared with others of their age, experience, or environment.
>
> These children and youth exhibit high performance capability in intellectual, creative, and/or artistic areas, possess an unusual leadership capacity, or excel in specific academic fields. They require services or activities not ordinarily provided by the schools.
>
> Outstanding talents are present in children and youth from all cultural groups, across all economic strata, and in all areas of human endeavor. (p. 26)

Unfortunately, it seems that expanding definitions have not been equally matched by broader identification methods. Despite well-intentioned policy statements (Coleman & Gallagher, 1995), underrepresentation of groups persists and general intelligence measures often prevail even in a climate of more complex views of intelligence (Jenkins-Friedman, 1982). Expanded definitions cannot be functional unless they are applied effectively to identify and serve those they recognize as gifted. Achieving meaningful impact from increasingly subtle, comprehensive, and inclusive definitions has proved remarkably difficult. (For further information on changing notions of giftedness, see Sternberg & Davidson, 1986, 2005.)

FROM DEFINITIONS TO IDENTIFICATION: SYSTEMIC CHALLENGES

For definitions of giftedness to become operational, a number of criteria must be met. Scientific models naturally demand empirical support and, even once established, experience an often-lengthy lag time between scholarly publication and permeation of the educational culture. Adoption of particular definitions by policy makers, and of equal importance, school administrators, still in no way guarantees that such definitions will be effectively adhered to in practice. If policy makers and educators do not properly align identification procedures and gifted services with definitions of giftedness, these definitions are, in effect, moot.

Although finding gifted curricula to complement a program's definition may be a fairly straightforward process, appropriate identification tools have proven more elusive. Callahan, Lundberg, and Hunsaker (1993) designed the Scale for the Evaluation of Gifted Identification Instruments (SEGII) to assist in the complex task of selecting such instruments. They posited that, "at a minimum, local school personnel should be aware of the psychometric appropriateness of using a particular instrument to assess the construct of giftedness they have adopted" (p. 137). When identification instruments do not reflect the preferred definition, schools will not identify the types of skills or types of students they intend to recognize and serve. Likewise, when services offered do not match the model for identification, identified students may not benefit as expected, and unidentified students who might have been well served by the program will not get this opportunity (Kwiatkowski & Sternberg, 2004).

Another challenge to the successful application of definitions in practice is the decentralization of the American education system. Although the delegation of educational decisions to the state and local levels may allow for greater accountability and diversity of educational practices, the responsibility for gifted programming often falls to each district, resulting in extreme variability in gifted education standards. To the extent that differences in gifted education reflect genuinely different values, needs, and goals of communities, such decentralization is beneficial. Yet, when communication between so many administrative bodies is difficult and best practices are only minimally shared, this system poses challenges to the optimal impact of well-matched giftedness definitions, identification methods, and programming. Anecdotally, local school officials value their autonomy but typically appreciate guidance, particularly in selecting appropriate methods for identification that allow for an effectively coordinated gifted education plan. Indeed, Hunsaker's (1994) national study of identification practices revealed that no district felt satisfied with the results of its efforts.

Identification instruments grounded in theories of giftedness that reflect the broad range of abilities presently recognized in popular definitions and that succeed in identifying these varied abilities in a diverse student population are invaluable to gifted program coordinators. Current practices have fallen short of achieving this ideal. The consideration of populations that remain persistently underrepresented in gifted programming highlights the extent of what policy makers have termed a "quiet crisis in educating talented students" (U.S. Department of Education, 1993, p. 5).

UNDERREPRESENTED POPULATIONS IN GIFTED PROGRAMMING

Correcting trends of underrepresentation and exclusion in no way necessitates nor should in any way involve a "lowering of the bar," but rather an expanded appreciation for what giftedness is. At least four populations of students are clearly underidentified for gifted programming through current practices: (1) minorities, particularly Black, Hispanic, and American Indian students; (2) children with simultaneous gifts and learning disabilities; (3) children from low-SES backgrounds; and (4) children with abilities not recognized by traditional assessment measures. The groups are not mutually exclusive and, for the most part, there is considerable awareness of and concern regarding their underrepresentation. The challenge, therefore, lies in finding validated, reliable, objective, and fair methods to identify these students. Such standards should be expected for criteria leading to any high-stakes educational decision, and gifted identification is no less than this type of decision.

As is evident in the definition of giftedness provided in the Javits Act cited earlier, the recognition of gifted children from traditionally underrepresented minority groups and low socioeconomic backgrounds has become a national priority. The literature is filled with examples of underrepresented minority groups and economically disadvantaged students' limited presence in gifted programming. This phenomenon is mirrored by overrepresentation in special education classrooms, and the challenges of correcting both imbalances are addressed in the National Research Council's (2002) report on *Minority Students in Special and Gifted Education*.

Reasons for underrepresentation are complex, and deserve attention. Gordon and Bridglall (2005) have written that, "for many students of color in the United States, the identification, assessment and nurturance of giftedness are complicated by limited opportunities to learn, psychological and social pressures, and racial and ethnic discrimination" (p. 120). A discussion of these important factors is beyond the scope of this chapter, but some of the most objective of these culprits are briefly considered here. The occasional persistence of narrow definitions of giftedness has been credited with overemphasis on middle-class, majority culture values that fail to recognize many important abilities (Frasier, 1987). Particular emphasis on verbal abilities leaves those with language differences between home and school at a significant disadvantage (Sisk, 1988). When recognition of giftedness is limited in these ways, many children effectively have reduced "cultural capital" in the school context and those that should receive gifted services are not readily identified. Perhaps the greatest criticism, though, is leveled at identification methods in particular.

Although charges of test bias typically are directed at intelligence quotient (IQ) tests, other standardized achievement batteries have been criticized as well (Mills & Tissot, 1995). Whether or not such bias is inherent, it is clear that traditional psychometric methods are not sufficiently able to identify the gifts of children from underrepresented populations. Certain testing possibilities do show considerable promise, however. Nonverbal instruments emphasizing fluid (rather than crystallized) intelligence, such as the Leiter International Performance Scale and the Ravens Progressive Matrices, have been shown to identify gifted minority students with relative success (Mills & Tissot, 1995; Ryan, 1983). Evidence suggests that minority and low-SES students perform better on spatial than on verbal and mathematical reasoning tasks (Naglieri, 1999). Torrance (1977) noted minority students' particular strengths in the figural area of his Torrance Tests of Creative Thinking. Identifying giftedness only with traditional tests of IQ and achievement with emphasis on verbal and mathematical abilities denies students with intellectual gifts invested in spatial and creative areas. Because minority and economically disadvantaged students benefit from assessments measuring this broader range of cognitive skills (see Sato, 1974; Stemler, Grigorenko, Jarvin, & Sternberg, 2006; VanTassel-Baska, Johnson, & Avery, 2002), the inclusion of such measures in gifted identification procedures not only would result in greater appreciation of important skills, but in greater program equity. We wish to emphasize here that test scores provide a measurement of an individual's performance on a test, an outcome influenced by complex factors including personal investment in particular skills over others, the influence of sociocultural background and educational opportunities, and measurement bias in addition to ability. Group differences always should be viewed in light of this understanding. Tests—and group tests in particular—should be valued only as limited if not utterly primitive tools of measurement. They also may be applied flexibly with special populations (e.g., to include but not exclude from gifted programming).

Students with learning disabilities (LD) are another group that is routinely overlooked in gifted education (for a review, see Newman & Sternberg, 2004). Learning disabilities are an elusive disorder, only recently characterized and still often misunderstood. Like giftedness, learning disabilities are characterized differently and constructed in different contexts. It has been particularly difficult, then, to identify students with both LD and giftedness, and many are excluded from gifted programming (Fall & Nolan, 1993). Although rarely jointly addressed, giftedness and learning disabilities are in no way contradictory or mutually exclusive. Because such disabilities are defined by "marked impairments in the development of specific skills" (American Psychiatric Association, 1994), the expansion of definitions of giftedness to include specific strengths makes the two constructs utterly compatible. Just as excelling in one area in no way guarantees remarkable ability in others, neither does a particular deficit preclude simultaneous gifts. Gifted/LD students also may experience alternating gifts and learning disabilities in related areas, such as reading and writing, or great discrepancies between potential and performance in a single area (Brody & Mills, 1997).

Finally, there are many students not included in the above categories who could benefit from gifted programming but currently are not being selected. The most common assessments of giftedness in schools today are IQ and achievement tests, whose purposes and effects are limited in comparison with popularly accepted (but poorly implemented) definitions of giftedness with greater scope. Such measures certainly are able to reflect a part of giftedness, but do not attempt to capture the creative skills or leadership capacity explicitly cited in the federal definition. Creativity is hardly revealed through a multiple-choice question, or practical ingenuity in a math problem. In the real world, such abilities are incredibly valuable, honored by society, and even lucrative. It is a shame that children with these skills are not encouraged to develop them further in academic settings, and, indeed, may even be prevented from important opportunities to do so (Sternberg, 1997). The broadening of definitions of giftedness to include these students is an important step, but without identification tools that successfully apply these definitions, they are only paper promises. Here we provide an overview of the most popular methods to paint a picture of the current state of gifted assessment, both its possibilities and limitations.

CLEANING OUT THE TOOLBOX: A LOOK AT CURRENT PRACTICES

"What is honored in a country will be cultivated there." Durden and Tangherlini (1993, p. 133) aptly conjure Plato as a preface to a discussion of gifted education with a quote that seems almost cautionary today. Do we indeed cultivate what we honor? That question is perhaps a good place to begin an evaluation of the most common current practices of gifted identification. Here we examine some of the most prevalently employed IQ and achievement tests with a consideration of their appropriate use, as well as both avoidable and unavoidable pitfalls. We also review alternative tests and the supplementation of more subjective measures. Finally, we summarize the "holes" in the dominant modes of identification and suggest a possible remedy, the Aurora Battery.

Achievement and IQ tests may be thought of as "first cousins" of a sort, with the former a narrower, subject-oriented version of the latter (Yarborough & Johnson, 1983). Standardized achievement tests are numerous and typically vary at the state level, but are largely comparable in substance. Most commonly administered in a group setting, they assess students' aptitude in subject areas and also are used to identify or screen for giftedness. IQ tests usually are administered individually, output numeric scores based on an average of 100, and aim to assess general cognitive ability. They are commonly used in schools for purposes of gifted identification and include (but are not limited to) the progressively updated Stanford-Binet (Roid, 2003) and Wechsler Intelligence Scale for Children–Revised (WISC, now in its fourth edition; Wechsler et al., 2004), as well as the Kaufman Assessment Battery for Children (K-ABC and K-ABC II; Kaufman & Kaufman, 1983, 2004).

There are good reasons for the use of IQ and achievement tests for gifted identification. First, they are stable and very well standardized, and IQ tests in particular follow additional guidelines for validity and reliability set by the Standards for Educational and Psychological Testing (AERA, APA, & NCME, 1999). They also are well known to predict academic performance in traditional settings, and can be useful in identifying students for rigorous or strict academic gifted programming. The value of objectivity also should not be underestimated. Although narrow reliance on these measures has resulted in overall underrepresentation of certain populations, there likely are some who benefit from this objectivity. IQ and achievement tests can provide opportunities to disprove classroom stereotypes regarding giftedness (Kaufman & Harrison, 1986), for gifted/LD students to evidence their strengths (Brody & Mills, 1997), and for others who don't match ideal perceptions of gifted behavior or performance to counter first impressions (Borland, 1986).

There are, however, many ways in which these measures can be abused. Misuses are, of course, correctable, but nevertheless continue to pervade the gifted education system. Both critics and defenders of these standardized instruments warn against setting strict cut-off scores to exclude students without regard for standard error; using scores to label children or make fine distinctions between them; considering only summed scores without regard for subtest abilities; employing scores without awareness of their variable sensitivity to race/ethnicity; and using scores alone to identify children for gifted programming (Borland, 1986; Callahan et al., 1993; Harrington, 1982; Kaufman & Harrison, 1986; Perrone, 1991; Robinson & Chamrad, 1986; Whitmore, 1981). Employing IQ and achievement tests as screening devices *only* guards against their most prevalent abuses. Hadaway and Marek-Schroer (1992) emphasized that high scores, much like high grades, warrant recognition, but that poor performance might be due to any number of factors unrelated to actual giftedness. These scores only should be used to include students.

Less avoidable flaws include low ceilings inherent in achievement measures (Harrington, 1982) and the failure of both types of measures to recognize divergent (or, more loosely, creative) thinking in addition to convergent thinking (Guilford, 1967). Most concerning to educators today is the stark failure of these instruments equitably to identify students, which has at times led them to effectively "enforce racial and socioeconomic segregation" (Borland, 1986, p. 163) in schools. Although nonverbal subtests and those with greater emphasis on fluid intelligence have been shown to more effectively identify students from underrepresented populations (as discussed earlier), such tests are not typically employed to select students for gifted programming. Many abilities thus remain functionally unrecognized.

Nontraditional assessments available for use in schools include measures that attempt to identify a broader range of gifts, but these also have received criticism. Popular creativity measures, such as the Torrance Tests of Creative Thinking (Torrance, 1984), are charged with demonstrating insufficient reliability (Anastasi, 1982) and measuring creativity in narrowly defined ways (Sternberg & Grigorenko, 2002). (For a more comprehensive collection of alternative instruments, as well as locally developed methods of identification, see the National Data Bank on Identification and Evaluation Methods introduced by Callahan and Caldwell [1993].) Neither traditional nor nontraditional instruments are immune to reproach, but these types of assessment receive greatly differing degrees of attention. As a result, the latter are applied sparsely, whereas schools continue to rely on the former. A reasonable response to imperfections in testing might be to use multiple types of instruments without giving too much or too little sway to any one in particular. More commonly, however, educators have sought to correct for deficiencies in traditional measures only with more subjective complements.

Survey studies have revealed the popularity of teacher and parental input as a supplement to traditional testing tools for gifted programming (Coleman & Gallagher, 1995; Yarborough & Johnson, 1983). Anecdotal accounts abound of teachers who believed in and championed underachieving students when no one else would, and of parents who successfully advocated for the recognition of children's gifts that have gone unnoticed at school, and there certainly are cases in which this has resulted in the rightful inclusion of unidentified students. Nevertheless, research suggests that on the whole, teachers and parents may not be the most effective judges of giftedness. Although parents seem to identify giftedness with greater accuracy than teachers, they still fail to recognize a significant proportion of gifted children (Ciha, Harris, Hoffman, & Potter, 1974; Jacobs, 1971). Teachers typically nominate only children with the most commonly expected characteristics of giftedness (Whitmore, 1980) and often base nomination directly on classroom performance and grades (Schack & Starko, 1990). Such children likely are to be the same children identified by traditional measures, which renders the supplemental value of parent and teacher input less robust. Finally, as Mills and Tissot (1995) point out, at their worst, subjective measures have the potential to be even less equitable in identifying minority students for gifted programming than are objective tools. The roles of teachers and parents then are likewise imperfect, and will be most effective only when nominators have been well educated with regard to under-identified populations and the broad range of giftedness recognized by definitions (Hadaway & Marek-Schroer, 1992).

Taken together, tests of IQ and achievement, along with alternative assessments and subjective means of identification for gifted programming, all are imperfect, as will be any conceivable method of gifted identification. In pursuit of ever-better instruments and procedures, we must recognize the particular ways in which current practices may be improved on for progress to be made. Some of today's shortfalls are correctable in relatively small ways, whereas others present remarkable challenges. Inappropriate application of IQ and achievement tests and restrictive criteria for subjective nominations can be curtailed by educating practitioners about common misuses. Less remediable is a narrowness of scope in identification methods, if not in actual definitions of giftedness (or programming, for that matter). This narrowness results in two undesirable outcomes. First, there is only limited qualification of different types and degrees of skills as score ceilings often remain low and measures of novel thinking are underrepresented. Second, valuable abilities go unrecognized and receive little encouragement, as evident in the underrepresentation of several populations. Closing the gap between theory and practice, and, more specifically, between broad definitions and identification methods, demands more than the curbing of current measures' misuse. We present the Aurora Battery as a theory-based instrument with promise for enhancing identification procedures and reducing the most glaring problems with selection for gifted programming today.

SUCCESSFUL INTELLIGENCE: A THEORETICAL FOUNDATION

Psychologist E. G. Boring (1923) described intelligence as that quality which intelligence tests measure. Boring's wry commentary also should be read as a warning. Even more so than intelligence, giftedness is a created category whose boundaries alternately are stretched and confined by political, social, and moral values. Yet, this construct hardly is conjured from nothing, and its present limitations are not artificial: There are children who benefit from and arguably are in need of gifted programming, significant potential is going unrecognized and untapped, and current identification systems often result in the exclusion of individuals with important abilities. The way in which giftedness is defined and thereby created is intended to reflect the discovery of actual truths. Bridging the gap between societal constructions of giftedness and their underlying foundation is theory. It is what orders our understanding, prevents our definitions of giftedness from being arbitrary, and can ultimately guard against the application of prejudicial and discriminatory beliefs. For these reasons, the tools used for identification of giftedness also should be based in validated scientific theory. To the extent that identification methods are anchored in this way, they are far more defensible, especially as sources of information for high-stakes decisions such as selection for gifted programming (Stemler et al., 2006). Theoretical grounding ensures that, to a certain extent, tests measure what giftedness is, and not just the other way around.

Sternberg's (2005) theory of successful intelligence offers a systems approach to intelligence in which different, interrelated aspects function together. Successful intelligence is most succinctly defined as

> the ability to succeed in life according to one's own definitions of success, within one's sociocultural context, by capitalizing on one's strengths and correcting or compensating for one's weaknesses; in order to adapt to, shape, and select environments; through a combination of analytical, creative, and practical abilities. (Sternberg & Grigorenko, 2002, p. 265)

This theory extends the scholarly discussion on intelligence through its emphasis on the importance of applying abilities in life. In this sense, no psychometric test can measure true successful intelligence, but it is very possible to imagine how measurable abilities other than those most commonly tested can contribute to success in life. The ultimate emphasis of the theory of successful intelligence on creative and practical skills, in addition to the analytical abilities most commonly recognized in schools, provides clear direction for the development of a theoretically based assessment for gifted identification. Support of the theory by confirmatory factor analysis and data from several countries (Sternberg, Castejón, Prieto, Hautamäki & Grigorenko, 2001; Sternberg, Grigorenko, Ferrari, & Clinkenbeard, 1999) further encourages the effort to create such an instrument. (For more details on the definition and development of the theory of successful intelligence, see Jensen, 1984, and Yarborough & Johnson, 1983). The three types of abilities that comprise the theory of successful intelligence are valuable and commonly synthesized in the real world, but are justly represented in schools to varying degrees. Relative to others, analytical abilities are easy to measure. They are used to analyze, compare and contrast, evaluate, judge, or classify. These are familiar classroom tasks and are the most widely represented skill set on IQ and achievement tests. Creative abilities are used to create, design, imagine, discover, hypothesize, or invent. Tasks that require these skills do not necessarily demand divergent thinking, but are almost always relatively novel. Although these abilities are valued in school and often are a central part of gifted programming, they are used less commonly for purposes of gifted identification and measured objectively only rarely. Practical abilities are used to apply, implement, or put into practice in real-world contexts. They also may be equated with common sense or tacit knowledge—that which is acquired without explicit instruction, or even conscious awareness, but is highly relevant to real-world performance. Even when not explicitly recognized, these skills are incredibly important in school, as well as nearly every setting, but almost never assessed. Research on applications of the theory of successful intelligence has been conducted using problems developed to measure all three of these ability types at the high school level and has yielded very promising results.

Two studies are particularly important indicators of the potential value of a gifted identification assessment because they evidence the ability of such a test to predict school success, close achievement gaps between racial and ethnic groups, and qualify varied student profiles. The Rainbow Project (Sternberg, The Rainbow Project Collaborators, & The University of Michigan Business School Project Collaborators, 2004; Sternberg & The Rainbow Project Collaborators, 2005, 2006) employed an assessment battery consisting of analytical, practical, and creative items to supplement the SAT. Adding assessments of creative and practical skills roughly doubled the power of the SAT alone to predict first-year college grades, thereby demonstrating the value of these skills even in an academic setting not specially designed to reward them. Furthermore, racial and ethnic performance differences decrease with the supplemental battery of analytical, creative, and practical skills relative to the SAT. The achievement gap between White and Black students on measures of creative, as opposed to analytical skills, was reduced substantially (by about .5 SD).

Similar results were found in another study augmenting Advanced Placement (AP) exams in psychology and statistics with assessments of memory, analytical, creative, and practical abilities (Stemler et al., 2006). Augmented exams in both subjects reduced differences between groups. This study also indicated the ability of such a test to assess an individual's variable levels of abilities. A subset of students exhibited extreme differences in performance between measurements of skill types, scoring at the lowest levels in one area and the highest in another. Taken together, these findings at the high school level point to the potential for an instrument based on the theory of successful intelligence to correct problems of limited ability assessment and underrepresentation in gifted identification procedures.

THE AURORA BATTERY: PUTTING THEORY INTO PRACTICE

A shining light bulb long has been the symbolic representation of clever ideas in cartoons and comics. The activity of the human brain is far more complex than such an image suggests, and is perhaps best invoked by the multifarious display of light that is an aurora. Complex interactions between electrons, gas atoms, and the earth's magnetic field are generated by solar wind to create the spectacular displays known as the northern and southern lights. It is in the interests of a better metaphor, and in honor of this shimmering spectrum, that the Aurora Battery so has been named.

Two parts comprise the battery under current development, a newly designed, augmented part (Aurora-*a* or Aurora-*a* battery) and a more conventional, intelligence-based part (Aurora-*g* or Aurora-*g* battery). Both are paper-and-pencil assessments intended for group administration to students at the elementary to middle school levels at which gifted programming is most prevalent. The augmented assessment is more substantial and is grounded in the theory of successful intelligence as presented earlier. The conventional assessment of general intellectual ability has been developed as a supplement. Of greatest importance and significance is the former, which, accordingly, we discuss more extensively here.

In designing the augmented assessment, we used a basic grid structure to depict graphically the broad range of item types to be developed. Analytical, creative, and practical domains are depicted as columns and figural, verbal, and quantitative modes as rows (see Figure 1). Subtests are created such that their dominant properties fulfill the criteria of each cell of the grid (for another example of such item development, see Sternberg & Clinkenbeard, 1995). Resulting are nine different types of subtests that together assess each combination of domain and modal specificity. This design is implemented for three reasons: to anchor the assessment securely in the theory of successful intelligence, to allow students balanced opportunities to demonstrate multiple and

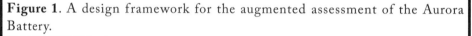

Domains: / Modes:	Analytical	Creative	Practical
Figural			
Verbal			
Quantitative			

Figure 1. A design framework for the augmented assessment of the Aurora Battery.

varied abilities, and to serve as a clear guide for assessing abilities across and between domains and modes.

Augmented assessment items differ in ways beyond the categorical properties of the grid. Difficulty varies from subtest to subtest, and from item to item within these. A central goal of task creation is the elimination of ceilings on each subtest to the extent possible (and reasonable) without compromising the capacity of the assessment to be given not only to students already thought to be gifted but to whole student populations without generating undue distress or anxiety. Both subtests and tasks range in length and individual questions take many forms. Some items require receptive answers (those chosen from a discrete set of options) and others require productive answers, generated by the student with varying degrees of constraint. Among other variations, there are multiple choice and fill-in-the-blank questions answered, math problems solved, lists generated, short selections written, pieces of information classified and ordered, money allocated, paths drawn, and subjective decisions made. The assessment includes photographs, arrangements of numbers, drawings, short paragraphs, and computer generated images.

Progressing across the grid of the Aurora-*a* battery, reading the cells from left to right and then top to bottom, example subtests are described. Floating Boats allows students to match patterns of connected toys whose arrangement changes from one photograph to another. Book Covers allows students to gen-

Task Types: Modes:	Analogy	Series Completion	Classification
Figural			
Verbal			
Quantitative			

Figure 2. A design framework for the *g*-factor assessment of the Aurora Battery.

erate a brief story plot to describe somewhat abstract pictures described as children's book covers. Toy Shadows allows students to choose the shadow that is made by a toy oriented in a particular way in relation to a light. Strange Metaphors allows students to generate a link between two somewhat unrelated nouns. Inanimate Conversations allows students to imagine what certain objects might say to each other, including humorous statements, if they could speak. Tough Decisions allows students to categorize given information in pro or con lists to make an everyday choice. Letter Math allows students to find numerical solutions to math problems with letters in place of some "missing" values. Number Talk allows students to explain the reason for a social interaction briefly described and illustrated between two cartoon numbers. Logistics Mapping allows students to compare different routes to destinations based on incremental distances provided.

As a supplement to the analytical, creative, and practical measures described above, a *g*-factor assessment also has been developed (the so-called Aurora-*g* battery). Its design is likewise guided by a grid structure with identical modes, but with task types rather than skill domains informing the second axis (see Figure 2). These are analogy, series completion, and classification tasks—all typical traditional measures of general intelligence. Analogies require students to analyze a relationship between a pair of stimuli (images, words, or numbers) and extend this relationship to a second, unfinished pair by choosing the correct stimulus from choices. Series completion items require students to evaluate the logic of a progressive series of stimuli (images, words, or numbers) and choose the next stimulus in the series from choices. Finally, classification tasks require students to compare and contrast the properties of a list of stimuli (images, words, or numbers) and select the one that conforms least to the others.

The two sections that make up the Aurora Battery are intended to complement each other by reserving a place for traditionally valued *g*-factor skills while expanding the scope of identification methods to recognize less formally appreciated creative and practical skills with the augmented assessment. The inclusion of both tests grants schools the ability to demonstrate the relative effectiveness of each for assessing the abilities valued in their stated definitions of giftedness and fostered through their programming.

Depending on the variable definitions of giftedness adopted, types of programs offered, and particular concerns of gifted educators, the Aurora Battery may be viewed as a series of assessments and therefore employed in several ways. Because the *g*-factor assessment (*g* battery) is intended as a supplement, the use of only this portion of the battery is likely to offer schools little beyond what is already available. Conversely, the augmented assessment is designed to allow for several alternative uses. First, schools uninterested in or discouraged by the performance of traditional instruments with their population might use the *a* battery independent of the *g* battery. Alternatively, schools seeking to better identify only a particular skill, either as a complement to existing identification measures, or for selection for more specialized gifted programming, might use only part of the Aurora-*a* assessment. For example, creativity subtests, or only those dealing with figures as opposed to verbal and numerical modes, might be administered alone.

SUCCESSFUL IMPLEMENTATION: HOPES, LIMITS, AND NEW DIRECTIONS

The Aurora Battery, with its explicit goals to avoid ceiling effects, allows for expression of abilities in different domains, and assesses creative and practical skills in addition to traditional analytical skills. It offers promise that a greater variety of gifted children will be more successfully identified. Students whose strengths lie in important domains that rarely are assessed may now be recognized. Those whose profiles are varied, perhaps even children who are gifted/ LD, may see their abilities better qualified and understood. Minority and low-SES students may receive greater recognition for their strengths. Research on the sources of current trends in the underrepresentation of these students, and the promise of assessments grounded in the theory of successful intelligence, suggest that just such outcomes of the Aurora Battery are not beyond reasonable hopes. Its design and flexibility will at a minimum allow gifted educators to better match the abilities of students with the gifted programming offered, arguably one of the most crucial features of effective gifted programming (see, for example, Hansen & Linden, 1990).

The Aurora Battery is not offered as a panacea for current gifted education ills. No test can assess all of the subtle abilities that may comprise giftedness as we recognize it. Nor can any test assess any ability perfectly or completely describe the strengths and weaknesses of any one person. Group tests in particular do not allow for the important subjective input or personal attention possible with individually administered assessments. For these reasons, the Aurora Battery should serve as a thorough screening tool, considered along with other sources of input to make educational choices. In this capacity, it may have great value without falling subject to misuse.

Other means of applying the theory of successful intelligence for more comprehensive gifted assessment also are entering the development phase. A scored parental interview, teacher rating scale, and observation schedule for use by professional educators and clinicians have been conceived as additions to the paper-and-pencil battery. These supplemental instruments provide exciting avenues for further research and development.

Different fish bite at different lures, just as different abilities are revealed in different contexts. If all of the fish caught are identical when there is an abundance of different species, the fly fisherman in search of variety does not simply use more of the same lure. This only would result in more of the same fish and an effective lowering of the bar on the catch. Instead, new lures are cast, and new fish bite. Extended metaphors aside, there are better ways to recognize diverse abilities than to keep using the same methods. IQ scores, achievement test results, classroom grades, and teacher nominations based on student reputations in effect may all recognize the same abilities and therefore identify the same students for gifted programming. Although all of these children may very well be gifted, there doubtless are many going unidentified. It's time to start casting new lures to identify a broader spectrum of abilities. The Aurora Battery may allow us to do just that.

REFERENCES

American Educational Research Association, American Psychological Association, & National Council on Measurement in Education. (1999). *Standards for educational and psychological testing.* Washington, DC: Authors.

American Psychiatric Association. (1994). *Diagnostic and statistical manual of mental disorders* (4th ed.). Washington, DC: Author.

Anastasi, A. (1982). *Psychological testing.* New York: Macmillan.

Boring, E. G. (1923). Intelligence as the tests test it. *New Republic, 35,* 35–37.

Borland, J. H. (1986). IQ tests: Throwing out the bathwater, saving the baby. *Roeper Review, 8,* 163–167.

Borland, J. H. (2005). Gifted education without gifted children. In R. J. Sternberg & J. Davidson (Eds.), *Conceptions of giftedness* (2nd ed., pp. 1–19). New York: Cambridge University.

Brody, L. E., & Mills, C. J. (1997). Gifted children with learning disabilities: A review of the issues. *Journal of Learning Disabilities, 30,* 282–296.

Callahan, C. M., & Caldwell, M. S. (1993). Establishment of a national data bank on identification and evaluation instruments. *Journal for the Education of the Gifted, 16,* 201–219.

Callahan, C. M., Lundberg, A. C., & Hunsaker, S. L. (1993). Development of the scale for the evaluation of gifted identification instruments (SEGII). *Gifted Child Quarterly, 37,* 133–140.

Callahan, C. M., & Miller, E. M. (2005). A child-responsive model of giftedness. In R. J. Sternberg & J. Davidson (Eds.), *Conceptions of giftedness* (2nd ed., pp. 38–51). New York: Cambridge University.

Carroll, J. B. (1996). A three-stratum theory of intelligence: Spearman's contributions. In I. Dennis & P. Tapsfield (Eds.), *Human abilities: Their nature and measurement* (pp. 1–17). Mahwah, NJ: Erlbaum.

Ciha, T. E., Harris, R., Hoffman, C., & Potter, M. W. (1974). Parents as identifiers of giftedness, ignored but accurate. *Gifted Child Quarterly, 18,* 191–195.

Coleman, M. R., & Gallagher, J. J. (1995). State identification policies: Gifted students from special populations. *Roeper Review, 17,* 268–275.

Cross, T. L., & Coleman, L. J. (2005). School-based conception of giftedness. In R. J. Sternberg & J. Davidson (Eds.), *Conceptions of giftedness* (2nd ed., pp. 1–19). New York: Cambridge University.

Durden, W. G., & Tangherlini, A. E. (1993). *Smart kids: How academic talents are developed and nurtured in America.* Seattle, WA: Hogrefe & Huber.

Ericsson, K. A. (2005). Recent advances in expertise research: A commentary on the contributions to the special issue. *Applied Cognitive Psychology, 19,* 223–241.

Feldhusen, J. F. (1986). A conception of giftedness. In R. E. Sternberg & J. E. Davidson (Eds.), *Conceptions of giftedness* (pp. 112–127). New York: Cambridge University.

Fall, J., & Nolan, L. (1993). A paradox of personalities. *Gifted Child Today, 16*(1), 46–49.

Frasier, M. (1987). The identification of gifted Black students: Developing new perspectives. *Journal for the Education of the Gifted, 10,* 155–180.

Freeman, J. (2005). Permission to be gifted: How conceptions of giftedness can change lives. In R. J. Sternberg & J. Davidson (Eds.), *Conceptions of giftedness* (2nd ed., pp. 80–97). New York: Cambridge University Press.

Gagné, F. (1995). From giftedness to talent: A developmental model and its impact on the language of the field. *Roeper Review, 18,* 103–111.

Gardner, H. (1983). *Frames of mind.* New York: Basic Books.

Gordon, E. W., & Bridglall, B. L. (2005). Nurturing talent in gifted students of color. In R. J. Sternberg & J. Davidson (Eds.), *Conceptions of giftedness* (2nd ed., pp. 120–146). New York: Cambridge University.

Guilford, J. P. (1967). *The nature of human intelligence.* New York: McGraw-Hill.

Hadaway, N., & Marek-Schroer, M. F. (1992). Multidimensional assessment of the gifted minority student. *Roeper Review, 15,* 73–77.

Hansen, J. B., & Linden, K. W. (1990). Selecting instruments for identifying gifted and talented students. *Roeper Review, 13,* 10–15.

Harrington, R. G. (1982). Caution: Standardized testing may be hazardous to the education programs of intellectually gifted children. *Education, 103*(2), 112–117.

Hothersall, D. (1984). *History of psychology.* New York: Random House.

Hunsaker, S. L. (1994). Adjustments to traditional procedures for identifying under-served students: Successes and failures. *Exceptional Children, 61*, 72–76.

Jacobs, J. (1971). Effectiveness of teacher and parent identification of gifted children as a function of school level. *Psychology in the Schools, 8*, 140–142.

Jenkins-Friedman, R. (1982). Myth: Cosmetic use of multiple selection criteria! *Gifted Child Quarterly, 26*, 24–26.

Jensen, A. R. (1984). The Black–White difference on the K-ABC: Implications for future tests. *Journal of Special Education, 18*, 377–408.

Kaufman, A. S., & Harrison, P. L. (1986). Intelligence tests and gifted assessment: What are the positives? *Roeper Review, 8*, 154–159.

Kaufman, A. S., & Kaufman, N. L. (1983). *K-ABC: Kaufman Assessment Battery for Children: Interpretive manual.* Circle Pines, MN: American Guidance Service.

Kaufman, A. S., & Kaufman, N. L. (2004). *Kaufman Assessment Battery for Children* (2nd ed.). Circle Pines, MN: American Guidance Service.

Kwiatkowski, J., & Sternberg, R. J. (2004). Getting practical about gifted education. In D. Boothe & J. C. Stanley (Eds.), *In the eyes of the beholder: Critical issues for diversity in gifted education* (pp. 227–235). Waco, TX: Prufrock Press.

Marland, S. (1972). *Education of the gifted and talented: Report to the Congress of the United States by the U. S. Commissioner of Education.* Washington, DC: U.S. Government Printing Office.

Mills, C. J., & Tissot, S. L. (1995). Identifying academic potential in students from under-represented populations: Is using the Ravens Progressive Matrices a good idea? *Gifted Child Quarterly, 39*, 209–217.

Mönks, F. J. (1992). Development of gifted children: The issue of identification and programming. In F. J. Mönks & W. A. M. Peters (Eds.), *Talent for the future* (pp. 191–202). Assen, The Netherlands: Van Gorcum.

Mönks, F. J. (2005). Giftedness and gifted education. In R. J. Sternberg & J. Davidson (Eds.), *Conceptions of giftedness* (2nd ed., pp. 187–200). New York: Cambridge University.

Naglieri, J. A. (1999). *The essentials of CAS assessment.* New York: Wiley.

National Commission on Excellence in Education. (1983). *A nation at risk: The imperative for educational reform: A report to the nation and the Secretary of Education, United States Department of Education.* Washington, DC: Government Printing Office.

National Research Council. (2002). *Minority students in special and gifted education.* Washington, DC: Author.

Newman, T., & Sternberg, R. J. (Eds.). (2004). *Students with both gifts and learning disabilities: Identification, assessment, and outcomes.* Boston: Kluwer.

Perrone, V. (1991). On standardized testing. *Childhood Education, 67*, 131–142.

Plucker, J. A., & Barab, S. A. (2005). The importance of contexts in theories of giftedness: Learning to embrace the messy joys of subjectivity. In R. J. Sternberg & J. Davidson (Eds.), *Conceptions of giftedness* (2nd ed., pp. 201–216). New York: Cambridge University Press.

Renzulli, J. (1978). What makes giftedness? Reexamining a definition. *Phi Delta Kappan, 60*, 180–184.

Robinson, N. M., & Chamrad, D. L. (1986). Appropriate uses of intelligence tests with gifted children. *Roeper Review, 8*(3), 160–163.

Roid, G. H. (2003). *Stanford-Binet Intelligence Scales* (5th ed.). Itasca, IL: Riverside.

Ryan, J. (1983). Identifying intellectually superior Black children. *Journal of Educational Research, 76,* 153–156.

Sato, I. S. (1974). The culturally different gifted child: The dawning of his day? *Exceptional Children, 40,* 572–576.

Schack, G. D., & Starko, A. (1990). Identification of gifted students: An analysis of criteria preferred by preservice teachers, classroom teachers, and teachers of the gifted. *Journal for the Education of the Gifted, 13,* 346–363.

Sisk, D. A. (1988). Children at risk: The identification of the gifted among the minority. *Gifted Education International, 5,* 138–141.

Spearman, C. (1927). *The abilities of man.* New York: Macmillan.

Stanley, J. C. (1974). Intellectual precocity. In J. C. Stanley, D. P. Keating, & L. H. Fox (Eds.), *Mathematical talent: Discovery, description, and development* (pp. 1–22). Baltimore: Johns Hopkins University.

Stanley, J. C. (1976). Use of tests to discover talent. In D. P. Keating (Ed.), *Intellectual talent: Research and development* (pp. 3–22). Baltimore: Johns Hopkins University.

Stemler, S. E., Grigorenko, E. L., Jarvin, L., & Sternberg, R. J. (2006). Using the theory of successful intelligence as a basis for augmenting AP exams in psychology and statistics. *Contemporary Educational Psychology, 31,* 344–376.

Sternberg, R. J. (1984). Toward a triarchic theory of human intelligence. *Behavioral and Brain Sciences, 7,* 269–287.

Sternberg, R. J. (1985). *Beyond IQ: A triarchic theory of human intelligence.* New York: Cambridge University.

Sternberg, R. J. (1997). *Successful intelligence.* New York: Plume.

Sternberg, R. J. (1999). The theory of successful intelligence. *Review of General Psychology, 3,* 292–316.

Sternberg, R. J. (2005). The triarchic theory of successful intelligence. In D. P. Flanagan & P. L. Harrison (Eds.), *Contemporary intellectual assessment* (2nd ed., pp. 103–119). New York: Guilford.

Sternberg, R. J., Castejón, J. L., Prieto, M. D., Hautamäki, J., & Grigorenko, E. L. (2001). Confirmatory factor analysis of the Sternberg Triarchic Abilities Test in three international samples: An empirical test of the triarchic theory of intelligence. *European Journal of Psychological Assessment, 17,* 1–16.

Sternberg, R. J., & Clinkenbeard, P. R. (1995). The triarchic model applied to identifying, teaching, and assessing gifted children. *Roeper Review, 17,* 255–260.

Sternberg, R. J., & Davidson, J. E. (Eds.). (1986). *Conceptions of giftedness.* New York: Cambridge University.

Sternberg, R. J., & Davidson, J. E. (Eds.). (2005). *Conceptions of giftedness* (2nd ed.). New York: Cambridge University.

Sternberg, R. J., & Grigorenko, E. L. (2002). The theory of successful intelligence as a basis for gifted education. *Gifted Child Quarterly, 46,* 265–277.

Sternberg, R. J., Grigorenko, E. L., Ferrari, M., & Clinkenbeard, P. (1999). A triarchic analysis of an aptitude-treatment interaction. *European Journal of Psychological Assessment, 15,* 1–11.

Sternberg, R. J., The Rainbow Project Collaborators, & The University of Michigan Business School Project Collaborators. (2004). Theory-based university admissions testing for a new millennium. *Educational Psychologist, 39,* 185–198.

Sternberg, R. J., & The Rainbow Project Collaborators. (2005). Augmenting the SAT through assessments of analytical, practical, and creative skills. In W. Camara &

E. Kimmel (Eds.), *Choosing students. Higher education admission tools for the 21st century* (pp. 159–176). Mahwah, NJ: Erlbaum.

Sternberg, R. J., & The Rainbow Project Collaborators. (2006). The Rainbow Project: Enhancing the SAT through assessments of analytical, practical, and creative skills. *Intelligence, 34,* 321–350.

Tannenbaum, A. J. (1983). *Gifted children: Psychological and educational perspectives.* New York: Macmillan.

Terman, L. M. (1925). *Genetic studies of genius: Vol. 1. Mental and physical traits of a thousand gifted children.* Stanford, CA: Stanford University.

Torrance, E. P. (1970). Broadening concepts of giftedness in the 70s. *Gifted Child Quarterly, 14,* 199–208.

Torrance, E. P. (1977). Your style of learning and thinking, forms A and B: Preliminary norms, abbreviated technical notes, scoring keys, and selected references. *Gifted Child Quarterly, 21,* 563–573.

Torrance, E. P. (1984). *Torrance Tests of Creative Thinking.* Bensenville, IL: Scholastic Testing.

Trentham, L. L., & Hall, E. G. (1987). The relationship between scores on the gifted student screening scale and scores on IQ tests. *Roeper Review, 9,* 229–231.

U.S. Department of Education. (1993). *National excellence: A case for developing America's talent.* Washington, DC: Author.

VanTassel-Baska, J., Johnson, D., & Avery, L. D. (2002). Using performance tasks in the identification of economically disadvantaged and minority gifted learners: Findings from Project STAR. *Gifted Child Quarterly, 46,* 110–123.

Wechsler, D., Kaplan, E., Fein, D., Kramer, J., Morris, R., Delis, D., et al. (2004). *Wechsler Intelligence Scale for Children* (4th ed.). San Antonio, TX: The Psychological Corporation.

Whitmore, J. R. (1980). *Giftedness, conflict, and underachievement.* Boston: Allyn & Bacon.

Whitmore, J. R. (1981). Gifted children with handicapping conditions: A new frontier. *Exceptional Children, 48,* 106–114.

Yarborough, B. H., & Johnson, R. A. (1983). Identifying the gifted: A theory–practice gap. *Gifted Child Quarterly, 27,* 135–138.

Zeigler, A. (2005). The Actiotope Model of Giftedness. In R. J. Sternberg & J. Davidson (Eds.), *Conceptions of giftedness* (2nd ed., pp. 411–436). New York: Cambridge University.

AUTHOR NOTE

The authors wish to thank Karen Jensen Neff, without whose generous support this project never could have happened. Thanks are also due the members of the Aurora Project team, including Linda Jarvin, Jens Beckmann, Tina Newman, and Jonna Kwiatkowski. The authors also wish to thank Robyn Rissman for her valuable editorial assistance. Correspondence regarding this chapter should be sent to Elena L. Grigorenko at Child Study Center, Yale University, 230 South Frontage Road, New Haven, CT 06519-1124 (elena. grigorenko@yale.edu).

Chapter 21

Intelligences Outside the Normal Curve: Co-Cognitive Traits that Contribute to Giftedness

Joseph S. Renzulli and Rachel E. Sytsma Reed

Background

s conceptions of giftedness expanded (Albert, 1975; Bloom & Sosniak, 1981; Csikszentmihalyi, 1996; Gardner, 1983; Renzulli, 1978, 2002; Sternberg, 1986), researchers provided support for views of giftedness that went beyond high cognitive potential, and more persons became interested in affective issues, moral and ethical development, and what we will describe as intelligences outside the normal curve.[1] A better understanding of people who

---

1   This chapter describes recent theoretical development and related research that is an extension of what is known popularly as the three-ring conception of giftedness (above average but not necessarily superior ability, creativity, and task commitment). The three rings were embedded in a houndstooth background that represents the interactions between personality and environment. The current three-ring conception and research related to elaboration of personality and environment focuses on a scientific examination of some of the co-cognitive background components necessary in order for us to understand the sources of gifted behaviors and more importantly, the ways in which people transform their gifted assets into constructive action. These factors form the basis for the development of Operation Houndstooth, which is described in more detail in Renzulli, J. S., Sytsma, R. E., & Berman, K. B. (2003). Ampliando el concepto de superdotación de cara a educar líderes para una comunidad

use their gifts in socially constructive ways can help us create conditions that expand the number of people who contribute to the growth of social as well as economic capital.

What Is Social Capital and Why Is It Important?

Social capital is a set of intangible assets that address the collective needs and problems of other individuals and our communities at large. The notion of social capital evolved out of empirical research contributing to developing theories of capital in the 1970s and 1980s (Bourdieu & Passeron, 1970/1977). What may best be described as a "strategic approach" to social capital is espoused by Bourdieu, wherein his conceptualization parallels that of economic capital. Social capital is viewed as a resource that provides power or "credit" to an individual through interactive relationships among individuals within a collective group. These relationships provide influence and power to the individual where she may not have held influence on her own, thereby making membership in a group valuable (Bourdieu, 1986). While group membership can certainly become exclusionary, acceptance within and cohesiveness of many social groups (e.g., families, activist associations including political affiliation) is guided by common values, behavior patterns, and ideology, which may be utilized to strengthen civic duty and promotion of social welfare. Essentially, the idea of group membership is viewed with broad, socially-constructive boundaries that move "membership" away from an act of exclusion toward an inclusive act of social improvement and increased civic awareness.

Another perspective with regard to social capital may be considered a "functional approach." LaBonte (1999) bridges the "functional-strategic" gap somewhat when he defines social capital as:

> Something going on "out there" in peoples' day-to-day relationships that is an important determinant to the quality of their lives, if not society's healthy functioning. It is the "gluey stuff" that binds individuals to groups, groups to organizations, citizens to societies. (p. 431)

LaBonte's "gluey stuff" resembles Bourdieu's interactive relationships. Yet, the social capital that LaBonte conceptualizes focuses on general enhancement of community life and the network of obligations we have to one another, as opposed to Bourdieu's emphasis on collective power and group membership as a vehicle for any concomitant socially constructive product. A functional approach highlights investments in social capital because of their benefit to society as a whole through creation of the values, norms, networks, and social trust that facilitate coordination and cooperation geared toward the greater public good.

global. In J. A. Alonso, J. S. Renzulli, & Y. Benito (Eds.), *Manual internacional de superdotación* (pp. 71–88). Madrid, Fundamentos Psicipedagogicos.

The functional approach to social capital is supported by more empirical research than a strategic approach such as Bourdieu's (Healy, 2004). More aligned with a functional approach, Putnam (1993) initially defined social capital as "features of social organizations such as networks, norms, and social trust that facilitate coordination and cooperation for mutual benefit (p. 67), but later suggested that social trust is an outcome of social capital (2000). Putnam (1993, 1995) pointed out that the aggregation of social capital has contributed to economic development. He found that widespread participation in group activities, social trust, and cooperation created conditions for both good government and prosperity. Putnam traced the roots of investments in social capital to medieval times and concluded that communities did not become civil because they were rich, but rather they became rich because they were civil. Other researchers have concluded that social capital is simultaneously a cause and an effect leading to positive outcomes such as economic development, good government, reduced crime, greater participation in civic activities, and cooperation among diverse members of a community (Portes, 1998). Investments in *both* economic and social capital can result in greater prosperity and improved physical and mental health, as well as a society that honors freedom, happiness, justice, civic participation, and the dignity of a diverse population.

Researchers who have studied social capital have examined it mainly in terms of its impact on communities at large, but they also point out that it is created largely by the actions of individuals. Healy (2004) provides a summation of social capital that includes the creation of benefits over time, where "benefits" encompasses intangible assets such as improved human condition for individuals; he supports the idea that social capital resources exist in the form of social networks of obligation, which harkens back to Bourdieu's strategic approach. Researchers also have reported that leadership is a necessary condition for the creation of social capital. Although numerous studies and a great deal of commentary about leadership have been discussed in the gifted education literature, no one has yet examined the relationship between the characteristics of gifted leaders and their motivation to use their gifts for the production of social capital.

Gifted Education and Social Capital

Academic success typically occurs within classroom and school contexts. Classes and schools are social networks and, as such, cannot elude discussion of group membership. Membership in a social network and the access to social capital affiliated with that membership have the potential to fulfill many aspects of the "deficiency needs" in Maslow's hierarchy of needs (1987). The four deficiency needs (i.e., physiological, safety, love and belonging, esteem) are actually satisfied more easily by participating in a group than they are attained individually. Maslow's hierarchy requires that all deficiency needs (satisfied only by external sources such as inclusion in a group) must be met before an individual can embark on an intrinsically motivated path of growth and development—a path toward self-actualization. Self-esteem needs are often met through peer associations, and Bourdieu's concept of social capital suggests that the ongoing process of recognition in a group repeatedly affirms self-esteem through an ongoing cycle of support confirming that a member is worthy of being a member. Therefore, social capital is valuable strategically in nurturing individuals as learners and is valuable functionally for the learning context, wherein social values and civic duties may take center stage in the management of the classroom, in student–student relationships, and in academic tasks. This rationale resembles Sternberg's (2005) notion of wisdom and its role in his proposed learning theory, WICS (wisdom, intelligence, creativity, synthesized). He emphasizes the need for leaders to move beyond mere skills and attitudes toward wisdom, which he describes as an individual's ability to use his intelligence, creativity, and experience for a common good, necessitating a focus on the interests of others in addition to one's own interests (Sternberg, 1998).

Research on the characteristics of gifted individuals has addressed the question: What causes some people to use their intellectual, motivational, and creative assets in ways that lead to outstanding manifestations of creative productivity, while others with similar or perhaps even more considerable assets fail to achieve high levels of accomplishment? Perhaps an even more important question so far as the production of social capital is concerned is: What causes some people to mobilize their interpersonal, political, ethical, and moral realms of being in such ways that they place human concerns and the common good above materialism, ego enhancement, and self-indulgence? The abundance of folk wisdom, research literature, and biographical and anecdotal accounts about creativity and giftedness are nothing short of mind boggling, and yet we are still unable to answer these fundamental questions about persons who have devoted their lives to improving the human condition. Several writers (Gagné, 1985; Gardner, 1993; Mönks, 1991; Renzulli, 1978; Sternberg, 1986; Tannenbaum, 1986) have speculated about the necessary ingredients for giftedness and creative productivity. These theories have called attention to important components and conditions for high-level accomplishment, but they have failed to explain how the confluence of desirable traits result in commitments for making the lives of all people more rewarding, environmentally safe, peaceful, and politically free. Our future leaders will come from the pool of our gifted young people, so improving our understanding of and ability to affect socially constructive attitudes, ideologies, and civic commitments among all students—but particularly among those gifted individuals who will have leadership roles in our society—is critical.

In the sections that follow, we examine the scientific research that defines several categories of personal characteristics that have been associated with such commitments and form the basis for Operation Houndstooth Theory: Optimism, Courage, Romance With a Topic or Discipline, Sensitivity to Human Concerns, Physical/Mental Energy, and Vision/Sense of Destiny. These factors and their subcomponents are portrayed in Figure 1. We will refer

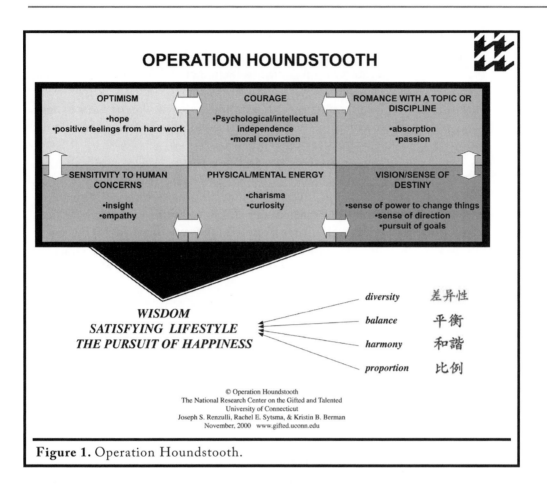

Figure 1. Operation Houndstooth.

to these traits as *co-cognitive factors* because they interact with and enhance the cognitive traits that we ordinarily associate with the development of human abilities. Moon (2000) suggested that constructs of this type, including social, emotional, and inter/intra-personal intelligence, are related to each other and are independent from traditional measures of ability. The two-directional arrows in this diagram are intended to point out the many interactions that take place between and among the factors.

Optimism. The most widely investigated component is optimism, defined as a mood or attitude associated with an expectation about a future that one regards as socially desirable—either to the individual's advantage or for the individual's pleasure (Tiger, 1979). Peterson (2000) described optimism as an amoeba-like, "velcro" concept to which many attitudes, behaviors, and performance seem to adhere for reasons that are not entirely obvious. The reason for optimism's amoebic and adhesive nature is its complexity.

Optimism appears to have evolutionary benefits (Tiger, 1979) and is susceptible to alteration. Something we all have to a certain degree, optimism is a personal, dispositional trait that appears to mediate between external events and individual interpretation of those events (Seligman & Csikszentmihalyi,

2000). However, work by Seligman and his colleagues have illustrated that optimistic behaviors or mindsets can be modified (learned) through reflective self-awareness and intervention strategies (Seligman, 1991; Seligman, Reivich, Jaycox, & Gillham, 1995). Aspinwall and Brunhart (2000) note that while optimism may be based on one's sense of competence or learned ways of coping, it may also be rooted in a variety of beliefs in powers that transcend the individual, such as spiritual or religious beliefs.

Much research also exists on "hope," a subcomponent of optimism (Snyder, 1995; Snyder, Sympson, Michael, & Cheavens, 2001; Snyder, Sympson, Ybasco, Borders, Babyak, & Higgins, 1996). Distinguishing hope from optimism, however, and understanding their respective effects on individuals remains challenging because of the high degree of overlap between the two. Much can be inferred about hope and optimism through the study of hopelessness, which has been shown to correlate with depression, anxiety, and a more external locus of control (Beck, Weissman, Lester, & Trexler, 1974).

Ample literature exists explaining optimism's positive benefits to well-being, coping, perseverance, health, and happiness, and it is therefore essential that we expand our understanding of the power of optimism in the development of talent. Perhaps those students with high measures of optimism in combination with other co-cognitive factors are the very students most likely to develop into the creative producers and eminent leaders of tomorrow.

Courage. The co-cognitive factor courage comprises three subsets: moral, psychological, and physical. Both moral and psychological courage are correlated with creativity in the literature (MacKinnon, 1978). Putman (1997) describes moral courage as the maintenance of moral integrity in fearful situations. Moral courage is strongly correlated with other co-cognitive factors such as empathy, altruism, and sensitivity to human concerns. The concept of sensitivity to human concerns combines these concepts into action in that through heartfelt feeling for another's plight, one will act courageously for the benefit of others, even in the face of societal disapproval. Psychological courage (Putman, 1997) is required for independence and is therefore likely to correlate positively with such abilities as exploring controversial questions, generating "outside the box" solutions to problems, and tenacity (maintaining focus despite difficulty). Ryff and Singer (2003) appear to equate psychological courage with autonomy—the capacity to stand alone—and cite it as one of six dimensions integral to psychological well-being. This definition of autonomy links psychological courage to risk-taking, which is integral to success through goal setting and attainment, intrinsic motivation (autonomous control), and self-determination theory, as well as studies associated with achievement motivation (Elliot & Church, 1997; Harackiewicz & Elliot, 1998; Locke & Latham, 2002; Nix, Ryan, Manly, & Deci, 1999; Ryan & Deci, 2000).

Courage has also been discussed in connection with the emergence of creativity, so much so that MacKinnon (1978) recognized it as the most significant characteristic of a creative person. This includes questioning what's accepted, being open to new experiences, listening to one's own intuition, imagining the impossible, and standing with, or against, the group if necessary.

Often the creative person must grapple with internal blocks or fears that must be overcome in order to seek and express the truths of new ideas, popular or not. Many people are blocked when they find themselves in psychological servitude, or under the emotional manipulation of another being. Psychological courage must be developed to live a normal life, separating from parents, and developing healthy relationships that do not interfere with independent functioning. A strong basis of psychological courage is necessary for making good decisions—decisions that establish positive conditions for the productive functioning of the individual rather than decisions based in denial of problems or for instant gratification (Putman, 1997).

One can also understand the significance of courage by examining its antithesis—lack of courage. For example, self-handicapping may exemplify the absence of intellectual courage, psychological courage, or both. Self-handicapping (purposefully acquiring or displaying impediments to success for protection of a desired self-image) is motivated by self-preservation concerns and threats to self-esteem (Rhodewalt, Morf, Hazlett, & Fairfield, 1991). Research conducted by Rhodewalt et al. investigated the relationship between self-esteem and self-handicapping; because if one can posit a correlation between self-esteem and autonomy, one can also see how psychological courage or risk-taking and self-esteem may relate. Courage, therefore, is integral to resilience because it demands that one is capable of facing obstacles, which are inevitable occurrences along any road to success or goal-attainment (Dweck & Leggett, 1988).

Romance With a Topic or Discipline. The concept of romance with a topic can be explored through the notions of passion, peak experience, or flow. This relates to physical and mental energy in that intrinsic motivation exists in the context of topics that have appeal or ones that arise from personal interest (Ryan & Deci, 2000). When all of these elements are present, the original meaning of the word passion becomes relevant. The Latin root of the word is *pati,* meaning to suffer. One is willing to suffer for that which one loves. The concept of suffering also implies the connection with effort, exertion, and intense action (Kaufmann, 2000).

Flow, as described by Csikszentmihalyi (1990), occurs when one becomes thoroughly engaged in an activity in which the balance of ability and challenge meshes, and the resulting experience is one of total absorption and self-actualization. In Csikszentmihalyi's research (1996), participants' activities that stimulated the feeling of flow were often "painful, risky, difficult activities that stretched the person's capacity and involved an element of novelty and discovery" (p. 110). The activity became almost automatic yet with a high focus of consciousness.

In the study of creative and eminent adults, the love of a topic has usually begun at an early age and blossomed under nurturing circumstances. Talent, personality, and ability often are not enough to succeed without the ingredient of the labor of love (Amabile, 1983). Locke and Latham (2002), whose work focuses on goal setting and task motivation, say that the relationship between goals and performance is strongest when people are committed to what they are doing; that is, commitment to one's goals facilitates performance. Effortful engagement in a task requires a valued goal and a sufficient level of confidence that the goal can be met (Carver & Scheier, 2003). What is important to note, with regard to utilizing passion or romance with a topic to facilitating goal attainment is that, "People do not take up goals that don't matter to them, and if they did, they wouldn't persist when things got difficult. The greater the goal's value, the greater the person's commitment to it" (Carver & Scheier, p. 88).

Across domains and across time, eminence has demanded extensive dedication of energy and time; humans commit at this level to things they love. Therefore, it is not surprising to find that eminent individuals experience a sort of intimacy with, or passion for, the field in which they thrive (Cullum, 1997; Gardner, 1993).

Sensitivity to Human Concerns. Sensitivity to human concerns includes the concepts of empathy and altruism and combines these concepts into action in that, through heartfelt feeling for another's plight, one will act for the benefit of others. A meta-analysis of studies involving the relationship between empathy and prosocial behavior, which is malleable and may be manifested as altruism, shows inconsistent results in the relationship. This result may be attributable to assessment methods. However, generally, the strength of the association increases with age. Implications lead to the question of whether or not these traits can be influenced by environment; that is, can we teach sensitivity? Danish and Kagan (1971) found significant changes on the Scale of Affective Sensitivity in a control group after an intensive counseling intervention.

Other researchers have found a relationship between empathic or altruistic tendencies and helping or prosocial behaviors (Eisenberg & Miller, 1987; Eisenberg & Wang, 2003; Eisenberg-Berg, 1979; Mehrabian & Epstein, 1972; Reis, 1995). This connection suggests the importance of developing ways to increase empathic tendencies if sensitivity to human concerns is a trait of value. Most psychologists now agree that empathy is a primary determinant of prosocial and altruistic behavior and that empathy and altruism engender certain behaviors, which may be considered moral.

Research suggests that the environment can influence the nurturing of the traits associated with this co-cognitive factor, sensitivity to human concerns (Battistich, Watson, Solomon, Schaps, & Solomon, 1991; Berman, 1997; Danish & Kagan, 1971; Zahn-Waxler & Radke-Yarrow, 1982).

Physical and Mental Energy. Physical and mental energy are more difficult to define, and are best understood in the context of several related factors that have been discussed in the research literature. The nature of charisma, defined often as nonverbal emotional expressiveness and the ability to inspire followers with admiration (Lindholm, 1990), implies a high level of physical and mental energy. Curiosity, or inquisitiveness, also manifests itself in high levels of energy or intensity. In her study of eminent older women, Reis (1995) found a sense of vitality and energy to be an essential personal characteristic.

The importance of this energy level to creative production has been identified and described by several different theorists. John-Steiner (1997) states: "Creativity requires a continuity of concern, an intense awareness of one's active inner life combined with sensitivity to the external world . . . intensity is then the one universal given in this account of creative thinking" (p. 219).

General agreement exists that gifted individuals are typically enthusiastic, absorbed in their work, and energetic (Goertzel, Goertzel, & Goertzel, 1978; Piechowski, 1986; Reis, 1998); when charisma is combined with intelligence and socially constructive giftedness, it has the potential to be a very powerful, positive force.

Curiosity or inquisitiveness can be yet another component of physical and mental energy, fueling one's desire for learning even when the application of knowledge is not readily apparent. This suggests an investigation of self-determination theory and the concept of intrinsic motivation (Ryan & Deci, 2000). Findings show that these are related to three psychological needs: competence, autonomy, and relatedness. When these conditions are met, the result is increased motivation and mental health; when hindered, these conditions lead to diminished well-being. Extensive curiosity can lead to dangerous behaviors as well, yet studies also show a more predominant positive relationship between curiosity and creativity (Padhee & Das, 1987). Identification of social or environmental factors that nurture these traits concerns many researchers. Nonpunitive environments open to exploration rather than those which exert excessive control, provide low levels of challenge, and lack connectedness have been shown to optimize potential in the expression of physical and mental energy (Berman, 1997; Ryan & Deci, 2000).

Vision/Sense of Destiny. Vision/Sense of Destiny pertains to one's feeling or perception that there is a plan for one's life, regardless of whether that plan is dictated by fate, self, or a superhuman (e.g., supernatural) being. It is literally a vision for how one's life will proceed—a sense that there is a destiny that one must fulfill. This co-cognitive factor is the least researched component of Operation Houndstooth, yet the life histories of individuals eminent in their respective fields strongly suggest that vision and a sense of destiny are integral to the development of extraordinarily high levels of performance and success. While identification and description of the characteristics setting these individuals apart from simple performance or success is difficult, the manifestation of those characteristics is quite obvious. Given the difficulty in identifying and describing characteristics that highlight the contributions and level of commitment of such individuals, it is not surprising that quantifying and defining those characteristics are far from accomplished.

Despite the dearth of research literature in these areas, possible components of these factors seem to be emerging from a few well-researched areas of psychology and education. These include achievement motivation, competence motivation, locus of control, intrinsic motivation, self-determination theory, and self-regulation theory (Ambrose, 2000; Rea, 2000; Rotter, 1966; Ryan & Deci, 2000; Schwartz, 2000; Wicker, Lambert, Richardson, & Kahler, 1984; Williams, 1998; Wong & Csikszentmihalyi, 1991). Internal locus of control (Rotter, 1990) and competence motivation (White, 1959) appear to lead to intrinsic motivation and self-determination theory (Ryan & Deci, 2000). Almost all of the research on gifted contributors to all walks of life points out that eminent individuals possess an urge not to settle, conform, or become complacent. In fact, having a sense of direction, destiny, or purpose was found to be integral in studies of gifted women who achieved eminence (Reis, 1995, 1998). Research on eminent individuals consistently recognizes the task commitment of these individuals for continuing their efforts, sometimes under the most adverse circumstances.

Work with self-determination theory has highlighted a positive correlation with vitality (Nix et al., 1999), emphasizing the interrelationship between having a sense of destiny, or purpose, and possessing or being willing to commit to high levels of energy. However, it is important to note that some researchers, such as Schwartz (2000), see excessive emphasis on self-determination as indicative of too much freedom—too much focus on the individual. The result is lack of cultural constraints and perhaps lack of social connection. Critics such as Schwartz cite excessive self-determination as a plausible correlate with dissatisfaction with life and with increased incidences of clinical depression.

Finally, Bandura (1997) suggested that people have the power to use purposeful thought to actively control their lives. He says that this power includes the abilities to program and re-program the subconscious, to select goals, and to filter—in a discriminating way—what gets pulled from the subconscious into the conscious realm.

In summary, these six co-cognitive factors and the connections they hold with social capital, life satisfaction, success, well-being, and happiness are essential to fully understanding the development of potential. The co-cognitive factors are influenced by personality, ultimately limited by cognitive ability, and simultaneously influence and respond to life's circumstances, while they function, in consort with cognition and self-perception, as vehicles for high levels of performance and success.

RESEARCH ON CO-COGNITIVE FACTORS

Sytsma (2003) found that scale scores for mental/physical energy and optimism were significantly correlated ($.49, p < .01; N = 533$) which is similar to what Snyder (1995) found in his work with hope. Student participation in community-oriented extracurricular activities consistently correlated with courage and sensitivity to human concerns. Interestingly, vision/sense of destiny was inversely related to grade point average (GPA). The full set of six co-cognitive factors was least able to predict GPA in follow-up regression analyses. Given that research has indicated GPA as an unreliable predictor for life success (Renzulli, 1978; Sternberg, 1986), the results from Sytsma's 2003 study may represent the first indication that such unreliability may be empirically corroborated with research on co-cognitive factors. Finally, the study provided initial quantitative evidence that the set of co-cognitive factors is capable of predicting motivation and happiness among high school students. This finding and results from the studies described above point to the fact that the role of co-cognitive factors cannot be ignored when considering what motivates students, what drives commitment, and how abilities can be honed or nurtured

INTERVENTION

The research reviewed in this chapter generally focuses on school-related opportunities and alternatives for the development of positive changes in the development of those co-cognitive factors discussed above. Based on literature reviews, we have divided these approaches into six areas, ranging from what research indicates are the least powerful to the most powerful approaches for making strong attitudinal and behavioral changes in students (Vess & Halbur, 2003). Before reviewing the six approaches, it is important to point out that each approach may contribute in varying degrees to positive growth. Although the first interventions discussed have less power to promote internalization, they may have value as part of a chain of experiences that maximize the effect of each individual level of intervention.

The Rally-Round-the-Flag Approach

This approach, sometimes referred to by others as "the cheerleading method," involves visual displays (posters, banners, bulletin boards) featuring certain values, slogans, or examples of virtuous or desired behaviors. Also included are verbal slogans delivered over the schools' public address system or presented orally in classrooms and at assemblies.

The Gold Star Approach

This approach is not unlike the ways in which we traditionally have rewarded students for good academic work. The approach makes use of techniques such as providing positive reinforcement through merit badges, placement on "citizen-of-the-week" lists, extolling good behavior at award assemblies or other events, and even having students earn points, gold stars, or other tokens that can be exchanged for prizes or privileges. Based on classic behaviorism, the rationale underlying this approach is that positive reinforcement for desirable behaviors will increase the frequency of these behaviors. One prevalent program that utilizes the Gold Star Approach is the Girl Scouts of America. Research regarding the effectiveness of Girl Scouts is varied. Some studies claim that the program helps to enable moral development, while other studies question the efficacy of the program (Dubas & Snider, 1993; Smalt, 1997).

The Teaching-and-Preaching Approach

The direct teaching of noncognitive material is probably the most frequently used method to promote attitudes and behaviors related to character and value development. This approach resembles the kinds of training commonly used over the centuries in religious instruction and in situations in which allegiance to particular ideologies is the goal of persons responsible for the curriculum. The direct teaching approach spans a broad range of techniques ranging from recitation and drills about desirable beliefs and behaviors that require students to repeat back slogans or answer in prescribed ways ("What is meant by honesty?"), to dialogue, discussions, and debate about character- or value-laden issues. The direct teaching approach might include discussions based on fiction, films and videos, or examinations of personal characteristics or decision points in the lives of noteworthy persons portrayed in biographies, autobiographies, or other nonfiction genres.

The Vicarious Experience Approach

This approach is often used as an extension of direct teaching; however, it uses techniques that place students in situations in which they are expected to experience a particular personal or emotional reaction to situations where a specified noncognitive goal is being pursued. Role-playing, dramatization, and simulations of significant or critical incidents are examples of the Vicarious Experience Approach. The rationale underlying this approach is that deep and enduring effects on attitudes, values, or character must be experienced at a more active and participatory level than merely learning about them through general awareness or direct teaching.

Direct Involvement—I

Many people believe that the best way to internalize noncognitive characteristics is to provide young people with experiences in which they come into direct contact with situations and events where affective behaviors are taking place. Commonly referred to as "service-learning," it includes community service, internships that deal with provisions for helping others or remediating injurious events, and participation in events where social or political action is being formulated or taking place.

Direct Involvement—II

This type of direct involvement consists of situations in which young people take an *active leadership role* to bring about some kind of positive social, educational, environmental, or political change—especially change that promotes justice, peace, or more harmonious relations between individuals and groups. In most instances, the fact that a young person has made a personal commitment to pursue a change-oriented course of action means that certain positive attitudes or values are already present, but putting the values or character traits into action helps to solidify and deepen the commitment to particular beliefs. The rationale for this type of involvement is that a deep internalization of positive attitudes and attendant behaviors has a more enduring influence on developing wisdom, a satisfying lifestyle, and a lifelong value system than quick-fix behavioral changes that may result from experiences that do not culminate in personally fulfilling activities based on action-oriented involvement.

CONCLUSION

Research in psychology, sociology, and anthropology clearly indicates that these co-cognitive traits can be assessed (at varying levels of precision) and that the environment in general, and schooling in particular, can nurture and influence the co-cognitive traits we have identified in Operation Houndstooth. Economists have pointed out the benefits of a reciprocal relationship between material and social capital, and many social, political, spiritual, and educational commentators have indicated that nurturing these traits must become an imperative.

REFERENCES

Albert, R. S. (1975). Toward a behavioral definition of genius. *American Psychologist, 30,*140–151.

Amabile, T. (1983). *The social psychology of creativity*. New York: Springer Verlag.

Ambrose, D. (2000). World-view entrapment: Moral-ethical implications for gifted education. *Journal for the Education of the Gifted, 23,* 159–186.

Aspinwall, L. G., & Brunhart, S. M. (2000). What I do know won't hurt me: Optimism, attention to negative information, coping, and health. In J. E. Gillham (Ed.), *The science of optimism and hope: Research essays in honor of Martin E. P. Seligman* (pp. 163–200). Philadelphia: US Press.

Bandura, A. (1997). *Self-efficacy: The exercise of control.* New York: Freeman.

Battistich, B., Watson, M., Solomon, D., Schaps, E., & Solomon, J. (1991). The child development project: Program for the development of prosocial character. In W. Kurtines & J. Gewirtz (Eds.), *Handbook of moral behavior and development, Volume 3: Application* (pp. 1–34). Hillsdale, NJ: Lawrence Erlbaum.

Beck, A. T., Weissman, A., Lester, D., & Trexler, L. (1974). The measurement of pessimism: The hopelessness scale. *Journal of Consulting and Clinical Psychology, 42,* 861–865.

Berman S. (1997). *Children's social consciousness and the development of social responsibility.* Albany: State University of New York Press.

Bloom, B. S., & Sosniak, L. A. (1981). Talent development vs. schooling. *Educational Leadership, 38,* 86–94.

Bourdieu, P. (1986). The forms of capital. In J. G. Richardson (Ed.), *Handbook of theory and research for the sociology of education* (pp. 241–258). New York: Greenwood Press.

Bourdieu, P., & Passeron, J. (1977). *Reproduction in education, society and culture* (R. Nice, Trans.). London: Sage. (Original work published 1970)

Carver, C. S., & Scheier, M. F. (2003). Three human strengths. In L. G. Aspinwall & U. M. Staudinger (Eds.), *A psychology of human strengths: Fundamental questions and future directions for a positive psychology* (pp. 87–102). Washington, DC: American Psychological Association.

Csikszentmihalyi, M. (1990). *Flow: The psychology of optimal experience.* New York: HarperCollins.

Csikszentmihalyi, M. (1996). *Creativity: Flow and the psychology of discovery and invention.* New York: HarperCollins.

Cullum, L. (1997). *Genius came early: Creativity in the twentieth century.* Fredericksburg, TX: Windsor House.

Danish, S. J., & Kagan, N. (1971). Measurement of affective sensitivity: Toward a valid measure of interpersonal perception. *Journal of Counseling Psychology, 18,* 51–54.

Dubas, J. S., & Snider, B. A. (1993). The role of community-based youth groups in enhancing learning and achievement through nonformal education. In R. M. Lerner (Ed.), *Early adolescence: Perspectives on research, policy, and intervention* (pp. 159–174). Hillsdale, NJ: Lawrence Erlbaum Associates.

Dweck, C. S., & Leggett, E. L. (1988). A social-cognitive approach to motivation and personality. *Psychological Review, 95,* 256–273.

Eisenberg, N., & Miller, P. A. (1987). The relation of empathy to prosocial and related behaviors. *Psychological Bulletin, 101,* 91–119.

Eisenberg, N., & Wang, V. O. (2003). Toward a positive psychology: Social developmental and cultural contributions. In L. G. Aspinwall & U. M. Staudinger (Eds.), *A psychology of human strengths: Fundamental questions and future directions for a positive psychology* (pp. 117–131). Washington, DC: American Psychological Association.

Eisenberg-Berg, N. (1979). Development of children's prosocial moral judgment. *Developmental Psychology, 15,* 128–137.

Elliot, A. J., & Church, M. A. (1997). A hierarchical model of approach and avoidance achievement motivation. *Journal of Personality and Social Psychology, 72,* 218–232.

Gagné, F. (1985). Giftedness and talent: Reexamining a reexamination of the definitions. *Gifted Child Quarterly, 29*, 103–112.

Gardner, H. (1983). *Frames of mind: The theory of multiple intelligences*. New York: Basic Books.

Gardner, H. (1993). *Creating minds: An anatomy of creativity seen through the lives of Freud, Einstein, Picasso, Stravinsky, Eliot, Graham, and Gandhi*. New York: Basic Books.

Goertzel, M. G., Goertzel, V., & Goertzel, T. G. (1978). *Three hundred eminent personalities: A psychosocial analysis of the famous*. San Francisco, CA: Jossey-Bass.

Harackiewicz, J. M., & Elliot, A. J. (1998). The joint effects of target and purpose goals on intrinsic motivation: A mediational analysis. *Personality and Social Psychology Bulletin, 24*, 675–690.

Healy, T. (2004). Social capital: Old hat or new insight? *Irish Journal of Sociology, 13*(1), 5–8.

John-Steiner, V. (1997). *Notebooks of the mind: Explorations of thinking*. New York: Oxford University Press.

Kaufmann, F. (2000). Gifted education and romance of passion. *Communicator, 31*(3), 1.

LaBonte, R. (1999). Social capital and community development: Practitioner emptor. *Australian and New Zealand Journal of Public Health, 23*, 430–433.

Lindholm, C. (1990). *Charisma*. Cambridge, MA: Basil Blackwell.

Locke, E. A., & Latham, G. P. (2002). Building a practically useful theory of goal setting and task motivation. *American Psychologist, 57*, 705–717.

MacKinnon, D. W. (1978). *In search of human effectiveness*. Buffalo, NY: Creative Education Foundation.

Maslow, A. H. (1987). *Motivation and personality* (3rd ed.). New York: Harper & Row.

Mehrabian, A., & Epstein, N. (1972). A measure of emotional empathy. *The Journal of Personality, 40*, 525–543.

Mönks, F. J. (1991). Kann wissenschaftliche argumentation auf aktultät verzichten? [Are scientific arguments dispensable in the discussion on identification of the gifted?] *Zeitschrift für Entwicklungspsychologie und Pädagogische Psychologie, 23*, 232–240.

Moon, S. M. (2000, May). *Personal talent: What is it and how can we study it?* Paper presented at the Fifth Biennial Henry B. and Joycelyn Wallace National Research Symposium on Talent Development, Iowa City, IA.

Nix, G. A., Ryan, R. M., Manly, J. B., & Deci, E. L. (1999). Revitalization through self-regulation: The effects of autonomous and controlled motivation on happiness and vitality. *Journal of Experimental Social Psychology, 35*, 266–284.

Padhee, B., & Das, S. (1987). Reliability of an adapted curiosity scale. *Social Science International, 3*(2), 27–30.

Peterson, C. (2000). The future of optimism. *American Psychologist, 55*, 44–55.

Piechowski, M. M. (1986). The concept of developmental potential. *Roeper Review, 8*, 190–197.

Portes, A. (1998). Social capital: Its origins and applications in modern sociology. *Annual Review of Sociology, 24*, 1–24.

Putnam, R. (1993). *Making democracy work: Civic traditions in modern Italy*. Princeton, NJ: Princeton University Press.

Putnam, R. (1995). Bowling alone: America's declining social capital. *Journal of Democracy, 6*(1), 65–78.

Putman, D. (1997). Psychological courage. *Philosophy, Psychiatry, & Psychology 4*(1), 1–11.

Putnam, R. D. (2000). *Bowling alone: The collapse and revival of American community.* New York: Simon and Schuster.

Rea, D. W. (2000). Optimal motivation for talent development. *Journal for the Education of the Gifted, 23,* 187–216.

Reis, S. M. (1995). Older women's reflections on eminence: Obstacles and opportunities. *Roeper Review, 18,* 66–72.

Reis, S. M. (1998). *Work left undone: Choices and compromises of talented females.* Mansfield Center, CT: Creative Learning Press.

Renzulli, J. S. (1978). What makes giftedness? Re-examining a definition. *Phi Delta Kappan, 60,* 180–184.

Renzulli, J. S. (2002). Expanding the conception of giftedness to include co-cognitive traits and to promote social capital. *Phi Delta Kappan, 84*(1), 33–40, 57–58.

Rhodewalt, R., Morf, C., Hazlett, S., & Fairfield, M. (1991). Self-handicapping: The role of discounting and augmentation in the preservation of self-esteem. *Journal of Personality and Social Psychology, 61,* 122–131.

Rotter, J. B. (1966). Generalized expectancies for internal versus external control of reinforcement. *Psychological Monographs, 81*(1, Whole No. 609).

Rotter, J. B. (1990). Internal versus external control of reinforcement: A case history of a variable. *American Psychologist, 45,* 489–493.

Ryan, R. M., & Deci, E. L. (2000). Self-determination theory and the facilitation of intrinsic motivation, social development, and well-being. *American Psychologist, 55,* 68–78.

Ryff, C. D., & Singer, B. (2003). Ironies of the human condition: Well-being and health on the way to mortality. In L. G. Aspinwall & U. M. Staudinger (Eds.), *A psychology of human strengths: Fundamental questions and future directions for a positive psychology* (pp. 271–288). Washington, DC: American Psychological Association.

Schwartz, B. (2000). Self-determination: The tyranny of freedom. *American Psychologist, 55,* 79–88.

Seligman, M. E. P. (1991). *Learned optimism.* New York: Knopf.

Seligman, M. E. P., & Csikszentmihalyi, M. (2000). Positive psychology. *American Psychologist, 55,* 5–14.

Seligman, M. E. P., Reivich, K., Jaycox, L., & Gillham, J. (1995). *The optimistic child.* New York: Houghton Mifflin.

Smalt, R. H. (1997). *The influence of Girl Scouting as a character-building organization on the moral development of young Girl Scouts.* Unpublished doctoral dissertation, Fordham University.

Snyder, C. R. (1995). Conceptualizing, measuring, and nurturing hope. *Journal of Counseling and Development, 73,* 355–360.

Snyder, C. R., Sympson, S. C., Michael, S. T., & Cheavens, J. (2001). Optimism and hope constructs: Variants on a positive expectancy theme. In E. C. Chang (Ed.), *Optimism and pessimism: Implications for theory, research, and practice* (pp. 101–125). Washington, DC: American Psychological Association.

Snyder, C. R., Sympson, S. C., Ybasco, F. C., Borders, T. F., Babyak, M. A., & Higgins, R. L. (1996). Development and validation of the state hope scale. *Journal of Personality and Social Psychology, 70,* 321–335.

Sternberg, R. J. (1986). Triarchic theory of intellectual giftedness. In R. J. Sternberg & J. E. Davidson (Eds.), *Conceptions of giftedness* (pp. 223–243). New York: Cambridge University Press.

Sternberg, R. J. (1998). A balance theory of wisdom. *Review of General Psychology, 2*, 347–365.

Sternberg, R. J. (2005). WICS: A model of giftedness in leadership. *Roeper Review, 28*, 37–44.

Sytsma, R. E. (2003). *Co-cognitive factors and socially-constructive giftedness: distribution, abundance, and relevance among high school students.* Unpublished doctoral dissertation, University of Connecticut, Storrs.

Tannenbaum, A. J. (1986). Giftedness: A psychosocial approach. In R. J. Sternberg & J. E. Davidson (Eds.), *Conceptions of giftedness* (pp. 21–52). New York: Cambridge University Press.

Tiger, L. (1979). *Optimism: The biology of hope.* New York: Simon & Schuster.

Vess, K. A., & Halbur, D. A. (2003). *Character education: What counselor educators need to know.* Greensboro, NC: ERIC Counseling and Student Services Clearinghouse. (ERIC Document Reproduction Service No. ED475389)

White, R. (1959). Motivation reconsidered: The concept of competence. *Psychological Review, 66*, 297–333.

Wicker, F. W., Lambert, F. B., Richardson, F. C., & Kahler, J. (1984). Categorical goal hierarchies and classification of the human motives. *Journal of Personality, 52*, 285–305.

Williams, J. (1998). Self-concept–performance congruence: An exploration of patterns among high-achieving adolescents. *Journal for the Education of the Gifted, 21*, 415–422.

Wong, M. M., & Csikszentmihalyi, M. (1991). Motivation and academic achievement: The effects of personality traits and the quality of experience. *Journal of Personality, 59*, 539–574.

Zahn-Waxler, C., & Radke-Yarrow, M. (1982). The development of altruism: Alternative research strategies. In N. Eisenberg-Berg (Ed.), *The development of prosocial behavior* (pp. 109–37). New York: Academic.

Chapter 22

LEVELS OF SERVICE

Stephen T. Schroth

INTRODUCTION

chool leaders elect to implement particular gifted education program models with the belief they are to provide an enhanced education to the gifted and talented students with whom they work. Indeed, although many question the value of providing gifted services, studies consistently have demonstrated that gifted students who receive *any* level of services achieve at higher levels than their gifted peers who receive none (Delcourt, Loyd, Cornell, & Goldberg, 1994; Kulik, 2003). But, the question of the effectiveness of various gifted program models persists. The questions that emerge from both the practitioner and the research literature include:

- Do particular gifted program models have better-documented student outcomes than others?
- Are some gifted program models more effective with certain populations of students than others?

- Have some program models worked better with younger, or older, age groups than others?

A substantial amount of research has been conducted addressing these questions, but with uneven attention to some of the variables. This chapter shall examine the research on the following categories of gifted education services: integrated classroom support, cluster grouping, pull-out programs, special classes for gifted students, and special schools. Because each gifted program model can lead to different results, decision-makers should review the results with their goals in mind.

INTEGRATED CLASSROOM SUPPORT

Integrated classroom support refers to those gifted education services that are provided by the students' regular classroom teacher, with or without the assistance of a gifted education specialist. Integrated classroom support, also known as *within-class services*, has enjoyed a recent surge in popularity for a variety of reasons, including the goals of improving nongifted students' access to quality resources (Tomlinson et al., 2002), increasing the proportion of time during which gifted students' receive services (Landrum, 2001), and achieving cost savings through reducing the number of specialized personnel needed to serve the gifted (VanTassel-Baska, 1992). Such goals make integrated classroom support an attractive option to many school leaders.

Although the motives of its proponents are compelling, integrated classroom support has a weak research base to support its use. Indeed, an extensive study concerning integrated classroom support found that all other levels of service (pull-out, special classes, or special schools) demonstrated higher academic achievement amongst gifted students (Delcourt et al., 1994). Gifted students in pull-out programs, special classes, or special schools, "showed higher levels of achievement than students from within-class programs" (Delcourt et al., 1994, p. 4). Historically, many attempts to eliminate gifted education have later been reversed due to the failures of some teachers to adequately accommodate gifted students (McDaniel, 2002). Learning environments that neglect to offer an appropriate level of challenge have been cited in self-reported surveys of gifted students as a reason for low motivation (Gentry & Springer, 2002).

In making decisions to choose integrated classroom support, school leaders should be cognizant of the paucity of research supporting this position. In addition, the call for heterogeneous grouping as an antidote to inequities, for example, is based on ethnographic studies rather than experimental studies of effects (see, e.g., Oakes, 1985; Sapon-Shevin, 1994, 1996; Wells & Oakes, 1996). The curricular and instructional differences that are observed in those reports that are critical of other grouping arrangements may "represent appropriate responses to the different educational and emotional needs of different school children" (Kulik, 2003, p. 277). Although certain case studies and evaluations have highlighted individual schools where in-class services were effective, these schools have used out-of-the-classroom collaborative resource teachers who worked with regular classroom teachers to craft instruction for gifted students (Kane & Henning, 2004; Landrum, 2001).

Providing within-class gifted services theoretically demands teachers skilled at working with gifted students in *every* classroom, or at least in every classroom to which gifted students are assigned. Callahan (2001) suggested that provision of high-quality education to gifted learners in the regular classroom demands: (1) serious commitment of time, energy, and funds; (2) teacher expertise in, and in-depth understanding of, the discipline content, processes, and products; (3) administrative commitment; and (4) a focus on the needs of all gifted students. Very little research documents the existence of these abilities across the teacher population, and some research indicates that teachers lack the skill and/or the will to provide such services (Moon, Callahan, & Tomlinson, 1995).

Robinson (1990, 1991, 2003) noted some negative effects of heterogeneous grouping options in her observations that gifted students grow tired of the expectations that they must "carry" other students assigned to their groups and engage in coping mechanisms to avoid this. Specifically, studies have demonstrated that gifted students respond to the *sucker effect*, or the understanding that they are carrying a greater share of the group's work, by reducing their own efforts for subsequent projects (Robinson, 2003).

CLUSTER GROUPING

Cluster grouping, a specific refinement of the integrated classroom support or pure heterogeneous grouping model, refers to the program model where gifted students receive services grouped with other gifted students in a regular education classroom. In several studies, cluster grouping has resulted in benefits for gifted students (Delcourt & Evans, 1994; Feldhusen & Moon 1992; Kulik & Kulik, 1992; Reis, Gentry, & Maxfield, 1998; Schuler, 1998). In correlational analyses of multiple studies of cluster grouping, within-class programs in elementary and middle schools resulted in increased achievement scores for gifted students, as well as the other students in the classroom (Kulik, 1992, 2003). Cluster grouping also may have financial benefits, as it allows for increased services for gifted students without the additional cost of a gifted education specialist *if* all teachers are sufficiently trained and willing to work with groups of gifted students in their classrooms (Gentry & Owen, 1999; LaRose, 1986; Winebrenner & Devlin, 1998). Schools that use cluster grouping also witness an increase in the number of students identified as gifted, which may indicate that some students thrive when higher ability peers are not in the classroom (Gentry & Owen, 1999).

Implementing cluster grouping at a school involves going through a three-step process (Gentry, 1999; Gentry & Owen, 1999). Guidelines that have evolved from the study of cluster grouping include:

1. school administrators place three to ten students, identified as gifted, high-achieving, or high-ability, in a single classroom (Gentry & Owen, 1999);
2. the classroom teacher and students must accept that the grouping has been made so that differentiation may occur (Gentry & Owen, 1999);
3. teachers who serve high-ability clusters should demonstrate the background, training, experience, and expertise to work with gifted students (Gentry & Owen, 1999; Winebrenner & Devlin, 1998).

Each step in the process must be in place for cluster grouping to be effective (Gentry, 1999; Gentry & Keilty, 2004; VanTassel-Baska, 1992).

The notion of cluster grouping offends some teachers, who insist that nongifted students need to work with gifted students so they will have a "model" for their own work and behaviors (Schunk, 1987; VanTassel-Baska, 1992). Such beliefs have been reinforced by supporters of heterogeneous grouping, such as Slavin (1986a), who hypothesized a "Robin Hood" effect for low-ability students working with more-able peers, where the gifted students serve others less fortunate in the learning process. This belief, although passionately held, has not been documented—low-ability students do *not* model their behavior or learning on the behaviors or learning strategies of gifted students (Schunk, 1987). Indeed, nongifted students also show positive benefits from cluster grouping, perhaps because such grouping also allows them to work at *their* instructional levels (Kulik, 1992, 2003; Rogers, 1991). Unfortunately, teacher attitudes can result in cluster grouping failing to serve gifted students adequately even when official policy favors grouping the gifted together (Blanksby, 1999). Planning and preparation on the part of school leaders can correct such attitudes, however. At one school where cluster grouping was studied, for example, its effectiveness was enhanced when increased planning time and professional development were provided to the classroom teachers responsible for its implementation (Blanksby, 1999).

PULL-OUT PROGRAMS

Pull-out programs, where students leave their regular classroom to work with a specialist trained in gifted education in a separate room, represent a common form of gifted education (Swiatek & Lupkowski-Shoplik, 2003). In a survey of more than 4,500 third through sixth graders scoring at or above the 95th percentile on standardized achievement tests, for example, 40% of these students received pull-out services, more than any other type of service (Swiatek & Lupkowski-Shoplik, 2003). Although pull-out programs often are criticized as elitist and unnecessary, a meta-analysis conducted by Vaughan, Feldhusen, and Asher (1991) showed significantly greater gains for students enrolled in such programs in achievement and thinking skills than did their gifted peers who received no services (Feldhusen & Moon, 1992; Vaughan et al., 1991). Pull-out programs also are seen as a way of supporting gifted students' social and emotional needs, especially when those are not met in the general education classroom (Peine, 2003; Robinson, 2003; Silverman, 1997). Each of these benefits will be addressed.

How pull-out programs affect gifted students' academic performance has been the focus of numerous studies (e. g., Kulik, 1992, 2003; Rogers, 1991). After examining many studies related to pull-out programs, for example, Rogers (1991) concluded that such grouping produced an academic *effect size*[1] of .65, which is reflected in general achievement, creativity, and critical thinking skills. Similarly, Kulik (1992) examined 25 studies that explored the use of enrichment pull-out programs for gifted and talented students. Gifted and talented students who enjoyed such pull-out sessions outperformed gifted and talented students who did not participate in pull-out programs by ".41 standard deviations, equivalent to about four months on a grade-equivalent scale," as measured by standardized achievement tests (Kulik, 2003, p. 275). Additionally, because the pull-out sessions focused on enrichment, rather than acceleration, Kulik's (2003) findings suggest that gifted and talented students have a need for instruction that focuses on depth and complexity, rather than mere skill-focused exercises. This buttresses other studies, which have found that gifted and talented students learn better in less-structured environments and prosper when indirect and unstructured teaching methods are used (Feldhusen & Moon, 1992; National Research Council, 2000; Snow, 1989).

Interacting with others with similar intellectual skills as provided by pull-out programs has been documented in case study reports as important for gifted and talented students' social and emotional development. In a qualitative study of 16 students enrolled in a pull-out program for the gifted and talented, students articulated dissatisfaction with the pace and depth of instruction in their regular classroom and also emphasized that they welcomed the opportunity to work with cognitive peers, which reduced feelings of isolation and frustration (Peine, 2003). These feelings of isolation are especially sensitive and complex for gifted students who are members of ethnic or language minority groups (Kyburg, 2006), who may relish the intellectual compatibility, but have difficulty with racial isolation. Recent examinations of Advanced Placement (AP) and International Baccalaureate (IB) programs, for example, provided some evidence of the particular issues faced by minority students when grouped separately, particularly when the minority group is not well-represented (Kyburg, 2006). Although "minority students in this study reported that they especially liked being in classes with intellectual peers," they also "expressed an apprecia-

---

1   Examining effect size is the preferred means for reporting research results (Paul & Plucker, 2004). Effect size was described by Cohen (1988) as small, medium, and large, with each category being approximately .20, .50, and .80 respectively. Large effect sizes, however, are generally not encountered in educational studies, where a .30 is considered substantial (Pedhazur & Schmelkin, 1991).

tion of having fellow minority students in their classes (Kyburg, 2006, p. 127). Those making decisions that involve removing minority students from their regular classroom setting would be well served to consider, and plan for, these dual social pressures.

Pull-out groups may reduce the negative impact of heterogeneous grouping that Robinson noted (see above) at least for that time gifted students are working with their cognitive peers and forced to produce more due to increased group standards for performance and/or competition (Robinson, 1990, 2003).

Popular belief relates that pull-out programs make students enrolled feel "odd" and out of place with classmates (Davis & Rimm, 2003). When Cohen, Duncan, and Cohen (1994) examined 53 gifted students, however, their findings indicated positive affective results for students enrolled in pull-out programs. The gifted students enrolled in pull-out programs were, relative to classmates, evaluated positively by peers, more aware of the demands of friendship, and perceived less often as victims or aggressors by classmates (Cohen et al., 1994). Similar studies also have indicated better family and home–school relationships resulted for those students enrolled in gifted pull-out programs (Moon, 1995; Moon, Feldhusen, & Dillon, 1994). The self-concept of gifted students, however, is affected when gifted students are placed in situations where they work with their cognitive peers—those gifted students who regularly work with other gifted students have lower self-concept than those gifted students who spend their time in a regular classroom (Marsh, Chessor, Craven, & Roche, 1995; Marsh, Plucker, & Stocking, 2001; Plucker, Taylor, Callahan, & Tomchin, 1997). Such a reaction is not necessarily a bad thing, and indeed can improve gifted students' work ethic (Marsh et al., 1995; Plucker & Stocking, 2001). Further, lower self-concept does not translate into poor self-concept.

SPECIAL CLASSES FOR THE GIFTED

Special classes for gifted students have been used to refer to a wide variety of options, including pull-out groups or Saturday and summer programs. Usually, however, the term is used to describe classes that provide either enriched or accelerated curriculum for more able learners, such as honors or Advanced Placement (AP) or International Baccalaureate (IB) classes (Kulik, 2003). Special classes can refer to self-contained classrooms made up almost exclusively of gifted and talented students at the elementary level (Tsai & Shih, 1997); however, in practice they tend to be used mostly with middle and high school students (Adams-Byers, Whitsell, & Moon, 2004; Gentry & Owen, 2004). Special classes are unpopular with critics of gifted education (Oakes, 1985; Sapon-Shevin, 1996). The literature on special classes presents evidence of both positive academic and social and emotional benefits for gifted students and also raises questions about the impacts of these classes (Adams-Byers et al., 2004; Gentry & Owen, 2004).

In one study of gifted students in special classes, they reported feeling less capable in their level of achievement, greater reluctance to work independently, and less willing to seek challenge than their peers in within-class or pull-out programs (Delcourt et al., 1994). Another study involving 24 gifted fourth- and fifth-grade students found that a self-contained class provided a challenging learning environment to all students, but that not all students responded positively to this challenge (Moon, Swift, & Schallenberger, 2002). Such mixed findings are perhaps predictable, because studying with cognitive peers certainly would increase the performance levels of the gifted children's peers and present new and unfamiliar challenge.

Special classes can, of course, focus on acceleration, enrichment, or both (Kulik, 2003). More than 23 studies have focused on accelerated classes where the entire class received moderate acceleration (Kulik, 2003). These were *not* cases where individuals received tailored instruction, but classes that moved at a faster pace (Kulik, 2003). In all of the cases examined by Kulik (1992), gifted students in accelerated classes performed one full standard deviation better on achievement tests than their gifted peers who did not receive acceleration. This amounted to accelerated gifted students outperforming gifted nonaccelerated students by a full year's progress on a grade-equivalent scale (Kulik, 1992). Such results greatly strengthen the argument for those advocating for special classes for gifted students. Indeed, with gifted students removed from the mix, *all* classes are able to provide instruction better linked to students' zones of proximal development (Kulik, 1992, 2003). Rather than impede those students who are not in special classes, such offerings improve the instruction offered to all students.

SPECIAL SCHOOLS

The term *special schools* generally refers to public schools set up to focus on a specific disciplinary area such as math, science, technology, or the performing arts (although all subjects are taught; Borland, Schnur, & Wright, 2000; Sethna, Wickstrom, Boothe, & Stanley, 2001; Subotnik, 2002). Some of these schools may be residential. Other special schools also have been specifically established to meet the learning needs of the gifted in the broad educational realm (Borland et al., 2000; Coleman, 2005). Many recent studies examining these schools often have been qualitative in nature, with an emphasis on how interacting with other gifted children on a daily basis changes students' experiences and motivation. Other studies also have examined aspects of special schools and how studying or teaching in one affects students' learning experiences.

As measured by achievement tests, gifted students enrolled in special schools outperform all of their gifted peers in other learning environments except those students enrolled in special classes, who perform equally well (Delcourt et al., 1994; Kulik, 2003). In terms of achievement, a major study of special schools found that gifted children attending special schools for gifted students performed better than gifted peers not in programs (Delcourt et al., 1994). Other studies, conducted in a variety of settings, also illustrate that gifted students enrolled in special or magnet schools frequently perform at a high level of achievement (see, e.g., Clark & Zimmerman, 2001, 2002; Evered & Nayer, 2000; Sullivan & Rebhorn, 2002). Some of these studies are limited, however, in not using control groups that could provide stronger experimental evidence of the effects of enrollment at the special school and a high level of performance. Recent qualitative studies *have* suggested that, for the students enrolled at the schools studied, students' educational opportunities seem to be improved through attendance at special or magnet schools.

Gifted students enrolled in special schools report experiencing greater levels of challenge than gifted students in other settings (Gentry, Rizza, & Owen, 2002) A recent study examined the level of challenge presented to gifted learners in regular classrooms as opposed to that provided in special or magnet schools (Gentry et al., 2002). Students from both settings, at both the elementary and middle school level, were asked to report their perceptions of the level of challenge required by their classroom activities (Gentry et al., 2002). Although elementary students did not report a significant difference in the level of challenge received between regular and special or magnet schools, middle school students at special or magnet schools reported significantly more challenge than did their peers enrolled in regular middle schools (Gentry et al., 2002). Such findings are limited, of course, by the nature of self-report data and the risk that students have heard parents, administrators, or teachers refer to their schools' "high level of challenge," and merely repeated these comments in response to questions regarding their placements. Despite this, the qualitative studies provide descriptive evidence of the types of experiences that can happen as a result of a special school.

Coleman (2005), for example, spent a year at a state-sponsored residential school for students gifted in math, science, and technology, conducting ethnographic research relating to the students' experiences at the school. After observing, interviewing, and analyzing the school, Coleman determined that academic rigor and diversity available only in a special environment changed students' lives. Specifically, Coleman found that gifted students enrolled at the special school were better able to meet and tackle new ideas than were their peers enrolled in regular high school settings.

Coleman (2005) also concluded openness and acceptance were related to academic rigor and diversity and were significant due to the novelty of rigor and diversity for most of the special school's students. Rigorous academic demands threw many students off balance, because "many have never had to study and few really know how to do it" (Coleman, 2005, p. 27). As one student explained, "At home I did my homework all in class and I got straight A's. Here, I do homework and I study and I get mostly B's" (p. 36). The unyielding demands of homework and studying caused students at the school to adjust their outlooks and work patterns (Coleman, 2005). Student perspectives relating to the value of such schools are valuable, especially because special schools' critics often attack demonstrated achievement as being the result of selection practices (cf. Oakes, 1985; Sapon-Shevin, 1994). Special schools *can* result in environments where test scores and achievement are valued above other accomplishments (see, e.g., Humes, 2003). Where a general education setting has proven inadequate for certain gifted students' learning needs, however, special schools seem a valid and appropriate option.

Special schools enjoy limited appeal because, except for very large or very wealthy school districts, they are impractical in terms of expense and logistics. It is important to note that students enrolled in special classes within a school essentially enjoy the same boost in achievement. With the recent focus on smaller schools at the middle and secondary levels, such schools may be more practicable for many districts that have not been able to make such an investment to date.

FUTURE RESEARCH

More research is necessary regarding how differing levels of services affect certain groups. Little or no data, for example, exists that examines how differences in student ethnic groups, age, or sex influence the appropriateness of a given option for certain students. Although certain studies, such as those of Delcourt et al. (1994), specifically controlled for student ability levels, many studies that examine grouping or service options do not (e.g., Slavin, 1986b). Statements made about certain options often do not delineate their appropriateness for certain populations of gifted students. Those making program decisions also must consider the resources and realities of a given school district. Choices made must vary from district to district due to variations in population, funding, organizational structure, community values, personnel, and school culture. As a result, some of the options with the least research support may be the most appropriate option for one district, while other options, although proven, are not a good fit for its particular population.

QUESTIONS THAT REMAIN

Although important decisions made about the levels of service provided to gifted students often are based on philosophical or fiscal reasons, most of the research conducted to date indicates that gifted students in separate classes or special schools outperform their gifted peers in all other settings (Delcourt et al., 1994). Gifted students who receive any type of gifted services, however, outperform their gifted peers who do not receive such services (Kulik, 2003). Much research needs to be conducted, including,

- Do newer models for within-class gifted services perform better than earlier models that attempted to provide this?

- What are the relative costs of the levels of service when compared to the results they deliver?
- Is there a relationship between the models and identification of gifted students, and the effects of differing program and identification models?
- Are gifted students from various subgroups affected differentially by different levels of service?
- Are special schools and classes more "successful" because they use a different identification process?
- Do differing levels of staff development relate to differing outcomes in each level of service?
- Which methods of supporting classroom teachers who serve gifted students in any program model would provide the greatest achievement within class or pull-out programs?
- What training relates to positive effects in schools with special classes for the gifted or in districts with special schools?
- Do teachers and school leaders possess the skills to effectively serve gifted learners in the regular education classroom, and can they learn and implement those skills given the current pressures on the general education program?

Although the extant research provides a wealth of information regarding levels of service, much more remains to be done. Part of the reason the research is spotty is because until very recently, schools did not focus extensively on research-based practices. With the recent sea change regarding the role of research in selecting program models, much needs to be done to justify many practices currently in vogue.

REFERENCES

Adams-Byers, J., Whitsell, S. S., & Moon, S. M. (2004). Gifted students' perceptions of the academic and social/emotional effects of homogeneous and heterogeneous grouping. *Gifted Child Quarterly, 48*, 7–20.

Blanksby, D. C. (1999). Not quite eureka: Perceptions of a trial of cluster grouping as a model for addressing the diverse range of student abilities in a junior secondary school. *Educational Studies, 25*(1), 79–88.

Borland, J. H., Schnur, R., & Wright, L. (2000). Economically disadvantaged students in a school for the academically gifted: A postpositivist inquiry into individual and family adjustment. *Gifted Child Quarterly, 44*, 13–32.

Callahan, C. M. (2001). Fourth down and inches. *Journal of Secondary Gifted Education, 12*, 148–156.

Clark, G., & Zimmerman, E. (2001). Identifying artistically talented students in four rural communities in the United States. *Gifted Child Quarterly, 45*, 104–144.

Clark, G., & Zimmerman, E. (2002). Tending the special spark: Accelerated and enriched curricula for highly talented art students. *Roper Review, 24*, 161–168.

Cohen, J. (1988). *Statistical power analysis for the behavioral sciences* (2nd ed.). Hillsdale, NJ: Lawrence Erlbaum.

Cohen, R., Duncan, M., & Cohen, S. (1994). Classroom peer relations of children participating in a pull-out enrichment program. *Gifted Child Quarterly, 38,* 33–37.

Coleman, L. J. (2005). *Nurturing talent in high school: Life in the fast lane.* New York: Teachers College Press.

Davis, G. A., & Rimm, S. B. (2003). *Education of the gifted and talented* (5th ed.). Needham Heights, MA: Allyn & Bacon.

Delcourt, M. A. B., & Evans, K. (1994). *Qualitative extension of the learning outcomes study* (Research Monograph No. 94110). Storrs: National Research Center on the Gifted and Talented, University of Connecticut.

Delcourt, M. A. B., Loyd, B. H., Cornell, D. G., & Goldberg, M. D. (1994). *Evaluation of the effects of programming arrangements on student learning outcomes* (Research Monograph No. 94108). Storrs: National Research Center on the Gifted and Talented, University of Connecticut.

Evered, L., & Nayer, S. (2000). Novosibirsk's school for the gifted: Changing emphases in the new Russia. *Roeper Review, 23,* 22–24.

Feldhusen, J. F., & Moon, S. M. (1992). Grouping gifted students: Issues and concerns. *Gifted Child Quarterly, 36,* 63–67.

Gentry, M. L. (1999). *Promoting student achievement and exemplary classroom practices through cluster grouping: A research-based alternative to heterogeneous elementary classrooms.* Storrs: National Research Center on the Gifted and Talented, University of Connecticut.

Gentry, M., & Keilty, B. (2004). Rural and suburban cluster grouping: Reflections on staff development as a component of program success. *Roeper Review, 26,* 147–155.

Gentry, M., & Owen, S. V. (1999). An investigation of the effects of total school flexible cluster grouping on identification, achievement, and classroom practices. *Gifted Child Quarterly, 43,* 224–243.

Gentry, M., & Owen, S. V. (2004). Secondary student perceptions of classroom quality: Instrumentation and differences between advanced/honors and nonhonors classes. *Journal of Secondary Gifted Education, 16,* 20–29.

Gentry, M., Rizza, M. G., & Owen, S. V. (2002). Examining perceptions of challenge and choice in classrooms: The relationship between teachers and their students and comparisons between gifted students and other students. *Gifted Child Quarterly, 46,* 145–155.

Gentry, M., & Springer, P. M. (2002). Secondary student perceptions of their class activities regarding meaningfulness, challenge, choice, and appeal: An initial validation study. *Journal of Secondary Gifted Education, 13,* 192–204.

Humes, E. (2003). *School of dreams: Making the grade at a top American high school.* Orlando, FL: Harcourt.

Kane, J., & Henning, J. E. (2004). A case study of the collaboration in mathematics between a fourth-grade teacher and a talented and gifted coordinator. *Journal for the Education of the Gifted, 27,* 243–266.

Kulik, J. A. (1992). *An analysis of the research on ability grouping: Historical and contemporary perspectives* (Research Monograph No. 9204). Storrs: National Research Center on the Gifted and Talented, University of Connecticut.

Kulik, J. A. (2003). Grouping and tracking. In N. Colangelo & G. A. Davis (Eds.), *Handbook of gifted education* (2nd ed., pp. 268–281). Boston: Allyn & Bacon.

Kulik, J. A., & Kulik, C. C. (1992). Meta-analytic findings on grouping programs. *Gifted Child Quarterly, 36,* 73–77.

Kyburg, R. M. (2006). *Minority adolescents in Advanced Placement and International Baccalaureate programs.* Doctoral dissertation, University of Virginia.

Landrum, M. S. (2001). An evaluation of the catalyst program: Consultation and collaboration in gifted education. *Gifted Child Quarterly, 45,* 139–151.

LaRose, B. (1986). The lighthouse program: A longitudinal research project. *Journal for the Education of the Gifted, 9,* 224–232.

Marsh, H. W., Chessor, D., Craven, R., & Roche, L. (1995). The effects of gifted and talented programs on academic self-concept: The big fish strikes again. *American Educational Research Journal, 32,* 285–319.

Marsh, H. W., Plucker, J., & Stocking, V. B. (2001). The Self-Description Questionnaire II and gifted students: Another look at Plucker, Taylor, Callahan & Tomchin's (1997) "Mirror, mirror on the wall." *Educational and Psychological Measurement, 61,* 976–996.

McDaniel, T. R. (2002). Mainstreaming the gifted: Historical perspectives on equity and excellence. *Roeper Review, 24,* 112–114.

Moon, S. M. (1995). The effects of an enrichment program on the families of participants: A multiple-case study. *Gifted Child Quarterly, 39,* 198–208.

Moon, T. R., Callahan, C. M., & Tomlinson, C. A. (1995). *Academic diversity in the middle school: Results of a national survey of middle school administrators and teachers* (Research Monograph No. 95124). Storrs: National Research Center on the Gifted and Talented, University of Connecticut.

Moon, S. M., Feldhusen, J. F., & Dillon, D. R. (1994). Long-term effects of an enrichment program based on the Purdue three-stage model. *Gifted Child Quarterly, 38,* 38–48.

Moon, S. M., Swift, M., & Schallenberger, A. (2002). Perceptions of a self-contained class for fourth- and fifth-grade students with high to extreme levels of intellectual giftedness. *Gifted Child Quarterly, 46,* 64–79.

National Research Council. (2000). *How people learn: Brain, mind, experience, and school.* Washington, DC: National Academy Press.

Oakes, J. (1985). *Keeping track: How schools structure inequality.* New Haven, CT: Yale University Press.

Paul, K. M., & Plucker, J. (2004). Two steps forward, one step back: Effect size reporting in gifted education research from 1995–2000. *Roeper Review, 26,* 68–72.

Pedhazur, E. J., & Schmelkin, L. P. (1991). *Measurement, design, and analysis: An integrated approach.* Hillsdale, NJ: Lawrence Erlbaum.

Peine, M. E. (2003). Doing grounded theory research with gifted students. *Journal for the Education of the Gifted, 26,* 184–200.

Plucker, J., & Stocking, V. (2001). Looking outside and inside: Self-concept development of gifted adolescents. *Exceptional Children, 67,* 535–548.

Plucker, J. A., Taylor, J. W., V, Callahan, C. M., & Tomchin, E. M. (1997). Mirror, mirror, on the wall: Reliability and validity evidence for the Self Description Questionnaire–II with gifted students. *Educational and Psychological Measurement, 57,* 704–713.

Reis, S. M., Gentry, M., & Maxfield, L. R. (1998). The application of enrichment clusters to teachers' classroom practices. *Journal for the Education of the Gifted, 21,* 310–334.

Robinson, A. (1990). Cooperation or exploitation? The argument against cooperative learning for talented students. *Journal for the Education of the Gifted, 14*(1), 9–27.

Robinson, A. (1991). *Cooperative learning and the academically talented student* (Research-Based Decision Making Series No. 9106). Storrs: National Research Center on the Gifted and Talented, University of Connecticut.

Robinson, A. (2003). Cooperative learning and high-ability students. In N. Colangelo & G. A. Davis (Eds.), *Handbook of gifted education* (2nd ed., pp. 282–292). Boston: Allyn & Bacon.

Rogers, K. B. (1991). *The relationship of grouping practices to the education of the gifted and talented learner* (Research Monograph No. 9102). Storrs: National Research Center on the Gifted and Talented, University of Connecticut.

Sapon-Shevin, M. (1994). *Playing favorites: Gifted education and the disruption of community*. Albany, NY: State University of New York Press.

Sapon-Shevin, M. (1996). Beyond gifted education: Building a shared agenda for school reform. *Journal for the Education of the Gifted, 19*, 194–214.

Schuler, P. A. (1998). *Cluster grouping coast-to-coast*. Storrs: National Research Center on the Gifted and Talented, University of Connecticut.

Schunk, D. H. (1987). Peer models and children's behavioral change. *Review of Educational Research, 52*, 149–174.

Sethna, B. N., Wickstrom, C. D., Boothe, D., & Stanley, J. C. (2001). The Advanced Academy of Georgia: Four years as a residential early-college entrance program. *Journal of Secondary Gifted Education, 13*, 11–21.

Silverman, L. S. (1997). The construct of asynchrony. *Peabody Journal of Education, 72*(3–4), 36–58.

Slavin, R. E. (1986a). Best-evidence synthesis: An alternative to meta-analytic and traditional reviews. *Educational Researcher, 15*(9), 5–11.

Slavin, R. E. (1986b). *Ability grouping and student achievement in elementary schools: A best-evidence synthesis*. Baltimore, MD: Center for Research on Elementary and Middle Schools.

Snow, R. E. (1989). Aptitude treatment interaction as a framework for research on individual differences in learning. In P. L. Ackerman, R. J. Sternberg, & R. Glaser (Eds.), *Learning and individual differences* (pp. 513–591). New York: W. H. Freeman.

Subotnik, R. F. (2002). Talent developed: Conversations with the masters in the arts and sciences—Eliot Feld. *Journal for the Education of the Gifted, 25*, 290–302.

Sullivan, S. C., & Rebhorn, L. (2002). PEGS: Appropriate education for exceptionally gifted students. *Roeper Review, 24*, 221–225.

Swiatek, M. A., & Lupkowski-Shoplik, A. (2003). Elementary and middle school student participation in gifted programs: Are gifted students underserved? *Gifted Child Quarterly, 47*, 118–130.

Tomlinson, C. A., Kaplan, S. N., Renzulli, J. S., Purcell, J., Leppien, J., & Burns, D. (2002). *The parallel curriculum: A design to develop high potential and challenge high-ability learners*. Thousand Oaks, CA: Corwin Press.

Tsai, D. M., & Shih, Y. S. (1997). *Gifted education in Taiwan: Services, problems and challenges* (Report No. DGE-EC-305626). Reston, VA: The Council for Exceptional Children. (ERIC Document Reproduction Service No. ED346082)

VanTassel-Baska, J. (1992). Educational decision making on acceleration and grouping. *Gifted Child Quarterly, 36*, 68–72.

Vaughan, V. L., Feldhusen, J. F., & Asher, J. W. (1991). Meta-analyses and review of research on pull-out programs in gifted education. *Gifted Child Quarterly, 35*, 92–105.

Wells, A. S., & Oakes, J. (1996). Potential pitfalls of systemic reform: Early lessons from research on detracking [Special issue]. *Sociology of Education, 69,* 135–143.

Winebrenner, S., & Devlin, B. (1998). Cluster grouping of gifted students: How to provide full-time services on a part-time budget. *Teaching Exceptional Children, 30*(3), 62–65.

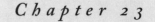

Chapter 23

LIFE EVENTS

Trudy L. Clemons

DEFINITIONS

ignificant life changes (e.g., marriage, divorce, death of a loved one, loss of a job, relocation) are often referred to as major life events or life stressors in the literature (Myers, 1995). Literature and research on life events of children tend to focus on the following: parental divorce, death of a parent, death of a grandparent, death of a sibling, and relocation.

MAJOR QUESTIONS ADDRESSED

There is a minimal amount of research related to the impact of significant life changes on gifted children, therefore limiting the number and types of research questions that are addressed. Researchers have sought to answer the following questions related to gifted students and death in the family, parental divorce, and relocation:

- What is the perceived stressfulness of life stressors such as death in the family and parental divorce among a group of gifted adolescents?
- What is the relationship between parental divorce, longevity, and cause of own death in a group of gifted adults?
- What are the social, emotional, and academic impacts of moving on gifted children?
- What is the relationship between major life events in childhood and adult eminence or creativity?

There is also one review of the literature that looks at research on gifted students to determine the incidence of divorce in families with gifted children (Rogers & Nielson, 1993).

In addition to the research on significant life changes in gifted populations, there is research on the adjustment of gifted students, as well as coping strategies used by gifted students (Derevensky & Coleman, 1989; Reynolds & Bradley, 1983; Scholwinski & Reynolds, 1985; Sowa, McIntire, May, & Bland, 1994; Tomchin, Callahan, Sowa, May, 1996; Tong & Yewchuk, 1996). Findings from research on gifted children's coping strategies could be used to direct research on the impact of significant life events on gifted children. However, the research does not directly address adjustment or coping strategies related to events such as death in the family, relocation, or parental divorce, so these will not be discussed in this chapter.

Clinical reports and case studies are also available, which provide discussions related to counseling gifted students and their families to address developmental issues such as parental loss/divorce and relocation. These reports can lead to theories regarding the needs of gifted children; however, they are not empirical in nature. Some of the reports do provide some detail of family therapy models that have been reported as successful in addressing developmental issues (Moon & Hall, 1998; Moon, Nelson, & Piercy, 1993; Moon & Thomas, 2003).

CONCLUSIONS THAT CAN BE DRAWN FROM THE RESEARCH

In comparison to the research on the impact of life events on all children, the empirical research on the impact of life events on gifted children is very limited. Very few, if any, conclusions can be drawn from research on gifted children. The research that does exist for the gifted population is either dated or based on small and/or very specific populations and therefore it is not generalizable. Due to the limited findings from research on the impact of life events on gifted children, a summary of findings from the general school-age population will be presented along with the findings related to gifted children. The findings from the general school-age population are presented because they may have implications for the types of questions that need to be researched related to the gifted population.

Divorce and Death in the Family

Gifted Students. Karnes and Oehler-Stinnett (1986) investigated 53 seventh-grade gifted students' responses on the Life Events Scale for Adolescents and the Adolescent Life Change Event Scale. The students rated death of parent or sibling as one of the most stressful events. However, the students rated "not being able to take a courses you want" as a more stressful event than remarriage of a parent.

In their review of the literature of studies of families of gifted children, Rogers and Nielson (1993) found that few studies reported information on parents' marital status. Of the studies that did report this information, low rates of divorce and/or separation were found. Only one of the studies included in the review was conducted after the 1970s (it was completed in 1989). Depending on the information provided in the study, the authors present divorce and/or separation rates and/or percentage of children living with both parents for each of the reported studies. Divorce and/or separation rates in the reported studies ranged from 6.3% to 12.5%. Percentage of gifted children living with both parents ranged from 85% to 100%.

Friedman et al. (1995) conducted a follow-up study on the sample of gifted children studied by Terman and Oden (1947). The Friedman et al. (1995) study employed survival analysis to predict the longevity and cause of death in this sample from parental divorce during childhood, unstable marriages in adulthood, and other possible mediating health variables. Their analysis revealed a significant relationship among parental divorce and longevity; the median age at death of men whose parents divorced was 76, whereas men whose parents did not divorce had a median age at death of 80. Women lived to 82 and 86 respectively. The analysis did not reveal a relationship between death of a parent and longevity, but did suggest an interaction among parental divorce, personality, and family stability as related to longevity. This interaction suggests that parental divorce is not the only variable that affects longevity; rather, longevity is related to an interaction among several variables that may include parental divorce.

General School-Age Population. Research suggests that children whose parents divorce are more likely than children from intact families to experience a decrease in academic achievement, an increase in behavior problems, and an increase in emotional problems, and also have a decreased likelihood of attending college (Amato, 1993; Amato & Keith 1991a, 1991b; Zill, Morrison, & Coiro, 1993). The extent to which children of divorced parents experience these adverse affects depends on many factors, such as the stress of the breakup, the relationship of the parents after the divorce, parent-child relationships, peer support, family economic status, and parental resources (Acock & Demo, 1994; Morrison & Cherlin,

1995; Peris & Emery, 2004; Rogers & Rose, 2002; Vandervalk, Spruijt, De Goede, Meeus, & Maas, 2004). The findings from this research suggest that divorce may impact children in many different ways depending on several factors.

Children who experience a death in the family are also impacted in different ways depending on several family factors. They are at greater risk for depression, anxiety, behavior problems, forced increases in maturity, school performance problems, sleep problems, medical problems, and mental health problems (Christ et al., 1993; Christ, Siegel, & Sperber, 1994; Harris, 1991; Lewinsohn, Rohde, & Seeley, 1996; Siegel et al., 1992; Siegel, Raveis, & Karus, 1996; Silverman & Worden, 1992; Valente, Saunders, & Street, 1988; Weller, Weller, Fristad, & Bowes, 1991; Worden, 1996; Worden, Davies, & McCown, 1999). The effect that the death of a family member has on a child varies depending on the level of warmth of the caregiver, the degree to which the child is capable of coping with stress, the parents' coping strategies, changes in health of a family member, additional adults coming to live in the household, the caregiver's mental health, the events that follow the death (i.e., family moves, economic status), and the cause of the family member's death (Elizur & Kaffman, 1982; Raveis, Siegel, Karus, 1999; Silverman & Worden, 1992; Thompson, Kaslow, Price, Williams, & Kingree, 1998; West, Sandler, Pillow, Baca, & Gersten, 1991; Worden, 1996).

Relocation

Gifted Students. In their study of five military families, Plucker, Hill, and Yecke (1999) interviewed parents and children who had moved frequently. The findings suggest that in this sample, although short-term social difficulties were experienced by gifted children, frequent moves had no long-term social, emotional, or academic effects on gifted children. Parents reported frustrations with the inconsistencies in the gifted programming in the different schools, and had developed strategies to cope with difficulties related to their children's education, such as getting to know at least one staff member well at the school.

General School-Age Population. Research suggests a relationship between frequent moves and decreased academic achievement, increased likelihood of dropping out of high school, negative parent–child relationships, increased promiscuity, negative impact on friendship networks, and increased behavioral problems (Haveman, Wolfe, & Spaulding, 1991; Myers, 2005; Pittman & Bowen, 1994; Pribesh & Downey, 1999; South & Haynie, 2004, Stack, 1994). However, many of these relationships are confounded by other variables such as age of the child when he or she experiences the move, level of mobility in the school that the child attends, gender, reason for relocation, structure of family (i.e., two-parent vs. one-parent homes), and parents' attitude about relocating (Myers, 2005; Norford & Medway, 2002; South & Haynie, 2004; Tucker, Marx, & Long, 1998).

Eminence and Creativity

Using historiometric methods, several researchers have suggested a relationship between creativity and/or eminence and traumatic life events, such as loss of a parent (Albert, 1971; Berry, 1981; Eisenstadt, 1978; Eisenstadt, Haynal, Rentchnick, & De Senarclens, 1989; Goertzel, Goertzel, & Goertzel, 1978; Martindale, 1972; Silverman, 1974; Simonton, 1986; Woodward, 1974). Historiometry is "a scientific discipline in which nomothetic hypotheses about human behavior are tested by applying quantitative analyses to data concerning historical individuals" (Simonton, 1990, p. 3). These studies are conducted in order to find trends in history without regard to whether the findings can be generalized to other populations. Researchers using historiometric methods have found that many of the individuals who have been identified as eminent suffered a childhood trauma; however, this relationship was not found in all talent domains. This finding suggests that childhood traumatic events may contribute to the development of some creative potential.

LIMITATIONS OF RESEARCH ON THIS TOPIC

This biggest limitation in research related to significant life changes in gifted populations is the lack of empirical research available on the topic. As stated previously, the findings from the research have limited generalizability due to the date, sample, and methodology of the research. Specifically, there is limited literature or research on the topic published within the last 10 years. Many of the studies use small samples or a sample of children with specific characteristics that may not be found in the general population of gifted children. The studies are also generally descriptive in nature with no comparison groups to determine if gifted children have behaviors different from other children when experiencing life events such as parental divorce, death in the family, or relocation.

PRACTICAL AND RESEARCH IMPLICATIONS

Because the current findings are very limited, there are few practical implications related to the findings, however, there are implications for future research. Further research may lead to findings that have implications for counseling gifted students, gifted student achievement, and identification of gifted students. Research related to the impacts that parental divorce and death in the family have on gifted children may lead to a better understanding of how gifted children cope with these traumatic events, and what, if any, long-term social, emotional and academic effects these events have on gifted children. Findings about gifted children's coping have implications for counselors and therapists working with gifted children. Findings related to social, emotional, and academic affects have implications for teachers and parents of gifted children.

Research on the general school-age population has suggested that students who move more often exhibit lower levels of achievement (United States General Accounting Office, 1994). Also, students from lower income families are more likely to move frequently (Barton, 2003; U.S. Census Bureau, 2003). Therefore, students from lower income families may exhibit lower levels of achievement due to frequent moves. The lower level of achievement of these students may limit their chances of being identified for gifted programming. One finding suggests that as few as 9% of students in gifted programs are in the bottom quartile of family income, whereas 47% are in the top quartile (U.S. Department of Education, 1993). The connection between lower income, relocation, and lower levels of achievement has implications for teachers working with students new to their schools. Teachers must become familiar with these students' prior learning and make sure that any gaps in the students' learning are closed in order to assure that they are successful. Further research is needed in order to determine if students' mobility may be related to identification for gifted programming, and, if so, what can be done to overcome this obstacle.

MAJOR RESOURCES AND REFERENCES

There are only a few major resources on significant life events as related to gifted children. There are a few resources on adolescent grieving and coping with stress that might provide some direction for working with gifted children, and a few resources that provide overviews of relocation with gifted children and counseling gifted children. These include:
- *Handbook of Adolescent Death and Bereavement* (Corr & Balk, 1996);
- *Adolescent Coping: Theoretical and Research Perspectives* (Frydenberg, 1997);
- *"We're Moving Again?" Starting Your Gifted Child in a New School* (Plucker et al., 1998); and
- *Counseling Families* (Moon, 2003).

WHAT THE RESEARCH TELLS US

The following findings are based on research on all school-age children:
- Children may experience adverse consequences in response to the death of a family member, parental divorce, and/ or relocation.

- The extent to which children experience these adverse consequences is dependent on a number of factors related to biological factors, as well as children's school and home environment.

The following finding is based on research on gifted children:
- Gifted children may have different methods of coping with relocation, and therefore may have different experiences related to relocation.

IDEAS FOR FUTURE RESEARCH

The following list contains suggestions for future research:
- Relationship between identification for gifted programming and student mobility: Does the relationship between mobility and lower levels of achievement have an impact on the identification of children from lower level incomes?
- Research with comparison groups in order to determine whether the ability level of a student affects the student's response to life events.
- More multidimensional research that considers the relationship among several variables (i.e., income, gender, age) and the affects of life events.
- More research on students' actual responses to life events rather than perceived responses.

REFERENCES

Acock, A. C., & Demo, D. H. (1994). *Family diversity and well-being.* Thousand Oaks, CA: Sage.

Albert, R. S. (1971). Cognitive development and parental loss among the gifted, exceptionally gifted and the creative, *Psychological Reports, 29,* 19–26.

Amato, P. R. (1993). Children's adjustment of divorce: Theories, hypotheses, and empirical support. *Journal of Marriage and Family, 55,* 23–38.

Amato, P. R., & Keith, B. (1991a). Parental divorce and adult well-being: A meta-analysis. *Journal of Marriage and Family, 53,* 43–58.

Amato, P. R., & Keith, B. (1991b). Parental divorce and the well-being of children: A meta-analysis. *Psychological Bulletin, 110,* 26–46.

Barton, P. E. (2003). *Parsing the achievement gap: Baselines for tracking progress.* Princeton, NJ: Policy Information Center Educational Testing Service.

Berry, C. (1981). The Nobel scientists and the origins of scientific achievement. *British Journal of Sociology, 32,* 381–391.

Christ, G., Siegel, K., Freund, B., Langosch, D., Henderson, S., Sperber, D., et al. (1993). Impact of parental terminal cancer on latency-age children. *American Journal of Orthopsychiatry, 63,* 417–425.

Christ, G., Siegel, K., & Sperber, D. (1994). Impact of parental terminal cancer on adolescents. *American Journal of Orthopsychiatry, 64,* 604–613.

Corr, C. A., & Balk, D. E. (Eds.). (1996). *Handbook of adolescent death and bereavement.* New York: Springer.

Derevensky, J., & Coleman, E. B. (1989). Gifted children's fears. *Gifted Child Quarterly, 33,* 65–68.

Eisenstadt, J. M. (1978). Parental loss and genius. *American Psychologist, 33,* 211–223.

Eisenstadt, J. M., Haynal, A., Rentchnick, P., & De Senarclens, P. (1989). *Parental loss and achievement.* Madison, CT: International Universities Press.

Elizur, E., & Kaffman, M. (1982). Children's reactions following death of the father: The first four years. *Journal of the American Academy of Child Psychiatry, 21,* 474–480.

Friedman, H. S., Tucker, J. S., Schwartz, J. E., Tomlinson-Keasey, C., Martin, L. R., Wingard, D. L., et al. (1995). Psychological and behavioral predictors of longevity: the aging and death of the Termites. *American Psychologist, 50,* 69–78.

Frydenberg, E. (1997). *Adolescent coping: Theoretical and research perspectives.* New York: Routledge.

Goertzel, M. G., Goertzel, V., & Goertzel, T. G. (1978). *Three hundred eminent personalities: A psychosocial analysis of the famous.* San Francisco: Jossey-Bass.

Harris, E. (1991). Adolescent bereavement following the death of a parent: An exploratory study. *Child Psychiatry and Human Development, 21,* 267–281.

Haveman, R., Wolfe, B. L., & Spaulding, J. (1991). Childhood events and circumstances influencing high school completion. *Demography, 28,* 133–157.

Karnes, F. A., & Oehler-Stinnett, J. J. (1986). Life events as stressors with gifted adolescents. *Psychology in the Schools, 23,* 406–414.

Lewinsohn, P. M., Rohde, P., & Seeley, J. R. (1996). Adolescent suicidal ideation and attempts: Prevalence, risk factors, and clinical implications. *Clinical Psychology: Science and Practice, 3,* 25–46.

Martindale, C. (1972). Father absence, psychopathology, and poetic eminence. *Psychological Reports, 31,* 843–847.

Moon, S. M. (2003). Counseling families. In N. Colangelo & G. Davis (Eds.), *Handbook of gifted education* (3rd ed., pp. 388–402). Boston: Allyn & Bacon.

Moon, S., & Hall, A. (1998). Family therapy with intellectually and creatively gifted children. *Journal of Marital and Family Therapy, 24,* 59–80.

Moon, S. M., Nelson, T. S., & Piercy, F. P. (1993). Family therapy with a highly gifted adolescent. *Journal of Family Psychotherapy, 4*(3), 1–16.

Moon, S., & Thomas, V. (2003). Family therapy with gifted and talented adolescents. *Journal of Secondary Gifted Education, 14,* 107–113.

Morrison, D. R., & Cherlin, A. J. (1995). The divorce process and young children's well-being: A prospective analysis. *Journal of Marriage and the Family, 5,* 800–812.

Myers, D. G. (1995). *Psychology* (4th ed.). New York: Worth.

Myers, S. M. (2005). Childhood and adolescent mobility and adult relations with parents. *Journal of Family Issues, 26,* 350–379.

Norford, B. C., & Medway, F. J. (2002). Adolescents' mobility histories and present social adjustment. *Psychology in the Schools, 39,* 51–62.

Peris, T. S., & Emery, R. E. (2004). A prospective study of the consequences of marital disruption for adolescents: Predisruption family dynamics and postdisruption adolescent adjustment. *Journal of Clinical Child and Adolescent Psychology, 33,* 694–704.

Pittman, J. F., & Bowen, G. L. (1994). Adolescents on the move: Adjustments to family relocation. *Youth and Society, 26,* 69–91.

Plucker, J. A., Hill, C., & Yecke, C. P. (1998, March). "We're moving again?" Starting your gifted child in a new school. *Parenting for High Potential, 23,* 31.

Plucker, J. A., & Yecke, C. P. (1999). The effect of relocation on gifted students. *Gifted Child Quarterly, 43,* 95–106.

Pribesh, S., & Downey, D. B. (1999). Why are residential and school moves associated with poor school performance? *Demography, 36,* 521–534.

Raveis, V., Siegel, K., & Karus, D. (1999). Children's psychological distress following the death of a parent. *Journal of Youth and Adolescence, 28,* 165–180.

Reynolds, C. R., & Bradley, M. (1983). Emotional stability of intellectually superior children versus nongifted peers as estimated by chronic anxiety levels. *School Psychology Review, 12,* 190–194.

Rogers, J. A., & Nielson, A. B. (1993). Gifted children and divorce: A study of the literature on the incidence of divorce in families with gifted children. *Journal for the Education of the Gifted, 16,* 251–267.

Rogers, K. B., & Rose, H. A. (2002). Risk and resiliency factors among adolescents who experience marital transitions. *Journal of Marriage and Family, 64,* 1024–1037.

Scholwinski, E., & Reynolds, C. R. (1985). Dimension of anxiety among high IQ children. *Gifted Child Quarterly, 29,* 125–130.

Siegel, K., Mesagno, F., Karus, D., Christ, G., Banks, G., & Moynihan, R. (1992). Psychosocial adjustment of children with a terminally ill parent. *Journal of the American Academy of Child/Adolescent Psychiatry, 31,* 327–333.

Siegel, K., Raveis, V., & Karus, D. (1996). Patterns of communication with children when a parent has cancer. In L. Baider, C. Cooper, & A. DeNour (Eds.), *Cancer in the family* (pp. 109–128). New York: John Wiley & Sons.

Silverman, S. M. (1974). Parental loss and scientists. *Science Studies, 4,* 259–264.

Silverman, R. R., & Worden, W. (1992). Children's reactions in the early months after the death of a parent. *American Journal of Orthopsychiatry, 62,* 93–104.

Simonton, D. K. (1986). Biographical typicality, eminence and achievement style. *Journal of Creative Behavior, 20,* 14–22.

Simonton, D. K. (1990). *Psychology, science, and history: An introduction to historiometry.* New Haven, CT: Yale University.

Sowa, C. J., McIntire, J., May, K. M., & Bland, L. (1994). Social and emotional adjustment themes across gifted children. *Roeper Review, 17,* 95–98.

South, S. J., & Haynie, D. L. (2004). Friendship networks of mobile adolescents. *Social Forces, 83,* 315–350.

Stack, S. (1994). The effect of geographic mobility on premarital sex. *Journal of Marriage and the Family, 56,* 204–208.

Terman, L. M., & Oden, M. H. (1947). *Genetic studies of genius: The gifted child grows up, Vol. 4.* Stanford, CA: Stanford University.

Thompson, M. P., Kaslow, N. J., Price, A. W., Williams, K., & Kingree, J. B. (1998). Role of secondary stressors in the parental death–child distress relation. *Journal of Abnormal Child Psychology, 26,* 357–366.

Tomchin, E. M., Callahan, C. M., Sowa, C. J., & May, K. M. (1996). Coping and self-concept: Adjustment patterns in gifted adolescents. *Journal of Secondary Gifted Education, 8,* 16–27.

Tong, J., & Yewchuk, C. (1996). Self concept and sex-role orientation in gifted high school students. *Gifted Child Quarterly, 40,* 15–23.

Tucker, C. J., Marx, J., & Long, L. (1998). "Moving on": Residential mobility and children's school lives. *Sociology of Education, 71,* 111–129.

U.S. Census Bureau. (2003). *Geographic mobility: 2003* (Detailed Tables for P20-549). Washington, DC: U.S. Government Printing Offices.

U.S. Department of Education, Office of Educational Research and Improvement. (1993). *National excellence: A case for developing America's talent.* Washington, DC: U.S. Government Printing Office.

United States General Accounting Office. (1994). *Elementary school children: Many change schools frequently, harming their education.* Washington, DC: Health, Education, and Human Services Division.

Vandervalk, I., Spruijt, E., De Goede, M., Meeus, W., & Maas, C. (2004). Marital status, marital process, and parental resources in predicting adolescents' emotional adjustment: A multilevel analysis. *Journal of Family Issues, 25,* 291–317.

Valente, S. M., Saunders, J., & Street, R. (1988). Adolescent bereavement following suicide: An examination of relevant literature. *Journal of Counseling and Development, 67,* 174–177.

Weller, E. B., Weller, R. A., Fristad, M. A., & Bowes, J. M. (1991). Depression in recently bereaved prepubertal children. *American Journal of Psychiatry, 148,* 1536–1540.

West, S., Sandler, I., Pillow, D., Baca, L., & Gersten, J. (1991). The use of structural equation modeling in generative research: Toward the design of a preventive intervention for bereaved children. *American Journal of Community Psychology, 19,* 459–480.

Woodward, W. R. (1974). Scientific genius and loss of a parent. *Science Studies, 4,* 265–277.

Worden, J. W. (1996). *Children and grief: When a parent dies.* New York: Guilford Press.

Worden, J. W., Davies, B., & McCown, D. (1999). Comparing parent loss with sibling loss. *Death Studies, 23,* 1–15.

Zill, N., Morrison, D. R., & Coiro, M. J. (1993). Long-term effects of parental divorce on parent-child relationships, adjustment, and achievement in young adulthood. *Journal of Family Psychology, 7,* 91–103.

Chapter 24

MATCHING INSTRUCTION AND ASSESSMENT

*Linda Jarvin, Tina Newman, Judi Randi,
Robert J. Sternberg, and Elena L. Grigorenko*

n the United States, the Individuals with Disabilities Education Improvement Act (IDEA; 1990) requires state and local education agencies to provide children with disabilities opportunities to be educated with children who are not disabled to the greatest extent possible. This requirement has led to an increase in the number of inclusive classrooms in public schools. These inclusive classrooms serve children with different educational needs, ranging from low-ability children with learning disabilities to high-ability gifted students; they also present teachers with the challenge of providing a learning environment where each child is working at his or her level of potential. As the push for inclusive education continues, the task will be to refine how we can best help regular classroom teachers with little or no training in gifted or special education meet the needs of *all* of their students and provide them with challenging learning opportunities. If instructional practices are enhanced to meet the needs of a wide range of students, we must also ensure that classroom assessment practices are equally inclusive to provide

the teacher with a truthful overview of students' strengths and weaknesses. How can we assist teachers in making sure that instruction and assessment are matched and provide an adequate picture of all students' knowledge and skills? This chapter will illustrate how one team of researchers and curriculum developers designed a program addressing the needs of different learner profiles that enabled teachers to serve—and assess—all of the students in their classroom, including gifted students. The program was not designed for the exclusive use in gifted classrooms, but rather, offers a model for teaching that will benefit both gifted students and children not identified as such.

First, we provide a brief review of existing definitions of giftedness. We then present the principles of Teaching for Successful Intelligence (TSI) and show how this instructional approach can help teachers meet the needs of students of varying levels of ability. Finally, we present concrete examples from an elementary school intervention based on TSI.

DEFINITIONS OF GIFTEDNESS

We propose that current conceptions of giftedness can be categorized into three main models: the analytical intelligence model, the analytical and creative model, and the analytical, creative, and practical model (see also Sternberg & Davidson, 2005). Each one is described below.

Model I: The Analytical Intelligence (g-Based) Model

The analytical (g-based) model of intelligence and giftedness dates back to Spearman (1904, 1927; see also Jensen, 1998), who argued that individual differences in human intelligence can be understood primarily in terms of differences in a general factor of intelligence (the g factor), which Spearman believed to be mental energy. The most well-known study of giftedness, the Terman study (Terman & Oden, 1940a, 1940b), explored the transition between childhood and adulthood giftedness by following up on the participants once they had grown into adults. Participants were recruited in medium and large urban areas of California, and were aged 3 to 19 during the first wave of testing (in 1921–1922). Participants' IQ scores generally exceeded 140, which is to say they were 2.5 standard deviations above the population mean. Participants were divided into three groups—A, B, and C—depending on their IQs. Although IQ is not equivalent to psychometric g, it is highly correlated with it. We refer to these as measures of *analytical intelligence*, to use a uniform terminology in describing the three models. Terman and his colleagues compared the achievements of individuals in the three groups as adults. The A's generally reached higher levels of achievement than did the C's, with the B's in between. But, the differences were not large and there were many A's who were not particularly successful and C's that were.

Terman's study was followed up on the East Coast by Subotnik, Kassan, Summers, and Wasser (1994), who investigated the life trajectories of Hunter College Elementary School graduates who had initially been identified as gifted primarily on the basis of IQ-based abilities. Subotnik et al.'s East Coast study replicated Terman's West Coast study in a key respect: In both samples, individuals were notable for their overall success in terms of the outcomes' societal value (money, fame, and to a much lesser extent, power). But, they also were notable for the lack of truly outstanding success of the kind that leads to Nobel Prizes or the highest levels of major recognition in their fields. Some participants reached the heights of their professions, but their numbers were surprisingly small if one took these samples to represent the most gifted children to be found on the two coasts of the United States. Notably, the large majority of participants in these studies were White and middle class. Relatively few were from underrepresented minorities, suggesting that the means used to identify the students as gifted may have been skewed.

Model II: The Analytical + Creative Intelligence Model

A second model emphasizes the importance not only of conventional (analytical) intelligence but of creative intelligence as well (or, in more conventional terminology, intelligence plus creativity). Renzulli (1984), for example, has distinguished between "schoolhouse gifted" children and "creative–productive gifted" children. The former are notable for their good test scores, grades, and ability to achieve at the highest levels in a variety of academic settings. The latter are notable for their creative products, such as artwork, musical compositions, poems, short stories, science projects, or other forms of creative production. Renzulli has pointed out that these groups of children, although they may overlap, are by no means the same. Many schoolhouse-gifted children are not creatively–productively gifted, and many children who do outstanding creative work are not particularly valued by their teachers and schools.

Bamberger (1986) has taken a related point of view in her studies of musically gifted individuals. She has suggested that there appears to be a marked transition between what it takes to be gifted as a musician in childhood and what is required to be a gifted musician in adulthood. Specifically, musically gifted children tend to do what others do and do it extremely well. In a sense, their giftedness is reproductive or imitative. Gifted adults, however, need to go beyond what others have done, and great skill in childhood therefore does not necessarily predict great or even distinctive skill as an adult. Subotnik and Jarvin (Jarvin & Subotnik, 2006; Subotnik & Jarvin, 2005; Subotnik, Jarvin, Moga, & Sternberg, 2003) reached similar conclusions in their investigations of top East Coast conservatories.

A problem with many studies of creative individuals is that they examine persons who have become creatively accomplished, meaning that the individuals had the *opportunity* to become creatively accomplished. Members of underserved minority groups who might have become creatively accomplished but lacked the necessary opportunity never make it into these samples. These individuals often do not have a chance to attain the educational credentials that might enable them to reach the point where they can contribute creatively. Other studies may examine more diverse children but use psychometric tests of creativity (such as the Torrance tests) that historically have favored members of the dominant majority group from middle to upper socioeconomic levels.

Model III: The Analytical + Creative + Practical Model of Successful Intelligence

A third model emphasizes the importance not only of analytical and creative intelligence, but of practical intelligence as well. This model, proposed by Sternberg (1985, 1988, 1997, 1999a), suggests that even individuals who are analytically and creatively gifted will not necessarily possess the abilities to make it as creative adults. For example, they may be able to produce creative artwork but not know how to get it exhibited, or write creative stories but not know how to get them published, or compose creative musical arrangements but not know how to get them played. They may fail in later transitions of giftedness because they are ineffective at promoting their ideas.

Csikszentmihalyi (1996) provides a relevant distinction between the domain and the field in which an individual works. *Domain* refers to the kind of work one does (musical composition, biological research, painting, writing novels), whereas *field* refers to the social organization of the domain—the entire network of people who both create and judge the products of creators. In terms of the present model, one may be successful in the domain through a combination of analytical and creative intelligence but not particularly successful in the field because of a lack of practical intelligence. Or, one may be successful in the field and achieve great recognition, at least in the short term, for work that is mediocre in terms of its creative impact.

There is research suggesting the usefulness of this model. Sternberg et al. (2000) have shown in studies of individuals in dozens of pursuits around the world that people who are high in practical intelligence are not necessarily high in analytical intelligence, and vice versa. Moreover, practical intelligence predicts real-world job success about as well as or even better than does IQ. Moreover, Sternberg, Grigorenko, Ferrari, and Clinkenbeard (1999) have shown that the analytical, creative, and practical aspects of intelligence are relatively distinct. Sternberg and Lubart (1995) have shown, as have others (see essays in Sternberg, 1999b), that analytical and creative intelligence, although not necessarily independent, are only weakly related. It is often suggested that creative work requires some minimum level of IQ (120), but that after roughly that level, IQ fails to matter or matters much less (Simonton, 1997).

The authors of this chapter subscribe to the third model of intelligence and giftedness, and from now on in using the term *giftedness*, we refer to individuals who (a) demonstrate excellence in their work, (b) possess this excellence relative to peers, (c) are able to display this excellence through some kind of tangible performance, (d) can repeat this performance multiple times, and (e) excel in a way that is socially valued.

Now, having stated our explicit definition of giftedness, we discuss a possible approach for teaching children who meet this definition.

Teaching for Successful Intelligence

Students learn in different ways: Some learn best when given an opportunity to think analytically; others excel when given the chance to learn creatively and/or practically.

Teaching for Successful Intelligence (TSI) is based on Sternberg's (1985, 1997, 1999a) triarchic theory, which posits that three components of intelligence, in addition to memory, are needed for success both in and beyond the classroom: (1) *analytical*, characterized by cognitive processes such as analysis, evaluation, or comparison (e.g., when students are asked to solve a math problem or take a stand and argue their point in writing a persuasive text); (2) *practical*, characterized by application of knowledge in situation-specific tasks (e.g., students may be asked to apply their knowledge of fractions to musical notes or use their vocabulary words in conversation); and (3) *creative*, characterized by original thinking, design, invention, or imagination (e.g., a student may be asked to create a system of measurement or imagine a change in a story and recreate the ending). Studies in which TSI instruction was infused into regular curriculum content taught by the regular classroom teacher showed that students who received the TSI approach to instruction generally demonstrated greater gains than did students who received traditional memory-based instruction (see Grigorenko, Jarvin, & Sternberg, 2002).

There are three principles of TSI instruction that explain how this approach works to afford all students learning opportunities. TSI (1) provides learners opportunities to encode the material in multiple ways, (2) allows students to capitalize on their strengths to maximize learning, and (3) motivates students to engage in content in meaningful and interesting ways.

First, TSI enables students to use different strategies to encode the material to be learned. That is, instead of simply memorizing, students are taught to encode information analytically, creatively, and practically as well. When students encode information in multiple ways and then elaborate on the encodings in meaningful experiences, there are many traces through the subject matter content (Grigorenko et al., 2002). Multiple means of encoding material and demonstrating knowledge, especially when the encodings are meaningful to the student, provide the basis for many more retrieval cues to be effective.

Second, because TSI draws on three components of intelligence in addition to memory, for most students there is at least some instruction that is compatible with their strengths, enabling them to bring these strengths to bear on the work at hand. Aptitude-treatment interaction (ATI) research reviewed in the 1970s (see Cronbach & Snow, 1977) demonstrated that in many cases the same treatments produce different effects in different student populations and at different points in time. For example, Corno and Snow (1986) described ATI studies of curriculum interventions in which students were assigned to treatments based on analysis of their aptitudes. Results of these studies showed that students performed better when the treatments were matched to their particular aptitudes. TSI has also been successfully evaluated from an ATI perspective (Sternberg et al., 1999). In the inclusive classroom, however, it is not always realistic and feasible for the teacher to individually tailor the instruction and to provide aptitude-matched instruction for each student.

Third, TSI motivates student learning. Just as students have different strengths and learning preferences, there are also individual differences in motivation (Kanfer, 1990). A great deal of research supports the importance of motivation in learning and differences in motivation levels often account for differences in student achievement (e.g., Naceur & Schiefele, 2005). Gifted students in an inclusive classroom are particularly at risk for decreased motivation because of a lack of appropriate challenge (Stepanek, 1999). TSI inherently includes components that address students' different interests and offers activities of varying degrees of challenge. For example, the practical component emphasizes real-life applications that are immediately relevant. Likewise, the creative component adds interest by allowing students to "play" with ideas and concepts. Past evaluation of TSI (Grigorenko et al., 2002; Sternberg, Torff, & Grigorenko, 1998) has showed that TSI instruction was found to be more motivating as reported by students. In one study, elementary students were administered a self-assessment questionnaire in which they were asked how much they liked the course, how much they thought they learned in the course, and how well they thought they did in the course. The students in the TSI group generally gave significantly higher ratings than did the students taught with traditional approaches (Sternberg, Grigorenko, & Jarvin, 2001).

Overall, TSI has been empirically validated in three types of studies: (1) in ATI paradigms (Sternberg et al., 1999); (2) in the regular classroom with infused off-the-shelf curricula (Sternberg et al., 2001), and (3) in both regular and special classrooms with stand-alone curricula (Grigorenko et al., 2002). After exploring why TSI can lead to enhanced student performance and motivation, we examine concrete examples of how curricula and their matching assessments can be infused with the principles of TSI.

APPLYING THE PRINCIPLES OF TSI IN THE INCLUSIVE CLASSROOM

To illustrate how TSI can assist teachers in providing adequate levels of challenge for all students, including gifted ones, in their inclusive classrooms, we take examples from a study conducted by the Sternberg research group at the PACE Center (Grigorenko, Jarvin, Sternberg, Newman, & Randi, 2007). In this study, stand-alone curriculum units were developed within the context of a large-scale intervention study comparing three modes of instruction (TSI, critical thinking instruction that employed primarily analytical activities, and traditional memory-based instruction). The units were designed for implementation in fourth-grade classrooms in three subject areas: language arts, mathematics, and science. They were not designed for gifted classrooms alone, but were used both in inclusive (gifted and nongifted) and in gifted classrooms.

Curriculum materials were developed for each experimental condition, targeting the same content but taught through different modes of instruction depending on the condition. That is, one version focused on memory-based instruction, one version focused on critical-thinking-based instruction, and one version focused on TSI-based instruction. Each unit consisted of a pre-intervention assessment, instructional materials, and a post-intervention assessment. The instructional materials consisted of a teacher guide containing background content information and instructional guidelines, as well as an activity workbook for students. Each unit spanned approximately 2 to 3 weeks of instructional time.

In language arts, five thematic units, including matching pre- and post-intervention assessments, were developed in each of the three conditions: (1) How and Why Nature Tales, (2) Informative Nonfiction, (3) Biography, (4) Quest Literature, and (5) Mystery. Five math units were designed in each of the three conditions: (1) Equivalent Fractions, (2) Measurement, (3) Geometry, (4) Data Analysis and Representation, and (5) Number Sense and Place Value. In science, four thematic units were developed in each of the three conditions: (1) Light, (2) Magnetism, (3) Electricity, and (4) Ecology. In all subject areas, the content taught and assessed in each of the three versions was identical.

One goal of the curriculum development was to accommodate a wide range of learners. Teachers in this study reported having gifted students (receiving pull-out gifted instruction), students with special needs (as per their IEP), bilingual students (as reported by teachers), and nonreaders (as reported by teachers and/or determined in students' IEP). Fifty teachers (approximately one fourth of all participants) taught specifically to gifted students. The design of this curriculum serves as an example of how a single curriculum can be adapted by teachers to accommodate learner differences and enable all students to participate fully in the learning experiences, and of how matching assessments provide a more nuanced and representative picture of students' knowledge and skills.

As stated earlier, TSI provides all learners opportunities to encode the material in multiple ways, which allows students to capitalize on their strengths to maximize learning and motivates students to engage in the content in meaningful and interesting ways. Next, we provide specific examples from the curriculum to illustrate these three principles of TSI instruction, and show how teachers can develop curricula containing more and less challenging activities to meet the varying needs of their students.

Multiple Encodings Assist Memory

One principle of TSI curriculum design is to provide a balance of creative, analytical, and practical activities (in addition to memory) in which all students must participate, regardless of their particular strengths and weaknesses. In our fourth-grade curriculum, each unit included a balanced proportion of each type of activity. Let us look at an example in language arts. Table 1 shows how three different types of activities are used to lead students toward an objective in the introductory lesson of a unit focusing on "how and why" tales as a genre of literature. These different creative, practical, and analytical activities provide students multiple entries into the same content, and offer varying levels of challenge to meet different students' needs.

It is important to note that each student was required to participate in all types of activities, thus promoting multiple encodings of the general concept taught in the unit. This does not mean that the same exact activity was repeated three times, however, or that students in the TSI intervention received three times more instruction on a given topic than did students in the other conditions, as the example in Table 1 shows. The curriculum is designed such that a balance of creative, practical, and analytical activities—in addition to memory tasks—are employed across a unit.

In the language arts unit on mystery, students learned about the conventions of mystery as the teacher read aloud, modeled literary analysis, and discussed the mystery *From the Mixed-Up Files of Mrs. Basil E. Frankweiler*. Concurrently, students independently read a mystery of their choice and completed a variety of activities based on their independent reading. To learn about detective character traits, for example, students applied their knowledge of character analysis to different types of activities. The following are examples from one student who read the fantasy mystery *Bunnicula*. The analytical activity required students to analyze character traits and identify the textual evidence for detective behaviors (e.g., Harold, the "detective" dog, is a watchdog, listens closely, gets close to see, and is a mind-reader). The practical component required students to make a text–self connection (e.g., Harold the watchdog reminded the student of his mom; the mind-reader, of his dad). The creative activity encouraged students to generate elaborated similes (e.g., A good detective is like a shovel because he digs for clues; a good detective is like a train because he follows lots of tracks). It should be noted that activities may not be

TABLE 1

Multiple Encodings: Sample Activities From "How and Why Tales"

Objective	Analytical	Creative	Practical
Students will be introduced to tales of wonder (how and why tales) through poetry. In the first lesson, they read a poem and are brought to understand that one function of poetry is to convey a sense of wonder. Students will understand how poetry uses sounds and images to convey a sense of wonder.	Focused reading with teacher-guided comprehension questions and thinking questions.	Students add a verse to the poem they have read in class.	Students begin a Wonder Journal to identify their own wonders.
Variations for Individual Student Differences	**Less Challenging** For a mini-phonics lesson, the poem provides the opportunity to teach/review the homophones (bear, bare) and rhyming words that are spelled differently (deep, cheap, cheep).	**Less Challenging** Students generate pairs of words that rhyme.	**Less Challenging** Non-writers can record their wonders on audio-tape.
	More Challenging Guide students to notice the alliterations ("winter winds" and "fall fast") or the play on words (bare bear feet)..	**More Challenging** Students add a verse in the same literary format as the one used by the author.	**More Challenging** Students find out what the term "pourquoi" means.

purely analytical, practical, or creative. For example, the creative simile activity necessarily involves some analysis or logic, and all of the activities depend on memory, or, in this case, knowing what a character trait is. This is an example of how many tasks—in school and in life—tend to require a combination of abilities for successful completion.

Let us take another example, this time from a math unit on measurement: One day, students might measure things with a ruler, a broken ruler, a piece of string, a tape measure, and footsteps (analytical). The teacher could add a measurement puzzle as a more challenging activity for advanced students (see Figure 1).

Another day, the teacher may use an activity in which students determine the type of measuring instrument and unit of measurement for everyday items (practical). An optional, more challenging activity for gifted students might be to have them play a measurement game in which the objective is to convert measurements within units of measurement. Students play in groups of 2 to 4 players. The first player rolls a set of number cubes and moves the number of spaces indicated by the cubes on a game board. Each square on the game board presents a conversion problem (e.g., "2,000 cm = _____ m). If the player can make the conversion on the space landed, he or she can stay; if not, the player must return to his or her original space. The other students check to make sure the conversion is correct. The first player home wins.

Another day, a teacher may have students create their own system of measurement (creative). A more challenging activity for advanced students may be to have students measure some items in the classroom and then imagine that something happened to make these objects shrink to one third of their original sizes. Students must then figure out the new measurements for the items they just measured.

Each of these regular and more challenging analytical, practical, and creative activities works toward the objective of building students' understanding of measurement; however, they are not repeating the same material in three different ways. Nor are the more gifted students just asked to do "more of the same" (i.e., five problem sets instead of one); rather, they are challenged in different ways.

The design of the curriculum thus ensured full student participation by allowing teachers to substitute alternative activities to meet individual student needs. Below are some more examples of regular and more challenging activities drawn from a science unit focused on magnets. Students are given a tray full of various materials (e.g., wood, metal, cloth, etc.) and three magnets and asked to use as many items from the tray as they can to create a sculpture that contains as many different nonmetallic objects as possible. Students can only use objects in the tray. After students finish building their sculptures, the teacher records the number of nonmetallic objects students were able to incorporate. The teacher also asks students to share the different methods they used for connecting the different nonmetallic objects and asks them to come up with a name for each method.

Measurement Crossword

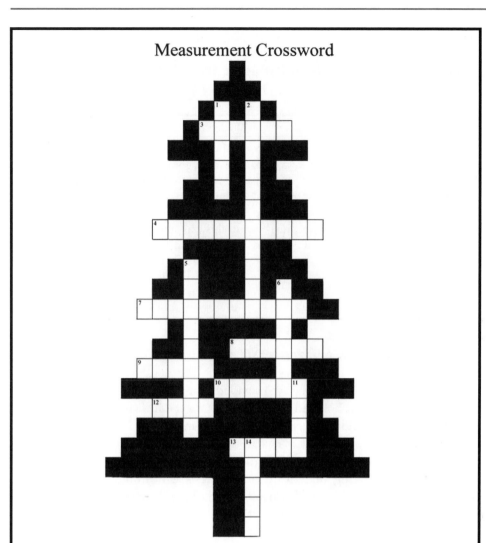

Across

3. This word means 'line' and could be a measure of length, width, or height.
4. This measuring instrument is like a ruler, but you can roll it up when you are done.
7. This measuring instrument can tell you how hot it is outside.
8. If you are measuring how tall you are, you are getting a measure of this.

9. This measuring tool is used to take linear measures and is shorter than a yard or meter stick.
10. When you want to know how heavy something is, you take this kind of measure.
12. If you wanted to know how much floor space there was in your room, you would take this measure.
13. If you wanted to know how much something weighs,

you would use this measuring instrument.

Down

1. This is a measure of how wide something is.
2. When you want to know how hot it is outside, you would take this kind of measure.
5. This is a measure of the distance around the outside of something.

6. This is a measure of how long something is.
11. You may use a clock or a stopwatch to get this kind of measure.
14. This is what you would use if you wanted to know what time it is.

Figure 1. Measurement puzzle.

T A B L E 2

Challenging Students to Broaden Their Learning Repertoire: Science Unit on Light

Verbal Activity	Spatial Activity
Using your knowledge of refraction, write a story about a light beam and its travels. Imagine what types of surfaces the beam encounters on its journey, and use your understanding of refraction to explain how the beam could bend. Feel free to use drawings to illustrate most of the story.	Using your knowledge of mirrors, you are now going to design an exhibit for a Mirror Exploratorium. An exploratorium is a place where you can explore phenomena through hands-on activities. In this exploratorium, you want to set up exhibits that let kids discover the magical world of mirrors. Kids in your exploratorium should be able to do something that is fun, and hands-on. Think of wacky ways you can use mirrors.

TSI Capitalizes on Students' Strengths

The TSI curriculum not only provided students with appropriate levels of challenge but also included activities that drew on different abilities (i.e., analytical, creative, and practical, in addition to memory). The TSI curriculum is based on the assumption that not all students learn best by memory. Some gifted students learn best when afforded opportunities for creative thinking, others learn by thinking analytically, and others learn through practical applications. Although all students learned the content in three ways, some students tended to benefit more from instruction in their area of strength. In most classrooms, it is not feasible to teach only to a student's strengths, and we do not advocate assessing students for only their strengths, but rather for teachers to broaden their instructional repertoire to reach a larger number of students. High-ability students can have gifts in different areas (i.e., analytical, practical, or creative), and a broadened curriculum can help them increase their performance in all three, presenting them with the challenge of broadening their learning styles repertoire.

For example, in a science unit on light, all students were taught the concept of reflection and that the angle of incidence is equal to the angle of reflection. Students with strong spatial abilities and lower verbal skills were challenged to show their understanding of refraction by writing a story about a light beam and its travels and encounters with different surfaces, whereas students with strong verbal skills and lower spatial skills were encouraged to strengthen those skills by building a mirror exploratorium. All students are thus taught the same concepts, but they increase and demonstrate their understanding of them through different means (see Table 2).

T A B L E   3

Sample Activities From a Language Arts Unit on Biographies

Analytical Activity:	Practical Activity:	Creative Activity:
Look at two pictures of Abraham Lincoln and decide in which picture Lincoln looked most handsome. Write a paragraph in which you describe how Lincoln appeared in each picture and how you decided in which picture Lincoln looked most handsome.	Think of a student in your class. Write a paragraph that describes this student. Then, share your description with at least three other students and ask them to guess which student you described. Consider your description successful if the other students could determine which student you described.	Lincoln was said to appear quite animated when he gave speeches. Imagine that you could go back in time, attend one of Lincoln's speeches, and capture his expressions on camera. Draw a series of pictures that your camera took. Caption each picture with a one-sentence description of Lincoln's appearance.

TSI increases students' repertoire of learning styles while concurrently allowing students to demonstrate their understanding of concepts through their strengths. Thus, assessments are more valid because they evaluate understanding of the targeted concepts without penalizing students for lack of understanding (or lack of interest) in other areas. In language arts, for example, those with poor writing skills were allowed to dictate their stories so that teachers could judge students' understanding of story structure. Similarly, gifted students may fail to demonstrate understanding in "test" situations or they may fail to put in effort on "easy" tasks. One way of differentiating assessment (and instruction) is to provide options and allow students to choose to demonstrate understanding in their area of strength.

Consider, for example, the activities in Table 3 from which students may choose to demonstrate their understanding of descriptive vocabulary, from a language art unit on biographies.

Another example shows how creative thinking can be included in the mathematics curriculum. This activity assessed students' understanding of dimensions by asking students to imagine their day as a two-dimensional person (see Figure 2).

TSI Motivates Students to Achieve

Motivating students to succeed is an important component of TSI, and a problem frequently faced by gifted students who feel that they are not sufficiently challenged in the inclusive classroom.

Imagine that one day you woke up and in your sleep you had become 2-dimensional. In other words, you were flat!!! What would your life be like? Write a story about you as a 2-dimensional person.

One day when I woke up everything seemed normal except I felt a little strange. When I sleepily walked into the bathroom and looked in the mirror, I was almost knocked flat! I saw that I was in 2-D! I rubbed my eyes to see if I was still sleeping, but I wasn't. When my little sister saw me, she just screamed and ran down stairs. When she ran, she made a gust of wind that pulled me down the stairs too. I was scared silly. I was falling like a piece of paper down the stairs. When I got to the bottom, my brother was there and said, " Mom, Caitlin's been leaving her paper dolls around again."

You could guess how the rest of my family reacted when they found out I was 2-D. They were so surprised. They were happy in a way though because they didn't have to feed me at all. My brother Paul dropped his bouncy ball under the couch. Since I was as thin as paper, I slipped under the couch and got his bouncy ball for him. When my sister snuck up on me and jumped on me, she ripped out half of my hair. I liked being 2-D for two reasons. One I could open my mouth and my sister could use me as a beanbag game. The other reason is I could be very good at playing hide and seek because if I turned to my side all you could see of me is a straight line. The next day when I went to school everone was crowding around me because they thought it was so cool.

Figure 2. Sample student response (student grammar and spelling uncorrected).

One way that TSI motivates students is by providing different types of learning experiences, including optional more or less challenging activities that enable the teacher to teach the same concepts to all of the students in her class, while at the same time ensuring that individual student activities are appropriately challenging. Students are encouraged to think of practical activities focusing on real-life applications. For example, in a math unit on equivalent fractions, students engaged in real-life problem-solving tasks such as discussing how to share a graham cracker equally among four students or using measuring cups to determine equivalent measures of ingredients for a candy recipe. In language arts, students were asked to relate the literature they read to real life. For example, students compare themselves to story characters and decide what they might do in similar situations. In the language arts unit on biographies, students interviewed family members and created photo biographies. In a unit on journeys, students were taught useful skills such as organizing for writing and persistence in difficult tasks by learning to emulate the qualities of quest heroes.

An example from one student in the class of a teacher who implemented all five language arts units illustrates how TSI encourages practical application. In the language arts unit on journeys, students were asked to compare the writing process to a quest. Students were required, for example, to think of obstacles the writing process presented to them and how they might overcome those obstacles in the manner of a quest hero. Quest heroes typically seek help from others, draw on their own strengths and cunning, and find opportunities in available resources. In one activity linking the writing process to quest hero strategies, students were asked to identify others from whom they might seek help (e.g., the teacher, parents and grandparents, older siblings, the media specialist), their own strengths (e.g., thinking, trying, revising, turning in my work on time), and available resources they might draw on (e.g., dictionary, computer, thesaurus, grammar book). The journeys unit culminated in a direct writing assessment in which students wrote an original quest tale. One student who identified "thinking of ideas" as an obstacle to writing chose to write his quest tale by revising, embellishing, and expanding the mystery story he had begun in a previous unit. The result was a 10 "chapter" Herculean-type quest tale, complete with a series of challenging tasks and obstacles assigned by "Deliah," who had agreed to reveal the mystery's solution to the hero who performed her tasks. Written in the first person, the tale ends when Deliah reveals who stole the punch bowl from the town's historic mansion. Clearly this student overcame his expressed "lack of ideas" by drawing on his strengths and available resources (in this case, the model quest, *Hercules*, and his own previous writing).

In addition to these practical activities, creative activities also served to motivate through interest and novelty. In math, for example, students were asked to write a creative story for how ¾ became ⅜. One student wrote the following (spelling corrected):

> ¾ came walking down the street. They were the happiest people alive until they saw a rubber band. The 2 got scared and fainted, but the 4 was safe on top of the line. The rubber band felt bad, so he twisted himself into an 8 and put himself under the line. That's how ¾ became ⅜.

Another creative activity asked students to imagine that fractions were secret agents and that they needed to assume aliases (equivalent names). In language arts, students were engaged in creative activities such as story writing, interviewing story characters, coining words, generating original word puzzles, and creating new titles and endings to stories.

We believe that the instructional approach described here can help teachers in the inclusive classroom solve the conundrum of having to meet the needs of students with various levels of ability and challenge. Employing TSI gives students with many different learning styles the opportunity to learn new information and demonstrate their knowledge through creative, practical, and analytical activities, and even through the traditional memory domain. By adding more and less challenging activities, the teacher can pick and choose to be able to serve all of her students at the appropriate level.

ALIGNING INSTRUCTION AND ASSESSMENT

As stated in the introduction to this chapter, it is essential that teachers match instruction and assessment. If pedagogy and curriculum are enhanced to meet the needs of a wider range of learners, then corresponding assessments that enable all students to build on their strengths to express their knowledge and skills must be offered. In other words, if we teach for TSI, we should assess for TSI. Many teachers who are able to incorporate creative and practical activities in their teaching may feel at loss when it comes to assessing creative or practical skills and end up assessing students only for their memory and analytical skills. There are two consequences to that action. The first is an imbalance between what is taught and what is assessed; students will quickly feel that some classroom activities (the creative and practical ones) are not as important as others (the analytical and memory ones) because they never appear on the test. Students will not feel encouraged to take all activities as seriously.

The second consequence is that not all students will be able to capitalize on their strengths to learn better and experience a rewarding feeling of success in the classroom. We are not promoting the idea that some kids are solely creative and should not be taught and assessed for memory or analytical skills. We do believe, however, that the "creative kid" will benefit from a teaching style that addresses several skills and be able to capitalize on the areas of strength to remediate areas of weakness. Similarly, by being assessed in a domain of strength (e.g., for creative skills), the student will be able to display strengths and have a more positive experience than if the student were assessed in an area of weakness alone. Based on our belief in the necessity of matching instruction and assessment, we developed pre- and post-assessments for each thematic unit that contained creative and practical questions in addition to the analytical and memory items. How do these types of items differ? Memory items require students to recall and/or recognize who did certain things (e.g., Who was the hero in the story?); what things they did (e.g., What did the bear do when his tail froze in the ice?); how certain things are done (e.g., how two fractions are added); or when certain things are done (e.g., when plants reject carbon dioxide). Analytical items require students to analyze (e.g., the plot of a story); critique (e.g., the design of a science experiment); evaluate (e.g., whether a certain formula is appropriate for solving a mathematical problem); or compare and contrast (e.g., the attitudes of two characters in a story). Creative items require students to create (e.g., a comic strip summarizing a story they've read); imagine (e.g., a new ending to a story); invent (e.g., a science experiment); or suppose (e.g., what would happen if everything was twice the size it is now). Practical items require students to apply (e.g., the lesson of a story to a real-life event); use (e.g., a ruler to measure length); or apply what has been learned (e.g., the six big steps in library research).

Each test was composed of a blend of multiple-choice and open-ended items addressing different levels of ability so as to be suitable for all students in the inclusive classroom. For each skill type (memory, analytical, creative, and practical skills) and in each subject area domain (language arts, science, and mathematics), we developed a 5-point proficiency scale. This scale illustrates what an easy (1-point) item should assess, what a slightly higher level 2-point item should assess, and so forth, as illustrated in Table 4 for the domain of mathematics, and so on.

In designing assessments, we thus made sure to (1) match assessment and instruction by including assessment items for creative and practical abilities in addition to analytical and memory items, and (2) address and challenge a range of student abilities by including assessment items of varying difficulty levels. The illustrations in this chapter were drawn from an elementary school curriculum, but we believe that the principles and guidelines for instruction and assessment described here can be implemented in any subject area and at any grade level.

T A B L E 4

Sample Proficiency Scales in the Domain of Mathematics

Items Assessing *Memory* Skills	Items Assessing *Analytical* Skills
Level 1. The task requires recognition of one term, or vocabulary word or its definition. The terms and definitions have been explicitly taught and applied throughout the unit (e.g., recognizing a line with an arrow at one end as a ray, given a list of choices).	*Level 1.* The question or task has one concept. This concept has only one critical attribute that the student must recognize and be able to use in providing their response (e.g., using the knowledge that perimeter is the length of all sides added together, placing a series of polygons in order of smallest to largest perimeter).
Level 2. The task requires cued recall of one term, vocabulary word, or its definition (e.g., identifying a right angle from among a set of angles).	*Level 2.* The question or task has two or more pieces of information or concepts, but the student is asked to determine only 1 relationship between those concepts or pieces of information (e.g., identifying corresponding measures in the metric and customary systems).
Level 3. The task requires active recall of concepts, terms, vocabulary words or their definitions (e.g., drawing an example of lines that intersect).	*Level 3.* The student must identify critical attributes of a concept and evaluate which fits (e.g., given a rectangle, identifying the sides that are congruent).
Level 4. The task requires active recall of a list or the identification of missing pieces of information in a sequenced or unsequenced list (e.g., describing the sequence of tasks when conducting data collection and analysis).	*Level 4.* The student must provide basic explanations of their responses or the student must show some evidence of reasoning (e.g., given a circle, drawing the shape they would see if the circle was folded along a line of symmetry).
Level 5. The task requires production of paraphrase, summary, or synonym; requires application of skills (e.g., describing what you are measuring when you measure the volume of something).	*Level 5.* The student must provide more extended explanations of their responses and justify their responses (e.g., providing an example of when it would be better to use a tape measure than a ruler and explaining why the tape measure would be better to use in this situation).

Items Assessing *Creative* Skills	Items Assessing *Practical* Skills
Level 1. The student must provide a slight elaboration/modification of presented material (e.g., given a house made up of rectangles, redrawing it using other shapes of their choice).	*Level 1.* The student must grasp the main message of the material with regard to his or her own life—that is, to identify a possible application of the concept to the students' activities and actions (e.g., identifying two pieces of food that are shaped like a sphere).
Level 2. The student is asked to provide a novel variation given an existing example or framework—new ideas based on prior experience (e.g., following a data collection unit, coming up with an interesting question of their own to investigate).	*Level 2.* The student must incorporate new knowledge while taking the context into account (e.g., determining one question they may want to collect data on when inviting the whole class to a party).
Level 3. The student is given a change in the situation and they must create the consequences of this change (e.g., imagining schools were made of spheres instead of prisms, what might be the biggest problem).	*Level 3.* The student must find an optimal solution to a situation (that might originate in the student's personal experience), assuming that all necessary data are available in the item administered. In addition, students are expected to transfer the knowledge to new contexts (e.g., determining what measuring tools are needed to find out if you meet the qualifying time for a 100 meter race for a track and field event).
Level 4. The student is asked to make an extension or fill in missing information—no framework provided (e.g., coming up with an equivalent fraction alias for the space explorer ⅓ and describing a time the alias is useful).	*Level 4.* The student must process the information, take a position, and formulate a convincing explanation of why the information obtained has (or does not have) a practical value (e.g., describing one way to measure the length of the room and convince another person that this is a good way to measure it).
Level 5. The student is asked to devise, create, or originate novel situations (e.g., imagining that they are in an unexplored section of space, with no gravity, and they weigh nothing at all. They must describe something new that they can do now that they weigh nothing that they could not do on earth).	*Level 5.* The student must assimilate information for transformation to clearly express his or her position and advise someone else in a situation resembling (but not identical to) the one in the item (e.g., describing to a friend how to measure the circumference of a tree trunk using a ruler and a piece of string).

REFERENCES

Bamberger, J. (1986). Cognitive issues in the development of musically gifted children. In R. J. Sternberg & J. E. Davidson (Eds.), *Conceptions of giftedness* (pp. 388–413). New York: Cambridge University Press.

Corno, L., & Snow, R. E. (1986). Adapting teaching to individual differences among learners. In M. Wittrock (Ed.), *Third handbook of research on teaching* (pp. 605–629). New York: Macmillan.

Cronbach, L. & Snow, R. (1977). *Aptitudes and instructional methods: A handbook for research on interactions.* New York: Irvington Publishers.

Csikszentmihalyi, M. (1996). *Creativity.* New York: Harper Collins.

Grigorenko, E. L., Jarvin, L., & Sternberg, R. J. (2002). School-based tests of the triarchic theory of human intelligence: Three settings, three samples, three syllabi. *Contemporary Educational Psychology, 27,* 167–208

Grigorenko, E. L., Jarvin, L., Sternberg, R. J., Newman, T., & Randi, J. (2007). *Applying the theory of successful intelligence in the classroom: An empirical study.* Manuscript in preparation.

Individuals with Disabilities Education Act, 20 U.S.C. §1401 et seq. (1990).

Jarvin, L., & Subotnik, R. (2006). Academic and musical talent development: From basic abilities to scholarly performance. In F. A. Dixon & S. M. Moon (Eds.), *The handbook of secondary gifted education* (pp. 203–220). Waco, TX: Prufrock Press.

Jensen, A. R. (1998). *The g factor: The science of mental ability.* Westport, CT: Praeger/ Greenwood.

Kanfer, R. (1990). Motivation and individual differences in learning: An integration of developmental, differential, and cognitive perspectives. *Learning and Individual Differences, 2,* 221–239.

Naceur, A., & Schiefele, U. (2005). Motivation and learning—The role of interest in construction of representation of and long-term retention: Inter- and intraindividual analyses. *European Journal of Psychology of Education, 20,* 155–170.

Renzulli, J. S. (1984). *Technical report of research studies related to the revolving door identification model* (Rev. ed.). Storrs: Bureau of Educational Research, University of Connecticut.

Simonton, D. K. (1997). *Genius and creativity: Selected papers.* Norwood, NJ: Ablex.

Spearman, C. (1904). "General intelligence," objectively determined and measured. *American Journal of Psychology, 15,* 201–293.

Spearman, C. (1927). *The abilities of man.* London: Macmillan.

Stepanek, J. (1999). *The inclusive classroom. Meeting the needs of gifted students: Differentiating mathematics and science instruction.* Portland, OR: Northwest Regional Educational Laboratory.

Sternberg, R. J. (1985). *Beyond IQ: A triarchic theory of human intelligence.* New York: Cambridge University Press.

Sternberg, R. J. (1988). *The triarchic mind: A theory of human intelligence.* New York: Viking.

Sternberg, R. J. (1997). *Successful intelligence.* New York: Plume.

Sternberg, R. J. (1999a). The theory of successful intelligence. *Review of General Psychology, 3,* 292–316.

Sternberg, R. J. (Ed.). (1999b). *Handbook of creativity.* New York: Cambridge University Press.

Sternberg, R. J., & Davidson, J. E. (Eds.). (2005) *Conceptions of giftedness* (2nd ed.). New York: Cambridge University Press.

Sternberg, R. J., Forsythe, G. B., Hedlund, J., Horvath, J., Snook, S., Williams, W. M., et al. (2000). *Practical intelligence in everyday life.* New York: Cambridge University Press.

Sternberg, R. J., Grigorenko, E. L., & Jarvin, L. (2001). Improving reading instruction: The triarchic model. *Educational Leadership, 58*(6), 48–52.

Sternberg, R. J., Grigorenko, E. L., Ferrari, M., & Clinkenbeard, P. (1999). A triarchic analysis of an aptitude–treatment interaction. *European Journal of Psychological Assessment, 15*(1), 1–11.

Sternberg, R. J., & Lubart, T. I. (1995). *Defying the crowd: Cultivating creativity in a culture of conformity.* New York: Free Press.

Sternberg, R. J., Torff, B., & Grigorenko, E. L. (1998). Teaching triarchically improves school achievement. *Journal of Educational Psychology, 90,* 374–384.

Subotnik, R., & Jarvin, L. (2005). Beyond expertise: Conceptions of giftedness as great performance. R. J. Sternberg & J. E. Davidson (Eds.), *Conceptions of giftedness* (2nd ed., pp. 343–357). New York: Cambridge University Press.

Subotnik, R. F., Jarvin, L., Moga, E., & Sternberg, R. J. (2003). Wisdom from gate-keepers: Secrets of success in music performance. *Bulletin of Psychology and the Arts, 4*(1), 5–9.

Subotnik, R. F., Kassan, L. D., Summers, E. S., & Wasser, A. B. (1994). *Genius revisited: High IQ children grown up.* Norwood, NJ: Ablex.

Terman, L. M., & Oden, M. (1940a). The significance of deviates. II. Status of the California gifted group at the end of sixteen years. *Yearbook of the National Society for the Study of Education, 39,* 67–74.

Terman, L. M., & Oden, M. (1940b). The significance of deviates. III. Correlates of adult achievement in the California gifted group. *Yearbook of the National Society for the Study of Education, 39,* 74–89.

AUTHOR NOTE

Preparation of this chapter was supported by Grant REC-9979843 from the National Science Foundation and R206R00001 from the Javits Act Program administered by the Institute for Educational Sciences, U.S. Department of Education. Grantees undertaking such projects are encouraged to express freely their professional judgment. This chapter, therefore, does not necessarily represent the position or policies of the National Science Foundation or the Institute for Educational Sciences, U.S. Department of Education, and no official endorsement should be inferred. We are grateful to all of the teachers and school administrators for their participation in this program, as well as to the postdoctoral associates who assisted with designing the instructional materials. The authors also wish to thank Ms. Robyn Rissman for her valuable editorial assistance.

Chapter 25

MATHEMATICS, ELEMENTARY

M. Katherine Gavin and Jill L. Adelson

his chapter addresses the major issues facing educators, administrators, and parents in nurturing mathematical talent in students at the elementary level. The focus is on presenting relevant research and guidance on the application of this research so that the reader will be able to make informed decisions that will benefit young mathematically gifted students. Providing appropriate curriculum for mathematically gifted students is complex, in part because the definition of mathematical giftedness is not universal. How one defines mathematical giftedness in turn affects how students are identified for services and how the actual services, including the curriculum, are rendered. Thus, to get a true picture of the research associated with curriculum for elementary mathematics gifted education, several areas need to be addressed. To varying degrees, the research addresses the following questions related to providing appropriate curriculum for mathematically gifted elementary students:

- How can we identify students who are mathematically gifted?
- What kinds of programming options for these students have research support?
- What instructional approaches and grouping models work best for these options?
- What research-based curriculum is appropriate for mathematically gifted elementary students?

THE DEFINITION OF MATHEMATICAL GIFTEDNESS

Prior to examining any questions on identification or programming for mathematically gifted students, it is crucial to begin with the knowledge of what mathematical giftedness means and how it is manifested in elementary students. This definition is the underlying construct that should drive identification, programming, and curriculum for gifted mathematics students.

In reviewing the literature, it is apparent that there is no one agreed upon definition of mathematical giftedness, and in fact, there are different schools of thought. Often it is defined empirically as an outcome of a score on an ability, aptitude, or achievement test, such as an IQ test, the SAT-M, or the mathematics sections of the Iowa Tests of Basic Skills (ITBS). Although testing provides an easy means for identification, it really skirts the issue of what mathematical giftedness is.

Renzulli (1988), Sternberg (1986), and Gardner (1983), among others, believe that giftedness is comprised of multiple talents rather than one general ability. In the area of mathematics, Benbow and Minor (2004) have shown that mathematically precocious students differ from those who are verbally precocious. In their study of 144 thirteen-year-old gifted children, students with gifts in the verbal domain scored higher on verbal and general knowledge kinds of tests whereas mathematical talent was associated with spatial and nonverbal abilities.

Yet, there has been little research conducted on what constitutes mathematical giftedness. What has been done relates to the characteristics displayed by mathematically gifted children. The Russian psychologist V. A. Krutetskii (1968/1976) conducted the seminal work in this field when he did a number of observational studies of what he labeled "not capable," "capable," and "very capable" students from ages 6 to 16. Similar to the methodology employed by Jean Piaget, he spent a great deal of time observing these students as they worked on mathematical problems. His goal was to differentiate the talents of these students in order to provide a structure of abilities that constitutes mathematical giftedness. He outlined his results in *The Psychology of Mathematical Abilities in Schoolchildren* (1968/1976), creating a rather detailed and complicated structure.

Usiskin (1999) condensed Krutetskii's structure into four major components: flexibility, curtailment, logical thought, and formalization. Flexibility is being able to switch strategies in solving a problem easily and many times in order to make sense of the problem. Curtailment means being able to skip explicit steps in the logical thought process as though looking at the solution to a problem as a whole instead of as linearly connected logical steps. This may be one reason why some students have difficulty in explaining their reasoning; they literally cannot go back and retrace their steps because they did not follow a step-by-step process to get the answer. Krutetskii (1968/1976) also found that students who are gifted mathematically follow a logical thought process, even if they are able to skip some steps. They look at the world from a logical perspective and filter all incoming data through this lens. They often think in mathematical symbols. The fourth component of mathematical giftedness is formalization, the ability to see the overall structure of a problem and to make generalizations very quickly from only a few examples.

One reason that the definition of mathematical giftedness is elusive is that there are different types of talent within the domain itself. Along with Krutetskii (1968/1976), other researchers in the Soviet Union found mathematically talented students exhibited a variety of characteristics and not all the same ones (Ivanitsyna, 1970, as cited in Sriraman, 2004; Menchinskaya, 1959; Shapiro, 1965, as cited in Sriraman, 2004; Yakimanskaya, 1970, as cited in Sriraman, 2004). In discussing the mathematical cast of mind that these students possess, these researchers stated that some students have an "algebraic cast of mind" and tend to be very abstract, interpreting even geometric problems in an algebraic way, whereas others are more "geometric" and have facility with visualizing problems pictorially. Then, there are some who possess a "harmonic" mind with a combination of both algebraic and geometric casts of mind. Krutetskii's work with elementary-aged children, in particular, found that more of them were of the harmonic type. It is important to note that Krutetskii specifically identified swiftness, computational ability, memory for formulas, and other details as "not obligatory" though useful characteristics of mathematical giftedness (Krutetskii, 1968/1976; Sowell, Bergwell, Zeigler, & Cartwright, 1990).

In more recent studies, Davidson and Sternberg (1984) worked with fourth-, fifth-, and sixth-grade students to determine how insight skills were related to intellectual giftedness. They found that mathematically gifted students use three processes: selective encoding, which involves sifting out relevant information from a problem situation; selective combination, which involves synthesizing the relevant information; and selective comparison, which involves comparing the information synthesized to other relevant information. They pointed out that speed in doing mathematics is important but is secondary to insight. According to Davidson and Sternberg, one can be exceptionally insightful but not a quick problem solver and still be considered gifted in mathematics; however, one cannot be gifted if speed is the only element present. Other characteristics of gifted mathematics students include their focus on conceptual understanding (Sheffield,

Bennet, Berriozabal, DeArmond & Wertheimer, 1999), their ability to abstract and generalize (Krutetskii, 1968/1976; Shapiro, 1965, as cited in Sriraman, 2004; Sriraman, 2002), and their persistence and ability to make decisions in problem-solving situations (Frensch & Sternberg, 1992).

In the United States, in particular, the definition of mathematical gift-edness becomes complicated because of students' varying levels of exposure to mathematics due to different home and school experiences. The National Council of Teachers of Mathematics (NCTM) established a task force in 1994 to examine issues on the development of mathematically talented students and to make recommendations regarding identification and programming. The task force purposely chose the word *promising* rather than *gifted* or *talented* to emphasize the goal of including students who have previously been excluded because of lack of opportunity or experience. Their definition was an outgrowth of the broadened definition of giftedness issued by the federal government after the passage of the Javits Gifted and Talented Education Act in 1988. The task force defined promising students as "those who have the potential to become leaders and problem solvers of the future" (Sheffield et al., 1999, p. 310). More specifically, they stated:

> We see mathematical promise as a function of
> * ability,
> * motivation,
> * belief, and
> * experience or opportunity.
>
> This definition includes the students who have been traditionally iden-tified as gifted, talented, precocious, and so on, and it adds students who have been traditionally excluded from rich mathematical oppor-tunities. This definition acknowledges that students who are math-ematically promising have a large range of abilities and a continuum of needs that should be met. (p. 310)

Practical Implications

The research cited above clearly indicates that mathematical giftedness is not a single construct nor is it the same for all those who possess this gift. It is multidimensional and can be displayed in a variety of ways. It is important to note that computational ability, memorization of formulas, and speed are not required to be mathematically gifted (Davidson & Sternberg, 1984; Krutetskii, 1968/1976). This needs to be carefully considered when establishing an iden-tification process and consequently providing an appropriate curriculum of study for identified students. Using the research on mathematical giftedness to understand what it really means can change the way we identify and serve gifted students.

Limitations

Research conducted in the area of defining mathematical giftedness has not been extensive and is dated. The field needs more recent qualitative studies in which students are observed in the process of creative problem solving and interviewed about their thinking in order to help us understand what this construct entails. A word of caution to the reader is important here. There are many articles written on describing the characteristics of gifted young children with a list of observable characteristics that are often used as checklists for identification. Most of these articles are not research-based and are written from the experiences of the authors. The major substantive work on defining the characteristics of mathematically talented students has been done by Krutetskii, and his process of interviews and observations has been used by Russian educators for more than 50 years (Sowell et al., 1990).

HOW CAN WE IDENTIFY STUDENTS WHO ARE MATHEMATICALLY GIFTED?

The discussion of what it means to be mathematically gifted leads directly to identification. It is difficult to separate the definition of mathematical giftedness from identification and, in turn, isolate identification from the curriculum and instruction provided to students. Defining mathematical giftedness should naturally lead to identifying students with these gifts, and educators should identify students to match services to develop their talent, which includes curriculum and its delivery model. Furthermore, identification and the services provided for students should inform one another in an ongoing process to provide an optimal match between the two. If these are not aligned, the effectiveness of any one component is clearly diminished. Figure 1 provides a visual presentation of this process.

Quantitative Measures for Identification

Perhaps because standardized intelligence, aptitude, and achievement tests are norm-referenced with the statistical assurances of reliability and validity, they are the most widely used quantitative measure for identifying gifted students (Callahan, Hunsaker, Adams, Moore, & Bland, 1995). This includes mathematically gifted students (Sowell et al., 1990). However, Sheffield (1994) pointed out that standardized achievement tests may not identify students who are truly gifted in mathematics because they concentrate on low-level tasks that do not require students to think and reason in ways that Krutetskii observed as defining attributes of mathematical giftedness. Romberg and Wilson (1992) examined the mathematics sections of six different standardized achievement

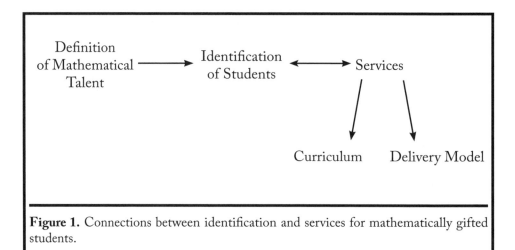

Figure 1. Connections between identification and services for mathematically gifted students.

tests and found that 62–82% of the items tested the topic of number and operations, with very few items dealing with other mathematical content areas, such as probability, geometry, and algebraic reasoning. In the area of number and operations, 62–91% of the items focused on computation. They found that 84–96% of the items dealt with following procedures, a low-level skill, with only 2–16% of the items testing higher level mathematics concepts.

Most of the research on the identification of mathematically gifted students has been done with students in middle and high school who are exceptionally talented. The Study for Mathematically Precocious Youth (SMPY), which was begun by Julian Stanley of Johns Hopkins University in 1971, is a well-known, systematic longitudinal study that initially focused on these upper-grade-level students and has followed them through their schooling to track their performance (Lubinski & Benbow, 2006). Students in these grade levels who score in the top 3% on a standardized achievement test at their current grade level are invited to take an out-of-level test. Highly talented students require this type of test because of the ceiling effect on regular grade-level testing. In fact, we do not know how high these students can achieve because the test is basically too easy.

Extending the SMPY talent search concept to elementary students, researchers from various universities, including Johns Hopkins University, Carnegie Mellon University, University of Iowa, and University of North Texas, have investigated the effectiveness of using out-of-level tests on younger students who score in the top 3% on standardized achievement tests. These out-of-level tests include the lower level of the Secondary School Admission Test (SSAT-L), the PLUS test designed specifically as an above-level test for fifth and sixth graders, and most recently, the EXPLORE test developed by ACT. These tests are used specifically to identify highly talented elementary students for participation in their Elementary Student Talent Search. Results showed that this method eliminated the ceiling effect for at least 98% of the students and the very top students from this sample were able to be identified (Assouline & Lupkowski-

Shoplik, 2005; Lupkowski-Shoplik & Assouline, 1993). Sheffield (1994) offered a word of caution on using this procedure as the sole means of identifying the talent pool. She stated that there is an inherent problem with this identification procedure in that the initial screening uses the standardized achievement test score. Because these initial tests are not testing high-level reasoning or creative problem solving, some talented students may be missed.

Other researchers have found that reliance on global indicators of intelligence may exclude too many nonverbal students. Benbow and Minor (1986) found support for using the Raven's Progressive Matrices Test for identification of mathematically gifted students because the Raven's test scores predicted performance of gifted students in a fast-paced mathematics class. They concluded that there should be a "multiple-talents approach to identification" with selection based on the intent of the program and not an overall ability test score. Identification should be aligned with programming and curriculum.

There are other ability, achievement, and aptitude tests that are not associated with a particular programming model or study but are available to identify mathematically gifted elementary students. Researchers and programs alike have used many of these to find a broader talent pool of students than SMPY or other talent searches are identifying. For a review of these tests, including an analysis of their construction and statistical strengths, refer to Assouline and Lupkowski-Shoplik's (2005) discussion in their book *Developing Math Talent: A Guide for Educating Gifted and Advanced Learners in Math*. Research is needed on the effectiveness of these tests as identification tools, whether alone or in combination with other measures.

Limitations. Most of the tests mentioned above are generally not free of charge and thus may not be available to economically disadvantaged students, although some scholarships are offered. Programs using these tests are generally looking for students who are extremely precocious, the top 1–2% of the population. There is a range of talent in the area of mathematical giftedness, as there is in any domain, and these tests are meant to select only the very top. The use of out-of-level achievement or aptitude tests as a sole means of identification is questioned by the National Council of Teachers of Mathematics. Recommendations made by the National Task Force on the Mathematically Promising show the concern for missing students who do not have exposure to accelerated curriculum and/or who traditionally do not do well on standardized timed tests. The Task Force makes the following statement:

> Traditional methods of identifying gifted and talented mathematics students, such as standardized test scores, are designed to limit the pool of students identified as mathematically promising. . . . To avoid bias in the selection process, identification procedures should include a wide variety of measures to identify the broadest number of both females and males from diverse cultural and socioeconomic backgrounds. (Sheffield et al., 1999, p. 311)

Qualitative Measures for Identification

Rating Scales. To help with the identification process, researchers have developed checklists and rating scales. The reader should be cautious of using such instruments that have no research backing. With that in mind, teacher rating scales can help identify behavioral characteristics of students who are mathematically promising and, in fact, help teachers think differently about the possibility of mathematical talent in many of their students. There are a variety of rating scales on the market for teachers to identify students with gifted characteristics, including the Gifted Education Scale, Second Edition (GES–2; McCarney & Anderson, 1998); the Pfeiffer-Jarosewich Gifted Rating Scale (GRS; Jarosewich, Pfeiffer, & Morris, 2002); and the Gifted and Talented Evaluation Scales (GATES; Gilliam, Carpenter, & Christensen, 1996). The Scales for Rating the Behavioral Characteristics of Superior Students (SRBCSS; Renzulli, Smith, White, Callahan, & Hartman, 1976) were one of the earliest scales. These scales have undergone several revisions and are still one of the most widely used rating scales. In the area of elementary mathematics, researchers recently have added a new set of scales to the set (Renzulli et al., 2004). This scale builds on the lists of characteristics cited by leading mathematics educators and researchers for this age group, yet also has the strength of statistical testing. Content experts in the fields of gifted education, mathematics education, and mathematics, including resource teachers and university faculty, evaluated the scale. Teachers piloted the scale by rating more than 735 students in grades 4–6 in urban, suburban, and rural settings. Statistical analysis revealed very high reliability; thus, the scales have solid research backing. Furthermore, there also is a teacher-training component that helps ensure reliability for individual administration.

Interviews and Observation. The use of informal observation during performance tasks and follow-up interviews may help to ensure an inclusive and valid identification process. Clinical investigations of problem-solving processes comparing mathematically gifted students with average-ability students show that gifted students think differently about problems, employing Krutetskii's structure of mathematical thinking (Krutetskii, 1968/1976; Span & Overtoom-Corsmit, 1986; Stonecipher, 1987). In other studies, researchers found gifted students to be quick to identify the nature of problems and rely on mental rather than paper-and-pencil problem solving (Catron, 1985; Mandell, 1980). Using observational studies and interviews should enable teachers to better complete the rating scales, which include such characteristics as the ability to switch strategies easily when appropriate and the ability to solve problems abstractly.

In the area of identifying very young students at the primary level, there is a paucity of research. However, researchers have conducted some work with regard to parent identification from observations of their children. Interestingly, research has shown that parents of young children are relatively accurate in identifying general giftedness in their children (Colligan, 1976; Robinson, Dale, & Landesman, 1990; Silverman, Chitwood, & Waters, 1986), even more so than their teachers (Ciha, Harris, Hoffman, & Potter, 1974; Jacobs, 1971). Using questionnaires completed by 120 parents of kindergarten students, Pletan, Robinson, Berninger, & Abbott (1995) found that these parents not only were good at identifying very young children as mathematically gifted but also were accurate in describing them in terms of a general intelligence factor, a memory factor, a spatial reasoning factor, and a specific relational knowledge factor.

Limitations. When using qualitative techniques, there is always an inherent bias of the person who is observing or interviewing. However, these techniques can add an important dimension to the identification process. When using them to identify mathematically gifted students, teachers should employ a problem-solving focus in their instruction to encourage the traits of talented students to emerge. Teachers may also need training in observation and interview skills in order to recognize how mathematically gifted students solve problems. With these two things in place, qualitative instruments can be effective as identification tools and should be used in conjunction with other measures. Having analyzed research on identification procedures, Sowell et al. (1990) concluded that the use of more than one instrument is desirable. The NCTM Task Force on the Mathematically Promising (Sheffield et al., 1999) concurred and pointed out that it is especially important to use a variety of identification tools to target students from disadvantaged backgrounds with mathematics potential.

WHAT KINDS OF PROGRAMMING OPTIONS FOR THESE STUDENTS HAVE RESEARCH SUPPORT?

The Optimal Match

The first consideration in deciding about programming and curriculum for talented students is to focus on the optimal match (Assouline & Lupkowski-Shoplik, 2005; Waxman, Robinson, & Mukhopadhyay, 1996). This means assessing the student's academic ability and achievements and matching them to the most appropriate level and type of curriculum and instruction. In doing this, educators should consider various research-based programming options. In the area of mathematics, researchers conducted most of the studies on middle, high school, and college students, and many of these studies are associated with the research conducted by talent searches with students at these age levels. Nevertheless, some studies have been conducted at earlier grades.

Acceleration

Despite decades of research on the positive effects of acceleration for gifted students, it is still a hotly contested subject in educational circles. The Templeton National Report on Acceleration, *A Nation Deceived: How Schools Hold Back America's Brightest Students* (Colangelo, Assouline, & Gross, 2004), is a comprehensive review of the literature on acceleration, with experts in the field advocating for its use as an excellent and cost-effective measure to meet the needs of talented students. This report lists 18 different types of acceleration, provides the research support, and discusses social-emotional issues, long-term effects, and public policy. The entire report is available online at http://www.nationdeceived.org. Acceleration for gifted elementary students includes early entrance to kindergarten, grade skipping, and subject-based acceleration.

Early Entrance and Grade Skipping

Research has shown that early entrance to kindergarten or first grade is an efficient and effective way to meet the needs of young gifted students (Robinson & Weimer, 1991; Rogers, 1992). Students gained an additional half a year's growth in all academic areas as compared to their gifted age peers (Rogers, 1992). With regard to their mathematical development, early entrance is the easiest and smoothest solution because gaps in skills and knowledge are minimized. Research has also shown grade skipping to be an effective form of acceleration for students who are advanced in many content areas, not just mathematics (Kulik, 1992; Kulik & Kulik, 1984; Rogers, 1992; Rogers & Kimpston, 1992). Note that research has shown that both these types of acceleration do not hamper a child's social or emotional development (Rankin & Vialle, 1996; Robinson & Weimer, 1991; Rogers, 1992). Instruments, such as the Iowa Acceleration Scale developed by Assouline, Colangelo, Lupkowski-Shoplik, Lipscomb, and Forstadt (2003), are available to help parents and educators determine whether acceleration is the appropriate academic option.

Subject–Matter Acceleration

In subject-matter acceleration, most of the studies have, in fact, been in the area of mathematics; however, most of them center on skipping middle school grades in order to take algebra in seventh or eighth grade. In 17 studies on mathematics acceleration ranging in grade levels from 2 to 12, Rogers (1992) found three fifths of a year of accelerated growth in mathematics, demonstrating the positive effects of moving ahead in mathematics. Case studies conducted by Lupkowski-Shoplik and Assouline (1994) with extremely mathematically gifted children in first grade and younger have found evidence that either grade skipping or subject acceleration were the best options for these children. However, in a case study of two highly gifted preschoolers, Lewis (2002) found that acceleration alone was not enough. She suggested that three key components—assessment, flexible scheduling, and counseling—are critical. In the area of mathematics, she suggested early acceleration may be appropriate in the hands of skilled teachers who are strong in content and pedagogy. Longitudinal studies tracking these students are necessary to chart student progress through the grade levels, as has been done with older students in SMPY. The results of SMPY suggest that acceleration does not harm gifted students academically and often helps them establish a long-lasting interest in mathematics. The students studied expressed high levels of satisfaction with college and with their experiences with acceleration (Swiatek, 2002).

Distance Learning

The Education Program for Gifted Youth (EPGY) at Stanford University has developed and offers computer-based courses in mathematics for high-ability students in grades kindergarten through high school. These are individualized programs in which a student moves through the curriculum at a fast pace. Results of their research (Tock & Suppes, 2002) have shown that students who work through this curriculum at a pace and schedule most suited to their needs advance their understanding beyond their current grade level, often advancing several levels.

Extracurricular Programs

Some programs offer acceleration outside of the regular school curriculum. Many universities that conduct talent searches, such as Carnegie Mellon, University of Iowa, Northwestern University, and Johns Hopkins, offer weekend and more intense academic summer programs for highly talented students in elementary through high school. Mills, Ablard, and Gustin (1994) conducted research on one such program for third through sixth graders. In this program, developed by the Center for Talented Youth (CTY) at Johns Hopkins University, highly talented mathematics students who had completed at least one year of the flexibly paced mathematics course gained as much as 46 percentile points from pre- to posttesting, with third graders showing the greatest gains. These students also outperformed a comparison group of older students.

Enrichment

There has been a great deal of debate over the years in terms of acceleration versus enrichment as the best means to meet the academic needs of gifted mathematics students. Those in favor of enrichment are concerned that acceleration alone will not provide a rich curriculum for students to investigate deep and complex mathematical concepts and will encourage students to learn mathematics in a rapid, superficial manner. Proponents of acceleration are afraid that enrichment alone is not enough for mathematically gifted students who can reason abstractly and are able to master concepts more easily than their grade-level peers.

There are far more studies on acceleration than enrichment in mathematics. In a review of the research on programs for mathematically gifted students, Sowell (1993) found that five studies focusing solely on mathematics enrichment had mixed results. In the two studies involving younger children (preschool and grades 4–6), preschoolers and fourth graders outperformed the control groups on cognitive measures, and the fourth graders improved in attitude toward mathematics, as well. However, the fifth and sixth graders were not significantly different from the control group in attitude or achievement.

Practical Implications

The answer to the most appropriate program for mathematically talented students is perhaps a combination of both acceleration and enrichment in programming, keeping in mind that the optimal match must be considered for each student. Research on the use of both acceleration and enrichment is promising, albeit limited. Moore and Wood (1988) found that students in grades 3–7 learned mathematics more quickly using this combined approach than they would have if they were in the regular school curriculum. In studying the effects of the Model Mathematics Program that used both an accelerated and enriched mathematics curriculum with students of varying high-ability levels, Miller and Mills (1995) found that students in second through sixth grade made dramatic gains in mathematics achievement. Gavin (2005) found that third- and fourth-grade students in an enriched and accelerated mathematics program made significant achievement gains and maintained positive attitudes towards mathematics.

WHAT INSTRUCTIONAL APPROACHES AND GROUPING MODELS WORK BEST FOR THESE OPTIONS?

Instructional Approaches

Differentiation Within the Regular Classroom. Because mathematically talented students are able to skip steps in the logical thought process, use problem-solving strategies flexibly, and have a mathematical cast of mind, they require differentiated instruction and curriculum. Tomlinson (1995) developed a working definition of differentiating instruction: "consistently using a variety of instructional approaches to modify content, process, and/or products in response to learning readiness and interest of academically diverse learners" (p. 80).

In a study on the effects of grouping and curricular practices on fourth- and fifth-grade students' mathematics achievement, Tieso (2002) found that "an enhanced or differentiated mathematics unit can create significant achievement gains over the students' regular textbook unit" (p. 22). Furthermore, quantitative analyses indicated that this was true for students with middle or high levels of prior knowledge and for students from all socioeconomic backgrounds.

Unfortunately, research has shown that differentiation for high-ability students is not a common practice in elementary classrooms. In a national survey, fourth- and fifth-grade teachers in public and private schools responding to the Classroom Practices Questionnaire (CPQ) stated that they made only minor modifications in the regular curriculum and in their instruction to meet the needs of gifted learners (Archambault et al., 1993). These results were consistent for the four regions of the United States (Northeast, South, West, and North Central) and for teachers in rural, urban, and suburban schools. Likewise, Westberg, Archambault, Dobyns, and Salvin (1993) found that teachers in 46 third- and fourth-grade classrooms provided no form of differentiation in 84% of the activities (across all five subject areas) for the targeted gifted students the researchers observed and that these students spent the majority of their time on passive activities, such as written assignments and participating in review/recitation activities.

Curriculum Compacting. Curriculum compacting (Reis, Burns, & Renzulli, 1992; Renzulli & Reis, 1985) is an instructional strategy to streamline the learning activities for students who demonstrate proficiency on concepts and skills prior to teaching. Teachers then are able to provide students with enriched and/or accelerated experiences in lieu of the regular curriculum. Schultz (1991) conducted a study on the mathematics achievement of 132 fourth graders using curriculum compacting and found no significant differences on student achievement in mathematics as measured by the ITBS between the students whose curriculum was compacted and those who did not have this treatment. This means that students whose curriculum was compacted still achieved comparable scores on the fourth-grade ITBS to students who spent the majority or all of their time on the regular fourth-grade curriculum. In a national study, Reis et al. (1993) found that elementary teachers in three treatment groups were able to compact on average 39–49% of the regular mathematics curriculum for high-ability students. Again, they measured student pre- and postachievement using the ITBS, and results indicated that the achievement test scores of students whose curriculum was compacted were not significantly different from students whose curriculum was not compacted. Overall, in a review and analysis of gifted education research and literature, Rogers (2005) found curriculum compacting in the specific subject areas of mathematics, science, and foreign language to be very effective.

Diagnostic Testing → *Prescriptive Instruction Model.* The Diagnostic Testing → Prescriptive Instruction Model (DT→PI) is an instructional plan developed by Julian Stanley and based on a series of above-grade-level diagnostic tests to identify mathematically gifted students' strengths and weaknesses and determine areas in which they need work. Students work with a mentor on topics that they do not understand and take a posttest. They then reenter the process at the next higher level of achievement. Because a mentor is employed in this model, it is actually used outside of regular classroom instruction, and there is a cost to pay the mentors. Research with older students has shown that these students are able to move through courses much more quickly, some completing an entire year's worth of material in just 75 hours (Olszewski-Kubilius, Kulieke, Willis, & Krasney, 1989). This model has been adopted for use with younger students (Lupkowski & Assouline, 1992) and various university-based programs, such as Carnegie Mellon and Johns Hopkins, use it with elementary students. More research on the effectiveness of this model with younger children is needed.

Practical Implications

The findings from the curriculum compacting studies are important because they show that gifted students can eliminate up to half of the regular mathematics curriculum and still achieve the same results on standardized tests as their counterparts who have spent the majority or all of their time working with the regular curriculum (Reis et al., 1993). Yet, studies have shown that teachers are not making the modifications necessary to provide the enhanced instruction needed for talented students (Archambault et al., 1993; Westberg et al., 1993). In addition to not being provided modified curriculum and instruction, mathematically talented students spend much of their time reviewing (Reis et al., 1993). Although more research is needed, results to date are promising on the use of differentiated instruction and the Diagnostic Testing→Prescriptive Instruction model. Using research-based models to make instructional and curriculum decisions will help teachers provide appropriate educational opportunities for mathematically talented elementary students.

Grouping for Instruction

Gifted learners need some form of grouping by ability to effectively accomplish several educational goals, including appropriately broadened, extended, and accelerated curricula. They must be in groups so that their school curriculum may be appropriately broadened and extended. The pacing of instruction, the depth of content, and advancement in knowledge fields, which these students must have, cannot be effectively facilitated without a variety of ability grouping arrangements. (Rogers, 1993, p. 12)

Although she was commenting on gifted learners in general, the conclusions that Rogers (1993) drew ring true for mathematically talented students. Because they can learn mathematics at a faster rate and are able to compact nearly half of the regular curriculum, mathematically gifted elementary students would benefit from ability grouping when working on skill development or when the class is reviewing material they have already learned (Stepanek, 1999). Much of the research on ability grouping has not been specific to mathematics. However, the authors thought it important to review the research findings on different types of ability grouping because these may be used as strategies to meet the needs of mathematically gifted students. In particular, Kulik (1992) noted that "within-class and cross-grade programs are almost invariably single-subject programs in which group assignment is based on a specific skill" (p. 33); thus, these types of ability grouping may be particularly appropriate for meeting the needs of students who are specifically talented in mathematics.

Within-Class Grouping. Within-class grouping takes place in a heterogeneous classroom in which students are grouped with like-ability peers. This is perhaps the most widely used form of grouping. McPartland, Coldiron, and Braddock (1987) found that 90% of Pennsylvania schools used within-class ability grouping at the primary level and that 85–90% of Pennsylvania schools used it at the upper elementary level.

Kulik (1992) reviewed the research on within-class grouping. In 9 of the 11 studies he examined, students who were grouped within their class had higher overall achievement than those who were not grouped. In regard to within-class grouping specifically in mathematics, Slavin (1987) examined the research literature and found some evidence of substantial academic gains for students of all ability levels who participated.

Between-Class Grouping. In between-class grouping, students at a single grade level are divided into high-, middle-, and low-ability groups and instructed in separate classrooms for either the entire day or for a single subject. The high, middle, and low groups in many of these programs use the same text materials and follow the same curriculum. McPartland et al. (1987) found between-class grouping also to be used frequently in Pennsylvania elementary schools. They reported that almost 70% of Pennsylvania elementary schools used between-class grouping for at least one subject.

In order to determine the effects of between-class grouping on students, Kulik (1992) examined the research literature and found 25 studies in which grouping began during elementary school (grades 1–6). Results show a slight advantage for students in terms of achievement gains in high-ability groups and no difference for students in middle and low groups as compared to students who are heterogeneously grouped. However, only nine of these studies indicated that the curriculum and instructional methods were differentiated based on the ability of the groups, and only two of them indicated flexible movement between groups. Kulik concluded that the main problem with between-class grouping in the studies he examined was the lack of differentiated curriculum. He stated that these programs are "programs of differential placement but not differential treatment" (Kulik, 1992, p. xii).

Regrouping for mathematics with differentiated curriculum is a different story. Rogers' (1992) findings showed that the academic achievement of students regrouped for specific instruction in mathematics is significantly increased. In a study on the effects of grouping and curricular practices specifically on fourth- and fifth-grade students' mathematics achievement, Tieso's (2002) results revealed that high-achieving students make significant achievement gains when grouped by ability with differentiated instruction. Additionally, Gavin et al. (in press) found that between-class grouping in combination with a curriculum created specifically for high-ability students resulted in significant growth in conceptual understanding for third- and fourth-grade students identified as having mathematical talent.

Cross-Grade Grouping. Kulik (1992) also examined research on cross-grade grouping and reported that 11 of the 14 studies found that students achieved more when taught in cross-grade grouping. Like within-class grouping, cross-grade grouping usually involves differentiation of curriculum and instruction to group level.

Supporting Kulik's (1992) findings and applying directly to mathematics, Slavin (1987) reported substantial academic gains for elementary students of all ability levels who participated in cross-grade grouping in mathematics. Likewise, Mills et al. (1994) studied a flexibly paced mathematics course that placed students in groups based on entering achievement level without regard to age or grade level. Students in the program made achievement gains "far beyond the normative gains expected over a one-year gain" (p. 455) and greater than gains made by students several grade levels higher.

Pull-Out Programs. In some elementary schools, mathematically gifted programs are conducted as "pull-out" programs, where children are grouped for special instruction one or more days a week. Delcourt, Loyd, Cornell, and Goldberg (1994) studied pull-out programs for a variety of subject areas. They found that when the curriculum is sufficiently deepened, as well as differentiated from and advanced beyond that of the regular curriculum to accommodate the needs of the children, this type of instructional method can be very effective. However, Waxman et al. (1996) point out that many of these programs tend to offer students fun puzzles, logic problems, and field trips to keep interest high rather than advanced mathematics content to challenge talented students.

Student and Teacher Enjoyment of Grouping. In a study of 31 fourth- and fifth-grade classrooms, Tieso (2002) found statistically significant results that students enjoy participating in a variety of small groups:

> Students in all groups had positive reactions to the grouping arrangements. All of the students interviewed enjoyed changing classes or working in small groups for math even though they understood that they might be working on different assignments. The students also believed that all of their peers liked the grouping as well. (p. 27)

The students not only enjoyed working in a variety of different grouping arrangements, but the qualitative findings also suggested that the grouping arrangements did not damage students' self-esteem or self-efficacy. Likewise, the qualitative findings from Tieso's (2002) study suggested that "teachers preferred having students change classrooms for mathematics" (p. 29).

Summary of Ability Grouping. Kulik (1992) found that "a careful re-analysis of findings from all the studies on different types of grouping showed once again that higher aptitude students benefit academically from ability grouping" (p. 41). Likewise, after conducting an extensive review of research on grouping practices, Rogers (1991) concluded the following:

> It is very clear that the academic effects of a variety of long and short-term [homogeneous] grouping options for both the purposes of enrichment and acceleration are extremely beneficial for students who are academically or intellectually gifted or talented. There is *no* body of evidence that "the research says" otherwise! (pp. 25–26)

Practical Implications

Research shows that mathematically talented students benefit from being grouped together if curriculum and instruction are differentiated to meet their needs. In particular, ability grouping allows teachers to more effectively differentiate the curriculum and instruction to meet the different learning paces of students and the levels of complexity that they need. Depending on the school structure, this need can be met by within-class grouping, between-class grouping, cross-grade grouping, or pull-out programs.

Limitations

Some limitations need to be mentioned with regard to differentiation and ability grouping. Much of the literature on differentiation in mathematics provides recommendations for teachers (see Johnson, 2000; and Stepanek,

1999), but does not provide a research base for those recommendations. Also, much of the research on ability grouping and curriculum compacting that has been conducted is not focused on mathematics education in the elementary school. More research is needed to determine the effectiveness of differentiation, curriculum compacting, and ability grouping on the achievement of mathematically talented elementary students and to determine how these instructional approaches and grouping options can best be combined to meet their needs.

WHAT RESEARCH-BASED CURRICULUM IS APPROPRIATE FOR MATHEMATICALLY GIFTED ELEMENTARY STUDENTS?

In reviewing curriculum and instruction for gifted elementary students, it is important to note that curricular materials and instruction are dependent on the teacher's and/or district's perspective of what that curriculum should be. Should mathematically gifted students be studying skills and their application at a fast pace so as to advance through the levels of computation from kindergarten to algebra quickly? Or, should these students be studying advanced mathematical concepts and be required to think deeply about the mathematics while learning mathematical skills as a means to understand the concepts better?

Skills-Based Curriculum Approaches

Researchers focused on a positive response to the first question are generally advocates of an individualized mathematics program that allows students to master skills and move ahead based on mastery. Accelerated Math (Renaissance Learning, 1998) is one such program that is a curriculum-based instructional management system for elementary mathematics. It involves assessment of student skill level and provision of instruction matched to skill level, personalized goal setting, significant amounts of practice time using an "Algorithm Problem Generator," and provision of direct and immediate feedback to students and teachers regarding performance. Ysseldyke, Tardrew, Betts, Thill, and Hannigan (2004) studied the effectiveness of this program in improving test scores on mathematics skills in relation to numeric concepts, computation, and mathematics applications. Results showed that gifted students in grades 3–6 using the program scored significantly higher on these skills than gifted students who were not using the program.

Concepts-Based Curriculum Approaches

Although it is important for mathematically gifted students to master skills and their applications, NCTM (2000) stresses the importance of studying a variety of content strands, as well as a strong focus on the process strands of problem solving, communication, reasoning, connections, and representations. In order to develop the variety of abilities that have been observed in mathematically gifted students, curriculum must extend far beyond computation skills. In fact, NCTM (1980, 2000) states that problem solving should be the focus of the curriculum and especially so for gifted mathematics students (Sheffield, 1994; Wheatley, 2004). Sheffield (1994) stated that all students should follow the core curriculum outlined in the NCTM standards, and goes on to emphasize that top students should do more—they should "explore topics in more depth, draw more generalizations, and create new problems and solutions related to each topic" (p. 21).

In this vein, Gavin, Sheffield, Chapin, and Dailey developed Project M[3]: Mentoring Mathematical Mind (Project M[3], 2005). This curriculum focuses on students thinking and acting like mathematicians within a classroom culture of verbal and written discussion, as opposed to individual work on mastering skills (Gavin et al., in press). The Mentoring Mathematical Minds series combines the core content promoted by NCTM with exemplary practices of gifted education. There is a strong focus on in-depth study of advanced math concepts, mathematical creativity, motivating students, and appealing to their interests as recommended by Renzulli (2001).

Research (Carroll, 2004, 2005, 2006) on the effectiveness of this curriculum has shown statistically significant gains on the ITBS. In addition, students have made significant gains on open-ended questions that assess mathematical understanding of concepts and the ability to communicate mathematically. Participating students have outperformed a comparison group of gifted students from the same schools on these measures, as well.

Practical Implications

Elementary teachers have many challenges in meeting the needs of gifted mathematics students. One of the biggest is finding appropriate curriculum to challenge and motivate these students. There are excellent books with suggestions for topics to be studied by talented students (see Johnson, 2000; Sheffield, 1994; and VanTassel-Baska & Stambaugh, 2006) and resources available that stimulate these students (see Findell, Gavin, Greenes, & Sheffield, 2000; and Sheffield, 2003).

Some individualized programs, such as Accelerated Math, have been effective in accelerating skill development in gifted elementary students. Other curriculum such as Project M[3]: Mentoring Mathematical Minds, focuses on mathematical reasoning and creativity along with conceptual understanding.

Research results show students have made statistically significant gains in mathematical understanding and have outperformed a comparison group of like ability. These results show promise for this curriculum. More research on its longitudinal effects is in progress.

There are also extracurricular opportunities for talented elementary students of which teachers should be aware. Those that are research-based are for exceptionally talented students and offered by universities through talent searches, as mentioned earlier. In addition, there are competitions for elementary students conducted at the school level, including Mathematical Olympiads for Elementary and Middle Schools (http://moems.org), the Math League (http://www.mathleague.com), the Continental Math League (http://www.continentalmathematicsleague.com). Teachers often coach students as part of an afterschool program or mathematics club in preparing students for these competitions. Although there is no research to date on the effectiveness of these competitions, many students participate nationally (more than 87,000 students in the 2004–2005 Math Olympiads elementary division; R. Kalman, personal communication, January 9, 2006), and the material is quite challenging.

SUMMARY

Meeting the needs of mathematically gifted elementary students is a complex and multifaceted process. In planning an appropriate model, educators must consider the definition of mathematical giftedness, identification procedures, programming, curriculum, instruction, and delivery. The following bullet points summarize the authors' research-based recommendations to educators involved in serving mathematically gifted students.

- Mathematical giftedness is not a single construct, nor is it the same for all those who posses this gift. It is multidimensional and can be displayed in a variety of ways.
- The ability to compute swiftly or memorize formulas is not necessary for one to be mathematically gifted.
- In order to identify mathematically gifted students at the elementary level, a variety of measures should be used including standardized tests, school performance, and rating scales or questionnaires based on observations by teachers and/or parents.
- Educators need to find the optimal match between the needs of the student and the programming model, curriculum, and instruction provided.
- Acceleration at the elementary level in the form of early entrance to school and grade skipping has been used effectively to advance students who are mathematically gifted.

- A combination of acceleration and enrichment should be used to provide programming that is appropriately challenging for gifted elementary students.
- Differentiating the content, process, and/or products based on the readiness and interest of students in order to meet their needs has been shown to result in significant achievement gains for mathematically talented students.
- Research has indicated that mathematically talented students still achieve mastery on grade-level objectives when their curriculum is compacted. Nearly 50% of the regular mathematics curriculum can be streamlined for high-ability students.
- Ability grouping has academic benefits on the mathematics achievement of high-ability students. This can be achieved through within-class grouping, between-class grouping, cross-grade grouping, or a pull-out program. Within-class and cross-grade grouping have shown the greatest benefits.
- Curriculum that is both conceptually oriented and focused on advanced reasoning, problem solving, and creativity has been shown to improve the achievement of mathematically gifted elementary students.

RESEARCH-BASED RESOURCES

Assouline, S., & Lupkowski-Shoplik, A. (2005). *Developing math talent: A guide for education gifted and advanced learners in math.* Waco, TX: Prufrock Press.

Colangelo, N., Assouline, S. G., & Gross, M. U. M. (2004). *A nation deceived: How schools hold back America's brightest students* (Vols. 1 & 2). Iowa City, IA: The Connie Belin & Jacqueline N. Blank International Center for Gifted Education and Talent Development.

Gavin, M. K. (2001). *Encouraging talented girls in mathematics: A practitioner's guide for educators.* Storrs: National Research Center on the Gifted and Talented, University of Connecticut.

National Council of Teachers of Mathematics (NCTM). (2000). *Principles and standards for school mathematics.* Reston, VA: Author.

Sheffield, L. J. (1994). *The development of gifted and talented mathematics students and the National Council of Teachers of Mathematics Standards* (Research Monograph No. 9404). Storrs: National Research Center on the Gifted and Talented, University of Connecticut.

Sheffield, L. J. (Ed.). (1999). *Developing mathematically promising students.* Reston, VA: National Council of Teachers of Mathematics.

Waxman, B., Robinson, N. M., & Mukhopadhyay, S. (1996). *Parents nurturing math-talented young children* (Research Monograph No. 96228). Storrs: National Research Center on the Gifted and Talented, University of Connecticut.

RESEARCH-BASED CURRICULUM FOR MATHEMATICALLY TALENTED ELEMENTARY STUDENTS

Gavin, M. K., Chapin, S. H., Dailey, J., & Sheffield, L. J. (2006a). *Awesome algebra: Looking for patterns and generalizations.* Dubuque, IA: Kendall/Hunt.

Gavin, M. K., Chapin, S. H., Dailey, J., & Sheffield, L. J. (2006b). *Unraveling the mystery of the MoLi stone: Place value and numeration.* Dubuque, IA: Kendall/Hunt.

Gavin, M. K., Chapin, S. H., Dailey, J., & Sheffield, L. J. (2007a). *Analyze this! Representing and interpreting data.* Dubuque, IA: Kendall/Hunt.

Gavin, M. K., Chapin, S. H., Dailey, J., & Sheffield, L. J. (2007b). *Factors, multiples and leftovers: Linking multiplication and division.* Dubuque, IA: Kendall/Hunt.

Gavin, M. K., Chapin, S. H., Sheffield, L. J., & Dailey, J. (2007). *At the mall with algebra: Working with variables and equations.* Dubuque, IA: Kendall/Hunt.

Gavin, M. K., Dailey, J., Chapin, S. H., & Sheffield, L. J. (2007). *Getting into shapes.* Dubuque, IA: Kendall/Hunt.

Gavin, M. K., Sheffield, L. J., Chapin, S. H., & Dailey, J. (2006a). *Digging for data: The search within research.* Dubuque, IA: Kendall/Hunt.

Gavin, M. K., Sheffield, L. J., Chapin, S. H., & Dailey, J. (2006b). *What's the ME in measurement all about?* Dubuque, IA: Kendall/Hunt.

WEB SITES TO SUPPORT DEVELOPING MATHEMATICAL TALENT IN GIFTED STUDENTS

College of William and Mary, Center for Gifted Education Resource Guide to Mathematics Curriculum Material for High-Ability Learners, Grades K–8
http://www.cfge.wm.edu/documents/Resource_Guide_to_Mathematics_Curriculum_Materials.pdf

Northern Kentucky University, Dr. Linda Jensen Sheffield Resources for Parents, Teachers and Gifted, Talented, Creative and Promising Mathematics Students
http://www.nku.edu/~mathed/gifted.html

University of Connecticut, Neag Center for Gifted Education & Talent Development, Project M³: Mentoring Mathematical Minds and Other Curriculum Resources
http://www.gifted.uconn.edu/projectm3

Schoolwide Enrichment Model Curriculum Resources for Talent Development
http://www.gifted.uconn.edu/sem/bestofbest/tdsubjec.html

REFERENCES

Archambault, F. X., Westberg, K. L., Brown, S. W., Hallmark, B. W., Emmons, C. L., & Zhang, W. (1993). *Regular classroom practices with gifted students: Results of a national survey of classroom teachers* (Research Monograph No. 93102). Storrs: National Research Center on the Gifted and Talented, University of Connecticut.

Assouline, S., Colangelo, N., Lupkowski-Shoplik, A., Lipscomb, J., & Forstadt, L. (2003). *Iowa Acceleration Scale: Manual, form, and summary and planning sheet.* Scottsdale, AZ: Great Potential Press.

Assouline, S., & Lupkowski-Shoplik, A. (2005). *Developing math talent: A guide for educating gifted and advanced learners in math.* Waco, TX: Prufrock Press.

Benbow, C. P., & Minor, L. L. (1986). Mathematically talented students and achievement in the high school sciences. *American Educational Research Journal, 23,* 425–426.

Benbow, C. P., & Minor, L. L. (2004). Cognitive profiles of verbally and mathematically precocious students: Implications for identification of the gifted. In S. M. Reis (Series Ed.) & J. S. Renzulli (Vol. Ed.), *Identification of students for gifted and talented programs: Vol. 2. Essential readings in gifted education* (pp. 87–100). Thousand Oaks, CA: Corwin Press.

Callahan, C. M., Hunsaker, S. L., Adams, C. M., Moore, S. D., & Bland, L. C. (1995). *Instruments used in the identification of gifted and talented students* (Research Monograph No. 95130). Storrs: National Research Center on the Gifted and Talented, University of Connecticut.

Carroll, S. R. (2004). *Mentoring Mathematical Minds (M³): Evaluation of program year two (PY2).* Torrington, CT: Words & Numbers Research.

Carroll, S. R. (2005). *Mentoring Mathematical Minds (M³): Evaluation of program year three (PY3).* Torrington, CT: Words & Numbers Research.

Carroll, S. R. (2006). *Mentoring Mathematical Minds (M³): Evaluation of program year four (PY4).* Torrington, CT: Words & Numbers Research.

Catron, R. M. (1985). The effects of an intensive summer program on the SAT scores of gifted seventh graders. *Dissertation Abstracts International, 46,* 322B. (University Microfilms No. 385-29786)

Ciha, T. E., Harris, R., Hoffman, S., & Potter, M. W. (1974). Parents as identifiers of giftedness, ignored but accurate. *Gifted Child Quarterly, 18,* 191–195.

Colangelo, N., Assouline, S. G., & Gross, M. U. M. (2004). *A nation deceived: How schools hold back America's brightest students* (Vol. 2). Iowa City, IA: The Connie Belin & Jacqueline N. Blank International Center for Gifted Education and Talent Development.

Colligan, R. C. (1976). Prediction of kindergarten reading success from preschool report of parents. *Psychology in the Schools, 13*, 304–308.

Davidson, J. E., & Sternberg, R. J. (1984). The role of insight in intellectual giftedness. *Gifted Child Quarterly, 28*, 58–64.

Delcourt, M. A. B., Loyd, B. H., Cornell, D. G., & Goldberg, M. D. (1994). *Evaluation of the effects of programming arrangements on student learning outcomes* (Research Monograph No. 94018). Storrs: National Research Center on the Gifted and Talented, University of Connecticut.

Findell, C. R., Gavin, M. K., Greenes, C. E., & Sheffield, L. J. (2000). *Awesome math problems for creative thinking*. Chicago: Creative Publications.

Frensch, P., & Sternberg, R. (1992). *Complex problem solving: Principles and mechanisms*. Hillsdale, NJ: Erlbaum.

Gardner, H. (1983). *Frames of mind*. New York: Basic Books.

Gavin, M. K. (2005, Fall/Winter). Are we missing anyone? Identifying mathematically promising students. *Gifted Education Communicator, 24*–29.

Gavin, M. K., Casa, T. M., Adelson, J. L., Carroll, S. R., Sheffield, L. J., & Spinelli, A. (in press). Project M[3]: Mentoring mathematical minds: A research-based curriculum for talented elementary students. *Journal of Advanced Academics*.

Gilliam, J. E., Carpenter, B. O., & Christensen, J. R. (1996). *Gifted and Talented Evaluation Scales*. Austin, TX: PRO-ED.

Jacobs, J. C. (1971). Effectiveness of teacher and parent identification of gifted children as a function of school level. *Psychology in the Schools, 8*, 140–142.

Jarosewich, T., Pfeiffer, S. I., & Morris, J. (2002). Identifying gifted students using teacher rating scales: A review of existing instruments. *Journal of Psychoeducational Assessment, 20*, 322–336.

Johnson, D. T. (2000). *Teaching mathematics to gifted students in a mixed-ability classroom* (Report No. EDO-EC-00-03). Reston, VA: ERIC Clearinghouse on Disabilities and Gifted Education. (ERIC Document Reproduction Service No. ED441302)

Krutetskii, V. A. (1976). *The psychology of mathematical abilities in schoolchildren* (J. Teller, Trans.). Chicago: University of Chicago Press. (Original work published 1968)

Kulik, J. A. (1992). *An analysis of the research on ability grouping: Historical and contemporary perspectives* (Research Monograph No. 9204). Storrs: National Research Center on the Gifted and Talented, University of Connecticut.

Kulik, J. A., & Kulik, C. C. (1984). Effects of acceleration on students. *Review of Educational Research, 54*, 409–425.

Lewis, G. (2002). Alternatives to acceleration for the highly gifted child. *Roeper Review, 24*, 130–133.

Lubinski, D., & Benbow, C. P. (2006). Study of Mathematically Precocious Youth after 35 years: Uncovering antecedents for the development of math-science expertise. *Perspectives on Psychological Science, 1*, 316–346.

Lupkowski, A. E., & Assouline, S. G. (1992). *Jane and Johnny love math: Recognizing and encouraging mathematical talent in elementary students*. Unionville, NY: Trillium Press.

Lupkowski-Shoplik, A. E., & Assouline, S. G. (1993). Identifying mathematically talented elementary students: Using the lower level of the SSAT. *Gifted Child Quarterly, 37*, 118–123.

Lupkowski-Shoplik, A. E., & Assouline, S. G. (1994). Evidence of extreme mathematical precocity: Case studies of talented youths. *Roeper Review, 16*, 144–151.

Mandell, A. (1980). Problem-solving strategies of sixth-grade students who are superior problem solvers. *Science Education, 64*, 203–211.

McCarney, S. B., & Anderson, P. D. (1998). *The Gifted Evaluation Scale (2nd ed.): Technical manual.* Columbia, MO: Hawthorne Educational Services.

McPartland, J. M., Coldiron, J. R., & Braddock, J. H. (1987). *School structures and classroom practices in elementary, middle, and secondary schools.* Baltimore: Center for Research on Elementary and Middle Schools, Johns Hopkins University. (ERIC Document Reproduction Service No. ED 291703)

Menchinskaya, N. A. (1959). *Psychology of the mastery of knowledge in school.* Moscow: APN Press.

Miller, R., & Mills, C. (1995). The Appalachia Model Mathematics Program for gifted students. *Roeper Review, 18*, 138–141.

Mills, C. J., Ablard, K. E., & Gustin, W. C. (1994). Academically talented students' achievement in a flexibly paced mathematics program. *Journal for Research in Mathematics Education, 25*, 495–511.

Moore, N. D., & Wood, S. S. (1988). Mathematics in elementary school: Mathematics with a gifted difference. *Roeper Review, 10*, 231–234.

National Council of Teachers of Mathematics. (1980). *An agenda for action: Recommendations for school mathematics of the 1980s.* Reston, VA: Author.

National Council of Teachers of Mathematics. (2000). *Principles and standards for school mathematics.* Reston, VA: Author.

Olszewski-Kubilius, P., Kulieke, M. J., Willis, G. B., & Krasney, N. (1989). An analysis of the validity of SAT entrance scores for accelerated classes. *Journal for the Education of the Gifted, 13*, 37–54.

Pletan, M. D., Robinson, N. M., Berninger, V. W., & Abbott, R. D. (1995). Parents' observations of kindergartners who are advanced in mathematical reasoning. *Journal for the Education of the Gifted, 19*, 30–44.

Project M³. (2005). *Project M³: Mentoring mathematical minds.* Retrieved January 9, 2006, from http://www.projectm3.org

Rankin, F., & Vialle, W. (1996). Early entry: A policy in search of practice. *Australian Journal of Early Childhood, 21*, 6–11.

Reis, S. M., Burns, D. E., & Renzulli, J. S. (1992). *Curriculum compacting: The complete guide to modifying the curriculum for high ability students.* Mansfield Center, CT: Creative Learning Press.

Reis, S. M., Westberg, K. L., Kulikowich, J., Caillard, F., Hébert, T., Plucker, J., et al. (1993). *Why not let high ability students start school in January? The curriculum compacting study* (Research Monograph No. 93106). Storrs: National Research Center on the Gifted and Talented, University of Connecticut.

Renaissance Learning. (1998). *Accelerated math* [Computer software]. Wisconsin Rapids, WI: Author (http://www.renlearn.com).

Renzulli, J. S. (1988). A decade of dialogue on the three-ring conception of giftedness. *Roeper Review, 11*, 18–25.

Renzulli, J. S. (2001). *Enrichment curriculum for all students.* Arlington Heights, IL: SkyLight Training and Publishing.

Renzulli, J. S., & Reis, S. M. (1985). *The schoolwide enrichment model: A comprehensive plan for educational excellence.* Mansfield Center, CT: Creative Learning Press.

Renzulli, J. S., Smith, L. H., White, A. J., Callahan, C. M., & Hartman, R. K. (1976). *Scales for rating the behavioral characteristics of superior students.* Mansfield Center, CT: Creative Learning Press.

Renzulli, J. S., Smith, L. H., White, A. J., Callahan, C. M., Hartman, R. K., Westberg, K. L., et al. (2004). *Scales for rating the behavioral characteristics of superior students—online version*. Mansfield Center, CT: Creative Learning Press.

Robinson, N. M., Dale, P. S., & Landesman, S. J. (1990). Validity of Stanford-Binet IV with young children exhibiting precocious language. *Intelligence, 14,* 173–176.

Robinson, N. M., & Weimer, L. J. (1991). Selection of candidates for early admission to kindergarten and first grade. In W. T. Southern & E. D. Jones (Eds.), *The academic acceleration of gifted children* (pp. 29–73). New York: Teachers College Press.

Rogers, K. B. (1991). *The relationship of grouping practices to the education of the gifted and talented learner* (Research Monograph No. 9102). Storrs: National Research Center on the Gifted and Talented, University of Connecticut.

Rogers, K. B. (1992). A best-evidence synthesis of the research on acceleration options for gifted learners. In N. Colangelo, S. G. Assouline, & D. L. Ambroson (Eds.), *Talent development: Proceedings from the 1991 Henry B. and Jocelyn Wallace National Research Symposium on Talent Development* (pp. 406–409). Unionville, NY: Trillium.

Rogers, K. B. (1993). Grouping the gifted and talented: Questions and answers. *Roeper Review, 16,* 8–12.

Rogers, K. B. (2005, November). *A content analysis of gifted education research and literature*. Paper presented at the annual convention of the National Association for Gifted Children, Louisville, KY.

Rogers, K. B., & Kimpston, R. D. (1992). Acceleration: What we do vs. what we know. *Educational Leadership, 50,* 58–61.

Romberg, T. A., & Wilson, L. D. (1992). Alignment of tests with the standards. *Arithmetic Teacher, 39,* 18–22.

Schultz, C. B. (1991). *The effects of curriculum compacting upon student achievement in fourth grade mathematics*. Unpublished master's thesis, University of Northern Iowa, Cedar Falls.

Sheffield, L. J. (1994). *The development of gifted and talented mathematics students and the National Council of Teachers of Mathematics Standards* (Research Monograph No. 9404). Storrs: National Research Center on the Gifted and Talented, University of Connecticut.

Sheffield, L. J. (Chair), Bennett, J., Berriozabal, M., DeArmond, M., & Wertheimer, R. (1999). Report of the task force on the mathematically promising. In L. J. Sheffield (Ed.), *Developing mathematically promising students* (pp. 309–316). Reston, VA: National Council of Teachers of Mathematics.

Sheffield, L. J. (2003). *Extending the challenge in mathematics: Developing mathematical promise in K–8 students*. Thousand Oaks, CA: Corwin Press.

Silverman, L. K., Chitwood, D. G., & Waters, J. L. (1986). Young gifted children: Can parents identify giftedness? *Topics in Early Childhood Special Education, 6*(1), 23–28.

Slavin, R. E. (1987). Ability grouping: A best-evidence synthesis. *Review of Educational Research, 57,* 293–336.

Sowell, E. J. (1993). Programs for mathematically gifted students: A review of empirical research. *Gifted Child Quarterly, 37,* 124–129.

Sowell, E. J., Bergwell, L., Zeigler, A. J., & Cartwright, R. M. (1990). Identification and description of mathematically gifted students: A review of empirical research. *Gifted Child Quarterly, 34,* 147–154.

Span, P., & Overtoom-Corsmit, R. (1986). Information processing by intellectually gifted pupils solving mathematical problems. *Educational Studies in Mathematics, 17,* 273–295.

Sriraman, B. (2002). How do mathematically gifted students abstract and generalize mathematical concepts? *NAGC 2002 Research Briefs, 16,* 83–87.

Sriraman, B. (2004). Gifted ninth graders' notions of proof: Investigating parallels in approaches of mathematically gifted students and professional mathematicians. *Journal for the Education of the Gifted, 27,* 267–292.

Stepanek, J. (1999). *The inclusive classroom: Meeting the needs of gifted students: Differentiating mathematics and science instruction.* Retrieved January 5, 2006, from http://www.nwrel.org/msec/just_good/9/gifted.pdf

Sternberg, R. J. (1986). Identifying the gifted through IQ: Why a little bit of knowledge is a dangerous thing. *Roeper Review, 8,* 143–147.

Stonecipher, L. D. (1987). A comparison of mathematical problem solving processes between gifted and average junior high students: A clinical investigation. *Dissertation Abstracts International, 47,* 3347A-3348A. (University Microfilms No. 3387-00653)

Swiatek, M. A. (2002). A decade of longitudinal research on academic acceleration through the study of mathematically precocious youth. *Roeper Review, 24,* 141–144.

Tieso, C. L. (2002). *The effects of grouping and curricular practices on intermediate students' math achievement* (Research Monograph No. 02154). Storrs: National Research Center on the Gifted and Talented, University of Connecticut.

Title 5, Part D. [Jacob K. Javits Gifted and Talented Students Education Act of 1988], Elementary and Secondary Education Act of 1988 (2002), 20 U.S.C. Sec. 7253 et seq.

Tock, K., & Suppes, P. (2002). *The high dimensionality of students' individual differences in performance in EPGY's K6 computer-based mathematics curriculum.* Retrieved January 12, 2006, from http://epgy.stanford.edu/research/trajectories.html

Tomlinson, C. A. (1995). Deciding to differentiate instruction in middle school: One school's journey. *Gifted Child Quarterly, 39,* 77–87.

Usiskin, Z. (1999). The mathematically promising and the mathematically gifted. In L. J. Sheffield (Ed.), *Developing mathematically promising students* (pp. 57–69). Reston, VA: National Council of Teachers of Mathematics.

VanTassel-Baska, J., & Stambaugh, T. (2006). *Comprehensive curriculum for gifted learners* (3rd ed.). Boston: Allyn & Bacon.

Waxman, B., Robinson, N. M., & Mukhopadhyay, S. (1996). *Teachers nurturing math-talented young children* (Research Monograph No. 96228). Storrs: National Research Center on the Gifted and Talented, University of Connecticut.

Westberg, K. L., Archambault, F. X., Dobyns, S. M., & Salvin, T. J. (1993). *An observational study of instructional and curricular practices used with gifted and talented students in regular classrooms* (Research Monograph No. 93104). Storrs: National Research Center on the Gifted and Talented, University of Connecticut.

Wheatley, G. H. (2004). A mathematics curriculum for the gifted and talented. In S. M. Reis (Series Ed.) & J. VanTassel-Baska (Vol. Ed.), *Essential readings in gifted education: Vol. 4. Curriculum for gifted and talented students* (pp. 137–146). Thousand Oaks, CA: Corwin Press.

Ysseldyke, J., Tardrew, S., Betts, J., Thill, T., & Hannigan, E. (2004). Use of an instructional management system to enhance math instruction of gifted and talented students. *Journal for the Education of the Gifted, 27,* 293–319.

Chapter 26

MATHEMATICS, SECONDARY

Bharath Sriraman and Olof Bjorg Steinthorsdottir

INTRODUCTION

he reported research on talent development in mathematics education is limited, particularly at the secondary level. If one conducts a literature search in educational research journals using possible combinations of key words such as *mathematics*, *secondary*, *gifted education*, *highly able*, and *high achieving*, this results in only a relatively small proportion of articles focused on talent development/secondary mathematics gifted education in comparison to the total number of articles. This suggests that although the research output in the field has been steadily increasing, scant attention has been paid to mathematics talent development/gifted education at the secondary level.

In the U.S., the curriculum at the secondary level is typically enriched with honors and/or Advanced Placement courses. However this one-size-fits-all approach leaves much to be desired in terms of meeting the needs of mathematically gifted students with cognitive and affective traits different from the general group. In this chapter, we report and synthesize the major findings in the specific domain of mathematics with direct implications for the secondary curriculum. We draw on the relevant literature from international journals in mathematics education, gifted education, and philosophy.

A BRIEF REVIEW OF DEFINITIONS

There is no agreed upon definition of the term *mathematically gifted*. A synthesis of the body of studies on mathematical giftedness and characteristics of mathematical thinking show that mathematically gifted and talented students are different than their peers in:

1. the ability to abstract, generalize and discern mathematical structures (Kiesswetter, 1985, 1992; Krutetskii, 1976; Shapiro, 1965; Sriraman, 2002, 2003);
2. data management (Greenes, 1981; Yakimanskaya, 1970);
3. the ability to master principles of logical thinking and inference (Goldberg & Suppes, 1972; Suppes & Binford, 1965);
4. analogical, heuristic thinking, and posing related problems (Kiesswetter, 1985);
5. flexibility and reversibility of mathematical operations and thought (Krutetskii, 1976);
6. an intuitive awareness of mathematical proof (Sriraman, 2004c, 2004d);
7. independent discovery of mathematical principles (Sriraman, 2004a, 2004b);
8. decision-making abilities in problem-solving situations (Frensch & Sternberg, 1992; Sriraman, 2003);
9. the ability to visualize problems and/or relations (Presmeg, 1986); and
10. the ability to distinguish between empirical and theoretical principles (Davydov, 1988, 1990).

Some terms used within the existing research literature relevant for this chapter on secondary mathematics are: (1) contest problem training; (2) curriculum compacting; (3) curriculum differentiation; (4) heterogeneous and/or homogeneous grouping; (5) higher order mathematical processes (abstraction, generalization, discovering mathematical structures and problem solving); (6) radical acceleration; and (7) summer programs.

Contest problem training is used to refer to specific mathematical techniques from the areas of algebra, analysis, combinatorics, geometry, and number theory, which are useful to solve a wide variety contest problems (e.g., Fomin, Genkin & Itenberg, 1996).

Curriculum compacting simply means eliminating previously mastered work (typically involving routine computations and procedures) to condense the regular curriculum for gifted learners (Reis & Westberg, 1994).

Curriculum differentiation as defined by various theorists means tailoring the curriculum to meet the specific needs of learners of varied abilities. Although this term was initially used to refer to the varied needs of gifted learners, it has mutated into tailoring the curriculum and the classroom environment to create different learning experiences for all students (Tomlinson, 2004; VanTassel-Baska, 1985).

Homogeneous grouping refers to the grouping of learners at the same ability level, whereas heterogeneous grouping allows for learners of mixed-ability levels to work together on ongoing class activities, projects, and the like. Sometimes the term *exclusive grouping* is used to refer to homogeneous or same ability grouping.

Abstraction is defined as the process of delineating a certain quality as a common one and separating it from other qualities, which allows one to convert the general quality into an independent and particular object of subsequent actions (Piaget, 1987). On the other hand, generalization is the process by which one derives or induces from particular cases. It includes identifying commonalties in the structure of a given class of problems (Polya, 1954) and expanding domains of validity (Davydov, 1990). Simply put, the mental processes involved in the process of mathematical generalization work can be described as follows. First, a general method or structure is derived from a set of particular examples (Skemp, 1986). This method or structure is then applicable to other examples. The method/structure is then formulated explicitly and considered as an entity by itself, and its structure is analyzed (Piaget, 1987); this structure is then used to further encompass examples of different types, without making changes to the original method (Skemp, 1986). This process results in the formulation of new theorems, discovery of new proof techniques, and making deep connections within mathematics.

Radical acceleration refers to the practice of grade skipping and early university entrance for profoundly[1] gifted learners.

Summer programs are typically 1–4 week courses held on university campuses in which mathematically gifted students are exposed to new topics in mathematics, as well as its far-reaching applicability and relevance to the everyday world.

MAJOR RESEARCH QUESTIONS AND FINDINGS

Having defined some of the frequently used terms, we are now in a position to better understand the aims and the scope of the major research carried out in this area. Given the impossibility of listing every research question addressed, a synthesis of the literature reveals the following clusters of ques-

---

1   The "profoundly" gifted label is used for those with IQ scores of more than 180 (see Gross, 1993, 1994, 1995, 1997, 1998.)

tions around which talent development/gifted education research has focused. Some of the major research questions found in the literature are:

1. Can curriculum compacting, differentiation, and acceleration be effectively implemented in the secondary level mathematics?
2. What are the benefits of homogenous and/or heterogeneous grouping at the secondary level?
3. Which higher order mathematical processes should be cultivated at the secondary level?
4. What are the characteristics of mathematical tasks that offer the maximum benefits to gifted and talented learners?
5. Do mathematical contests offer an adequate challenge for mathematically gifted and talented students?
6. How appropriate are problem solving and modeling activities for mathematically gifted and talented students?
7. What are the benefits of radical acceleration and summer programs for secondary school students?
8. What impact have Advanced Placement and International Baccalaureate programs made on the secondary mathematics curriculum?

Before conveying the findings of the research, it is important for the reader to be aware that "what the research" in this area says is a function of three variables, namely what researchers consider to be (a) relevant mathematics (pure or applied or a combination), and (b) mathematical thinking at the secondary level (i.e., which processes are valued?), and (c) the nature of the battery used for testing (a) and (b). Therefore in a sense, the results are subjective and dependent to an extent on what the researchers consider mathematics is and what they are measuring, namely pure mathematical abilities or applied mathematical abilities. An example will help illustrate this important point. Kiesswetter (1992) has developed the so-called Hamburg Model in Germany, which is more focused on allowing gifted students to engage in problem posing activities, followed by time for exploring viable and nonviable strategies to solve the posed problems. This approach in a sense captures an essence of the nature of professional mathematics, where the most difficult task is to often to correctly formulate the problem (theorem). Some extant models within the U.S. such as those used in the Center for Talented Youth (CTY) tend to focus on accelerating the learning of concepts and processes from the regular curriculum, thus preparing students for advanced coursework within mathematics (Barnett & Corazza, 1993). With this caveat, the remainder of this chapter focuses on a synthesis of research related to curriculum compacting, differentiation, acceleration and radical acceleration, mixed-ability and/or exclusive grouping, math contests (Olympiad training methods), relevant mathematics content and contemporary curricula, mathematical processes, and characteristics of mathematical tasks.

Given the previously stated differences in mathematical abilities, curriculum compacting, differentiation, and acceleration can be effectively applied to secondary mathematics curriculum to meet the needs of the mathematically gifted students. There exists compelling evidence from longitudinal studies conducted in the former Soviet Union (Krutetskii, 1976; Shapiro, 1965) that mathematically gifted students are able to abstract and generalize mathematical concepts at higher levels of complexity and more easily than their peers in the context of arithmetic and algebra. These results were recently extended for the domains of combinatorics and number theory (Sriraman, 2002, 2003). Further, the research literature presents evidence that mathematically gifted individuals have complex problem-solving abilities (Frensch & Sternberg, 1992; Sriraman, 2003, 2004a, 2004b). Numerous studies (e.g., Kolitch & Brody, 1992; Kulik & Kulik, 1992) have shown that acceleration is perhaps the most effective way of meeting gifted student programming needs. Mathematics unlike any other discipline lends itself to acceleration because of the sequential developmental nature of many elementary concepts. The very nature of acceleration suggests that the principles of curriculum compacting are applied to trim out the excessive amount of repetitive tasks. Differentiation occurs naturally as acceleration allows gifted students with the opportunity to get through the "typical" traditional high school curriculum of geometry, algebra 2, precalculus, and calculus much faster than the norm of 4 years. Kolitch and Brody's (1992) report on mathematically gifted students who were exposed to this form of acceleration from the late middle school (seventh grade) onward were successful in completing calculus 2.5 years earlier than their peers. In this endeavor, exclusive-ability grouping as opposed to mixed-ability grouping has been found to particularly effective (Kulik & Kulik, 1992).

Julian Stanley's landmark Study of Mathematically Precocious Youth (SMPY) and the more than 250 papers produced in its wake, provides excellent empirical support for the effectiveness of curriculum acceleration and compaction in mathematics. Benbow, Lubinski, and Sushy (1996) have taken the findings from SMPY to argue for the benefits of this approach for profoundly gifted students. The longitudinal SMPY started by Julian Stanley at Johns Hopkins in 1971 generated a vast amount of empirical data gathered over the last 30 years, and has resulted in many findings about the types of curricular (e.g., acceleration, compacting) and affective interventions that foster the pursuit of advanced coursework in mathematics.

In addition, the effectiveness of radical acceleration and exclusive-ability grouping, as extensively reported by Gross (1993, 1994, 1995, 1997) in her longitudinal study of exceptionally and profoundly gifted students in Australia, indicates that the benefits far outweigh the risks of such an approach. Most of the students in Gross's studies reported high levels of academic success in addition to normal social lives (e.g., Gross, 1998). Simply put, the purpose of curricular modifications such as acceleration, compacting, and differentiation for mathematically gifted students is to tailor materials that introduce new topics at a faster pace that allow for high-level thinking and independence reminiscent of research in the field of mathematics.

Besides the use of curriculum compacting, differentiation, and acceleration techniques, many school programs offer *all* students opportunities to participate in math clubs, in local, regional and statewide math contests. Typically, the mathematically talented students benefit the most from such opportunities. In many countries (such as Hungary, Romania, Russia, and the U.S.), the objective of such contests is to typically select the best students to eventually move on to the national and international rounds of such competitions. The pinnacle of math contests are the prestigious International Math Olympiads (IMO) where teams of students from different countries work together to solve challenging math problems. Although the IMO is an example of an exclusive math contest, numerous countries such as France host the Le Kangourou des Mathématiques, in which large numbers of students from France and Europe participate. In general, contest problem training methods are highly dependent on the level in which the students are participating. Good Olympiad problems capture the essence of creating new mathematics during the solution process and convey to the student a "feel" of professional mathematics. At the local and regional levels, problems typically require mastery of concepts covered by a traditional high school curriculum with the ability to employ/connect methods and concepts flexibly. However, at the Olympiad levels, students in many countries are trained in the use of undergraduate-level algebraic, analytic, combinatorial, graph theoretic, number theoretic, and geometric principles. Any sampling of contest training books (e.g., Andreescu & Gelca, 2001; Erickson & Flowers, 1999; Fomin et al., 1996; Lozansky & Rousseau, 1996) reveals increasing use of contest problems involving discrete mathematics (as opposed to continuous mathematics).

The rationale for the increasing use of discrete mathematics in contest problems is that discrete mathematics, unlike continuous mathematics, is accessible to students, starting at the elementary levels because it builds from simple enumerative techniques. In an often quoted survey article in the literature, Kapur (1970) argued for the inclusion of combinatorial mathematics in the school curriculum for the following reasons:

1. its independence from calculus;
2. its usefulness to teach "concepts of enumeration, making conjectures, generalizations, optimization . . . and systematic thinking" (p. 114);
3. numerous applications to the physical, natural, and computing sciences, probability, number theory, and topology;
4. the opportunities created for using computing tools, but also illustrating the limitations of such tools (For instance, several families of numbers such as binomial coefficients, the Fibonacci numbers, and partition numbers are derived from recurrence relations. Conjectures and some plausible proofs of such conjectures can be constructed without advanced mathematical training.); and

5. discrete mathematics and their applications illustrate recent develop-
    ments in mathematics, thereby allowing students to develop a feel-
    ing for how mathematics grows. A synthesis of the body of studies
    on combinatorial thinking and discrete mathematics in general (e.g.,
    Sriraman & English, 2004) supports the successful use of such prob-
    lems within the mathematics curriculum, with significant benefits
    for the abstraction and generalization capabilities of mathematically
    gifted students (e.g., Sriraman, 2002).

In fact *all* of the National Science Funding (NSF) funded reform-based
mathematics projects in the 1990s, which resulted in the writing of integrated
mathematics curricula, include a heavy dose of discrete mathematics. In particular, high school curricula such as the Core Plus Mathematics Project (CPMP)
developed at Western Michigan University and The Systemic Initiative for
Montana Mathematics and Science (SIMMS) developed at the University of
Montana, are based on the premise of situating mathematics in authentic real-
world contexts, which require the modeling of a given situation, which in turn
motivates or creates the need for the use of mathematical techniques and concepts. Unlike the traditional high school curricula with calculus at its pinnacle,
these two authentic integrated mathematics curricula introduce students to
discrete mathematics, combinatorics, transformational geometry, matrix algebra, statistics, modeling techniques, and informatics.

In the U.S., the urgency of preparing today's students adequately for
future-oriented fields is increasingly being emphasized at the university level.
Steen (2005) writes that "as a science biology depends increasingly on data,
algorithms and models; in virtually every respect it is becoming . . . more
mathematical" (p. xi). Both the National Research Council (NRC) and the
National Science Foundation (NSF) in the U.S. is increasingly funding universities to initiate interdisciplinary doctoral programs between mathematics
and the other sciences with the goal of producing scientists who are adept at
"mathematizing" reality. Secondary mathematics is usually the gateway for an
exposure to both breadth and depth of mathematical topics. However, most
traditional mathematics curricula are still anchored in the traditional treatment of mathematics, as opposed to an interdisciplinary and modeling-based
approach of mathematics used in the real world. Sheffield, Bennett, Berriozabal,
DeArmond, & Wertheimer (1995) lamented that not much had changed in
terms of mathematics curriculum as of that point in time and remarked that
gifted students of mathematics were the ones that were the most shortchanged
and unable to utilize their "precious societal resource" invaluable to maintain
leadership in a technologically changing world. High school mathematics also
serves as the gatekeeper for many areas of advanced study (Kerr, 1997) and the
traditional treatment of mathematics with little or no emphasis on modeling-
based activities that require teamwork and communication have historically
left gifted girls from pursuing 4 years of high school mathematics. This deficit
is difficult to remediate at the undergraduate level and results in the effect

of low numbers of students capable of graduate-level work in interdisciplin-ary fields such as mathematical biology and bio-informatics (see Steen, 2005). Any educator with a sense of history foresees the snowball effect or the cycle of blaming inadequate preparation to high school onto middle school onto the very elementary grades, which suggests we work bottom up. That is, initiate and study the modeling of complex systems that occur in real-life situations from the very early grades. In projects such as Purdue University's Gender Equity in Engineering Project, when students' abilities and achievements were assessed using tasks that were designed to be simulations of "real-life" problem-solving situations, the understandings and abilities that emerged as being critical for success included many that are not emphasized in traditional textbooks or tests. Thus, the importance of a broader range of deeper understandings and abilities, and a broader range of students naturally emerged as having extraor-dinary potential. Surprisingly enough, these students also came from popula-tions (females and minorities) that are highly underrepresented in fields that emphasize mathematics, science, and technology, and this was true precisely because their abilities were previously unrecognized (Lesh & Sriraman, 2005; Lesh, Hamilton, & Kaput, 2007).

Numerous studies involving students of mixed abilities on the effectiveness of a modeling-based integrated mathematics high school curricula (Hirsch & Weinhold, 1999; Schoen & Hirsch, 2003a, 2003b; Schoen & Ziebarth, 1997) offer empirical evidence that students learning mathematics through such curricula

> perform particularly well (and better than the comparison students) on measures of conceptual understanding, interpretation of mathemati-cal representations and calculations, and problem solving in applied contexts. Their performance is also relatively strong in content areas like statistics and probability that are emphasized in the curriculum. On measures of algebraic manipulative skills, CPMP students usually, but not always, score as well as students in more traditional curricula. (Schoen & Hirsch, 2003a, p. 114)

Similar locally based reform efforts by the gifted education community such as Project Ga-GEMS (Georgia's Project for Gifted Education in Math and Science) have investigated the effectiveness of placement in an integrated math-science curriculum on the achievement of academically talented high school students (Tyler-Wood, 2000). Tyler-Wood (2000) reported that after 2 years in the integrated math-science (discovery-based) program, at the end of the 10th grade

> Ga-GEMS participants and a control group were given the math-ematics and science sections of the ACT . . . [t]he Ga-GEMS students scored significantly higher on the Science Math Total, Pre-Algebra/ Elementary Algebra, Intermediate Algebra/Coordinate Geometry and

Plane Geometry/Trigonometry sections of the ACT. To determine if the Ga-GEMS students retained their higher scores throughout high school the SAT scores of both groups were compared as the students exited high school. Significant differences in the areas of total score and mathematics were noted. (p. 266)

These studies offer empirical support for the use of authentic integrated mathematics curricula that make rich connections with the sciences and relevant real-world applicable learning opportunities all students, mathematically talented or otherwise.

Finally, a chapter purporting to address curricular issues related to secondary mathematics gifted education would be incomplete without addressing Advanced Placement (AP) and International Baccalaureate (IB) programs. AP mathematics courses were never explicitly designated as courses for mathematically gifted students with adequate programming considerations for the needs of gifted students. Instead, they were historically meant to be college courses offered at the high school level available for motivated seniors to take such courses. The IB, on the other hand, was specifically designed as a pre-university preparatory program for academically gifted students with six areas of study (including mathematics), a capstone course on epistemology, and a senior "thesis" (essay). As previously stated, AP courses have unfortunately become a convenient one-size-fits-all approach to meet to the needs of mathematically gifted students without any attention to research on programming techniques for these students. The same is unfortunately true for IB programs. What is even more shocking is the lack of research on the long-term effectiveness of AP and IB programs for the curricular needs of mathematically gifted students. The National Research Council report of 2002 (National Research Council, Gollub, Bertenthal, Labov, & Curtis, 2002) assessed the effectiveness of AP and IB programs currently in place in the U.S. For the context of this chapter, the findings of the committee especially relevant are:

1. *Conceptual understanding is often not emphasized.* Although AP and IB programs espouse an emphasis on concepts and key ideas, this commitment is largely unrealized in the science disciplines. Excessive breadth of coverage and insufficient focus on key concepts in the final assessments in all fields contribute significantly to the problem.

2. *Collaborative projects are not emphasized.* Teamwork and collaborative investigation can enhance learning and is especially important in advanced study . . . better use of technologies for collaborative learning is needed.

3. *Contextual shortcomings.* The AP and IB programs currently do not emphasize interdisciplinary connections sufficiently or assess students' abilities to apply their knowledge in varying formats or in new situations.

4. *Validity of measurement instruments.* What do the examinations actually measure? In particular, little is known about the kinds of thinking

elicited by the examinations . . . certain kinds of validity research are lacking, including attention to the social consequences (or consequential validity) of assessments.

It therefore comes as no surprise that the synthesis of the vast body of literature conducted in this chapter corroborate the findings of the NRC particularly for the gifted segment of the population.

CONCLUDING POINTS

In conclusion, the vast body of research literature synthesized and reported in this chapter indicates that there are indeed major differences in the mathematical abilities between the mathematically gifted and talented students and their peers, and that these differences can be addressed both in the mixed-ability or exclusive-ability classroom via the use of appropriate programming techniques such as curriculum acceleration, compacting, and differentiating. In certain instances, radical acceleration offers the best intellectual opportunities for the profoundly gifted students. The literature also shows that the nature of mathematics itself has changed over time. The experiential world of the 21st-century student and teacher is characterized by complex systems such as the Internet, multimedia, sophisticated computing tools, global markets, virtual realities, and access to online educational environments, and emerging fields such as bio-informatics and mathematical genetics, cryptography, and mathematical biology that call for different mathematical skills such as the ability to model complex systems and problem solving (Sriraman, 2005; Sriraman & Dahl, in press). Authentic integrated mathematics curricula such as those reported in this chapter offer all students opportunities to experience the relevance and applicability of mathematics to the world around them. Contests offer the more able students opportunities to learn and apply mathematical principles to both pure and applied math problems and create a sound foundational base for advanced coursework in mathematics at the university level. The free availability of resources and access to researchers via the Internet offer a multitude of possibilities for the classroom practitioner to both enrich and adapt traditional mathematics curricula to make it relevant for today's world. It is hoped that practitioners, with the help of researchers, can effectively transform the extant research into effective classroom and curricular practice, with students ultimately benefiting from such a symbiosis.

REFERENCES

Andreescu, T., & Gelca, R. (2001). *Mathematical Olympiad challenges*. Boston: Birkhäuser.

Barnett, L. B., & Corazza, L. (1993). Identification of mathematical talent and programmatic efforts to facilitate development of talent. *European Journal for High Ability, 4*, 48–61.

Benbow, C. P., Lubinski, D., & Sushy, B. (1996). The impact of SMPY's educational programs from the perspective of the participant. In C. P. Benbow & D. Lubinski (Eds.), *Intellectual talent* (pp. 266–300). Baltimore: Johns Hopkins University Press.

Davydov, V. V (1988). The concept of theoretical generalization and problems of educational psychology. *Studies in Soviet Thought, 36*, 169–202.

Davydov, V. V. (1990). Type of generalization in instruction: Logical and psychological problems in the structuring of school curricula. In J. Kilpatrick (Ed.), *Soviet studies in mathematics education* (Vol. 2). Reston, VA: National Council of Teachers of Mathematics.

Erickson, M. J., & Flowers, J. (1999). *Principles of mathematical problem solving*. New Jersey: Prentice Hall.

Fomin, D., Genkin, S., & Itenberg, I. (1996). *Mathematical circles: Russian experience*. Washington, DC: American Mathematical Society.

Frensch, P., & Sternberg, R. (1992). *Complex problem solving: Principles and mechanisms*. Mahwah, NJ: Lawrence Erlbaum and Associates.

Goldberg, A., & Suppes, P. (1972). A computer assisted instruction program for exercises on finding axioms. *Educational Studies in Mathematics, 4*, 429–449.

Greenes, C. (1981). Identifying the gifted student in mathematics. *Arithmetic Teacher, 28*(6),14–17.

Gross, M. U. M. (1993). Nurturing the talents of exceptionally gifted children. In K. A. Heller, F. J. Mönks, & A. H. Passow (Eds). *International handbook of research and development of giftedness and talent* (pp. 473–490). Oxford, England: Pergamon Press.

Gross, M. U. M. (1994). Radical acceleration: Responding to academic and social needs of extremely gifted adolescents. *Journal of Secondary Gifted Education, 5*(4), 27–34.

Gross, M. U. M. (1995). Seeing the difference and making the difference for highly gifted students. *Tempo, 15*(1), 1, 11–14.

Gross, M. U. M. (1997). How ability grouping turns big fish into little fish—or does it? Of optical illusions and optimal environments. *Australasian Journal of Gifted Education, 6*(2), 18–30.

Gross, M. U. M. (1998). Fishing for the facts: A response to Marsh and Craven, 1998. *Australasian Journal of Gifted Education, 7*(1), 16–28.

Hirsch, C. R., & Weinhold, M. L. W. (1999). Everybody counts—including the mathematically promising. In L. Sheffield (Ed.), *Developing mathematically promising students* (pp. 233–241). Reston, VA: National Council of Teachers of Mathematics.

Kapur, J. (1970). Combinatorial analysis and school mathematics. *Educational Studies in Mathematics, 3*,111–127.

Kerr, B. A. (1997). Developing talents in girls and young women. In N. Colangelo & G. A. Davis (Eds.), *Handbook of gifted education* (2nd ed., pp. 483–497). Boston: Allyn & Bacon.

Kiesswetter, K. (1985). Die förderung von mathematisch besonders begabten und interessierten Schülern- ein bislang vernachlässigtes sonderpädogogisches problem. *Der mathematische und naturwissenschaftliche Unterricht, 38,* 300–306.

Kiesswetter, K. (1992). Mathematische begabung. Über die komplexität der phänomene und die unzulänglichkeiten von punktbewertungen. *Mathematik-Unterricht, 38,* 5–18.

Kolitch, E. R., & Brody, L. E. (1992). Mathematics acceleration of highly talented students: An evaluation. *Gifted Child Quarterly, 36,* 78–86.

Krutetskii, V. A. (1976). *The psychology of mathematical abilities in school children.* (J. Teller, Trans. and J. Kilpatrick & I. Wirszup, Eds.). Chicago: University of Chicago Press.

Kulik, J. A., & Kulik, C. C. (1992). Meta-analytic findings on grouping programs. *Gifted Child Quarterly, 36,* 73–77.

Lesh, R., Hamilton, E., & Kaput, J. (Eds.). (2007). *Models and modeling as foundations for the future in mathematics education.* Mahwah, NJ: Lawrence Erlbaum.

Lesh, R., & Sriraman, B. (2005). John Dewey revisited: Pragmatism and the models-modeling perspective on mathematical learning. In A. Beckmann, C. Michelsen, & B. Sriraman (Eds.), *Proceedings of the 1st International Symposium on Mathematics and its connections to the arts and Sciences* (pp. 32–51). Gmuend, Germany: Franzbecker Verlag.

Lozansky, E., & Rousseau, C. (1996). *Winning solution: Problem books in mathematics.* New York: Springer-Verlag.

National Research Council (Corporate Author), Gollub, J. P., Bertenthal, M. W., Labov, J. B., & Curtis, P. C. (Eds.). (2002). *Learning and understanding: Improving advanced study of mathematics and science in US high schools.* Washington, DC: National Academy Press.

Piaget, J. (1987). *Possibility and necessity: The role of necessity in cognitive development* (Vols. 1 & 2). Minneapolis: University of Minnesota Press.

Polya, G. (1954). *Mathematics and plausible reasoning: Induction and analogy in mathematics* (Vol. II). Princeton, NJ: Princeton University Press.

Presmeg, N. C. (1986). Visualization and mathematical giftedness. *Educational Studies in Mathematics, 17,* 297–311.

Reis, S. M., & Westberg, K. L (1994). The impact of staff development on teachers' ability to modify curriculum for gifted and talented students. *Gifted Child Quarterly, 38,* 127–135.

Schoen, H. L., & Hirsch, C. R. (2003a). Responding to calls for change in high school mathematics: Implications for collegiate mathematics. *American Mathematical Monthly, 110,* 109–123. Retrieved August 7, 2005, from http://www.wmich.edu/cpmp/bibliography.html

Schoen, H. L., & Hirsch, C. R. (2003b). The Core-Plus Mathematics Project: Perspectives and student achievement. In S. Senk & D. Thompson (Eds.), *Standards-oriented school mathematics curricula: What are they? What do students learn?* (pp. 311–344). Hillsdale, NJ: Lawrence Erlbaum Associates.

Schoen, H. L., & Ziebarth, S. W. (1997). A progress report on student achievement in the Core-Plus Mathematics Project field test. *NCSM Journal of Mathematics Education Leadership, 1*(3), 15–23.

Shapiro, S. I. (1965). A study of pupil's individual characteristics in processing mathematical information. *Voprosy Psikhologii, 2.*

Sheffield, L. J., Bennett, J., Berriozabal, M., DeArmond, M., & Wertheimer, R. (1995). *Report of the task force on the mathematically promising.* Reston, VA: National Council of Teachers of Mathematics.

Skemp, R. (1986). *The psychology of learning mathematics.* New York: Penguin Books.

Sriraman, B. (2002). How do mathematically gifted students abstract and generalize mathematical concepts? *NAGC 2002 Research Briefs, 16,* 83–87.

Sriraman, B. (2003). Mathematical giftedness, problem solving, and the ability to formulate generalizations. *Journal of Secondary Gifted Education, 14,* 151–165.

Sriraman, B. (2004a). Reflective abstraction, uniframes and the formulation of generalizations. *Journal of Mathematical Behavior, 23,* 205–222.

Sriraman, B. (2004b). Discovering a mathematical principle: The case of Matt. *Mathematics in School, 33*(2), 25–31.

Sriraman, B. (2004c). The characteristics of mathematical creativity. *The Mathematics Educator, 14*(1), 19–34.

Sriraman, B. (2004d). Gifted ninth graders' notions of proof. Investigating parallels in approaches of mathematically gifted students and professional mathematicians. *Journal for the Education of the Gifted, 27,* 267–292.

Sriraman, B. (2005). Are mathematical giftedness and mathematical creativity synonyms? A theoretical analysis of constructs. *Journal of Secondary Gifted Education, 17,* 20–36.

Sriraman, B., & Dahl, B. (in press). On bringing interdisciplinary ideas to gifted education. In L. V. Shavinina (Ed.), *The international handbook of giftedness.* New York: Springer Science.

Sriraman, B., & English, L. (2004). Combinatorial mathematics: Research into practice. *The Mathematics Teacher, 98,* 182–191.

Steen, L. A. (2005). *Math & Bio 2010: Linking undergraduate disciplines.* Washington, DC: Mathematical Association of America.

Suppes, P., & Binford, F. (1965). Experimental teaching of mathematical logic in the elementary school. *The Arithmetic Teacher, 12,* 187–195.

Tomlinson, C. A. (2004). Introduction to differentiation for gifted and talented students. In S. M. Reis (Ed.), *Essential readings in gifted education* (Vol. 5, pp. xxiii–xxxiv). Thousand Oaks, CA: Corwin Press.

Tyler-Wood, T. (2000). An effective mathematics and science curriculum option for secondary gifted education. *Roeper Review, 22,* 266–270.

VanTassel-Baska, J. (1985). Appropriate curriculum for the gifted. In J. Feldhusen (Ed.), *Toward excellence in gifted education* (pp. 175–189). Denver, CO: Love.

Yakimanskaya, I. S. (1970). Individual differences in solving geometry problems on proof. In J. Kilpatrick & I. Wirszup (Eds.), *Soviet studies in the psychology of learning and teaching mathematics* (Vol. 4). Stanford, CA: School Mathematics Study Group.

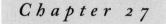
MENTORING

Carolyn M. Callahan and Robin Kyburg Dickson

INTRODUCTION

entorships are offered as a programming option for gifted and talented students and youth predicated on the observation that these individuals are unique in their cognitive, educational, social, and emotional developmental needs and the assumption that involvement of gifted individuals in these special instructional relationships will be beneficial to both their cognitive and affective development. In some cases, such as the performing arts, they may also be beneficial to psychomotor development (e.g., musical performance, dance).

DEFINITIONS

Prodigies

Within the more general population of gifted students, and of particular importance in the study of mentoring gifted students, is the very select and narrow subpopulation labeled *prodigies*. Prodigies are defined by researchers as children age 10 or younger who already are performing at an adult professional's level of skill in a cognitively complex area such as chess, music, or mathematics (Feldman, 1979, 1991). Retrospective biographical analysis and case studies of prodigies have formed the basis of the literature on mentoring for these students.

Mentorship

Within the literature on gifted education, the term *mentorship* as applied to gifted students has been as narrowly defined as a teacher who "models learning skills daily to a student to encourage life-long learning" (Bisland, 2001, p. 22) and broadly defined as a "guide, advisor, model, counselor, and friend who helps advance the student's knowledge of a particular field" (Silverman, 1993, p. 225). In most literature describing the effects of mentorships and mentoring programs, definitions of mentoring go beyond the tutor/teacher concept to include attention to the full development of the individual in areas ranging from career development, to learning about the commitment to the discipline and personal adjustment issues. Nash, Haensly, Rodgers, & Wright (1993) summarized the functions of mentors of the gifted as: role modeling, nurturing creativity, providing career exploration opportunities, providing content-based enrichment in an area of special interest of the student, and aiding in student personal growth—particularly self-awareness.

Formal vs. Informal Mentorships

Formal school mentoring programs are organized by school personnel with goals focusing on career development, support for recognition and acceptance of talents, and initiation into the typical lives of professionals. A typical goal statement reads: "opportunities for learner access to expertise in the community, offer[ing] real life experiences by providing an experientially based framework for enriching the curriculum, and present[ing] traditional and non-traditional role models of competence in pursuit of commitment to excellence" (Swassing & Fichter, 1991, p. 181). Most of these mentoring programs (with a few notable exceptions that will be reviewed) are aimed at high school students.

Typically, the extraschool or extracurricular mentorships are sought out and established by parents of students who are prodigies or students who exhibit other extremely precocious potential with the purpose of helping the student develop particular skills and advanced performance expertise in areas not served at exceptional levels within the school environment. Parents of prodigies will seek out mentors for their children outside of the school setting, and sometimes even outside the local community, as the child's progress accelerates for purposes of instruction in the skills of the discipline and for performance opportunities. Typically, the areas of musical, dance, or artistic performance and performance in athletics (swimming, track and field, tennis, etc.) fall in this category and the descriptions of these mentorships have been elaborated on by Bloom (1985) and Feldman (1991).

MENTORSHIP AS DISTINCT FROM INDEPENDENT STUDY OR INTERNSHIP

One clear attribute of mentorship that distinguishes it from traditional options outside the regular classroom, such as an independent study or an internship, is the expectation that there will be a relationship between the mentor and protégé that goes beyond a structured learning goal. Independent study relies on a set of goals and related activities carried out by a student with oversight on the academic/cognitive dimension of the student's achievements. In an internship, the student is expected to perform prearranged tasks at a stated level of proficiency or standards for performance or to demonstrate growth through a set of developmental stages of expertise. In internship situations, a student is generally assigned to an organization or an institution with a supervisor. Finally, the expectation for long-term commitments and enduring relationships are absent from internship and independent study assignments (Zorman, 1993). The internship arrangement may, in fact, result in relationships between the student and the supervisor that evolve into mentorships, but the experience is not designed to realize that goal.

MENTORSHIP CHARACTERISTICS

An underlying assumption of mentorships is an expected hierarchical relationship. Those relationships have ranged from professionals in the community assuming mentoring roles, to older students serving as tutors or teachers, role models, and supports for younger students (Bisland, 2001). Although experts (e.g., Pleiss & Feldhusen, 1995; Shandley, 1989) stress that matching a mentor to the gifted protégé—particularly on attitudes, values, and lifestyles—is a critical step in establishing the mentorship, research on matching characteristics of the gifted students in terms of those variables or interest, personality, stage of development of the students and the mentor, gender, and race is lacking. Research questions or analyses relating to gender, for example, are missing from studies due to a paucity of available females mentors in leadership positions until recent times.

In the sections that follow, we summarize the theory and rationale offered for providing mentorships to gifted students, review extant research literature, provide guidelines for establishing mentorships for this special population of students, and finally, offer suggestions for future research.

THEORY AND RATIONALE UNDERLYING MENTORSHIPS FOR GIFTED STUDENTS

Reasons for Mentors for the Gifted

The rationale for either school mentorships or extracurricular mentorships is the advanced knowledge or performance level of gifted students, the more eclectic and/or unusual interest areas and passions of these students for learning in general or for a specific discipline or performance area, and the challenges they face in their social and emotional adjustment. Advanced knowledge or performance levels of the student may require exposure to higher levels of instruction and different forms of instruction than the school environment can afford to offer. Boston (1976), Gray and Gray (1988) and Reis and Burns (1987) stress the importance of mentorships for providing activities that are inquiry-related and incorporate opportunities to develop higher level thinking skills as applied in actual disciplines. The need for intense learning experiences beyond the level of instructional content and strategies available in traditional school environments requires the provision of opportunities to engage in learning and performance routines that exceed those that typical school level instructors have experienced and/or can provide in the school environment. Such intense experiences are best accomplished in professional settings in the company of already-established experts in the field and often entail use of cutting-edge equipment, texts, or resources outside the reach of most school districts (Grybek, 1997; Pizzini, 1985). Intense interest in advanced-level learning and performance may also require student and instructor time commitments beyond those that can be accommodated within the schedule of a school setting or by an individual school instructor. A mentorship also provides the opportunity to address the highly focused and goal-directed nature of gifted students (Grybek, 1997) not possible in other settings.

Shore, Cornell, Robinson, and Ward (1991) concluded that there is strong research support for career education for the gifted population in general. Like all students, they need understandings of why people work and the benefits of working. Hence, a mentorship based on interests and talents for career exploration has been the basis of many programs for mentoring gifted students. Students who clearly exhibit talents in areas that are unique and not part of the usual school experience can use mentorship programs for exposure to careers that extend beyond those that might be presented to and discussed with the general population. Further, gifted students who exhibit many different areas of strength may be helped through the exploration of the degree of commitment and interest they have to several areas for potential career development.

However, Shore et al. (1991) also noted that gifted students need to understand the lifestyles associated with the kinds of work that talented individuals may do, the moral issues they may face in their careers, and the impact of high aspirations, focus, and dedication to careers that may be extremely demanding, and the impacts of these factors on their lives in general. Gifted students, therefore, may especially benefit from opportunities to develop relationships with those who have that level of experience in the discipline and associated careers within their area(s) of interest and talent. As Cross (1998) has pointed out, mentors may provide models for learning about pathways to the fulfillment of talent potential.

Gifted students who have been accelerated (e.g., early entrance to college, grade skipping) may be in positions where they face decisions about college, about majors, or even graduate school at an unusually early age. Although learning about their own commitments to a discipline may be helpful outcomes of a mentorship for these students, the mentors may also help these gifted students (as well as other gifted students) negotiate "major transitions in academic life, from high school to college, from college to graduate school, and from school to work" (Grybek, 1997, p. 116).

Others have stressed the importance of the mentorship in the social and emotional adjustment of the gifted students. Gifted students may not be secure in the recognition and acceptance of the importance of their talents because of ridicule that stems from classmates and a lack of knowledge on the part of educators on how to affirm students' evolving expertise, particularly when it surpasses their own (Edlind & Haensly, 1985). Not only does the establishment of the mentorship provide an opportunity for affirming abilities for the student, it provides a message that the talent is worth developing to its fullest (Batten & Rogers, 1993). Finally, Gardner (1993) notes that because the creative individual's highly developed sensitivity may lead to critical evaluations of self and others, a refusal to accept authority, and boredom with routine tasks, the mentor can provide the needed emotional support, as well as technical challenge stretching the gifted individual who is at that point in his or her career where a creative breakthrough is pending. He contends that the gifted individual at that point may, in fact, need dual mentors.

Further, because gifted students are also often faced with confirmation that they are "different" from other students, they may worry about not fitting in and/or being successful socially with peers, a significant adolescent developmental challenge. The mentor can provide a model of adjustment, demonstrating pathways to negotiate complicated social interactions, showing the way to the gifted students, and providing assurances of the satisfaction both emotionally and socially whilst nonetheless pursuing high-level performance goals.

Mentors as Teachers

Many authors who advocate mentorships for gifted students or who describe the mentorships that have influenced gifted students have focused on the teaching role of the mentorship (e.g., Bisland, 2001; Lupkowski, Assouline, & Stanley, 1990). However, even within that role identified as teaching, levels of formality of the relationships vary considerably. Simply modeling the learning skills daily in order to encourage lifelong learning has been labeled mentoring by some (e.g., Davalos & Haensly, 1997); others describe intensive, prescriptive instruction or tutoring only (Lupkowski et al., 1990). Most, however, would view the role of mentor as much more complex even when associated with the teaching function. Bloom (1985) stressed the importance of the early mentor of the young talented students as teaching with a stress on making the study interesting, playful, and fun; the teacher in middle childhood as providing instruction with stress on precision and accuracy, but also providing encouragement and supporting a commitment to the field; and finally, during adolescence, helping the student achieve the highest level of performance, but also helping the student identify and develop a unique, personal style.

Prodigies who exhibit unusually advanced talents in areas such as musical performance or composition may need teachers who have skills in the discipline and skill in developing advanced levels of performance that are beyond those of the school. In nearly all of these cases, these teachers are or become mentors. For example, while Feldman's (1991) study of prodigies emphasized the teacher as mentor and mentor as teacher, he noted that the role is much more than simple and somber skill transfer. While watching a mentor work with a student in choosing paper, ruling neat staffs on paper, arranging pages, and selecting the perfect pen and ink for writing scores, he observed:

> I had the sense of a craft being passed on from one generation to another, in a way that can never be done by reading a book or simply observing. This aspect of the composer's craft was treated with the same care and love as the more musical and technical aspects of the domain. (p. 138)

CRITICAL RESEARCH QUESTIONS

The research on mentoring can be summarized as addressing these four critical questions:

1. What effect does mentoring have on the development and learning of gifted and talented students?

2. Are there particular, differentiated effects for subpopulations of gifted students (gifted females, gifted students from minority populations, very young gifted students, gifted handicapped students, gifted students from impoverished environments, underachieving gifted)?
3. Do gifted students need particular types of teachers and/or mentors at different points in their development?
4. Are there any potential negative effects of mentoring?

RESEARCH

The very limited empirical literature on the roles that mentorships have played in the lives of gifted individuals and the effects of mentor relationships relies on post-hoc analyses of biographical data, case study analyses, and/or retrospective questionnaire data. Experimental studies of the effects of programs or specific types of mentorships for gifted students do not exist. While the data from the existing studies are often only reflective, highly subjective, and self-report, thus limiting generalizability, these studies do provide some beginning evidence of benefits that accrue from mentorships and ways in which particular decisions in setting up mentorship programs have affected perceived success.

Effects of Mentor Relationships

Pleiss and Feldhusen (1995) report that students involved in mentorships perceive these relationships to be beneficial in the further development of interests and motivation and provide a sense of the lifestyle of a career, as well as the specific roles, functions, activities, and goals of individuals who are accomplished in those careers. Similarly, Arnold's (1995) study of valedictorians and salutatorians verified that mentorships help students to understand the role of a professional in the field, to learn about conducting research in the field, to become socialized in the field, and to develop a belief in self-efficacy.

Beck's (1989) survey of students who had participated in a high school mentoring program confirmed significant differences between classroom experiences and mentorships on student perceptions of their opportunity and willingness to

> take risks, develop talents, learn about advanced subject matter, work independently, utilize technical skills, utilize research skills, investigate job routines and responsibilities, find out about career entrance requirements, examine lifestyles and characteristics of professionals, see how professionals interact, and make contacts and network. (p. 24)

Effects of Mentoring on Special Populations of Gifted Students

Gifted Females. The positive effects of mentorships on gifted females and career choice have been documented by Arnold (1995), Beck (1989), Kaufmann, Harrel, Milam, Woolverton, & Miller (1986), Kerr (1991), and Reilly and Welch (1994–1995). Female valedictorians and salutatorians in Arnold's study were motivated to pursue careers associated with the mentorships in science—a less traditional field for women—because of the ways they "saw graduate students and department faculty **doing** science and leading their lives" (p. 121). Arnold concluded from her case studies that "for women, however, personal sponsorship into testing opportunities was necessary for high career aspirations. Role models, guides, and sponsors all connected women to nonacademic opportunities where their success and enjoyment of professional challenge made career futures seem real" (p. 125). Similarly, Packard and Nguyen (2003) found that women who chose to pursue and remain in careers in science, math, and technology noted that mentors played a key role in their decision to continue in those careers. Kerr's (1991) study of eminent women led her to conclude that in her sample mentors were an important factor in the confluence of factors influencing their career choices and success. Three times as many female students as male students in a school mentoring program surveyed by Reilly and Welch (1994–1995) reported that they made focused career decisions as a result of their mentoring experience. In a related finding, significantly more females in Beck's (1989) survey claimed that mentorships contributed to helping them examine ways to integrate career and family. Further, female mentors were perceived as contributing more to helping students take risks and work independently. Achor and Morales (1990) identified mentoring as the second most significant factor affecting the success of Chicano women who earned doctorates. At a more pragmatic level, Kaufmann et al. (1986) found that female Presidential Scholars who had mentors earned salaries equal to those of males, whereas females in the overall sample earned significantly less than the males.

Students From Minority Groups and/or Low Socioeconomic Backgrounds. Arellano and Padilla (1996) found Latino university students (73% of whom had been identified as gifted in elementary school) reflected that mentors were of great importance to them in setting and achieving academic goals. These students whose parents "possessed less 'cultural capital'" (p. 501) also identified the importance of mentors in helping them access information that they would not have otherwise obtained. Rodriguez (1986), in comparing traditional counseling with mentor relationships among college students from lower socioeconomic groups, concluded that the mentoring program was more effective in assisting students in social and academic integration in the college community and in increasing student commitment to achievement in college.

Wright and Borland (1992) established mentoring opportunities for a small number (eight) of poor, minority kindergarten students using older, adolescent academically gifted students from the same city and culture as mentors based on the assumption that interactions with "an indisputable living example of an intelligent young person who has achieved academic success in spite of the odds . . . can mitigate the effects of an absent adult or the negative role model offered as typical of urban minority culture by the media" (p. 25). Paired on traits of similar interest, commonalities of background, and evidence of "clicking," mentors participated with the children during a summer program in specific informal (play and talking time) and formal activities (including coaching in successful school behaviors and basic skills, a writer's workshop, and a mathematics laboratory). The mentors also were involved in the extended day component of the program after school ended. The kindergartners, interviewed at the end of the summer experience, were enthusiastic about the chance to have a "special friend" and the authors concluded from the interview data that "it was clear [the kindergartners] derived a sense of being somehow special as a result . . . it is probably safe to conclude that their self esteem was positively affected as a result of receiving so much attention for someone so highly regarded" (pp. 128–129).

Tomlinson, Callahan, and Lelli (1997) conducted case studies of very young students (K–3) from low-income backgrounds and minority groups who had been nominated as "successful" or "unsuccessful" in an intervention program and found that for the successful students the assignment of a mentor was perceived as extremely positive. Although the mentors were identified as contributing in many ways, most importantly they served as a safety net for students who were not supported by either parents or teachers.

Underachieving Gifted. Positive effects of mentors on reversing the underachievement of three adolescent males (improved school behaviors and academic achievement) were documented by Hébert and Olenchak (2000). The specific characteristics of the successful relationships for these young men were consistent social and emotional support and advocacy that supplemented the more direct instructor/student relationship. Notably, the mentors also worked with the students to help them identify barriers to developing their creative productivity and helped them develop and test strategies for overcoming those barriers.

Need for Different Types of Mentors at Different Stages of Development

Both Gardner (1993) and Bloom (1985) have examined the development of successful prodigies and correlated success of the child with a succession of mentors having different characteristics with consequent different goals. The successful mentor for the young child was a guide who encouraged exploration and having fun with the discipline. They cautioned that mentors who demand mastery in the early years may discourage talent development. Successive developmental stages required different mentoring types: first, a mentor who teaches more advanced technical skills of the discipline and begins to impart the sense of discipline and commitment to the field and then, a leader in the field who is a model of expected proficiency.

Feldman (1991) concluded from his study of prodigies that while all gifted individuals may need to experience these stages of mentorship, the prodigy may go through these stages at a much earlier age and may need several mentors at the final stages of development with ever increasing levels of proficiency.

Functions of the Mentor in Late Adolescent/Adult Gifted Individuals. Three categories of functions fulfilled by mentors emerged from a survey of Presidential Scholars approximately 10–15 years after their high school graduation (Kaufmann et al., 1986). The role-model function, which encompassed being an exemplar, enhancing job-related or professional skills, and transmitting professional value and attitudes, was described most frequently as having an influence. This was followed closely by professional or personal support and encouragement. The last category, professional socialization and support, included the functions of providing opportunities for increased visibility and career opportunities; teaching the protégé to play the game; defending, protecting, or advocating for the protégé; or introducing the protégé to influential people. While the literature on other populations suggests that professional socialization through such activities as networking are extremely valuable, this population reported less benefit from such functions, but rather placed far greater significance on the transmission of attitudes and values such as passion for the discipline or profession.

Potential Detrimental Effects of Mentoring

Although most literature on mentoring emphasizes the potential positive outcomes of mentorships for gifted individuals, there are indications from retrospective studies of eminent individuals (e.g., Gardner, 1993; Simonton, 2000) and case studies of prodigies (Feldman, 1991) that the inappropriate matching of mentors or inappropriate behaviors of mentors may have detrimental effects on the protégé. For example, Simonton (2000) notes that if the mentors are "past their prime, and thus . . . less receptive to new ideas" (p. 117), they may stifle the creativity of the gifted students. He further cautions that when the underlying motivations of the mentors are focused on creating clones of themselves through their students, the effect may be injurious by limiting the development of the student's unique talents. For this reason, Simonton recommends that highly able students be given the opportunity to experience multiple mentors. Gardner (1993) concluded that a mentor who demands mastery at a level too advanced for the child too early may discourage the student from pursuing a particular talent.

Finally, several authors have addressed the dangers in inappropriate termination of the mentor relationship. Because gifted students may be isolated due to the differences in performance levels from their peers, they may develop strong attachments to mentors and become distressed when the mentoring relationship ends (Grybek, 1997).

Synthesis and Future Directions

Synthesis

Mentors have served the unique population of gifted individuals for as long as anyone has tracked the development of talent. However, it has only been recently that educators have formally created programs for gifted students focused on mentoring concepts or studied the impacts of mentors and mentor programs on gifted students. Further, the lack of experimental research on mentoring programs for the gifted results in limited knowledge of the benefits and dangers associated with this programming option. Although qualitative and quantitative, nonexperimental approaches give some guidance, the applicability of the findings rely on triangulation of results across a wide variety of samples, approaches, and mentoring approaches. Given those limitations, we have drawn tentative conclusions about the effects of mentoring programs.

Recommendations for Research

Key to advancing the literature on mentoring programs for gifted students is the development and design of experimental research programs that are based on sound empirical research principles:

1. Design specific mentoring programs with experimental research protocols incorporated into the design allowing for identification and documentation of the effects of specific components.
2. Carefully design experimental interventions with specific populations of gifted students that are clearly defined and documented. Use the experimental designs to allow for studying the varying effects of differing mentorship goals and interventions by cognitive level of the student, talent development stage, and social and emotional status of the students.
3. Develop and validate new measures of the outcomes of the mentoring relationship for the gifted student. Relying on survey reports of satisfaction is not sufficient and available measures of achievement designed for the average population are inadequate because of ceiling effects. Examining such outcome measures as enrollment in Advanced Placement courses or college courses, production of advanced-level

products or engagement in advanced-level performance, heightened career awareness and goals, improved sense of self-efficacy, or other measures based on the stated outcome goals and population served is critical.

4. Create specific experimental research programs that capitalize on the increased numbers of minority men and minority and Caucasian women in professional roles to study the effects of gender and racial matching.

5. Create experimental designs that allow for examination of the importance of matching on values and attitudes rather than career interests as suggested by the literature.

REFERENCES

Achor, S., & Morales, A. (1990). Chicanas holding doctoral degrees: Social reproduction and cultural ecological approaches. *Anthropology & Education Quarterly, 21,* 269–287.

Arellano, A. R., & Padilla, A. M. (1996). Academic invulnerability among a select group of Latino university students. *Hispanic Journal of Behavioral Sciences, 18,* 485–508.

Arnold, K. D. (1995). *Lives of promise.* San Francisco: Jossey-Bass.

Batten, J., & Rogers, J. (1993). Response to "Mentoring: Extending learning for gifted students." In C. J. Maker (Ed.), *Critical issues in gifted education: Programs for the gifted in regular classrooms* (pp. 331–341). Austin, TX: PRO-ED.

Beck, L. (1989). Mentorships: Benefits and effects on career development. *Gifted Child Quarterly, 33,* 22–28.

Bisland, A. (2001). Mentoring—an educational alternative for gifted students. *Gifted Child Today, 24*(4), 22–25, 64–65.

Bloom, B. S. (Ed.). (1985). *Developing talent in young people.* New York: Ballantine Books.

Boston, B. O. (1976). *The sorcerer's apprentice: A case study in the role of the mentor.* Reston, VA: The Council for Exceptional Children. (ERIC Document Reproduction Service No. ED126671)

Cross, T. (1998). Working on behalf of gifted students. *Gifted Child Today, 21*(3), 21–22.

Davalos, R. A., & Haensly, P. A. (1997). After the dust has settled: Youth reflect on their high school mentored research experience. *Roeper Review, 19,* 204–207.

Edlind, E. P., & Haensly, P. A. (1985). Gifts of mentorships. *Gifted Child Quarterly, 29,* 55–60.

Feldman, D. H. (1979). The mysterious case of extreme giftedness. In A. H. Passow (Ed.), *The gifted and talented: Their education and development: The seventy-eighth yearbook of the national society for the study of education* (pp. 335–351). Chicago: University of Chicago.

Feldman, D. H. (1991). *Nature's gambit: Child prodigies and the development of human potential.* New York: Teachers College Press.

Gardner, H. (1993). *Creating minds.* New York: Basic Books.

Gray, M. M., & Gray, W. A. (1988). Mentor-assisted enrichment projects: A proven way of carrying out Type III triad projects and of promoting higher-level thinking in GTC student-protégés. In M. M. Gray & W. A. Gray (Eds.), *Proceedings of the First International Mentoring Conference* (Vol. 1, pp. 1–8). Vancouver, BC: International Association for Mentoring.

Grybek, D. D. (1997). Mentoring the gifted and talented. *Preventing School Failure, 41,* 115–118.

Hébert, T. P., & Olenchak, F. R. (2000). Mentors for gifted underachieving males: Developing potential and realizing promise. *Gifted Child Quarterly, 44,* 196–207.

Kaufmann, F. A., Harrel, G., Milam, C. P., Woolverton, N., & Miller, J. (1986). The nature, role, and influence of mentors in the lives of gifted adults. *Journal of Counseling and Development, 64,* 576–578.

Kerr, B. A. (1991). Educating gifted girls. In N. Colangelo & G. A. Davis (Eds.), *Handbook of gifted education* (pp. 402–415). Boston: Allyn & Bacon.

Lupkowski, A. E., Assouline, S. G., & Stanley, J. C. (1990). Applying a mentor model for young mathematically talented students. *Gifted Child Today, 13*(2), 15–17.

Nash, W. R., Haensly, P. A., Rodgers, V. J. S., & Wright, N. L. (1993). Mentoring: Extending learning for gifted students. In C. J. Maker (Ed.), *Critical issues in gifted education: Programs for the gifted in regular classrooms* (Vol. 3, pp. 313–330). Austin, TX: PRO-ED.

Packard, B. W., & Nguyen, D. (2003). Science career-related possible selves of adolescent girls: A longitudinal study. *Journal of Career Development, 29,* 251–263.

Pizzini, E. L. (1985). Improving science instruction for gifted high school students. *Roeper Review, 7,* 231–234.

Pleiss, M. K., & Feldhusen, J. F. (1995). Mentors, role models, and heroes in the lives of gifted children. *Educational Psychologist, 30,* 159–169.

Reilly, J. M., & Welch, D. B. (1994–1995). Mentoring gifted young women: A call to action. *Journal of Secondary Gifted Education, 6,* 120–128.

Reis, S. M., & Burns, D. E. (1987). A school-wide enrichment team invites you to read about methods for promoting community and faculty involvement in a gifted program. *Gifted Child Today, 10*(2), 27–32.

Rodriguez, R. (1986). Effects of two counseling approaches on institutional integration and persistence of high risk college students (Doctoral dissertation, Fordham graduate school of education, 1986). *Dissertation Abstracts International-A, 47/05,* 1625.

Shandley, T. C. (1989). The use of mentors for leadership development. *NASPA Journal, 27,* 59–66.

Shore, B. M., Cornell, D. G., Robinson, A., & Ward, V. S. (1991). *Recommended practices in gifted education: A critical analysis.* New York: Teachers College Press.

Silverman, L. K. (1993). Career counseling. In L. K. Silverman (Ed.), *Counseling the gifted and talented* (pp. 215–238). Denver, CO: Love.

Simonton, D. K. (2000). Genius and giftedness: Same or different? In K. A. Heller, F. J. Mönks, R. J. Sternberg & R. F. Subotnik (Eds.), *International handbook of giftedness and talent* (pp. 111–122). Amsterdam: Elsevier.

Swassing, R. H., & Fichter, G. R. (1991). University and community-based programs for the gifted adolescent. In M. Bireley & J. Genshaft (Eds.), *Understanding the gifted adolescent—educational, developmental, and multicultural issues* (pp. 176–186). New York: Teachers College Press.

Tomlinson, C. A., Callahan, C. M., & Lelli, K. M. (1997). Challenging expectations: Case studies of high-potential, culturally diverse young children. *Gifted Child Quarterly, 41,* 5–17.

Wright, L., & Borland, J. H. (1992). A special friend: Adolescent mentors for young economically disadvantaged, potentially gifted students. *Roeper Review, 14,* 124–129.

Zorman, R. (1993). Mentoring and role modeling programs for the gifted. In K. A. Heller, F. J. Mönks, & A. H. Passow (Eds.), *International handbook of research and development of giftedness and talent* (pp. 727–741). Oxford, England: Pergamon.

Chapter 28

MOTIVATION

Joyce M. Alexander and Angela K. Schnick

ifted students have presented many a parent or teacher with a conundrum. Here is a very smart young person, motivated to pursue his or her own interests outside of school yet sometimes those high-level intellectual skills are not applied to daily work in the classroom. Other parents or teachers may see a gifted child doing quite well in school, but the child still seems bored or seems satisfied with less than he or she could really do. With all the advantages gifted students have, why do we still see motivational problems? The present chapter explores these issues by beginning with a bigger question: How do a gifted student's motivational beliefs interact with the context of the classroom to produce favorable or unfavorable motivational and learning outcomes? To truly understand motivational problems and triumphs, we must realize that gifted students find themselves in contexts that are supportive and not so supportive of their learning and motivational needs. This chapter will explore this issue in some detail.

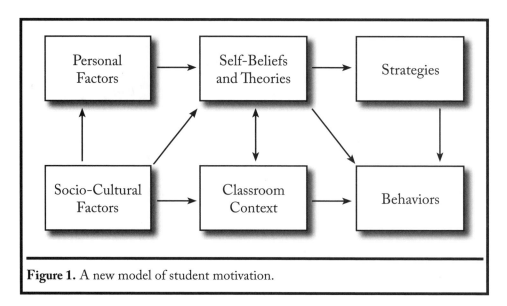

Figure 1. A new model of student motivation.

Achievement motivation has been studied from multiple theoretical orientations. Clinkenbeard (1996) has suggested that there have been two types of motivation research concerning gifted students: the first concentrating on motivation as a personality characteristic or trait, and the second concentrating on motivation as something that is specific to the environment in which the individual finds him- or herself. Conclusions from the first type of research might lead us to say that an individual is highly intrinsically motivated; conclusions from the second type of research might lead us to say that a particular classroom is a highly motivating environment. We find each approach to motivation too simple to explain the true complexities in behavior. A more integrative model, based on social-cognitive perspective, is necessary to truly reflect how individual traits are engendered in specific learning contexts. The model presented in Figure 1 builds on previous work by Dai, Moon, and Feldhusen (1998), Eccles (1983, 2005), Rhodewalt and Tragakis (2002), and Dweck and Molden (2005), but more explicitly represents the role of the context and focuses on gifted students' particular motivational needs. The model also stresses the interactive nature of the individual in the context. Thus, the beliefs individuals bring to a learning situation will affect how they react to aspects of the context in which they find themselves.

To preview the model, personal factors affect motivation, including long-held beliefs about abilities in certain situations, personality, temperament, or present aptitude. In addition, we believe a series of socio-cultural factors affect both the classroom context and past motivational history of the individual. Together, the socio-cultural factors and personal factors contribute to the development and maintenance of a series of self-beliefs and theories.

Self-beliefs and theories act as a filter for incoming information from the context (i.e., teacher comments, feedback) and affect how individuals will react in the situation, including the strategies they might use to facilitate their learning, as well as affective reactions to feedback, assignments, or grouping practices. The context, along with the concomitant choices a teacher makes about competition, feedback, rewards, and activities affects how the self-beliefs play out on a day-to-day basis. Finally, all of these factors affect achievement behaviors such as effort, persistence, engagement, and challenge-seeking. Each of these factors will be reviewed more fully below.

Personal Factors

Each individual learner brings to a learning situation a host of personal characteristics that will interact with self-beliefs and contextual variables. For example, individual aptitude, temperament, and personality traits will all affect how an individual responds to feedback, classroom activities, and learning situations. Additionally, the individual brings a storehouse of self-beliefs to each learning situation. As we will review below, these "trait-like" self-beliefs affect how individuals react in any given situation. A fuller examination of how these personal factors interact with self-beliefs and classroom contextual factors will be reviewed below.

Socio-Cultural Factors

Socio-cultural factors are the deep-rooted values that are expressed in our everyday educational and societal interactions. These values may be socialized or may be inherently different in individuals. Regardless, they form a backdrop against which our ideas of competence and motivation develop.

The very definition of competence is a culturally determined factor. The meaning of competence in American classrooms is tied directly to our conception of competence in adulthood. Students (and adults) should be quick, able to express their ideas, and be good problem solvers. We should be able to see their "wheels turning" as they move beyond difficulties presented (Plaut & Markus, 2005). Thus, for Americans, being competent is located in the individual and in the mind. Other cultures, such as east Asian cultures, emphasize the goal of maintaining relations with others and developing competence through relations with others (Azuma & Kashiwagi, 1987; Shapiro & Azuma, 2004). Other cultures use different definitions of competence. For example, Ugandans believe that competence is slow, careful, and straightforward. Competence, according to Ugandans, is also "friendly" and "public" (Wober, 1974). Thus, the very definition of competence is affected by the cultures in which we find ourselves.

Gender role socialization is a second major socio-cultural factor. In a review of the literature pertaining to gender differences in intrinsic aptitude for mathematics and science, Spelke (2005) concluded that males and females share the same set of biological capacities for scientific and mathematical reasoning throughout the lifespan (also see Hyde, 2005). She maintains that societal factors ultimately must drive gender inequities in scientific careers. Dweck and Molden (2005) report research illustrating that females in a domain dominated by males (in this case mathematics), are likely to experience stereotype threat. Stereotype threat occurs when the presence of a negative stereotype about a group's ability poses a threat because it calls into question the competence of group members and makes them concerned about confirming the stereotype of low ability (Aronson & Steele, 2005). Being that stereotypes arise from cultural attitudes and beliefs, stereotype threat has also been shown to affect African American and other minority groups (Aronson, Fried, & Good, 2002; Aronson & Steele, 2005).

Gifted students in the Unites States certainly conform to our culturally determined expectations related to competence. Some have argued, however, that labeling an individual as "gifted" perpetuates a focus on one's fixed ability, rather than a focus on how one can improve over time (an entity theory of ability rather than an incremental theory of ability; Dweck, 2002). Dweck has argued that an entity theory of ability might predispose one to want to "look smart" and avoid looking incompetent. This may mean some gifted students may avoid difficult learning tasks simply to preserve their label of "giftedness." Interestingly, negative effects of labeling have not always been found (Feldhusen & Dai, 1997; Hershey & Oliver, 1988).

Others have argued that the labeling process for gifted students also contributes to social divisiveness (Sapon-Shevin, 1994) and negative peer reactions (Steinberg, 1996). This may present a type of stereotype-threat to gifted students. The stereotype of always having to be smart may conflict with gifted students' social goals as they grow older (Manaster, Chan, Watt, & Wiehe, 1994; Manor-Bullock, Look, & Dixon, 1995). There may be particular dangers for high-achieving women in traditional male domains, such as math or science (Hyde, 2005; Spelke, 2005). Thus, overarching socio-cultural factors likely affect the self-beliefs and behaviors of gifted students.

SELF-BELIEFS AND THEORIES

As children get older, they compare themselves to their peers and form theories about their level of competence based on these comparisons. This perceived level of competence forms the basis or the core of self-beliefs and motivational constructs, which in turn influences behavior (see Figure 1). Perceived competence provides information for the development of self-concept and self-efficacy, a foundation for the functioning of self-theories and meaning systems, and the core for achievement goals. Each of these will be reviewed below.

Academic Self-Concept

Bracken and Howell (1991) defined academic self-concept as a student's perceptions of self as learner. Marsh and Shavelson (1985) argued that self-concept is a multidimensional concept with both academic and nonacademic aspects. The present chapter focuses on academic self-concept, as research has repeatedly shown it is related to academic achievement and other motivational constructs (e.g., Hattie, 1992). Besides influencing academic achievement, self-concept influences student effort, engagement, persistence, and career choice (Felson, 1984).

Bong and Skaalvik (2003) discuss the sources of academic self-concept information in depth. Some sources particularly relevant to the research on gifted students include (a) mastery experiences/prior successes in the environment, (b) reflected appraisals from or relationships with significant others, and (c) frames of reference/social comparison. Each will be reviewed below.

High levels of prior achievement or mastery experiences should facilitate high levels of academic self-concept in gifted students. In fact, gifted students demonstrate higher academic self-concepts than typically achieving or underachieving gifted students, although the structure and function of self-concept is similar across the groups (McCoach & Siegle, 2003; Van Boxtel & Mönks, 1992). Research on the related concept of self-efficacy suggests gifted students have higher perceived competence than typically achieving students (Chan, 1996), with gifted girls demonstrating higher academic competence beliefs than gifted boys (Chan, 1996; Freeman, 2003). The significant difference between research on self-concept and self-efficacy has been the disagreement over whether these self-beliefs are domains specific (Siegle & Reis, 1998). Self-efficacy has been argued to be specific to a task (Bandura, 1997). Thus, one feels competent or not competent at two-digit multiplication. Self-concept on the other hand, is a more global feeling of how good one believes one is in math (Marsh & Shavelson, 1985). Both types of self-beliefs affect engagement and effort.

Another way students form their self-concept is through appraisals from significant others. In fact, relationships that students have with teachers (Ryan & Patrick, 2001), parents (Grolnick, Ryan, & Deci, 1991), classmates (Goodenow, 1993), and friends (Wentzel, 2005) play an important role in academic success and the development of academic self-concept. Students gain important feedback within these relationships about their abilities. Students' academic self-concept may also be influenced by social appraisal within the larger context (Nelson-Haynes, 1996; Phillips, 1992).

Gifted students' academic self-concept is likely affected by their most salient social comparison group. When other gifted students serve as the referent group for comparison, self-concept typically lowers. This is termed the big-fish-little-pond effect (BFLPE) and will be discussed in more detail later in the chapter. Interestingly, research has shown that students not only use social groups as referents for comparison, they use themselves, too. A student's self-concept for a particular subject or domain may be affected in reference to how that student performs in a different subject (Plucker & Stocking, 2001). For example, a student's self-concept in math may be negatively affected if that student performs at a higher level in reading.

Research has shown that positive academic self-concept is related to many different positive student outcomes. In a meta-analysis, Valentine, DuBois, and Cooper (2004), found a significant relation between self-beliefs and later achievement even after controlling for prior achievement. Eccles, Alder, and Meece (1984) suggest that academic self-concept affects "a variety of behaviors including academic performance, task persistence, task choice" (p. 27). In a longitudinal study, Guay, Larose, and Boivin (2004) revealed that academic self-concept predicted educational attainment level 10 years later over and above prior achievement even after controlling for socioeconomic status (SES) and family structures.

Beliefs About Ability and Self-Theories: Incremental Views vs. Entity Views

Some of the strongest self-beliefs that affect motivation are beliefs about ability. People tend to hold either an incremental view of ability or an entity view of ability (Dweck, 2002). An incremental view perceives ability as unstable, changeable, and controllable. Ability is something that can grow and develop, dependent on the amount of work and effort an individual puts forth. An entity view perceives ability as stable, unchangeable, uncontrollable, and unequally distributed among individuals.

Dweck and Molden (2005) discuss how these views of ability give rise to self-theories or meaning systems (a network of beliefs) that operate to affect motivation and behavior by valuing either competence acquisition (mastery or learning goals) or competence validation (performance or ego goals). Incremental self-theorists value competence acquisition, whereas entity self-theorists value competence validation in which one's level of competence is displayed to others. In fact, research has demonstrated that people with incremental theories take pleasure in things they have to work hard to master over time, whereas people with entity theories may not enjoy something unless they are good at it right away (Butler, 2000). Research also suggests that individuals with entity theories may experience negative affective responses to failure, but individuals with incremental theories may not (Niiya, Crocker, & Bartmess, 2004). Importantly, research has demonstrated that these self-theories may be malleable and can be influenced by the context in which the individual finds him- or herself (see Figure 1).

Very little research has examined the prevalence of entity versus incremental theorists among gifted students. Dai and Feldhusen (1996; Feldhusen & Dai, 1997) suggested that gifted students tend to hold incremental views of abilities. However, these results were collected from a sample of gifted students voluntarily enrolled in a summer enrichment program. These students are likely highly motivated to begin with and may not be representative of the gifted population in general. The field has very little information about how these theories play out in the day-to-day world of the classroom.

Overall, self-theories of ability have been shown to determine the types of attributions individuals make about successes and failures, affect the level of effort individuals put forth and strategies used, and determine the type of achievement goals an individual may set. Given their importance in determining goals and behavior, this is clearly an area for future research.

Attributions. In order to understand their successes and failures, students will make attributions. Some researchers view students' attributions as being fairly stable beliefs that are developed from past experiences (Graham, 1991). Attributions will affect motivation and behavior depending on the characteristics of the attributions made. For instance, it is better if students attribute successes and failures to unstable and changeable factors, like the amount of effort or ineffective strategies as compared to unchangeable factors (Weiner, 2000). It is no surprise that individuals with incremental theories of ability tend to make attributions that positively influence effort and persistence, whereas individuals with entity theories tend to make attributions that negatively affect those individuals' self-perceptions (Dweck & Molden, 2005). Gifted students tend to attribute successes and failures to amount of effort invested, while typically achieving students are more likely to attribute successes and failures to luck (Chan, 1996). Gifted students are also more likely to attribute failure to use of ineffective strategies rather than a lack of ability (Chan, 1996). These results suggest that gifted students tend to perceive greater control over their successes and failures than typically achieving students, providing evidence that these students may hold a more incremental view of ability. Though, as noted above, more research is clearly needed in this area.

Effort and Strategies. Self-theories of ability affect students' views about effort. Research reported in Dweck and Molden (2005) indicates that for incremental theorists, effort and persistence are means of increasing knowledge. For entity theorists, the need for effort and persistence acts as an indicator of lack of ability—one should not have to work hard if one is smart. Additionally, students with incremental theories tend to modify their strategies as needed to master a task, whereas students with entity theories tend to give up on tasks that they do not initially master. Given that little research highlights the differences in gifted and typically achieving students' views about effort and strategies, it is worth keeping in mind that maladaptive patterns of achievement behavior may be related to students' views about the need for effort and strategies. If one has an entity theory of ability, one should not have to work hard to achieve one's goals. This kind of attitude could lead a gifted child down a difficult path of not trying, although possibly still succeeding without effort, and learning nothing about learning strategies or the use of effort until confronted (maybe even until college).

Achievement Goals

Goal orientations are patterns of beliefs about goals that arise from a person's self-theories and are related to motivation and achievement (Locke & Latham, 2002). A person who holds an incremental view of ability is more likely to set mastery or learning goals, whereas a person who holds an entity view of ability is more likely to set performance goals (Dweck & Molden, 2005). Students who set mastery goals focus on learning and do not focus on their performance as compared to others. Students who set performance goals care about demonstrating their ability to others and are likely to focus on getting good grades or winning (Stipek, 2002).

Recently, Elliot (2005) has added the new dimension of approach-avoidance to the two main dimensions of achievement goals to create a 2x2 framework. Thus, achievement goals can fall into four distinct patterns: mastery-approach, mastery-avoidance, performance-approach, and performance-avoidance. Competence can be evaluated either by task or self-references ("How am I doing?" mastery goals), or by norm references ("How are others doing?" performance goals). Second, goals can be delineated according to whether the goal focuses on approaching the possibility of competence or whether the goal focuses on avoiding the possibility of incompetence.

Although past research suggests that performance goals have negative outcomes (e.g., task avoidance), whereas mastery goals have positive outcomes (e.g., challenge seeking), the current framework allows for more flexible evaluations of the different achievement goals. Recent research indicates that performance-approach goals are also related to positive outcomes, although not as strongly as mastery goals (Elliot, 2005). In addition, some research highlights that high-achievement-oriented students benefit from maintaining performance-approach achievement goal orientations. Elliot (2005) also suggests that perfectionists may be likely to adopt mastery-avoidance goals such as striving to avoid making any mistakes. Currently, more research is needed in the gifted literature on this new distinction. Are gifted students more likely to hold performance-approach goals than typically achieving students? Do gifted students hold mastery-avoidance goals? In other words, are they afraid of losing the mastery they have already gained in particular areas?

Perfectionism. Perfectionism is the tendency for an individual to need to get "everything right" about an assignment. Although sometimes this can lead to a high-quality product, other times it can result in procrastination or other motivational difficulties, because the pressure of being perfect is just too intense. Orange (1997) found that gifted students scored high on a perfectionism quiz (and high in procrastination) although scores were not compared to a typically achieving cohort. Additionally, Schuler (2000) also reported a tendency for gifted students to be perfectionistic with 58% of the sample in the healthy range of perfectionism (focusing on order and organization) and 30% of the sample in the neurotic range (focusing on making mistakes).

On the other hand, Parker and Mills (1996) suggested that perfectionism may not be a common characteristic of gifted students. In addition, LoCicero and Ashby (2000) compared levels of perfectionism of gifted middle school students with a typically achieving cohort using the Almost Perfect Scale. The results indicated that gifted students have higher levels of adaptive perfectionism (holding high personal standards) and lower levels of maladaptive perfectionism (distress resulting from a discrepancy between personal standards and performance). These researchers suggest that gifted students are likely to strive for perfection as suggested in past literature, but gifted students may not experience the negative outcomes associated with perfectionism.

Some of the negative outcomes linked to perfectionism are underachievement (Davis & Rimm, 1994; Reis, 1987), loss of self-esteem (Delisle, 1990), procrastination (Adderholdt-Elliot, 1987), and depression (Delisle, 1990). Empirical evidence of these associations is not conclusive. One explanation for the inconclusive results may be the inconsistent definition of perfectionism used by various researchers. Researchers have moved from one-dimensional definitions of perfectionism to more multidimensional definitions (Adler, 1956; Frost, Marten, Lahart, & Rosenblate, 1990; Hamacheck, 1978; Pacht, 1984; Slaney & Ashby, 1996), and have argued that some dimensions may lead to negative outcomes whereas other dimensions may lead to positive outcomes.

Currently, the available research in perfectionism does not explain the developmental course of perfectionism (Parker & Adkins, 1995) or explain the mechanisms by which gifted individuals may be more prone to perfectionism than the general population. Some suggested precursors of the development of perfectionism may be high personal standards, achievement goal orientations, birth order, parental relations, and pressure from teachers and peers (Adderholdt-Elliot, 1991; Speirs Neumeister, 2004; Schuler, 2000). However, future research is needed to understand more fully how these precursors contribute to the development of this motivational construct. In addition, research suggesting ways to prevent these perfectionistic tendencies from becoming unhealthy would be important for the gifted population.

STRATEGIES

Chan (1996) has stated that personal motivation factors energize self-regulating, executive skills necessary for strategy selection, implementation, and monitoring (Borkowski, Carr, Rellinger, & Pressley, 1990; Borkowski & Muthukrishna, 1992). In a series of reviews of previous research, gifted students have been shown to have more well-developed metacognitive abilities (Alexander, Carr, & Schwanenflugel, 1995; Alexander & Schwanenflugel,

1996; Carr, Alexander, & Schwanenflugel, 1996). Gifted students are also more likely with age to use a variety of both simple and complex strategies for learning and carry out those strategies more effectively (Alexander et al., 1995; Risemberg & Zimmerman, 1992), although the overarching metacognitive superiority of gifted over typically achieving students has been difficult to establish (Alexander et al., 1995; Chan, 1996).

Strategies also likely interact with self-beliefs (see Figure 1). For example, Mangels and Dweck (as cited in Dweck, Mangels, & Good, 2004) examined how long individuals focused their attention for feedback about the correctness of an answer followed by informative feedback. Entity theorists only wanted to know the right answer and stopped attending before informative feedback was given. Incremental theorists paid attention to both types of information. In a second example, Dweck and Molden (2005) reported research showing that mastery learning goals (as opposed to performance goals) predict learning and the use of self regulated learning (SRL) strategies including deep level study strategies, time management, and self-regulation of emotion and motivation.

Chan (1996) found that gifted and typically achieving students who believed that school success was under their personal control were likely to have a larger repertoire of strategies and more effectively use them. Neber and Schommer-Aikins (2002) found high correlations between SRL strategies and motivational beliefs with a gifted sample of elementary and high school students. They also found that task goal orientation was the strongest predictor of self-regulated learning strategies. Interestingly, strategy use among gifted students may differ by gender, with girls using more strategies and being more mastery goal oriented than boys (Ablard & Lipschultz, 1998).

Thus, although gifted students typically are more self-regulating of their strategy use than typically achieving students, it is likely that the effective use of these strategies interacts with self-beliefs and self-theories. Students with entity and incremental theories prefer different strategies to aid their learning. In addition, task goal orientation is a good predictor of the self-regulation of strategies. Importantly, the interplay of these self-beliefs has yet to be studied in the classroom and seems an important area for future research.

CLASSROOM CONTEXT

Teachers' instructional practices affect student motivation. The tasks teachers choose, the types of assessments they give, and how they deal with diverse learners in the classroom all affect student motivation, particularly their intrinsic motivation to learn (or learning for the sake of learning). Research has documented that gifted students spend a significant portion of their time in classrooms feeling bored (Kunkel, Chapa, Patterson, & Walling, 1992; Larson & Richards, 1991) or unchallenged (Feldhusen & Kroll, 1991; Gallagher, Harradine, & Coleman, 1997). In fact, a real hunger for challenge is typical of gifted students from preschool to high school (Hilliard, 1993; Kanevsky, 1992; Plucker & McIntire, 1996).

Others have argued that intellectually gifted students are generally high in intrinsic motivation (Gottfried & Gottfried, 1996; Vallerand, Gagné, Senécal, & Pelletier, 1994). Unfortunately, this may not always generalize to motivated classroom behavior (Hoekman, McCormick, & Gross, 1999; Janos & Robinson, 1985; Robinson & Noble, 1991). As gifted learners become bored or unchallenged in class, they may turn to other pursuits to fill the challenges they seek (Kanevsky & Keighley, 2003; Plucker & McIntire, 1996).

Why does boredom happen and how can we encourage intrinsic motivation in gifted students? To explore these questions, we review research examining the interplay between personal beliefs and four main areas of the classroom context: teachers' choices for classroom tasks, teachers' chosen assessment practices, relationships with teachers and peers, and classroom structure factors (see Figure 1).

Classroom Tasks

The choices teachers make about classroom tasks will influence rates of boredom and intrinsic motivation. As Kanevsky and Keighley (2003) have noted, the opposite of boredom is learning. Learning can alleviate almost any boredom. Most research on intrinsically motivated learning concurs that learning should be under the control of the student (or self-determined), may be an innate inclination of the human species (i.e., we are born to seek competence), occurs best when tasks are challenging and matched optimally to our ability levels, and occurs most naturally when tasks are novel or somewhat discrepant from what we expect as they make us curious or interested. Research in each of these areas will be reviewed more thoroughly below.

Self-Determination. Deci and his colleagues (Deci & Moller, 2005; Deci & Ryan, 1991) have argued that when individuals self-determine, or are in control of their own behavior, intrinsic motivation is higher. Self-determination has been shown to play a large role in gifted students' feelings about classroom learning (Kanevsky & Keighley, 2003). Self-determination can be seen most readily in classrooms when teachers give students choices and individualize learning in terms of timelines, content, or depth.

Competence and Challenge. White (1959) has argued that seeking competence is adaptive from an evolutionary standpoint. Also, people derive pleasure for increasing mastery, but only when mastering moderately difficult tasks (based on individual prior histories). Csikszentmihalyi (1993) has argued that "the basic requirement for a milieu supportive of optimal psychological growth is that at the appropriate moment in the child's maturation, it should provide neither too many, nor too few opportunities for action in relation to the child's developing capacities to act" (p. 41). Csikszentmihalyi and Csikszentmihalyi (1988) found that high-IQ students were able to handle about twice as many challenging tasks as average-IQ students. Thus, gifted students may be prepared to handle more frequent challenging tasks or may need larger steps between projects. As a result, a relatively greater increase in skill development can result than for typically achieving students (Kanevsky, 1992).

Novelty, Curiosity, and Interest. Novelty is the concept at the heart of intrinsic motivation. According to Vygotsky's and Csikszentmihalyi's theories (Csikszentmihalyi, Abuhamdeh, & Nakamura, 2005; Vygotsky, 1978), optimal learning is facilitated when educational opportunities are not only responsive to students' interests, abilities, and individual differences, but actually extend their prior knowledge. As Hunter and Csikszentmihalyi (2003) have argued, students who experience interest as opposed to boredom are more likely to have positive psychological well-being. Piaget (1952) and others (Berlyne, 1966; Hunter, Ames, & Koopman, 1983) have argued that individuals are predisposed to derive pleasure and curiosity from moderately surprising, incongruent, or moderately discrepant events. Interestingly, these variables may present unique challenges for teachers of gifted students. In a mixed-ability setting, activities that are novel or curious to gifted students may be too far outside the range of other students' abilities.

Assessment

Assessment choices made by teachers in the classroom can easily undermine intrinsic motivation. Some examples might include:

- Putting emphasis on the assessment (particularly isolated knowledge kinds of assessments) rather than on learning itself.
- Emphasizing the grades, rather than informative feedback.
- Not sharing grading criteria, or making it less than clear to students, making students feel less in control of their own performance.
- Providing external rewards for tasks that students are already intrinsically motivated to do (this makes the behavior less likely to be repeated, as the reward becomes expected).
- Using rewards simply to control the "doing" of a behavior, not the quality of learning (e.g., giving students high marks for simply working during a time period, not producing quality work; this lowers the meaning of a high mark in the students' eyes).

Assessments, should, on the other hand, enhance learning and motivation. Thus, they should promote meaningful learning (allowing for larger ideas to be explored) such as project-based learning, match the use of information in a real-world setting (or be based on a "real" and authentic problems), and easily measure affective reactions, as well as knowledge. In addition, assessment should provide clear and immediate feedback about information learned and allow self-appraisal of skills, and/or goal setting for future assessments. In sum, the goal of classroom assessments should be to help the student concentrate on his or her own growing mastery of material and to facilitate the acceptance of mastery goals and an incremental view of ability.

The literature also suggests that it is best when there is a fit between the types of achievement goals held by the student and the goals for assessment emphasized by the context (Dai et al., 1998; Elliot, 2005). Gifted students prefer individual or competitive learning environments over cooperative learning environments (Clinkenbeard, 1989; Li & Adamson, 1992; Tomlinson, 1994), *even based on different reasons.* although individual students may vary as to why they prefer competitive learning situations. Some students like competition because it allows them to outperform others (competition outcome); others see competition as an energizing factor for learning (competition process; Feldhusen, Dai, & Clinkenbeard, 2000; Subotnik, Kassan, Summers, & Wasser, 1993). These individual differences highlight the multifaceted roles achievement goals play in competence motivation.

Relationships

With Teachers. Alexander and Murphy (1998) have argued that when teachers acknowledge students' personal goals and interests and learners perceive the academic climate to be supportive and encouraging, they are more likely to perform well. Kanevsky and Keighley (2003) argued that, for gifted students, a caring teacher can overcome deficits in what they call "the other 4 C's" (control, choice, challenge, complexity). In their study, gifted students valued teachers for their professional commitment and because they were fair yet flexible. These teachers respected the students' need to talk, to question, to challenge, and to dig deeper. These teachers gave students some control over aspects of their learning and showed a concern for all individuals' well-being. In sum, these teachers were enthusiastic about interacting with gifted students.

Csikszentmihalyi, Rathunde, and Whalen (1993) described similar responses to teachers in their study of talented teens. "More than most teens, they reach high school already interested in a particular domain and its subjective rewards. This awareness makes them . . . particularly intolerant of teachers who go through the motions" (p. 185). Thus, teachers may play an important supportive role for gifted students, even if it must be a college instructor because the student has advanced beyond what the high school can offer (Mingus & Grassl, 1999).

Kanevsky and Keighley (2003) have highlighted a situation that seems to result from years of difficulties between gifted students and teachers—nonproducers. Nonproducers are not at risk psychologically, but they are academically. These individuals are self-assured and have chosen purposefully not to attend classes or complete boring or irrelevant school assignments. Nonproducers believe that they are taking the honorable approach to their learning by disengaging from the curriculum. Each of these students also noted, as we mentioned above, that a caring teacher can help alleviate many of these difficulties.

With Peers. By early adolescence, students become increasingly aware of the social costs involved with high academic achievement. As a result, some high-achieving students experience social isolation (Brown & Steinberg, 1990), although this may differ depending on whether the student is placed in an academically gifted classroom or a mixed-ability classroom. Academically gifted students with personal friendship groups that hold anti-academic norms or whose cultural expectations for competence are different from those espoused in the mainstream may be particularly at risk (Gross, 1989; Phelan, Davidson, & Cao, 1991; Tannenbaum, 1983). Recent research examining student engagement may help shed light on these issues with gifted students (Carini, Kuh, & Klein, 2006).

Gifted students who stay in mixed-ability classrooms have to contend with other difficult social issues including teasing and bullying (Moon, Nelson, & Piercy, 1993), being misunderstood or unappreciated (Baker, Bridger, & Evans, 1998), or being rejected or ostracized (Gross, 1989). Sometimes gifted students deal with these difficulties by hiding their exceptional abilities (Clasen & Clasen, 1995; Gross, 1993; Silverman, 1993). Research by Ford (1992, 1993, 1996) shows that this phenomenon is particularly likely with minority students. As many as 79% of minority gifted students report hiding their academic abilities (Borland, 2004; Ford, 1992). Supporters of mixed-ability classes have argued that gifted students are provided with good opportunities for social development when a wide range of individuals are dealt with (Oakes, 1985; Slavin, 1987).

Students themselves agree. They prefer heterogeneous grouping over high-ability grouping for social/emotional reasons (Adams-Byers, Whitsell, & Moon, 2004). However, as Adams-Byers et al. (2004) note, gifted students do not, in the long run, advantage themselves when they build their "houses upon sand" by defining their self-worth in relation to less-able peers. They suggest that grouping gifted students with heterogeneous peer groups may actually encourage a performance goal orientation and be detrimental, in the long run, to the student's motivation.

Classroom Structure

Gifted students find themselves in many different service arrangements in order to meet their unique needs. Gifted students are sometimes serviced with pull-out programs, separate gifted classrooms, special "academies" or course options, or simply within heterogeneous groups in the classroom. The motivational implications for each are discussed below.

Academically Selective Programs. Research has documented both positive and negative effects when gifted students are placed in an academically selective program. Positive motivational effects come from increased collegiality. Negative motivational effects come from threats to self-concept and emphasis on performance goals within highly competitive environments.

Plucker et al. (2004) have argued that "being in the company of like-minded peers with whom one can related, converse, and argue is a critical component of intellectual and social development" (p. 269). Adams-Byers et al. (2004) have noted that gifted students were happy to be in a homogenous ability class where their peers understood what they were saying, played important roles in classroom conversations, and "talked their language." In addition, Gross (1993, 1998) found that gifted students' reluctance to work with classmates dissipates when they are placed with peers of equal ability.

On the other hand, research by Marsh and his colleagues (Marsh, Chessor, Craven, & Roche, 1995; Marsh & Hau, 2003; Lüdtke, Köller, Marsh, & Trautwein, 2005) documents drops in academic self-concept as gifted students move to academically selective programs or schools (known as the big-fish-little-pond effect, or BFLPE). The BFLPE model has been replicated with gifted adolescents (Plucker & Stocking, 2001). This means that for at least half of the students in the class of gifted students, they would no longer by considered the most academically gifted students (or the "biggest fish") in the immediate social comparison group. Some have argued this drop in self-concept is temporary (Gibbons, Benbow, & Gerrard, 1994; Plucker et al., 2004). Plucker et al. (2004) suggest that self-concept may be reduced but still remain at a fairly high level. Thus, self-concept might actually be resetting to a more realistic level.

Research by Lockwood and Kunda (1997) suggests that how individuals react in the BFLPE situation may be dependent on their views of ability (incremental vs. entity) and other personal factors. For example, Lockwood and Kunda (1997) found that exposure to a highly successful fourth-year student led first-year accounting students with incremental views of ability to have higher self-ratings on career success than those with a fixed view of ability. Typically, according the BFLPE, upward social comparison should result in a lower level of self-concept. Thus, personal factors seem to be moderating these effects.

Finally, academically selective programs may have negative effects on motivation because of the increased emphasis on competitiveness in self-contained gifted education programs (Udvari & Schneider, 2000). An increased emphasis on competitiveness increases the likeliness of students adopting performance goals as compared to mastery goals. As noted earlier, performance-goal orientation is correlated with an increase in work avoidance (Thorkildsen, 1988) and performance-goal oriented gifted students are less well liked by peers and considered overly competitive (Udvari, Schneider, & Tassi, 1997). These studies suggest that performance goals, particularly in environments where teachers are trying to stress mastery, may make it difficult for gifted students to "fit in."

In sum, more work clearly needs to be done in the gifted literature on both the positive and negative motivational effects of academically selective programs and how self-beliefs interact with these classroom contexts. Future work on the newly hypothesized performance-approach goals versus performance-avoidance goals split (Elliot, 2005) will also be important for understanding how these variables affect each other. Finally, understanding how social comparisons develop across the multiple contexts in which gifted students tend to be serviced (school, after-school programs, summer programs, weekend enrichment programs) will be important.

Heterogeneous Grouping Within a Single Classroom. With the move away from homogeneous ability grouping over the past two decades, high-ability students have been increasingly used as peer tutors and group leaders in heterogeneous classrooms. Although research indicates that high-ability students are typically good peer tutors (Feldhusen & Treffinger, 1985; Paradis & Peverly, 1994; Peterson, Janicki, & Swing, 1981; Webb, Meckstroth, & Tolan, 1982), gifted students do not report feeling like they have learned the material better, particularly when the peer they are working with is of low ability (Matthews, 1992). Many gifted students express frustration and feelings of exploitation because of their tutoring role. As Adams-Byers et al. (2004) note, "this arrangement can incite hostility toward gifted students placed in the (teaching) role, rather than engender cooperation and teamwork" (p. 17).

On the positive side, Fuchs et al. (1996) documented a well-established link between constructing explanations and achievement for the providers of those explanations. Similarly, Adams-Byers et al. (2004) found that gifted students enjoyed knowing more and being able to do more than their peers in heterogeneously grouped classes when placed in tutoring roles. They also like to help others because it makes them feel good about their abilities. Unfortunately, Matthews (1992) has noted that gifted students tend to take over groups rather than provide shared leadership and sometimes lack the knowledge about how to explain well without giving answers.

Thus, balancing cognitive and social needs for gifted students' work in groups can be difficult for a teacher. Robinson (1990) and Matthews (1992) suggested that gifted students be grouped together to work within heterogeneous classrooms or they be placed in mixed-ability groups only for learning something in their area of weakness. Other models of cooperative learning such as jigsaw (Aronson, Blaney, Stephan, Sikes, & Snapp, 1978; Slavin, 1983), where each student must become an "expert" in part of the project before coming together, may be another viable alternative (Matthews, 1992).

RESEARCH SUMMARY

Are academically gifted students more motivated than typically achieving students? The answer is—*it depends on the context*. In many ways, gifted students react like typically achieving students to motivational factors in situations.

- They bring self-beliefs about their abilities to the classroom context. Teachers' actions, feedback, assignments, and classroom configurations give the student information to facilitate the formation and modification of those self-beliefs.
- Self-beliefs affect the kinds of strategies students will use in a learning situation, resulting in greater persistence, attention, effort, and engagement.
- At the same time, different classroom contexts arising from teachers' own beliefs about learning and motivation afford different kinds of engagement, challenge-seeking, and attention.

In other ways, gifted students have specific unique motivational issues.
- The personal resources gifted students bring to the classroom context present a challenge for the teacher. Their ability to process information, their need for challenge, and need to question may not match well with the teacher's views about learning tasks and assessments.
- Gifted students may be more likely to show both healthy and unhealthy levels of perfectionism, exacerbating the need for an environment matched to their learning goals.
- As gifted students grow older, they may experience, sometimes for the first time, challenges in academic tasks that undermine their self-beliefs in their abilities. Self-beliefs interact with the context such that they may begin to doubt their own abilities.
- Finally, classroom contexts present unique challenges for teachers of gifted students, as the very nature of challenges differ for these students from typically achieving students. Gifted students have a high incidence rate of boredom in classrooms. Teachers need to respond to these challenges by setting goals that help move the gifted student toward mastery goals and incremental views of ability, as these have been shown to have the strongest connections to life-long learning and motivation.

PRIORITIES FOR FUTURE RESEARCH

Our review of the research examining gifted student motivation has clearly identified some priorities for future research. We include them here to encourage researchers to explore these issues as thoroughly as possible. The field needs:
- A better understanding of the prevalence of entity vs. incremental theories in the gifted student population and how these theories are affected by activity and assessment choices in the day-to-day world of the classroom.

- A more thorough exploration of how theories of ability connect to the attributions gifted students make, and the consequences those attributions have for engagement and effort.
- An understanding of the developmental course of perfectionism and the negative consequences of perfectionism (or certain dimensions of perfectionism). We also need to understand the mechanisms by which gifted individuals may be more prone to perfectionism than the general population. More importantly, we need to suggest ways to prevent these perfectionistic tendencies from becoming unhealthy.
- An exploration of the 2x2 Achievement Goal Framework (Elliot, 2005). The field needs to explore most particularly the prevalence of performance-approach and mastery-avoid goals in gifted students.
- To determine whether the newly developing concept of "engagement" can offer explanations about how gifted students maintain engagement over time in classes, especially in their relationships to peers and others in school.
- To examine the interplay between self-regulation and gifted students' self-beliefs and self-theories in the classroom. Do certain self-theories lead to particular kinds of self-regulation skills (or lack thereof)? If identified as a difficulty, we also need to explore how these difficulties can be remediated.
- An understanding how social comparisons develop across the multiple contexts in which gifted students tend to be serviced (school, after-school programs, summer programs, weekend enrichment programs).
- An evidence-based plan for reconnecting nonproducers to the classroom, or preventing the development of nonproducers in the first place.
- A more general understanding of both the positive and negative motivational effects of academically selective programs and how self-beliefs interact with these selective classroom contexts.

REFERENCES

Ablard, K. E., & Lipschultz, R. E. (1998). Self-regulated learning in high-achieving students: Relations to advanced reasoning, achievement goals, and gender. *Journal of Educational Psychology, 90,* 94–101.

Adams-Byers, J., Whitsell, S. S., & Moon, S. M. (2004). Gifted students' perceptions of the academic and social/emotional effects of homogeneous and heterogeneous grouping. *Gifted Child Quarterly, 48,* 7–20.

Adderholdt-Elliot, M. R. (1987). *Perfectionism: What's bad about being too good?* Minneapolis, MM: Free Spirit.

Adderholdt-Elliot, M. R. (1991). Perfectionism and the gifted adolescent. In M. Bireley & J. Genshaft (Eds.), *Understanding the gifted adolescent: Educational, developmental, and multicultural issues* (pp. 65–75). New York: Teachers College Press.

Adler, A. (1956). Striving for superiority. In H. L. Ansbacher & R. Ansbacher (Eds.), *The individual psychology of Alfred Adler: A systematic presentation in selections from his writings* (pp. 101–125). New York: Harper & Row.

Alexander, J. M., Carr, M., & Schwanenflugel, P. J. (1995). Development of metacognition in gifted children: Directions for future research. *Developmental Review, 15,* 1–37.

Alexander, J. M., & Schwanenflugel, P. J. (1996). Development of metacognitive concepts about thinking in gifted and nongifted children: Recent research. *Learning and Individual Differences, 8,* 305–325.

Alexander, P. A., & Murphy, P. K. (1998). The research base for APA's learner-centered principles. In N. M. Lambert & B. L. McCombs (Eds.), *How students learn: Reforming schools through learner-centered education* (pp. 25–60). Washington, DC: American Psychological Association.

Aronson, E., Blaney, N., Stephan, C., Sikes, J., & Snapp, M. (1978). *The jigsaw classroom.* Beverly Hills, CA: Sage.

Aronson, J., Fried, C., & Good, C. (2002). Reducing the effects of stereotype threat on African American college students by shaping theories of intelligence. *Journal of Experimental Social Psychology, 38,* 113–125.

Aronson, J., & Steele, C. M. (2005). Stereotypes and the fragility of academic competence, motivation, and self-concept. In A. J. Elliot & C. S. Dweck (Eds.), *Handbook of competence and motivation* (pp. 436–456). New York: Guilford Press.

Azuma, H., & Kashiwagi, K. (1987). Descriptors for an intelligent person: A Japanese study. *Japanese Psychological Research, 29*(1), 17–26.

Baker, J. A., Bridger, R., & Evans, K. (1998). Models of underachievement among gifted preadolescents: The role of personal, family, and school factors. *Gifted Child Quarterly, 42,* 5–15.

Bandura, A. (1997). *Self-efficacy: The exercise of control.* New York: WH Freeman.

Berlyne, D. E. (1966). Lyuboznatel'nost' i poisk informatsii [Curiosity and the quest for information]. *Voprosy Psychologii, 3*(3), 54–60.

Bong, M., & Skaalvik, E. M. (2003). Academic self-concept and self-efficacy: How different are they really? *Educational Psychology Review, 15,* 1–40.

Borkowski, J., & Muthukrishna, N. (1992). Moving metacognition into the classroom: "Working models" and effective strategy teaching. In M. Pressley, K. R. Harris & J. T. Guthrie (Eds.), *Promoting academic competence and literacy in school* (pp. 477–501). San Diego, CA: Academic Press.

Borkowski, J. G., Carr, M., Rellinger, E., & Pressley, M. (1990). Self-regulated cognition: Interdependence of metacognition, attributions, and self-esteem. In B. F. Jones & L. Idol (Eds.), *Dimensions of thinking and cognitive instruction.* (pp. 53–92). Hillsdale, NJ: Lawrence Erlbaum Associates.

Borland, J. (2004). *Issues and practices in the identification and education of gifted students from under-represented groups.* Storrs: National Research Center on the Gifted and Talented, University of Connecticut.

Bracken, B. A., & Howell, K. K. (1991). Multidimensional self concept validation: A three-instrument investigation. *Journal of Psychoeducational Assessment, 9,* 319–328.

Brown, B. B., & Steinberg, L. (1990). Skirting the "brain-nerd" connection: Academic achievement and social acceptance. *The Education Digest, 55,* 57–60.

Butler, R. (2000). Making judgments about ability: The role of implicit theories of ability in moderating inferences from temporal and social comparison information. *Journal of Personality and Social Psychology, 78*, 965–978.

Carini, R., Kuh, G., & Klein, S. (2006). Student engagement and student learning: Testing the linkages. *Research in Higher Education, 47*, 1–32,

Carr, M., Alexander, J. M., & Schwanenflugel, P. J. (1996). Where gifted children do and do not excel on metacognitive tasks. *Roeper Review, 18*, 212–217.

Chan, L. K. S. (1996). Motivational orientations and metacognitive abilities of intellectually gifted students. *Gifted Child Quarterly, 40*, 184–193.

Clasen, D. R., & Clasen, R. E. (1995). Underachievement of highly able students and the peer society. *Gifted and Talented International, 10*, 67–76.

Clinkenbeard, P. R. (1989). The motivation to win: Negative aspects of success at competition. *Journal for the Education of the Gifted, 12*, 293–305.

Clinkenbeard, P. R. (1996). Research on motivation and the gifted: Implications for identification, programming and evaluation. *Gifted Child Quarterly, 40*, 220–221.

Csikszentmihalyi, M. (1993). Contexts of optimal growth in childhood. *Daedalus, Journal of American Academy of Arts and Sciences, 122*, 31–56.

Csikszentmihalyi, M., Abuhamdeh, S., & Nakamura, J. (2005). Flow. In A. J. Elliot & C. S. Dweck (Eds.), *Handbook of competence and motivation* (pp. 598–608). New York: Guilford Press.

Csikszentmihalyi, M., & Csikszentmihalyi, I. S. (Eds.). (1988). *Optimal experience: Psychological studies of flow in consciousness.* New York: Cambridge University Press.

Csikszentmihalyi, M., Rathunde, K. R., & Whalen, S. (1993). *Talented teenagers.* New York: Cambridge University Press.

Dai, D. Y., & Feldhusen, J. F. (1996). Goal orientations of gifted students. *Gifted and Talented International, 11*, 84–88.

Dai, D. Y., Moon, S. M., & Feldhusen, J. F. (1998). Achievement motivation and gifted students: A social cognitive perspective. *Educational Psychologist, 33*(2), 45–63.

Davis, G., & Rimm, S. (1994). *Education of the gifted and talented.* Englewood Cliffs, NJ: Prentice Hall.

Deci, E. L., & Moller, A. C. (2005). *The concept of competence: A starting place for understanding intrinsic motivation and self-determined extrinsic motivation.* New York: Guilford Publications.

Deci, E. L., & Ryan, R. M. (1991). A motivational approach to self: Integration in personality. In R. A. Dienstbier (Ed.), *Nebraska symposium on motivation: Vol. 38. Perspectives on motivation* (pp. 237–288). Lincoln: University of Nebraska Press.

Delisle, J. R. (1990). The gifted adolescent at risk: Strategies and resources for suicide prevention among gifted youth. *Journal for the Education of the Gifted, 13*, 212–228.

Dweck, C. S. (2002). Beliefs that make smart people dumb. In R. J. Sternberg (Ed.), *Why smart people can be so stupid* (pp. 24–41). New Haven, CT: Yale University Press.

Dweck, C. S., Mangels, J., & Good, C. (2004). Motivational effects on attention, cognition, and performance, In D. Y. Dai & R. J. Sternberg (Eds.), *Motivation, emotion, and cognition: Integrated perspectives on intellectual functioning* (pp. 41–56). Mahwah, NJ: Erlbaum.

Dweck, C. S., & Molden, D. C. (2005). Self theories: Their impact on competence motivation and acquisition. In A. J. Elliot & C. S. Dweck (Eds.), *Handbook of competence and motivation* (pp. 122–140). New York: Guilford Press.

Eccles, J., Alder, T., & Meece, J. L. (1984). Sex differences in achievement: A test of alternate theories. *Journal of Personality and Social Psychology, 46,* 26–43.

Eccles, J. D. (1983). Courses for gifted young writers. *Gifted Education International, 2*(1), 49–51.

Eccles, J. S. (2005). Subjective task value and the Eccles et al. model of achievement-related choices. In A. J. Elliot & C. S. Dweck (Eds.), *Handbook of competence and motivation* (pp. 105–121). New York: Guilford Press.

Elliot, A. J. (2005). A conceptual history of the achievement goal construct. In A. J. Elliot & C. S. Dweck (Eds.), *Handbook of competence and motivation* (pp. 52–72). New York: Guilford Press.

Feldhusen, J. F., & Dai, D. Y. (1997). Gifted students' attitudes and perceptions of the gifted label, special programs, and peer relations. *Journal of Secondary Gifted Education, 9,* 15–20.

Feldhusen, J. F., Dai, D. Y., & Clinkenbeard, P. R. (2000). Dimensions of competitive and cooperative learning among gifted learners. *Journal for the Education of the Gifted, 23,* 328–342.

Feldhusen, J. F., & Kroll, M. D. (1991). Boredom or challenge for the academically talented in school. *Gifted Education International, 7,* 80–81.

Feldhusen, J. F., & Treffinger, D. J. (1985). *Creative thinking and problem solving in gifted education.* Dubuque, IA: Kendall-Hunt.

Felson, R. B. (1984). The effect of self-appraisals of ability on academic performance. *Journal of Personality and Social Psychology, 47,* 944–952.

Ford, D. Y. (1992). Determinants of underachievement as perceived by gifted, above average and average Black students. *Roeper Review, 14,* 130–136.

Ford, D. Y. (1993). An investigation of the paradox of underachievement among gifted Black students. *Roeper Review, 16,* 78–84.

Ford, D. Y. (1996). *Reversing underachievement among gifted Black students.* New York: Teachers College Press.

Freeman, J. (2003). Gifted children grown up. *British Journal of Educational Psychology, 73,* 141–142.

Frost, R. O., Marten, P., Lahart, C., & Rosenblate, R. (1990). The dimensions of perfectionism. *Cognitive Therapy and Research, 14,* 449–468.

Fuchs, L. S., Fuchs, D., Karns, K., Hamlett, C. L., Dutka, S., & Karzakroff, M. (1996). The relation between student ability and the quality and effectiveness of explanations. *American Educational Research Journal, 33,* 631–664.

Gallagher, J., Harradine, C. C., & Coleman, M. R. (1997). Challenge or boredom? Gifted students' views on their schooling. *Roeper Review, 19,* 132–141.

Gibbons, F. X., Benbow, C. P., & Gerrard, M. (1994). From top dog to bottom half: Social comparison strategies in response to poor performance. *Journal of Personality and Social Psychology, 67,* 638–652.

Goodenow, C. (1993). Classroom belonging among early adolescent students: Relationships to motivation and achievement. *Journal of Early Adolescence, 13,* 21–43.

Gottfried, A. E., & Gottfried, A. W. (1996). A longitudinal study of academic intrinsic motivation in intellectually gifted children: Childhood through early adolescence. *Gifted Child Quarterly, 40,* 179–183.

Graham, S. (1991). A review of attribution theory in achievement contexts. *Educational Psychology Review, 3*, 5–39.

Grolnick, W. S., Ryan, R. M., & Deci, E. L. (1991). Inner resources for school achievement: Motivational mediators of children's perceptions of their parents. *Journal of Educational Psychology, 83,* 508–517.

Gross, M. U. M. (1989). The pursuit of excellence or the search for intimacy? The forced-choice dilemma of gifted youth. *Roeper Review, 11,* 189–194.

Gross, M. U. M. (1993). *Nurturing the talents of exceptionally gifted individuals.* Elmsford, NY: Pergamon Press.

Gross, M. U. M. (1998). The "me" behind the mask: Intellectually gifted students and the search for identity. *Roeper Review, 20,* 167–174.

Guay, F., Larose, S., & Boivin, M. (2004). Academic self-concept and educational attainment level: A ten-year longitudinal study. *Self and Identity, 3,* 53–68.

Hamacheck, D. E. (1978). Psychodynamics of normal and neurotic perfectionism. *Psychology, 15,* 27–33.

Hattie, J. (1992). *Self-concept.* Hillsdale, NJ: Erlbaum.

Hershey, M., & Oliver, E. (1988). The effects of the label gifted on students identified for special programs. *Roeper Review, 11,* 33–34.

Hilliard, S. A. D. (1993). Who's in school? Case studies of highly creative adolescents. *Dissertation Abstracts International, 54*(6), 2110.

Hoekman, K., McCormick, J., & Gross, M. U. M. (1999). The optimal context for gifted students: A preliminary exploration of motivational and affective considerations. *Gifted Child Quarterly, 43,* 170–193.

Hunter, J. P., & Csikszentmihalyi, M. (2003). The positive psychology of interested adolescents. *Journal of Youth and Adolescence, 32,* 27–35.

Hunter, M. A., Ames, E. W., & Koopman, R. (1983). Effects of stimulus complexity and familiarization time on infant preferences for novel and familiar stimuli. *Developmental Psychology, 19,* 338–352.

Hyde, J. S. (2005). The gender similarities hypothesis. *American Psychologist, 60,* 581–592.

Janos, P. M., & Robinson, N. M. (1985). The performance of students in a program of radical acceleration at the university level. *Gifted Child Quarterly, 36,* 175–179.

Kanevsky, L. (1992). The learning game. In P. S. Klein, & A. J. Tannenbaum (Eds.), *To be young and gifted* (pp. 204–241). Westport, CT: Ablex Publishing.

Kanevsky, L., & Keighley, T. (2003). To produce or not to produce? Understanding boredom and the honor in underachievement. *Roeper Review, 26,* 20–28.

Kunkel, M. A., Chapa, B., Patterson, G., & Walling, D. D. (1992). Experience of giftedness: "Eight great gripes" six years later. *Roeper Review, 15,* 10–14.

Larson, R. W., & Richards, M. H. (1991). Boredom in the middle school years: Blaming schools versus blaming students. *American Journal of Education, 99,* 418–443.

Li, A. K., & Adamson, G. (1992). Gifted secondary students' preferred learning style: Cooperative, competitive, or individualistic? *Journal for the Education of the Gifted, 16,* 46–54.

LoCicero, K. A., & Ashby, J. S. (2000). Multidimensional perfectionism in middle school age gifted students: A comparison to peers from the general cohort. *Roeper Review, 22,* 182–185.

Locke, E. A., & Latham, G. P. (2002). Building a practically useful theory of goal setting and task motivation: A 35-year odyssey. *American Psychologist, 57,* 705–717.

Lockwood, P., & Kunda, Z. (1997). Superstars and me: Predicting the impact of role models on the self. *Journal of Personality and Social Psychology, 73*, 91–103.

Lüdtke, O., Köller, O., Marsh, H. W., & Trautwein, U. (2005). Teacher frame of reference and the big-fish-little-pond effect. *Contemporary Educational Psychology, 30*, 263–285.

Manaster, G. J., Chan, J. C., Watt, C., & Wiehe, J. (1994). Gifted adolescents' attitudes toward their giftedness: A partial replication. *Gifted Child Quarterly, 38*, 176–178.

Manor-Bullock, R., Look, C., & Dixon, D. N. (1995). Is giftedness socially stigmatizing? The impact of high achievement on social interactions. *Journal for the Education of the Gifted, 18*, 319–338.

Marsh, H. W., Chessor, D., Craven, R., & Roche, L. (1995). The effect of gifted and talented programs on academic self-concept: The big fish strikes again. *American Educational Research Journal, 32*, 285–319.

Marsh, H. W., & Hau, K. (2003). Big-fish-little-pond effect on academic self-concept: A cross-cultural (26-country) test of the negative effects of academically selective schools. *American Psychologist, 58*, 364–376.

Marsh, H. W., & Shavelson, R. (1985). Self-concept: Its multifaceted, hierarchical structure. *Educational Psychologist, 20*, 107–123.

Matthews, M. (1992). Gifted students talk about cooperative learning. *Educational Leadership, 49(2)*, 48–50.

McCoach, D. B., & Siegle, D. (2003). The structure and function of academic self-concept in gifted and general education students. *Roeper Review, 25(2)*, 61–65.

Mingus, T. T. Y., & Grassl, R. M. (1999). What constitutes a nurturing environment for the growth of mathematically gifted students? *School Science and Mathematics, 99*, 286–293.

Moon, S. M., Nelson, T. S., & Piercy, F. P. (1993). Family therapy with a highly gifted adolescent. *Journal of Family Psychotherapy, 4(3)*, 1–16.

Neber, H., & Schommer-Aikins, M. (2002). Self-regulated science learning with highly gifted students: The role of cognitive, motivational, epistemological, and environmental variables. *High Ability Studies, 13(1)*, 59–74.

Nelson-Haynes, L. (1996). The impact of the student conflict resolution program in Dallas Public Schools. *Dissertation Abstracts International Section A: Humanities and Social Sciences, 56(9-A)*, 3458.

Niiya, Y., Crocker, J., & Bartmess, E. N. (2004). From vulnerability to resilience: Learning orientations buffer contingent self-esteem from failure. *Psychological Science, 15*, 801–805.

Oakes, J. (1985). *Keeping track: How schools structure inequality.* New Haven, CT: Yale University Press.

Orange, C. (1997). Gifted students and perfectionism. *Roeper Review, 20*, 39–41.

Pacht, A. R. (1984). Reflections on perfection. *American Psychologist, 39*, 386–390.

Paradis, L. M., & Peverly, S. (1994, April). *The effects of knowledge and task on students' peer-directed questions in modified cooperative learning groups.* Paper presented at the Annual Meeting of the American Educational Research Association, New Orleans, LA. (ERIC Document Reproduction Service No. ED371027)

Parker, W. D., & Adkins, K. K. (1995). Perfectionism and the gifted. *Roeper Review, 17*, 173–176.

Parker, W. D., & Mills, C. J. (1996). The incidence of perfectionism in gifted students. *Gifted Child Quarterly, 40*, 194–199.

Peterson, P. L., Janicki, T. C., & Swing, S. R. (1981). Ability x treatment interaction effects on children's learning in large-group and small-group approaches. *American Educational Research Journal, 18*, 453–473.

Phelan, P., Davidson, A. L., & Cao, H. T. (1991). Students' multiple worlds: Negotiating the boundaries of family, peer, and school cultures. *Anthropology & Education Quarterly, 22*, 224–250.

Phillips, R. T. (1992). A study of the relationships of academic self-concept, student perceptions of school climate, ethnicity, gender, and achievement in science. *Dissertation Abstracts International, 53*(6-A), 1755.

Piaget, J. (1952). *The origins of intelligence in children.* New York: W. V. Norton.

Plaut, V. C., & Markus, H. R. (2005). The "inside" story: A cultural-historical analysis of being smart and motivated, American style. In A. J. Elliot & C. S. Dweck (Eds.), *Handbook of competence and motivation* (pp. 457–488). New York: Guilford Press.

Plucker, J. A., & McIntire, J. (1996). Academic survivability in high-potential, middle school students. *Gifted Child Quarterly, 40*, 7–14.

Plucker, J. A., Robinson, N. M., Greenspon, T. S., Feldhusen, J. F., McCoach, D. B., & Subotnik, R. F. (2004). It's not how the pond makes you feel, but rather how high you can jump. *American Psychologist, 59*, 268–269.

Plucker, J. A., & Stocking, V. B. (2001). Looking outside and inside: Self-concept development of gifted adolescents. *Exceptional Children, 67*, 535–548.

Reis, S. M. (1987). We can't change what we don't recognize: Understanding the special needs of gifted females. *Gifted Child Quarterly, 31*(2), 83–89.

Rhodewalt, F., & Tragakis, M. W. (2002). Self-handicapping and school: Academic self-concept and self-protective behavior. In J. Aronson (Ed.), *Improving academic achievement: Impact of psychological factors on education* (pp. 109–134). San Diego, CA: Academic Press.

Risemberg, R., & Zimmerman, B. J. (1992). Self-regulated learning in gifted students. *Roeper Review, 15*, 98–101.

Robinson, A. (1990). Does that describe me? Adolescents' acceptance of the gifted label. *Journal for the Education of the Gifted, 13*, 245–255.

Robinson, N. M., & Noble, K. D. (1991). *Social-emotional development and adjustment of gifted children.* Elmsford, NY: Pergamon Press.

Ryan, A. M., & Patrick, H. (2001). The classroom social environment and changes in adolescents' motivation and engagement during middle school. *American Educational Research Journal, 38*, 437–460.

Sapon-Shevin, M. (1994). *Playing favorites: Gifted education and the disruption of community.* Albany, NY: State University of New York Press.

Schuler, P. A. (2000). Perfectionism and the gifted adolescent. *Journal of Secondary Gifted Education, 11*, 183–196.

Shapiro, L. J., & Azuma, H. (2004). *Intellectual, attitudinal, and interpersonal aspects of competence in the United States and Japan.* Washington, DC: American Psychological Association.

Siegle, D., & Reis, S. M. (1998). Gender differences in teacher and student perceptions of gifted students' ability and effort. *Gifted Child Quarterly, 42*, 39–47.

Silverman, L. K. (1993). Social development, leadership, and gender issues. In L. K. Silverman (Ed.), *Counseling needs and programs for the gifted* (pp. 292–327). Elmsford, NY: Pergamon Press.

Slaney, R. B., & Ashby, J. S. (1996). Perfectionists: Study of a criterion group. *Journal of Counseling & Development, 74,* 393–398.

Slavin, R. (1983). *Cooperative learning.* New York: Longman.

Slavin, R. (1987). Ability grouping and student achievement in the elementary schools: A best evidence synthesis. *Review of Educational Research, 57,* 293–336.

Spelke, E. S. (2005). Sex differences in intrinsic aptitude for mathematics and science?: A critical review. *American Psychologist, 60,* 950–958.

Speirs Neumeister, K. L. (2004). Understanding the relationship between perfectionism and achievement motivation in gifted college students. *Gifted Child Quarterly, 48,* 219–231.

Steinberg, L. (1996). *Beyond the Classroom.* New York: Simon & Schuster.

Stipek, D. (2002). *Motivation to learn: Integrating theory and practice.* Boston: Allyn & Bacon.

Subotnik, R., Kassan, L., Summers, E., & Wasser, A. (1993). *Genius revisited: High IQ children grown up.* Norwood, NJ: Ablex Publishing.

Tannenbaum, A. J. (1983). *Gifted children: Psychological and educational perspectives.* New York: Macmillan.

Thorkildsen, T. A. (1988). Theories of education among academically able adolescents. *Contemporary Educational Psychology, 13,* 323–330.

Tomlinson, C. A. (1994). Gifted learners: The boomerang kids of middle school? *Roeper Review, 16,* 177–182.

Udvari, S. J., & Schneider, B. H. (2000). Competition and the adjustment of gifted children: A matter of motivation. *Roeper Review, 22,* 212–216.

Udvari, S. J., Schneider, B. H., & Tassi, F. (1997, April). *Chinese-Canadian and English-Canadian children's competitive behavior: Implications for peer relations.* Poster presented at the biennial meeting of the Society for Research in Child Development, Washington, DC.

Valentine, J. C., DuBois, D. L., & Cooper, H. (2004). The relation between self-beliefs and academic achievement: A meta-analytic review. *Educational Psychologist, 39,* 111–133.

Vallerand, R. J., Gagné, F., Senécal, C., & Pelletier, L. G. (1994). A comparison of the school intrinsic motivation and perceived competence of gifted and regular students. *Gifted Child Quarterly, 38,* 172–175.

Van Boxtel, H. W., & Mönks, F. J. (1992). General, social, and academic self-concepts of gifted adolescents. *Journal of Youth and Adolescence, 21,* 169–186.

Vygotsky, L S. (1978). *Mind in society: The development of higher psychological process.* Cambridge, MA: Harvard University Press.

Webb, J. T, Meckstroth, E. A., & Tolan, S. S. (1982). *Guiding the gifted child: A practical source for parents and teachers.* Columbus: Ohio Psychology.

Weiner, B. (2000). Intrapersonal and interpersonal theories of motivation from an attributional perspective. *Educational Psychology Review, 12,* 1–14.

Wentzel, K. R. (2005). Peer relationships, motivation, and academic performance at school. In A. J. Elliot & C. S. Dweck (Eds.), *Handbook of competence and motivation* (pp. 279–296). New York: Guilford Press.

White, R. W. (1959). Motivation reconsidered: The concept of competence. *Psychological Review, 66,* 297–333.

Wober, M. (1974). Towards an understanding of the Kiganda concept of intelligence. In J. W. Berry & P. R. Dasen (Eds.), *Culture and cognition: Readings in cross-cultural psychology* (pp. 261–280). London: Methuen.

Chapter 29

MUSICAL TALENT

Joanne Haroutounian

s the concept of intelligence and talent broadens to embrace artistic ways of knowing, there is a growing need for the development of effective procedures to identify students who show potential, as well as demonstrated, musical talent. The development of musical talent relies on instruction reaching beyond school walls, through private lessons and specialized schooling. The combination of individualized instruction early on, the availability of challenging curricular options within school, and opportunities to expand curricular challenges through community offerings can provide a solid educational framework for musically talented students (Haroutounian, 1995, 1998, 2002; Howe & Sloboda, 1991; Sloboda & Howe, 1991; Sosniak, 1985a). Challenges facing those pursuing research across the fields of gifted education and music include the diminishing role of music, in general, in school curricula nationwide, the exclusion of the arts in talent identification procedures, and the emphasis of bringing basic music education to all, de-emphasizing the role of recognizing and developing talent within the field of music education.

PERSPECTIVES OF MUSICAL TALENT AS DEFINED IN RESEARCH

The topic of musical talent has been examined, researched, and debated by experts across the fields of music psychology, music performance, and music education since the turn of the 20th century and well before. Terminology plays a key role in determining viewpoints of musical talent from specialists across these musical fields.

Music Aptitude

Music aptitude describes the *discrimination of sound through fine-tuned perception* and defines musical talent to the music psychologist. The scientific analysis and measurement of human perception and discrimination of sounds began in the late 1800s, establishing the field of music psychology (Eagle, 1980; Shuter-Dyson & Gabriel, 1968).

Carl Seashore (1919, 1938), considered the most influential pioneer in the field of music psychology, describes musical talent as a hierarchy of attributes stemming from inborn sensory capacities that function from early childhood (Seashore, 1938). According to Seashore, children display these capacities at an early age and a reliable measurement of music aptitude can be made by the age of 10. After this age, Seashore contends that music aptitude becomes stabilized. Future training can enhance existing aptitude but not extend these capacities (Seashore, 1938, p. 8). Gordon (1986) bases measurement of music aptitude on "audiation" or internal listening capacities, with stabilization in his measures set at the age of 9.

Musical Intelligence

Musical intelligence describes the *process of cognitive-developmental learning through music*, which distinguishes it from music aptitude, which is based primarily on natural musical capacities. The concept of musical intelligence most likely dates back to the early Chinese and Greek theories of music and is included in the texts of Carl Seashore (1938). The renaissance of the term can be credited to Howard Gardner (1983), who included musical intelligence as one of the separate intelligences described in *Frames of Mind: The Theory of Multiple Intelligences*. The attention given to this theory has allowed the idea of a specific musical intelligence to extend to an audience well beyond the specialized field of music psychology, with the field of gifted education taking particular notice of curricular inclusion through musical domains.

Musical Ability—Performance

A musician communicates potential talent through musical performance. The mainstay of the identification of musical talent lies in the assessment of musical performance. Performance ability requires training and development with early detection of talent often reliant on rapid skill development of performance abilities. A student may have a high music aptitude, but the development of musical talent relies on student commitment, physical capabilities, and teacher guidance (Manturszewska, 1990; Sloboda 1994, 1996; Sosniak, 1985a, 1985b). Musical performance research areas that directly relate to musical talent and giftedness deal with expressivity and expertise in performance (Sloboda, 1994, 1996, 2005; Sloboda, Davidson, & Howe, 1994).

Musical Creativity—Creative Interpretation

The musical creative process involves realizing sounds internally and communicating to others in a unique way. Musical creativity is realized generatively through improvisation and composition. It can also be realized through the creative interpretative process in performance and, expanding parameters further, through creative listening and critique. Musical creativity communicated through these different venues to an astute listener often defines the "spark" of musical talent.

Musical talent, as creativity, can be witnessed at the earliest stages of musical learning, through early childhood and elementary levels of musical improvisation or play. Webster's studies (1979, 1987, 1992) of creative thinking in music show evidence of musical extensiveness, flexibility, originality, and syntax in musical tasks that reflect behaviors similarly measured in creative testing in general. Evidence of creative interpretation in performance and in listening are more complex to identify and measure but are also an integral part of the profile of musical talent (Feinberg, 1974; Haroutounian, 2002; Rodriguez & Webster 1997; Sloboda, 1996).

Musical Giftedness

Musical giftedness defines exceptional talent in music. The prodigy portrays giftedness in music in the clearest way, with students at age 10 exhibiting musical capabilities equal to those of a highly trained adult. Unique examples of musical giftedness in the savant or those with Williams Syndrome portray isolated advanced musical abilities in a mind with low cognitive reasoning capabilities (Levitin & Bellugi, 1998; Miller, 1989; Morelock & Feldman, 1993). Studies of prodigies specify exceptional abilities within the domain of music that do not necessarily extend to academic areas, clarifying the need to define talent identification appropriately within musical contexts (Feldman, 1993). The fascination of understanding musical intelligence as it emanates in individuals with chromosomal disorders further defines the uniqueness of giftedness in music.

Use of the term *musically gifted* versus *musically talented* to define the student with outstanding musical abilities is problematic in the literature because it unearths the never-ending conflict of nature vs. nurture—accepting the idea of innate musical "giftedness" versus the ongoing role of practice, commitment, and training in the development of musical talent. Gagné's Differentiated Model of Giftedness and Talent (1995) renews the debate across gifted and musical fields.

MAJOR ISSUES ADDRESSED IN MUSICAL TALENT RESEARCH

Music Aptitude Measurement

The field of music psychology has researched the measurement of music aptitude through the development of tests of aural discrimination of pitch, rhythm, and dynamic attributes of music beginning in the late 1800s. The Seashore Measures of Musical Talent (1919) set the precedent for music aptitude measurement. Boyle and Radocy (1987) and Shuter-Dyson and Gabriel (1968) offer a complete description of validity and reliability statistics of these measures and other early test measurements.

Over the next 30 years, the field abounded with research on the development of music aptitude tests, all variations of the basic standards of measurement established by Seashore (Bentley, 1966; Gaston, 1957; Grashel, 1996; Kwalwasser & Dykema, 1931; Wing, 1939). Haroutounian (2002) offers a chart of test contents and reliability and validity statistics of music aptitude measures from 1919 to 1989.

The most comprehensive music aptitude tests in use today were developed from 1965 through 1989 by Edwin Gordon. Gordon has developed many different tests that span assessment of music aptitude from age 7 through adult. The Primary Measures of Music Audiation (PMMA; 1979b) measures normal music aptitude in grades K–3. Gordon recommends the Intermediate Measures of Music Audiation (IMMA; 1979a) for the identification of high music aptitude in elementary grades. If seeking exceptional levels of aptitude in these grades, the Musical Aptitude Profile (1965) can be used as early as 4th grade with an extended ceiling including measurement through 12th-grade levels.

Reliability of these measures vary from .72 to .96 in different test components, with validity compared with instrumental achievement ratings ranging from .67 to .73. Grashel (1996) noted 16 studies published in the *Journal of Research in Music Education* during the 1980s utilized Gordon's measures.

Studies show the use of music aptitude testing in schools and research settings were prevalent during the 1970s and 1980s, gradually dwindling to sporadic use from the 1990s to present day. These tests are still used in research studies as a measurable instrument of discriminative listening in musical cognition and as a component of musical talent (Grashel, 1996; Hassler, Birbaumer, & Feil, 1992; Nelson, Barresi, & Barrett, 1992).

Musical Talent Identification

Research on the appropriate criteria and procedures for the identification of musical talent is a prevalent topic for research. What are the basic characteristics of musical talent that can be used as criteria in the development of identification instruments? What type of performance assessment can include potential, as well as demonstrated musical talent, in this identification procedure? What role does the use of music aptitude testing play in the identification process?

There are minimal resources currently available to assist gifted and talented coordinators or music administrators seeking formal identification of musical talent in their schools. Most measures are locally devised, working closely with music teacher nominations and performance assessment and achievement in music classes. The most common observational rating scales are the musical scales found within the Scales for Rating the Behavioral Characteristics of Superior Students (SRBCSS; Renzulli, Smith, White, Callahan, & Hartman, 1976). These ratings were recently revised, basically expanding the number of weighted ratings from four to six (Abeel, Callahan, & Hunsaker, 1994). There is a crucial need for the development of valid identification instruments that include more specialized musical talent criteria and appropriate performance assessment procedures that can be easily generalized to different school settings.

Arts Connection's research (1992) included a Music Identification Tally Sheet with criteria categorized into three areas: skills (rhythm, perception of sound, coordination); motivation (enthusiasm, ability to focus, perseverance); and creativity (expressiveness, composition, and improvisation). The identification procedures include several weeks of specialized classes taught by consulting music specialists with classroom teachers and music teachers observing student behaviors in a class setting.

Haroutounian's identification study (1995, 2000b) includes the Indicators of Potential Talent observation scale based on 10 basic characteristics of talent under areas of aptitude and ability (perception of pitch, rhythm, contextual differentiation, performance ease); creative interpretation (experimenting with sounds, discriminative listening, personal expression), and commitment (perseverance and focus, refinement and critique). The resulting identification framework includes observation of specific curricular activities across these criteria that highlight potential talent in a classroom or small group setting.

Haroutounian's (1995) analysis of identification procedures from the National Research Center on the Gifted and a survey of procedures used in specialized performing arts schools, G/T school programs, and summer programs from 23 states found minimal use of music aptitude testing as part of the identification procedure, with no use of the IMMA, recommended for measurement of high music aptitude in the elementary grades. This survey revealed evidence of the mismatched use of general testing of aptitude, creativity, and achievement for musical talent identification.

Musical Intelligence—Multiple Intelligence Theory Research

Research conducted through Project Zero at Harvard University focused on the cognitive process of learning and understanding, based on the concept of multiple ways of knowing. Those working in multiple intelligence (MI) studies focus attention on the *process* of learning within and across intelligences rather than the psychometric measurement of basic capacities of these intelligences.

MI research in elementary classrooms emphasizes learning situations that require students to work through problem-solving activities within the domain, encouraging conceptual understanding rather than rote learning of factual material. According to Davidson and Scripp (1989), "learning occurs with the development of problem-solving strategies required for resolving cognitive conflicts in the environment. We see the child solving musical problems through inventive means" (p. 61). MI's research focuses on learning that results in active change in patterns of thinking that unfold with cognitive development (Davidson, 1990; Davidson & Scripp, 1989).

Bamberger's studies (1986, 1995) of musically talented students at MIT indicate that these students require a shift between different representations of a musical task (performing, reading a score, listening), with talented students more adept in this cognitive/perceptive shift. Research and curriculum development that embraces the substantive meaning of musical intelligence for the gifted student requires emphasis on problem solving across different representations within the domain of music.

Musical Performance Research

Music psychologists specializing in the research of expertise and expressivity in musical performance bring the element of practice and commitment into play rather than the "folk psychology of talent" that believes in innately determined differences in people's capacity for musical accomplishment and genetically programmed superiority in musical abilities (Sloboda, 1994, 1996, 2005; Sloboda et al., 1994). Studies by Ericsson et al. in the arts and sciences and sports found that the role of deliberate practice over many years developed expertise in performance, with outstanding musical ability developed through training and a supportive environmental context (Ericsson, 1996; Ericsson, Krampe, & Tesch-Romer, 1993; Manturszewska, 1990).

Studies show that the assessment of musical performance is problematic because of its inherent interpretive/subjective nature (Boyle & Radocy, 1987; Warnick, 1985). Gifted identification procedures in music will require development of an effective assessment form for musical performance at the informal classroom level, as well as at an individualized audition level for more specialized screening (Haroutounian, 2002; Wenner, 1985).

Musical Talent Development

Musical talent development requires focus beyond the school walls and starts as early as infancy. What are the earliest signs of musical talent? What stages does this development take? What is the most effective way to develop this talent, inside school and out?

Signs of perceptual sound awareness and discrimination begin before birth, with infants as early as a few days able to discriminate a mother's voice or a song heard before birth. A wealth of prenatal and infant studies are found in Irene Deliege and John Sloboda's (1996) *Musical Beginnings: Origins and Development of Musical Competence.*

The development of early musical abilities has been researched and analyzed in depth since Moog's (1976) studies of 500 children from 3 months to 3 years. Preschool studies by Project Zero examined the child's process of building a range of melodic pitches towards stabilized melodies sung by age 6 (Gardner, 1982). A number of other preschool music studies examined creative musical "gestures" and creative musical environment stimulation (Davidson & Scripp, 1994; McKernon, 1979; Ries, 1982).

Bloom's (1985) study of the development of talent in young people included three basic stages of development—the early stage of "play and romance," followed by "precision and discipline," and then advancing to "individuality and insight." Hargreaves' (1996) stages of general musical development reflect those of Piaget, from the sensorimotor "babbling stage," to figural stages of understanding a single line or pitch contour, to added dimensions and conservation of musical properties. Development finally leads to the reflective metacognitive professional stage beyond age 15.

The literature recommends educational guidance of this development through a combination of school curricular options, private instruction, and community involvement to provide suitable challenges for full musical talent development (Haroutounian, 1998, 2000a, 2003; Uszler, 1990). There is a growing number of reference books for parents that provide guidance for talented children through their musical education from birth through secondary school (Cutietta, 2001; Haroutounian, 2002, 2003; Machover & Uszler, 1996).

Studies by Haroutounian (2000a) and Baum, Owen, and Oreck (1997) provide an impetus for further research on the value of ongoing musical training of talented disadvantaged youth.

Nature vs. Nurture

The age-old question of musical talent as innate or developmental remains of interest to researchers across musical and gifted fields. A survey conducted by Evans, Bickel, and Pendarvis (2000) found different perspectives from teachers, students, and parents, showing a combination of innate ability and hard work contributing to musical success.

Gagné's Differentiated Model of Giftedness and Talent (1995) distinguishes gifts (innate abilities) and talents (performance), creating controversy with Sloboda and Howe, music researchers of performance expertise whose studies show that the influence of practice, teacher-student relationships, and parental influence played a decided role in high musical achievement. Howe (1996) even argues the case of Mozart's genius and its development as partly reliant on these factors. In a reply to Gagné, Sloboda and Howe (1999) state that "their 1991 study did not conclusively rule out genetic contributions to individual differences in musical achievement; however there was no evidence of findings which make it necessary to accept specific differences caused by genetic differences" (p. 54). Sloboda (2005) does conclude that the vast majority of the population shows evidence of a "common receptive musical ability" by the first decade of life, regardless of any formal musical education of training (p. 266), which reflects Gordon's idea of music aptitude.

Music and the Brain

New connections between musical functioning and brain research has spawned great interest in the possibilities of using music to enhance spatial reasoning and understanding of the neurological underpinnings of "musical knowing" that may unlock the mysteries of the musical giftedness of savants and William Syndrome individuals.

The widely popular "Mozart effect" research conducted by Rauscher and Shaw (1998) suggested that listening to music (Mozart in particular) helps to "organize temporarily, the cortical firing patterns for spatial temporal processes" (p. 836). Improvement was uniquely confined to spatial-temporal tasks that involve inner imagery and not spatial-recognition tasks, which involve the less complex ability to classify physical similarities among objects. An eruption of research resulted from these suggested findings, some misaligned to seek findings in more generalized spatial functioning, others using different stimuli and approaches to disprove the effect (Chabris, 1999; Nantais & Schellenberg, 1999; Newman et al., 1995; Steele, Brown, & Stoecker, 1999; Rideout, Dougherty, & Wernert, 1997). Further studies by Rauscher and colleagues (Rauscher, Shaw, & Ky, 1995; Rauscher, Shaw, Levine, & Wright, 1997) showed the connection of active music-making (versus listening) and the development of spatial-temporal reasoning.

Seeking a biological basis for musical talent, neurological research has discarded the notion of "right-brained" musicians, discovering that musicians have a more pronounced left hemisphere dominance than nonmusicians (Bower, 1994; Hodges, 1996; Leng & Shaw, 1991; Malina, 1990; Schlaug, Jancke, Huang, & Steinmetz, 1995). Neurological research also shows that the planum temporal of musicians with absolute pitch was enlarged on the left side. This area also takes up a higher proportion of the brain of individuals with Williams Syndrome, who all possess absolute pitch. Ongoing research seeks to discover ways these unique connections may help us understand the intricacies of the musical mind (Lenhoff, 1998; Lenhoff, Wang, Greenberg, & Bellugi, 1997; Levitin, 2006; Levitin & Bellugi, 1998).

Music and Academic Achievement

The field of music education seeks ongoing research on the connections of learning music and improvement in academic achievement in school, largely as leverage to secure the continuation of school music programs. Various studies connect the study of music with improvements in reading, language skills, mathematics, general creativity, and concerns such as self-esteem, social skills, and reduction of dropout rates (Cutietta, Hamann, & Walker, 1995; Trusty & Oliva, 1994; Winner & Hetland, 2000). One of the more publicized findings showed that students engaged in musical instruction scored higher than the national average in both verbal and math scores on the SAT over a period of at least 7 years (Cutietta et al., 1995).

The field of gifted education has embraced the arts in the academic classroom as a result of incorporating multiple intelligences in gifted curricula. Research is just emerging seeking answers to the effectiveness of teachers to incorporate artistic learning in the classroom (Oreck, 2000).

CONCLUSIONS FROM MUSICAL TALENT RESEARCH

The fields of music education, music psychology, and musical performance have examined the perceptive/cognitive musical mind in detail since the 1800s. We are well equipped in scientifically measuring perceptive capacities of children from infancy, including multiple tests of aural discrimination through music aptitude tests. Examination of the studies found in books by Seashore (1938), Gordon (1986), and Deliege and Sloboda (1996) establish ample empirical evidence that can measure outstanding capacities that reflect musical talent or giftedness.

The field of cognitive psychology, merging with music psychology, offers myriad studies that examine the inner functioning of the musical mind. Sloboda's (e.g., 1994, 1996, 2005) well-established research history matched with Bamberger's MIT studies and those conducted by the music researchers of Project Zero (e.g., Gardner, 1982) provide empirical evidence of how musical intelligence can be assessed and how musically talented students cognitively/perceptively work through musical tasks. The perceptive workings of the musically creative mind has also been examined, with studies using emerging technology as a way to tap into potential creative musical talent beyond performance abilities (Davidson, 1990; Webster, 1992).

Neurological research has opened new vistas of research in understanding how the musical mind biologically functions. We can conclude that the links between musical functioning and other forms of reasoning will be determined through this ongoing research. These findings will be of vital importance to those interested in working with learning impaired students with unusual gifts, such as those with Williams Syndrome (Reis et al., 2000).

Although music has been included in gifted identification and development mandates since the 1970s, its inclusion in G/T identification procedures has been largely ignored. A 1987 survey of large cities in 10 north-central states (population more than 50,000) found no provision for musical talent within their gifted programs. Nationally, only four states required visual and performing arts identification at that time (Atterbury, 1991; Richert, 1985, 1991; Richert, Alvino, & McDonnel, 1982). Active development of research-based identification instruments based on valid indicators of musical talent, with procedures comfortable for most school settings, may be the catalyst needed to change this predicament.

This development requires bringing practitioners who work in specialized arts schools, music educators who see talent developed through performance-based programs in their schools, and gifted specialists in music and the arts together to formulate workable identification instruments and talent development programs that are feasible in the current educational climate.

Now it is time for the field of gifted education to take notice of "musical ways of knowing" in the development of challenging curriculum that utilizes problem solving in music, working across multiple dimensions. The gifted field specializes in this curricular approach. Research and development that brings G/T curriculum experts together with gifted/music specialists can build effective guidelines for gifted programs in music beyond the performance-based programs that are the norm in most schools.

LIMITATIONS AND PRACTICAL APPLICATIONS OF THE RESEARCH ON MUSICAL TALENT

The educational pendulum has swung away from interest on talent identification and development in general, with arts talent development always finding difficulty in establishing a research niche in the field of gifted education. A search of the RILM and ERIC databases with the keyword "musical talent" finds no new studies directly related to musical talent identification and development since 2000. However, there are growing state mandates that include the arts in talent identification. Practically, the time has come for active development of identification instruments and workable procedures from existing research that will mesh with the realistic educational limitations of funding and specialist availability in music and gifted fields.

The field of music education has a philosophy that de-emphasizes the term "talent" to dissuade administrators from limiting musical offerings only to those deemed talented, thus working against their goal of establishing music as part of the core curriculum for all students. The National Standards for Arts Education does include specific inclusion of "special experiences designed for gifted and talented students according to their abilities and interests" (National Association for Music Education, 1994, p. 7) in curricular guidelines (Music Educators National Conference, 1994). Establishing gifted music programs may be problematic to implement when schools are continually battling to keep music in the schools in general. Practically, implementation of gifted music programs will include curricular options beyond school, through independent study, private instruction options, internships, and other community opportunities.

CONCLUSION

What we know:
- Musical talent emanates very early and requires environmental nurturing before the age of 10–12.
- Musical talent requires specialized training that may extend beyond normal school offerings.
- Musical talent may manifest itself through creative expression in performance, listening, improvisation, composition, or critique in all genres.
- Studies of music and the brain are revealing important connections between music-making and spatial-temporal functioning and language development.
- The majority of our schools are not including the identification of musical talent or the arts in their gifted/talented identification procedures.

What we need:
- Valid identification instruments and talent development programs for music that will be feasible and effective.
- Further research seeking empirical evidence of practices used in specialized arts schools or successful school music programs that include gifted differentiation.
- Further research of the effectiveness of musical talent development through training for underserved populations.

MAJOR RESOURCES AND REFERENCES FOR MUSICAL TALENT DEVELOPMENT

The following are basic reference texts about musical knowing and talent development.

Bamberger, J. (1995). *The mind behind the musical ear: How children develop musical intelligence.* Cambridge, MA: Harvard University Press.

Bloom, B. (Ed.). (1985). *Developing talent in young people.* New York: Ballantine Books.

Boardman, E. (Ed.). (1989). *Dimensions of musical thinking.* Reston, VA: Music Educators National Conference.

Deliege, I., & Sloboda, J. (1996). *Musical beginnings: Origins and development of musical competence.* Oxford, England: Oxford University Press.

Deliege, I., & Sloboda, J. (1997). *Perception and cognition of music.* East Sussex, England: Psychology Press Ltd.

Gardner, H. (1983). *Frames of mind: The theory of multiple intelligences.* New York: Basic Books.

Gordon, E. (1986). *The nature, description, measurement, and evaluation of music aptitudes.* Chicago: G.I.A. Publications.

Haroutounian, J. (2002). *Kindling the spark: Recognizing and developing musical talent.* New York: Oxford University Press.

Seashore, C. E. (1938). *Psychology of music.* New York: McGraw Hill.

Shuter-Dyson, R., & Gabriel, C. (1968). *The psychology of musical ability.* London: Methuen & Co.

Sloboda, J. (1985). *The musical mind: The cognitive psychology of music.* Oxford, England: Oxford University Press.

Sloboda, J. (1988). *Generative processes in music.* Oxford, England: Clarendon Press.

Sloboda, J. (2005). *Exploring the musical mind.* Oxford, England: Oxford University Press.

The following are major studies and articles on musical knowing and talent development.

Bamberger, J. (1977). In search of a tune. In D. Perkins & B. Leondar (Eds.), *The arts and cognition* (pp. 284-317). Baltimore: Johns Hopkins Press.

Bamberger, J. (1982). Growing up prodigies: The mid-life crisis. In D. Feldman (Ed.), *Developmental approaches to giftedness and creativity* (pp. 265–279). San Francisco: Jossey-Bass.

Bamberger, J. (1986). Cognitive issues in the development of musically gifted children. In R. Sternberg & J. Davidson (Eds.), *Conceptions of giftedness* (pp. 389–413). New York: Cambridge University Press.

Davidson, J. W., Howe, M. J. A., Moore, D. G., & Sloboda, J. A. (1996). The role of parental influences in the development of musical ability. *British Journal of Developmental Psychology, 14,* 399–412.

Davidson, J. W., Howe, M. J. A., Moore, D. G., & Sloboda, J. A. (1998). Characteristics of music teachers and the progress of young instrumentalists. *Journal of Research in Music Education, 46,* 141–160.

Davidson, L., & Scripp, L. (1989). Education and development in music from a cognitive perspective. In D. Hargreaves (Ed.), *Children and the arts* (pp. 59–86). Philadelphia: Open University Press.

Davidson, L., & Scripp, L. (1992). Surveying the coordinates of cognitive skills in music. In R. Colwell (Ed.), *Handbook of research on music teaching and learning* (pp. 392–400). New York: Schirmer Books.

Davidson, L., & Scripp, L. (1994). Conditions of giftedness: Musical development in the preschool and early elementary years. In R. F. Subotnik & K. D. Arnold (Eds.), *Beyond Terman: Contemporary longitudinal studies of giftedness and talent* (pp. 155–185). Norwood, NJ: Ablex.

Ericsson, K. A., Krampe, R. T., & Tesch-Romer, C. (1993). The role of deliberate practice in the acquisition of expert performance. *Psychological Review, 100,* 363–406.

Haroutounian, J. (1995). *The assessment of potential talent in musical behavior/performance: Criteria and procedures to consider in the identification of musically gifted and talented students.* Unpublished doctoral dissertation, University of Virginia.

Haroutounian, J. (1995). Talent identification and development in the arts: An artistic/educational dialogue. *Roeper Review, 18,* 112–117

Haroutounian, J. (1998). Drop the hurdles and open the doors: Fostering talent development through school and community collaboration. *Arts Education Policy Review, 99*(6), 15–25.

Haroutounian, J. (2000). The delights and dilemmas of the musically talented teenager. *Journal of Secondary Gifted Education 12,* 3–16.

Haroutounian, J. (2000). MusicLink: Nurturing potential and recognizing achievement. *Arts Education Policy Review, 101*(6), 12–20.

Haroutounian, J. (2000). Perspectives of musical talent: A study of identification criteria and procedures. *High Ability Studies, 11,* 137–160.

Howe, M., & Sloboda, J. (1991). Young musician's accounts of significant influences in their early lives. II. Teachers, practicing and performing. *British Journal of Music Education, 7*, 53–63.

Sloboda, J. (1996). The acquisition of musical performance expertise: Deconstructing the 'talent' account of individual differences in musical expressivity. In K. A. Ericsson (Ed.), *The road to excellence: The acquisition of expert performance in the arts and sciences, sports, and games* (pp. 107–127). Mahwah, NJ: Lawrence Erlbaum Associates.

Sloboda, J., & Howe, M. (1991). Biographical precursors of musical excellence: An interview study. *Psychology of Music, 19*, 3–21.

Sosniak, L. A. (1985). Learning to be a concert pianist. In B. Bloom (Ed.), *Developing talent in young people* (pp. 19–67). New York: Ballantine Books.

Sosniak, L. A. (1985). Phases of learning. In B. Bloom (Ed.), *Developing talent in young people* (pp. 409–438). New York: Ballantine Books.

Webster, P. (1987). Refinement of a measure of creative thinking in music. In C. Madsen & C. Pricket (Eds.), *Applications of research in music behavior* (pp. 257–271). Tuscaloosa: University of Alabama Press.

Webster, P. (1992). Research on creative thinking in music: The assessment literature. In R. Colwell (Ed.), *Handbook of research on music teaching and learning* (pp. 266–280). New York: Schirmer Books.

REFERENCES

Abeel, L., Callahan, C., & Hunsaker, S. (1994). *The use of published instruments in the identification of gifted students*. Washington, DC: National Association for Gifted Children.

Arts Connection. (1992). *Talent beyond words: Identifying and developing talent through music and dance in economically disadvantaged, bilingual, and handicapped children.* Report submitted to the United States Department of Education Jacob Javits Gifted and Talented Program. Brooklyn, NY: Author.

Atterbury, B. W. (1991). The musically talented: Aren't they also gifted? *Update: Applications of Research in Music Education, 9*(3), 21–23.

Bamberger, J. (1986). Cognitive issues in the development of musically gifted children. In R. Sternberg & J. Davidson (Eds.), *Conceptions of giftedness* (pp. 389–418). New York: Cambridge University Press.

Bamberger J. (1995). *The mind behind the musical ear: How children develop musical intelligence.* Cambridge, MA: Harvard University Press.

Baum, S., Owen, S., & Oreck, B. (1997). Transferring individual regulation process from arts to academics. *Arts Education Policy Review, 98*(4), 32–39.

Bentley, A. (1966). *Musical ability in children and its measurement*. New York: October House.

Bloom, B. S. (Ed.). (1985). *Developing talent in young people.* New York: Ballantine.

Bower, B. (1994, April). Brain images reveal cerebral side of music. *Science News, 145*, 260.

Boyle, J. D., & Radocy, R. E. (1987). *Measurement and evaluation of music experiences.* New York: Schirmer.

Chabris, C. F. (1999). Prelude or requiem for the 'Mozart effect'? *Nature, 400,* 826–827.

Cutietta, R. A. (2001). *Raising musical kids: A guide for parents.* New York: Oxford University Press.

Cutietta, R., Hamann, D. L., & Walker, L. M. (1995). *Spin-offs: The extra-musical advantages of a musical education.* Elkhart, IN: United Musical Instruments.

Davidson, L. (1990). Tools and environments for musical creativity. *Music Educators Journal, 76*(9), 47–51.

Davidson, L., & Scripp, L. (1989). Education and development in music from a cognitive perspective. In D. Hargreaves (Ed.), *Children and the arts* (pp. 59–86). Philadelphia: Open University Press.

Davidson, L., & Scripp, L. (1994). Conditions of giftedness: Musical development in the preschool and early elementary years. In R. Subotnik & K. D. Arnold (Eds.), *Beyond Terman: Contemporary longitudinal studies of giftedness and talent* (pp. 155–185). Norwood, NJ: Ablex.

Deliege, I., & Sloboda, J. (1996). *Musical beginnings: Origins and development of musical competence.* Oxford, England: Oxford University Press.

Eagle, C. T. (1980). An introductory perspective of music psychology. In D. A. Hodges (Ed.), *Handbook of music psychology* (pp. 1–15). Lawrence, KS: National Association for Music Therapy.

Ericsson, K. A. (1996). *The road to excellence: The acquisition of expert performance in the arts and sciences, sports, and games.* Mahwah, NJ: Laurence Erlbaum.

Ericsson, K. A., Krampe, R. T., & Tesch-Romer, C. (1993). The role of deliberate practice in the acquisition of expert performance. *Psychological Review, 100,* 363–406.

Evans, R. J., Bickel, R., & Pendarvis, E. (2000). Musical talent innate or acquired? Perceptions of students, parents, and teachers. *Gifted Child Quarterly, 44,* 80–90.

Feinberg, S. (1974). Creative problem-solving and the music listening experience. *Music Educators Journal, 61*(1), 53–59.

Feldman, D. (1993). Child prodigies: A distinctive form of giftedness. *Gifted Child Quarterly, 37,* 188–193.

Gagné, F. (1995). From giftedness to talent: A developmental model and its impact on the language of the field. *Roeper Review, 18,* 103–111.

Gardner, H. (1982). *Art, mind, and brain: A cognitive approach to creativity.* New York: Basic Books.

Gardner, H. (1983). *Frames of mind: The theory of multiple intelligences.* New York: Basic Books.

Gaston, E. T. (1957). *Test of musicality.* Lawrence, KS: Odell's Instrumental Service.

Gordon, E. E. (1965). *Musical aptitude profile.* Boston: Houghton Mifflin.

Gordon, E. E. (1979a). *Intermediate measures of music audiation.* Chicago: G.I.A. Publications.

Gordon, E. E. (1979b). *Primary measures of music audiation.* Chicago: G.I.A. Publications.

Gordon, E. E. (1986). *The nature, description, measurement, and evaluation of music aptitudes.* Chicago: G.I.A. Publications.

Grashel, J. (1996). Test instruments used by *Journal of Research in Music Education*: Authors from 1980–1989. *Update: Applications of Research in Music Education, 14*(2), 24–30.

Hargreaves, D. (1996). The development of artistic and musical competence. In I. Deliege & J. Sloboda (Eds.), *Musical beginnings: Origin and development of artistic and musical competence* (pp. 145–170). Oxford, England: Oxford University Press.

Haroutounian, J. (1995). *The assessment of potential talent in musical behavior/performance: Criteria and procedures to consider in the identification of musically gifted and talented students.* Unpublished doctoral dissertation, University of Virginia.

Haroutounian, J. (1998). Drop the hurdles and open the doors: Fostering talent development through school and community collaboration. *Arts Education Policy Review, 99*(6), 15–25.

Haroutounian, J. (2000a). The delights and dilemmas of the musically talented teenager. *Journal of Secondary Gifted Education, 12,* 3–16.

Haroutounian, J. (2000b). Perspectives of musical talent: A study of identification criteria and procedures. *High Ability Studies, 11,* 137–160.

Haroutounian, J. (2002). *Kindling the spark: Recognizing and developing musical talent.* New York: Oxford University Press.

Haroutounian, J. (2003). Musical talent: Nurturing potential and guiding development. In P. Olszewski-Kubilius, L. Limburg-Weber, & S. Pfeiffer (Eds.), *Early gifted: Recognizing and nurturing children's talents* (pp. 83–102). Waco, TX: Prufrock Press.

Hassler, M., Birbaumer, N., & Feil, A. (1992). Musical talent and visual-spatial abilities: A longitudinal study. *Psychology of Music, 20,* 99–113.

Hodges, D. (1996). Neuromusical research: A review of the literature. In D. Hodges (Ed.), *Handbook of music psychology* (2nd ed., 197–284). San Antonio, TX: IMR Press.

Howe, M. (1996). The childhoods and early lives of geniuses: Combining psychological and biographical evidence. In K. A. Ericsson (Ed.), *The road to excellence: The acquisition of expert performance in the arts and sciences, sports, and games* (pp. 255–270). Mahwah, NJ: Laurence Erlbaum.

Howe, M., & Sloboda, J. (1991). Young musician's accounts of significant influences in their early lives, II: Teachers, practicing and performing. *British Journal of Music Education 7,* 53–63.

Kwalwasser, J., & Dykema, P. (1931). *Kwalwasser-Dykema music tests.* New York: Carl Fischer.

Leng, X., & Shaw, G. (1991). Toward a neural theory of higher brain function using music as a window. *Concepts in Neuroscience, 2,* 229–258.

Lenhoff, H. M. (1998). Information sharing: Insights into the musical potential of cognitively impaired people diagnosed with Williams Syndrome. *Music Therapy Perspectives, 16*(1), 33–36.

Lenhoff, H. M., Wang, P. P., Greenberg, F., & Bellugi, U. (1997). Williams Syndrome and the brain. *Scientific American, 277*(6), 68–73.

Levitin, D. (2006). *This is your brain on music: The science of a human obsession.* New York: Dutton Pub.

Levitin, D., & Bellugi, U. (1998). Musical abilities in individuals with Williams Syndrome. *Music Perception, 15,* 357–389.

Machover, W., & Uszler, M. (1996). *Sound choices: Guiding your child's musical experiences.* New York: Oxford University Press.

Malina, D. (1990). Cerebral symphony. *Harvard Medical Alumni Review, 73*(1), 20–27.

Manturszewska, M. (1990). A biographical study of the life-span development of professional musicians. *Psychology of Music, 18*, 112–139.

McKernon, P. E. (1979). The development of first songs in young children. *New Directions in Child Development, 3*, 43–58.

Miller, L. K. (1989). *Musical savants: Exceptional skill in the mentally retarded.* Hillsdale, NJ: Laurence Erlbaum.

Moog, H. (1976). *The musical experience of the pre-school child* (C. Clarke, Trans.). London: Schott.

Morelock, M., & Feldman, D. H. (1993). Prodigies and savants: What they have to tell us about giftedness and human cognition. In K. Heller, F. Mönks, & H. Passow (Eds.), *International handbook of research and development of giftedness and talent* (pp. 161–169). Oxford, England: Pergamon Press.

Music Educators National Conference. (1994). *National standards for arts education.* Reston, VA: Author.

Nantais, K. M., & Schellenberg, G. (1999). The Mozart effect: An artifact of preference. *Psychological Science, 10*, 370–373.

National Association for Music Education. (1994). *Opportunity-to-learn standards for music instruction, grades preK–12.* Lanham, MD: Rowman & Littlefield Education.

Nelson, F., Barresi, A., & Barrett, J. (1992). Musical cognition within an analogical setting: Toward a cognitive component of music aptitude in children. *Psychology of Music and Music Education, 20*, 70–79.

Newman, J., Rosenbach, J., Burns, K., Latimer, B., Matocha, H., & Vogt, E. R. (1995). An experimental test of "The Mozart effect": Does listening to his music improve spatial ability? *Perceptual and Motor Skills, 81*, 1379–1387.

Oreck, B. (2000, April). *Artistic choices: How and why teachers use the arts in the classroom.* Paper presented at the Annual Meeting of the American Educational Research Association, New Orleans, LA.

Rauscher, F., Shaw, G., & Ky, K. (1995). Music and spatial task performance. *Nature, 365*, 611.

Rauscher, F. H., Shaw, G., Levine, L., & Wright, E. (1997). Music training causes long-term enhancement of preschool children's spatial-temporal reasoning. *Neurological Research, 19*, 2–8.

Rauscher, F. H., & Shaw, G. L. (1998). Key components of the Mozart effect. *Perceptual and Motor Skills, 86*, 835–841.

Renzulli, J. S., Smith, L., White, A., Callahan, C., & Hartman, R. (1976). *Scales for rating the behavior of characteristics of superior students.* Mansfield Center, CT: Creative Learning Press.

Richert, S. (1985). Identification of gifted students: The need for pluralistic assessment. *Roeper Review, 8*, 68–72.

Richert, S. (1991). Rampant problems and promising practices in identification. In N. Colangelo, & G. Davis, G. (Eds.), *Handbook of gifted education* (pp. 81–96). Boston: Allyn & Bacon.

Richert, S., Alvino, L., & McDonnel, R. (1982). *National report on identification: Assessment and recommendations for comprehensive identification of gifted and talented youth.* Sewell, NJ: U.S. Department of Education, Educational Information Resource Center.

Rideout, B., Dougherty, S., & Wernert, L. (1997, April). *The effect of music on spatial performance: A test of generality*. Paper presented at the Eastern Psychological Association, Washington, DC.

Ries, N. L. (1982). *An analysis of the characteristics of infant-child singing expressions*. Unpublished doctoral dissertation, Arizona State University.

Reis, S. M., Schader, R., Shute, L. Don, A., Milne, H., Stephens, R., et al. (2000, Fall). Williams Syndrome: A study of unique musical talents in persons with disabilities. *The National Research Center on the Gifted and Talented Newsletter, 3*.

Rodriguez, C. X., & Webster, P. R. (1997). Development of children's verbal interpretive responses to music listening. *Bulletin of the Council for Research in Music Education, 134*, 9–30.

Seashore, C. E. (1919). *The psychology of musical talent*. New York: Silver Burdett.

Seashore, C. E. (1938). *Psychology of music*. New York: McGraw Hill

Schlaug, G., Jancke, L., Huang, Y., & Steinmetz, H. (1995). In vivo evidence of structural brain asymmetry in musicians. *Science, 267*, 699–701.

Shuter-Dyson, R., & Gabriel, C. (1968). *The psychology of musical ability*. London: Methuen.

Sloboda, J. (1994). Music performance: Expression and the development of excellence. In R. Aiello & J. Sloboda (Eds.), *Musical perceptions* (pp. 153–169). Oxford, England: Oxford University Press.

Sloboda, J. (1996). The acquisition of musical performance expertise: Deconstructing the "talent" account of individual differences in musical expressivity. In K. A. Ericsson (Ed.), *The road to excellence: The acquisition of expert performance in the arts and sciences, sports, and games* (pp. 107–127). Mahwah, NJ: Lawrence Erlbaum.

Sloboda, J. (2005). *Exploring the musical mind: Cognition, emotion, ability, and function*. New York: Oxford University Press.

Sloboda, J., Davidson, J., & Howe, M. (1994). Is everyone musical? *Psychologist, 7*, 153–169.

Sloboda, J., & Howe, M. (1991). Biographical precursors of musical excellence: An interview study. *Psychology of Music, 19*, 3–21.

Sloboda, J., & Howe, M. (1999). Musical talent and individual differences in musical achievement: A reply to Gagné. *Psychology of Music, 27*, 52–54.

Sosniak, L. A. (1985a). Learning to be a concert pianist. In B. Bloom (Ed.), *Developing talent in young people* (pp. 19–67). New York: Ballantine Books.

Sosniak, L. A. (1985b). Phases of learning. In B. Bloom (Ed.), *Developing talent in young people* (pp. 409–438). New York: Ballantine Books.

Steele, K., Brown, J. D., & Stoecker, J. A. (1999). Failure to confirm the Rauscher and Shaw description of recovery of the Mozart effect. *Perceptual and Motor Skills, 88*, 843–848.

Trusty, J., & Oliva, G. M. (1994). The effect of arts and music education on students' self concept. *Update: Application of Research in Music Education, 11*(1), 23–27.

Uszler, M. (1990). Musical giftedness. *American Music Teacher, 41*(4), 20–21.

Warnick, E. (1985). Overcoming measurement and evaluation phobia. *Music Educators Journal, 71*(8), 33–40.

Webster, P. (1979). Relationship between creative behavior in music and selected variables as measured in high school students. *Journal of Research in Music Education, 27*, 227–242.

Webster, P. (1987). Refinement of a measure of creative thinking in music. In C. Madsen & C. Pricket (Eds.), *Applications of research in music behavior* (pp. 257–271*).*Tuscaloosa: University of Alabama Press.

Webster, P. (1992). Research on creative thinking in music: The assessment literature. In R. Colwell (Ed.), *Handbook of research on music teaching and learning* (pp. 266–280). New York: Schirmer Books.

Wenner, E. (1985). Discovery and recognition of the artistically talented. *Journal for the Education of the Gifted, 18*, 221–238.

Wing, H. D. (1939). *Standardized tests of musical intelligence.* Sheffield, England: City of Sheffield Training College.

Winner, E., & Hetland, L. (2000, Fall). The arts and academic improvement: What the evidence shows. *Journal of Aesthetic Education, 3*.

Chapter 30

NEURAL BASES OF GIFTEDNESS

Sharlene D. Newman

INTRODUCTION

What does it mean to be gifted? Is there something different about the neurobiology of a gifted person compared to us average people? If so, what is it? These are questions that have been debated for years and ones that I have attempted to address here. Even though giftedness seems to be a characteristic that we all think we know when we encounter it, there is no agreed upon definition. One of the earliest definitions was provided by Terman (1925): Someone is gifted if he or she is in the top 1% of general intellectual ability. Based on this definition, giftedness is synonymous with high intelligence or IQ. There have been many who have argued that this definition is limiting. As such, broader definitions have been proposed. One such definition of giftedness provided by Kalbfleisch (2004) is

> when their aptitude/IQ measures approximately two
> standard deviations above the norm (~130) on psycho-

metric measures of intelligence and when they display certain behaviors or traits such as creativity, exceptional memory, rapid processing speed, high motivation, an affinity for learning, and optimal cognitive performance in one or more domains. (p. 21)

However, in most definitions of giftedness, intelligence is a major factor. Intelligence, like giftedness, is very difficult to define, and in fact, there is little consensus among scientific researchers as to what is meant by it (Jensen, 1998). A general definition provided by Sternberg and Salter (1982) that we will use here is goal-directed adaptive behavior. Intelligent behavior is adaptive in that it changes to confront and meet successfully with challenges. An intelligent person does not continue to use a strategy that is not working or that is not very efficient. Because it is not enough for intelligent behavior to simply be adaptive, it is also thought to be goal-directed, or purposeful. However, it is the adaptive nature of intelligence and how it contributes to giftedness that will be the primary focus of this chapter.

The focus of previous studies that have examined the neural basis of giftedness, as well as intelligence, has been to determine the underlying neural signature that causes giftedness. This research has taken a number of directions, from genetic/heritability studies (Kalbfleisch, 2004; Posthuma, de Geus, & Boomsma, 2001; Posthuma, Mulder, Boomsma, & de Geus, 2002), to attempting to localize general intelligence to a specific brain region (Duncan et al., 2000), to determining whether gifted individuals rely more heavily on the brain's right hemisphere during mathematical tasks (O'Boyle, 2005). The approach discussed in the current chapter is somewhat different and takes into consideration a number of general neural operating principles that may be used to guide future studies of giftedness.

Before discussing the general operating principles of the neural system, it is important to discuss the role of the frontal lobe in giftedness. Both intellectual ability and the frontal lobe have often been linked to executive functions such as control processing, strategy formulation, planning, and monitoring the contents of working memory (Duncan, Emslie, & Williams, 1996; Luria, 1966; Newman, Carpenter, Varma, & Just, 2003; Norman & Shallice, 1980; Snow, 1981). As a result of the significant overlap, some have suggested that intelligence is localized to the prefrontal cortex (e.g., Duncan et al., 2000). I do not dispute that the frontal lobes play an important role in problem solving and intelligence, but suggest instead that the biological basis of intelligence extends well beyond the frontal lobe. In fact, intact frontal functions have been found to be somewhat unrelated to intelligence, as measured by psychometric tests (Teuber, 1972). In addition, in a recent study examining the correlation between IQ and gray matter volume, the correlation was significant in a number of regions extending beyond the frontal lobe (Haier, Jung, Yeo, Head, & Alkire, 2004). These findings and others suggest that attempting to localize giftedness to a single aspect of the neuroanatomy or a single neural process is limiting.

Neural Operating Principles

In this chapter I present a theory of neural processing that is derived from the use of functional neuroimaging, particularly functional magnetic resonance imaging (fMRI). fMRI has the potential to provide a clearer characterization of the neural bases of giftedness. A key contribution of fMRI is its ability to provide information about several important properties of the large-scale neural networks that underlie cognition. These properties include the specification of the processing taking place within a brain region, the temporal profile of that processing, and the degree of synchronization between pairs of activated regions (or functional connectivity).

The theory of neural processing presented is discussed in such a way as to provide a possible explanation for giftedness. Given that there has been little investigation of the neural bases of giftedness, the following discussion is intended to open up the discussion and hopefully lead to future studies that will better characterize this phenomena. The major proposal of this chapter is that how well the neural system can adapt to changes in the environment will affect the quality and efficiency of its processing, thereby constituting a major source of individual differences in cognitive processing. Adaptability is assessed here by examining neural efficiency, the malleability of processing networks, and functional connectivity. These measures are used because how well someone can adapt to fluctuations in the computational demands is thought to be correlated with these measures. The theory described here is composed of a set of operating principles for cortical computation put forth by Newman and Just (2005) and Just and Varma (in press); please refer to them for more details.

Neural Efficiency

Have you ever encountered a problem that was so difficult to solve that you felt like your head was going to explode? It was almost as though you could feel all the blood in your body rushing to your brain to help you solve it. So, the statement that energy is consumed during the performance of cognitive tasks is a little obvious. But, it is related to the first operating principle of neural processing: The amount of resources required to perform any cognitive task varies as a function of effort. What this means practically is that one person may find a problem easy and put forth little effort (resulting in little brain activation), whereas someone else may find the same problem very difficult and put forth a lot of effort (resulting in significantly more brain activation). Support for this principle can been found in the many studies that have found that the amount of brain activation increases with increasing computational demands using cognitive tasks such as sentence comprehension (Just, Carpenter, Keller, Eddy, & Thulborn, 1996; Keller, Carpenter, & Just, 2001; Röder, Stock, Neville, Bien, & Rosler, 2002), working memory (Braver, Cohen, Jonides, Smith, & Noll, 1997; Rypma, Prabhakaran, Desmond, Glover, & Gabrieli, 1999), and mental

Neural Efficiency Differences Between High- and Low-Capacity Readers

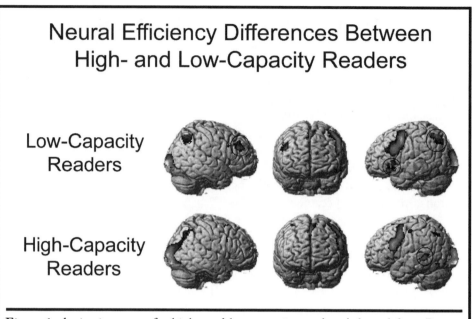

Low-Capacity Readers

High-Capacity Readers

Figure 1. Activation maps for high- and low-capacity readers (adapted from Prat et al., in press). As shown, the activation maps for these two groups of participants reveal significant differences. Overall, the low-capacity readers show greater levels of activation, particularly in the left parietal region. In addition, the pattern of activation is different for the two groups. The low-capacity group show right hemisphere activation that is not present in the high-capacity group while the high-capacity group show left hemisphere temporal and inferior frontal activation that is not present in the low-capacity group.

rotation tasks (Carpenter, Just, Keller, Eddy, & Thulborn, 1999; Just, Carpenter, Maquire, Diwadkar, & McMains, 2001).

One of the implications of the resource consumption approach is that individuals may differ in resource efficiency. In other words, those with above-average performance may use the available resources more efficiently. There is evidence that lends support to this efficiency hypothesis (Just, Carpenter, Mijake, 2003; Haier et al., 1988; Newman et al., 2003; Parks et al., 1988, 1989; Reichle, Carpenter, & Just, 2000). One example study compared the brain activation of low-capacity readers (individuals with a small working memory capacity) with high-capacity readers during a sentence comprehension task (Prat, Keller, & Just, in press). As shown in Figure 1, the low-capacity readers, on average, recruited more of the brain to perform the same sentence comprehension task than high-capacity readers. However, this increase in recruitment was not all over the brain, but in specific, circumscribed regions. Although giftedness is much more than having a large working memory capacity, studies like those conducted by Prat and colleagues may be able to provide some insight into how individuals process information differently.

One potential next step is to examine possible differences in the cognitive strategies used by gifted individuals. For example, when examining the activation maps for the high and low-capacity readers it is noted that the low-capacity group activated a region of the inferior frontal gyrus that is not activated in the high-capacity group, while the high-capacity group activated a region in the temporal cortex that is not activated in the low-capacity group. One explanation is that the two groups of readers may use different strategies to perform the same task with the strategy adopted by the high-capacity group being more efficient. With the use of novel neuroimaging and behavioral experiments it may be possible to learn much more about how gifted individuals think.

Malleability of Processing Networks

We mentioned earlier that intelligent behavior is adaptive. In other words, when a task becomes too difficult for the strategy initially used, a new one is "devised." For neural processing, that means that when using one strategy to solve a problem, a specific set, or network, of brain regions is involved, and when the strategy switches, the network of brain regions also changes. The ability to switch strategies and dynamically change the cortical landscape related to a given task may contribute to individual differences in task performance. In fact, Garlick (2002) showed that an artificial neural network that was better able to adapt its connections to the environment learned to read faster, accommodated information from the environment better, and scored higher on fluid intelligence tests. Each of these properties is characteristic of highly intelligent individuals.

The question left for researchers to address now is how can neuroimaging methods be used to explore individual differences in the malleability of neural networks. Unfortunately, there are few studies that examine dynamic strategy switching. There are, however, studies that have compared easier and harder versions of the same task. These studies revealed that the recruitment of brain regions during a task is incremental, not all-or-none, providing for just-in-time, as-needed, neural support for cognitive processing (Newman, Just, & Carpenter, 2002). However, how this incremental recruitment varies as a function of ability has yet to be studied.

Functional Connectivity

No one brain region performs a cognitive task alone; it requires a network of brain regions. For example, as you read this chapter, visual processing is taking place in occipital brain regions, semantic processing is taking place in temporal regions, and phonological processing is taking place in parietal regions. Because brain regions work together to accomplish a task, the processing taking place in these regions must be coordinated, possibly by passing information back and forth. A third neural processing operating principle is that there are variations in the degree of synchronization or efficiency of the communication between regions across individuals that may contribute to giftedness. The hypothesis to be tested is that gifted individuals have better, more efficient inter-regional communication. One possible consequence of better inter-regional communication is adaptive behavior; it is easier to switch processing strategies when the communication between regions is efficient. Again, inter-regional communication is measured by the synchronization of brain regions, or functional connectivity in the context of brain imaging. This refers to indirect evidence of communication or collaboration between various brain areas (Hampson, Peterson, Skudlarski, Gatenby, & Gore, 2002; Horwitz, Rumsey, & Donohue, 1998).

There are only a handful of studies that have examined the influence of individual differences on functional connectivity measures (Just, Cherkassky, Keller, Kana, & Minsher, 2007; Kana, Keller, Cherkassky, Minshew, & Just, 2006; Kana, Keller, Minshew, & Just, 2007; Osaka et al., 2003; Prat et al., in press). In the Prat study, mentioned above, individual differences in functional connectivity were examined. There, as predicted, it was found that high-capacity readers showed activation that was more synchronized across regions compared to low-capacity readers, suggesting that inter-regional communication is better. Even more interesting, it was found that as demand of any kind increased, high-capacity readers were able to either maintain or increase functional connectivity, while low-capacity readers often showed decreases in functional connectivity with increasing demand. Again, this difference suggests that, at least within the language comprehension network, high-capacity readers have more efficient inter-regional communication than low-capacity readers and that this more efficient communication results in better task performance. Additionally, this finding demonstrates that individual differences are not confined to a particular brain region, but are instead distributed throughout the brain and may be a characteristic of the co-functioning or cooperation of each region within a network of brain regions.

Summary

Although many research approaches have attempted to localize differences in intelligence to an elementary cognitive process (Jensen, 1993; Kane, 2003; Kyllonen & Christal, 1990), we suggest a different approach in this chapter by examining the properties of the neural system that underlies intelligent behavior. Based on the principles and findings discussed, it can be concluded that the neural basis of giftedness is not located in a particular region of the brain. Instead, the neural basis of giftedness is distributed throughout the brain and giftedness emerges as a consequence of having a neural system that is adaptive and malleable.

There are some limitations to the principles outlined here. The major limitation being that they were derived from fMRI research. Although fMRI is a very exciting technology, it should be noted that it does not measure neural processing directly. It instead measures changes in blood oxygenation (see Kwong et al., 1992, or Ogawa, Lee, Kay, & Tank, 1990, for a review). Therefore, there may be problems with making inferences regarding the properties of neural networks based on measures of blood oxygenation. This being said, using fMRI as a way to begin to develop and test theories of giftedness is not a fruitless endeavor and may lead to great advances in our understanding of this phenomena.

Future Directions

To date, there has been little use of fMRI to study giftedness. The list of operating principles discussed here is not intended to be comprehensive but is instead intended to be a springboard from which exciting new studies and theories of giftedness can emerge. With fMRI, and other neuroimaging methodologies, we have the capability to explore the brain in its active state. With innovative experimental paradigms, there is the possibility to learn much more about what is different about the gifted brain.

The next major question that this line of research can, and should address is whether and then how we can train someone to become gifted. If it turns out that giftedness really emerges as a consequence of having a neural system that is adaptive and malleable, can we train someone to have a more adaptive neural system? Incorporating both neuroimaging and behavioral learning paradigms will be essential to addressing this question.

References

Braver, T., Cohen, J. D., Jonides, J., Smith, E. E., & Noll, D. C. (1997). A parametric study of prefrontal cortex involvement in human working memory. *NeuroImage, 5*, 49–62.

Carpenter, P. A., Just, M. A., Keller, T., Eddy, W. F., & Thulborn, K. R. (1999). Graded functional activation in the visuospatial system with the amount of task demand. *Journal of Cognitive Neuroscience, 11*, 9–24.

Duncan, H., Emslie, H., & Williams, P. (1996). Intelligence and the frontal lobe: The organization of goal-directed behavior. *Cognitive Psychology*, 30, 257–303.

Duncan, J., Seitz, R. J., Kolodny, J., Bor, D., Herzog, H., Ahmed, A., et al. (2000). A neural basis for general intelligence. *Science, 289*, 457–460.

Garlick, D. (2002). Understanding the nature of the general factor of intelligence: The role of individual differences in neural plasticity as an explanatory mechanism. *Psychological Review, 109*, 116–136.

Haier, R. J., Siegel, B. V., Neuchterlein, K. H., Hazlett, E., Wu, J. C., Paek, J., et al. (1988). Cortical glucose metabolic rate correlates of abstract reasoning and attention studied with Positron Emission Tomography. *Intelligence, 12*, 199–217.

Haier, R. J., Jung, R. E., Yeo, R. A., Head, K., & Alkire, M. T. (2004). Structural brain variation and general intelligence. *NeuroImage, 23*, 425–433.

Hampson, M., Peterson, B. S., Skudlarski, P., Gatenby, J. C., & Gore, J. C. (2002). Detection of functional connectivity using temporal correlations in MR Images. *Human Brain Mapping, 15,* 247–262.

Horwitz, B., Rumsey J. M., & Donohue, B. C. (1998). Functional connectivity of the angular gyrus in normal reading and dyslexia. *Proceedings of the National Academy of Sciences USA, 95,* 8939–8944.

Jensen, A. R. (1993). Why is reaction time correlated with psychometric g? *Current Directions in Psychological Science, 2,* 53–56.

Jensen, A. R. (1998). *The g factor the science of mental ability.* Westport, CT: Praeger.

Just, M. A., Carpenter, P. A., & Miyake, A. (2003). Neuroindices of cognitive workload: Neuroimaging, pupillometric, and event-related potential studies of brain work. *Theoretical Issues in Ergonomics, 4,* 56–88.

Just, M. A., Carpenter, P. A., Keller, T. A., Eddy, W. F., & Thulborn, K. R. (1996). Brain activation modulated by sentence comprehension. *Science, 274,* 114–116.

Just, M. A., Carpenter, P. A., Maguire, M., Diwadkar, V., & McMains, S. (2001). Mental rotation of objects retrieved from memory: An fMRI study of spatial processing. *Journal of Experimental Psychology: General, 130,* 493–504.

Just, M. A., Cherkassky, V. L., Keller, T. A., Kana, R. K., & Minshew, N. J. (2007). Functional and anatomical cortical underconnectivity in autism: Evidence from an fMRI study of an executive function task and corpus callosum morphometry. *Cerebral Cortex, 17,* 951–961.

Just, M. A., & Varma, S. (in press). The organization of thinking: What functional brain imaging reveals about the neuroarchitecture of complex cognition. *Cognitive, Affective, and Behavioral Neuroscience.*

Kalbfleisch, M. L. (2004). The functional neural anatomy of talent. *The Anatomical Record, 277B,* 21–36.

Kana, R. K., Keller, T. A., Cherkassky, V. L., Minshew, N. J., & Just, M. A. (2006). Sentence comprehension in autism: Thinking in pictures with decreased functional connectivity. *Brain, 129,* 2484–2493.

Kana, R. K., Keller, T. A., Minshew, N. J., & Just, M. A. (2007). Inhibitory control in high functioning autism: Decreased activation and underconnectivity in inhibition networks. *Biological Psychiatry, 62,* 198–206.

Kane, M. J. (2003). The intelligent brain in conflict. *Trends in Cognitive Sciences, 7,* 375–377.

Kwong, K. K., Belliveau, J. W., Chesler, D. A., Goldberg, I. E., Weisskoff, R. M., Poncelet, B. P., et al. (1992). Dynamic magnetic resonance imaging of human brain activity during primary sensory stimulation. *Proceedings of the National Academy of Sciences, 89,* 5675–5679.

Keller, T. A., Carpenter, P. A., & Just, M. A. (2001). The neural bases of sentence comprehension: An fMRI examination of syntactic and lexical processing. *Cerebral Cortex, 11,* 223–237.

Kyllonen, P. C., & Christal, R. E. (1990). Reasoning ability is (little more than) working-memory capacity?! *Intelligence, 14,* 389–433.

Luria, A. R. (1966). *Higher cortical functions in man.* London: Tavistock.

Newman, S. D., Just, M. A., & Carpenter, P. A. (2002). Synchronization of the human cortical working memory network. *NeuroImage, 15,* 810–822.

Newman, S. D., Carpenter, P. A., Varma, S., & Just, M. A. (2003). Frontal and parietal participation in problem solving in the Tower of London: fMRI and computational modeling of planning and high-level perception. *Neuropsychologia, 41*, 1668–1682.

Newman, S. D., & Just, M. A. (2005). The neural bases of intelligence: A perspective based on functional neuroimaging. In R. J. Sternberg & J. Pretz (Eds.), *Cognition and intelligence: Identifying the mechanisms of the mind* (pp. 88–103). New York: Cambridge University Press.

Norman, D. A., & Shallice, T. (1980). *Attention to action: Willed and automatic control of behavior* (Report No. 8006). San Diego: University of California, Center for Human Information Processing.

O'Boyle, M. W. (2005). Some current findings on brain characteristics of the mathematically gifted adolescent. *International Education Journal, 6*, 247–251.

Ogawa, S., Lee, T., Kay, A., & Tank, D. (1990). Brain magnetic resonance imaging with contrast dependent blood oxygenation. *Proceedings of the National Academy of Sciences, 87*, 9868–9872.

Osaka, N., Osaka, M., Kondo, H., Morishita, M., Fukuyama, H., & Shibasaki, H. (2003). The neural basis of executive function in working memory: an fMRI study based on individual differences. *NeuroImage, 21*, 623–631.

Parks, R. W., Crockett, D. J., Tuokko, H., Beattie, B. L., Ashford, J. W., Coburn, K. L., et al. (1989). Neuropsychological "systems efficiency" and positron emission tomography. *Journal of Neuropsychiatry, 1*, 269–282.

Parks, R. W., Lowenstein, D. A., Dodrill, K. L., Barker, W. W., Yoshii, F., Chang, J. Y., et al. (1988). Cerebral metabolic effects of a verbal fluency test: A PET scan study. *Journal of Clinical and Experimental Neuropsychology, 10*, 565–575.

Posthuma, D., de Geus, E. J. C., & Boomsma, D. I. (2001). Perceptual speed and IQ are associated through common genetic factors. *Behavior Genetics, 31*, 593–602.

Posthuma, D., Mulder, E. J. C. M., Boomsma, D. I., & De Geus, E. J. C. (2002). Genetic analysis of IQ, processing speed and stimulus-response incongruency effects. *Biological Psychology, 61*, 157–182.

Prat, C. S., Keller, T. A., & Just, M. A. (in press). Individual differences in sentence comprehension: An fMRI investigation of syntactic and lexical processing demands. *Journal of Cognitive Neuroscience.*

Reichle, E. D., Carpenter, P. A., & Just, M. A. (2000). The neural basis of strategy and skill in sentence-picture verification. *Cognitive Psychology, 40*, 261–295.

Röder, B., Stock, O., Neville, H., Bien, S., & Rosler, F. (2002). Brain activation modulated by the comprehension of normal and pseudo-word sentences of different processing demands: A functional magnetic resonance imaging study. *NeuroImage, 15*, 1003–1014.

Rypma, B., Prabhakaran, V., Desmond, J. E., Glover, G. H., & Gabrieli, J. D. E. (1999). Load-dependent roles of frontal brain regions in the maintenance of working memory. *NeuroImage, 9*, 216–226.

Snow, R. E. (1981). Toward a theory of aptitude for learning. I. Fluid and crystallized abilities and their correlates. In M. P. Friedman, J. P. Das, & N. O'Connor (Eds.), *Intelligence and learning* (pp. 345–362). New York: Macmillan.

Sternberg, R. J., & Salter, W. (1982). Conceptions of intelligence. In R. J. Sternberg (Ed.), *Handbook of human intelligence* (pp. 3–28). Cambridge, England: Cambridge University Press.

Terman, L. (1925). *Mental and physical traits of a thousand gifted children: Genetic studies of genius, Vol. 1.* Stanford, CA: Stanford University Press.

Teuber, H.-L. (1972). Unity and diversity of frontal lobe functions. *Acta Neurobiologiae Experimentalis, 32,* 615–656.

Chapter 31

PARENTING

Robin M. Schader

here is a wealth of information available on parenting gifted children, as the briefest of Internet searches instantly reveals. Abundant anecdotal accounts, as well as volumes of advice invoking "research," offer strategies for success that appear to be based on authoritative studies. However, the ease of accessing seemingly valid and reliable information can be misleading. Many summaries that begin with "Research shows . . ." do not provide support or even clues about the data from which they are derived. Consequently, parents without experience evaluating research studies risk forming opinions and making decisions based on unfounded information, misinformation, or even disinformation.

Researchers, as well, may be cautioned that even results from solid studies often provide little clarity and few generalizable conclusions about the topic of how parents can best meet their gifted child's needs. Why? A major reason may be one of terminology. Within current research and resources, the word parenting is rarely operationally defined. Rather, parenting is an agglomeration: a term broadly used to hold multiple concepts including combinations of various family, nature, and/or nurture variables. Consider these three points.

First, the broad umbrella terminology of "parenting gifted children" covers information on wholly separate issues that are not easily disaggregated, such as data on demographics of the parents of gifted or talented children (who the parents are), data on the influence of parents in talent development (how parents might impact the process), and data related to various aspects of making good decisions about parenting gifted children (information helpful for parents).

Second, as such, a scan of parenting research offers a mix of information from distinctly different research questions but, because the data involves parents, it may suggest conclusions, comparisons, or interpretations across the studies. These interpretations may erroneously suggest conclusions about parenting or parents of gifted children because they appear to synthesize results coming from research with very different contexts or purposes. In addition, many of the individual studies use limited samples. Much research on parenting, in fact, consists of studies of small populations, even case studies, necessary and valuable starting points, but far from empirically valid benchmarks.

Third, another major difficulty with discussing research on parenting gifted children is that discussions and/or analysis of parental influences are frequently embedded within other research agendas, making it difficult to uncover and assess. This suggests there may be more pertinent information available about the role of parenting gifted children than previously reported; however, as stated previously, many of these individual studies draw from small, specific samples targeted for the primary topic. Consider that findings about parents within studies of high-achieving women (Kitano, 1997; Reis, 1999; Rimm, 1999), research on artistic development (Berman, 2002; Oreck, Baum, & McCartney, 2000), and studies of factors contributing to perfectionism or underachievement (Peterson, 2002; Schuler, 1999; Siegle & Schuler, 2000; Speirs Neumeister, 2004) each offer clues into the role of parental influence, but within very distinct frameworks.

What is particularly striking about reviewing the current research is that parenting within the field of gifted education does not have an established terminology nor is there yet a scholarly consensus for a comprehensive research agenda.

To establish a framework for this chapter, the studies are divided into two main sections. The first, "Research About Parents," includes demographic information and characteristics of GT parents. The second, "About Parenting," covers parenting practices and parental input within representative studies from the past 10 years of research. The heading "About Parenting" also includes factors such as types of information a parent might acquire, as well as their relationships with children and teachers, perceptions, and beliefs and values that effect the environmental conditions within or surrounding the three domains of home, education, and the talent development process.

RESEARCH ABOUT PARENTS

Who are the parents? Parents of gifted children are described as having unique characteristics that set them apart when compared to the general population (e.g., intelligent, independent, self-sufficient, critical, assertive, and persistent; Gockenbach, 1989), much as their children are noted as "different" within the realm of a regular classroom. Summaries of parent and family characteristics, such as Olszewski, Kulieke, and Buescher's (1987) review of literature related to multiple dimensions of families of gifted individuals (e.g., composition, structure, environmental characteristics, parenting styles, parental values), Gockenbach's (1989) discussion of the personality factors in parents of gifted children, and Goertzel and Goertzel's (1962) work on eminent individuals, provide significant insight into the parents who have nurtured exceptional abilities.

Yet, there are no recent comparable studies. This raises two important questions. First, decades have passed since the individual studies described within those works were conducted. In that time, the world's population, as well as family structure and composition, has dramatically changed. Second, these studies drew from largely middle class, Western European samples that did not encompass what is now recognized as the "many faces of gifted." For example, economically disadvantaged parents are not well represented in the literature on parenting gifted children (Robinson, Lanzi, Weinberg, Ramey, & Ramey, 2002; Robinson, Weinberg, Redden, Ramey, & Ramey, 1998), and although current federal research in the field of gifted specifies attention on ways to identify and support underserved populations (U.S. Department of Education, 2001), we lack current comprehensive information about the characteristics of parents and families of gifted students within this demographic. As Olszewski et al. (1987) noted, data on parents and families "while seemingly superficial, are indications of important psychological processes and environmental conditions that facilitate the growth of gifted individuals and the development of specific talents" (p. 12).

ABOUT PARENTING

If success at school and in life begins at home, then all parents need knowledge about what they can do to fulfill their critical roles in the home, in academics, and in providing talent development opportunities and support. Friends, relatives, and neighborhood and community groups serve as sounding boards for young families; however, for parents of gifted children (who by definition do not fit the norm), there is a need for empirically based pertinent information to offset inconsistent, unreliable folk "wisdom."

As Ruf (2005) points out from her interviews with parents of 78 gifted children, "Most parents of gifted children go through a similar process of discovering that their children are different from others . . ." (p. 23), but then they do not know where to find reliable information about how to support their child's development. This observation is confirmed by analysis of parent e-mail (n = 2,872) received by the National Association for Gifted Children (NAGC) from 2001–2004 (Schader, 2004). The majority comes from first-time parents who want to optimize their child's potential and are not familiar with or are confused by contradictions in current literature. Thirty-six percent of the e-mail asks for general information about recognizing and enriching a gifted child. "My child is different than others her age. How can I find out if she's gifted?" and "How I can help my child develop his exceptional abilities and assure they don't go to waste" are common themes. The second highest set of questions (27%) requests information about schools, programs, options, and regulations. "What kind of program is best for a gifted child?" and "How can I make sure my child is adequately challenged in school?" are recurrent themes. Achievement issues, including problems with boredom, underachievement, and twice-exceptionalities account for 13% of the inquiries. Other concerns include social and emotional needs (9%), identifying information about resources for specific topics such as music, math, reading, science, history (8%), and advocacy (7%). Of the inquiries with the age of child included, nearly half (48%) were about children 5 years old or younger.

Parenting in the Home

Research that records the experiences of parents of gifted children serves to help parents and educators better understand the diverse range of gifted, as well as become aware of what others have faced and solutions they have found. However, as a whole, the only conclusion to be drawn from studies to date is there is not one superior type of parenting, nor one identifiable set of family dynamics that leads to the fulfillment of a child's potential. Within the literature, one can find both discussion of a supportive, cohesive family as an important component of talent development, as well as conclusions that a tense, challenging home is a contributor to high levels of achievement. Although parent variables such as educational attainment, economic status, parenting style, and energy devoted to talent development appear to explain achievement in some children, the results are not consistent, even within families (Feldman & Piirto, 2002; Freeman, 2001; Hertzog & Bennett, 2004; Huff, 2002; Robinson et al., 1998; Ruf, 2005). Similar circumstances, including the shared genetic background of siblings, can have notably different outcomes (Crozier, 2003; Feldman & Piirto, 2002; Sulloway, 1996), leading to further questions concerning the relationship and responsiveness of parents in the nurturing of a child's gifts.

In addition, studies of the impact of parental conceptions of giftedness on choices about supporting a child's abilities provide further dimension to the picture of family influence (Solow, 2001). Although current research continues to produce reports of how parents deal with a gifted child in the home, the findings are again limited by sample demographics and sampling methods. With few exceptions, conclusions are drawn from self-report and retrospective views, which may have been altered by time: "For example, the girl I interviewed while she was a university student in the 1980s told me at the time how unhappy she was and so often in tears, but in 2001 she described her student years as all fun" (Freeman, 2001, p. 195).

Each of the studies cited opens the door to better understanding of parent and family influences yet, at the same time, calls for further work with larger samples from a broader range. For example, parental influences are often discussed when investigating the multidimensional topic of perfectionism. From research of the topic with 127 sets of parents (87% White), as well as their sixth-grade children participating in a talent search, it was concluded that children with parents who focused on performance goals (as opposed to learning goals) had higher expectations of themselves and felt more pressure, which placed them at risk for dysfunctional perfectionism (Ablard & Parker, 1997). Information from Schuler's (1999) multiple case study design of rural students (n = 20) and Speirs Neumeister's (2004) study of college-age women (n = 12) points to the impact of parents and teachers in socially prescribed and self-oriented perfectionism. Many of the subjects reported a need to reflect their parents' values of doing their "personal best" and wanting to please. Although parenting factors were not of primary consideration in the research, they surfaced as important contributors in the overall findings. Continued research into the impact of parental expectations and the interpretation of expectations as pressure serve to guide both parents and educators in understanding that relationship and its manifestations.

The need to incorporate diverse groups of participants is a common theme today across the overarching topic of parenting gifted children. Recent work has brought attention to ethnic group differences among parents and how their underlying beliefs and values affect children's educational achievement (Dwairy, 2004; Kim & Park, 2006; Kitano, 1997, 1998; Okagaki & Frensch, 1998). Among recent doctoral research studies, there are inroads in accounting for parental factors within a particular culture, in particular African American, Arab, Asian American, Korean, Latina, Mexican American, and Chinese (Borelli, 1996; Campbell, 1999; Henderson, 2001; Huff, 2002; Yang, 2004), while a limited number compare parenting variables across cultures.

Through a few studies targeting the impact of family experiences such as television viewing or relocation (Abelman & Gubbins, 1999; Plucker & Yecke, 1999), we find that parents of gifted children discuss and explain rather than direct. Although there has been research that addresses family functioning in the affective realm and its impact on achievement, the findings call for continued exploration in the area (Peterson, 2002; Siegle & Schuler, 2000; Speirs Neumeister, 2004). In particular, groundbreaking investigations of social and emotional issues such as suicide of a gifted child may lead to counter-interpretation if not extended and/or replicated (Cross, Gust-Brey, & Ball, 2002).

Gender-specific studies also provide varying perspectives of the role of parents. Through demographic and retrospective reports and interviews, participants (both male and female) reveal the importance of having high standards set by the adults in their lives (Hébert, 1998; Kitano, 1997, 1998; Reis, 1999; Rimm, 1999; Runco & Albert, 2005; Speirs Neumeister, 2002).

There is a need for further research into topics such as community support of parents of gifted children, parents as identifiers of giftedness, and effects of training for parents in recognizing and working with social and emotional aspects of giftedness.

Feldman and Piirto (2002) note in the opening of their chapter on parenting talented children, "Although few would sympathize with parents who find themselves trying to raise a child with exceptional intellectual talent, it is in fact one of the most daunting and often discouraging challenges that family life has to offer" (p. 195). In many ways, the challenges faced by parents of gifted children are distinct from general parenting issues, much as teachers find the needs of gifted children in the classroom are quite different from those of the majority of students.

Parenting in Education

Not only are parents recognized as a child's first teachers, their responsibility does not end when the child enters the classroom. In practical terms, parents need to balance their child's learning needs with family obligations, available resources, and in light of available and possible educational options. This becomes more of an issue for parents of a gifted child for three reasons: available school options may not sufficiently challenge (Ruf, 2005; Webb, Gore, Amend, & DeVries, 2007); talent development opportunities may be costly (Bloom, 1985; Davidson, Howe, Moore, & Sloboda, 1996; Schader, 2001); and families may include other siblings with their own range of needs. Educated and involved parents of gifted children will search for options and opportunities for their very young child; however, parents of at-risk gifted children may not know where to begin (Robinson, 1998). Throughout their child's school career, the involved, aware, educated parents continue to question, often to the discomfort of those teachers who may not have either experience or education in the field of gifted, themselves (Hertzog & Bennett, 2004; Sankar-DeLeeuw, 1999). Parents of at-risk gifted students may not know there are alternatives to an inappropriate classroom situation (Robinson et al., 1998; Robinson et al., 2002), while parents with means can and do provide educational opportunities beyond public school offerings (Hertzog & Bennett, 2004; Ruf, 2005). What happens to the gifted child whose parent cannot afford lessons, tutoring, materials, or private school, if necessary? To be effective and useful, research in this area must be current, realistic, ongoing, and reflect best practices for the wide continuum of parents and teachers.

There are few empirically based studies reflecting the direct educational impact of those parents who provide specific educational interventions for their gifted children in the home. For example, what are the findings about homeschooling gifted children? Are there differences among and between children whose parents who provide additional lessons or tutoring and those who do not when a gifted child is very young? In what way and to what degree does "professional development" of parents play a part in a gifted child's ability to thrive in school? There are no published studies that address topics such as the effectiveness of classes for parents in supporting their gifted child, learning about educational programming options, or advocacy.

Data from an ongoing longitudinal research of former Head Start children who continue to achieve despite family conditions are striking (Robinson et al., 1998; Robinson et al., 2002): Among the at-risk families, those with academically achieving students placed high value on school and education as shown through their involvement in school and support of their child, even though the educational level of the parents was not necessarily higher nor was English the primary language spoken at home. The students in the study were not as readily identified within classrooms; yet, with their continued achievement of at least one to four grade levels higher than their current grade level, it is likely that, as they mature, they will require curricular modifications to both maintain their enthusiasm for school and continue to achieve at high levels (Robinson et al., 2002).

Although parent and family variables such as parenting style, energy devoted to talent development, educational attainment, and economic status appear to explain achievement in some children, the results are not consistent, even within families (Feldman & Piirto, 2002; Freeman, 2001; Hertzog & Bennett, 2004; Huff, 2002; Robinson et al., 1998; Ruf, 2005). With regard to achievement orientation, parents' beliefs and behaviors differ across ethnic groups (Okagaki & Frensch, 1998); for example, parents of gifted Arab children tended to be more authoritative (Dwairy, 2004).

Studies with information about parent factors and preschool children reveal three areas for further exploration. First, parents do observe developmental differences among children and can provide useful insight into early signs of giftedness. Secondly, although parent observations may not mirror teacher accounts, they offer beneficial insights into identifying and nurturing emerging gifts. Third, there may not be established channels to collect and share information between home and school (Hertzog & Bennett, 2004; Hodge & Kemp, 2000).

As noted above, parent attitudes toward school and achievement impact the educational choices they make (or do not know they need to make). Recognizing those attitudes can help professionals better understand how a child's learning can be supported both at school and at home. Hertzog and Bennett (2004) conclude,

> It is apparent from the findings of this study that parents desire partnerships with school personnel because they believe this will help their children to thrive. This is even more important when a child has more than one exceptionality. Communication between school personnel and the family is key to developing partnerships and having ongoing discussions about goals for the child's education. This is important despite the resourcefulness of many families in providing activities for their children outside of school. (p. 102)

Despite findings such as these, there has been little investigation into if and how the educational needs of gifted children can be met in partnership with the family and school. As one study revealed, teacher perceptions of parents made communication about programming difficult (Saunders, 2004). In addition, there is no body of research on professional development for either preservice or experienced teachers regarding effective ways they can work with parents of gifted children. Woven within findings from previous studies are clues to the importance of building such a relationship, yet a recent textbook for student teachers states:

> We know it is difficult to work in a community where you expect educated parents to support your efforts but instead perceive themselves as experts and question your professional expertise. It is important for teachers, and especially beginning teachers, to realize that their professional knowledge is distinct and not interchangeable with the knowledge that educated parents may have. It may be a misnomer to call parents "educated" when they are disrespectful of teachers. We alert you to the existence of these parents but also reassure you that the truly educated parent will value and respect you as a teacher. (Olsen & Fuller, 2003, p. 99)

Not only are parents vitally important in supporting academic opportunities for their gifted child, they can also play an integral role as advocates for gifted programming. Although it is only a single case, the promising in-depth study of one district shows that contributions from concerned and well-informed parents had major impact in expanding gifted programming, even in the face of the other district cutbacks or curtailments across the state (Kennedy, 2003). According to Kennedy, "The parents have actively sought a knowledge base in gifted education in order to promote appropriate differentiation for their individual children, and they have also worked to support the program" (p. 90).

The federal publication "A Nation at Risk" gave parents this advice more than 25 years ago: "You have the right to demand for your children the best our schools and colleges can provide. Your vigilance and your refusal to be satisfied with less than the best are the imperative first step" (National Commission on Excellence in Education, 1983). There are few studies to support parents in its implementation. While parents are told what they *should* do, there is little substantive information in the field of gifted about *how* to accomplish this. In contrast, parents within the field of special education are increasingly recognized as experts. A study of 723 Dutch parents of special needs students found that parents are the providers of essential information about education options for their children as a result of their experience and personal search for knowledge (de Geeter, Poppes, & Vlaskamp, 2002). Although the "parents' increase in knowledge and experience appeared to lead to a change in their demands and expectations" (de Geeter et al., p. 451), the position of the parent needs to be understood by those within the school. "When professionals consider parents as experts, they must develop a suitable working method to allow them to take advantage of that expertise" (de Geeter et al., p. 452). To what degree would the development of a plan for formally involving parents of gifted children impact variables such as satisfaction with school, achievement, and program effectiveness?

A case study in the field of gifted education (Cooper, Ness, & Smith, 2004) highlights the critical role of a persistent parent over a 6-year time span, concluding that academic gains made by the dual-exceptional child resulted from a combination of parental advocacy and trained school personnel. Another study investigated differing perspectives of parents and teachers concerning the effectiveness and importance of certain strategies within the classroom (Saunders, 2004). Both reveal the need for further research into the effectiveness of linking parent and teacher information.

Parenting in Talent Development

In this review of parenting research, the term *talent development* is used as a heading for gifts beyond the academic realm such as painting, sculpture, animation, dance, music, or drama. Inarguably, within the realm of environmental influences, parents serve as positive or negative catalysts for their child's talent development process (Gagné, 2004), and, as shown though studies in pre-1996 gifted literature, parents and family have had substantial influence in the lives of eminent adults. Historically, Bloom's (1985) study of family interactions of 120 young adults who had reached world-class acclaim was groundbreaking, extracting crucial variables in the talent development of eminent artists, academicians, and athletes. Overall, Bloom concludes that these individuals would not have reached such high levels had they not had the support of their families in terms of time and financial investment. Although his findings were important and well documented, there is little variation beyond upper middle class demographics and values (i.e., being raised in traditional, intact, nuclear families). Bloom's work has served well as an initial baseline study; nonetheless, today's pool of talent is growing up in significantly different family conditions and configurations. Would a study of representative eminent young adults replicate his findings in our rapidly evolving society?

Early domain-specific interests have been linked to the development of expertise, with parents and family playing an active role in providing an environment in which interests can reveal themselves (Rathunde, 2001). Factors such as provisions for free play time, positive emphasis toward achievement, consistency of talent development, communication of information about interest areas, and prioritization of a child's interests all contribute to the emergence of interests within cognitive domains (Johnson, Alexander, Spencer, Leibham, & Neitzel, 2004).

Much pertinent research about sustaining and developing talent in exceptionally talented children has come from within such specific domains as chess, biotechnology, medicine, music, or sports. This information is not necessarily cross referenced within gifted education (e.g., Berman, 2002; Davidson et al., 1996; Schader, 2001). As a result, useful information for parents could be easily overlooked (e.g., children who become successful musicians generally have parents who take an active part in lessons, support practice through listening, and themselves become more involved in musical activities (Davidson et al., 1996) or, in a study of elite female athletes, environmental catalysts including the support of parents, were considered to be important; however, they were not judged by the athletes to be as essential as other factors. Instead, athletes indicated the primary contributing factors to success (such as persistence and practice) were in the hands of the elite athlete herself, and the most important parental role was that of "opportunity maker" (Schader, 2001).

What motivates parents to provide extracurricular opportunities for their children? Because, in the younger years, opportunities for a child to participate in out-of-school activities depend on parental input, information into the reasons (including underlying beliefs and values) offers clues into supporting the development of emerging abilities (Dai & Schader, 2001, 2002; Olszewski & Lee, 2004). Other important insights for parents and educators can be found in studies of expertise, motivation, achievement, resilience, and leadership even though some of this work is drawn from limited samples. For example, the provocative and widely discussed conclusion that the performance level and motivation of children praised for their intelligence decreased compared to children praised for their effort was drawn solely from single event studies of fifth graders (Mueller & Dweck, 1998).

GENERAL CONCERNS

Readers need to be cautious in interpreting the results of studies or sets of studies about parenting. Foremost, beyond studies employing large databases such as the National Head Start/Public School Early Childhood Transition Demonstration Project, much research is based on relatively small sample sizes. For example, the median sample for dissertation studies mentioned above is 20 participants, and the mode is 12: Neither number is sufficient to establish confidence beyond the scope of the actual study. Although there may be valuable information and prompts for future direction among the findings, parents, educators, and other professionals who work with gifted children should be made aware that results from the research may not generalize. In terms of future overview, it would be useful to compare or combine research on parenting variables, yet it cannot currently be accomplished, as many studies do not delineate definitions or characteristics of the sample "gifted" population studied.

Moreover, causal links are often implied but not necessarily substantiated. In addition, the bulk of studies in the area of parent and family factors are split between self-report survey and variations of interview methodologies for data collection. A look at the instruments used indicates that not all have established reliability and validity with gifted populations. Most data are retrospective. Taken together, many of these inherent limitations are not disclosed to the lay reader, the person who has the greatest interest in accurate interpretation of the results.

FUTURE DIRECTION

Single, disconnected snapshots of parenting gifted children are simply no longer sufficient. In all other disciplines, the ability or inability to duplicate the results is given great importance and, although there are replicated empirical studies of parenting, few deal with the gifted. The parenting of gifted children is a research area with promise of rich rewards. Ongoing effort in the development of a multidimensional research agenda can benefit educators, other professionals, parents, and the children with whom we live and work. If an effective family model can be articulated to provide clarity about how parents can best meet their gifted child's needs, both within and beyond the classroom walls, it will only emerge when the role of parents is examined from the various critical perspectives required by the diversity of our society.

REFERENCES

Abelman, R., & Gubbins, E. J. (1999). Preaching to the choir: TV advisory usage among parents of gifted children. *Roeper Review, 22*, 56–64.

Ablard, K. E., & Parker, W. D. (1997). Parents' achievement goals and perfectionism in their academically talented children. *Journal of Youth and Adolescence, 26*, 651–667.

Berman, K. B. (2002). *Successful stage directors: Journeys in talent development and creative process.* Unpublished doctoral dissertation, University of Connecticut, Storrs.

Bloom, B. S. (1985). *Developing talent in young people.* New York: Ballantine.

Borelli, M. (1996). *Gender, ethnicity, and bilingual gifted education: A qualitative study of supportive Mexican-American families in Chicago.* Unpublished doctoral dissertation, Illinois State University, Normal.

Campbell, T. L. (1999). *Academically gifted African-American inner-city children: Comparisons with an average sample on whole family functioning, closeness with father figures, and child psychosocial behavior.* Unpublished doctoral dissertation, California School of Professional Psychology.

Cooper, E. E., Ness, M. & Smith, M. (2004). A case study of a child with dyslexia and spatial-temporal gifts. *Gifted Child Quarterly, 48,* 83–94.

Cross, T., Gust-Brey, K., & Ball, B. (2002). A psychological autopsy of the suicide of an academically gifted student: Researchers' and parents' perspectives. *Gifted Child Quarterly, 46,* 247–264.

Crozier, W. R. (2003). Individual differences in artistic achievement: A within-family case study. *Creativity Research Journal, 15,* 311–319.

Dai, D., & Schader, R. M. (2001). Parents' intrinsic/extrinsic reasons for supporting their child's musical training, *Roeper Review, 24,* 23–26.

Dai, D. Y., & Schader, R. M. (2002). Decisions regarding music training: Parental beliefs and values. *Gifted Child Quarterly, 46,* 135–144.

Davidson, J. W., Howe, M. J., Moore, D. G., & Sloboda, J. A. (1996). The role of parental influences in the development of musical performance. *British Journal of Developmental Psychology, 14,* 399–412.

de Geeter, K. I., Poppes, P., & Vlaskamp, C. (2002). Parents as experts: The position of parents of children with profound multiple disabilities. *Care, Health and Development, 28,* 443–453.

Dwairy, M. (2004). Parenting styles and mental health of Arab gifted adolescents. *Gifted Child Quarterly, 48,* 275–286.

Feldman, D., & Piirto, J. (2002). Parenting talented children. In M. Bornstein (Ed.), *Handbook of parenting: Vol.5. Practical issues in parenting* (pp. 195–219). Mahwah, NJ: Lawrence Erlbaum.

Freeman, J. (2001). *Gifted children grown up.* London: David Fulton.

Gagné, F. (2004). Transforming gifts into talents: The DMGT as a developmental theory. *High Ability Studies, 15,* 119–147.

Gockenbach, L. B. (1989). A review of personality factors in parents of gifted children and their families: Implications for research. *Journal of Clinical Psychology, 45,* 210–213.

Goertzel V., & Goertzel, M. G. (1962). *Cradles of eminence.* Boston: Little, Brown.

Hébert, T. P. (1998). Gifted Black males in an urban high school: Factors that influence achievement and underachievement. *Journal for the Education of the Gifted, 21,* 385–414.

Henderson, M. E. (2001). *Achievement: An exploration of parental influences on gifted and talented females from culturally diverse backgrounds.* Unpublished doctoral dissertation, Fielding Graduate Institute, Santa Barbara.

Hertzog, N. B., & Bennett, T. (2004). In whose eyes? Parents' perspectives on the learning needs of their gifted children. *Roeper Review, 26,* 96–104.

Hodge, K. A., & Kemp, C. R. (2000). Exploring the nature of giftedness in preschool children. *Journal for the Education of the Gifted, 24,* 46–73.

Huff, R. E. J. (2002). *The experiences of parents of gifted African American children: A phenomenological study.* Unpublished doctoral dissertation, Azusa Pacific University.

Johnson, K. E., Alexander, J. M., Spencer, S., Leibham, M. E., & Neitzel, C. (2004). Factors associated with the early emergence of intense interests within conceptual domains. *Cognitive Development, 19,* 325–343.

Kennedy, D. M. (2003). Custer, South Dakota: "Gifted's" last stand. *Gifted Child Quarterly, 47*, 82–93.

Kim, U., & Park, Y. S. (2006). Indigenous psychological analysis of academic achievement in Korea: The influence of self-efficacy, parents, and culture. *International Journal of Psychology, 41*, 287–292.

Kitano, M. K. (1997). Gifted Asian American women. *Journal for the Education of the Gifted, 21*, 3–37.

Kitano, M. K. (1998). Gifted Latina women. *Journal for the Education of the Gifted, 21*, 131–159.

Mueller, C. M., & Dweck, C. S. (1998). Praise for intelligence can undermine children's motivation and performance. *Journal of Personality and Social Psychology, 75*, 33–52.

National Commission on Excellence in Education. (1983, April). *A nation at risk: The imperative for educational reform*. Retrieved June 30, 2006, from http://www.ed.gov/pubs/NatAtRisk/recomm.html

Okagaki, L., & Frensch, P. A. (1998). Parenting and children's school achievement: A multiethnic perspective. *American Educational Research Journal, 35*, 123–144.

Olsen, G., & Fuller, M. L. (2003). *Home-school relations: Working successfully with parents & family*. Boston: Allyn & Bacon.

Olszewski, P., Kulieke, M., & Buescher, T. (1987). The influence of the family environment on the development of talent: A literature review. *Journal for the Education of the Gifted, 11*, 6–28.

Olszewski, P., & Lee, S. (2004). The role of participation in in-school and outside-of-school activities in the talent development of gifted students. *Journal of Secondary Gifted Education, 15*, 107–123.

Oreck, B., Baum, S., & McCartney, H. (2000). *Artistic talent development for urban youth: The promise and the challenge* (Research Monograph No. 00144). Storrs: National Research Center on the Gifted and Talented, University of Connecticut.

Peterson, J. S. (2002). A longitudinal study of post-high-school development in gifted individuals at risk for poor educational outcomes. *Journal of Secondary Gifted Education, 14*, 6–18.

Plucker, J. A., & Yecke, C. P. (1999). The effect of relocation on gifted students. *Gifted Child Quarterly, 43*, 95–106.

Rathunde, K. (2001). Family context and the development of undivided interest: A longitudinal study of family support and challenge and adolescents' quality of experience. *Applied Developmental Science, 5*, 158–171.

Reis, S. M. (1999). *Work left undone: Choices and compromises of talented females*. Mansfield, CT: Creative Learning Press.

Rimm, S. B. (1999). *See Jane win: The Rimm report on how 1000 girls became successful women*. New York: Crown Publishers.

Robinson, N. M. (1998). Synergies in the families of gifted children. In M. Lewis & C. Feiring (Eds.), *Families, risk, and competence* (pp. 309–324). Mahwah, NJ: Lawrence Erlbaum.

Robinson, N. M., Lanzi, R. G., Weinberg, R. A., Ramey, S., & Ramey, C. (2002). Family factors associated with high academic competence among former Head Start children at third grade. *Gifted Child Quarterly, 46*, 278–290.

Robinson, N. M., Weinberg, R. A., Redden, D., Ramey, S., & Ramey, C. (1998). Family factors associated with high academic competence among former Head Start children. *Gifted Child Quarterly, 42*, 148–156.

Ruf, D. (2005). *Losing our minds: Gifted children left behind.* Scottsdale, AZ: Great Potential Press.

Runco, M. A., & Albert, R. S. (2005). Parents' personality and the creative potential of exceptionally gifted boys. *Creativity Research Journal, 17,* 355–367.

Sankar-DeLeeuw, N. (1999). Gifted preschoolers: Parent and teacher views on identification, early admission and programming. *Roeper Review, 21,* 174–179.

Saunders, K. (2004). *Parents' and teachers' differing views of group work with gifted students.* Unpublished doctoral dissertation, McGill University.

Schader, R. M. (2001). *Perceptions of elite female athletes regarding success attributions and the role of parental influence on talent development.* Unpublished doctoral dissertation, University of Connecticut.

Schader, R. M. (2004). *Parent resource specialist report for the board of the National Association for Gifted Children.* Unpublished manuscript.

Schuler, P. A. (1999). *Voices of perfectionism: Perfectionistic gifted adolescents in a rural middle school* (Research Monograph 99140). Storrs: National Research Center on the Gifted and Talented, University of Connecticut.

Siegle, D., & Schuler, P. (2000). Perfectionism differences in gifted middle school students. *Roeper Review, 23,* 39–44.

Solow, R. (2001). Parents' conceptions of giftedness. *Gifted Child Today, 24*(2), 14–22.

Speirs Neumeister, K. L. (2002) Shaping an identity: Factors influencing the achievement of newly married, gifted young women. *Gifted Child Quarterly, 46,* 291–305.

Speirs Neumeister, K. L. (2004). Factors influencing the development of perfectionism in gifted college students. *Gifted Child Quarterly, 48,* 259–274.

Sulloway, F. J. (1996). *Born to rebel: Birth order, family dynamics, and creative lives.* New York: Random House.

United States Department of Education. (2001). Jacob K. Javits Gifted and Talented Students Education Act. Retrieved August 16, 2006, from http://www.ed.gov/programs/javits/legislation.html

Webb, J. T., Gore, J. L., Amend, E. R., & DeVries, A. R. (2007). *A parent's guide to gifted children.* Scottsdale, AZ: Great Potential Press.

Yang, W. (2004). *Perceptions of high socio-economic Chinese-American parents about their children's academic achievement, home environment, and Chinese language proficiency.* Unpublished doctoral dissertation, University of Connecticut.

Chapter 32

PERSONAL TALENT

Sidney M. Moon and Saiying Hu

WHAT IS PERSONAL TALENT?

The Construct

ersonal talent has been defined as exceptional ability to select and achieve difficult goals that are a good fit with a person's unique profile of interests, abilities, values, and social contexts (Moon, 2003a, 2003b). Personal talent is high ability in an unstructured life domain that can be learned informally through experience or formally through systematic instruction in combination with deliberate practice. The personal domain is like more familiar domains such as science or athletics in that it includes both content (knowledge) and processes (skills). The development of talent in any domain, including the personal domain, involves acquiring knowledge and developing skill. However, the personal domain is different from domains like science and athletics because the knowledge and skills that

make up the domain are less well-structured and sometimes self-referenced. Thus, we currently know less about how individuals can develop personal talent than we do about how they develop scientific or athletic talent.

Personal talent has five components that relate to the knowledge and skills of underlying personal domain:

- *Self-knowledge*—knowledge of one's own interests, abilities, values, personality traits, psychological vulnerabilities, and the like.
- *Environmental knowledge*—knowledge of the world in which the individual lives, his or her immediate context, and the unconscious sociocultural conditioning that one has received.
- *Psychological knowledge*—knowledge of the psychology of goal selection and attainment, which includes knowledge about dispositions that influence well-being and achievement, such as optimism and hope.
- *Personal decision making skills*—skill in making effective decisions for one's own life, including big decisions like selecting a career, as well as the small, moment-by-moment decisions an individual makes on a daily basis.
- *Self-regulation skills*—skill in achieving the large and small goals one sets for oneself through effective planning, implementation, monitoring, and evaluation.

The construct of personal talent was developed from a thorough review of the psychological literature on intrapersonal factors that facilitate adaptive goal selection, achievement, and well-being (Moon, 2003b). There was strong empirical support in that literature for the importance of the five components of personal talent in helping individuals select appropriate goals for their lives and achieve the goals they set.

Research conducted since the publication of Moon's initial paper continues to support the validity of the construct and the importance of the various subcomponents (Moon & Ray, 2006). For example, 35 years of data on students who participated in the Study of Mathematically Precocious Youth (SMPY) strongly supports the importance of value and ability profiles in career decision making among highly talented youth (Lubinski & Benbow, 2006). Similarly, research on the self-concordance model has demonstrated that goal selection processes that are intrinsic and consistent with personal values enhance well-being in adults (Judge, Bono, Amir, & Locke, 2005). In addition, ongoing research from research programs on related constructs such as *successful intelligence* (Sternberg, 1996, 2002); *wisdom* (Baltes & Staudinger, 2000; Sternberg, 2000); *self-determination theory* (Baard, Deci, & Ryan, 2004; Ratelle, Vallerand, Chantal, & Provencher, 2005; Sheldon, Ryan, Deci, & Kasser, 2004); *selection, optimization, and compensation (SOC) theory* (Wiese, Freund, & Baltes, 2002); *emotional intelligence* (Cherniss & Goleman, 2001; Mayer, Salovey, & Caruso, 2000); and *social/emotional learning* (Elias et al., 1997; Zins, Bloodworth, Weissberg, & Walberg, 2004) provide further empirical support for the existence and importance of the construct of personal talent.

Future research in the field of gifted and talented studies on personal talent might focus on (a) development of ways to assess levels of personal talent, especially among gifted children and adolescents; (b) identifying the areas of the brain that contribute to personal talent development; and (c) specifying the extent to which personal talent is correlated with related abilities such as traditional intelligence, creativity, practical intelligence, emotional intelligence, leadership skills, and wisdom.

Personal Talent Theory. Personal talent theory includes testable propositions related to the construct of personal talent and implies new research questions for the field of gifted education. For example, personal talent theory predicts that individuals with personal talent will be more likely than those who lack personal talent to experience happiness and/or achieve eminence in their fields. In this chapter, we will present the evidence for two of the most important propositions of personal talent theory:

- Personal talent facilitates achievement and promotes well-being.
- Personal talent can be learned and developed.

For each theoretical proposition, we summarize what we can conclude with confidence from the research, and note where additional research is needed.

Facilitating Achievement and Well-Being

The psychological literature undergirding personal talent indicates that personal talent is associated with positive outcomes such as better performance on tasks, improved health, or enhanced well-being (Moon, 2003b). Skill in *self-regulation* has strong empirical support in the general psychological literature for positive outcomes at all levels of development (Schunk & Zimmerman, 1994). Self-regulation appears to be especially important for achievement outcomes. For example, a study of highly successful Finnish scientists revealed that these high-achieving adults had taken control of their lives and created their own career paths, shaping events to fit their goals and purposes (Koro-Ljungberg, 2002). These scientists also set their own short- and long-term goals, persisted in the face of obstacles, and took advantage of opportunities. In other words, they exhibited very high levels of self-regulation. In addition, studies of gifted students who underachieve suggest many of these students have deficits in self-regulation (Hébert, 2001; McCoach & Siegle, 2003).

There is also strong empirical evidence from a variety of research programs in the field of positive psychology that adaptive dispositions such as optimism, hardiness, and hope are associated with improved achievement and well-being outcomes (Snyder & Lopez, 2002). Personal talent theory proposes that individuals with personal talent develop and exhibit these adaptive dispositions as one aspect of their self-regulatory abilities. Similarly, the gifted and talented studies literature has provided empirical evidence that adaptive dispositions associated with personal talent, such as "belief in self" (Hébert, 2000), self-oriented perfectionism (Hébert, 2000; Speirs Neumeister, 2004), and optimism (Hoekman, McCormick, & Barnett, 2005) promote achievement, while maladaptive dispositions associated with lack of personal talent, such as defensiveness, procrastination, and pervasive, mixed-maladaptive, and socially prescribed perfectionism, inhibit achievement (Dixon, Lapsley, & Hanchon, 2004; Hébert, 2001; Speirs Neumeister, 2004). There is also evidence that parenting styles can influence the development of adaptive self-regulatory skills (Csikszentmihalyi, Rathunde, & Whalen, 1993; Rathunde, 1996; Speirs Neumeister & Finch, 2006). More specifically, authoritative, permissive, and complex parenting styles seem to promote the development of personal talent skills.

The empirical support for the impact of *environmental knowledge* on achievement and well-being is strong, as well. For example, gender stereotyping has been shown to have a negative impact on the development of talent in females, but females who are made aware of gender stereotyping can be immunized against its deleterious effects (Arnold, Noble, & Subotnik, 1996; Reis, 1998). There is also good evidence that individuals who develop tacit knowledge about their daily environments achieve at higher levels than persons who lack such tacit knowledge (Sternberg et al., 2000; Wagner & Sternberg, 1985).

Until recently, there had been less research on the *self-awareness* and *personal decision making* components of personal talent. Self-awareness is hard to observe and assess. The outcomes of personal decisions may be unclear initially or evaluated differently at different time periods or by different observers. For example, it can take several years to determine whether a decision to marry or pursue a career in biochemistry was a wise decision. However, a recent study on mindfulness not only provided support for the importance of enhanced self-awareness in promoting well-being, it also demonstrated that such awareness enhances the personal talent skill of self-regulation (Brown & Ryan, 2003). Research on career development has provided support for the importance of self-awareness in career decision making. For example, a study of a career development intervention for at-risk girls with talent in the sciences appears to have increased the girls' achievement motivation (Kerr, Kurpius, & Harkins, 2005; Kurpius, Kerr, & Harkins, 2005). The interventions in this study included values and interest assessments along with activities to make the girls aware of the many opportunities available to them. Similarly, self-knowledge has been identified as a key variable for exceptional achievement among women (Noble, Subotnik, & Arnold, 1999) and the intellectually gifted participants in Terman's longitudinal study (Zuo & Cramond, 2001).

With regard to *personal decision making*, several studies from the perspective of self-determination theory have shown that both performance and well-being are enhanced when people perceive coaches, teachers, or work supervisors encourage personal autonomy in decision making; these studies have also shown that motivation becomes more self-determined, self-regulated, and persistent in environments that simultaneously promote autonomy, competence, and relatedness (Levesque, Blais, & Hess, 2004; Pelletier, Fortier, Vallerand, & Briere, 2001; Rousseau & Vallerand, 2000). Finally, there is strong empirical support for the hypothesis that negative outcomes occur when self-awareness and personal decision-making abilities are compromised by injuries to the frontal lobes (Damasio, 1994), biochemical disorders that affect the frontal lobes such as depression or ADHD (Brown, 1999), or brain disorders such as Asperger's syndrome (Neihart, 2000).

Developing Personal Talent

Indirect Interventions. The existing literature suggests that some individuals seem to be able to develop personal talent through adverse life experiences. For example, the resiliency literature has demonstrated that some children who experience very adverse environments develop some of the components of personal talent through a combination of temperament and interactions with a caring, mentoring adult (Masten, 2001; Masten & Marie-Gabrielle, 2002). These children are called "resilient" because of their ability to overcome adversity. They may or may not have other components of personal talent, such as the ability to set high-level goals consistent with their abilities, interests, and values, but they do have the self-regulatory abilities to overcome obstacles and recover quickly from setbacks. Several scholars in gifted education have summarized the factors that tend to be associated with the development of resilience such as intelligence, curiosity, problem-solving ability, engagement in productive activities, sense of humor, high self-efficacy, internal locus of control, a positive sense of self, and a good relationship with at least one caring adult (Bland, Sowa, & Callahan, 1994; Kitano & Lewis, 2005; Neihart, 2002; Reis, Colbert, Hébert, 2004). By definition, gifted children possess some of these characteristics, such as intelligence and problem-solving ability. It is unclear, however, why some gifted children who face adverse circumstances develop resilience while others do not. Personal talent theory predicts that targeted interventions to build the self-regulation skills needed to cope with failure and adversity might increase the number of resilient gifted children. This prediction is supported by a recent study that found that deliberate practice activities for swimmers needed to include an emphasis on facilitative coping skills in order to develop swimming talent to elite levels (Johnson, Tenenbaum, & Edmonds, 2006).

As noted above, the talent development literature provides evidence that the process of developing talent may have the indirect benefit of identifying and developing personal talent because those who are successful often develop personal talent skills such as self-knowledge, resilience, and expertise in self-regulation (Dai & Renzulli, 2000). For example, a recent study that analyzed responses of 50 college students to questions about their perceptions of the effects of their prior participation in gifted and talented programming found that they perceived numerous benefits related to personal talent such as learning how to study, developing a stronger work ethic, improved time management skills, and the ability to accomplish difficult tasks (Hertzog, 2003). There is also evidence in the gifted education literature that specific strategies such as creative problem solving (Moon, Feldhusen, & Dillon, 1994), independent projects (Delcourt, 1994; Freeman, 2003), mentorships (Grantham, 2004; Hébert & Olenchak, 2000; Koro-Ljungberg, 2002), and service learning (Terry, 2003) provide indirect, experiential stimuli for the development of integrated personal talent skills (Moon, 2003a).

Finally, there is empirical support for peer modeling and adaptive feedback as indirect methods of developing personal talent skills in children and adolescents. Among the general population, coping models appear to be more effective than mastery models for students learning new skills (Kitsantas, Zimmerman, & Cleary, 2000; Zimmerman & Kitsantas, 2002). Social feedback during performance has been found to assist college students in acquiring writing, revision, and self-regulation skills (Zimmerman & Kitsantas, 2002). In the gifted education research literature, the most substantial program of research of this type has used both peer modeling and teacher feedback strategies to create more adaptive attributional patterns among gifted females enrolled in competitive, secondary science classes (Ziegler & Heller, 1997, 2000; Ziegler, Monika, & Grassinger, 2005; Ziegler & Stoeger, 2004). The interventions have had several positive effects on gifted females including the development of more adaptive attributions, enhanced self-efficacy, improved science achievement, and increased cooperation.

Direct Interventions. Almost no studies have examined the effects of explicit, direct interventions to develop personal talent among academically gifted students. The general psychological literature includes a few studies of interventions designed to increase one or more components of personal talent (Moon, 2003b). These studies generally report positive results from such interventions. Many more examples of successful interventions to develop components of personal talent can be found in the sports psychology literature (Hardy, Jones, & Gould, 1996). For example, a Finnish researcher has developed an intervention called Individual Zone of Optimal Functioning (IZOF) that helps individual athletes identify, monitor, and change their emotional states to facilitate optimal performance (Robazza, Pellizzari, & Hanin, 2004). This intervention was unusual because it was focused directly on emotional regulation and completely self-referenced. It is an excellent example of a creative and direct intervention to enhance personal talent by teaching individuals to identify and modify their internal states in order to accomplish their goals.

AREAS OF NEEDED RESEARCH

The study of personal talent raises some thorny methodological issues. For example, some personal talent processes, such as goal setting, are self-referenced; that is, they are evaluated not with reference to objective, external standards but with reference to their suitability for the individual and his or her context. A goal that is appropriate for one person may be completely inappropriate for another. It is challenging to design research to investigate personal talent because it is phenomenological in nature. In addition, the same personal talent skills can be applied to the achievement of very different outcomes including well-being, a balanced life, high-level achievement in a domain, and/or groundbreaking creative productivity. Some of these outcomes are private; others are public. Some require the achievement of multiple goals in multiple domains; others require single-minded focus in one domain. Most current research on talent development processes focuses on high-level achievement in one discipline such as math. Comprehensive research on personal talent will require a more complex conceptualization of outcome variables.

Research on personal talent is in its infancy, especially with respect to gifted and talented individuals. The purpose of this section is to discuss four promising approaches to future personal talent research in the field of gifted and talented studies: process research, case studies, developmental studies, and intervention research.

Process Research

Process research is useful for investigating and further refining the personal talent construct. Process researchers investigate the processes that make up personal talent and increase the knowledge base of the personal talent domain. Extensive programs of research on personal talent constructs and processes currently exist in several fields including personal and social psychology (Carver & Scheier, 1998, 2000; Dweck, 1999; J. S. Peterson, 2000) and educational psychology (Ames, 1992; Schunk & Zimmerman, 1994, 1998). These research programs have investigated processes related to personal talent such as interactions among goals, affect, and self-regulation (Martin & Tesser, 1996). This type of research is valuable and necessary in order to create the psychological knowledge base of the personal domain. However, at least three additional emphases must be added in order to study talent in this domain. First, these constructs will need to be conceptualized as knowledge that can be acquired and/or skills that can be learned rather than as static personality traits, so studies can be designed that investigate how such knowledge and skills are acquired. Second, researchers can investigate how individuals who have developed these skills to very high levels differ from those who are less talented in the personal domain. Third, investigators can study the ways that high levels of personal talent affect the life course. Positive psychology (Seligman & Csikszentmihalyi, 2000) is a step in the right direction but it doesn't go far enough. The study of personal talent is the study of *optimal psychology*— the study of how some individuals are able to utilize personal talent to optimize their lives in self-selected directions.

The self-referenced nature of personal talent creates unique challenges for process researchers. Most of the existing research on personal talent processes has been carried out with traditional between-person comparison designs using either experimental or predictive methods. To fully understand personal talent processes, investigators must focus on self-referenced, within-person growth processes, as well as other-referenced, between-person comparisons. Individual growth modeling (Willett, 1997), a quantitative approach to the study of within-person change processes, holds promise for investigations of growth in personal talent processes over time within individuals. The IZOF research program cited above has utilized innovative, single-subject designs to address the self-referenced and individualized nature of personal talent. Qualitative methods (Miles & Huberman, 1994; Strauss & Corbin, 1990) may be helpful in illuminating some self-referenced personal talent processes, such as how individuals decide whether a particular goal is a good match for their interests and abilities. Diary studies (Gagne, Ryan, & Kelly, 2003), experience sampling studies (Csikszentmihalyi et al., 1993), and studies of student perceptions (Gentry, Gable, & Springer, 2000; Gentry, Rizza, & Gable, 2001; Gentry, Rizza, & Owen, 2002) may be helpful in determining whether students perceive their classroom environments to have the characteristics that have repeatedly been demonstrated to promote personal talent development. Finally, new methods will need to be developed specifically for the purpose of investigating self-referenced personal talent issues such as whether a particular goal is a good match for a particular individual in a particular context.

Case Study Research

Case study research is useful for investigating the propositions of personal talent theory that are the focus of this chapter; that is, personal talent facilitates achievement, promotes well-being, and can be developed. Case study research has been used to investigate many aspects of talent development psychology (Arnold, 1995; Bloom, 1985; Feldman, 1986; Gardner, 1997; Gruber, 1989; Moon & Dillon, 1995). Two types of case study research are especially promising for research on personal talent: exemplar studies and negative case studies. To provide a complete picture of personal talent, exemplar studies will need to include individuals who focus their lives in the private sphere, as well as those focused on the public sphere; outcomes related to family relationships, as well as career achievements; and balanced excellence in multiple domains, as well as concentrated excellence in a single domain.

Negative case studies take the opposite approach from the exemplar studies—they look for individuals where a dearth of personal talent prevents goal achievement. Case studies of gifted children with ADHD (Moon, Zentall, Grskovic, Hall, & Stormont, 2001; Zentall, Moon, Hall, & Grskovic, 2001) or gifted underachievers (Hébert, 2001; J. S. Peterson, 2000, 2001; Reis, Hébert, Diaz, Maxfield, & Ratley, 1995) are examples of negative case studies. Negative case studies are effective in identifying the impact of a lack of personal talent on both well being and achievement in other domains.

Developmental Research

Developmental research is especially useful for illuminating how personal talent develops over time, naturally and informally, without intervention. It is also useful for examining the ways the personal talent impacts achievement and well-being. Developmental issues are central in all talent development processes. Developmental research can be qualitative or quantitative, cross-sectional or longitudinal. Several existing developmental studies in the field of talent development psychology have at least tangentially explored issues related to personal talent. For example, Arnold's (1995) qualitative study of high school valedictorians revealed that life outcomes for valedictorians depend, in part, on the life goals selected by the individual. Valedictorians whose focus was on achieving balance between work and family created very different lives from valedictorians whose focus was primarily on high-level professional achievement. Another example is Hany's (1994) 3-year longitudinal study of the development of creative talent in technological domains among 11- and 13-year-olds. This study highlighted the importance of interest in domain-specific talent development. Hany found interest in science and technology was a more powerful predictor of participation in scientific/technical activities than spatial reasoning ability, especially among high-ability students. The Fullerton Longitudinal Study has determined that academic intrinsic motivation predicts academic achievement, self-concept, and classroom functioning independently of IQ and represents a form of giftedness (Gottfried, Gottfried, Cook, & Morris, 2005). As a final example, a recent reexamination of Terman's longitudinal study of high-IQ children from the perspective of identity development theory demonstrated the importance of personal talent on life outcomes for gifted individuals (Zuo & Cramond, 2001). These studies are examples of developmental research that illustrate the influence of personal talent variables on the development of talent in more traditional domains.

Also needed are developmental studies that focus more specifically on how people develop awareness of their interests, decide what outcomes to pursue in life, and go about achieving those outcomes. Developmental research is essential to understanding age-related differences in the abilities that are prerequisites for the development of high-level talent in the personal domain, individual and group patterns in the development of personal talent over the lifespan, and the effects of the environment on the development of personal talent, especially in children and adolescents.

Intervention Research

To fully understand the ways that individuals develop personal talent, researchers need to investigate interventions designed to increase personal talent. There are many possible avenues for the design of interventions in the personal domain. Indeed, a few such studies have already been conducted. For example, the Practical Intelligence for Schools Project demonstrated that teaching students tacit knowledge related to the school context improves students' performance in reading, writing, homework assignments, and testing taking (Gardner, Krechevsky, Sternberg, & Okagaki, 1994). This study suggests that interventions that increase the *environmental knowledge* component of personal talent can facilitate achievement.

There is even more support for the value of interventions to increase the *self-regulation component* of personal talent. Schunk and his colleagues have demonstrated through a series of studies that interventions such as cognitive modeling (Schunk, 1981; Schunk & Hanson, 1985; Schunk, Hanson, & Cox, 1987), verbalization of self-regulatory strategies (Schunk, 1982; Schunk & Cox, 1986), and effort feedback (Schunk, 1981; Schunk & Cox, 1986) can improve the self-efficacy and academic achievement of elementary students. Similarly, an intervention program using strategies from cognitive-behavioral therapy to teach grade-school children to be more optimistic has shown that optimism training can reduce the incidence of depression in such students (Gillham, Reivich, Jaycox, & Seligman, 1995; C. Peterson, 2000). Taken together, these studies support personal talent theory because they suggest that personal talent knowledge and skills can be developed even in young children, and that developing personal talent can have a positive effect on both cognitive and affective outcomes.

There is also some evidence that gifted students need interventions to promote self-regulation because they do not develop all aspects of self-regulation naturally. For example, gifted high school students have been shown to have higher scores on adaptability and lower scores on stress management than normative samples, suggesting that interventions to build personal talent in gifted adolescents should emphasize stress management skills (Lee & Olszewski-Kubilius, 2006). Similarly, moderately and mildly gifted students in mathematics have been shown to have different attributional patterns, with the more highly gifted students having the least adaptive pattern (Nokelainen, Tirri, & Merenti-Valimaki, 2007). Interventions to promote adaptive attributional patterns in mathematics may be most necessary for the most highly talented students. Likewise, gifted students in regular sixth-grade mathematics classrooms have been shown to have weaker strategy use than comparison students (Dresel & Haugwitz, 2005), suggesting that gifted students in regular mathematics classrooms may have greater need for interventions to develop effective self-regulated learning strategies than their less talented chronological peers. Finally, gifted students appear to need interventions to develop social coping skills and positive peer relationship in order to enhance their well-being (Chan, 2005).

Most of the studies cited above focused on self-regulation skills for goals selected by others—teachers, parents, coaches, or researchers. Personal talent researchers must also develop and test individualized training programs that facilitate the achievement of goals selected by participating individuals. In other words, intervention studies are needed that focus on goal selection, personal decision making, and the self-regulation of progress toward self-selected goals. Applied fields that have developed interventions to enable individuals to make better personal decisions and achieve self-selected goals include sports psychology and lifestyle coaching. Sports psychology has pioneered the development of individualized personal talent coaching to facilitate peak performance (Hardy et al., 1996). Sports psychology consultants work with individual athletes to help them maximize their athletic performance by developing personal talent skills such as goal setting, relaxation, mental rehearsal, strategies for developing specific efficacy expectations, anxiety management, self-determination, high levels of both intrinsic and extrinsic motivation, stress management, concentration, and coping strategies (Hardy et al., 1996). Similarly, the emergent field of lifestyle coaching helps individuals define self-selected goals such as weight loss, career success, relational success, and then helps those individuals design strategies for achieving their goals. Training programs and certification programs are currently being developed for this emerging profession. Research on the efficacy of services provided by both sports psychology consultants and lifestyle coaches is another potential avenue for enhancing our understanding of personal talent interventions.

A final approach to research on interventions to build personal talent comes from the field of gifted and talented education, where educators have traditionally emphasized instructional strategies that require *integrated application of all of the components of personal talent*. For example, several well-known models of gifted programming provide students with opportunities to conduct long-term independent study projects (Betts, 1985; Feldhusen & Kolloff, 1986; Moon, 1993; Renzulli & Reis, 1985). Academically talented students who successfully complete an independent study project develop personal talent as they master tasks such as identifying their interests, selecting one or more goals for their project, developing a plan for accomplishing these self-selected goals, monitoring their progress over a long period of time, and self-evaluating the results. Hence, educators interested in helping students develop personal talent may find it helpful to investigate educational strategies such as independent study or problem-based learning that require comprehensive coordination of multiple personal talent processes.

Summary

The facilitative and self-referenced qualities of personal talent, combined with the large number of outcomes that can be influenced by this type of talent, are challenges for personal talent research. Promising approaches for addressing these challenges have been suggested within the process, case study, developmental, and intervention research traditions. Ideally, these approaches will be combined in programmatic research agendas on personal talent. A good model for the type of programmatic research that is needed is the research program currently being conducted at the Max Planck Institute for Human Development (Baltes & Staudinger, 2000). This creative research program on the construct of wisdom is explicitly oriented towards understanding exceptional human functioning in an unstructured domain related to personal talent. Baltes and his colleagues have investigated wise persons (exemplar case study approach; Baltes, Staudinger, Maercker, & Smith, 1995), developmental trends in the acquisition of wisdom-related knowledge (developmental approach; Pausupathi, Staudinger, & Baltes, 1999), and wisdom-related processes such as whether people's performance on wisdom tasks improves when they discuss the task with a significant other versus when they work alone (process approach; Staudinger & Baltes, 1996). Similar programmatic research with gifted and talented children combining multiple approaches is needed to build our understanding of personal talent in the gifted population.

PRACTICAL IMPLICATIONS

The construct of personal talent has substantial implications for the field of gifted education. Many of these implications have already been discussed. Listed below are 10 recommendations for gifted educators flowing from the propositions of personal talent theory discussed in this chapter:

1. Identify gifted children with deficits in one or more of the five components of personal talent as early as possible and work with school counselors to design individualized programs to help them overcome those deficits.
2. Identify individuals with high levels of personal talent in combination with strong interest in the domain for domain-specific talent development programs even if they do not meet traditional selection criteria based on test scores.
3. Help gifted children and adolescents develop a deep understanding of their interests, abilities, and values.
4. Create classroom environments that promote adaptive and resilient dispositions in young gifted children.
5. Emphasize experiential instructional strategies that build personal talent skills such as simulations, problem-based learning, service-learning, creative problem solving, and independent projects.
6. Provide professional development workshops for teachers on personal talent knowledge, skills, and dispositions.
7. Develop curricula to enable upper elementary and middle school teachers to provide gifted and talented children with direct instruction in key personal talent skills such as goal setting and time management.

8. Include an exposure to careers that are related to the content area in high school honors or AP classes, and promote the development of the domain-specific personal talent skills required for career success in those fields.

9. Encourage gifted adolescents to become involved in one or more extracurricular activities.

10. Help gifted adolescents learn life management skills that will enable them to simultaneously achieve strong personal relationships, high-level career goals, robust identities, and personal happiness.

REFERENCES

Ames, C. (1992). Classrooms: Goals, structures, and student motivation. *Journal of Educational Psychology, 84*, 261–271.

Arnold, K., Noble, K. D., & Subotnik, R. F. (1996). *Remarkable women: Perspectives on female talent development*. Cresskill, NJ: Hampton Press.

Arnold, K. D. (1995). *Lives of promise: What becomes of high school valedictorians? A 14-year study of achievement and life choices*. San Francisco: Jossey-Bass.

Baard, P. P., Deci, E. L., & Ryan, A. M. (2004). Intrinsic need satisfaction: A motivational basis of performance and well-being in two work settings. *Journal of Applied Psychology, 34*, 2045–2068.

Baltes, P. B., & Staudinger, U. M. (2000). Wisdom: A metaheuristic (pragmatic) to orchestrate mind and virtue toward excellence. *American Psychologist, 55*, 122–136.

Baltes, P. B., Staudinger, U. M., Maercker, A., & Smith, J. (1995). People nominated as wise: A comparative study of wisdom-related knowledge. *Psychology and Aging, 10*, 155–166.

Betts, G. T. (1985). *Autonomous learner model for the gifted and talented*. Greeley, CO: ALPS.

Bland, L. C., Sowa, C. J., & Callahan, C. M. (1994). An overview of resilience in gifted children. *Roeper Review, 17*, 77–80.

Bloom, B. S. (Ed.). (1985). *Developing talent in young people*. New York: Ballantine.

Brown, K. W., & Ryan, R. M. (2003). The benefits of being present: Mindfulness and its role in psychological well-being. *Journal of Personality and Social Psychology, 84*, 822–848.

Brown, T. E. (1999, August). *Inattention and executive functions: New understandings of the ADD syndrome*. Paper presented at the American Psychological Association, Boston.

Carver, C. S., & Scheier, M. F. (1998). *On the self-regulation of behavior*. New York: Cambridge University Press.

Carver, C. S., & Scheier, M. F. (2000). *Perspectives on personality* (4th ed.). Boston: Allyn & Bacon.

Chan, D. W. (2005). Emotional intelligence, social coping, and psychological distress among Chinese gifted students in Hong Kong. *High Ability Studies, 16*, 163–178.

Cherniss, C., & Goleman, D. (Eds.). (2001). *The emotionally intelligent workplace: How to select for, measure, and improve emotional intelligence in individuals, groups, and organizations*. San Francisco: Jossey Bass.

Csikszentmihalyi, M., Rathunde, K., & Whalen, S. (1993). *Talented teenagers.* Cambridge, England: Cambridge University Press.

Dai, D. Y., & Renzulli, J. S. (2000). Dissociation and integration of talent development and personal growth: Comments and suggestions. *Gifted Child Quarterly, 44,* 247–251.

Damasio, A. R. (1994). *Descartes' error: Emotion, reason, and the human brain.* New York: Avon.

Delcourt, M. A. (1994). Characteristics of high-level creative productivity: A longitudinal study of students identified by Renzulli's three-ring conception of giftedness. In R. F. Subotnik & K. D. Arnold (Eds.), *Beyond Terman: Contemporary longitudinal studies of giftedness and talent* (pp. 401–437). New York: Ablex.

Dixon, F. A., Lapsley, D. K., & Hanchon, T. A. (2004). An empirical typology of perfectionism in gifted adolescents. *Gifted Child Quarterly, 48,* 95–106.

Dresel, M., & Haugwitz, M. (2005). The relationship between cognitive abilities and self-regulated learning: Evidence for interactions with academic self-concept and gender. *High Ability Studies, 16,* 201–218.

Dweck, C. S. (1999). *Self-theories: Their role in motivation, personality, and development.* Philadelphia: Psychology Press.

Elias, M. J., Zins, J. E., Weissberg, R. P., Frey, K. S., Greenberg, M. T., Haynes, N. M., et al. (1997). *Promoting social and emotional learning: Guidelines for educators.* Alexandria, VA: Association for Supervision and Curriculum Development.

Feldhusen, J. F., & Kolloff, P. B. (1986). The Purdue Three-Stage Enrichment Model at the elementary level. In J. S. Renzulli (Ed.), *Systems and models for developing programs for the gifted and talented* (pp. 126–152). Mansfield Center, CT: Creative Learning Press.

Feldman, D. H. (1986). *Nature's gambit.* New York: Basic Books.

Freeman, J. (2003). Gender differences in gifted achievement in Britain and the U.S. *Gifted Child Quarterly, 47,* 202–211.

Gagne, M., Ryan, R. M., & Kelly, B. (2003). Autonomy support and need satisfaction in the motivation and well-being of gymnasts. *Journal of Applied Psychology, 15,* 372–390.

Gardner, H. (1997). *Extraordinary Minds.* New York: Basic Books.

Gardner, H., Krechevsky, M., Sternberg, R. J., & Okagaki, L. (1994). Intelligence in context: Enhancing students' practical intelligence for school. In K. McGilly (Ed.), *Classroom lessons: Integrating cognitive theory and classroom practice* (pp. 105–127). Cambridge, MA: Bradford Books.

Gentry, M., Gable, R. K., & Springer, P. (2000). Gifted and nongifted middle school students: Are their attitudes toward school different as measured by the new affective instrument, My Class Activities? *Journal for the Education of the Gifted, 24,* 74–95.

Gentry, M., Rizza, M. G., & Gable, R. K. (2001). Gifted students' perceptions of their class activities: Differences among rural, urban, and suburban student attitudes. *Gifted Child Quarterly, 45,* 115–129.

Gentry, M., Rizza, M. G., & Owen, S. V. (2002). Examining perceptions of challenge and choice in classrooms: The relationship between teachers and their students and comparisons between gifted students and other students. *Gifted Child Quarterly, 46,* 145–155.

Gillham, J. E., Reivich, K. J., Jaycox, L. H., & Seligman, M. E. P. (1995). Prevention of depressive symptoms in schoolchildren: Two-year follow-up. *Psychological Science, 6,* 343–351.

Gottfried, A. W., Gottfried, A. E., Cook, C. R., & Morris, P. E. (2005). Educational characteristics of adolescents with gifted academic intrinsic motivation: An longitudinal investigation of school entry through early adulthood. *Gifted Child Quarterly, 49,* 172–186.

Grantham, T. C. (2004). Multicultural mentoring to increase Black male representation in gifted programs. *Gifted Child Quarterly, 48,* 232–245.

Gruber, H. E. (1989). The evolving systems approach to creative work. In D. B. Wallace & H. E. Gruber (Eds.), *Creative people at work* (pp. 3–24). New York: Oxford University Press.

Hany, E. A. (1994). The development of basic cognitive competence of technical creativity: A longitudinal comparison of children and youth with high and average intelligence. In R. F. Subotnik & K. D. Arnold (Eds.), *Beyond Terman: Contemporary longitudinal studies of giftedness and talent* (pp. 115–154). Norwood, NJ: Ablex.

Hardy, L., Jones, G., & Gould, D. (1996). *Understanding psychological preparation for sport: Theory and practice of elite performers.* Chichester, England: John Wiley.

Hébert, T. P. (2000). Defining belief in self: Intelligent young men in an urban high school. *Gifted Child Quarterly, 44,* 91–114.

Hébert, T. P. (2001). "If I had a new notebook, I know things would change": Bright underachieving young men in urban classrooms. *Gifted Child Quarterly, 45,* 174–194.

Hébert, T. P., & Olenchak, F. R. (2000). Mentors for gifted underachieving males: Developing potential and realizing promise. *Gifted Child Quarterly, 44,* 196–207.

Hertzog, N. B. (2003). Impact of gifted programs from the students' perspectives. *Gifted Child Quarterly, 47,* 131–143.

Hoekman, K., McCormick, J., & Barnett, K. (2005). The important role of optimism in a motivational investigation of gifted adolescents. *Gifted Child Quarterly, 49,* 99–110.

Johnson, M. B., Tenenbaum, G., & Edmonds, W. A. (2006). Adaptation to physically and emotionally demanding conditions: The role of deliberate practice. *High Ability Studies, 17,* 117–136.

Judge, T. A., Bono, J. E., Amir, E., & Locke, E. A. (2005). Core self-evaluations and job and life satisfaction: The role of self-concordance and goal attainment. *Journal of Applied Psychology, 90,* 257–268.

Kerr, B., Kurpius, S., & Harkins, A. (Eds.). (2005). *Handbook for counseling girls and women: Talent development* (Vol. 2). Mesa, AZ: Nueva Science Press.

Kitano, M. K., & Lewis, R. B. (2005). Resilience and coping: Implications for gifted children and youth at risk. *Roeper Review, 27,* 200–205.

Kitsantas, A., Zimmerman, B. J., & Cleary, T. (2000). The role of observation and emulation in the development of athletic self-regulation. *Journal of Educational Psychology, 92,* 811–817.

Koro-Ljungberg, M. (2002). Constructions of high academic achievement through the analysis of critical events. *Gifted Child Quarterly, 46,* 209–223.

Kurpius, S., Kerr, B., & Harkins, A. (Eds.). (2005). *Handbook for counseling girls and women: Talent, risk, and resiliency.* Mesa, AZ: Nueva Science Press.

Lee, S., & Olszewski-Kubilius, P. (2006). The emotional intelligence, moral judgment, and leadership of academically gifted adolescents. *Journal for the Education of the Gifted, 30*, 29–67.

Levesque, M., Blais, M. R., & Hess, U. (2004). Motivation, discretionary organizational behaviors, and wellbeing in an African setting: When is it a duty? *Canadian Journal of Behavioural Science, 36*, 321–332.

Lubinski, D., & Benbow, C. P. (2006). Study of mathematically precocious youth after 35 years: Uncovering the antecedents for the development of math-science expertise. *Perspectives on Psychological Science, 1*, 316–345.

Martin, L. L., & Tesser, A. (Eds.). (1996). *Striving and feeling*. Mahwah, NH: Lawrence Erlbaum.

Masten, A. S. (2001). Ordinary magic: Resilience processes in development. *American Psychologist, 56*, 227–238.

Masten, A. S., & Marie-Gabrielle, J. (2002). Resilience in development. In C. R. Snyder (Ed.), *Handbook of positive psychology* (pp. 74–88). London: Oxford University Press.

Mayer, J. D., Salovey, P., & Caruso, D. R. (2000). Emotional intelligence as zeitgeist, as personality, and as a mental ability. In R. Bar-On & D. A. Parker (Eds.), *The handbook of emotional intelligence: Theory, development, assessment, and application at home, school, and in the workplace* (pp. 92–117). San Francisco: Jossey Bass.

McCoach, D. B., & Siegle, D. (2003). Factors that differentiate underachieving gifted students from high-achieving gifted students. *Gifted Child Quarterly, 47*, 144–154.

Miles, M. B., & Huberman, A. M. (1994). *Qualitative data analysis*. Thousand Oaks, CA: Sage.

Moon, S. M. (1993). Using the Purdue Three-Stage Model: Developing talent at the secondary level. *Journal of Secondary Gifted Education, 5*(2), 31–35.

Moon, S. M. (2003a). Developing personal talent. In F. J. Mönks & H. Wagner (Eds.), *Development of human potential: Investment into our future. Proceedings of the 8th Conference of the European Council for High Ability (ECHA). Rhodes, October 9–13, 2002* (pp. 11–21). Bad Honnef, Germany: K.H. Bock.

Moon, S. M. (2003b). Personal talent. *High Ability Studies, 14*(1), 5–21.

Moon, S. M., & Dillon, D. R. (1995). Multiple exceptionalities: A case study. *Journal for the Education of the Gifted, 18*, 111–130.

Moon, S. M., Feldhusen, J. F., & Dillon, D. R. (1994). Long-term effects of an enrichment program based on the Purdue Three-Stage Model. *Gifted Child Quarterly, 38*, 38–48.

Moon, S. M., & Ray, K. (2006). Personal and social talent development. In F. A. Dixon & S. M. Moon (Eds.), *The handbook of secondary gifted education* (pp. 249–280). Waco, TX: Prufrock Press.

Moon, S. M., Zentall, S. S., Grskovic, J. A., Hall, A., & Stormont, M. (2001). Emotional and social characteristics of boys with AD/HD and/or giftedness: A comparative case study. *Journal for the Education of the Gifted, 24*, 207–247.

Neihart, M. (2000). Gifted children with Asperger's syndrome. *Gifted Child Quarterly, 44*, 222–230.

Neihart, M. (2002). Risk and resilience in gifted children: A conceptual framework. In M. Neihart, S. M. Reis, N. M. Robinson & S. M. Moon (Eds.), *The social and emotional development of gifted children: What do we know?* (pp. 113–122). Waco, TX: Prufrock Press.

Noble, K. D., Subotnik, R. F., & Arnold, K. D. (1999). To thine own self be true: A model of female talent development. *Gifted Child Quarterly, 43*, 140–149.

Nokelainen, P., Tirri, K., & Merenti-Valimaki, H.-L. (2007). Investigating the influence of attribution styles on the development of mathematical talent. *Gifted Child Quarterly, 51*, 64–81.

Pausupathi, M., Staudinger, U. M., & Baltes, P. B. (1999). *The emergence of wisdom-related knowledge and judgment during adolescence.* Berlin: Max Planck Institute for Human Development.

Pelletier, L. G., Fortier, M. S., Vallerand, R. J., & Briere, N. M. (2001). Associations among perceived autonomy support, forms of self-regulation, and persistence: A prospective study. *Motivation and Emotion, 25*, 279–306.

Peterson, C. (2000). The future of optimism. *American Psychologist, 55*, 44–55.

Peterson, J. S. (2000). A follow-up study of one group of achievers and underachievers four years after high school graduation. *Roeper Review, 22*, 217–224.

Peterson, J. S. (2001). Successful adults who were adolescent underachievers. *Gifted Child Quarterly, 45*, 236–250.

Ratelle, C. F., Vallerand, R. J., Chantal, Y., & Provencher, P. (2005). Cognitive adaptation and mental health: A motivational analysis. *European Journal of Social Psychology, 34*, 459–476.

Rathunde, K. (1996). Family context and talented adolescents' optimal experience in school-related activities. *Journal of Research on Adolescence, 6*, 605–628.

Reis, S. M. (1998). *Work left undone: Choices and compromises of talented females.* Mansfield Center, CT: Creative Learning Press.

Reis, S. M., Colbert, R. D., & Hébert, T. P. (2004). Understanding resilience in diverse, talented students in an urban high school. *Roeper Review, 27*, 110–120.

Reis, S. M., Hébert, T. P., Diaz, E. I., Maxfield, L. R., & Ratley, M. E. (1995). *Case studies of talented students who achieve and underachieve in an urban high school* (Research Monograph No. 95120). Storrs: National Research Center on the Gifted and Talented, University of Connecticut.

Renzulli, J. S., & Reis, S. M. (1985). *The schoolwide enrichment model: A comprehensive plan for educational excellence.* Mansfield Center, CT: Creative Learning Press.

Robazza, C., Pellizzari, M., & Hanin, Y. (2004). Emotion self-regulation and athletic performance: An application of the IZOF model. *Psychology of Sport and Exercise, 5*, 379–404.

Rousseau, F. L., & Vallerand, R. J. (2000). Does motivation mediate the influence of social factors on educational consequences. *Psychological Reports, 87*, 812–814.

Schunk, D. H. (1981). Modeling and attributional effects on children's achievement: A self-efficacy analysis. *Journal of Educational Psychology, 73*, 93–105.

Schunk, D. H. (1982). Verbal self-regulation as a facilitator of children's achievement and self-efficacy. *Human Learning, 1*, 265–277.

Schunk, D. H., & Cox, P. D. (1986). Strategy training and attributional feedback with learning disabled students. *Journal of Educational Psychology, 78*, 201–209.

Schunk, D. H., & Hanson, A. R. (1985). Peer models: Influence of peer-model attributes on children's beliefs and learning. *Journal of Educational Psychology, 81*, 54–61.

Schunk, D. H., Hanson, A. R., & Cox, P. D. (1987). Peer model attributes and children's achievement behaviors. *Journal of Educational Psychology, 79*, 54–61.

Schunk, D. H., & Zimmerman, B. J. (Eds.). (1994). *Self-regulation of learning and performance.* Hillsdale, NJ: Lawrence Erlbaum.

Schunk, D. H., & Zimmerman, B. J. (Eds.). (1998). *Self-regulated learning: From teaching to self-reflective practice*. New York: Guilford.

Seligman, M. E. P., & Csikszentmihalyi, M. (2000). Positive psychology: An introduction. *American Psychologist, 55*(1), 5–14.

Sheldon, K. M., Ryan, R. M., Deci, E. L., & Kasser, T. (2004). The independent effects of goal contents and motives on well-being: It's both what you pursue and why you pursue it. *Personality and Social Psychology, 30,* 475–486.

Snyder, C. R., & Lopez, S. J. (Eds.). (2002). *Handbook of positive psychology*. Oxford, England: Oxford University Press.

Speirs Neumeister, K. L. (2004). Understanding the relationship between perfectionism and achievement motivation in gifted college students. *Gifted Child Quarterly, 48,* 219–231.

Speirs Neumeister, K. L., & Finch, H. (2006). Perfectionism in high-ability students: Relational precursors and influences on achievement motivation. *Gifted Child Quarterly, 50,* 238–251.

Staudinger, U. M., & Baltes, P. B. (1996). Interactive minds: A facilitative setting for wisdom-related performance. *Journal of Personality and Social Psychology, 71,* 746–762.

Sternberg, R. J. (1996). *Successful intelligence*. New York: Simon & Schuster.

Sternberg, R. J. (2000). Wisdom as a form of giftedness. *Gifted Child Quarterly, 44,* 252–260.

Sternberg, R. J. (2002). The theory of successful intelligence as a basis for gifted education. *Gifted Child Quarterly, 46,* 265–277.

Sternberg, R. J., Forsythe, G. B., Hedlund, J., Horvath, J. A., Wagner, R. K., Williams, W. M., et al. (2000). *Practical intelligence in everyday life*. Cambridge, England: Cambridge University Press.

Strauss, A., & Corbin, J. (1990). *Basics of qualitative research*. Newbury Park, CA: Sage.

Terry, A. W. (2003). Effects of service learning on young, gifted adolescents and their communities. *Gifted Child Quarterly, 45,* 295–308.

Wagner, R. K., & Sternberg, R. J. (1985). Practical intelligence in real-world pursuits: The role of tacit knowledge. *Journal of Personality and Social Psychology, 49,* 436–458.

Wiese, B. S., Freund, A. M., & Baltes, P. B. (2002). Subjective career success and emotional well-being: Longitudinal predictive power of selecting, optimization, and compensation. *Journal of Vocational Behavior, 60,* 321–335.

Willett, J. B. (1997). Measuring change: What individual growth modeling buys you. In E. Amsel & K. A. Renninger (Eds.), *Change and development: Issues of theory, method, and application* (pp. 213–243). Mahwah, NJ: Lawrence Erlbaum.

Zentall, S. S., Moon, S. M., Hall, A. M., & Grskovic, J. A. (2001). Learning and motivational characteristics of boys with AD/HD and/or giftedness: A multiple case study. *Exceptional Children, 67,* 499–519.

Ziegler, A., & Heller, K. A. (1997). Attribution retraining for self-related cognitions among women. *Gifted and Talented International, 12,* 36–41.

Ziegler, A., & Heller, K. A. (2000). Effects of an attribution retraining with female students gifted in physics. *Journal for the Education of the Gifted, 23,* 217–243.

Ziegler, A., Monika, F., & Grassinger, R. (2005). Predicators of learned helplessness among average and mildly gifted girls and boys attending initial high school physics instruction in Germany. *Gifted Child Quarterly, 49,* 7–18.

Ziegler, A., & Stoeger, H. (2004). Evaluation of an attributional retraining (modeling technique) to reduce gender differences in chemistry instruction. *High Ability Studies, 15,* 63–83.

Zimmerman, B. J., & Kitsantas, A. (2002). Acquiring writing revision and self-regulatory skill through observation and emulation. *Journal of Educational Psychology, 94,* 660–668.

Zins, J. E., Bloodworth, M. E., Weissberg, R. P., & Walberg, H. J. (2004). The scientific base linking social and emotional learning to school success. In J. E. Zins, R. P. Weissberg, M. C. Want, & H. J. Walberg (Eds.), *Building academic success on social and emotional learning: What does the research say?* (pp. 3–22). New York: Teachers College Press.

Zuo, L., & Cramond, B. (2001). An examination of Terman's gifted children from the theory of identity. *Gifted Child Quarterly, 45,* 251–259.

AUTHOR NOTE

Work on this chapter was partially supported by a Purdue University Ross Fellowship to the second author. The chapter is based on papers presented by the first author at the 5th Biennial Henry B. and Joycelyn Wallace National Research Symposium on Talent Development, the University of Iowa, Iowa City, IA, May, 2000, and the 8th Conference of the European Council for High Ability (ECHA), Rhodes, October, 2002.

Chapter 33

POLICY AND ADVOCACY

James J. Gallagher

WHAT RESEARCH SHOWS

O f the various topics in the education of gifted students, policy and advocacy remains among the most silent when the question of "What does the research tell us?" is raised. *Policy* means the rules and standards by which scarce resources are allocated to almost unlimited social needs (Gallagher, 2004). *Advocacy* refers to those initiatives that attempt to influence policy decisions and policy decision makers.

The limited research base is not the result of a decision or conclusion regarding the importance of these areas. To the contrary, many in the field of gifted education declare that the future of the nation literally depends upon the next generation of gifted and talented students and the programs we design for them (see Gallagher, 2005; Renzulli, 2005). For example,

> If we believe, or act as if we believe, that our national security depends on how many nuclear weapons we

have stockpiled or how many divisions under arms we maintain, instead of nurturing the intellectual resources of coming generations, we may well tremble for the future of our nation. (Gallagher, 2005, p. 40)

As limited as our research knowledge of gifted students, their instruction, and their teachers may be, the investigations into the lack of needed policies—and the ways to advocate for those policies—that will best address the most effective and efficient means of providing essential resources to meet the educational and developmental needs of students who are gifted are even more absent. Why is there such a limited policy research base? The answer lies in public policy that allocates scarce research resources to other, more immediate priorities, or priorities that seem to be more in line with current cultural values. In the classic policy battle between *equity* and *excellence*, equity seems to be dominant in the current political environment. But, why have advocacy efforts not been more effective in establishing a higher priority for these gifted students and their education?

Investigating Social and Educational Change

Although traditional educational research focuses on children, their families, schools, and the like, policy research addresses the rules and standards, and the forces that impact on their development and use.

Engines of Change

For us to utilize policy studies and direct our advocacy, we need to focus on the traditional engines of change (Gallagher, 2002): *legislation, court decisions, administrative rule making* and *professional initiatives*, and see how they apply to gifted students and what investigations have been made or should be made of these initiatives.

Legislation. The preponderance of legislation on the education of gifted students can be found at the state level. Currently, 22 states have legislation relating to the establishment of programs—often as part of "exceptional children" legislation, a fact that has been financially favorable to those programs (Baker & Friedman-Nimz, 2000).

These findings can be compared with the field of educating children with disabilities where federal legislation has a major impact through such laws as PL 94-142 (the Education for All Handicapped Children Act of 1975), now IDEA (the Individuals with Disabilities Education Act, 1990). This legislation, and its subsequent amendments, has changed the shape of American education. In contrast, the only identifiable federal legislation for gifted students is the Javits Act (2002), a small demonstration program with limited funding (around 10 million dollars for the entire U.S.) for model projects and to support the National Research Center on the Gifted and Talented. Even so, the Javits priorities on minority children with giftedness have sharply increased the interest of this issue within gifted education.

Court Decisions. In contrast to children with disabilities, where the courts have delivered a multitude of decisions impacting on American education (see, e.g., *Pennsylvania Association for Retarded Children v. Commonwealth of Pennsylvania*, 1972, which guaranteed a free and appropriate public education for all children with disabilities), only a limited number of court cases have had major impact on gifted students. The most telling of these court actions, or threatened court actions, has been the work of the Office of Civil Rights that identified the lack of minority students in programs for the gifted as a possible breach of civil rights (Karnes & Marquardt, 2000). These actions or threatened actions have caused school systems to examine identification and programming procedures with the goal of providing gifted services to greater numbers of minority students (Ford & Harris, 1999).

Administrative Rule Making. When legislation and court actions are translated into practical rules for school systems, these administrative rules written to implement policy become extremely important influences on practice. For example, schools may have a rule that students cannot be enrolled prior to the age of 5, which effectively limits schools from using early admission to kindergarten as a means of serving a rapidly developing young child. North Carolina has passed legislation (see Section 115-364d) allowing schools to admit students to kindergarten early, essentially overruling local school limitations. Unfortunately, the rules requiring parents to collect the data required to receive permission is so time consuming that the child may be old enough to enter kindergarten under the traditional policy before permission for early admission is granted.

Professional Initiatives. Research initiatives can influence policy by purposefully designing studies that will yield information to impact educational policy. Table 1 shows some of the data-gathering devices used singularly or in combination in policy studies. Because policy relies heavily on perception and attitudes of key players in policy development or maintenance, such perceptions are often the target of these studies and qualitative analysis is used to generate results.

One example of policy studies that have been driven by investigators who wish to use the results to influence existing policies is the major literature review on educational acceleration by Colangelo, Assouline, and Gross (2004). They focus on debunking some of the common ideas about the dangers of educational acceleration and synthesizing the literature that is strongly positive on the benefits of acceleration. This is research that can be used to encourage increased use of policies supporting acceleration.

T A B L E   1

Data Gathering Devices for Policy Studies

Document Analysis

The analysis of state or local legislation, rules and regulations, or policy documents on issues such as eligibility and transitions.

Structured Interviews

A structured interview format by which large numbers of persons in state departments, universities, and local programs can give their viewpoints on a set of common issues.

Focus Groups

An interview with 8–10 persons with common experiences or background on a prearranged topic. Especially designed to bring forth barriers to effective policy implementation and solutions.

Case Studies

The collection of interview data, survey data, and documents review to determine the effects of policy on a particular program, community, or state. Many different sources of data are synthesized and triangulated to create an overall portrait.

Surveys

A set of carefully designed questions that focuses on determining what may be happening in given programs, communities, or states. More useful in determining what is going on than the dynamics of why something is happening.

Synthesis of Related Data

In many instances, there are relevant data sources that can be useful in addressing a policy issue, even if the data has been collected for other purposes (e.g., statewide head counts, financial data on special and regular education).

Literature Reviews

A drawing together of existing literature around a particular policy (e.g., inclusion). Major effort will usually be made to draw in literature from other related fields (e.g., Head Start, maternal and child health, policy implementation, general finance issues).

Program development combined with research is another important professional initiative for policy and advocacy in gifted education. For example, the Study of Mathematically Precocious Youth (SMPY) created by Julian Stanley to identify middle school age students gifted in the area of mathematics using the Scholastic Aptitude Test established a baseline, which was then expanded to multiple sites (Stanley, 1997). Stanley designed extra learning opportunities for gifted youth in schools and summer programs that have continued for 40 years, with continuing research on the students and their achievements (see Pyryt, 2000).

When the middle school professional associations led a movement to develop policies that impacted negatively on gifted students, such as eliminating ability grouping (see George, 1988), Gallagher, Coleman, and Nelson (1995) used a survey strategy to compare the attitudes of middle school teachers with those of educators of gifted students. Results of the responses of a random selection of 100 teachers from the membership lists of the Middle School Association, the Association for Supervision and Curriculum Developmental, and the National Association for Gifted Children revealed major differences in attitudes between the two groups of teachers. Middle school teachers believed that identifying students as gifted caused social difficulty for them, that the regular curriculum challenged gifted students more than the teachers of the gifted believed, and that gifted children did not benefit from being grouped together. Major gaps in the attitudes of the two groups of teachers were used to encourage interaction between professional groups, resulting in articles exchanged between journals and meetings to help gain a common vision of gifted students.

Purcell (2004) reported on a case study of the effects of the elimination of programming for gifted students. Through parent interviews, document analysis, and teacher interviews, she found a sharp increase in boredom and an increase in disruptive behavior by gifted students after the elimination of special programming. Half of the parents said they were considering other placements outside the public schools.

Document analysis was also the strategy used in a review of textbooks by Renzulli and Reis (2004). Their analysis identified a "dumbing down of the curriculum." Textbooks have been simplified so that they can be mastered by the great majority of students, even those having trouble in reading so they present little challenge to the gifted and talented.

ADVOCACY INITIATIVES

Some of the attempts to change the priorities for gifted students have been the publication of major reports from scholarly panels or from international test results. In 1983, the report "A Nation at Risk" (National Commission on Excellence in Education, 1983) declared that the nation was committing "unthinking unilateral educational disarmament" (¶ 2) in its ignoring the education of gifted students. A decade later another report "National Excellence" (U.S. Department of Education, Office of Educational Research and Improvement, 1993) reported that "Most regular classroom teachers make few, if any, provisions for gifted and talented students. These youngsters spend most of their time working on grade level assignments" (p. 2). It also pointed out that only 1-cent out of every $100 spent on K–12 education in the U.S. is spent on special opportunities for talented students.

A report of Trends in International Mathematics and Science study (TIMSS; Mullis, Martin, & Foy, 2005) stressed the low performance of American students. Students in the United States in advanced calculus and physics classes were only able to perform at the level of average students from other countries in these subjects. These reports and studies were designed to alert the American public and its public decision makers, on the unfavorable status of our most advanced students. Such reports have not had major policy impact at the present time.

Another advocacy attempt to influence policy in general education rested on the outlining of the benefits to all students that come from educating gifted children (Tomlinson & Callahan, 1992). They pointed to the increased emphasis on such curricular ideas as advanced thinking processes (problem solving and problem finding) and metacognitive processes (planning and strategies for attacking problems) that were first identified as components of curriculum for gifted students and later adopted by general education. In addition, the emphasis in gifted education on multiple modes of instruction, standards of excellence in content fields, and seeking hidden talent through unconventional methods (e.g., portfolios) all influence general education programs. In this fashion, we illustrate the value to all students of the education of gifted students.

Another device to influence public policy has been the development of standards by professional groups. In *What Every Special Educator Must Know*, The Association for the Gifted (TAG), a division of the Council for Exceptional Children, provided a statement on "Knowledge and Skills" that should form the basis for educating teachers of the gifted (CEC, 2000). The National Association for Gifted Children has also developed a set of program standards (Landrum, Callahan, & Shaklee, 1999) to guide local and state educators in the program development and curricular differentiation for gifted and talented students. Such standards can provide a base for discussions with general educators or public decision makers on quality education for gifted students.

SUGGESTIONS FOR FUTURE POLICY STUDIES

Although the policy and advocacy initiatives described above have been presented as means of influencing the education of gifted children, data on the effectiveness of the policies, research efforts, and advocacy efforts have not been the subject of systematic policy analysis. This leaves a scarcity of good guidelines for what works or best influences change in policy or programs. The shortage of studies on policy and advocacy should be of concern to activists in gifted education. Such studies can point the way to identify effective strategies to help advocate for further public action. The following are a few suggested policy studies.

Document Analysis

A comprehensive analysis of the effects of education regulations at the state level should be conducted to identify specific mention of the needs of gifted students. Suggested standards to local school systems for increased personnel preparation and resources for gifted students can help guide further program differentiation. Comparison of these policies and their effectiveness to the standards, such as those offered by NAGC can be used as the basis for advocacy for change in the direction of meeting needs of gifted students.

Demographic Studies

Analysis of the impact of policy directives relating to the inclusion of culturally different gifted students in programs for the gifted and charting the subsequent increase in such children in special programs and their success can be used to assess the relative effects of such changes in policy. The question underlying this type of policy study lies in assessing impact and change at the local level (in increasing diversity in programs) as a result of this increased state interest.

Synthesis of Related Data

Analysis of scores of gifted students who have participated in the National Assessment of Educational Progress (NAEP) may be used to ascertain the proportion who attained the Advanced (not just the Proficient) level in content fields. Any substantial number not achieving the highest score would indicate shortcomings in challenging these students.

Case Study

Creation of case studies of school systems identified as having excellent services for gifted students using teacher and parent surveys, interviews of administrators, and the like can be used to document the means through which they were able to create these programs and operate them efficiently. Such studies can provide guidance in policy creation and advocacy based on the factors associated with success.

Focus Groups

Interviews with representatives of the media can be used to explore why gifted and talented students and their education have not warranted more attention in the media.

The results of such studies and those like them could provide a strong base for advocacy and policy improvement for gifted and talented students. Such focus groups could also be used to suggest more appropriate ways to approach media outlets on the topic of educating children with special gifts.

NEEDED ADVOCACY RESEARCH

One of the missing components in research on gifted students has been the absence of attempts to investigate the effectiveness of advocacy efforts on their behalf. We can be reasonably certain that the Sputnik scare of the 1950s began some strong advocacy for changed curriculum that resulted in the major curriculum initiatives supported by the National Science Foundation (e.g., Physical Science Study Committee, Biological Sciences Curriculum Study) of the 1960s, but there is no data available to show how and why such advocacy paid off.

For example, identification of a specific goal such as major changes in state legislation for gifted students, and subsequent tracking of the various individual and organizational advocacy efforts, can serve as the basis of analysis of advocacy effectiveness. If the advocacy initiatives are successful, interviews with key decision makers on which of these efforts was most influential on their decisions would identify relatively influential strategies.

Even more important might be a study as to why advocacy for programs for gifted students turns out to be pallid and hesitant compared to other advocacy efforts. What is the reluctance to launch strong advocacy efforts on such issues that many observers agree are vital to our society? Is it the fear of being labeled an elitist? Is it the fact that these students are doing pretty well anyway and so the pressure for change is not as great as it would be for parents of students with disabilities? Is it fear that they will be accused of creating unfair advantage for their own children?

Without research on the effects of policy initiatives, the field has little substantive guidance on the relative methods for advocating for policy at the local, state, or national level. Then, if effective policy can be identified, the research on advocacy provides little guidance in how to effectively advocate for their enactment. Research initiatives are needed to guide those seeking guidance in addressing both policy and advocacy.

REFERENCES

Baker, B., & Friedman-Nimz, R. (2000). *State policies and equal opportunity: The example of gifted education.* Lawrence: University of Kansas.

Colangelo, N., Assouline, S. G., & Gross, M. U. M. (2004). *A nation deceived: How schools hold back America's brightest students* (Vol. 1). Iowa City, IA: The Connie Belin & Jacqueline N. Blank International Center for Gifted Education and Talent Development.

Council for Exceptional Children. (2000). *What every special educator must know.* Reston, VA: Prentice Hall.

Ford, D., & Harris, J. (1999). *Multicultural gifted education.* New York: Teachers College.

Gallagher, J. J. (2002). *Society's role in educating gifted students: The role of public policy* (Research Monograph No. 02162). Storrs: National Research Center on the Gifted and Talented, University of Connecticut.

Gallagher, J. (Ed.). (2004). *Public policy in gifted education.* Thousand Oaks, CA: Corwin Press.

Gallagher, J. (2005, May 25) National security and educational excellence. *Education Week, 40,* 32–33.

Gallagher, J. J., Coleman, M. R., & Nelson, S. (1995). Perceptions of educational reform by educators representing middle schools, cooperative learning, and gifted education. *Gifted Child Quarterly, 39,* 66–76.

George, P. (1988). Tracking and ability grouping: Which way for the middle school? *Middle School Journal, 20,* 21–28.

Individuals With Disabilities Education Act, 20 U.S.C. §1401 et seq. (1990).

Karnes, F., & Marquardt, R. (2000). *Gifted children and legal issues: An update.* Scottsdale, AZ.: Gifted Psychology Press.

Landrum, M., Callahan, C. M., & Shaklee, B. (Eds.). (1999). *Aiming for excellence: Gifted program standards: Annotations to the NAGC pre-K–grade 12 gifted program standards.* Waco, TX: Prufrock Press.

Mullis, I. V. S., Martin, M. O., & Foy, P. (2005). *IEA's TIMSS 2003 international report on achievement in the mathematics cognitive domains.* Chestnut Hill, MA; International Association for the Evaluation of Educational Achievement.

National Commission on Excellence in Education. (1983). *A nation at risk.* Retrieved July 13, 2007, from http://www.ed.gov/pubs/NatAtRisk/risk.html

Pennsylvania Association for Retarded Children v. Commonwealth of Pennsylvania, 334 F. Supp. 1257 (1972).

Pyryt, M. (2000). Talent development in science and technology. In K. Heller, F. Mönks, R. Sternberg, & R. Subotnik (Eds.), *International handbook of gifted and talented* (pp. 427–438). Oxford, England: Elsevier.

Purcell, J. H. (2004). The effects of the elimination of gifted and talented programs on participating students and their parents. In J. J. Gallagher (Ed.), *Public policy in gifted education* (pp. 71–93). Thousand Oaks, CA: Corwin Press.

Renzulli, J. S. (2005, May 25). A quiet crisis clouding the future of R & D. *Education Week, 24,* 32–33, 40.

Renzulli, J. S., & Reis, S. M. (2004). The reform movement and the quiet crisis in gifted education. In J. J. Gallagher (Ed.), *Public policy in gifted education. Essential readings in gifted education* (pp. 1–19). Thousand Oaks, CA: Corwin Press.

Stanley, J. C. (1997). In the beginning: The study of intellectually precocious youth in C. Benbow & D. Lubinski (Eds.), *Intellectual talent: Psychometric and social issues* (pp. 225–235). Baltimore: Johns Hopkins University Press.

Title 5, Part D. [Jacob K. Javits Gifted and Talented Students Education Act of 1988], Elementary and Secondary Education Act of 1988 (2002), 20 U.S.C. Sec. 7253 et seq.

Tomlinson, C. A., & Callahan, C. M. (1992). In the public interest: Contributions of gifted education to general education in a time of change. *Gifted Child Quarterly, 36*, 183–189.

U.S. Department of Education, Office of Educational Research and Improvement. (1993). *National excellence: A case for developing America's talent.* Washington, DC: U.S. Government Printing Office.

Chapter 34

PRODIGIES

David Henry Feldman

rodigies have fascinated and amazed people for centuries; have played major roles in cultural, political, and religious movements in many cultures; have provoked controversy, as well as admiration; and have raised questions about issues concerning intelligence, the role of genes in development, general versus specific talents, creativity, and many other topics relevant to giftedness. In spite of the longstanding public interest in prodigies and their development, there has been relatively little research done that might help answer the many questions raised about them (Baumgarten, 1930; Feldman, 1986/1991; Radford, 1990a, 1990b; Winner, 1996, 2000; Wrightsman, 1983). In this chapter, I will summarize what is now known about child prodigies based on systematic research, organized around the questions often asked about them.

For the purposes of this chapter, a *child prodigy* is considered to be a child who performs and is recognized for performing at an adult professional level in a valued, highly demanding domain. This definition, while not accepted by all scholars, is used by most scholars who study child prodigies (Kenneson, 1998; Shavinina, 1999).

Before turning to the questions and the research, it is important to note that the word *prodigy* has a long history that extends beyond its current reference to children of extreme accomplishment in highly valued fields. The earliest known meaning of the prodigy was of a portent, or sign, that change was coming or that the natural order was about to transform. *Webster's Third International Dictionary* (Gove, 1961) defines a prodigy as "a monstrosity; something out of the usual course of nature, like a comet or meteor." This broader meaning of the term prodigy may help account for the complex reactions often found when encountering child prodigies and, perhaps, might help account for the paucity of research found in the literature. For example, a television commentary on a child prodigy (Adragon DeMello, a precocious college graduate from California) began as follows: "If child prodigies make you sick . . ." (BBC *Breakfast Time*, June 17, 1988; as cited in Radford, 1990a, p. 213).

HOW MANY STUDIES HAVE BEEN DONE ON CHILD PRODIGIES?

Although it is not possible to say with confidence, the number of studies of child prodigies is small, fewer than in most other areas of the study of giftedness (Feldman, 1993). At the end of the 19th and first two decades of the 20th century, there were several studies of children whose achievements in mathematics, music, chess, and writing would qualify as prodigious, culminating in two book-length works, one on a single musical prodigy (Revesz, 1925/1971), the other (Baumgarten, 1930) on nine children whose prodigiousness showed itself in several domains: chess, dance, drawing, geography, and music (five of the children were involved in music). Both of these works were by European psychologists and were originally published in German (Morelock & Feldman, 2003).

Few studies of prodigies appeared in the research literature between 1917 and 1986, the year when the first of two recent book-length research studies on prodigies was published (Feldman, 1986/1991; Kenneson, 1998). A search of Web-based PsychINFO yielded a total of 24 references, several of which were not primarily about child prodigies, and several others reported variations on the same material. This is an infinitesimal amount of research on a topic that would appear to be of great interest to the professional and nonprofessional communities alike.

Although not research per se, a number of popular books on prodigies have been published in the past two decades. These works, generally done by journalists, contain rich materials on the lives of individual cases like cyberneticist Norbert Wiener (Conway & Siegelman, 2005) and mathematicians William James Sidis (Wallace, 1986) and Srinivasa Ramanujan (Kanigel, 1991). NOVA television documentaries have been produced on Ramanujan, Andrew Wiles, and Einstein, among others, providing important materials that may be useful in future research (Morelock & Feldman, 2003).

WHAT FIELDS PRODUCE THE MOST PRODIGIES?

Music, chess, and mathematics, in that order, account for most cases of prodigies historically, although greater numbers seem to be appearing in art and literature (especially poetry) in recent years. A Web search using *Wikipedia* (an online encyclopedia) listed prodigies in 14 fields, including art, music, mathematics, physics, literature, medicine, sports, academics, mental calculators, computing, military, languages, and politics. The vast majority of reported cases have been boys, but in recent decades the numbers of girl prodigies has increased dramatically (Feldman, 1986/1991; Goldsmith, 2000). Several of the fields in the *Wikipedia* list are not typically included as sources of prodigies in research studies (e.g., politics, military, sports, medicine), and the definition of what constitutes a prodigy in that publication is not necessarily consistent with the research literature (see Edmunds & Noel, 2003). Still, 94 individuals (living and deceased) are listed on the site as child prodigies. As information becomes shared more easily around the world, numbers of reported prodigy cases are likely to increase, although definitional issues and shifting cultural interests and preoccupations no doubt will continue to play a role in what kinds of phenomena are reported and labeled prodigious (Edmunds & Noel, 2003; Shavinina, 1999).

There are, for example, cultures that depend on child prodigies for their identity and continuity, such as the Tibetan form of Buddhism, which seeks its spiritual leaders among very young (2- or 3-year-old) children (Powers, 1995; Thurman, 1995). Within these cultural contexts, it is a matter of great importance that the right children be identified, and specialized techniques have been developed to carry out searches for future leaders, typically within a reincarnation framework (Stevenson, 1977). In the West, there has been increased interest in spiritual prodigies, with studies on "moral exemplars" at the adult level revealing interesting qualities about their childhood experiences (Colby & Damon, 1992; Schwartz, 2005; Stevenson, 1977).

Domains that produce prodigies tend to be those that are: (1) highly rule bound; (2) have relatively transparent knowledge structures; (3) have developed technologies and/or techniques for transmission of their knowledge; (4) have criteria for excellence that are either transparent or accessible; and (5) able to be adapted to the capabilities of the very young child (Feldman, 1986/1991; Winner, 1996, 2000). Small-scale musical instruments like the ½- and ¾-size cello and violin are examples of a domain providing specialized artifacts that give greater access to that domain's knowledge. Computers have evolved to be ever more "user friendly," making it likely this domain will soon be producing prodigies if it has not already done so (Feldman, 1986/1991). Therefore, the domains that produce prodigies apparently are not a fixed set, but rather are domains that share certain qualities and characteristics. How a culture values a particular domain also will affect the likelihood that it will be a fertile context for developing prodigies (Feldman, 1986/1991, 1993).

HOW MUCH OF A CHILD PRODIGY'S TALENT IS INBORN?

Questions concerning the role of natural talent in prodigies have been raised frequently in recent decades (Ericsson & Charness, 1994; Ericsson & Faivre, 1988; Ericsson, Krampe, & Tesch-Romer, 1993; Feldman & Katzir, 1998; Shanks, 1999; Winner, 2000). Previously, supernatural sources were widely assumed to cause prodigies, and in some cultures still are (Stevenson, 1977). In the past two centuries, as other phenomena have become more naturalized, claims about biological and/or genetic causes more often have been invoked.

For much of the last century, a very high IQ was taken to be a source of prodigious talent, and so the ability of the prodigy was perceived to be mostly biological (e.g., Hollingworth, 1942). More recently, some researchers have claimed that natural or inborn talent plays no significant role in the remarkable performance that marks the prodigy. The prodigy's feats are, in this view, a function of training and practice (Ericsson & Charness, 1994; Shanks, 1999). There have been challenges and counter claims to the radical environmental point of view (e.g., Feldman & Katzir, 1998; Winner, 1996, 2000), and the issue remains controversial. At this point, most scholars would endorse an interactionist perspective, acknowledging that nature makes a powerful contribution to the possibility of being a child prodigy, but nurture must play its role or that potential will not fulfill its promise (Feldman, 1986/1991).

Most of the work to date on child prodigies has been case study research, done prior to the availability of direct assessment of brain and neurological structure and at an age that would make conclusions about genetic differences, or even early biological sources, nearly impossible to discover. There have been few studies of brain anatomy and neurological structure of child prodigies; the closest have been studies of musicians versus nonmusicians (Baeck, 2002; Banich, 1997; Popp, 2004; Schlaug, 2001); of autistic individuals who have performed at remarkable levels in various domains (Gardner, 1993; Policastro & Gardner, 1988; Selfe, 1977; Synder, 2001; Snyder & Thomas, 1997); and of brain damaged and/or learning-disabled individuals (Geschwind & Galaburda, 1985; Winner, 2000).

Research on the so-called "Mozart effect," a movement that promotes the idea that early exposure to classical music may enhance intellectual development, also has been interpreted as evidence that exceptional development may require intense early stimulation (Jones & Zigler, 2002; Rauscher & Shaw, 1998; Rauscher, Shaw, & Ky, 1993). Very controversial and largely done with older children and young adults, research on the Mozart effect so far has contributed little to the question of natural, biological causes as the source of child prodigies, even in music (e.g., Jones & Zigler, 2002; Steele, Brown, & Stoecker, 1999; see Shaw, 2000).

A more systems-based explanation for prodigies has been offered by Feldman (Feldman, 1986/1991; Radford, 1990b); this framework, called "co-incidence," keys on the interplay among several kinds of influences that must be coordinated over time to produce remarkable early achievement. Included are biological and genetic advantages, family, teachers, a receptive society, a culture that offers opportunities for development of the specific talent, and a period of history where the domain is sufficiently developed to be optimal for the child. Other versions of this notion of interplay among vectors or dimensions that include chance and other variables have been proposed, but not for prodigies specifically (e.g., Radford, 1990a, 1990b; Simonton, 1997; Sternberg, 1999).

HOW IMPORTANT ARE TEACHERS AND FAMILIES IN THE DEVELOPMENT OF CHILD PRODIGIES?

Given that the data base for child prodigies is extremely small and spread out over more than a century, with fewer than two large-scale studies during each decade, it is difficult to reach firm conclusions about the role that teachers and families play in the development of child prodigies (Radford, 1990a, 1990b).

In one of the most recent book-length studies (Feldman, 1986/1991), six boys were followed for several years as they pursued mastery in chess (two cases), mathematics, writing, and music (two cases). The boys were as young as 3½, and as old as 9 when recruited to the study. In every case, family resources put into the child's development in his area of interest were substantial, and all families were relatively affluent. Families reoriented and organized their lives around the child's talent, and one of the parents (mothers in all cases except for the two chess players, where fathers were central) became deeply involved in fostering the child's opportunities for appropriate challenges and access to optimal instructional resources. The families were striking in their focus and determination to foster the child's gifts, putting large proportions of their resources into the development (and sometimes the promotion) of the child's talents.

Howe (1982, 1988, 1999) and Radford (1990a) have raised questions about the wisdom of such "hot housing" of children to maximize their early achievements, but the empirical evidence supports the conclusion that such efforts are the rule rather than the exception with prodigies. The main concerns are that putting such intense pressure on young children may work counter to the likelihood that they will later fulfill their great potential, or that the over-zealous efforts of parents themselves may impact the process of development in their field or domain in unfavorable ways. Others have questioned the use of the term *prodigy* itself as too emotionally loaded, preferring "precocious" as a better label for the remarkable early progress of children in certain domains (Edmunds & Noel, 2003).

As for teachers, very deep commitments and attachments to teachers were found across all six cases. Families tended to place great trust in the teachers of their children and gave over much of the responsibility for the child's prog-ress to the teacher. When progress diminished, or when there arose conflicts between families and teachers, great efforts were made to compromise and adjust so as to sustain the teacher/student relationship.

If and when it became clear to parents and/or their children that a teacher could no longer foster the child's progress optimally, they would look for another instructional environment (Bloom, 1985; Feldman, 1986/1991). In all cases, sustained instruction and appropriate opportunities to challenge the child's skills were essential to the child being labeled a prodigy. In all cases, the children were passionate about learning in their chosen area, and their progress was often astonishingly rapid, but based on current research, it appears that the ancient belief that prodigies are born with their abilities full-blown and that they require no assistance from more knowledgeable others is not based on systematic data, at least among Western prodigies.

Traditions that seek children as young as one year old to be future religious leaders maintain a belief that the capabilities for reaching the highest levels of practice in the relevant religious domain are in the child when he or she is born (Powers, 1995; Thurman, 1995). Even in these situations, though, the future religious leader or *lama* goes through one of the most intense and all-encom-passing educational programs imaginable, typically spanning several decades (Thurman, 1995). In these cases, families are required to all but withdraw from the process and turn over their children to religious mentors and special insti-tutions (Mackenzie, 1988, 1995). To date, little systematic empirical research has been carried out with children identified as being future religious leaders in Western or non-Western cultural contexts.

WHAT IS THE RELATIONSHIP BETWEEN BEING A PRODIGY AND BEING CREATIVE?

It is important to recognize that the prodigy is not necessarily creative. Research to date has shown that most prodigies do not become major cre-ative contributors to their fields; their distinctive characteristics are very rapid mastery of existing knowledge and skill, but relatively rarely does a prodigy transform a domain in a significant way (Csikszentmihalyi, 1999; Feldman, 1986/1991; Gardner, 1983; Gruber & Wallace, 1999; Winner, 1996, 2000). One of the conclusions of research is that creativity and prodigiousness may be related in certain fields (e.g., in music it is rare for a successful classical composer to have not been a music prodigy), but the two are nonetheless quite distinct. Prodigiousness refers to the highly precocious mastery of an existing domain, whereas creativity refers to the transformation of that domain in ways that are embraced by the field (Csikszentmihalyi, 1999; Feldman, Csikszentmihalyi, & Gardner, 1994; Winner, 2000).

The fact that, especially in the West, Mozart often is seen as the quintessential child prodigy probably has contributed to the tendency to conflate prodigiousness with creative contribution. Mozart was a relatively rare case, even among prodigies, in that his drive to transform was powerful from his earliest years (Feldman, 1994). Even so, Mozart's first major work to be included in many classical repertoires (the Piano Concerto No. 9, K. 271) was written when he was about 16 (Weisberg, 1999; Winner, 2000). Mozart's case also confirms what is often called the "10 year rule" (Gardner, 1993; Hayes, 1989), which shows that across many fields it takes at least 10 years of sustained, organized, and guided effort to reach world-class levels of performance.

WHAT ARE THE MAJOR AREAS FOR FUTURE RESEARCH ON CHILD PRODIGIES?

With such a small number of studies of prodigies, and with all of the major studies using a form of case study methodology, there are clearly many questions for future research. Only a few dozen cases have been studied systematically, the majority in music, in more than three quarters of a century. Here are some challenges for future research on child prodigies:

1. Are there specific brain structures involved in the activity of prodigies in different fields (Gardner, 1983, 1993)? For example, do music prodigies use different parts of their brains to do music than chess prodigies use to do chess? Do music prodigies use different parts of their brains than other trained musicians who started their training later (say, after age 10)?

2. Are there brain activity and brain usage differences between child prodigies in various fields and individuals with exceptionally high IQs who perform at approximately the same levels (Morelock, 1995)? What about brain activity and usage differences between prodigies and mono savants (Treffert, 1989) in the same fields (e.g., mathematics, drawing, music)?

3. Do prodigies simply move more quickly through levels of expertise in their domains, or are the processes of development qualitatively distinct (Feldman, 1986/1991)?

4. Why have girl prodigies started to appear in certain fields in the West (and in a few instances, the East) much more frequently than has been true historically (Goldsmith, 1987)? In music, chess, poetry, art, and mathematics, there are girls who are reaching astonishing levels of performance. Why?

5. Is the prodigy phenomenon universal? Do all cultures have versions of child prodigies? In the same fields? What roles do prodigies play in various cultural contexts (e.g., in Nepalese culture, prodigies are central to religious and spiritual life, whereas in the West prodigies serve more as exemplars of early achievement and exceptional promise; Mackenzie, 1988, 1995)?

6. Do fields that have produced prodigies have common characteristics? Are there new fields (e.g., computer science) where prodigies are likely to (or have already begun to) appear, and others where it is less likely that new prodigies will emerge (Feldman, 1986/1991)? Related, how much do shifts in cultural resources and values influence the number and diversity of prodigy cases?

7. Are the cognitive, emotional, and physical developmental processes of prodigies the same as those in other children (but accelerated), or are there processes unique to the prodigy? What unique challenges, if any, confront parents, teachers, and other stakeholders in the prodigy's development (Feldman, 1986/1991)?

8. What kinds of theoretical frameworks are likely to be most productive in helping guide future research with prodigies? Should there be an integrative framework that compares and contrasts various kinds of extreme cases (prodigies, savants, high-IQ cases; Morelock & Feldman, 2003), or an even broader framework that includes all forms of development (Feldman & Fowler, 1997), or a special theory to account for the specific characteristics of the child prodigy phenomenon itself? In other words, what kind of framework will best guide future research efforts?

From these many questions awaiting future work, it should be evident that research with prodigies has just begun, contrasting dramatically with the prodigies themselves who seemingly fly through their domains. We may hope the pace of research will gain momentum in the coming decades, and it will shed greater light on this venerable, elusive, and fascinating topic.

WHAT WE KNOW

- There is relatively little research on child prodigies. Only a few dozen cases have been studied during the past century.

- There is only a partial consensus on what the definition of a child prodigy should be. From its original meaning of "something out of the usual course of nature," the prodigy has come to be defined as a child who performs at an adult professional level in a demanding and valued field.

- Until recently, there were very few girl prodigies in the literature. A major cultural shift has occurred in the past few decades. Girl prodigies have now appeared in all of the fields where prodigies occur.

- Until recently, there were few prodigies in the visual arts and poetry. These fields were seen as inaccessible to the prodigy, but several cases (boys and girls) have shown that these fields are not excluded, although they are still rare.

- Prodigies are the product of natural talents and favorable environmental circumstances. Most contemporary explanations of the prodigy are based on systems principles, which emphasize how several dimensions must interact productively over at least 10 years to produce what we call a prodigy.

- There is as yet no evidence that provides information on the brains of child prodigies versus other children. Although brain research has dramatically increased in recent years, few studies of child prodigies have been carried out to date.

REFERENCES

Baeck, E. (2002). The neural networks of music. *European Journal of Neurology, 9*, 449–456.

Banich, M. T. (1997). *Neuropsychology: The neural bases of mental function*. Boston: Houghton Mifflin.

Baumgarten, F. (1930). *Wunderkinder: Psychologische unterschungen*. Leipzig, Germany: Johann Ambrosius Barth.

Bloom, B. S. (1985). *Developing talent in young people*. New York: Ballantine Books.

Colby, A., & Damon, W. (1992). *Some do care: Contemporary lives of moral commitment*. New York: The Free Press.

Conway, F., & Siegelman, J. (2005). *Dark hero of the information age: In search of Norbert Wiener, the father of cybernetics*. New York: Basic.

Csikszentmihalyi, M. (1999). Implications of a systems perspective for the study of creativity. In R. J. Sternberg (Ed.), *Handbook of creativity* (pp. 313–335). Cambridge, England: Cambridge University Press.

Edmunds, A. L., & Noel, K. A. (2003). Literary precocity: An exceptional case among exceptional cases. *Roeper Review, 25*, 185–194.

Ericsson, K. A., & Charness, N. (1994). Expert performance: Its structure and acquisition. *American Psychologist, 49*, 725–747.

Ericsson, K. A., & Faivre, R. I. (1988). What's exceptional about exceptional abilities? In L. Obler & D. Fein (Eds.), *The exceptional brain: Neuropsychology of talent and special abilities* (pp. 436–473). New York: Guilford Press.

Ericsson, K. A., Krampe, R., & Tesch-Romer, C. (1993). The role of deliberate practice in the acquisition of expert performance. *Psychological Review, 100*, 363–406.

Feldman, D. H. (with Goldsmith, L. T.). (1991). *Nature's gambit: Child prodigies and the development of human potential.* New York: Teachers College Press. (Original work published 1986)

Feldman, D. H. (1993). Child prodigies: A distinctive form of giftedness. *Gifted Child Quarterly, 37*, 188–193.

Feldman, D. H. (1994). Mozart and the transformational imperative. In J. M. Morris (Ed.), *On Mozart* (pp. 52–71). Cambridge, England: Cambridge University Press.

Feldman, D. H., Csikszentmihalyi, M., & Gardner, H. (1994). *Changing the world: A framework for the study of creativity.* Westport, CT: Praeger/Greenwood.

Feldman, D. H., & Fowler, C. (1997). The nature(s) of developmental change: Piaget, Vygotsky and the transition process. *New Ideas in Psychology, 15*, 195–210.

Feldman, D. H., & Katzir, T. (1998). Natural talents: An argument for the extremes. *Behavioral and Brain Sciences, 21*, 414.

Gardner, H. (1983). *Frames of mind.* New York: Basic Books.

Gardner, H. (1993). *Creating minds.* New York: Basic Books.

Geschwind, N., & Galaburda, A. M. (1985). *Cerebral lateralization: Biological mechanisms, associations, and pathology.* Cambridge, MA: MIT Press.

Goldsmith, L. T. (1987). Girl prodigies: Some evidence and some speculations. *Roeper Review, 10*, 74–82.

Goldsmith, L. T. (2000). Tracking trajectories of talent: Child prodigies growing up. In R. C. Friedman & M. B. Shore (Eds.), *Talents unfolding: Cognition and development* (pp. 89–118). Washington, DC: American Psychological Association.

Gove, P. B. (Ed.). (1961). *Webster's third new international dictionary.* Springfield, MA: G. & C. Merriam.

Gruber, H., & Wallace, D. (1999). The case study method and evolving systems approach for understanding unique creative people at work. In R. J. Sternberg (Ed.), *Handbook of creativity* (pp. 93–115). Cambridge, England: Cambridge University Press.

Hayes, J. R. (1989). Cognitive processes in creativity. In J. A. Glover, R. Ronning, & C. Reynolds (Eds.), *Handbook of creativity* (pp. 135–145). New York: Plenum.

Hollingworth, L. (1942). *Children above 180 IQ.* New York: Arno Press.

Howe, M. J. A. (1982). Biological evidence and the development of outstanding individuals. *American Psychologist, 37*, 1071–1081.

Howe, M. J. A. (1988). Intelligence as an explanation. *British Journal of Psychology, 79*, 349–360.

Howe, M. J. A. (1999). Prodigies and creativity. In R. J. Sternberg (Ed.), *Handbook of creativity* (pp. 431–446). Cambridge, England: Cambridge University Press.

Jones, S. M., & Zigler, E. (2002). The Mozart effect: Not learning from history. *Applied Developmental Psychology, 23*, 355–372.

Kanigel, R. (1991). *The man who knew infinity: A life of the genius Ramanujan.* New York: Pocket Books.

Kenneson, C. (1998). *Musical prodigies: Perilous journeys, remarkable lives.* Portland, OR: Amadeus Press.

Mackenzie, V. (1988). *The boy lama.* New York: Harper & Row.

Mackenzie, V. (1995). *Reborn in the west.* London: Bloomsbury.

Morelock, M. J. (1995). *The profoundly gifted child in family context*. Unpublished doctoral dissertation, Tufts University, Medford, MA.

Morelock, M. J., & Feldman, D. H. (2003). Extreme precocity: Prodigies, savants and children of extraordinarily high IQ. In N. Colangelo & G. A. Davis (Eds.), *Handbook of gifted education* (3rd ed., pp. 455–469). Boston: Allyn & Bacon.

Policastro, E., & Gardner, H. (1988). From case studies to robust generalizations: An approach to the study of creativity. In R. J. Sternberg (Ed.), *Handbook of creativity* (pp. 213–225). Cambridge, England: Cambridge University Press.

Popp, A. J. (2004). Music, musicians, and the brain: An exploration of musical genius. *Journal of Neurosurgery, 101*, 895–903.

Powers, J. (1995). *Introduction to Tibetan Buddhism*. Ithaca, NY: Snow Lion Publications.

Radford, J. (1990a). *Child prodigies and exceptional early achievers*. New York: The Free Press.

Radford, J. (1990b). The problem of the prodigy. In M. J. A. Howe (Ed.), *Encouraging the development of exceptional skills and talents* (pp. 32–48). Leicester, UK: BPS Books.

Rauscher, F., & Shaw, G. L. (1998). Key components of the Mozart Effect. *Perceptual and Motor Skills, 86*, 835–841.

Rauscher, F., Shaw, G. L., & Ky, K. N. (1993). Music and spatial task performance. *Nature, 365*, 611.

Revesz, G. (1971). *The psychology of a musical prodigy*. Freeport, NY: Books for Libraries Press. (Original work published 1925)

Schlaug, G. (2001). The brain of musicians: A model for functional and structural adaptation. *Annals of the New York Academy of Science, 930*, 281–299.

Schwartz, A. (2005, June). *Spiritual prodigies*. Paper presented at the The Piaget Society, Vancouver, BC.

Selfe, L. (1977). *Nadia: A case of extraordinary drawing ability in an autistic child*. London: Academic Press.

Shanks, D. R. (1999). Outstanding performers: Created, not born [Electronic version]? *Science Spectra, 18*, 28–34. Retrieved June 8, 2006, from http://www.psychol.ucl.ac.uk/david.shanks_expertise.html

Shavinina, L. V. (1999). The psychological essence of the child prodigy phenomenon: Sensitive periods and cognitive experience. *Gifted Child Quarterly, 43*, 25–38.

Shaw, G. L. (2000). *Keeping Mozart in mind*. San Diego, CA: Academic Press.

Simonton, D. K. (1997). Creative productivity: A predictive and explanatory model of career trajectories and landmarks. *Psychological Review, 104*, 66–89.

Snyder, A. (2001). Paradox of the savant mind. *Nature, 413*, 251–252.

Snyder, A., & Thomas, M. (1997). Autistic artists give clues to cognition. *Perception, 29*, 93–96.

Steele, K. M., Brown, J. D., & Stoecker, J. A. (1999). Failure to confirm the Rauscher and Shaw description of recovery of the Mozart effect. *Perceptual and Motor Skills, 88*, 843–848.

Sternberg, R. J. (Ed.). (1999). *Handbook of creativity*. Cambridge, England: Cambridge University Press.

Stevenson, I. (1977). The explanatory value of the idea of reincarnation. *Journal of Nervous and Mental Disease, 164*, 305–326.

Thurman, R. A. F. (1995). *Essential Tibetan Buddhism*. San Francisco: Harper.

Treffert, D. A. (1989). *Extraordinary people: Understanding "idiot savants."* New York: Harper & Row.

Wallace, A. (1986). *The prodigy: A biography of William James Sidis, America's greatest child prodigy.* New York: E. P. Dutton.

Weisberg, R. W. (1999). Creativity and knowledge: A challenge to theories. In R. J. Sternberg (Ed.), *Handbook of creativity* (pp. 226–250). Cambridge, England: Cambridge University Press.

Winner, E. (1996). *Gifted children: Myths and realities.* New York: Basic Books.

Winner, E. (2000). The origins and ends of giftedness. *American Psychologist, 55*(1), 159–169.

Wrightsman, C. C. (1983). *Encouraged precocity in American children from 1800 to the present: A study of attempts by certain American parents to develop high intelligence in their children.* Unpublished doctoral dissertation, Emory University, Atlanta.

Chapter 35

PROFESSIONAL DEVELOPMENT

E. Jean Gubbins

or several decades, professional development and its implementation has been the subject of debate. Educators, parents, and community members wondered why school hours were shortened to have teachers convene for "training." Didn't teachers have enough training? All had 4 years of college, many had advanced degrees, and they interacted with colleagues regularly. They also had access to journals, teacher manuals, and newsletters dealing with current educational trends, issues, and curriculum updates. Efforts to promote professional development continued, even when the impacts were not fully articulated or studied under experimental conditions. Approaches to professional development have expanded and the associated accountability is more evident. Educators recognize the importance of professional development. "In fact, one constant finding in the research literature is that notable improvements in education almost never take place *in the absence* of professional development" (Guskey, 2000, p. 4). Professional development may be a necessary, but not sufficient ingredient, for changes in teachers' classroom strategies, practices, and curricula.

DEFINING THE TERMS AS USED IN THE RESEARCH

The research and experiential learning described herein do not require an in-depth understanding of statistical or educational terms. However, it is important to discuss the extent to which professional development in gifted and talented education is a major or minor educational research topic and to offer definitions of professional development as background for this chapter.

Professional development, *staff development*, and *in-service* are common descriptors referring to opportunities to engage in different types of educational experiences linked to pedagogy, instruction, curriculum, or classroom management. A check of these three terms resulted in little or no indications in the subject indices in gifted and talented education textbooks published in the last 5 years (Colangelo & Davis, 2003; Coleman & Cross, 2005; Davis & Rimm, 2004; Karnes & Bean, 2005; Rogers, 2002). Another search revealed that there was less than one full page in Colangelo and Davis (2003) under the subject of "teacher, professional development for."

This lack of text dedicated to a discussion of professional development is somewhat ironic, given that authors' textbooks set the stage for understanding the characteristics of gifted and talented students, identifying students who need services, describing curricular models, and explaining program and student evaluation techniques. Essentially, the authors' objective is to help readers learn about educating gifted and talented students through their presentation of research and practice. Illustrative examples provide guidance for the interpretation and application of recommended practices. In many ways, these textbooks do offer informal "professional development" for anyone who chooses to review the chapters. This informal textbook option is somewhat limiting, which leads to the following question: How do teachers access research-based knowledge about effective professional development opportunities in gifted and talented education?

Two definitions are offered for professional development. In the 1970s, the National Staff Development Council (NSDC) started with a few members and it has grown substantially with its membership, newsletters, and *Journal of Staff Development*. Staff development, as their preferred term, is the "means by which educators acquire or enhance the knowledge, skills, attitudes, and beliefs necessary to create high levels of learning for all students" (NSDC, 2001, p. 2). This definition posits the dual responsibilities of educators by emphasizing what they must accomplish and how their learning should affect students.

There are many other definitions of professional development; some are more implicit than explicit. In professional development research conducted by

The National Research Center on the Gifted and Talented (NRC/GT; 1996), a broad definition of professional development was created: "Professional development is a planned program of learning opportunities to improve the performance of the administrative and instructional staff" (Gubbins et al., 2002, p. 163). Although this definition lacks detail, it does emphasize performance. Unlike the NSDC definition, it does not mention the ultimate impact on student learning.

WHAT ARE THE MAJOR QUESTIONS ADDRESSED IN THE RESEARCH ON THIS TOPIC?

Several researchers have incorporated effective approaches to gifted and talented education by using professional development as a critical component for their innovations focusing on strategies, practices, and curricula. Three key questions are addressed in this chapter on professional development and gifted and talented education. Questions 1 and 2 reflect the general professional development literature. Question 3 is specific to how professional development is the "vehicle" for sharing innovative strategies, practices, and curricula in gifted and talented education.

1. What are effective professional development formats?
2. How is professional development linked to the change process?
3. How does professional development in gifted and talented education promote innovative strategies, practices, and curricula?

Responses to these questions are based on research and experiential data. Professional development is a "field of study" in which researchers and educators test, describe, comment, and create a considerable amount of written material to inform multiple audiences. Some of the findings emerge from sound research studies using quantitative and qualitative methodologies; other findings are experiential data evolving from daily, weekly, monthly, or yearly practices codified by researchers and practitioners. The experiential data may be considered lessons learned. These lessons may not be viewed as research in an empirical sense; however, well-documented strategies, practices, and curricular approaches may be very informative and eventually lead to future empirical research studies.

Linkages between professional development, educational reform, teacher performance, and student achievement are evident in research literature, media, journalism, and laws. The federal No Child Left Behind Act (NCLB; 2001) requires school districts to develop systematic professional development plans that center on teacher performance and student achievement. In the future, professional development may be considered as a synonym for accountability. For now, current knowledge related to the three key questions will be presented.

WHAT CAN WE CONCLUDE WITH SOME CONFIDENCE FROM THE RESEARCH?

Large- and small-scale quantitative and qualitative studies exist about professional development in general education (Garet, Porter, Desimone, Birman, & Yoon, 2001). There are even more theoretical and practical perspectives that have emerged through educators' experiential wisdom gained from daily classroom interactions. "Despite the size of the body of literature, however, relatively little systematic research has been conducted on the effects of professional development on improvements in teaching or on student outcomes" (Garet et al., 2001, p. 917). Bransford, Brown, and Cocking (1999) concluded:

> Research studies are needed to determine the efficacy of various types of professional development activities, including pre-service and in-service seminars, workshops, and summer institutes. Studies should include professional development activities that are extended over time and across broad teacher learning communities in order to identify the processes and mechanisms that contribute to the development of teachers' learning communities. (p. 240)

There are even less research data on the effectiveness of alternative formats of professional development in gifted education as outcome variables, unless the data are part of intervention strategies to support, improve, or extend strategies, practices, or curricula tailored to students' academic needs. To gain the knowledge and understanding of "what works in professional development," educators must review the research literature and professional practices. Therefore, the general research literature on professional development is highlighted first, followed by a focus on the change process, and, finally, professional development in gifted and talented education is presented.

Effective Professional Development

The National Staff Development Council contends that staff development improves the learning of all students, when context, process, and content standards are supported and implemented. These standards offer guidance at very global levels. They were not traced to one or more specific research studies; however, the NSDC stated that they were "grounded in research" (NSDC, 2001, p. 2) and organized in a context/process/content schema. The research-based standards represent "good practices" and substantiate the "endgame" of professional development as student achievement. Standards include recommendations for organizing adults into learning communities with goals aligned with the needs of the school and district; promoting the use of disaggregated student data to design effective teaching and learning strategies; and deepening educators' content knowledge.

The National Staff Development Council extended each standard and provided specific outcomes for practice. They developed continua of behaviors using Hall and Hord's (2001) Innovation Configuration maps to ensure educators would have a clear vision of the standards in action; use the vision to design professional development; create systematic plans and allocate resources to implement the standards; and assess implementation of the standards. The maps are designed specifically for teachers, principals, superintendents, central office staff, and school board members (Roy & Hord, 2003).

Professional Development Formats

What are appropriate perspectives on professional development in the general education literature? Is professional development a solitary, group, or community process? Professional development of individuals, professional development of groups, and professional development within a learning community are all possible approaches to learning. Professional development may be a solitary or group experience. Reading articles from journal subscriptions, reviewing new curriculum manuals, and practicing learned skills are possible without interacting with others. Potential topics vary according to the person's professional interests or needs. A solitary approach must be sustained, as it honors individual needs, talents, and abilities. It also must be recognized that professional development for the group is an " . . . essential and indispensable part of the school improvement process" (Cawelti, 1995, p. 168).

Lowden (2006) developed a survey to determine the effectiveness and impact of professional development. Workshops, observations, and assessments by supervisors did not change attitudes and beliefs about teaching and learning. Recommended practices included job-embedded professional development, and opportunities for reflection, practice, and discussion. Smith, Hofer, Gillespie, Solomon, and Rowe (2003) confirmed the importance of practice and discussion resulting from professional development opportunities. Knowledge, skills, attitudes, and beliefs needed to evolve as more was learned and actually practiced in familiar classroom settings. It also was critical to be able to share progress in applying what was learned through additional professional development. Joyce and Showers (1988, 1995) asserted that implementing new classroom practices requires continued support. Professional development was not about waiting for something different to happen in education; professional development was designed to integrate knowing, understanding, thinking, and doing.

Cawelti's (1995) review of extant research supported the importance of providing "generous opportunities for teacher learning and collaboration, and by altering the culture and structures of the schools in which they work, teachers can and will improve teaching and learning in ways that truly benefit all students" (p. 168). Teacher learning and collaboration with others are equally important. Lewis (2002) noted characteristics of professional development critical to improving teacher learning. If teachers note how professional development is integral to innovations, and if they have time to practice, reflect, ask questions, and share their learning, there is a stronger likelihood of success with integrating the innovation into the school system.

Planning professional development in response to identified needs of schools goes well beyond topics. Strategic professional development plans must be carefully designed and executed. The organization, timing, objectives, and explicit links to innovations are important considerations. Guskey (2000) determined, "At the core of each and every successful educational improvement effort is a thoughtfully well conceived, well designed, and well supported professional development component" (p. 4).

Sustained Professional Learning

Educators recognize the benefits of having students actively involved with learning; the same opportunity for learning must be provided for educators. Lieberman (1995) believes traditional approaches to professional development fall short of this goal, indicating that it is somewhat ironic that the educational needs of educators are not viewed in the same way as they are for students. According to Lieberman (1995):

> What everyone appears to want for students—a wide array of learning opportunities that engage students in experiencing, creating, and solving real problems, using their own experiences, and working with others—is for some reason denied to teachers when they are learners. (p. 591)

Donovan and Pellegrino (2004) offered sage advice about "targets of learning": "Learning is as complex an undertaking when the teacher is the target as it is when the student is the target" (p. 22). They also identified several barriers to sustained professional learning. "Even when change is effectively instituted with the help of program developers, it is frequently not sustained when the developer departs" (pp. 22–23). Relying on external experts alone without building expertise within schools will ultimately be a disadvantage. Local "champions" with high levels of expertise in implementing the innovation need to assume leadership roles in maintaining the innovation. Integrating the innovation into the school's mission statement is critical; otherwise, changes in staffing may result in a lack of support for effective innovations (Moffett, 2000).

Relationship Between Professional Development and the Change Process

Views of professional development certainly have changed over time. Sparks and Hirsh (1997) offered a new vision of professional development. The success of schooling is judged by what students "actually know and can do as a result of their time in school" (p. 4), and "knowledge is not simply transmitted from teacher to student, but instead is constructed in the mind of the learner" (p. 9). The days of viewing a student as a "tabula rasa" and believing that teachers were the "transmitters" of knowledge were over. Sparks and Hirsh documented the changing views of professional development (see Table 1), reflecting research and experiences. To make substantial change, professional development must be focused on the goals of the schools and districts as effective organizations. Creating achievable strategic plans maintains the focus on what schools and districts have defined as next steps to achieve their goals.

Focusing at the district level was important for overall goals. However, school-focused professional development promoted ownership of the goals and provided opportunities to fine-tune and witness missteps and successes of on-the-job behaviors supporting student learning outcomes. Encouraging discussions, observations, questions, and sharing what worked and what did not work for individual teachers made job-embedded learning a reality.

Moving professional development and professional developers closer to implementation sites of the adapted or adopted strategies, practices, or curricula made it apparent that the ultimate impact of professional development was to promote continuous improvement in performance for "...everyone who affects student learning" (Sparks & Hirsh, 1997, p. 16).

Describing and Understanding Change

Change theory continues to receive considerable attention in the research literature. Some of the impetus for understanding change is associated with the recognition of a somewhat faulty belief: provide options for professional development, encourage teachers to participate, and observe what was learned in classrooms. A linear approach to change proved unrealistic and too simplistic.

The research literature evidences explicit and implicit links between professional development and the change process. All formats for professional development, whether informal or formal, should promote thinking about changing strategies, practices, and curricula. With appropriate experiences, support, and resources, professional development provokes action. The action might include:
- embedding performance assessment tasks in curricula in response to analyzing desired outcomes of educational experiences (Hibbard et al., 1996);

TABLE 1

Changing Views of Professional Development

Former Perspective	Recommended Perspective
1. Individual development	Individual development and organizational development
2. Fragmented, piecemeal improvement efforts	Coherent, strategic plan for the district, schools, and departments
3. District-focused approaches	School-focused approaches
4. Adult needs and satisfaction	Student needs and learning outcomes, and changes in on-the-job behaviors
5. Training conducted away from the job	Multiple forms of job-embedded learning
6. Transmission of knowledge and skills to teachers by "experts"	The study by teachers of the teaching and learning processes
7. Generic instructional skills	Combination of generic and content-specific skills
8. Staff developers who function primarily as trainers	Staff developers who provide consultation, planning, and facilitation services, as well as training
9. Staff development provided by one or two departments	Staff development as a critical function and major responsibility performed by all administrators and teacher leaders
10. Staff development directed toward teachers as the primary recipients	Continuous improvement in performance for everyone who affects student learning
11. Staff development as a "frill" that can be cut during difficult financial times	Staff development as an indispensable process without which schools cannot hope to prepare children for citizenship and productive employment

Note. Adapted from Sparks and Hirsh (1997).

- learning and applying multiple intelligences (linguistic, logical-mathematical, musical, spatial, bodily-kinesthetic, interpersonal, intrapersonal, and naturalist) to curricula (Baum, Viens, & Slatin, 2005); or
- using analytical, creative, and practical intelligences to master concepts and essential principles of psychology (Sternberg, Ferrari, Clinkenbeard, & Grigorenko, 1996).

Professional Development As Learning

Professional development should equal learning. The most parsimonious definition of learning follows: learning is a change in behavior. This statement sounds simplistic, but years of research and practice confirmed the complexities associated with changing human behavior (Fullan, 1993, 2001, 2005; Fullan, Cuttress, & Kilcher, 2005; Hall & Hord, 1987, 2001; Hord, Rutherford, Huling-Austin, & Hall, 1987; Joyce, 1990; Joyce & Showers, 1988, 1995; Joyce, Wolf, & Calhoun, 1993; Killion, 2002; Killion, Munger, Roy, & McMullen, 2003). Hall and Hord's research resulted in the identification of 12 principles of change:

- *Change Principle 1:* Change Is a Process, Not an Event
- *Change Principle 2:* There Are Significant Differences in What Is Entailed in Development and Implementation of an Innovation
- *Change Principle 3:* An Organization Does Not Change Until the Individuals Within it Change
- *Change Principle 4:* Innovations Come in Different Sizes
- *Change Principle 5:* Interventions Are the Actions and Events That Are Key to the Success of the Change Process
- *Change Principle 6:* Although Both Top-Down and Bottom-Up Change Can Work, a Horizontal Perspective Is Best
- *Change Principle 7:* Administrator Leadership Is Essential to Long-Term Change Success
- *Change Principle 8:* Mandates Can Work
- *Change Principle 9:* The School Is the Primary Unit for Change
- *Change Principle 10:* Facilitating Change Is a Team Effort
- *Change Principle 11:* Appropriate Interventions Reduce the Challenges of Change
- *Change Principle 12:* The Context of the School Influences the Process of Change (Hall & Hord, 2001, pp. 4–15)

These change principles require self-study to fully understand theoretical and practical perspectives. Moving from an early 1970s assumption that learning was an event to the recognition that learning was a process was a long journey. The journey paralleled or influenced myriad approaches to professional development. Hall and Hord (2001) described one administrator's event mentality regarding the first year of implementation of a project: "What do you mean that teachers need more training? We bought them the books? Can't they read?" (p. 6). The researchers confirmed the importance of planning for change. Hall and Hord (2001) asserted, "most changes in education take three to five years to be implemented at a high level" (p. 4). They learned that

change means developing new understandings and doing things in new ways. If faculty are going to use new curricular programs or instructional practices, they must learn how to do that. Thus, *learn-*

ing is the basis of and the corollary to change. Formal training and other forms of staff and personal development, then, are essential to prepare implementors for the change. Such learning opportunities for the implementors should be ongoing as they develop more expertise in using the identified change. (p. 111; italics in original)

The change principles confirm the complexities of the change process. Maintaining the status quo of current strategies, practices, curricula, and beliefs is much easier and, essentially, more comfortable. Learning new approaches is not always embraced. Many teachers are reluctant to adopt or adapt instructional and curricular strategies that challenge long-held beliefs about teaching and learning.

Acceleration as Implicit Professional Development in Gifted Education

The title of an article by Julian Stanley (2000), a preeminent researcher who studied acceleration for decades, is the most succinct objective of acceleration: "Helping Students Learn What They Don't Already Know." Acceleration offers options for learning at a younger age than typically associated with age/grade status operating in most schools, and it provides students opportunities for variable rates of learning as needed in one or more subject areas (Colangelo, Assouline, & Gross, 2004). Southern and Jones (1991, 2004) identified 18 types of acceleration, including grade skipping, subject matter acceleration, and early entrance to school or college. Acceleration types differ on five dimensions:
1. pacing or rate of instruction;
2. salience or the degree to which various types of acceleration are apparent to others;
3. social separation from age and grade-level peers;
4. level of access to different types due to size of schools/districts or resources; and
5. timing or the age at which accelerative types are offered or available.

In retrospective, current, and longitudinal studies of acceleration and its impact on students, formal or informal professional development opportunities may have occurred, but are not described. In publications, the research findings shift to the impact of acceleration types. Educators involved in the decision-making process about acceleration types most likely engaged in informal or formal professional development, as discussions about appropriate options occurred.

Robinson (2004) and Colangelo, Assouline, and Lupkowski-Shoplik (2004) focused attention on the decision-making process. They contended that decisions about optimal timing for adopting grade-based or subject-based acceleration must be made with knowledge of cognitive and affective strengths, learner readiness, and school and home support to ensure that changes in options for learning were most appropriate. These researchers, along with Rogers (2004), also confirmed that decisions about acceleration types for individual students need revision periodically to maintain the challenge level and to reflect the needs and readiness levels of candidate students. Therefore, acceleration types usually include implicit approaches to professional development, even if not explicitly stated or described.

With this inference in mind, the definitive research on acceleration highlighted below offers additional examples of effective strategies and practices. Kulik's (2004) meta-analytic results concluded:

> Bright students almost always benefit from accelerated programs of instruction. Two major findings support this conclusion. First, on achievement tests, bright, accelerated youngsters usually perform like their bright, older non-accelerated classmates. Second, the accelerated youngsters usually score almost one grade-level higher on achievement than bright, same-age non-accelerated students, do. (p. 20)

Acceleration allowed students to experience education typically available to older students. Some educators still harbor concerns about accelerative options. Lubinski (2004) summarized recent longitudinal findings from the Study of Mathematically Precocious Youth (SMPY). He examined the data to determine adults' reactions to their accelerative options as intellectually precocious youth. He stated:

> Being responsive to individual differences in learning rates facilitates achievement and learning, and the subjective impressions of intellectually precocious participants who experienced such opportunities view them positively well into adulthood. Indeed, when the curriculum moves at a slow pace, boredom and discontent frequently ensue. (p. 34)

Several researchers spent decades reviewing the learning trajectories of students who needed the acceleration options and their findings supported the positive academic outcomes. Robinson (2004) confirmed the effectiveness of acceleration:

> The overwhelming evidence suggests that all forms of acceleration constitute viable options of any attempts to provide an optimal educational and social match for gifted students. None of the options has been shown to do psychosocial damage to gifted students as a group; when effects are noted, they are usually (but not invariably) in a positive direction. (p. 64)

Formal or informal professional development approaches were not described in the research highlighted above. However, acceleration as a topic necessitates careful study and reflection when decisions are to be made about changing students' educational programs, which is professional development for all involved in the decision-making process.

Explicit Professional Development in Gifted and Talented Education

There is increasing interest in the outcomes of professional development as it relates to gifted and talented education (Dettmer & Landrum, 1998). Croft (2003) connected the principles of professional development to gifted and talented education and viewed professional development opportunities as a "confluence of several streams of expertise" (p. 567), which included the following:

- a balance of pedagogical theory and practices in gifted education and in subject areas;
- advanced content in subject areas, including complex performance goals reflected in national standards;
- links among teachers' existing knowledge, schools' program objectives, and best practices for differentiating curricula to meet the needs of intellectually gifted learners;
- historical and contemporary issues in gifted education from the nature of intelligence and its assessment to the continuum of essential services for diverse gifted students, taught through direct instruction, videos, individualized and independent learning, small-group discussions, field experiences, and peer coaching; and
- observations of gifted teachers facilitating the development of the extraordinary abilities of gifted students. (p. 567)

Instructional and curricular strategies often are the research focus in the field of gifted and talented education (Renzulli, Gubbins, & Koehler, 2003). Reis et al. (1993) conducted an experimental study of curriculum compacting, which is a technique of eliminating mastered curriculum and substituting more challenging curricula to extend and enhance students' skills and abilities. Experimental teachers received different levels of professional development (videotapes, books, and articles; simulations; and peer coaches) to determine if the intensity made a difference in applying learned teaching strategies supported by curriculum compacting. They documented mastery of students' learning and eliminated between 40–50% of curriculum across several content areas (Reis, Westberg, Kulikowich, & Purcell, 1998). Results indicated that teachers effectively learned and implemented curriculum compacting and the impact on students' achievement, content area preferences, and attitudes toward learning was very positive (Reis & Westberg, 1994; Reis et al., 1993).

Curriculum compacting is viewed as one approach to modifying the grade-level curriculum, which, in many cases, lacks the challenge and rigor necessary for gifted and talented students to continue learning. There are several ways to modify, differentiate, and enrich curriculum. Gubbins et al. (2002) conducted a national study of professional development, which provided teachers opportunities to become local experts by studying and implementing the professional development module developed by The National Research Center on the Gifted and Talented, which emphasized:

- modification of curriculum to increase challenge, authenticity, and active learning;
- differentiation to improve the match between learners' characteristics and various curriculum components emphasizing depth and breadth of learning; and
- enrichment strategies to promote investigative activities and artistic productions in which the learner assumes the role of a first-hand inquirer and a practicing professional. (Burns et al., 2002; Gubbins et al., 2002)

Quantitative and qualitative data confirmed the effectiveness of developing the expertise of local liaisons who used professional development sessions, demonstration lessons, coaching opportunities, and mentoring to guide local teachers as they responded to the academic needs of all of their students in general education classrooms. This study identified several principles as requisites of effective professional development:

- recognition of the importance of a personal and professional commitment to make a change in existing strategies and practices;
- identification of school-level, grade-level, small group, or individual need;
- emphasis on knowledge acquisition and implementation of new learning;
- promotion of practice, feedback, and reflection; and
- collection, analysis, and application of school-level and district-level data to make informed decisions. (adapted from Gubbins et al., 2002, pp. 151–152)

Tomlinson (1999, 2005) conducted several studies of differentiation, offering another perspective on what teachers need to meet the varying academic needs of students. Tomlinson (1999) posited that differentiating instruction was

> not an instructional strategy or a teaching model. It's a way of thinking about teaching and learning that advocates beginning where individuals are rather than with a prescribed plan of action, which ignores student readiness, interest, and learning profile. It is a way of thinking that challenges how educators typically envision assessment, teaching, learning, classroom roles, use of time, and curriculum. (p. 108)

In response to students' readiness, interests, and learning profiles to increase the rigor, complexity, and depth and breadth of curriculum, research on differentiation provided critical information about teaching and learning (Tomlinson, 1995; Tomlinson et al., 2003). Tomlinson (1995) conducted an exploratory qualitative case study of a district interested in providing differentiated instruction for middle school students and concluded that teachers who moved toward differentiated classrooms were inquirers about students. Tomlinson (1995) found that "change among faculty at large during the first year of differentiated instruction . . . supports the idea that people are more likely to act their way into belief than to believe their way into acting" (pp. 85–86). Earlier research by Guskey (1986) and Reis and Westberg (1994) corroborated Tomlinson's finding that success was more effective in fostering changes in teachers' behavior than trying to convince them of the usefulness of the strategies, practices, and curricula.

For some teachers, however, witnessing success in using innovations was not sufficient because of long-held beliefs. Brighton (2003) researched the similarities and differences between middle school teachers' espoused beliefs and how they learned how to differentiate instruction and assessment in general education classrooms. Qualitative data included interviews with teachers, administrators, and students; classroom observations; student products; and teachers' planning and instructional materials. Data analyses indicated that

> . . . despite their stated positions, a significant gap existed between teachers' verbal enthusiasm and the practices observed and discussed in their classrooms. This chasm seemed filled with teachers' deeply held beliefs about the nature of middle school, the role of teacher in the middle school, and students' natural proclivities toward challenging learning. (Brighton, 2003, p. 186)

Brighton (2003) concluded that changing teachers' beliefs and practices to accommodate academic diversity in classrooms was a difficult goal. Teachers whose espoused beliefs and actions were similar to those suggested in the innovation differentiated strategies, practices, content, and assessments. Other teachers whose words and actions were counter to the differentiation efforts resisted change.

Converting teachers who resist change overtly or covertly may be very difficult. It must be recognized that during the implementation of any innovation, each person must work out his or her own reality of what it means in the classroom. Fullan (2005) stated, "Smooth implementation is often a sign that not much is really changing" (p. 6). Resistors to change may harbor valid points that must be addressed.

Learning is sometimes more easily recognized as developmental when the subjects are children rather than adults. Changes in strategies, practices, or curricula require multiple stages of understanding, practicing, reflecting, and integrating into current content pedagogy and instructional repertoires. It also is important to establish a clear vision of what the strategies, practices, and curricula look like in classrooms so teachers can assess their own progress (National Foundation for the Improvement of Education, 1996; Stigler & Hiebert, 1999). Landrum, Callahan, and Shaklee (2001) met this challenge by providing annotated standards and sample outcomes related to program design, program administration and management, socioemotional guidance and counseling, student identification, curriculum and instruction, professional development, and program evaluation. Exemplary standards may be regarded as markers of excellence in program design, development, and implementation.

Integration of Content, Strategies, and Practices

Research on professional development is often targeted to specific content areas. Attention to key content areas is increasing, as is the importance of determining the relationship between and among teacher content knowledge and understanding, effective pedagogy and instructional practices, and student learning to promote educational reform. Highlights of professional development in mathematics, reading/language arts, and social studies are presented.

Project M³ (Mentoring Mathematical Minds; Project M³, n.d.) employed multiple professional development techniques to increase teachers' mathematical knowledge and to promote enrichment learning and mathematical discourse with students in grades 3–5. Core objectives for teachers and students were linked to ensure that newly developed curriculum, strategies, and practices would be implemented as designed. The objectives emphasized creating challenging curriculum units, providing sustained professional development, increasing math achievement, and promoting positive attitudes toward math.

The professional development model used in Project M³ combined several effective formats: sustained opportunities to explore the curriculum with experts; multiple resources available through print and technology; interactions between and among teachers and researchers; and access to periodic updates of students' progress. There were statistically significant gains on teachers' perceptions of an increase in their knowledge base and skills as a result of training and statistically significant gains on a pre- and postinstrument used to measure actual content acquisition.

Other recent research studies focused on reading and language arts. High-quality children's literature served as the core content for the Schoolwide Enrichment Model Reading Study (SEM-R). Reis et al. (2005) investigated the effects of a reading program on students' reading fluency, comprehension, and attitude toward reading. The Schoolwide Enrichment Reading Model provides

> enriched reading experiences by exposing students to exciting, high interest books, encouraging them to increase daily independent reading of appropriately challenging, self-selected books through individualized reading instruction, and providing interest-based choice opportunities in reading. (p. i)

Teachers were involved in professional development and coaching opportunities throughout the research study. The effectiveness of the professional development, coaching, and resource materials was confirmed through teacher observations and focus groups. It also was beneficial for teachers to access data indicating changes in student achievement. They recognized that students in SEM-R treatment classrooms outperformed control group students in reading fluency, reading comprehension, and reading attitude, and these results were confirmed through data analyses.

The College of William and Mary developed language arts and social studies curricula. Project Athena (VanTassel-Baska, 2003a), focusing on language arts, was implemented in several school districts (grades 3–5). As in the research studies described above, professional development was a stated objective: "To develop and implement professional training models for teachers, administrators, and broader school communities" (p. 5). Classroom observations and on-site coaching or technical assistance helped teachers maintain their focus on accomplishing the project's objectives. These observations were informative for researchers as they recognized the need to further emphasize the application of complex thinking strategies throughout the language arts units.

Given the availability of the language arts units that offered detailed content, strategies, and practices, they, too, should be regarded as professional development opportunities for individuals or groups as a self-study approach. Of course, involvement in professional development with the experts provided firsthand knowledge of how to maintain the fidelity of implementation as originally designed by the researchers. Additionally, *A Guide to Implementation of Project Athena* (VanTassel-Baska, 2003a) documents all phases of the project in action and describes the principals' critical role in the implementation process, which is a form of professional development leadership. Principals can ensure the effective implementation of the program by monitoring involvement with training and implementation of the lessons, promoting communication with parents about the program, supporting the administration of assessments for literary analysis and interpretation and writing, and seeking implementation support from a local coordinator.

To gain further knowledge of the impact of language arts units, VanTassel-Baska, Zuo, Avery, and Little (2002) launched a curriculum study of gifted-student learning in language arts using four College of William and Mary units: *Journeys and Destinations, Literary Reflections, Autobiographies,* and *The 1940s: A Decade of Change.* These units were based on the Integrated Curriculum Model (VanTassel-Baska, 1995, 2003b), emphasizing the development of analytical and interpretive literature skills, persuasive writing skills, linguistic competency, listening/oral communication skills, and reasoning skills. Researchers found that the use of the language arts units "made a difference in student learning in regard to both literary analysis and interpretation skills and persuasive writing skills . . ." (VanTassel-Baska et al., 2002, p. 41).

Researchers from the College of William and Mary also created Project Phoenix, focusing on the development and implementation of social studies units for students in grades 2–8. Teachers were involved in professional development related to American history, world history, and government. Teachers made significant gains in their implementation of critical thinking strategies incorporated in each unit. Students in the treatment group also made gains documented by the content assessments (Little, 2002). Once again, the researchers understood the importance of providing the topical content, strategies, and practices in a series of units that were piloted and refined during the research study.

Formal and informal approaches to professional development were critical to informing educators about the innovations, codifying all aspects of the innovations, and monitoring their implementation. Due to the uniqueness of each innovation, it was not possible to select one professional development approach over another as most effective. There is no formula that directs educators in determining how much, how often, or what professional development formats will work best.

WHAT ARE THE LIMITATIONS OF THE RESEARCH ON THIS TOPIC?

Teachers interested in professional development as it relates to gifted and talented students may find limited attention to the topic. Dettmer and Landrum (1998) are the only authors who dedicated a book to gifted education staff development. Landrum et al. (2001) presented professional development as one of the critical and essential criteria in gifted education programming. Guiding principles, standards, and sample outcomes are delineated for the chapter on staff development in *Aiming for Excellence: Gifted Program Standards* (Landrum et al., 2001). A few years later, Imbeau (2006) prepared a chapter on professional development for the recent book entitled, *Designing Services and Programs for High Ability Learners: A Guidebook for Gifted Education* (Purcell & Eckert, 2006). Fortunately, many findings from the general research and experiential data on effective professional development plans can provide appropriate guidance.

Understanding "what works" in professional development is critical. Unfortunately, educators have " . . . simply not done a very good job of documenting the positive effects of professional development, nor of describing precisely which aspects of professional development most contribute to its effectiveness . . ." (Guskey, 2000, p. 4). To truly measure the effectiveness of professional development, the documentation of potential impact has to be conceived of as occurring across years, not days or months. Time is often a limitation in any research study. More time to introduce or practice strategies may be desirable, but limited resources may make it prohibitive.

The reality of such continuous documentation, reflection, and application of learning is beyond the scope of many research plans. Therefore, researchers spend time and energy at the start-up phase of professional development and follow the progress according to a preset schedule. Researchers might return to the settings to gain additional data retrospectively to assess the extent to which innovations were sustained. Although long-term research on professional development may be difficult to achieve, there are some built-in responsibilities for schools and districts to evaluate the impact of innovations. Professional development and its links to teacher learning and, ultimately, student learning are critical to successful schools.

Another research limitation is related to the innovations. Several studies had their own unique innovations based on researchers' interests and theoretical perspectives that required testing in schools as naturalistic settings. Innovation-specific and situation-specific innovations honored the researchers' theoretical and practical work. To ensure that other interested researchers will be able to replicate the research studies, it is imperative that future studies incorporating professional development are documented carefully, and strategies, practices, or curricula are described in detail. In addition, future research studies need to maintain professional development formats as outcome variables to illuminate the impacts on teachers and students.

Given that studying professional development implies that researchers need to work with schools and teachers, it is important to understand that some variables cannot be controlled in naturalistic settings. Multiple research methods were used to collect data in the highlighted studies. Some were experimental studies with random assignment and control groups; others were surveys; and still others were observations, interviews, or case studies. All of the methodologies have assets and limitations, which are well understood.

The research summarized above focused on teachers, rather than administrators. It is assumed that administrative leadership was key to several research studies because administrators can be supporters or gatekeepers to the actual implementation of research. It is recognized that administrators are acutely aware of the accountability of all educational practices; they understand the investment of time for introducing, practicing, and using the strategies, practices, or curricula. As Moffett (2000) declared, "Changing structures is necessary but not sufficient for sustainable change. Changing the professional structure is key" (p. 2). Administrators, teachers, and students all contribute to the professional, organizational, and academic structures of schools.

WHAT ARE THE PRACTICAL IMPLICATIONS OF THE RESEARCH ON THIS TOPIC?

The highlighted research focused on effective professional development formats, professional development and the change process, and professional development for innovations in gifted and talented education related to strategies, practices, and curricula. Cited research studies led to several implications for educators and researchers.

Professional development must be conceived as *professional learning* with one major goal: improved educational outcomes for teachers and students. The continuous learning process means that working with strategies, practices, and curricula requires commitment to the theoretical and philosophical underpinnings of the innovations. Such a commitment cannot be sustained if programs and services for gifted and talented students are marginalized. Because the identified population of gifted and talented students usually represents a small percentage of the total student population, articulated connections to school and district mission statements must be evident. The availability of programs and services based on the academic needs of gifted and talented students should be considered sound educational practices necessary for quality educational systems.

Professional learning must be part of an overall multiyear strategic plan. Knowledgeable educators with the ability to marshal instructional and material resources and expertise with the innovations must be in charge of strategic, professional development plans. Time, energy, and resources must be devoted to professional learning to make a difference for teachers and students. It is evident that connections between teacher learning and student learning need further exploration. The National Education Commission on Time and Learning (1994) declared: "If experience, research, and common sense teach nothing else, they confirm the truism that people learn at different rates, and in different ways with different subjects" (p. 4). More information is available about how people learn, but there are elements of the learning process that are not fully understood. Donovan and Pellegrino (2004) indicated:

> The typical learning trajectory for teachers, and how it changes with learning opportunities, also requires empirical investigation. Much that teachers need to know cannot be learned apart from practice. This raises several questions for inquiry: Under what conditions can teachers best learn while engaged in practice? What knowledge and skill must teachers acquire at the beginning of their careers? What knowledge and skill is best acquired once they enter the profession? What organizational, material, and human resources are necessary to support and sustain teacher learning over time? (p. 22)

Donovan and Pellegrino unmasked the disconnections between research and practice and proposed questions for teaching and learning to direct future research on students and teachers as learners in environments that must be responsive to change (see Table 2).

To summarize what is currently known about professional development in gifted and talented education, three questions were addressed through a review

TABLE 2

Schematic Questions for Teaching and Learning

	Student Learner	Teacher as Learner
Destination	What should he or she know and/or be able to do (regarding the discipline or topic)?	What should he or she know about the discipline or topic? What should he or she know about student learning of, and the teaching of, the discipline or topic?
Point of departure	What are the typical preconceptions and informal understandings that students bring to the topic?	What are the teacher's existing understandings about the topic and about student learning?
Route	What is the expected progression of understanding, and what are the predictable points of difficulty or hurdles?	What are the typical pre-service and in-service learning trajectories and what difficulties are likely to be encountered?
Vehicle	What curriculum/pedagogy and classroom norms and practices facilitate learning?	What factors/experiences facilitate learning?
Checkpoints/ course corrections	How can identified student progress be monitored and instructional activities matched to current understanding?	How can progress be monitored and instructional activities matched to current understanding?

Note. From Donovan and Pellegrino (2004, p. 15).

of the research and experiential data. The following conclusions are in response to each question.

What Are Effective Professional Development Formats?
- Professional development should be viewed as an ongoing process to practice what was learned, to share ideas and thinking, and to reflect on progress.
- Professional development should include job-embedded opportunities so teachers can experience the strategies, practices, or curricula in naturalistic settings.
- Differentiated professional development (e.g., collegial coaching, mentorships, conferences) should be in response to the identified needs of individuals and groups within schools and districts.

How Is Professional Development Linked to the Change Process?
- Professional development is the "vehicle" of educational reform.
- Professional development must be conceived of as *professional learning* with one major goal: improved educational outcomes for teachers and students.
- Professional development objectives must be articulated clearly to ensure that expected outcomes are attained.
- Systematic professional development plans must be based on identified needs of schools, districts, and educators who work with students on a daily basis.

How Does Professional Development in Gifted and Talented Education Promote Innovative Strategies, Practices, and Curricula?
- Professional development offers educators opportunities to learn and practice innovative strategies, practices, and curricula to meet students' varying academic needs.
- Professional development must be carefully articulated in innovative strategies, practices, and curricula to ensure that potential impacts can be traced to the most effective approaches.

Researchers studied delivery systems for professional development and provided principles to guide the creation of effective approaches. The nature, type, and frequency of professional development were considered "inputs." As researchers examined professional development as mechanisms for changing current strategies, practices, and curricula, they became acutely aware that offering professional development did not necessarily mean that changes or "outputs" would ensue.

Conclusions

The beneficiaries of effective professional development should be administrators, teachers, students, and learning communities. It is important for teachers to understand that they are the change agents in multiple, educational "laboratories" known as schools. Providing job-embedded opportunities to learn, practice, reflect, and adjust new strategies, practices, and curricula is critical to the change process. Numerous political, societal, and educational forces can inhibit the adoption of effective strategies, practices, or curricula. Some teachers return to the status quo because they determine that too much time, work, and resources are required. Therefore, it is imperative that systematic professional development be devoted to effective innovations integral to the teaching/learning cycle.

Professional development is part of the argot of educational communities. The term should evoke the goal of professional learning for all involved with education. Educators have to go beyond the idea of viewing professional development as the eternal journey of Sisyphus from Greek mythology who continually rolled a boulder uphill that, just before it reached the top, would roll back down. Professional learning is a continuous process of setting and meeting goals that leads to changes in knowledge, skills, attitudes, and beliefs that improve desired educational outcomes.

MAJOR RESOURCES AND REFERENCES ON PROFESSIONAL DEVELOPMENT

In selecting resources related to professional development and gifted and talented education, two questions guided the process:

1. Which professional development resources provide practical guidance to help educators reach the goals of schools and districts?
2. Which resources describe effective strategies, practices, and curricula that make a difference for students and teachers?

A few suggested references are listed below.

Eisenhower National Clearinghouse, and National Staff Development Council. (2002). *By your own design: A teacher's professional learning guide* [CD-ROM]. Columbus, OH: Author.

The "By Your Own Design" CD-ROM includes articles from the Eisenhower National Clearing House, National Staff Development Council, and other resources to help educators plan, develop, and implement effective professional development that is responsive to educators' needs. Many articles have discussion and reflection tools highlighting key points and suggesting additional resources for further reflection. Professional learning can be accomplished by using the CD-ROM with individuals or groups.

Burns, D. E., Gubbins, E. J., Reis, S. M., Westberg, K. L., Dinnocenti, S. T., & Tieso, C. L. (2004). *Applying gifted education pedagogy in the general education classroom: Professional development module* [CD-ROM]. Storrs: National Research Center on the Gifted and Talented, University of Connecticut.

Educators can learn how to apply gifted education pedagogy in their classrooms. The professional development module focuses on conceptions of giftedness, curriculum modification, curriculum differentiation, and enrichment. Information is presented using PowerPoint slides with notes, suggestions to promote audience involvement, and recommended resources. The content of the CD-ROM provides an opportunity to develop the expertise of local educators who may become professional developers within their own schools or districts.

Dettmer, P. A., & Landrum, M. S. (Eds.). (1998). *Staff development: The key to effective gifted education programs.* Waco, TX: Prufrock Press.

This is the only book on staff development created specifically to address gifted education programs. The authors note the dearth of specific books and articles merging the topics. They present guidance on how to plan, implement, monitor, and evaluate gifted education staff development.

Landrum, M. S., Callahan, C. M., & Shaklee, B. D. (Eds.). (2001). *Aiming for excellence: Gifted program standards: Annotations to the NAGC pre-K–grade 12 gifted education program standards.* Waco, TX: Prufrock Press.

The authors present seven elements critical to programming for gifted and talented students: program design, program administration and management, socioemotional guidance and counseling, student identification, curriculum and instruction, professional development, and program evaluation. Guiding principles, rationale, benefits, and potential barriers are described in detail, followed by descriptions of minimum and exemplary standards. Educators may use this book as a guide to assess the quality of their programs and services and to chart new directions.

National Staff Development Council. (2001). *National Staff Development Council's standards for staff development: Advancing student learning through staff development* (Rev. ed.). Oxford, OH: Author.

The National Staff Development Council developed 12 content, process, and product standards to guide educators as they develop plans of action. All standards have an ultimate goal of improving student learning. The format for each standard includes a rationale, case study, discussion questions, next steps, and selected references. The appendix includes a self-assessment tool with specific statements related to each standard. Educators can review each statement and determine the extent to which there is agreement or disagreement. Ratings are summarized in a Self-Assessment Scoring Guide. Resulting scores aid educators in developing their personalized staff development plans. An annotated bibliography also is provided.

Roy, P., & Hord, S. (2003). *Moving NSDC's staff development standards into practice: Innovation configurations.* Oxford, OH: National Staff Development Council.

The National Staff Development Council's standards are beneficial for educators who want to improve professional learning opportunities for everyone in the educational community. To fully explicate what the standards would look like in action, Roy and Hord (2003) developed Innovation Configuration maps. Each map states the desired outcome for the standard and delineates six levels of implementation, indicating the quality and fidelity of the standard in action. The high (Level 1) to low (Level 6) implementation levels provide a rating system that offers specific, measurable guidance to improve the levels of use of the standards.

REFERENCES

Baum, S., Viens, J., & Slatin, B. (2005). *Multiple intelligences in the elementary classroom: A teacher's toolkit.* New York: Teachers College Press.

Bransford, J. D., Brown, A. L., & Cocking, R. R. (1999). *How people learn: Brain, mind, experience, and school.* Washington, DC: National Academy Press.

Brighton, C. (2003). The effects of middle school teachers' beliefs on classroom practices. *Journal for the Education of the Gifted, 27,* 177–206.

Burns, D. E., Gubbins, E. J., Reis, S. M., Westberg, K. L., Dinnocenti, S. T., & Tieso, C. L. (2002). *Applying gifted education pedagogy in the general education classroom: Professional development module* [CD-ROM]. Storrs: National Research Center on the Gifted and Talented, University of Connecticut.

Cawelti, G. (Ed.). (1995). *Handbook of research on improving student achievement.* Arlington, VA: Educational Research Service.

Colangelo, N., Assouline, S. G., & Gross, M. U. M. (2004). *A nation deceived: How schools hold back America's brightest students* (Vol. II). Iowa City, IA: The Connie Belin & Jacqueline N. Blank International Center for Gifted Education and Talent Development.

Colangelo, N., Assouline, S. G., & Lupkowski-Shoplik, A. E. (2004). Whole-grade acceleration. In N. Colangelo, S. G. Assouline, & M. U. M. Gross (Eds.), *A nation deceived: How schools hold back America's brightest students* (Vol. II, pp. 77–86). Iowa City, IA: The Connie Belin & Jacqueline N. Blank International Center for Gifted Education and Talent Development.

Colangelo, N., & Davis, G. A. (Eds.) (2003). *Handbook of gifted education* (3rd ed.). Boston: Allyn & Bacon.

Coleman, L. J., & Cross, T. L. (2005). *Being gifted in school: An introduction to development, guidance, and teaching* (2nd ed.). Waco, TX: Prufrock Press.

Croft, L. (2003). Teachers of the gifted: Gifted teachers. In N. Colangelo & G. A. Davis, *Handbook of gifted education* (3rd ed., pp. 558–571). Boston: Allyn & Bacon.

Davis, G. A., & Rimm, S. B. (2004). *Education of the gifted and talented* (5th ed.) Boston: Allyn & Bacon.

Dettmer, P. A., & Landrum, M. S. (Eds.). (1998). *Staff development: The key to effective gifted education programs.* Waco, TX: Prufrock.

Donovan, M. S., & Pellegrino, J. W. (Eds.). (2004). *Learning and instruction: A SERP research agenda.* Washington, DC: National Academies Press.

Fullan, M. (1993). *Change forces: Probing the depths of educational reform.* London: The Falmer Press.

Fullan, M. (2001). *The new meaning of educational change* (3rd ed.). New York: Teachers College Press.

Fullan, M. (2005, November). 10 do and don't assumptions about change. *The Learning Principal, 1*(3), 1, 6–7.

Fullan, M., Cuttress, C., & Kilcher, A. (2005). 8 forces for leaders of change. *Journal of Staff Development, 26*(4), 54–58, 64.

Garet, M. S., Porter, A. C., Desimone, L., Birman, B. F., & Yoon, K. S. (2001). What makes professional development effective? Results from a national sample of teachers. *American Educational Research Journal, 38,* 915–945.

Gubbins, E. J., Westberg, K. L., Reis, S. M., Dinnocenti, S. T., Tieso, C. L., Muller, L. M., et al. (2002). *Implementing a professional development model using gifted education strategies with all students.* Storrs: National Research Center on the Gifted and Talented, University of Connecticut.

Guskey, T. R. (1986). Staff development and the process of teacher change. *Educational Researcher, 15*(5), 5–12.

Guskey, T. R. (2000). *Evaluating professional development.* Thousand Oaks, CA: Corwin Press.

Hall, G. E., & Hord, S. M. (1987). *Change in schools: Facilitating the process.* Albany: State University of New York.

Hall, G. E., & Hord, S. M. (2001). *Implementing change: Patterns, principles, and potholes.* Needham Heights, MA: Allyn & Bacon.

Hibbard, K. M., Van Wagenen, L., Lewbel, S., Waterbury-Wyatt, S., Shaw, S., Pelletier, K., et al. (1996). *A teacher's guide to performance-based learning and assessment.* Alexandria, VA: Association for Supervision and Curriculum Development.

Hord, S. M., Rutherford, W. L., Huling-Austin, L., & Hall, G. E. (1987). *Taking charge of change.* Alexandria, VA: Association for Supervision and Curriculum Development.

Imbeau, M. B. (2006). Designing a professional development plan. In J. H. Purcell & R. D. Eckert (Eds.), *Designing services and programs for high ability learners: A guidebook for gifted education* (pp. 183–194). Thousand Oaks, CA: Corwin Press.

Joyce, B. (Ed.). (1990). *Changing school culture through staff development.* Alexandria, VA: Association for Supervision and Curriculum Development.

Joyce, B., & Showers, B. (1988). *Student achievement through staff development.* White Plains, NY: Longman.

Joyce, B., & Showers, B. (1995). *Student achievement through staff development* (2nd ed.). White Plains, NY: Longman.

Joyce, B., Wolf, J., & Calhoun, E. (1993). *The self-renewing school.* Alexandria, VA: Association for Supervision and Curriculum Development.

Karnes, F. A., & Bean, S. M. (Eds.). (2005). *Methods and materials for teaching the gifted* (2nd ed.). Waco, TX: Prufrock Press.

Killion, J. (2002). *Assessing impact: Evaluating staff development.* Oxford, OH: National Staff Development Council.

Killion, J., Munger, L., Roy, P., & McMullen, P. (2003). *Training manual for assessing impact: Evaluating staff development.* Oxford, OH: National Staff Development Council.

Kulik, J. A. (2004). Meta-analytic studies of acceleration. In N. Colangelo, S. G. Assouline, & M. U. M. Gross (Eds.), *A nation deceived: How schools hold back America's brightest students* (Vol. II, pp. 13–22). Iowa City, IA: The Connie Belin & Jacqueline N. Blank International Center for Gifted Education and Talent Development.

Landrum, M. S., Callahan, C. M., & Shaklee, B. D. (Eds.). (2001). *Aiming for excellence: Gifted program standards: Annotations to the NAGC pre-K–grade 12 gifted education program standards.* Waco, TX: Prufrock Press.

Lewis, A. C. (2002). School reform and professional development. *Phi Delta Kappan, 83,* 488–489.

Lieberman, A. (1995). Practices that support teacher development. *Phi Delta Kappan, 76,* 591–596.

Little, C. (2002, Spring). Project Phoenix year 3 results. *Systems Newsletter, 10*(2), 8.

Lowden, C. (2006). Reality check. *Journal of Staff Development, 27*(1), 61–64.

Lubinski, D. (2004). Long-term effects of educational acceleration. In N. Colangelo, S. G. Assouline, & M. U. M. Gross (Eds.), *A nation deceived: How schools hold back America's brightest students* (Vol. II, pp. 23–37). Iowa City, IA: The Connie Belin & Jacqueline N. Blank International Center for Gifted Education and Talent Development.

Moffett, C. A. (2000). Sustaining change: The answers are blowing in the wind. *Educational Leadership, 57*(7), 1–7.

National Education Commission on Time and Learning. (1994). *Prisoners of time.* Washington, DC: Author.

National Foundation for the Improvement of Education. (1996). *Teachers take charge of their learning: Transforming professional development for student success.* West Haven, CT: Author.

National Research Center on the Gifted and Talented. (1996). *Professional development practices in gifted education: Gifted education survey.* Storrs: National Research Center on the Gifted and Talented, University of Connecticut.

National Staff Development Council. (2001). *National Staff Development Council's standards for staff development: Advancing student learning through staff development* (Rev. ed.). Oxford, OH: Author.

No Child Left Behind Act, 20 U.S.C. §6301 (2001).

Project M³. (n.d.) *Project M³: Mentoring mathematical minds.* Retrieved July 17, 2007, from http://www.gifted.uconn.edu/projectm3

Purcell, J. H., & Eckert, R. D. (Eds.). (2006). *Designing services and programs for high ability learners: A guidebook for gifted education.* Thousand Oaks, CA: Corwin Press.

Reis, S. M., Eckert, R. D., Schreiber, F. J., Jacobs, J., Briggs, C., Gubbins, E. J., et al. (2005). *The schoolwide enrichment model reading study.* Storrs: National Research Center on the Gifted and Talented, University of Connecticut.

Reis, S. M., & Westberg, K. L. (1994). The impact of staff development on teachers' ability to modify curriculum for gifted and talented students. *Gifted Child Quarterly, 38,* 127–135.

Reis, S. M., Westberg, K. L., Kulikowich, J., Caillard, F., Hébert, T., Plucker, J., et al. (1993). *Why not let high ability students start school in January? The curriculum compacting study* (Research Monograph No. 93106). Storrs: National Research Center on the Gifted and Talented, University of Connecticut.

Reis, S. M., Westberg, K. L., Kulikowich, J. M., & Purcell, J. H. (1998). Curriculum compacting and achievement test scores: What does the research say? *Gifted Child Quarterly, 42,* 123–129.

Renzulli, J. S., Gubbins, E. J., & Koehler, J. (2003). The National Research Center on the Gifted and Talented: Recent studies and a look at the future of research in our field. *Journal for the Education of the Gifted, 27,* 107–118.

Robinson, N. M. (2004). Effects of academic acceleration on the social-emotional status of gifted students. In N. Colangelo, S. G. Assouline, & M. U. M. Gross (Eds.), *A nation deceived: How schools hold back America's brightest students* (Vol. II, pp. 47–57). Iowa City, IA: The Connie Belin & Jacqueline N. Blank International Center for Gifted Education and Talent Development.

Rogers, K. B. (2002). *Re-forming gifted education: Matching the program to the child.* Scottsdale, AZ: Great Potential Press.

Rogers, K. B. (2004). The academic effects of acceleration. In N. Colangelo, S. G. Assouline, & M. U. M. Gross, *A nation deceived: How schools hold back America's brightest students* (Vol. II, pp. 59–67). Iowa City, IA: The Connie Belin & Jacqueline N. Blank International Center for Gifted Education and Talent Development.

Roy, P., & Hord, S. (2003). *Moving NSDC's staff development standards into practice: Innovation configurations.* Oxford, OH: National Staff Development Council.

Smith, C., Hofer, J., Gillespie, M., Solomon, M., & Rowe, K. (2003). *How teachers change: A study of professional development in adult learners.* Cambridge, MA: National Center for the Study of Adult Learning and Literacy, Harvard Graduate School of Education.

Southern, W. T., & Jones, E. D. (1991). *The academic acceleration of gifted children.* New York: Teachers College Press.

Southern, W. T., & Jones, E. D. (2004). Types of acceleration: Dimensions and issues. In N. Colangelo, S. G. Assouline, & M. U. M. Gross, *A nation deceived: How schools hold back America's brightest students* (Vol. II, pp. 5–12). Iowa City, IA: The Connie Belin & Jacqueline N. Blank International Center for Gifted Education and Talent Development.

Sparks, D., & Hirsh, S. (1997). *A new vision for staff development.* Alexandria, VA: Association for Supervision and Curriculum Development.

Stanley, J. (2000). Helping students learn what they already don't know. *Psychology, Public Policy, and the Law, 6,* 216–222.

Sternberg, R. J., Ferrari, M., Clinkenbeard, P., & Grigorenko, E. L. (1996). Identification, instruction, and assessment of gifted children: A construct validation of a triarchic model. *Gifted Child Quarterly, 40,* 129–137.

Stigler, J., & Hiebert, J. (1999). *The teaching gap: Best ideas from the world's teachers for improving education in the classroom.* New York: Free Press.

Tomlinson, C. A. (1995). Deciding to differentiate instruction in middle school: One school's journey. *Gifted Child Quarterly, 39,* 77–87.

Tomlinson, C. A. (1999). *The differentiated classroom: Responding to the needs of all learners.* Alexandria, VA: Association for Supervision and Curriculum Development.

Tomlinson, C. A. (2005). Traveling the road to differentiation in staff development. *Journal of Staff Development, 26*(4), 8–12.

Tomlinson, C., Brighton, C., Hertberg, H., Callahan, C., Moon, T., Brimijoin, K., et al. (2003). Differentiating instruction in response to student readiness, interest, and learning profile in academically diverse classrooms: A review of the literature. *Journal for the Education of the Gifted, 27,* 119–145.

VanTassel-Baska, J. (1995). The development of talent through curriculum. *Roeper Review, 18,* 98–102.

VanTassel-Baska, J. (Ed.). (2003a). *A guide to implementation of Project Athena.* Williamsburg, VA: College of William and Mary, Center for Gifted Education.

VanTassel-Baska, J. (2003b). *Curriculum planning & instructional design.* Denver, CO: Love.

VanTassel-Baska, J., Zuo, L., Avery, L. D., & Little, C. A. (2002). A curriculum study of gifted student learning in the language arts. *Gifted Child Quarterly, 46,* 30–44.

Chapter 36

SCIENCE, ELEMENTARY

Cheryll M. Adams and Rebecca L. Pierce

n the late 1980s, efforts to make schools accountable for the academic success of their students resulted in a wave of school reform. Two very similar works are excellent guides for what students should know in science. Project 2061's *Benchmarks for Science Literacy* (American Association for the Advancement of Science, 1993) and the *National Science Education Standards* (National Research Council [NRC], 1996) form the basis for many of the state and district standards developed for school systems across the country. However, gifted and high-ability students are addressed only marginally in these works with such statements as "providing opportunities for those students interested in and capable of moving beyond the basic program" (NRC, 1996, p. 221).

Paul Brandwein (1995) reviewed the state of science education and concluded that it was nearly the same as it was in 1983. In that year, the National Science Teachers Association identified a number of recurring issues in the teaching of science. Some of the issues identified were an almost exclusive use of textbook-based science programs, lack of instructional strategies other than lecture; lack of a "real-world" focus; severe lack of supplies, equipment, and resources in most classrooms; and lack of content in elementary school science. In general, science is just becoming a tested subject on statewide standardized tests, and, until now, teachers have spent much of their time covering mathematics and reading skills that were the focus of most statewide testing programs. At a time when minimal competency, not maximal achievement, is the focus and science is just beginning to appear in most state accountability plans, little emphasis is given to science in the elementary classroom. In addition, as a result of the No Child Left Behind Act (2001), schools are placing an emphasis on low-achieving students in an effort to close the achievement gap. Consequently, little research has been or is being conducted concerning elementary science curriculum for gifted and high-ability students.

MAJOR QUESTIONS ADDRESSED IN THE RESEARCH

Creativity and Science: Finding Science Talent

Identifying science talent is not a simple process. Gardner (1995) has identified the naturalist intelligence and Fliegler (1961) developed a comprehensive 21-item checklist to assist with finding science talent. Brandwein (1988) suggested that creativity and process play essential roles when attempting to identify those students who are gifted and talented in science. These researchers advise that scientific talent may not easily be found by using standard paper-and-pencil creativity tests and traditional IQ tests because personality factors, competency in science, and a student's previous opportunities to practice the skills of a scientist are not reflected in the scores on these tests. Brandwein (1988) recommended that a better way to find science talent is to watch students actually working through the process of science as a scientist does and completing an experimental design.

Adams (2003) provided the following list of personality traits of scientists compiled from the works of early researchers in the area of scientific creativity (see MacKinnon, 1968; Mansfield, 1981; Roe, 1952; Ypma, 1968):

- risk-taker,
- autonomous,
- unconventional,
- original,
- persistent,
- looks at unusual details,
- independent,
- playful,

- rational,
- dislikes ambiguity,
- interest in art/humanities,
- energetic,
- broad aptitude,
- curious,
- intellectual courage, and
- daring. (p. 25)

In a recent study of Westinghouse finalists and members of the National Academy of Science, Feist (2006) determined that a commonality among both groups was an early realization that each wanted to be a scientist. According to Feist, his investigation served to "confirm the importance of early recognition of science talent if creative potential is to become actual creative achievement in adulthood" (p. 32). Clearly, finding science talent in the elementary grades will depend on keen observations by teachers and challenging, hands-on, inquiry-based activities to make those observations possible.

Attitudes Toward Science

Problems With Attitude Research in Science Education. Attitude research has been criticized in science education in several respects. In 1979, Peterson and Carlson admonished, "Attitude research is chaotic. . ." (p. 500). The construct of attitude has been defined in vague and ambiguous terms, resulting in inconsistent outcomes (Baker, 1985; Germann, 1988; Shrigley, 1990). Much of the research has been conducted without a theoretical model (Germann, 1988). Investigators seem to have arbitrarily chosen a plethora of variables rather than using a theoretical basis for including particular variables in the research (Germann, 1988; Haladyna & Shaughnessy, 1982; Peterson & Carlson, 1979). In a meta-analysis of 49 studies dealing with attitudes toward science, Haladyna and Shaughnessy (1982) concluded there is a "strong tendency to choose variables in a haphazard way without regard for the theoretical significance of any choice" (p. 557). Even the attitude instruments themselves are suspect (Fraser, 1977; Germann, 1988; Munby, 1983; Pearl, 1973).

The chaotic state of attitude research in science education makes analysis and interpretation of studies difficult. In an attempt to prevent the continuation of haphazard attitude research in science, Munby (1983) identified four categories of attitudes toward science: (1) scientific attitudes (scientific attitudes, scientific processes, scientific curiosity); (2) attitudes to science instruction (teaching science, science subject preference, science interests/activities, science in school); (3) attitudes to science itself; and (4) attitudes to science careers (career preference, occupational interests). If a study neither defines the construct nor provides a description of the instrument, however, there is virtually no way to determine which attitude toward science was measured. It is on this cautionary note that the discussion of attitudes toward science proceeds.

Research on Attitudes Toward Science. There are few meta-analyses of attitudes toward science since work completed in the 1980s and there are even fewer studies that looked at gifted elementary students. An early study of attitude toward science in intellectually gifted students (IQ > 140) was undertaken by Hansen & Neujahr (1974). The study focused on attitudes toward science, defined as interest in pursuing science as a career and involvement in science outside of school. Although the population was chosen for both its high interest in and aptitude for science, gifted females showed less positive attitudes toward science and less interest in pursuing a career in science. As a result of their work with attitudes toward science, Farenga and Joyce (1998) recommended that "efforts to increase achievement must be accompanied by efforts to improve attitudes toward science and may need to be tailored for gender" (p. 250).

In a quantitative synthesis of attitude research in science, Haladyna and Shaughnessy (1982) found attitudes (defined as attitudes toward the subject of science) more predictable if the unit of analysis was class rather than student. This lends support to the notion that the teacher and the learning environment contribute heavily to attitude development. Simpson and Oliver (1990) reported similar findings from their 10-year longitudinal study to determine the salient influences on attitude toward science (global definition). Their results suggest classroom environment is a strong influence on students' attitudes toward science (46% to 73% of variance explained). The basic feelings students formulate toward science and toward their future involvement with science courses appear to be mediated by the science classroom.

In looking at students' attitudes toward science over 21 years, Weinburgh (1995) found a moderate correlation between attitude toward science and achievement in science. The correlation was stronger for girls than for boys, suggesting that having a positive attitude towards science may be essential for girls to achieve at high levels.

Most research on attitudes toward science has been conducted using students of middle school age through college (see DeBaz, 1994). In informal interviews with science majors and nonscience majors, Evans (Gould, Weeks, & Evans, 2003) found that many of the nonscience majors cited a negative experience in elementary school science as a reason for their lack of interest in science. The work of Farenga and Joyce (1998) indicated that attitudes toward science predicted science course selection to a greater degree in young high-ability girls (aged 9–13) than in boys. In a study of highly gifted elementary and high school students, Neber and Schommer-Aikins (2002) found that these high-ability students required a science learning environment in which exploration and discovery learning were strong components. Perhaps now that science is becoming a tested subject in many states we will see attitude research in science increase to the pre-1990 level.

Curriculum Issues

Despite an emphasis on using basal textbooks in science, we could find little evidence of studies about effectiveness with any students, including those who are gifted or of high ability. In fact, Lockwood (1992) notes that most textbook publishers fail to address the texts' effectiveness and those adopting the textbooks generally take the word of the publisher that the books are effective.

A meta-analysis of the reform science curriculum of the 1970s concluded that, in addition to achievement scores, testing other outcomes such as attitude and creativity was essential in evaluating a curricular instructional model (Bredderman, 1978). Based on their research in science classrooms of high-ability students aged 5 to 11 years, Coates and Wilson (2001) suggested that when challenging these students, "teachers do not necessarily need to look towards the amount of work that is done, but rather to the cognitive demands that it makes upon the children" (p. 17). Opportunities need to be planned for critical and higher level thinking skills to be accessed. Scientific investigations, open-ended questions, and problem solving are ways for this type of thinking to occur. In a study of self-regulated learning among elementary science students and high school physics students at a school for gifted students, Neber and Schommer-Aikins (2002) found that the high school students felt the learning environment was less conducive to possibilities for their own investigations than did the elementary students. Elementary students seemed to hold the belief that success did not require work, suggesting that they were not experiencing enough challenge. Neber and Schommer-Aikins proposed that learning environments in science should be designed to provide time for more self-initiated investigations if students are to become self-regulated learners.

Results of Wood's (2002) study of girls' extracurricular science activities suggested that most science classrooms offer little hands-on, inquiry-based science. In an attempt to increase teacher efficacy in relation to science, Wood recommended compulsory science in-service training for teachers and subject-specific teachers in grades 3–6, as well as adequate equipment and supplies for teaching science. According to Wood, "a teacher's love or fear of science is contagious, and in-services may not be enough" (p.39). Callahan, Tomlinson, Reis, and Kaplan (2000) urge schools to appraise their current science offerings at all levels to be sure the curriculum is challenging and provides opportunities to cover topics in depth, rather than the "mile-wide inch-deep" approach currently in place.

A review of the literature from approximately the last 25 years on elementary science curriculum for gifted and high-ability students revealed one book, a resource, and 139 articles that we classified into three different categories. Unfortunately, 53 of the 139 did not address all three areas (i.e., elementary, science, and gifted/high ability). For example, computer science was often the focus rather than science. In the Curriculum Compacting Study (Reis et. al., 1993), teachers compacted in science only when students demonstrated very high ability in science. However, the replacement material given to these students was not necessarily related to science and no specific description of the materials was reported. An analysis of single-subject acceleration across 21 studies covering grades 2–12 revealed three fifths of a year's additional growth in the subject accelerated. However, only two of the studies dealt with science acceleration (Rogers, 1992).

The resources and additional references are listed at the end of this chapter. The book *Gifted Young in Science: Potential Through Performance* (Brandwein & Passow, 1988) describes purposes, principles, and programs for developing science talent and teaching science to gifted and high-ability students. While a valuable reference, most chapters are conceptual in nature.

Of the three categories mentioned above, the majority (n = 60) addressed activities or projects that authors proposed as good curriculum ideas and/or carried out in their own classrooms. In general, any data that were gathered from these addressed whether the students liked the material or enjoyed the lessons/experiences. A second category (n = 18) addressed conceptual ideas about science education for gifted and high-ability students and professional development for teachers. For the most part, these works did not include any data gathered from implementation of the ideas.

The third category (n = 8) consists of a relatively small number of research-based papers about effectiveness of a particular curriculum. Three were concerned with the units developed by Joyce VanTassel-Baska and her William and Mary colleagues. One paper dealt with the IDEAS model, one dealt with the Individual Progress Program, and three were reports for the Jacob K. Javits grants, Project SPRING and Project SPRING II.

CONCLUSIONS FROM THE RESEARCH

The most frequently mentioned question in the first type of work was, "Was this material/project/curriculum successful?" In the majority of the studies, success was measured through surveys or interviews that addressed user satisfaction. For example, a frequent question was, "Did you like this unit?" Not surprisingly, all of the studies reported very positive results. The second type of work didn't pose any type of research questions and could be characterized mainly as literature reviews or the author's ideas about what should be included in elementary science curriculum for gifted and high-ability students.

The third type of work collected real data on the effectiveness of the curriculum based on pre- and posttest data, standardized achievement data, or case study methodology using multiple data sources. Because the number of pertinent papers is so small, below we discuss the conclusions from each of them in chronological order.

Individual Progress Program (IPP)

The IPP (Norsen & Wick, 1983) was begun in 1978 at one elementary school in Seattle, WA, with students in grades 1–5 who were functioning two to four or more grade levels above their age-appropriate grade. The curriculum was delivered at an accelerated pace in what appears to be clusters of like-ability students. As a cost-effective measure, the curriculum model was to adapt already existing material whenever possible. The curriculum was developed with an interdisciplinary, thematic approach using student learning objectives and the district's core objectives. Three themes—patterns, origins, and systems—were the focus and were implemented on a 3-year rotation. The science curriculum dealt specifically with higher order science process skills, laboratory activities, critical thinking, and complex problem solving. It was a hands-on, activity-oriented program.

The effectiveness of the program was evaluated through comparison with a control group matched by gender, ethnicity, grade, and ability level. Both groups were tested using reading comprehension, language mechanics, and math computation subtests of the California Achievement Tests 2 years above grade level. Statistically significant higher scores were reported for the IPP students in all three areas. However, the IPP did not measure science achievement and did not adequately describe the curriculum model used in science beyond the fact that it was based on the district scope and sequence, making it difficult to judge its merits.

Special Populations Rural Information Network for the Gifted (Project SPRING and Project SPRING II)

Project SPRING served special populations of gifted students in Indiana, Illinois, and Ohio. Through this project, researchers demonstrated ways to identify these students, assisted teachers in designing and implementing curriculum for them, and provided in-service training for teachers (Spicker & Aamidor, 1993). The purpose of Project SPRING II (Spicker, 1996) was to identify and serve underserved rural gifted children in grades 3–8 from African American, Mexican American, Mescalero Apache, and Appalachian populations in three states: Indiana, South Carolina, and New Mexico. Science curriculum and teaching strategies for developing their talents were designed during the SPRING project and were modified by two states for implementation during the SPRING II project. Two units were described from Project SPRING II: water and forestry. The interdisciplinary water unit was developed for Project SPRING and was used again for Project SPRING II. This unit also was the model for the forestry unit (used only at the Indiana site). The units were unique in that they considered the cultural and geographical characteristics of the areas in which Project SPRING II was implemented (rural students in Indiana, South Carolina, and New Mexico). The units addressed the National Science Standards and were designed using Bloom's taxonomy and Gardner's theory of multiple intelligences to provide interdisciplinary and differentiated curriculum. Teachers wrote lessons that provided opportunities for students to think critically through open-ended responses, promoting rich discussions. Inquiry-based lessons capitalized on students' curiosity and allowed the students to develop an understanding of the scientific process. For specific information about the units, see Spicker and Aamidor (1996).

The effectiveness of this science curriculum for elementary students in South Carolina and New Mexico was evaluated through the Test of Basic Process Skills (BAPS) and/or the science portion of a standardized achievement test. Findings relevant to elementary science curriculum indicated the intervention significantly improved the scientific problem-solving skills of the identified students. In South Carolina, students showed significant gains as measured by the BAPS and a slight nonsignificant increase in their science grades, but their achievement tests scores dropped. In New Mexico, students also showed significant gains as measured by the BAPS, but no results were reported based on grades or achievement test scores. Although the Project SPRING II science curriculum manual provided information to replicate the curriculum, science achievement decreased between pre- and posttesting even though science problem-solving skills improved, indicating further modification to the curriculum might be warranted.

The William and Mary Curriculum

Although there are seven science units that have been developed by colleagues at the College of William and Mary, we could find research addressing only three: *Acid, Acid Everywhere*; *Electricity City*; and *What a Find*. The first two titles were developed for grades 4–6 and the last title for grades 2–4.

Acid, Acid Everywhere (VanTassel-Baska, Bass, Ries, Poland, & Avery, 1998) was implemented in 45 classes across 15 school districts in 7 states at grade levels 4–6. The unit is based on the Integrated Curriculum Model (ICM) designed specifically for gifted learners and developed at the Center for Gifted Education at the College of William and Mary. *Acid, Acid Everywhere* is a 20–36-hour problem-based learning unit in which students explore the concepts of acids and bases in chemistry, as well as model the scientific processes that a practicing scientist would use. The overarching scientific concept is *systems*.

The effectiveness study added 17 comparison classrooms, making the total number of students in both groups 1,471. To determine the effectiveness of the unit, the Diet Cola Test (Adams & Callahan, 1995; Fowler, 1990) was used as a student outcome measure because it may be used as an evaluation tool for science process skills. Statistically significant differences between the posttest means of the experimental and comparison groups were shown using an analysis of covariance (F = 32.86; p < .001). The effect size was reported to be 1.30. Although the results for this unit indicated significant gains for students in the experimental group when compared to the control group not using the unit, no data was reported for the other six units that have been developed.

Evaluation of the Implementation of the Units. One study (VanTassel-Baska, Avery, Little, & Hughes, 2000) dealt with two sites, A and B, which had been using the William and Mary curriculum units at the elementary levels for at least 3 years. Although both sites implemented the language arts units, only site A implemented the science units. Site A used the science units at the elementary and middle schools with gifted and nongifted students.

Case-study methodology was used in two elementary classrooms for the *Electricity City* unit. Although the article describes using several data sources, the science curriculum is only mentioned specifically under classroom observation and the teachers were observed to be using the curriculum appropriately. Although case study methodology provided pertinent information about the units in general, adding quantitative data may have provided a better picture of the effectiveness of particular units.

Longitudinal Assessment of the Units. In a longitudinal study (Feng, VanTassel-Baska, Quek, Bai, & O'Neill, 2005) of the effects of the William and Mary curriculum units over a period of 6 years, results indicated that students showed strong enhanced achievement patterns. The science units in the study were *Acid, Acid, Everywhere*; *What a Find*; and *Electricity City*. The 973 students in the study ranged from grades 3 to 9, with most students having been involved with the units for 3 years during grades 3, 4, and 5. The Diet Cola Test (Adams & Callahan, 1995) mentioned previously had been used during the time students participated in the study to assess their learning. Paired-samples t tests were used to measure students' achievement over time. Effect sizes using Cohen's d index ranged from 1.00 (grade 5) to 1.37 (grade 3), indicating both significant and important gains academically. The repeated exposure effect is perhaps the most important aspect of this study: Students who used the curriculum all 3 years had the highest pre- and posttest mean scores on the Diet Cola Test. The researchers underscore the need for consistency in using research-based curriculum with gifted learners rather than changing the curriculum repeatedly in favor of the latest novel approach.

In-Depth Expanded Applications of Science (IDEAS)

Across a 5-year period, the IDEAS model (Romance & Vitale, 2001) was implemented in a variety of classrooms with average, above-average, and at-risk students in grades 2–5. The IDEAS model replaces traditional reading/language arts instruction with a daily 2-hour time block focused on science concept instruction in an effort to combat the lack of adequate instructional time for teaching science in the elementary grades. During this time, reading comprehension and language arts skills are taught via science.

The Metropolitan Achievement Test–Science (MAT–Science) was used to measure science achievement to determine the model's effectiveness. Effects of .93 to 1.6 grade equivalents on the MAT-Science were found over the 5 years. However, the achievement scores were not disaggregated according to average, above-average, and at-risk populations. Therefore, while the model seems effective with students in general, we can not determine its effectiveness for gifted and high-ability students in particular.

IDEAS did not provide separate achievement data for average, above-average, and at-risk students. Thus, we have no way of knowing which group made the greatest gains and for whom the curriculum was most appropriate. In addition, curriculum specifics were not given; however, general steps for planning IDEAS instruction were included.

LIMITATIONS OF THE RESEARCH

Of the five research-based papers, four had major limitations with respect to effectiveness and/or replication of the curriculum. Elements that were consistently missing were science achievement measurements, inadequate descriptions of the model used, lack of quantitative data, and failure to identify results by student ability levels. Even though the William and Mary science units are well respected in the field of gifted education, the effectiveness studies we found focused only on three of the units. Additionally, when reviewing the literature using the names of the other science units, no effectiveness studies were found.

PRACTICAL IMPLICATIONS OF THE RESEARCH

If you are looking for appropriate elementary science curriculum there are several that provide enough detail to allow a teacher to begin implementing them. In particular, the William and Mary units and the Project SPRING II curriculum manual are well documented. The appendix to the IDEAS report provides a framework and some description of a few activities but not in enough detail to implement the curriculum.

From the research standpoint, educators looking for high-quality curriculum whose effectiveness has been well documented would find very little on elementary science curriculum for gifted and high-ability learners. Hence, this is an area open to further studies focusing on the effectiveness of existing elementary science curriculum with gifted and high-ability learners, as well as the design, development, and implementation of new curriculum for this population.

There have been some extracurricular programs that show promise, such as a museum science program (Melber, 2003) and an afterschool science enrichment program for girls (Wood, 2002). Results from both programs indicate that students prefer inquiry-based science activities and would welcome these activities in the classroom.

Identifying science talent requires, in part, challenging science curriculum. If science reform is to be successful, teachers will need a wide range of resources and tools such as modular materials, rather than basal texts that are not conducive to inquiry-based teaching, and training that focuses on content-based pedagogy using high-quality material. In addition, the curriculum must be monitored to ensure that it is being implemented appropriately (VanTassel-Baska, 1999).

To identify other factors, more research is needed into the development of science talent over time, as well as its relationship to creativity. Feist (2006) suggests measuring "the change and growth in scientific interest, motivation, and ability from childhood through adulthood," (p. 34) similar to what has been done with mathematical talent (Benbow & Minor, 1986; Benbow & Stanley, 1982; Benbow, Lubinski, Shea, & Eftekhari-Sanjani, 2000).

Johnson, Boyce, and VanTassel-Baska (1995) undertook a study of science textbooks and curricular material in an attempt to find challenging material for high-ability learners. Their findings indicate that there is no basal science program that is appropriate for gifted students at the elementary or junior high level. These results, taken with the issues presented earlier, suggest that these school factors do not provide a setting conducive to nurturing science talent. According to Adams (2003),

> particularly at the elementary level, there are far too many instances where unqualified, uninterested teachers are leaving the study of science to Friday afternoons, thirty minutes before school is out rather than doing an exemplary job of preparing future scientists and scientifically literate citizens, exposing students to a variety of real-world issues and problems to solve, and providing opportunities for using critical and creative thinking skills. (p. 22)

She offers the following as nonnegotiables for an elementary science program that nurtures science talent:

1. Children are exposed to science in some way every day.
2. The classroom contains a rich collection of books, manipulatives, and other materials, both natural and man-made.
3. Children have time each day to pursue their interest in science by reading books with a science focus, investigating their own self-selected projects, and/or spending time with science-related materials.

4. Science investigations are inquiry-based, student-centered, and open-ended.
5. A broad range of ability and reading levels are addressed by the materials used in the science classroom.
6. The teacher has advanced knowledge of the science topics taught at the particular grade level.
7. There are provisions for enrichment and acceleration in each topic studied.
8. The science content is taught using concepts, principles, issues, and themes.
9. There are opportunities to work in homogenous groups.
10. Assessment includes both traditional paper-and-pencil tests and alternative assessment options (e.g., performance assessments, portfolios, student-selected projects). (p. 25)

WHAT WE KNOW

- There are very few research studies that focus on the effectiveness of existing elementary science curriculum for gifted and high-ability learners.
- Few research studies focus on the design and development of science curriculum for elementary gifted and high-ability learners.
- Curriculum for gifted and high-ability learners should model the habits of mind and approaches of real scientists.
- Additional research is needed to verify the effectiveness of existing and/or newly developed curriculum that goes beyond "Students liked it!"

MAJOR RESOURCES AND REFERENCES

Listed below are a few resources focusing on both elementary science issues and gifted and high-ability learners. However, due to the paucity of articles on elementary science curriculum for gifted and high-ability learners that mention research, no credible resources are available for research on this topic.

Brandwein, P. F. (1995). *Science talent in the young expressed within ecologies of achievement* (Research-Based Decision Making Series No. 9510). Storrs: National Research Center on the Gifted and Talented, University of Connecticut.

Brandwein, P. F., & Passow, A. H. (Eds.). (1988). *Gifted young in science: Potential through performance.* Washington, DC: National Science Teachers Association.

Center for Gifted Education. (1997). *Guide to teaching a problem-based science curriculum.* Dubuque, IA: Kendall-Hunt.

Johnson, D. T., Boyce, L. N., & VanTassel-Baska, J. (1995). Science curriculum review: Evaluating materials for high-ability learners. *Gifted Child Quarterly, 39,* 36–43.

REFERENCES

Adams, C. M. (2003). Talent development in science. In P. Olszewski-Kubilius, L. Limburg-Weber, & S. Pfeiffer (Eds.), *Early gifts: Recognizing and nurturing children's talents* (pp. 19–38). Waco, TX: Prufrock Press.

Adams, C. M., & Callahan, C. M. (1995). The reliability and validity of a performance task for evaluating science process skills. *Gifted Child Quarterly, 39,* 14–20.

American Association for the Advancement of Science. (1993). *Benchmarks for science literacy.* New York: Oxford University Press.

Baker, D. R. (1985). Predictive value of attitude, cognitive ability, and personality to science achievement in the middle school. *Journal of Research in Science Teaching, 22,* 103–113.

Benbow, C. P., & Minor, L. L. (1986). Mathematically talented students and achievement in the high school sciences. *American Educational Research Journal, 23,* 259–282.

Benbow, C. P., & Stanley, J. C. (1982). Consequences in high school and college of sex differences in mathematical reasoning ability: A longitudinal perspective. *American Educational Research Journal, 19,* 598–622.

Benbow, C. P., Lubinski, D., Shea, D. L., & Eftekhari-Sanjani, H. E. (2000). Sex differences in mathematical reasoning ability at age 13: Their status 20 years later. *Psychological Sciences, 11,* 474–480.

Brandwein, P. (1988). Science talent: In an ecology of achievement. In P. Brandwein & A. H. Passow (Eds.), *Gifted young in science: Potential through performance* (pp. 73–103). Washington, DC: National Science Teachers Association.

Brandwein, P. F. (1995). *Science talent in the young expressed within ecologies of achievement* (Research-Based Decision Making Series No. 9510). Storrs: National Research Center on the Gifted and Talented, University of Connecticut.

Brandwein, P. F., & Passow, A. H. (Eds.). (1988). *Gifted young in science: Potential through performance.* Washington, DC: National Science Teachers Association.

Bredderman, T. (1978). Elementary school process curricula—A meta-analysis. Albany: State University of New York. (ERIC Document Reproduction Service No. ED170333)

Callahan, C. M., Tomlinson, C. A., Reis, S. M., & Kaplan, S. N. (2000). TIMSS and high-ability students. *Phi Delta Kappan, 81,* 787–790.

Coates, D., & Wilson, H. (2001, November). Science masterclasses for able six-year-old children: Do we underestimate able students' abilities? *Australian Science Teachers Association, 4,* 17–20.

DeBaz, T. P. (1994). *Meta-analysis of the relationship between students' characteristics and achievement and attitudes toward science.* Unpublished doctoral dissertation, Ohio State University.

Farenga, S. J., & Joyce, B. A. (1998). Science-related attitudes and science course selection: A study of high-ability boys and girls. *Roeper Review, 20,* 247–251.

Feist, G. J. (2006). The development of scientific talent in Westinghouse finalists and members of the National Academy of Sciences. *Journal of Adult Development, 13,* 23–35.

Feng, A. X., VanTassel-Baska, J., Quek, C., Bai, W., & O'Neill, B. (2005). A longitudinal assessment of gifted students' learning using the integrated curriculum model (ICM): Impacts and perceptions of the William and Mary language arts and science curriculum. *Roeper Review, 27,* 78–83.

Fliegler, L. A. (1961). *Curriculum planning for the gifted.* Englewood Cliffs, NJ: Prentice Hall.

Fowler, M. (1990). The diet cola test. *Science Scope, 13*(4), 32–34.

Fraser, B. (1977). Selection and validation of attitudes scales for curriculum evaluation. *Science Education, 6,* 317–329.

Gardner, H. (1995, November). Reflections on multiple intelligences: Myths and messages. *Phi Delta Kappan, 77,* 202–209.

Germann, P. J. (1988). Development of the attitude toward science in school assessment and its use to investigate the relationship between science achievement and attitude toward science in school. *Journal of Research in Science Teaching, 25,* 689–703.

Gould, J. C., Weeks, V., & Evans, S. (2003). Science starts early. *Gifted Child Today, 26*(3), 38–41

Haladyna, T., & Shaughnessy, J. (1982). Attitudes toward science: A quantitative synthesis. *Science Education, 66,* 547–563.

Hansen, R., & Neujahr, J. (1974). Career development of males and females gifted in science. *The Journal of Educational Research, 68,* 43–45.

Johnson, D. T., Boyce, L. N., & VanTassel-Baska, J. (1995). Science curriculum review: Evaluating materials for high-ability learners. *Gifted Child Quarterly, 39,* 36–43.

Lockwood, A. (1992). Whose knowledge do we teach? *Focus on Change, 6,* 3–7.

MacKinnon, D. W. (1968). Childhood variables and adult personality in two professional samples: Architects and research scientists. In F. E. Williams (Ed.), *Creativity at home and in school: A report of the Conference on Child Rearing Practices for Developing Creativity* (pp. 125–160). St. Paul, MN: Macalester College.

Mansfield, R. G. (1981). *The psychology of creativity and discovery: Scientists and their work.* Chicago: Nelson Hall.

Melber, L. M. (2003). Partnerships in science learning: Museum outreach and elementary gifted education. *Gifted Child Quarterly, 47,* 251–258.

Munby, H. (1983). Thirty studies involving the Scientific Attitude Inventory: What confidence can we have in this instrument? *Journal of Research in Science Teaching, 20,* 141–162.

National Research Council. (1996). *National science education standards.* Washington, DC: National Academy Press.

Neber, H., & Schommer-Aikins, M. (2002). Self-regulated science learning with highly gifted students: The role of cognitive, motivational, epistemological, and environmental variables. *High Ability Studies, 13,* 59–74.

No Child Left Behind Act, 20 U.S.C. §6301 (2001).

Norsen, B. G., & Wick, C. (1983). *Individual progress program for the extremely gifted student in the greater Seattle area.* Seattle, WA: Seattle Public Schools. (ERIC Reproduction Services No. ED232347)

Pearl, R. E. (1973). The present status of science attitude measurement: History, theory and availability of measurement instruments. *School Science and Mathematics, 73,* 375–381.

Peterson, R. W., & Carlson, G. R. (1979). A summary of research in science education—1977. *Science Education, 63,* 497–500.

Reis, S. M., Westberg, K. L., Kulikowich, J., Caillard, F., Hébert, T., Plucker, J., et al. (1993). *Why not let high ability students start school in January?: The curriculum compacting study* (Research Monograph 93106). Storrs: National Research Center on the Gifted and Talented, University of Connecticut.

Roe, A. (1952). *The making of a scientist.* New York: Dodd, Mead.

Rogers, K. B. (1992). A best-evidence synthesis of the research on acceleration options for gifted learners. In N. Colangelo, S. G. Assouline, & D. L. Ambroson (Eds.), *Talent development: Proceedings from the 1991 Henry B. & Jocelyn Wallace national research symposium on talent development* (pp. 406–409). Unionville, NY: Trillium.

Romance, N. R., & Vitale, M. R. (2001). Implementing an in-depth expanded science model in elementary schools: Multi-year findings, research issues, and policy implications. *International Journal of Science Education, 23,* 373–404.

Shrigley, R. L. (1990). Attitudes and behaviors are correlates. *Journal of Research in Science Teaching, 27,* 97–113.

Simpson, R. D., & Oliver, J. S. (1990). A summary of major influences on attitude toward and achievement in science among adolescent students. *Science Education, 74,* 1–18.

Spicker, H. H. (1996). *Project SPRING II final report.* Bloomington: Indiana University. (ERIC Document Reproduction Service No. ED404789)

Spicker, H., & Aamidor, S. (1993). Educational modifications: Project SPRING: Special populations resource information network for the gifted. Bloomington: Indiana University. (ERIC Document Reproduction Service No. ED365066)

Spicker, H., & Aamidor, S. (1996). *Project SPRING II: Science curriculum modifications for rural disadvantaged gifted students.* Retrieved March 24, 2007, from http://www.eric.ed.gov/ERICDocs/data/ericdocs2/content_storage_01/0000000b/80/25/2c/20.pdf

VanTassel-Baska, J. (1999). Science education for gifted and talented children. *The ERIC Review, 6*(2), 50–51.

VanTassel-Baska, J., Avery, L. D., Little, C., & Hughes, C. (2000). An evaluation of the implementation of the curriculum innovation: The impact of the William and Mary units on schools. *Journal for the Education of the Gifted, 23,* 244–272.

VanTassel-Baska, J., Bass, G., Ries, R., Poland, D., & Avery, L. D. (1998). A national study of science curriculum effectiveness with high ability students. *Gifted Child Quarterly, 42,* 200–211.

Weinburgh, M. (1995). Gender differences in student attitudes toward science: A meta-analysis. *Journal of Research in Science Teaching, 32,* 387–98.

Wood, S. (2002). Perspectives of best practices for learning gender-inclusive science: influences of extracurricular science for gifted girls and electrical engineering for women. *Journal of Women and Minorities in Science and Engineering, 8,* 25–40.

Ypma, E. G. (1968). Prediction of the industrial creativity of research scientists from biographical information. (Doctoral Dissertation, Purdue University, 1968). *Dissertation Abstracts International, 30,* 5731.

Chapter 37

SCIENCE, SECONDARY

Joyce VanTassel-Baska and Bronwyn MacFarlane

INTRODUCTION

cience education continues to experience several major and interrelated problems in this country. Major curriculum reform efforts such as the National Science Education Standards, and those emanating from several disciplines, have highlighted the need for curriculum change. The recommended science reform standards emphasize a hands-on, minds-on approach to learning scientific processes, inquiry, and content. "Learning science is something that students do, not something that is done to them" (National Research Council, 1996, p. 2). The council also recommends the importance of the use of cognitive science-based research strategies in the teaching of science that include the development of concepts and concept mapping, metacognition, higher level thinking, and articulation of scientific understandings in visual and oral forms (Donovan & Bransford, 2005; National Science Resources Center, 2006).

Yet, in general, school organizational structures at all grade levels remain too inflexible to accommodate serious science study. Laboratory time and hands-on classroom experiments require longer time periods than typically are allocated, and complication with costs and proper equipment are paramount. Most middle school teachers rely heavily on textbook worksheets and canned experiments for conveying science (VanTassel-Baska & Stambaugh, 2006), appropriate mentors are frequently unavailable, and secondary school officials may give inappropriate guidance (Subotnik & Steiner, 1993). Meanwhile, international data clearly indicate that our top students are not ready to compete at world-class levels in science (Smith, Martin, Mullis, & Kelly, 2000). It is critical that high-ability students have a functional knowledge of science, even if they do not enter careers directly related to scientific research or teaching. Yet, empirical research on interventions for teaching science to secondary gifted students is limited.

TEACHING SCIENCE TO ALL LEARNERS

Minstrell and Kraus (2005) emphasized the importance of science learning experiences needing to develop from firsthand, concrete experiences to the more distant or abstract. Ideas develop from experiences, and technical terms develop from the ideas and operations that are rooted in those experiences. Students need opportunities to see where ideas come from, and they need to be held responsible for knowing and communicating that knowledge. They also need opportunities to learn to inquire in the disciplines, a skill best developed by teachers modeling the sorts of questions that the students later will ask themselves and by teachers providing guided inquiry.

A recent study of Westinghouse finalists (Feist, 2006b) suggests that increasing the number of gifted scientists will require deepening the experiences of such students in the critical transition years of ages 11–22, which bridge the years Westinghouse winners identify science as a major interest and when they matriculate into a career in science or a related area. The nature of such intervention was not explicitly explored in the study, but "motivation to do science" was cited by 79% of the sample as the major reason for continuing in the discipline. Few gender differences were found except for causes of motivation for doing science, with females citing altruistic reasons and males citing their own curiosity about how the world works as primary rationales.

In a related study, Feist (2006a) examined retrospectively early life predictors of lifetime achievement and eminence in science for members of the National Academy of Sciences (NAS). The study confirmed that early interest in science, early publications, and high productivity all set the stage for eminence. The group also self-identified the top three reasons for their success in science as being scientific intuition, intelligence, and drive/persistence, all qualities associated in earlier studies with high performance in science (Simonton, 1988; Subotnik & Steiner, 1994; Zuckerman, 1996).

GENDER ISSUES IN SCIENCE EDUCATION

Gender issues and girls' attitudes toward science are unique areas of concern to the discipline of scientific study. According to the U.S. Department of Education's National Center for Education Statistics (Rohrer & Welsch, 1998), although almost half of the American labor force are women (ages 25–64), they comprise only 8% of all of the United States' engineers, 27% of the natural scientists, 32% of the mathematical and computer scientists, and only 9% of the physicists. In science, notable women who exhibit precocity have been encouraged by parents and teachers (Filippelli & Walbert, 1997). Factors that tend to influence success in science courses and scientific careers include attitude (Farenga & Joyce, 1998; Swiatek & Lupkowski-Shoplik, 2000), perception of ability (Li & Adamson, 1995), and accessibility to mentors (Subotnik & Steiner, 1993; Subotnik, Stone, & Steiner, 2001). Attitudes are particularly important predictors for young women who take advanced courses (Farenga & Joyce, 1998; Joyce & Farenga, 2000). Factors affecting engagement in science then appear to differ along gender lines.

GENDER ISSUES AMONG THE GIFTED

Many studies have been conducted regarding the teaching of science to high-ability learners at the secondary level. Findings of these studies focus on gender differences and teaching practices best suited to gifted learners.

Farenga and Joyce (1998) examined science-related attitudes and science course selection among high-ability boys and girls. The sample consisted of 111 high-achieving students between the ages of 9 and 13 who completed the Test of Science-Related Attitudes and the Course Selection Sheet. They found girls' science-related attitudes to be important predictors of the number of science courses they select, and encouraged educators to make science appealing through hands-on, inquiry-based activities.

Reis and Park (2001) found more high-achieving males than females in a sample of math and science high-achieving students from the National Education Longitudinal Study of 1988. The researchers examined gender differences between high-achieving students in math and science and found that high-achieving males feel better about themselves than do high-achieving females. Olszewski-Kubilius and Yasumoto (1995) found that females who are high achieving in math and science are more influenced by teachers and families than are males. These data appear to indicate that supportive environments, both at home and school, can make a significant difference in encouraging gifted students, particularly young girls, in pursuing math and science careers.

Researchers Joyce and Farenga (2000) examined a sample of high-ability and average 9–13-year-old girls in science regarding their academic ability, perceptions, and future participation in science. The authors concluded that selection of science courses may be related more to gender than to academic abilities.

Using a sample of 656 middle school students who participated in a summer academic program, researchers Olszewski-Kubilius and Yasumoto (1995) found that gender influences the course-taking choices in math and science courses over verbal courses, favoring males. Parental attitudes, previous educational experiences, and ethnicity (in this study Asian American) also exerted a positive influence on the selection of math and science courses over verbal courses. The importance that parents place on mathematics and science for their child's future also may have the most powerful influence on a child's selection of mathematics and science courses.

Rohrer and Welsch (1998) designed a summer program for female middle school students in math and science to provide a nonthreatening, all-female environment where young girls could work with female scientists and teachers and ultimately encourage continuing education in science and math. Students reported increased confidence in their abilities to succeed at mathematics and science as a result of program activities and interaction with female peers. Rohrer and Welsch suggest the implications for schools include (1) encouraging high-ability female students to work together on science projects, (2) the identification of female mentors and role models, (3) providing guided practice with equipment prior to using it in class, (4) the maintenance of a psychologically safe environment for reflection and discussion, (5) opportunities for question exploration and problem solving within and beyond class time, and (6) increased teacher awareness of their classroom pattern interactions, with an emphasis on the connections between math and science and daily life.

High-stakes testing may be a barrier to gifted girls in science (Rebhorn & Miles, 1999). In explaining the different scores achieved by boys and girls on standardized tests in science, Rebhorn and Miles discuss possible explanations to include gender bias in tests and expectations held by parents and teachers. All solutions proposed by the authors fit into one of two categories, (1) modify the testing and (2) provide supportive school and home environments.

TEACHING SCIENCE TO GIFTED LEARNERS

The Third International Math and Science study (TIMSS; Mullis et al. 1998) compared a sample of the best science students in the United States to the best students in other countries. U.S. 12th graders outperformed only 2 of the 21 participating countries in mathematics and science. The TIMSS data emphasize the need to examine how curriculum for advanced students is presented and the types of programs secondary gifted students need to facilitate their acquisition of higher level science curriculum (Tyler-Wood, Mortenson, Putney, & Cass, 2000).

Special science residential and day schools for the gifted have been a traditional model for serving the gifted in Russia since the 1960s (Donoghue, Karp, & Vogeli, 2000). Student selection for admissions were tied to performance on the prestigious Olympiads conducted in every region of the Soviet Union. The curricula and mode of instruction with two to three Ph.D.-level teachers in science in every classroom were standard. In this country, similar schools exist, with varying modes of admission and delivering curriculum, yet common issues such as the nature and rigor of the science curriculum, the amount of laboratory time in science, and the accessibility of science mentors from national laboratories and other facilities continue to be fluid in service delivery. Furthermore, many residential campuses engage in outreach activities impacting public service regionally to improve science education for students and teachers beyond the residential setting (Cross & Miller, 2007).

Mentorships and internships offer structured program opportunities for gifted students to appreciate the nature of collaborative work in the sciences. In science, one of the requirements is usually to have a mentor in the field (Subotnik & Steiner, 1993; VanTassel-Baska & Subotnik, 2004). Csikszentmihalyi (1996) found that highly creative persons who made a significant contribution in science often had a mentor or someone to guide them in the processes, culture, and accepted practices of the field. Yet, availability of mentors to collaborate with students is limited. Mentors in the scientific field may be needed at different times and usually in different transition periods of a gifted student's talent development journey (Subotnik & Steiner, 1993).

Studies of science Olympiad winners have emphasized the importance of the role of the mentoring experience in a gifted student's productivity in science (Feng, 2007). Highly talented science students and winners of the Westinghouse/Intel competition indicated highly regarded mentors imparted tacit knowledge about a domain of science to their protégé (Subotnik et al., 2001). Mentors serve as role models in which the gifted learner can see "an idealized self and in that sense realize possibilities for future accomplishments" (VanTassel-Baska, 1998, p. 493). In a recent study of mentorship programs for high-ability science students, the most effective mentors were reported to have qualities including (1) a genuine interest in the mentee as an individual, (2) well-versed in the field, and (3) passion for the subject/field. A good mentor was also reported to "know when to help and when to let a mentee work independently and create opportunities to give the mentee more exposure in the field" (Quek, 2005, p. 199).

Understanding the need for pacing, optimal instructional conditions, and ability grouping also are important aspects of science education for gifted students. Just as in mathematics, accelerated summer courses affect entrance examination science achievement scores (Lynch, 1992). In both math and science, students who participate in fast-paced summer courses receive credit in their home schools (Mills & Ablard, 1993). To involve more inner city students, summer programs in math and science may increase confidence with mentors critical to the program's success (Miserandino, Subotnik, & Ou, 1995).

Residential math and science high schools (Stephens, 1998–1999) and special-ized math and science curriculum (Tyler-Wood et al., 2000) do appear to make a difference in gifted student performance by exposing students to advanced content when they are academically ready for the challenge.

Science curriculum for gifted students provides a foundation for them to become knowledge producers, having internalized the scientific skills such as observation, experimentation, and measurement, as well as adoption of an atti-tudinal mind-set that views the world through the lens of a scientist, which can be used as a framework for research in all fields. To ensure gifted students have this ability, it is essential to have five key components in a science K–12 cur-riculum: (1) opportunities for laboratory experimentation and original research work, (2) high-level content-based curriculum, (3) opportunities for interac-tions with practicing scientists, (4) a strong emphasis on inquiry processes, and (5) inclusion of science topics that focus on technological applications of science in the context of human decision making and social policy (VanTassel-Baska, Gallagher, Bailey, & Sher, 1993; VanTassel-Baska & Kulieke, 1987).

For students to develop understanding in any scientific discipline, teachers and curriculum developers must attend to a set of complex and interrelated components, including the nature of practice in particular scientific disciplines, students' prior knowledge, and the establishment of a collaborative environ-ment that engages students in reflective scientific practice. These design com-ponents allow educators to create curriculum and instructional materials that help students learn about science as inquiry (Stewart, Cartier, & Passmore, 2005).

Cooper, Baum, and Neu (2004) presented a successful model for identi-fying and developing scientific talent in gifted students. The emphasis of the model focused on helping students become creative producers, featuring a strong mentoring component that included role-modeling and problem solv-ing within specific scientific domains and provided students with authentic, experiential, advanced-level subject matter of the domain. The means of assess-ing student achievement focused on a student's performance in class and the product he or she created, not on test scores.

The National Science Education Standards do not simply suggest that science teachers incorporate inquiry in classrooms; rather, they demand that teachers embrace inquiry in order to (1) plan an inquiry-based science program for their students, (2) focus and support inquiry while interacting with stu-dents, and (3) create a setting for student work that is flexible and supportive of science inquiry by modeling and emphasizing the skills, attitudes, and values needed (NRC, 2000). Johnson, Boyce, and VanTassel-Baska (1995) evaluated existing science materials using national science standards and needs of high-ability learners as a set of criteria. The authors suggested that many existing basal textbooks failed to meet new science curriculum standards, while modu-lar programs and supplementary materials were generally found to be superior in emphasizing such inquiry-based approaches.

Riley and Karnes (2007) described the plethora of competitive opportunities for secondary gifted students that have multiplied over the years. Many of the options are specifically targeted in the areas of mathematics and science, such as Math Counts, Math-letes, Talent Search Math Olympiad, JETS, science fairs, Science Olympiad, Future Problem Solving bowls, and Odyssey of the Mind. Many of these competitions also are group-oriented, consistent with research breakthroughs being made by scientific teams made up of individuals with specialized backgrounds that require combinational knowledge from several areas (Simonton, 2004).

RESEARCH ON TEACHING GIFTED LEARNERS

Early access to advanced science content appears to be a desirable option for gifted learners. Cross and Coleman (1992) surveyed gifted high school students and found their main complaint about general science instruction was frustration at being held back by the pace and content of the course. In a 6-year study of middle-school-age gifted learners enrolled in biology, chemistry, or physics during a 3-week summer program, Lynch (1992) found that these younger learners outperformed high school students who were enrolled in the courses for a full year. Follow-up questionnaires further found continued success in science among participating students regarding placement and credit in science in the academic year following the fast-paced summer science course, thereby suggesting a need for high-school-science-level courses to commence at earlier levels with course flexibility for students who can master the content in less time.

Academically talented adolescents attending a residential science high school in Korea reported statistically significant differences in school life satisfaction, favoring the science high school sample over their contemporaries attending a regular high school. The results further indicated that the gifted students attending the science high school appreciated the advanced curriculum and the expertise of their teachers. They also reported satisfactory relationships with teachers and peers and overall suggested that the residential science high school was meeting the educational needs of talented Korean students, at least better than the traditional high school. The study provides empirical support for the value of special high schools in creating satisfaction with school life among academically talented youth and suggests special high schools create a more positive climate for students with talents in the sciences, even in cultures where peers are generally quite supportive of academic achievement (Jin & Moon, 2006).

A recent longitudinal study tracking 1,110 adolescents identified as mathematically precocious in middle school with plans for a math-science undergraduate major found that participants' high school educational experiences, abilities, and interests predicted whether their attained undergraduate degrees were within math-science or nonmath-nonscience areas. More women than men eventually completed undergraduate degrees outside math-science, but many individuals who completed nonmath-nonscience degrees ultimately chose math-science occupations (Webb, Lubinski, & Benbow, 2002).

RESEARCH ON INSTRUCTIONAL APPROACHES

A variety of studies have been conducted on what works in teaching secondary science to gifted students. In an action research study of the effectiveness of problem-based learning in promoting the acquisition and retention of knowledge, Dods (1997) compared the effects of problem-based learning (PBL), traditional lecture (L), and a combination of the two (PBL+L) on student retention of the major concepts in an elective biochemistry course taught at a school for talented students. Findings suggested that in-depth understanding was increased by the PBL experience whereas content coverage was promoted by lecture.

In examining the effects of problem-based learning on problem solving, Gallagher, Stepien, and Rosenthal (1992) studied 78 students enrolled in a residential high school for students talented in mathematics and science. Participating students in the study received a problem-based course that incorporated social science, physics, and mathematics: Science, Society, and the Future. The experimental group became significantly better at problem finding and performed better than the comparison group on fact finding, problem finding, and solution finding. Interestingly, the researchers found that prior experience with problem solving did not appear to affect the results.

Integrating technology with computer-based mathematics and physics for gifted students has been found to be a useful teaching technique. A group of 27 middle and high school students took computer-based advanced math classes at a middle school in which a tutor provided assistance that included correcting off-line work, grading tests, and certifying performance in the course. The vast majority of these students (88%–100%, depending on the course) received scores of 4 or 5 on Advanced Placement tests. The computer courses were designed at the Education Program for Gifted Youth (EPGY) at Stanford University. Ravaglia, Suppes, Stillinger, and Alper (1995) concluded that computer-based education makes it possible for gifted and talented middle and early high school students to complete advanced courses in mathematics and physics earlier than expected and to do as well as older students on a high-stakes test.

Lynch (1992) conducted a 6-year study of fast-paced high school science for academically talented students, 12 to 16 years old, who completed a one-year course in high school biology, chemistry, or physics in 3 weeks at a residential summer program. Students demonstrated subject mastery by taking College Entrance Examination Board science achievement tests. Their mean scores were higher than those of high school juniors and seniors. Follow-up studies indicated that students also performed well in subsequent science courses. The study suggested that academically talented students could begin high school sciences earlier than is currently allowed in most American schools. Yet, such opportunities may be met with resistance by schools. Researchers Mills and Ablard (1993) surveyed 892 academically talented students about academic credit and/or course placement for their participation in a precalculus or fast-paced science course during the summer. They found that upon successful completion of the coursework, only 39% of the math students and only 38% of the science students received credit in their schools.

Stephens (1998–1999) examined residential math and science high schools by providing an informative profile of the students, faculty, and curricula of each of the 11 state-supported, residential math and science high schools. The curricula offered both acceleration and enrichment models, with all allowing for the study of advanced-level content. The program models were more comparable to colleges and universities than to traditional high schools. Stephens concluded that these high schools offer comprehensive, challenging, and innovative educational programs for gifted secondary students in the sciences, as well as other fields. A more recent analysis reported similar results (Cross & Miller, 2007).

Tyler-Wood et al. (2000) found that a program involving 32 secondary students in a 2-year interdisciplinary math/science program that incorporated higher level thinking skills and more real-life laboratory experiences produced important learning gains. Researchers found that the participants in this new program performed significantly better on the ACT in the areas of science, math, prealgebra, algebra, geometry, and trigonometry than did comparison students.

VanTassel-Baska, Bass, Ries, Poland, and Avery (1998) conducted a national study of science curriculum effectiveness with high-ability students. The study examined the effects of problem-based learning William and Mary units used with students from grades 2–8. The curriculum used the national science standards and stressed advanced content, higher level thinking, and problem-solving processes, and the understanding of the concept of systems. The authors found that students who used the units made small, but significant gains on an assessment of experimental design when compared to students who did not use the units. The teachers cited that the hands-on, problem-based, and student-centered aspects of the units supported their teaching and motivated students and themselves to excel.

In a study linking high-ability students to marine scientists in a summer camp setting, Schenkel (2002) found that many aspects of the summer program aligned with elements that are considered essential for high-ability learners. Students reported positive change in feelings and opinions about science and scientists. Students also reported that the camp setting provided them opportunities to conduct field and laboratory research and work with quality equipment and technology not always available to them in their school classroom settings.

Science assessment tools have also been examined to test their appropriateness for use with gifted learners. Adams and Callahan (1995) evaluated the reliability of the Diet Cola Test and its validity for identifying gifted students. They tested 180 students in grades 4–8 in 6 states. The data supported the use of the Diet Cola Test for assessing science process skills as part of an instructional program or evaluation.

RELATED STUDIES ON WORKING WITH GIFTED STUDENTS IN THE SCIENCES

Concern over the underrepresentation of minorities in natural sciences, mathematics, and engineering led to a longitudinal study of high-ability minority students. Grandy (1998) found that (1) whether students had parents with Ph.D.s or parents who had not completed high school had very little effect on their success in science and engineering fields, (2) females, slightly more than males, attended 4-year colleges and universities, (3) science achievement in high school was not a factor in persistence, (4) social development in high school had some small but notable effects on students' pathways through college, and (5) grades in science and engineering had less effect on outcome than did interest and commitment.

The role of gender and familial influence, however, has been found to be a contributing factor in gifted students' science achievement in other studies. Differential achievement patterns between gifted male and gifted female high school students were noted by Verna and Campbell (1999) in their study. The study investigated the factors that contributed to gifted high schools students' mathematics achievement at the secondary level. A sample of 225 highly gifted students (109 males and 116 females), ages 16–18, were semifinalists or finalists in the Westinghouse Talent Search. The students and their parents completed the Inventory of Parental Influence and the Self-Confidence Attribute Attitude Scale. Males perceived more parental pressure than females to achieve in math. Being in a two-parent family was more important for gifted males than gifted females in academic achievement. Higher socioeconomic status (SES) was associated with higher achievement for females. High SES also was associated with higher self-concept and math self-concept for males, although high SES had no significant effect on self-concept for females.

Adult manifestations of adolescent talent in science were examined in a study of the 146 men and women who were among the 300 semifinalists and finalists of the 1983 Westinghouse Science Talent Search. Subotnik and Steiner (1993) found that at 26 years of age, 49 of the 60 male participants and 25 of the 38 female participants could be categorized as scientists or mathematicians because of their study or employment. The 11 men and 13 women who left science had, for the most part, found careers in other disciplines. They left the scientist's lifestyle for several reasons, including (a) other fields were more attractive, (b) mentors in science were unavailable, (c) parents and secondary school officials gave inappropriate guidance, or (d) undergraduate science instruction was of low quality. In a related study examining the variables that led to the retention and attrition of talented men and women in science, Subotnik et al. (2001) analyzed the lost generation of elite talent in science. The sample included 85 Westinghouse Science Talent Search winners who completed a questionnaire and interviews. The researchers found that accessibility to a mentor increased the individual's status, eliciting further resources and recognition. Women tended to forgo high-powered careers for a more balanced life with family. Access to grants and senior faculty positions played a significant role in determining the satisfaction and level of opportunity for these gifted scientists.

WHAT WE KNOW AND NEED FOR FURTHER RESEARCH

It is evident that science education for the gifted at the secondary level has received some research attention, especially related to the importance of key program components, instructional techniques, and the role of individuals such as mentors and teachers in the process of talent development. Data from the College Board Advanced Placement Program continue to show increased participation in science courses, yet with modest gains in scores as more students, both gifted and nongifted, access the coursework and testing. Major findings from the research base to date on successful interventions in science with gifted learners suggest:

- Gifted learners at secondary levels appear to benefit from sustained and personalized attention in learning science from a mentor or an encouraging teacher over a period of time, especially in producing a science project of high merit.
- Gifted learners at secondary levels benefit from advanced instruction in science, consistent with their levels of functioning in the subject, but beyond the typical level of science offered by the school.
- Gifted learners at secondary levels profit from real-world internships in laboratories, hospitals, and other research settings that allow them to see and participate in science being done professionally.
- Summer experiences provide an important context for learning science that brings together high-powered resources in an intensive time frame for learning that is stimulating for gifted students.

What we still do not know in secondary science education for the gifted is a reasonable trajectory of opportunities necessary to keep gifted students in the science pipeline, especially during the critical years of middle school and early high school before advanced opportunities begin. Moreover, we have not yet studied sufficiently the outcomes of specific curriculum and instructional approaches on science learning, or the impact of different science domains on gifted student involvement.

REFERENCES

Adams, C. M., & Callahan, C. M. (1995). The reliability and validity of a performance task for evaluating science process skills. *Gifted Child Quarterly, 39*, 14–20.

Cooper, C. R., Baum, S. M., & Neu, T. W. (2004). Developing scientific talent in students with special needs: An alternative model for identification, curriculum, and assessment. *Journal of Secondary Gifted Education, 15*, 162–169.

Csikszentmihalyi, M. (1996). *Creativity: Flow and the psychology of discovery and invention.* New York: Harper Collins.

Cross, T. L., & Coleman, L. J. (1992). Gifted high school students' advice to science teachers. *Gifted Child Today, 15*(5), 25–26.

Cross, T., & Miller, K. (2007). An overview of three models of publicly funded residential academies for gifted adolescents. In J. VanTassel-Baska (Ed.), *Serving gifted learners beyond the traditional classroom: A guide to alternative programs and services* (pp. 81–104). Waco, TX: Prufrock Press.

Dods, R. F. (1997). An action research study of the effectiveness of problem-based learning in promoting the acquisition and retention of knowledge. *Journal for the Education of the Gifted, 20*, 423–437.

Donoghue, E. F., Karp, A., & Vogeli, B. R. (2000). Russian schools for the mathematically and scientifically talented: Can the vision survive unchanged? *Roeper Review, 22*, 121–122.

Donovan, M. S., & Bransford, J. D. (Eds.). (2005). *How students learn: History, mathematics, and science in the classroom.* Washington, DC: The National Academies Press.

Farenga, S. J., & Joyce, B. A. (1998). Science-related attitudes and science course selection: A study of high-ability boys and girls. *Roeper Review, 20*, 247–251.

Feist, G. J. (2006a). How development and personality influence scientific thought, interest, and achievement. *Review of General Psychology, 10*, 163–182.

Feist, G. J. (2006b). The development of scientific talent in Westinghouse finalists and members of the National Academy of Sciences. *Journal of Adult Development, 13*(1), 23–35.

Feng, A. (2007). Developing personalized learning experiences: Mentoring for talent development. In J. VanTassel-Baska (Ed.), *Serving gifted learners beyond the traditional classroom: A guide to alternative programs and services* (pp. 189–212). Waco, TX: Prufrock Press.

Filippelli, L. A., & Walbert, H. J. (1997). Childhood traits and conditions of eminent women scientists. *Gifted Child Quarterly, 41*, 95–103.

Gallagher, S. A., Stepien, W., & Rosenthal, H. (1992). The effects of problem-based learning on problem solving. *Gifted Child Quarterly, 36*, 195–200.

Grandy, J. (1998). Persistence in science of high-ability minority students: Results of a longitudinal study. *Journal of Higher Education, 69*, 589–620.

Jin, S., & Moon, S. M. (2006). A study of well-being and school satisfaction among academically talented students attending a science high school in Korea. *Gifted Child Quarterly, 50*, 169–184.

Johnson, D. T., Boyce, L. N., & VanTassel-Baska, J. (1995). Science curriculum review: Evaluating materials for high-ability learners. *Gifted Child Quarterly, 39*, 36–43.

Joyce, B. A., & Farenga, S. J. (2000). Young girls in science: Academic ability, perceptions and future participation in science. *Roeper Review, 22*, 261–262.

Li, A. K. S., & Adamson, G. (1995). Causal attributions of siblings of gifted secondary school students for science, mathematics, and English performance. *Journal of Secondary Gifted Education, 6*, 229–232.

Lynch, S. J. (1992). Fast-paced high school science for the academically talented: A six-year perspective. *Gifted Child Quarterly, 36*, 147–154.

Mills, C. J., & Ablard, K. E. (1993). Credit and placement for academically talented students following special summer courses in math and science. *Journal for the Education of the Gifted, 17*, 4–25.

Minstrell, J., & Kraus, P. (2005). Guided inquiry in the science classroom. In S. M. Donovan & J. D. Bransford (Eds.), *How students learn: History, mathematics, and science in the classroom* (pp. 475–513). Washington, DC: National Academies Press.

Miserandino, A., Subotnik, R., & Ou, K. (1995). Identifying and nurturing mathematical talent in urban school settings. *Journal of Secondary Gifted Education, 6*(4), 245–257.

Mullis, I., Martin, M., Beaton, A., Gonzalez, E., Kelly, D., & Smith, T. (1998). *The mathematics and science achievement in the final years of secondary school: IEA's Third International Mathematics and Science Study (TIMSS)*. Chestnut Hill, MA: International Study Center, Lynch School of Education, Boston College.

National Research Council. (1996). *National science standards*. Washington, DC: National Academies Press.

National Research Council, Committee on Science and Mathematics Teacher Preparation. (2000). *Educating teachers of science, mathematics, and technology: New practices for the new millennium*. Washington, DC: National Academies Press.

National Science Resources Center, National Academies. (2006). *Delivering excellence in science education: National Science Resources Center 2005 annual report*. Retrieved February 1, 2007, from http://www.nsrconline.org/pdf/2005ar.pdf

Olszewski-Kubilius, P., & Yasumoto, J. (1995). Factors affecting the academic choices of academically talented middle school students. *Journal for the Education of the Gifted, 18*, 298–318.

Quek, C. (2005). *A national study of scientific talent development in Singapore*. Unpublished doctoral dissertation, College of William and Mary, Williamsburg, VA.

Ravaglia, R., Suppes, P., Stillinger, C., & Alper, T. M. (1995). Computer-based mathematics and physics for gifted students. *Gifted Child Quarterly, 39*, 7–13.

Rebhorn, L. S., & Miles, D. D. (1999). High-stakes testing: Barrier to gifted girls in mathematics and science. *School Science and Mathematics, 99*, 313–319.

Reis, S. M., & Park, S. (2001). Gender differences in high-achieving students in math and science. *Journal for the Education of the Gifted, 25*, 52–73.

Riley, T., & Karnes, F. A. (2007). Competitions for gifted and talented students: Issues of excellence and equity. In J. VanTassel-Baska (Ed.), *Serving gifted learners beyond the traditional classroom: A guide to alternative programs and services* (pp. 145–168). Waco, TX: Prufrock Press.

Rohrer, J., & Welsch, S. (1998). The Lake Tahoe watershed project: A summer program for female middle school students in math and science. *Roeper Review, 20,* 288–290.

Schenkel, L. A. (2002). Hands on and feet first: Linking high-ability students to marine scientists. *Journal of Secondary Gifted Education, 13,* 173–191.

Simonton, D. (1988). *Scientific genius: A psychology of science.* Cambridge, England: Cambridge University Press.

Simonton, D. K. (2004). *Creativity in science: Chance, logic, genius, and zeitgeist.* New York: Cambridge University Press.

Smith, T., Martin, M., Mullis, I., & Kelly, D. (2000). *The profiles in student achievement in science at the TIMSS international benchmarks.* Chestnut Hill, MA: International Study Center, Lynch School of Education, Boston College.

Stephens, K. R. (1998–1999). Residential math and science high schools: A closer look. *Journal of Secondary Gifted Education, 10,* 85–92.

Stewart, J., Cartier, J., & Passmore, C. (2005). Developing understanding through model-based inquiry. In S. M. Donovan & J. D. Bransford (Eds.), *How students learn: History, mathematics, and science in the classroom* (pp. 515–555). Washington, DC: National Academies Press.

Subotnik, R. F., & Steiner, C. L. (1993). Adult manifestations of adolescent talent in science. *Roeper Review, 15,* 164–169.

Subotnik, R., & Steiner, C. L. (1994). Adult manifestations of adolescent talent in science: A longitudinal study of 1983 Westinghouse Science Talent Search winners. In R. F. Subotnik & K. D. Arnold (Eds.), *Beyond Terman: Contemporary longitudinal studies of giftedness and talent* (pp. 52–76). Norwood, NJ: Ablex.

Subotnik, R. F., Stone, K. M., & Steiner, C. (2001). Lost generation of elite talent in science. *Journal of Secondary Gifted Education, 13,* 33–43.

Swiatek, M. A., & Lupkowski-Shoplik, A. (2000). Gender differences in academic attitudes among gifted elementary school students. *Journal for the Education of the Gifted, 23,* 360–377.

Tyler-Wood, T. L., Mortenson, M., Putney, D., & Cass, M. A. (2000). An effective mathematics and science curriculum option for secondary gifted education. *Roeper Review, 22,* 266–269.

VanTassel-Baska, J. (1998). Counseling the gifted. In J. VanTassel-Baska (Ed.), *Excellence in educating the gifted* (pp. 489–510). Denver, CO: Love.

VanTassel-Baska, J., Bass, G., Ries, R., Poland, D., & Avery, L. D. (1998). A national study of science curriculum effectiveness with high ability students. *Gifted Child Quarterly, 42,* 200–211.

VanTassel-Baska, J., Gallagher, S., Bailey, J., & Sher, B. (1993). Scientific experimentation. *Gifted Child Today, 16*(5), 42–46.

VanTassel-Baska, J., & Kulieke, M. (1987). The role of the community-based scientific resources in developing scientific talent: A case study. *Gifted Child Quarterly, 30,* 111–115.

VanTassel-Baska, J., & Stambaugh, T. (2006). *Comprehensive curriculum for gifted learners* (3rd ed.). Boston: Allyn & Bacon.

VanTassel-Baska, J., & Subotnik, R. (2004, November). *World-class talent development: What does it look like and what does it mean for the future of gifted education?* Paper presented at the National Association of Gifted Children, Denver, CO.

Verna, M. A., & Campbell, J. R. (1999). Differential achievement patterns between gifted male and gifted female high school students. *Journal of Secondary Gifted Education, 10*, 184–194.

Webb, R. M., Lubinski, D., & Benbow, C. P. (2002). Mathematically facile adolescents with math-science aspirations: New perspectives on their educational and vocational development. *Journal of Educational Psychology, 94*, 785–794.

Zuckerman, H. (1996). *Scientific elite* (2nd ed.). New York: Free Press.

Chapter 38

SELF-CONCEPT

Michael C. Pyryt

THE CONSTRUCT OF SELF-CONCEPT

n psychology, interest in self-concept can be traced to the writings of William James (1890). Self-concept has been viewed as an integral component of the self-system (Epstein, 1973; Harter, 1993; James, 1890; Mönks & Ferguson, 1983) and as a precursor to eminent achievement (Feldhusen, 1986; Foster, 1983). Shavelson, Hubner, and Stanton (1976) envisioned self-concept as the organization of an individual's perceptions of oneself in terms of many facets such as academic self-concept, social self-concept, emotional self-concept, and physical self-concept. Self-concept facets such as academic self-concept can be further subdivided into math self-concept and verbal self-concept. Math self-concept can be subdivided into decimal self-concept, fraction self-concept, statistics self-concept, and so forth. These facets or dimensions are hypothesized to be hierarchical in nature. General self-concept is at the top of the hierarchy. Situation-specific self-concept such as decimal self-concept is at the bottom of the hierarchy. Whereas general self-concept is thought to be relatively stable, situation-specific self-concept is hypothesized to vary across time and situation. The dimensions of self-concept are viewed as differentiating over the lifespan, and as having both descriptive and evaluative elements. Much empirical support (Byrne, 1984; Marsh, 1990a, 1990b; Marsh, Byrne, & Shavelson, 1988; Marsh & Hocevar, 1985; Shavelson & Bolus, 1982) exists for this conception of self-concept. Byrne (1996) noted that one construct controversy involves the distinction between self-concept and self-esteem. Although it is possible to view self-concept in terms of description of one's capability and self-esteem as the evaluation of this description, it is difficult to empirically differentiate self-concept and self-esteem. A similar controversy relates to the overlap between self-concept facets and self-efficacy facets. Using the Shavelson et al. (1976) conceptualization of self-concept, math self-efficacy easily could be seen in terms of situation-specific self-concept that falls at the base of the hierarchical model. Byrne (1996) provides numerous synonyms for self-concept (self-perception, self-image, self-identity, self-awareness) and self-esteem (self-regard, self-worth, self-evaluation, self-acceptance). To understand self-concept requires familiarity with the research literature related to these various terms as well.

Understanding the construct of self-concept also involves understanding the factors that affect its development. Mendaglio and Pyryt (2003) have described three major theories of self-concept development: reflected appraisals, social comparison, and attribution. Based on the pioneering work of Cooley (1902) and Mead (1934), the reflected appraisals approach proposes that self-concept formation is based on the perceived appraisals of significant others. Festinger's (1954) social comparison theory situates self-concept development in terms of an individual's comparison with peers. Attribution theory (Heider, 1958; Kelley, 1967, 1973) examines factors that impact an individual's willingness to explain behavior due to ability rather than effort, task difficulty, or luck. Marsh's (1986) internal/external frame of reference model suggests that effort mediates the likelihood of an individual making an ability attribution. A student who excels at both math and language arts but works harder in mathematics will have a more positive verbal self-concept.

Although there are multiple theories of gifted individuals' self-concept development (Mendaglio & Pyryt, 2003), recent attention has focused on the role of social comparison processes (Dai, 2004; Marsh & Hau, 2003, 2004; Plucker et al., 2004). This approach suggests that self-concept develops in relation to our observed comparison with peers on comparison measures. If we see ourselves as performing better at academic tasks (by making better grades), then we see ourselves as smart. To understand an individual's self-concept from the social comparison perspective, it is essential to understand the individual's reference or comparison group. A gifted student in a heterogeneous classroom environment might develop an inflated academic self-concept by comparing oneself with less able peers. A gifted student in a homogeneous classroom environment might develop a depressed academic self-concept by comparing oneself to equally able peers. In the first scenario, the student becomes a "big fish in a little pond." In the second scenario, the student becomes a "little fish in a big pond." Marsh, Chessor, Craven, and Roche (1995) have found that gifted programs may negatively impact the academic self-concepts of students in them. Marsh and Hau (2003) examined the cross-cultural generalizability of the big-fish-little-pond effect (BFLPE) in a monumental study of 103,558 fifteen-year-olds from 26 countries. The mean regression coefficient for school-average achievement was -.20, indicating that students' academic self-concepts were negatively affected by attending academically selective schools. Researchers in gifted education have noted that other factors including individual achievement are more important than average school achievement in influencing self-concept (Dai, 2004; Plucker et al., 2004; Pyryt & Mendaglio, 2006).

There appear to be minimal differences in the self-concept ratings of gifted males and gifted females. Pyryt and Richwein (in press) conducted a meta-analysis of 35 studies comparing the self-concepts of gifted males and females. Participants in the 35 studies included 5,599 males and 5,611 females from 9 countries (Australia, Canada, China, Finland, Germany, Korea, New Zealand, Sweden, United States). For the most part, gender differences in self-concept among gifted samples reflect self-concept differences in the general population. Males have more positive athletic self-concepts than females, and have more positive math and science self-concepts than females. Males have lower verbal self-concepts than females.

RESEARCH QUESTIONS REGARDING SELF-CONCEPT AND GIFTED STUDENTS

The major research question related to self-concept and gifted students is the extent to which the self-concept facets of gifted students are comparable to the self-concept of average-ability students. A related question involves the extent to which giftedness interacts with the process of self-concept development. A third research question relates to the impact of placement of intellectually gifted students in gifted programs on their self-concept facets. A fourth research question focuses on the congruity between self-concept ratings and demonstrated accomplishments. A final research question relates to the generalizability of findings across various subgroups of gifted students (gifted females, culturally diverse gifted, students with gifts and disabilities, creatively gifted students).

RESEARCH FINDINGS REGARDING GIFTEDNESS AND SELF-CONCEPT

Results of a meta-analysis of self-concept research comparing gifted and average-ability students (Hoge & Renzulli, 1993) and a narrative review (Dixon, 1998) indicate that gifted students display greater academic self-concept scores than average-ability peers. This is particularly true when the instruments used in the research use a single indicator of academic self-concept (Pyryt & Mendaglio, 1999). When multiple indicators are used, Marsh's (1986) internal/external frame of reference processes seem to operate. Perceptions of ability are determined by intrapersonal comparisons rather than by external markers of achievement. Research with gifted populations (Plucker & Stocking, 2001; Williams & Montgomery, 1995) has shown general support for Marsh's frame of reference theory. Although there is a statistically significant correlation between gifted students' achievement on standardized achievement tests of mathematics and language arts, the correlation between their math and verbal self-concept is close to zero. This indicates that gifted students use effort as a mediator in evaluating self-concept.

LIMITATIONS IN THE RESEARCH

Initial research comparing gifted and average-ability students typically focused on global self-concept. Such studies failed to take into account the multi-dimensionality of self-concept, however (Friedman, 1992; Schneider, 1987). Although recent studies take a multidimensional perspective, methodological limitations such as sampling problems also have been noted (Hoge & Renzulli, 1991; Olszewski-Kubilius, Kulieke, & Krasney, 1988). The description of the characteristics of the sample in terms of intellectual ability often is quite limited. Instrumentation often precludes any type of developmental comparison because separate test instruments are constructed for various developmental stages. There is a critical need for longitudinal studies to better examine how a gifted individual's self-concepts change over time, particularly when gifted students are placed in specialized settings. Although much of the writing on self-concept assumes that the higher the self-concept, the better, Dabrowski's Theory of Positive Disintegration provides another framework for evaluating self-concept. From a Dabrowskian perspective, self-concept is linked to an individual's level of development (Mendaglio & Pyryt, 1996). Individuals at Level III (Spontaneous Multilevel Disintegration) experiencing feelings of inferiority, shame, and guilt should have poor self-concepts. Individuals at Level IV (Organized Multilevel Disintegration) experiencing self-awareness, self-control, and empathy should have positive self-concepts. There also is a need to better understand the congruity of self-concept with accomplishment.

PRACTICAL IMPLICATIONS

The major practical implication of the research on self-concept and the gifted is that, contrary to stereotypes (Robinson & Clinkenbeard, 1998), gifted students are not socially isolated misfits. Their social self-concept is similar to that of their peers. Another practical implication is that self-concept is a complex construct. Attempts to enhance self-concept will require examining an individual's communication with significant others, comparisons with reference groups, experiences of success, and perceived ability across various domains.

RESOURCES FOR RESEARCH IN SELF-CONCEPT

The starting point for research on the gifted should be Hoge and Renzulli's (1993) meta-analytic review of comparisons between gifted and average-ability students. Their review provides a solid base for understanding the diversity of studies that have been conducted. The narrative review by Dixon (1998) also provides an excellent description of research comparing the self-concept of gifted and average-ability students. Mendaglio and Pyryt (2003) provide an introduction to the theoretical foundations of self-concept development. Byrne (1996) is a critical resource for understanding the conceptual and psychometric properties of a wide variety of self-concept instruments. Important assessment information, as well as state-of-the art reviews of the literature, can be found in the various chapters of Bracken's (1996) *Handbook of Self-Concept*.

REFERENCES

Bracken, B. A. (Ed.). (1996). *Handbook of self-concept: Developmental, social, and clinical considerations*. New York: Wiley.

Byrne, B. M. (1984). The general/academic self-concept nomological network: A review of construct validation research. *Review of Educational Research, 54*, 427–456.

Byrne, B. M. (1996). *Measuring self-concept across the lifespan: Issues and instrumentation*. Washington, DC: American Psychological Association.

Cooley, C. H. (1902). *Human nature and the social order*. New York: Scribner's.

Dai, D. Y. (2004). How universal is the big-fish-little-pond effect? *American Psychologist, 59*, 267–268.

Dixon, F. A. (1998). Social and academic self-concepts of gifted adolescents. *Journal for the Education of the Gifted, 22*, 80–94.

Epstein, S. (1973). The self-concept revisited: Or a theory of a theory. *American Psychologist, 28*, 404–416.

Feldhusen, J. F. (1986). A conception of giftedness. In R. J. Sternberg & J. E. Davidson (Eds.), *Conceptions of giftedness* (pp. 112–127). New York: Cambridge University Press.

Festinger, L. (1954). A theory of social comparison processes. *Human Relations, 7,* 117–140.

Foster, W. (1983). Self-concept, intimacy, and the attainment of excellence. *Journal for the Education of the Gifted, 6,* 20–29.

Friedman, R. (1992). Zorba's conundrum: Evaluative aspects of self-concept in talented individuals. *Quest, 3*(1), 1–5.

Harter, S. (1993). Developmental perspectives on the self-system. In E. M. Hetherington (Ed.), *Socialization, personality, and social development: Handbook of child psychology* (Vol. 4, pp. 275–385). New York: Wiley.

Heider, F. (1958). *The psychology of interpersonal relations.* New York: Wiley.

Hoge, R. D., & Renzulli, J. S. (1991). *Self-concept and the gifted child.* Storrs: National Research Center on the Gifted and Talented, University of Connecticut.

Hoge, R. D., & Renzulli, J. S. (1993). Exploring the link between giftedness and self-concept. *Review of Educational Research, 63,* 449–465.

James, W. (1890). *Principles of psychology.* New York: Holt.

Kelley, H. H. (1967). Attribution theory in social psychology. In D. Levine (Ed.), *Nebraska symposium on motivation* (pp. 191–241). Lincoln: University of Nebraska Press.

Kelley, H. H. (1973). The process of causal attribution. *American Psychologist, 28,* 107–128.

Marsh, H. W. (1986). Verbal and math self-concepts: An internal/external frame of reference model. *American Educational Research Journal, 23,* 129–149.

Marsh, H. W. (1990a). Confirmatory factor analysis of multitrait-multimethod data: The construct validation of multidimensional self-concept responses. *Journal of Personality, 58,* 661–691.

Marsh, H. W. (1990b). Multidimensional, hierarchical self-concept: Theoretical and empirical justification. *Educational Psychology Review, 2,* 77–172.

Marsh, H. W., Byrne, B., & Shavelson, R. J. (1988). A multifaceted academic self-concept: Its hierarchical structure and its relation to academic achievement. *Journal of Educational Psychology, 80,* 366–380.

Marsh, H. W., Chessor, D., Craven, R. G., & Roche, L. (1995). The effects of gifted and talented programs on academic self-concept: The big fish strikes again. *American Educational Research Journal, 32,* 285–319.

Marsh, H. W., & Hau, K.-T. (2003). Big-fish-little-pond effect on academic self-concepts: A cross-cultural (26 country) test of the negative effects on academically selective schools. *American Psychologist, 58,* 364–376.

Marsh, H. W., & Hau, K.-T. (2004). The big-fish-little-pond effect stands up to scrutiny. *American Psychologist, 59,* 269–272.

Marsh, H. W., & Hocevar, D. (1985). The application of confirmatory factor analysis to the study of self-concept: First and higher order factor structure and their invariance across age groups. *Psychological Bulletin, 97,* 562–582.

Mead, G. H. (1934). *Mind, self, and society.* Chicago: University of Chicago Press.

Mendaglio, S., & Pyryt, M. C. (1996). Self-concept and the gifted: A Dabrowskian perspective. In B. Tillier (Ed.), *Perspectives on the self: The second biennial conference on Dabrowski's theory of positive disintegration* (pp. 38–51). Banff, AB, Canada: Dabrowski Conference.

Mendaglio, S., & Pyryt, M. C. (2003). Self-concept and giftedness: A multi-theoretical perspective. *Gifted and Talented International, 18,* 76–82.

Mönks, F. J., & Ferguson, T. J. (1983). Gifted adolescents: An analysis of their psychosocial development. *Journal of Youth and Adolescence, 12,* 1–18.

Olszewski-Kubilius, P., Kulieke, M. J., & Krasney, N. (1988). Personality dimensions of gifted adolescents: A review of the empirical literature. *Gifted Child Quarterly, 32,* 347–352.

Plucker, J. A., Robinson, N. M., Greenspon, T. S., Feldhusen, J. F., McCoach, D. B., & Subotnik, R. F. (2004). It's not how the pond makes you feel, but rather how high you can jump. *American Psychologist, 59,* 268–269.

Plucker, J. A., & Stocking, V. B. (2001). Looking outside and inside: Self-concept development of gifted adolescents. *Exceptional Children, 67,* 535–548.

Pyryt, M. C., & Mendaglio, S. (1999, April). *The academic self-concept of gifted and average-ability students: A meta-analytic review.* Paper presented at the meeting of the American Educational Research Association, Montreal.

Pyryt, M. C., & Mendaglio, S. (2006, May). *Big-fish-little-pond effect: Methodological and empirical perspectives.* Paper presented at the eighth biennial Henry B. and Jocelyn Wallace National Research Symposium on Talent Development, Iowa City.

Pyryt, M. C., & Richwein, M. (in press). Self-concept comparisons between gifted males and females: A meta-analytic review. *Korean Educational Development Institute Journal.*

Robinson, A., & Clinkenbeard, P. R. (1998). Giftedness: An exceptionality examined. *Annual Review of Psychology, 49,* 117–139.

Schneider, B. H. (1987). *The gifted child in peer group perspective.* New York: Springer-Verlag.

Shavelson, R. J., & Bolus, R. (1982). Self-concept: The interplay of theory and methods. *Journal of Educational Psychology, 74,* 33–17.

Shavelson, R. J., Hubner, J. J., & Stanton, G. C. (1976). Self-concept: Validation of construct interpretations. *Review of Educational Research, 46,* 407–441.

Williams, J. E., & Montgomery, D. (1995). Using frame of reference theory to understand the self-concept of academically able students. *Journal for the Education of the Gifted, 18,* 400–409.

Chapter 39

SOCIAL STUDIES

Jessica A. Hockett

n the late 1980s, the quality of social studies education tion garnered widespread attention with the publication of several books and reports that called for educational reform (Bloom, 1987; Cheney, 1987; Hirsch, 1987; Ravitch & Finn, 1987). Individually, these publications highlighted students' limited knowledge and understanding of history, geography, and culture. Collectively, they further motivated a public and political examination of what American students were learning in school, and how (Marzano, Kendall, & Gaddy, 1999). The extent to which social studies curricular and instructional quality has changed due to these efforts is questionable. For example, although significantly more high school students are taking geography courses today than 15 years ago (Shettle et al., 2007), 12th graders' performance on national geography assessments has remained stagnant (Weiss, Lutkus, Hildebrant, & Johnson, 2002). Still, social studies is an area of educational research that has proliferated over the past two decades.

By contrast, social studies has received little attention in gifted education research, especially compared with other subject areas. There are at least two possible reasons this is the case. The first is attributable to the sheer number and nature of subjects and disciplines encompassed by the term *social studies*. According to the National Council for the Social Studies (NCSS; 1994), "social studies is the integrated study of the social sciences and humanities to promote civic competence" (¶ 1). This includes, but is not limited to, anthropology, archaeology, economics, geography, history, law, philosophy, political science, psychology, religion, and sociology. Selected content from the humanities, mathematics, and natural sciences also might be relevant (NCSS, 1994). Because social studies is more a category than it is a discipline, it may be difficult to define or pinpoint for educational research purposes.

A second likely reason for the lack of attention to social studies in gifted education research is that most school-based programs and services for gifted learners are rooted in math, science, or language arts. Less common are programs that identify students for services that develop abilities related to social studies. This may be symptomatic of less instructional attention overall to social studies than to other subjects in the general education classroom, at least in the elementary grades. According to the National Center for Education Statistics (2002), more than 50% of 4th graders received less than 24 minutes per day of social studies instruction. Research also suggests that the increased emphasis on accountability testing in math, reading, and science may prompt some elementary teachers to devote less time to social studies than their districts require (Bailey, Shaw, & Hollifield, 2006; Christensen et al., 2001), or less time than they were prior to the No Child Left Behind Act (NCLB; 2001), especially in high-poverty districts (Center on Education Policy, 2006). If social studies are suffering from relative neglect in some gifted and general education programs, then their comparative absence from empirical study in gifted education is unsurprising.

GIFTED LEARNERS IN THE REGULAR SOCIAL STUDIES CLASSROOM

Although there is a shortage of research focused intentionally on social studies and gifted learners, findings from studies with broader purposes indicate that highly able learners may not consistently experience differentiated curriculum or instruction in their social studies classes. In a survey of more than 850 students identified as academically talented, 60% of elementary and secondary students reported that their social studies courses were challenging, and 40% of middle school students reported high challenge in the subject[1] (Gallagher, Harradine, & Coleman, 1997). Some of these middle school stu-

---

1   The middle schools involved in this study grouped students heterogeneously for social studies classes.

dents indicated in open-ended responses that they spend much of their social studies class time copying information and regurgitating facts.

Beyond student perceptions, two seminal studies that examined how elementary teachers address the academic needs of their highly able students suggest that social studies may not be a primary subject teachers consider differentiating for gifted learners. In a study that relied on researcher observations of 46 third- and fourth-grade classrooms, Westberg, Archambault, Dobyns, and Salvin (1993) discovered that, 95% of the time, identified gifted students were not involved in differentiated learning experiences during social studies—the highest rate among the five subject areas observed. Similarly, Reis and Purcell (1993) found that fewer teachers chose to compact social studies content for advanced learners than they did math, language arts, and spelling content. The mean percent of social studies curriculum compacted for the gifted students in the study was 35%, less than science (38%), language arts (47%), math (43%), or spelling (55%)[2]. When the teachers did compact social studies curriculum, they did so for students who demonstrated very high ability or interest.

Many teachers who participated in these two studies did not use a variety of instructional configurations during social studies to support differences in students' readiness. For example, 15% of teachers with heterogeneously grouped classes reported using cluster grouping (Reis et al., 1993). This was equal to the percentage of teachers who reported using it in science, but far fewer than those who said they used cluster grouping in math (51%) and language arts (56%). Likewise, Westberg et al. (1993) observed heterogeneous instructional groupings in almost all social studies classes, with students spending almost 80% of social studies instructional time in whole-group configurations. These findings echo those of the National Center for Education Statistics (NCES; 1999), which reported that 61% of elementary and secondary teachers used small-group instruction during social studies—the lowest percentage of the four core subject areas.

Students with advanced abilities also may be limited by the range of instructional strategies and types of materials used in some social studies classes. According to one national report, social studies teachers were less likely than math, English, and science teachers to deviate from whole-class instruction (NCES, 1999). Among common approaches used in teaching social studies are listening to lectures, reading the textbook, answering questions, and defining vocabulary (Bailey et al. 2006; NCES, 1999; Westberg et al., 1993). These strategies are not surprising given that social studies curricula often are organized topically or chronologically—contrary to research-based and theoretical advice urging a concept-based framework geared toward developing historical understanding (Brophy, 1990; Erickson, 2002; National Research Council, 1998; Twyman, McCleery, & Tindal, 2006).

The quality of social studies textbooks also might hinder talent development in social studies. Analyses of history textbooks claim that many are not aligned with national curriculum standards (Foster, Morris, & Davis, 1996);

---

2   These and all percentages cited in this chapter have been rounded.

portray events in an unbalanced, inaccurate manner (Sewall, 2004); or fail to reflect the way historians think and work (Paxton, 1997, 1999). Given evidence that social studies teachers rely heavily on textbooks for both classwork and homework (NCES, 1999, 2002), poor textbook quality likely affects the caliber of curriculum and instruction for many students, including those who are gifted.

Coupled with other research on teachers' reported and observed instructional practices with gifted learners in academically diverse settings across subjects (Archambault et al., 1993; Brighton, Hertberg, Moon, Tomlinson, & Callahan, 2005; Moon, Callahan, & Tomlinson, 1995; Moon, Callahan, Tomlinson, & Miller, 2002), these findings collectively conclude that at least some students with advanced abilities are not challenged regularly in their social studies classes.

SOCIAL STUDIES INSTRUCTION THAT WORKS WITH GIFTED LEARNERS

Gifted education literature is replete with *advice* on how to optimize social studies for gifted learners; yet, *research* on the effectiveness of social-studies-specific instructional strategies and curricular approaches for gifted learners is limited. It is beyond the scope of this chapter to review the substantial body of research on what constitutes high-quality, effective social studies curriculum and instruction in general, but there is little doubt that a broad, engaging set of instructional strategies aimed at delivering discipline-based, authentic curriculum benefits all learners, including those who are gifted.

However, independent of other important "ingredients" (e.g., purposeful objectives, modifications for an individual learner's needs), a strategy does not necessarily promise positive results. For example, using multiple texts to help students develop historical understanding is widely endorsed in social studies education (e.g., Holt, 1990; Ravitch, 1992; Wineburg, 1991). Stahl, Hynd, Britton, McNish, and Bosquet (1996) investigated this recommended practice with students in two AP U.S. History classes[3], and concluded that students are not likely to benefit from exploring multiple documents—especially when they present conflicting accounts of events—without explicit instruction in *how* to read and evaluate them. So, although gifted learners probably do benefit from reading and analyzing primary and secondary source documents, assuming they do not need scaffolding and guidance in the process could render an otherwise authentic task ineffective.

Likewise, a strategy or approach is not inherently sound or unsound for a certain group of learners. In their large-scale study of curriculum compacting, Reis et al. (1993) found the social studies achievement test scores of gifted students whose curriculum had been compacted in the subject did not differ from

---

3   Study participants were 44 tenth graders described as "high achieving students who were expecting to attend college" (Stahl et al., 1996, p. 7). The study did not identify students as gifted.

gifted students whose curriculum was not compacted. This finding preempts opposition to the strategy on the grounds that student achievement will suffer unless they experience every facet of the curriculum, including content and skills they have already mastered. But, these results do not indicate that the strategy is *uniquely* appropriate to learners identified as gifted.

PROBLEM-BASED LEARNING IN SOCIAL STUDIES AND GIFTED LEARNERS

Problem-based learning (PBL) in the context of social studies has received some attention in gifted education research. Broadly defined, problem-based learning is "apprenticeship for real-life problems" (Stepien, Gallagher, & Workman, 1993, p. 342). Typically, PBL involves a provocative, loosely structured problem that approximates or simulates a past, present, or future challenge likely to be faced by real stakeholders (e.g., professionals in a field, citizens of a community). Seeking viable solutions, students assume the role of problem solvers, with the teacher acting as facilitator or coach (Gallagher, 2000). In this review, research on problem-based learning and gifted learners includes problem-based instructional activities and curricular units, the Future Problem Solving Program, and service-learning.

Problem-Based Instructional Activities and Curricular Units in Social Studies

Skeptics of PBL as an academically effective approach to use with gifted learners in social studies may question whether students learn as much content as they would with a traditional instructional format (e.g., lecture and note-taking). Gallagher and Stepien (1996) compared the performance of gifted students[4] across four American studies courses, one of which devoted half of the year to problem solving "post-holes."[5] (Teachers in the other three sections of the course relied on instructor presentations, discussions prompted by higher order questioning, and textbook reading.) Results from the multiple-choice pre- and posttest indicated that the students in the PBL class had the highest mean gains. This was statistically higher than the mean gains of two of the other classes, although the gains for all four classes were small. Nevertheless, the students exposed to the problem-based activities did not appear to have acquired less information than their peers who received traditional instruction.

---

4   Defined as students attending a 3-year, state-supported residential school for students with advanced abilities in math and science.

5   A series of days within a unit when instruction transitions from traditional pedagogy and tasks to problem-based investigation (Stepien et al., 1993).

There is evidence that problem-based social studies units could be an effective approach for eliciting talent in disadvantaged students who have not been identified as gifted. Gallagher (2000) used a problem-based curriculum model focused on ill-structured problems, advanced content, complex reasoning, and authentic assessment to guide teachers in creating and pilot-testing six units. The units addressed challenges faced by disadvantaged people in history and were used in regular U.S. History, world history, and government classes.[6] Observations, analyses of student work, and student reflections revealed that the PBL units increased student engagement and challenged students' and teachers' previous conceptions about which students were gifted. Although formally identified gifted students performed better than other students on unit assessments, many students' written responses were not commensurate with the level of their responses during class discussions.

The Future Problem Solving Program

Often advocated for gifted learners, the Future Problem Solving Program (FPSP) is a school-based program that integrates problem-based learning in two of its components. In Team Problem-Solving, students solve a situational futuristic challenge about social or scientific issues; Community Problem-Solving requires students to identify and solve a problem in their own school, community, or state. A district or school might offer FPSP as an extracurricular activity open to all students; others may integrate it with their gifted program curriculum.

Some studies have investigated how well FPSP achieves its goals. Tallent-Runnels (1993) compared the performance of gifted learners who had participated in FPSP for 6 months with gifted learners who had not participated in a mock FPSP competition. The participants outperformed the nonparticipants, suggesting that the students who had been exposed to instruction in the program and processes[7] were better able to solve a futuristic problem. Surveying participants in state-level FPSP competition[8], Frasier, Lee, & Winstead (1997) found that students and their coaches felt the program was accomplishing its goals, particularly in how it developed creative thinking abilities. Although both groups reported positive perceptions, the coaches felt more strongly than the students about the program's efficacy. This difference might be attributable to the coaches having a better understanding of FPSP's goals (Frasier et al., 1997).

Investigating potential long-term impacts of FPSP, Volk (2006) surveyed former FPSP participants in Australia, most of whom had been involved with

---

6   Regular classes were chosen because it was thought that gifted disadvantaged students were more likely to be in those contexts than in honors courses.

7   FPSP teaches a six-step process: (1) identify challenges; (2) select an underlying problem; (3) produce solution ideas; (4) generate and select criteria; (5) apply criteria; and (6) develop an action plan (FPSP, 2001).

8   Participants were not identified as gifted or nongifted.

the program for 2 years or longer. A strong majority of respondents agreed that FPSP had helped improve their research and communication skills; strengthened their teamwork abilities; bolstered their confidence in approaching critical and analytical thinking tasks; increased their capacity to address complex social issues; and positively influenced their capacity to develop original ideas.

It is reasonable to expect a program focused on solving problems of the future to influence how students perceive the future. Tallent-Runnels & Yarbrough (1992) found that gifted students involved in FPSP felt they had a greater sense of control over the future than did gifted students not involved in the program. When prompted to ask 20 questions concerning the future, gifted FPSP participants asked a greater number of questions than statistically predicted about topics further removed from their experiences, such as world affairs, war and energy sources, and the economy. Unlike gifted and nongifted students who were not in FPSP, personal concerns were not among the top five question categories for the gifted FPSP participants. In other words, it appeared the FPSP students might have had a more "global" outlook on the future. This makes sense given the types of problems used in the Future Problem Solving component of FPSP.

A majority of Volk's (2006) former FPSP participants (64%) agreed that their interest in the future had been increased as a result of the program, but only 46% agreed that it had influenced their confidence in being able to instigate changes in the future, and roughly one third said they were uncertain about whether the program had affected their confidence in this regard.

Taken together, this research on the Future Problem Solving lends credibility to teaching students to use an explicit process for solving ill-structured problems that often have a basis in or require skills associated with social studies. Whether the program or its processes increases the likelihood that students will be able to transfer the skills they learn to real-world and discipline-specific contexts has not yet been investigated empirically.

Service-Learning

If a major goal of social studies is to develop responsible, well-informed citizens (NCSS, 1994), then research on service-learning and gifted learners is appropriate to consider in this chapter. The National Commission on Service-Learning (NCSL) defines service-learning as "a teaching and learning approach that integrates community service with academic study to enrich learning, teach civic responsibility, and strengthen communities" (2002, p. 3). Service-learning also can be viewed as a type of problem-based learning. Guided by well-articulated and authentic learning goals, students identify and respond to a community need through research and decision-making processes (NCSL, 2002). Because serving-learning encourages students to identify, research, and solve real-world problems that are important to them and their communities, it is well-aligned with some learning outcomes articulated by gifted education experts (e.g., Renzulli & Reis, 1997; Tomlinson, 2005; VanTassel-Baska & Little, 2003).

Case study research on gifted learners and service-learning indicates that projects directed toward community change can have numerous benefits (Terry, 2000, 2003). The students in these studies reported having a sense of accomplishment and new respect for their communities as a result of the community action projects they conceived and completed in their gifted program class. As they explored the problem and sought solutions, their commitment to the projects increased. Possibly due in part to being able to identify and choose the outlet for the project, engaging in service-learning empowered the students, strengthening their beliefs that change was possible and that they could make it happen. The students selected for the case study were mindful of how working cooperatively, using creative problem solving methods, receiving teacher guidance as needed, and having opportunities to reflect on their work combined for successful, meaningful experiences.

There are a number of out-of-school programs for gifted students with a service-learning basis or component. A recent study investigated how one such program impacted the development of civic attitudes and behaviors of its academically gifted participants (Lee & Olszewski-Kubilius, 2007). The researchers administered three surveys to both groups of students, which measured civic responsibility, civic behavior, and leadership skills, respectively. Students who participated in the service-learning program indicated a higher level of civic responsibility before and after the program compared to students in an academically accelerated program. In particular, the service-learning participants evidenced a greater awareness of civic issues and a stronger connection and commitment to the community. The two groups of students did not differ on the civic behaviors and leadership measures after participation in their respective programs.

DEVELOPING SOCIAL STUDIES ABILITY: MOVING STUDENTS TOWARD EXPERTISE

A considerable amount of research has been devoted to expertise in the discipline of history[9]. These studies reveal that working historians rely less on factual knowledge than they do on heuristics and schema for assimilating, organizing, and evaluating information. Most, if not all, students are *capable* of thinking historically (Foster & Yeager, 1999), although the level at which an individual student is to able do so may be limited by his or her reading ability, prior knowledge, or a poorly designed instructional task (Foster & Yeager, 1999; Stahl et al., 1996; VanSledright & Kelly, 1998).

Identifying talent in social studies subjects, then, is not simply a matter of discovering who has memorized or been previously exposed to rote information.

9   See Voss & Wiley, 2006, for a complete review.

There is limited value, for example, in viewing talent in geography as knowing the names and locations of 50 state capitals prior to a unit on American regions. Certainly, the student who already can label a U.S. map—or who can do so quickly or without much guidance—should not be subjected to instruction or tasks that needlessly reinforce what he already knows. However, a professional geographer's work involves asking and answering geographic questions, as well as obtaining and analyzing geographic information (Geography Education Standards Project, 1994). It is reasonable, therefore, to conclude that spotting and developing talent in social studies subjects calls for curriculum that reflects the nature of what experts do.

WHAT WE KNOW AND WHAT WE NEED TO KNOW

The following conclusions are supported by existing research related to gifted learners and social studies:

- Many gifted learners do not receive differentiated curriculum and instruction in their social studies classes.
- There may be limited instructional time devoted to social studies in some general education elementary classrooms. This may stifle opportunities for students with special aptitude for or interest in social studies to explore and demonstrate their talents.
- Talent development in social studies also may be hindered when teachers do not employ a range of instructional strategies or materials.
- Gifted learners do not learn less from problem-based curriculum and instruction in social studies than they might from traditional curriculum and instruction.
- The Future Problem Solving Program has a positive influence on gifted learners who participate in it. From the participants' perspectives, the program is internally consistent; strengthens numerous social, academic, and personal skill areas; and helps them think about the future in a positive way.
- Service-learning can provide productive, motivating opportunities for gifted learners to affect change through problem solving.
- Teaching social studies as a set of facts to be memorized and skills to be mastered is not conducive to developing the kind of sophisticated understanding that characterizes the way experts in the social sciences think and work.
- Discovering and developing talent in social studies is best viewed as a process of moving students toward the thinking and skills characteristic of professionals who work in the fields of history, geography, economics, and so on.

Future research might begin with these inquiries:

- What does giftedness in social studies "look like"? Might it look different in various social studies disciplines (e.g., history and geography)? How does it manifest itself in and beyond the classroom?
- How many in-school programs and services for gifted learners incorporate social studies subjects?
- How do teachers conceptualize talent in social studies?
- How should curriculum and instruction for eliciting talent in the social studies be designed?
- Are there approaches to social studies curriculum and instruction that are *more* beneficial for gifted learners than they are for other learners?

There is little reason to believe that, given the prevailing educational and political climate, researchers in gifted education will feel compelled to give *exclusive* attention to investigating these and other questions on social studies and gifted learners. More realistically, researchers intentionally can include social studies subjects in studies that examine curriculum models, instructional strategies, gifted programs, talent development, and how teachers make adjustments for a range of learner needs. Another possibility is for gifted education researchers to collaborate with experts in social studies education to purposely identify and include gifted learners in analyses of innovative or widely advocated approaches to social studies curriculum and instruction.

REFERENCES

Archambault, F. X., Westberg, K. L., Brown, S. W., Hallmark, B. W., Emmons, C. L., & Zhang, W. (1993). *Regular classroom practices with gifted students: Results of a national survey of classroom teachers* (Research Monograph No. 93102). Storrs: National Research Center on the Gifted and Talented, University of Connecticut.

Bailey, G., Shaw, E. L., & Hollifield, D. (2006). The devaluation of social studies in the elementary grades. *Journal of Social Studies Research, 30*(2), 18–29.

Bloom, A. J. (1987). *The closing of the American mind: How higher education has failed democracy and impoverished the souls of today's students.* New York: Simon & Schuster.

Brighton, C. M., Hertberg, H. L., Moon, T. R., Tomlinson, C. A., & Callahan, C. M. (2005). *The feasibility of high-end learning in a diverse middle school* (Research Monograph No. 05210). Storrs: National Research Center on the Gifted and Talented, University of Connecticut.

Brophy, J. E. (1990). Teaching social studies for understanding and higher-order applications. *The Elementary School Journal, 90,* 351–417.

Cheney, L. V. (1987). *American memory: A report on the humanities in the nation's public schools.* Washington, DC: National Endowment for the Humanities.

Center on Education Policy. (2006). *From Capitol to the classroom: Year 4 of the No Child Left Behind Act.* Washington, DC: Author.

Christensen, L. M., Wilson, E. K., Anders, S. K., Dennis, M. B., Kirkland, L., Beacham, M., et al. (2001). Teachers' reflections on their practice of social studies. *The Social Studies, 92,* 205–208.

Erickson, H. L. (2002). *Concept-based curriculum and instruction: Teaching beyond the facts.* Thousand Oaks, CA: Corwin.

Foster, S., Morris, J. W., & Davis, O. L. (1996). Prospects for teaching historical analysis and interpretation: National curriculum standards for history meet current history textbooks. *Journal of Curriculum and Supervision, 11,* 367–385.

Foster, S. J., & Yeager, E. A. (1999). "You've got to put together the pieces": English 12-year-olds encounter and learn from historical evidence. *Journal of Curriculum and Supervision, 14,* 286–317.

Frasier, M., Lee, J., & Winstead, S. (1997). Is the Future Problem Solving Program accomplishing its goals? *Journal of Secondary Gifted Education, 8,* 157–163.

Future Problem Solving Program. (2001). *Future Problem Solving Program coach's handbook.* Lexington, KY: Author.

Gallagher, J., Harradine, C. C., & Coleman, M. R. (1997). Challenge or boredom? Gifted students' views on their schooling. *Roeper Review, 19,* 132–136.

Gallagher, S. A. (2000). Project P-BLISS: An experiment in curriculum for disadvantaged high school students. *NASSP Bulletin, 84*(615), 47–57.

Gallagher, S. A., & Stepien, W. J. (1996). Content acquisition in problem-based learning: Depth versus breadth in American studies. *Journal for the Education of the Gifted, 19,* 257–275.

Geography Education Standards Project. (1994). *Geography for life: National geography standards 1994.* Washington, DC: National Geographic Research & Exploration.

Holt, T. (1990) *Thinking historically: Narrative, imagination and understanding.* Chicago: College Entrance Examination Board.

Hirsch, E. D. (1987). *Cultural literacy: What every American needs to know.* Boston: Houghton Mifflin.

Lee, S. Y., & Olszewski-Kubilius, P. (2007, April). *The development of civic attitudes and behaviors of gifted adolescents through service learning.* Paper presented at the American Educational Research Association, Chicago, IL

Marzano, R., Kendall, J., & Gaddy, B. (1999). *Essential knowledge: The debate over what American students should know.* Aurora, CO: McREL.

Moon, T. R., Callahan, C. M., & Tomlinson, C. A. (1995). *Academic diversity in the middle school: Results of a survey of middle school administrators and teachers* (Research Monograph No. 95124). Storrs: National Research Center on the Gifted and Talented, University of Connecticut.

Moon, T. R., Callahan, C. M., Tomlinson, C. A., & Miller, E. M. (2002). *Middle school classrooms: Teachers' reported practices and student perceptions* (Research Monograph No. 02164). Storrs: National Research Center on the Gifted and Talented, University of Connecticut.

National Center for Education Statistics. (1999). *What happens in classrooms? Instructional practices in elementary and secondary schools, 1994–1995.* Washington, DC: U.S. Department of Education.

National Center for Education Statistics. (2002). *The nation's report card: U.S. History 2001.* (NCES 2002-483). Washington, DC: U.S. Department of Education, Office of Educational Research and Improvement.

National Commission on Service-Learning. (2002). *Learning in deed: The power of service-learning for American schools.* Retrieved on March 14, 2007, from http://learningindeed.org/slcommission/learningindeed.pdf

National Council for the Social Studies. (1994). *Expectations of excellence: Curriculum standards for social studies.* Retrieved July 6, 2007, from http://www.ncss.org/standards

National Research Council. (1998). *How people learn: Brain, mind, experience, and school.* Washington, DC: National Academy Press.

No Child Left Behind Act, 20 U.S.C. §6301 (2001).

Paxton, R. J. (1997). "Someone with like a life wrote it": The effects of a visible author on high school history students. *Journal of Educational Psychology, 89,* 235–250.

Paxton, R. J. (1999). A deafening silence: History textbooks and the students who read them. *Review of Educational Research, 69,* 315–339.

Ravitch, D. (1992). *The democracy reader.* New York: HarperCollins.

Ravitch, D., & Finn, C. E. (1987). *What do our 17-year-olds know? A report on the First National Assessment of History and Literature.* New York: Harper & Row.

Reis, S. M., & Purcell, J. H. (1993). An analysis of content elimination and strategies used by elementary classroom teachers and the curriculum compacting process. *Journal for the Education of the Gifted, 16,* 147–170.

Reis, S., Westberg, K., Kulikowich, J., Caillard, F., Hébert, T., Plucker, J., et al. (1993). *Why not let high ability students start school in January?: A research monograph on the curriculum compacting study* (Research Monograph No. 93106). Storrs: National Research Center on the Gifted and Talented, University of Connecticut.

Renzulli, J. S., & Reis, S. M. (1997). *The Schoolwide Enrichment Model: A how-to guide for educational excellence.* Mansfield Center, CT: Creative Learning Press.

Sewall, G. T. (2004). *World history textbooks: A review. A report of the American Textbook Council.* Retrieved March 16, 2007, from http://www.historytextbooks.org/world.htm

Shettle, C., Roey, S., Mordica, J., Perkins, R., Nord, C., Teodorovic, J., et al. (2007). *The nation's report card: America's high school graduates* (NCES 2007- 467). Washington, DC: U.S. Government Printing Office.

Stahl, S., Hynd, C., Britton, B., McNish, M., & Bosquet, D. (1996). What happens when students read multiple source documents in history? *Reading Research Quarterly, 31,* 430–456.

Stepien, W. J., Gallagher, S. A., & Workman, D. (1993). Problem-based learning for traditional and interdisciplinary classrooms. *Journal for the Education of the Gifted, 16,* 338–357.

Tallent-Runnels, M. K. (1993). The Future Problem Solving Program: An investigation of effects on problem-solving ability. *Contemporary Educational Psychology, 18,* 382–388.

Tallent-Runnels, M. K., & Yarbrough, D. W. (1992). Effects of the Future Problem Solving program on children's concerns about the future. *Gifted Child Quarterly, 36,* 190–194.

Terry, A. W. (2000). An early glimpse: Service learning from an adolescent perspective. *Journal of Secondary Gifted Education, 11,* 115–135.

Terry, A. W. (2003). Effects of service learning on young, gifted adolescents and their community. *Gifted Child Quarterly, 47,* 295–308.

Tomlinson, C. A. (2005). Quality curriculum and instruction for highly able students. *Theory Into Practice, 44,* 160–166.

Twyman, T., McCleery, J., & Tindal, G. (2006). Using concepts to frame history content. *Journal of Experimental Education, 74,* 331–349.

VanSledright, B. A., & Kelly, C. (1998). Reading American history: The influence of multiple sources on six fifth graders. *Elementary School Journal, 98,* 239–265.

VanTassel-Baska, J., & Little, C. (2003). *Content-based curriculum for high ability learners.* Waco, TX: Prufrock Press.

Volk, V. (2006). Expanding horizons—Into the future with confidence! *Roeper Review, 28,* 175–178.

Voss, J. F., & Wiley, J., (2006). Expertise in history. In K. A. Ericsson, N. Charness, P. J. Feltovich, & R. R. Hoffman (Eds.), *The Cambridge handbook of expertise and expert performance* (pp. 569–584). New York: Cambridge University Press.

Weiss, A. R., Lutkus, D., Hildebrant, B. S., & Johnson, M. S. (2002). *The nation's report card: Geography 2001* (NCES 2002-484). Washington, DC: U.S. Department of Education.

Westberg, K. L., Archambault, F. X., Dobyns, S. M., & Salvin, T. J. (1993). The classroom practices observation study. *Journal for the Education of the Gifted, 16,* 120–146.

Wineburg, S. S. (1991). Historical problem solving: A study of the cognitive processes used in the evaluation of documentary and pictorial evidence. *Journal of Educational Psychology, 83,* 73–87.

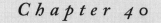

Chapter 40

SPECIAL SCHOOLS

Kelly E. Rapp

Since the establishment of the first state-supported residential high school for academically gifted students in North Carolina in 1978, a growing number of specialized schools—most with an emphasis in the areas of math and science—continue to serve the nation's gifted (Stephens, 1998). The National Association for Gifted Children (NAGC; n.d.) reports that public high schools or academies for advanced students in math, science, and to a lesser extent, the arts and humanities, currently exist in 13 states[1]. Although many specialized programs or Governor's Schools are offered to gifted students during the summer months, the scope of this chapter will be limited to schools operating during the traditional academic year.

---

1   The Advanced Academy of Georgia, a public residential early-college-entrance program for gifted juniors and seniors, is not considered a high school because students "exclusively take regularly scheduled university classes taught by university professors" (Advanced Academy of Georgia, n.d., ¶ 2). Likewise, several private residential early-college-entrance programs exist (Boothe, Sethna, Stanley, & Colgate, 1999) but are not considered within this chapter.

The majority of the public secondary schools for the gifted serve students from across a state and are necessarily residential; however, a notable exception is the 16 regional, nonresidential Academic-Year Governor's Schools in Virginia (Virginia Department of Education, n.d.). Existing literature on specialized secondary schools for the gifted (Boothe et al., 1999; Green, 1993a, 1993b; Stephens, 1998) is limited to residential high schools and cannot be assumed to generalize to the nonresidential experiences at the Governor's Schools in Virginia. Because of the lack of data on these nonresidential high schools, discussion in this chapter does not include the Virginia schools.

In 1998 (the most recent date of a comprehensive statistic), total legislative budgets among 11 math and science residential schools ranged from $1,356,000 to $13,150,500, with most budgets falling in the $3 million to $7 million range. Additionally, some schools received additional funding through grants or other external sources (Stephens, 1998). Typically, the entire cost of tuition and boarding at residential academies is covered by the state, although some academies charge activity or other miscellaneous fees. In many instances, the school is located on a college campus (NAGC, n.d.).

These specialized residential schools offer academically gifted students who are selected for admission the accelerated study of advanced subjects through an extensive curriculum often augmented by the resources of a partnering university (Green, 1993b). Employing a hybrid high school/college approach, the social atmosphere at these schools resembles that of high school, and the curriculum is college-level (Jones, Fleming, Henderson, & Henderson, 2002).

Many smaller, rural, or underprivileged traditional public schools may not be able to offer sufficient programming for gifted students; therefore, a centralized, public site of instruction allows equal access to all gifted students across a state. Furthermore, at a specialized school, students have the opportunity to thrive both emotionally and academically through interactions with a supportive, similar-ability peer group in a community that values high achievement (Green, 1993b; Stephens, 1998).

Several articles and reports offer a description of the public residential academies for the gifted, but few recent empirical studies have been conducted in order to determine impacts of these schools on academic outcomes. In fact, only the multisite longitudinal study of Thomas and Love (2002) investigates the effects of attendance at a residential math and science academy on students' postgraduation experiences. The majority of empirical studies with this population focus on psychological characteristics and adjustment patterns of the students in the residential high schools. Existing literature on state-supported specialized schools for the gifted addresses the following questions: (1) What do these schools look like? and (2) What are the psychosocial and academic impacts of attending these schools?

DESCRIPTIVE LITERATURE

From the opening of the first public residential academy for the gifted and the advent of the movement to establish more such schools (Stanley, 1987), several journal articles (e.g., Boothe et al., 1999; Cox & Daniel, 1983; Feldhusen & Boggess, 2000; Stephens, 1998), organizational reports (e.g., Green, 1993b; Jarwan & Feldhusen, 1993), and book chapters (e.g., Kolloff, 1997; Swassing & Fichter, 1992) have been written, summarizing characteristics across these schools. Additionally, many articles and reports exist that describe curricular approaches at particular schools (e.g., Eilber, 1987; Green, 1993a; Lewis, 1993; Lyublinskaya, 1997; Milner & Milner, 1986; Stanley, 1991). Below are key themes from the literature across multiple residential schools that describe similarities in students, faculty, admissions, and curriculum.

Students and Student Life

As of 1998, the size of the 11 existing residential math and science high schools ranged from 125 to 631 students (Stephens, 1998). In 1993, the average entering SAT score (taken by 8th-, 9th-, or 10th-grade students) across 9 residential academies for the gifted was 1200 (Green, 1993b). Although most of the nine schools in Green's (1993b) study reported specifically targeting recruitment of populations and geographic regions traditionally underrepresented in their programs, actual enrollment data reflected that Hispanics, African Americans, and Native Americans were largely underrepresented, and Asian Americans were overrepresented in comparison to state profiles (Green, 1993b; Jarwan & Feldhusen, 1993; Stephens, 1998). However, Stephens (1998) reported that the residential academies exhibited varying degrees of success in representing geographic regions of the state depending on the emphasis or lack of emphasis placed on this factor during the admission process. Additionally, there were approximately the same number of males and females across all 11 schools profiled (Stephens, 1998).

At the public residential high schools, students are offered a variety of extracurricular experiences such as intramural or interscholastic athletics and service and academic clubs and honor societies (Green, 1993b; Stephens, 1998). None of the public academies that offer early entrance to college allow the students to join fraternities or sororities (Boothe et al., 1999), and the National Collegiate Athletic Association prohibits students who have not graduated from high school from participating on the college athletic teams. However, students at the residential academies are allowed to participate in collegiate physical education classes and intramural programs.

Green (1993b) adds that on college campuses, students may participate in the cultural life of the campus, including lectures, plays, and art exhibits. Additionally, the residential component allows students to collaborate with each other, rather than working in isolation like many may have done in their home schools. Living in common residences facilitates group projects, peer tutoring, and group study sessions (Green, 1993b).

Faculty

According to Stephens (1998), the majority of faculty at the 11 math and science academies had advanced degrees, either a master's or a doctorate, with the percentage of teachers at a given school holding a doctorate ranging from 19% to 73%. Despite these credentials, Green (1993b) found that teacher salaries at the public residential academies were lower than at traditional public schools, and most academies did not have tenure systems. At many of the math and science academies, part-time faculty also hold teaching positions at local colleges and universities. In fact, the Texas Academy of Math and Science (TAMS) employs faculty entirely from University of North Texas rather than hiring its own teachers. Additionally, many of the residential schools profiled in both Green (1993b) and Stephens (1998) have visiting teacher or scholar programs, where instructors come to the campus from business or industry, universities, or other public secondary schools.

Teacher certification requirements for the public residential high schools are flexible (Stephens, 1998), and none of the nine academies profiled in Green (1993b) require that the teachers have teaching licenses. The primary focus is on recruiting individuals with advanced knowledge and expertise in specific content areas (Green, 1993b; Stephens, 1998). Most academies require their teachers to have previous teaching experience, preferably with high-ability students, but as of 1993, none required formal training in the education of the gifted (Green, 1993b).

Admissions Procedures

Generally, the state-supported specialized residential schools are open to juniors and seniors in high school (the notable exception being the Illinois Mathematics and Science Academy [IMSA], which accepts students as sophomores; IMSA, n.d.). Because the applications for admission typically exceed available spots in the academies, competitive formal admissions processes involving multiple criteria for reviewing applications are used to select students (Green, 1993b). In the nine states housing schools profiled in Green (1993b), enabling legislation states that the schools must focus on admitting academically talented students.

The recruiting and application process usually begins in the fall for the next academic year. Recruiting strategies at most residential academies discourage generating large application pools that would result in large numbers of students being denied admission (Green, 1993b). Transcripts from as early as seventh grade, as well as standardized test scores, are considered, although only a small number of schools mention specific cut-off test scores or grade point averages required for admission. Often, written essays highlighting special talents, accomplishments, and awards; letters of recommendation; interviews; and portfolios also are considered (Green, 1993b; Stephens, 1998). Additionally, 7 of the 11 math and science academies profiled in Stephens (1998) explicitly cite an interest in science and math as a requirement.

In addition to academic requirements, many of these schools assess a student's social and emotional maturity to enter a residential academy, based on recommendations from high school personnel and student and parent interviews (Boothe et al., 1999). Each student in the four residential public schools profiled in Boothe et al. (1999) is thoroughly assessed so that the admitting institution can be certain that the student is ready for such a move and that this decision is the student's desire rather than solely pressure from a parent or mentor. Additionally, residential school admissions committees often look for indicators of commitment to learning, motivation, and self-discipline necessary to succeed in a rigorous program away from home (Green, 1993b).

Curriculum and Program Models

The research-based acceleration and enrichment models used in the state-supported specialized residential schools accommodate the characteristics of gifted adolescents who learn at faster rates and are more capable of problem solving and of abstract thought (Green, 1993b). The curriculum, at least at the nine residential schools profiled in Green (1993b) and likely at most of the schools, affords students the opportunity for accelerated study of advanced subjects not commonly offered at traditional high schools, enrichment activities, and experiences outside of the classroom, including apprenticeships with university researchers, seminars, academic field trips, or intense mini-courses (Green, 1993b). Most of the public high schools for advanced students emphasize math and science (NAGC, n.d.) but not to the exclusion of the arts and humanities. In fact, many of the schools with a math or science focus offer interdisciplinary courses to connect the domains (Green, 1993b).

The curriculum at public academies for advanced students is more comparable to college than to high school and allows gifted students to pursue their particular educational interests (Boothe et al., 1999). Indeed, the academies located on a college campus incorporate undergraduate college courses to complement their own courses, with the exception of the Texas Academy of Math and Science, at which students enroll solely in college courses in order to complete the last 2 years of high school (in absentia) and the first 2 years of college simultaneously (Green, 1993b; Stephens, 1998). Schedules at public high schools for advanced students often mimic college schedules, with courses spaced throughout the day and in many cases only meeting 4 days a week (Stephens, 1998).

EMPIRICAL STUDIES

Psychosocial and academic impacts of attending a residential academy for the gifted are best determined through empirical studies. The majority of existing empirical studies use one academy as the population of inquiry, however, preventing conclusions from being drawn across multiple academies. Many of the existing studies examine psychosocial characteristics of students and their adjustment to the schools but do not examine the long-term academic outcomes of the students. Evaluations of specific academies exist (i.e., Virginia Department of Education, 1989) but often are not available to the public, and even fewer studies examine academic outcomes across multiple schools.

The Psychosocial Dimension

Researchers have used existing scales (Minnesota Multiphasic Personality Inventory for Adolescents [MMPI-A]; Myers-Briggs Type Indicator [MBTI]), as well as original instruments and data from interviews and observations with a combination of quantitative (descriptive statistics, *t*-tests, ANOVA, MANOVA, regressions) and qualitative (ethnographic and phenomenological inquiry; Coleman 2001, 2002, 2005) analyses, in order to determine psychological characteristics, social support structures, and adjustment patterns of gifted students attending state-supported specialized residential schools.

Regarding the experiences of students at residential public academies for the gifted, findings are mixed. Students in Hawkins's (1997) study appreciated being in the majority of personality type—many for the first time in their academic career—and studying with so many other students with common interests. However, Coleman (2002, 2005) found that the rigorous academic requirements and homework demands at one state-funded public residential high school for the gifted were a shock to students. The students in Coleman's ethnographic study struggled to cope with the surprise of learning that they often did not have adequate study skills and were ill-prepared for the demands of the academy due to the lack of emphasis placed on homework in the traditional schools.

Many factors, such as social support from peers, family, or the school staff, contribute to adolescent adjustment to public residential academies (Dunn, Putallaz, Sheppard, & Lindstrom, 1987). Dunn et al. (1987) found interactions among sex of the student, source of support, and nature of the adjustment problem at one residential school. For example, successful overall adjustment to the school environment was related to perceived support from family, whereas psychological adjustment showed a clear relation to perceived support in general. Additionally, parents and students may perceive adjustment to the residential schools differently (Dorsel & Wages, 1993). Parents in survey research conducted by Dorsel and Wages (1993) generally expressed more positive attitudes, feelings, and beliefs than their students, exhibiting more pride and hope and less doubt, anger, disappointment, and worry. Throughout the course of the school year, both groups became less optimistic about the impact of the residential school on the students' potential for getting into better colleges, but they all reported that personality and ability to cope improved (Dorsel & Wages, 1993).

In addition to the above-mentioned studies on the psychosocial experiences of gifted students at residential academies, research also has been conducted on psychological characteristics of students at these academies. Cross, Adams, Dixon, and Holland (2004) found that the psychological characteristics (as measured by the MMPI-A) of gifted adolescents in the academy were similar to a normative group of (not necessarily gifted) adolescents on the MMPI-A. However, Hawkins (1997) found that his sample of 966 gifted students in a public residential academy from 1990–1995 had different psychological types, as measured by the MBTI, than a sample of traditional (not necessarily gifted) high school students drawn from the MBTI Atlas of Type Tables. Additionally, Hawkins compared personality types of gifted students in a specialized residential school to other gifted students not attending a residential school and found that both groups had similar personality types.

In contrast to studies that investigate the perspectives of residential academy students, Jones et al. (2002) surveyed gifted nonapplicants to the Texas Academy of Mathematics and Science in order to determine reasons that qualified students were hesitant to apply to this early-college-entrance program. Results indicated that students were confident in their ability to meet admission requirements; however, they were unwilling to leave home 2 years earlier than usual and to abandon a variety of athletic and other extracurricular activities. Although students who lived farther away did cite distance as a concern, students who lived closer to the campus were no more likely to apply (Jones et al., 2002).

Academic Outcomes

The National Consortium for Specialized Secondary Schools of Mathematics, Science, and Technology (NCSSSMST) has conducted the only longitudinal study of graduates of public academies for advanced students to date (Thomas & Love, 2002). Data collection for this study began in the spring of 1999 with consortium schools interviewing graduates who had been out of high school for one year and those who had been out for 4 years. Findings indicate that, as of the 2001 data collection point, graduates consistently were satisfied with their high school experiences. Additionally, a large number of these graduates were entering into or had completed majors related to math and science, were active in campus activities and leadership roles, and had earned many academic honors as undergraduates (Thomas & Love, 2002). The relationship between attendance at the math and science academies cannot be determined with certainty, however, because a control group was not used. Furthermore, responses regarding satisfaction may be biased due to the fact that the schools themselves collected the data.

Jarwan and Feldhusen (1993), through the National Research Center on the Gifted and Talented, investigated the relationship between admissions selections procedures and academic outcomes of seven state-supported residential high schools for mathematics and science through a combination of qualitative (interviews with administrators) and quantitative (multiple regression analyses) analyses. Results indicated that students' home-school adjusted grade point average was the best predictor and SAT test scores the second best predictor of first- and second-year grade point averages. Overall, the researchers found that statistical prediction of academic outcomes was superior to professional prediction by interview or rating of complete files. However, rather than abandon the practice of using multiple data sources in identification and selection of gifted students, the researchers recommended adequate training of committee members involved in the selection process in order to increase cross-rater or cross-interviewer reliability (Jarwan & Feldhusen, 1993).

CONCLUSIONS, LIMITATIONS, AND IMPLICATIONS FOR FUTURE STUDY

State-supported residential high schools for the gifted fill an important programming need for gifted and talented students in the United States (Stephens, 1998). Students attending these advanced academies have the opportunity to interact with intellectual peers of the same age, conduct meaningful research, and experience college life and college-level studies early. For many of the students, feeling free to interact and express ideas without fear of ridicule and being removed from the sometimes anti-intellectual environment of a traditional high school can be a welcome relief (Boothe et al., 1999). Based on the existing literature on residential high schools for the gifted—not including summer academies, on which there are numerous writings, as well—the following conclusions are warranted:

- African American and Hispanic students are underrepresented in comparison to the state profile in these specialized schools, and degree of equal geographic representation from areas of the state varies among the high schools.
- Students are offered a variety of extracurricular experiences, and the residential high schools associated with a college or university are able to provide additional cultural experiences through campus activities.
- Curriculum and scheduling at these academies resemble what is found in college rather than high school. Additionally, most academies incorporate experiences such as research, seminars, mentorship, and community service.

- The rigorous academic requirements and homework demands at the residential high schools may be a shock to students due to the lack of emphasis placed on homework in the traditional schools.
- Successful adjustment to the residential school environment is related to perceived social support.

Despite some commonalities, it must be remembered that summarizing across such unique programs presents difficulties for homogenizing individual traits. Additionally, the most recent published summary of the schools is from 2000 (Feldhusen & Boggess); therefore, a more current representation of specialized schools for the gifted is needed.

What we know about student experiences cannot be adequately summarized into bullet points that represent the entirety of residential public academies. However, for a thorough account of experiences at one residential high school, interested readers should consult the 2005 book by Laurence J. Coleman, *Nurturing Talent in High School: Life in the Fast Lane*. Coleman lived among the students at one school and gained an in-depth perspective of how the environment interacted with the students' talents to impact their development.

Although findings of individual studies are generally positive (i.e., gifted students at the academies seem to be adjusting well to social and academic demands and have similar MMPI-A scores as a normative group of adolescents), results must be interpreted with caution, as each study was conducted at a single site and the corresponding results may not be generalizable.

Although a longitudinal study of postgraduation experiences of students attending math and science academies for the gifted has been conducted (Thomas & Love, 2002), there is a dearth of literature that comprehensively and empirically (rather than anecdotally) evaluates current experiences and long-term effects of residential public academies both for math and science and the humanities. Indeed, more research utilizing both quantitative and qualitative methods and spanning multiple sites is needed in order to address what we still do not know about these schools. The following questions remain:

- What are the long-term impacts on alumni of the schools? How do the academic outcomes of these students compare to control groups of gifted students who did not enroll in residential schools?
- What are the perceptions of and impacts on parents, faculty, administrators, other students, and teachers throughout the state who receive outreach from the academies?
- Are there any differences in academic outcomes when measured by alternative assessments such as portfolios, surveys, and interviews rather than standardized test scores?
- Are the residential public academies meeting the needs of students, parents, teachers, and other stakeholders in the state?
- Are there any market influences on traditional schools as a result of the existence of the public residential academies?

- What is the role of the teacher in these specialized schools? Are certified teachers more effective than noncertified teachers? As public schools, how are the academies being affected by the highly qualified teacher provisions of the No Child Left Behind Act of 2001 (NCLB) which states, in part, that all teachers in schools receiving Title I funds must be certified in the subject matter they teach?

The current paucity of literature is certainly due, at least in part, to problems inherent in evaluating programs for the gifted. Gifted students do not fit typical paradigms for evaluating educational programs—they already score in the highest ranges on standardized tests, so academic improvement as traditionally measured is difficult to show. Green (1993b) attributed the lack of evaluations of residential academies for the gifted to the fact that the movement was fairly recent and there had not been time; however, 14 years have passed since the publication of Green's report, and only one evaluative study on outcomes has been conducted.

In order to have the greatest impact on sustenance and improvement of the specialized school movement, research in this area must evolve from its primarily descriptive focus. Research with an evaluative focus that emphasizes practical implications of the findings will make the most difference in reforming the organization of or service delivery within these schools.

REFERENCES

Advanced Academy of Georgia. (n.d). *Welcome to the Advanced Academy of Georgia*. Retrieved July 3, 2007, from http://www.advancedacademy.org

Boothe, D., Sethna, B. N., Stanley, J. C., & Colgate, S. D. (1999). Special opportunities for exceptionally able high school students: A description of eight residential early-college-entrance programs. *Journal of Secondary Gifted Education, 10*, 195–202.

Coleman, L. J. (2001). A "rag quilt": Social relationships among students in a special high school. *Gifted Child Quarterly, 45*, 164–173.

Coleman, L. J. (2002). A shock to study. *Journal of Secondary Gifted Education, 14*, 39–52.

Coleman, L. J. (2005). *Nurturing talent in high school: Life in the fast lane*. New York: Teachers' College Press.

Cox, J., & Daniel, N. (1983). Specialized schools for high ability students. *Gifted Child Today, 28*, 2–9.

Cross, T. L., Adams, C., Dixon, F., & Holland, J. (2004). Psychological characteristics of academically gifted adolescents attending a residential academy: A longitudinal study. *Journal for the Education of the Gifted, 28*, 159–181.

Dorsel, T. N., & Wages, C. (1993). Gifted, residential education: Outcomes are largely favorable, but there are some cautions. *Roeper Review, 15*, 239–242.

Dunn, S. E., Putallaz, M., Sheppard, B. H., & Lindstrom, R. (1987). Social support and adjustment in gifted adolescents. *Journal of Educational Psychology, 79*, 467–473.

Eilber, C. R. (1987). The North Carolina School of Science and Mathematics. *Phi Delta Kappan, 68*, 772–777.

Feldhusen, J. F., & Boggess, J. (2000). Secondary schools for academically talented youth. *Gifted Education International, 14,* 170–176.

Green, J. E. (1993a). *A multidimensional curriculum for academically gifted students: Educating the whole person at the Indiana Academy.* Muncie, IN: Ball State University. (ERIC Document Reproduction Service No. ED365010)

Green, J. E. (1993b). *State academies for the academically gifted* (Fastback 349). Bloomington, IN: Phi Delta Kappa Educational Foundation. (ERIC Document Reproduction Service No. ED357596)

Hawkins, J. (1997). Giftedness and psychological type. *Journal of Secondary Gifted Education, 9,* 57–67.

Illinois Mathematics and Science Academy. (n.d.). *About IMSA.* Retrieved March 6, 2006, from http://www2.imsa.edu/about

Jarwan, F. A., & Feldhusen, J. F. (1993). *Residential schools of mathematics and science for academically talented youth: An analysis of admission programs* (Collaborative Research Study, CRS93304). Storrs: National Research Center on the Gifted and Talented, University of Connecticut. (ERIC Document Reproduction Service No. ED379851)

Jones, B. M., Fleming, D. L., Henderson, J., & Henderson, C. E. (2002). Common denominators: Assessing hesitancy to apply to a selective residential math and science academy. *Journal of Secondary Gifted Education, 13,* 164–172.

Kolloff, P. B. (1997). Special residential high schools. In N. Colangelo & G. A. Davis (Eds.), *Handbook of gifted education* (pp. 198–206). Needham Heights, MA: Allyn & Bacon.

Lewis, G. (1993). Keeping the options open: Curriculum at the Louisiana School for Math, Science, and the Arts. *Journal for the Education of the Gifted, 16,* 387–399.

Lyublinskaya, I. (1997). Optical instrumentation for an interdisciplinary student research course. *Journal of Secondary Gifted Education, 9,* 76–82.

Milner, J. O., & Milner, L. M. (1986). A comprehensive approach to the humanities. *Clearing House, 60,* 183–186.

National Association for Gifted Children. (n.d.). Public high schools for advanced students. Retrieved March 6, 2006, from http://www.nagc.org/index.aspx?id=974

No Child Left Behind Act, 20 U.S.C. §6301 (2001).

Stanley, J. C. (1987). State residential high schools for mathematically talented youth. *Phi Delta Kappan, 68,* 770–773.

Stanley, J. C. (1991). A better model for residential high schools for talented youths. *Phi Delta Kappan, 72,* 471–473.

Stephens, K. R. (1998). Residential math and science high schools: A closer look. *Journal of Secondary Gifted Education, 10,* 85–92.

Swassing, R. H., & Fichter, G. R. (1992). Residential, regional, and specialized schools. In *Challenges in gifted education: Developing potential and investing in knowledge for the 21ˢᵗ century.* Columbus, OH: Ohio Department of Education. (ERIC Document Reproduction Service No. ED344402)

Thomas, J., & Love, B. L. (2002). NCSSSMST longitudinal study of graduates: A three-year analysis of college freshmen and college seniors. *NCSSSMT Journal, 7*(2), 4–8.

Virginia Department of Education. (1989). *Evaluation of the Virginia Governor's Schools.* Richmond, VA: Author. (ERIC Document Reproduction Service No. ED330144)

Virginia Department of Education. (n.d.). *Virginia Governor's School program.* Retrieved March 6, 2006, from http://www.pen.k12.va.us/VDOE/Instruction/ Govschools

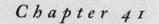

Chapter 41

SUICIDE

Tracy L. Cross

uicide rates among adolescents and young adults (individuals aged 15–24) increased more than 240% between 1955 and 1995 (American Association of Suicidology, 2004). Although there was a decline in the rates of suicide in the general population between 1994 and 2000 (from 13.8 in 1994 to 9.9 in 2002 suicides per 100,000), prevalence rates increased to 10.4 in 2004. Suicide still ranks as the third leading cause of death among adolescents (American Association of Suicidology, 2004). The rates of suicide for children younger than 14 years reflect a similar pattern, but with a steeper increase over time. The rates for this group in some way are difficult both to comprehend and to interpret (National Center for Health Statistics, 2006). Are children as young as 5 or 6 years old actually killing themselves? Yes. The fact that this phenomenon is so startling to imagine is one of the reasons the rates of this group are hard to interpret (Mishara, 1999). Because the possibility of children killing themselves was not something Americans seriously studied more than 50 years ago, the data collected on this age group likely underestimates the actual rates between 1950 and approximately 1970. These prevalence rates are a concern. However, the American Association for Suicidology (AAS; 2004) estimates that for every successful attempt, there are as many as 25 unsuccessful attempts.

TERMS AND DEFINITIONS

To fully understand the suicidal behaviors of gifted students, several terms and concepts must be understood. Suicidal behavior actually represents at least four categories of behaviors. The first group of behaviors is called *suicide ideation*. Suicide ideation is thinking about killing oneself. We label people who engage in these behaviors *ideators*. The second group of behaviors is described as *suicidal gestures*. These efforts have been determined not to be serious efforts of people to end their lives, per se (Muehlenkamp & Gutierrez, 2004). Those who engage in these behaviors are called *gesterors*. The third group of behaviors consists of individuals' bona fide efforts to kill themselves, which result in failure. These behaviors are labeled *suicidal attempts*, and those who engage in them are called *attemptors*. The fourth set of behaviors is those that end in the death of the people making the attempts, or *suicide completions*. Suicidologists call victims of suicide completions *completers*.

To conduct their research and to discuss suicidal behavior, suicidologists rely on prevalence rates rather than numbers of completions to discuss suicidal behavior. The primary reason for this reliance is that the age groups that are reported on vary significantly in absolute numbers. Therefore, typically, prevalence rates reflecting a proportion of those who die out of 100,000 people within the age group (e.g., 5–14, 15–24, 25–34, 45–54, 55–64, 65–74, 75–84, 85+) are reported and emphasized. This approach has yielded numerous important findings. For example, although adolescents and young adults (15–24 years old) have the highest number of completed suicides in a given year, in actual prevalence rates, they rank third from last. The three oldest groups (65–74, 75–84, 85+) have higher prevalence rates of suicide completions.

This situation illustrates that even when dealing with the most concrete questions associated with suicide, answers are hard to achieve. When the remaining three categories of suicidal behavior are factored in—ideation, gestures, attempts—where an obvious range exists in the ease with which the behaviors can be known, one can easily see how much more complicated understanding this phenomenon actually is. Figure 1 illustrates some of the complexities associated with the relationships among the four categories of suicidal behaviors. The first important fact to note is that suicidal ideation is generally believed to exist at some level before a gesture, attempt, or completion takes place. One study reported that 85% of suicide attemptors had revealed suicidal ideation in advance (Pinto, Whisman, & McCoy, 1997). Second, there are many more people who think about suicide than who gesture, attempt, or complete. Some people engage only in ideation, whereas others ideate and make gestures and

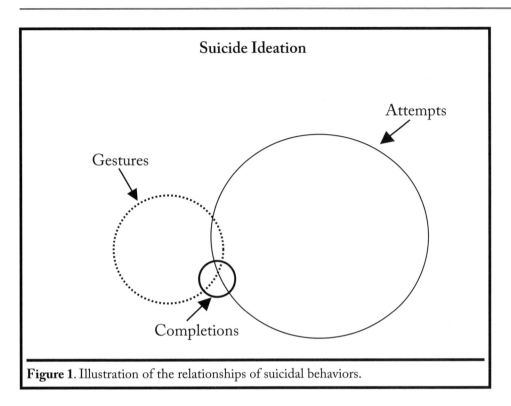

Figure 1. Illustration of the relationships of suicidal behaviors.

that is as far as they go. Still others ideate and make only failed attempts and stop. Some ideate and then complete. A very small percentage may engage in all four sets of behaviors. To put this into perspective, about 10 in 100,000 15- to 24-year-olds complete suicide annually in the U.S. If the AAS is correct in their estimation that there are 25 times more attempts to completions, that rate would be approximately 250 of every 100,000 15- to 24-year-olds making suicide attempts. Unfortunately, evidence of gestures is quite limited, and evidence that does exist seems unreliable (Muehlenkamp & Gutierrez, 2004). Consequently, a dotted line is used to illustrate the uncertainty associated with this category of suicidal behavior.

WHAT DOES THE RESEARCH SUPPORT?

Because there is virtually no research that demonstrates that the patterns of suicidal behavior of the general population of children are different from those of gifted children, important findings about suicidal behavior for all children will be reported first. Later, the salient studies of gifted children will be included. Davidson & Linnoila (1991) have described the 10 significant risk factors associated with the suicides of adolescents:

1. psychiatric disorders such as depression and anxiety,
2. drug and alcohol abuse,
3. genetic factors,

4. family loss or disruption,
5. friend or family member of suicide victim,
6. homosexuality,
7. rapid sociocultural change,
8. media emphasis on suicide,
9. impulsiveness and aggressiveness, and
10. ready access to lethal methods. (Davidson & Linnoila, 1991)

Other suicidologists have attempted to classify the characteristics that place individuals at greater risk of suicide (Shneidman, 1993, 1996). Stillion and McDowell's (1996) conceptualization summarizes the orientations that have been offered from various dimensions of psychological thought. Their Suicide Trajectory Model summarized four primary categories of risk factors: (a) biological (e.g., depression, gender, genetics); (b) psychological (e.g., poor self-esteem, depression, feelings of hopelessness); (c) cognitive (e.g., poor problem solving, inflexible thinking, low coping strategies); and (d) environmental (e.g., family experiences, life events, presence of deadly weapons). The interactions among these factors are important when determining the likelihood of suicidal risk (Stillion & McDowell, 1996). Holmes (1991) claimed that, in the face of extreme perceived stress (environmental/psychological), adolescents often will view suicide as an escape. Under conditions of stress, poor problem-solving strategies (cognitive) are typically displayed, leading to inflexible thinking and fixation on a limited selection of potential solutions to the problem. Once suicide is generated as a possible solution to the perceived problem, the individual is likely to perseverate on suicidal thoughts and tendencies until an attempt is made (Holmes, 1991). Consequently, the probability of suicide completion is heightened when firearms are readily available (environmental) and particularly when depression (biological) is a factor.

Epidemiological researchers have demonstrated that the incidence rates of attempted suicide vary among groups of adolescents and young adults. For example, it has been reported that as many as 10% of all adolescents (Smith & Crawford, 1986), 33% of troubled adolescents (Tomlinson-Keasey & Keasey, 1988), and 61% of juvenile offenders (Alessi, McManus, Brickman, & Grapentine, 1984) attempt suicide. Males have higher rates of completed suicide at nearly every age level and are at greatest risk for attempting suicide in the 15–24 age group (Holinger, Offer, Barter, & Bell, 1994).

Holinger et al. (1994), in a review of research on suicide, reported that most adolescents who kill themselves meet criteria for diagnosable psychiatric disorders. They reported comorbidity of affective disorders at 25% to 75% and/or personality disorders at 25% to 40%. Comorbidity of affective disorders, personality disorders, and/or substance abuse appears to be particularly lethal. In addition, 25% to 50% of adolescents completing suicide have a family history of psychiatric disorders and/or suicides, and 25% to 50% have made previous attempts to take their own life. Not surprisingly, the number and lethality of attempts also are found to correlate with completed suicide. When firearms exist within the home, a large increase in the risk of suicide is observed. Gender identity issues (i.e., homosexuality) also have been correlated with the risk of suicide among adolescents.

STATE OF CURRENT RESEARCH ON GIFTED STUDENT SUICIDE

Given the fact that the field of suicidology has grown considerably over the past 50 years, what do we know about the suicide of gifted students? Arguably the most important question is this: What are the prevalence rates of suicide completion among gifted adolescents and young adults and children and youth below 14 years of age? At this time, the answer to this question is that we cannot know given the paucity of research that addresses this question on the subject. There are several reasons for the limited number of studies conducted on the suicides of gifted students. One is the widespread belief among members of society that students with gifts and talents can take care of themselves. Others include the following:

1. The current data collected nationally about adolescent suicide do not include whether the victims were gifted.
2. The varying definitions of the terms *gifted* and *talented* used across the U.S. make it difficult to know whether the children and adolescents who committed suicide were similarly gifted.
3. Issues of confidentiality limit access to data.
4. Conducting psychological autopsies of suicide victims is an expensive endeavor in terms of time and money.
5. The fact that more adolescents than preadolescents commit suicide, combined with the fact that secondary schools are not as actively engaged in identifying gifted students, makes conducting research on this topic difficult.
6. The terminal nature of suicide requires certain types of information to be garnered after the event. (Cross, 1996, p. 46).

A few studies have examined the prevalence of suicide ideation, depression, and/or significant amounts of stress among gifted adolescents. Baker (1995) examined the prevalence and nature of depression and suicide ideation in two groups of gifted students. The first group (exceptionally gifted) scored above 900 on the Scholastic Aptitude Test (SAT) at age 13; the second group included those in the upper 5% of their class rankings or scoring above the 95th percentile on standardized achievement tests. A comparison group was composed of students identified as having average abilities. The three groups completed the Reynolds Adolescent Depression Scale (RADS) and Suicidal Ideation Questionnaire (SIQ). No significant difference was found among the three groups on either the RADS or SIQ. In addition, no significant difference was found concerning the nature of depression among "exceptionally" gifted, gifted, or academically average students. Twelve percent of the "exceptionally" gifted adolescents, 8% of gifted adolescents, and 9% of average adolescents experienced significant levels of depression. Baker (1995) determined that the incidence of depression and suicide ideation was similar for gifted and average adolescents. She offered the following implications of her findings for educators of the gifted:

> . . . educators of the gifted should be alerted that approximately 10% of their students may be suffering from clinically significant levels of depression. This finding supports the need for faculty to receive training in recognizing and intervening with depressed students in their classrooms . . . gifted students, like their average peers, could benefit from preventive affective education or from support to understand their affective development and to cope with stressors and psychological distress. Given the incidence of depressive symptomatology in adolescents, school-based curricula seem warranted to address the mental health needs of high school students. (p. 223)

Baker's study provides evidence that some gifted adolescents seriously consider taking their own lives while at the same time manifesting evidence of depression, the most common suicide correlate.

In another study, Hayes and Sloat (1990) examined the prevalence of suicide among gifted students and studied the "attempted" and "completed" suicide rate among 69 schools in a four-county area. They reported that 19% (8) of the 42 reports of suicide-related occurrences were among gifted students. However, no completed suicides were recorded. They described their results as preliminary because of the lack of a clear definition of giftedness among the schools sampled.

A recent study (Cross, Cassady, & Miller, 2006) explored the question of whether gifted adolescents were more likely to be at risk for suicidal ideation than the general population of adolescents. Gender effects in the gifted sample also were considered. The results confirmed that, like the normal population, gifted males present with statistically significant lower levels of suicidal ideation than gifted females. As a consequence, all analyses exploring suicidal ideation included gender as an independent variable. Using the norming sample tables provided by Reynolds (1987), the gifted adolescents in this study were shown to have normal levels of suicidal thoughts.

From these studies, it is reasonable to conclude that there is no compelling evidence that being gifted places a student at risk for suicidal ideation, gestures, attempts, or completions at this time. A more measured conclusion would be that there is too little evidence to address the question.

BEYOND PREVALENCE RATES

Despite the fact that recent studies do not support the myth that gifted adolescents are more suicidal than their nongifted peers, it is possible that the two groups differ in the suicidal structure or in the manifestation of suicidal tendencies. A study that attempts to understand the psychology of gifted adolescents relative to personality types and suicidal ideation recently was completed. When examining psychological type profiles of gifted adolescents as measured by the Myers-Briggs Type Indicator and compared to the normal sample, Cross et al. (2006) found that gifted students differed on all four dichotomies (Extraversion/Introversion, Intuition/Sensing, Thinking/Feeling, Judging/Perceiving), with a strong preference for intuitive-perception profiles. These variations in the psychological profiles of gifted adolescents do not appear to modify the overall rate of suicidal intent, thoughts, or attempts. However, sensitivity to differential conceptions of self are necessary to ensure that the identifiers of suicide risk are applied appropriately to the gifted population. This study found that 18% of the variance associated with suicidal ideation was predicted by students characterized on the MBTI as introverted and perceiving types.

In a follow-up study, Cassady and Cross (2006) examined the factorial representation for suicidal ideation among the academically gifted population by comparing its scores on the Suicide Ideation Questionnaire with the general norming group's scores. The results revealed a difference in the underlying structure of suicidal ideation for the gifted sample when compared to the norming sample. The differences support the need for additional research to be conducted in this area and may prove important to more fully understanding the psychological nature of suicidal ideation among gifted students.

RESEARCH USING PSYCHOLOGICAL AUTOPSIES

Another category of research on gifted and suicidal behavior was conducted using a case study approach to research called *psychological autopsy* (PA). PA was originally developed as a research approach to solve equivocal deaths and is a process designed to assess the behaviors, thoughts, feelings, and relationships of individuals who are deceased (Ebert, 1987). The approach includes interviews of family members, friends, or significant others; reviews of records from school, physician, or psychologist/psychiatrist; and cataloging and analysis of books read, music listened to, video games played, and so forth. Data from all of these sources are analyzed. Over the years, psychological autopsies of four gifted adolescents and young adults have been reported (Cross, Cook, & Dixon, 1996; Cross, Gust-Brey, & Ball, 2002). From these studies several consistencies have been found.

In these case studies of suicide completions, several similarities among the gifted adolescents were found that can be aligned with the Suicide Trajectory Model. First, all four were males, and incidences of depression were noted in select cases (biological). Second, the young men had minimal social outlets, experienced intense emotions that they desired to be rid of, and reported conflict, pain, and confusion at times due to peer ridicule and rejection (psychological and environmental). Third, they all engaged in discussion of suicide as an honorable or viable solution and maintained hierarchical, polarized, egocentric value systems (cognitive). Although these psychological autopsies hold great promise for understanding suicidal behaviors of gifted students, given the small number of cases discussed to date, one should generalize the results only cautiously.

SUMMARY

The current research base concerned with suicidal behavior of gifted students can answer virtually no questions in a compelling fashion that are specific to gifted youth, adolescents, or young adults. More specifically, we cannot know what the prevalence rates are for suicidal ideation, gestures, attempts, or completions at this time. However, a small body of research has reported that suicide ideation does not appear to be markedly different from that of the general population of same-age peers. Therefore, it is prudent to assume that the prevalence rates are similar to the general population. This assumption can be made until or unless it is proven to be incorrect. Until that time, the signatures or correlates of suicide, such as the presence of depression when suicidal behaviors are engaged in, should be used to identify those in need of assistance. Plus, models such as the Suicide Trajectory Model hold promise for identifying those needing care, while at the same time providing evidence of the etiology of the problem.

The deeper psychological nature of the suicidal ideation process may prove to be somewhat different between the general population and gifted students. If so, then approaches to dealing with suffering gifted students may need to be amended. Research clearly needs to be continued in this area.

Although not fully answered with direct research-based evidence, the question about whether being gifted makes a person more likely to engage in suicidal behavior may be addressed through a combination of study types. For example, multiple recent studies and reviews of literature have drawn the same basic conclusions: gifted students do not show greater incidences of depression, significant mental health problems, or suicide ideation than the general population of same-aged peers. Given the relationships among depression, suicide ideation, issues of comorbidity, and suicidal behavior, it is reasonable to assume that it is highly unlikely that being gifted makes one more susceptible to falling prey to suicide.

Good news and some direction for the future exist among this dearth of research. Without compelling evidence to the contrary, conventional efforts to identify and treat the general population of people struggling with suicidal behaviors should guide practice when helping students with gifts and talents. Moreover, aberrant behaviors that manifest among gifted children should not be explained away as "just the way the gifted kids behave." Given the lack of substantial research on any of the four categories of suicidal behavior, perhaps the best advice when facing potentially suicidal gifted children is "When in doubt, do something!" (Cross, Cook, & Dixon, 1996).

To end this chapter, a synopsis of what we know on this topic, based on research, will be followed by a description of research that needs to be conducted to address the critical research questions still unanswered.

WHAT WE KNOW

- Gifted children and young adults engage in suicidal behaviors: ideation, gesturing, attempts, and completions.
- Claims in the literature about prevalence rates are speculative at best.
- The actual prevalence rates are not known at this time.
- There has yet to be any substantial evidence that gifted students are more prone to suicidal behaviors than are their nongifted counterparts.
- Some new research (Cross et al., 2006) has reported lower rates of suicide ideation than expected among samples of the adolescent gifted population.
- Correlates of suicide (e.g., depression, access to lethal means, homosexuality, other psychological maladies) are the best means of identifying students in distress.
- Best practice at this time for assisting potentially suicidal students with gifts and talents is to treat them in the same manner as their nongifted counterparts who are at risk for suicide.

FUTURE RESEARCH

To know more about the suicidal behavior of students with gifts and talents, studies in the following areas should be conducted:
- National studies should focus on prevalence rates that include an indication of whether the victims were students with gifts and talents.
- Studies focusing on ideation in varying settings need to be conducted.
- Studies using in-depth case-study approaches need to be conducted that focus on the lived experience of being a student with gifts and talents who has engaged in suicidal behavior (i.e., ideation, gesture, attempts) and survived.

- Studies using methods and procedures of psychological autopsy need to be conducted for students with gifts and talents who complete suicide.

REFERENCES

Alessi, N. E., McManus, M., Brickman, A., & Grapentine, W. L. (1984). Suicidal behavior among serious juvenile offenders. *American Journal of Psychiatry, 141,* 286–287.

American Association of Suicidology. (2004). *U.S.A. suicide: Official 2002 data.* Retrieved July 25, 2005, from http://www.suicidology.org/associations/1045/files/2002FinalData.pdf

Baker, J. A. (1995). Depression and suicidal ideation among academically talented adolescents. *Gifted Child Quarterly, 39,* 218–223.

Cassady, J. C., & Cross, T. L. (2006). A factorial representation of gifted adolescent suicide. *Journal for the Education of the Gifted, 29,* 290–304.

Cross, T. L. (1996). Examining claims about gifted children and suicide. *Gifted Child Today, 18*(3), 46–48.

Cross, T. L., Cassady, J. C., & Miller, K. A. (2006). Suicide ideation and personality characteristics among gifted adolescents. *Gifted Child Quarterly, 50,* 295–358.

Cross, T. L., Cook, R. S., & Dixon, D. N. (1996). Psychological autopsies of three academically talented adolescents who committed suicide. *Journal of Secondary Gifted Education, 7,* 403–409.

Cross, T. L., Gust-Brey, K., & Ball, P. B. (2002). A psychological autopsy of the suicide of an academically gifted student: Researchers' and parents' perspectives. *Gifted Child Quarterly, 46,* 247–264.

Davidson, L., & Linnoila, M. (Eds.). (1991). *Risk factors for youth suicide.* New York: Hemisphere.

Ebert, B. W. (1987). Guide to conducting a psychological autopsy. *Professional Psychology: Research and Practice, 11*(1), 52–56.

Hayes, M., & Sloat, R. (1990). Suicide and the gifted adolescent. *Journal for the Education of the Gifted, 13,* 229–244.

Holinger, P. C., Offer, D., Barter, J. T., & Bell, C. C. (1994). *Suicide and homicide among adolescents.* New York: Guilford Press.

Holmes, D. (1991). *Abnormal psychology.* New York: HarperCollins.

Mishara, B. L. (1999). Conceptions of death and suicide in children ages 6–12 and their implications for suicide prevention. *Suicide and Life Threatening Behavior, 29,* 105–118.

Muehlenkamp, J. J., & Gutierrez, P. M. (2004). An investigation of differences between self-injurious behavior and suicide attempts in a sample of adolescents. *Suicide and Life-Threatening Behavior, 34,* 12–23.

National Center for Health Statistics. (2006). *Causes of death report.* Retrieved December 20, 2006, from http://www.cdc.gov/ncipc/wisqars

Pinto, A., Whisman, M. A., & McCoy, K. J. M. (1997). Suicidal ideation in adolescents: Psychometric properties of the suicidal ideation questionnaire in a clinical sample. *Psychological Assessment, 9,* 63–66.

Reynolds, W. M. (1987). *Reynolds Adolescent Depression Scale.* Odessa, FL: Psychological Assessment Resources.

Shneidman, E. S. (1993). *Suicide as psychache: A clinical approach to self-destructive behavior*. Northvale, NJ: Jason Aronson.

Shneidman, E. S. (1996). *The suicidal mind*. Oxford, England: Oxford University Press.

Smith, K., & Crawford, S. (1986). Suicidal behavior among "normal" high school students. *Suicide and Life Threatening Behavior, 16*, 313–325.

Stillion, J. M., & McDowell, E. E. (1996). *Suicide across the life span*. Washington, DC: Taylor & Francis.

Tomlinson-Keasey, C., & Keasey, C. B. (1988). "Signatures" of suicide. In D. Capuzzi & L. Golden (Eds.), *Preventing adolescent suicide* (pp. 213–245). Muncie, IN: Accelerated Development. (ERIC Document Reproduction Service No. ED344145)

Chapter 42

TALENT SEARCH PROGRAMS

Michael S. Matthews

DEFINING THE TERMS

he term *talent search* is used in two ways. In the generic sense, as in "the talent search model," the term describes a particular evaluative approach. This approach uses a standardized test designed for older students to determine the degree to which younger students' abilities and/or achievements exceed those that can be assessed using grade-level tests (Charlton, Marolf, & Stanley, 2002; Olszewski-Kubilius, 1998b). Students with whom this approach is useful generally already have scored among the top 3–5% of students at their grade level. They often have obtained perfect or near perfect scores on one or more grade-level standardized tests that may be referred to as *qualifying tests*, because scores on these assessments qualify students for out-of-level assessment.

Tests used in the talent search model usually have been designed for learners 2 to 5 years above the talent search students' grade level (e.g., Stanley, 1976). By providing this *above-*

level testing or *out-of-level testing*, talent searches allow parents and schools to determine how much a child's level of performance differs from the performance of other above-average students at a given age or grade level, and therefore, to determine which potential curricular modifications might be most appropriate for meeting the child's individual educational needs. Talent search testing is most appropriate for students who can answer correctly all or nearly all of the questions on their grade-level tests. These students are said to have reached the test's *ceiling*, which is the highest level that any particular test can measure. Because above-level tests are written for older students, they provide more difficult items and, hence, a greater range of measurement is possible at the higher end of achievement than on grade-level tests. In other words, above-level tests allow a more accurate assessment of the upper levels at which the child can achieve.

When capitalized, "Talent Search" refers to testing that follows this model but is administered through a particular organization, for example, the Duke University Talent Identification Program (Duke TIP) Talent Search. The Scholastic Assessment Test, or SAT (formerly known as the Scholastic Aptitude Test), a college entrance exam, is the standardized test most commonly utilized by these organizations. The American College Testing program (ACT) assessment is a close second, and the EXPLORE test[1] (used with younger students) also is widely offered. Scores obtained on the SAT and ACT tests by seventh graders who participate in talent search programs exhibit the same distribution obtained by college-bound high school seniors (Bleske-Rechek, Lubinski, & Benbow, 2004). In the United States there are four regional-level Talent Search programs, as well as other smaller programs that operate primarily within single states (Lee, Matthews, & Olszewski-Kubilius, in press).

Talent search programs are the special educational offerings, particularly summer residential programs, that are administered by the various talent search organizations (for an overview, see Lee et al., in press). Summer programs offer students the opportunity to study content that is equivalent to a year of high school, or a college-level course in a single discipline, during approximately 3 weeks of intensive study. Educational programs available to younger students are of shorter duration, often a single day or weekend, and tend more toward enrichment with less emphasis on the academic acceleration than the summer programs customarily offer for older participants.

MAJOR QUESTIONS AND FINDINGS OF TALENT SEARCH RESEARCH

The philosophy behind the talent search movement is grounded in the individual differences tradition in psychology. Rather than seek commonalities

---

1   Although the EXPLORE test customarily is written using all capital letters, it apparently has never been an acronym, according to an ACT customer service representative (personal communication, December 6, 2005).

among all learners, this point of view favors identifying and meeting the needs of individual students at differing levels of ability (VanTassel-Baska, 1997).

Much of the research conducted at the talent searches has been designed to inform this goal of meeting individual needs, in particular by examining the effectiveness of various aspects of the talent search testing process and the programs' associated educational offerings. Major areas examined have included talent search screening criteria; affective characteristics of participating students; accelerated instruction, particularly as delivered via fast-paced homogeneously grouped summer programs; and the long-term outcomes of participation in these programs.

Screening Criteria for Selecting Talent Search Participants

Several studies have examined the score criteria used to identify those students eligible for further talent search assessment. The desired outcome of screening is to be as inclusive as possible, given the uncertainty in measurement that occurs with scores near the test ceiling, while minimizing the potential for any harm that might be done if students participated who were not ready for above-level testing. Although each talent search organization independently sets its own criteria, studies generally concur in judging seventh-grade students to be ready for above-level testing when screening criteria are set at or above the 95th percentile on grade-level tests (Ebmeier & Schmulbach, 1989; Lupkowski-Shoplik & Swiatek, 1999; Stanley & Brody, 1989).

Other studies have concluded that the 95th percentile or above on a grade-level test also is an appropriate screening criterion for student applicants in grades 4–6. In talent search testing, these students are administered above-level tests designed for eighth and ninth graders, such as the Secondary School Admissions Test (SSAT) and the EXPLORE test. Talent search participants' scores on these tests also are normally distributed, and their mean scores are approximately equal to or slightly above the mean scores obtained by students at the grade levels for which these tests were designed (Lupkowski-Shoplik & Assouline, 1993; Lupkowski-Shoplik & Swiatek, 1999; Mills & Barnett, 1992).

Although studies such as these offer research-based guidelines for screening test performance, in practice each Talent Search ultimately sets its own screening criteria. Because each state or even each district has adopted its own regimen of standardized testing, it can be difficult or impossible to determine the actual grade-level screening test used by any individual talent search participant (see, e.g., Lupkowski-Shoplik, 2001). Although the Talent Searches generally approve screening tests on the basis of a content match with the above-level test to be given (e.g., both have verbal or math components), the goal of screening is to identify potential; consequently, the screening measures that are considered acceptable can vary quite widely.

Screening criteria also vary slightly from one year to the next depending on external factors such as the particular grade-level tests adopted by states or districts, how scores on these tests are reported to students, and how many students actually obtain scores at a particular level of performance. In response to such variation, screening test score requirements are reexamined regularly, and may differ from one year to the next as one component of Talent Search efforts to manage enrollment.

Affective Dimensions

Talent search studies also have demonstrated that the above-level testing experience is neither too difficult nor too stressful for the students who are identified for further testing using the 95th percentile qualifying criteria described above. Jarosewich and Stocking (2003b) surveyed more than 900 talent search participants and their parents about their experience, and concluded that the overall experience was a positive one: "Students and parents reported higher levels of positive feelings (i.e., pride, confidence, excitement, and smartness) and lower levels of negative feelings (i.e., nervousness, apprehension, worry, stress, and frustration) while students took the [talent search] tests" (p. 149). The response rate in this study was below 24%, so selection effects may have had a strong influence on these results.

In another study, frustration was defined as correctly answering fewer than 25% of the items in a given section of the EXPLORE test (Lupkowski-Shoplik, 2001). This study included all test takers, minimizing potential selection effects. Although nearly one third of tested third graders obtained scores in the frustration range, only 1.6% of fifth graders and none of the participating sixth graders scored in this range on the math portion of the test, which was the most difficult section. Based on an examination of students' grade-level test scores, the author concluded that the 95th percentile was an appropriate screening criterion to minimize frustration on this above-level test for students in the fifth and sixth grade. By checking to ensure that the testing is not too stressful, these and other studies demonstrate that those who run the Talent Searches are committed to the social and emotional welfare of their participating students.

Other studies of talent search participants' affective characteristics and needs have considered student satisfaction (Rogers, Schatz, & Dykstra, 2001); self-concept (Plucker & Stocking, 2001; Swiatek, 2005); and attitudes toward school (Matthews & McBee, 2007).

As is the case among other summer programs for academically talented students (e.g., Worrell, Szarko, & Gabelko, 2001), talent search educational program attendees report that the social opportunities provided by these programs contribute to their reported satisfaction above and beyond the contribution made by these programs' academic aspects (Rogers et al., 2001). Summer program attendees are the most able among the talent search students, as measured by above-level test scores, so it seems plausible that their satisfaction is due at least in part to the fact that these students encounter few intellectual peers outside of the summer program context (Barnett & Corazza, 1998).

Even though participants assign great value to social interaction in the summer programs, other studies of talent search program attendees confirm that they are healthier than average, both emotionally and physically. Parker (1996) administered the Brief Symptom Inventory to 274 talent search students attending a summer precalculus class and found that overall these students were exceptionally well-adjusted. Matthews and McBee (2007) found that factors predictive of underachievement in the regular school setting did not predict academic or behavioral problems among 440 students in the summer program setting. They attributed this finding to the summer program's ability to meet both the academic and social needs of these students. In another study, Jarosewich and Stocking (2003a) examined the medical records of more than 1,900 students attending a summer residential talent search program. Jarosewich and Stocking documented low rates of psychological disorders, medication use, and counseling needs in this talent search population. Further research is needed to determine the degree to which selection effects are responsible for these studies' findings.

Studies of talent search students' academic self-concept have sought to understand whether this construct functions in the same manner for gifted students as it does for mainstream children. Plucker and Stocking (2001) suggested that for the most part, it does. One point of difference noted in this and other studies conducted with talent search populations (Olszewski-Kubilius & Turner, 2002; Swiatek, 2005) suggests that academic self-concept among these gifted students may vary more across subjects or domains than is the case among academically average students. This line of research is important because academic self-concept is believed to influence academic achievement and course-taking patterns, both of which are particularly relevant for gifted populations.

These favorable reports should be tempered by the strong likelihood that selection biases strongly affect these populations, so this picture of health cannot provide an accurate reflection of the much larger populations of gifted students who participate in only the testing portion of the talent searches, who do not participate in them at all, or who drop out of the programs. However, in a recent study, Matthews (2006) reported an extremely low school dropout rate among a statewide population of talent search students, the majority of whom participated only in the testing aspect of the talent search. Although this study did not compare talent search students with nonparticipating gifted students, findings suggest that in comparison with mainstream students, talent search participants who do not attend summer programs also appear to have relatively stable personal lives.

Accelerated Instruction

Research strongly supports the success of students enrolled in accelerated curricula as a result of selection via the talent search model. The extent to which this is due to the above-level testing rather than to selection effects on motivation or other nonacademic characteristics remains unknown. Stanley and Stanley (1986) documented that talent search students could complete basic high school science coursework in chemistry and biology 2 years earlier than their peers, learning a year of high school coursework during an intensive 3-week summer session. At the end of these classes, test scores of participating students were comparable to those made by their classmates, 2 years later, who had taken a conventional year-long high school course in the subject.

Lynch (1992) followed more than 900 high schools students who took a year of high school science during a 3-week summer program. These students had few problems mastering the material, as evidenced by their similar performance on the College Entrance Examination Board science achievement tests, in comparison with the students who took the courses at the usual time and pace. The accelerated students achieved these results an average of 2 years earlier than they would have if they had taken the courses in school. Other studies report similar successes with the intensive summer program model (e.g., Mills, Ablard, & Lynch, 1992; Olszewski-Kubilius, 1998a; Stocking & Goldstein, 1992; Swiatek, 2002).

Fewer studies of accelerated instruction have been conducted with younger students, possibly because these students only have been included in talent searches in relatively recent years. In one such study, Mills, Ablard, & Gustin (1994) documented the successful implementation of a flexibly paced program of accelerated mathematics instruction that was completed by more than 300 third- through sixth-grade talent search students during the regular school year. Depending on grade level, 87% to 95% of these participants exceeded expected score gains on a nationally-normed standardized math test.

Long-Term Outcomes of Talent Search Participation

Talent search summer programs also yield academic benefits that extend beyond simply moving students more rapidly through the high school curriculum. Schiel (1998; Schiel & Stocking, 2001) found that summer program participation explained academic performance in high school above and beyond the variance accounted for by students' seventh-grade ACT scores. Students who participated in a math course offered by a summer talent search program scored higher on the ACT Math assessment at the end of high school, in comparison with their peers with comparable seventh-grade scores who did not attend the summer program. Schiel (1998) reported a Cohen's *d* effect size of 0.45. This suggests that summer program math classes increased the average participant's high school ACT Math score by nearly half of a standard deviation (i.e., approximately two points on the ACT's 36-point scale) in comparison to the average score of talent search students who did not attend the program. Other long-term studies concur with regard to the effectiveness of acceleration in meeting the academic and affective needs of students identified through the talent search model (e.g., Richardson & Benbow, 1990; Swiatek & Benbow, 1991).

Other studies have examined what happens to talent search students once they return to school, after having attended summer programs run by the talent search organization. Generally, such studies have concluded that schools are not particularly responsive to these students' needs. Schools rarely use talent search test results or summer program coursework to make curricular or placement decisions (VanTassel-Baska, 1998), and when they do, students report that the school courses seem less challenging by comparison (Mills et al., 1992). Schools appear to be more likely to recognize summer coursework if the summer program has been accredited by an agency such as the North Central Association of Colleges and Schools, although petitioning and other factors can increase the likelihood of schools awarding credit for work completed through a nonaccredited program (Lee & Olszewski-Kubilius, 2005; Olszewski-Kubilius, Laubscher, Wohl, & Grant, 1996; Swiatek & Lupkowski-Shoplik, 2003). Methods of encouraging public schools to recognize work completed in Talent Search programs and other extracurricular contexts should be subject to additional study, as this lack of articulation across a student's educational experiences constitutes an important limitation of the talent search model as presently implemented.

SMPY and Sex Differences in Mathematical Performance

In 1971, Julian Stanley began the Study of Mathematically Precocious Youth (SMPY), a planned 50-year longitudinal research program whose objective is "to develop a better understanding of the unique needs of intellectually precocious youth and the determinants of the contrasting developmental trajectories they display over the lifespan" (SMPY, 2007, ¶ 1). Stanley's efforts to locate youth who reasoned exceptionally well mathematically for the SMPY pioneered what has since become known as the talent search approach. Because SMPY (Stanley, 1988, 1996) is the primary longitudinal investigation of its type, the majority of longitudinal studies of talent search students have been conducted by SMPY researchers. The SMPY literature is extensive (more than 300 publications as of this writing); however, several SMPY studies merit specific mention here because SMPY is so closely tied to the talent search model. The talent search at Johns Hopkins University is now run by the Center for Talented Youth, founded by Stanley for this purpose in 1979 (Stanley, 2002), and researchers based at Vanderbilt University now continue the SMPY study (SMPY, 2007).

The study of male/female differences among talented populations has been a major interest within the Study of Mathematically Precocious Youth. A large body of research has examined these differences among students with extremely high levels of mathematical ability (e.g., Benbow, Lubinski, Shea, & Eftekhari-Sanjani, 2000; Benbow & Stanley, 1983). In a seminal paper, Benbow (1988) detailed the hypothesis that both biological and environmental causes might explain why many more males than females produced talent search math scores at the very highest levels. In commentaries published with this article, many other researchers suggested that only environmental explanations are necessary. Perhaps the most compelling of these counterarguments suggests that greater variation in math ability among males would explain the greater numbers of males found at both the high and low ends of the ability spectrum. This issue remains contentious.

LIMITATIONS OF THE RESEARCH

Relatively little research conducted with talent search populations has been performed by unaffiliated and neutral individuals. Although there are no grounds for suspecting that researchers' affiliations might have biased these results, the relatively small number of researchers in the field has perhaps led to a certain degree of repetition in the research questions that have been considered. As in other areas of education, there have been few randomized, experimental-control research designs, and the self-selection inherent in talent search testing and programming likely limits the extent to which such designs could be implemented in these areas. Talent Search programs have unrivaled access to large numbers of highly gifted students; yet, budgetary and other concerns often mean that only limited research is conducted with these learners. If these programs were to allow access to qualified external researchers, it would offer the field a tremendous opportunity to learn more about such students.

Another serious limitation of this body of research is that the populations that participate in talent searches do not tend to be diverse, either in terms of ethnicity, socioeconomic status, or cultural or linguistic background. The talent search model has been extremely effective in meeting the needs of the specific subgroup of the academically gifted population the model serves, that is, predominantly culturally mainstream students from middle to upper middle class economic backgrounds, but the very test scores that the model relies upon to yield such effectiveness tend also to limit diversity among the students who participate.

Although financial obstacles may limit participation in summer programs to those who can afford it, substantial scholarship money is awarded by the talent searches each year. Fee grants or waivers for talent search testing are widely available at the different Talent Searches, and often scholarships to attend academic programs are awarded based on test performance, so financial concerns are not always as insurmountable as they may at first appear. However, talent search summer program participants at this time continue to be primarily middle to upper middle class and predominantly White. Therefore, the degree to which talent search findings may be generalized to other gifted populations is unknown. Anecdotal evidence suggests that perhaps there may be a participation threshold above which underrepresented students would feel more comfortable attending talent search summer programs, but empirical data are lacking to address this question. Talent search staff members appear to be developing an awareness of these diversity issues, and in recent years some programs have begun targeting their resources to increase participation by members of traditionally underrepresented groups (Lee et al., in press).

One other limitation of the talent search model is that it relies upon a narrow view of giftedness that is closely coupled with high-stakes testing. In particular, a child's score on a single one of the two to four sections of a test can define the child as eligible for program benefits (recognition, educational programming, even scholarship money in some cases). Rather than considering potential ability as in some other models of giftedness, it is this expressed ability, measured as a test score, that defines a gifted child in the talent search model (Stanley, 1997).

To address the needs of students who may not express their abilities well on the first try, the talent searches have developed accommodations through which students may test again at a later date. Often such retesting is coupled with higher score requirements for program participation. Despite these provisions, in this respect the talent search model is quite similar to early psychometric views that considered giftedness to be determined by an IQ test score alone.

PRACTICAL IMPLICATIONS OF TALENT SEARCH RESEARCH

The practical implications of these studies are several. The talent search approach appears to offer an effective intervention for a narrowly defined group of highly able students whose academic and especially social needs are not fully met in most regular school settings. These students, particularly those who attend summer programs administered by the talent searches, are as a whole characterized by high levels of academic performance, the ability to display these abilities on standardized tests, and apparently by generally well-adjusted personal lives.

Since the inception of the talent search model, approximately 1 of every 20 students who have participated in talent search testing have gone on to attend one or more of the educational programs administered by a talent search organization (Lee et al., in press). Yet for the majority of students—those who participate in talent search testing yet do not subsequently attend summer educational programs—the testing experience alone also appears to have value.

Above-level testing offers students the chance to learn more about their own abilities, provides them with a glimpse of a future peer group, and publicizes appropriate educational resources that help these students make informed decisions about their future lives.

MAJOR RESOURCES

The Web sites of the talent searches themselves, particularly the more established programs, offer a valuable resource for locating relevant research. The Web site for the Johns Hopkins Center for Talented Youth or CTY (http://www.jhu.edu/~gifted/research/research.html) stands out in offering citations and descriptive information about studies conducted by CTY staff. The Duke TIP Web site offers a bibliography of selected publications at http://www.tip.duke.edu/about/research. Limited information about research is available online at this time from the other talent search programs. Web sites of the Talent Identification Program (http://www.tip.duke.edu) and Center for Talent Development (http://www.ctd.northwestern.edu) offer program contact information, and research personnel at these organizations may be able to address specific questions about their work. Finally, the PsychINFO database, which is available through most university libraries, also indexes most of the references cited in this chapter.

WHAT WE KNOW

- Above-level testing as used in the talent search model is quite effective in identifying gifted students who can benefit from academic acceleration.
- Above-level testing is not overly stressful for students who meet the screening criteria established by Talent Search programs.
- Accelerated instruction, as offered through talent search summer educational programs, is effective in moving highly able students more rapidly through the school curriculum.
- Schools generally fail to take advantage of the information that talent search testing and educational programs could provide about their students.

WHAT WE NEED TO KNOW

- In what specific, quantifiable ways do talent search participants differ from the academically gifted individuals who do not participate in these programs?

- What factors limit the participation of currently underrepresented populations in talent search testing and educational programs, and what interventions are effective in promoting these students' participation?

REFERENCES

Barnett, L. B., & Corazza, L. (1998). Identification of mathematical talent and programmatic efforts to facilitate development of talent. *High Ability Studies, 9*, 48–61.

Benbow, C. P. (1988). Sex differences in mathematical reasoning ability among the intellectually talented: Their characterization, consequences, and possible explanations. *Behavioral and Brain Sciences, 11*, 169–183.

Benbow, C. P., Lubinski, D., Shea, D. L., & Eftekhari-Sanjani, H. (2000). Sex differences in mathematical reasoning ability: Their status 20 years later. *Psychological Science, 11*, 474–480.

Benbow, C. P., & Stanley, J. C. (1983). Sex differences in mathematical reasoning ability: More facts. *Science, 222*, 1029–1031.

Bleske-Rechek, A., Lubinski, D., & Benbow, C. P. (2004). Meeting the educational needs of special populations: Advanced Placement's role in developing exceptional human capital. *Psychological Science, 15*, 217–224.

Charlton, J. C., Marolf, D. M., & Stanley, J. C. (2002). Follow-up insights on rapid educational acceleration. *Roeper Review, 24*, 145–151.

Ebmeier, H., & Schmulbach, S. (1989). An examination of the selection practices used in the talent search program. *Gifted Child Quarterly, 33*, 134–143.

Jarosewich, T., & Stocking, V. B. (2003a). Medication and counseling histories of gifted students in a summer residential program. *Journal of Secondary Gifted Education, 14*, 91–99.

Jarosewich, T., & Stocking, V. B. (2003b). Talent Search: Student and parent perceptions of out-of-level testing. *Journal of Secondary Gifted Education, 14*, 137–150.

Lee, S-Y., Matthews, M. S., & Olszewski-Kubilius, P. (in press). A national picture of talent search and talent search educational programs. *Gifted Child Quarterly*.

Lee, S.-Y., & Olszewski-Kubilius, P. (2005). Investigation of high school credit and placement for summer coursework taken outside of local schools. *Gifted Child Quarterly, 49*, 37–50.

Lupkowski-Shoplik, A. (2001). Carnegie Mellon Elementary Student Talent Search: Establishing appropriate guidelines for qualifying test scores. In N. Colangelo & S. G. Assouline (Eds.), *Talent development IV: Proceedings from the 1998 Henry B. and Jocelyn Wallace National Research Symposium on Talent Development* (pp. 379–385). Scottsdale, AZ: Great Potential Press.

Lupkowski-Shoplik, A., & Assouline, S. (1993). Identifying mathematically talented elementary students: Using the lower level of the SSAT. *Gifted Child Quarterly, 37*, 118–123.

Lupkowski-Shoplik, A., & Swiatek, M. A. (1999). Elementary student talent searches: Establishing appropriate guidelines for qualifying test scores. *Gifted Child Quarterly, 43*, 265–272.

Lynch, S. J. (1992). Fast-paced high school science for the academically talented: A six-year perspective. *Gifted Child Quarterly, 36*(3), 147–154.

Matthews, M. S. (2006). Gifted students dropping out: Recent findings from a Southeastern state. *Roeper Review, 28*, 216–223.

Matthews, M. S., & McBee, M. T. (2007). School factors and the underachievement of gifted students in a talent search summer program. *Gifted Child Quarterly, 51*, 167–181.

Mills, C. J., Ablard, K. E., & Gustin, W. C. (1994). Academically talented students' achievement in a flexibly paced mathematics program. *Journal for Research in Mathematics Education, 25*, 495–511.

Mills, C. J., Ablard, K. E., & Lynch, S. J. (1992). Academically talented students' preparation for advanced-level coursework after individually-paced precalculus class. *Journal for the Education of the Gifted, 16*, 3–17.

Mills, C. J., & Barnett, L. B. (1992). The use of the Secondary School Admission Test (SSAT) to identify academically talented elementary students. *Gifted Child Quarterly, 36*, 155–159.

Olszewski-Kubilius, P. (1998a). Research evidence regarding the validity and effects of talent search educational programs. *Journal of Secondary Gifted Education, 9*, 134–142.

Olszewski-Kubilius, P. (Ed.). (1998b). Talent Search—Purposes, rationale, and role in gifted education [Special issue]. *Journal of Secondary Gifted Education, 9*(3).

Olszewski-Kubilius, P., Laubscher, L., Wohl, V., & Grant, B. (1996). Issues and factors involved in credit and placement for accelerated summer coursework. *Journal of Secondary Gifted Education, 8*, 5–15.

Olszewski-Kubilius, P., & Turner, D. (2002). Gender differences among elementary school-aged gifted students in achievement, perceptions of ability, and subject preference. *Journal for the Education of the Gifted, 25*, 233–268.

Parker, W. D. (1996). Psychological adjustment in mathematically gifted students. *Gifted Child Quarterly, 40*, 154–157.

Plucker, J. A., & Stocking, V. B. (2001). Looking outside and inside: Self-concept development of gifted adolescents. *Exceptional Children, 67*, 535–548.

Richardson, T. M., & Benbow, C. P. (1990). Long-term effects of acceleration on the social-emotional adjustment of mathematically precocious youths. *Journal of Educational Psychology, 82*, 464–470.

Rogers, K. B., Schatz, E., & Dykstra, M. (2001). The effects of content, cognitive congruence, and camaraderie on talented students' attitudes toward academically accelerated residential programs. In N. Colangelo & S. G. Assouline (Eds.), *Talent development IV: Proceedings from the 1998 Henry B. and Jocelyn Wallace National Research Symposium on Talent Development* (pp. 415–417). Scottsdale, AZ: Great Potential Press.

Schiel, J. L. (1998). *Academic benefits in high school of an intensive summer program for academically talented seventh graders* (No. 98-4, ACT Research Report Series). Iowa City, IA: ACT.

Schiel, J. L., & Stocking, V. B. (2001). Benefits of TIP summer residential program participation, as reflected by subsequent academic performance in high school. In N. Colangelo & S. G. Assouline (Eds.), *Talent development IV: Proceedings from the 1998 Henry B. and Jocelyn Wallace National Research Symposium on Talent Development* (pp. 435–438). Scottsdale, AZ: Great Potential Press.

SMPY. (2007). *The Study of Mathematically Precocious Youth.* Retrieved July 5, 2007, from http://www.vanderbilt.edu/Peabody/SMPY

Stanley, J. C. (1976). Test better finder of great math talent than teachers are. *American Psychologist, 31*, 313–314.

Stanley, J. C. (1988). Some characteristics of SMPY's "700–800 on SAT-M before age 13 group": Youths who reason extremely well mathematically. *Gifted Child Quarterly, 32*, 205–209.

Stanley, J. C. (1996). In the beginning: The Study of Mathematically Precocious Youth. In C. P. Benbow & D. Lubinski (Eds.), *Intellectual talent: Psychometric and social issues* (pp. 225–235). Baltimore: Johns Hopkins University Press.

Stanley, J. C. (1997). Varieties of intellectual talent. *Journal of Creative Behavior, 31*, 93–119.

Stanley, J. C. (2002). *Reflections from Julian Stanley: Supplementing the education of children with exceptional mathematical or verbal reasoning ability.* Retrieved December 15, 2005, from http://www.jhu.edu/~gifted/set/jcs-apa.html

Stanley, J. C., & Brody, L. E. (1989). Comment about Ebmeier and Schmulbach's "An examination of the selection practices used in the talent search program." *Gifted Child Quarterly, 33*, 142.

Stanley, J. C., & Stanley, B. S. (1986). High-school biology, chemistry, or physics learned well in three weeks. *Journal of Research in Science Teaching, 23*, 237–250.

Stocking, V. B., & Goldstein, D. (1992). Course selection and performance of very high ability students: Is there a gender gap? *Roeper Review, 15*, 48–51.

Swiatek, M. A. (2002). A decade of longitudinal research on academic acceleration through the study of mathematically precocious youth. *Roeper Review, 24*, 141–144.

Swiatek, M. A. (2005). Gifted students' self-perceptions of ability in specific subject domains: Factor structure and relationship with above-level test scores. *Roeper Review, 27*, 104–109.

Swiatek, M. A., & Benbow, C. P. (1991). Ten-year longitudinal follow-up of ability-matched accelerated and unaccelerated gifted students. *Journal of Educational Psychology, 83*, 528–538.

Swiatek, M. A., & Lupkowski-Shoplik, A. (2003). Elementary and middle school student participation in gifted programs: Are gifted students underserved? *Gifted Child Quarterly, 47*, 118–130.

VanTassel-Baska, J. (1997). Response to "Varieties of intellectual talent." *Journal of Creative Behavior, 31*, 125–130.

VanTassel-Baska, J. (1998). A critique of the talent searches. *Journal of Secondary Gifted Education, 9*, 139–144.

Worrell, F. C., Szarko, J. E., & Gabelko, N. H. (2001). Multi-year persistence of nontraditional students in an academic talent development program. *Journal of Secondary Gifted Education, 12*, 80–89.

Chapter 43

TALENTED READERS

Sally M. Reis

ittle research has focused on identifying and teaching talented readers, or using the pedagogy of gifted education (e.g., critical and creative problem solving and thinking; acceleration; curriculum modification and differentiation; independent study; advanced content; self-selected, interest-based opportunities) to encourage and develop advanced, continuous reading progress in talented readers (Jackson & Roller, 1993; Renzulli & Reis, 1989). Recently, Reis et al. (2004) synthesized research[1] in this area and suggested that talented readers can be defined by four characteristics: reading early and at advanced levels, using advanced processing in reading, reading with enthusiasm and enjoyment, and demonstrating advanced language skills (oral, reading, and written).

Talented readers need appropriately challenging instruction and curricular content that helps them make continuous progress in reading. They have differentiated talents and

---

1 (Baskin & Harris, 1980; Catron & Wingenbach, 1986; Dooley, 1993; Halsted, 1994; Jackson, 1988; Kaplan, 1999; Renzulli & Reis, 1989; Southern & Jones, 1992; Stanley, 1989; Trezise, 1978; Vacca, Vacca, & Grove, 1991; VanTassel-Baska, 1996)

instructional needs that require advanced learning opportunities to challenge and extend their abilities, to enable them to read content above their current reading level, to engage and think about complex texts, and to extend conventional basal reading instruction, which is usually below their chronological grade level. In one study, 40–50% of the regular reading curriculum was eliminated for academically talented students with strengths in reading, without any decline in reading achievement as measured by the Reading Comprehension subtests of the Iowa Tests of Basic Skills (Reis et al., 1993).

QUESTIONS ADDRESSED IN THE RESEARCH ABOUT TALENTED READERS

Research questions pertinent to talented readers relate to the level of differentiated instruction and instructional and curricular practices used to meet their needs in regular classrooms, the perceptions that teachers have about whether they are meeting the needs of this population, the types of processing and self-regulated behaviors talented readers use when interpreting text, and, most importantly, the optimal strategies educators should use to maximize these students' reading experience. Four essential questions emerge in a review of the related research and discourse in this area:

1. How are talented readers defined, and what types of processes do these students use when reading at different stages of reading development and maturity?
2. Do teachers use differentiated teaching practices to challenge talented readers?
3. What instructional or curriculum strategies or practices can ensure that talented readers make continuous progress in reading?
4. What ramifications occur when the academic needs of talented readers are not addressed?

TALENTED READERS: DEFINITIONS AND CHARACTERISTICS

Identifying the characteristics of and defining talented readers is challenging because no consensus exists in the research or anecdotal case studies literature. Not all academically gifted students read at high levels, and not all talented readers will be identified as academically gifted because of the variation of abilities in this population (Durkin, 1990; Jackson, 1988). Characteristics of talented readers have been described anecdotally, but little empirical research has focused on this population. Dole and Adams (1983) defined talented readers as "reading approximately two or more years above grade level as measured by a standardized reading test and identified as intellectually gifted with potential for high reading performance" (p. 66). Kaplan (1999) described talented readers as avid, enthusiastic, voracious readers who use reading differently for different purposes. Others have described them as spending more time reading than their peers, and reading a greater variety of literature (Collins & Aiex, 1995; Halsted, 1990). Stainthorp and Hughes (2004) found that talented readers often teach themselves to read prior to any instruction at home or in school. Halsted (1994) found that talented readers understand language subtleties, use language for humor, write words and sentences early, and produce superior creative writing. Additionally, some talented students automatically integrate prior knowledge and experience into their reading; utilize higher order thinking skills such as analysis, synthesis, and evaluation; and successfully communicate these ideas (Catron & Wingenbach, 1986). They may display verbal ability in self-expression, use colorful and descriptive phrasing, demonstrate advanced understanding of language, have an expansive vocabulary, perceive relationships between and among characters, and grasp complex ideas (Catron & Wingenbach, 1986; Dooley, 1993; Levande, 1993).

Anecdotal information suggests that talented readers display an advanced ability to understand a variety of texts (Bonds & Bonds, 1983; Halsted, 1994; Levande, 1993; Vacca et al., 1991) and have other language-related abilities, such as the ability to retain a large quantity of information, advanced comprehension, varied interests and curiosity in texts, and high-level language development and verbal ability (Clark, 1997). Talented readers understand books to be a way to acquire information, clarify ideas, stimulate the imagination, and deepen understanding (Halsted, 1994). Kaplan (1999) reported that highly able readers often have preferences for science, history, biography, travel, poetry, and informational texts such as atlases, encyclopedias, and how-to books. Jackson (1988) identified advanced readers as using complex processes made up of many subskills that vary in students. Halsted (1994) found a pattern that exists in some of these readers: They initially teach themselves how to read before they start school, are independent readers by second grade, know their favorite authors by third grade, and have well-established reading patterns by fifth grade. Unfortunately, current research also demonstrates that the reading levels of these students may decline by the time they reach upper elementary as a result of an absence of challenge in reading in school (Reis & Boeve, 2007). If these patterns are set (Halsted, 1994), negative outcomes may ensue.

Reis et al.'s (2004) summary of the characteristics and descriptors of talented readers from the extant, primarily anecdotal, literature identified four characteristics that most often have been applied to talented readers: reading early and at advanced levels, using advanced processing in reading, reading with enthusiasm and enjoyment, and demonstrating advanced language skills (oral, reading, and written). Using a random national sample of teachers, Reis (2003) validated the Scale for Rating the Superior Characteristics of Superior Students–Reading, a teacher rating scale for talented readers (an extension of the Scales for Rating the Behavioral Characteristics of Superior Students

T A B L E   1

Characteristics of Talented Readers

The student . . .

- eagerly engages in reading related activities
- applies previously learned literary concepts to new reading experiences
- focuses on reading for an extended period of time
- pursues advanced reading material
- demonstrates tenacity when posed with challenging reading
- shows interest in reading other types of interest-based reading materials

Note. From Reis (2003).

[SRBCSS]). The resulting stems used in the scale (see Table 1) for talented readers yielded an alpha reliability of .96.

CURRENT CLASSROOM READING EXPERIENCES OF TALENTED READERS

Over the last two decades, limited research has addressed the classroom reading skills and subsequent experiences of talented readers. Taylor and Fry (1988) found that 78% to 88% of 5th- and 6th-grade average and above-average readers could pass pretests on basal comprehension skills before the material was covered. The average readers performed at approximately 92% accuracy, while the advanced readers performed at 93% accuracy on the comprehension skills pretest, suggesting that both talented and average readers may be spending time in school doing work that they already know.

A series of studies using the Classroom Practices Survey identified a disturbing pattern of minimal challenge (Archambault et al., 1993). Classroom teachers reported making only *minor* modifications in the regular curriculum to meet the needs of gifted students. In a follow-up observation study, Westberg, Archambault, Dobyns, and Salvin (1993) observed gifted and average achieving students in 46 classrooms, finding that third- and fourth-grade classroom teachers used little differentiation in instructional and curricular practices for gifted and talented students. In particular, gifted and talented or high-ability students experienced no instructional or curricular differentiation in 80% of the observed instructional activities in reading. A decade later, Reis et al. (2004) confirmed findings from the Westberg et al. study. In-depth qualitative comparative case studies were used to study 12 third- and seventh-grade reading classrooms in urban and suburban schools. Observations of daily practices in reading classrooms to determine frequency and type of various differentiation practices, such as curriculum compacting, interest or instructional-level grouping arrangements, acceleration opportunities, and the nature of independent reading or work completed by talented readers indicated that talented readers received some minimal levels of differentiated reading instruction in only 3 of the 12 classrooms. In the other 9 classrooms, no challenging reading material or advanced instruction was provided for talented readers during regular classroom reading instruction. Appropriately challenging books were seldom made available for talented students, and they rarely were provided with more challenging work. Different patterns did emerge across urban and suburban school districts; the three classroom teachers who provided some level of differentiation taught in suburban schools. Richards (2003) found a similar pattern in a national random sample of grade 3–7 teachers' perceptions about whether they provided levels of challenge for talented readers—the majority of classroom teachers believed that additional challenge was unnecessary and/or that they were simply unable to provide challenging reading instruction for talented students.

A pervasive finding emerging from the limited research or discussions on instructional practices for talented readers is that regular reading instruction often is too easy for talented readers (Chall & Conard, 1991; Collins & Aiex, 1995; Dole & Adams, 1983; Reis, Hébert, Diaz, Maxfield, & Ratley, 1995; Renzulli & Reis, 1989; Shrenker, 1997). Chall and Conard (1991) also found that the talented readers they studied were not adequately served in school, explaining that "their reading textbooks, especially, provided little or no challenge, since they were matched to students' grade placement, not their reading levels" (p. 111). Many students were aware of this, according to Chall and Conard, who said that in interviews, students commented that they preferred harder books because they learned harder words and ideas from them.

Chall and Conard (1991) stated that when there is a match between a learner's abilities and the difficulty of the instructional work, learning is enhanced. If, however, "the match is not optimal, learning is less efficient and development may be halted" (p. 19). Using textbooks that are several years below students' reading level may result in arrested development, as well as motivational problems for talented readers. In a longitudinal study of academically talented students who either achieved or underachieved in a large urban high school (Reis et al., 1995), underachieving students consistently acknowledged that the easy curriculum they encountered in elementary and middle school failed to prepare them for the rigors of challenging classes in high school, and most mentioned a lack of challenge in reading. In a recent study of talented readers in an after-school program, Reis and Boeve (2007) found that many had never been challenged in reading and when asked to read even slightly above grade level, encountered frustration and gave up trying after only minutes of effort. In summary, the research on classroom reading experiences of talented readers suggests that although they can benefit from appropriately challenging levels of reading, they seldom receive it.

WHAT INSTRUCTIONAL AND CURRICULAR STRATEGIES DO WORK?

Allington (2002) concluded that all students need to interact with appropriately complex books. Renzulli and Reis (1989) found many talented readers reap no benefit from conventional instruction in readings and would benefit from appropriately challenging levels of reading, but seldom receive it.

Methods for differentiating curriculum and instruction for talented readers exist, and some research supports the effectiveness of specific instructional and curricular strategies with talented readers. Some strategies, when implemented well, can modify reading instruction for talented readers. Reis et al. (1993) found that with only 1–2 hours of training, teachers could compact curriculum for talented students. When teachers eliminated 49% of regular reading curricular content for gifted and talented students identified in their classrooms, no differences were found between treatment and control groups on posttest achievement scores in reading comprehension. However, teachers had difficulty replacing the compacted curriculum with high-quality, challenging work, because doing so would require increased levels of support.

The use of instructional-level grouping with talented readers has resulted in increased understanding and enjoyment of literature (Gentry, 1999; Levande, 1993). In general, grouping academically talented students together for instruction has been found to produce positive achievement outcomes when the curriculum content and instruction provided to students in different groups is appropriately differentiated to be challenging (Gentry, 1999; Kulik & Kulik, 1991; Rogers, 1991). It is the challenging content and instruction that occur within groups that makes grouping an effective instructional strategy (Kulik & Kulik, 1991; Rogers, 1991). In one study of advanced literature use with academically talented students, VanTassel-Baska, Zuo, Avery, and Little (2002) found that using curricular units that stressed the application of reasoning to reading and writing, the creation of high-quality products, and the organization of learning around a major concept or theme produced significant differences in favor of treatment groups compared to control groups. This treatment was effective with students from both low and high socioeconomic groups.

Although little specificity is found on the nature of reading comprehension strategy instruction that should be provided to talented readers, one study suggests that there are differences in the type of strategies that gifted readers use as compared to their nongifted peers (Fehrenbach, 1991). The skills more often used by gifted readers were rereading, inferring, analyzing structure, watching or predicting, evaluating, and relating information to content area. Accordingly, educators suggest that a differentiated reading program should enable students to interact with advanced content that has both depth and complexity (Kaplan, 1999), focus on developing higher level comprehension skills (Collins & Aiex, 1995), and engage students with advanced reading skills instruction (Reis et al., 2005). The use of higher level questioning and opportunities can be incorporated into reading experiences to enable talented readers to apply advanced reading strategies to challenging reading. These reading strategies incorporate higher order thinking skills that should be a foundational component in the instruction of talented readers (Brown & Rogan, 1983; Catron & Wingenbach, 1986; Dole & Adams, 1983; Reis et al., 2005; Renzulli & Reis, 1989).

In one data-based study, Lamb and Feldhusen (1993) identified reading instruction strategies reported by teachers for advanced first-grade readers: grouping in the classroom (90%), higher level basal readers (70%), independent reading (95%), computers (89%), and in descending order of use, content acceleration to a higher grade level for reading, independent research, and using teaching materials other than basals. In contrast, a decade later, Richards (2003) found teachers reporting fairly minimal curricular differentiation for talented readers in a study of reading classroom practices. In another recent study about differentiated classroom practices for talented readers (Reis et al., 2004), researchers spent more than 100 days in classrooms finding that only 25% of 3rd- and 7th-grade teachers actually used any differentiation strategies on some occasions to challenge talented readers. The methods used by the minority of teachers who did implement a few of these strategies included compacting (25%), within-class grouping (25%), use of advanced instruction (25%), use of higher level questioning skills (25%), use of challenging content (25%), and the use of technology during reading class (18%). Conflicting research exists about strategies teachers report using and the practices they actually are observed implementing to differentiate instruction for talented readers in their classrooms.

A more optimistic view, however, extends to how teachers can learn to provide appropriate levels of challenge for all students, including those who are academically talented. Current research on the Schoolwide Enrichment Model–Reading Framework (SEM–R; Reis et al., 2005) using a randomized, control group design found that participating students improved their attitudes toward reading, and increased reading comprehension and oral fluency. The goals of the SEM–R are to increase reading achievement and self-regulation strategies through increased interest and motivation. In phase 1, teachers stimulate interest in reading by engaging students through book talks and interesting read alouds of a variety of genres, followed by scaffolding of higher level questions. During phase 2, also called supported independent reading, students read silently from self-selected materials at appropriate levels of challenge and teachers conduct individualized, differentiated reading conferences with students. During this time, teachers assess students' comprehension using higher order questions and ensure that students are reading books that are adequately challenging. The third phase enables students to choose a pleasurable reading activity or project based on their interests from a menu of choices, such as independent study, creativity training activities, books on tape or CD, reading alone or with a friend, using technology, or doing interesting self-selected short-term projects. The SEM–R has been implemented in three studies (Reis et al., 2005), two of which included the use of a cluster-randomized design. In the first study, randomly assigned urban elementary classrooms participated in direct instruction in reading. Experimental classrooms then participated in the SEM–R program, while the control group continued to participate in the traditional remedial reading and test preparation program. Significant differences favoring the treatment group were found in attitudes toward reading, reading comprehension, and reading fluency (Reis et al., 2005). During the second study, the SEM-R was implemented in two additional schools, one urban and one suburban, and in another school as an afterschool enrichment reading program (Reis & Boeve, 2007). Researchers found significant differences favoring the treatment group in reading fluency and/or comprehension, as well as increases in students' self-regulation to read for extended periods of time.

In summary, talented readers will benefit from challenging materials in reading based on their interests and from meeting together for a block of time on a daily basis (Kulik & Kulik, 1991; Rogers, 1991). They can be assigned appropriately challenging substitute books that offer depth and complexity (Kaplan, 1999) and challenge their comprehension and fluency. Talented readers also can be given opportunities to complete different creative products and participate in alternative writing assignments (Renzulli & Reis, 1989) and can be encouraged to bring prior knowledge and insight into their interpretations of challenging text (Reis et al., 2005). They can use technology to access Web sites of authors, read challenging books online, and interact with talented readers from other schools using literature circle discussion strategies. Technology also can be used to access advanced content, to create concept maps and other technological products, to write and revise stories, chapters, and even books (Reis et al., 2005).

Differentiation for talented readers has met with varied results. Differentiation attempts to address the variations among learners in the classroom through multiple approaches that enrich, modify, and adapt instruction and curriculum to match students' individual needs (Renzulli, 1977, 1988; Tomlinson, 1995). Differentiation of instruction and curriculum suggests that students can be provided with materials and work of varied levels of difficulty through scaffolding, enrichment, acceleration, diverse kinds of grouping, and different time schedules (Tomlinson, 1995). In a current research study, Reis and Boeve (2007) found that with only 12 afterschool sessions using challenging self-selected reading materials with talented readers, culturally diverse academically talented readers in third and fourth grade could achieve as much fluency growth as most readers make in a year. In this study, however, researchers found that these students did have difficulties participating in above-grade-level reading, due to an elementary school reading program that was consistently too easy. These talented urban readers were accustomed to expending minimal effort and had few self-regulation strategies to employ and few advanced reading strategies that they could use when they were asked to read material that was slightly above their grade level.

TABLE 2

Differentiated Instructional or Curricular Strategies to Challenge Talented Readers

Curriculum compacting	Reis, Burns, & Renzulli, 1992; Reis et al., 2005
Acceleration	Southern & Jones, 1992
Substitution of regular reading material with more advanced trade books	Reis et al., 2005; VanTassel-Baska, 1996
Appropriate use of technology for talented readers	Alvermann, Moon, & Hagood, 1999; Reis et al., 2005
More complex reading and writing	Reis et al., 2004; VanTassel-Baska et al., 2002
Independent reading choices	Reis et al., 2005; Renzulli & Reis, 1989
Independent writing options	VanTassel-Baska et al., 2002
Independent study and project opportunities	Reis et al., 2005; Renzulli & Reis, 1989, 1997; VanTassel-Baska et al., 2002
Grouping changes (within or across classes)	Kulik & Kulik, 1991; Reis et al., 2005; Rogers, 1991
Thematic instructional changes for talented readers (tiered reading for thematic units)	VanTassel-Baska et al., 2002
Substitution of regular instructional strategies with other options	Reis & Renzulli, 1989; Reis et al., 2005; VanTassel-Baska et al., 2002
Advanced questioning skills and literary skills	Reis et al., 2005
Interest assessment and interest-based reading opportunities	Reis et al., 2005

The strategies suggested in Table 2 are research-supported methods for differentiating instruction and curriculum for talented readers that can be used in combination to provide an enriching, advanced reading program. For example, curriculum compacting uses assessment that may lead to advanced content and products for students. This strategy, however, requires teachers to find appropriately challenging resources and materials, and also may require classroom changes, such as the creation of a space for students to work together and for providing advanced content materials.

All students should have opportunities to participate in appropriately challenging learning experiences, and differentiated instruction can be used to ensure that all learners experience continuous progress in reading. Teaching reading with materials that the majority of students in a heterogeneous classroom can read may create boredom for talented readers (Renzulli & Reis, 1989) and contribute to diminished achievement in reading, particularly in urban areas or low socioeconomic areas, where remedial and direct instruction often are used.

WHAT RESEARCH-BASED CONCLUSIONS CAN BE MADE ABOUT TALENTED READERS?

Talented readers are placed at risk in many schools. Many are not challenged and, therefore, their reading development can be delayed or even halted. If instructional and independent reading materials are not above the students' level of knowledge or understanding, learning is less efficient and reading development may be delayed or stopped. It is, for example, not surprising to find that an academically talented first grader in an urban school who reads on a fifth-grade level is still reading at that level when he or she enters fifth grade. Some talented readers never learn to exert effort in reading and consequently, acquire poor work habits. The following four conclusions emerged in this review of the research.

1. Four characteristics are most often used to describe talented readers: reading early and at advanced levels, using advanced processing in reading, reading with enthusiasm and enjoyment, and demonstrating advanced language skills (oral, reading, and written).

2. A summary of information on the current classroom reading experiences of talented readers suggests that although they can benefit from appropriately challenging levels of reading, they seldom receive it.

3. Methods for differentiating curriculum and instruction for talented readers exist, and teachers can learn to differentiate. Some research supports the effectiveness of specific instructional and curricular strategies with talented readers, particularly curriculum compacting, grouping, acceleration, the use of advanced literature and challenging reading, and using the Schoolwide Enrichment Model–Reading Framework.

4. Some talented readers grow accustomed by third or fourth grade to expending minimal effort and learn few self-regulation strategies and few advanced reading strategies that they can use when they have to read more challenging content that is only slightly above grade level.

Important research on talented readers remains to be done and this research should include implementation of various forms of programming, including what would happen if accelerated and in-depth reading programs were offered to talented readers from first grade and throughout the rest of elementary and middle school. Also, research on talented readers who receive differentiated reading programs based on interest as opposed to replacement of advanced content selected for them should be conducted.

WHAT ARE THE PRACTICAL IMPLICATIONS OF THE EXTANT RESEARCH?

If talented readers are going to be challenged, the process will require high levels of professional development, new curricular and instructional options, and the use of materials that eliminate or extend basal reading programs and provide high levels of challenge. Unfortunately, current standards, as well as some of the regulations and practices that are inherent or imagined in the federal legislation No Child Left Behind (NCLB; 2001) have led to the adoption of more remedial or direct instruction programs in reading, which may hold back talented readers even more than the research reviewed in this article suggests. To challenge talented readers, we must compact their regular reading instruction, provide challenging alternate materials, give opportunities for acceleration, and find other ways to stimulate their potential. Promising strategies, such as the research reported on SEM–R, suggests that there are ways that this can be accomplished in public school classrooms.

REFERENCES

Allington, R. L. (2002). What I've learned about effective reading instruction from a decade of studying exemplary classroom teachers. *Phi Delta Kappan, 83,* 740–747.

Alvermann, D. E., Moon, J. S., & Hagood, M. C. (1999). *Popular culture in the classroom: Teaching and researching critical media literacy.* Newark, DE: International Reading Association.

Archambault, F. X., Westberg, K. L., Brown, S., Hallmark, B. W., Emmons, C. L., & Zhang, W. (1993). *Regular classroom practices with gifted students: Results of a national survey of classroom teachers* (Research Monograph No. 93102). Storrs: National Research Center on the Gifted and Talented, University of Connecticut.

Baskin, B. H., & Harris, K. H. (1980). *Books for the gifted child.* New York: R. R. Bowker.

Bonds, C., & Bonds, L. T. (1983). Teacher, is there a gifted reader in first grade? *Roeper Review, 5*(3), 4–6.

Brown, W., & Rogan, J. (1983). Reading and young gifted children. *Roeper Review, 5*(3), 6–9.

Catron, R. M., & Wingenbach, N. (1986). Developing the potential of the gifted reader. *Theory Into Practice, 25,* 134–140.

Chall, J. S., & Conard, S. S. (1991). *Should textbooks challenge students? The case for easier or harder textbooks.* New York: Teachers College Press.

Clark, B. (1997). *Growing up gifted* (5th ed.). Columbus, OH: Charles E. Merrill.

Collins, N. D., & Aiex, N. K. (1995). *Gifted readers and reading instruction.* Bloomington, IN: ERIC Clearinghouse on Reading, English and Communication.

Dole, J. A., & Adams, P. J. (1983). Reading curriculum for gifted readers: A survey. *Gifted Child Quarterly, 27,* 64–72.

Dooley, C. (1993). The challenge: Meeting the needs of gifted readers. *Reading Teacher, 46,* 546–551.

Durkin, D. (1990). Matching classroom instruction with reading abilities: An unmet need. *Remedial and Special Education, 11*(3), 23–28.

Fehrenbach, C. R. (1991). Gifted/average readers: Do they use the same reading strategies? *Gifted Child Quarterly, 35,* 125–127.

Gentry, M. L. (1999). *Promoting student achievement and exemplary classroom practices through cluster grouping: A research-based alternative to heterogeneous elementary classrooms* (Research Monograph No. 99138). Storrs: National Research Center on the Gifted and Talented, University of Connecticut.

Halsted, J. W. (1990). *Guiding the gifted reader.* Retrieved September 5, 2007, from http://kidsource.com/kidsource/content/guiding_gifted_reader.html

Halsted, J. W. (1994). *Some of my best friends are books: Guiding gifted readers from preschool to high school.* Dayton, OH: Ohio Psychology Press.

Jackson, N. E. (1988). Precocious reading ability: What does it mean? *Gifted Child Quarterly, 32,* 200–204.

Jackson, N. E., & Roller, C. M. (1993). *Reading with young children* (Research Monograph No. 9302). Storrs: National Research Center on the Gifted and Talented, University of Connecticut.

Kaplan, S. (1999). Reading strategies for gifted readers. *Teaching for High Potential, 1*(2), 1–2.

Kulik, J. A., & Kulik, C.-L. C. (1991). Ability grouping and gifted students. In N. Colangelo & G. A. Davis (Eds.), *Handbook of gifted education* (pp. 179–196). Boston: Allyn & Bacon.

Lamb, P., & Feldhusen, J. F. (1993). Recognizing and adapting instruction for early readers. *Roeper Review, 15,* 108–110.

Levande, D. (1993). Identifying and serving the gifted reader. *Reading Improvement, 30,* 147–150.

No Child Left Behind Act, 20 U.S.C. §6301 (2001).

Reis, S. M. (2003). *Scales for Rating the Behavioral Characteristics of Superior Students–Reading.* Storrs: Neag Center for Gifted Education and Talent Development, University of Connecticut.

Reis, S. M., & Boeve, H. (2007). *Appropriate challenge for academically gifted and talented readers in an urban elementary school.* Manuscript submitted for publication.

Reis, S. M., Burns, D. E., & Renzulli, J. S. (1992). *Curriculum compacting.* Mansfield Center, CT: Creative Learning Press.

Reis, S. M., Eckert, R. D., Jacobs, J., Coyne, M., Richards, S., Briggs, C. J., et al. (2005). *The Schoolwide Enrichment Model—Reading Framework.* Storrs: National Research Center on the Gifted and Talented, University of Connecticut.

Reis, S. M., Gubbins, E. J., Briggs, C., Schreiber, F., Richards, S., Jacobs, J., et al. (2004). Reading instruction for talented readers: Few opportunities for continuous progress. *Gifted Child Quarterly, 48,* 315–338.

Reis, S. M., Hébert, T. P., Diaz, E. I., Maxfield, L. R., & Ratley, M. E. (1995). *Case studies of talented students who achieve and underachieve in an urban high school* (Research Monograph No. 95120). Storrs: National Research Center on the Gifted and Talented, University of Connecticut.

Reis, S. M., Westberg, K. L., Kulikowich, J. K., Caillard, F., Hébert, T. P., Plucker, J., et al. (1993). *Why not let high ability students start school in January? The curriculum compacting study* (Research Monograph No. 93106). Storrs: National Research Center on the Gifted and Talented, University of Connecticut.

Renzulli, J. S. (1977). The enrichment triad model: A plan for developing defensible programs for the gifted and talented: II. *Gifted Child Quarterly, 21,* 227–233.

Renzulli, J. S. (1988). The multiple menu model for developing differentiated curriculum for the gifted and talented. *Gifted Child Quarterly, 32,* 298–309.

Renzulli, J. S., & Reis, S. M. (1989). Providing challenging programs for gifted readers. *Roeper Review, 12,* 92–97.

Renzulli, J. S., & Reis, S. M. (1997). *The schoolwide enrichment model: A how-to guide for educational excellence.* Mansfield Center, CT: Creative Learning Press.

Richards, S. (2003). Current reading instructional practices for average and talented readers. Unpublished doctoral dissertation, University of Connecticut, Storrs.

Rogers, K. B. (1991). Grouping the gifted and talented: Questions and answers. *Roeper Review, 16,* 8–12.

Shrenker, C. E. (1997). Meeting the needs of gifted students within whole group reading instruction. *Ohio Reading Teacher, 31*(3), 70–74.

Southern, T. W., & Jones, E. D. (1992). The real problems with academic acceleration. *Gifted Child Today, 15*(2), 34–38.

Stainthorp, R., & Hughes, D. (2004). An illustrative case study of precocious reading ability. *Gifted Child Quarterly, 48,* 107–120.

Stanley, J. C. (1989). A look back at educational non-acceleration: An international tragedy. *Gifted Child Today, 12*(4), 60–61.

Taylor, B. M., & Fry, B. J. (1988). Pretesting: Minimize time spent on skill work for intermediate readers. *Reading Teacher, 42,* 100–104.

Tomlinson, C. A. (1995). *How to differentiate instruction in mixed-ability classrooms.* Alexandria, VA: Association for Supervision and Curriculum Development.

Trezise, R. L. (1978). What about a reading program for the gifted? *Reading Teacher, 31,* 742–747.

Vacca, J. L., Vacca, R. T., & Grove, M. K. (1991). *Reading and learning to read.* New York: HarperCollins.

VanTassel-Baska, J. (1996). Effective curriculum and instructional models for talented students. *Gifted Child Quarterly, 30,* 164–169.

VanTassel-Baska, J., Zuo, L., Avery, L. D., & Little, C. A. (2002). A curriculum study of gifted-student learning in the language arts. *Gifted Child Quarterly, 46,* 30–44.

Westberg, K. L., Archambault, F. X., Jr., Dobyns, S. M., & Salvin, T. J. (1993). *An observational study of instructional and curricular practices used with gifted and talented students in regular classrooms* (Research Monograph No. 93104). Storrs: National Research Center on the Gifted and Talented, University of Connecticut.

Chapter 44

TEACHER CHARACTERISTICS

Ann Robinson

eacher characteristics have been the subject of research in general education for several decades; their hypothesized link to student outcomes, particularly academic achievement, assures that research on them will play a continued role in educational policy debates. In gifted education, the research on teacher characteristics focuses on a variety of background variables such as grade levels taught, years of experience, preparation status (e.g., preservice or in-service, trained or untrained in gifted education), personality attributes (e.g., need to achieve, sense of humor), and attitudes toward high-ability learners. The literature on teacher characteristics in gifted education is informed by the general teacher literature, but the variables of interest are not entirely the same.

DEFINING THE TERMS IN THE LITERATURE ON TEACHER CHARACTERISTICS

Research studies on teacher characteristics take several forms. Four clusters of variables appear in the gifted education research literature: teacher demographics, status of teacher academic and pedagogical preparation, teacher competencies and teaching behaviors, and teacher personality attributes and attitudes.

Teacher Demographics

The research on teacher characteristics in gifted education reports general grade levels taught (elementary versus secondary), specific grade levels of the teacher sample, years of experience, gender, and infrequently, ethnicity.

Teacher Academic and Pedagogical Preparation

The variables of interest in terms of academic and pedagogical preparation include preservice or in-service status, and certification, licensure, or length and nature of exposure to professional development in gifted education.

Teacher Competencies and Teaching Behaviors

Teaching competencies and behaviors are an amalgam of variables believed to be modifiable through training (Feldhusen, 1997). Examples include knowledge of the nature and needs of high-ability learners, skill in promoting higher level thinking, and the ability to facilitate independent study with gifted students.

Teacher Personality Attributes and Attitudes

Teacher learning styles and attitudes toward giftedness and toward provisions for high-ability learners are the most frequently researched variables in this cluster. Examples include the teachers' need for achievement, intellectual interests, enthusiasm, ability to relate to gifted students, and the level of support expressed for instructional and program provisions for high-ability learners.

MAJOR QUESTIONS ADDRESSED IN THE RESEARCH ON TEACHER CHARACTERISTICS

The major question addressed in the research on teacher characteristics in general education focuses on the relationship of specific teacher characteristics to student achievement (Wayne & Youngs, 2003). In contrast, the question of student achievement is tangentially addressed in the literature on teacher characteristics and high-ability learners. For example, Bloom's (1985) retrospective study of highly proficient young adults drew inferences about teachers who effectively develop talents across the lifespan, but did not focus on teachers in the school context, nor specific characteristics of teachers influential in the development of talent. Rather than establishing links between teacher characteristics and student achievement in schools, the research literature in gifted education focuses on describing and documenting teacher characteristics identified by students, supervisors, and experts in gifted education as desirable for high-ability learners.

In gifted education, research on teacher characteristics is anchored by two distinct but related issues. As is the case in general education, there is a belief that teachers who are particularly effective in teaching some groups of students are not necessarily effective in teaching other groups (Brophy & Good, 1986). Large-scale studies documenting that few adaptations are made for high-ability learners in the classroom appear to confirm that their academic needs are not met by general education teachers (Archambault et al., 1993; Westberg, Archambault, Dobyns, & Salvin, 1993). Fueled by steady parental and practitioner commentary, the field of gifted education is concerned that some teachers are ineffective with high-ability learners (Ferrell, Kress, & Croft, 1988). Second, the research literature on teacher attitudes and dispositions toward high-ability learners documents moderately positive attitudes in some cases (Buttery, 1978; Megay-Nespoli, 2001), but also documents disinterest or negative attitudes in other samples (Cramond & Martin, 1987). Thus, concerns about the differential effectiveness of teachers and the restrained enthusiasm teachers express for high-ability learners in some studies have led researchers to focus on the following questions:

1. What characterizes successful teachers of high-ability learners according to gifted students?
2. What characterizes successful teachers of high-ability learners according to expert judgment?
3. Which teacher characteristics are correlated with positive attitudes toward high-ability learners and service provisions for them?

CONCLUSIONS FROM THE RESEARCH ON TEACHER CHARACTERISTICS AND HIGH-ABILITY LEARNERS

The empirical research on teacher characteristics can be divided into three general areas: (a) studies of high-ability student preferences for teachers with specific characteristics, (b) studies of expert or supervisory judgment of teachers and teacher behaviors believed to be effective with high-ability learners, and (c) studies of teacher attitudes toward high-ability learners.

Student Preferences

In terms of student preferences, an early influential study by Bishop (1968) sought to characterize successful secondary teachers of high-ability learners. Bishop surveyed high school seniors from 65 different districts and identified 109 teachers who were nominated by one or more gifted students as "most successful." A comparison group of 97 teachers who also taught the adolescents, but were not identified by them, were randomly selected from a pool of 500 educators from the same districts. Both groups were surveyed, administered a measure of verbal intelligence, and observed in their classrooms; a subsample was also interviewed. Bishop concluded that intelligence, cultural interests, subject matter expertise, and a strong need for achievement characterized the successful teachers. In terms of teacher attitudes, the successful teachers were more often praised by their students for positive attitudes, and the teachers reported they preferred to teach high-ability learners.

Buser, Stuck, and Casey (1974) surveyed approximately 500 high- and low-achieving high school students and found that among both high and low achievers, the knowledge of subject and a sense of humor were the highest rated characteristics for teachers. In terms of preferred teacher behaviors, both high- and low-achieving students identified "listens to students" as the highest ranked behavior. There were, however, differences between the preferences between the two groups of students. For example, the teacher's attendance at extraclass activities, availability for out-of-class discussions, enthusiasm for the subject, and ability to react favorably to student criticism were more important to high achievers than to low achievers.

Four studies have investigated the preferences of high-ability students through the use of instruments that contrast the relative importance of cognitive and intellectual characteristics to personal and social characteristics of teachers. Milgram (1979) conducted the first of these studies with 459 Israeli students in grades 4–6 who attended afternoon enrichment classes. She constructed a scale, Student Perception of Teachers (SPOT), that asked students to choose among preferred teacher behaviors in the cognitive domain, in the creative domain, and in the personal domain. In the second part of the scale, the forced choice was removed and students were allowed to rate the absolute importance of each domain separately. Overall, students valued all three domains, but preferred teachers who were in command of their subject, a characteristic in the cognitive domain. In contrast, Maddux, Samples-Lachmann, and Cummings (1985) found that American students in grades 7–9 preferred the personal-social domain over the cognitive. Using a different instrument, the Preferred Instructor Characteristics Scale (PICS), Dorhout (1983) surveyed 279 randomly selected gifted students in grades 5–12 and their teachers. Students expressed a preference for personal and social attributes. A decade later, Abel and Karnes (1994) partially replicated the Dorhout study with rural, low-income and suburban, advantaged gifted students in grades 6–12. Both groups of students preferred the personal and social attributes of teachers, although the personal-social preferences were stronger for rural, low-income high-ability learners than for advantaged, suburban students.

Finally, the interest in the personalities of gifted students is mirrored in studies of teachers' styles. Mills (2003) investigated 63 exemplary teachers of gifted students in an accelerative talent search program. Her interest was in the self-reported personality styles of the teachers who had been identified as exemplary by program administrators over a 2-year period and who had received outstanding ratings from students participating in the program. Students rated teachers on the dimensions of content knowledge, preparedness, concern for individual learning, and openness to differing opinions. As expected, the sample of talent search teachers included college and university personnel, as well as Pre-K–12 teachers and therefore generalizing from this sample should be done cautiously. Mills found that on the Myers-Briggs Type Inventory (MBTI) exemplary teachers were more likely to prefer intuition (abstract, symbolic, and hypothetical reasoning, rather than reasoning from facts) and thinking (logical, analytical decision making, rather than subjective and interpersonal) than the normative sample. In this regard, Mills concluded, they resembled their gifted, adolescent students

Across the studies of student preferences with respect to teacher characteristics and behaviors, researchers have found some commonalities. Students do identify intellectual characteristics as important, but they also value personal attributes like a sense of humor, enthusiasm, and respect for students. In three of the four forced-choice studies, student preferences were focused on the personal and social domain.

Studies of Expert Judgment

Two decades after Bishop's initial investigation of student preferences, Whitlock and DuCette (1989) built a model of characteristics of outstanding teachers of high-ability learners through intensively interviewing 10 outstanding and 10 average teachers of the gifted. Initially, a panel of experts generated a list of personal characteristics, abilities, and skills of outstanding teachers. In the second phase of the study, a pool of outstanding teachers were nominated by panel members familiar with them. Next, a random sample of 10 outstanding teachers and 10 average teachers underwent intensive interviews. Finally, a survey was sent to the full sample of 65 teachers from which the 10 outstanding and 10 average teachers were nominated and drawn. The survey asked the larger sample of teachers to respond to the importance of the characteristics generated by the panel of experts, and the results were used to check agreement with the model developed from the interviews. There were statistically significant differences between outstanding and average teachers of the gifted on six dimensions, several of which are characteristics rather than competencies. Specifically, the outstanding teachers were characterized by greater enthusiasm, self-confidence, achievement orientation, and commitment. They also were more likely to describe their teaching role as one of facilitation, to report building program support, and to apply their theoretical, experiential, and observational knowledge in the descriptions of their jobs.

Structured interviews were used by Ferrell et al. (1988) to determine if they could discriminate between 30 teachers from a large urban gifted program and nominated as successful with high-ability learners by their principals and gifted coordinators and a randomly selected control group of 46 teachers who were faculty in the regular academic program. The instrument used to guide the discussion, the Teacher Perceiver Interview, resulted in six themes that discriminated between the two groups: Focus (sees teaching as a life-long career), Gestalt (sets a high standard of achievement), Innovation (uses new approaches and strives to develop creativity), Mission (views teaching as improving society), Rapport (builds relationship with students and exhibits personal warmth), and Investment (derives satisfaction from student learning). Of these themes, the researchers noted that three are commonly found in the lists of characteristics of effective teachers of the gifted generated by experts. These were Gestalt, Innovation, and Rapport. The researchers noted that other characteristics that commonly appeared on expert-generated lists such as intellectualism and knowledge of subject matter were not assessed by the Teacher Perceiver Interview protocol.

In addition to the survey and interview methodologies, two studies included observation in their expert judgment investigations of successful teachers. These studies depend on small samples and are practice-based examinations rather than rigorously controlled designs. Feldhusen and Hansen (1988) reported on procedures for selecting faculty for the Purdue Super Saturday program using teacher characteristics found in the literature. Informed by the work of Maker (1975), Hultgren and Seeley (1982), and others, a checklist of characteristics (e.g., well-organized, willing to put in extra work) and competencies (e.g., understand gifted students characteristics and needs, knows how to lead students in independent study) was used to guide the selection of teachers for the campus-based enrichment program. During a spring semester, teachers were observed with an early version of the Purdue Teacher Observation Form (TOF). Of the 34 teachers in the sample, the researchers reported that 27 (79%) received outstanding or high ratings from their supervisors; the remaining individuals, satisfactory. Feldhusen and Hansen (1988) concluded that their informal selection with a checklist and accompanying supervision resulted in effective classroom teaching behaviors for high-ability learners.

Wendel and Heiser (1989) conducted an ethnographic analysis of three videotaped teachers nominated by their principals as most effective with gifted junior high school students. The teachers were drawn from a rural, a suburban, and an urban district. The researchers selected 10 observable behaviors from the expert literature on effective teachers of the gifted and used them as a template for a panel of experts viewing the videotaped instruction. The 10 behaviors included: (a) flexibility, (b) sense of humor, (c) allows independent study based on student choice, (d) develops positive and close relationship with students, (e) is process oriented, (f) is enthusiastic, (g) is creative, (h) respects students, (i) insists on high-quality work, and (j) is firm and fair. The three behaviors noted most frequently by the observers were sense of humor, respect for students, and cares about students, which Wendel and Heiser noted are affective in nature. Two additional behaviors not part of the initial observational template surfaced in the videotape analysis; these were (a) maintaining a close physical presence to students and (b) using probing questions to stimulate discussion. The researchers concluded that these two specific behaviors were related to developing a positive and close relationship with students and to a process orientation to teaching.

Across the studies of teacher characteristics relying on expert judgment and/or observation, the literature identifies a combination of both characteristics and competencies. The importance of rapport and respect for students emerged in all studies reviewed in the section on teacher characteristics investigated through the lens of expert judgment. Because expert judgment studies are "bounded" by the qualities, characteristics, or variables previously identified from the expert opinion literature, these trends are expected. Like the items on student preference surveys, the nature of the interview or observation instrument circumscribes what characteristics the researchers target. Given the complexity of classroom interactions between teachers and their students, the circumscribed lists of preferred teacher characteristics and behaviors are unlikely to capture the full richness of effective teachers.

Teacher Attitudes Toward High-Ability Learners

In addition to studies of generated lists of successful teacher characteristics, the literature on teachers also focuses on studies of their attitudes toward high-ability learners. For example, Cramond and Martin (1987) replicated Tannenbaum's (1962) classic study of adolescent attitudes toward academic brilliance with a sample of in-service and preservice teachers. Like adolescents 25 years earlier, teachers tended to rate athletic students most positively and the brilliant, studious, and nonathletic students the least positively. Cramond and Martin (1987) correlated the SAT scores of preservice teachers with their attitudes toward the students and found no relationship; high-ability preservice teachers were no more positive about brilliant and studious nonathletes than were others. However, years of experience, the teacher characteristic investigated in the in-service sample, also was correlated with teacher attitude and teachers with more experience rated students more positively overall.

In contrast to Cramond and Martin (1987), other studies of teacher attitude find a modestly positive disposition toward high-ability learners. For preservice teachers, Buttery (1978), Morris (1987), and Megay-Nespoli (2001) investigated samples of 32, 250, and 64 teachers respectively and found moderately positive attitudes toward gifted learners following exposure and training. House (1979) and Rubenzer and Twaite (1978) reported a similar finding with in-service educators. House (1979) investigated 24 in-service teachers in a master's program in gifted education and found them to be positive. Rubenzer and Twaite (1978) surveyed 1,200 teachers and reported that positive attitudes were related to the degree of exposure to gifted education reported by the respondents.

Most of these studies constitute an aging research base on teacher attitudes toward high-ability learners and provisions for them. However, they are relatively consistent. Teachers are moderately positive toward students, and their positive attitudes toward the students and specialized provisions for them are related to the presence or absence of experience and preparation. More experienced teachers are more positive; teachers with exposure to preparation or professional development in gifted education also tend to be positive.

SUMMARY OF RESEARCH ON TEACHER CHARACTERISTICS IN GIFTED EDUCATION

In summary, the research on teacher characteristics in gifted education has focused on teachers identified as successful by gifted students, and by panels of experts and supervisors. In addition, the literature on characteristics includes studies of teacher attitudes toward these learners. In general, the research indicates that the characteristics that reoccur across the studies of exemplary teachers of the gifted include: intellectualism, subject matter expertise, a personal rapport with high-ability learners, and enjoyment in teaching them.

LIMITATIONS OF THE RESEARCH ON TEACHER CHARACTERISTICS AND HIGH-ABILITY LEARNERS

The limitations of the research on teacher characteristics and talent development include the small number of empirical studies that directly address teacher characteristics, the difficulty in conceptually clarifying the difference between teacher characteristics and teacher competencies, methodological challenges in linking achievement and motivational outcomes for high-ability learners with teacher characteristics, and the lack of a well-defined teaching force to permit investigations of workforce demography, availability, and preparedness.

First, a small number of empirical studies directly address teacher characteristics. Baldwin, Vialle, and Clarke (2000); Croft (2003); Feldhusen (1997); Ford and Trotman (2001); Heath (1997); and Robinson and Kolloff (2006) have reviewed the literature that includes teacher characteristics, but the reviews reflect that research on teachers in gifted education generally is approached from a broader perspective—one that includes teacher preparation, as well as characteristics such as demographics and personal attributes. Without exception, the studies reviewed in this chapter mix demographics, preparation variables, personal attributes, and competencies in an effort to tease out practical lessons about effective teachers of high-ability learners.

Second, clearly delineating between characteristics of successful teachers in general and successful teachers of high-ability learners is difficult. The lists generated in both literatures read like "the ideal educator." In particular, the difference between characteristics and competencies is not always easy to define. Although certain demographic characteristics such as age, gender, ethnicity, years in teaching, and certification status are straightforward, others are not. For example, subject matter expertise, skill in meeting the instructional needs of gifted learners, or dispositions toward teaching them can be developed. Would deploying such knowledge, skills, and dispositions effectively be a competency or a characteristic? Which are amenable to training and therefore should be connected explicitly to the curricular experiences in teacher preparation programs?

Third, little attention has been paid to linking high-ability student achievement or motivational outcomes with specific teacher characteristics. In this regard, the literature in gifted education differs from the literature on teacher characteristics in general education. General education research has sought to tie teacher characteristics like certification status to student learning, particularly as it relates to culturally diverse children and children attending low-income schools. In gifted education, research does not focus on establishing linkages between teacher characteristics and the achievement of high-ability learners. It may be that the same methodological challenges of establishing program efficacy for high-ability learners with standard measures of achievement apply to the design of studies that investigate the relationship between teacher characteristics and student achievement outcomes.

Finally, no large-scale studies have sought to identify and describe the teaching force as it relates to high-ability learners. This may be the function of the difficulty with determining the teaching force responsible for high-ability students, and therefore collecting data meaningfully on them. Most high-ability learners spend the majority of their time in general classrooms rather than being taught by specialists in gifted education. Thus, how does the field define its teaching force and what demography should be reported? At present, little is known about the age; years in teaching; gender, ethnic, or linguistic diversity; or geographic distribution of teachers responsible for the education of high-ability learners either in general classrooms or in specialized programs.

IMPLICATIONS

The research in general education affords teachers a central place in importance (Hammerness et al., 2005). The same can be said of gifted education (Cramer, 1991; Croft, 2003; Feldhusen, 1997; Renzulli, 1969). It does matter who teaches, but practical prescriptions for action are difficult to tease out of current literature on teacher characteristics and high-ability learners. For example, no tidy checklist or efficient interview protocol for the selection of effective teachers of the gifted has been validated with subsequent performance measures in rigorously controlled field studies. Nevertheless, some specific guidance is available from the literature.

- First, the research on successful teachers and on teacher attitudes toward high-ability learners confirms the importance of both cognitive factors such as intellectualism and subject matter expertise and affective factors such as respect for high-ability learners and enthusiasm for teaching them. School leaders seeking faculty responsive to high-ability learners can be guided by interview protocols that tap these factors and should consider these factors when making personnel decisions.

- Second, the field is concerned about the attitudes of teachers toward their gifted students and has focused on preparation and professional development as a means to increase teacher awareness of and willingness to provide for these learners. Given the studies that indicate that both preservice and in-service teachers are aware of the needs of gifted learners, but are unable to translate their awareness into differentiated instruction in general classrooms, the focus on preparation remains a key issue in gifted education (Archambault et al., 1993; Tomlinson et al., 1994; Westberg et al., 1993). Teacher preparation specific to high-ability learners matters; districts and states should adopt policies that acknowledge the importance of specialized preparation.

- Third, the field retains an interest in developing models of successful teachers of high-ability learners. However, the models have not increased in sophistication nor have they been extensively researched through observational studies. A promising area of research for developing these models focuses on investigating teacher beliefs about the construct of high ability, about students who have been identified as high-ability learners, and about their willingness to meet the needs of these learners in their classrooms.

- Fourth, the field of gifted education has little information on its teaching workforce. A key task for future research is to define the teacher workforce in the field and to collect demographic and preparation data on them. Policy makers cannot prepare for the future if they do not have information about who currently teaches high-ability learners.

REFERENCES

Abel, T., & Karnes, F. A. (1994). Teacher preferences among the lower socioeconomic rural and suburban advantaged gifted students. *Roeper Review, 17*, 52–53.

Archambault, F. X., Westberg, K. L., Brown, S. W., Hallmark, B. W., Zhang, W., & Emmons, C. L. (1993). Classroom practices used with gifted third and fourth grade students. *Journal for the Education of the Gifted, 16*, 103–119.

Baldwin, A. Y., Vialle, W., & Clarke, C. (2000). Global professionalism and perceptions of teachers of the gifted. In K. A. Heller, F. J. Mönks, R. J. Sternberg, & R. Subotnik (Eds.), *International handbook of giftedness and talent* (2nd ed., pp. 565–572). Amsterdam: Elsevier.

Bishop, W. E. (1968). Successful teachers of the gifted. *Exceptional Children, 34*, 317–325.

Brophy, J. E., & Good, T. L. (1986). Teacher behavior and student achievement. In M. C. Wittrock (Ed.), *Handbook of research on teaching* (pp. 328–375). New York: Macmillan.

Bloom, B. S. (Ed.). (1985). *Developing talent in young people.* New York: Ballantine.

Buser, R. A., Stuck, D. L., & Casey, J. P. (1974). Teacher characteristics and behaviors preferred by high school students. *Peabody Journal of Education, 51*, 119–123.

Buttery, T. J. (1978). Pre-service teachers' attitude regarding gifted children. *College Student Journal, 12*, 288–289.

Cramer, R. H. (1991). The education of gifted children in the United States: A delphi study. *Gifted Child Quarterly, 35*, 84–91.

Cramond, B., & Martin, C. E. (1987). Inservice and preservice teachers' attitudes toward the academically brilliant. *Gifted Child Quarterly, 31*, 15–19.

Croft, J. (2003). Teachers of the gifted: Gifted teachers. In N. Colangelo & G. A. Davis, (Eds.), *Handbook of gifted education* (3rd ed., pp. 558–571). Boston: Allyn & Bacon

Dorhout, A. (1983). Student and teacher perceptions of preferred teacher behaviors among the academically gifted. *Gifted Child Quarterly, 27*, 122–125.

Feldhusen, J. F. (1997). Educating teachers for work with talented youth. In N. Colangelo & G. A. Davis (Eds.). *Handbook of gifted education* (2nd ed., pp. 547–552). Boston: Allyn & Bacon.

Feldhusen, J. F., & Hansen, J. (1988). Teachers of the gifted: Preparation and supervision. *Gifted Education International, 5*(2), 84–89.

Ferrell, B., Kress, M., & Croft, J. (1988). Characteristics of teachers in a full day gifted program. *Roeper Review, 10*, 136–139.

Ford, D. Y., & Trotman, M. F. (2001). Teachers of gifted students: Suggested multicultural characteristics and competencies. *Roeper Review, 23*, 235–239.

Hammerness, K., Darling-Hammond, L., Bransford, J. (with Berliner, D., Cochran-Smith, M., McDonald, M., & Zeichner, K.). (2005). How teachers learn and develop. In L. Darling-Hammond & J. Bransford (Eds.), *Preparing teachers for a changing world: What teachers should learn and be able to do* (pp. 358–389). San Francisco: Jossey-Bass.

Heath, W. J. (1997). *What are the most effective characteristics of teachers of the gifted?* (ERIC Document Reproduction Service No. ED411665)

House, P. A. (1979). Through the eyes of their teachers: Stereotypes of gifted pupils. *Journal for the Education of the Gifted, 2*, 220–224.

Hultgren, H. M., & Seeley, K. R. (1982). *Training teachers of the gifted: A research monograph on teacher competencies.* Denver, CO: University of Denver School of Education.

Maddux, C., Samples-Lachmann, I., & Cummings, R. (1985). Preferences of gifted students for selected teacher characteristics. *Gifted Child Quarterly, 29*, 160–163.

Maker, C. J. (1975). *Training teachers for the gifted and talented: A comparison of models.* Reston, VA: Council for Exceptional Children.

Megay-Nespoli, K. (2001). Beliefs and attitudes of novice teachers regarding instruction of academically talented learners. *Roeper Review, 23*, 178–182.

Milgram, R. M. (1979). Perception of teacher behavior in gifted and non-gifted children. *Journal of Educational Psychology, 71*, 125–128.

Mills, C. J. (2003). Characteristics of effective teachers of gifted students: Teacher background and personality styles of students. *Gifted Child Quarterly, 47*, 272–281.

Morris, S. K. (1987). Student teachers' attitudes toward gifted students. *Creative Child and Adult Quarterly, 12*, 112–114.

Renzulli, J. S. (1969). Identifying key features in programs for the gifted. *Exceptional Children, 35*, 217–221.

Robinson, A., & Kolloff, P. B. (2006). Preparing teachers to work with high-ability youth at the secondary level: Issues and implications for licensure. In F. Dixon & S. Moon (Eds.), *The handbook of secondary gifted education* (pp. 581–610). Waco, TX: Prufrock Press.

Rubenzer, R. L., & Twaite, J. A. (1978). Attitudes of 1,200 educators toward the education of the gifted and talented: Implications for teacher preparation. *Journal for the Education of the Gifted, 2*, 202–213.

Tannenbaum, A. J. (1962). *Adolescent attitudes toward academic brilliance.* New York: Teachers College Bureau of Publications.

Tomlinson, C. A., Tomchin, E. M., Callahan, C. M., Pizzat-Tinnin, P., Cunningham, C. M., Moore, B., et al. (1994). Practices of preservice teachers related to gifted and other academically diverse learners. *Gifted Child Quarterly, 38*, 106–114.

Wayne, A. J., & Youngs, P. (2003). Teacher characteristics and student achievement gains: A review. *Review of Educational Research, 73*, 89–122.

Wendel, R., & Heiser, S. (1989). Effective instructional characteristics of teachers of junior high school gifted students. *Roeper Review, 11*, 151–153.

Westberg, K. L., Archambault, F. X., Dobyns, S. M., & Salvin, T. J. (1993). The classroom practices observation study. *Journal for the Education of the Gifted, 16*, 120–146.

Whitlock, M. S., & DuCette, J. P. (1989). Outstanding and average teachers of the gifted: A comparative study. *Gifted Child Quarterly, 33*, 15–21.

Chapter 45

TEACHER
PREPARATION

Alane Jordan Starko

hen I was asked to write a chapter reviewing the research on preparation of teachers for gifted and talented students, my first thought was, "That's going to be a very short chapter." Research on teacher preparation in general is rich with questions and short on clear-cut answers, long on hypotheses and short on data. So, too, are the results of my review within this subsection of the field. As such, the chapter will first overview the range of questions originally considered, discuss data available to address those questions, and end with a new collection of questions raised by both the data and the complexity of the field.

A straightforward—but also little-researched—question would be, "How are teachers prepared to teach gifted and talented students (however one may define those terms)?" A more interesting question is, "What kinds of preparation allow teachers to successfully teach gifted and talented students?" To which we might add, "How will we recognize such success when we see it?" This approach places questions regarding preparation for teachers of gifted students as a wheel within the revolving wheel of questions about teacher preparation in general.

Currently, the world of teacher preparation is embroiled in a series of policy, theory, and research debates as to how general education teachers should be prepared, and, in particular, what types of teacher preparation are linked to better student achievement. Achievement, in today's political climate if not in the research literature, generally is defined as improved standardized test scores. Some writers suggest that little or no preparation beyond content knowledge is necessary or appropriate for any prospective teachers (Abell Foundation, 2001; Kanstoroom & Finn, 1999; U.S. Department of Education, 2002, 2003). Recent years have been marked by several significant efforts to collect and analyze research on the impact of teacher preparation programs, each raising more questions than it answers (Allen, 2003; Cochran-Smith & Zeichner, 2005; Darling-Hammond & Bransford, 2005; Levine, 2006; Wilson & Floden, 2003).

It is noteworthy that the idea of specialized knowledge or skills to teach subsets of the student population has not been a major topic in the teacher preparation debates. For example, Cochran-Smith and Zeichner's (2005) *Studying Teacher Education: The Report of the AERA Panel on Research and Teacher Education*, the result of a multiyear analysis by some of the top teacher preparation researchers in the country, contains a chapter on preparing special education teachers but does not contain the word "gifted" in its index, nor presumably on any of its other 757 pages. This absence brings to mind the "unthinkable thought" raised by Gallagher in 2000. Faced with a communication from the National Board for Professional Teaching Standards stating that the Board did not recognize teaching gifted students as a distinctive specialty area, Gallagher raised the question, "Is there such an entity as special personnel preparation for teachers of gifted students?" (2000, p. 8). To that query I add, "If so, do we have evidence to suggest that specific types of teacher preparation make a difference in the experiences or achievements of high-ability students?" A truthful response at this date would be, "To suggest it? Probably. To demonstrate it with reasonable degrees of confidence? Not yet."

To many, the idea that individuals preparing to teach particular populations of students ought to have specialized knowledge regarding the characteristics, needs, and learning styles of those students appears to be such common sense that it would not seem a productive avenue for research. That, it now appears, has been one of the major mistakes made by researchers in general education. It has, to many, seemed so obvious that teachers are better off with preparation for the profession than without it, that when conservative think-tanks began asking the question, "Where is the research that demonstrates that teachers who have completed preparation programs are more successful than 'teachers' who have no such training?," the response could not be as immediate and clear as educators might hope. I have argued elsewhere (Starko, 2002) that such a question is akin to asking how well graduates of a first-aid class do in an emergency room as compared to professional nurses. Do we have evidence that nurses do better? I'd be willing to bet we do not, because the research would be too dangerous to the patients. Still, and despite parallel risks to students, questions regarding the need for teacher preparation of any kind continue to be raised.

It is in this context that we examine the logic behind specialized preparation for teachers of the gifted. It is important to remain mindful that although the logic may seem straightforward, data, rather than logic, is the essential currency in the politics of today's teacher preparation.

WHAT DOES LOGIC SUGGEST?

Any discussion of teacher preparation for gifted and talented students must define the teacher population to be addressed. There are, in fact, at least two different pools of teachers to be considered. First, there are teachers who specialize in teaching gifted and talented students (TAG teachers or G/T specialists). These are the teachers who, in the states where such are available, may earn special credentials as a teacher of the gifted and/or work as a specialized TAG teacher. They may teach highly able learners in targeted classes or provide support within heterogeneous classes in an inclusion model. But, also essential to the success of most bright young people are the general education teachers in whose classrooms most gifted and talented students spend the majority of their time. Research provides ample documentation that differentiation in such classrooms is minimal (Archambault et al., 1993; Westberg, Archambault, Dobyns, & Salvin, 1993; Westberg & Daoust, 2003). This leads to two questions to be considered: (1) What types of preparation are appropriate for specialists in gifted and talented education and (2) what types of preparation regarding gifted and talented education should be required of all teachers preparing to teach heterogeneous classes?

A well-reasoned case for personnel preparation specific to gifted education can be made, even with the paucity of available data (see, e.g., Feldhusen, 1997; Gallagher, 2001). Sternberg and Horvath's (1995) analysis identified three essential dimensions of expert teaching in any population: the knowledge base, efficiency in using the knowledge base, and insight in solving problems. Logic might suggest that those teaching gifted and talented students would require both a knowledge base of the exceptional characteristics/needs associated with such students and the ability to bring that knowledge to bear on specific student problems. That is, sterile knowledge of characteristics of gifted students will have little impact if it is not coupled with the ability to recognize when and where those characteristics require intervention with particular students in particular environments. The ability to use information in multidimensional problem situations requires a depth of understanding beyond what is likely to be acquired through general life experiences, or even through a casual mention in a textbook or class lecture. There is some evidence to suggest that teachers assigned to work with gifted students have more knowledge regarding appropriate instruction for gifted learners, but it is not always clear how they gained such knowledge.

Teachers who have been identified as successful teachers of the gifted (TAG teachers) use strategies commonly cited in gifted education literature, for example, higher level thinking and facilitating independence (Hansen & Feldhusen, 1994; Silverman, 1982; Story, 1985). Starko and Schack (1989) found that TAG teachers were more confident in their abilities to use, and more likely to use, strategies recommended for gifted students than were general classroom teachers. While the TAG teachers in that study had completed significantly more workshops and courses in gifted education than the classroom teachers, few specifics about their preparation are available. Brown et al. (2005) determined that TAG teachers and G/T consultants were more likely to favor flexible identification standards, use multiple criteria, and take into account context and cultural factors when identifying students for gifted programs than were classroom teachers or other administrators. Again, the flexible and complex view of assessment mirrors recommended practice, but it is impossible to tell how the TAG teachers gained their views. We may hope they had some preparation for their jobs, but we have no data to support that assumption.

Similarly, Siegle and Powell (2004) found that when nominating students for special programs, G/T specialists (who, again we assume, had some preparation) valued mental computations and problem solving more than did classroom teachers. In no case did classroom teachers rate a student higher than did the G/T specialists. Siegle and Powell hypothesized that classroom teachers' focus on remediating student problems may make it less likely for them to identify strength areas. This could be problematic when classroom teachers are key gatekeepers in nomination processes, particularly if bright students display their gifts in nontraditional or inconvenient ways (see, e.g., Elhoweris, Mutua, Alsheikh, & Holloway, 2005; Joseph & Ford, 2006; Lee, Cramond, & Lee, 2004; Masten & Plata, 2000). Although all teachers need multicultural competencies, such competencies may be of particular import when teachers are responsible for identifying and nurturing exceptional talents in diverse populations (Ford & Trotman, 2003; Moore, Ford, & Milner, 2005). It seems reasonable to suggest that understanding of characteristics and needs of gifted students across varied populations should be an essential component of all teachers' preparation, as well as that of specialists. Certainly this meets the expectations of professionals in the field.

National Association for Gifted Children's (NAGC; 1998) *Pre-K–Grade 12 Gifted Program Standard*s include a Professional Development section that specifies that to meet even minimal standards, all personnel working with gifted learners must be aware of the unique learning differences and needs of gifted learners at the grade level they are teaching and receive appropriate staff development in that area. Minimal recommended standards for specialists in gifted education require that teachers hold or be working toward certification in gifted education or its equivalent. In 1994, NAGC released a position paper delineating the competencies needed by teachers of gifted and talented students. These included:

- a knowledge and valuing of the origins and nature of high levels of intelligence, including creative expressions of intelligence;
- a knowledge and understanding of the cognitive, social and emotional characteristics, needs, and potential problems experienced by gifted and talented students from diverse populations;
- a knowledge of and access to advanced content and ideas;
- an ability to develop a differentiated curriculum appropriate to meeting the unique intellectual and emotional needs and interests of gifted and talented students; and
- an ability to create an environment in which gifted and talented students can feel challenged and safe to explore and express their uniqueness.

It was noted that these competencies were in addition to those required for good teaching and learning in general, such as modeling openness, curiosity, and enthusiasm.

In 2006, The National Association for Gifted Children (NAGC) and the Council for Exceptional Children (CEC) culminated a 3-year collaboration to develop "revised, research-based standards" for teacher preparation in gifted education (National Association for Gifted Children, 2006; see also Parker, 1996; VanTassel-Baska, 2005). The research base undergirding the standards is a global base on theory and practice in education of the gifted, rather than a research base on preparation of teachers of the gifted *per se*. Still, it represents a major step forward in the development of scholarly consensus regarding the knowledge and skills necessary to teach highly able students. The standards include requirements in foundations of the field, development and characteristics of gifted learners, differentiated instruction and assessment, and professional and collaborative practice. They include a substantial emphasis on diversity that spans all major areas of the standards.

WHAT DO WE KNOW ABOUT HOW TAG TEACHERS ARE PREPARED?

No national study examines the preparation of teachers currently assigned to teach gifted and talented students. It is, however, possible to examine what states require for teachers in those assignments. The *State of the States Gifted and Talented Education Report, 2004–2005* (NAGC) reported the following:

- Only one state, Washington, required coursework in gifted education for regular classroom teachers.
- Twenty-three states required that teachers working in specialized programs for gifted and talented have taken graduate courses or received

a teaching certificate in gifted education (two fewer than cited by Landrum, Katsiyannis, and DeWaard in 1998).

- In states with certification in gifted and talented education, requirements ranged from six credit hours (Arizona and South Carolina), to a master's degree with at least 24 credit hours in specified gifted curriculum (Colorado).
- More than 50% of the state respondents identified professional development initiatives in gifted education (providing practical training for classroom teachers) as the most positive force affecting services for gifted students.

This data is paralleled by Seeley (1998), who cites a study in which Seeley and Hultgren surveyed a large sample of practitioners active in the field of gifted education ($N = 528$) to determine the competencies judged essential for teachers of the gifted, and the types of experiences that had prepared individuals for those competencies. The most common options for teachers were in-service classes and workshop opportunities. Half the sample, primarily administrators and support personnel, held graduate degrees in gifted education.

The emphasis on workshop presentations as vehicles for preparation may be related to the limited options for graduate study in gifted education. VanTassel-Baska (2005) noted that only 2% of the universities in the United States have graduate programs in gifted and talented education. In most cases, only a single faculty member is assigned to the program. Limitations of available preparation, combined with limited (or no) state requirements, result in too many beginning teachers of the gifted like the one described by Joffe (2003), by all accounts a fine young teacher but with absolutely no preparation in the area of gifted and talented. He graduated midyear, worked as a substitute for a short period of time, and became a teacher of the gifted when a teacher became ill, selected from an applicant pool in which no candidate had specialized expertise.

It should be noted that lack of preparation options and lack of state requirements can combine in a dysfunctional cycle. In places where no preparation is required, it is very difficult for colleges and universities to entice teachers into graduate programs in the field. In the current fiscal environments in higher education, low-enrollment graduate programs are difficult or impossible to maintain. And yet, when states consider the creation of certification programs or mandated services, one of the considerations is the availability of high-quality preparation. Thus, in my own state I've participated in numerous discussions that could be summarized as follows.

> Advocate: "We aren't serving gifted students well. We need to require that teachers be better prepared."
> Department of Education Personnel: "We can't require teachers be prepared; we don't have enough university programs to prepare them."

Universities: "But, we can't offer programs without students. Until there are requirements that will bring students to our classes, we can't offer the programs."

Sadly, and not surprisingly, in my home state we continue to have few options for preparation and no endorsement opportunities for teachers.

WHAT DO WE KNOW ABOUT THE EFFECTIVENESS OF PREPARATION FOR TEACHERS WORKING WITH GIFTED STUDENTS?

Hansen and Feldhusen (1994) conducted the only study located that examined differences in practice between trained and untrained teachers of the gifted (TAG teachers). Defining a "trained" teacher as one with a minimum of four graduate courses in gifted education, the study concluded that trained teachers were more likely to demonstrate:

- fast pacing of instruction,
- emphasis on creativity and thinking skills,
- teacher–student interactions,
- appropriate motivational techniques,
- student-directed activities, and
- use of media and models in teaching.

These differences were noted both through direct observation and through student reports. Feldhusen (1997) described the trained teachers' performance as "highly superior" (p. 550). In contrast, Mills (2003) found that of 63 effective instructors in intensive summer classes for gifted students, 79% had never had a course in gifted education and less than ⅓ were certified teachers. Many were college instructors with advanced degrees in their content area.

There is slightly more literature regarding general education teachers working with gifted students in heterogeneous classrooms. Westberg and Archambault's (1995, 1997) multisite case study of successful classroom practices for high-ability students examined general education teachers' strategies for meeting the needs of gifted students within their classrooms. They found that while teachers applied concepts from in-service training to their classrooms, those with graduate degrees in gifted education or special education were more likely to individualize instruction than those without such preparation. In this case, "successful classroom practices" were defined to mean accommodation for individual differences, including those of gifted students, within heterogeneous elementary classrooms.

Westberg and Daoust (2003), in a survey of 1,366 third- and fourth-grade teachers in two states, also found that teachers who had taken graduate courses in gifted education provided curriculum modifications more frequently. Teachers who had degrees in gifted education were significantly more likely to provide challenge and choice for both gifted and average students, as well as to modify the curriculum to meet individual needs. Of course, there is no way to know whether the increased attention to the needs of gifted and talented students is a result of the graduate classes or if some third factor—for example, interest and motivation regarding the field—caused teachers both to select relevant graduate courses and to implement strategies studied.

There is evidence that workshops can facilitate classroom teachers' modification of teaching practice for gifted students. Reis and Westberg (1994) found that teachers who received varied levels of staff development were able to successfully individualize through curriculum compacting. The more intense the intervention, the higher the judged quality of differentiation planned. Cashion and Sullenger (2005) reported that after attending a summer institute on giftedness, teachers reported they changed their attitudes toward giftedness. The strategies used to accommodate gifted learners were more complex in the second year after the institute than in the first. Participants reported feeling better about themselves as teachers, and better about their students' learning. They also reported struggles with limited support, resources, and autonomy.

On the other hand, workshop experiences were more limited in their impact on preservice teachers. Although workshops and associated mentoring raised preservice teachers' awareness of academically diverse students, they had limited impact on beginning teacher practice (Moon, Callahan, & Tomlinson, 1999; Tomlinson et al., 1995; Tomlinson et al., 1997; Tomlinson et al., 1994).

WHAT RESEARCH IS YET TO COME? WHAT DO WE DO IN THE MEANTIME?

In summary, available research supports the following conclusions.

1. Teachers who are identified as teachers of the gifted use curriculum strategies recommended for use with gifted learners more regularly than do general education teachers. They also are likely to use more flexible identification strategies and to take into account cultural and contextual variables when identifying potentially gifted learners. In half of the states, TAG teachers are required to have some specialized training. One study suggests that TAG teachers with at least four graduate courses in the field use appropriate strategies more frequently than those without such courses.

2. General education teachers who have taken graduate courses in gifted education are more likely to differentiate to meet the needs of gifted learners than teachers who have not taken such courses. Those who

have degrees in gifted education provide more complex differentiation than those who have only a few courses.

3. General education teachers who have high-quality staff development on strategies for diversifying curriculum can adapt curriculum to better meet the needs of highly able learners. Without such programs, differentiation for gifted learners is unlikely to occur.

4. Preparing beginning general education teachers to differentiate curriculum is challenging. The type of workshop format that can be effective with practicing teachers is less effective in changing the behaviors of student teachers, who are dealing with many new and complex variables.

5. The most common way for teachers to learn about the characteristics and needs of gifted learners is though in-service staff development.

These results sum to the not-surprising conclusion that the more knowledgeable teachers are about the characteristics and needs of gifted learners, the more likely they are to respond to those needs in ways the literature deems appropriate. However, this leaves unanswered the million dollar question, "Can we demonstrate that better preparation is linked to some type of positive outcome for the students involved?" The answer to date is, we cannot. All of the research results cited describe changes in *teacher* behavior. Except by inference, we do not have evidence that better-prepared teachers' behavior results in something better for students. This is gifted education's parallel to the general teacher education challenge that asks, "Can you demonstrate that fully prepared teachers result in students learning more?" Relying on logic to respond to that question is a luxury we can no longer afford.

In gifted education, the student-outcomes question is confounded because, to an even greater degree than in general education, there is no clear consensus on what the target outcomes are. In some ways, this is parallel to the creativity research dilemma that Treffinger, Renzulli, and Feldhusen identified in 1971. In that case, the authors demonstrated the difficulty of validating measures of creativity without agreement on some standard of creativity to which they could be compared. When examining education of the gifted, it is difficult to demonstrate that teachers with appropriate preparation do "better" without an agreement on what "better" looks like.

In the case of general education teachers working with gifted students, the operational definition to date has been that "better" entails differentiating instruction based on individual needs, in ways that parallel gifted education literature (e.g., curriculum compacting, more complex assignments, opportunities for individual investigations). However, in the case of TAG teachers, the desired outcomes vary considerably from program to program. For example, it may be appropriate to measure the impact of an intensive summer math program via a test on the advanced content. On the other hand, if elementary students are participating in a program focused on independent research, content tests will not be appropriate outcome measures. And, of course, all of this is further confounded by the typical assessment problems for exceptionally able learners, particularly ceiling effects. When examining outcomes for bright students, whatever measures are used must provide sufficient discriminating power among students to make comparisons possible.

In order to provide research support for the professional development standards already recommended, a number of research procedures and problems will need to be addressed.

1. In any study comparing teaching practices in different populations, particularly gifted education specialists, it is essential to describe the types of preparation experienced by participants. If classroom teachers behave one way and teachers of the gifted behave differently, it is important to know if some of the differences may be attributed to differing preparation. Preparation standards vary so widely across the states that no conclusions can be drawn without data.

2. In educational research, the bottom line of any investigation is its impact on students. When comparing varying types of teacher preparation, it is essential to examine outcomes beyond what teachers do. This can be done either by gathering the student data as part of the study or by citing earlier research that already demonstrates the connection between teacher behavior A and student outcome B. Differing teacher behaviors really don't matter at all unless we can demonstrate that they have different impacts on students.

3. Examining student outcomes will require a more complex view of the types of outcomes sought for specific groups of students, and what preparation is appropriate for those circumstances. For example, seeming conflicts between studies cited earlier are explained easily (at least hypothetically) by the differing populations and desired outcomes. Hansen and Feldhusen's (1994) subjects were deemed significantly more effective after completing four graduate courses. The large majority of those individuals were teaching in elementary school gifted programs. Most of Mills' (2003) successful teachers were content specialists who had no preparation in gifted education—most were not even certified teachers. That group was teaching in an intensive summer program for advanced high school students. It is not hard to imagine that different types of preparation would facilitate excellent teaching in those differing circumstances. More generally, it seems highly likely that the types of preparation that best facilitate gifted learners will be different for learners at different stages of development and/or different subject areas. Landvogt (2001) notes the need for different types of teachers at different stages of students' development, echoing Bloom's (1985) descriptions of different types of instruction needed throughout the phases of talent development. Research that seeks to tie teacher preparation to its impact on students will need to be quite specific about the types of impact sought for a particular student population.

4. In examining the impact of teacher preparation on gifted learners, it seems wise to examine linkages to questions being asked in more general teacher preparation. Such examinations may bring to light areas in which standards and preparation should be similar and where they may be different when preparing specialists to teach gifted learners. Questions might include the impact of advanced content knowledge, pedagogical knowledge specific to gifted learners, specific personal characteristics (e.g., would teachers do better if they would qualify for the programs they teach?), and the impact of certification.

While we await the results of research-yet-to-come, it is possible to be guided by logic and existing data. These would suggest that graduate programs have value, both for gifted education specialists and for classroom teachers who teach gifted students within their classrooms. Helping those programs remain viable when the political pendulum swings away from interest in gifted education is an important goal. Expanding options, particularly distance options that can be available in areas that otherwise could not access appropriate courses, also is vital. For teachers hoping to be gifted education specialists, in-depth preparation is the best recommendation to date.

However, the limited availability of graduate programs in gifted education makes it equally important to examine flexible options for high-quality professional development, both for general classroom teachers and for specialists without graduate school opportunities. Gallagher (2001) cites examples such as certification modules, academies, distance learning, and summer institutes that can be used to bring essential information to a wider audience.

Finally, those of us who are responsible for preparing new teachers must look long and hard at how we can help beginning teachers think about the varied populations of students before them and find ways to differentiate instruction that are not so overwhelming as to seem impossible. This is likely to require that planning for diverse populations be part of teacher preparation from the beginning, rather than a topic addressed after "regular" planning has been covered. Such a shift will be enormously challenging as it moves novice educators immediately into advanced levels of curriculum planning. And yet, the additional stress of early complex planning tasks may well pale when compared to the confidence to plan appropriately for real students, who are all counting on their teachers to see them, understand them, and help them learn.

REFERENCES

Abell Foundation. (2001). *Teacher certification reconsidered: Stumbling for quality.* Retrieved October 10, 2005 from http://www.abell.org/publications

Allen, M. B. (2003). *Eight questions on teacher preparation: What does the research say?* Denver, CO: Education Commission of the States.

Archambault, F. X., Jr., Westberg, K. L., Brown, S. W., Hallmark, B. W., Emmons, C. L., & Zhang, W. (1993). *Regular classroom practices with gifted students: Results of a national survey of classroom teachers* (Research Monograph 93102). Storrs: National Research Center on the Gifted and Talented, University of Connecticut.

Bloom, B. (1985). *Developing talent in young people.* New York: Ballantine.

Brown, S. W., Renzulli, J. S., Gubbins, E. J., Siegle, D., Zhang, W., & Chen, C. (2005). Assumptions underlying the identification of gifted and talented students. *Gifted Child Quarterly, 49,* 68–79.

Cashion, M., & Sullenger, K. (2005). "Contact us next year": Tracing teachers' use of gifted practices. *Roeper Review, 23,* 18–21.

Cochran-Smith, M., & Zeichner, K. M. (Eds.). (2005). *Studying teacher education: The report of the AERA panel on research and teacher education.* Washington, DC: American Educational Research Association.

Darling-Hammond, L., & Bransford, J. (2005). *Preparing teachers for a changing world; What teachers should learn and be able to do.* San Francisco: Jossey-Bass.

Elhoweris, H., Mutua, K., Alsheikh, N., & Holloway, P. (2005). Effect of children's ethnicity on teachers' referral and recommendation decisions in gifted and talented programs. *Remedial and Special Education, 26*(1), 25–31.

Feldhusen, J. F. (1997). Educating teachers for work with talented youth. In N. Colangelo & G. A. Davis (Eds.), *Handbook of gifted education* (2nd ed., pp. 547–552). Boston: Allyn & Bacon.

Ford, D. Y., & Trotman, M. D. (2003). Teachers of gifted students: Suggested multicultural characteristics and competencies. *Roeper Review, 23,* 235–239.

Gallagher, J. J. (2000). Unthinkable thoughts: Education of gifted students. *Gifted Child Quarterly, 44,* 5–12.

Gallagher, J. J. (2001). Personnel preparation and secondary education programs for the gifted. *Journal of Secondary Gifted Education, 12,* 133–138.

Hansen, J. B., & Feldhusen, J. F. (1994). Comparison of trained and untrained teachers of gifted students. *Gifted Child Quarterly, 38,* 115–123.

Joffe, W. (2003). Investigating the acquisition of pedagogical knowledge: Interviews with a beginning teacher of the gifted. *Roeper Review, 23,* 219–226.

Joseph, L. M., & Ford, D. Y. (2006). Nondiscriminatory assessment: Considerations for gifted education. *Gifted Child Quarterly, 50,* 42–51.

Kanstoroom, M., & Finn, C. (1999). *Better teachers, better schools.* Washington, DC: Thomas Fordham Foundation.

Landrum, M. S., Katsiyannis, A., & DeWaard, J. (1998). A national survey of current legislative and policy trends in gifted education: Life after the national excellence report. *Journal for the Education of the Gifted, 21,* 352–371.

Landvogt, J. (2001). Affecting eternity: Teaching for talent development. *Roeper Review, 23,* 190–196.

Lee, S., Cramond, B., & Lee, J. (2004). Korean teachers' attitudes toward academic brilliance. *Gifted Child Quarterly, 48,* 42–53.

Levine, A. (2006). *Educating school teachers.* Washington, DC: The Education School Project.

Masten, W. G., & Plata, M. (2000). Acculturation and teacher ratings of Hispanic and Anglo-American students. *Roeper Review, 23,* 45–46.

Mills, C. J. (2003). Characteristics of effective teachers of gifted students: Teacher background and personality styles of students. *Gifted Child Quarterly, 47,* 272–281.

Moon, T., Callahan, C., & Tomlinson, C. (1999). Effects of mentoring relationships on preservice teachers' attitudes toward academically diverse students. *Gifted Child Quarterly, 43*, 56–62.

Moore, J. L., Ford, D. Y., & Milner, H. R. (2005). Recruitment is not enough: Retaining African American students in gifted education. *Gifted Child Quarterly, 49*, 51–67.

National Association for Gifted Children. (1994). *Position paper: Competencies needed by teacher of gifted and talented students.* Washington, DC: Author.

National Association for Gifted Children. (1998). *Pre–K–grade 12 gifted program standards.* Washington, DC: Author. Retrieved October 12, 2005, from http://www.nagc.org/index.aspx?id=546

National Association for Gifted Children. (2004–2005). *The big picture.* Retrieved February 28, 2007, from http://www.nagc.org/index.aspx?id=532

National Association for Gifted Children. (2006). *Teacher preparation standards in gifted and talented education.* Retrieved February 28, 2007, from http://www.nagc.org/index.aspx?id=1862

Parker, J. (1996). NAGC standards for personnel preparation in gifted education: A brief history. *Gifted Child Quarterly, 40,* 158–164.

Reis, S. M., & Westberg, K. L. (1994). The impact of staff development on teachers' ability to modify curriculum for gifted and talented students. *Gifted Child Quarterly, 38,* 127–135.

Seeley, K. (1998). Facilitators for talented students. In J. VanTassel-Baska (Ed.), *Excellence in educating gifted and talented learners* (3rd ed., pp. 471–488). Denver, CO: Love.

Siegle, D., & Powell, T. (2004). Exploring teacher biases when nominating students for gifted programs. *Gifted Child Quarterly, 48,* 21–29.

Silverman, L. K. (1982). The gifted and talented. In E. L. Meyen (Ed.), *Exceptional children and youth* (pp. 184–190). Denver, CO: Love.

Starko, A. J. (2002, Spring). *Diverse viewpoints: Extensive pedagogy training essential to teacher education. Michigan Education Report.* Retrieved October 14, 2005, from http://www.mackinac.org/pubs/mer/article.asp?ID=4376

Starko, A. J., & Schack, G. D. (1989). Perceived need, teacher efficacy, and teaching strategies for the gifted and talented. *Gifted Child Quarterly, 33,* 118–122.

Sternberg, R., & Horvath, J. A. (1995). A prototype view of expert teaching. *Educational Researcher, 24*(6), 9–17.

Story, C. M. (1985). Facilitator of learning: A microethnographic study of the teacher of the gifted. *Gifted Child Quarterly, 29,* 155–159.

Tomlinson, C. A., Callahan, C. M., Moon, T., Tomchin, E. M., Landrum, M., Imbeau, M., et al. (1995). *Preservice teacher preparation in meeting the needs of academically diverse learners* (Research Monograph 95134). Storrs: National Research Center on the Gifted and Talented, University of Connecticut.

Tomlinson, C. A., Callahan, C. M., Tomchin, E. M., Eiss, N., Imbeau, M., & Landrum, M. (1997). Becoming architects of communities of learning: Addressing academic diversity in contemporary classrooms. *Exceptional Children, 63,* 269–282.

Tomlinson, C. A., Tomchin, E. M., Callahan, C. M., Cunningham, C., Moore, B., Lutz, L., et al. (1994). Practices of preservice teachers related to gifted and other academically diverse learners. *Gifted Child Quarterly, 38,* 106–114.

Treffinger, D. J., Renzulli, J. S., & Feldhusen, J. F. (1971). Problems in the assessment of creative thinking. *Journal of Creative Behavior, 5,* 104–112.

U.S. Department of Education (2002). *Meeting the highly qualified teacher challenge: The Secretary's annual report on teacher quality.* Washington, DC: Author.

U.S. Department of Education (2003). *Meeting the highly qualified teacher challenge: The Secretary's annual report on teacher quality.* Washington, DC: U.S. Department of Education, Office of Post Secondary Education.

VanTassel-Baska, J. (2005, October). *The development of an NCATE conceptual framework, research base, and standards for gifted education.* Presentation at Winthrop University, Charlotte, NC.

Westberg, K. L., & Archambault, F. X. (Eds.). (1995). *Profiles of successful practices for high ability students in elementary classrooms* (Research Monograph 95122). Storrs: National Research Center on the Gifted and Talented, University of Connecticut.

Westberg, K. L., &, Archambault, F. X. (1997). A multi-site case study of successful classroom practices for high-ability students. *Gifted Child Quarterly, 41,* 42–51.

Westberg, K. L., & Daoust, M. E. (2003, Fall). *The results of the replication of the classroom practices survey: Replication in two states.* Retrieved October 17, 2005, from http://www.gifted.uconn.edu/nrcgt/newsletter/fall03/fall032.html

Westberg, K. L., Archambault, F. X., Dobyns, S., & Salvin, T. J. (1993). *An observational study of instructional and curricular practices used with gifted and talented students in regular classrooms* (Research Monograph 93104). Storrs: National Research Center on the Gifted and Talented, University of Connecticut.

Wilson, S. M., & Floden, R. E. (2003). *Creating effective teachers: Concise answers to hard questions.* New York: AACTE Publications.

Chapter 46

THINKING AND LEARNING STYLES

David Yun Dai

ill Gates, the cofounder and CEO of Microsoft, is, without doubt, a highly intelligent person. But, does he think in some unique ways? Does he approach learning and performance tasks in a manner that is qualitatively, rather than quantitatively, different from most of us? Is his style of thinking more innovative than most people, regardless of domains or contents involved? These are a set of questions typically addressed under the rubric of thinking and learning styles.

WHAT DO WE MEAN BY THINKING/LEARNING STYLES?

Style, in a broad sense, refers to a distinctive manner of behaving, conducting, or expressing oneself. To the extent that individuals habitually and consistently display certain ways of thinking or certain manners of mastery, we call them thinking or learning styles. Thinking and learning styles often are grouped together because the two concepts overlap with each other: Efforts of learning involve thinking, and thinking often leads to new learning. Various style can be classified based on different facets of cognitive functions. For example, *cognitive style* concerns *modality* (e.g., auditory vs. visual learners), *encoding* (e.g., image vs. verbal representation of learning material), and *mode of information processing* (e.g., holistic vs. analytic). Learning styles concern characteristic ways of processing new information (e.g., learning as reproducing what is learned vs. transforming it into a form that allows flexible use), and organizing new information (relying on externally provided structure vs. imposing structure of one's own). Some styles have clear personality underpinnings, such as impulsivity vs. reflectivity, legislative vs. judicial, and liberal vs. conservative, while others indicate specific preferences for a particular type of work or activity; for instance, some prefer activities that involve reflective observation of what is out there, and others may prefer engagement in active experimentation; some prefer to pursue theoretical ideas and others like solving practical matters better.

Teachers often like to invoke the concept of style in explaining individual differences they observe in their students. Yet, people typically don't differentiate the scientific concepts of thinking and learning styles from related folk beliefs. Although not all folk beliefs are wrong, these beliefs often remain implicit and unexamined. For example, some people do not differentiate style and ability; for them, multiple intelligences are synonymous to multiple thinking styles. Some believe that styles work like personality traits or fixed characteristics of the person, rather than one's characteristic way of dealing with a specific type of task environment. Although these assumptions are not necessarily "wrong," they are nevertheless oversimplistic.

WHAT DOES THE RESEARCH TELL US ABOUT THINKING AND LEARNING STYLES?

One question people often ask is whether gifted children as a group have unique thinking and learning styles. The research evidence is mixed regarding this question. In general, we should think of gifted children as diversely inclined in terms of their habitual ways of thinking and learning, although some stylistic dimensions might be viewed as "gifted" par excellence. The following are some conclusions and principles that represent current thinking and the state of knowledge:

- Gifted learners (as defined by IQ) are more "legislative" and tend to impose structure on learning materials, rather than relying on structure provided by adults, including educators (Snow, 1994; Sternberg & Grigorenko, 1993). They also are more field-independent, that is, not easily distracted by irrelevant background information (Davis, 1991).

A related claim partly supported by research is that gifted children tend to be *intuitive* learners; that is, they tend to see the intangible and envision connections and possibilities that are not obvious (see Piirto, 1998, pp. 108–109).

- Some children distinguish themselves from others in showing a characteristic tendency toward divergent thinking; that is, they tend to deviate from "conventional" ways of thinking and produce thoughts that go in many directions, although it is still uncertain as to whether children's divergent thinking is associated with creative productivity in adulthood (Runco, 2005).

- Style and ability have a complex relationship; some stylistic dimensions, such as field dependence-independence and cognitive complexity-simplicity, have ability underpinnings (Davis, 1991); we still don't know how to tease apart the stylistic and ability aspects of intellectual functioning, although attempts have been made (see Lohman & Bosma, 2002).

- People often assume that thinking and learning styles must be based on simple individual differences, just like people differ in intellectual abilities and skills. However, it may be intra-individual differences (strengths and weaknesses within the person) rather than interindividual differences (differences between individuals) that help explain why, say, one person tends to rely on verbal representation of learning materials, and another relies on spatial representation (Lohman, 1994). Patterns of strengths and weaknesses involve various configurations of abilities, which reveal intricate style-ability interaction (Renzulli & Dai, 2001).

- Personality factors, such as intellectual risk taking and perfectionism, play a role in one's stylistic functioning, as far as individuals consistently show these dispositions across learning or performance situations. These dispositions are affective in nature: whether one experiences dissatisfaction with anything less than perfect versus being realistic about oneself and others, or toward failure aversion versus adventuring into the unknown. These personality and affective variables may not have a consistent relationship with psychometrically defined abilities, but may influence intellectual development over time (Dweck, 1999).

- Some domains (e.g., arts vs. sciences, or history vs. chemistry) may require specific styles of functioning; for instance, Labouvie-Vief (1990) suggested two modes of meaning that shape differential developmental trajectories: in the *mythos* mode (speech, narrative, plot, or dialogue), experience is holistic and based on close identification between the self and the object of thought, whereas in the *logos* mode (reckoning, explanation, rule, principle, reason), knowing is objective and detached, and can be rendered purely analytic, mechanical, and computable. As a result, some children will find a better match between their styles of functioning and some privileged domains. There may be gender differences in stylistic preferences that predispose them to choose differing career paths, with males leaning toward inorganic fields and females toward organic ones (Lubinski & Benbow, 1992).

WHAT ARE PRACTICAL IMPLICATIONS OF THINKING AND LEARNING STYLES AS WE KNOW THEM?

Why is the matter of style important for gifted education? The concept of thinking/learning style broadens our conceptions of giftedness beyond what we see as "abilities." It allows us to go beyond structural or faculty views of talent, intelligence, or creativity. The concept of ability differences addresses the quantitative question of *how well or how much*, whereas the concept of stylistic differences tackles the qualitative question of *how*: characteristic ways in which individuals think and learn, and how these specific styles of ways of thinking can be cultivated, developed, or matched with proper instructional designs, and sometimes modified to advance their courses of talent and career development (Grigorenko & Sternberg, 1997).

First, consider style as reflecting higher order principles of self-organization of cognitive resources in dealing with academic or other challenges (cf. Gardner, 1953). For example, Lohman (1994) hypothesized that it is within-person, rather than absolute between-person, ability differences that give rise to characteristic modes of functioning. This line of thinking can be easily extended to *multiple exceptionalities*, as the title of Lohman's article, "Spatially Gifted, Verbally Inconvenienced," points to (see also Miller, 1996; West, 1991). There is ample evidence that ability profiles of many gifted children are diverse and show unique strengths and weaknesses (e.g., Wilkinson, 1993; see Winner, 2000, for a discussion). Gifted educators need to be aware of students' cognitive profiles (i.e., various combinations of strengths and weaknesses) in order to develop an educational plan that optimizes their developmental pathways.

Second, style as reflecting the principle of self-organization in dealing with challenges has its affective, as well as cognitive, dimensions; that is, how people experience and manage their affect and motivation in the face of challenge, success, and failure. Messick (1994) proposed *defensive style* as consistent ways of maintaining positive affect in cognition (see also Labouvie-Vief & Gonzalez, 2004). We might add *novelty seeking* (Zuckerman, 2004), *perfectionism* (Schuler, 2002) and *intellectual risk taking* (Kogan, 1983) as some self-organizing principles of learning and development. The importance of these personality-centered styles for talent development cannot be overestimated, as they are concerned, one way or another, with approach vs. avoidance, self-expanding vs. self-maintaining personal tendencies (Dai, 2000). Gifted educators need to be aware of these personality- or affect-based stylistic functioning as indicative of *aptitude* or *inaptitude* for challenges in general or a specific line of work in particular.

Third, in light of the view of style as reflecting self-organizing principles, various thinking/learning style typologies (e.g., Kolb, 1971; Kolb, Boyatzis, & Mainemelis, 2001) can be very useful for gifted counseling. Similar to the distinction between the mythos and logos modes of thinking identified by Labouvie-Vief (1990), Snow (1967) identified two cultures (humanism vs. scientism) in the professional communities, which suggests that (a) certain domains and fields may require specific modes of functioning, for instance, analytic versus holistic; (b) certain ability/interest/style constellations may indicate specific niche potential and career trajectories; and (c) matching the learner's styles with curricular goals or helping the learner adapt to new styles of functioning is an important teaching strategy. Thus, various style concepts can be used, not as a tool to pigeonhole students, but as a heuristic device in counseling and guidance sessions to raise self-awareness, clarify options, and facilitate students'/clients' academic and career decision making.

Finally, given the fact that the nature of various styles proposed in the literature is not completely understood, teachers and parents need to keep three points in mind when using the concept of style as an intellectual tool for guiding practice and making educational decisions:

1. Be aware of possible biological underpinnings of a specific style. Some neurological research using EEG measures has yielded interesting findings regarding enhanced right hemispheric functions in gifted male adolescents (e.g., O'Boyle, Benbow, & Alexander, 1995). Although whether it has to do with style issues remains to be seen, it yields important clues about *qualitative* differences in cognitive functions (i.e., a matter of *how*). Evidence from gifted individuals with dyslexia and other learning disabilities implicates stylistic functioning of these individuals, suggesting a mechanism of *compensation* may underlie the unique *self-organization* of brain functions.

2. Be aware of the role of socialization. Pedagogical practices may reinforce certain style but suppress expressions of other styles, for better or for worse. For example, a preference for sequential, procedural learning, instead of constructing mental models in mathematics, may be reinforced by good grades due to its procedural precision, to the detriment of a deep understanding of mathematical principles and further learning of mathematics. One also can ask how frequently teachers encourage intellectual risk taking by facilitating "educated guesses," instead of expecting "correct answers" in classroom. Besides, findings from Bamberger (1986) and Lubinski and Benbow (1992) suggest that certain styles may be developed as a result of domain constraints and the norm of a field or subfield (e.g., professional psychologists vs. experimental psychologists). Thus, style is not only a matter of individual differences; it is developmentally shaped through experience.

3. Be aware of the dynamic nature of style; that is, style also reflects adaptivity (or the lack thereof) in a functional context. It is probably maladaptive to indiscriminately respond to situations with the

same style. There is a feedback control in which the learner gauges the effectiveness of certain strategies and makes adjustments accordingly (e.g., win-stay, lose-shift), resulting in a style that is better attuned to demands of a specific situation (Pask, 1976, 1988). Of course, individuals also develop their own unique strategies and styles in dealing with challenges. For the concept of style to illuminate gifted potential, not only should its dispositional aspect be explored, so should the socialization/internalization and adaptivity aspects. The utility of the concept of style for understanding and serving gifted children lies in its potential to shed light on how brilliant minds work in specific functional contexts, and how we might facilitate their development.

WHAT ARE SOME CHALLENGES IN UNDERSTANDING THINKING AND LEARNING STYLE?

There are three challenges inherent in the style research. The first is to differentiate style from ability. The initial impetus of the style research is dissatisfaction with the ability research, which measures differences in performance *outcomes* and *levels* but does not seem to yield much insight into differences in *processes*. Unlike ability constructs, style is about *performance*, rather than *competence* (Lohman & Bosma, 2002). To be useful and nonredundant, style concepts have to be empirically and theoretically distinguished from ability concepts. Style concerns *how* a task is performed, and ability addresses *how well* a task is performed. Given a problem, two persons may perform equally well, yet display different ways of accomplishing the task; for example, some may enlist images while others use verbal representations, and some may grasp the problem holistically while others break the task down to several components. We infer competence (i.e., ability) from performance outcomes, and style from underlying processes (e.g., dispositions). *Ability* indicates *quantitative* differences (degrees and levels), and *style* indicates *qualitative* differences (different manners and patterns of strategies used). Intelligence can be seen both as a capacity (competence) and as a style. As Cronbach (1977) argued, "intelligence is not a thing; it is a style of work" (p. 275). Although there is a distinction, it is not easy empirically to separate style and ability in performance-based measures, which tend to elicit maximal performance (ability) rather than typical engagement (style). Measurement innovations are needed to advance this line of research (see Lohman & Bosma, 2002).

The second challenge is to reconcile two traditions of the style research. In general, the *cognitive style* research is rooted in the long objective-analytic tradition and typically uses performance measurements (e.g., Witkin & Goodenough, 1981), whereas the *learning style* research takes a more phenomenological approach, assuming an experiential basis for learning preferences and relying on self-report and interview data (e.g., Boulton-Lewis, Marton, & Wilss, 2001). Compared to their cognitive style counterparts, researchers on learning style tend to be more pragmatic, concerned with different learners' preferences for various learning activities and contexts (e.g., Dunn, Dunn, & Price, 1989). Thus, while performance-based cognitive styles are criticized for being close to abilities (Sternberg & Grigorenko, 2001), learning style theories are criticized for relying on introspective self-report measures, which are in many ways flawed (Kline, 1995). Learning styles, though often intuitively accessible to lay audiences, also are criticized for the lack of a solid psychological foundation and empirical support (e.g., Ramsay, 1995).

The third challenge, probably most critical, is to grasp the nature of a style, and the question of how it functions. Some researchers believe that cognitive styles are hardwired in one's personality and therefore are fairly fixed, and even has a physiological substrate (Riding, 2001). Others treat style as reflecting how the person interacts with a class of tasks, and thus cannot be separated from specific functional environments; in other words, style is sensitive to context and subject to change (Biggs, 2001). Whether we consider style as a baggage one brings to performance or learning contexts or as an emergent characteristic inherently contextual has profound implications for how we measure and assess styles in research, and how we provide proper instruction and counseling in practical settings. Given that various styles may have their unique origins and developmental trajectories, it is possible that some styles have an *innate* quality, and is thus more stable and invariant across situations, whereas others may be emergent and dynamic, reflecting both the person and the task involved. For instance, Pask's (1976) *versatile style* of shifting strategies based on task demands show the adaptive side of style. Understanding the nature of specific style construct, its adaptive value, and its stability and change becomes crucial if we are to give it a more privileged status in guiding education. Yet, we know precious little about this matter.

LIMITATIONS OF THE STYLE RESEARCH

Most of the style research in the field has used gifted and "nongifted" comparative designs. Kanevsky (1995) cautioned that "the pursuit of consistent group differences that can be used to distinguish gifted and non-gifted students will continued to be frustrated by the uniqueness of innate abilities and experiences" (p. 63). This caution also applies to research on style issues in the field. Group comparisons between gifted and nongifted are still a dominant design in research. It can easily lead to simplistic but unwarranted conclusions (Kanevsky, 1995). Group comparison designs also sabotage the impetus for style research, which initially was intended to break a mental set or fixation with differential conceptions and measurements of ability in that psychometric measures only assess *products*, not *processes*, assuming competence as reflecting *capacity*, not *performance*. Although links between specific ability and style constructs can be made through investigation, the unqualified, default assumption that intellectually gifted students based on IQ or achievement are a homogeneous group and differ from the rest of students in terms of cognitive and learning styles is unwarranted. Comparative research will do well to bear in mind within-group variations when investigating between group differences. Ultimately, to investigate style is to examine an intimate form of individuality that can only be observed through carefully designed tasks and settings.

There also is a lack of integration between research on style and broader issues of gifted education and talent development. Taken together, the style research in the field is largely descriptive, sporadic, and isolated. If this trend continues, it is inevitable that style will become a peripheral concern in the field, as it is always a difficult topic to research, and its relevance and importance to giftedness and gifted education will remain opaque.

MAJOR RESOURCES AND REFERENCES

Messick (1994) provided an overview of the style construct in the history of psychological research. Riding and Rayner (1998) gave a more comprehensive treatment on the topic of cognitive and learning styles. For more recent, updated reviews of mainstream perspectives on thinking and learning styles, see an edited volume by Sternberg and Zhang (2001) and a coauthored book by Zhang and Sternberg (2006). Of particular interest to giftedness, Kogan (1983) provided a developmental view on cognitive style, with a focus on risk taking and creativity. Milgram, Dunn, and Price (1993) published an edited volume entitled *Teaching and Counseling Gifted and Talented Adolescents: An International Learning Style Perspective*, although it was criticized for making many claims that are not empirically supported (Ramsay, 1995).

SUMMARY OF MAIN POINTS

- Style reflects self-organizing principle in one's interaction with the environment, rather than mere description of isolated, static personal characteristics.
- Stylistic functioning in learning and achievement settings can have both cognitive and affective origins, and can be cognition-based, motivation-based, or personality-based.
- Style and ability have an intricate relationship. Some styles may have an ability component; certain stylistic functioning may result from a unique configuration of abilities, and can be seen as showing gifted potential relative to specific lines of work or study.

- Gifted children defined by test scores are not homogeneous in terms of stylistic functioning; two children with identical IQ scores may nevertheless have very different thinking and learning styles.
- Instructional adaptations should include considerations of students' stylistic functioning; match and mismatch of the learner's and teacher's style affects educational outcomes.
- Some domains and fields may demand specific modes of functioning, and therefore one should see style as a pervasive factor in talent development.
- There are many unanswered questions due to conceptual and methodological difficulties involved in the style research.
- A complete understanding of stylistic functioning involves integration of biological disposition, socialization, and dynamics of person-situation (or task) fit.

REFERENCES

Bamberger, J. (1986). Cognitive issues in the development of musically gifted children. In R. J. Sternberg & J. E. Davidson (Eds.), *Conceptions of giftedness* (pp. 388–413). New York: Cambridge University Press.

Biggs, J. (2001). Enhancing learning: A matter of style or approach? In R. J. Sternberg & L. Zhang (Eds.), *Perspectives on thinking, learning, and cognitive styles* (pp. 73–102). Mahwah, NJ: Lawrence Erlbaum.

Boulton-Lewis, G. M., Marton, F., & Wilss, L. A. (2001). The lived space of learning: An inquiry into indigenous Australian university students' experiences of studying. In R. J. Sternberg & L. Zhang (Eds.), *Perspectives on thinking, learning, and cognitive styles* (pp. 137–164). Mahwah, NJ: Lawrence Erlbaum.

Cronbach, L. J. (1977). *Educational psychology* (3rd ed.). New York: Harcourt Brace Jovanovich.

Dai, D. Y. (2000). To be or not be (challenged), that is the question: Task and ego orientations among high-ability, high-achieving adolescents. *Journal of Experimental Education, 68,* 311–330.

Davis, J. K. (1991). Educational implications of field dependence-independence. In S. Wapner & J. Demick (Eds.), *Field dependence-independence: Cognitive style across the life span* (pp. 149–176). Hillsdale, NJ: Lawrence Erlbaum.

Dunn, R., Dunn, K., & Price, G. E. (1989). *Learning style inventory.* Lawrence, KS: Price Systems.

Dweck, C. S. (1999). *Self theories: Their role in motivation, personality, and development.* Philadelphia: Psychology Press.

Gardner, R. W. (1953). Cognitive styles in categorizing behavior. *Journal of Personality, 22,* 214–233.

Grigorenko, E. L., & Sternberg, R. J. (1997). Styles of thinking, abilities, and academic performance. *Exceptional Children, 63,* 295–312.

Kanevsky, L. (1995). Learning potentials of gifted students. *Roeper Review, 17,* 157–163.

Kline, P. (1995). A critical review of the measurement of personality and intelligence. In D. H. Saklofske & M. Zeidner (Eds.), *International handbook of personality and intelligence* (pp. 505–524). New York: Plenum Press.

Kogan, N. (1983). Stylistic variations in childhood and adolescence: Creativity, metaphor, and cognitive style. In J. H. Flavell & E. M. Markman (Eds.), *Handbook of child psychology: Cognitive development* (4th ed., Vol. 3, pp. 630–706). New York: Wiley.

Kolb, D. A. (1971). *Individual learning styles and the learning process.* Cambridge, MA: MIT Press.

Kolb, D. A., Boyatzis, R. E., & Mainemelis, C. (2001). Experiential learning theory: Previous research and new directions. In R. J. Sternberg & L. Zhang (Eds.), *Perspectives on thinking, learning, and cognitive styles* (pp. 227–247). Mahwah, NJ: Lawrence Erlbaum.

Labouvie-Vief, G. (1990). Wisdom as integrated thoughts: Historical and developmental perspectives. In R. J. Sternberg (Ed.), *Wisdom: Its nature, origins, and development* (pp. 52–83). Cambridge, England: Cambridge University Press.

Labouvie-Vief, G., & Gonzalez, M. M. (2004). Dynamic integration: Affect optimization and differentiation in development. In D. Y. Dai & R. J. Sternberg (Eds.), *Motivation, emotion, and cognition: Integrative perspectives on intellectual functioning and development* (pp. 237–272). Mahwah, NJ: Lawrence Erlbaum.

Lohman, D. F. (1994). Spatially gifted, verbally inconvenienced. In N. Colangelo, S. G. Assouline, & D. L. Ambroson (Eds.), *Talent development* (Vol. 2, pp. 251–263). Dayton: Ohio Psychology Press.

Lohman, D. F., & Bosma, A. (2002). Using cognitive measurement models in the assessment of cognitive styles. In D. N. Jackson & H. I. Braun (Eds.), *The role of constructs in psychological and educational measurement* (pp. 127–146). Mahwah, NJ: Lawrence Erlbaum.

Lubinski, D., & Benbow, C. P. (1992). Gender differences in abilities and preferences among the gifted. *Current Directions in Psychological Science, 1,* 61–66.

Messick, S. (1994). The matter of style: Manifestations of personality in cognition, learning, and teaching. *Educational Psychologist, 29,* 121–136.

Milgram, R. M., Dunn, R. S., & Price, G. E. (1993). *Teaching and counseling gifted and talented adolescents: An international learning style perspective.* Westport, CT: Praeger.

Miller, A. I. (1996). *Insights of genius: Imagery and creativity in science and art.* New York: Springer-Verlag.

O'Boyle, M. W., Benbow, C. P., & Alexander, J. E. (1995). Sex differences, hemispheric laterality, and associated brain activity in the intellectual gifted. *Developmental Neuropsychology, 11,* 415–443.

Pask, G. (1976). Styles and strategies of learning. *British Journal of Educational Psychology, 46,* 128–148.

Pask, G. (1988). Learning strategies, teaching strategies, and conceptual and learning style. In R. R. Schmeck (Ed.), *Learning strategies and learning styles* (pp. 83–100). New York: Plenum.

Piirto, J. (1998). *Understanding those who create* (2nd ed.). Dayton, OH: Gifted Psychology Press.

Ramsay, M. C. (1995). Teaching and counseling gifted and talented adolescents: An international learning style perspective. *PsycCRITIQUES, 40*(2).

Renzulli, J. S., & Dai, D. Y. (2001). Abilities, interests, and styles as aptitudes for learning: A person-situation interaction perspective. In R. J. Sternberg & L. Zhang (Eds.), *Perspectives on thinking, learning, and cognitive styles* (pp. 23–46). Mahwah, NJ: Lawrence Erlbaum.

Riding, R. (2001). The nature and effects of cognitive style. In R. J. Sternberg & L. Zhang (Eds.), *Perspectives on thinking, learning, and cognitive styles* (pp. 47–72). Mahwah, NJ: Lawrence Erlbaum.

Riding, R. J., & Rayner, S. G. (1998). *Cognitive styles and learning strategies: Understanding style differences in learning and behavior*. London: D. Fulton.

Runco, M. A. (2005). Creative giftedness. In R. J. Sternberg & J. E. Davidson (Eds.), *Conceptions of giftedness* (2nd ed., pp. 295–311). New York: Cambridge University Press.

Schuler, P. (2002). Perfectionism in gifted children and adolescents. In M. Neihart, S. M. Reis, N. M. Robinson, & S. M. Moon (Eds.), *The social and emotional development of gifted children: What do we know?* (pp. 71–79). Waco, TX: Prufrock Press.

Snow, C. P. (1967). *The two cultures and a second look*. London: Cambridge University Press.

Snow, R. E. (1994). Aptitude development and talent achievement. In N. Colangelo, S. G. Assouline, & D. L. Ambroson (Eds.), *Talent development* (Vol. 2, pp. 101–120). Dayton: Ohio Psychology Press.

Sternberg, R. J., & Grigorenko, E. L. (1993). Thinking styles and the gifted. *Roeper Review, 16*, 122–130.

Sternberg, R. J., & Grigorenko, E. L. (2001). A capsule history of theory and research on styles. In R. J. Sternberg & L.-F. Zhang (Eds.), *Perspectives on thinking, learning, and cognitive styles* (pp. 1–21). Mahwah, NJ: Lawrence Erlbaum Associates.

Sternberg, R. J., & Zhang, L.-F. (2001). *Perspectives on thinking, learning, and cognitive styles*. Mahwah, NJ: Lawrence Erlbaum.

West, T. G. (1991). *In the mind's eye: Visual thinkers, gifted people with learning difficulties, computer images, and the ironies of creativity*. Buffalo, NY: Prometheus Books.

Wilkinson, S. C. (1993). WISC-R profiles of children with superior intellectual ability. *Gifted Child Quarterly, 37*, 84–91.

Winner, E. (2000). The origins and ends of giftedness. *American Psychologist, 55*, 159–169.

Witkin, H. A., & Goodenough, D. R. (1981). *Cognitive styles: Essence and origins—Field dependence and field independence*. New York: International Universities Press.

Zhang, L.-F., & Sternberg, R. J. (2006). *The nature of intellectual styles*. Mahwah, NJ: Lawrence Erlbaum.

Zuckerman, M. (2004). The shaping of personality: Genes, environments, and chance encounters. *Journal of Personality Assessment, 82*, 11–22.

Chapter 47

TWICE-EXCEPTIONAL LEARNERS

M. Layne Kalbfleisch and Carolyn M. Iguchi

he field has held a long interest in the gifted child with learning disabilities (Elkind, 1973; Whitmore,1980; Whitmore & Maker, 1985). These children often are referred to as *paradoxical learners* (Tannenbaum, 1983; Tannenbaum & Baldwin, 1983) because they may demonstrate inefficiency with basic types of cognitive processes, yet function intellectually at very high and even superior levels of skill and expertise. Despite this interest, much of what we understand about the twice-exceptional learner comes from observations in clinical and counseling settings, research within specific areas of talent, and observations from the classroom. Little is known about the physiological origins of twice-exceptionality, an area of research that has the greatest potential to contribute to our understanding of this special population and how to best serve their needs. The defining characteristic of a twice-exceptional learner is evidence of high performance or potential in a gift, talent, or ability combined with a disability that suppresses the student's ability to achieve according to his or her potential (Brody & Mills, 1997).

GIFTEDNESS ACROSS DISABILITIES

The first disability that comes to mind when describing a twice-exceptional student is a learning disability. Other types of disorders contributing to the inability of gifted students to reach their potential include but are not limited to: dyslexia, auditory processing problems, visual processing deficits, emotional and behavioral disabilities, and autism spectrum disorders. Another chapter (see Kalbfleisch and Banasiak, ADHD chapter, this volume) provides a separate elaboration on giftedness and Attention Deficit/Hyperactivity Disorder (ADHD).

Learning Disabilities

Although specific disabilities and their definitions follow in this discussion, a general list of descriptors for twice-exceptional learners with learning disabilities includes the following (McEachern & Bornot, 2001; Silverman, 1989):
- above-grade-level and extensive vocabulary;
- good listening comprehension skills;
- strong verbal expression;
- poor or illegible handwriting;
- struggle with spelling basic words;
- difficult time sitting still (hyperactivity, impulsivity, inattentiveness);
- can become deeply immersed in special interests and creative activities;
- reason abstractly and solve complex problems;
- may display sophisticated sense of humor;
- display divergent thinking skills;
- use novel problem-solving strategies;
- can be easily bored and frustrated with grade-level school work in subjects where they are strong;
- dislike rote memorization;
- difficult time engaging in social aspects of the classroom;
- low self-concept;
- confusion caused by mix of special abilities that can lead to frustration and a sense of isolation and unhappiness; and
- teachers may perceive them as more quiet, asocial, and less accepted by others than gifted students.

The Wechsler Intelligence Scale for Children, Third Edition (WISC-III), a widely utilized IQ test, has 13 subtests with scores ranging from 1 to 19. The mean for each subtest is 10 and the standard deviation is 3. The scores of the individual subtests are averaged to create a Verbal IQ, a Performance IQ, and a Full Scale IQ. Typically, a 9-point discrepancy between the highest and lowest scores on the subtest indicates that a student has a learning disability and justifies the allocation of remedial services for a given student. However, a gifted student with a 9-point discrepancy may not receive services because the lower score is still within the "normal" range (Silverman, 2000).

From the research on the psychometric characterization of these types of students, we know that there will be more discrepancies and variability on the WISC subtests than that of a student who is only gifted or who only has a learning disability (Barton & Starnes, 1988; Schiff, Kaufman, & Kaufman, 1981; Waldron & Saphire, 1990, 1992). This is a highly heterogeneous population. For instance, in one study, higher IQ boys exhibited behaviors resembling boys with learning disabilities (Shaywitz et al., 2001).

These students tend to exhibit strengths in the verbal domain rather than the performance domain and are marked by average or substandard performance on WISC Freedom from Distractibility subtests such as Digit Span and Coding, which characterize cognitive and motor sequencing ability. Gifted and talented learning-disabled (GT/LD) students often are referred for evaluation or special services much later than average children who exhibit learning problems. Further, most of these referrals come from parents, because teachers do not tend to refer these types of students because they achieve at or above the norm in the classroom.

Dyslexia

Dyslexia is a disorder that impacts both the ability to read and write. Though many understand dyslexia to be a disorder that greatly hampers school learning, others argue that the traits evidenced in dyslexics are mental processes that can serve as valuable gifts (Cooper, Ness, & Smith, 2004; Geschwind & Galaburda, 1987; Winner, Casey, Dasilva, & Hayes, 1991; Winner et al., 2001). Although the classic GT/LD student exhibits higher verbal aptitude scores versus performance skills when assessed psychometrically, gifted students with dyslexia will display the opposite tendencies. Gifted students with dyslexia may experience difficulty with the sequencing and verbal abilities that would make them proficient readers, but they excel with performance-based tasks that require facility with blocks, visual design, and spatial activities. Functional neuroimaging studies have begun to document the physiological mechanisms of dyslexia in the human brain (Pammer, Hansen, Holliday, & Cornelissen, 2006; Shaywitz et al., 1998; Zeffiro & Eden, 2000). A structural neuroimaging study of the brains of one family with a high incidence of dyslexia and concomitant visual spatial talent provides evidence of differences in the parietal operculum (the auditory association cortex), an area of the brain involved in language processing (Craggs, Sanchez, Kibby, Gilger, & Hynd, 2006). Although this study is conducted within one family, it suggests a correlational relationship between the presence of dyslexia, superior nonverbal performance IQ, and atypical development in this area of the brain.

Auditory Processing Problems

Central auditory processing disorder (CAPD) is defined as the inability to attend to, discriminate, recognize, remember, or comprehend auditory information, despite normal intelligence and hearing ability (Arehole & Rigo, 1999). Gifted children with auditory processing problems have been shown to have short-term auditory memory, and difficulty with auditory sequencing and auditory discrimination. These types of difficulties can impact their formal language abilities. An electrophysiological study by Arehole and Rigo (1999) revealed that low-achieving gifted students were significantly different from high-achieving gifted students in the way their brains discriminated auditory information. This finding validates this type of twice-exceptional student and is useful to researchers who seek to develop identification procedures for this population based on electrophysiological measures.

Visual Processing Deficits

A visual processing deficit affects the way the brain sorts out visual information. Individuals with visual perception disabilities often have difficulty recognizing, organizing, interpreting, and remembering visual images, even though an eye exam will show 20/20 vision. This particular disability is especially challenging in elementary school because the type of learning emphasized in the early years is centered on symbolic images such as letters and numbers. Students who show discrepancies between verbal and performance scores on the WISC-III often are referred for problems with visual processing deficits. Despite tendencies to progress more slowly in intellectual performance, creative production, and general cognitive development, gifted children with visual processing deficits may demonstrate superior abilities in their rates of learning, memory, communication skills and vocabulary, problem-solving skills, creativity, ease in learning Braille, persistence, motivation, and concentration (Hutchins, 2000; Whitmore & Maker, 1985).

Emotional and Behavioral Disabilities

Despite negative and problematic characteristics of the students with emotional and behavior disabilities (EBD), those who are gifted display high academic ability and creative thought (Morrison, 2001). There are currently no controlled studies that examine the profiles of these types of students in depth.

Autism

Autism is a severely incapacitating developmental disability that affects the brain and appears in the first 3 years of life. Autistic symptoms are observed in an estimated 15 of every 10,000 births. Although there is a higher incidence in boys, autism is not confined to any racial, ethnic, or social background. Despite the belief in the early 20th century that autism was caused by a cold mother-child relationship, it has not been linked to psychological factors in the environment of the child (Cash, 1999).

Autism has been described as a spectrum disorder, meaning that the symptoms occur in a range of severity and every case is unique. This is true of the intelligence levels of people with autism, as well; intelligence in this group ranges from mentally challenged to highly gifted with some people showing savant abilities. Along the autistic spectrum, symptoms have been grouped into several different types: Asperger's syndrome, Kanner-type autism, Pervasive Developmental Disorder, and Regressive/Epileptic-type autism. By definition, the autistic savant and Asperger's syndrome are the two types of autism present with giftedness. Savants have extraordinary abilities in the areas of mathematics or music in the face of other extremely severe social, emotional, and cognitive deficits (Heaton & Wallace, 2004; Kalbfleisch, 2004). In contrast, the mildest form of autism, Asperger's syndrome, can be characterized by poor motor coordination, late mobility, formal speech with adult-like qualities, hypersensitivity to certain sensory stimuli, obsessive-compulsive tendencies, and signs of little or no Theory of Mind, the ability to read social cues and perceive the thoughts and emotions of others (Frith, 2004). Strengths typically associated with Asperger's syndrome that may coexist with giftedness include visual-spatial ability, exceptional memory, and intellectual obsessiveness on specific idiosyncratic topics of interest (Neihart, 2000).

Recent public interest in autism, along with higher rates of identification of the disorder, has increased research interest in this field. However, few studies have examined individuals with autism and concurrently high IQ. The rare incidence of individuals with autism exhibiting IQ scores in the gifted range may account for the paucity of research. That said, emergence of research using magnetic resonance imaging (MRI) and functional magnetic resonance imaging (fMRI) are helping elucidate the autistic brain. Of note are imaging studies that explore brain connectivity, brain structure, and activation of brain regions during cognitive tasks for individuals with autism spectrum disorders (Cherkassky, Kana, Keller, & Just, 2006; Dichter & Belger, 2007; Hardan, Muddasani, Vemulapalli, Keshavan, & Minshew, 2006; Just, Cherkassky, Keller, Kana, & Minshew, 2007; Kana, Keller, Minshew, & Just, 2007; Kennedy, Redcay, & Courchesne, 2006; Turner, Frost, Linsenbardt, McIlroy, & Müller, 2006).

One connectivity study by Cherkassky and colleagues (2006) examined the resting brain in individuals with high-functioning autism compared with matched controls. They determined that although both groups have similar resting-state neural networks (brain activation associated with a relaxed awake resting state) relating to volume and organization, the networks of individuals with autism were more loosely connected. In a study on executive function, participants completed tasks requiring planning and goal-management abilities. Individuals with autism displayed less brain connectivity compared to matched controls resulting in lower degree of information integration (Just et al., 2007). Turner and colleagues (2006) examined systems in the brain known as the caudate nuclei, a motor area of the brain associated with aspects of attention, learning, and memory. For individuals with autism, these systems were less pronounced or altogether absent, compared to matched controls.

Differences in brain structure may explain the issue of less coherent brain connectivity. A structural MRI study by Hardan and colleagues (2006) observed greater total cerebral sulcal and gyral thickness in children with autism compared to healthy controls. The researchers hypothesize this cortical thickness contributes to the increased gray matter volume and brain size observed in children with autism.

Functional magnetic resonance imaging (fMRI) enables researchers to examine the areas of the brain called into action during cognitive processing. This technology reveals several functional abnormalities present in autism. Dichter and Belger (2007) used the flanker task to examine executive function and attentional control in subjects with autism and Asperger's syndrome. In this task, participants are required to indicate the direction of the center arrow in a series as quickly as possible without sacrificing accuracy. Sometimes same-direction arrows (i.e., < < $\underline{<}$ < <) and sometimes opposite-direction arrows (> > $\underline{<}$ > >) flank the center arrow (underlined). In this study, the participants completed the classic version of the task, as well as a version where faces looking left or right replaced the arrows. During the arrow condition, participants with autism and Asperger's syndrome exhibited similar brain activation as healthy controls. The neurotypical subjects recruited the same brain regions for the "face" task as the arrow task, but participants with autism showed markedly reduced activation in the face version of the task. The authors conclude that social-cognitive stimuli (in this case, faces) interfere with brain functioning during cognitive control tasks for individuals with autism.

In a similar study, Kana et al. (2007) found that for a task of response inhibition (the ability to withhold or refrain from giving a response), participants with autism showed less brain activation in areas of the brain known to be active in inhibition tasks, but more activation in the premotor cortex. This indicates that individuals with autism may call upon different areas of the brain to perform tasks compared with neurotypical individuals. Continuing this line of research, Kennedy et al. (2006) examined brain activity during rest compared to activity during cognitively challenging tasks. There are several areas of the brain that are known to activate more highly during rest, then deactivate during active cognitive processing. However, for participants with autism, the state of activation remained constant. Kennedy and colleagues believe this lack of deactivation contributes to the social and emotional deficits in autism.

In sum, brain imaging studies are just beginning to allow us inside the brains of individuals with autism and are providing evidence for the structural and functional differences behind autistic behaviors. Future research may help us to understand whether gifted individuals with autism use strategies to overcome atypical brain function, or if their brain processes are more similar to those of neurotypical individuals.

KEY ISSUES

Theory and research in the area of twice-exceptionality has focused on three key areas: (1) appropriate identification, (2) instruction in compensation strategies and disability remediation, and (3) the need for social and emotional support and talent development.

Appropriate Identification

For many gifted students with learning disabilities, their giftedness and disability merge to create the illusion of an average student. It has been found that 41% of gifted students with various learning disabilities are not diagnosed until college (McEachern & Bornot, 2001). A commonly used method of identification for twice-exceptional students that warrants caution is profile analysis. Profile analysis is the practice of interpreting differences among subtests of intelligence scales as evidence of a differential and distinct pattern of cognitive function in a student (McCoach, Kehle, Bray, & Siegle, 2001). This practice can be misleading because IQ tests may not be sensitive enough to determine significant discrepancies between subtest scores, particularly for gifted populations (Kavale & Forness, 1984). A student's giftedness may mask a major area of weakness and vice versa.

Tallent-Runnels and Sigler (1995) surveyed gifted program coordinators in Texas to determine if students were being identified properly. They found 19.7% of the districts reported having gifted students with learning disabilities. Of those districts, approximately 75% had made modifications to the selection process in order to identify these students. The districts reporting an overall lower percentage of gifted students were less likely to identify gifted children with learning disabilities among their gifted population. Linking appropriate assessment and identification to programmatic strategies for intervention and talent development remains a challenge at both local and state levels (Brody & Mills, 2004; Coleman & Gallagher, 1995; Weinfeld, Barnes-Robinson, Jeweler, & Shevitz, 2002; Yewchuck & Lupart, 2000).

Compensation and Remediation

Twice-exceptional learners can be puzzling students. They are particularly vulnerable during transitions from one level of education to the next. One program in New Mexico was designed to follow students from the elementary level through high school (Nielsen, Higgins, Wilkinson, & Wiest Webb, 1994). The program consisted of three key components: (1) the creation of a transition plan to emphasize giftedness, as well as the need for remediation; (2) an emphasis on collaboration among high school professionals including a case manager who was responsible for facilitating communication between counselors, special educators, gifted educators, and general educators, connecting the students with resources and technology tools to compensate for their weaknesses, and working with the general education teachers to provide appropriate modifications for their students; and (3) the provision of unique course options for twice-exceptional students that provided them with access to magnet high school math, science, and summer courses to aid transition from middle to high school.

Reis and Neu (1994) sought to understand the types of educational interventions, assistance programs, and strategies that help make twice-exceptional students successful in college. They found that all of the students used compensation strategies such as talking to professors, using other student's notes to supplement their own, taking fewer classes, taking advantage of extended time for testing, and consistently utilizing technology to compensate for their weaknesses. Parental support was found to be most important to all of the students in the study, as was participation in a university learning-disability program. Finally, all of these students attributed their success to their willingness to work harder than their peers to obtain the same level of results.

Social and Emotional Support

Students who are gifted and have learning disabilities are at a greater risk for social isolation and poor self-esteem due to poor performance and frustration. Dole (2000) studied the resiliency and risk factors of twice-exceptional students. The factors placing students in this population at risk are a poor self-concept, poor self-efficacy, hypersensitivity, emotionality, and high levels of frustration, anxiety, or self-criticism. The characteristics that seem to buffer twice-exceptional students are personality factors such as self-esteem and high self-efficacy, the exercise of the student's abilities, parental characteristics that foster self-esteem in the child, the presence of other supportive adults, and opportunities at major life transitions.

IMPLICATIONS

Research on twice-exceptional learners holds great promise for students who struggle to reach their potential because of a limiting disability. Although the literature provides characterizations and suggestions for meeting the needs of these types of individuals, there is a paucity of empirical evidence informing what we know about this population. Well-controlled studies are still needed to determine the effectiveness of intervention strategies already in use for twice-exceptional learners. There is a great need for the medical and psychological fields to broaden their definition of atypical function to include the twice-exceptional (Gilger & Kaplan, 2001; Kalbfleisch, in press). Fundamental, empirical research on twice-exceptionality and the cognitive and neurobiological factors that define each type could aid in greater recognition of this special group by mainstream educators and educational policy makers.

WHAT WE KNOW ABOUT TWICE-EXCEPTIONALITY

- Behavioral observation and clinical, psychometric assessment are the basis of much of what is understood about twice-exceptionality.
- Emerging neuroscientific evidence denotes the advent of our ability to understand the physiological underpinnings for high-ability dyslexia and central auditory processing disorder. This type of evidence is necessary to further legitimize the presence of these concomitant profiles in children.
- It is important to broaden the identification and service processes for twice-exceptional students. Even when proper identification occurs, many state policies do not permit schools to be reimbursed twice for one student, thus restricting access to available services.

DIRECTIONS FOR FUTURE STUDY OF TWICE-EXCEPTIONALITY

- Epidemiological studies are needed to document the prevalence of twice-exceptional students in the nation's schools, both public and private.
- Because of lack of agreement on basic definitions of giftedness, a general framework would aid inquiry into instances of twice-exceptionality (Gilger & Wilkins, in press).
- Hypothesis-driven, large-sample, longitudinal, and cross-sectional studies are needed in order to continue to examine the physiological

foundations of these disorders as they are expressed in high-achieving populations.

- As emerging findings from the neurosciences mature, funding mechanisms for translational research will be required to innovate identification procedures, interventions, and school policies that will recognize these types of students for strategic academic and affective support.

SUGGESTED RESOURCES

Kay, K. (2000). *Uniquely gifted: Identifying and meeting the needs of the twice-exceptional student*. Gilsum, NH: Avocus.

Newman, T. M., & Sternberg, R. J. (2004). *Students with both gifts and learning disabilities: Identification, assessment, and outcomes*. New York: Kluwer Academic/Plenum.

Olenchak, F. R. (1994). Talent development: Accommodating the social and emotional needs of secondary gifted/learning disabled students. *Journal of Secondary Gifted Education, 5*(3), 40–52.

Reis, S. M., & Ruban, L. M. (2004). Compensation strategies used by high ability students with learning disabilities. In T. A. Newman & R. J. Sternberg (Eds.), *Students with both gifts and learning disabilities: Identification, assessment, and outcomes* (pp. 155–198). New York: Springer.

Winebrenner, S. (2003). Teaching strategies for twice exceptional students. *Intervention in School and Clinic, 38*(3), 131–137.

REFERENCES

Arehole, S., & Rigo, T. G. (1999). Auditory evoked potentials in low-achieving gifted adolescents. *Roeper Review, 22*, 51–56.

Barton, J. M., & Starnes, W. T. (1988). Identifying distinguishing characteristics of gifted and talented/learning disabled students. *Roeper Review, 12*, 23–29.

Brody, L. E., & Mills, C. J. (1997). Gifted children with learning disabilities: A review of the issues. *Journal of Learning Disabilities, 30*, 282–297.

Brody, L. E., & Mills, C. J. (2004). Linking assessment and diagnosis to intervention for gifted students with learning disabilities. In T. M. Newman & R. J. Sternberg (Eds.), *Students with both gifts and learning disabilities: Identification, assessment, and outcomes* (pp. 73–94). New York: Kluwer Academic/Plenum.

Cash, A. B. (1999). A profile of gifted individuals with autism: The twice-exceptional learner. *Roeper Review, 22*, 22–27.

Cherkassky, V. L., Kana, R. K., Keller, T. A., & Just, M. A. (2006). Functional connectivity in a baseline resting-state network in autism. *NeuroReport, 17*, 1687–1690.

Coleman, M. R., & Gallagher, J. J. (1995). State identification policies: Gifted students from special populations. *Roeper Review, 17*, 268–275.

Cooper, E. E., Ness, M., & Smith, M. (2004). A case study of a child with dyslexia and spatial-temporal gifts. *Gifted Child Quarterly, 48*, 83–94.

Craggs, J. G., Sanchez, J., Kibby, M. Y., Gilger, J. W., & Hynd, G. W. (2006). Brain morphology and neuropsychological profiles in a family displaying dyslexia and superior nonverbal intelligence. *Cortex, 42*, 1107–1118.

Dichter, G. S., & Belger, A. (2007). Social stimuli interfere with cognitive control in autism. *NeuroImage, 35*, 1219–1230.

Dole, S. (2000). The implications of the risk and resilience literature for gifted students with learning disabilities. *Roeper Review, 23*, 91–96.

Elkind, J. (1973). The gifted child with learning disabilities. *Gifted Child Quarterly, 17*, 96–97.

Frith, U. (2004). Emanuel Miller Lecture: Confusions and controversies about Asperger syndrome. *Journal of Child Psychology and Psychiatry, 45*, 672–686.

Geschwind, N., & Galaburda, A. M. (1987). *Cerebral lateralization: Biological mechanisms, associations, and pathology.* Cambridge, MA: MIT Press.

Gilger, J. W., & Kaplan, B. J. (2001). Atypical brain development: A conceptual framework for understanding developmental learning disabilities. *Developmental Neuropsychology, 20*, 465–481.

Gilger, J., & Wilkins, M. (in press). Neurodevelopmental variation as a cause of learning disabilities. In M. Mody & E. Silliman (Eds.), *Language impairment and reading disability: Interactions among brain, behavior, and experience.* New York: Guilford Press.

Hardan, A. Y., Muddasani, S., Vemulapalli, M., Keshavan, M. S., & Minshew, N. J. (2006). An MRI study of increased cortical thickness in autism. *American Journal of Psychiatry, 163*, 1290–1292.

Heaton, P., & Wallace, G. L. (2004). Annotation: The savant syndrome. *Journal of Child Psychology and Psychiatry, 45*, 899–911.

Hutchins, R. E. (2000). Visual processing deficits in the gifted. In K. Kay (Ed.), *Uniquely gifted: Identifying and meeting the needs of the twice-exceptional student* (pp. 166–168). Gilsum, NH: Avocus.

Just, M. A., Cherkassky, V. L., Keller, T. A., Kana, R. K., & Minshew, N. J. (2007). Functional and anatomical cortical underconnectivity in autism: Evidence from an fMRI study of an executive function task and corpus callosum morphometry. *Cerebral Cortex, 17*, 951–961.

Kalbfleisch, M. L. (2004). The functional anatomy of talent. *The Anatomical Record (Part B: The New Anatomist), 277B*, 21–36.

Kalbfleisch, M. L. (in press). The neural plasticity of giftedness. In L. Shavinina (Ed.), *Handbook on giftedness.* New York: Springer Science.

Kana, R. K., Keller, T. A., Minshew, N. J., & Just, M. A. (2007). Inhibitory control in high-functioning autism: Decreased activation and underconnectivity in inhibition networks. *Biological Psychiatry, 62*, 198–206.

Kavale, K. A., & Forness, S. R. (1984). A meta-analysis of the validation of Wechsler Scale profiles and recategorizations: Patterns or parodies? *Learning Disabilities Quarterly, 7*, 136–156.

Kennedy, D. P., Redcay, E., & Courchesne, E. (2006). Failing to deactivate: Resting functional abnormalities in autism. *Proceedings of the National Academy of Sciences of the United States of America, 103*, 8275–8280.

McCoach, D. B., Kehle, T. J., Bray, M. A., & Siegle, D. (2001). Best practices in the identification of gifted students with learning disabilities. *Psychology in the Schools, 38*, 403–411.

McEachern, A. G., & Bornot, J. (2001). Gifted students with learning disabilities: Implications and strategies for school counselors. *Professional School Counseling, 5*(1), 34–41.

Morrison, W. F. (2001). Emotional/behavioral disabilities and gifted and talented behaviors: Paradoxical or semantic differences in characteristics? *Psychology in the Schools, 38,* 425–431.

Neihart, M. (2000). Gifted children with Asperger's syndrome. *Gifted Child Quarterly, 44,* 222–229.

Nielsen, M. E., Higgins, L. D., Wilkinson, S. C., & Wiest Webb, K. (1994). Helping twice-exceptional students to succeed in high school: A program description. *Journal of Secondary Gifted Education, 5*(3), 35–39.

Pammer, K., Hansen, P., Holliday, I., Cornelissen, P. (2006). Attentional shifting and the role of the dorsal pathway in visual word recognition. *Neuropsychologica, 44,* 2926–2936.

Reis, S. M., & Neu, T. W. (1994). Factors involved in the academic success of high ability university students with learning disabilities. *Journal of Secondary Gifted Education, 5*(3), 60–74.

Schiff, M. M., Kaufman, A. S., & Kaufman, N. L. (1981). Scatter analysis of WISC-R profiles for learning disabled children with superior intelligence. *Journal of Learning Disabilities, 14,* 400–404.

Shaywitz, S. E., Shaywitz, B. A., Pugh, K. R., Fulbright, R. K., Constable, R. T., Einar Mencl, W. E., et al. (1998). Functional disruption in the organization of the brain for reading in dyslexia. *Proceedings of the National Academy of Sciences, 95,* 2636–2641.

Shaywitz, S. E., Holahan, J. M., Freudenheim, D. A., Fletcher, J. M., Makuch, R. W., & Shaywitz, B. A. (2001). Heterogeneity within the gifted: Higher IQ boys exhibit behaviors resembling boys with learning disabilities. *Gifted Child Quarterly, 45,* 16–23.

Silverman, L. K. (1989). Invisible gifts, invisible handicaps. *Roeper Review, 12,* 37–42.

Silverman, L. K. (2000). The two-edged sword of compensation: How the gifted cope with learning disabilities. In K. Kay (Ed.), *Uniquely gifted: Identifying and meeting the needs of the twice-exceptional student* (pp. 153–165). Gilsum, NH: Avocus Publishing.

Tallent-Runnels, M. K., & Sigler, E. A. (1995). Gifted students with learning disabilities: The status of the selection of gifted students with learning disabilities for gifted programs. *Roeper Review, 17,* 246–247.

Tannenbaum, A. J. (1983). *Gifted children: Psychological and educational perspectives.* New York: Macmillan.

Tannenbaum, A. J., & Baldwin, L. J. (1983). Giftedness and learning disability: A paradoxical combination. In L. H. Fox, L. Brody, & D. Tobin (Eds.), *Learning-disabled gifted children: Identification and programming* (pp. 11–36). Baltimore: University Park Press.

Turner, K. C., Frost, L., Linsenbardt, D., McIlroy, J. R., & Müller, R. A. (2006). Atypically diffuse functional connectivity between caudate nuclei and cerebral cortex in autism. *Behavioral and Brain Functions, 2*(34). Retrieved March 22, 2007, from http://www.behavioralandbrainfunctions.com/content/2/1/34

Waldron, K. A., & Saphire, D. G. (1990). An analysis of WISC-R factors for gifted students with learning disabilities. *Journal of Learning Disabilities, 23,* 491–498.

Waldron, K. A., & Saphire, D. G. (1992). Perceptual and academic patterns of learning-disabled/gifted students. *Perceptual and Motor Skills, 74,* 599–609.

Weinfeld, R., Barnes-Robinson, L., Jeweler, S., Shevitz, B. (2002). Academic programs for gifted and talented/learning disabled students. *Roeper Review, 24,* 226–233.

Whitmore, J. R. (1980). *Giftedness, conflict, and underachievement.* Boston: Allyn & Bacon.

Whitmore, J., & Maker, C. J. (1985). *Intellectual giftedness in disabled persons.* Austin, TX: PRO-ED.

Winner, E., Casey, M. B., Dasilva, D., & Hayes, R. (1991). Spatial abilities and reading deficits in visual art students. *Empirical Studies of the Arts, 9,* 51–63.

Winner, E., Von Károlyi, C., Malinsky, D., French, L., Seliger, C., Ross, E., et al. (2001). Dyslexia and visual-spatial talents: Compensation and deficit model. *Brain and Language, 76,* 81–110.

Yewchuck, C., & Lupart, J. (2000). Inclusive education for gifted students with disabilities. In K. A. Heller, F. J. Mönks, R. J. Sternberg, & R. F. Subotnik (Eds.), *International handbook of giftedness and talent* (2nd ed., pp. 659–670). Oxford, England: Elsevier Science.

Zeffiro, T., & Eden, G. (2000). The neural basis of developmental dyslexia. *Annals of Dyslexia, 50,* 3–23.

Chapter 48

UNDERACHIEVERS

D. Betsy McCoach and Del Siegle

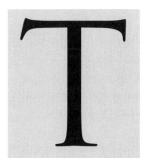he underachievement of academically able students frustrates both parents and teachers. How many gifted and talented students are underachieving and who are they? Why do some gifted and talented students fail to perform at a level commensurate with their abilities? What happens to underachieving gifted students in occupational settings if they do not achieve academically? How can parents and educators help these students reach their potential? Unfortunately, there is no magic solution to the problem of underachievement. This chapter will review the state of research related to these questions, mention several promising practices, and suggest fertile areas for future research.

WHO ARE THE GIFTED UNDERACHIEVERS?

A certain degree of controversy surrounds the processes of defining underachievement and identifying underachieving gifted students. Although no universally agreed upon definition of underachievement currently exists, the most common component of the various definitions of underachievement in gifted students involves identifying a discrepancy between ability or potential (expected performance) and achievement (actual performances; Baum, Renzulli, & Hébert, 1995a; Butler-Por, 1987; Dowdall & Colangelo, 1982; Emerick, 1992; Redding, 1990; Reis & McCoach, 2000; Rimm, 1997a, 1997b; Supplee, 1990; Whitmore, 1980; Wolfle, 1991).

Reis and McCoach (2000) published an extensive review of literature on gifted underachievers and proposed an operational definition of underachievement adopted in several recent empirical studies (Matthews & McBee, 2007; McCoach & Siegle, 2003b; Siegle et al., 2006). They asserted that

> Underachievers are students who exhibit a severe discrepancy between *expected achievement* (as measured by standardized achievement test scores or cognitive or intellectual ability assessments) and *actual achievement* (as measured class grades and teacher evaluations). To be classified as an underachiever, the discrepancy between expected and actual achievement must not be the direct result of a diagnosed learning disability and must persist over an extended period of time. Gifted underachievers are underachievers who exhibit superior scores on measures of expected achievement (i.e., standardized achievement test scores or cognitive or intellectual ability assessments). (p. 157)

Although grades provide less evidence of reliability than standardized measures of academic achievement, they provide the most valid indication of a student's current level of achievement within a classroom environment. Further, students with high ability and low standardized achievement test scores may be underachievers, or they may suffer from undiagnosed learning disabilities. Therefore, gifted students with low standardized achievement test scores should be screened for learning disabilities prior to treating these students as underachievers (Moon & Hall, 1998).

Lau and Chan (2001) compared three statistical methods of identifying underachievers with teacher and peer nominations: (1) *arbitrary absolute split method* (underachievers are defined as students who score higher than a certain minimum measure of ability, but score lower than a certain minimum measure of performance), (2) *simple difference score method* (underachievers are defined as students with a given discrepancy score that is obtained by subtracting a standardized performance score from a standardized ability score), and (3) *regression method* (students who deviate more than one standard error of estimate difference from the regression of achievement on ability). These three methods identified similar students as underachievers. However, teacher and peer nominations identified different students. Lau and Chan concluded that the arbitrary absolute split method was most suitable for studying gifted underachievers because it specifically targets high-ability students. They cautioned that teacher nominations can overlook very high-ability students with average achievement because these students do not perform poorly enough to be recognized as underachievers.

Although many gifted children with high scores on ability measures fail to demonstrate comparable school achievement (Pirozzo, 1982), this is not necessarily unexpected. Ability and achievement are not correlated perfectly (Thorndike, 1963). Intelligence test scores explain only 25% of the variance in school grades (Neisser et al., 1996). This leaves 75% of the fluctuation in achievement test scores unaccounted for by IQ scores. Based on this relationship, a student with an IQ score of 145 (three standard deviations above the mean) would have a predicted achievement of only 1.5 standard deviations above the mean. Therefore, we should expect gifted students to be above average in terms of their achievement, but we should not necessarily expect their achievement to be as exceptionally high as their ability.

EXTENT AND PERSISTENCE OF THE PROBLEM

Without a commonly accepted definition of gifted underachievement, it is impossible to determine how prevalent underachievement is among gifted students. Speculation ranges from 10% to more than 50% (Hoffman, Wasson, & Christianson, 1985; Richert, 1991). The issue is further confused when considering underachievement in academics versus underachievement in non-academic areas (many of which are essential for original contributions to a field; Richert, 1991). Any estimation of the number of gifted underachievers is therefore speculation at best.

How persistent is the problem of underachievement? Although some underachievers become achievers later in their academic or occupational careers, some students maintain a chronic pattern of underachievement. The onset of underachievement often occurs in middle school or junior high school and often persists into high school (Peterson & Colangelo, 1996). A study of academically gifted underachievers and achievers examined the school records of 153 gifted students and analyzed trends in their achievement throughout their secondary school careers (Peterson & Colangelo, 1996). In this study, 45% of the students who were underachieving in grade 7 continued to underachieve throughout junior high and high school. Peterson (2000) conducted a follow-up study of these achievers and underachievers 4 years after high school graduation. High school and college academic achievement were strongly related; the correlation between high school and college achievement was .64. All achievers attended college; 83% of the achievers finished 4 years of college. In contrast, 87% of underachievers attended college; only 52% finished 4 years. The most extreme high school underachievers completed the fewest years of college (mean = 1.33 years). Of the high school underachievers who attended college, 41% improved academically, approximately 44% remained about the same, and 15% experienced a decline in their academic performance.

In the largest longitudinal study of underachievers conducted to date, McCall, Evahn, and Kratzer (1992) found that 13 years after high school, the educational and occupational status of high school underachievers paralleled their grades in high school, rather than their abilities. They also found that underachievers appeared to have greater difficulty completing college and remaining in their jobs and marriages than other students did. In conclusion, although some students are able to reverse their underachievement, many students who become underachievers in junior high school remain underachievers throughout high school, and the effects of this underachievement may persist into college and even into their adult occupations. Therefore, it is imperative that educators and researchers focus on prevention and early intervention of underachievement.

CHARACTERISTICS OF GIFTED UNDERACHIEVERS

Much of the recent research in the area of underachievement has explored the characteristics of underachievers. Although there appear to be several different types of underachievers, factors commonly associated with underachievement include:

- low academic self-perceptions (Freedman, 2000; Matthews & McBee; 2007; Schunk, 1998; Supplee, 1990; Whitmore, 1980) or low self-efficacy (Siegle & McCoach, 2005);
- low self-motivation; low effort toward academic tasks (Albaili, 2003; Baslanti & McCoach, 2006; Lacasse, 1999; Matthews & McBee; 2007; McCoach & Siegle, 2003b; Rayneri, Gerber, & Wiley, 2003; Weiner, 1992);
- external attributions (Carr, Borkowski, & Maxwell, 1991; Siegle & McCoach, 2005);
- low goal-valuation (Baslanti & McCoach, 2006; Freedman, 2000; Lacasse, 1999; Matthews & McBee; 2007; McCall et al., 1992; McCoach & Siegle, 2003b),
- negative attitudes toward school and teachers (Colangelo, Kerr, Christensen, & Maxey, 1993; Ford, 1996; McCoach & Siegle, 2003b; Rimm, 1995); and

- low self-regulatory or metacognitive skills (Carr et al., 1991; Krouse & Krouse, 1981; Yu, 1996).

However, underachievers appear to be a fairly heterogeneous group. Although some underachievers may display low levels of the characteristics named above, other underachievers score high on these measures. Moreover, the variability of motivational and attitudinal measures within samples of underachievers tends to be higher than the variability for comparison groups of average or high achievers. For example, groups of gifted underachievers tend to display significantly more variability on self-report measures of motivation, perceptions, and attitudes than gifted achievers do (McCoach & Siegle, 2003b). The large amount of variability suggests that although underachievers may share some common characteristics, they are not a homogeneous population of students. Each student may underachieve for a somewhat unique combination of reasons; therefore, it is possible that gifted underachievers may be low on only one or two of the many characteristics commonly ascribed to underachievers, and may be average or even high in all other areas. Given the variability among underachievers, several researchers in the area of underachievement have proposed specific subtypes of underachievers (e.g., Mandel & Marcus, 1988, 1995; Rimm, 1995, 1997b; Siegle & McCoach, 2005). Interestingly, some research suggests that underachieving gifted students share more common characteristics with underachievers in general than they do with achieving gifted students (Dowdall & Colangelo, 1982; McCall et al., 1992; You-Lim, 1995).

Generally, underachievers are more likely to be male than female. Across a number of studies of underachievers, the ratio of male underachievers to female underachievers appears to be at least 2:1 (Baker, Bridger, & Evans, 1998; Matthews & McBee, 2007; McCall, 1994; McCoach, 2002; McCoach & Siegle, 2003a, 2003b; Peterson & Colangelo, 1996; Richert, 1991; Siegle et al., 2006). However, Richert suggested twice as many males as females underachieve academically in school, but "over an individual's lifetime, females as a group are the greater underachievers" (1991, p. 145).

FAMILY DYNAMICS

The limited empirical research conducted on the family characteristics of underachieving gifted students suggests that certain types of home environments may be related to the development of students' underachievement patterns (Baker et al., 1998; Brown, Mounts, Lambourn, & Steinberg, 1993; Rimm & Lowe, 1988; Zilli, 1971). For example, inconsistent parenting techniques appear to occur more frequently in the homes of underachieving children (Rimm & Lowe, 1988). Rimm and Lowe studied the family environments of 22 underachieving gifted students. In 95% of the families, one parent emerged as the disciplinarian, and the other parent acted as a protector. Often, opposition between parents increased as the challenger became more authoritarian and the rescuer became increasingly protective. Parents of underachievers tend to be either overly lenient or overly strict (Pendarvis, Howley, & Howley, 1990; Weiner, 1992), or they may vacillate between lenient and strict. In addition, bestowing adult status on a child at too young an age may contribute to the development of underachievement (Fine & Pitts, 1980; Rimm & Lowe, 1988). Therefore, Rimm and Lowe emphasized the importance of maintaining consistency across parents.

Do students underachieve because they come from families in conflict, does the underachievement of the child create problems in the family unit, or is there a dynamic interaction between the underachiever and the family? One qualitative study of gifted urban underachievers and achievers reported that achievers seemed to come from happier homes, whereas the homes of underachievers tended to exhibit more conflict (Reis, Hébert, Diaz, Maxfield, & Ratley, 1995). However, another study comparing the families of underachievers and achievers found families with underachieving gifted students were not any more likely to be dysfunctional than families with achieving gifted students (Green, Fine, & Tollefson, 1988). Interestingly though, dysfunctional families with achieving gifted students reported greater satisfaction with their family lives than did dysfunctional families of underachieving students.

THE INFLUENCE OF PEERS

Peer issues also may contribute to the achievement and underachievement of adolescents. Reis et al. (1995) found high-achieving peers had a positive influence on gifted students who began to underachieve in high school and contributed to some students' reversal of their underachievement. Likewise, negative peer attitudes often relate to underachievement (Clasen & Clasen, 1995; Weiner, 1992). Underachieving students frequently report peer influence as the strongest force impeding their achievement. In one study, 66% of high-ability students named peer pressure or the attitude of the other kids, including friends, as the primary force against getting good grades (Clasen & Clasen, 1995). Several studies with nongifted students also suggest the importance of peer influences on achievement in secondary school. In a national longitudinal study of secondary students (NELS:88), students with friends who cared about learning demonstrated better educational outcomes than those in less educationally oriented peer groups (Chen, 1997). Berndt (1999) measured students' grades and behavior in the fall and spring of one academic year. Berndt found that students seemed to more closely resemble their friends at the end of the school year than they did at the beginning of the school year; students' grades decreased between fall and spring if their friends had lower grades in the fall. Although peer achievement levels do relate to students' academic achievement, it is unclear whether the choice to associate with other nonachievers is a cause or a result of gifted students' underachievement.

UNDERACHIEVEMENT AND SPECIAL POPULATIONS OF GIFTED STUDENTS

The construct of underachievement in gifted students differs across cultures. Unfortunately, limited research has focused specifically on culturally diverse underachievers (Ford, 1992, 1996; Reis et al., 1995). Culturally diverse students face unique barriers to their achievement for several reasons. Minority students are often underrepresented in programs for the gifted and talented (Ford, 1996; Tomlinson, Callahan, & Lelli, 1997). Culturally diverse students continue to face unintentional bias at school and in society at large (Ford, 1996). Further, the definition of achievement in a particular subculture may be very different from that of the dominant culture. Researchers and educators may need to adjust their views of both giftedness and underachievement when attempting to both identify and address the phenomenon within a culturally diverse student population.

Equality of educational opportunity also affects underachievement. Unfortunately, what is viewed as achievement in a poor school may be viewed as underachievement by a more competitive school or by society at large. Students who are not given adequate opportunities to develop their talents often become "involuntary underachievers." Research suggests that quality of schooling (Anderson & Keith, 1997; Baker et al., 1998) and completion of academic coursework (Anderson & Keith, 1997) appear to be significant predictors of achievement for at-risk high school students; each additional academic course results in an increase of one eighth of a standard deviation in predicted academic achievement test scores (Anderson & Keith, 1997).

Researchers have begun to probe the relationships between underachievement, attention deficit disorders, and learning disabilities (Hinshaw, 1992a, 1992b). Students who seem unmotivated may have attention deficits (Busch & Nuttall, 1995) or hidden learning disabilities. Recent research indicates that many twice-exceptional students underachieve in school, and high-ability students also may have learning problems (Barton & Starnes, 1988; Baum, Owen, & Dixon, 1991; Bireley, 1995) or attention deficits (Baum, Olenchak, & Owen, 1998) that may result in low academic achievement.

A recent study compared the prevalence of inattention and impulsivity/hyperactivity on the ADHD home and school rating scales (DuPaul, Power, Anastapoulos, & Reid, 1998) in a sample of 178 gifted underachievers to published norms for the instrument (McCoach, Siegle, Mann, & Moore, 2005). The prevalence rate of inattention was more than 7.4 times higher than the norm sample on the ADHD home scale and more than 4 times higher than the norm sample on the school scale. However, for both the parent and teacher rating scales, the prevalence of clinically significant hyperactive/inattentive behavior actually was lower than it was in the norm group. More than half of the students in the sample met the criteria for ADHD-primarily attentive type based on teacher reports, and almost a third of the students in the sample met the criteria for ADHD-primarily attentive type based on parent reports. These results suggest that although the prevalence of hyperactivity and impulsivity within the underachieving sample may be similar to that of a typical school-aged population, the prevalence of inattention may be much higher (McCoach et al., 2005).

Distinguishing between a chronic underachiever and a gifted student who has learning disabilities, attention deficits, or psychological problems is crucial because the interventions appropriate for these subgroups may be radically different (Reis & McCoach, 2000).

INTERVENTIONS

Characteristics of gifted underachievers have received considerable attention in recent research literature; however, intervention research aimed at reversing students' underachievement remains scarce. Very few researchers have attempted to utilize true or quasi-experimental designs to study the efficacy of various interventions, and most of the intervention research reported in the literature is at least 10 years old (Baum, Renzulli, & Hébert, 1995b; Supplee, 1990; Whitmore, 1980). In addition, the results of these studies have been somewhat mixed. Therefore, researchers know very little how to most effectively combat underachievement.

Most interventions intended to reverse underachievement fall into two general categories: counseling and instructional interventions (Butler-Por, 1993; Dowdall & Colangelo, 1982). Counseling interventions, including individual, group, and/or family counseling, concentrate on changing the personal and/or family dynamics that contribute to a student's underachievement (Jeon, 1990). Many early attempts to improve underachievers' academic achievement through counseling treatments were unsuccessful (Baymur & Patterson, 1965; Broedel, Ohlsen, Proff, & Southard, 1965).

The most well-known educational interventions for gifted underachievers established either part-time or full-time special classrooms for gifted under-achievers (e.g., Butler-Por, 1987; Fehrenbach, 1993; Supplee, 1990; Whitmore, 1980). In these self-contained classrooms, educators strive to create a favorable environment for student achievement by altering the traditional classroom organization through a smaller student/teacher ratio, less conventional types of teaching and learning activities, student choice, and encouragement to utilize different learning strategies. The most well-known classroom interventions include Whitmore's full-time and Supplee's part-time classes for gifted elementary underachievers. Both programs addressed affective education, designed student-centered classroom environments, and provided some anecdotal and qualitative evidence success. However, neither study used a comparison group of untreated underachievers; therefore, it is unclear whether the students' achievement might have improved in the absence of the intervention.

Students' strengths and interests may provide one route to reversing underachievement (Emerick, 1992). One study utilized self-selected Type III enrichment projects as a systematic intervention for underachieving gifted students (Baum et al., 1995b). This enrichment-based approach specifically targeted student strengths and interests to reverse academic underachievement (Baum et al., 1995b). Most of the students who completed Type III investigations showed some positive gains in either behavior or achievement during the course of the school year. Eleven of the 17 participants showed improved achievement, 13 of the 17 students appeared to exert more effort within their classes, and 4 of the 17 students showed marked improvement in their classroom behavior. In a qualitative study of this intervention technique, relationship with the teacher, use of self-regulation strategies, opportunity to investigate topics related to their underachievement, opportunity to work on an area of interest in a preferred learning style, and time to interact with an appropriate peer group appeared to improve achievement (Baum et al., 1995b).

AREAS FOR FUTURE RESEARCH

No one type of intervention appears to be effective for the full range of underachieving gifted students. Because the factors influencing the development and manifestation of underachievement vary, a continuum of strategies and services may be necessary if we are to systematically address this problem. Model-based interventions provide an internal consistency between diagnostic and prescriptive elements. Therefore, future researchers in this field should posit coherent, complete models of gifted underachievement and design interventions in accordance with their proposed models.

First, researchers should begin to explore the relationship between classroom practices and academic underachievement. Reis (1998) observed that there appears to be a relationship between unchallenging or inappropriate curriculum in elementary school and underachievement in middle or high school. If unchallenging scholastic environments produce underachieving gifted students, then providing intellectual challenge and stimulation at all grade levels should decrease underachievement. Do schools that differentiate instruction for high-ability students have fewer incidences of underachievement among the gifted? Does providing part or full-time gifted programming reduce the occurrence of academic underachievement among the gifted? Is providing intellectual challenge especially critical during any particular age range? Research exploring the impact of differentiation, acceleration, enrichment, and other curricular modifications on patterns of achievement and underachievement could provide important information for educators. Further, the long-term effects of interventions remain underexplored. Do underachievement interventions have enduring effects on student motivation and achievement? What happens when the student is once again faced with nonstimulating schoolwork? These and many other questions remain unanswered.

The National Research Center on the Gifted and Talented is completing a 5-year study of underachievers (Siegle et al., 2006) based on the Achievement-Orientation Model (Siegle & McCoach, 2005), which provides different interventions for different types of underachievers. Further research should focus on developing and testing multiple approaches to both preventing and reversing underachievement. Different types of underachievers may require different combinations of counseling, self-regulation training, and instructional or curricular modifications; therefore, successful interventions should incorporate both proactive and preventative counseling and innovative instructional interventions.

Finally, research should examine the effectiveness of family oriented interventions, such as family counseling and home and school partnerships, as well as school-based interventions. Given the complexity and intractability of underachievement behaviors, interventions that combine school and family based components may prove to be most successful in reversing underachievement.

CONCLUSIONS

Gifted underachievers seem to be a diverse group of students who share some common motivational and attitudinal characteristics, such as low motivation, low self-regulation, and low value for school and academic tasks. In general, inadequate research has examined the interventions aimed at reversing underachievement. Further research is needed in this area in order to unravel the mystery of why gifted students underachieve and how we can help them to succeed. The research literature mentions only a small number of interventions; the field needs more outcome data on clearly defined interventions for gifted underachievers of differing types. These interventions should probably involve counseling and some form of curricular modification or differentiation. Future research should evaluate the efficacy of both instructional and counseling treatments for reversing underachievement, as well as the ability of curricular modifications to prevent academic underachievement in academically gifted students.

REFERENCES

Albaili, M. A. (2003). Motivational goal orientations of intellectually gifted achieving and underachieving students in the United Arab Emirates. *Social Behavior and Personality, 31,* 107–120.

Anderson, E. S., & Keith, T. Z. (1997). A longitudinal test of a model of academic success for at-risk high school students. *Journal of Educational Research, 90,* 259–268.

Baker, J. A., Bridger, R., & Evans, K. (1998). Models of underachievement among gifted preadolescents: The role of personal, family, and school factors. *Gifted Child Quarterly, 42,* 5–14.

Barton, J. M., & Starnes, W. T. (1988). Identifying distinguishing characteristics of gifted and talented learning disabled students. *Roeper Review, 12,* 23–29.

Baslanti, U., & McCoach, D. B. (2006). Gifted underachievers and factors affecting underachievement. *Roeper Review, 28,* 210–215.

Baum, S. M., Owen, S. V., & Dixon, J. (1991). *To be gifted and learning disabled: From identification to practical intervention strategies.* Mansfield, CT: Creative Learning Press.

Baum, S. M., Olenchak, F. R., & Owen, S. V. (1998). Gifted students with attention deficits: Fact and/or fiction? Or, can we see the forest for the trees? *Gifted Child Quarterly, 42,* 96–104.

Baum, S. M., Renzulli, J. S., & Hébert, T. P. (1995a). *The prism metaphor: A new paradigm for reversing underachievement* (CRS95310). Storrs: National Research Center on the Gifted and Talented, University of Connecticut.

Baum, S. M., Renzulli, J. S., & Hébert, T. P. (1995b). Reversing underachievement: Creative productivity as a systematic intervention. *Gifted Child Quarterly, 39,* 224–235.

Baymur, F., & Patterson, C. H. (1965). Three methods of assisting underachieving high school students. In M. Kornrich (Ed.), *Underachievement* (pp. 501–513). Springfield, IL: Charles C. Thomas.

Berndt, T. J. (1999). Friends influence on students' adjustment to school. *Educational Psychologist, 34,* 15–28.

Bireley, M. (1995). *Crossover children: A sourcebook for helping students who are gifted and learning disabled.* Reston, VA: Council for Exceptional Children.

Broedel, J., Ohlsen, M., Proff, F., & Southard, C. (1965). The effects of group counseling on gifted underachieving adolescents. In M. Kornrich (Ed.), *Underachievement* (pp. 514–528). Springfield, IL: Charles C. Thomas.

Brown, B. B., Mounts, N., Lamborn, S. D., & Steinberg, L. (1993). Parenting practices and peer group affiliation in adolescence. *Child Development, 64,* 467–482.

Busch, B., & Nuttall, R. L. (1995). Students who seem to be unmotivated may have attention deficits. *Diagnostique, 21*(1), 43–59.

Butler-Por, N. (1987). *Underachievers in school: Issues and intervention.* Chichester, England: John Wiley and Sons.

Butler-Por, N. (1993). Underachieving gifted students. In K. A. Heller, F. J. Mönks, & A. H. Passow (Eds.), *International handbook of research and development of giftedness and talent* (pp. 649–668). Oxford, England: Pergamon.

Carr, M., Borkowski, J. G., & Maxwell, S. E. (1991). Motivational components of underachievement. *Developmental Psychology, 27,* 108–118.

Chen, X. (1997). *Students' peer groups in high school: The pattern and relationship to educational outcomes* (NCES 97-055). Washington, DC: U.S. Department of Education.

Clasen, D. R., & Clasen, R. E. (1995). Underachievement of highly able students and the peer society. *Gifted and Talented International, 10*(2), 67–75.

Colangelo, N., Kerr, B., Christensen, P., & Maxey, J. (1993). A comparison of gifted underachievers and gifted high achievers. *Gifted Child Quarterly, 37,* 155–160.

Dowdall, C. B., & Colangelo, N. (1982). Underachieving gifted students: Review and implications. *Gifted Child Quarterly, 26,* 179–184.

DuPaul, G. J., Power, T. J., Anastapoulos, A. D., & Reid, R. (1998). *ADHD Rating Scale IV*. New York: Guilford Press.

Emerick, L. J. (1992). Academic underachievement among the gifted: Students' perceptions of factors that reverse the pattern. *Gifted Child Quarterly, 36,* 140–146.

Fehrenbach, C. R. (1993). Underachieving students: Intervention programs that work. *Roeper Review, 16,* 88–90.

Fine, M. J., & Pitts, R. (1980). Intervention with underachieving gifted children: Rationale and strategies. *Gifted Child Quarterly, 24,* 51–55.

Ford, D. Y. (1992). Determinants of underachievement as perceived by gifted, above average, and average Black students. *Roeper Review, 14,* 130–136.

Ford, D. Y. (1996). *Reversing underachievement among gifted Black students.* New York: Teacher's College Press.

Freedman, J. (2000). *Personal and school factors influencing academic success or underachievement of intellectually gifted students in middle childhood.* Unpublished doctoral dissertation, Yale, New Haven, CT.

Green, K., Fine, M. J., & Tollefson, N. (1988). Family systems characteristics and underachieving gifted males. *Gifted Child Quarterly, 32,* 267–272.

Hinshaw, S. P. (1992a). Academic underachievement, attention deficits, and aggression: Comorbidity and implications for intervention. *Journal of Consulting and Clinical Psychology, 60,* 893–903.

Hinshaw, S. P. (1992b). Externalizing behavior problems and academic underachievement in childhood and adolescence: Causal relationships and underlying mechanisms. *Psychological Bulletin, 111,* 127–155.

Hoffman, J. L., Wasson, F. R., & Christianson, B. P. (1985). Personal development for the gifted underachiever. *Gifted Child Today, 8*(3), 12–14.

Jeon, K. (1990, August). *Counseling and guidance for gifted underachievers.* Paper presented at the First Southeast Asian Regional Conference on Giftedness, Manila, Philippines. (ERIC Document Reproduction Service No. ED328051)

Krouse, J. H., & Krouse, H. J. (1981). Toward a multimodal theory of underachievement. *Educational Psychologist, 16,* 151–164.

Lacasse, M. A. (1999). *Personality types among gifted underachieving adolescents: A comparison with gifted achievers and non-gifted underachievers.* Unpublished doctoral dissertation, York University, Toronto, Ontario, Canada.

Lau, K.-L., & Chan, D. W. (2001). Identification of underachievers in Hong Kong: Do different methods select different underachievers? *Educational Studies, 27,* 187–200.

Mandel, H. P., & Marcus, S. I. (1988). *The psychology of underachievement.* New York: Wiley & Sons.

Mandel, H. P., & Marcus, S. I. (1995). *Could do better.* New York: Wiley & Sons.

Matthews, M. S., & McBee, M. T. (2007). School factors and the underachievement of gifted students in a talent search summer program. *Gifted Child Quarterly, 51,* 167–181.

McCall, R. B. (1994). Academic underachievers. *Current Directions in Psychological Science, 3,* 15–19.

McCall, R. B., Evahn, C., & Kratzer, L. (1992). *High school underachievers: What do they achieve as adults?* Newbury Park: Sage.

McCoach, D. B. (2002). A validity study of the School Attitude Assessment Survey (SAAS). *Measurement and Evaluation in Counseling and Development, 35,* 66–77.

McCoach, D. B., & Siegle, D. (2003a). The SAAS-R: A new instrument to identify academically able students who underachieve. *Educational and Psychological
Measurement, 63,* 414–429.

McCoach, D. B., & Siegle, D. (2003b). The structure and function of academic self-
concept in gifted and general education samples. *Roeper Review, 25,* 61–65.

McCoach, D. B., Siegle, D., Mann, R., & Moore, M. (2005, November).
Underachievement or ADHD? Paper presented at the annual meeting of the
National Association of Gifted Children Annual Conference, Louisville, KY.

Moon, S. M., & Hall, A. S. (1998). Family therapy with intellectually and creatively
gifted children. *Journal of Marital and Family Therapy, 24,* 59–80.

Neisser, U., Boodoo, G., Bouchard, T. J., Boykin, A. W., Brody, N., Ceci, S. J., et al.
(1996). Intelligence: Knowns and unknowns. *American Psychologist, 51,* 77–101.

Pendarvis, E. D., Howley, A. A., & Howley C. B. (1990). *The abilities of gifted children.*
Englewood Cliffs, NJ: Prentice Hall.

Peterson, J. S. (2000). A follow-up study of one group of achievers and underachievers
four years after high school graduation. *Roeper Review, 22,* 217–225.

Peterson, J. S., & Colangelo, N. (1996). Gifted achievers and underachievers: A comparison of patterns found in school files. *Journal of Counseling and Development,
74,* 399–406.

Pirozzo, R. (1982). Gifted underachievers. *Roeper Review, 4,* 18–21.

Rayneri, L. J., Gerber, B. L., & Wiley, L. P. (2003). Gifted achievers and gifted underachievers: The impact of learning style preferences in the classroom. *Journal of
Secondary Gifted Education, 14,* 197–204.

Redding, R. E. (1990). Learning preferences and skill patterns among underachieving
gifted adolescents. *Gifted Child Quarterly, 34,* 72–75.

Reis, S. M. (1998). Underachievement for some—Dropping out with dignity for others. *Communicator, 29*(1), 1, 19–24.

Reis, S. M., Hébert, T. P., Diaz, E. P., Maxfield, L. R., & Ratley, M. E. (1995). *Case
studies of talented students who achieve and underachieve in an urban high school*
(Research Monograph No. 95120). Storrs: National Research Center for the
Gifted and Talented, University of Connecticut.

Reis, S. M., & McCoach, D. B. (2000). The underachievement of gifted students: What
do we know and where do we go? *Gifted Child Quarterly, 44,* 158–170.

Richert, E. S. (1991). Patterns of underachievement among gifted students. In J. H.
Borland (Series Ed.) & M. Bireley & J. Genshaft (Vol. Eds.), *Understanding the
gifted adolescent* (pp. 139–162). New York: Teacher College Press.

Rimm, S. (1995). *Why bright kids get poor grades and what you can do about it.* New York:
Crown Trade Paperbacks.

Rimm, S. (1997a). An underachievement epidemic. *Educational Leadership, 54*(7),
18–22.

Rimm, S. (1997b). Underachievement syndrome: A national epidemic. In N. Colangelo
& G. A. Davis (Eds.), *Handbook of gifted education* (2nd ed., pp. 416–435). Boston:
Allyn & Bacon.

Rimm, S., & Lowe, B. (1988). Family environments of underachieving gifted students.
Gifted Child Quarterly, 32, 353–358.

Schunk, D. H. (1998, November). *Motivation and self-regulation among gifted learners.* Paper presented at the annual meeting of the National Association of Gifted
Children, Louisville, KY.

Siegle, D., & McCoach D. B. (2005). *Motivating gifted students*. Waco, TX: Prufrock Press.

Siegle, D., Reis, S. M., McCoach, D. B., Mann, R. L., Greene, M., & Schreiber, F. (2006). [The National Research Center on the Gifted and Talented increasing academic achievement study]. Unpublished raw data.

Supplee, P. L. (1990). *Reaching the gifted underachiever*. New York: Teachers College Press.

Thorndike, R. L. (1963). *The concepts of over and underachievement*. New York: Teachers College Press.

Tomlinson, C. A., Callahan, C. M., & Lelli, K. M. (1997). Challenging expectations: Case studies of culturally diverse young children. *Gifted Child Quarterly, 41*, 5–17.

Weiner, I. B. (1992). *Psychological disturbance in adolescence* (2nd ed.). New York: John Wiley & Sons.

Whitmore, J. R. (1980). *Giftedness, conflict, and underachievement*. Boston: Allyn & Bacon.

Wolfle, J. A. (1991). Underachieving gifted males: Are we missing the boat? *Roeper Review, 13*, 181–184.

You-Lim, E. (1995). *Underachievement: Consistency across academic subjects and relationships with attribution, self-concept, and self-regulation*. Unpublished doctoral dissertation, State University of New York, Albany.

Yu, S. (1996). *Cognitive strategy use and motivation in underachieving students*. Unpublished doctoral dissertation, University of Michigan, Ann Arbor.

Zilli, M. G. (1971). Reasons why the gifted adolescent underachieves and some of the implications of guidance and counseling to this problem. *Gifted Child Quarterly, 15*, 279–292.

Chapter 49

VISUAL AND PERFORMING ARTS

Bess B. Worley II

DEFINING THE TERMS: WHAT ARE THE ARTS?

here are many interpretations of the term *arts* in the research and literature in the field of gifted education. Traditionally, *fine arts* is used to describe any of various art forms "produced or intended primarily for beauty rather than utility" (American Heritage Dictionaries, 2000), including sculpture, painting, and music. *Visual art* specifies any physical work of art, such as painting, photography, or sculpture, that can be seen and that "typically exists in permanent form" (American Heritage Dictionaries, 2000). *Performing arts* refers to dance, drama, and music because they are arts that are performed before an audience. The National Standards for Arts Education (Consortium of National Arts Education Associations, 1994) identifies four disciplines as areas for focus within the arts: visual arts, music, dance, and theater.

The national and state definitions for gifted education programs vary in their use of the terms *gifted*, *talent*, *artistically talented*, and *artistic capacity* (Stephens & Karnes, 2000; U.S. Department of Education, 1993). The research on giftedness and talent in the arts typically reflects the categories of the national standards for arts education, focusing specifically on the performing and visual arts. *Musical talent* typically reflects skill and mastery of an instrument or the voice, and the term *talent* within theater arts and dance is generally limited to performance as an actor or dancer, respectively. However, there are other areas in addition to performance talent that are a part of the domains of music, theater, and dance. These areas include composition, arranging, writing, choreography, directing, and criticism. *Artistically talented*, although often used to refer to students who are gifted or talented in the visual arts, will be used here to refer to talented students in all four arts areas, and *arts* will be used to refer to all four areas of focus. *Gifted*, *giftedness*, and *talent* will be used interchangeably, similar to the use of the terms within the field of gifted education (Gagné, 1995), except as the term is specifically used in the research studies reported—with clarification as necessary.

In keeping with an empirically grounded approach, the research reviewed for this chapter was limited primarily to peer-reviewed publications of empirical research. However, seminal publications of research studies as books and reports also were considered when peer-reviewed publications of research studies were not available. Further, reviews of relevant research were included to provide information on certain strands of inquiry not represented in databases for peer-reviewed publications. Published and unpublished theses and dissertations within the relevant arts areas are noted even though they have not transitioned to the peer-reviewed literature when they represent additional empirical findings not otherwise available.

CONCLUSIONS FROM THE RESEARCH ON GIFTEDNESS AND TALENT IN THE ARTS

Nature of Giftedness/Talent in the Arts

Study of the nature of talent in the visual and performing arts has focused mainly on the domains of music and the visual arts. Haroutounian (2002) examined the research and literature regarding musical talent and identified several perspectives of the nature of musical talent: measurement of sensory capacities (e.g., hearing and interpreting sound; Gordon, 1989; Seashore, 1938), behaviors of musical ability and musical learning (e.g., Bamberger, 1995; Gardner, 1983), skills of talented musical performance (e.g., Davidson, Howe, Moore, & Sloboda, 1996), musical creativity (e.g., Csikszentmihalyi, Rathunde, & Whalen, 1993; Sloboda, 1985), and musical giftedness (e.g., Feldman, 1993).

Gardner (1993a), using historical analysis, has studied the nature of ability and creativity within dance, music, and the visual arts in addition to understanding, describing, and supporting the development of musical intelligence (Gardner, 1983, 1993b). Haroutounian's (2002) work confirms that most experts still gauge the level of musical talent based on the ability to perform music on an instrument or with the voice whereas Gardner's (1983) work focuses on mastery of the language of music within the Western tonal system.

Clark and Zimmerman (1988, 1994, 2001) have engaged in extensive study of the nature of giftedness and talent as it relates to identification of talent within the domain of the visual arts. Findings from these studies, mostly of adolescents participating in a summer gifted program, indicate gifted and talented students in the visual arts attribute their identification as gifted or talented to hard work (Clark & Zimmerman, 1994) and report devoting a lot of time and energy to their artistic ability (Clark & Zimmerman, 1988). The students in this population also recognized an early interest and superior ability in the visual arts as compared to their age peers (Clark & Zimmerman, 1988).

The arts are perceived by some researchers as being similar to other areas of giftedness and talent (Bloom, 1985; Freeman, 1999; Gagné, 1993); others disagree as to the exact nature of the cognitive processes involved in the creation of artistic products or performances (Bamberger, 1995; Gardner, 1983; Haroutounian, 2002; Zimmerman, 2004). Bloom (1985), in his introduction to the studies included in landmark research on talent development, explains the selection of two talent areas within aesthetic fields focusing on sensory and aesthetic perception, motor coordination, and training to respond to sights and sounds. Although the areas selected—concert pianists and sculptors—require different learning experiences and development than athletic or cognitive fields, Bloom acknowledged that each talent area was not "pure" and that "other qualities and characteristics" are included to an extent to achieve success in an artistic area (p. 10). The research of Bamberger (1995) and Gardner (1983) examined musical ability and musical cognition in isolation from other cognitive processes. Zimmerman (2004) outlined these conflicting perspectives in an introduction to a volume of the 2004 Essential Readings from the journal *Gifted Child Quarterly* focused on artistically and musically talented students. These conflicts address the correlation of achievement in academics and the arts, the assumed and perceived incompatibility of arts performance and intelligence, and the lack of agreement on the definition of the terms *talent, giftedness,* and *creativity* or "relationships among these terms" (Zimmerman, 2004, p. xxxi).

Some artists report early recognition of their own abilities (Clark & Zimmerman, 1988; Freeman, 1999) whereas other artists, as well as their parents and teachers, did not consider their artistic abilities to be innate or with them from birth (Dai & Schader, 2002; Evans, Bickel, & Pendarvis, 2000; Sloane & Sosniak, 1985). Other studies indicate talent is perceived differently based on gender (Gagné, 1993; Zimmerman, 1995) and the support of talent development is related to how ability is perceived by both the artist and his or her environment (Dai & Schader, 2002; Evans et al., 2000). Although suggestions have been made that the arts play a role in the development of the intellectual or academic gifts and abilities (Berman, 2003; Hartshorn, 1960; Smutny, 2002; White & Sprague, 2002; Ziegfeld, 1961), empirical evidence could not be located.

Interpersonal traits and skills also are related to giftedness and talent. The ability to persist within an area of interest (Csikszentmihalyi et al., 1993; Zimmerman, 1997) and to understand and work within a domain from a creative perspective (Clark & Zimmerman, 1988; Getzels & Csikszentmihalyi, 1976) seems to contribute to talent development in the arts.

IDENTIFYING GIFTEDNESS/TALENT IN THE ARTS

The work of Clark and his colleagues within the domain of the visual arts suggests that talent in this area can be identified using measurements of drawing ability (Clark, 1989; Clark & Wilson, 1991) as one of several measures in a screening process (Clark & Zimmerman, 2001). Specifically, Clark's Drawing Abilities Test (CDAT) correlates significantly with teachers' ratings of students in a summer visual arts program (Clark & Wilson, 1991) and has been subsequently used to identify and serve talented students in the visual arts in multiple schools and programs (Clark & Zimmerman, 2001). Observations by professional artists or trained researchers of the artistic process (Getzels & Csikszentmihalyi, 1976) or the products created by artists are other tools used to identify talent in the visual arts (Clark & Zimmerman, 1983). Initial analysis of the Clark's Drawing Abilities Test also indicated student performance and age were unrelated (Clark, 1989), but subsequent piloting and analysis indicate a possible relationship between drawing ability and either maturation or instruction and training in drawing (Clark & Wilson, 1991).

The Talent Identification Instruments (TII), now known as the Talent Assessment Process in Dance, Music and Theater (D/M/T TAP; Oreck, 2004, 2005; Oreck, Owen, & Baum, 2003), have been developed in music and dance based on Renzulli's (1978) three-ring conception of giftedness (Baum, Owen, & Oreck, 1996). Initial interrater reliability for the TII ranged from .65 to .79 for music and .78 to .82 for dance (Baum et al., 1996). Evidence for validity suggests the TII scales do not correlate with measures of academic achievement and each scale describes a single construct of Music Talent or Dance Talent. Recent research has incorporated the TII in identifying and serving academically underachieving artistically gifted students (Pearson, 2005). Outside the field of gifted education, the Multidimensional Assessment Instrument in Dance (MAiD; Warburton, 2002) assesses content-related understanding in dance, opening the domain of dance beyond a performance-only focus.

Full-time specialized schools are identified as the gold standard for providing high-level instructional opportunities for high-ability students with intense motivation in specific domains such as the visual and performing arts (Cox, Daniel, & Boston, 1985; Haroutounian, 2000; Kolloff, 2002). A survey of secondary performing arts schools indicated that the number of such schools increased from 5 schools in 1970 to 55 in 1980 and almost 100 schools in 1985 (Curtis, 1986). Of the 55 schools included in the survey, most indicated that they were located in urban areas because of the large number of potentially talented students and the cultural resources available to the school's participants. These schools also shared an initial purpose of their creation to provide specialized arts training and/or to develop magnet schools related to integrating diverse racial and socioeconomic populations (Curtis, 1986). These schools include traditional secondary academic subjects while providing a minimum of 10 hours per week of specialized training in the arts areas addressed by their mission.

Many of these specialized schools for the arts have been established to provide instruction for a population of students who meet selection criteria and represent the state or local area for which the school is designated (Kolloff, 2002). Identification often involves a combination of objective and subjective assessment, including academic commitment, audition, and an interview (Kolloff, 2002; LaGuardia Arts!, n.d.; Nelson, 1987). Information on selection of candidates for specialized schools has been described in professional presentations and often is available from the sponsoring educational agency (Byrnes & Parke, 1982; Elam & Doughty, 1988).

These schools seek professionals with experience in their fields, as well as visiting artists to supplement the experiences of students (Kolloff, 2002). These specialized schools also mirror the suggested program elements found in the field of gifted education (Daniel & Cox, 1985). Internships, mentor programs, and college course credit and study are a few of the curricular elements that address the needs of gifted and talented students in the arts (Daniel & Cox, 1985; VanTassel-Baska, 2005). A recent study of specialized secondary schools for the performing arts examined teacher behaviors and classroom practices within these schools. Findings indicate some application of the concept of differentiation within these schools but a limited articulation of differentiation as a tool to meet the needs of high-ability students in the arts (Worley, 2006).

Factors Supporting Artistic Talent Development

Studies of talented individuals and their peers and families indicate that both parents and peers play an important role in the talent development process for artists (Bloom, 1985; Cox et al., 1985; Csikszentmihalyi et al., 1993; Freeman, 2000; Patrick et al., 1999). Supportive parents who provide access to teachers who stimulate both learning and interest encourage the development of advanced abilities (Bloom, 1985; Csikszentmihalyi et al., 1993). Peers with similar interests and abilities help adolescents maintain interest in and commitment to developing their abilities (Cox et al., 1985; Patrick et al., 1999). A home environment that fosters interest in and provides exposure to the arts area also is indicated as important to the development of artistic ability (Freeman, 2000).

More recent research on musically talented high school students continues to illustrate their need for support from family members, friends, and teachers (Chin & Harrington, 2007). Types of support include instrumental support, such as physical resources, emotional support, and support of musical activities. Instrumental support through financial support for equipment and lessons and transportation to lessons and rehearsals are crucial for success as a musician. Emotional support from teachers, parents, and friends in the form of encouragement is essential to help young musicians when they are discouraged. Young musicians also can be inspired by the musical and nonmusical accomplishments of others. Support specific to musical activities includes the attendance of family and friends at musical performances and active participation in a musical community. These three areas of support can be extended to all of the visual and performing arts as mechanisms to encourage the development of talent in a young artist.

The amount of time spent working within the area of talent to improve performance and technical abilities, specifically in the development of musical talent, also is well-supported (Davidson et al., 1996; Ericsson & Charness, 1994; Ericsson, Krampe, & Tesch-Romer, 1993). Practice leads to improvement. However, the inclination to spend large amounts of time on practice seems to be dependent upon several interpersonal and contextual factors (Csikszentmihalyi et al., 1993; Evans et al., 2000; Getzels & Csikszentmihalyi, 1976; Zimmerman, 1995). These factors include interest in the artistic area and the ability to be successful and receive support for artistic talent (Csikszentmihalyi et al., 1993; Evans et al., 2000; Getzels & Csikszentmihalyi, 1976). In the case of female adolescents in the visual arts, concern for how others viewed their ability combined with a greater concern for academic success might contribute to decreased time spent working in the talent area (Zimmerman, 1995).

School-based activities, individual instruction, and special programs for talent development in the arts tend to be successful in providing students with training in their talent area (Adams, 1992; Clark & Zimmerman, 1988; Kay & Subotnik, 1994; Oreck, Baum, & McCartney, 2000; Renfrow, 1983; Wilson & Clark, 2000). School-based programs that provide instruction in the talent area may be most important for talented students who lack the financial and emotional support structures (Oreck et al., 2000).

The development of talent also is dependent upon exposure to effective teachers for artistically talented students (Bloom, 1985; Oreck et al., 2000; Yeatts, 1980; Zimmerman, 1997) and support from peers with similar interests (Clark & Zimmerman, 1988; Patrick et al., 1999). Several studies in the visual and performing arts suggest teacher knowledge within the talent area (Bloom,

1985; Clark & Zimmerman, 1994; Sloane & Sosniak, 1985; Sosniak, 1985; Zimmerman, 1988, 1997) and teacher knowledge of the talent development process (Bloom, 1985; Yeatts, 1980; Zimmerman, 1992) are important to the development of high levels of ability.

Specifically, certain types of teachers may be more effective at certain stages of the talent development process (Bloom, 1985; Clark & Zimmerman, 1988; Zimmerman, 1997). Bloom's (1985) studies of several talent areas, including music and sculpture, suggest that effective teachers in the early stages of talent development cultivate an individual's interest in and passion for the art area. Effective teachers in the middle stages provide challenging instruction (Bloom, 1985) and connect technique and expression (Bloom, 1985; Clark & Zimmerman, 1988). In the third stage, the role of the master teacher for the pianists in Bloom's (1985) study was to identify imperfections in the musician's performance and help them through difficulties while they developed an individual style and a depth of understanding of their domain and repertoire. However, ethnographies of classical musical and dance training caution that rules and norms inherent to these specific artistic systems might interfere with the development of artistic potential by stifling personal creativity and self-esteem (Kingsbury, 1988; Lakes, 2005; Persson; 2000; Robson, Book, & Wimerding, 2000).

LIMITATIONS OF THE RESEARCH

The research concerning giftedness and talent within the visual and performing arts is limited by the range of the studies across the four arts areas, with visual art and music addressed often, and dance and theater lacking empirical studies (Seidel, 2002; Zimmerman, 2004). Further, the previous research has relied on quasi-experimental (e.g., Freeman, 2000), longitudinal (e.g., Csikszentmihalyi et al., 1993), correlational (e.g., Dai & Schader, 2002), and descriptive designs (Clark & Zimmerman, 1988, 2001) without supporting experimental design validation. And, the research is limited by small sample size and use of instruments with unknown or questionable reliability and validity. Although the research suggests directions for implementation in identifying talented arts students and providing educational opportunities to develop artistic talent, many of the studies are limited to one program (Clark & Zimmerman, 1988) or to one or two areas of the arts (Bloom, 1985; Clark & Zimmerman, 1988; Csikszentmihalyi et al., 1993).

APPLYING THE RESEARCH

There is much that remains to be known about the nature and development of giftedness and talent in the visual and performing arts. The definition of artistic talent varies across the arts areas and among researchers in this field (Baum et al., 1996; Clark & Zimmerman, 2001; Haroutounian, 2000; Zimmerman, 2004). Although most researchers advocate for the use of multiple measures to identify giftedness and talent in the arts (Baum et al., 1996; Clark & Wilson, 1991; Clark & Zimmerman, 2001; Haroutounian, 2002), there is no agreement on what combination of measures works best. There does seem to be consensus that the criteria for identification needs to consider the specific artistic domains individually because the needs of each arts area vary, especially between the visual and performing arts (e.g., Clark & Zimmerman, 2001; Haroutounian, 2002; Zimmerman, 2004).

There also is consensus that instruction in the arts is important to the development of talent in the arts (Bloom, 1985; Clark & Zimmerman, 1988; Kay & Subotnik, 1994; Oreck et al., 2000; Wilson & Clark, 2000). Specific prescriptions for this instruction, including how often, with whom, and what kind of instruction, do not exist at this time due to the limited research base. Teacher knowledge of the arts area and their ability to guide artistic development is indicated as one important piece of the instructional process for music and the visual arts (Bloom, 1985; Clark & Zimmerman, 1988).

To paraphrase and underscore the conclusion of Zimmerman (2004), a research agenda within the field of gifted education *must* be developed to "provide important information for improving educational opportunities" for talented arts students (p. xxxii). Although the visual arts and music have been explored across the categories examined here (nature of talent, identification, and services), this review supports previous conclusions about a lack of research and literature for developing giftedness and talent in theater and dance (Seidel, 2002; Zimmerman, 2004). More research is needed in each of the four main arts, as well as within each of the artistic domains. The areas of music, dance, and theater have focused primarily on the performance aspects of these domains while each domain also incorporates talent areas that require creativity in front of and away from an audience. More research also is needed outside the aesthetic branches of the arts in areas such as the folk or popular arts. For example, within music, how is exceptional talent and achievement developed in the genres of Jazz or Bluegrass? What interpersonal and environmental factors influence the development of talent in choreography, theatrical direction, musical composition, and musical recording? Although a few of these areas have been addressed by dissertations in theater (Berman, 2002), music (Kinney, 1990; Rexroad, 1985), and dance (Kim, 1998), the peer-reviewed literature, and, thus, the solid foundation of empirically based educational research, remains limited.

WHAT WE KNOW

- Students identified as gifted/talented in the visual arts recognized an early interest and ability but attribute their success to hard work and dedication.

- Specific measures of art ability such as Clark's Drawing Abilities Test for the visual arts and the Talent Assessment Process in Dance, Music, and Theater demonstrate some evidence of validity and reliability to identify students in these areas.
- Instruction in the arts area of talent/giftedness is essential for the development of potential gifts and talents.
- Arts teachers for the artistically gifted and talented need appropriate levels of knowledge and skill within the arts area, as well as understanding of the development of artistic gifts and talents.

AREAS FOR FUTURE RESEARCH

- Nature of giftedness/talent in all arts areas but specifically dance and theater/drama.
- Developing instruments to identify giftedness and talent in all areas, but especially theater/drama.
- Cross-validation of identification processes with other new and existing processes.
- Testing of identification process with a variety of populations and artistic styles.
- Longitudinal studies of students identified as potentially talented and involved in arts instruction.
- Blind review of talent identification processes by outside experts.
- Control group studies providing similar instructional opportunities to both talented and "normal" students.
- Appropriate types of services to develop giftedness and talent in all four areas of the visual and performing arts, including instructional strategies and professional development for arts teachers.

REFERENCES

Adams, R. T. (1992). *Improving characterization in scene study, in a magnet middle school, through learning directing skills.* New York: National Arts Education Research Center. (ERIC Document Reproduction Service No. ED367006)

American Heritage Dictionaries. (2000). *The American heritage dictionary of the English language* (4th ed.). New York: Houghton Mifflin. Retrieved June 1, 2005, from http://www.bartleby.com/61

Bamberger, J. (1995). *The mind behind the musical ear: How children develop musical intelligence.* Cambridge, MA: Harvard University Press.

Baum, S., Owen, S. V., & Oreck, B. A. (1996). Talent beyond words: Identification of potential talent in dance and music in elementary students. *Gifted Child Quarterly, 40,* 93–101.

Berman, K. B. (2002). Successful stage directors: Journeys in talent development and creative process (Doctoral dissertation, University of Connecticut, 2002). *Dissertation Abstracts International, 63,* 08A. (UMI No. AAI3062070)

Berman, K. (2003). The benefits of exploring opera for the social and emotional development of high-ability students. *Gifted Child Today, 26*(2), 46–53.

Bloom, B. S. (Ed.). (1985). *Developing talent in young people.* New York: Ballantine Books.

Byrnes, P., & Parke, B. (1982, April). *Creative Products Scale: Detroit Public Schools.* Paper presented at the Annual International Convention of the Council for Exceptional Children, Baltimore, MD.

Chin, C. S., & Harrington, D. M. (2007). Supporting the development of musical talent. *Gifted Child Today, 30*(1), 40–47, 65.

Clark, G. (1989). Screening and identifying students talented in the visual arts: Clark's Drawing Abilities Test. *Gifted Child Quarterly, 33,* 98–105.

Clark, G. A., & Wilson, T. (1991). Screening and identifying gifted/talented students in the visual arts with Clark's Drawing Abilities Test. *Roeper Review, 13,* 92–97.

Clark, G., & Zimmerman, E. (1983). At the age of six, I gave up a magnificent career as a painter: Seventy years of research about identifying students with superior abilities in the visual arts. *Gifted Child Quarterly, 27,* 180–184.

Clark, G., & Zimmerman, E. (1988). Views of self, family background, and school: Interviews with artistically talented students. *Gifted Child Quarterly, 32,* 340–346.

Clark, G., & Zimmerman, E. (1994). What do we know about artistically talented students and their teachers? *Journal of Art and Design Education, 13,* 275–286.

Clark, G., & Zimmerman, E. (2001). Identifying artistically talented students in four rural communities in the United States. *Gifted Child Quarterly, 45,* 104–114.

Consortium of National Arts Education Associations. (1994). *National standards for arts education.* Reston, VA: Music Educators National Conference. Retrieved October 6, 2002, from http://artsedge.kennedy-center.org/artsedge.html

Cox, J., Daniel, N., & Boston, B. O. (1985). *Educating able learners: Programs and promising practices.* Austin, TX: University of Texas Press.

Csikszentmihalyi, M., Rathunde, K., & Whalen, S. (1993). *Talented teenagers: The roots of success and failure.* Cambridge, England: Cambridge University Press.

Curtis, T. E. (1986, April). *Current status of performing arts secondary schools in the United States.* Paper presented at the annual meeting of the American Educational Research Association, San Francisco, CA.

Dai, D. Y., & Schader, R. M. (2002). Decisions regarding music training: Parental beliefs and values. *Gifted Child Quarterly 46,* 135–144.

Daniel, N., & Cox, J. (1985). Providing options for superior students in secondary schools. *NASSP Bulletin, 69*(482), 25–30.

Davidson, J. H., Howe, M. J. A., Moore, D. G., & Sloboda, J. A. (1996). The role of parental influences in the development of musical performance. *British Journal of Developmental Psychology, 14,* 399–412.

Elam, A., & Doughty, R. (1988). *Guidelines for the identification of artistically gifted and talented students* (Rev. ed.). Columbia, SC: South Carolina State Department of Education.

Ericsson, K. A., & Charness, N. (1994). Expert performance: Its structure and acquisition. *American Psychologist, 49,* 725–747.

Ericsson, K. A., Krampe, R. T., & Tesch-Romer, C. (1993). The role of deliberate practice in the acquisition of expert performance. *Psychological Review, 100,* 363–406.

Evans, R. J., Bickel, R., & Pendarvis, E. D. (2000). Musical talent: Innate or acquired? Perceptions of students, parents, and teachers. *Gifted Child Quarterly, 44*, 80–90.

Feldman, D. (1993). Child prodigies: A distinctive form of giftedness. *Gifted Child Quarterly, 37*, 188–193.

Freeman, C. (1999). The crystallizing experience: A study in musical precocity. *Gifted Child Quarterly, 43*, 75–85.

Freeman, J. (2000). Children's talent in fine art and music—England. *Roeper Review, 22*, 98–101.

Gagné, F. (1993). Sex differences in the aptitudes and talents of children as judged by peers and teachers. *Gifted Child Quarterly, 37*, 69–77.

Gagné, F. (1995). From giftedness to talent: A developmental model and its impact on the language of the field. *Roeper Review, 18*, 103–111.

Gardner, H. (1983). *Frames of mind: The theory of multiple intelligences.* New York: Basic Books.

Gardner, H. (1993a). *Creating minds: An anatomy of creativity seen through the lives of Freud, Einstein, Picasso, Stravinsky, Eliot, Graham, and Gandhi.* New York: Basic Books.

Gardner, H. (1993b). *Multiple intelligences: The theory in practice.* New York: Basic Books.

Getzels, J. W., & Csikszentmihalyi, M. (1976). *The creative vision: A longitudinal study of problem-finding in art.* New York: Wiley Interscience.

Gordon, E. (1989). *Advanced measures of music audiation.* Chicago: GIA.

Haroutounian, J. (2000). Teaching talented teenagers at the Interlochen arts academy (Interview). *Journal of Secondary Gifted Education, 12*(1), 39–42.

Haroutounian, J. (2002). *Kindling the spark: Recognizing and developing musical talent.* Oxford, England: Oxford University Press.

Hartshorn, W. C. (1960). *Music for the academically talented student in the secondary school.* Washington, DC: National Education Association. (ERIC Document Reproduction No. ED001712)

Kay, S. I., & Subotnik, R. F. (1994). Talent beyond words: Unveiling spatial, expressive, kinesthetic, and musical talent in young children. *Gifted Child Quarterly, 38*, 70–74.

Kim, J. (1998). The effects of creative dance instruction on creative and critical thinking of seventh-grade female students in Seoul, Korea. (Doctoral dissertation, New York University, 1998). *Dissertation Abstracts International, 59*, 05A. (UMI No. 9832748)

Kingsbury, H. (1988). *Music, talent, and performance: A conservatory cultural system.* Philadelphia: Temple University Press.

Kinney, M. (1990). Perceptions of developmental influences as contributing factors to the motivation for musical creativity of eminent twentieth century living American composers [Abstract]. (Doctoral dissertation, Syracuse University, 1990). *Dissertation Abstracts International, 52*, 02A.

Kolloff, P. B. (2002). State-supported residential high schools. In N. Colangelo & G. A. Davis (Eds.), *Handbook of gifted education* (3rd ed., pp. 238–246). Boston: Allyn & Bacon.

LaGuardia Arts! (n.d.). Retrieved August 1, 2005, from http://www.laguardiahs.org/about/history.html

Lakes, R. (2005). The messages behind the methods: The authoritarian pedagogical legacy in Western concert dance technique training and rehearsals. *Arts Education Policy Review, 106*(5), 3–18.

Nelson, J. R. (1987). Yes, we dance on the tables. *Gifted Child Today, 10*(5), 55–56.

Oreck, B. (2004) Assessment of potential theater arts talent in young people: The development of a new research-based assessment process. *Youth Theater Journal, 18*, 146–163.

Oreck, B. (2005). A powerful conversation: Teachers & artists collaborate in performance-based assessment. *Teaching Artist Journal, 3*, 220–227.

Oreck, B., Baum, S., & McCartney, H. (2000). *Artistic talent development for urban youth: The promise and the challenge* (Research Monograph Series). Storrs: National Research Center on Giftedness and Talent, University of Connecticut. (ERIC Document Services No. ED451665)

Oreck, B., Owen, S., & Baum, S. (2003). Validity, reliability and equity issues in an observational talent assessment process in the performing arts. *Journal for the Education of the Gifted, 27*, 62–94.

Patrick, H., Ryan, A. M., Alfeld-Liro, C., Fredricks, J. A., Hruda, L. Z., & Eccles, J. S. (1999). Adolescents' commitment to developing talent: The role of peers in continuing motivation for sports and the arts. *Journal of Youth and Adolescence, 28*, 741–763.

Pearson, L. (2005, November). *Funding and helping academically underachieving artistically gifted students*. Presented at the annual meeting of the National Association for Gifted Children, Louisville, KY.

Persson, R. S. (2000). Survival of the fittest or the most talented? *Journal of Secondary Gifted Education, 12*, 25–38.

Renfrow, M. J. (1983). Accurate drawing as a function of training of gifted children in copying and perception. *Educational Research Quarterly, 8*, 27–32.

Renzulli, J. S. (1978). What makes giftedness? Reexamining a definition. *Phi Delta Kappan, 60*, 180–184, 261.

Rexroad, E. F. (1985). Influential factors on the musical development of outstanding professional singers [Abstract]. (Doctoral dissertation, University of Illinois at Urbana-Champaign, 1985). *Dissertation Abstracts International, 46*, 04A.

Robson, B. E., Book, A., & Wimerding, M. V. (2000). Psychological stresses experienced by dance teachers: "How can I be a role model when I never had one?" *Medical Problems of Performing Artists, 17*, 173.

Seashore, C. E. (1938). *Psychology of music*. New York: McGraw-Hill.

Seidel, K. (2002). A review of research in theater, dance, and other performing arts education. In R. Colwell & C. Richardson (Eds.), *The new handbook of research on music teaching and learning* (pp. 977–985). Oxford, England: Oxford University Press.

Sloane, K. D., & Sosniak, L. A. (1985). The development of accomplished sculptors. In B. Bloom (Ed.), *Developing talent in young people* (pp. 90–138). New York: Ballantine.

Sloboda, J. A. (1985). *The musical mind: The cognitive psychology of music*. Oxford, England: Oxford University Press.

Smutny, J. F. (2002). *Integrating the arts into the curriculum for gifted students* (ERIC Digest Report No. EDO-EC-02-9). Washington, DC: Office of Educational Research and Improvement.

Sosniak, L. A. (1985). Learning to be a concert pianist. In B. Bloom (Ed.), *Developing talent in young people* (pp. 19–67). New York: Ballantine.

Stephens, K. R., & Karnes, F. A. (2000). State definitions for the identification of gifted and talented revisited. *Exceptional Children, 66*, 219–238.

U.S. Department of Education, Office of Educational Research and Improvement. (1993). *National excellence: A case for developing America's talent.* Washington, DC: U.S. Government Printing Office.

VanTassel-Baska, J. (2005). Gifted programs and services: What are the nonnegotiables? *Theory Into Practice, 44*(2), 90–97.

Warburton, E. C. (2002). From talent identification to multidimensional assessment: Toward new models of evaluation in dance education. *Research in Dance Education, 3*, 103–121.

White, D. A., & Sprague, C. (2002). "The Bohemian life": Opera and gifted education. *Gifted Child Today, 25*(3), 34–39, 64.

Wilson, T., & Clark, G. (2000). Looking and talking about art: Strategies of an experienced art teacher. *Visual Arts Research, 52*(2), 33–39.

Worley, B. B., II. (2006). Talent development in the performing arts: Teacher characteristics, behaviors, and classroom practices. (Doctoral dissertation, College of William and Mary, 2006). *Dissertation Abstracts International, 67*, 03A. (UMI No. AAT3209553)

Yeatts, E. H. (1980). The professional artist: A teacher for the gifted. *Gifted Child Quarterly, 24*, 133–137.

Ziegfeld, E. (1961). *Art for the academically talented student.* Washington, DC: National Education Association. (ERIC Document Reproduction No. ED001709)

Zimmerman, E. (1988). Rembrandt to Rembrandt: A case study of a memorable painting teacher for artistically talented 13 to 16 year old students. *Roeper Review, 13*, 76–81.

Zimmerman, E. (1992). A comparative study of two painting teachers of talented adolescents. *Studies in Art Education, 33*, 174–185.

Zimmerman, E. (1995). Factors influencing the art education of artistically talented girls. *Journal of Secondary Gifted Education, 6*, 103–112.

Zimmerman, E. (1997). I don't want to sit in the corner cutting out valentines: Leadership roles for teachers of talented art students. *Gifted Child Quarterly, 41*, 33–41.

Zimmerman, E. (Ed.). (2004). *Artistically and musically talented students.* Thousand Oaks, CA: Corwin Press.

Chapter 50

WRITING

Joyce VanTassel-Baska
and Bronwyn MacFarlane

INTRODUCTION

On a recent trip to China, the first author was struck by the powerful approach employed by special writing institutes to produce gifted writers during the preadolescent years. The formula involved (1) self-identification and follow-up writing samples to establish a threshold level of written language competency, (2) online tutorials with writers and educators who provided structured feedback to nurture revision, and (3) encouragement to publish through a company earmarked for young writer publications. The other variable in China used to promote gifted writers was intensive mentoring with students over time. Adele, a young 14-year-old writer we met, talked about her two books of fiction, published by her 14th birthday, and noted that her development was due to the caring teacher who had worked with her for 4 years to enhance her writing.

Our research on writing in the United States in school-based programs suggests a less coherent response to promoting writing development at the secondary level, defined as grades 7–12, and our national proficiency results also would suggest that our growth gains in this area of learning are limited. In the 1980s, two National Assessment of Educational Progress (NAEP) publications, *The Writing Report Card* (Applebee, Langer, & Mullis, 1986b) and *The Reading Report Card* (Applebee, Langer, & Mullis, 1986a), found that the percentage of students who could go beyond minimally adequate written responses or intermediate comprehension was found to be disturbingly low. The writing assessment of the most recent NAEP 2002 *Nation's Report Card on Writing* showed students' average scores on the NAEP writing assessment increased between 1998 and 2002 at grades 4 and 8; however, no significant change was detected in the performance of 12th graders between the two assessment years. Gains were observed among the middle- and high-performing students at grade 8, but at grade 12, only the score at the 90th percentile increased since 1998 (National Center for Education Statistics, 2002).

Researchers have known for a long time that testing drives the school curriculum (Madaus, 1988). Hillocks (2003) pointed out that writing is not immune to this maxim. In analyzing writing assessments across 5 states through the use of interviews with educators, examination of materials related to assessment used at the local and state levels, and writing assessments across 43 states, Hillocks (2003) found that writing assessments stipulate the kinds of writing that should be taught, set standards for what counts as good writing, and set the conditions under which students must demonstrate their proficiency and what they should learn. He also found that writing assessment differs greatly, from 40-minute assessment prompts in Illinois, to portfolio assessments in Kentucky. The Hillocks study found that more than 70% of Illinois teachers across grades 2–10 use the five-paragraph theme for teaching writing structure. One third-grade teacher reported, "We pound it, pound it, pound it!" Although testing assures that what is tested is taught, the tests cannot assure that things are taught well. For teaching of writing to improve, states will have to intervene to provide teachers more opportunities to learn effective procedures for teaching writing (Hillocks, 2002).

This chapter will focus on several strands of research including general findings on the teaching of writing for all learners, interdisciplinary connections that can be made in reading and language arts, specific strategies for teaching writing, the integration of technology with writing instruction, teaching writing to gifted learners, and working with learning-disabled gifted writers. A final section discusses questions that remain about what we know from the research on teaching writing.

TEACHING WRITING TO ALL LEARNERS

To assess the literature on writing for gifted learners, it is essential to examine the general literature and research on teaching writing to all learners because the teaching of process skills typically involves similar techniques. In identifying practices used across the ability spectrum, we are able to see which techniques may be especially impacting positively or negatively upon gifted student performance.

Mark Twain once wrote, "The difference between the right word and nearly the right word is the same as that between lightning and the lightning bug." Good writers are skillful in the use of a variety of descriptive words in their writing to convey their point to an audience. Research indicates that in order for students to perform well in writing, reading, and speaking, they must possess a rich vocabulary (Ediger, 1999; Laflamme, 1997; Manning, 1999). It has been suggested even that descriptive writing necessitates a larger vocabulary than reading (Smith, 2003). A comprehensive vocabulary development program should include regular emphasis on interesting words encountered, direct instruction of techniques or procedures to develop a varied vocabulary, connected learning, and intensive practice and repetition (Brabham & Villaume, 2002; Laflamme, 1997).

One of the challenges in teaching writing is that the writing process is a much more subjective area to teach than reading (Marzano, Pickering, & Pollock, 2001; Smith, 2003). Yet, the research on teaching writing offers insight into how improvement is best accomplished. Hillocks (1986) examined four approaches to teaching writing, described as follows: (1) presentation: The teacher explains what good writing is and gives examples; (2) natural process: The teacher has students engage in a great deal of free writing, individually and in groups; (3) focused practice: The teacher structures writing tasks to emphasize specific aspects of writing; and (4) skills: The teacher breaks down writing into its component parts and then provides practice, sometimes in isolation, on each part. Focused practice produced the strongest learning, with high effect sizes. Simply explaining to students what good writing is (i.e., the presentation approach) resulted in the lowest effect size in these studies. Furthermore, the natural process approach in which teachers simply had students writing a great deal, and the skills approach, which had students practice the components and subcomponents in isolation, were found to have small effect sizes also.

A second emphasis that enhances writing is the use of metacognitive strategies (Scardamalia & Bereiter, 1985). Guided practice should be amply provided by having students use metacognition control strategies for as many appropriate tasks as possible, providing reinforcement and feedback on how students can improve their execution of the strategies (Marzano et al., 2001; Pressley, Goodchild, Fleet, Zajchowski, & Evans, 1989; Pressley & Woloshyn, 1995) Students need to self-monitor their performance when using the strategies, and teachers need to encourage generalization of the strategies by having students use them with different types of materials in a variety of content areas (Pressley & Woloshyn, 1995). Moreover, all students need teachers to explain writing task expectations clearly and fully. The three processes identified as being critical to effective writing instruction are planning, writing, and revision (Warger, 2002).

INTERDISCIPLINARY CONNECTIONS IN READING AND LANGUAGE ARTS

Writing fosters learning in all disciplines. It is a tool for thinking, which makes it integral to every subject at every scholastic level. Skill in writing is developed and refined through practice, which means students should have frequent opportunities to write across the curriculum (Langer, 2001). The integration of reading and writing tasks has produced learning benefits for students (Henry & Roseberry, 1996; Newell, 1996). Specifically, the combination of incorporating inquiry through advanced questioning, analyzing, and responding in writing to literature, prewriting, and communicating specific criteria as expectations for learners have been found to be effective strategies that produce higher achievement gains in learners (Sadoski, Willson, & Norton, 1997). Feedback based on writing also produces higher achievement gains if specific instructional objectives are manifest (Appleman, 2000).

In 1999–2000, a field study of eight North Carolina schools was conducted; four senior project schools and four control schools were selected. Researchers identified four treatment schools that had institutionalized senior projects for at least 4 years, with all seniors participating in them and with all the program components (research paper, product, portfolio, presentation) in place (Egelson, Harman, & Bond, 2002). Control schools were selected to match each senior project school based on staff size, student body, percent of students in the federal free lunch program, percent of minority students enrolled at the school, overall performance in the state testing program, and urbanicity. A variety of measures, including focus groups, writing assessments, achievement test scores, and surveys were used to examine possible differences between senior project and control schools. Results of the study indicated several significant differences between experimental and control schools. Students who participated in the senior project indicated a more positive association with the following specific skills than did their counterparts at the control schools: writing a research paper, preparing and presenting a speech, carrying out a plan, and conducting interviews. Moreover, they perceived the skills of preparing and presenting a speech, conducting research, and locating appropriate references to have been reinforced more in their classes than the students at control schools did.

Interdisciplinary connections in reading and writing can span other content disciplines, as well. Students need to develop literary habits of mind that encourage them to use resources appropriately and effectively. Researching relevant issues of significance can be one avenue to develop such skills. By exploring an issue of real-world relevance and interest to the learner, students can learn how to organize data to support an argument, how to develop an argument, how to evaluate various perspectives on an issue, and how to present their findings in oral and written forms. Because many students may be engaged in conducting research during their school years, it is important that they have the appropriate tools to frame a written research report based on important issues and questions they have defined. Thus, teaching them the fundamental skills necessary for doing successful research work should include writing (VanTassel-Baska & Stambaugh, 2006).

Correlational studies consistently show that writing ability is strongly related to reading ability and to the availability of reading material in the home (Applebee et al., 1986a); students inevitably draw on the knowledge of language conventions and discourse structures (i.e., conversational models) they gain through reading when they write.

STRATEGIES FOR TEACHING WRITING

Research has suggested that teachers need opportunities to learn more effective procedures for teaching writing (Hillocks, 2002). The direct teaching of focused and intensive writing techniques appears to be more successful than relying on general process techniques. Carlin-Menter and Shuell (2003) found that when the organizational skills necessary for successful writing were emphasized throughout a unit, there was a significant increase in students' scores on the organizational quality of their essay writing from the pretest to the posttest, especially for students who received low scores on the pretest. In assessing the value of writing journals, Skerritt (1995) found that most students not only found journals to be worthwhile, but also believed they helped them in various other aspects of the English curriculum.

In a survey conducted by Cox (1995), results showed that writing assessment activities tended to be a mix of traditional paper-and-pencil activities and formal writing assignments. Although paper-and-pencil activities appeared to dominate the classroom, in terms of regular and routine use, writing activities carried more weight when teachers computed course grades. In that study, writing portfolios were not found to be in general use. In an NAEP survey to teachers and students, peer review was reported to be a common assessment practice in more than two thirds of eighth-grade classrooms (Greenwald, Persky, Campbell, & Mazzeo, 1999).

In regard to teacher feedback about student writing, the importance of it on student learning does not correlate with the degree of feedback offered to students. Data collected from 55 middle school English classes indicated that incidents of high-quality instructional feedback and individualized instruction occurred in a small number of smaller classrooms and never occurred in larger classrooms. Teacher qualifications (years of experience and credential status) were unrelated to this teaching practice, nor did reduced class sizes directly impact the use of this teacher practice in secondary classrooms (Gilstrap, 2003).

Varied packaged programs to teach writing are readily available for schools to use and have yielded impressive gains for consistent use. Grossen (2002) collected data on schools that have implemented the Reach System and found that when schools implemented the comprehension program of Corrective

Reading and/or Reasoning and Writing with all of their students, there were strong SAT-9 gains on the California statewide assessments. Research-based teaching units produced by the College of William and Mary Center for Gifted Education have been found to show significant achievement gains in both gifted and nongifted students at the secondary level in the area of persuasive writing, using performance-based assessments, modeled after NAEP assessment measures. Assessment results suggested that continued emphasis on the elaboration of ideas was an implication for writing instruction (VanTassel-Baska, Zuo, Avery, & Little, 2002).

INTEGRATING TECHNOLOGY WITH WRITING INSTRUCTION

As technology options have increased and developed, the integration and use of technology in instructional practices for teaching writing must be expanded in developing young writers. In a study focusing upon the use of technology, Fouts and Stuen (1997) found that writing skills were the most directly affected by the use of laptops, followed by communication and presentation skills. Furthermore, Fouts and Stuen found that overall teachers, parents, and students generally were positive about the use of laptops for learning.

MacArthur (1996) pointed out that although research on assistive technology for writing still is limited, the direction of current research and the evolving technology is promising. Promising areas in which technology can help support student writing include:

- software may assist with the basic processes of transcription and sentence generation (e.g., spellchecker, speech synthesis, word prediction, and grammar and style checkers);
- application can support the cognitive processes of planning (e.g., prompting programs, outlining and semantic mapping software, and multimedia applications); and
- computer networks can support collaboration and communication, which are important elements of the writing process.

Schunk and Swartz (1993) investigated how goal setting and feedback on progress affect self-efficacy and writing achievement, finding that self-efficacy was highly predictive of writing skill and strategy use. Students who received feedback on their progress achieved better writing outcomes and transfer of their writing abilities to other areas than students who did not. The students judged their self-efficacy for writing improvement higher than other students.

Recent studies suggest that high-stakes testing can shift instruction away from feedback and revision aspects of writing, thereby leading to a reductive approach to writing (Ketter & Pool, 2001; Scherff & Piazza, 2005). Yet, problems still abound with the use of performance-based approaches, as well. Even with a valid rubric, the interpretation of individual evaluators shapes assessment (Novak, 1996), and consistent use of assessment data for instruction appears limited (VanTassel-Baska, 2002).

Writing has not received the widespread research attention accorded to reading, but the number of research studies has been growing. Middle-school-age students do reasonably well with simple writing tasks, but the research is less clear with respect to students' ability to adjust the nature of their writing to address different types of audiences. In short, writing skills are developing somewhat during this period of time; however, there is substantial room for improving these skills among early adolescents (Pikulski, 1991).

TEACHING WRITING TO GIFTED LEARNERS

In Plato's *Phaedrus*, Socrates challenges bad writing and inquires whether it is possible to distinguish another form of communication to be the equal peer of written speech. Indeed the closer writing can come to "revealing and explicating the complexities and ambiguities of its own meaning," the closer it comes to writing "on the soul of the hearer" and carrying the condition for understanding (Hillocks, 2002).

Writing is a thinking process. So, through writing experiences, the gifted child can develop excellence in the capacity to think, as well as to write. The fundamental skills associated with a process writing approach need to be used with gifted learners at all stages of development. Specifically these are (a) pre-writing, (b) paragraph development, (c) theme development (literary generalizations), (d) development of introductions and endings, (e) work on supporting details, (f) effective use of figures of speech, (g) editing, (h) teacher and peer conferencing, (i) revising, and (j) rewriting (VanTassel-Baska & Stambaugh, 2006).

Consideration also needs to be given to the type of writing that gifted students are encouraged to master. Balance between creative writing forms and analytic expository writing forms, including persuasive writing, is needed. Writing with gifted students should include exposure to good writing through extensive reading, critique of others' writing, and many opportunities to practice their own writing skills (VanTassel-Baska & Stambaugh, 2006).

One form of such practice comes through writing competitions, which are readily available for secondary students online and in reference materials. Williams (1998) suggested that writing instruction for students attending residential public schools for gifted students must be tailored to their unique needs. Using both collaborative and direct instructional approaches, writing programs should include the writing conventions of various disciplines, writing for the general public, writing across the curriculum, technical writing, expressive writing, and persuasive writing.

Distance learning opportunities have dramatically increased options for meeting the needs of gifted students in writing. Programs such as the Johns Hopkins Writing Tutorials, as well as online high school and college courses, including online Advanced Placement (AP) classes, are challenging curriculum opportunities for students who demonstrate proficiency with grade-level material (Capurro, 2003).

Various studies have shed light on which teaching techniques specifically work well with teaching writing to gifted secondary students. In a study examining the use of strategy instruction and self-regulation to improve gifted students' creative writing, Albertson and Billingsley (2001) found that following application of a writing instructional package, participants wrote longer stories, increased writing fluency, included more story elements, and wrote higher quality stories. As was expected, students whose teachers have special training in writing instruction performed significantly better than those with untrained teachers (Pritchard & Marshall, 1994).

When a graphic organizer was used to teach persuasive writing, explicitly using a rubric, and teacher feedback consistently was provided, gifted learners showed significant improvement in persuasive writing at secondary levels from grades 6–11 (VanTassel-Baska et al., 2002).

LEARNING-DISABLED GIFTED WRITERS

By distinguishing instructional techniques to use with twice-exceptional learners, teachers can address both the gift and the disability through the use of appropriate interventions. In describing experiences in teaching writing skills to elementary gifted students with learning disabilities, journal writing and word processing were found to be powerful tools in improving student writing while increasing students' self-confidence. Guest speakers, daily reading aloud by the teacher, and field trips to enrich students' experiences also were found to be useful (Doney, 1995).

MacArthur (1996) found that students with learning disabilities produced better essays when dictating to either scribes or speech recognition systems than they did when writing them by hand. Despite the potential benefits, speech recognition systems place specific demands on students. For example, users must be trained to use the system, which includes speaking clearly without extraneous sounds, pronouncing punctuation, and correcting errors—all of which may interfere with the student's ability to compose. Simply having access to word processing has little impact on the revising behaviors of students with learning disabilities, yet instruction in revision combined with word processing can significantly increase the amount and quality of revision by such students.

In a meta-analysis of research on teaching expressive writing to students with learning disabilities, virtually every intervention analyzed was multifaceted and involved students writing every day as part of the curriculum (ERIC Clearinghouse on Disabilities and Gifted Education, 2002). The meta-analysis identified several themes critical to effective writing instruction: (1) adherence to a basic framework of planning, writing, and revision; (2) explicit instruction of critical steps in the writing process, as well as the features and conventions of the writing genre or text structure; and (3) provision of feedback guided by the information explicitly taught.

WHAT WE KNOW AND QUESTIONS THAT REMAIN

The literature base is rich with information on how to write, what should be included in teaching writing in the classroom, and suggested models for writing programs that could transfer to the learning needs of gifted students. However, extensive studies examining the effective teaching of writing methods to gifted students at the secondary level is limited. Use of packaged writing programs, technology tools, having an abundance of opportunities to write using a structured model, and receiving teacher feedback all have been found to be effective in increasing writing skills among all students. Evidence does not suggest that teaching writing to the gifted should be perceived as a different enterprise from teaching it to all learners. Differentiation appears to be most needed in diagnosing the level of written proficiency at the beginning of instruction and providing follow-up assistance appropriate to that knowledge of functional level. Moreover, the personalization of the writing process through the feedback that teachers provide allows for individual differences to be accommodated.

What we know then about teaching writing to the gifted, based on research, suggests the following implications for classroom practice:

- Gifted students benefit from practice in writing, using a structured model in the particular form being practiced. Models can come from a variety of sources, including using the style of great writers.
- Gifted students learn writing in much the same way as all learners, by focused practice with form, critical feedback from teachers, and meaningful revision.
- Instruction in writing for gifted learners should match their "grade level" of knowledge rather than their age level.
- Special populations of gifted learners, especially learning-disabled students, benefit from the use of technology and journaling to enhance writing skills.
- Teaching gifted students techniques for metacognitive control may enhance the overall quality of writing because it coalesces with the crucial stages of the writing process.

What we do not know about working with the gifted in writing centers around the following questions:

- What developmental differences emerge in teaching writing to the gifted?
- What are the most effective models for teaching narrative and technical writing?
- How can we most effectively assess and provide feedback to gifted writers?
- What are the technological options for improving writing through journaling, portfolios, and other written scenarios and the implications for using them?
- How can we provide ongoing intensive writing experiences that motivate gifted learners to consistently produce high-quality work?

Hopefully, new research will be able to address these issues.

REFERENCES

Albertson, L. R., & Billingsley, F. F. (2001). Using strategy instruction and self-regulation to improve gifted students' creative writing. *Journal of Secondary Gifted Education, 12*, 90–101.

Applebee, A., Langer, J., & Mullis, I. (1986a). *The reading report card: Progress toward excellence in our schools.* Princeton, NJ: Educational Testing Service.

Applebee, A., Langer, J., & Mullis, I. (1986b). *The writing report card: Writing achievement in American schools.* Princeton, NJ: Educational Testing Service.

Appleman, D. (2000). *Critical encounters in high school English: Teaching literary theory to adolescents language and literacy series.* New York: Teachers College Press.

Brabham, E. G., & Villaume, S. K. (2002). Vocabulary instruction: concerns and visions. *Reading Teacher, 56*, 264–268.

Carlin-Menter, S., & Shuell, T. (2003). Teaching writing strategies through multimedia authorship. *Journal of Educational Multimedia and Hypermedia, 12*, 315–335.

Capurro, M. (2003). *Successful strategies for teaching gifted learners.* Retrieved July 10, 2007, from http://www.gt-cybersource.org/Record.aspx?NavID=2_0&rid=11201

Cox, K. B. (1995). *What counts in English class? Selected findings from a statewide study of California high school teachers.* (ERIC Document Reproduction Service No. ED384051)

Doney, C. J. (1995). Creating opportunities, or what is it like to be a WHALE? *Journal of Learning Disabilities, 28*, 194–195.

Ediger, M. (1999). Reading and vocabulary development. *Journal of Instructional Psychology, 26*, 7–15.

Egelson, P., Harman, S., & Bond, S. (2002, April). *A preliminary study of senior project programs in selected southeastern high schools.* Paper presented at the annual meeting of the American Educational Research Association, New Orleans. (ERIC Document Reproduction Service No. ED466336)

ERIC Clearinghouse on Disabilities and Gifted Education. (2002, Winter). Strengthening the second "R": Helping students with disabilities prepare well-written compositions. *Research Connections in Special Education, 10.*

Fouts, J. T., & Stuen, C. (1997). *Copernicus Project: Learning with laptops: Year 1 evaluation report.* Seattle, WA: Seattle Pacific University.

Gilstrap, S. C. (2003). *An evaluation of the effectiveness of federal class size reduction in the Los Angeles unified school district: Does class size influence teacher-student interaction in secondary classrooms?* Los Angeles: Los Angeles Unified School District Programming and Research Branch. (ERIC Document Reproduction Service No. LAUSDPARD141)

Greenwald, E. A., Persky, H. R., Campbell, J. R., & Mazzeo, J. (1999). *NAEP 1998 writing: Report card for the nation and the states.* Washington, DC: National Center for Education Statistics.

Grossen, B. (2002). *Direct instruction model for secondary schools: The research base for the REACH system.* (ERIC Document Reproduction Service No. ED481390)

Henry, A., & Roseberry, R. L. (1996). A corpus-based investigation of the language and linguistic patterns of one genre and the implications for language teaching. *Research in the Teaching of English, 30,* 472–489.

Hillocks, G. (1986). *Research on written composition.* Urbana, IL: ERIC Clearinghouse on Reading and Communication Skills and National Conference on Research in English.

Hillocks, G. (2002). *The testing trap: How state writing assessments control learning.* New York: Teachers College Press.

Hillocks, G. (2003). Fighting back: Assessing the assessments. *The English Journal, 92*(4), 63–70.

Ketter, J., & Pool, J. (2001). Exploring the impact of a high-stakes direct writing assessment in two high school classrooms. *Research in the Teaching of English, 35,* 344–393.

Laflamme, J. G. (1997). The effect of the multiple exposure vocabulary method and the target reading/writing strategy on test scores. *Journal of Adolescent and Adult Literacy, 40,* 372–384.

Langer, J. A. (2001). Beating the odds: Teaching middle and high school students to read and write well. *American Educational Research Journal, 38,* 837–880.

MacArthur, C. (1996). Using technology to enhance the writing processes of students with learning disabilities. *Journal of Learning Disabilities, 29,* 344–354.

Madaus, G. F. (1988). The influence of testing on the curriculum. In L. Tanner (Ed.), *Critical issues in curriculum* (pp. 83–121). Chicago: University of Chicago Press.

Manning, M. (1999). Helping words grow. *Teaching PreK–8, 29*(4), 103–105.

Marzano, R. J., Pickering, D., & Pollack, J. (2001). *Classroom instruction that works: Research-based strategies for increasing student achievement.* Alexandria, VA: Association for Supervision and Curriculum Development.

National Center for Education Statistics. (2002). *The nation's report card: Writing.* Retrieved July 13, 2007, from http://nces.ed.gov/nationsreportcard/writing/results2002

Newell, S. T. (1996). Practical inquiry: Collaboration and reflection in teacher education reform. *Teaching and Teacher Education, 12,* 567–576.

Novak, J. R. (1996). Establishing validity for performance-based assessments: An illustration for collections of student writing. *Journal of Educational Research, 89,* 220–233.

Pikulski, J. (1991). The transition years: Middle school. In J. Flood, J. Jensen, D. Lapp, & J. Squire (Eds.), *Handbook of research on teaching the English language arts* (pp. 303–319). New York: Macmillan.

Pressley, M., Goodchild, F., Fleet, J., Zajchowski, R., & Evans, E. D. (1989). The challenges of classroom strategy instruction. *Elementary School Journal, 89,* 301–342.

Pressley, M., & Woloshyn, V. (1995). *Cognitive strategy instruction that really improves children's academic performance.* Cambridge, MA: Brookline Books.

Pritchard, R. J., & Marshall, J. C. (1994). Evaluation of a tiered model for staff development in writing. *Research in the Teaching of English, 28,* 259–285.

Sadoski, M., Willson, V., & Norton, D. (1997). The relative contributions of research-based composition activities to writing improvement in the lower and middle grades. *Research in the Teaching of English, 31,* 120–151.

Scardamalia, M., & Bereiter, C. (1985). Fostering the development of self-regulation in children's knowledge processing. In S. F. Chipman, J. W. Segal, & R. Glaser (Eds.), *Thinking and learning skills: Vol. 2. Research and open questions* (pp. 563–577). Hillsdale, NJ: Lawrence Erlbaum.

Scherff, L., & Piazza, C. (2005). The more things change the more they stay the same. *Research in the Teaching of English, 39,* 271–304.

Schunk, D. H., & Swartz, C. W. (1993). Writing strategy instruction with gifted students: Effects of goals and feedback on self-efficacy and skills. *Roeper Review, 15,* 225–230.

Skerritt, M. E. (1995). *Early secondary students' views on the writing journal's ability to be a self motivator in writing.* (ERIC Document Reproduction Service No. ED481390)

Smith, C. (2003). *Vocabulary's influence on successful writing.* Bloomington, IN: ERIC Clearinghouse on Reading, English, and Communication. (ERIC Document Reproduction Service No. ED412506)

VanTassel-Baska, J. (2002). Assessment of gifted student learning in the language arts. *Journal of Secondary Gifted Education, 13*(2), 67–72.

VanTassel-Baska, J., & Stambaugh, T. (2006). *Comprehensive curriculum for gifted learners* (3rd ed.). Boston: Allyn & Bacon.

VanTassel-Baska, J., Zuo, L., Avery, L. D., & Little, C. A. (2002). A curriculum study of gifted-student learning in the language arts. *Gifted Child Quarterly, 46,* 30–44.

Warger, C. (2002). *Helping students with disabilities succeed in state and district writing assessments.* (ERIC Document Reproduction Service No. EDOEC0203)

Williams, A. S. (1998). Writing in public residential schools: A position paper. *Journal of Secondary Gifted Education, 9*(2), 83–88.

ABOUT THE EDITORS

Jonathan A. Plucker is professor of educational psychology and cognitive science at Indiana University, where he also directs the Center for Evaluation and Education Policy. After receiving his doctorate in educational psychology from the University of Virginia, he taught for 5 years at the University of Maine before moving to Indiana University, where he is entering his 11th year on the faculty. He is a past-chair of the Research and Evaluation Division of the National Association for Gifted Children, and he currently serves as president of American Psychological Association Division 10, the Society for the Psychology of Aesthetics, Creativity, and the Arts. Dr. Plucker has published more than 100 articles, chapters, and book reviews, and he has served on the editorial boards of *Gifted Child Quarterly*, *Roeper Review*, *Creativity Research Journal*, *Journal of Creative Behavior*, *Journal of Research on Science Teaching*, and *Psychology of Aesthetics, Creativity, and the Arts*. He has received numerous awards for his research on giftedness, talent, and creativity, including the NAGC Early Scholar Award, the NAGC Paul Torrance Award, and the APA Division 10 Berlyne Award.

Carolyn M. Callahan is Commonwealth Professor in the Curry School of Education at the University of Virginia. At the University of Virginia, she developed the graduate program in gifted education, the summer and Saturday program for gifted students, and is the director of the University of Virginia site of the National Research Center on the Gifted and Talented. Her research has resulted in more than 175 refereed articles and 40 book chapters across topics including program evaluation, the development of performance assessments, and curricular and programming options for highly able students. She has received recognition as Outstanding Faculty Member in the Commonwealth of Virginia, Outstanding Professor of the Curry School of Education, and Distinguished Higher Education Alumnae of the University of Connecticut, and was awarded the Distinguished Scholar Award and the Distinguished Service Award from the National Association for Gifted Children. She is a past-president of The Association for the Gifted and the National Association for Gifted Children.

ABOUT THE AUTHORS

Cheryll M. Adams is the director of the Center for Gifted Studies and Talent Development at Ball State University. She teaches graduate courses for the license in gifted education and previously taught math and science in public and private schools. Dr. Adams has authored or coauthored numerous publications in professional journals, as well as several book chapters and a book. She serves on the editorial review board for *Roeper Review* and *Gifted Child Quarterly*. She has served on the Board of Directors of the National Association for Gifted Children, has been president of the Indiana Association for the Gifted, and currently serves on the board of The Association for the Gifted, Council for Exceptional Children.

Jill L. Adelson is a doctoral student, research associate, and adjunct faculty member in educational psychology at the University of Connecticut. Her three areas of concentration are gifted education; measurement, evaluation, and assessment; and mathematics education, and she also is working on her quantitative research methods certification. Prior to coming to UConn, Jill taught in a self-contained gifted and talented fourth-grade classroom and earned her master's degree in curriculum and instruction with an emphasis in gifted education from the College of William and Mary. Jill's research interests include mathematics talent development, particularly in elementary and middle school students and in females, attitudes toward mathematics, research using large-scale national databases like the ECLS-K, and instrument design.

Joyce M. Alexander is associate professor of educational psychology at Indiana University. She graduated with her M.S. and Ph.D. in educational psychology from the University of Georgia. In addition to writing numerous articles and book chapters, Joyce has been involved in several grants from the National Science Foundation focused on the development of interest and motivation. She currently is serving as chair of the Department of Counseling and Educational Psychology.

Meredith Banasiak is an instructor in the College of Architecture and Planning at the University of Colorado. Her research interest lies in exploring the dialogue between the human factors of a building and the designed environment. As a research associate with the Academy of Neuroscience for Architecture (ANFA), Meredith engaged in cognitive neuroscience research with KIDLAB at the Krasnow Institute of Advanced Studies, George Mason University, where she used behavioral paradigms and functional magnetic resonance imaging (fMRI) to investigate environmental context effects on cognitive processes across the life cycle. Currently, Meredith is engaged in research with the Center for Youth and Environments (CYE) examining how links with outdoor nature play can affect children's physical and cognitive well-being.

Ronald A. Beghetto is assistant professor of educational studies at University of Oregon. He received his Ph.D. in educational psychology from Indiana University with an emphasis in learning, cognition, and instruction and organizational behavior. Dr. Beghetto's scholarship focuses on examining the K–12 schooling experiences of students (with respect to student creativity, learning, and motivation) and the influence of prospective teachers' past schooling experience on their beliefs, images, and assumptions about teaching, learning, and schooling.

James H. Borland is professor of education and coordinator of programs in gifted education at Teachers College, Columbia University. He is author of *Planning and Implementing Programs for the Gifted* and the editor of *Rethinking Gifted Education*, as well as numerous articles and book chapters. He is editor of the *Education and Psychology of the Gifted* series from Teachers College Press, and he is past editor of the section on Teaching, Learning, and Human Development of the *American Educational Research Journal*. He has twice won the Paper of the Year award from *Gifted Child Quarterly* and the Award for Excellence in Research from the Mensa Education and Research Foundation. He has consulted with more than 100 school districts and other organizations concerning gifted education.

Hilary Chart received her master's degree in international education policy from Stanford University in 2006 and is currently a doctoral student at the Harvard Graduate School of Education. She has worked as a teacher and educational researcher in both the United States and Africa (South Africa and Zambia). Her research interests include the influence of assessments on schooling, the interaction of local cultures with global trends in education policy and practice, the relationship between school outcomes and geographic mobility, and post-colonial studies.

Trudy L. Clemons received her doctorate in educational psychology from the University of Virginia. She currently works at Albemarle County School District in the Department of Assessment and Information Services. Trudy previously worked as a research assistant at the National Research Center on the Gifted and Talented and the Reading First Evaluation. Trudy serves as an instructor for online graduate-level courses offered through the University of Virginia. She has presented at state and national conferences, and has worked as an evaluator with a local school district in Virginia and for a statewide initiative in Maine, as well as assisting in several district-level evaluations.

Tracy L. Cross, George and Frances Ball Distinguished Professor of Gifted Studies, serves Teachers College at Ball State University as the Associate Dean for Graduate Studies, Research and Assessment. For 9 years he served as the executive director of the Indiana Academy for Science, Mathematics, and Humanities, Indiana's public residential academy for intellectually gifted adolescents. He is the editor of the *Journal for the Education of the Gifted*, and former editor of *Gifted Child Quarterly*, *Journal of Secondary Gifted Education*, *Roeper Review*, and *Research Briefs*. He has published two books—both in their second editions, 70 juried articles and chapters, and made approximately 200 presentations at national and international conferences. He has been awarded the National Association for Gifted Children Early Leader Award and Early Scholar Award and recently, both the NAGC and The Association for the Gifted of the Council for Exceptional Children Distinguished Service Awards.

David Yun Dai is an associate professor in the Department of Educational and Counseling Psychology, at University at Albany, State University of New York. He received his Ph.D. from Purdue University, with John Feldhusen as his advisor, and worked as a postdoctoral fellow at the National Research Center on the Gifted and Talented under the tutelage of Joseph Renzulli. His research interests include gifted children and talent development.

Robin Kyburg Dickson received her Ph.D. in educational psychology/gifted education at the University of Virginia after spending nearly a quarter of a century in Europe. Her current research interests focus on developing innovative ways to serve underserved populations of advanced learners. She directs

Michigan's Virtual University's development of unique online summer experiences for middle school students in math and science, as well as develops courses for Michigan State University's technology specialization for K–12 teachers.

Felicia A. Dixon is professor of psychology in the Department of Educational Psychology at Ball State University. She directs the master's degree program in educational psychology and the license/endorsement in gifted education. She received her doctorate from Purdue University and specializes in gifted education. Author of more than 30 articles and chapters, Felicia Dixon coedited the important *The Handbook of Secondary Gifted Education* in 2006 and received the Early Scholar Award from NAGC in 2004. She has served as a member of the Board of Directors of NAGC and currently is chairperson of the Task Force on Secondary Gifted Education of NAGC. Her research interests include critical thinking, cognitive abilities, self-concept of gifted adolescents, perfectionism, and curriculum. Her special interest is in the advancement of gifted education for secondary students.

David Henry Feldman is professor of developmental psychology at Tufts University. He also has served on the faculties of the University of Minnesota and Yale University. Recipient of several grants and fellowships, Feldman was a Fulbright Scholar at Tel Aviv University and Scholar of the Year of the National Association for Gifted Children. Author of nearly 200 publications, including the books *Changing the World* with Mihaly Csikszentmihalyi and Howard Gardner, and *Nature's Gambit* with Lynn Goldsmith, Feldman currently is working on projects on the development of expertise, creativity, and a theory of nonuniversal cognitive development.

James J. Gallagher has been active in the field of special education for more than a half century. He currently is Kenan Professor of Education Emeritus at the University of North Carolina. In 1970s–1980s, he served for 17 years as director of the Frank Porter Graham Child Development Center at the University of North Carolina at Chapel Hill. He was the first director of the Bureau of Education for the Handicapped in the U.S. Office of Education in 1967–1970. Among his more than 200 books, monographs, and articles are *Teaching the Gifted Child*, coauthored with his daughter, Dr. Shelagh Gallagher, and *Driving Change in Special Education* (2006). He has served as president of TAG, NAGC, and the World Council on Gifted and Talented.

M. Katherine Gavin is associate professor in educational psychology at the University of Connecticut where she serves as the math specialist at the Neag Center for Gifted Education and Talent Development. Kathy has more than 30 years of experience in education as a mathematics teacher, department chair, and curriculum coordinator; elementary assistant principal; and assistant professor of mathematics education. She presently is writing and field testing curriculum units for talented elementary students, coauthoring a middle school mathematics textbook series, and is a member of the writing team for the National Council of Teachers of Mathematics *Navigations* series. Her research interests include gifted mathematics education for elementary and middle school students and gender issues in mathematics education.

Marcia Gentry serves as associate director of the Gifted Education Resource Institute at Purdue University, where she also directs the doctoral program in gifted education. Her research interests include student attitudes toward school and the connection of these attitudes toward learning and motivation; the use of gifted education pedagogy as a means of improving learning and teaching; the use of cluster-grouping and differentiation to promote student achievement; the use of nontraditional settings for talent development such as Career and Technical Education; and the development and recognition of talent among underserved populations. She frequently contributes to the gifted education literature, actively participates in NAGC and AERA, and regularly speaks at conferences and workshops from the local to international level. Prior to her work in higher education, Marcia spent 12 years in K–12 education as a teacher and administrator.

Elena L. Grigorenko received her Ph.D. in general psychology from Moscow State University, Russia, in 1990, and her Ph.D. in developmental psychology and genetics from Yale University in 1996. Currently, Grigorenko is associate professor of child studies and psychology at Yale and associate professor of psychology at Moscow State University. Grigorenko has published more than 200 peer-reviewed articles, book chapters, and books. She has received awards for her work from five different divisions of the American Psychological Association (Divisions 1, 7, 10, 15, and 24). In 2004, she won the APA Distinguished Award for an Early Career Contribution to Developmental Psychology. Grigorenko's research has been funded by NIH, NSF, DOE, Cure Autism Now, the Foundation for Child Development, the American Psychological Foundation, and other federal and private sponsoring organizations.

Miraca U. M. Gross is professor of gifted education and director of the Gifted Education Research, Resource and Information Centre at the University of New South Wales in Sydney, Australia. Her research interests include: socio-affective development in gifted children and adolescents; the highly gifted; short- and long-term outcomes of ability grouping and acceleration; and teacher attitudes toward gifted children and gifted education. Miraca's awards for research include: the Hollingworth Award for Excellence in Research in the Education and Psychology of the Gifted (1987), Mensa International Education and Research Foundation Awards for Excellence (1988 and 1990), and the National Association for Gifted Children's Early Scholar Award (1995) and Distinguished Scholar Award (2005). In 1997, the Australian Federal Government honored her with the inaugural Australian Award for University

Teaching in Education. In 2003, the Australian College of Educators honored her with the Sir Harold Wyndham Medal for outstanding service to Australian education.

E. Jean Gubbins is associate professor of educational psychology at the University of Connecticut and associate director of the National Research on the Gifted and Talented, which is a federally funded grant from the United States Department of Education. In her current position, she works with a team of researchers who design and implement quantitative and qualitative studies throughout the country. Her main areas of interest are research, evaluation, and service projects in the field of gifted and talented education. Gubbins teaches graduate courses; consults at the local, state, regional, national, and international levels; conducts formative and summative evaluations locally and nationally; and shares her expertise at invitational workshops, conferences, and symposia.

Joanne Haroutounian enjoys a career across the fields of music, arts education, and gifted education as a teacher, performer, lecturer, writer, and consultant. Haroutounian serves on the piano faculty of George Mason University where she oversees the piano pedagogy program. She consults nationally in the areas of musical talent, gifted/arts development, and creative teaching strategies in music. She conceived and developed the MusicLink Foundation based on her research and expertise on musical talent identification and development. She currently serves as its executive director, overseeing more than 100 programs nationally that have provided ongoing musical training to more than 2,500 promising students in need across the country. Haroutounian is the author of *Kindling the Spark: Recognizing and Developing Musical Talent* published by Oxford University Press, as well as many music editions and teaching publications offered by Neil A. Kjos Music.

Holly Hertberg-Davis is assistant professor in the Curry School of Education at the University of Virginia and a principal investigator for the National Research Center on the Gifted and Talented. Her research interests include advanced curriculum and instruction for middle school and high school learners, differentiation of instruction, and the efficacy of staff development. She is a former middle school and high school English teacher.

Jessica A. Hockett is a doctoral student in educational psychology (gifted education emphasis) at the University of Virginia. She has a M.A.T. in secondary education from National-Louis University and a M.A. in gifted and talented education from the University of Connecticut. A former secondary teacher in the Chicago area, Jessica taught English, social studies, and math for academically talented students. She works as a consultant on differentiated instruction to schools across the U.S. and in Canada.

Pau-San Hoh teaches linguistics and writing at Marist College, where she also is known by her married name, Pau-San Haruta. She received her Ph.D. in linguistics from the University of Delaware in 1992. She particularly is interested in cross-disciplinary linkages and has written papers on language and cognition, as well as on contributions of linguistics to giftedness research. She also has presented her work on using writing as a tool for mathematical learning at national and international conferences. Her current research interests include the study of linguistic intelligence and the verbal abilities of exceptional populations. She is the director of EduNational, LLC, which provides academic counseling to children with special needs in New York.

Saiying Hu is a doctoral candidate in the Department of Educational Studies at Purdue University, West Lafayette, IN. Her ongoing research interests include talent development and psychology of the gifted, life experiences and career development of creative individuals, scientific productivity of creative individuals and organizations, positive emotion and engagement of creative persons, and quantitative research methodology.

Carolyn M. Iguchi is a doctoral student in the College of Education and Human Development at George Mason University in Fairfax, VA. She completed her master's degree in educational psychology at George Mason University in 2005. Iguchi's research interests include self-regulation and self-determination for students with cognitive disabilities and the role of churches in creating inclusive environments for people with disabilities.

Linda Jarvin is associate research professor in Tufts University's Department of Education and the deputy director of the Center for Psychology of Abilities, Competencies, and Expertise (PACE) and Tufts Center for Enhancing Learning and Teaching (CELT). Her research interests focus on curriculum and assessment development, and she has published numerous articles on these topics.

M. Layne Kalbfleisch is both an educational psychologist and a cognitive neuroscientist. As a transdisciplinary scientist, she has two overarching goals: (1) to investigate the relationship between talent and disability (particularly in twice-exceptional children) and (2) to pioneer methods for better representing real-world cognition in the artificial functional MRI environment. Her laboratory, KIDLAB, does this using behavioral studies, psychometrics, and functional magnetic resonance imaging (fMRI) to investigate the neural bases of reasoning and attention processes in adults and children. Comparing reasoning and attention permits her to inquire scientifically about historical definitions of intelligence, expertise, creativity, and learning. Studies to date involve collaborations with architects and computer scientists to explore environmental effects on learning. She seeks to contribute new insight into how the brain develops, learns, creates, and solves problems throughout the lifespan during typical development and in the cases of giftedness, Attention-Deficit Hyperactivity Disorder, autism, and dyslexia.

Margie K. Kitano serves as associate dean of the College of Education and professor of special education at San Diego State University (SDSU). She codeveloped and works with the San Diego Unified School District collaborative certificate in gifted education and SDSU's graduate certificate and master's degree program in developing gifted potential. Her research and publications focus on improving services to gifted individuals diverse in culture, language, economic status, and gender.

Robert Kunzman is assistant professor in the Indiana University School of Education, where he teaches courses in secondary education and moral and civic education. He recently has concluded a multiyear project funded by the Spencer Foundation and National Academy of Education exploring homeschooling policies, practices, and philosophies across the United States. He also is author of *Grappling With the Good: Talking About Religion and Morality in Public Schools* (SUNY, 2006).

Brenda Linn is a doctoral candidate and lecturer in the Department of Education and Counselling Psychology at McGill University in Montreal, Canada. She has taught at the elementary, secondary and postsecondary level, and has worked in particular with gifted dyslexic students in both school and clinical settings. Her current research examines possible differences in thinking dispositions between cognitive psychologists and teacher-educators, and explores the way these differences may affect their interpretation of recent research in the field of reading.

Bronwyn MacFarlane works at the Center for Gifted Education as research assistant to the executive director and is a doctoral student at the College of William and Mary in the educational policy, planning, and leadership program with a concentration in gifted education administration. She holds a M.Ed. in counseling from Stephens College, a private women's college in Missouri. Bronwyn earned her master's degree in curriculum and instruction with a minor in literacy and her bachelor's degree in secondary education at the University of Missouri-Columbia. Bronwyn currently serves as the nationally elected student representative to the SIG Board of Research on Gifted and Talented within the American Educational Research Association (AERA) and is the academic dean for the Summer Institute for the Gifted at Princeton University.

Matthew C. Makel is a graduate student in educational psychology at Indiana University studying giftedness, creativity, and expertise. His research interests span from the theoretical underpinnings of human cognitive performance, to the applications of empirical work in educational settings, as well as policy decisions affecting education and the evaluation of programs to facilitate cognitive development. He received his master's degree in developmental psychology from Cornell University and his bachelor's degree in psychology from Duke University.

Michael S. Matthews is an assistant professor of gifted education at the University of South Florida. He is the author of two books, *Working With Gifted English Language Learners* and *Encouraging Your Child's Science Talent: The Involved Parents' Guide*. Matthews taught science at a public high school, and then completed his Ph.D. at the University of Georgia in 2002. Prior to his appointment at USF, Matthews held a postdoctoral appointment with the TIP Talent Search at Duke University. He presents frequently at local and national conferences and writes regularly on gifted education topics. His research interests relate to cultural and linguistic diversity in gifted education, with particular attention to assessment and identification issues. Associated areas include science and math education, gifted education policy, and underachievement among gifted learners.

D. Betsy McCoach is an assistant professor in the Educational Psychology Department in the Neag School of Education at the University of Connecticut, where she teaches graduate courses in measurement, educational statistics, and research design. Her methodological research interests include hierarchical linear modeling, instrument design, factor analysis, structural equation modeling, longitudinal analysis, and quantitative research methodology. Betsy's substantive research interests include the underachievement of academically able students and issues related to academic growth and achievement. Betsy is the coeditor of a new book, *Multilevel Modeling of Educational Data*, available in the Fall of 2007, and she is the coeditor of the *Journal of Advanced Academics*.

Erin Morris Miller is a full-time stay-at-home parent and an adjunct professor at James Madison University. She currently instructs online continuing education courses for teachers wishing to study gifted education. Her research interests include thinking and reasoning processes, the cognitive and emotional development of gifted students, and exploring the social construction of giftedness.

Sidney M. Moon is director of the Gifted Education Resource Institute and Associate Dean for Learning and Engagement in the College of Education at Purdue University. She has been involved in the field of gifted education for almost 25 years. In that time, she has contributed more than 75 books, articles, and chapters to the field. Her most recent book is *The Handbook of Secondary Gifted Education*. Sidney is active in the National Association for Gifted Children, where she has served as chair of the Research and Evaluation Division and a member of the Board of Directors. Her research interests include talent development in the STEM disciplines (science, technology, engineering, and mathematics), underserved populations of gifted students, and personal talent development.

Tonya R. Moon is associate professor at the Curry School of Education at the University of Virginia and a principal investigator for the National Research Center on the Gifted and Talented. She has a Ph.D. in educational measurement, research, and evaluation. At the university, she actively is engaged in teaching and research. Her interests focus on issues of testing and accountability and their implication on practice, establishing appropriate standards and benchmarks, research methodology, and gifted education. In addition, she also is the chair of the University's Institutional Review Board, a board responsible for oversight of all research conducted at the university.

Sharlene D. Newman earned her bachelor's degree from Vanderbilt University in 1993 and her Ph.D. from the University of Alabama at Birmingham in 1999. Newman currently is assistant professor in the Department of Psychological and Brain Sciences at Indiana University. Her research uses functional magnetic resonance imaging as a tool to explore language comprehension and planning/problem solving. Her language comprehension research focuses primarily on the study of syntactic analysis and attempts to explore the working memory system's contribution to comprehension. Dr. Newman's second line of research, planning/problem solving, is designed to better characterize the neural architecture that supports planning, focusing particularly on the role of the prefrontal cortex.

Tina Newman has worked as an associate research scientist and child psychologist at the Yale University Department of Psychology and the Child Study Center at Yale University. She currently is a child psychologist at Sunny Hill Health Center for Children, British Columbia Children's Hospital. She is interested in both research and practice with children who have special needs.

Stuart N. Omdal is associate professor in gifted education in the School of Special Education at the University of Northern Colorado. He is the assistant director of the Center for the Education and Study of the Gifted, Talented, Creative and the education director for the Summer Enrichment Program. Interests include the underachievement of high-ability students, the development of appropriate curriculum for high-ability students, and the role of creativity in gifted and talented education.

Jean Sunde Peterson, associate professor and coordinator of the school counseling program at Purdue University, was a longtime classroom and gifted education teacher before entering the counseling field. She is past chair of the Counseling and Guidance Division of NAGC and has been a regular convention presenter for more than 20 years. Her workshops, convention presentations, and award-winning qualitative and longitudinal research reflect her interest in the social and emotional development and counseling concerns of gifted youth. She is a national award winner in group work, and her books on group work, including *The Essential Guide for Talking with Gifted Teens*, are used internationally. Among her many publications is the coedited *Models of Counseling Gifted Children, Adolescents, and Young Adults*.

Rebecca L. Pierce is associate professor of mathematical sciences at Ball State University and fellow at the Center for Gifted Studies and Talent Development. She teaches undergraduate and graduate courses in mathematics and statistics and previously taught mathematics to elementary, middle school, and high school students. Pierce directs the Ball State Institute for the Gifted in Mathematics. She has authored or coauthored numerous publications in professional journals, as well as several book chapters and a book. She serves as a reviewer for *Roeper Review*, *Gifted Child Quarterly*, and the *Teacher Educator*.

Michael C. Pyryt is director of the Centre for Gifted Education and associate professor of applied psychology at the University of Calgary. He specialized in gifted education in the United States at both the master's (Johns Hopkins University) and doctoral level (University of Kansas.) He has a wide range of research interests in gifted education including identification approaches, creativity, instructional planning and several aspects of social-emotional development including self-concept, perfectionism, personality development, and career planning. He has made more than 150 presentations at national and international conferences and has more than 60 publications related to giftedness. His work appears in both editions of the *International Handbook on Giftedness and Talent* and the *Handbook of Gifted Education*. He is coeditor of *AGATE*, journal of the Gifted and Talented Education Council of the Alberta Teachers' Association, and serves on the editorial advisory board of the *Journal for the Education of the Gifted*, *Gifted Child Quarterly*, and *PsycCRITIQUES-Contemporary Psychology: APA Review of Books*.

Kelly E. Rapp is an affiliate of the Center for Evaluation and Education Policy (CEEP) at Indiana University where she previously worked as a research associate. She is working toward her Ph.D. in educational psychology with an emphasis on inquiry methodology. Rapp's research interests include charter schools and gifted education policy.

Judi Randi is associate professor of education at the University of New Haven. Her research focuses on how educational research and theories are translated into practice in actual classrooms. She has authored and coauthored articles on teacher innovation, teacher professional learning, and teachers as self-regulated learners. She recently has served as guest editor of the Autumn 2007 special issue of *Theory into Practice*, focusing on "Research in the Service of Practice."

Rachel E. Sytsma Reed holds a master's degree in astrobiogeochemistry and a Ph.D. in educational psychology from the University of Connecticut; is principal investigator and program coordinator for TRIAGE, a National Science Foundation Academy for Young Scientists; and is assistant professor of education at Calvin College. Her research interests have taken her from the Caribbean coast, where she studied methane cycling as a member of NASA's Astrobiology Institute, to schools, school districts, and classrooms in New England and Michigan, where she consulted about and evaluated gifted programs and science education. Rachel currently is developing a Student Research Institute, which combines her experience with gifted education and laboratory and field research. Her current research focuses on co-cognitive factors and giftedness in the context of science education.

Joseph S. Renzulli is a UConn Distinguished Professor at the University of Connecticut, where he also serves as director of the National Research Center on the Gifted and Talented and holds an Honorary Doctor of Laws Degree from McGill University. His research has focused on the identification and development of creativity and giftedness in young people, and on curricular and organizational models for differentiated learning environments that contribute to total school improvement. The American Psychological Association named Renzulli among the 25 most influential psychologists in the world. He is the founder of the summer Confratute program at UConn, which began in 1978, and has served more than 20,000 educators from around the world. His most recent work is a computer-based assessment of student strengths integrated with an Internet-based search engine that matches enrichment activities and resources with individual student profiles (http://www.renzullilearning.com).

Sally M. Reis is professor and the past department head of Educational Psychology Department at the University of Connecticut, where she also serves as a principal investigator for the National Research Center on the Gifted and Talented. She was a teacher for 15 years, 11 of which were spent working with gifted students at the elementary, junior high, and high school levels. She has authored more than 140 articles, 11 books, 50 book chapters, and numerous monographs and technical reports. Her research interests are related to special populations of gifted and talented students, including students with learning disabilities, gifted females, and diverse groups of talented students. She is a past president of the National Association for Gifted Children. She recently was honored with the highest award in her field, Distinguished Scholar of the National Association for Gifted Children, and named a Board of Trustees Distinguished Professor at the University of Connecticut.

M. R. E. Richards is an educational consultant in gifted education, curriculum design, and differentiation and is an adjunct professor at the University of Northern Colorado in science education. Her background in science and education allows her to understand the needs of both fields and design curriculum to meet the educational growth of a diverse student population while including the background content and skills in science that are needed in high school and postsecondary education.

Anne N. Rinn is assistant professor of psychology at Western Kentucky University. She holds a Ph.D. in educational psychology from Indiana University. Her research focuses on the academic, social, and emotional development of gifted adolescents and college students, as well as the effects of gifted programming on student development as a whole.

Ann Robinson is professor of education and founding director of the Center for Gifted Education at the University of Arkansas at Little Rock. She is a former editor of the *Gifted Child Quarterly*, serves on the Board of Directors of the National Association for Gifted Children as the vice president, and received the Early Leader, the Early Scholar, and Distinguished Service Awards from the association. In 2004, she and coauthor Sidney Moon received the *Gifted Child Quarterly* Paper of the Year Award for "The National Study of State and Local Advocacy in Gifted Education." With Shore, Cornell, and Ward, Ann coauthored *Recommended Practices in Gifted Education: A Critical Analysis*, identified as one of the 50 most influential works in gifted education by the Research and Evaluation Division of the National Association for Gifted Children. Her most current publication is *Best Practices in Gifted Education: An Evidence-Based Guide* recently released by Prufrock Press and coauthored with Bruce Shore of McGill University and Donna Enersen of Purdue University.

Nancy M. Robinson is Professor Emerita of Psychiatry and Behavioral Sciences at the University of Washington and former director of what is now known as the Halbert and Nancy Robinson Center for Young Scholars. Formerly known for her work in mental retardation, her research interests on gifted children have focused on effects of marked academic acceleration to college, adjustment issues of gifted children, intellectual assessment, and verbal and mathematical precocity in very young children. Robinson chairs advisory committees to the U.S. State Department Office of Overseas Schools and the Advanced Academy of Georgia. She received the 1998 Distinguished Scholar Award from the National Association for Gifted Children.

Robin M. Schader is assistant research professor in the Neag Center for Gifted Education and Talent Development at the University of Connecticut, where she teaches courses titled "Parenting for Talent Development" and "Collaborating With Parents and Community in Gifted Education." Her work focuses on talent development, particularly with respect to the role of parents, and successful ways to match educational programs to students' needs. She also serves as the parent resource specialist for the National Association for Gifted Children. Robin has presented at regional, national, and international conferences. Her publications include a regular column in *Parenting for High Potential*, and the newsletter *Connecting for High Potential*, as well as numerous articles.

Angela K. Schnick is a doctoral student in educational psychology at Indiana University. Her interests include cognitive development, exceptional students, and motivation. Angela currently is working as an assistant instructor for the Department of Counseling and Educational Psychology at Indiana University.

Stephen T. Schroth teaches in the Educational Studies Department at Knox College in Galesburg, IL. He possesses a bachelor's degree from Macalester College, a JD from the University of Minnesota Law School, a master's degree from Teachers College at Columbia University, and a Ph.D. in education from the University of Virginia. Prior to enrolling at UVA, he served as a classroom teacher for 6 years and a literacy coach for 2 years with the Los Angeles Unified School District, teaching a variety of elementary grades and serving as a gifted, Title I, and bilingual coordinator. His research interests include talent development of diverse students, evaluation of gifted education programs, effective instructional and leadership practices, integration of technology in the classroom, and working with English-language development.

Bruce M. Shore is professor of educational psychology in the Faculty of Education at McGill University in Montreal, where he also has served as chair of the department and dean of students. His research has addressed the ways in which gifted students think and learn differently from other students, how the development of giftedness parallels that of expertise, and understanding learning processes in inquiry-driven environments. He and his graduate students currently are focused on such topics as interprofessional education and practice, inquiry in teacher education and undergraduate science education, how research ideas arise, and the identification and evaluation of the outcomes of inquiry-based teaching and learning. He has a BSc in mathematics and chemistry (with psychology), a teaching diploma in secondary mathematics and science, a master's degree in education from McGill University, and a Ph.D. in educational psychology from The University of Calgary.

Del Siegle is associate professor of educational psychology in the Neag School of Education at the University of Connecticut. He currently teaches classes in creativity, principles of educational research, and enhancing personal creativity with digital photography. He recently was recognized for his outstanding teaching by being honored as a university teaching fellow. Prior to earning his Ph.D., Del worked as a gifted and talented coordinator in Montana. He is president of the National Association of Gifted Children and serves on the board of directors of The Association for the Gifted (CEC-TAG). He is coeditor of the *Journal of Advanced Academics* and authors a technology column for *Gifted Child Today*. Del's research interests include teaching with technology, motivation of gifted students, and teacher bias in the identification of students for gifted programs.

Bharath Sriraman is associate professor of mathematics at The University of Montana, with a wide range of eclectic research interests including mathematical creativity, innovation, gifted education, and talent development. He received his Ph.D. from the department of mathematics at Northern Illinois University. Bharath is the editor of the *Montana Mathematics Enthusiast*, associate editor of *ZDM—*the *International Journal on Mathematics Education* (formerly known as *Zentralblatt fŸr Didaktik der Mathematik*), consulting editor of *Interchange: A Quarterly Review of Education*, and reviews editor of *Mathematical Thinking & Learning*, as well as *ZDM*. He serves on the editorial boards of *Gifted Child Quarterly*, the *Journal of Advanced Academics*, and several other journals. He holds very active research ties with researchers working in his domains of interest in Australia, Canada, Cyprus, Denmark, Germany, Iceland, India, Turkey, and the United States.

Alane Starko is professor in the Department of Teacher Education of Eastern Michigan University, where she teaches the areas of educational psychology and curriculum. Her current research interests are creativity, classroom differentiation, and the development of teacher thinking.

Olof Bjorg Steinthorsdottir currently is assistant professor of mathematics education in the School of Education at University of North Carolina–Chapel Hill. A former mathematics classroom teacher in her native country of Iceland, Steinthorsdottir teaches mathematics education courses in the elementary education and culture, curriculum and change programs. Her scholarly interests include the teaching and learning of mathematics among students in pre-Kindergarten through middle school, specifically students' understanding of mathematics and how teachers can use that understanding to make instructional decisions, talent development, and social justice. Steinthorsdottir also serves on the planning committee for the First School Initiative of the Frank Porter Graham Child Development Institute, a proposed school for 3-year-olds through third graders. Her work addresses the curriculum and instruction to be implemented in the First School and ways to incorporate continual professional development into the format. She is active in the mathematics education profession locally, nationally, and internationally. In collaboration with educators in the North Carolina Partnership in Mathematics and Science (NCPIMS), she developed and implemented professional development materials for elementary teachers that focus on the pedagogical and content perspectives of algebraic reasoning.

Robert J. Sternberg is dean of the School of Arts and Sciences and professor of psychology at Tufts University. Prior to accepting this position, he was IBM professor of psychology and Education in the Department of Psychology, professor of management in the School of Management, and director of the Center for the Psychology of Abilities, Competencies, and Expertise at Yale University. Sternberg also was the 2003 President of the American Psychological Association. He is the author of more than 1,100 journal articles, book chapters, and books, and has received more than $20 million in grants and contracts for his research that has been conducted on 5 continents. The central focus of his research is on intelligence, creativity, and wisdom, and he also has studied love and close relationships, as well as hate.

Adrian T. Thomas is a doctoral candidate in Purdue's educational psychology program. She has worked on grants concerning the problem of underrepresented populations in gifted programs and the literacy of young children from low-income families. Her research interests include student–teacher relationships, racial socialization, minority children, and the development of talent in multicultural children.

Carol Ann Tomlinson is professor of educational leadership, foundations, and policy at the University of Virginia's Curry School of Education. Prior to her university work, she was a public school teacher for 21 years, teaching in preschool, middle school, and high school. Her research and writing most often focus on effective instruction for academically diverse student populations. She works with educators around the world who want to learn more about differentiated instruction.

Joyce VanTassel-Baska is the Jody and Layton Smith Professor of Education and executive director of the Center for Gifted Education at the College of William and Mary in Virginia, where she has developed a graduate program and a research and development center in gifted education. She is a past president of the National Association for Gifted Children. Dr. VanTassel-Baska has published 22 books and more than 500 refereed journal articles, book chapters, and scholarly reports. She has received numerous awards including the National Association for Gifted Children's Early Leader Award in 1986, the State Council of Higher Education in Virginia Outstanding Faculty Award in 1993, the Phi Beta Kappa faculty award in 1995, the National Association for Gifted Children Distinguished Scholar Award in 1997, and the President's Award, World Council on Gifted and Talented Education in 2005. Her research interests are on the talent development process and effective curricular interventions with the gifted. She holds B.A., M.A., M.Ed., and Ed.D. degrees from the University of Toledo.

Bess B. Worley II is the director of gifted education services for Gloucester County Public Schools, in Gloucester, VA, where she also supports and coordinates the K–12 visual and performing arts programs. She has served as a K–8 general music teacher, middle school choir teacher, elementary gifted education specialist, assistant managing editor for *Gifted Child Today*, and as a graduate and research assistant at the College of William and Mary and Baylor University. Bess has served on the Board of Directors for the Virginia Association for the Gifted and currently is serving on the Board for the Virginia Consortium of Gifted Education Administrators. She is Chair of the Arts Division of the National Association for Gifted Children for 2005–2007.

INDEX